DISNEY **A**to**Z**

Th **Official Encyclopedia** Third Edition

Dave Smith

EDITIONS

New York

For information address Disney Editions, 114 Fifth Avenue, New York, New York 10011-5690.
Editorial Director: Wendy Lefkon
Senior Editor: Jody Revenson
Editorial Assistant: Jessica Ward

The book's producers would like to extend special thanks to Carole Brandi, Guy Cunningham, Diane Hodges, Sharon Krinsky, Jenny Langsam, and Jessica Ward.

The following are some of the trademarks, registered marks, and service marks owned by Disney Enterprises, Inc.: Adventureland® Area; Audio-Animatronics® Figure; Big Thunder Mountain® Railroad; Blizzard Beach Water Park; California Screamin'; Circle-Vision; Critter Country®; DinoLand, U.S.A. Area; Dinosaur! Attraction; Discovery Island® Area; Discoveryland; Disney®; Disneyland®; Disneyland® Hotel; Disneyland® Park; Disneyland® Resort; Disneyland® Resort Paris; Disney-MGM Studios; Disney's Animal Kingdom® Theme Park; Disney's California Adventure® Park; Disney's Typhoon Lagoon Water Park; Epcot®; Expedition EVEREST; Fantasyland® Area; FASTPASS® Service; Fort Wilderness; Frontierland® Area; Future World; Golden State; Hong Kong Disneyland® Park; Imagineering; Imagineers; "it's a small world"; It's Tough To Be A Bug!® Attraction; Kali River Rapids® Attraction; Kilimanjaro Safaris® Expedition; Magic Kingdom® Park; Maharajah Jungle Trek® Attraction; Main Street, U.S.A., Area; Mickey's Toontown® Fair; Mission: SPACE; monorail; New Orleans Square®; Orbitron; Paradise Pier; Primeval Whirl; Rock 'N Roller Coaster® Attraction; Space Mountain® Attraction; Splash Mountain® Attraction; Tokyo Disneyland® Park; Tokyo Disneysea®; Tomorrowland® Area; Toontown®; Walt Disney World® Resort; World Showcase

A Bug's Life; Cars; Finding Nemo; The Incredibles; Monsters, Inc.; and Toy Story characters; and Buzz Lightyear Astro Blasters and Buzz Lightyear Space Ranger Spin © Disney Enterprises, Inc./Pixar Animation Studios

©The Baby Einstein Company, LLC. All Rights Reserved. Baby Einstein, Little Einsteins, and the Boy's Head logo are trademarks of The Baby Einstein Company, LLC. All Rights Reserved. EINSTEIN and ALBERT EINSTEIN are trademarks of The Hebrew University of Jerusalem. All Rights Reserved.

Walt Disney's Bambi is based on the original story by Felix Salten.

Captain Eo; Indiana Jones™ Adventure, Indiana Jones™ Adventure: Temple of the Crystal Skull, Indiana Jones™ and the Temple of Peril: Backwards!, Indiana Jones™ Epic Stunt Spectacular!, and Star Tours © Disney/Lucasfilm, Ltd.

Dumbo is based on the Walt Disney motion picture Dumbo, suggested by the story Dumbo, the flying elephant, by Helen Aberson and Harold Pearl. Copyright © 1939 by Rollabook Publishers.

Mary Poppins is based on the Walt Disney motion picture Mary Poppins, based on the series of books by P. L. Travers.

Mr. Potato Head® and Mrs. Potato Head® are registered trademarks of Hasbro, Inc. Used with permission. © Hasbro Inc. All rights reserved.

MUPPETS mark & logo and characters are trademarks of Muppets Holding Company, LLC. © Muppets Holding Company, LLC. Muppet*Vision 3D™ & © 2004 Muppets Holding Company.

One Hundred and One Dalmatians is based on the book by Dodie Smith, published by Viking Press.

Oswald the Rabbit Copyright © by Universal City Studios, Inc. Courtesy of Universal Studios Publishing Rights. All Rights Reserved.

Roger Rabbit characters © Walt Disney Pictures/Amblin Entertainment, Inc.

Slinky® Dog © James Industries.

TARZAN'S TREEHOUSE® is a registered trademark of Edgar Rice Burroughs, Inc. All rights reserved. Trademark TARZAN Owned by Edgar Rice Burroughs, Inc. Used by permission.

The Twilight Zone® is a registered trademark of CBS, Inc., and is used pursuant to a license from CBS, Inc.

Winnie the Pooh characters based on the "Winnie the Pooh" works by A. A. Milne and E. H. Shepard.

Academy Award® and Oscar® are registered trademarks of the Academy of Motion Picture Arts and Sciences.

Emmy is a registered trademark of the Academy of Television Arts and Sciences. Golden Globe(s)® is the registered trademark of the Hollywood Foreign Press Association. Grammy is a registered trademark of the National Academy of Recording Arts and Sciences, Inc.

IMAX® is a registered trademark of IMAX Corporation.

Tony Award is the registered trademark of American Theatre Wing, Inc.

Library of Congress Cataloging-in-Publication Data on file.
ISBN: 0-7868-4919-3
Printed in the United States of America
This book was set in Simoncini Garamond.
Designed by Michael Farmer
First Edition
10 9 8 7 6 5 4 3 2 1

Introduction

Disney *A to Z: The Official Disney Encyclopedia* is the first of its kind, a unique reference book. When it was originally published in 1996, it contained over 5,200 entries in alphabetical order. Now, in its third edition, the encyclopedia's total number of entries is up to 6,500. It has been eight years since the second edition in 1998. During those years, The Walt Disney Company has expanded greatly, from $23 billion in annual revenues to the current $30 billion-plus. Disney has made great strides: launching a second cruise ship; releasing 144 new feature films; adding exciting park attractions, hotels, restaurants, and shops; debuting 77 new television series; celebrating the Millennium and the 100th anniversary of Walt Disney's birth; producing new stage shows in Berlin, London, and on Broadway; and opening new theme parks in Florida, California, France, Japan, and Hong Kong, not to mention celebrating the 50th anniversary of the first Disney theme park—Disneyland. This growth has required not only almost a thousand new entries, but also more than 1,250 changes to existing entries, as awards are won, television shows end, attractions close and make way for new ones, and executives move on to new positions.

Everything you might want to look up about Disney is available in this book, in an easy-to-use form. The encyclopedia attempts to list all Disney theatrical shorts and features; all Disney television shows, series, and specials; all Disney educational and nontheatrical films; all Disney park attractions, along with the major park resorts, restaurants, and shops; key Disney company personnel; primary actors in Disney films and television productions; important songs; and many other elements that make up the world of Disney. The primary coverage is from the beginnings of the company up through 2005. Under the film entries one can learn when the film was released, who starred in it, who directed it, what its running time was, where it was filmed, what it was about, and any interesting facts about its production. The park entries tell you when a particular attraction or restaurant opened, along with its closing date if it is no longer there. The actor and actress entries tell what films the person starred in, and the role he or she played, along with any television appearances. There are special lists of Disney Academy Awards and Emmy Awards, animated features, cartoons starring the major characters, Mouseketeers through the years, feature films in chronological order, the Disney Channel Premiere Films, and television series.

The genesis of this encyclopedia project was in January 1994. The day after the 6.8 earthquake hit Los Angeles, I had a meeting scheduled at the Walt Disney Studio with Bob Miller of Hyperion Books to discuss possible future Disney-themed books that they might publish. As the building housing the Walt Disney Archives received major structural damage in the earthquake, everything was in disarray and we had to have our meeting at an outdoor table at the nearby studio commissary. As we sat there talking, one book I mentioned was one I had always felt would be of great interest to readers everywhere—a Disney encyclopedia. While I knew the book would be useful, I also knew that it would take a tremendous amount of research and writing. While it was something I would be very interested in attempting, I explained that this might be a project that I would probably only be able to undertake after I retired.

As the months went on, however, I continued to think about the encyclopedia, and I realized that I did not want to wait for my retirement. The book would be of great help to those of us in the Walt Disney Archives because it would combine detailed information from any number of different files. Everything would be in one alphabet, easy to look up when someone called with a question on the telephone. So, in June 1994, I decided to begin the compilation of the encyclopedia. Since I had no extra time during my workday, it would have to be done on my own time, at home on my own computer. The research phase took more than 380 hours of my time over the next six months, not to mention the additional hours put in by research assistants.

I want to extend special thanks to four people who have spent many hours helping me to compile the needed information. Michael Troyan acted as my research assistant on the theatrical films, ferreting out little-known facts and helping to draft the entries. Steven Clark and David Mumford helped with park-related items, fleshing out a number of the entries. Brian Hoffman, Shelly Graham, and Michael Buckhoff on my staff helped compile and process the photographs for

this new edition. Thanks also go to the rest of my staff at the Walt Disney Archives (and Photo Library)—Robert Tieman, Rebecca Cline, Collette Espino, Ed Squair, and Andrea Recendez-Carbone. I could never have compiled this book had it not been for the indexes, lists, bibliographies, and catalogs prepared in the Walt Disney Archives over the past 35 years of its existence. For that reason, I extend my deepest thanks to former staff members Carol Svendsen, Les Perkins, John Cawley, Robert McGrath, Paula Sigman, Karen Brower, Jennifer Hendrickson, Rose Motzko, Joanne Warren, Jan Loveton, Adina Lerner, Steve Rogers, Lizza Andres, and Brigitte Dubin. Support and advice have also come from Tony Anselmo, Dean Barickman, Russell Brower, Kerry Caldwell, Steven Cannady, Bryan Castleberry, Jonathan Clough, Bill Cotter, Carol Davis-Perkins, Jerry Edwards, Tyson Ervin, Will Herbig, Richard Jordan, Anders Krantz, Julian Lowy, Tom McKee, Michael Maney, Stacia Martin, John Mauro, Trevor Nelson, Clay Shoemaker, Russell Schroeder, Andrew Swailes, Tracy Terhune, and Steve Vagnini. At Hyperion and Disney Editions, I extend my gratitude to Bob Miller, Wendy Lefkon, and Jody Revenson.

Because encyclopedias such as this tend to become dated rapidly, my aim is to keep the information up to date, and provide that supplement on a monthly basis for publication on the official Disney Internet Web site. I always welcome suggestions of new entries, along with changes or revisions. You can write me at the Walt Disney Archives, 500 S. Buena Vista St., Burbank, CA 91521-3040, or by e-mail to dave.smith@disney.com.

Dave Smith
Archives Director
The Walt Disney Company
Spring 2006

A

Aames, Willie Actor; appeared on television in *Twister*, *Bull from the Sky*, and *Runaway on the Rogue River*.

A&E Network With the acquisition of Capital Cities/ABC in 1996, Disney obtained a 37.5 percent ownership of the A&E Network, known for its *Biography* series and high-profile specials and original dramas.

Abbate, Nancy Mouseketeer from the 1950s television show.

Abbott, Chuck Legendary attractions host and foreman at Disneyland for 36 years, beginning in 1955. He was named a Disney Legend in 2005.

ABC See American Broadcasting Company.

ABC Commissary Restaurant at Disney-MGM Studios; opened on December 16, 1990, as The Commissary. Loosely patterned after a movie studio commissary, it features movie and television awards on display. It became the ABC Commissary on July 1, 1997.

ABC Family New channel created from  the old Fox Family Channel, after its acquisition by Disney on October 24, 2001. It targets adults aged 18–34, featuring original movies and specials.

ABC Kids The ABC-TV network's Saturday morning programming block of shows  for kids, beginning on September 14, 2002. It includes programming also featured on Disney Channel, Toon Disney, and ABC Family.

ABC of Hand Tools, The (film) Training film showing the proper use and care of common hand tools, as well as the type of work performed by each tool; made for General Motors Corporation and delivered to them on February 5, 1946. Directed by Bill Roberts. General Motors continued to use the film and several editions of the accompanying booklet for many years as part of its training course.

ABC Soap Opera Bistro Restaurant at Hollywood Pictures Backlot at Disney's California Adventure, opened February 8, 2001, and closed November 4, 2002.

ABC Sound Studio Sound effects demonstration attraction, titled One Saturday Morning, opening July 1, 1997, and closing February 20,

1999, at Disney-MGM Studios at Walt Disney World Resort, formerly the Monster Sound Show. Seven guests add sound effects to a *One Hundred and One Dalmatians* cartoon and then the audience watches the humorous results. A new show, Sounds Dangerous, starring Drew Carey as gumshoe Charlie Foster, opened on April 22, 1999.

ABC Sound Studio: Sounds Dangerous
Sound effects attraction at Disney-MGM Studios; opened April 22, 1999. (See also Monster Sound Show and ABC Sound Studio.)

ABC1 The first ABC-branded international television channel debuted in the United Kingdom in September 2004 and airs acquired programming as well as ABC shows from the United States.

Abner Country mouse in *The Country Cousin* (1936).

Absent-Minded Inventors and the Search for Flubber (television) Half-hour television special, airing on ABC on November 21, 1997. A humorous look at strange inventions of the past and a promo for the release of *Flubber*. Hosted by Bill Nye.

Absent-Minded Professor, The (film) For the third time, Professor Ned Brainard of Medfield College is so engrossed in a scientific experiment he fails to show up for his wedding with pretty Betsy Carlisle. But although he loses his girl to rival Professor Shelby Ashton, his absent-mindedness pays off with the creation of Flubber, a rubbery substance with an antigravity agent. With his new invention he is able to make the puny Medfield basketball team win against Rutland College, prevent a crook, Alonzo Hawk, from stealing Flubber, and win back Betsy, flying on a Flubberized Model T to Washington to give the powerful creation to a grateful government. Released on March 16, 1961.

Directed by Robert Stevenson in black and white. 96 min. Stars Fred MacMurray (Ned Brainard), Nancy Olson (Betsy Carlisle), Keenan Wynn (Alonzo Hawk), Ed Wynn (Fire Chief), Tommy Kirk (Biff Hawk), Leon Ames (Rufus Daggett), Edward Andrews (Defense Secretary), and Elliott Reid (Shelby Ashton). The special effects were created by Robert A. Mattey and Eustace Lycett, who were nominated for an Academy Award, and included the sodium screen matte process, as well as miniatures and wire-supported mock-ups. The film's "Medfield Fight Song" was written by Richard M. Sherman and Robert B. Sherman, their first song for a Disney feature. The motion picture, made on a small budget, did fine business at the box office, led to a sequel, *Son of Flubber*, and had theatrical reissues in 1967 and 1974. Released on video in black and white in 1981 and 1993, and in a colorized version in 1986, after an airing on The Disney Channel in March of that year. This was the first Disney film to be colorized, but the process was still in its infancy and the results were less than spectacular. In 1988–89, two television episodes based on the film were produced, starring Harry Anderson. (See also *Flubber*.)

Absent-Minded Professor, The (television) Henry Crawford, an absent-minded professor, programs his computer, named Albert in honor of Albert Einstein, to remind him of his girlfriend's poetry reading. But the computer was also programmed to analyze some old papers Henry found in his attic, and just before leaving for the poetry reading, he tests one formula. When an experiment goes awry, the result is a sort of flying rubber, called Flubber. The girlfriend, Ellen Whitley, does not share Henry's enthusiasm for his new substance, which he uses on some shoes and his Model T Ford. Albert is stolen by some teenagers, but Henry manages to get it back and patch things up with Ellen. Aired on November 27, 1988. Directed by Robert Sheerer. Stars Harry Anderson (Henry Crawford), Mary Page Keller (Ellen Whitley), Cory Danziger (Gus), David Paymer (Oliphant), James Noble (Dr. Blount), Bibi Osterwald (Mrs. Nakamura), Stephen Dorff (Curtis), Jason Zalder (Greg). Roughly based on the 1961 feature film.

Absent-Minded Professor, The: Trading Places (television) Henry Crawford is persuaded by ex-roommate Jack Brooker to switch places. Henry will go to work at the top secret Rhinebloom Labs, and Jack will teach Henry's classes. What Henry doesn't know is that Jack is worried that the lab may be involved in something illegal. When Henry tries to find out what is going on by using his computer, Albert, a virus is put into the computer. Henry and Jack learn the project is a weapons system, and, by using Flubber, they are able to sabotage a demonstration. Aired on February 26, 1989. Directed by Bob Sweeney. Stars Harry Anderson (Henry Crawford), Mary Page Keller (Ellen), Ed Begley, Jr. (Jack Brooker), James Noble (Dean Blount), Richard Sanders (Dr. Dark), Ron Fassler (Hacker). A sequel to the 1988 television episode *The Absent-Minded Professor*.

Abu Aladdin's monkey friend, "voiced" by Frank Welker.

Academy Award Review of Walt Disney Cartoons (film) Compilation of five Oscar-winning cartoons, *Flowers and Trees*, *Three Little Pigs*, *The Tortoise and the Hare*, *Three Orphan Kittens*, and *The Country Cousin*, released on May 19, 1937, partly to herald the forthcoming release of Walt's first feature-length animated film, *Snow White and the Seven Dwarfs*.

Academy Awards As of 2005, Disney has won a total of 86 Academy Awards, but the impressive number is that of these, 32 were won by Walt Disney personally. This is by far the record, and Walt Disney is in the Guinness *Book of World Records*.

(Second in line is Cedric Gibbons, the MGM art director, with 11 awards, and tied for third is costume designer Edith Head and the composer Alan Menken with eight.) Most of Walt Disney's awards came to him as producer of a film. He also won the prestigious Irving Thalberg Award, given by the Academy of Motion Picture Arts and Sciences. Animated Disney characters have occasionally appeared on the Academy Awards show. While Minnie, Donald, and Daisy watched from the audience, Mickey Mouse interacted with Tom Selleck in 1988, an animated Belle and Beast appeared in 1992, Snow White in 1993, and Woody and Buzz from *Toy Story* in 1996. The use of a live Snow White in an uncomplimentary musical number with Rob Lowe in 1989 led to an immediate lawsuit by Disney, which was dropped after the Academy offered an apology.

The awards, listed by the year in which they were presented, are as follows:

1932
1)* *Flowers and Trees* (Cartoon Short Subject, 1931–32)
2)* Special Award to Walt Disney for the creation of Mickey Mouse

1934
3)* *Three Little Pigs* (Cartoon Short Subject, 1932–33)

1935
4)* *The Tortoise and the Hare* (Cartoon Production, 1934)

* presented to Walt Disney

1936

5)* *Three Orphan Kittens* (Cartoon Production, 1935)

1937

6)* *The Country Cousin* (Cartoon Short Subject, 1936)

1938

7)* *The Old Mill* (Cartoon Short Subject, 1937)

8)* Top Technical Award to Walt Disney Productions for the design and application to production of the Multi-Plane Camera, 1937

1939

9)* *Ferdinand the Bull* (Cartoon Short Subject, 1938)

10)* Special Award to Walt Disney for *Snow White and the Seven Dwarfs*—recognized as a significant screen innovation which has charmed millions and pioneered a great new entertainment field for the motion picture cartoon

1940

11)* *The Ugly Duckling* (Cartoon Short Subject, 1939)

1941

12) *Pinocchio* (Song, 1940: "When You Wish Upon A Star" by Leigh Harline and Ned Washington)

13) *Pinocchio* (Original Score, 1940, by Leigh-Harline, Paul J. Smith, and Ned Washington)

1942

14)* Irving Thalberg Memorial Award to Walt Disney for "the most consistent high quality of production achievement by an individual producer." (This is not an Oscar but a special award in the form of a bust of Thalberg.)

15)* Special Technical Award for "outstanding contribution to the advancement of the use of sound in motion pictures through the production of *Fantasia*"

16)* *Lend a Paw* (Cartoon Short Subject, 1941)

17) Special Award to Leopold Stokowski and associates for their achievement "in the creation of a new form of visualized music" (*Fantasia*)

18) *Dumbo* (Original Score, 1941, by Frank Churchill and Oliver Wallace)

1943

19)* *Der Fuehrer's Face* (Best Cartoon Short Subject, 1942–43)

1947

20) Special Technical Award to Members of the Walt Disney Studio Sound Department, for a process of checking and locating noise in sound tracks

1948

21) *Song of the South* (Song, 1947: "Zip-A-Dee-Doo-Dah"; Music by Allie Wrubel, Lyrics by Ray Gilbert)

22) *Song of the South* (Honorary Award to James Baskett, for his "able and heartwarming characterization of Uncle Remus, friend and storyteller to the children of the world")

1949

23)* *Seal Island* (Two-Reel Short Subject, 1948)

1950

24) Honorary Award to Bobby Driscoll, outstanding juvenile actor of 1949 (performances included *So Dear to My Heart*)

1951

25)* *In Beaver Valley* (Two-Reel Short Subject, 1950)

1952

26)* *Nature's Half Acre* (Two-Reel Short Subject, 1951)

1953

27)* *Water Birds* (Two-Reel Short Subject, 1952)

1954

28)* *The Living Desert* (Documentary Feature, 1953)

29)* *Bear Country* (Two-Reel Short Subject, 1953)

30)* *The Alaskan Eskimo* (Documentary Short Subject, 1953)

31)* *Toot, Whistle, Plunk and Boom* (Cartoon Short Subject, 1953)

1955

32)* *The Vanishing Prairie* (Documentary Feature, 1954)

33)* *20,000 Leagues Under the Sea* (Achievement with Special Effects, 1954)

34) *20,000 Leagues Under the Sea* (Achievement in Art and Set Decoration, 1954; John Meehan and Emile Kuri)

1956

35)* *Men Against the Arctic* (Documentary Short Subject, 1955)

1958

36)* *The Wetback Hound* (Live-Action Short Subject, 1957; Walt Disney, executive producer; Larry Lansburgh, producer)

1959

37)* *White Wilderness* (Documentary Feature, 1958)

38)* *Grand Canyon* (Live-Action Short Subject, 1958)

39)* *Ama Girls* (Documentary Short Subject, 1958; Walt Disney, executive producer; Ben Sharpsteen, producer)

1960

40) Special Technical Award to Ub Iwerks for the design of an improved optical printer for special effects and matte shots

1961

41)* *The Horse With the Flying Tail* (Documentary Feature, 1960; Walt Disney, executive producer; Larry Lansburgh, producer)

42) *Pollyanna* (Honorary Award to Hayley Mills for the most outstanding juvenile performance during 1960)

1965

43) *Mary Poppins* (Actress, 1964; Julie Andrews)

44) *Mary Poppins* (Song, 1964: "Chim-Chim Cheree" by Richard M. Sherman and Robert B. Sherman)

45) *Mary Poppins* (Musical Score, Original, 1964, by Richard M. Sherman and Robert B. Sherman)

46) *Mary Poppins* (Film Editing, 1964; Cotton Warburton)

47) *Mary Poppins* (Special Visual Effects, 1964; Peter Ellenshaw, Hamilton Luske, and Eustace Lycett)

48) Special Technical Award to Peter Vlahos, Wadsworth Pohl, and Ub Iwerks for conception and perfection of techniques of color traveling matte composite cinematography [*Mary Poppins*]

1969

49)* *Winnie the Pooh and the Blustery Day* (Cartoon Short Subject, 1968; Walt Disney, executive producer)

1970

50) *It's Tough to Be a Bird* (Cartoon Short Subject, 1969; Ward Kimball, producer)

1972

51) *Bedknobs and Broomsticks* (Special Visual Effects, 1971; Danny Lee, Eustace Lycett, and Alan Maley)

1986

52) Technical Achievement Award to David W. Spencer for the development of an Animation Photo Transfer process (APT)

1987

53) *The Color of Money* (Actor, 1986; Paul Newman)

1989

54) *Who Framed Roger Rabbit* (Award for Special Achievement in Animation Direction to Richard Williams)

55) *Who Framed Roger Rabbit* (Film Editing, 1988; Arthur Schmidt)

56) *Who Framed Roger Rabbit* (Sound Effects Editing, 1988; Charles L. Campbell, Louis L. Edemann)

57) *Who Framed Roger Rabbit* (Visual Effects, 1988; Ken Ralston, Richard Williams, Edward Jones, George Gibbs)

1990

58) *Dead Poets Society* (Original Screenplay, 1989; Tom Schulman)

59) *The Little Mermaid* (Original Score, 1989; Alan Menken)

60) *The Little Mermaid* (Best Song, 1989: "Under the Sea"; Music by Alan Menken, Lyrics by Howard Ashman)

1991

61) *Dick Tracy* (Makeup, 1990; John Caglione, Jr., Doug Drexler)

62) *Dick Tracy* (Art Direction/Set Decoration, 1990; Richard Sylbert [art]; Rick Simpson [set])

63) *Dick Tracy* (Best Song, 1990: "Sooner or Later [I Always Get My Man]"; Music and Lyrics by Stephen Sondheim)

1992

64) Scientific/Technical Award to Members of the Walt Disney Feature Animation Department, for CAPS (Computer Animated Production System), showcased in *Beauty and the Beast*. The system enables the seamless combination of hand-drawn and computer animation. Disney employees receiving awards: Randy Cartwright, David B. Coons, Lem Davis, James Houston, Mark Kimball, Thomas Hahn, Peter Nye, Michael Shantzis, and David F. Wolf

65) Scientific/Technical award to YCM Laboratories for the motion picture restoration process with liquid gate and registration correction on a contact printer, as used in the restoration of *Fantasia*

66) *Beauty and the Beast* (Original Score, 1991; Alan Menken)

67) *Beauty and the Beast* (Best Song, 1991: "Beauty and the Beast"; Music by Alan Menken, Lyrics by Howard Ashman)

1993

68) *Aladdin* (Original Score, 1992; Alan Menken)

69) *Aladdin* (Best Song, 1992: "A Whole New World"; Music by Alan Menken, Lyrics by Tim Rice)

1995

70) *Ed Wood* (Supporting Actor, 1994; Martin Landau)

71) *Ed Wood* (Makeup, 1994; Rick Baker, Ve Neill, Yolanda Toussieng)

72) *The Lion King* (Original Score, 1994; Hans Zimmer)

73) *The Lion King* (Best Song, 1994: "Can You Feel the Love Tonight"; Music by Elton John, Lyrics by Tim Rice)

1996

74) Special Achievement Oscar, 1995, to John Lasseter, director and co-writer of *Toy Story*, for "the development and inspired application of techniques that have made possible the first feature-length computer-animated film"

75) *Pocahontas* (Original Musical or Comedy Score, 1995; Alan Menken and Stephen Schwartz)

76) *Pocahontas* (Best Song, 1995: "Colors of the Wind"; Music by Alan Menken, Lyrics by Stephen Schwartz)

1997

77) *Evita* (Best Song, 1996: "You Must Love Me"; Music by Andrew Lloyd Webber, Lyrics by Tim Rice)

2000

78) *Tarzan* (Best Song, 1999: "You'll Be in My Heart"; Music and lyrics by Phil Collins)

79) Scientific/Technical Award to Hoyt H. Yeatman, Jr. of Dream Quest Images and John C. Brewer of Eastman Kodak for the identification and diagnosis leading to the elimination of the "red fringe" artifact in traveling matte composite photography.

2002

80) *Monsters, Inc.* (Best Song, 2001: "If I Didn't Have You"; Music and lyrics by Randy Newman)

81) *Pearl Harbor* (Best Sound Editing; George Watters II, Christopher Boyes)

2003

82) Scientific/Technical Award to Eric Daniels, George Kanatics, Tasso Lappas, and Chris

Springfield (Feature Animation) for the development of the Deep Canvas rendering software, which was used first in *Tarzan* and more extensively in *Treasure Planet*.

83) *Spirited Away* (Best Animated Feature, Hiyao Miyazaki, producer)

2004

84) *Finding Nemo* (Best Animated Feature, Andrew Stanton, producer)

2005

85) *The Incredibles* (Best Animated Feature, Brad Bird, writer-director)

86) *The Incredibles* (Best Sound Editing, Randy Thom, Michael Silvers)

According to Jim (television) A contemporary comedy half-hour series on ABC, premiering on September 26, 2001. Jim, a contractor in a design firm, is an all-American guy, with a smart and sophisticated wife, and three kids. He struggles with the issues of how to achieve the picket-fence ideal life, yet keep a firm grip on his manhood. Stars Jim Belushi (Jim), Courtney Thorne-Smith (Cheryl), Kimberly Williams (Dana), Larry Joe Campbell (Andy), Taylor Atelian (Ruby), Billi Bruno (Gracie). Produced by Touchstone Television in association with Brad Grey Television.

Ackerman, Josh Actor; appeared on the *Mickey Mouse Club* on The Disney Channel, beginning in 1989.

Acorn Ball Crawl Attraction opened in Mickey's Toontown at Disneyland on January 24, 1993. Kids can plunge and burrow into a huge pile of red and yellow balls.

Acting Sheriff (television) Unsold television pilot (30 min.) airing on CBS on August 17, 1991. Directed by Michael Lembeck. A small-time movie actor applies for the job of sheriff of a small Northern California town. Stars Robert Goulet, John Putch, Hillary Bailey Smith.

Adès, Lucien (1920–1992) French music publisher who pioneered sing-along books in the 1950s. He was named a European Disney Legend in 1997.

Admiral Joe Fowler Riverboat Frontierland attraction in Magic Kingdom Park at Walt Disney World, operated from October 2, 1971 until the fall of 1980, when it was retired from the waterways. Its sister ship, the *Richard F. Irvine*, remained. The *Admiral Joe Fowler* was named after the retired admiral who was in charge of construction of both Disneyland and Walt Disney World.

Adrian, Iris (1913–1994) Character actress; appeared in *That Darn Cat!* (landlady), *The Love Bug, Scandalous John, The Apple Dumpling Gang* (Poker Patty), *The Shaggy D.A.* (manageress), *Freaky Friday* (bus passenger), *Herbie Goes Bananas*.

Adventure in Art, An (television) Television show, aired April 30, 1958. Directed by Wilfred Jackson and C. August Nichols. Walt, using Robert Henri's book, *The Art Spirit*, as a reference, explains how people see art in different ways, including the history of silhouettes, and he has four of his artists, each with a different style, paint one tree. That segment, featuring Marc Davis, Eyvind Earle, Joshua Meador, and Walt Peregoy, was later released as an educational film entitled *4 Artists Paint 1 Tree*. The show also emphasizes how music can be an inspiration to artists, as in Bach's *Toccata and Fugue in D Minor* from *Fantasia*.

Adventure in Color, An/Mathmagic Land (television) The first television show of *Walt Disney's Wonderful World of Color*, when the series moved to NBC, changed its title from *Walt Disney Presents*, and began telecasting in color. Aired on September 24, 1961. Directed by Hamilton S. Luske. The show introduced the new character, Professor Ludwig Von Drake, who gives a comic lesson about color. The kaleidoscopic opening, set to the new title song, "The Wonderful World of Color," by Richard M. Sherman and Robert B. Sherman, helped show off color television sets, and make other viewers think, "Oh, how great this must look in color," to the obvious glee of RCA, one of the sponsors. Veteran voice actor, Paul Frees, provided Von Drake's voice. The show concluded with *Donald in Mathmagic Land*.

Adventure in Dairyland (television) Serial on the *Mickey Mouse Club* during the 1956–57 season. Annette Funicello and Sammy Ogg visit a Wisconsin dairy farm. The first Disney appearance of Kevin Corcoran, here playing Moochie McCandless. Also stars Herb Newcombe, Fern Persons, Glen Graber, Mary Lu Delmonte. Directed by William Beaudine. 8 episodes.

Adventure in Satan's Canyon (television) Television show; aired November 3, 1974. Directed by William Beaudine, Jr. A young man tries to master the kayak, and becomes a hero in helping to save his coach, who is badly injured in an accident. To accomplish this feat, the young man has to navigate some very dangerous rapids in his kayak, giving himself confidence. The show was filmed in the wilds of the Pacific Northwest, and along the Stanislaus River in California. Stars Richard Jaeckel, David Alan Bailey, Larry Pennell.

Adventure in the Magic Kingdom, An (television) Television show; aired April 9, 1958. Directed by Hamilton S. Luske. Tinker Bell leads a guided tour of Disneyland, which includes a live performance of the Mouseketeers in Holidayland and a sampling of fun and entertainment throughout the park. The show ends with the spectacular fireworks display in the sky above the castle.

Adventure in Wildwood Heart (television) Television show; aired September 25, 1957. Directed by Hamilton S. Luske. Producer Winston Hibler explains how *Perri*, Disney's first and only True-Life Fantasy, was filmed. The film crew was so entranced by their setting in Utah, that it became known among them as Wildwood Heart. It took almost three years to film the adventures of the squirrels.

Adventure Isle Area in Adventureland at Disneyland Paris; opened April 12, 1992, with secret

caves, grottos, waterfalls, a floating bridge, and a suspension bridge.

Adventure Story, The (television) Television show, aired March 20, 1957. Directed by Wolfgang Reitherman. The story of the exploits of the Goofy family through the ages. New animation of fictional Goofy relatives was used to tie together five Goofy cartoons made between 1945 and 1953.

Adventure Thru Inner Space Tomorrowland attraction at Disneyland, from August 5, 1967 to September 2, 1985. Sponsored by Monsanto. Guests sat in an Atomobile and were transported through a giant microscope to see what the inside of an atom might be like. The attraction was removed to make way for Star Tours.

Adventureland One of the original lands of Disneyland, most noted for the Jungle Cruise, which takes up most of its space. The land was suggested by Walt's True-Life Adventure series. Also in Magic Kingdom Park at Walt Disney World, at Tokyo Disneyland, at Disneyland Paris, and at Hong Kong Disneyland.

Adventureland Bazaar Shop in Adventureland at Disneyland, featuring leather, wood-carvings, jewelry, ceramics, and other exotic wares from around the world. Opened on July 17, 1955. A number of years later, the designers working on a rehab of this shop dug around in the warehouses at Disneyland and found two of the old ticket booths that used to be in front of Disneyland attractions, which they then disguised as sales counters. They were removed during a major remodeling in 1994. Also at Tokyo Disneyland; opened April 15, 1983.

Adventureland Veranda Restaurant in Magic Kingdom Park at Walt Disney World; opened on October 1, 1971, serving fast food with a tropical flavor (such as teriyaki sauce and a pineapple ring on a hamburger). Sponsored by Kikkoman beginning October 5, 1977. It closed in 1994.

Adventurer's Club Nightclub at Pleasure Island at Walt Disney World; opened on May 1, 1989. Features memorabilia supposedly from Merriweather Adam Pleasure's trips around the world, including some curios which interact with guests.

Adventures by Disney Travel program with tours to Wyoming and Hawaii beginning in May 2005. Planned as an immersive experience for a family, each tour for about 30 guests will have two Disney tour guides. Activities in the weeklong vacation will be planned around stories, much as are many of the Disney park attractions.

Adventures in Babysitting (film) Seventeen-year-old Chris Parker's babysitting assignment turns to bedlam when a frightened friend calls her from a bus station. Packing her charges into the family station wagon, they head for downtown Chicago to save the friend. They find themselves caught up in a comic nightmare in the urban jungle of the big city, a place very different from the suburbia which they know, tangling with car thieves, bums, and other unsavory characters. Released on July 1, 1987. Directed by Chris Columbus. A Touchstone film. 102 min. Stars Elisabeth Shue (Chris), Maia Brewton (Sara), Keith Coogan (Brad), Anthony Rapp (Daryl). Released on video in 1988. Coogan, under the name, Keith Mitchell, had provided the voice of the young Tod in *The Fox and the Hound* in 1981. Filmed on location in Chicago and Toronto. Released in England as *A Night on the Town*.

Adventures in Babysitting (television) Pilot for a television series based on the 1987 Touch-

stone feature; aired on CBS on July 7, 1989. 30 min. Directed by Joel Zwick. The babysitter takes her charges to a convenience store, which is then robbed. Stars Jennifer Guthrie, Joey Lawrence, Courtney Peldon, Brian Austin Green.

Adventures in Fantasy (television) Television show, aired November 6, 1957. Directed by Bill Justice. Tells how the inanimate can be brought to life through animation, with examples from the stories of *Johnny Fedora and Alice Bluebonnet; The Little House; Susie, the Little Blue Coupe;* and *Little Toot*.

Adventures in Music: Melody (film) Special cartoon; released on May 28, 1953. Directed by Charles Nichols and Ward Kimball. Professor Owl tries to teach his class about melody. Includes the song "The Bird and the Cricket and the Willow Tree." First cartoon ever filmed in 3-D. It was shown in the Fantasyland Theater at Disneyland as part of the *3D Jamboree*. The 3-D process never really caught on with theater audiences because of the need to wear the polarized glasses, but the show remained a novelty at Disneyland for several years. This film was the first in a proposed series of shorts where Professor Owl would teach musical principles to his class, but only one more, *Toot, Whistle, Plunk and Boom*, was made.

Adventures in Wonderland See *Disney's Adventures in Wonderland*.

Adventures of Bullwhip Griffin, The (film) At the time of the California Gold Rush, a young boy from Boston runs away to California to try and restore his family's fortune, pursued by the very proper family butler. The butler, Griffin, as the result of a lucky punch, becomes mistakenly renowned as a boxer. In a series of adventures, both boy and butler tangle with a crook who uses many disguises. But they find their fortune, and the staid butler becomes his own man and marries the boy's attractive older sister. Released on March 3, 1967. Directed by James Neilson. 110 min. Stars Bryan Russell (Jack Flagg), Roddy McDowall (Bullwhip Griffin), Suzanne Pleshette (Arabella Flagg), Karl Malden (Judge Higgins), Harry Guardino (Sam Trimble), Richard Haydn (Quentin Bartlett), Hermione Baddeley (Irene Chesney). Haydn had 16 years earlier voiced the Caterpillar in *Alice in Wonderland*. Released on video in 1986. Based on the book, *By the Great Horn Spoon*, by Sid Fleischman. Ward Kimball was credited with "titles and things," which included some inventive animation tidbits.

Adventures of Chip 'n Dale, The (television) Television show, aired February 27, 1959. Directed by Bill Justice. Chip and Dale as guest hosts present several cartoons in which they star. Retitled for a 1978 rerun as *Mixed Nuts* and for later reruns as *The Misadventures of Chip 'n Dale*.

Adventures of Clint and Mac, The (television) Serial on the *Mickey Mouse Club* during the 1957–58 season. Directed by Terrence Fisher. Two boys become involved with thieves in England who have stolen a famous manuscript from the British Museum. Stars Neil Wolfe, Jonathan Bailey, Sandra Michaels, John Warwick, Dorothy Smith, Bill Nagy, Mary Barclay. Narrated by Tim Considine. 15 episodes.

Adventures of Huck Finn, The (film) A carefree boy who hates his stifled existence under adoption to the Widow Douglas and Miss Watson fakes his own murder and sets off down the Mississippi with a runaway slave, Jim, as a companion. Jim dreams of traveling downriver to Cairo, Illinois, to buy his wife and children out of bondage. Along the way, Huck and Jim escape a deadly feud between two neighboring families and meet up with two crafty con men, the King and the Duke. When these two attempt to steal the family fortune of the wealthy Wilks family, Huck cannot stand for it, and he tries to destroy their plot. His success brings him the gratitude of the Wilks sisters, who help Jim buy back his family. Based on the Mark Twain book. Released on April 2, 1993. Directed by Stephen Sommers. 108 min. Stars Elijah Wood (Huck), Courtney B. Vance (Jim), Robbie Coltrane (The Duke), Jason Robards (The King). Primary filming took place in the vicinity of Natchez, Mississippi. Released on video in 1993.

Adventures of Ichabod and Mr. Toad, The (film) The film begins in a library with actor Basil Rathbone telling the tale of *The Wind in the Willows* (from the book by Kenneth Grahame), about Mr. Toad, Squire of Toad Hall, whose love for transportation vehicles was insatiable. His friends, Rat, Mole, and MacBadger try to help him when his mania leads to the loss of the deed to Toad Hall and a charge of car theft. Toad is thrown in jail, but on escaping, he learns Winkie, the tavern-keeper, and the weasels have taken over Toad Hall, and with his friends, Toad redeems his good name by recovering the deed to the estate and promises to reform, until he eyes a 1908 biplane. Back in the library, singer Bing Crosby picks up with *The Legend of Sleepy Hollow* (by Washington Irving), in which Ichabod Crane, a new school-teacher, arrives in Sleepy Hollow and captures every lady's heart except for Katrina Van Tassel, daughter of a wealthy farmer. Ichabod has his eye on the Van Tassel wealth, but his attempts to woo Katrina disturb her bold suitor, Brom Bones, who tries to scare Ichabod away with the tale of the Headless Horseman. As Ichabod rides home that Halloween evening, he encounters the terrifying phantom and is mysteriously missing the next morning. While the townspeople spread rumors of Ichabod's whereabouts, Katrina weds Brom. Released October 5, 1949. Directed by Jack Kinney, Clyde Geronimi, and James Algar. 68 min. Voices in the *Mr. Toad* segment included Eric Blore as Toad, J. Pat O'Malley as Cyril, his horse, and Claud Allister and Collin Campbell as his friends, Rat and Mole. Disney composer and this film's music director, Oliver Wallace, himself took the role of Winkie. Songs include "Ichabod," "Katrina," "The Headless Horseman," and "The Merrily Song." This was the last of the several package pictures of the 1940s, during which the Walt Disney Studio had deep economic problems. Expenses were lowered by reusing animation cycles from *The Old Mill* (1937) and by patterning Katrina closely on Grace Martin from *The Martins and the Coys*. Henceforth, Walt Disney would be able to finance the production of regular, one-story, animated features, beginning the next year with *Cinderella*. Its success ensured the continuation of animation at the Studio. The entire film of *The Adventures of Ichabod and Mr. Toad* was never released on video cassette, but the two parts were released separately. The complete feature was released on laser disc in 1992, and on video in 1999.

Adventures of J. Thaddeus Toad, The (film) Educational title of the featurette released theatrically as *The Madcap Adventures of Mr. Toad* and *Wind in the Willows*, released in September 1980. Originally part of *The Adventures of Ichabod and Mr. Toad*.

Adventures of Mickey Mouse, The (television) Television show; aired October 12, 1955.

Directed by Jack Hannah and Bill Roberts. Walt discusses the career of Mickey Mouse, showing several cartoons, including *Mickey and the Beanstalk*. Retitled for 1980 reruns as *Mickey's Greatest Adventures*, and edited for syndication as *Adventures with Mickey*.

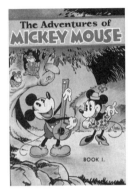

Adventures of Mickey Mouse, The The very first hardback Disney book, published by David McKay in 1931. The story names a number of the barnyard animals, among them Donald Duck. The character of Donald Duck was not actually created until three years later. The book was preceded only by the slim, paper-covered *Mickey Mouse Book*, published by Bibo-Lang in 1930.

Adventures of Pollyanna, The (television) Television show, aired on April 10, 1982, based on the theatrical film, *Pollyanna*. Directed by Robert Day. Stars Shirley Jones, Patsy Kensit, Edward Winter, Beverly Archer, Lucille Benson, John Putch. Pollyanna's Aunt Polly wants the girl to spend her time studying, but Pollyanna has other ideas. She joins a secret club with a group of orphans, and they spy on a mysterious new resident in town, only to learn that her standoffishness is because of her desire to shield a retarded son. Pollyanna helps the town accept the boy and his mother. The town square set at the Studio became the town of Harrington; it had been built for *Something Wicked This Way Comes*, and was later the last backlot set at the Studio to be torn down, in July 1994.

Adventures of Spin and Marty, The (television) Serial on the *Mickey Mouse Club* during the 1955–56 season, starring David Stollery and Tim Considine, about a spoiled rich kid, Marty

(Stollery), who goes to a summer boys' camp. Spin (Considine), who was the most popular kid from the previous summer, is back, and the two don't get along because Marty so obviously hates the camp. The summer climaxes with a big rodeo, and the boys eventually end their feud. Directed by William Beaudine, Sr. Also stars Roy Barcroft, Harry Carey, Jr., Lennie Geer, J. Pat O'Malley, B. G. Norman, Tim Hartnagel, Roger Broaddus, Sammy Ogg, Sammee Tong. 25 episodes. Episodes of the serial were edited together and shown on The Disney Channel as *Spin and Marty: The Movie* in October 1995. See also *The Further Adventures of Spin and Marty* and *The New Adventures of Spin and Marty.*

Adventures of the Great Mouse Detective, The 1992 reissue title of *The Great Mouse Detective.*

Adventures of the Gummi Bears See *Disney's Adventures of the Gummi Bears.*

Adventures of Tom Thumb & Thumbelina, The (film) Direct-to-video release on August 6, 2002, of an animated feature produced by Hyperion Studio. Thumbelina, a young teenage girl, is only six inches tall. She meets Tom Thumb, a teenager just a little shorter than herself, and the two embark on a fantastic quest together, leading them to the comically villainous Mole King. Directed by Glenn Chaika. Voices include Jennifer Love Hewitt (Thumbelina), Elijah Wood (Tom Thumb), Peter Gallagher (Mole King), Bebe Neuwirth (Queen Mother), Michael Chiklis (Roman), Robert Guillaume (Ben).

Adventures with Mickey (television) Syndicated, edited television version of *The Adventures of Mickey Mouse.*

Advice on Lice (film) Educational film, released in September 1985. Facts about the symptoms, transmission, treatment, and prevention of head lice.

Aesop's Hare and the Tortoise (film) Educational film, released in September 1986. 14 min.

Walt Disney introduces an animated overview of Aesop's life, by way of footage from one of his television lead-ins, followed by the popular fable. Retitled in 1987 as *An Introduction to Aesop.*

Affleck, Ben Actor; appeared in *Armageddon* (A.J. Frost) and *Pearl Harbor* (Rafe McCawley). He was also co-executive producer, with Matt Damon, on *Push, Nevada.*

Africa Before Dark (film) Oswald the Lucky Rabbit cartoon; released on February 20, 1928.

African Diary (film) Goofy bungles his way on safari in deepest Africa. The safari ends abruptly when a rhino chases Goofy and his safari all the way back to their ship on the Ivory Coast.

African Lion, The (film) True-Life Adventure feature, released on September 14, 1955. Directed by James Algar, with a notable musical score by Paul Smith. The photography team of Alfred and Elma Milotte spent three years in Africa studying the realm of the king of beasts, and came up with some fascinating footage of not only lions but giraffes, rhinoceroses, elephants, and baboons. The effects of a drought on the animals and the eventual tropical storms that end it round out the motion picture. The cost of film was not a major factor; the Milottes shot until they got the footage that would make an interesting film. Eventually only about six percent of the film they shot was used in the final production. The movie's theme of the annual life cycle would years later be echoed in "The Circle of

Life" in *The Lion King.* 72 min. See *His Majesty, King of the Beasts* for the abridged 1958 television

airing. For behind-the-scenes footage, see *Beaver Valley/Cameras in Africa*.

African Lion and His Realm, The (film) Portion of *The African Lion*, released on 16mm for schools in May 1969. A study of the lion reveals little-known facts about his domain and about other predators and grazers that live there.

After You've Gone (film) A segment of *Make Mine Music*, with the Benny Goodman Quartet, using the song by Henry Creamer and Turner Leighton; a surreal episode with anthropomorphic musical instruments.

Age of Not Believing, The Song from *Bedknobs and Broomsticks*, written by Richard M. Sherman and Robert B. Sherman. Nominated for an Academy Award.

Agrabah Fictional home of Aladdin.

Agrati, Don Mouseketeer from the 1950s television show. He was later known as Don Grady on *My Three Sons* and other shows.

Aguilera, Christina Actress; appeared on the *Mickey Mouse Club* on The Disney Channel, beginning in 1993. She became a top-selling pop vocalist, and sings the pop version of the song "Reflection" in *Mulan*.

Agutter, Jenny (1918–2005) Actress; appeared in *Amy* (Amy Medford), and on television years earlier as a child dancer in *Ballerina*.

Ahmanson, Caroline Leonetti Member of the Disney board of directors from 1975 to 1992.

Aida Stage musical version of the Aida story, with 19 new songs by Elton John and Tim Rice, opened as *Elaborate Lives: The Legend of Aida* at the Alliance Theater in Atlanta on October 7, 1998. This was the first cooperation between The Walt Disney Company and a nonprofit resident theater company. The title of the musical was shortened to *Aida* in 1999, when a CD of the sound track was released. The show played at Chicago's Palace Theatre from November 12, 1999 to January 9, 2000, and opened at the Palace Theatre on Broadway on March 23, 2000, after a month of previews, closing after a successful run on September 5, 2004. The story is about a love triangle between Aida, a Nubian princess forced into slavery, Amneris, an Egyptian princess, and Radames, the soldier they both love.

AIDS (film) Educational film, released in September 1986. 18 min. Facts on the human immune system and the AIDS virus. The film was revised a year later, with updated information.

AIDS: What Do We Tell Our Children? (film) Educational film, released in August 1987. 20 min. The facts about AIDS presented to children.

AIDS: You've Got to Do Something (film) Educational film, released in June 1992. 19 min. Narrated by Mayim Bialik. Provides teens with important facts about HIV and AIDS, with peer discussion and role-playing used to encourage them to become aware of individual and social responsibilities to help stop the spread of the disease.

Ainsley Harriott Show, The (television) Britain's television chef extraordinaire began a syndicated run from Buena Vista Television on January 10, 2000, of an entertainment-talk-cooking show produced in New York. The show ended on September 15, 2000. Stars Ainsley Harriott.

Air Bud (film) An aspiring 12-year-old basketball player, Josh Framm, trying to deal with the death of his father, moves with his family to the sleepy town of Fernfield, Washington, where he has no friends and is too shy to try out for the school basketball team. One day, he finds a runaway golden retriever while practicing on an abandoned court. The amazing thing about Buddy, the dog, is that he can accurately shoot hoops! Soon the two make the school basketball team and astound the media. But, there are problems when Buddy's bad-guy former owner, Norm Snively, discovers what is happening and comes up with a scheme to cash in on the dog's popularity. Josh and Buddy must keep one step ahead of Snively while rallying the town's school team as they aim for the state basketball finals. Directed by Charles Martin Smith. Released on August 11, 1997. Stars Kevin Zegers (Josh Framm), Michael Jeter (Norm Snively), Wendy Makkena (Jackie Framm), Eric Christmas (Judge Cranfield), Brendan Fletcher (Larry Willingham). 98 min. The dog, Buddy, was  discovered by his trainer, Kevin DiCicco, when he crawled out of the woods near DiCicco's cabin in the mountains near Yosemite National Park. The abused year-old dog was dirty and hungry, and DiCicco worked many months to get him back into shape, eventually discovering his talents. Buddy was soon making regular appearances, including two on David Letterman's "Stupid Pet Tricks." The town of Fernfield was created by the filmmakers in the environs of Vancouver, British Columbia. A sequel, *Air Bud: Golden Receiver*, starring Kevin Zegers (Josh Framm) and directed by Richard Martin, was released by Buena Vista Home Entertainment. There were three further video sequels: *Air Bud: World Pup*; *Air Bud: Seventh Inning Fetch*; and *Air Bud Spikes Back*.

Air Bud: Golden Receiver (film) Sequel to 1997's *Air Bud*; released on August 14, 1998. The basketball-playing dog, Buddy, helps out his best friend, Josh, by demonstrating that he also has amazing football talents to help Josh's team win the state championship. Directed by Richard Martin. Stars Kevin Zegers (Josh Framm), Cynthia Stevenson (Jackie), Gregory Harrison (Patrick). 90 min. Produced by Keystone Pictures and Dimension Films; released on video labeled "Disney Presents" by Buena Vista Home Entertainment.

Air Bud: Seventh Inning Fetch (film) The fourth film in the series, produced by Keystone Entertainment and released direct-to-video on June 18, 2002, by Walt Disney Home Entertainment. Andrea Framm joins the junior high school baseball team to escape the tedium of her home life. While she is not very good, her dog Buddy is a natural. But scientists interested in cloning kidnap the dog just before the big game. Directed by Robert Vince. Stars Caitlin Wachs (Andrea Framm), Richard Karn (Patrick), Cynthia Stevenson (Jackie), Kevin Zegers (Josh). 90 min.

Air Bud Spikes Back (film) Direct-to-video sequel produced by Keystone Entertainment; released on June 24, 2003, by Walt Disney Home Entertainment. Andrea Framm's best friend is moving out of town, so, to make new friends, she and Buddy join the local beach-volleyball team. Directed by Robert Vince. Stars Katija Pevec (Andrea), Jake D. Smith (Noah), Tyler Boissonnault (Connor), Cynthia Stevenson (Jackie), Edie McClurg (Grandma). 87 min.

Air Bud: World Pup (film) Direct-to-video sequel to *Air Bud* (1997) and *Air Bud Golden Receiver* (1998); released on December 12, 2000. Buddy's owner, Josh Framm, falls in love with his sister's new soccer coach, Emma, who also happens to be the only female on his high school's soccer team. Josh and Buddy join the soccer team, and Buddy himself falls in love with Emma's golden retriever, Molly. After some drama with kidnapped puppies, Buddy helps the team win the championship. Directed by Bill Bannerman. Stars Kevin Zegers (Josh Framm), Brittany Paige Bouck (Emma Putter), Caitlin Wachs (Andrea), Dale Midkiff (Patrick Framm). Several U.S. women's soccer players make cameo appearances. An *Air Bud* television series from Keystone Entertainment was not a Disney project.

Air Up There, The (film) Assistant college basketball coach Jimmy Dolan is a competitive sportsman with a goal of taking over when his boss, Coach Ray Fox, retires. However, in order to be considered for the position, Jimmy needs to prove that he knows how to recruit star talent. Since all the best players are signing with competing schools, the chances for Jimmy's advancement look bleak until he gets the wild idea to scout for a wonder player in Africa. In Kenya he discovers a tall Winabi warrior, Saleh, who cannot be dazzled by fast-talking recruiting techniques and promises of wonderful gifts and flashy cars. Jimmy's high-pressure techniques clash with the local customs, but he is finally able to prove himself when the tables are turned and he himself is recruited by the Winabi to help coach their misfit team so they can beat the team of a neighboring tribe, the Mingori, in a game with extremely high stakes—the Winabi's land, their cattle, and the future of the tribe. As a reward, Jimmy is able to draft the star player he needs. Directed by Paul M. Glaser. Released on January 7, 1994. A Hollywood Pictures film, in association with Interscope Communications. 107 min. Stars Kevin Bacon (Jimmy Dolan), Charles Gitonga Maina (Saleh), Yolanda Vazquez (Sister Susan), Winston Ntshona (Urudu). The filmmakers utilized the Samburu tribe of Northern Kenya, but transported them to the primary location in Hoedspruit, South Africa, for the filming. Other filming took place in Canada and Kenya. Released on video in 1994.

Ajax Title character in *Donald Duck and the Gorilla* (1944).

Akershus See Restaurant Akershus.

Aladdin (film) Animated feature about a street-smart young thief in the mythical city of Agrabah who meets and falls in love with the Sultan's beautiful daughter, Jasmine, a liberated young

lady who seeks to escape her present lifestyle. Help comes when the evil vizier, Jafar, plots to get a magic lamp for his own rise to power, and decides he needs Aladdin, a true "diamond in the rough," to seek the lamp in the Cave of Wonders.

Aladdin and his friend, the monkey Abu, gain the lamp and the wise-cracking Genie inside for themselves. The Genie changes Aladdin into a prince so he can woo the princess, but the deception fails to impress Jasmine. As his true self, however, he uses his cunning and courage, with the help of the Genie, to defeat Jafar and his evil plans, in the end earning a princely title and the princess. Initial release on November 11, 1992; general release on November 25, 1992. Directed by John Musker and Ron Clements. 90 min. Aladdin has a speaking voice provided by Scott Weinger and a singing voice by Brad Kane. Other voices are Robin Williams (Genie), Jonathan Freeman (Jafar), Linda Larkin (Jasmine speaking), Lea Salonga (Jasmine singing), and Gilbert Gottfried (Iago). The idea of adapting the Aladdin story as a Disney animated musical was first proposed by Howard Ashman in 1988 when he and Alan Menken were still working on *The Little Mermaid*. He wrote an initial treatment and collaborated on six songs with Menken, including "Arabian Nights," "Friend Like Me," and "Prince Ali." After Ashman's death in 1991, Tim Rice came onboard to write some additional songs, notably "One Jump Ahead" and "A Whole New World." The art directors were influenced by Persian miniatures and Arabian calligraphy. Supervising animator Eric Goldberg, who created the Genie, was the first animator to work on the project. He was heavily influenced by the curved, fluid caricature style of artist Al Hirschfeld. Computer-generated imagery enabled the filmmakers to create the amazing magic carpet ride through the Cave of Wonders, the intricately patterned carpet itself, and the stunning tiger-head cave. The film won Academy Awards for Best Song ("A Whole New World") and Best Original Score. The film became the highest grossing animated film to date, earning over $200 million domestically. The video release in 1993 also set records. There were two made-for-video sequels—*The Return of Jafar* and *Aladdin and the King of Thieves*.

Aladdin (television) Animated television series based on the characters from the motion picture began on Disney Channel on February 6, 1994, in syndication on September 5, 1994, and ended August 29, 1997, and on CBS on September 17, 1994, where it ended on August 24, 1996. Follows the magical and often hilarious escapades of Aladdin, Jasmine, and the others within and beyond the land of Agrabah. Voices include Val Bettin (Sultan), Dan Castellaneta (Genie), Gilbert Gottfried (Iago), Scott Weinger (Aladdin), Linda Larkin (Jasmine), Jason Alexander (Abis Mal), Bebe Neuwirth (Mirage), Michael Jeter (Runtar), Julie Brown (Saleen). 86 episodes.

Aladdin: A Musical Spectacular Elaborate, Broadway-caliber live musical stage show presented in the Hyperion Theater at Disney's California Adventure, beginning in December 2002, with an official debut on January 17, 2003. Generally, the show follows the plot of the movie, though Alan Menken composed one new song, "To Be Free," for Jasmine.

Aladdin and the King of Thieves (film) Animated motion picture; released exclusively on video on August 13, 1996. The wedding of the century turns into a great adventure, as the legendary Forty Thieves spoil the party in their search for the mysterious Hand of Midas—a magic treasure that turns all things to gold. Aladdin soon learns that his long-lost father is still alive and the quest to find him leads directly to the secret den of the King of Thieves. This is the second made-for-video sequel to *Aladdin*, following *The Return of Jafar*. A major new character is added to the story, Cassim, Aladdin's father. Directed by Tad Stones. Voices, many returning from the original cast, include Val Bettin, Jim Cummings, Gilbert Gottfried, Linda Larkin, Jerry Orbach (Sa'luk), John Rhys-Davies (Cassim), Scott Weinger, Frank Welker, and Robin Williams.

Aladdin on Ice (television) Television special; aired on CBS on November 17, 1995. Directed by Steve Binder. Videotaped on location in Cairo, Egypt. Stars Kurt Browning (Aladdin), Kristi Yamaguchi (Jasmine).

Aladdin's Oasis Taking the place of the Tahitian Terrace at Disneyland on July 2, 1993, and tied in

with the release of *Aladdin*, this dinner theater presented an *Aladdin*-themed show and featured "Americanized" Middle Eastern cuisine. The show was discontinued after a few years, but the restaurant opened during peak periods, and beginning in 1997, the venue was used for storytelling.

Aladdin's Royal Caravan Parade at Disneyland from April 2, 1993 to June 1994, and at Disney-MGM Studios from December 21, 1992 to August 27, 1995, featuring the "Prince Ali" song. On one float golden camels turned their heads from side to side and "spit" into the crowd lining the street. It was actually kind of refreshing on a summer day if you happened to be in a direct line for the expectorating beasts.

Alamo, The (film) An epic retelling of the 1836 battle in San Antonio de Bexar where less than 200 men, led by James Bowie, Lt. Col. William B. Travis, and the legendary Davy Crockett, try to hold the small, ruined mission, the Alamo, against the much larger forces of Mexican general Antonio López de Santa Anna. The Texans and their deeds would pass into history as General Sam Houston's rallying cry for Texas independence and into legend for their symbolic significance. Released on April 9, 2004, after a March 27 world premiere in San Antonio.  Directed by John Lee Hancock. A Touchstone Picture. Stars Dennis Quaid (Sam Houston), Billy Bob Thornton (Davy Crockett), Jason Patric (Jim Bowie), Patrick Wilson (Col. William B. Travis), Jordi Mollá (Juan Seguín), Emilio Echevarria (Santa Anna). 137 min. Filmed in CinemaScope on location in Texas, with a 45-acre set of the Alamo and its courtyard built on a private ranch west of Austin. With 70 structures on 51 acres, it was the largest freestanding set ever built in North America. Released on video in 2004.

Alan Smithee Film, An: Burn Hollywood Burn (film) This satirical story of the behind-the-scenes intrigue of a big budget action/adventure Hollywood film reveals director Alan Smithee's bizarre odyssey through a series of interviews with real celebrities and fictional characters. The machinations and agendas of everyone and anyone in filmmaking—from the producer to the makeup artists—are revealed. Smithee makes his directorial debut on the biggest budget action film in Hollywood history, but when he becomes distraught over choices forced upon him by his producer, he takes the master negative hostage. A Hollywood Picture in association with Cinergi. Released on February 27, 1998. Directed by Alan Smithee. Stars Ryan O'Neal (James Edmunds), Coolio (Dion Brothers), Chuck D. (Leon Brothers), Richard Jeni (Jerry Glover), Eric Idle (Alan Smithee), and special appearances by Sylvester Stallone, Whoopi Goldberg, Jackie Chan. The screenplay is by Joe Eszterhas. "Alan Smithee" is a name that has historically been applied to Hollywood films when the director has asked to have his name removed. 86 min.

Alaska: Dances of the Caribou (television) Highlights the caribou's annual trek to the magnificent North Slope of the Brooks Range, and the pageant of life summertime brings to this breathtaking yet forbidden landscape. Aired in syndication beginning February 14, 2000, as a New True Life Adventure. Produced by Bruce Reitherman. 45 min.

Alaskan Eskimo, The (film) People and Places featurette, released on February 18, 1953. Directed by James Algar. 27 min. Utilized footage shot in Alaska by the team of Alfred and Elma Milotte, depicting the everyday home life of the families in a typical Eskimo village. The building and hunting activities of the summer, the winter activities underground when the blizzards come, and the celebration of spring with the "mask dance" are all shown. Walt Disney originally sent the Milottes to Alaska to film anything they found of interest, but when he selected their footage of the seals (for *Seal Island*) and wanted to present it with no indication of man's presence, there was no use for the rest of their film. So, some of the footage detailing the everyday home life of Eski-

mos in a typical village was edited together to become this first People and Places featurette, the forerunner of a number of such travelogues. The project was as successful as *Seal Island* had been, for *The Alaskan Eskimo* also won an Academy Award.

Alaskan Gold Rush, The (film) Sixteen-mm release in June 1973 of television film from *A Salute to Alaska*. Historical photos in a family album tell the story of the hardy pioneers in the Alaskan gold rush.

Alaskan Sled Dog (film) Featurette, released on July 3, 1957. Directed by Ben Sharpsteen. Filmed in CinemaScope. 18 min. The story of an Eskimo father and son who train and groom a sled dog team. When the father is lost on an ice floe, the son takes the unproven team on the search, and succeeds in finding his father.

Alaska's Bush Pilot Heritage (film) Sixteen-mm release in June 1973 of television film. The story of the special breed of pilot who has challenged the perilous Alaskan landscape.

Alberoni, Sherry See Allen, Sherry.

Albert, Eddie (1906–2005) Actor; appeared in *Miracle of the White Stallions* and *Escape to Witch Mountain* (Jason), and on television in *Beyond Witch Mountain* and *The Barefoot Executive* (Herbert Gower).

Albertson, Jack (1910–1981) Character actor; appeared in *The Shaggy Dog* (reporter), *Son of Flubber* (Mr. Barley), *A Tiger Walks* (Sam Grant), and provided the voice of Amos Slade in *The Fox and the Hound*.

Albright, Milt Joined Disney in 1947 as a junior accountant, and was promoted in 1954 to manager of accounting for Disneyland. He became the manager of Holidayland in 1957 and in 1958 founded the Magic Kingdom Club. He was instrumental in beginning the Grad Nites in 1961. He was named a Disney Legend in 2005.

Alcoholism: Who Gets Hurt? (film) Educational film using sequences from *Follow Me, Boys!* In the Questions!/Answers? series, released in October 1975. Shows a youngster's dilemma in dealing with the problem of an alcoholic parent.

Alda, Alan Actor/director; appeared in *Betsy's Wedding* (Eddie Hopper).

Alden, Norman He voiced Sir Kay in *The Sword in the Stone*, appeared in *Ed Wood* (Cameraman Bill), and on television in *Sunday Drive* (John Elliott).

Alexander, Jane Actress; appeared in *Night Crossing* (Doris Strelzyk), and on The Disney Channel in *A Friendship in Vienna* (Hannah Dornenwald).

Alexander, Jason Actor; appeared in *Pretty Woman* (Philip Stuckey), and on television in *Rodgers & Hammerstein's Cinderella* (Lionel) and *Bob Patterson* (title role), and provided the voice of Abis Mal in the *Aladdin* television series and *The Return of Jafar*, Hugo in *The Hunchback of Notre Dame*, and Lightning in *101 Dalmatians II: Patch's London Adventure.*

Alexander, Stanley Voice of the young Flower in *Bambi*.

Alford, Phillip Actor; appeared on television in *Bristle Face*.

Alfredo's See L'Originale Alfredo di Roma Ristorante.

Algar, James (1912–1998) He joined Disney in 1934 as an animator and worked on *Snow White and the Seven Dwarfs*. Later became animation director on *The Sorcerer's Apprentice* and sequences of *Bambi* and *The Adventures of Ichabod and Mr. Toad*. Directed several of the True-Life

Adventures, and produced *The Gnome-Mobile* and numerous television shows and park films, such as the Circle-Vision productions. He was honored as a Disney Legend in 1998.

Alias (television) One-hour drama on ABC television, premiering September 30, 2001, exploring the double life of Sydney Bristow, a 26-year-old graduate student secretly working as a CIA agent. Stars Jennifer Garner (Sydney Bristow), Victor Garber (Jack Bristow), Ron Rifkin (Arvin Sloane), Michael Vartan (Agent Vaughn), Carl Lumbly (Agent Dixon), Kevin Weisman (Marshall), Greg Grunberg (Eric Weiss), Mia Maestro (Nadia Santos). Produced by Touchstone Television.

Alice and the Dog Catcher (film) Alice Comedy, released on July 1, 1924.

Alice and the Three Bears (film) Alice Comedy, released on December 1, 1924.

Alice at the Carnival (film) Alice Comedy, released on February 7, 1927.

Alice at the Rodeo Alternate title, see *Alice's Rodeo*.

Alice Bluebonnet Girlfriend of Johnny Fedora in the segment about the romance between two hats in *Make Mine Music*.

Alice Cans the Cannibals (film) Alice Comedy, released on January 1, 1925.

Alice Charms the Fish (film) Alice Comedy, released on September 6, 1926.

Alice Chops the Suey (film) Alice Comedy, released in 1925.

Alice Comedies Series of 56 silent cartoons made by Walt Disney between 1924 and 1927, with a live girl acting in Cartoonland. Walt first hired four-year-old Virginia Davis and then Margie Gay, Dawn O'Day, and Lois Hardwick to be the little Alice romping in a cartoon world.

Enthusiastically, he sent out the first unfinished pilot film, *Alice's Wonderland*, to cartoon distributors in New York. One of them, Margaret Winkler, agreed to distribute the series, with payment

beginning at $1,500 per reel. The pilot film was made in Kansas City; all 56 of the remaining films in the series were made in Hollywood. Miss Winkler married Charles Mintz, and he continued the dealings with Walt Disney until 1927 when Disney tired of combining live action and animation and they switched instead to the Oswald the Lucky Rabbit series.

Alice Cuts the Ice (film) Alice Comedy, released on November 1, 1926.

Alice Foils the Pirates (film) Alice Comedy, released on January 24, 1927.

Alice Gets in Dutch (film) Alice Comedy, released on November 1, 1924.

Alice Gets Stung (film) Alice Comedy, released on February 1, 1925.

Alice Helps the Romance (film) Alice Comedy, released on November 15, 1926.

Alice Hunting in Africa (film) Alice Comedy, released on November 15, 1924.

Alice in the Alps (film) Alice Comedy, released on March 21, 1927.

Alice in the Big League (film) Alice Comedy, released on August 22, 1927.

Alice in the Jungle (film) Alice Comedy, released on December 15, 1925.

Alice in the Klondike (film) Alice Comedy, released on June 27, 1927.

Alice in the Wooly West (film) Alice Comedy, released on October 4, 1926.

Alice in Wonderland (film) Lewis Carroll's famous story of Alice and her adventures after falling down a rabbit hole. Following a White Rabbit, she meets such strange creatures as a talking doorknob, who helps her through a keyhole into Wonderland, Tweedledum and Tweedledee, who tell the story of "The Walrus and the Carpenter," the Caterpillar, and the Mad Hatter and the March Hare celebrating an unbirthday at their tea party. Finally Alice has a showdown with the Queen of Hearts and her army of playing cards. The whole thing becomes such a nightmare that Alice awakens from her dream to the recitations of her sister and the purring of her cat, Dinah. Alice is voiced by Kathryn Beaumont. Other voices include Verna Felton (Queen), Bill Thompson (White Rabbit), Ed Wynn (Mad Hatter), Jerry Colonna (March Hare), and Sterling Holloway (Cheshire Cat). Premiered in England

on July 26, 1951, and released in the U.S. two days later. Directed by Clyde Geronimi, Hamilton Luske, and Wilfred Jackson. Songs include "All in the Golden Afternoon," and "I'm Late," by Bob Hilliard and Sammy Fain, and "The Unbirthday Song," by Mack David, Al Hoffman, and Jerry Livingston. 75 min. Nominated for an Academy Award for Best Scoring of a Musical

Picture. This animated feature had been on Walt Disney's mind since 1933, when he considered a live-action version starring Mary Pickford. He shelved the project after Paramount made a version, but later had artist David Hall, a Hollywood artist and designer, create some concepts for an all-animated film. World War II intervened, and it was not until the late 1940s that work began again in earnest. One of Walt's big problems with this film was that here he was dealing with a highly regarded classic, and what was charming and appropriately bizarre in book form seemed oddly out of place on the motion picture screen. Walt's feeling, expressed in later years, was that Alice had no "heart." An edited version aired on television on November 3, 1954. The film was rediscovered by the psychedelic generation, when it was made available on 16mm for schools, and it was re-released in theaters in 1974 and 1981. Released on video in 1981 and 1986 and kept in release.

Alice in Wonderland Fantasyland dark ride attraction at Disneyland, opened on June 14, 1958. Closed from September 6, 1982 to April 13, 1984 for a major remodeling. Kathryn Beaumont, who provided the voice for Alice in the 1951 motion picture, was brought back at that time to record narration tracks for the attraction.

Alice in Wonderland: A Lesson in Appreciating Differences (film) Educational film, released in September 1978. The film stresses appreciating others for their differences is an important quality in mature young people.

Alice Loses Out (film) Alice Comedy, released in 1925.

Alice on the Farm (film) Alice Comedy, released on January 1, 1926.

Alice Picks the Champ (film) Alice Comedy, released in 1925.

Alice Plays Cupid (film) Alice Comedy, released on October 15, 1925.

Alice Rattled by Rats (film) Alice Comedy, released on November 15, 1925.

Alice Solves the Puzzle (film) Alice Comedy, released on February 15, 1925.

Alice Stage Struck (film) Alice Comedy, released in 1925.

Alice the Beach Nut (film) Alice Comedy, released on August 8, 1927.

Alice the Collegiate (film) Alice Comedy, released on March 7, 1927.

Alice the Fire Fighter (film) Alice Comedy, released on October 18, 1926.

Alice the Golf Bug (film) Alice Comedy, released on Janaury 10, 1927.

Alice the Jail Bird (film) Alice Comedy, released on September 15, 1925.

Alice the Lumber Jack (film) Alice Comedy, released on December 27, 1926.

Alice the Peacemaker (film) Alice Comedy, released on August 1, 1924.

Alice the Piper (film) Alice Comedy, released on December 15, 1924.

Alice the Toreador (film) Alice Comedy, released on January 15, 1925.

Alice the Whaler (film) Alice Comedy, released on July 25, 1927.

Alice Wins the Derby (film) Alice Comedy, released in 1925.

Alice's Auto Race (film) Alice Comedy, released on April 4, 1927.

Alice's Balloon Race (film) Alice Comedy, released on January 15, 1926.

Alice's Brown Derby (film) Alice Comedy, released on December 13, 1926.

Alice's Channel Swim (film) Alice Comedy, released on June 13, 1927.

Alice's Circus Daze (film) Alice Comedy, released on April 18, 1927.

Alice's Curious Labyrinth Maze attraction in Fantasyland at Disneyland Paris; opened April 12, 1992, in which guests try to find their way through the hedgerows to a castle, encountering various surprises along the way.

Alice's Day at Sea (film) First of the Alice Comedies, released on March 1, 1924. The first six Alice Comedies had extensive live-action beginnings, then went into the cartoon. Beginning with the seventh cartoon, Walt Disney dispensed with the long live-action introductions. In this first film, Alice goes to the seashore with her dog and falls asleep in a rowboat. The cartoon segment features a shipwreck, and battles with fish, birds, and an octopus.

Alice's Egg Plant (film) Alice Comedy, released in 1925.

Alice's Fishy Story (film) Alice Comedy, released on June 1, 1924.

Alice's Knaughty Knight (film) Alice Comedy, released on May 2, 1927.

Alice's Little Parade (film) Alice Comedy, released on February 1, 1926.

Alice's Medicine Show (film) Alice Comedy, released on July 11, 1927.

Alice's Monkey Business (film) Alice Comedy, released on September 20, 1926.

Alice's Mysterious Mystery (film) Alice Comedy, released on February 15, 1926.

Alice's Orphan (film) Alice Comedy, released in 1926. An alternate title was *Alice's Ornery Orphan*.

Alice's Picnic (film) Alice Comedy, released on May 30, 1927.

Alice's Rodeo (film) Alice Comedy, released on February 21, 1927. *Alice at the Rodeo* is an alternate title.

Alice's Spanish Guitar (film) Alice Comedy, released on November 29, 1926.

Alice's Spooky Adventure (film) Alice Comedy, released on April 1, 1924.

Alice's Tea Party Attraction in Fantasyland at Tokyo Disneyland, opened on March 8, 1986.

Alice's Three Bad Eggs (film) Alice Comedy, released on May 16, 1927.

Alice's Tin Pony (film) Alice Comedy, released in 1925.

Alice's Wild West Show (film) Alice Comedy, released on May 1, 1924.

Alice's Wonderland (film) Pilot film for the Alice Comedy series made by Walt Disney in Kansas City in 1923. Alice visits an animation studio. Later she dreams that she goes to Cartoonland, dances for the animals, and is chased by lions that escape from the zoo. This film was never released as part of the series. Virginia Davis starred as Alice in this initial effort, and when Walt Disney moved to California and was able to sell a series based on this pilot film, he persuaded the Davis family to move west also, bringing young Virginia to continue in the role of Alice.

Alien Encounter See The ExtraTERRORestrial Alien Encounter.

Alien Encounters from New Tomorrowland (television) Syndicated television special; aired on February 27, 1995. Directed by Andy Thomas. Robert Urich hosts a pseudo-documentary on the history of UFO sightings, which is used to introduce a brief look at The ExtraTERRORestrial Alien Encounter attraction and the newly remodeled New Tomorrowland at Walt Disney World. Produced by Walt Disney World.

Aliens of the Deep (film) In this documentary, a team of young oceanographers and NASA scientists study, among other things, an ecosystem, two and a half miles below the surface of the ocean, that has hypothermal vents at its core. Directed by James Cameron. Released on January 28, 2005. A Walt Disney Pictures and Walden Media presentation of an Earthship production. For large format/IMAX theaters, filmed in 70mm. 47 min. Released on DVD in 2005.

Alive (film) In 1972, an airplane carrying a rugby team of Uruguayan college students crashes in the Andes en route to a game in Chile. Flying in poor visibility, the plane's wing clipped the side of a mountain, and the aircraft came to rest on the snow-covered Tinguiririca volcano at 11,500 feet. Several of the passengers and most of the crew died instantly, but the majority survived and waited to be rescued. On the eighth day they learned via transistor radio that official search operations had been abandoned. Soon their food and drink was gone, and facing a certain future of starvation and death, they resorted to cannibalism. Finally, after ten weeks, two men, Nando and Roberto, left camp and bravely traveled over the Andes where they were able to find help. Directed by Frank Marshall. Released on January 15, 1993. A Touchstone film, being a co-production with Paramount Pictures, with the latter handling foreign distribution. Based on the book by Piers Paul Read. 126 min. Stars Ethan Hawke (Nando Parrado), Vincent Spano (Antonio Balbi), Josh Hamilton (Roberto Canassa). The producers were

able to obtain the usage of the exact type of aircraft involved in the crash—a Fairchild F-227 twin-engined turboprop. The plane crash was one of the most realistic ever filmed. Doubling for the actual location, the filmmakers used the Delphine glacier at an altitude of 9,500 feet in the Columbia Mountains near Panorama, British Columbia. The actual survivors of the crash were consulted to make the production as accurate as possible, and one of them, Nando Parrado, served as technical adviser. Released on video in 1993. A special video entitled *Alive: 20 Years Later* was also released in 1993.

All About Magic (television) Television show, aired January 30, 1957, with Walt using the Magic Mirror to act as emcee to explain about magic. Directed by Hamilton S. Luske. Stars Hans Conried as the Magic Mirror, which had made its debut in *Snow White and the Seven Dwarfs*. The Mirror shows two magic-themed cartoons, as well as the "Bibbidi-Bobbidi-Boo" sequence from *Cinderella* and *The Sorcerer's Apprentice* from *Fantasia*.

All About Weightlessness (film) Sixteen-mm educational release of a portion of *Man in Space*, released in September 1964. Humans experience many unique problems as they venture into outer space.

All-American College Band Program begun at Disneyland in 1971 and Walt Disney World in 1972 that allows talented college musicians from across the country to perform at one of the parks for the summer season. The name was changed to the Collegiate All-Star Band in 1998 but reverted to the original name in 2002. 2003 marked Al Bartner's 25th year in conducting the band at Disneyland. The Walt Disney World program was canceled after the summer of 2000, with the exception of a one-time group of five musicians in the summer of 2001.

All-American Girl (television) Television series, debuted on September 14, 1994, and ran until March 22, 1995. Explores the cultural and generational conflicts that arise between a free-spirited, completely assimilated Korean-American college student, Margaret Kim, and her more conservative, traditional family. Stars Margaret Cho (Margaret Kim), Jodi Long (Mother), Clyde Kusatsu (Dad), Amy Hill (Grandma), Maddie Corman (Ruthie).

All Because Man Wanted to Fly (film) Lighthearted look at early human efforts to fly, hosted by Orville, the albatross, for the pre-show of PSA's Circle-Vision attraction at Disneyland. Opened on July 4, 1984, and ran for five years.

All in a Nutshell (film) Donald steals Chip and Dale's nuts for his nut-butter shop, which is shaped like a giant walnut. The chipmunks think the shop is a real nut. After they crack open the roof, they steal the nut butter, with Donald chasing after them. When Donald runs into a tree and knocks himself silly, Chip and Dale load him into a log like a cannonball and drop a hornets' nest into the log to "shoot" Donald into a nearby lake.

All New Adventure of Disney's Sport Goofy, An; Featuring Sport Goofy in Soccermania (television) Television special on NBC, airing on May 27, 1987. 60 min. Directed by John Klawitter. Several Goofy and Mickey Mouse cartoons are shown, followed by *Sport Goofy in Soccermania*, a new Goofy cartoon, which debuted here. Uncle Scrooge agrees to sponsor the Nephews' soccer team in order to get back a valuable trophy, which he mistakenly donated. The Beagle Boys are also after the trophy, and it is up to Sport Goofy to save the day. This cartoon was directed by Matt O'Callaghan.

All Star Cafe Two hundred forty-seat restaurant which opened at Disney's Wide World of Sports complex at Walt Disney World on February 26, 1998. It was originally operated by Planet Hollywood International, but Disney took over the lease in March 2000.

All-Star Resorts Moderate-priced hotel at Walt Disney World, with the first unit, devoted to surfing, opening on April 29, 1994. The units of the All-Star Sports Resort are Surf's Up, Hoops Hotel (basketball), Touchdown (football), Home Run Hotel (baseball), and Center Court (tennis). Includes the End-Zone Food Court and Sport Goofy Gifts & Sundries. Center Court was the last unit opened, on August 11, 1994. The All-Star Music Resort began opening in November 1994, one unit at a time. The units are named Calypso, Jazz, Rock Inn, Country Fair, and Broadway. The All-Star Movies Resort was added in 1999, with the first units opening on January 15. The units were themed to *The Mighty Ducks*, *One Hundred and One Dalmatians*, *The Love Bug*, *Fantasia*, and *Toy Story*.

All the Cats Join In (film) Segment of *Make Mine Music* featuring Benny Goodman and his Orchestra, with an animated pencil drawing a

group of lively teenagers having a jitterbug session at the local malt shop. The song is by Alec Wilder, Ray Gilbert, and Eddie Sauter.

All Together (film) Shows the advisability and necessity of purchasing Canadian war bonds. Made for the National Film Board of Canada and delivered to them on January 13, 1942. Mickey and the gang, including Pinocchio and Geppetto, lead a parade to help sell the war bonds.

All Wet (film) Oswald the Lucky Rabbit cartoon; released on October 31, 1927.

Allan-a-Dale Rooster narrator of *Robin Hood*; voiced by Roger Miller.

Allen, Barbara Jo (1906–1974) Voiced Fauna in *Sleeping Beauty*, Goliath's mother in *Goliath II*, and the scullery maid in *The Sword in the Stone*.

Allen, Bob (1932–1987) Beginning at Disneyland in 1955 as a ride operator, he later spent two years as the manager of the Celebrity Sports Center in Denver and as a project manager for the proposed Mineral King resort. He became director of General Services at Disneyland in 1968, two years later moving to Walt Disney World with the same title. In Florida he soon became vice president of Resorts, and on January 1, 1977, he was promoted to vice president of Walt Disney World, a position he held until his untimely death in 1987. He was named a Disney Legend posthumously in 1996.

Allen, Rex (1920–1999) Actor/singer, with his distinctive, homey western voice, narrated such features and television shows as *The Legend of Lobo; The Incredible Journey; An Otter in the Family; Run, Appaloosa, Run; Cow Dog; Ringo, the Refugee Raccoon; Seems There Was This Moose; My Family Is a Menagerie.* He was named a Disney Legend in 1996.

Allen, Sherry Mouseketeer from the 1950s television show. Her real name was Sherry Alberoni.

Allen, Tim Actor/comedian; starred in *The Santa Clause* (Scott Calvin), *Jungle 2 Jungle* (Michael Cromwell), *Big Trouble* (Eliot Arnold) and *The Santa Clause 2* (Scott Calvin), and on television in *Home Improvement*. He also appeared in *Disney's Great American Celebration* and *The Dream Is Alive*. He provided the voice of Buzz Lightyear in *Toy Story* and *Toy Story 2*. He also provided the voice of Buzz again on television in *Buzz Lightyear of Star Command*. His book, *Don't Stand Too Close to a Naked Man*, was published in 1994 by Hyperion. For a time in 1994, he had the honor of being in the number-one television series, the number-one motion picture, and having the number-one book on the best seller lists. He was named a Disney Legend in 1999.

Allen, Woody Actor/director; appeared in *New York Stories* (Sheldon) and *Scenes from a Mall* (Nick).

Allers, Roger Storyman/director; joined Disney in 1985, was head of story for *Oliver & Company* and *Beauty and the Beast*. After working on the stories for other animated features, he made his feature film directing debut with Rob Minkoff on *The Lion King*.

Alley, Kirstie Actress; appeared in *Shoot to Kill* (Sarah), and hosted the television special *Wonderful World of Disney: 40 Years of Television Magic*. Also starred in *Toothless* on *The Wonderful World of Disney*.

Alley, Lindsey Actress; appeared in *Ernest Saves Christmas* (Patsy) and as a regular on the *Mickey Mouse Club* on The Disney Channel, beginning in 1989.

Alley Cats Strike! (television) Disney Channel Original Movie; premiered on March 18, 2000. Four hip teens are content with their nonconformist attitudes, retro styles of dress, and an interest in bowling and lounge music that have made them outcasts among their classmates at West Appleton Middle School. But when an annual interschool competition ends in a tie, the school has to turn to bowling to break it, and suddenly the four teens are thrust into the spotlight, with the most popular and athletic kid in school, who has never bowled, added to their team. The teens must set aside their differences and learn to work together. Directed by Rod Daniel. Stars Kyle Schmid (Alex Thompson), Robert Ri'chard (Todd McLemore), Kaley Cuoco (Elisa), Mimi Paley (Delia), Joey Wilcots (Ken).

Allwine, Wayne Former Disney sound effects technician who currently provides the voice of Mickey Mouse on a freelance basis. He learned his craft from veteran Disney sound-effects wizard, and previous voice of Mickey Mouse, Jim Macdonald.

Almost Angels (film) The young Toni Fiala is a boy born to sing, and his greatest desire is to be accepted as one of the members of the Vienna Boys Choir. His father, a railroad engineer, wants his son to learn a trade, but his mother knows her son must be given a chance to sing. The mother makes the opportunity possible and the boy wins his way into the choir. This story of the training, travel, and adventures of the boys within this famous institution is accompanied by the beautiful music of the choir. Toni's admiration for the oldest boy in the choir, Peter Schaefer, is tested when Peter's voice begins to change and Toni convinces the other members of the choir to cover for him. When Peter is finally found out, he is able to obtain a position as assistant conductor. Released on September 26, 1962. Directed by Steve Previn. The foreign release title was *Born to Sing*. 93 min. Stars Peter Weck (Max Heller), Sean Scully (Peter Schaefer), Vincent Winter (Toni Fiala), Denis Gilmore (Friedel Schmidt), Hans Holt (Elsinger), Fritz Eckhardt (Herr Fiala), Bruni Lobel (Frau Fiala), Gunther Philipp (Radio commentator), and the Vienna Boys Choir. The film was made on location in Austria. Released on video in 1986.

Almost Home (television) Television series, aired on NBC from February 6 to July 3, 1993. Continued the story of *The Torkelsons*. Seattle businessman Brian Morgan has offered home-spun Millicent Torkelson a job as the live-in nanny to his two rebellious teenagers, so the Torkelson clan packs up their small-town life in Pyramid Corners, Oklahoma, and heads for the big city. Blending the two families is as natural as mixing oil and water, but with her sunny approach to life, Millicent sets out to bridge the gap. Stars Connie Ray (Millicent Torkelson), Olivia Burnette (Dorothy Jane), Lee Norris (Chuckie Lee), Rachel Duncan (Mary Sue), Perry King (Brian Morgan), Brittany Murphy (Molly Morgan), Jason Marsden (Gregory Morgan).

Along the Oregon Trail (television) Television show; aired November 14, 1956, as a behind-the-scenes look at the filming of *Westward Ho the Wagons!* Directed by William Beaudine. Walt Disney describes the Oregon Trail, then turns to Fess Parker, one of the stars of the film, to give a behind-the-scenes look at the production and, with Jeff York, to show how the pioneers lived and the hardships they faced. Iron Eyes Cody and Sebastian Cabot, both also in the feature, tell how the Native Americans and the pioneers were suspicious of each other.

Alpine Climbers (film) Mickey Mouse cartoon; released on July 25, 1936. Directed by Dave Hand. In the mountains, Pluto and a friendly St. Bernard get drunk from the big dog's keg of brandy after Pluto is rescued, and Mickey runs afoul of a mother eagle, necessitating rescue by Donald Duck.

Alpine Gardens Flowers surround a pond between Tomorrowland and Fantasyland at Disneyland, once the site of the Monsanto Home of the Future. It became Triton Gardens in February 1996.

Aluminum Hall of Fame See Hall of Aluminum Fame.

Ama Girls (film) People and Places featurette, released on July 9, 1958. Directed by Ben Sharpsteen. A typical day in the life of a family of fisherfolk of Japan. The elder daughter is an Ama, or diving girl, who collects "Heaven Grass," a variety of seaweed, as a crop. The girls' training is studied as well as the teamwork and stamina needed to harvest this marine crop. Filmed in CinemaScope. 29 min. Academy Award winner. 16mm release as *Japan Harvests the Sea*.

Amazing Race, The (television) Reality adventure series pitting 11 teams against each other in a worldwide 30–40-day journey, with the first team to reach the final destination winning $1 million. Airing on CBS, it premiered on September 5, 2001. Hosted by Phil Keoghan. Produced by Touchstone Television in association with CBS Productions. The show won an Emmy for Reality-Competition Program in 2003 and 2004.

Amazon Awakens, The (film) Travelogue on the history and geography of the Amazon Basin, with information on the Ford Plantation at Fordlandia and the ambitious rubber program there. Produced under the auspices of the Coordinator of Inter-American Affairs. Delivered on May 29, 1944.

Ambassador Beginning with Julie Reihm in 1965, Disneyland has selected a young cast member each year to act as "Disneyland ambassador to the world." The ambassador travels to participate in parades, hospital visits, television and radio interviews, and other special events, and hosts special visitors to Disneyland. Walt Disney World continued the tradition beginning in 1971, as did Tokyo Disneyland in 1983, Disneyland Paris in 1992, and Hong Kong Disneyland in 2005. There is a detailed selection process annually among the cast members at each park, with each judged on such qualities as poise and personality. For 1995 the program was changed at Disneyland and Walt Disney World to allow for a team of ambassadors, and males were included for the first time.

Ambition: What Price Fulfillment? (film) Educational film, using sequences from *Third Man on the Mountain*. In the Questions!/Answers? series; released in 1976. A boy's greatest ambition is to climb the mountain that took his father's life; should he give up that dream to save the life of a man he hates?

Ambrose Kitten star of *The Robber Kitten* (1935).

Ambush at Laredo (television) Television show, part two of *Texas John Slaughter*.

Ambush at Wagon Gap (television) Television title of part one of *Westward Ho the Wagons!*

Ameche, Don (1908–1993) Actor; appeared in *The Boatniks* (Commander Taylor), *Oscar* (Father Clemente), on television in *Our Shining Moment*, and as the voice of Shadow in *Homeward Bound: the Incredible Journey*.

Amemiya, Hideo He spent 30 years with Disney in the area of hotel management, starting out with the Polynesian Hotel at Walt Disney World in 1971, working on the Tokyo Disneyland project, and ending his career as senior vice president of Disneyland Resort Hotels. He was named a Disney Legend in 2005.

America Gardens Amphitheater in front of The American Adventure in World Showcase at Epcot; opened October 1, 1982. Ethnic groups often present song-and-dance presentations tied to the countries of World Showcase. In 1993 it was remodeled temporarily for a Barbie show.

America on Parade Special American Bicentennial parade, at Walt Disney World from June 6, 1975 to September 6, 1976. Also at Disneyland from June 12, 1975 to September 12, 1976. Disney designers, led by entertainment head Bob Jani came up with special floats and a series of costumes featuring oversized heads that told the story of America's history, culture, and achievements, from its pioneers to the present, all marching to a sound track of American popular songs recorded from a band organ, the Sadie Mae. The parade was led by Mickey Mouse, Donald Duck, and Goofy as the "Spirit of '76."

America on Parade (television) Television special for the American Bicentennial starring Red Skelton, featuring the America on Parade pageant at Disneyland; aired on April 3, 1976. Directed by Clark Jones.

America Sings Tomorrowland attraction at Disneyland in the carousel theater originally built for the GE Carousel of Progress, from June 29, 1974 to April 10, 1988. The narrator was Sam the

Eagle, periodically interrupted by a pesky weasel. Taking the place of the Carousel of Progress when that attraction was moved to Walt Disney World, it featured over 100 characters in a history of American popular music in four separate scenes, each from a different era. The audience moved in turn to each of the scenes. When the attraction closed, many of the Audio-Animatronics characters that had populated it were moved to Critter Country to become part of Splash Mountain. America Sings is fondly remembered by many Disneyland guests.

America the Beautiful (film) Circarama (360-degree) film, which originally opened at the Brussels World's Fair in 1958 and was brought to Disneyland in 1960; a tour of the United States. 16 min. The film was reshot in 1967 as a Circle-Vision 360 film for the new Tomorrowland at Disneyland. The new film opened on June 25, 1967, and ran 18 min. It was revised again in 1975 to include sequences of Philadelphia for the American Bicentennial. It closed on January 3, 1984, to be followed by *American Journeys*. The film was shot with nine cameras, arranged on a circular stand. Shown in Tomorrowland in Magic Kingdom Park at Walt Disney World from November 25, 1971 until March 15, 1974, and from March 15, 1975 until September 9, 1984, and followed there also by *American Journeys*. *America the Beautiful* was released on 16mm film at normal screen size for educational use in 1980.

America Works . . . America Sings (film) Educational film, released in September 1982. A glimpse of everyday people whose daily lives gave birth to the folk songs that have enriched our history.

American Adventure, The Attraction in World Showcase at Epcot which celebrates the American spirit, from its earliest days right up to the present, originally sponsored jointly by American Express and Coca-Cola; opened October 1, 1982. It features some of the most sophisticated Audio-Animatronics figures produced by Disney, including one character, Benjamin Franklin, that for the first time appears to climb several steps.

The sound track music was recorded by the Philadelphia Orchestra. While guests wait to enter the theater, in the lobby area they are often entertained by the Voices of Liberty, an a capella singing group whose renditions of American folk and patriotic songs are thrilling. If you want to catch an architectural mistake, take a look at the columns in the rotunda. Their capitals have been placed on them sideways. Coca-Cola ceased their participation in 1998 and American Express in 2002.

American Broadcasting Company In 1954, Walt Disney agreed to produce a regular television series for the network, if they would help him out by investing in Disneyland. So, with a $500,000 investment and guarantee of an additional $4.5 million in loans, ABC became a one-third owner of Disneyland. The television series began in the fall and Walt was able to use it to help promote the park he was building in Anaheim. On July 17, 1955, ABC produced the largest live television broadcast to date, with the grand opening of the park. Disney remained on ABC until 1961; a year earlier they had bought out the ABC investment in Disneyland for $7.5 million. Four decades later, on July 31, 1995, Disney and Capital Cities/ABC announced a $19 billion merger of the two companies. After necessary government approvals, the merger was completed on February 9, 1996. With the deal, Disney acquired, among other enterprises, 9 VHF and 1 UHF television stations; 11 AM and 10

FM radio stations; a percentage of ESPN, The History Channel, A&E Network, and Lifetime Television; and a publishing group including 85 trade journals, 18 shopping guides, 2 consumer magazines, 21 weeklies, and 7 daily newspapers. Much of the publishing group was later sold.

American Dog (film) CG-animated feature planned for release in 2007. Even though he is stranded in the desert, a canine celebrity thinks that he is still on his television show. Directed by Chris Sanders.

American Dragon: Jake Long (television) Animated series debuting on Disney Channel on January 21, 2005. Jake Long is a 13-year-old Chinese American kid in New York who discovers he is descended from dragons. When he transforms into a fire-breather, it is his duty to protect the other groups of magical creatures living secretly among Gotham's famous landmarks. But the teen also has to confront the usual teenage conflicts, including a crush on Rose, the new girl in school. Voices include Dante Basco (Jake Long), Jeff Bennett (Jake's father), Amy Bruckner (Haley Long), Daveigh Chase (Rose Paxton), Lauren Tom (Jake's mother), Marlowe Gardiner-Heslin (David Long).

American Egg House Restaurant on Main Street at Disneyland, open from July 14, 1978 to September 30, 1983. Sponsored by the American Egg Board. Later Town Square Cafe. Featuring alfresco and indoor dining, it was the first restaurant one encountered on entering the park, so it was popular for breakfast.

American Journeys (film) Circle-Vision presentation capturing the many facets of America. Opened on July 4, 1984, at Disneyland, sponsored by PSA. In 1989, Delta took over the sponsorship. It ended its run on July 7, 1996. It opened in Tomorrowland at Walt Disney World beginning September 15, 1984 and ending on January 9, 1994. Shown in Tomorrowland at Tokyo Disneyland from May 17, 1986 to August 31, 1992.

American Pottery See Evan K. Shaw Ceramics.

American Teacher Awards, The Created by Disney as an annual salute to America's teachers and aired on The Disney Channel beginning November 4, 1990. Top stars are on hand to pass out awards to teachers in a dozen categories, and then those winners themselves pick the Teacher of the Year. Short video pieces on each nominee show them in their classrooms and creating rapport with their students. The awards program evolved from a Disney Channel series entitled *The Disney Channel Salutes the American Teacher*, which began in 1989. The Outstanding Teacher of 1990 was Sylvia Anne Washburn; in 1991 it was Edward M. Schroeder; in 1992, Rafe Esquith; in 1993, Patricia Ann Baltz and Leta Andrews shared the honor; in 1994, Huong Tran Nguyen; in 1995, Richard Ruffalo; in 1996, Phoebe Irby. For the first three years, the ceremony was held at the Pantages Theater in Hollywood; in 1993 it moved to the American Adventure Theater in World Showcase at Epcot, and in 1994 and 1995 it was held in Washington, D.C. In 1996, the ceremony returned to the Pantages Theater. There were no awards in 1997. The 1998 winner, Ray E. Chelewski, received his award at the Dorothy Chandler Pavilion in Los Angeles, and 1999 winner, Terri Lindner, received hers at the Pantages Theater. In 2000, the awards moved to the Shrine Auditiorium in Los Angeles, and were shown on the Lifetime cable network. The winner was Ron Clark. The 2001 winner, also on Lifetime, and announced at CBS Television City, was Ben Wentworth III. There was no awards ceremony in 2002. In 2003, the winner was John Passarini, in a ceremony at the Disneyland Hotel, announced on *The Wayne Brady Show*, and the 2004 winner was Jeffrey Thompson, honored at Disney's Grand Californian Hotel. The name was changed to the DisneyHand Teacher Awards in 2003. The 2005 award was presented to David Vixie at the Disneyland Hotel. The show won an Emmy Award for Music Direction in 1991.

American Werewolf in Paris, An (film) Three young American college graduates, Andy, Brad, and Chris, traveling across Europe on a self-styled "Daredevil Tour," descend upon Paris seeking some serious fun and adventure. While planning a bungee jump from the Eiffel Tower, Andy sees the woman of his dreams, the beautiful and mysterious Serafine, intent on committing suicide. He makes the split-second decision to jump to save her, which he does, but he is injured and knocked unconscious and she escapes. In searching for her, he discovers that, when the moon is full, she turns into a werewolf, and it is happening to him too. A Hollywood Pictures release, in association with Cometstone Pictures and J&M Entertainment. Released on December 25, 1997. Directed by Anthony Waller. Stars Tom Everett Scott (Andy), Julie Delpy (Serafine), Vince Vieluf (Brad), Phil Buckman (Chris), Julie Bowen (Amy), Pierre Cossi (Claude), Tom Novembre (Inspector LeDuc), Thierry Lhermitte (Dr. Pigot). 98 min. Based on the characters created by John Landis in *An American Werewolf in London* (1981). Filmed on location in France, Luxembourg, and Holland.

Americana's Dutch Resort See Grosvenor Resort.

America's Heart & Soul (film) In this documentary, filmmaker Louis Schwartzberg emphasizes that it is the people that make America so special. Audiences meet ordinary Americans with extraordinary stories, and learn their values, dreams, and passion. The unusual, captivating, inspiring, and emotional stories make us into something more than a collection of individuals. Released on July 2, 2004. Features the original song, "The World Don't Bother Me None," by John Mellencamp. 88 min. Released on video in 2005.

Ames, Leon (1903–1993) Actor; appeared as President Rufus Daggett in both *The Absent-Minded Professor* and *Son of Flubber*, also as the judge in *The Misadventures of Merlin Jones* and *The Monkey's Uncle*.

Amos The "me" in *Ben and Me* (1953), a mouse who advises Ben Franklin and helps him come up

with many of his great inventions; voiced by Sterling Holloway.

Amos, John Actor; appeared in *The World's Greatest Athlete* (Coach Sam Archer).

Amos Slade Farmer who hated foxes in *The Fox and the Hound*; voiced by Jack Albertson.

Amsberry, Bob (Uncle Bob) (1928–1957) Adult Mouseketeer; used as a utility man on the 1950s television show.

Amy (film) Amy is a young mother who has recently lost her cherished deaf son. She leaves her domineering and insensitive husband to go to a school to teach the deaf to speak in an era when sign language was considered the only feasible means of communication. In helping her students to overcome their handicaps, she herself learns to be independent and self-reliant. Released on March 20, 1981. Directed by Vincent McEveety. 99 min. Stars Jenny Agutter (Amy), Barry Newman (Dr. Ben Corcoran), Kathleen Nolan (Helen), Chris Robinson (Elliott), Lou Fant (Lyle), Margaret O'Brien (Hazel), Nanette Fabray (Malvina). The characters of the deaf children were played by students from the California School for the Deaf. A shortened educational film version (31½ minutes) was titled *Amy-on-the-Lips*, which was the working title of the feature. Released on video in 1981 and 1985.

Anaheim When Walt Disney was searching for a location for Disneyland, he hired the Stanford Research Institute to do the survey for him, and their preferred location turned out to be Anaheim, California. So, Walt's agents negotiated on the purchase of a parcel of land where Harbor Boulevard intersects the Santa Ana Freeway (Interstate 5), and it was there that he built Disneyland in 1955. The success of Disneyland acted as a catalyst for the major growth of Anaheim that took place over the ensuing decades.

Anaheim Angels The California Angels baseball team changed its name to the Anaheim Angels in November 1996, and unveiled new team colors and logos for the 1997 season. For the 1998 season, Anaheim Stadium, where the team plays its home games, was renamed Edison International Field of Anaheim. In October 2002, the Angels won the World Series championship for the first time, beating the San Francisco Giants. Disney came to an agreement with businessman Arte Moreno in April 2003 to sell the team for $185 million; the deal was finalized on May 22. See also California Angels.

Anaheim Sports, Inc. Disney operating entity that previously owned the Mighty Ducks and the Anaheim Angels. Formerly (before December 1996) known as Disney Sports Enterprises.

Anastasia One of Cinderella's evil stepsisters; voiced by Lucille Bliss.

Anderson, Bill (1911–1997) Producer of television programs (58 of the *Zorro* shows, *Texas John Slaughter*, *Daniel Boone*, *The Swamp Fox*) and motion pictures (*Third Man on the Mountain*, *Swiss Family Robinson*, *The Happiest Millionaire*, *Superdad*, *The Strongest Man in the World*, *The Shaggy D.A.* and others). Bill began at Disney in 1943 in the production control department. He was promoted to production manager for the Studio in 1951 and vice president of Studio operations in 1956. He was elected to the board of directors in 1960 and remained a member until 1984. He was named a Disney Legend posthumously in 2004.

Anderson, Harry Actor; appeared on television in *The Absent-Minded Professor* (Henry Crawford), *The Magical World of Disney*, and *The Disney-MGM Studios Theme Park Grand Opening.*

Anderson, John (1922–1992) Actor; appeared on television in *Shadow of Fear*, *For the Love of Willadean*, and *I-Man*. He also did the voices of Mark Twain and Franklin Delano Roosevelt in the American Adventure at Epcot.

Anderson, Ken (1909–1993) Artist; began his Disney career in 1934, contributing to many animated classics as art director beginning with

Snow White and the Seven Dwarfs. Since he had an architectural background, he came up with innovative perspective on such Silly Symphony cartoons as *Goddess of Spring* and *Three Orphan Kittens*. Specializing in character design in later years, he designed such characters as Shere Khan in *The Jungle Book* and Elliott in *Pete's Dragon*. He was production designer on such films as *Sleeping Beauty*, *One Hundred and One Dalmatians*, and *The Aristocats*. He also designed many parts of Disneyland, including major portions of Fantasyland, the Storybook Land Canal Boats, and others. He retired in 1978, but continued to consult at WED Enterprises. He was honored with the Disney Legends award in 1991.

Anderson, Michael, Jr. Actor; appeared in *In Search of the Castaways* (John Glenarven).

Andrews, Edward (1915–1985) Actor; appeared as the Secretary of Defense in both *The Absent-Minded Professor* and *Son of Flubber*, he also starred in *A Tiger Walks* (governor), *$1,000,000 Duck* (Morgan), *Now You See Him, Now You Don't* (Mr. Sampson), and *Charley and the Angel* (banker), and on television in *The Whiz Kid and the Mystery at Riverton* (Mayor Massey) and *The Young Loner* (Bert Shannon)

Andrews, Julie Actress; appeared in the title role of *Mary Poppins*, for which she won the Academy Award for Best Actress, and in *The Princess Diaries* and *The Princess Diaries 2: Royal Engagement* (Queen Clarisse Renaldi). She appeared on television in *Eloise at the Plaza* and *Eloise at Christmastime* (Nanny). She also appeared on the *Grand Opening of Walt Disney World* television special in 1971, and in *The Cat that Looked at a King*. She was a company spokesperson for Disneyland for its 50th anniversary in 2005. She was named a Disney Legend in 1991.

Andrews' Raiders (television) Two-part television show, airing on May 7 and 14, 1961, the television version of *The Great Locomotive Chase*. The two episodes were titled *Secret Mission* and *Escape to Nowhere*.

Andy Burnett See *The Saga of Andy Burnett*.

Angel, Heather Actress; voiced the sister in *Alice in Wonderland* and Mary Darling in *Peter Pan*.

Angelopoulos, Angel (1907–1990) He helped develop Disney merchandising in Greece, Yugoslavia, Turkey, and Egypt. Presented a European Disney Legends award in 1997.

Angels in the Endzone (television) Two-hour made-for-television movie which aired on *The Wonderful World of Disney* on November 9, 1997. Al the angel visits a small town, altering the losing tradition of the Westfield High School Angels football team, and changing the lives of two young brothers who are devastated by the sudden loss of their father. Directed by Gary Nadeau. Stars Christopher Lloyd (Al), Matthew Lawrence (Jesse Harper), David Gallegher (Kevin Harper), Paul Dooley (Coach Buck). Vancouver College (British Columbia, Canada) doubled for the fictional Westfield High, though their football field had to be re-marked for the movie; Canadian football is played on a 110-yard-long field, and American audiences would have been surprised by the presence of a 55-yard-line.

Angels in the Infield (television) Two-hour television movie; airing on *The Wonderful World of Disney* on April 9, 2000. Big-league pitcher Eddie Everett is on a losing streak but his estranged young daughter, Laurel, wants to help restore his self-confidence. She prays for help, and along it comes in the guise of an angel, Bob Bugler, who still hasn't earned his wings, and a bunch of inept angel helpers. Directed by Robert King. Stars: Patrick Warburton (Eddie Everett), Brittney Irvin (Laurel), Kurt Fuller (Simon), Rebecca Jenkins (Claire Everett), Duane Davis (Randy Fleck), David Alan Grier (Bob Bugler). Released on video in 2000.

Angels in the Outfield (film) Foster child Roger is told with grim humor that there is about as much chance for his family getting back together as there is for the last-place Angels baseball team to win the pennant. But miracles do happen. When 11-year-old Roger prays for divine intervention, a band of real angels, including one named Al, answers the call. Although nobody except Roger can see or hear these heaven-sent guardians, it is not long before hot-tempered and skeptical team manager George Knox sees the extraordinary evidence of something magical helping his team out of the basement and into the playoffs. With the angels' presence being felt on and off the field, the players and young Roger discover the power of believing in dreams and finding the courage never to give up hope. Released on July 15, 1994. Directed by William Dear. Produced in association with Caravan Pictures. 103 min. Stars Danny Glover (George Knox), Tony Danza (Mel Clark), Brenda Fricker (Maggie Nelson), Ben Johnson (Hank Murphy), Jay O. Sanders (Wanch Wilder), Christopher Lloyd (Al), Joseph Gordon-Levitt (Roger). Many of the baseball stadium sequences were filmed at the Oakland Coliseum. The film was a remake of a 1951 MGM film starring Paul Douglas. Released on video in 1995.

Angie (film) Born and raised in the tight-knit neighborhood of Bensonhurst, Brooklyn, Angie has a growing need for personal fulfillment that expresses itself in ways her family and best friend Tina cannot understand. When Angie becomes pregnant by her longtime boyfriend, Vinnie, and

begins an affair with Noel, a successful lawyer in Manhattan, everyone is aghast, increasingly so when Angie decides not to marry Vinnie but still have the baby. After the child is born and her affair with Noel ends, Angie embarks on a journey of self-discovery facing her family's darkest secrets, and learning to take responsibility for herself and her new baby. Released on March 4, 1994. Filmed in CinemaScope. Directed by Martha Coolidge. A Hollywood Picture, in association with Caravan Pictures. Adapted from Avra Wing's novel, *Angie, I Says*. 108 min. Stars Geena Davis (Angie), James Gandolfino (Vinnie), Aida Turturro (Tina), Philip Bosco (Frank), Stephen Rea (Noel). Location shooting took place in the Bensonhurst section of Brooklyn.

Angus MacBadger The accountant at Toad Hall in *The Adventures of Ichabod and Mr. Toad*; voiced by Campbell Grant.

Animagique Black light show based on the greatest moments from Disney classics; opened at Walt Disney Studios Paris on March 16, 2002.

Animal Kingdom, Disney's Disney's largest park, at 500 acres, opened as part of the Walt Disney World complex on April 22, 1998. Filled with thrilling rides, lush landscaping, and dramatic animal encounters, the park entertains and educates guests about creatures ranging from live animals to dinosaurs. As part of the Kilimanjaro Safaris attraction, guests view at close range a multitude of animals including giraffes, zebras, antelopes, hippos, and elephants roaming a savanna larger than the entire Disneyland Park. Lowland gorillas can be viewed on the Pangani Forest Exploration Trail. In all, there are approximately 1,000 animals, representing 200 species. The hub of the park contains Safari Village, with the giant Tree of Life, intricately carved with more than 300 animal images and including a

special-effects show about insects, *It's Tough to Be a Bug*. Guests can take the Wildlife Express train ride to Rafiki's Planet Watch, to learn about

animal conservation and become aware of animal issues. To view animals of the past, guests can visit DinoLand U.S.A., with its Dinosaur! attraction. An Asia area, featuring the Maharajah Jungle Trek and the Kali River Rapids, opened March 1, 1999.

Animal Kingdom Lodge Elegant 1,307-room resort that opened next to Disney's Animal Kingdom at Walt Disney World on April 16, 2001. The hotel features three savannas where guests can observe animals from their room balconies and three restaurants—Jiko, Boma, and Mara.

Animals at Home in the Desert (film) Segment from *The Living Desert*; released on 16mm for schools in November 1974. Shows how desert animals have adapted to the region.

Animals of the South American Jungle (film) Segment from *Jungle Cat*, released on 16mm for schools in December 1974. Tells of such Amazon jungle animals as the monkeys, marmosets, sloths, jaguars, and boa constrictors.

Animated Atlas of the World, The (film) Short animated film telling of the geological and meteorological aspects of the ocean, for showing in Seabase Alpha in The Living Seas, Epcot.

Opened on January 15, 1986. Directed by Mike West.

Animated features, classic The major Disney full-length animated features produced by Walt Disney Feature Animation have been deemed Disney Classics. This list does not include direct-to-video features, theatrical features made by Disney Television Animation, stop-motion animated features (such as *Tim Burton's The Nightmare Before Christmas*) or computer animated features (such as *Toy Story*). The films are as follows:

1. *Snow White and the Seven Dwarfs* (1937)
2. *Pinocchio* (1940)
3. *Fantasia* (1940)
4. *Dumbo* (1941)
5. *Bambi* (1942)
6. *Saludos Amigos* (1943)
7. *The Three Caballeros* (1945)
8. *Make Mine Music* (1946)
9. *Fun and Fancy Free* (1947)
10. *Melody Time* (1948)
11. *The Adventures of Ichabod and Mr. Toad* (1949)
12. *Cinderella* (1950)
13. *Alice in Wonderland* (1951)
14. *Peter Pan* (1953)
15. *Lady and the Tramp* (1955)
16. *Sleeping Beauty* (1959)
17. *One Hundred and One Dalmatians* (1961)
18. *The Sword in the Stone* (1963)
19. *The Jungle Book* (1967)
20. *The Aristocats* (1970)
21. *Robin Hood* (1973)
22. *The Many Adventures of Winnie the Pooh* (1977)
23. *The Rescuers* (1977)
24. *The Fox and the Hound* (1981)
25. *The Black Cauldron* (1985)
26. *The Great Mouse Detective* (1986)
27. *Oliver & Company* (1988)
28. *The Little Mermaid* (1989)
29. *The Rescuers Down Under* (1990)
30. *Beauty and the Beast* (1991)
31. *Aladdin* (1992)
32. *The Lion King* (1994)
33. *Pocahontas* (1995)
34. *The Hunchback of Notre Dame* (1996)
35. *Hercules* (1997)
36. *Mulan* (1998)
37. *Tarzan* (1999)
38. *Fantasia/2000* (2000)
39. *The Emperor's New Groove* (2000)
40. *Atlantis: The Lost Empire* (2001)
41. *Lilo & Stitch* (2002)
42. *Treasure Planet* (2002)
43. *Brother Bear* (2003)
44. *Home on the Range* (2004)

Animated features, computer The first film to extensively use computer technology was *Tron* in 1982, though it was primarily a live-action motion picture. Beginning with *The Black Cauldron*, digital elements found their way into the classic animated features, and computers soon simplified the inking and painting tasks. Eventually, some animated features were made primarily with computer imagery. They are:

1. *Toy Story* (1995)
2. *a bug's life* (1998)
3. *Toy Story 2* (1999)
4. *Dinosaur* (2000)
5. *Monsters, Inc.* (2001)
6. *Finding Nemo* (2003)
7. *The Incredibles* (2004)
8. *Chicken Little* (2005)
9. *Cars* (2006)

Animated features; live-action features with animated characters or segments

1. *The Reluctant Dragon* (1941)
2. *Victory Through Air Power* (1943)
3. *Song of the South* (1946)
4. *So Dear to My Heart* (1949)
5. *Mary Poppins* (1964)
6. *Bedknobs and Broomsticks* (1971)
7. *Pete's Dragon* (1977)
8. *Who Framed Roger Rabbit* (1988)

Animated features, other Beginning in 1990, Disney had its Television Animation division (later DisneyToon Studios) produce a series of animated features, which debuted in movie theaters then immediately made the transition to video. (See *Video* for direct-to-video animated features.) These films were:

1. *Ducktales: The Movie, Treasure of the Lost Lamp* (1990)—released as a Disney Movietoon
2. *A Goofy Movie* (1995)
3. *Doug's 1ˢᵗ Movie* (1999)
4. *The Tigger Movie* (2000)
5. *Recess: School's Out* (2001)
6. *Return to Never Land* (2002)
7. *The Jungle Book 2* (2003)—from Disney-Toon Studios
8. *Piglet's Big Movie* (2003)
9. *Teacher's Pet* (2004)
10. *Pooh's Heffalump Movie* (2005)

Animated features, stop-motion

1. *Tim Burton's The Nightmare Before Christmas* (1993)
2. *James and the Giant Peach* (1996)

Animation Building The major building at the Disney Studio when it was built in 1939–40, designed by architect Kem Weber. Divided into separate wings, the three-story structure was earthquake resistant and provided space for the different animation units and the executive offices. It was one of the first major buildings to be air-conditioned in Southern California, and was designed so that all of the offices had windows and the artists could get outside light. Walt Disney's office was located on the third floor. Over the years, as live-action production and other company activities encroached on animation, less and less of the building was used for that purpose. Finally, in 1985, all the animation offices moved to a building near Walt Disney Imagineering in Glendale. In late 1994, a newly constructed animation building opened at the Disney Studio, just across Riverside Drive, and the animators made a triumphant return to the lot. The original Animation Building has been seen in several live-action Disney films, often doubling as a college building.

Animation Courtyard Area at Walt Disney Studios Paris, featuring a 60-foot-high Sorcerer's hat.

Animation Gallery Shop opened at Disney-MGM Studios on May 1, 1989. Located at the end of the Animation Tour, it features a selection of Disney cels and other artwork, along with books on animation.

Animation photo transfer process A process, known as APT, which was first used at the Disney Studio during the production of *The Black Cauldron*, whereby photography was used in the production of cels. David Spencer of the Studio's Still Camera Department won an Academy Award in 1986 for the development of the process. The computer, however, would soon render the APT obsolete.

Animation Tour Opened at Disney-MGM Studios on May 1, 1989. For the first time, guests could watch story personnel, animators, layout artists, background artists, and ink-and-paint technicians at work producing animated motion pictures. Large windows, and explanatory television monitors, enabled guests walking through the department to see some of the intricate work that goes into the making of an animated film, while not disturbing the artists. Guests found it fascinating. The animation staff in Florida contributed numerous scenes to the Disney animated features, and produced *Off His Rockers*, *Trail Mix-up*, and *Roller Coaster Rabbit* totally on their own. In the mid-1990s, they geared up to produce a complete animated feature, *Mulan*, by themselves. The Florida Studio was also primarily responsible for *Lilo & Stitch* and *Brother Bear*; it closed in 2004.

Anka, Paul Actor/singer; appeared in *Captain Ron* (Donaldson).

Ann-Margret Actress; appeared in *Newsies* (Medda Larkson).

Anna (television) Unsold pilot for a television series; a feisty elderly white woman and a struggling African American actor share an apartment in New York City. Aired on NBC on August 25,

1990. 30 min. Directed by Noam Pitlik. Stars Maria Charles, Keith Diamond, Tom LaGrua, Dennis Lipscomb, Bill Macy, Herb Edelman.

Annakin, Ken For Disney, he directed *The Story of Robin Hood and His Merrie Men*, *The Sword and the Rose*, *Swiss Family Robinson*, and *Third Man on the Mountain*. He was named a Disney Legend in 2002.

Annapolis (film) After winning admission to the Naval Academy at Annapolis, Jake Huard wonders if a regular kid from a poor blue-collar family can fit into the Academy's pressure-cooker atmosphere. Barely making the grade as a plebe, Jake has one last shot at proving he has what it takes to become an officer—he decides to enter the notoriously fierce Navy boxing competition known as the Brigade Championships, and face off against his archnemesis, Midshipman Lt. Cole. Everything Jake has ever hoped for stands in the balance: the chance to make his father proud, validate his lieutenant's faith in him, stand up for his fellow plebes, and, most of all, forge a different future. Released on January 27, 2006. Directed by Justin Lin. Stars James Franco (Jake Huard), Tyrese Gibson (Cole), Jordana Brewster, Donnie Wahlberg (Lt. Cmdr. Burton), Chi McBride, Vicellous Reon Shannon, Wilmer Calderon. Began filming in October 2004, in Philadelphia.

Anne Frank (television) Four-hour television miniseries, airing on ABC on May 20–21, 2001. Based on Melissa Müller's book, *Anne Frank: A Biography*. Anne Frank, a Jew living in Amsterdam during World War II, goes into hiding with her family to escape the Nazis. This miniseries encompasses her idyllic childhood before the war, her adolescence in Amsterdam, and her last months in captivity. Anne's diary, which she left behind, presents a moving narrative of Jews during the Holocaust. Produced by Milk and Honey Productions, in association with Dorothy Pictures, Inc., for Touchstone Television. Directed by Robert Dornhelm. Stars Ben Kingsley (Otto Frank), Brenda Blethyn (Auguste Van Pels), Hannah Taylor Gordon (Anne Frank). Released on video in 2001.

Anne of Avonlea: The Continuing Story of Anne of Green Gables (television) Movie on The Disney Channel, airing in four parts on four consecutive weeks. Directed by Kevin Sullivan. Premiered on May 19, 1987. Anne is now a teacher in Avonlea, but she leaves town for another job because she feels she cannot marry Gilbert Blythe. When she returns on vacation, she eventually patches things up with Gilbert. 238 min. Stars Megan Follows, Colleen Dewhurst, Dame Wendy Hiller, Frank Converse, Jonathan Crombie, Patricia Hamilton.

Annette (film) Serial on the *Mickey Mouse Club* during the 1957–58 season. Directed by Charles Lamont. Country girl Annette goes to visit her town relatives and finds romance in the local school, but is also accused of theft. Stars Annette Funicello, Tim Considine, David Stollery, Judy Nugent, Richard Deacon, Sylvia Field, Mary Wickes, Roberta Shore, Doreen Tracy, Shelley Fabares, Sharon Baird, Tommy Cole. Based on the book *Margaret*, by Janette Sebring Lowrey. 20 episodes.

Annette's Diner Restaurant in Disney Village at Disneyland Paris; opened on April 12, 1992.

Annie (television) Two-hour television movie, airing on *The Wonderful World of Disney* on November 7, 1999. A new production of the classic musical about the little redheaded orphan who finds a permanent, loving home with the big-hearted billionaire, Daddy Warbucks, much to the chagrin of her mean-spirited orphanage matron, Miss Hannigan. Directed by Rob Marshall. Stars Kathy Bates (Miss Hannigan), Alicia Morton (Annie), Alan Cumming (Rooster Hannigan), Audra McDonald (Grace Farrell), Kristin Chenoweth (Lily St. Regis), Victor Garber (Oliver Warbucks). Based on the Broadway musical written by Thomas Meehan, with music and lyrics by Charles Strouse and Martin Charnin. Andrea McArdle, who played Annie on Broadway 20 years previously, has a cameo role as "Star-to-Be." Filmed entirely on location in Los Angeles. The show won Emmys for choreography (Rob Marshall) and music direction (Paul Bogaev). Released on video in 2002.

Annual passports Special year-long admission passes to the Disney parks, introduced at Walt Disney World on September 28, 1982, and at Disneyland in June 1983.

Another Stakeout (film) In this sequel to *Stakeout*, Las Vegas police lose an important witness when their hideout is blown up by the criminals who want the witness dead. The search for the witness moves to Seattle where two police detectives are joined by a female assistant DA in staking out a couple on Bainbridge Island; the trio pose as father, mother, and son, and have as much trouble getting along with each other as they do with their surveillance. Released on July 23, 1993. Directed by John Badham. A Touchstone film. 109 min. Stars Richard Dreyfuss (Chris Lecce), Emilio Estevez (Bill Reimers), Rosie O'Donnell (Gina Garrett), Cathy Moriarty (Lu Delano), Dennis Farina (Brian O'Hara), Marcia Strassman (Pam O'Hara). Location filming took place in Las Vegas and in the vicinity of Vancouver, British Columbia, Canada. Released on video in 1994.

Ansara, Michael Actor; appeared in *The Bears and I* (Oliver Red Fern), and narrated *Shokee, the Everglades Panther*.

Anselmo, Tony Animator; joined Disney in 1980, and the current voice of Donald Duck, he apprenticed with Clarence Nash for three years and then took over after Nash's death in 1985.

Antarctica Directed by Frank Marshall. A Touchstone Pictures/Mandeville Films production. Stars Paul Walker, Jason Biggs, Bruce Greenwood, Moon Bloodgood. Filming began in Canada on February 21, 2005.

Antarctica—Operation Deepfreeze (television) Television show; aired on June 5, 1957, continues *Antarctica—Past and Present*, with the efforts to explore Antarctica during the International Geophysical Year. Produced, directed, and narrated by Winston Hibler. The efforts to build bases at McMurdo Sound and Little America are chronicled.

Antarctica—Past and Present (television) Television show; aired on September 12, 1956,

begins with a history of attempts to reach the South Pole, and continues with the Operation Deepfreeze operation of the Navy. Directed and narrated by Winston Hibler. See also *To the South Pole for Science* for the third program in the Antarctica trilogy.

Anwar, Gabrielle Actress, appeared in *Wild Hearts Can't Be Broken* (Sonora Webster) and *The Three Musketeers* (Queen Anne).

Anything Can Happen Day Wednesday on the 1950s *Mickey Mouse Club*.

Apache Friendship (television) Television show, part ten of *Texas John Slaughter*.

Apocalypto (film) Directed by Mel Gibson. Planned for release in summer 2006.

Apollo God of the sun in the *Pastoral* segment of *Fantasia*.

Appearances (television) Unsold pilot for a television series; appearances are deceiving in the story of a "perfect" American family, at home and at work. Aired on NBC on June 17, 1990. 120 min. Directed by Win Phelps. Stars Scott Paulin,

Wendy Phillips, Casey Biggs, Matt McGrath, Ernest Borgnine, Robert Hooks.

Apple Dumpling Gang, The (film) In 1879, gambler Russel Donavan arrives in Quake City, California, always looking for a profitable poker game. But despite his frequent losses, he ends up with a shipment of valuables consigned to a local ne'er-do-well who has lit out for San Francisco. The "valuables"—the Bradley orphans Bobby, 12, Clovis, 7, and Celia, 5—arrive aboard a stagecoach driven by pretty "Dusty" Clydesdale. Desperate, Russel tries to unload the brood, who discover a huge gold nugget in a nearby mine, causing unwelcome interest by the bumbling Hash Knife Outfit. As Russel rewards the now-famous orphans with their favorite meal of apple dumplings, the numbskull desperadoes try to steal the gold, but, as usual, are caught. However, the dangerous Stillwell gang also plan a bank heist, but are undone when the children and the Hash Knife Outfit, aided by Russel and Dusty, break into the holdup. Russel and Dusty marry, uniting the happy new family now known as "The Apple Dumpling Gang." Released on July 4, 1975. Directed by Norman Tokar. 100 min. Stars Bill Bixby (Russel Donavan), Tim Conway (Amos), Don Knotts (Theodore), Susan Clark (Magnolia), David Wayne (Col. T. T. Clydesdale), Slim Pickens (Frank Stillwell), Harry Morgan (Homer McCoy), John McGiver (Leonard Sharpe), Don Knight (John Wintle), Clay O'Brien (Bobby Bradley), Brad Savage (Clovis Bradley), Stacy Manning (Celia Bradley). The story was based on the book by Jack M. Bickham. The song "The Apple Dumpling Gang" was written by Shane Tatum and sung by Randy Sparks and The Back Porch Majority. While planning the sets for the film at the Disney Studio, the set designers decided that three copies of the bank had to be built. One was indoors on a soundstage (featuring exterior *and* interior sets), and two matching exteriors were built outdoors on the backlot, one of them roofless and with burned beams exposed, showing the aftermath of an explosion. Location filming took place at the Tropico gold mine in Rosamond, California, and in the Los Padres and Deschutes National Forests in Oregon. The pair-

ing of Tim Conway and Don Knotts worked so well that they were teamed in several later Disney films. The great popularity of the film spawned a sequel in 1979, *The Apple Dumpling Gang Rides Again.* Released on video in 1980, 1985, and 1992. See *Tales of the Apple Dumpling Gang* for a television remake, along with the series *Gun Shy*.

Apple Dumpling Gang Rides Again, The (film) Theodore and Amos, trying to quietly live down their checkered past as part of the Apple Dumpling Gang, find themselves caught up in still another series of hilarious misadventures. Major Gaskill will lose his command of Fort Concho if he cannot stop the raids on his supply wagons, and it is up to Theodore and Amos to bungle their way to a triumphant finale, breaking up a dastardly smuggling ring. Released on June 27, 1979. Directed by Vincent McEveety. 89 min. Stars Tim Conway (Amos), Don Knotts (Theodore), Tim Matheson (Pvt. Jeff Reid), Kenneth Mars (Marshal), Elyssa Davalos (Millie), Jack Elam (Big Mac), Robert Pine (Lt. Jim Ravencroft), Harry Morgan (Major Gaskill), Ruth Buzzi (Tough Kate), Audrey Totter (Martha Osten). The film was shot on location in Sonora, California; Kanab, Utah; and at the Disney Studio in Burbank. Released on video in 1981 and 1985.

Appreciating Differences (film) Educational film, in the Songs for Us series, released in September 1989. 10 min. The film teaches children to value people of different ages, races, sexes, and people with disabilities.

April, May, and June Daisy had three nieces, April, May, and June, in the comic books, making their first appearance in *Walt Disney's Comics and Stories* #149 in February 1953. They never appeared in a film.

Aquamania (film) Goofy cartoon; released on December 20, 1961. Directed by Wolfgang Reitherman. Nominated for an Academy Award, this cartoon looks at how boatsman Goofy and his son spend a weekend. When Goofy demonstrates the art of water-skiing, his son is so impressed he quickly gets them into a championship race,

where Goofy has all sorts of misadventures, including everything from an octopus to a roller coaster. Finally, Goofy manages to win the race and the cup.

Aquarela do Brasil (film) Segment of *Saludos Amigos*, in which José Carioca teaches Donald Duck to dance the samba. Re-released as a short on June 24, 1955.

Aquatopia Attraction at Tokyo DisneySea; opened on September 4, 2001. Guests have a wild ride across the waters of Port Discovery on a hydro-glider water vehicle, which spins and twirls across a shallow pool through a maze of fountains, rock formations, and whirlpools.

Arachnophobia (film) Fed up with the frustrations of big-city living, Dr. Ross Jennings moves his wife and two kids to the sleepy community of Canaima, California. They soon learn that they are not the only recent arrivals. Jennings discovers a deadly spider, accidentally imported from the Amazon jungles, that has mated and set thousands of offspring loose on the unsuspecting populace. Teamed up with exterminator Delbert McClintock, Jennings is forced to confront his past in the spine-tingling showdown. Released on July 18, 1990. Directed by Frank Marshall. The first film from Hollywood Pictures, in cooperation with Amblin Entertainment. 109 min. Stars Jeff Daniels (Ross Jennings), Harley Jane Kozak (Molly Jennings), John Goodman (Delbert McClintock), Julian Sands (Dr. James Atheron). The publicity for the film was highlighted by the phrase, "eight legs, two fangs, and an attitude."

The lead spider was an Amazonian bird-eating tarantula, and the actors had to become accustomed, or at least less reticent, in working with the intimidating (and shockingly large) arachnids. Locations included a remote jungle region of Venezuela near Angel Falls, and the town of Cambria, California. Released on video in 1991. See also *Thrills, Chills & Spiders: The Making of Arachnophobia.*

Aracuan Bird Pesky character who bothers Donald Duck in *The Three Caballeros, Clown of the Jungle,* and *Melody Time.*

Aramaki, Hideo "Indian" He began work at Disneyland as chef at the Tahitian Terrace in 1964, and two years later was promoted to executive chef over all the food facilities in Disneyland, a position which he held until his retirement in 1985. He was named a Disney Legend in 2005.

Arau, Alfonso Actor; appeared in *Scandalous John* (Paco) and *Run, Cougar, Run* (Etie).

Arcata d'Antigiani Shop in Italy in World Showcase at Epcot, opened October 1, 1982, and closed September 30, 1989. Became Delizie Italiane.

Archimedes Wise owl friend of Merlin in *The Sword in the Stone*; voiced by Junius C. Matthews.

Arctic Antics (film) Silly Symphony cartoon; released on June 27, 1930. Directed by Ub Iwerks. Polar bears, seals, and penguins perform on cakes of ice and in the water.

Arctic Region and Its Polar Bears, The (film) Part of *White Wilderness*, released on 16mm for schools in September 1964. In the unmapped valleys, the annual thaw brings forth the walrus to confront his mortal enemy, the polar bear.

Arden, Eve (1912–1990) Actress; appeared in *The Strongest Man in the World* (Harriet).

Ariel Mermaid heroine of *The Little Mermaid*; voiced by Jodi Benson. Her sisters are Aquata, Andrina, Arista, Attina, Adella, and Alana.

Ariel's Seafood restaurant with a nautical motif at the Beach Club Resort at Walt Disney World. It opened on November 19, 1990, and closed on May 3, 1997.

Ariel's Grotto Restaurant at Paradise Pier at Disney's California Adventure; opened December 20, 2002. Formerly Avalon Cove. Also a character greeting area in Fantasyland at Magic Kingdom Park at Walt Disney World; opened in October 1996.

Ariel's Playground Attraction in Mermaid Lagoon at Tokyo DisneySea; opened on September 4, 2001. It consists of Fishermen's Nets, Kelp Forest, Galleon Graveyard, Ariel's Grotto, Cave of Shadows, Sea Dragon, Ursula's Dungeon, Starfish Playpen, and Mermaid Sea Spray. The playground is a fun-filled area created especially for children, where they can climb, crawl, interact, and explore in many colorful settings that feature locations and characters from *The Little Mermaid*.

Aristocats, The (film) Animated feature in which a pedigreed mother cat, Duchess, and her three kittens, Toulouse, Berlioz, and Marie, are catnapped by a greedy butler named Edgar who hopes to gain by getting the inheritance left to the family of cats by their owner, Madame Bonfamille. Things look hopeless for the cats until they are befriended by Thomas O'Malley, an easygoing alley cat. After the cats have many misadventures getting back to Paris, the villainous butler is frustrated when a gang of alley cats and a mouse named Roquefort join O'Malley to rescue Duchess and her kittens. Premiere in Los Angeles on December 11, 1970; general release on December 24, 1970. Directed by Wolfgang Reitherman. 78 min. Features the voices of Phil Harris (Thomas O'Malley), Eva Gabor (Duchess), Sterling Holloway (Roquefort), Scatman Crothers (Scat Cat), Paul Winchell (Chinese Cat), Lord Tim Hudson (English Cat), Vito Scotti (Italian Cat), Thurl Ravenscroft (Russian Cat), Dean Clark (Berlioz), Liz English (Marie), Gary Dubin (Toulouse), Nancy Kulp (Frou-Frou), Charles Lane (Georges Hautecourt), Hermione Baddeley (Madame Adelaide Bonfamille), Roddy Maude-Roxby (Edgar), Bill Thompson (Uncle Waldo), George Lindsey (Lafayette), Pat Buttram (Napoleon), Monica Evans (Abigail Gabble), Carole Shelley (Amelia Gabble), Pete Renoudet (French Milkman), and Maurice Chevalier, who sang the

title tune. This was the first feature-length animated cartoon completed without Walt Disney. The song "Ev'rybody Wants to Be a Cat," was written by Floyd Huddleston and Al Rinker. "Thomas O'Malley" was written by Terry Gilkyson, and Richard and Robert Sherman composed "The Aristocats," "She Never Felt Alone," and "Scales and Arpeggios." For the background musical score, George Bruns featured the accordionlike musette for French flavor and with his considerable background with jazz bands in the 1940s, provided a great deal of jazz music. The film was four years in the making, budgeted at over $4 million, and included more than 325,000 drawings made by 35 animators, with twenty main sequences to the film having 1,125 separate scenes using 900 painted backgrounds. The project employed some 250 people. The film was a box office success, earning reissues in 1980 and 1987. Released on video in 1996.

Arizona Sheepdog (film) Featurette; released on May 25, 1955. Directed by Larry Lansburgh. 22 min. Nick and Rock are two sheepdogs, belonging to a herder in Arizona, who must help him get the sheep from the dry lands of the plains up to the lush mountain pastures. Along the way, they have to search for lost sheep and ford mountain streams, and protect the herd from mountain lions. Later released on 16mm as *Nicky and Rock—Working Sheep Dogs.*

Arkin, Alan Actor; appeared in *The Rocketeer* (Peevy), *Indian Summer* (Unca Lou), *The Jerky Boys* (Ernie Lazarro), *Grosse Pointe Blank* (Dr. Oatman), and in the title role on the television series *Harry.*

Arlen, Richard (1905–1976) Actor; appeared on television in *The Sky's the Limit.*

Armageddon (film) An asteroid the size of Texas is heading directly toward Earth at 22,000 mph, with the potential to destroy the planet. NASA's executive director, Dan Truman, has only one option—to send up a crew to destroy the asteroid. He enlists the help of an unlikely hero, Harry S. Stamper—the world's foremost deep-core oil driller—and Stamper's roughneck team of drillers to land on the asteroid, drill 800 feet into its surface, and drop a nuclear device into the core. On this heroic journey, utilizing two space shuttles, *Freedom* and *Independence*, they face the most physically and emotionally challenging conditions ever encountered in order to save the world and prevent Armageddon. Directed by Michael Bay. A Touchstone Picture. Released on July 1, 1998, after a June 29 World Premiere screening at the Kennedy Space Center. Stars Bruce Willis (Harry Stamper), Billy Bob Thornton (Dan Truman), Liv Tyler (Grace Stamper), Ben Affleck (A.J. Frost), Will Patton (Chick Chapple), Peter Stormare (Lev Andropov), Keith David (General Kimsey), Owen Wilson (Oscar Choi), William Fichtner (Willie Sharp), Steve Buscemi (Rockhound). Filmed in CinemaScope. 151 min. NASA technical advisers who helped give some scientific accuracy to the project included their former director of advanced programs, Ivan Bekey, and former astronaut Joseph Allen. In order to experience some of the astronaut training firsthand, Willis and Affleck, along with members of the crew, spent several days at the Johnson Space Center in Texas, where the two actors were the first civilians to be allowed in the lab's neutral-bouyancy tank, where astronauts train to work in space suits. In order to construct the asteroid set on Stage 2 at the Disney Studios, one of the largest in Hollywood, craftsmen had to excavate up to 30 feet below the stage level, so there would be space for the tall set pieces. Exterior shots utilized vast terrain outside of Kadoka, South Dakota. NASA allowed the company to shoot actual shuttle launches at the Kennedy Space Center in Florida, and to film at the Johnson Space Center and Ellington Air Field in Texas (where they received a surprise visit from former President George H. Bush). *Armageddon* became Disney's highest-grossing film, until passed by *The Sixth Sense*. Released on video in 1998.

Armageddon: Les Effets Speciaux Attraction at Walt Disney Studios Paris; opened on March 16, 2002. Guests embark on a voyage through the history of special effects.

Armstrong, Louis (1900–1971) Trumpet virtuoso, first performed at Disneyland for the second Dixieland at Disneyland on September 30, 1961, and then returned in 1962 and 1964 through 1967. He also appeared on the television show *Disneyland After Dark*. In 1968, Buena Vista Records released an album: "Louis Armstrong—Disney Songs the Satchmo Way."

Armstrong, Sam (1893–1976) Storyman and background artist; worked at Disney from 1934 to 1941.

Army Mascot, The (film) Pluto cartoon; released on May 22, 1942. Directed by Clyde

Geronimi. Pluto yearns to be an Army mascot because of the good food they get, and he outwits a goat mascot to earn the job.

Around the World in 80 Days (film) Eccentric London inventor, Phileas Fogg has come up with the secrets of flight, electricity, and even Rollerblades, but the world has dismissed him as a crackpot. Desperate to be taken seriously, Fogg makes an outlandish bet with Lord Kelvin, the head of the Royal Academy of Science, to circumnavigate the globe in no more than 80 days. With his two sidekicks—Passepartout and femme fatale Monique—Fogg is headed on a frantic, heart-pounding, round-the-world race that takes our heroes to the world's most exotic places by land, sea, and air, facing many adventures and obstacles along the way. Directed by Frank Coraci. A Walt Disney Pictures/Walden Media film. Released on June 16, 2004. Stars Steve Coogan (Phileas Fogg),

Jackie Chan (Passepartout), Cécile De France (Monique), Jim Broadbent (Lord Kelvin). Cameos include Kathy Bates (Queen Victoria), Owen and Luke Wilson (the Wright Brothers), Arnold Schwarzenegger (Prince Hapi). 120 min. Based on the novel by Jules Verne. A remake of Mike Todd's classic 1956 film for United Artists starring David Niven and Cantinflas. Filmed in Super 35-Scope. Released on video in 2004.

Arquette, Rosanna Actress; appeared in *New York Stories* (Paulette) and *Gone Fishin'* (Rita).

Art Corner, The Shop located in Tomorrowland at Disneyland beginning late in 1955 that sold Disney animation art. In 1955 a cel from a recent Disney film cost two or three dollars; think what it would bring on the market today!

Art of Animation, The Tomorrowland display at Disneyland, from May 28, 1960 to September 5, 1966. Walt Disney created this display after making *Sleeping Beauty*, showing the history and development of animation and utilizing elements from *Sleeping Beauty* to explain the actual animation process. Two traveling versions of this exhibit went on tour throughout the United States beginning in 1958 and to the Far East and Europe. Author Bob Thomas wrote a useful book, entitled *The Art of Animation*, explaining the animation process and also using *Sleeping Beauty* as a basis. There was really nothing to compare with the exhibit until the Animation Tour opened at Disney-MGM Studios in 1989, 23 years later.

Art of Disney, The Shop in the Downtown Disney Marketplace at Walt Disney World, selling Disney prints, cels, and other collectibles. Opened on August 28, 1994. Another shop opened at Epcot on October 1, 2000.

Art of Self-Defense, The (film) Goofy cartoon; released on December 26, 1941. Directed by Jack Kinney. Goofy demonstrates, in his inimitable fashion, the arts of defense from the Stone Age to modern times, with the assistance of a narrator.

Art of Skiing, The (film) Goofy cartoon; released on November 14, 1941. Directed by Jack Kinney. In his typical clumsy fashion, Goofy demonstrates various skiing techniques with the aid of offscreen narration.

Artesanias Mexicanas Shop in Mexico in World Showcase at Epcot; opened on October 1, 1982. Sells glass-blown items, crafts, and art objects from Mexico. Presented by Arribas Brothers.

Arthur Young servant who becomes the king in *The Sword in the Stone*; voiced by Ricky Sorenson and Robert Reitherman. Also known as Wart.

Arthur, Bea Actress; appeared on television in *The Golden Girls* (for which she won the Emmy Award as Outstanding Lead Actress in a Comedy Series in 1988).

Artist Point Restaurant in the Wilderness Lodge at Walt Disney World; opened in May 1994. A specialty is salmon, served sizzling on a cedar plank.

Arvida Corporation One of the biggest real estate and development companies in Florida, specializing in planned communities. It was purchased by Disney in May 1984, for $200 million in Disney stock, with the Bass Brothers ending up with 5.9 percent of the Disney stock as a result of the transaction. Part of the reason for the purchase was to dilute the value of the stock, which was at that time being bought up by a corporate raider, Saul Steinberg. While some thought the marriage of the two companies was ideal because of Disney's large land holdings in Florida, others were not so happy, and after Michael Eisner and Frank G. Wells took over the management of Disney, Arvida was sold in 1987 to JMB Realty Corporation for $404 million.

Ashman, Howard (1951–1991) Lyricist, with his partner, Alan Menken, wrote songs for *The Little Mermaid*, *Beauty and the Beast*, and *Aladdin*. He posthumously received an Oscar for *Beauty and the Beast*, for he had died on March 14, 1991, at the age of 40. He was named a Disney Legend in 2001.

Ask Max (television) Television show, aired on November 2, 1986. Directed by Vincent McEveety. Young scientific genius Max tries to impress a girl but she ignores the overweight boy. By designing a special bicycle, which comes to the attention of a toy company, Max comes into great amounts of money, but he learns that money will not win him the girl. Instead, he becomes a hero by helping save an aircraft plant, which employs many locals, from closing. Stars Jeff B. Cohen, Ray Walston, Cassie Yates, Gino DeMauro.

Asner, Edward Actor; appeared in *Gus* (Hank Cooper) and *Perfect Game* (Billy Hicks), and on television in *The Christmas Star* and the series *Thunder Alley*. He appeared on The Disney Channel in *A Friendship in Vienna*. He provided a voice on *Gargoyles*.

Aspen Extreme (film) Two happy-go-lucky young men, Dexter and T.J., leave their humdrum jobs on the auto assembly lines of Detroit and head to Aspen to become ski instructors and win the famous Powder Eight competition. T.J. enjoys instant popularity, while Dexter finds Aspen life more difficult, and, after a disastrous rendezvous with the local drug ring, the two friends part. Their common dream of winning the Powder Eight reunites them until Dexter is accidentally killed during practice in a restricted zone. T.J. vows to win in memory of his partner, and, with an admiring pupil, wins the race. Released on January 22, 1993. A Hollywood Picture. 118 min.

Stars Paul Gross (T.J. Burke), Peter Berg (Dexter Rutecki), Finola Hughes (Bryce Kellogg), Teri Polo (Robin Hand). After opening shots in Detroit, Michigan, the motion picture was filmed on location in Aspen, Colorado, with ski sequences in the Monashee range of the Canadian Rockies in British Columbia. The story was based on real-life experiences of writer/director Patrick Hasburgh. Released on video in 1993.

Associate, The (film) Laurel Ayers, a bright financial analyst, is disgusted when she is passed over for a well-deserved promotion, so she creates a perception that she has formed a partnership with a powerful financial whiz. Fabricating and donning the persona of "Robert S. Cutty," a strutting, ponytailed, bass-voiced man, Laurel maneuvers a number of successful financial deals until her underhanded rival, Frank, attempts to unmask Cutty and appropriate the disguise for his own personal gain. Laurel eventually proves that men do not have a monopoly on creative enterprise. Released on October 25, 1996. Directed by Donald Petrie. A Hollywood Picture. Stars Whoopi Goldberg (Laurel Ayers), Dianne Wiest (Sally), Tim Daly (Frank), Bebe Neuwirth (Camille), Lainie Kazan (Cindy Mason), Austin Pendleton (Aesop), George Martin (Walter Manchester), Eli Wallach (Fallon). 114 min. Based on the French film, *L'Associé*, which was adapted from the novel *El Socio* by Jenaro Prieto. Filmed entirely on location for 11 weeks in New York. Special arrangements were required to accommodate a 130-person cast and crew team invading an active stock market trading floor (they shot on weekends). Academy Award–winning makeup artist Greg Cannom created the prosthetics to turn Goldberg into Cutty; it was a three-and-a-half-hour transformation process. Released on video in 1997.

Astin, John Actor; appeared in *Freaky Friday* (Bill Andrews), and on television in *Mr. Boogedy.* He hosted two episodes of *The Mouse Factory.*

Astin, Mackenzie Actor; appeared in *Iron Will* (Will Stoneman) and on television in *Selma, Lord, Selma* (Jonathan Daniels).

Astin, Sean Actor; appeared in *Encino Man* (Dave Morgan), and on television in *The B.R.A.T. Patrol.*

Astro-Jets Tomorrowland attraction at Disneyland, from March 24, 1956 to September 5, 1966. Also known, from 1964 to 1966 as Tomorrowland Jets; later became Rocket Jets. By manipulating the handle, you could make your jet rise and lower, giving yourself a bird's-eye view of Disneyland as the attraction rotated. At Walt Disney World the attraction was first known as Star Jets and later as Astro Orbiter.

Astro Orbiter New name (1995) for the attraction formerly known as Star Jets in the Walt Disney World Magic Kingdom. An Astro Orbitor

(with a new spelling) attraction, based on the Orbitron at Disneyland Paris, opened at Disneyland on May 22, 1998.

Astuter Computer Revue Show in Epcot Computer Central sponsored by Sperry, from October 1, 1982 to January 2, 1984. Superseded by Backstage Magic. Attempted to explain the workings of computers, by utilizing animation and the actual computers used to operate many of the Epcot attractions.

At Home with Donald Duck (television) Television show; aired on November 21, 1956. Directed by Jack Hannah. A compilation of cartoons for Donald's birthday. Includes a segment with Cubby O'Brien and the Firehouse Five Plus Two. A rerun in 1976 was titled *Happy Birthday Donald Duck*, and substituted footage from the new *Mickey Mouse Club* for the latter segment.

Atencio, Francis X He joined Disney in 1938 as an in-betweener and became an assistant animator on *Fantasia*. He worked on the inventive *Noah's Ark, Jack and Old Mac,* and *A Symposium on Popular Songs,* using stop-motion animation in collaboration with Bill Justice. In 1965, he moved to WED Enterprises, where he worked on Primeval World, Pirates of the Caribbean, Adventure Thru Inner Space, and The Haunted Mansion. For the Disneyland attractions, he wrote the lyrics for "Yo Ho (A  Pirate's Life for Me)" and "Grim Grinning Ghosts." (The X stands for Xavier, but he was called X ever since high school pals gave him that nickname.) He retired in 1984, and was named a Disney Legend in 1996.

Atkinson, Rowan Actor; voiced Zazu in *The Lion King*.

Atlanta Braves Walt Disney World announced in February 1996 that the Atlanta Braves would use Disney's Wide World of Sports for their spring training home beginning in 1998. However, they inaugurated the stadium at the sports complex with an exhibition game against the Cincinnati Reds on March 28, 1997.

Atlantic Dance Nightclub at the Board-Walk Resort at Walt Disney World; opened July 1, 1996. The club has experimented with different dance styles, including Latino and swing.

Atlantic Wear & Wardrobe Emporium Shop in the Beach Club Resort at Walt Disney World; opened on November 19, 1990. Gifts and souvenirs are themed to the Beach Club atmosphere. It closed on January 5, 2005, to be remodeled and reopened, on March 24, 2005, as Beach Club Marketplace (including grab 'n go food service).

Atlantis: Milo's Return (film) Milo, Kida, and their crew gear up for more action in this direct-to-video sequel to *Atlantis: The Lost Empire,* with the story beginning just a few months after the original film's conclusion. While Kida—now Atlantean queen—and explorer Milo Thatch have set about rebuilding the city and restoring greatness to the Atlantean culture as a center of knowledge and learning, they are surprised by the return of Team Atlantis with billionaire Preston Whitmore in tow. The team must leave Atlantis to discover what mysterious powers are causing trouble in a new, fantastic location. Directed by Tad Stones, Toby Shelton, and Victor A. Cook. Released May 20, 2003. Voices include James Taylor (Milo), Cree Summer (Kida), Don Novello (Vinny Santorini), Stephen Barr (Cookie), Jacqueline Obradors (Audrey), John Mahoney (Preston B. Whitmore), Corey Burton (Mole), Florence Stanley (Mrs. Packard), Phil Morris (Dr. Sweet). 80 min. From Walt Disney Television Animation.

Atlantis: The Lost Empire (film) In 1914, Milo Thatch, an inexperienced young museum cartographer and linguistics expert, joins up with a group of daredevil explorers in an expedition funded by an eccentric billionaire, Preston B. Whitmore, to find the legendary lost empire of Atlantis. Milo is continuing a quest begun by his late grandfather. Utilizing a long-lost journal, which provides new clues to the location, they embark in a state-of-the-art submarine, the *Ulysses,* under fearless but cunning Commander Rourke. But

what they find defies their expectations—crystal energy that has kept the Atlantis inhabitants alive. Rourke steals the crystals and kidnaps the Atlantean Princess Kida. It is up to Milo to come to the rescue, save the princess, and protect the city from certain doom. Directed by Kirk Wise and Gary Trousdale. Released in New York and Los Angeles on June 8, and nationwide on June 15, 2001. World premiere was at the El Capitan Theater in Hollywood on June 3. Voices include Michael J. Fox (Milo Thatch), James Garner (Commander Rourke), Cree Summer (Princess Kida), Leonard Nimoy (King of Atlantis), Phil Morris (Dr. Sweet), Jacqueline Obradors (Audrey Ramirez), Claudie Christian (Helga Sinclair), John Maloney (Preston B. Whitmore), Jim Varney (Cookie), David Ogden Stiers (Fenton Q. Harcourt), Don Novello (Vinny Santorini), Florence Stanley (Mrs. Packard). 96 min. James Newton Howard composed the film's epic score. The directors based the design on the style of cult comic book artist Mike Mignola, who served as an artistic consultant. For the Atlanteans, an original readable, speakable language was created by linguistics expert Marc Okrand. Filmed in CinemaScope. Released on video in 2002. See *Atlantis: Milo's Return* for sequel.

Atom, The: A Closer Look (film) Updated educational version of *Our Friend the Atom*, released in September 1980.

Atta Girl, Kelly! (television) Three-part television show; aired on March 5, 12, and 19, 1967. The three episodes were titled *K for Kelly*, *Dog of Destiny*, and *The Seeing Eye*. Directed by James Sheldon. Story of a seeing-eye dog, through its being raised as a puppy by a young boy who resists giving it up, to its rigorous training, and finally its placement with a blind attorney, who has lost a previous dog and finds it hard to trust the new one. Stars Billy Corcoran (Danny Richards), Beau Bridges (Matt Howell), Arthur Hill (Evan Clayton), J. D. Cannon, James Broderick, Jan Shepard.

Attmore, Billy "Pop" Actor; appeared in *Treasure of Matecumbe* (Thad), and as a Mouseketeer on the new *Mickey Mouse Club*. He was born

March 19, 1965. Billy was the only Mouseketeer to have earlier acted in a Disney movie.

Attwooll, Hugh Production manager and associate producer for a number of Disney films made in Europe beginning with *Kidnapped*. He also worked on such films as *Greyfriars Bobby*, *The Moon-Spinners*, *Candleshoe*, *In Search of the Castaways*, *The Three Lives of Thomasina*, *The Littlest Horse Thieves*, and *Watcher in the Woods*. He was named a Disney Legend in 2002.

Atwell, Roy (1880–1962) He voiced Doc in *Snow White and the Seven Dwarfs*.

Au Petit Café Restaurant in France in World Showcase at Epcot; opened on October 1, 1982. Lighter fare than one would find at Les Chefs de France or Le Bistro de Paris, but still tasty French cuisine served in typical French sidewalk café style.

Auberge de Cendrillon Quality sit-down restaurant in Fantasyland at Disneyland Paris; opened on April 12, 1992. Sponsored by Vittel.

Auberjonois, René Actor; appeared in *Inspector Gadget* (Artemus Bradford), on television in *The Christmas Star* (Mr. Summer) and *Geppetto* (Prof. Buonragazzo), and as the voice of Louis in *The Little Mermaid*.

Audio-Animatronics When Walt Disney found an antique mechanical singing bird in a shop in New Orleans when he was there on vacation, he was intrigued. He reasoned that he and his staff had been doing animation on film for years, but it would be fun to try some three-dimensional animation. He had Wathel Rogers and other studio technicians take the bird apart to see how it worked. Then work was started to come up with a prototype figure. Charles Cristodoro, a sculptor, modeled some human heads, utilizing actor Buddy Ebsen and staff members around the Studio as models, and experiments were made with cams, hydraulics, and other methods of enabling the figures to move realistically. One early concept was for a figure of Confucius who would interact with guests in a Chinese restaurant at Disneyland. The Chinese restaurant was never built, so the technicians turned instead to the nation's sixteenth president, Abraham Lincoln. When Robert Moses, in charge of the 1964–1965 New York World's Fair, saw the figure being tested at the Disney Studio, he knew that he had to have it for the Fair. Walt agreed to speed up development of Lincoln, and the state of Illinois came forward to act as sponsor. The exhibit opened in April 1964, to great acclaim. But, Audio-Animatronics had actually been used in a show that had opened at Disneyland the previous year. Less sophisticated figures of birds, flowers, and tiki gods populated the Enchanted Tiki Room. From then on, Audio-Animatronics would be an accepted part of many of the attractions at the Disney parks, reaching high degrees of complexity in Pirates of the Caribbean, the Haunted Mansion, America Sings, the Country Bear Jamboree, Spaceship Earth, The Hall of Presidents, and the American Adventure.

Audley, Eleanor (1905–1991) She voiced Lady Tremaine in *Cinderella* and Maleficent in *Sleeping Beauty*, and appeared on television in *The Swamp Fox*. At Disneyland, she provided the voice for the disembodied head of Madame Leota in the crystal ball in The Haunted Mansion.

Aumont, Jean Pierre (1911–2001) Actor; appeared in *Jefferson in Paris* (D'Hancarville), and on television in *The Horse Without a Head* (Inspector Sinet).

Aunt Jemima Pancake House Restaurant in Frontierland at Disneyland from August 9, 1955 to January 1962. Became Aunt Jemima's Kitchen (July 17, 1962 to 1970), Magnolia Tree Terrace (1970 to 1971), and then River Belle Terrace. In the early days of Disneyland, Aunt Jemima herself would greet guests outside her restaurant. Her cheerful disposition made her a well-loved fixture in Frontierland. The restaurant was operated by Quaker Oats from 1955 to 1967, then Disneyland took over the operation until 1970, though Quaker Oats remained as a sponsor.

Aunt Sarah Stern relative who comes to care for the baby in *Lady and the Tramp*; voiced by Verna Felton.

Autograph Hound, The (film) Donald Duck cartoon; released on September 1, 1939. Directed by Jack King. Despite a watchful security guard, Donald manages to sneak into a movie studio in his attempt to get autographs. But when the guard catches him and he gives his name, the stars, including Greta Garbo, Bette Davis, and Mickey Rooney, come to get *his* autograph. Includes caricatures of many movie stars.

Autopia Tomorrowland attraction at Disneyland; opened on July 17, 1955. Originally sponsored by Richfield (1955–1970). Redesigned in 1959, 1964, and 1968. Also a Discoveryland attraction in Disneyland Paris, opened on April 12, 1992. The Disneyland Autopia was closed from September 1999 to June 2000 for an extensive remodeling, reopening with Chevron as sponsor. For children and teenagers under the driving age, Autopia has always given them a chance to drive a car on a freeway, though it is continually a problem to convince them that this is not a carnival bumper-car attraction, especially when a friend, or parent, is in the car in front. People who were youngsters in the 1950s sometimes still have their Richfield Autopia driver's license, on which you could place your thumb print and biographical data necessary to make you a licensed Autopia driver. See also Fantasyland Autopia, Junior Autopia, and Midget Autopia. For the Walt Disney World attraction, see Grand Prix Raceway.

Autumn (film) Silly Symphony cartoon; released on February 15, 1930. Directed by Ub Iwerks. The animals get ready for winter by foraging and preparing for hibernation.

Aux Epices Enchantées Restaurant in Adventureland in Disneyland Paris; opened on April 12, 1992. Sponsored by Maggi. Became Restaurant Hakuna Matata in May 1995.

Avalon Cove Restaurant at Paradise Pier at Disney's California Adventure; opened February 8, 2001. Operated by Wolfgang Puck until September 30, 2001. It became Ariel's Grotto in 2002.

Ave Maria Composed by Franz Shubert, the sacred *Ave Maria*, the concluding segment of *Fantasia*, was used in juxtaposition to the profane *Night on Bald Mountain*.

Avonlea (television) Highly acclaimed weekly series on The Disney Channel, which began on March 5, 1990, and aired its last new episode on December 8, 1996. Based on the stories by Lucy Maud Montgomery, who wrote *Anne of Green Gables*. Sara Stanley comes to Avonlea on Prince Edward Island to live with her relatives, and Avonlea is never the same again. She lives with her aunt, the spinster schoolteacher, Hetty King, and constantly bickers with her cousin, Felicity. Stars Sarah Polley (Sara Stanley), Jackie Burroughs (Hetty King), Mag Ruffman (Olivia), Cedric Smith (Alec King), Lally Cadeau (Janet King), Gema Zamprogna (Felicity), Zachary Bennett (Felix), R. H. Thomson (Jasper), Michael Mahonen (Gus). The show won the Emmy Award as Best Children's Program in 1993, and another Emmy for a guest appearance of Christopher Lloyd.

Award Wieners Fast-food facility at Hollywood Pictures Backlot at Disney's California Adventure; opened February 8, 2001.

Aykroyd, Dan Actor; appeared in *Celtic Pride* (Jimmy Flaherty), *Grosse Pointe Blank* (Grocer), and *Pearl Harbor* (Capt. Thurmann), and on television in *Soul Man* (Mike Weber).

Ayres, Lew (1908–1996) Actor; appeared in *The Biscuit Eater* (Mr. Ames).

Azaria, Hank Actor; appeared in *Pretty Woman* (detective), *Quiz Show* (Albert Freedman), *Grosse Pointe Blank* (Lardner), *Cradle Will Rock* (Marc Blitzstein), *Mystery, Alaska* (Charles Danner), and on television in *Herman's Head* (Jay Nichols), *Imagine That* (Josh Miller), and *If Not for You* (Craig).

B

Babbitt, Art (1907–1992) Animator; started at Disney in 1932, and is recognized with escalating Goofy to stardom by giving the character unique mannerisms and a rather clumsy walk in such films as *Mickey's Service Station* and *Moving Day*. He is known for his animation of the Evil Queen in *Snow White and the Seven Dwarfs*, Geppetto in *Pinocchio*, the stork in *Dumbo*, and especially the mushrooms in the *Nutcracker Suite* segment of *Fantasia*. He was instrumental in helping begin art classes for the animators. As an active proponent of unions, he left Disney in 1941 at the time of the bitter strike, returning only briefly in 1946–47.

Babe, the Blue Ox Co-star of *Paul Bunyan* (1958).

Babes in the Woods (film) Silly Symphony cartoon; released on November 19, 1932. One of the first cartoons in color. Directed by Burt Gillett. Based on the Hansel and Gretel story. Two children wandering through a forest are lured into the house of a wicked witch, who lives with her collection of creatures. The boy is changed into a spider by a potion, and just as the girl is about to be changed into a rat, she is rescued by woodland dwarfs, and she finds a potion to transform her spider brother and the other creatures back into the children they once were. The children help the dwarfs turn the witch into stone with her own cauldron.

Babes in Toyland (film) Just as Tom and Mary are about to be married in Mother Goose Village, the villain, Barnaby, knowing Mary is to inherit a large sum of money when wed, has Tom kidnapped by his two henchman who are to toss Tom into the sea. The henchman then steal Mary's sheep, the sole support for her and the children she cares for. Just as it looks as if Mary will have to marry Barnaby, Tom, who has not really drowned at all, reappears, and takes off with Mary and the children to find the sheep. Traveling in the Forest of No Return, Tom's party ends up in Toyland, with Barnaby and his henchman not far behind. There Tom, Mary, and the kids help the Toymaker make toys for Christmas until the Toymaker's assistant, Grumio, invents a gun which reduces everything to toy-size. Barnaby gets hold of the gun, reduces Tom and the Toymaker, and forces the latter to marry him to Mary. Before the ceremony is completed, Tom, who has mobilized the toy armies, attacks. In the furious battle, Mary reduces Barnaby and Tom disposes of him in a duel. Grumio comes up with a restoring formula and all ends happily. Released on December 14, 1961. Directed by Jack Donohue. 106 min. Stars Ray Bolger (Barnaby), Tommy Sands (Tom Piper), Annette Funicello (Mary Contrary), Ed Wynn (Toymaker), Henry Calvin (Gonzorgo), Gene Sheldon (Roderigo), Tommy Kirk (Grumio), Kevin Corcoran (Boy Blue), Ann Jillian (Bo Peep). This was the Studio's first live-action musical fantasy, and featured numerous songs including "I Can't Do The Sum," "Castle In Spain," "Just A Whisper Away," "Forest of No Return," and "Toyland," by George Bruns and Mel Leven, based on the operetta by Victor Herbert and Glenn McDonough. The special effects, for many people the true highlight of the film, were by Eustace Lycett, Robert Mattey, Joshua Meador, Bill Justice, and X. Atencio. Fabulous toys, from wooden soldiers to golden-haired dolls, from guns that shoot to airships that fly, were specially designed for the exciting climax. Disney animation veteran Ward Kimball, himself a noted toy collector, headed the unit that created the mechanical toys. The film was promoted on the Disney television show, and pieces from the set were reconstructed at the Disneyland Opera House where they remained as an attraction from 1961 to 1963. Released on video in 1982. See also *Backstage Party*.

Babes in Toyland Exhibit Display of sets from the movie, shown in the Opera House at Disneyland from December 17, 1961 to September 30, 1963. Because *Babes in Toyland* contained some elaborate sets, Walt Disney thought they might be appealing on display at Disneyland, though their popularity never matched that of the *20,000 Leagues Under the Sea* sets that were displayed in Tomorrowland.

Baby Center Opened on Main Street, U.S.A., at Disneyland in July 1957, in response to requests from mothers for a place where they could change and care for their babies during a visit to Disneyland. Disneyland nurses had an unexpected event happen on July 4, 1979, when the first baby was born in the park—Teresa Salcedo weighed in at 6 lbs. 10½ oz. The happy but surprised parents were Rosa and Elias Salcedo of Los Angeles.

Baby Einstein Company LLC, The Award-winning creator of the infant developmental media category specifically designed for babies and toddlers. Through unique combinations of real-world objects, music, art, language, science, poetry, and nature, Baby Einstein products expose little ones to the world around them in playful and enriching ways. Originally founded by a mom, the company's videos, etc., encourage parent-child interaction. Subsidiary of the Walt Disney Company. Acquired by Disney in November 2001.

Baby Herman Cigar-smoking "baby" in *Who Framed Roger Rabbit* and the Roger Rabbit cartoons; voiced by Lou Hirsch.

Baby Mine Song from *Dumbo*, written by Ned Washington and Frank Churchill. Nominated for an Academy Award.

Baby . . . Secret of the Lost Legend (film) A young scientist discovers the existence of a family of dinosaurs in the jungles of Africa. With her husband, she attempts to rescue them from an evil scientist who, with government support, is trying to capture the creatures. Soldiers kill the father and capture the mother, but the scientist manages to save the baby brontosaurus. After a series of hair-raising adventures the couple defeats the evil scientist and reunites the infant with its mother. Released on March 22, 1985. Directed by B.W.L. Norton. A Touchstone film. 93 min. Stars William Katt (George Loomis), Sean Young (Sean Matthews-Loomis), Patrick McGoohan (Dr. Eric Kivist), Kyalo Mativo (Cephu). Central to the plot are the dinosaur characters designed and constructed by mechanical-effects experts Ron Tantin and Isidoro Raponi. These characters, among the largest and most complex ever created for the screen, required almost one full year of planning. The dinosaur models range in size from a full-scale father (70 feet long and 25 feet high) to a miniature baby (30 inches long and 10 inches high). The dinosaurs were sculpted and molded in the United States and reconstructed at two "dino bases" in the Ivory Coast. After a global search, the filmmakers settled on the Ivory Coast because of its tropical rain forest and primitive bush villages. The film crew, based in Abidjan (population 1.5 million), utilized locations in the nearby Parc National du Banco for tropical jungle scenes. Several villages within a 70-kilometer radius and situated along the Comoe River were also primary sites. Filming was completed at the Disney Studio in Burbank. Released on video in 1985, 1989, and 1993.

Baby Weems (film) Segment of *The Reluctant Dragon*, with the story of a precocious baby who creates a big sensation but then fades into obscurity, told in limited animation.

Bacchus God of wine in the *Pastoral* segment of *Fantasia*.

Back Home (television) A mother eagerly awaits the return of her daughter from the United States in post-World War II England, but her daughter's new American sensibility creates conflicts with her family. A Disney Channel Premiere Film, first aired on June 7, 1990. Directed by Piers Haggard. Stars Hayley Mills (Peggy). 103 min. Released on video in 1993.

Back to Hannibal: The Return of Tom Sawyer and Huckleberry Finn (television) Grown-up Tom and Huck return to Hannibal to save their friend Jim, accused of murdering Becky's husband. A Disney Channel Premiere Film, first aired on October 21, 1990. Directed by Paul Krasny. Stars Paul Winfield (Jim), Raphael Sbarge (Tom Sawyer), Mitchell Anderson (Huckleberry Finn), Ned Beatty (the Duke), Megan Follows (Becky Thatcher). 92 min. Released on video in 1992.

Back to Neverland [*sic*] (film) A "new" lost boy from *Peter Pan* gave guests a hilarious lesson in animation basics at the beginning of the Animation Tour, Disney-MGM Studios; opened on May 1, 1989, and closed on September 30, 2003. Stars Walter Cronkite and Robin Williams. 9 min.

Back to School with the Mickey Mouse Club See *Darkwing Duck Premiere*.

Backlot Area at the Disney Studio in Burbank beyond the office buildings, shops, and soundstages, where outdoor filming was done. Over the years, many different sets have occupied these various locations, which were hidden from the sight of passersby by large berms. The primary set areas were the *Zorro* set (featuring a town square, the fort, and Don Diego's home), the Western set (several streets with Western-type saloons, blacksmith shops, etc., constructed for *Elfego Baca* and *Texas John Slaughter*), the residential street (with the look of a normal Midwestern town, first used for *The Absent-Minded Professor*), and the business street (with shops and stores surrounding a town square, originally built for *The Ugly Dachshund* and *Follow Me, Boys*, and completely reconstructed for *Something Wicked This Way Comes*). Other areas could be made to resemble whatever

location was needed—a gold-rush town with stream (for *The Adventures of Bullwhip Griffin*), a colonial-era estate (for *The Swamp Fox*), a Maine waterfront (for *Pete's Dragon*), a Viking settlement (for *Island at the Top of the World*), an olive orchard (for *Monkeys, Go Home!*), or an English lane, yard, and cottage (for *Bedknobs and Broomsticks*). The backlot saw its primary usage from the late 1950s until the late 1970s. By then, backlots had lost some of their allure, as sophisticated audiences forced movie producers to seek out real, as opposed to the often fake-looking, sets. Besides, it became easier to go on location, with more portable equipment. Gradually, the seldom used backlot sets at the Disney Studio gave way to needed office buildings, warehouses, and parking garages.

Backlot Express Fast-food restaurant; opened at Disney-MGM Studios on May 1, 1989. Also a restaurant at Walt Disney Studios Paris; opened March 16, 2002.

Backstage Magic Show in Epcot Computer Central sponsored by Sperry, from February 4, 1984 to October 1, 1993. Superseded the Astuter Computer Revue.

Backstage Party (television) Television show, aired December 17, 1961, being a tour of the Disney Studio and a party celebrating the completion of *Babes in Toyland*. Directed by Jack Donohue. Annette Funicello hosts the final segment by introducing various cast members who perform. A special award, a Mousecar (Disney equivalent of an Oscar), is presented to Ed Wynn. Also starred Ray Bolger, Tommy Sands, Tommy

Kirk, Kevin Corcoran, Noah Beery, Jr., and others.

Backstage Studio Tour Opened at Disney-MGM Studios on May 1, 1989. One of the main reasons for building the Disney-MGM Studios was to give guests an opportunity to see what goes on behind the scenes during the making of a movie or television show. This tour began with a tram ride through production buildings, with windows showing costume and set construction areas. Then it was onto the backlot, with a ride down a residential street before entering Catastrophe Canyon for a special-effects demonstration. In the early days of the tour, the tram would drive guests around the New York Street area, but later they were welcome to stroll that area on their own. On exiting the tram, guests were encouraged to continue their tour to an area called Inside the Magic—Special Effects and Production Tour. Here were several special-effects locations, followed by a walk along an enclosed catwalk above the soundstages, where filming was often in progress. One of the primary residents of one of the soundstages was The Disney Channel's *Mickey Mouse Club*. A highlight on the tour was the viewing of a short film, called *The Lottery*, starring Bette Midler; then guests were directed through the sets of the film. In 1996, this last area was remodeled to show clips and sets from the live-action version of *101 Dalmatians*. The tour has changed throughout the years, with the residential section removed for the building of the Lights, Motors, Action attraction, 2005. See also Studio Tram Tour—Behind the Magic.

Backus, Jim (1913–1989) Actor; appeared in *Now You See Him, Now You Don't* (Timothy Forsythe) and *Pete's Dragon* (mayor).

Bacon, Kevin Actor; appeared in *The Air Up There* (Jimmy Dolan).

Bad Company (film) An out-of-favor CIA agent is caught in a maze of deadly intrigue when he is sent to infiltrate an industrial-espionage boutique and ends up being seduced by a master manipulator into taking over the operation. Their relationship erupts into uncontrollable passion, with greed proving to be the underlying motivation in this tale of espionage and ruthless double-crossing. Released on January 20, 1995. Directed by Damian Harris. Filmed in CinemaScope. A Touchstone Picture. 108 min. Written by the Edgar Award–winning mystery writer Ross Thomas. Stars Ellen Barkin (Margaret Wells), Laurence Fishburne (Nelson Crowe), Frank Langella (Vic Grimes), Michael Beach (Tod Stapp), David Ogden Stiers (Judge Beach).

Bad Company (film) A different film from the one released in 1995 with the same title. Gaylord Oakes, a veteran CIA agent, must transform sarcastic, streetwise punk Jake Hayes into a sophisticated and savvy spy to replace his murdered identical twin brother. He has only nine days to accomplish this mission, before having to negotiate a sensitive nuclear weapons deal with terrorists. Directed by Joel Schumacher. A Touchstone Picture from Jerry Bruckheimer Films. Released on June 7, 2002. Stars Anthony Hopkins (Gaylord Oakes), Chris Rock (Jake Hayes), Matthew Marsh (Dragan Adjanic), Gabriel Macht (Seale), John Slattery (Roland Yates), Peter Stormare (Adrik Vas), Kerry Washington (Julie), Garcelle Beauvais-Nilon (Nicole). 117 min. Working title was *Black Sheep*. Filmed in Super 35 wide-screen format in New York and Prague. Released on video in 2002.

Baddeley, Hermione (1906–1986) Character actress; appeared in *Mary Poppins* (Ellen), *The Adventures of Bullwhip Griffin* (Irene Chesny), *The Happiest Millionaire* (Mrs. Worth), and provided the voice of Madame Adelaide Bonfamille in *The Aristocats*.

Baer, Parley (1914–2002) Actor; appeared in *Those Calloways* (Doane Shattuck), *The Ugly Dachshund* (Mel Chadwick), *Follow Me, Boys* (Mayor Hi Plommer), and *The Adventures of Bullwhip Griffin* (chief executioner), and on television in *The Boy Who Stole the Elephant*, *The Strange Monster of Strawberry Cove*, and *Bristle Face*.

Baggage Buster (film) Goofy cartoon; released on March 28, 1941. Directed by Jack Kinney. In his efforts to load a magician's trunk, baggageman Goofy has a series of encounters with its contents, including rabbits, a bull, skeleton, and elephant.

Bagheera Sophisticated panther character in *The Jungle Book* voiced by Sebastian Cabot.

Bagnall, George (1896–1978) Member of the Disney board of directors from 1961 to 1974. His son, Michael, served for a time as the company's chief financial officer.

Baia (film) Segment of *The Three Caballeros* in which Donald Duck and José Carioca go to Baia, Brazil, and dance the samba.

Bailey, Pearl Singer/actress; voiced Big Mama in *The Fox and the Hound*.

Bailey (Turner), Grace (1904–1983) Began work at Disney in 1932 in the Ink and Paint Department, and in 1954 became its head. She remained in that position until her retirement in 1972, and received a posthumous Disney Legends award in 2000.

Bailey's Mistake (television) Two-hour television movie airing on *The Wonderful World of Disney* on March 18, 2001. Liz Donovan, recently widowed, discovers that her late husband, Paul, had secretly spent their life savings to purchase property on Bailey's Mistake, a small island off coastal Maine. She travels there with her two children, Dylan and Becca, determined to sell the property, but instead discovers a breathtakingly beautiful island with a touch of magic and mystery. Strange things happen, and there is a group of strange local residents. As Liz struggles with her dilemma, Dylan begins to display a magical gift for healing. The trip proves to be an emotional journey for the Donovans, as they come to terms with their loss and accept the gain of a "new" family. Directed by Michael M. Robin. Stars Linda Hamilton (Liz Donovan), Joan Plowright (Aunt Angie), Kyle Secor (Lowell Lenox), Jesse James (Dylan), Paz de la Huerta (Becca), Richard Burgi (Paul Donovan).

Baird, Sharon Mouseketeer from the 1950s television show, born August 16, 1943.

Bakalyan, Dick Disney regular; acted in *The Strongest Man in the World* (Cookie), *The Shaggy D.A.* (Freddie), *Return from Witch Mountain* (Eddie), *Follow Me, Boys* (umpire), *Never a Dull Moment* (Bobby Macon), *The Computer Wore Tennis Shoes* (Chillie Walsh), *Now You See Him, Now You Don't* (Cookie), and *Charley and the Angel* (Buggs); narrated *It's Tough to Be a Bird* (M.C. Bird) and provided the voice of Dinky in *The Fox and the Hound*. Appeared on television in *Way Down Cellar*, *The Whiz Kid and the Carnival Caper*, *The Young Runaways*, and *A Boy Called Nuthin'*.

Baker, Buddy (1918–2002) Composer; joined Disney in 1955 to help George Bruns write music for *Davy Crockett*, but later specialized in music for the Disney attractions at the 1964–1965 New York World's Fair, Disneyland, Walt Disney World, and Tokyo Disneyland. He wrote the music for The Haunted Mansion, and served as musical director for Epcot, where he worked on Universe of Energy, American Adventure, World of Motion, *Wonders of China*, Kitchen  Kabaret, Listen to the Land, and *Impressions de France*. He retired in 1983, the last staff composer at any major studio. He was honored as a Disney Legend in 1998.

Baker, Diane Actress; appeared in *The Horse in the Gray Flannel Suit* (Suzie Clemens) and *The Joy Luck Club* (Mrs. Jordan).

Baker's Field Bakery Shop at Disney's California Adventure; opened on February 8, 2001. The name is a play on the city named Bakersfield in Central California.

Bakersfield P.D. (television) Television series; airing on Fox beginning September 14, 1993, and ending January 4, 1994. An African American big-city detective tries to fit in with an all-white central California police department headed by a timid chief. Stars Giancarlo Esposito (Paul Gigante), Ron Eldard (Wade Preston), Brian Doyle-Murray (Phil Hampton), Chris Mulkey (Denny Boyer), Jack Hallett (Renny Stiles).

Baldwin, Alec Actor; appeared in *The Marrying Man* (Charley Pearl), *Pearl Harbor* (Jimmy Doolittle), and *The Last Shot* (Joe Devine), and narrated *The Royal Tenenbaums*.

Baldwin, Robert H. B. Member of the Disney board of directors from 1983 to 1985.

Baldwin, Stephen Actor; appeared in *Crossing the Bridge* (Danny Morgan).

Bale, Christian Young English actor; appeared in *Newsies* (Jack Kelly), *Swing Kids* (Thomas), and *Reign of Fire* (Quinn), and provided the voice of Thomas in *Pocahontas*.

Balk, Fairuza Actress; appeared in *Return to Oz* (Dorothy) and *The Waterboy* (Vicki Vallencourt).

Ballad of Davy Crockett, The One of the most popular songs to come out of a Disney production, with sixteen weeks at the top of the Hit Parade. It was written by George Bruns and Tom Blackburn, who dashed it off simply because the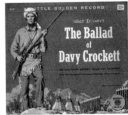

film was running short and something was needed to fill in the gaps.

Ballad of Hector the Stowaway Dog, The

(television) Two-part television show; aired on January 5 and 12, 1964. Directed by Vincent McEveety. The two parts were titled *Where the Heck is Hector?* and *Who the Heck is Hector?* A trained Airedale separated from his owner, who is the first mate on a freighter in Portugal. The sailor unwillingly gets mixed up in a jewel robbery, with the jewels sewn into Hector's collar. The dog manages to elude the thieves and aid the police in their capture, becoming a hero. Stars Guy Stockwell, Craig Hill, Eric Pohlmann. The two parts were edited together to become a foreign feature entitled *The Million Dollar Collar.*

Ballard, Kaye Actress; appeared in *Freaky Friday* (Coach Betsy).

Ballerina (television) Television show; aired in two parts on February 27 and March 6, 1966. Directed by Norman Campbell. Story of a young ballet student in Denmark who succeeds despite her mother's objections. Partly filmed at the Royal Theater in Copenhagen. Stars Kirsten Simone, Astrid Villaume, Ole Wegener, Poul Reichardt, Jenny Agutter. This film introduced 11-year old Jenny Agutter to American audiences; years later, she would appear in Disney's *Amy.*

Balloon Farm (television) Two-hour movie; airing on *The Wonderful World of Disney* on March 28, 1999. A peculiar farmer, Harvey H. Potter, arrives in the small town of Waterston where the families are facing financial ruin because of a drought. Potter's crop turns out to be a field of brilliantly colored balloon plants. The townsfolk are entranced, seeing magical properties in the balloons, but only a little girl, Willow, stands by Potter when mistrust overtakes the town. Directed by William Dear. Stars Rip Torn (Harvey Potter), Mara Wilson (Willow), Roberts Blossom (Wheezle), Laurie Metcalf (Casey Johnson). From the book *Harvey Potter's Balloon Farm*, by Jerdine Nolen. Released on video in 2000.

Baloo Happy-go-lucky bear who befriends Mowgli in *The Jungle Book*; voiced by Phil Harris. Baloo also stars on television in *Tale Spin* as a devil-may-care pilot for an air courier service.

Baloo's Dressing Room Special Fantasyland attraction at Disneyland until displaced by Toontown construction; open from March 15 to September 8, 1991. The attraction was inspired by a similar area in Mickey's Birthdayland at the Walt Disney World Magic Kingdom where guests were able to visit Mickey Mouse in his dressing room. Eventually, Toontown would provide the experience of directly meeting Mickey.

Bambi (film) Life story of a fawn, Bambi, who grows up, with friends Thumper the rabbit and Flower the skunk, to be the Great Prince of the Forest. But in the meantime he suffers through the death of his mother at the hand of hunters, falls in love with Faline, and barely escapes a catastrophic forest fire. World premiere in London on August 8, 1942; released in the U.S. on August 13, 1942. Based on the book by Felix Salten. The supervising director was David Hand. Voices include Bobby Stewart/Donnie Dunagan/Hardy Albright/John Sutherland (Bambi), Paula Winslowe (Bambi's mother), Cammie King/Ann Gillis (Faline), Fred Shields (Bambi's father), Bill Wright (Friend Owl), Stanley Alexander/Sterling Holloway/Tim Davis (Flower), Peter Behn/Tim Davis (Thumper). Includes the songs "Love Is a Song" and "Little April Shower," written by Frank Churchill and Edward H. Plumb. The film had been put into production as work on *Snow White and the Seven Dwarfs* was winding down. But the story of Bambi was different from anything else the Studio had ever attempted. It was more serious, and all the characters were animals. In striving for realism, the artists heard lectures from animal experts, made field trips to the Los

Angeles Zoo, watched specially filmed nature footage shot in the forests of Maine, and even studied the movements of two fawns that were donated to the Studio. The meticulous work was time-consuming; even taking care to see that the spots on the fawn's back remained constant meant fewer drawings could be finished in a day. The film moved exceedingly slowly through the production process, but Walt was delighted with the results he was seeing. "Fellas, this stuff is pure gold," he told the animators. *Bambi* was released at a difficult time, with the United States deep in World War II, so its initial profits were low, but the story of the little deer coming of age has endured, and today *Bambi* is universally regarded as one of Walt Disney's most charming films. The film received Academy Award nominations for Best Sound, Best Song ("Love Is a Song"), and Best Scoring of a Dramatic or Comedy Picture. 70 min. It was rereleased in theaters in 1942, 1947, 1957, 1966, 1975, 1982, 1988. Released on video in 1989 and 1997.

Bambi: A Lesson in Perseverance (film) Educational film; released in September 1978. Trying something new, like riding a bicycle, is not always successful the first time.

Bancroft, Tony He co-directed *Mulan* with Barry Cook, having joined Disney in 1989 as an animator and among other tasks supervised the animation of Pumbaa in *The Lion King.* His twin brother, Tom, was also a Disney animator, supervising the animation of Mushu, the dragon, in *Mulan.*

Band Concert, The (film) Mickey Mouse cartoon; the first one in color, released on February 23, 1935. From then on, with the exception of *Mickey's Service Station* and *Mickey's Kangaroo,* all the Disney cartoons would be in color. Directed by Wilfred Jackson. Mickey is a frustrated bandleader who must deal with obnoxious peanut vendor and flute player Donald Duck, who tries to persuade the band to play "Turkey in the Straw," and a cyclone before his concert of the "William Tell Overture" is completed. The cartoon was a major success, making Donald more popular than ever and was later included in *Milestones for Mickey* (1974). Conductor Arturo Toscanini called this cartoon his favorite.

Banderas, Antonio Actor; appeared in *Two Much* (Art), *Evita* (Che), *Miami Rhapsody* (Antonio), *Play It to the Bone* (Caesar Dominguez), and *The 13th Warrior* (Ahmed Ibn Fahdlan).

Bank of America The bank operated a branch on Main Street at Disneyland from July 17, 1955 to July 28, 1993. One of the longest-running participants at Disneyland, it was one of the only banks to have regular Sunday and holiday hours. It also sponsored "it's a small world" from 1966 to 1992. In the 1930s, Walt Disney depended on the Bank of America for funding, and it was Joe Rosenberg of the bank who was persuaded to come up with the money needed to finish *Snow White and the Seven Dwarfs.*

Banker's Daughter, The (film) Oswald the Lucky Rabbit cartoon; released on November 28, 1927.

Banks, Steven Actor; appeared on television in *The Steven Banks Show* and *Disney's Great American Celebration*.

Bannen, Ian (1928–1999) Actor; appeared in *The Watcher in the Woods* (John Keller) and *Night Crossing* (Josef Keller).

Banner in the Sky (television) Television airing of *Third Man on the Mountain*, in two parts on March 17 and 24, 1963, with episode titles of *To Conquer the Mountain* and *The Killer Mountain*.

Bar Girls (television) Unsold pilot for a television series; two mismatched women lawyers struggle to keep their law firm and the relationship afloat. Aired on CBS on July 5, 1990. 60 min. Directed by Eric Laneuville. Stars Joanna Cassidy, Marcy Walker, John Terlesky, Tom O'Brien.

Barash, Olivia Actress; appeared on television in *Child of Glass*.

Bardsley, Grant He voiced Taran in *The Black Cauldron*.

Bare Necessities, The Song from *The Jungle Book*, written by Terry Gilkyson. Nominated for an Academy Award.

Barefoot Executive, The (film) In the wacky world of television, an ambitious mailroom boy at the United Broadcasting Company, Steven Post, discovers that a chimpanzee being taken care of by his girlfriend, Jennifer, has an amazing talent—the chimp can pick programs that will become hits. Steven secretly uses the chimp to catapult himself into a vice presidency and a lush life, but the secret is revealed by jealous rivals. Steven loses both the chimp and his girlfriend until he changes his ways and wins out.

Released on March 17, 1971. Directed by Robert Butler. 96 min. Stars Kurt Russell (Steven Post), Joe Flynn (Wilbanks), Harry Morgan (Crampton), Wally Cox (Mertons), John Ritter (Roger), Heather North (Jennifer), Alan Hewitt (Farnsworth), Hayden Rorke (Clifford), Ruffles the Chimp. The film's song, "He's Gonna Make It," was written by Robert F. Brunner and Bruce Belland. The film was made with the cooperation of the National Academy of Television Arts and Sciences. A week of location shooting was done in Long Beach, California, with the rest of the shooting schedule completed at the Disney Studios. Released on video in 1985.

Barefoot Executive, The (television) Two-hour television movie; aired on ABC on November 11, 1995. A remake of the 1971 feature about the show business career of a young man who rises from mail boy to network vice president when he discovers a television-loving chimpanzee with an unfailing knack for picking hit series. Directed by Susan Seidelman. Stars Jason London (Billy Murdock), Eddie Albert (Herbert Gower), Michael Marich (Wayne), Jay Mohr (Matt), Terri Ivens (Lisa), Yvonne De Carlo (Norma), Julia Sweeney (Thelma), Chris Elliott (Jase Wallenberg).

Barks, Carl (1901–2000) Barks went to work at the Disney Studio in 1935 as an inbetweener and later worked on the story crew for several cartoons. In 1942, he began doing comic books, starting with "Donald Duck Finds Pirate Gold," and continuing with the duck comics until his retirement in 1966. His most famous creation, perhaps, is Uncle Scrooge, who made his debut in a 1947 comic book story, "Christmas on Bear Mountain." Barks became the most famous of all of the Disney comic book artists, with a loyal following all over the world. During his retirement in the 1970s, Barks prepared a number of paintings featuring Donald and the other ducks. He was named a Disney Legend in 1991. At the age of 93 (in 1994), he made a lengthy trip to Europe to meet with fans.

Barn Dance, The (film) The fourth Mickey Mouse cartoon. Released in 1929. Directed by

Walt Disney. When Mickey continually stomps on Minnie's feet during a dance, she spurns him for the better dancer, Pete. Mickey is left sitting on the floor, crying.

Barnes, Christopher Daniel Actor; appeared on television in *Exile*, *Just Perfect*, and *Disney's All-Star Comedy Circus*, and voiced Prince Eric in *The Little Mermaid* and Prince Charming in *Cinderella II: Dreams Come True*.

Barnstormer, The Roller coaster attraction at Goofy's Wiseacres Farm in Mickey's Toontown Fair at Walt Disney World; opened on October 1, 1996.

Barnyard Battle, The (film) Mickey Mouse cartoon; released in 1929. Directed by Walt Disney. Enduring a strenuous army physical, Mickey joins up to protect his home from enemy cats. At first he's one of many Mickey look-alike soldiers, as a machine gunner, using piano keys when he runs out of bullets. Mickey then fights alone against an army of cats, clobbering each with a hammer as they emerge from a tunnel. His fellow soldiers cheer him as a hero.

Barnyard Broadcast, The (film) Mickey Mouse cartoon; released on October 10, 1931. Directed by Burt Gillett. In this satire of radio broadcasting, Mickey runs the control room attempting to monitor the show and the audience. All goes well until howling cats spoil the broadcast and a chase ensues. In the pandemonium, the makeshift studio is destroyed, and Mickey signs off amid the debris.

Barnyard Concert, The (film) Mickey Mouse cartoon; released on April 10, 1930. Directed by Walt Disney. Mickey attempts to conduct a farmyard concert even though the various members of the band tend to drift off.

Barnyard Olympics (film) Mickey Mouse cartoon; released on April 15, 1932, to coincide with the Olympics in Los Angeles. Directed by Wilfred Jackson. Despite Pete's continual cheating in a cross country race, especially during the bicycle portion, Mickey ends up winning. A fun takeoff on Olympic events.

Barrie, Barbara Actress; appeared on television in *Child of Glass* and provided the voice of Alcmene in *Hercules*.

Barry of the Great St. Bernard (television) Two-part television show; aired January 30 and February 6, 1977. Directed by Frank Zuniga. An orphan at a hospice in the Alps trains a St. Bernard pup to become a rescue dog. He proves his worth with a daring rescue after an avalanche. Stars Jean Claude Dauphin (Martin), Pierre Tabard.

Barrymore, Drew Actress; appeared in *Mad Love* (Casey Roberts), and on television in *Disneyland's 30th Anniversary Celebration* and *EPCOT Center: The Opening Celebration*.

Bart, Roger Actor; appeared in *The Insider* (hotel manager), provided the voice of Young Hercules in *Hercules* and Scamp in *Lady and the Tramp II: Scamp's Adventure*, starred in *King David* (Jonathan), and appeared in *Desperate Housewives* (George Williams).

Barty, Billy (1924–2000) Actor; appeared in *Tough Guys* (Philly) and did the voice of the Baitmouse in *The Rescuers Down Under* and Figment in the Journey into Imagination at Epcot.

Baseball Fever (television) Television show; aired on October 14, 1979, being a group of baseball cartoons. Directed by Jack Kinney, Jack Hannah.

Bashful One of the Seven Dwarfs; voiced by Scotty Mattraw.

Basic Communication Skills (film) Educational film in the Skills for the New Technology: What a Kid Needs to Know Today series; released in September 1983. Teaches how communication skills are as important as ever in the computer age.

Basil Of Baker Street fame, the Sherlock Holmes mouse character in *The Great Mouse Detective*; voiced by Barrie Ingham.

Basinger, Kim Actress; appeared in *The Marrying Man* (Vicki Anderson).

Baskett, James (1904–1948) Actor; appeared in *Song of the South* as Uncle Remus and also provided the voice of Brer Fox. He received a special Academy Award in 1948 for his portrayal of the kindly storyteller, therefore becoming the first actor in a Disney film to be recognized by the Academy of Motion Picture Arts and Sciences.

Bassett, Angela Actress; appeared in *What's Love Got to Do with It?* (Tina Turner) and *Mr. 3000* (Mo Simmons), and provided the voice of Groove in *Whispers: an Elephant's Tale.*

Bates, Kathy Actress; appeared in *Dick Tracy* (Mrs. Green), *The War at Home* (Maureen Collier), *The Waterboy* (Mama Boucher), *Around the World in 80 Days* (Queen Victoria), and on television in *Annie* (Miss Hannigan).

Bath Day (film) Figaro cartoon; released on October 11, 1946. Directed by Charles Nichols. To his displeasure, Figaro is bathed and perfumed by Minnie. An alley cat, Lucifer, and his gang chase Figaro for being so prissy. The gang is fooled into thinking that Figaro has beaten up Lucifer in an alley, hidden from their view. Figaro returns home victorious, but the victory is short-lived when Minnie decides he needs another unwanted bath.

Bathing Time for Baby (film) Educational film in which a stork teaches the proper method for baby bathing, made for Johnson & Johnson and delivered to them on March 19, 1946.

Bathroom of Tomorrow See Crane Company Bathroom of Tomorrow.

Battle for Survival (television) Nature television show using time-lapse and close-up photography. This educational show features honeybees and grunion as plants, insects, and animals must all battle for survival. Directed by James Algar, this show aired April 9, 1961.

Baucom, Bill (1910–1981) He voiced Trusty in *Lady and the Tramp.*

Bauer, Cate She voiced Perdita in *One Hundred and One Dalmatians.*

Baxter, Tony Baxter began his Disney career in 1965 scooping ice cream on Main Street at Disneyland. His persistence and some intriguing ideas got him a job at WED Enterprises, where he worked up through the ranks to executive vice president in charge of design for the Disney parks. Some of his design projects include Big Thunder Mountain Railway, Splash Mountain, and Journey Into Imagination.

Bay Lake The 450-acre body of water east of the Contemporary Resort at Walt Disney World. During construction of Walt Disney World, one of the first tasks was to clear the muck out of Bay Lake. On doing so, Walt Disney World executives were delighted to discover that beautiful white sand was covering the bottom. This sand was utilized to create attractive beaches. Discovery Island, a nature preserve that could be visited by guests from 1974 to 1999, is located in Bay Lake. The lake is connected to the Seven Seas Lagoon in front of Magic Kingdom Park by a unique water bridge over the main road to the Contemporary Hotel. Hotel guests can rent various types of watercraft for cruising on the lake. The Fort Wilderness campground and Wilderness Lodge are located beside Bay Lake, as was the former River Country.

Bayou Boy (television) Two-part television show; aired on February 7 and 14, 1971. Directed by Gary Nelson. Two boys face danger, including a giant alligator, in searching for a lost silver church bell in Dead Man's Bayou. Stars John McIntire, Mitch Vogel, Mike Lookinland, Jeanette Nolan, Frank Silvera. A rerun of the show aired in 1979 as *The Boy from Deadman's Bayou*.

Be Our Guest Song from *Beauty and the Beast*; written by Howard Ashman and Alan Menken. Nominated for an Academy Award.

Beach, Adam Actor; starred in the title role in *Squanto: A Warrior's Tale*, and appeared in *Mystery, Alaska* (Galin Winetka).

Beach Club Marketplace See Atlantic Wear & Wardrobe Emporium.

Beach Club Resort Hotel; opened at Walt Disney World on November 19, 1990. Designed by Robert Stern, the hotel is situated next door to and connected to the Yacht Club Resort, and offers a short walk to an entrance to Epcot,

through the International Gateway next to France in World Showcase. Stormalong Bay, the 750,000 gallon, three-acre swimming pool common to the two hotels, with its meandering waterways with whirlpools, lagoons, and slides, is one of the most unusual in the world.

Beach Party, The (film) Mickey Mouse cartoon; released on November 5, 1931. Directed by Burt Gillett. A beach party with Mickey and the gang is interrupted by a disgruntled octopus accidentally pulled ashore by Pluto. After a free-for-all, Mickey gets rid of the octopus by lassoing it with a rope with an anchor attached.

Beach Picnic (film) Donald Duck cartoon; released on June 9, 1939. The first cartoon directed by Clyde ("Gerry") Geronimi. Donald, at the beach, teases Pluto with an inflatable rubber horse toy, but he gets a taste of his own medicine when an ant colony carries away his picnic food. Donald gets even angrier when he gets wrapped up in the flypaper he puts out to trap the ants.

Beaches (film) On a summer day in 1937, a remarkable and unlikely friendship begins on the beach at Atlantic City. Eleven-year-olds C.C. Bloom and Hilary Whitney are from different worlds; brash streetwise C.C. wants to be a famous singing star, while Hilary is a proper young lady from San Francisco. Although they go their separate ways, they vow to remain friends, and through letters they share each other's hopes, dreams, and frustrations. Years later, their lives again entwine when Hilary, now a lawyer, moves in with rising actress C.C. Their friendship is strained when C.C.'s director, John—with whom she is in love—falls for Hilary. When Hilary returns to California to take care of her ailing father, John turns to C.C. Hilary marries another lawyer who eventually leaves her. The strength of Hilary's and C.C.'s relationship sustains them through the successes and disappointments of their marriages and careers, through the birth of Hilary's daughter, and ultimately through a crisis that tests their love and teaches them the true meaning of friendship. Premiered in New York on December 21, 1988; general release on January 13, 1989. Directed by Garry Marshall. A Touchstone film. 120 min. Stars Bette Midler (C.C. Bloom), Barbara Hershey (Hilary Whitney Essex), John Heard (John Pierce), Lainie Kazan (Leona Bloom), Spalding Gray (Dr. Richard Milstein), Mayim Bialik (C.C., age 11). Filmed at over 42 locations in Los Angeles and New York. Released on video in 1989.

Beaches & Cream Soda Shop Café adjacent to Stormalong Bay at the Beach Club Resort at Walt Disney World, serving burgers and ice cream specialties.

Beagle Boys Convict characters (who wear their numbers around their necks); from the comic books and later *Ducktales*. They were created by artist Carl Barks and debuted in *Walt Disney's Comics and Stories* no. 134 in November 1951.

Beanblossom, Billie Jean Mouseketeer from the 1950s television show.

Bear Country (film) True-Life Adventure featurette; released on February 5, 1953. Directed by James Algar. Story of the American black bears from the time they are born and trained by their mothers, through the mating battles and finally the mother's abandonment of her young. Academy Award winner. 33 min.

Bear Country The seventh "land" at Disneyland, themed after rustic forest areas of the Northwest, opened in 1972 to house the Country Bear Jamboree, which had premiered at Magic Kingdom Park at Walt Disney World the year before; became Critter Country in 1988 during the construction of Splash Mountain.

Bear Family, The (film) Educational film made up from stock footage primarily from *Bear Country* and *White Wilderness*; released in April 1970. Depicts the lifestyle of the bear, emphasizing the Kodiak black bear and the Arctic polar bear.

Bear in the Big Blue House (television) Show on Disney Channel; debuting October 20, 1997, and featuring the friendly and furry Bear, who welcomes kids into his Big Blue House for fun playtime with his friends Tutter, an industrious mouse; Pip & Pop, mischievous otters; Treelo, a highly excitable lemur; and Ojo, an imaginative little girl bear. Produced by Jim Henson Productions in association with Disney Channel.

Bear in the Big Blue House Show, The Attraction at Disney-MGM Studios featuring Bear and other characters from his show; performed from July 4, 1999 to August 4, 2001. Replaced by Playhouse Disney—Live on Stage.

Bearly Asleep (film) Donald Duck cartoon; released on August 19, 1955. Directed by Jack Hannah. When Humphrey the bear is kicked out of his hibernation cave because of his snoring, he tries again and again to use Donald's house, ultimately disguising himself as an orphan bear to be taken back into the cave. Filmed in CinemaScope.

Bearly Country Shop in Frontierland in Magic Kingdom Park at Walt Disney World, from June 6, 1985 until February 25, 1991. Became Prairie Outpost Supply.

Bears and Bees, The (film) Silly Symphony cartoon; released on July 9, 1932. Directed by Wilfred Jackson. When little cubs are chased away from a honey-filled beehive by a big bear, who greedily begins to eat the honey, the bees give chase. Meanwhile, the cubs return and happily begin eating again.

Bears and I, The (film) Vietnam veteran Bob Leslie retreats into Indian territory, where he becomes a foster parent to three bear cubs and fights to preserve the dignity of the Bear Clan of the Taklute Indians. Red Fern believes it better the cubs be dead than captive, although Bob explains he is only protecting them until they reach maturity. Later, Sam Eagle Speaker wounds one bear and Bob promises to free him when he has recovered. Meanwhile, Bob solves the problem of the Indians being reluctant to give up their land for a National Park with his idea of making them all rangers—which is Bob's goal too. Released on July 31, 1974. Directed by Bernard McEveety. 89 min. Stars Patrick Wayne (Bob), Chief Dan George (Chief Peter), Andrew Duggan (Commissioner Gaines), Michael Ansara (Oliver Red Fern), Robert Pine (John), Val DeVargas (Sam Eagle Speaker), Hal Baylor (Foreman). John Denver composed and performed the song, "Sweet Surrender," for this film. The movie was shot in the scenic grandeur of the central British Columbian wilderness on Chilko Lake. The Nehemiah band of Chilcotin Indians, who lived there, were hired to appear in the film.

Beast Enchanted hero of *Beauty and the Beast*; voiced by Robby Benson.

Beast, The (television) One-hour television series; beginning on ABC on June 20, 2001, and ending July 18. Media mogul Jackson Burns builds a 24-hour broadcast news organization where the reporters not only cover the stories but are themselves covered as part of the story. Stars Frank Langella (Jackson Burns), Elizabeth Mitchell (Alice Allenby), Jason Gedrick (Reese McFadden), Peter Riegert (Ted Fisher).

Beasts of Burden Family, The (film) Educational film, released in June 1970. Details the use and usefulness of the working animals of the world that serve man, including huskies, elephants, burros, yaks, reindeer, and llamas.

Beatty, Warren Actor; played the title role in *Dick Tracy* and also directed the film.

Beaumont, Kathryn She voiced Alice in *Alice in Wonderland* and Wendy in *Peter Pan*, and appeared in *One Hour in Wonderland* and the *Walt Disney Christmas Show*. She was honored as a Disney Legend in 1998.

Beautiful Girl (television) Two-hour television movie; aired on ABC Family on October 19, 2003. A Touchstone Production. A young elementary school music teacher, about to get married, becomes an unlikely beauty-pageant contestant in order to win an Hawaiian trip for a honeymoon. Even though she doesn't exactly emulate society's vision of stick-thin perfection, she has an incredible voice and stage presence, natural style, and undeniable spunk. Stars Marissa Jaret Winokur (Becca Wasserman), Mark Consuelos (Adam), Fran Drescher (Amanda Wasserman), Reagan Pasternak (Libby Leslie), Sarah Manninen (Rachel), Amanda Brugel (Connie), Joyce Gordon (Nana), Brooke D'Orsay (Eve). Filmed in Toronto.

Beauty and the Beast (film) The beautiful Belle ignores her suitor, the vain Gaston, as she cares for her father, the eccentric Maurice. When Maurice stumbles upon a foreboding castle while lost in the woods, the servants, enchanted into household objects, try to make him welcome, but he is thrown into the dungeon by the Beast. Belle comes to rescue her father and agrees to remain in the castle as his substitute. In order to break the spell, Beast must learn to love another and to be loved in return. Belle seems a likely candidate, but it takes Beast a while to reign in his temper. Belle desperately misses her father, so Beast sadly allows her to leave. Gaston, realizing Beast is a rival for Belle's affection, leads the townsfolk to storm the castle. Belle rushes back in time to profess her love for Beast, and the spell is broken. Initial release in New York on November 13, 1991; general release on November 22, 1991. Directed by Gary Trousdale and Kirk Wise. 84 min. Voices include Paige O'Hara (Belle), Robby Benson (Beast), Richard White (Gaston), Jerry Orbach (Lumiere), David Ogden Stiers (Cogs-

worth), Angela Lansbury (Mrs. Potts), Jo Ann Worley (Wardrobe). Academy Award nominee in seven categories, including, for the first time for an animated feature, that of Best Picture, it won for Best Song ("Beauty and the Beast" by Howard Ashman and Alan Menken) and Best Original Score. Angela Lansbury sang the title song in the story, and Celine Dion and Peabo Bryson sang another rendition over the film's end credits. Since lyricist Howard Ashman had died earlier in the year, the film was dedicated to him: "To our friend, Howard, who gave a mermaid her voice and a beast his soul, we will be forever grateful." Production of the film took three and a half years and required the talents of nearly 600 animators, artists, and technicians. Portions of the film were animated at Disney's satellite facility at Disney-MGM Studios in Lake Buena Vista, Florida. Art directors working on the film traveled to the Loire valley in France for inspiration, and studied the great French romantic painters such as Fragonard and Boucher. It was Ashman who came up with the idea of turning the enchanted objects into living creatures with unique personalities. Glen Keane, the supervising animator on Beast, created his own hybrid beast by combining the mane of a lion, the beard and head structure of a buffalo, the tusks and nose bridge of a wild boar, the heavily muscled brow

of a gorilla, the legs and tail of a wolf, and the big and bulky body of a bear. Computer-generated imagery was used in several parts of the film, most notably in the "Be Our Guest" sequence and in the creation of a striking three-dimensional ballroom background, allowing dramatic camera moves on the animated characters as they danced. It became the most successful animated feature in motion picture history up to that time, with domestic box office revenues in excess of $140 million. Released on video in 1992. The film was reissued in IMAX and other giant screen theaters on January 1, 2002, featuring the song "Human Again" in a never-before-seen animated sequence. New running time 90 min.

Beauty and the Beast Show at Disney-MGM Studios beginning on November 22, 1991, and at Videopolis in Disneyland beginning on April 11, 1992, and closing April 30, 1995. The story of the film is presented onstage by Disney cast members using elaborate costumes and sets. The popularity of the show helped present an impetus for the creation of a *Beauty and the Beast* stage show for Broadway. The Disneyland stage show at Videopolis closed April 30, 1995.

Beauty and the Beast A stage version of the motion picture previewed in Houston and then played at the Palace Theater on Broadway from April 18, 1994. until September 5, 1999, when it moved to the Lunt-Fontanne Theater, opening

there on November 12, 1999. With a cast of 31, it includes one Ashman-Menken song written for but not used in the film ("Human Again") and several brand-new songs by Tim Rice and Alan Menken. Stars Susan Egan (Belle), Terrence Mann (Beast), Tom Bosley (Maurice), Burke Moses (Gaston), Gary Beach (Lumiere), Heath Lamberts (Cogsworth). The show received nine Tony nominations in 1994, which resulted in one award, to Ann Hould-

Ward for the costumes. A new production of the show opened at the Shubert Theater in Los Angeles on March 21, 1995, and there were later roadshow engagements in theaters throughout the world.

Beauty and the Beast (film) Educational production; released on videodisc in March 1995. Meant as a companion to a study of the Disney film version, the disc features an interview with the screenwriter, along with segments on medieval castles, stained glass, and the stages of animation.

Beauty and the Beast: Belle's Magical World See *Belle's Magical World*.

Beauty and the Beast: The Enchanted Christmas (film) Direct-to-video animated feature; released on November 11, 1997. Belle attempts to cheer up Beast by planning an elaborate Christmas celebration, though the malevolent Forte, a pipe organ, plots to prevent Beast from falling in love with Belle. When Belle leaves the castle with her friends to search for the perfect Christmas tree, Forte convinces Beast that she has run away. After he captures and imprisons her, he finds a gift she had made for him and realizes that she must have true feelings for him, so he determines to give Belle the best Christmas celebration ever. Directed by Andy Knight. Besides the voices from the original 1991 motion picture of Paige O'Hara (Belle), Robby Benson (Beast), Jerry Orbach (Lumiere), David Ogden Stiers (Cogsworth), and Angela Lansbury (Mrs. Potts), there are new characters of Angelique, voiced by Bernadette Peters, and Forte, voiced by Tim Curry. 80 min. Four new songs were composed by Rachel Portman and Don Black. This was the first made-for-video movie produced by Walt Disney Animation Canada, Inc., with studios in Toronto and Vancouver.

Beaver Valley (film) True-Life Adventure featurette; released on July 19, 1950. Directed by James Algar; photographed by Alfred Milotte; narrated by Winston Hibler; musical orchestra-

tions by Paul Smith. 32 min. Portrays the beaver as the leading citizen of the pond area in which he lives, sharing space with moose, deer, crayfish, raccoons, otters, frogs, and all kinds of birds. Winner of the Academy Award for Best Two-Reel Short Subject. Also known as *In Beaver Valley*.

Beaver Valley/Cameras in Africa (television) Television show; aired December 29, 1954, featuring the True-Life Adventure featurette along with some behind-the-scenes footage of Alfred and Elma Milotte filming rhinos, cheetahs, and other animals for *The African Lion*. Directed by Winston Hibler and James Algar. Rerun entitled *Cameras in Africa/Beaver Valley*.

Beckett, Neil (1923–1994) Disney merchandise representative in New Zealand from 1964 to 1989, he was named a Disney Legend in 2003.

Bedard, Irene Actress; appeared in *Squanto: A Warrior's Tale* (Nakooma) and provided the speaking voice for the title character in *Pocahontas*.

Bedford, Brian Actor; provided the voice of the title character in *Robin Hood*, and two decades later appeared in *Nixon* as Clyde Tolson. He appeared on television in *Mr. St. Nick* (Jasper).

Bedknobs and Broomsticks (film) In the autumn of 1940, an eccentric, ladylike spinster, Eglantine Price, becomes an apprentice witch, in hopes of finding a magic formula that will help England win the war against Nazi Germany. With the help of three London children, who she takes in to save them from the Blitz, she first seeks out her amusing but bogus professor of witchcraft, Emelius Brown, and then ventures into Portobello Road in search of the rare formula. Miss Price finally discovers that the words of the magical spell can be found on the legendary "Lost Isle of Naboombu," so she, Brown, and the children travel there, having adventures beneath the sea along the way. They discover the lion king of Naboombu is wearing a medallion with the words to the spell on it, which they have to obtain. All of this magical travel is possible with the aid of a magical bedknob. Returning home, Miss Price uses the formula to raise a ghostly army of armor from the local museum that routs a band of invading German commandos. Premiered in England on October 7, 1971; U.S. general release on December 13, 1971. Directed by Robert Stevenson. 117 min. for the original release version; whittled down to 98 min. for a 1979 reissue. Stars Angela Lansbury (Eglantine Price), Roddy McDowall (Mr. Jelk), David Tomlinson (Emelius

Brown), Sam Jaffe (Bookman), John Ericson (Col. Heller), Bruce Forsyth (Swinburne), Tessie O'Shea (Mrs. Hobday), Reginald Owen (Gen. Teagler), Ian Weighill (Charlie), Roy Snart (Paul), Cindy O'Callaghan (Carrie). The creative talent behind *Mary Poppins* joined forces again for this film, including producer-writer Bill Walsh, director Robert Stevenson, songwriters Richard M. Sherman and Robert B. Sherman, music supervisor Irwin Kostal, art director Peter Ellenshaw, and special-effects technician Eustace Lycett. The songs included: "The Old Home Guard," "Eglantine," "The Age of Not Believing," "Portobello Road," "The Beautiful Briny," and "Substitutiary Locomotion." One song sung by Angela Lansbury on the sound track record album, "A Step in the Right Direction," was edited out of the film just before its release. The screenplay was based on Mary Norton's book, with additions by Bill Walsh, who came up with the German invasion. The film was made entirely on the Disney Studio lot in Burbank, California, where outdoor sets included the town of Pepperinge Eye and Miss Price's seaview cottage, and indoor sets including a three-block section of London's legendary Portobello Road. Two hundred players jammed this set alone, which was filled with bric-a-brac and

such oddments as a Sicilian sedan chair, Limoges china, and gas masks from World War II. Among the performers and extras in the crowd were veterans of music halls, vaudeville, rep shows, radio, silent films, and early talkies. The ghostly medieval army's weapons and armor had originally been assembled in Spain for the film *El Cid*, and then were shipped to America to be used in the Warner Bros. musical *Camelot*. Ward Kimball was the director of the wonderful animation sequences on the Isle of Naboombu. Despite the effort, lavish budget, ingenuity, and special effects, the film was not a great box office success, causing the studio subsequently to edit the film. The editing was accomplished primarily to the detriment of musical numbers—large chunks of "Eglantine" and "With A Flair" were deleted. Academy Award winner for Best Special Visual Effects. The movie was nominated also for Best Art Direction/Set Direction, Best Song ("The Age of Not Believing"), Best Scoring, and Best Costume Design. The film remains a Disney favorite today, with a theatrical reissue in 1979 and releases on video in 1980, 1985, and 1989.

Bee at the Beach (film) Donald Duck cartoon; released on October 13, 1950. Directed by Jack Hannah. When Donald accidentally upsets a bee through a series of mishaps (and some deliberate provocation), the conflict worsens until the bee gets the ultimate revenge by ruining Donald's rubber raft, causing him to be chased by sharks.

Bee on Guard (film) Donald Duck cartoon; released on December 14, 1951. Directed by Jack Hannah. When Donald discovers bees taking honey from his flowers, he raids their beehive

dressed as a giant bee, fooling the bee on guard. The bee is banished in disgrace but is welcomed back as a hero after he wins a ferocious battle with Donald.

Beebe, Lloyd Nature photographer on the True-Life Adventures and field producer for a number of Disney animal films, including *Charlie the Lonesome Cougar*, *King of the Grizzlies*, and *The Footloose Fox*.

Beezy Bear (film) Donald Duck cartoon; released on September 2, 1955. Directed by Jack Hannah. Filmed in CinemaScope. Humphrey the

bear continually tries different ways to steal honey from Donald's beehives, resulting in conflicts between Donald and Ranger J. Audubon Woodlore when Donald wants the bears kept away.

Before and After (film) A respected, dedicated small town pediatrician, Carolyn Ryan finds her life thrown into turmoil when her teenage son, Jacob, disappears and is suspected of brutally murdering his girlfriend, whose body is found on an isolated snow-covered farm road. When Jacob returns home, Carolyn and her sculptor-husband, Ben, struggle to confront the tragedy and protect their son, even though the town and evidence is dead set against him. In doing so, they show how a family that is driven by love can survive such a catastrophe. A Hollywood Picture in association with Caravan Pictures. Directed by Barbet Schroeder. Released on February 23, 1996. Stars Meryl Streep (Carolyn Ryan), Liam Neeson (Ben Ryan), Edward Furlong (Jacob), Julia Weldon (Judith), Alfred Mol-

ina (Panos Demeris). 108 min. Filming took place primarily in the Berkshire County area of western Massachusetts, where an unseasonal lack of snow necessitated the bringing in of snowmaking machines from a local ski resort. Released on video in 1996.

Before It's Too Late: A Film on Teenage Suicide (film) Educational film; released in September 1985. The film shows ways to spot suicidal behavior and to help prevent teens from committing suicide.

Begley, Ed (1901–1970) Actor; appeared on television in *The Secrets of the Pirate's Inn*.

Begley, Ed, Jr. Actor; appeared in *Now You See Him, Now You Don't* (Druffle), *Charley and the Angel* (Derwood Moseby), and *Renaissance Man* (Jack Markin), and on television in *Tales of the Apple Dumpling Gang*, *The Absent-Minded Professor: Trading Places*, the remake of *The Shaggy Dog* (Mr. Daniels), *Murder She Purred: A Mrs. Murphy Mystery* (Fitz-Gilbert Hamilton), on Disney Channel in *Hounded* (Ward Van Dusen) and in the television series *Wednesday 9:30 (8:30 Central)* (Paul Weffler) and *Stephen King's Kingdom Hospital* (Dr. Jesse James).

Behind the Cameras in Lapland/Alaskan Eskimo (television) Television show; aired October 24, 1956, featuring the People and Places featurette about Alaska and the filming of one about the Lapps. Directed by Winston Hibler and James Algar.

Behind the Scenes of Walt Disney Studio
(film) Robert Benchley leads a tour of the Disney
Studio, as he tries to see Walt to sell him a story,
originally released as part of *The Reluctant Dragon*.
Released in 16mm in December 1952. 26 min.

Behind the Scenes with Fess Parker (television) Television show; aired on May 30, 1956.
Directed by Francis D. Lyon. Walt Disney talks

about trains and then introduces Fess Parker to
narrate a behind-the-scenes look at the filming
of *The Great Locomotive Chase*. Actor Jeffrey
Hunter and technical adviser Wilbur Kurtz join
in, and Peter Ellenshaw is shown creating matte
paintings. The actual filming of the chase is
shown taking place near Clayton, Georgia, on the
lines of the Tallulah Falls Railroad.

**Behind the True-Life Cameras/Olympic
Elk** (television) Television show; aired on September 21, 1955. Directed by Winston Hibler
and James Algar. Cameramen are shown filming
Secrets of Life in the desert and in the Everglades,
and trailing after animals near Mt. Kilimanjaro
for *The African Lion*.

Behn, Peter Child actor; voice of the young
Thumper in *Bambi*. In the 1980s, the Disney Studio tracked down Behn to help promote a re-issue
of *Bambi*; he was discovered working in the real
estate business in Vermont.

Being Right: Can You Still Lose? (film)
Educational film, using sequences from *Ride a*

Wild Pony. In the Questions!/Answers? series,
released in 1976. The dilemma of having a pony
decide between two former owners.

Beise, S. Clark (1898–1989) Executive with
the Bank of America and a member of the Disney
board of directors from 1965 to 1975.

Bejewelled (television) Four unlikely heroes
tackle the mystery of a fortune in missing jewels,
which disappeared while they were being transported to London for an exhibition. A Disney
Channel Premiere Film, first aired on January 20,
1991. Directed by Terry Marcel. Stars Emma
Samms (Stacey Orpington), Dirk Benedict (Gordon), Denis Lawson (Alistair Lord), Jade Magri
(Eloise Dubois), Aeryk Egon (Marvin Birnbaum).
94 min.

Bekins Van Lines The company operated a
locker area on Town Square at Disneyland from
1955 to 1962. The locker area was later sponsored by Global Van Lines and National.

Belafsky, Marty Child actor; appeared in
Newsies (Crutchy) and *Pearl Harbor* (Louie) and
on television in the series *Hull High*.

Believe . . . There's Magic in the Stars
Fireworks spectacular created for Disneyland's
45th anniversary, debuting on February 18, 2000,
taking the place of the long-running *Fantasy in
the Sky*. A holiday version, *Believe . . . in Holiday
Magic*, debuted on November 3, 2000, and featured a simulated snowfall at various areas in the
park. American Honda Motor Co. became the
sponsor in December 2004. For the 50th anniversary in 2005, the show changed to *Remember . . .
Dreams Come True*.

Believe You Can . . . and You Can! (television) Syndicated television special celebrating
the opening of the new Fantasyland at Disneyland, aired on April 21, 1983. Directed by
Lee Miller. Heather goes to Disneyland to find
magic to prevent her family from moving to
Minneapolis; instead, she discovers the park's

Fantasyland Problem Solver who shows her the new Fantasyland. Stars Morey Amsterdam, Heather O'Rourke, Lance Sloan, Mary Ann Seltzer.

Bell Telephone Science Series See *The Restless Sea*. Two other films in the series narrated by Dr. Frank Baxter, *Our Mister Sun* and *Hemo the Magnificent*, even though they contained animation, were not made by Disney.

Bella Notte Song from *Lady and the Tramp*; written by Peggy Lee and Sonny Burke.

Bellamy, Ralph (1904–1991) Actor; appeared in *The Good Mother* (grandfather) and *Pretty Woman* (James Morse), and on The Disney Channel in *Love Leads the Way*.

Bellboy Donald (film) Donald Duck cartoon; released on December 18, 1942. Directed by Jack

King. Soon after the hotel manager warns bellboy Donald about impoliteness to guests, Donald is taunted continually by Junior, Senator Pete's bratty son. Eventually, Donald ends up spanking Junior, after he has lost both his temper and his job.

Belle Beautiful heroine of *Beauty and the Beast*; voiced by Paige O'Hara. Also the title of a song by Howard Ashman and Alan Menken, nominated for an Academy Award.

Belle's Magical World (film) Direct-to-video release on January 13, 1998, of three animated films entitled *Perfect Word*, *Broken Wing*, and

Fifi's Folly featuring the characters from the *Beauty and the Beast* feature film. Reissued in 2003 as *Beauty and the Beast: Belle's Magical World*.

Belle's Tales of Friendship (film) Direct-to-video release on August 17, 1999. A compilation of live-action and animated characters, classic Disney storytelling, and five new-to-video songs. Directed by Jimbo Marshall. With Lynsey McLeod (Belle).

Beloved (film) A decade after the Civil War, Sethe, a woman who had escaped from slavery at the Sweet Home plantation, continues to live in its shadow. Living in a seemingly haunted house in rural Ohio at 124 Bluestone Road with her teenage daughter, Denver, Sethe receives a surprise visit from Paul D., another Sweet Home survivor. Denver resents the presence of Paul D., but the three have even more problems when a mysterious stranger named Beloved appears in their midst. Beloved was the name of Sethe's child, who had died at her hand years before, and Sethe believes this is that child revived. A Touchstone Picture. Directed by Jonathan Demme. Released on October 16, 1998. Stars Oprah Winfrey (Sethe), Danny Glover (Paul D.), Thandie Newton (Beloved), Kimberly Elise (Denver), Beah Richards (Baby Suggs). 172 min. Oprah Winfrey was the guiding light behind the film, having optioned the rights to the novel in 1988 for her production company, Harpo Films. Based on the Pulitzer Prize–winning novel by Toni Morrison. Production took place in rural areas of Maryland and Pennsylvania near Philadelphia. Released on video in 1999.

Belushi, James Actor; appeared in *Taking Care of Business* (Jimmy) and *Mr. Destiny* (Larry Burrows), and starred in the television series *According to Jim* (Jim).

Ben Ali Gator Lead alligator dancer in the *Dance of the Hours* segment of *Fantasia*.

Ben and Me (film) Special cartoon featurette, released on November 10, 1953. Directed by Hamilton Luske. Amos, a poor, little church

mouse, comes to live with the fabulous Ben Franklin and through Amos's suggestions the Franklin stove and bifocals are invented, electricity is discovered, and the opening words of the Declaration of Independence are provided. Franklin was voiced by Charlie Ruggles; Sterling Holloway voiced Amos; Hans Conried did Thomas Jefferson. Released by Buena Vista Distribution Company with *The Living Desert*. 21 min. Released on video in 1989.

Ben and Me/Peter and the Wolf (television) Television show; aired on November 15, 1964. Directed by Hamilton S. Luske and Clyde Geronimi. The television show aired both featurettes.

Ben Buzzard Crook who tries to sell Donald Duck a used airplane in *Flying Jalopy* (1943).

Benay-Albee Novelty Co. Company that introduced the Mickey Mouse ear hats for sale at Disneyland. The hats were patterned after those designed by Roy Williams and worn by the Mouseketeers on the *Mickey Mouse Club* television show. During the 1950s, along with the Davy Crockett coonskin caps, these were the preferred item of headwear for kids throughout America.

Benchley, Robert (1889–1945) Humorist; appeared in *The Reluctant Dragon*, taking a tour of the Disney Studio.

Benji the Hunted (film) Benji, the dog, becomes lost in the mountains after a fishing accident and is forced to become involved with animals that are normally a dog's mortal enemies, including a Kodiak bear, a black timber wolf, and a number of cougars. He aids some orphaned cougar cubs while trying to find his way back to civilization. Initial release in Dallas on June 5, 1987; general release on June 19, 1987. Directed by Joe Camp. An Embark Production in association with Mulberry Square Productions. 89 min. Filmed in Oregon and Washington. Released on video in 1988 and 1993. While there were other Benji motion pictures, this was the only one released by Disney.

Bennett, Rhona Actress; appeared on the *Mickey Mouse Club* on The Disney Channel, beginning in 1991. She also appears as Loquatia in *Homeboys in Outer Space*.

Bennett, Zachary Actor; appeared in *The Good Mother* (Young Bobby), and on Disney Channel in *Avonlea* (Felix King), *Back to Hannibal: the Return of Tom Sawyer* (Marcus), and *Looking for Miracles* (Sullivan Delaney).

Benny, Jack (1894–1974) Walt appeared on Jack Benny's television hour on November 3, 1965, in a skit where Jack asks Walt for 110 free passes to Disneyland for his crew.

Benny and the 'Roids (A Story About Steroid Abuse) (film) Educational film, released in March 1988. 25 min. A high school football player learns the dangers of steroid abuse.

Benny the Cab The anthropomorphic taxi in *Who Framed Roger Rabbit*; voiced by Charles Fleischer.

Benson, Jodi Actress; voiced Ariel in *The Little Mermaid* and provided the voice of Weebo in *Flubber*. She provided the voice for Ariel in *The Little Mermaid II: Return to the Sea*, Lady in *Lady and the Tramp II: Scamp's Adventure*, and Anita in *101 Dalmatians II: Patch's London Adventure*.

Benson, Robby Actor; voiced the Beast in *Beauty and the Beast*.

Bent-Tail Coyote character who appeared in four films, beginning with *The Legend of Coyote*

Rock (1945); he was joined by his son, Bent-Tail, Jr., in the next three films.

Berenger, Tom Actor; appeared in *Shoot to Kill* (Jonathan Knox).

Bergen, Edgar (1903–1978) Ventriloquist; appeared in *Fun and Fancy Free*, with his dummies Charlie McCarthy and Mortimer Snerd.

Berger, Richard (1939–2004) He served as the first president of the new company division called Walt Disney Pictures for two years beginning in 1982. He left the company when Jeffrey Katzenberg was brought in as chairman of Walt Disney Pictures.

Berlin, Irving, Inc. The composer's music publishing company acquired the rights to publish and license the use of the earliest Disney songs, from the Mickey Mouse and Silly Symphony songs of the early 1930s ("Who's Afraid of the Big Bad Wolf?" was the most famous) up to those of *Snow White and the Seven Dwarfs* and *Pinocchio*. Many of the songs became classics and have been kept in print to the present day, now published by Bourne.

Berlinger, Warren Actor; appeared in *Small and Frye* and in the title role on the *Kilroy* miniseries on television, and in the feature *The Shaggy D.A.* (Dip).

Berlioz Aspiring-musician kitten in *The Aristocats*; voiced by Dean Clark.

Bernard Male mouse lead in *The Rescuers*; voiced by Bob Newhart. Also in *The Rescuers Down Under.*

Bernardi, Herschel Actor; appeared in *No Deposit, No Return* and on television in *I-Man*.

Berry, Halle Actress; appeared in *Father Hood* (Kathleen Mercer), *The Program* (Autumn), and *The Rich Man's Wife* (Josie Potenza), and on television in *Oprah Winfrey Presents: Their Eyes Were Watching God* (Janie Crawford).

Berry, Ken Actor; starred in *Herbie Rides Again* (Willoughby Whitfield) and *The Cat from Outer Space* (Frank).

Bertha Mae Davy Crockett's keel boat in *Davy Crockett's Keel Boat Race*, also one of the Mike Fink Keel Boats at Disneyland and in Magic Kingdom Park at Walt Disney World.

Bertini, Antonio Joined Disney's Italian subsidiary in 1960 and headed it from 1963 until his retirement in 1990. He received a European Disney Legends Award in 1997.

Best Doggoned Dog in the World, The (television) Television show; aired on November 20, 1957. Walt shows how dogs and men have enjoyed a special relationship by showing scenes from *Old Yeller*, narrated by Dorothy McGuire, and the entire *Arizona Sheepdog* featurette. A 1961 rerun substituted *One Hundred and One Dalmatians* footage for *Old Yeller*.

Best of Country, The (television) Television special; aired on CBS on January 27, 1995.

Best of Country '92: Countdown at the Neon Armadillo (television) Television special on ABC; aired on December 10, 1992.

Best of Disney, The: 50 Years of Magic (television) Two-hour television special; aired on May 20, 1991, celebrating 50 years (actually 51) of the Disney Studio in Burbank. Directed by Don Mischer. With Harry Connick, Jr., Dick Van Dyke, Shelley Long, Daryl Hannah, Neil Patrick Harris, Annette Funicello, Teri Garr, Barbara Walters, Bill Campbell. The stars are called upon to reminisce about their favorite moments in Disney films.

Best of Disney Music, The: A Legacy in Song (television) Television special on CBS on February 3, 1993. Part 2 aired on May 21, 1993. 60 min. each. Angela Lansbury hosted the first part and Glenn Close the second. Directed by Don Mischer.

Best of Friends Song from *The Fox and the Hound*, written by Stan Fidel and Richard Johnston.

Best of Walt Disney's True-Life Adventures, The (film) Compilation feature released on October 8, 1975. Directed by James Algar. 89 min. Narrated by Winston Hibler, the film opens with a salute to Walt Disney as a pioneer in the nature films genre. Animals of all kinds and many species of insects are captured in dramatic and fascinating moments from the Amazon to the Arctic. Hibler's conclusion aptly states an underlying truth, making this True-Life Adventure collection ever popular: "as long as life goes on, nature and all her marvels will continue to fascinate mankind." Narration written by James Algar, Winston Hibler, Ted Sears. This film, with segments originally fashioned by Ben Sharpsteen and James Algar, is also a tribute to photographers Alfred G. and Elma Milotte, N. Paul Kenworthy, Jr., Robert H. Crandall, Hugh A. Wilmar, James R. Simon, Herb and Lois Crisler, Tom McHugh, Jack C. Couffer, John H. Storer, Stuart V. Jewell, Bert Harwell, Dick Borden, Alfred M. Bailey, Olin Sewall Pettingill, Jr., Karl H. Maslowski, Lloyd Beebe, William Carrick, Cleveland P. Grant, Murl Deusing, and many others who roamed remote regions of the earth to provide such memorable footage for the series. A variety of music scored for the series by Paul Smith, Oliver Wallace, and Buddy Baker is included.

BET Soundstage Club Opened June 10, 1998 at Downtown Disney Pleasure Island as the only nightclub in the country carrying the Black Entertainment Television name. Fans of R&B, hip-hop, and rap can watch performances by their favorite artists, while sampling drinks and Caribbean-style finger food. Took the place of the Neon Armadillo.

Betsy's Wedding (film) Eddie Hopper is determined to give his daughter, Betsy, a fantastic wedding with all the trimmings. Unfortunately, Betsy doesn't want a big wedding. Overextended financially and emotionally, Eddie finds the two families battling, with everyone pushing for their own favorite traditions in the ceremony. To make things worse, he gets into a questionable business deal with his unscrupulous brother-in-law. Everyone finds their lives changing as the pressures of the wedding mount. Released on June 22, 1990. Directed by Alan Alda. A Touchstone film. 94 min. Stars Alan Alda (Eddie Hopper), Joey Bishop (Eddie's father), Madeline Kahn (Lola Hopper), Molly Ringwald (Betsy Hopper), Catherine O'Hara (Gloria Henner), Joe Pesci (Oscar Henner), Ally Sheedy (Connie Harper), Burt Young (Georgie). The film was a personal project of Alda's, who also wrote the screenplay; he came up with the idea from the wedding of his own youngest daughter. Filmed in New York City and in the beautiful old coastal town of Wilmington, North Carolina. Released on video in 1990.

Better Way to Go, A: An Introduction to Non-Manipulative Selling (film) Educational film from The Nick Price Story of Non-Manipulative Selling series; released in February 1981. A salesman should be a skilled problem solver, not a persuader. By building trust, he can get repeat customers and increased sales.

Bettin, Val He voiced Basil's friend, Dr. Dawson, in *The Great Mouse Detective*, and provided the voice of the Sultan in versions of the *Aladdin* story after the original feature film.

Beverly Hills Family Robinson (television) Two-hour television movie; aired on January 25,

1997, on ABC. Bristling from being the family of Marsha Robinson, the star of a popular lifestyle television program, and having to live with her chic home decor and gourmet dinners, the entire Robinson family, head off for a vacation trip to Hawaii. When modern-day pirates take over their yacht, the family has to outwit them. Finding itself shipwrecked on a tropical island, the family builds a treehouse for shelter that Marsha proceeds to transform into a showcase for castaway living. Daughter Jane falls for a handsome Windsurfer, Digger, and the pirates return, causing the family to defend their tree house. Directed by Troy Miller. Stars Dyan Cannon (Marsha Robinson), Martin Mull (Dr. Doug Robinson), Sarah Michelle Gellar (Jane), Ryan O'Donohue (Roger), Josh Picker (Digger), Kevin Weisman (Brinks), Michael Edwards-Stevens (Claude), Nique Needles (Melvin). The "island" scenes were filmed in Queensland, Australia.

Beymer, Richard Actor; appeared in *Johnny Tremain* (Rab Silsbee), and provided a voice for *Boys of the Western Sea* on the *Mickey Mouse Club*.

Beyond Witch Mountain (television) Television show; aired on February 20, 1982. Directed by Robert Day. A pilot for a proposed series, based on the film, *Escape to Witch Mountain*. Tony and Tia leave Witch Mountain to look for their Uncle Bene, and they all fall into the clutches of the evil Deranian. They have to use their special powers to outwit him. Stars Eddie Albert, Tracey Gould, Andrew K. Freeman, J. D. Cannon, Noah Beery, Jr., Efrem Zimbalist, Jr. While Eddie Albert reprised his role as Jason O'Day from the motion picture, the rest of the cast was new.

Bialik, Mayim Actress; appeared in *Beaches* (C.C. Bloom at age 11), and in the title role on the television series *Blossom*. She narrated the educational film *AIDS: You've Got to Do Something.*

Bianca Goldfish who appeared in two cartoons, beginning with *Mickey's Parrot* (1938).

Bianca Female mouse lead in *The Rescuers*; voiced by Eva Gabor. Also in *The Rescuers Down Under*.

Bibbidi-Bobbidi-Boo Song from *Cinderella*, written by Jerry Livingston, Mack David, and Al Hoffman. Nominated for an Academy Award.

Bibo-Lang, Inc. Publisher in 1930 of the very first *Mickey Mouse Book*, a thin, green-colored pamphlet which contained a story written by Mr. Bibo's 8-year-old daughter, Bobette. The first hardback book, *The Adventures of Mickey Mouse*, was published the following year by David McKay.

Bicentennial Man (film) Andrew Martin, an android programmed to perform menial tasks, displays uncharacteristically human emotions and is curious and creative. Over time, he recognizes that he has a unique destiny—to become human. Through two centuries and generations in the Martin family, Andrew discovers the intricacies of life and love, and what it truly means to be a human being. Released on December 17, 1999. Directed by Chris Columbus. Stars Robin Williams (Andrew Martin), Sam Neill (Sir), Embeth Davidtz (adult Little Miss/Portia), Wendy Crewson (Ma'am), Oliver Platt (Rupert Burns), Hallie Kate Eisenberg (young Little Miss). 131 min. A co-production of Touchstone Pictures with Columbia Pictures, with Disney handling domestic distribution and Columbia handling international distribution. Based on the short story by Isaac Asimov, and the novel *The Positronic Man* by Asimov and Robert Silverberg. The production's set designers had to modernize the look of San Francisco from the near future to 200 years hence. The film received an Academy Award nomination for Best Makeup. Released on video in 2000.

Biehn, Michael Actor; appeared in *Tombstone* (Ringo) and *The Rock* (Charles Anderson).

Biergarten Restaurant in Germany in World Showcase at Epcot; opened on October 1, 1982. German entertainers yodel and play the

50-foot-long alphorns at regular intervals during the day to please the diners enjoying their bratwurst, sauerkraut, and apple strudel.

Big Bad Wolf, The Ferocious nemesis of the *Three Little Pigs* (1933), who went on to appear in seven additional films.

Big Bad Wolf, The (film) Silly Symphony cartoon; released on April 14, 1934. Directed by Burt Gillett. Red Riding Hood is warned by the Three Little Pigs about the wolf, who is waiting

for her at Grandmother's house. She is rescued in the nick of time by the Practical Pig, who gets rid of the wolf with hot coals and popcorn.

Big Bands at Disneyland (television) Series on The Disney Channel consisting of 12 episodes, premiering June 28, 1984, with bands such as the Count Basie Orchestra, the Glenn Miller Orchestra, the Bob Crosby Orchestra, Les Brown and His Band of Renown, and the Tommy Dorsey Orchestra, all performing in Plaza Gardens at Disneyland.

Big Brother Blues (film) Educational 16mm release in association with Metropolitan Life, 1992, 30 min. A young teen is shocked to learn that his mother and stepfather are about to have a baby. He is not sure how he feels about losing his status as the only child, but eventually he finds himself excited by the prospect of becoming a big brother.

Big Business (film) Two sets of twins, Rose and Sadie Shelton and Rose and Sadie Ratliff, are mixed up at birth. Years later the Sheltons are running a major corporation in New York, with Rose not caring for the corporate life, and the Ratliffs are living in a poor West Virginia town that relies on a local furniture company for its survival, with Sadie longing for the joys of the big city. When the Sheltons' company tries to sell off the furniture company (and town), the Ratliffs go to New York to protest. It is a major case of mistaken identities as all four ladies end up staying at the Plaza Hotel, pursued by their respective beaus. Released on June 10, 1988. Directed by Jim Abrahams. A Touchstone film. 98 min. Stars Bette Midler (Sadie Shelton/Sadie Ratliff), Lily Tomlin (Rose Shelton/Rose Ratliff), Fred Ward (Roone Dimmick), Edward Herrmann (Graham Sherbourne). The Plaza Hotel's lavish suites and distinctive lobby were re-created on a Disney soundstage, while exteriors and a scene in the Palm Court were filmed on location in New York. Released on video in 1989.

Big Council, The (television) Television show; the sixth episode of *The Saga of Andy Burnett.*

Big Fisherman, The (film) Not a Disney-produced film, but it was brought to the attention of Disney management in 1959, and they decided to release it through their Buena Vista Distribution Company. Based on the novel by Lloyd C. Douglas. Directed by Frank Borzage. Howard Keel portrays Simon Peter, the rough and skeptical fisherman of Galilee who eventually becomes Christ's chief disciple and founder of his church. Also stars Susan Kohner, John Saxon, Martha Hyer, Herbert Lom. Locations included Lake

Chatsworth and the Palm Springs area of Southern California. 180 min.

Big Game Safari Shooting Gallery See Safari Shooting Gallery.

Big Green, The (film) The arrival of British schoolteacher Anna Montgomery to the small town of Elma, Texas, and her determination to create a winning soccer team among the kids, creates many changes in the drab town. She is helped by sheriff Tom Palmer, who is anxious to best his rival, coach Jay Huffer from the big city. Directed by Holly Goldberg Sloan. A Walt Disney Picture, in association with Caravan Pictures. Released on September 29, 1995. Stars Steve Guttenberg (Tom Palmer), Olivia D'Abo (Anna Montgomery), Jay O. Sanders (Jay Huffer), John Terry (Edwin V. Douglas), Chauncey Leopardi (Evan Schiff), Patrick Renna (Larry Musgrove), Billy L. Sullivan (Jeffrey Luttrell). 100 min. Filmed on location around Austin, Texas, with the small town of Dale substituting for the fictional Elma. Since most of the child actors had no experience with soccer, the head coach of the University of Texas's varsity soccer team, Robert Parr, had to be called in to run a soccer camp.

Big Mama Motherly owl in *The Fox and the Hound;* voiced by Pearl Bailey.

Big Red (film) A boy's conviction that a handsome red setter can be handled and trained with love rather than harsh discipline brings him into conflict with Mr. Haggin, the owner of the kennel where he works. As an orphan hungering for love, he understands Big Red, who does not respond to Haggin's training methods. The boy's disobedience results in the dog being injured and the boy leaving. A series of adventures involving the dog, the boy, and Mr. Haggin brings about many valuable lessons to all and Mr. Haggin's eventual adoption of the youngster who will fill a vacuum that existed in the Haggin home since the death of an only son. Released on June 6, 1962. The first Disney film directed by Norman Tokar, who went on to direct many other Disney features in the 1960s and 1970s. 89 min. Stars Walter Pidgeon (James

Haggin), Gilles Payant (Rene Dumont), Emile Genest (Emile Fornet), Janette Bertrand (Therese Fornet). Besides interiors at the Disney Studio in Burbank, sequences were filmed on location near La Malbaie, Quebec, Canada, along the shore of the St. Lawrence, and at Big Bear Lake in California. The songs "Mon Amour Perdu" and "Emile's Reel" were written by Richard M. Sherman and Robert B. Sherman. Released on video in 1984.

Big Swindle, The (television) Television show; the second part of *The Further Adventures of Gallegher.*

Big Thunder Barbecue Outdoor restaurant in Big Thunder Ranch at Disneyland; opened on December 14, 1986. It was a unique eating place at the park with all the seating outdoors and the barbecued beef and chicken served from chuck wagons. It changed its name and theme on June 20, 1996, to become Festival of Foods. It reverted to Big Thunder Barbecue on May 30, 1997, and remained open until January 20, 2001.

Big Thunder Mountain Railroad Frontierland attraction at Disneyland; opened on September 2, 1979. Also Frontierland attraction in Magic Kingdom Park at Walt Disney World; opened September 23, 1980. Also in Westernland at Tokyo Disneyland; opened on July 4, 1987. A Disney-

land Paris version opened on April 12, 1992. For the original attraction at Disneyland, Disney designer Tony Baxter was intrigued by the scenery at Bryce Canyon National Park in Utah, so he designed the first Big Thunder Mountain to resemble it; the three later ones resemble scenery in Monument Valley. The mountain itself is completely manufactured, with Disney Imagineers becoming expert on using cement and paint to create realistic-looking rocks. To add atmosphere of the gold rush–era of the Old West, the designers scoured the ghost towns of the western states and came up with ore carts, cogwheels, buckets, and other authentic mining equipment. The roller coaster–like ride might seem tame to aficionados, but the addition of interesting themed detail everywhere makes the experience unique. Guests embark on a harrowing journey through dark caverns and deep sandstone gorges, encountering swarming bats, crashing landslides, and rumbling earthquakes along the way. Big Thunder Mountain replaced Rainbow Mountain and its Mine Train; some of that attraction's set pieces were retained for the new attraction.

Big Thunder Ranch Frontierland area at Disneyland near Big Thunder Mountain, a recreation of an 1880s working horse ranch, which included a petting area, ranch house, stable, and outdoor restaurant; opened on June 27, 1986. The Disneyland livestock had always been kept in the Pony Farm behind the Magic Kingdom, out of the sight of guests. Here, guests could now see and pet some of the horses, goats, and sheep, watch a blacksmith or harness-maker at work, and visit the ranch house. For several years, Mickey Moo, a cow with a Mickey Mouse–shaped mark on her back, was a highlight of a visit to Big Thunder Ranch. The ranch closed in February 1996, to make way for a medieval village for a *Hunchback of Notre Dame* show that closed on April 18, 1998. From 1998 to 2004, the area was used for corporate gatherings. On April 2, 2004, it reopened as Little Patch of Heaven to promote *Home on the Range*.

Big Trouble (film) An ensemble comedy about a mysterious suitcase which brings together, and changes, the lives of a divorced dad, an unhappy housewife, two hitmen, a pair of street thugs, two love-struck teens, two FBI men, and a psychedelic toad. Directed by Barry Sonnenfeld. A Touchstone Picture. Released on April 5, 2002. Stars Tim Allen (Eliot Arnold), Omar Epps (Seitz), Dennis Farina (Henry), Janeane Garofalo (Monica Romero), Jason Lee (Puggy), Stanley Tucci (Arthur Herk), Ben Foster (Matt Arnold), Heavy D (Greer), Patrick Warburton (Walter Kramitz), Zooey Deschanel (Jenny Herk), Johnny Knoxville (Eddie), Rene Russo (Anna Herk), Tom Sizemore (Snake), Jack Kehler (Leonard). 85 min. Based on a novel by Dave Barry. Filmed at various sites in the Miami area. Since the film plot includes terrorists and a bomb secreted on an airplane, release of the film was delayed six months due to sensitivities arising from the September 11, 2001, terrorist activities in New York and Washington, D.C. Released on video in 2002.

Big Wash, The (film) Goofy cartoon; released on February 6, 1948. Directed by Clyde Geronimi. Goofy tries to give a circus elephant, Dolores, a bath, but she proves elusive and ends up blowing

him into a mud puddle. Dolores was the name of Walt's secretary (Dolores Voght).

Bigfoot (television) Two-hour television show; aired on March 8, 1987. Directed by Danny Huston. A man and his intended bride take their respective children, who are not at all pleased with the impending marriage, camping, where they find a huge creature. The creature kidnaps the girl, and the others join a reclusive woman, Gladys, who has been studying the Sasquatch, in trying to rescue her. When the girl is rescued, she helps the others prevent the Sasquatch from being captured by a scientist. Stars Colleen Dewhurst, James Sloyan, Gracie Harrison, Joseph Maher, Adam Karl, Candace Cameron.

Bigle, Armand He started a Disney magazine in Belgium in 1947, but soon relocated to Paris and headed the French and eventually all European merchandising operations for the company until his retirement in 1988. Received a European Disney Legends Award in 1997.

Bill Lizard in *Alice in Wonderland* who is asked to get a huge Alice out of the White Rabbit's house. Voiced by Larry Grey.

Bill Nye, the Science Guy (television) Television series; syndicated beginning September 10, 1993. Nye demonstrates scientific principles and theories for kids, showing that science can be fun and exciting.

Billposters (film) Donald Duck cartoon; released on May 17, 1940. Directed by Clyde Geronimi. Donald and Goofy's plans to post bills fall apart when Goofy gets into trouble with a windmill and Donald meets his nemesis in an ornery goat.

Billy Bathgate (film) Young Billy, a streetwise kid from Bathgate Avenue in the Bronx, is convinced that success will come to him only if he is able to join mobster Dutch Schultz's gang. Starting out as a flunky for the crime ring, he soon graduates to trusted confidant only to find danger as his mentor's power and control wane. In an underworld populated by ruthless characters, it takes all of Billy's wits to survive and to save the life of Drew Preston, with whom he has his first love interest. Released on November 11, 1991. Directed by Robert Benton. A Touchstone film. Based on the acclaimed novel by E. L. Doctorow. 107 min. Stars Dustin Hoffman (Dutch Schultz), Nicole Kidman (Drew Preston), Loren Dean (Billy Bathgate), Bruce Willis (Bo Weinberg), Steven Hill (Otto Berman). The transformation of New York City locations into the 1930s milieu took a great deal of effort and extensive research. Shooting also took place at the Saratoga Race Track in upstate New York, the oldest track in America, and in Wilmington, Durham, and Hamlet, North Carolina, the last an almost perfectly intact likeness of a 1930s eastern community. Released on video in 1992.

Billy Bob's Country Western Saloon Bluegrass bands perform in Disney Village at Disneyland Paris.

Bing, Herman (1889–1947) Voice of the Ringmaster in *Dumbo*.

Birch, Thora Child actress; appeared in *Paradise* (Billie Pike) and *Hocus Pocus* (Dani).

Bird, Andy President of Walt Disney International, beginning in January 2004.

Bird and the Robot Humorous robot and film presentation in Transcenter in World of Motion at Epcot from 1982 to 1996, explaining how robots are used on the automobile assembly line.

Bird Store, The (film) Silly Symphony cartoon; released on January 16, 1932. Directed by Wilfred Jackson. When a crafty cat attempts to catch a baby canary, the other outraged birds force it into a large cage using a blowtorch. A spring in the cage sends the screaming cat through the roof and onto the flagpole of the local dog pound.

Birds, Baboons, and Other Animals—Their Struggle for Survival (film) Portion of *The African Lion*; released on 16mm for schools in May 1969. The telephoto lens helps one observe the habits of a veritable menagerie of strange and colorful creatures in the lion's domain.

Birds in the Spring (film) Silly Symphony cartoon; released on March 11, 1933. Directed by

Dave Hand. A baby bird, Otto, has many adventures when he runs away from home. He meets a hypnotic rattlesnake and runs into trouble with a hornets' nest. Rescued by his father and taken home, he is given a spanking.

Birds of a Feather (film) Silly Symphony cartoon; released on February 3, 1931. Directed by Burt Gillett. The peaceful serenity of birds flying through the sky is broken by a hawk that steals a baby chick. By attacking in airplane formation, the birds rescue the baby and return it to its mother.

Birthday Party, The (film) Mickey Mouse cartoon; released on January 7, 1931. Directed by Burt Gillett. The early Disney gang gives Mickey a surprise party that includes the gift of a piano. Mickey shows his gratitude by entertaining them with an energetic musical number.

Biscuit Barrel Shop in United Kingdom in World Showcase at Epcot, from October 1, 1982 to January 5, 1986. The Biscuit Barrel later became Country Manor.

Biscuit Eater, The (film) In the backcountry of Tennessee, Lonnie McNeil, the son of a tenant farmer, tries to train a young hunting dog, Moreover, who is thought inferior because of a "bad streak" in him. With the help of his best friend, Text, Lonnie maintains his faith in the dog. After overcoming serious obstacles, the dog proves that he has championship potential. Released on March 22, 1972. Directed by Vincent McEveety. 92 min. Stars Earl Holliman (Harve McNeill), Patricia Crowley (Mrs. McNeill), Lew Ayres (Mr. Ames), Johnny Whitaker (Lonnie), George Spell (Text Tomlin). Remake of a 1940 Paramount film. The dog that played Moreover was of a rare breed, a German wirehaired pointer. His real name was Rolph Von Wolfgang, and he was discovered playing with his master, who was working as a tree trimmer at Disney's Golden Oak Ranch.

Bistro de Paris Restaurant in France in World Showcase at Epcot, opened on June 3, 1984.

With the extreme popularity of Les Chefs de France, Epcot executives decided more eating space was needed in France. An upstairs area above Les Chefs was unused, so they turned it into the new restaurant, also specializing in gourmet French cuisine.

Bixby, Bill (1934–1993) Actor; appeared in *The Apple Dumpling Gang* (Russel Donavan).

Black, Shirley Temple Member of the Disney board of directors in 1974–75. As a child, she presented the special Academy Award to Walt Disney in 1939 for *Snow White and the Seven Dwarfs*, and years later she helped dedicate the Sleeping Beauty Castle attraction at Disneyland.

Black Arrow (television) A wealthy lord in medieval England plans to murder one ward, marry another, and take over the property of both, but he is outwitted by the notorious Black Arrow. A television movie for The Disney Channel, first aired on January 6, 1985. Directed by John Hough. Based on the Robert Louis Stevenson story. Stars Oliver Reed (Sir Daniel Brackley), Fernando Rey (Earl of Warwick), Benedict Taylor (Richard Shelton), Stephan Chase (Black Arrow), Georgia Slowe (Lady Joanna), Donald Pleasence (Oates). Filmed on location in Spain. Released on video in 1985.

Black Cauldron, The (film) Story of young Taran, a pig keeper, who attempts to rescue his clairvoyant pig, Hen Wen, from the Horned King's castle. The King tries to get Hen Wen to lead him to the mysterious Black Cauldron. Taran escapes with a young princess and a minstrel, and with the help of mischievous Gurgi, finds the Cauldron. Before they can destroy it, it is taken by the Horned King, who begins to unleash its awesome power of producing deathless warriors. Gurgi sacrifices himself to destroy the Cauldron's power and save his friends, but in the end, Taran defeats the Horned King and Gurgi is restored. Released on July 24, 1985. Directed by Ted Berman and Richard Rich. Filmed in 70mm stereo-surround Technirama. Features the voices of John Hurt (Horned King), Grant Bardsley

(Taran), John Byner (Gurgi), Susan Sheridan (Eilonwy), Freddie Jones (Dallben), Nigel Hawthorne (Fflewddur Flam), Phil Fondacaro (Creeper). 80 min. The production can be traced back to 1971, when the Disney Studio purchased the screen rights to Lloyd Alexander's *The Chronicles of Prydain*. The five-volume mythological fantasy had been published in the mid-1960s to critical acclaim and commercial success. Adapting Alexander's books with their numerous story lines and cast of over 30 major characters proved to be a time-consuming task. Several important writer/animators worked on the development of a screenplay through the 1970s until Joe Hale was

named producer in 1980. He rewrote the script, capsulizing the sprawling story and making some changes. For instance, the Horned King was a minor character in the series but since he had so many possibilities, Hale expanded his role, making the villain a composite of several characters from the books. Filmmakers took advantage of the latest technology, which became essential in the completion of the film. Video cameras gave animators and directors an immediate and inexpensive record of what their efforts might look like. Computers also made inroads in the manipulation of solid inanimate objects on-screen. The dimensions and volume of objects were fed into a computer and then their shapes were perfectly maintained as their movement was generated by programming. Disney's venerable multiplane cameras were updated with computers to expedite and control aperture settings and time exposures. Another technological breakthrough was the development of the APT (Animation Photo Transfer) process. The first major change in the Studio's method of transferring the artist's draw-

ings to a cel since photocopying replaced hand inking 20 years earlier, the APT greatly improved the quality of the animator's art. In all, the animated film was 12 years in the making—five years in actual production—at the cost of over $25 million. Over 1,165 different hues and colors were implemented and over 34 miles of film stock was utilized. This was the first animated Disney film made in cooperation with Silver Screen Partners II. The sheer lavishness of the production, however, did not guarantee huge grosses, and the film was a box office failure. David W. Spencer was awarded an Academy Award for his development of the APT process. Released on video in 1998.

Black Hole, The (film) The explorer craft USS *Palomino* is returning to Earth after a fruitless 18-month search for extraterrestrial life when the crew comes upon a supposedly lost ship, the magnificent USS *Cygnus*, hovering near a Black Hole. The ship is controlled by Dr. Hans Reinhardt and his monstrous robot companion, Maximillian. But the initial wonderment and awe the Palomino crew have for the ship, and its resistance to the power of the Black Hole, turns to horror as they uncover Reinhardt's plans, which involve turning his former crew into robots and flying through the Hole. As they try to escape, a meteorite shower damages the ship, and the survivors hang on as they are plunged into the most powerful force in the universe, heading toward the blinding light that holds whatever eternity awaits them. Premiered in London on December 18, 1979; U.S. premiere on December 20, 1979. Directed by Gary Nelson. First film made by the Disney Studio to receive a PG rating. 98 min. Stars Maximilian Schell (Dr. Hans Reinhardt), Anthony Perkins (Dr. Alex Durant), Robert Forster (Capt. Dan Holland), Ernest Borgnine (Harry Booth), Yvette Mimieux (Dr. Kate McCrae), Joseph Bottoms (Lt. Charles Pizer). The film was five years in development, 14 months in production, and cost $20 million. It failed to recoup its terrific cost, but wowed audiences with the dazzling special effects created by A.C.E.S. (Automatic Camera Effects Systems). All the soundstages at the Disney Studio were occupied by the production. Nearly 14 months of simultaneous and postproduction filming and processing were required by the studio's photographic process laboratory and special-effects departments. In some scenes, as many as 12 different photo processes were used simultaneously on the screen. Four Academy Award winners supervised the special effects: Peter Ellenshaw, production designer and director of special effects; Eustace Lycett and Art Cruickshank, special photographic effects; and Danny Lee, special visual effects. The film was nominated for Academy Awards for Cinematography (Frank Phillips) and Visual Effects. The film's original producer, Winston Hibler, died during production. Released on video in 1980 and 1983.

Black Holes: Monsters that Eat Space and Time (television) Syndicated television special about the mysterious black holes hosted by Durk Pearson, with footage from *The Black Hole*, aired in November 1979. Directed by Chuck Staley.

Blackbeard's Ghost (film) Upon his arrival in the tiny fishing town of Godolphin, where he will be track coach of the college team, Steve Walker inadvertently summons the ghost of the infamous Captain Blackbeard. The rascally old pirate causes him nothing but trouble, but, in the end, finally helps the coach win a track meet and a girlfriend and outwit some gangsters, which earns the ghost his desired eternal rest. Released on February 8, 1968. Directed by Robert Stevenson. 107 min. Stars Peter Ustinov (Blackbeard), Dean Jones (Steve Walker), Suzanne Pleshette (Jo Anne Baker), Elsa Lanchester (Emily Stowecroft), Joby Baker (Silky Seymour). This supernatural comedy re-teamed the popular Jones and Pleshette from *The Ugly Dachshund*, and with the spirited flamboyance of Ustinov as Blackbeard, made the film a box-office winner, with a reissue in 1976. The film was based on a book by Ben Stahl. Released on video in 1982 and 1990.

Blackberries in the Dark (film) Educational film about a grandmother and grandson learning to cope with a loved one's death. Released in March 1988. 27 min.

Blackie Mischievous little lamb in *The Legend of Coyote Rock* (1945).

Blades, Rubén Actor; appeared in *Disorganized Crime* (Carlos Barrios), *Color of Night* (police lieutenant), *Cradle Will Rock* (Diego Rivera), and on television in *Gideon's Crossing* (Max Cabranes).

Blair, Janet Actress; appeared in *The One and Only, Genuine, Original Family Band* (Katie Bower).

Blair, Mary (1911–1978) Started at Disney in 1940 as a color stylist and went on the 1941 Disney trip to Latin America with her husband, Lee. Many of her color concepts are obvious in *Saludos Amigos* and *The Three Caballeros*. She later moved over to WED Enterprises, where she was instrumental in the design of "it's a small world." She designed two large tile murals for Tomorrowland in Disneyland and another for the Contemporary Resort at Walt Disney World. She was named a Disney Legend posthumously in 1991.

Blame It on the Bellboy (film) A quirky bellboy in Venice, who has trouble with English homonyms, mixes up three guests in his hotel with similar-sounding names, Orton, Lawton, and Horton, causing chaos when each receives instructions meant for another. By the end of the film, everyone has realized the mistake and switches back—all the better for the experience. World premiere in London on January 24, 1992; U.S. release on March 6, 1992. Directed by Mark Herman. 78 min. Stars Dudley Moore (Melvyn Orton), Bryan Brown (Charlton Black), Bronson Pinchot (Bellboy), Patsy Kensit (Caroline Wright), Richard Griffiths (Maurice Horton), Andreas Katsulas (Scarpa), Alison Steadman (Rosemary Horton), Penelope Wilton (Patricia Fulford). A Hollywood Pictures film. Filmed on location in Venice, Italy, on the island of Murano, and at Lee International Studios near London. Released on video in 1992.

Blame It on the Samba (film) Segment of *Melody Time*, with the Dinning Sisters and Ethel Smith at the organ; Donald Duck is taught the samba by José Carioca. Re-released as a short on April 1, 1955.

Blanc, Mel (1908–1989) Voice artist who supplied a hiccup for the nonspeaking Gideon in *Pinocchio*, and provided several voices of his famous Warner Bros. characters for *Who Framed Roger Rabbit*.

Blanche-Neige et les Sept Nains Snow White attraction in Fantasyland at Disneyland Paris; opened April 12, 1992.

Blank Check (film) Eleven-year-old Preston Waters' rusty old bike is accidentally run over by a car driven by a crook named Quigley, who quickly dashes off a check to pay for the damages, but in his haste neglects to fill in the amount. Preston notices the oversight and boldly fills in an impressive amount—$1 million. Suddenly wealthy, Preston embarks on the wildest spending spree ever. He hires a personal chauffeur, buys a great house, and throws himself a spectacular 12th-birthday bash. But the party's over when the FBI along with Quigley and his thugs descend as uninvited guests, and Preston discovers how hard it is to hold on to his newfound riches. Released on February 11, 1994. Directed by Rupert Wainwright. 93 min. Stars Brian Bonsall (Preston Waters), Karen Duffy (Shay Stanley), Miguel Ferrer (Quigley), James Rebhorn (Fred Waters), Tone Loc (Juice), Jayne Atkinson (Sandra Waters), Michael Lerner (Biderman), Chris Demetral (Damian Waters). The motion picture was filmed on location in Austin, Texas. Released on video in 1994.

Blast to the Past Celebration with a parade at Disneyland in the spring of 1988 and 1989. The young Disneyland performers put on their (or perhaps their parents') attire from the 1950s, and presented a rousing salute to the era. There was a daily parade, with period cars adding to the ambiance, and a special show, the Main Street Hop, presented on Main Street and featuring five huge jukeboxes, hula hoops, Elvis, scooter riders, and confetti. Shows featured original entertainers from the 1950s and 1960s. As part of the event, Disneyland hosted the Super Hooper Duper event, smashing the world's record for the most persons hula-hooping at one time in one location—1,527 people gathered for the extravaganza in front of Sleeping Beauty Castle. See also *Disneyland Blast to the Past* for the syndicated television special.

Blaze (film) Set against the colorful backdrop of 1959–60 Louisiana, the scandalous liaison between Governor Earl K. Long and stripper Blaze Starr raised more than a few eyebrows. The governor's extramarital affair with the flamboyant redhead left Louisiana in a state of shock and rocked the very foundation of the Southern political machine. Released on December 13, 1989. Directed by Ron Shelton. A Touchstone film. 117 min. Stars Paul Newman (Earl Long), Lolita Davidovich (Blaze Starr), Jerry Hardin (Thibodeaux). Based on the book *Blaze Starr*, by Blaze Starr and Huey Perry. Filmed on location in Louisiana. Released on video in 1990.

Bletcher, Billy (1894–1979) Voiced the Big Bad Wolf and a host of other characters in the cartoons from 1933 to 1952.

Bliss, Lucille Voice of the stepsister Anastasia in *Cinderella*.

Blizzard Beach Sixty-six–acre water park at Walt Disney World. Opened April 1, 1995. The park has the atmosphere and equipment of a major ski resort, but with the paradox of being in the midst of a tropical lagoon. Mt. Gushmore rises more than 120 feet high, and features a variety of water slides. There is Summit Plummet, Shush Gusher, Teamboat Springs, Toboggan Racer, Snow Stormers, Runoff Rapids, Tike's Peak, Melt-Away Bay, and Cross Country Creek. Food is available at Lottawatta Lodge and souvenirs at Beach Haus.

Blood In, Blood Out: Bound by Honor Video release title of *Bound by Honor*.

Bloom, Orlando Actor; starred in *Pirates of the Caribbean: The Curse of the Black Pearl* and two sequels (Will Turner).

Blossom (television) Television series on NBC; beginning January 3, 1991, and ending on June 5, 1995. A teenage girl, Blossom Russo, experiences life in a household with her father and two quirky brothers: one, Anthony, recovered from drug addiction and the other, Joey, not too bright and at an age when girls are becoming a big part of his life. Stars Mayim Bialik (Blossom), Ted Wass (Nick), Joey Lawrence (Joey), Michael Stoyanov (Anthony), Jenna Von Oy (Six), David Lascher (Vinnie).

Blue Bayou (film) Segment of *Make Mine Music*, originally meant for *Fantasia* and utilizing Debussy's "Clair de Lune." The Ken Darby Chorus sings the song, written by Bobby Worth and Ray Gilbert.

Blue Bayou (television) Unsold pilot for a television series; a divorced real estate lawyer and her son face a new life in New Orleans, only to get involved in a murder case. Aired on NBC on January 15, 1990. 120 min. Directed by Karen Arthur. Stars Alfre Woodard, Mario Van Peebles, Ron Thinnes, Ashley Crow, Joseph Culp, Maxwell Caulfield, Elizabeth Ashley, Bibi Besch.

Blue Bayou Restaurant Restaurant in New Orleans Square at Disneyland; opened March 18, 1967. One of the most attractive dining areas at Disneyland, it is located inside the building that houses Pirates of the Caribbean. As guests embark in their boat on their Pirates adventure, they can look to the right and see the diners enjoying their meals in the Blue Bayou. The theming of a night sky, fireflies, and bayou sound effects provides a welcome respite on a hot day in the summer. Also in Adventureland at Tokyo Disneyland, opened on April 15, 1983. The equivalent at Disneyland Paris is the Blue Lagoon Restaurant.

Blue Fairy Character in *Pinocchio*; voiced by Evelyn Venable.

Blue Lagoon Restaurant Restaurant in Adventureland in Disneyland Paris; opened on April 12, 1992. The European equivalent of the Blue Bayou Restaurant at Disneyland, though the dining area is terraced to provide better views of the boats going by in the Pirates of the Caribbean attraction.

Blue Men of Morocco, The (film) People and Places featurette; released on February 14, 1957. Directed by Ralph Wright. 31 min. The theme for this subject is "going back in time." The action takes place in the Sahara Desert where the Blue Men of Morocco live today as they did in Biblical times. The film features their lifestyles, work, and journeys into Marrakech.

Blue Rhythm (film) Mickey Mouse cartoon; released on August 18, 1931. Directed by Burt Gillett. Musical beginning with Mickey playing

concert piano. Minnie sings the blues, Mickey joins her for a song and dance routine, then Mickey plays a clarinet solo imitating Ted Lewis. Finally, Mickey leads an orchestra of his gang, with the music getting so hot they eventually break through the floor.

Blue Ribbon Bakery Shop on Main Street at Disneyland from April 6, 1990. Took the place of the longtime Sunkist Citrus House. Moved into the former Carnation Ice Cream Parlor location in 1997.

Blue Yonder, The (television) A young boy travels back in time to meet his grandfather, a pioneer aviator. A movie for The Disney Channel, first aired on November 17, 1985. Directed by Mark Rosman. Stars Peter Coyote (Max Knickerbocker), Huckleberry Fox (Jonathan), Art Carney (Henry Coogan). Shown on the Disney anthology series later as *Time Flyer*. Released on video in 1986.

Bluegrass Special, The (television) Television show; aired on May 22, 1977. Directed by Andrew V. McLaglen. The story of Woodhill, an unruly racehorse, who catches the eye of Penny, a girl who wants to be a jockey. Penny uses kindness rather than the whip to train Woodhill and eventually prove that she and her horse are worthy to race in the Bluegrass Special. Stars William Windom, Celeste Holm, Davy Jones, Devon Ericson, James Gleason.

Blumberg, Barry He was named president of Walt Disney Television Animation in January 2003 after having served in positions of increasing responsibility in the division since 1994. He left the company in January 2006.

Bluth, Don Animator and director, came to Disney in 1955, working as an assistant animator on *Sleeping Beauty*. After being away for 14 years, he returned to animate on *Robin Hood* and *Winnie the Pooh and Tigger Too*, was a directing animator on *The Rescuers* and directed the animation for *Pete's Dragon*. He left the Studio in 1979 to form his own company in partnership with Gary Goldman and John Pomeroy.

Boag, Wally Longtime comedian from the Golden Horseshoe Revue at Disneyland, which put him into the Guinness *Book of World Records* for the most number of performances of a show. He was most known for creating characters out of balloons and for spitting out a seemingly inexhaustible number of his "teeth" (beans) after being hit in the mouth. He opened the show at Disneyland in 1955, took time out to get the same show started at the Diamond Horseshoe in Magic Kingdom Park at Walt Disney World in 1971, then returned to Disneyland for the remainder of his career. His last performance before his retirement was on January 28, 1982. Boag also had brief roles in *The Absent-Minded Professor*, *Son of Flubber*, and *The Love Bug*. He was named a Disney Legend in 1995.

BoardWalk The atmosphere of turn-of-the-century Atlantic City near Epcot at Walt Disney World; includes accommodations, entertainment, shopping, and dining (Spoodles, Flying Fish Cafe, Big River Grille & Brewing Works) along a boardwalk. There is the BoardWalk Inn, with 378 rooms, and the BoardWalk Villas with 532 rooms, along with convention facilities featuring a 20,000-square-foot convention center. Nightclubs include Jellyrolls, Atlantic Dance Club, and the ESPN Club. The resort, designed by Robert A. M. Stern, opened on July 1, 1996.

BoardWalk Bakery Bakery located at the BoardWalk Resort at Walt Disney World; opened July 1, 1996.

Boardwalk Candy Palace Candy shop on Main Street in Disneyland Paris; opened on April 12, 1992. It is hosted by Nestlé.

Boat Builders (film) Mickey Mouse cartoon; released on February 25, 1938. Directed by Ben

Sharpsteen. Mickey, Donald, and Goofy purchase a folding boat kit, but the boat is not as easy

to put together as they hoped. After much trouble, Minnie christens the boat; it is launched and promptly collapses, throwing them all into the water.

Boatniks, The (film) Newly assigned to duty in the Coast Guard at Newport Beach, California, ensign Thomas Garland soon faces the problems caused by Sunday sailors, those amateur boatniks who go down to the sea in ships. But the ensign also finds himself involved in romantic complications with Kate Fairchild, as well as with jewel thieves, whose careers are ended with the cooperation of Thomas and Kate. Released on July 1, 1970. Directed by Norman Tokar. 100 min. Stars Robert Morse (Ensign Garland), Stefanie Powers (Kate), Phil Silvers (Harry Simmons), Norman Fell (Max), Mickey Shaughnessy (Charlie), Wally Cox (Jason), Don Ameche (Commander Taylor). Released on video in 1984. The song, "The Boatniks," was written by Bruce Belland and Robert F. Brunner.

Boatwright's Dining Hall Restaurant in the Port Orleans Resort—Riverside at Walt Disney World; opened on February 2, 1992. The 200-seat full-service restaurant is patterned after a shipmaking facility.

Bob Patterson (television) Half-hour comedy series for ABC; premiered on October 2, 2001, and ended on October 31. Bob Patterson is a successful yet insecure motivational speaker who tries to manage his career and family life. A 20th Century Fox Television/Touchstone Television production. Stars Jason Alexander (Bob Patterson), Robert Klein (Landau), Jennifer Aspen (Janet), Chandra Wilson (Claudia), Phil Buckman (Vic), James Guidice (Jeffrey).

Bobo Title character in *Mickey's Elephant* (1936).

Bodenheimer, George He was named co-chair of Disney's Media Networks unit in 2004. He also serves as president of ABC Sports (since 2003) and president of ESPN, Inc. (since 1998). He had originally joined ESPN in 1981.

Body Wars Attraction in Wonders of Life in Future World at Epcot; opened October 19, 1989. Using the same simulator technology that made Star Tours possible, Disney designers designed an exciting miniaturized trip through the human body by way of the bloodstream.

Boiler Room Barbecue Restaurant at Tokyo Disneyland; opened on July 21, 1992,

Bolger, Ray (1904–1987) Actor; appeared in *Babes in Toyland* (Barnaby).

Bollenbach, Stephen F. Bollenbach joined The Walt Disney Company in 1995 as Senior Executive Vice President and Chief Financial Officer. He left the company in February 1996.

Bon Voyage (film) Harry Willard finally makes good his promise to take his bride of 20 years on a long-delayed trip by ship to Europe. They are accompanied by their 19-year-old son, Elliott, 18-year-old daughter, Amy, and an active 11-year-old son named Skipper. From the time they arrive at the dock, there follows an unending series of comedy adventures and romantic encounters that keep the family constantly involved until, exhausted but happy, they start for home with memories which will benefit them all in the years to come. Released on May 17, 1962. Directed by James Neilson. 132 min. Stars Fred MacMurray (Harry Willard), Jane Wyman (Katie Willard), Michael Callan (Nick O'Mara), Deborah Walley (Amy Willard), Tommy Kirk (Elliott Willard),

Kevin Corcoran (Skipper Willard), Jessie Royce Landis (La Contessa). This Disney family film ran into some criticism for including a prostitute who flirts with Harry and young Elliott Willard. The film is based on the book by Marrijane and Joseph Hayes, and was shot on location in Europe. It was nominated for Academy Awards for Best Costume Design, by Bill Thomas, and Best Sound, by Robert O. Cook. The title song was written by Richard M. Sherman and Robert B. Sherman. Released on video in 1987.

Bonanza Outfitters Frontierland shop selling western-themed clothing at Disneyland; opened on June 29, 1990, taking the place of the Pendleton Woolen Mills Dry Goods Store.

Bondi, Beulah (1892–1981) Actress; appeared in *So Dear to My Heart* (Granny Kincaid).

Bone Bandit (film) Pluto cartoon; released on April 30, 1948. Directed by Charles Nichols. Pluto's efforts to dig up a bone are frustrated by his allergy to goldenrod, and by a gopher who is using the bone to prop up his tunnel. Pluto and the gopher battle over the bone, ending up with the gopher also developing an allergy to goldenrod.

Bone Trouble (film) Pluto cartoon; released on June 28, 1940. The first cartoon directed by Jack Kinney. Pluto steals Butch's bone and gets chased

into a carnival hall of mirrors, but though he is frightened by the distortions, he uses them to his advantage in his escape from the bulldog.

Bones and Muscles Get Rhythm, The (film) Educational film in the Wonders of Life

series; released on January 26, 1990. 11 min. How bones and muscles work together, illustrated through dance.

Boneyard, The Playground for kids in Dinoland U.S.A. at Disney's Animal Kingdom, opened April 22, 1998. Kids can dig up dinosaur bones.

Bonfamille's Cafe Full-service restaurant at the Port Orleans Resort at Walt Disney World; opened on May 17, 1991, and closed on August 5, 2000.

Bongo (film) Segment of *Fun and Fancy Free*, narrated by Dinah Shore, with a young circus bear learning about romance. Re-released as a

featurette on January 20, 1971. 32 min. Released on video in 1982 and 1989.

Bonkers (television) Animated television series, premiered on The Disney Channel on February 28, 1993, and syndicated beginning September 6, 1993, and ending August 30, 1996. The show was introduced by a syndicated two-hour special, *Going Bonkers*. The character had been introduced in segments in *Raw Toonage* in the fall of 1992. Bonkers D. Bobcat becomes an off-the-wall, wildly enthusiastic recruit for the Hollywood Police Department—Toon Division. With his gruff, streetwise human partner, Detective Lucky Piquel, Bonkers tracks down cartoon criminals. Providing the voices are Jim Cummings (Bonkers, Piquel), Nancy Cartwright (Fawn Deer), Frank Welker (Fall Apart Rabbit). 65 episodes.

Bonnet Creek Golf Club Club; opened at Walt Disney World on January 23, 1992. The course includes the Eagle Pines and Osprey Ridge courses. In April 2005 the club's name changed to the Eagle Pines & Osprey Ridge Golf Club.

Bonsall, Brian Child actor; appeared in *Father Hood* (Eddie Charles) and *Blank Check* (Preston Waters).

Book of Pooh, The (television) Original series on Disney Channel beginning January 22, 2001. The Pooh characters are presented in stories uti-

lizing the 300-year-old art of Bunraku puppetry with computer-generated sets. Voices include Jim Cummings (Winnie the Pooh, Tigger), John Fiedler (Piglet), Ken Sansom (Rabbit), Peter Cullen (Eeyore), André Stojka (Owl), Stephanie D'Abruzzo (Kessie), Paul Tiesler (Christopher Robin).

Book of Pooh, The: Stories from the Heart (film) A direct-to-video movie featuring the Bunraku puppetry from the Disney Channel television series; released on July 17, 2001. Pooh and his pals are in Christopher Robin's room awaiting his return when they discover his favorite storybook filled with endearing tales written about them. They flip through the pages and the stories magically come to life. Developed by Mitchell Kriegman. With the same voices as in the television series.

Books The first Disney book was a *Mickey Mouse Book*, published by Bibo-Lang in 1930 and featuring a story written by Bobette Bibo, the young daughter of the publisher. It was followed in 1931 by *The Adventures of Mickey Mouse*, published in hardback and paperback by David

McKay, the first of several Disney books from that publisher. Blue Ribbon Books published some Disney pop-up books in 1933, but it was a contract with Whitman Books that same year that began a virtual flood of Disney titles. Whitman, later known as Western Printing and Lithographing and Western Publishing, headquartered in Racine, Wisconsin, remained one of the major publishers of Disney books for many years. Disney Little Golden and Big Golden Books are fondly remembered by many people; the books were kept in print many years after their original publication. A Wonderful World of Reading book club was begun by Random House in 1972, reaching millions of readers. In 1991, Disney set up its own publishing arm, with Hyperion, Hyperion Books for Children, Disney Press, and Mouse Works imprints. The Jump at the Sun imprint was added in 1998; it was the first children's book imprint devoted to celebrating the richness of African, African American, and Caribbean American culture. In 1999, Disney Editions took over as the imprint of nonfiction Disney-themed adult books, such as the "Making of" animated features books and Disney reference material. In 2005, Disney Editions added Disney-branded fiction to its list.

Boomerang, Dog of Many Talents (television) Two-part television show; aired on September 22 and 29, 1968. Directed by John Newland. A con man continually sells his dog, who then runs back to his owner. Then the con man himself is conned by a young widow into helping move a flock of 500 turkeys to market. Stars Darren McGavin, Patricia Crowley, Darby Hinton.

Booth, Nita Actress; appeared on the *Mickey Mouse Club* on The Disney Channel, beginning in 1991.

Boothe, Powers Actor; appeared in *Tombstone* (Curly Bill) and in *Nixon* (Alexander Haig).

Bootle Beetle (film) Donald Duck cartoon; released in August 1947. Directed by Jack Hannah. An elderly beetle scolds a young one for running away by telling him of the hazards of

meeting up with bug collector Donald. Donald, now elderly himself, still searches for the beetle. The title character was voiced by Dink Trout.

Border Collie (television) Serial on the *Mickey Mouse Club* during the 1955–56 season, starring Bobby Evans and Arthur N. Allen. Directed by Larry Lansburgh. Alvy Moore is the narrator. A boy trains his dog to be a sheepdog. 4 episodes.

Borgfeldt, George, & Co. Toy distributor who signed the first major contract to sell Disney character merchandise, in 1930. Borgfeldt was responsible for having the multitude of Disney bisque figurines, which were so popular in the 1930s, produced in Japan and imported into the United States for sale. They also handled games, wood figures, plush dolls, celluloid items, and many other types of novelties and toys.

Borgnine, Ernest Actor; appeared in *The Black Hole* (Harry Booth), on television in *Appearances*, and on The Disney Channel in *Love Leads the Way*.

Born to Run (television) Two-part television show; aired on March 25 and April 1, 1979. Directed by Don Chaffey. An Australian youngster who shares a love for harness racing with his grandfather, a farmer who is going broke, finds a colt with wonderful promise. Despite some near-disasterous incidents along the way, the colt gets trained and goes on to win a big race that saves the farm. Released theatrically abroad in 1977. Stars Tom Farley (Matthew Boyd), Robert Bettles (Teddy Boyd), Andrew McFarlane (Doone Boyd).

Born Yesterday (film) Billie Dawn, a former Las Vegas showgirl and current mistress of millionaire Harry Brock, is forced into the political limelight of Washington, D.C. While Harry conducts "a little tax business" he finds Billie to be a social hindrance, so he hires savvy journalist Paul Verrall to make her over. In the process, Billie learns to think on her own, and to understand the importance of her own individuality. When she falls in love with her handsome mentor, she decides to take matters into her own hands for the first time in her life and stand up to Harry. Learning that all of Harry's shady businesses are in her name, which gives her the real control, she turns the tables on him. Released on March 26, 1993. Directed by Luis Mandoki. A Hollywood Picture. 100 min. Stars Melanie Griffith (Billie Dawn), John Goodman (Harry Brock), Don Johnson (Paul Verrall), Edward Herrmann (Ed Devery). Based on the original Garson Kanin Broadway play from 1946, which starred Judy Holliday and Paul Douglas. Holliday repeated her performance in the 1950 screen version and won the Best Actress Academy Award. This remake was filmed partly on location at the Willard-Intercontinental Hotel in Washington, D.C., as well as at other local landmarks in our national capital, such as the Navy Memorial, Georgetown University, and the Library of Congress. Released on video in 1993.

Bosché, Bill (1922–1990) Artist, writer, and producer at the Disney Studio for 30 years. He wrote the landmark *Man in Space* television show and was writer/producer/director for *O Canada* at Epcot. He helped compile the *Walt Disney Story* film for the parks.

Boston Tea Party, The (film) Sixteen-mm release title of a portion of *Johnny Tremain*; released in May 1966. Dramatizes the significant role played by Johnny Tremain in Boston leading up to the Revolution. Also the title of part one when the motion picture was shown on television in two parts.

Bostwick, Barry Actor appeared on television in *Parent Trap III* and *Parent Trap Hawaiian*

Honeymoon, provided the voice of Thunderbolt in *101 Dalmatians II: Patch's London Adventure*, and appeared in *Spy Hard* (Norman Coleman).

Bottoms, Joseph Actor; appeared in *The Black Hole* (Lt. Charles Pizer) and on television in the title role in *Major Effects*.

Bottoms, Timothy Actor; appeared on The Disney Channel in *Love Leads the Way* (Morris Frank).

Boudin Bakery, The Attraction at Pacific Wharf at Disney's California Adventure; opened February 8, 2001, sponsored by Boudin Sourdough Bread Co. Guests learn how sourdough bread is made as they make their way through the bakery.

Boulangerie Patisserie Pastry shop in France in World Showcase at Epcot; opened on October 1, 1982. It was not long after the opening of Epcot that lines were snaking throughout the courtyard; word had gotten around that the French pastries were wickedly delicious. Imagineers quickly redesigned the shop to enable greater capacity.

Bound by Honor (film) Set against the background of East Los Angeles, the lives of three young men are traced during a 12-year span. When the half-Anglo, half-Chicano cousin, Miklo, of a barrio gang leader, Paco, arrives, he learns that the gang's motto is "blood in, blood out," which means to join the gang, one must spill the blood of a rival gang member. Amid increasing gang warfare, Miklo is arrested for killing an opposing gang leader and sent to prison where he also finds gangs are powerful. Paco becomes an undercover cop, and while the lives of Miklo, Paco, and their cousin, Cruz, go in different directions, they eventually realize that they must look out for each other, for they are truly "blood brothers." Initial release on January 27, 1993, in Las Vegas, Tucson, and Rochester, N.Y., under the title *Blood In, Blood Out*; general release on April 30, 1993. Directed by Taylor Hackford. A Hollywood Picture. 180 min. Video release under the title *Blood In, Blood Out: Bound by Honor*. Stars Damian Chapa (Miklo), Jesse Borrego (Cruz), Benjamin Bratt (Paco), Enrique Castillo (Montana). Filmed on location in the barrio of East Los Angeles, and in San Quentin State Prison in Northern California. Released on video in 1994.

Bounds, Lillian Maiden name of Walt Disney's wife. They were married at the home of her brother in Lewiston, Idaho, on July 13, 1925. See also under Lillian Bounds Disney.

Bourguignon, Phillippe Bourguignon began as senior vice president of real estate for Euro Disney and was promoted to president of the French park in 1992. In October 1996 he was given the additional title of executive vice president for The Walt Disney Company Europe. He left the company in February 1997.

Bowers, Reveta Franklin Became a member of the Disney board of directors in 1993, remaining until March 19, 2003.

Boxleitner, Bruce Actor; appeared in *Tron* (Alan Bradley, Tron), and on The Disney Channel in *Down the Long Hills* (Scott Collins).

Boy and the Bronc Buster, The (television) Two-part television show; aired on March 18 and 25, 1973. Directed by Bernard McEveety. An orphan boy joins a drifter on the rodeo circuit, where he learns to be a rodeo performer. But the drifter turns out to be wanted for murder, causing all sorts of complications. Stars Earl Holliman, Strother Martin, Vincent Van Patten, Jacqueline Scott, Lisa Gerritsen, Ken Swofford.

Boy Called Nuthin', A (television) Two-part television show; aired on December 10 and 17, 1967. Directed by Norman Tokar. A boy doesn't find the life he expects out West when he leaves Chicago to find his uncle. The West has changed— it is no longer "cowboys and Indians." He finds his uncle living in a shack, and in trying to be accepted and help out, the boy gets himself into all sorts of trouble, causing his uncle to refer to him as "good for nuthin'," a nickname that sticks. Eventually the two see that they need each other. Stars Forrest Tucker, Ronny Howard, John Carroll, Mary La Roche, Mickey Shaughnessy, Richard Bakalyan, Rafael Campos.

Boy from Deadman's Bayou, The See *Bayou Boy*.

Boy Meets World (television) Television series; airing on ABC beginning September 24, 1993, and ending September 8, 2000. A young junior high school student, Cory Matthews is an average teenager, struggling with the complications of growing up and the mysteries of life. He tries to get by on his wits, but is unfortunate to live next door to his teacher, Mr. Feeny. During the second season Cory heads to high school, where Feeny is now principal. Stars Ben Savage (Cory Matthews), William Daniels (Mr. Feeny), William Russ (Alan Matthews), Betsy Randle (Amy Matthews), Will Friedle (Eric Matthews), Rider Strong (Shawn), Tony Quinn (Jonathan Turner, second season). Alex Désert joined the cast in the 1995–96 season as teacher Eli Williams. Matthew Lawrence was added in 1997–98 as Jack, Eric's roommate at college, where Feeny now teaches. Eventually, Cory marries his girlfriend Topanga (Danielle Fishel).

Boy Who Flew with Condors, The (television) Television show; aired on February 19, 1967, about a California teenager who yearns to pilot a glider. His studies of the condors helps him with his gliding lessons. Stars Christopher Jury, Margaret Birstner, Fred W. Harris.

Boy Who Stole the Elephant, The (television) Two-part television show; aired on September 20 and 27, 1970. A boy working in a small traveling circus steals an elephant, Queenie, on loan from another circus to save her from being sold and return her to her rightful owner. Along the way, the elephant gets loose and causes havoc in a local town. Directed by Michael Caffey. Stars Mark Lester, David Wayne, June Havoc, Dabbs Greer, Parley Baer, Whitney Blake, Richard Kiel. Lester had recently received acclaim for starring

in the title role in the Academy Award–winning motion picture *Oliver!*

Boy Who Talked to Badgers, The (television) Two-part television show; aired on September 14 and 21, 1975. Directed by Gary Nelson. A boy, Ben, seems to prefer animals to people, and is even able to communicate with them, a trait that does not please his father. But when a badger helps save Ben's life after he falls in a creek and is carried away, the father comes to an understanding with his son. Stars Christian Juttner, Carl Betz, Salome Jens, Denver Pyle, Robert Donner, Stuart Lee.

Boyajian, Chuck (1917–2004) He was the first manager of custodial operations at Disneyland, and contributed to the reputation for high standards in cleanliness that the park would receive. He helped establish custodial functions at Walt Disney World and Tokyo Disneyland until his retirement in 1981. He was named a Disney Legend in 2005.

Boyd, Barton K. ("Bo") Boyd began with Disney in 1968 as an assistant supervisor in merchandise at Disneyland, then became a buyer and moved to Walt Disney World to help create the Merchandise Division there.  He later returned to the corporate headquarters in California and eventually became chairman of Disney Consumer Products. He retired in 2001.

Boyd, Carleton "Jack" (1916–1998) Effects animator at the Disney Studio, from 1939 to 1973, and again in 1981. He drew the Uncle Remus Sunday newspaper comic page from 1963 to 1972, and, as one of his projects, helped compile the *Walt Disney Story* film for the parks.

Boyer, Charles Artist, joined Disneyland in 1960 in the Marketing Art Department. He is noted for having created a number of lithographs of Disneyland subjects, beginning in 1976. One of his more well-known efforts is a "Triple Self-Portrait" of Walt Disney. He was named a Disney Legend in 2005.

Boys (film) High school senior, John Baker, Jr., is nearing graduation at a private school for boys and dreading the future, where he is expected to follow in his father's footsteps. When he has a chance encounter with a sophisticated woman, Patty Vare, who has fallen from her horse, he aids her and surreptitiously shields her from the police and his fellow students in his dorm room. They find a mutual attraction turning to romance, but are haunted by the unfolding story of a stolen car and a missing major league baseball pitcher. Directed by Stacy Cochran. A Touchstone Picture in association with Interscope Communications/PolyGram Filmed Entertainment. Released on May 10, 1996. Stars Lukas Haas (John), Winona Ryder (Patty), John C. Reilly (Kellogg Curry), James Le Gros (Fenton Ray), Skeet Ulrich (Bud Valentine). 86 min. Based on the short story "Twenty Minutes," by James Salter. St. John's College is Annapolis, Maryland, doubled for the Sherwood School for Boys in the movie. Released on video in 1996.

Boys of the Western Sea, The (television) Serial on the *Mickey Mouse Club* during the 1956–57 season. Life in a small fishing village in Norway, where the children have to help out. Some of the Mouseketeers joined other actors in dubbing the Norwegian voices into English. Stars Kjeld Bentzen, Anne Grete Hilding, Lars Henning-Jensen, Nette Hoj Hansen. Voices include Richard Beymer, Paul Frees, Billy Bletcher, Herb Vigran, Mary Lee Hobb, Tommy Kirk, Bobby Burgess, Lonnie Burr, Tommy Cole, Kevin Corcoran, David Stollery. 8 episodes.

Bracken, Eddie (1915–2002) Actor; appeared in *Oscar* (Five Spot Charlie).

Bradley, Milton, Co. Manufacturer of games that had a license for Disney character games from 1931 off and on to the present.

Bradley Time Company that took over the national license to manufacture Disney character watches in 1972 and produced hundreds of different varieties until 1987. They were a division of Elgin National Industries, Inc. See also Watches.

Brady, Wayne Actor; starred in *The Wayne Brady Show*, as the Magician Lazardo in *Geppetto*, and as Mr. Wyatt in *Going to the Mat*.

Braff, Zach Actor; appears on *Scrubs* (J.D. Dorian), and is the voice of the title character in *Chicken Little*.

Brahe Pedersen, Poul (1910–1978) He oversaw Disney publications in Scandinavia for Gutenberghus from 1955 to 1975, and was presented posthumously with a European Disney Legends Award in 1997.

Brain and the Nervous System Think Science, The (film) Educational film, in the Wonders of Life series, released on January 26, 1990. 11 min. How the brain and nervous system jointly control action and thought.

Brand New Life (television) Limited television series; aired in 1989–90. After a pilot episode aired on NBC, Disney picked up four episodes to air on its anthology series. Stars Barbara Eden, Don Murray, Shawnee Smith, Jennie Garth, Byron Thomes, Alison Sweeney, David Tom, Danny Nucci. A divorced mother of three meets a wealthy widower also with kids, and they soon marry. The series deals with the family's attempts to get along with each other.

Brand Spanking New Doug (television) Animated television series; premiered on ABC on September 7, 1996. Continuing the Nickelodeon series *Doug* which premiered in 1991, this series shows Doug Funnie growing up. He is approaching his 12th birthday in this exaggerated portrayal of a child muddling through the misadventures of growing up. Voices

include Thomas McHugh (Doug), Becca Lish (Theda Funnie, Judy Funnie, Connie Benge), Fred Newman (Skeeter Valentine, Ned Valentine, Mr. Dink), Chris Phillips (Roger Klotz), Alice Playten (Beebe Bluff), Connie Shulman (Patti Mayonnaise), Doug Preis (Chalky Studebaker, Bill Bluff, Phil Funnie, Lamar Bone). Produced by Jumbo Pictures in association with Walt Disney Television. The series moved to syndication beginning August 31, 1998, and changed its title to *Disney's Doug*. A feature film based on the series was *Doug's 1st Movie* (1999). 65 episodes.

Brandauer, Klaus Maria Actor; appeared in *White Fang* (Alex).

Brandis, Jonathan (1976–2003) Young actor; provided an "additional voice" for *Oliver & Company* and Mozenrath in *Aladdin*. He appeared in *Our Shining Moment* (Michael "Scooter" McGuire) and on television on *Blossom* (Stevie).

Brandy & Mr. Whiskers (television) Animated half-hour series on Disney Channel, premiering on August 21, 2004. Brandy, a pampered pooch, and Mr. Whiskers, an offbeat bunny, fall out of an airplane and are stranded in the lush Amazon rain forest. Joining them to become their jungle family are Lola Boa, a constrictor; Ed, a river otter; Cheryl & Meryl, sister toucans; Margo, a stick bug; and Gaspar LeGecko, the self-appointed king of the jungle. Voices include Kaley Cuoco (Brandy), Charlie Adler (Mr. Whiskers), Alanna Ubach (Lola Boa), Tom Kenny (Ed),

Sherri Shepherd (Cheryl & Meryl), Jennifer Hale (Margo), Andre Sogliuzzo (Gaspar LeGecko). 21 episodes.

B.R.A.T. Patrol, The (television) Two-hour television movie; aired on October 26, 1986. Directed by Mollie Miller. An unofficial club of children living on a marine base constantly antagonize a group of Junior Marines. They name themselves the B.R.A.T. Patrol, which stands for "Born, Raised, and Trapped." In competing for the base's Youth Service Award, the two groups spar, but the outcasts discover a plot to steal military supplies and eventually are able to prove their suspicions to the authorities and win the award. Stars Sean Astin, Tim Thomerson, Jason Presson, Joe Wright, Brian Keith, Stephen Lee, Billy Jacoby. The movie was filmed at the El Toro (California) Marine Corps Air Station.

Brave Engineer, The (film) Special cartoon; released on March 3, 1950. Directed by Jack Kinney. Casey Jones is determined to get his train to the station on time, in spite of train robbers, a flood, and a head-on collision with another train.

Although late, Casey finally arrives in the wrecked locomotive, with his watch reading "On Time . . . Almost."

Brave Little Tailor (film) Mickey Mouse cartoon; released on September 23, 1938. Directed by Bill Roberts. In a medieval setting, when tailor, Mickey, gleefully exclaims that he killed "seven with one blow," meaning flies that had been bothering him, the people in the medieval town, who had been talking about giants, assume him to be a gallant giant-killer and take him to the king. The king appoints Mickey to destroy a nearby giant, with the prize being a treasure of golden pazoozas and the hand of the fair Princess Minnie. Using his brain to outwit the giant's brawn,

Mickey defeats the hulking figure and becomes a hero. One of the most elaborate, and expensive, Mickey Mouse cartoons ever made. Its extremely high cost forced Walt to take a closer look at budgets for later cartoons. Nominated for an Academy Award.

Brave Little Toaster, The (film) Not a Disney animated film, but it aired on The Disney Channel in 1988, on the Disney anthology series in 1991, and was released on Disney's home-video label. A fantasy about five aging appliances who come to life and go in search of their missing master, from the novella by Thomas M. Disch. Directed by Jerry Rees. There were two, again non-Disney, direct-to-video sequels, *The Brave Little Toaster to the Rescue* and *The Brave Little Toaster Goes to Mars*.

Brave Little Toaster Goes to Mars, The (film) Not made by Disney, but released by Walt Disney Home Video under the "Disney Presents" label on May 19, 1998. The group of appliances from the original film are joined by others to take off on a trip to Mars to save the "Master's" new baby. Voices include Deanna Oliver (Toaster), Tim Stack (Lampy), Roger Kabler (Radio), Thurl Ravenscroft (Kirby), Eric Lloyd (Blanky), Farrah Fawcett (Faucet), Carol Channing (Fanny). The video for *The Brave Little Toaster to the Rescue* in 1999 did not include the "Disney Presents" label.

Brave New Girl (television) An ABC Family Original Movie, debuting on April 25, 2004. Directed by Bobby Roth. Holly has everything it takes to be a star—the voice, the dream, and the dedication—but she lacks the means to break away from her humble Texas upbringing. Then she gets the chance to attend a prestigious art and music school on the East Coast and her future suddenly looks bright though she must compete for the star spot with the snobby Angela. Luckily, Holly has the support of her mother and her roommate Ditz, who prove that being a star has nothing to do with fame and everything to do with faith, family, and friends. Stars Lindsey Haun (Holly), Virginia Madsen (Wanda), Jackie Rosenbaum (Ditz), Barbara Mamabolo (Angela).

Based on the novel *A Mother's Gift* by Britney and Lynne Spears.

Braverman, Alan Executive vice president and general counsel of The Walt Disney Company since 2003. He had originally joined ABC in 1993 as a vice president, before being promoted to senior vice president and general counsel in 1996 and executive vice president in 2000.

Braverman, Barry Imagineer at Walt Disney Imagineering since 1977. He worked on various projects, including Wonders of Life, and for a time headed the Epcot design effort. Then he turned his attentions to the West, where he headed the Disneyland Resort Development team, and led the design work on Disney's California Adventure.

Brayton's Laguna Pottery This manufacturer of figurines made a number of Disney items from 1938 to 1940 that are still popular with collectors. Some of their nicest items were characters from *Pinocchio* and *Ferdinand the Bull.*

Breakfast of Champions (film) Dwayne Hoover, the leader of a vast financial empire that controls Midland City, is on the verge of a midlife crisis. As his identity as the most respected man in the city begins to unravel in his own mind, he meets an impoverished writer, Kilgore Trout, in town for a fine-arts festival. Their worlds collide, and Midland City will never be the same. Directed by Alan Rudolph. Limited release in New York, Los Angeles, and Toronto on September 17, 1999. Stars Bruce Willis (Dwayne Hoover), Albert Finney (Kilgore Trout), Nick Nolte (Harry Le Sabre), Barbara Hershey (Celia Hoover), Glenne Headley (Francine Pefko), Omar Epps (Wayne Hoobler). 110 min. From the classic novel by Kurt Vonnegut, Jr. The filmmakers picked Twin Falls, Idaho, as the ideal location to be Midland City. Released on video in 2000.

Breakin' Through (film) Break-dancers and polished Broadway performers come together for a Broadway-bound musical, and the two groups have trouble adjusting to each other. An original video release in September 1985. Directed by Peter Medak. 73 min. Stars Ben Vereen, Donna McKechnie, Reid Shelton. This film had originally been planned for a Disney Channel release, but the company opted for a video release instead.

Brennan, Eileen Actress; appeared in *Stella* (Mrs. Wilkerson), and on television in *Kraft Salutes Walt Disney World's 10th Anniversary*, the remake of *Freaky Friday* (Principal Handel), and *Toothless* (board member).

Brennan, Walter (1894–1974) Actor; appeared in *Those Calloways* (Alf Simes), *The Gnome-Mobile* (D. J. Mulrooney; Knobby), and *The One and Only, Genuine, Original Family Band* (Grandpa Bower).

Brenner, Eve She voiced Queen Moustoria in *The Great Mouse Detective*.

Brer Bar Refreshment area, serving soft drinks and snacks, in Critter Country at Disneyland, renamed from Mile Long Bar on July 17, 1989. It closed in 2002.

Brer Bear Burly character in *Song of the South*, remembered for his threat "I'm gonna knock his head clean off"; voiced by Nicodemus Stewart.

Brer Fox Sly character always trying to get the best of Brer Rabbit in *Song of the South*; voiced by James Baskett (who also played Uncle Remus).

Brer Rabbit Happy-go-lucky character whose cockiness seems to get him in and out of trouble in *Song of the South*; voiced by Johnny Lee.

Breslin, Spencer Young actor; appeared in *Disney's The Kid* (Rusty Duritz), *The Santa Clause II* (Curtis), *Raising Helen* (Henry Davis), and *The Princess Diaries 2: Royal Engagement* (Prince Jacques), and on Disney Channel in *The Ultimate Christmas Present* (Joey Thompson) and *You Wish* (Stevie Lansing/Terrance Russell McCormack). He provided the voice of Crandall on *Teamo Supremo* and Cubby in *Return to Never Land*.

Brian's Song (television) Aired on *The Wonderful World of Disney* on December 2, 2001. A remake of the moving 1971 television film about the life and death of Chicago Bears fullback, Brian Piccolo, and his friendship with African American player, Gale Sayers. A production of Storyline Entertainment, distributed by Columbia Tristar Television. Directed by John Gray. Stars Sean Maher (Brian Piccolo), Mikhi Phifer (Gale Sayers), Ben Gazzara (George Halas), Paula Cale (Joy Piccolo), Elise Neal (Linda Sayers). Based on the book *I Am Third*, by Gale Sayers and Al Silverman.

Briar Patch, The Shop in Critter Country at Disneyland; opened in December 1988. Formerly Indian Trading Post. One of the unique architectural details is the presence of huge carrots, seemingly growing through the grass roof. In 2004 it became a hat shop.

Briar Rose Cottage Fantasyland shop at Disneyland, from May 29, 1987 to July 15, 1991. Sold Disney figurines and collectible merchandise. Preceded by Mickey's Christmas Chalet and succeeded by Disney Villains.

Bride of Boogedy (television) Two-hour television movie; aired on April 12, 1987. Directed by Oz Scott. A sequel to *Mr. Boogedy*, it continues the story of the Davis family and the evil spirit that visits it. The ghost returns and puts the father under his spell. Stars Richard Masur, Mimi Kennedy, Tammy Lauren, David Faustino, Joshua Rudoy.

Bridges, Beau Actor; appeared in *Night Crossing* (Gunter Wetzel) and *RocketMan* (Bud Nesbitt), and on television in *Atta Girl, Kelly*; *Thanksgiving Promise*; and *A Fighting Choice*. He appeared on The Disney Channel in *Nightjohn* (Clel Waller).

Bridges, Jeff Actor; appeared in *Tron* (Kevin Flynn, Clu), *White Squall*, and on television in *Thanksgiving Promise*.

Bridges, Lloyd (1913–1998) Actor; appeared in *Honey, I Blew Up the Kid* (Clifford Sterling), *Jane Austen's Mafia!* (Vincenzo Cortini), and on television in *Thanksgiving Promise* and *In the Nick of Time*.

Bright, Randy (1938–1990) Starting as an attraction host at Disneyland in 1959, he moved in 1965 to the Disney University, working at both Disneyland and later Walt Disney World. In 1976 he moved to Walt Disney Imagineering in the field of concepts and show development, executive producing film projects for Epcot and Tokyo Disneyland. In 1987 he wrote the first book of Disneyland history—*Disneyland: Inside Story*. He was named a Disney Legend in 2005.

Bright Lights (film) Oswald the Lucky Rabbit cartoon; released on March 19, 1928.

Brimley, Wilford Actor; appeared in *Country* (Otis).

Brimstone, the Amish Horse (television) Television show; aired on October 27, 1968. Directed by Larry Lansburgh. An Amish minister buys a crippled championship steeplechase horse and nurses him back to health. But the horse has not lost his yearning for the racetrack, a trait not appreciated in the strict Amish world. Stars Pamela Toll, Wallace Rooney, Phil Clark. Filmed on location in the Amish country of Pennsylvania.

Bringing Down the House (film) Peter Sanderson still loves his ex-wife and cannot understand what he did wrong to make her leave him. He is doing his best to move on, becoming smitten with a brainy, bombshell barrister he's been chatting with online. However, when she comes to the house for their first meeting, he quickly discovers she isn't refined, isn't Ivy League, and isn't even a lawyer. Instead, it's Charlene, a prison escapee, who proclaims her innocence and wants Peter to help clear her name. Charlene proceeds to turn Peter's perfectly ordered life upside down, jeopardizing his attempts to get back with his wife and woo a billion-dollar client. A Touchstone film. Directed by Adam Shankman. Released on March 7, 2003. Stars Steve Martin (Peter Sanderson), Queen Latifah (Charlene Morton), Eugene Levy (Howie Rottman), Joan Plowright (Mrs. Arness), Jean Smart (Kate), Kimberly J. Brown (Sarah Sanderson), Angus T. Jones (Georgey Sanderson), Missi Pyle (Ashley), Michael Rosenbaum (Todd Gendler), Betty White (Mrs. Kline). 105 min. Filmed in Super 35-Scope in the Los Angeles area, with Peter's house located in Pasadena. Released on video in 2003.

Bringing Out the Dead (film) A joint production from Touchstone and Paramount, this motion picture details the demanding job of a paramedic, showing how he comes into contact on a daily basis with the dead and dying. Frank Pierce, deeply troubled and becoming burned out with his job, is followed through a weekend of all-night duty. Directed by Martin Scorsese. Released on October 22, 1999. Stars Nicolas Cage (Frank Pierce), Patricia Arquette (Mary Burke), John Goodman (Larry), Ving Rhames (Marcus), Tom Sizemore (Tom Wolfe). 121 min. Disney handled the international distribution, with Paramount the domestic. Based on the novel by Joe Connelly.

Brink (television) A Disney Channel Original Movie, first aired on August 29, 1998. Andy Brinker ("Brink") is king of the "soul skaters" at the beach. He and his crew skate for the love of their sport, while their rivals, the X-Bladz are sponsored and skate for the money. When Brink discovers he needs extra money to help with his family, he faces a major decision and decides to desert his friends for Team X-Bladz. When he finds out that the captain of his new team is resorting to sabotage, he rejoins his original team in a tournament against the X-Bladz. Directed by Greg Beeman. Stars Erik von Detten (Andy), Patrick Levis (Peter), Asher Gold (Jordan), Christina Vidal (Gabriella), Sam Horrigan (Val). Released on video in 2002.

Bristle Face (television) Two-part television show; aired on January 26 and February 2, 1964. Directed by Bob Sweeney. In the rolling, wooded hills of Tennessee in the 1920s, a 14-year-old orphan, Jace, comes to town with his hound dog and tries to teach him to hunt. Bristle Face is unskilled, but he shows remarkable ability in tracking down foxes. Jace stays with a kindly shopkeeper who defends the boy and Bristle Face against the sheriff whom they have angered. Stars Brian Keith, Philip Alford (Jace Landers), Jeff Donnell, Wallace Ford, Parley Baer, Slim Pickens, George Lindsey.

Broadway at the Top Show in the Top of the World at the Contemporary Resort at Walt Disney World beginning on June 29, 1981, and running until September 1993. Many guests found the medley of show tunes from some of the greatest Broadway shows of all time sung by a quartet of talented performers one of the highlights of their stay at Walt Disney World. The bar featured an absolutely marvelous view over the Seven Seas Lagoon toward the Magic Kingdom.

Broadway Music Theater At Tokyo Disney-Sea, opening on September 4, 2001 with *Encore*, a 30-minute theatrical journey that presents the best in song and dance from Broadway's most popular shows.

Broadway Theater Formerly the Colony, this New York theater hosted the premiere of *Fantasia* on November 13, 1940, twelve years after *Steamboat Willie* had opened there. A plaque was installed in the lobby at the time of Mickey Mouse's 50th anniversary in 1978.

Broccoli & Co. Shop in The Land at Epcot; from December 1982 to October 25, 1993. A selection of merchandise was tied in with the Audio-Animatronics foodstuff characters performing in the nearby Kitchen Kabaret.

Broderick, James (1927–1982) Actor; appeared on television in *Atta Girl, Kelly*.

Broderick, Matthew Actor; voiced the adult Simba in *The Lion King*, portrayed the title character in *Inspector Gadget*, and starred in *The Last Shot* (Steven Schats). He starred on television as Professor Harold Hill in *The Music Man*.

Broggie, Roger E. (1908–1991) Broggie began his Disney career in 1939 in the Camera Department and later established the Disney Studio machine shop. Being interested in trains, he helped Walt Disney with his train hobby and engineered the layout for the scale-model train in Disney's Holmby Hills backyard. He later headed MAPO and retired in 1975. One of the locomotives on the Walt Disney World Railroad is named after him. He was named a Disney Legend in 1990.

Broken Toys (film) Silly Symphony cartoon; released on December 14, 1935. Directed by Ben Sharpsteen. Discarded toys at the city dump decide to repair themselves, including a sailor doll who restores the sight of a girl doll. The toys then march off to their new home, the local orphanage. Features caricatures of Hollywood stars as the toys.

Brom Bones Ichabod Crane's rival in *The Adventures of Ichabod and Mr. Toad*.

Brooks, Mylin Actress; appeared on the *Mickey Mouse Club* on The Disney Channel, beginning in 1990.

Brophy, Ed (1895–1960) He voiced Timothy Mouse in *Dumbo*.

Brother Against Brother (television) Television show, the second episode of *The Swamp Fox*.

Brother Bear (film) Set in the Pacific Northwest after the last Ice Age, this animated film tells the tale of three Native American brothers; Sitka, the eldest, Denahi, and Kenai, the youngest. After Sitka is accidentally killed by a bear, Kenai sets out on a quest of vengeance, only to be turned into a bear himself by the Great Spirits. As he discovers the world through the eyes of another, Kenai is befriended by a rambunctious bear cub named Koda and has a hilarious encounter with a pair of misguided moose, Tuke and Rutt. Kenai discovers that Denahi is attempting to avenge his death by trying to kill the bear that Kenai has become, believing that it is Kenai's killer. Before all is resolved, Kenai must decide whether he wants to change back into his human form or continue living as a bear. Released on November 1, 2003, after an October 24 limited release in New York and Los Angeles. Directed by Aaron Blaise and Robert Walker. Voices include Joaquin Phoenix (Kenai), Jeremy Suarez (Koda), Jason Raize (Denahi), Rick Moranis (Rutt), Dave Thomas (Tuke), D.B. Sweeney (Sitka), Michael Clarke Duncan (Tug), Joan Copeland (Tanana),

Estelle Harris (Old Lady Bear), Bumper Robinson (Chipmunks). 85 min. Jason Raize had originated the role of Simba in the Broadway production of *The Lion King*. Includes six songs by Phil Collins. Created at the Disney Feature Animation Studio in Florida. The last two thirds of the film, after Kenai is changed into a bear, are filmed in CinemaScope. The working title was

Bears. It received an Academy Award nomination as Best Animated Feature. Released on video in 2004.

Brotherly Love (television) Television series on NBC debuting with a sneak preview on September 16, 1995, before starting its regular Sunday night time slot September 24. Its last show on NBC was April 1, 1996. The show began a new season on the WB network on September 15, 1996. Life changes for the Roman family when Joe Roman trades his independent life on the road for the stability of a family he's never known. Coming to town to claim his share of a garage being run by his young widowed stepmother, Joe becomes a father figure for his two half-brothers. Stars real-life brothers Joey Lawrence (Joe Roman), Matthew Lawrence (Matt Roman), and Andrew Lawrence (Andy Roman), with Michael McShane (Lloyd), Liz Vassey (Lou), Melinda Culea (Claire Roman).

Broughton, Bob At Disney from 1937 to 1982, Broughton was a camera operator and camera-effects artist on both animated and live-action films, beginning with *Snow White and the Seven Dwarfs* and continuing to *The Black Hole*. He was named a Disney Legend in 2001.

Brown, Brandy Actress; appeared on the *Mickey Mouse Club* on The Disney Channel from 1989 to 1990.

Brown, Bryan Actor; appeared in *Cocktail* (Doug Coughlin) and *Blame It on the Bellboy* (Charlton Black).

Brown Derby See Hollywood Brown Derby.

Browne, Roscoe Lee Actor; voiced Francis in *Oliver & Company* and Mr. Arrow in *Treasure Planet*, and acted in *The World's Greatest Athlete* (Gazenga).

Bruckheimer, Jerry Prolific producer of films released by Disney/Touchstone. Titles have included *Con Air*, *Enemy of the State*, *Armageddon*, *Gone in Sixty Seconds*, *Remember the Titans*,

Coyote Ugly, Pearl Harbor, Bad Company, Pirates of the Caribbean: The Curse of the Black Pearl, Veronica Guerin, King Arthur. Earlier, with Don Simpson, he produced *The Ref, Crimson Tide, The Rock.*

Brunner, Bob Composer, hired by Disney in 1963, where for over 17 years he composed music for numerous television shows, and over a dozen features, including *That Darn Cat; Monkeys, Go Home!; Blackbeard's Ghost; Never a Dull Moment; The Barefoot Executive*; and *The Castaway Cowboy.* As a kid he had been a Talent Round Up guest on the Mickey Mouse Club.

Bruno The lazy dog in Cinderella's household.

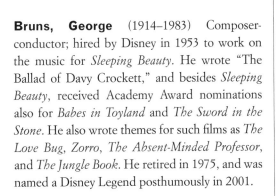

Bruns, George (1914–1983) Composer-conductor; hired by Disney in 1953 to work on the music for *Sleeping Beauty.* He wrote "The Ballad of Davy Crockett," and besides *Sleeping Beauty*, received Academy Award nominations also for *Babes in Toyland* and *The Sword in the Stone.* He also wrote themes for such films as *The Love Bug, Zorro, The Absent-Minded Professor*, and *The Jungle Book.* He retired in 1975, and was named a Disney Legend posthumously in 2001.

Brutally Normal (television) Half-hour comedy series on the WB Network, which debuted on January 24, 2000, and ended February 14. An introspective look at four teenage friends coming of age under the overwhelming pressures of high school. Stars Mike Damus (Robert "Pooh" Cutler), Lea Moreno (Anna Pricova), Eddie Kaye Thomas (Russell Wise), Tangie Ambrose (Dru Pope), Joanna Pacula (Gogi Pricova).

Bryan, Zachery Ty Actor; appeared in *First Kid* (Rob), and on television in *Home Improvement* (Brad) and *Principal Takes a Holiday* (John Scaduto).

Bryson, John E. Member of the Disney board of directors beginning September 19, 2000.

Bubble Bee (film) Pluto cartoon; released on June 24, 1949. Directed by Charles Nichols. After Pluto pounces on a "ball," which turns out to be a bubble gum machine, Pluto and a bee fight over the gum balls. After the bee stores the gum balls in its hive, Pluto destroys it, then uses the gum bubbles to keep the bee at bay until the bee wins by using the gum against Pluto.

Bubble Boy (film) Jimmy Livingston is a boy born without immunities and raised in a manufactured world provided by his well-intentioned but misguided mother. Jimmy is happy enough and has all the same experiences as other boys and girls growing up, except he lives in a bubble. When Jimmy realizes that he's in love with Chloe, the girl next door, he has no choice but to build a mobile "bubble suit" and set off across the country to stop Chloe's wedding. Directed by Blair Hayes. A Touchstone Picture. Released on August 24, 2001. Stars Jake Gyllenhaal (Jimmy Livingston), Swoosie Kurtz (Mrs. Livingston), Marley Shelton (Chloe), Danny Trejo (Slim), John Carroll Lynch (Mr. Livingston), Stephen Spinella (Chicken Man). 84 min. Filmed in CinemaScope. Released on video in 2002.

Buchanan, Stuart (1893–1973) Disney animation staff member; he voiced the Huntsman in *Snow White and the Seven Dwarfs.*

Bücherwurm, Der See *Der Bücherwurm.*

Buck Horse character in *Home on the Range*; voiced by Cuba Gooding, Jr.

Buddies (television) Series; debuted on ABC on March 5, 1996, and ended March 27, 1996 after four episodes. An interracial friendship, with its accompanying high jinks, between two young male filmmakers in Chicago, Illinois. Stars Dave Chappelle (Dave Carlisle), Christopher Gartin (John Bailey), Paula Cale (Lorraine Bailey), Tanya Wright (Phyllis Brooks), Richard Roundtree (Henry Carlisle), Judith Ivey (Maureen).

Buena Vista Club Golf club; opened at Lake Buena Vista on November 22, 1974, and closed on March 21, 1994. Also known as Lake Buena Vista Club. The restaurant in its country-club atmosphere featured the chef's specialty, a fantastic onion soup, with thick melted cheese overflowing the edges of the bowl. Renamed Disney Village Clubhouse in September 1988.

Buena Vista Distribution Company Founded by Disney in 1953 to distribute its films; its first release was *The Living Desert* (see more detail under that entry). The headquarters were located in New York until the 1970s, when they were moved to California. Irving Ludwig headed Buena Vista until his retirement, when Dick Cook took over. Later known as Buena Vista Pictures Distribution.

Buena Vista Games New parent in 2003 for Disney Interactive, the interactive games division of Disney Consumer Products. Buena Vista Games creates, markets, and distributes a broad portfolio of PC and multiplatform video games worldwide, as well as licensing Disney properties to other game publishers.

Buena Vista International Company incorporated in 1961 to handle the foreign distribution of Disney films. Occasionally, BVI will handle the foreign distribution of non-Disney films, including such titles as *Die Hard with a Vengeance*, *Face/Off*, *Starship Troopers*, and *Air Force One*.

Buena Vista Palace Hotel at Lake Buena Vista at Walt Disney World; opened on March 3, 1983. It became the Wyndham Palace Resort and Spa on November 1, 1998.

Buena Vista Pictures Distribution See Buena Vista Distribution Company.

Buena Vista Street Located in Burbank, California, where the Walt Disney Studios are located (500 South Buena Vista Street). At first, in the 1940s, the company used a 2400 W. Alameda address. The Studio lot is bordered on four sides by Buena Vista, Alameda, Keystone, and the Los Angeles River. Riverside Drive runs through the south end of the property. It was from the name of Buena Vista Street that Disney chose the name for its distribution company.

Buffalo, The—Majestic Symbol of the Plains (film) Part of *The Vanishing Prairie*, released on 16mm for schools in September 1962. Describes the appearance, habitat, and food of the buffalo and human's efforts to prevent their extinction.

Buffalo Bill's Wild West Show Dinner show at Disney Village at Disneyland Paris, where cowboys and Indians put on a pageant in a large arena reminiscent of Buffalo Bill's foray into France many decades earlier. Began April 12, 1992.

Buffalo Dreams (television) A Disney Channel Original Movie; debuted on March 11, 2005. Thomas Blackhorse, a Native American, rejects the customs of his Navajo tribe, much to his grandfather's chagrin. Josh Townsend, a Caucasian kid, newly relocated to New Mexico, takes a job on the buffalo preserve just so he can ride his mountain bike. Although Thomas is apprehensive, he allows Josh into his circle of friends, but soon feels betrayed when Josh makes the mistake of associating with local troublemakers who violate the restricted buffalo areas and desecrate sacred Navajo land. Directed by David Jackson. Stars Reiley McClendon (Josh Townsend), Simon R. Baker (Thomas Blackhorse), Graham Greene (John Blackhorse), George Newbern (Dr. Nick Townsend), Adrienne Bailon (Domino), Geraldine Keams (Abuela Rose), Christopher Robin Miller (Virgil), Seth Packard (Wylie), Jane Sibbett (Blaine Townsend), Tessa Vonn (Scout Blackhorse).

Bug Juice (television) Eighteen-episode documentary series on Disney Channel about a group of kids, aged 12 to 15, that goes off to summer camp at Camp Waziyatah in Waterford, Maine. Premiered on March 1, 1998, after a preview the previous night. A new camp, Camp Highlander near Asheville, North Carolina, was featured in a second series of 20 episodes premiering on March 5, 2000. The third season, premiering June 3, 2001, utilized Brush Ranch Camps near Santa Fe, New Mexico.

Bugs in Love (film) Silly Symphony cartoon; released on October 1, 1932. Directed by Burt Gillett. Nestled in a junk pile, a girl and boy bug are in love in their tiny village. When a crow captures the girl, the bugs sound the alarm and rescue her, imprisoning the crow in an old shoe.

bug's land, a Area featuring Flik's Fun Fair, attractions for children based on *A Bug's Life*, in Disney's California Adventure; opened on October 7, 2002. The attractions are Flik's Flyers, Tuck & Roll's Drive 'em Buggies, Heimlich's Chew Chew Train, Francis's Ladybug Boogie, and Princess Dot's Puddle Park. The area encompassed the previously opened It's Tough to Be a Bug and Bountiful Valley Farm.

bug's life, a (film) A hungry hoard of grasshoppers, led by Hopper, annually extort food from a timid ant colony. A klutzy but inventive worker ant, Flik, tries to increase production with a harvesting contraption, but his plans go awry, and he finds himself instead sent out of the colony to find a way to stop the grasshoppers. Flik recruits a bunch of inept flea-circus performers to rally against Hopper's raid. Working together, they plan for a climactic confrontation with the grasshoppers. Directed by John Lasseter and Andrew Stanton. Released in Los Angeles on November 20, 1998, and nationwide on November 25. Voices include Dave Foley (Flik), Kevin Spacey (Hopper), Julia Louis-Dreyfus (Princess Atta), Hayden Panettiere (Princess Dot), Phyllis Diller (The Queen), Richard Kind (Molt), David Hyde Pierce (Slim), Joe Ranft (Heimlich), Denis Leary (Francis), Jonathan Harris (Manny), Madeline Kahn (Gypsy), Bonnie Hunt (Rosie), Michael McShane (Tuck & Roll), John Ratzenberger (P.T. Flea), Brad Garrett (Dim), Roddy

McDowall (Mr. Soil). 95 min. CinemaScope. The second fully computer-animated film using *Toy Story*'s 3-D animation style to tell a story about the world of insects. Loosely based on Aesop's fable "The Ants and the Grasshopper," the film was a collaboration of Disney and Pixar Animation Studios. Released on video in 1999 with consumers getting a choice of five package covers (featuring Flik, Francis, Heimlich, Dot, or Hopper).

Building a Building (film) Mickey Mouse cartoon; released on January 7, 1933. Directed by Dave Hand. Mickey is a steam shovel operator at a construction site where Pete is the foreman; Minnie is selling box lunches. After Pete steals and eats Mickey's lunch, Minnie gives Mickey a box lunch. Pete attempts to kidnap Minnie, but Mickey and Minnie defeat him in a hot pursuit

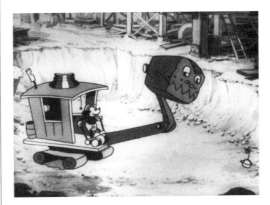

throughout the building. Mickey joins Minnie as co-operator of her box-lunch wagon, leaving Pete stuck in a cement mixer among fallen girders.

Building of a Tire, The (film) Educational film made for the Firestone Tire and Rubber Co.; delivered to them on February 14, 1946. Directed by Lou Debney. The film shows the cross section of a tire and demonstrates the manufacture of various parts, beginning at a rubber plantation and continuing to the finished tire.

Bujold, Genevieve Actress; appeared in *The Last Flight of Noah's Ark* (Bernadette Lafleur).

Bullock, Sandra Actress; appeared in *While You Were Sleeping* (Lucy) and *Gun Shy* (Judy Tipp).

Bumble Boogie (film) Segment from *Melody Time*, featuring Freddy Martin and His Orchestra, with Jack Fina at the piano; the fantasy of a bee's nightmare.

Burbank, California Home of The Walt Disney Company, at 500 South Buena Vista Street, at the corner of Buena Vista and Alameda, since 1940.

Burgess, Bobby Mouseketeer from the 1950s television show. Later went on to work with Lawrence Welk for many years.

Burke, Steve He joined Disney in 1985 as director of new business development, and in December 1987 he was promoted to vice president, The Disney Store, Inc. By 1990, he was executive vice president, specialty retailing, a post which he held until being selected as executive vice president, operations, for Euro Disney in late 1992. He was named president and chief operating officer of Euro Disney in February 1995. He left Paris on March 1, 1996, to become executive vice president of Capital Cities/ABC, Inc. after its merger with The Walt Disney Company, and was promoted to president of broadcasting in April 1997. He left the company in 1998.

Burley, Fulton He took over the role of the silver-toned tenor in the Golden Horseshoe Revue at Disneyland in 1962. His special brand of humor and authentic Irish-tenor voice made him an audience favorite, not only at Disneyland but also on publicity tours to promote upcoming movie releases. He was named a Disney Legend in 1995.

Burnett, Carol Actress; appeared in *Noises Off* (Dotty Otley), and on television in *Carol & Co.* and *The Carol Burnett Show*, *Great Moments in Disney Animation*, *The Dream Is Alive*, and *Once Upon a Mattress* (Queen Aggravain).

Burns, Harriet She joined the Disney Studio as a set and prop painter in 1955, and later was the first woman employed by WED Enterprises, where she helped design and build prototypes for theme park attractions, and then create

elements of the attractions themselves. She retired in 1986, and was named a Disney Legend in 2000.

Burr, Lonnie Mouseketeer from the 1950s television show. He went on to a career in writing and acting.

Bur-r-r Bank Ice Cream Shop at Disney's California Adventure; opened on February 8, 2001, with the name paying tribute to Burbank, where the Disney corporate headquarters are located.

Burstyn, Ellen Actress; appeared in *The Cemetery Club* (Esther Moskowitz), *When a Man Loves a Woman* (Emily), and *Roommates* (Judith), and on television on *The Ellen Burstyn Show* and in *Flash* (Laura Strong).

Burton, Corey Voice actor, doing many voices for Disney from 1986 to date. He voiced Gruffi Gummi in *Disney's Adventures of the Gummi Bears* after the death of Bill Scott, as well as Gladstone Gander in *Ducktales* and Zipper and Dale in *Chip 'n' Dale's Rescue Rangers*, and on television and at the parks, the roles of Ludwig Von Drake, Mr. Smee, Captain Hook, and others. He provided the voice of Onus in *Treasure Planet*.

Burton, Tim Hired by Disney as an artist in 1979, working on concepts for *The Black Cauldron*. During the five years he was at Disney, he prepared the inventive short films *Vincent* and *Frankenweenie*, but neither of them received broad releases. He left Disney in 1984 to eventually direct such hits as *Beetlejuice*, *Batman*, *Edward Scissorhands*, and *Batman Returns*. He returned to the Disney fold in the 1990s to produce *Tim Burton's The Nightmare Before Christmas* and direct *Ed Wood*.

Buscemi, Steve Actor; appeared in *New York Stories* (Gregory Stark), *Billy Bathgate* (Irving), *Con Air* (Garland Greene), *Armageddon* (Rockhound), and provided the voices of Randall in *Monsters, Inc.* and Wesley in *Home on the Range*.

Bush, George H.W. On September 30, 1991, President Bush presented medals to 575 persons being honored in The Daily Points of Light Celebration. The ceremony was televised live from America Gardens at Epcot on The Disney Channel.

Busy Beavers, The (film) Silly Symphony cartoon; released on June 30, 1931. As beavers busily attempt to build a dam, a storm breaks. The colony is saved by a clever little beaver who uses his teeth to saw a large tree, which blocks the flood. Directed by Wilfred Jackson.

Butch Macho bulldog who had a constant rivalry with Pluto; he appeared in 11 cartoons, beginning with *Bone Trouble* (1940).

Buttons, Red Actor; appeared in *Pete's Dragon* (Hoagy).

Buttram, Pat (1915–1994) He voiced Napoleon (*The Aristocats*), the Sheriff of Nottingham (*Robin Hood*), Luke (*The Rescuers*), and Chief (*The Fox and the Hound*).

Buyer Be Wise (film) Educational film; released in September 1982. Goofy makes common consumer errors, but Mickey Mouse and Donald Duck assist him in getting the best value for his money by setting priorities, comparing prices, and looking for sales.

Buzz Lightyear Character in Toy Story and Toy Story 2; voiced by Tim Allen.

Buzz Lightyear Astro Blasters Attraction in Tomorrowland in Disneyland and in Tokyo Disneyland, taking the place of the Circle-Vision Theaters. Buzz Lightyear Astro Blasters was based upon its counterpart, Buzz Lightyear's Space Ranger Spin, in Magic Kingdom Park at Walt Disney World. The attraction opened in Tokyo Disneyland (where it is known as Buzz Lightyear's Astro Blasters) on April 15, 2004, and at Disneyland on May 5, 2005, after soft opening in March. The Hong Kong Disneyland attraction, which opened September 12, 2005, is called Buzz

Lightyear Astro Blasters. There is also a Buzz Lightyear Astro Blasters Interactive Experience where online guests can team up with Disneyland park guests by lighting up special targets, enabling them to obtain higher scores. A Buzz Lightyear attraction is also planned for Disneyland Paris with an expected opening in 2006. The attractions are based on the Disney-Pixar film, *Toy Story 2*.

Buzz Lightyear of Star Command (television) Traditionally animated (not computer-animated) series, part of *One Saturday Morning*; debuted on October 14, 2000 (and also on weekdays on UPN and syndication, beginning October 2, 2000). Buzz Lightyear's adventures as he patrols the galaxy with his team of Space Rangers, battling evildoers "to infinity and beyond." Voices include Patrick Warburton (Buzz), Wayne Knight (Zurg), Adam Carolla (Nebula), Larry Miller (XR), Stephen Furst (Booster), Nicole Sullivan (Mira Nova). Based on the character in *Toy Story*. 65 episodes.

Buzz Lightyear of Star Command: The Adventure Begins (film) Direct-to-video release on August 8, 2000. The Evil Emperor Zurg captures a group of Little Green Men, in order to uncover the secret of their Uni-mind, which lets them think as one. As Zurg attacks their planet to steal the Uni-mind, he zaps the entire galaxy with a device that puts almost everyone under his evil control. When he unleashes his most dastardly henchman, Agent Z, Buzz Lightyear, the greatest space hero ever, working with three intergalactic crime-fighting rookies, Mira Nova, Booster, and XR, attempts to save the day—and the entire galaxy. Directed by Tad Stones. Voices include Tim Allen (Buzz Lightyear), Nicole Sullivan (Princess Mira Nova), Larry Miller (XR), Stephen Furst (Booster), Wayne Knight (Zurg). 70 min. A joint project of Walt Disney Home Video, Walt Disney Television Animation, and Pixar Animation Studios. William Shatner performs "To Infinity and Beyond" with the Star Command chorus under the final credits.

Buzz Lightyear's Space Ranger Spin Attraction in Tomorrowland in Magic Kingdom Park at Walt Disney World, taking the place of Take Flight. Guests travel through an interactive

adventure to the Gamma Quadrant, controlling their XP-37 space cruisers and firing at targets by use of a joystick. Direct hits trigger animation, sound, and light effects, with scores tallied on the cruiser's dashboard. It opened on October 7, 1998. See also *Buzz Lightyear Astro Blasters.*

Buzz on Maggie, The (television) Animated comedy debuting on Disney Channel on June 17, 2005. In the metropolis of Stickyfeet, Maggie Pesky, an unusually creative and expressive tweenage fly, is fun-loving and highly energetic, but she causes problems with her inspired antics in the conventional world of flies, which lead to consequences she did not anticipate. When she is faced with one of the many routines of everyday life, she devises a way to make it fresh and exciting. Voices include Jessica DiCicco (Maggie Pesky), David Kaufman (Aldrin Pesky), Thom Adcox (Pupert Pesky), Cree Summer (Rayna), Brian Doyle Murray and Susan Tolsky (Maggie's father and mother). Also aired on *ABC Kids* beginning September 17, 2005.

Buzz-Buzz Bee character in a number of Donald Duck cartoons, beginning with *Inferior Decorator* (1948); also known as Spike.

Buzzi, Ruth Actress; appeared in *Freaky Friday* (opposing coach), *The North Avenue Irregulars* (Dr. Rheems), and *The Apple Dumpling Gang Rides Again* (Tough Kate).

By the Book Alternate title of *Renaissance Man* for a short test run in Seattle.

Byner, John Actor; voiced Gurgi and Doli in *The Black Cauldron.*

C

Caan, James Actor; appeared in *Dick Tracy* (Spaldoni) and *The Program* (Coach Winters).

Cabane des Robinson, Le The Swiss Family Treehouse in Adventureland at Disneyland Paris; opened April 12, 1992.

Cabin Boy (film) On his way to a luxury ocean cruise, Nathanial Mayweather an insufferably spoiled rich kid mistakenly boards *The Filthy Whore*, a dilapidated fishing trawler populated by a crew of scurrilous old salts who turn his life of leisure into misery as their menial cabin boy. The crew encounter a bunch of quirky mythical creatures in a mysterious Pacific Ocean area known as Hell's Bucket before finding an island where they plan to repair their boat and rid themselves of Mayweather. But after killing the 50-foot giant shoe salesman jealous husband of the six-armed siren, Calli, Nathanial wins acceptance as well as the love of Trina, a long-distance swimmer. Reaching Hawaii, Nathanial discovers the pampered life no longer suits him, and he rejoins the crew. Released on January 7, 1994. A Touchstone film. Produced by Tim Burton and Denise DiNovi and directed by Adam Resnick. 80 min. Stars Chris Elliott (Nathanial Mayweather), Ritch Brinkley (Capt. Greybar), Brian Doyle-Murray (Skunk), James Gammon (Paps), Brion James (Big Teddy), Melora Walters (Trina). There is a cameo by David Letterman. Except for the fishing village, the movie was filmed almost entirely on soundstages in the Los Angeles area. Released on video in 1994.

Cable Car Bake Shop Restaurant on Main Street in Disneyland Paris; opened on April 12, 1992.

Cabot, Sebastian (1918–1977) Voiced Sir Ector in (and narrated) *The Sword in the Stone* and Bagheera in *The Jungle Book*; narrated *Winnie the Pooh*. Also played Bissonette in *Westward Ho the Wagons* and Jonathan Lyte in *Johnny Tremain*. Appeared on television in *Along the Oregon Trail*.

Cactus Kid, The (film) Mickey Mouse cartoon; released on May 15, 1930. Directed by Walt Disney. After a series of song and dance routines by Mickey, Minnie, and Pedro (Pete), Pedro kidnaps Minnie, with Mickey chasing them on horseback across the desert. Mickey defeats Pedro and rescues Minnie. Pedro tumbles over a cliff and is flattened by a rock, but manages to walk away "accordion" style, while Mickey, Minnie, and their horse jeer at him.

Cadet Kelly (television) A Disney Channel Original Movie, premiering on March 8, 2002. When the mom of carefree 14-year-old Kelly

Collins marries the new commandant at a military academy, Kelly is forced to become the school's newest recruit. Her independent spirit clashes with the conformity of the school, but she takes up the challenge, and even becomes a member of the drill team. Directed by Larry Shaw. Stars Hilary Duff (Kelly Collins), Gary Cole (Sir), Christy Carlson Romano (Jennifer Stone), Shawn Ashmore (Brad Rigby), Andrea Lewis (Carla Hall), Aimee Garcia (Gloria Ramos), Linda Kash (Samantha). 110 min. The film became the first Disney Channel movie to repeat on the ABC *Wonderful World of Disney*, on July 14, 2002.

Café des Cascadeurs Art Deco–style studio diner, seating 40 guests, at Walt Disney Studios Paris; opened June 6, 2002.

Café des Visionnaires In Discoveryland at Disneyland Paris; opened on April 12, 1992, and closed September 15, 1995.

Café Hyperion In Discoveryland at Disneyland Paris, opened on April 12, 1992.

Cafe Orleans In New Orleans Square at Disneyland; opened in 1972. Formerly called Creole Cafe. Guests can dine on New Orleans–style fare on the terrace under umbrellas facing the Rivers of America. Also in Adventureland at Tokyo Disneyland, opened on April 15, 1983.

Cage Nightclub at Pleasure Island at Walt Disney World, featuring music videos showing on 170 monitors. It opened on April 7, 1990, and closed in December 1992. Formerly Videopolis East; became 8 TRAX.

Cage, Nicolas Actor, appeared in *Fire Birds* (Jake Preston), *The Rock* (Stanley Goodspeed), *Con Air* (Cameron Poe), *Snake Eyes* (Rick Santoro), *Bringing Out the Dead* (Frank Pierce), *Gone in 60 Seconds* (Memphis Raines), and *National Treasure* (Ben Gates).

Caine, Michael Actor; appeared in *Mr. Destiny* (Mike), *Noises Off* (Lloyd Fellowes), *The Muppet Christmas Carol* (Scrooge).

Calame, Niketa Actress; voiced the young Nala in *The Lion King*.

CalArts See California Institute of the Arts.

Calendar Girls (film) A group of ladies attend dull weekly meetings at the Women's Institute branch in Knapely, Yorkshire, but two regulars, Chris Harper and Annie Clark, feel the institute needs a shakeup. Their plan is for the group of mature women to pose nude for a calendar to raise money for a local hospital. As a result, they become international celebrities. A Touchstone Picture in association with Harbour Pictures for Buena Vista International. Limited U.S. release on December 19, 2003, after a world premiere at the Locarno Film Festival on August 9 and a September 5 release in the U.K. Expanded release on January 1, 2004. Directed by Nigel Cole. Stars Helen Mirren (Chris Harper), Julie Walters (Annie Clark), John Alderton (John Clark), Linda Bassett (Cora), Annette Crosbie (Jessie), Philip Glenister (Lawrence), Ciaran Hinds (Rod), Celia Imrie (Celia), Geraldine James (Marie), Penelope Wilton (Ruth). 108 min. Filmed in Super 35-Scope on location in Yorkshire (with the village of Kettlewell standing in for the fictional Knapely) and London. Released on video in 2004.

California Adventure, Disney's Built on the parking lot of Disneyland, Disney's California Adventure is a 55-acre park that opened on February 8, 2001. It originally encompassed attractions, restaurants, and shopping in three districts—Golden State, Hollywood Pictures Backlot, and Paradise Pier. Golden State celebrates California's cultural diversity and natural beauty, with six themed areas—Condor Flats, Bountiful Valley Farm, Pacific Wharf, Bay Area, Grizzly Peak Recreation Area, and Golden Vine Winery. Grizzly Peak, a mountain in the shape of the head of a grizzly bear, features a flume ride attraction and is the icon for the park. Bountiful Valley Farm became part of a new district, a bug's land, in 2002. Hollywood Pictures Backlot focuses on the glitz and glamour of the Hollywood moviemaking and television mythos. Paradise Pier evokes the legendary California beach culture, styled after classic Pacific Coast amusement parks with high-tech rides and games of skill. Sitting on the boundary of the park is Disney's Grand Californian Hotel, and the Downtown Disney themed retail, dining, and entertainment complex. Along with Disneyland, the Disneyland Hotel, and the Paradise Pier Hotel, all of these areas make up the Disneyland Resort. For parking, the Resort constructed a 10,000-car parking structure, the largest in the world.

California Angels On May 18, 1995, Disney announced that it was purchasing 25 percent of the California Angels baseball team from owner Gene Autry. The remainder of the team would be acquired after Mr. Autry's death. The purchase took place on May 15, 1996, when Disney Sports Enterprises became Managing General Partner for the team. A $100 million renovation of Anaheim Stadium was completed in 1998. The team name was changed to the Anaheim Angels in November 1996, with new team colors and logos. After Gene Autry's death, Disney completed its purchase of the team on March 31, 1999. See also Anaheim Angels.

California Grill Restaurant on the top floor of the Contemporary Resort at Walt Disney World, taking the place of Top of the World. It opened on May 15, 1995. The restaurant features a stage kitchen with nine exhibition cooking areas, including a wood-burning pizza oven, grill and rotisserie, and three island stoves.

California Institute of the Arts Art school which was founded in 1962 combining the Chouinard Art Institute and the Los Angeles Conservatory of Music. Walt Disney had been a longtime supporter of Chouinard, because many of his artists had received training there, so he was an avid advocate for the new school. When he died in 1966, a large bequest from his estate helped finance the construction of the new campus for CalArts, as the school would be known, on a 60-acre site in Valencia, and Congress authorized the minting of a special commemorative medal, which could be sold to benefit the school's scholarship program. Eventually a character-animation curriculum would be established at CalArts, and many of the students would be selected to become Disney animators.

California Screamin' Roller coaster attraction in the Paradise Pier area of Disney's California Adventure opening on February 8, 2001. It is the world's longest steel looping roller coaster, at 6,000 feet, designed to mirror the wooden look of coasters of yesteryear but with twenty-first-century technology. Riders in 24-passenger cars are catapulted from zero to 55 mph in four seconds, and their ride includes a 360-degree loop.

Californy 'er Bust (film) Goofy cartoon; released on July 13, 1945. Directed by Jack Kinney. A covered wagon train populated with Goofy look-alikes is attacked by Indians, but an opportune cyclone appears to carry them over the Rockies.

Call, Brandon Actor; appeared on television in *The Richest Cat in the World* and provided the voice of one of the Fairfolk in *The Black Cauldron*.

Call It Courage (television) Television show; based on the book by Armstrong Sperry, aired on April 1, 1973. Directed by Roy Edward Disney. Filmed on Tahiti and Bora Bora, the story of a native boy, Mafatu, who, with his dog, tries to prove himself a man by setting sail in a small outrigger canoe. He is capsized in a storm and has to survive by his wits on an island inhabited by a fierce tribe. Stars Evan Temarii.

Callas, Charlie Actor; voiced Elliott the dragon in *Pete's Dragon*.

Calvin, Henry (1918–1975) Actor; appeared in *Zorro* (Sgt. Garcia), *Toby Tyler* (Ben Cotter), *Babes in Toyland* (Gonzorgo).

Camarata, Salvador "Tutti" (1913–2005) A musical supervisor, arranger, and conductor who joined Disney in 1956 to help found Disneyland Records. Over a five-year period he supervised recordings of over 300 Disney record albums, featuring stars such as Annette Funicello, for whom he created a special "Annette sound" utilizing an echo. He was named a Disney Legend in 2003.

Cambridge, Godfrey (1933–1976) Actor; appeared in *The Biscuit Eater* (Willie Dorsey).

Cameo by Night (television) Unsold pilot for a television series. A police-department secretary by day, secret-identity crime fighter by night, solves a murder mystery. Aired on NBC on July 12, 1987. 60 min. Directed by Paul Lynch. Stars Sela Ward, Justin Deas, Thomas Ryan, Art LaFleur.

Camera Center Shop on Main Street at Disneyland; opened July 17, 1955. Sponsored at various times by GAF, Polaroid, and now by Kodak. The shop moved its location in November 1994 to the former Carefree Corner site, and was known as Main Street Photo Supply. Also on Main Street in Magic Kingdom Park at Walt Disney World, opened October 1, 1971, and in World Bazaar at Tokyo Disneyland, opened April 15, 1983. The Walt Disney World shop moved into the Town Square Exhibition Hall on August 27, 1998.

Cameras in Africa/Beaver Valley (television) Rerun title of *Beaver Valley/Cameras in Africa*.

Cameras in Samoa/The Holland Story (television) Television show; aired on November 7, 1956. Directed and narrated by Winston Hibler. The story of problems that occur when the dikes are breached in Holland, along with a

visit behind the scenes with photographers Herbert and Trudi Knapp working on the People and Places film *Samoa*.

Cameron, Kirk Actor; appeared in the 1995 television remake of *The Computer Wore Tennis Shoes* (Dexter Riley) and in bit parts in *Beyond Witch Mountain* and the *Herbie, the Love Bug* miniseries. He appeared on Disney Channel in *You Lucky Dog* (Jack Morgan).

Camp Davy Crockett Campground at Disneyland Paris; opened on April 12, 1992. Name changed to Davy Crockett Ranch in May 1993.

Camp Dog (film) Pluto cartoon; released on September 22, 1950. Directed by Charles Nichols. While campers are away, Pluto must guard the campsite from two coyotes, Bent-Tail and his son, Junior. The coyotes try to steal food, with Junior complicating matters by "stealing" Pluto, whom he considers to be food. After a chase that destroys the camp, Pluto joins the coyotes in the hills rather than try to explain to the campers.

Camp Minnie-Mickey Area of Disney's Animal Kingdom at Walt Disney World set up to resemble an old-fashioned summer camp, where Mickey Mouse and his pals have come to visit. Special productions based on *The Lion King* (at Lion King Theater) and other animated films are featured.

Camp Nowhere (film) At the end of each school year, young Morris "Mud" Himmel and his friends are unceremoniously packed off by their wealthy parents to summer camps that specialize in computer programming, military training, or calorie counting. This summer, Morris and his clever cohorts have determined to create their own vacation haven. With help from out-of-work high school drama teacher, Dennis Van Welker—who passes himself off to each of the kids' parents as the owner of a different phony theme camp—the kids fabricate an elaborate scheme to create their own camp filled with video games and junk food. When Parents' Day approaches, the kids have to resort to even greater deceptions to try to fool the gullible parents. Released on August 26, 1994. Directed by Jonathan Prince. A Hollywood Pictures film. 96 min. Stars Christopher Lloyd (Dennis Van Welker), Jonathan Jackson (Morris "Mud" Himmel), Wendy Makkena (Dr. Celeste Dunbar), M. Emmet Walsh (T. R. Polk). Camp Nowhere was built on Disney's Golden Oak Ranch in Newhall. Released on video in 1995.

Campbell, Bill Actor; appeared in *The Rocketeer* (Cliff Secord), and on television in *The Best of Disney: 50 Years of Magic*, *Max Q* (Clay Jarvis), and in the series *Once and Again* (Rick Sammler).

Camping Out (film) Mickey Mouse cartoon; released on February 17, 1934. Directed by Dave Hand. When mosquitoes threaten Mickey, Minnie, Horace Horsecollar, and Clarabelle Cow's lazy summer day, Horace swats at them, which angers them and alerts more to form into an Army formation. Mickey saves the day by catching the swarm in Clarabelle's bloomers.

Campos, Rafael (1936–1985) Actor; appeared in *The Light in the Forest* (Half Arrow), *Tonka* (Strong Bear), and *Savage Sam* (Young Warrior), and on television in *A Boy Called Nuthin'* and *The Tenderfoot*.

Can of Worms (television) A Disney Channel Original Movie; aired on April 10, 1999. Fourteen-year-old Mike Pillsbury is a great storyteller who spins elaborate tales about imaginary aliens who he believes left him on a doorstep to be raised by earthlings. When a schoolmate humiliates him at a dance, he sends a plea into space begging for aliens to rescue him from Earth. Mike opens a can of worms when the aliens actually arrive, leaving him responsible for saving the world. Directed by Paul Schneider. Stars Michael Shulman (Mike Pillsbury), Marcus Turner (Scott), Erika Christensen (Katelyn), Adam Wylie (Nick), Andrew Ducote (Jay), Malcolm McDowell (voice of Barnabus). Filmed entirely on location in Vancouver, British Columbia.

Can You Feel the Love Tonight Academy Award–winning song from *The Lion King* by Elton John and Tim Rice.

Canada Pavilion in World Showcase at Epcot; opened October 1, 1982. The Hôtel du Canada evokes a feeling of French Canada, while rocky cliffs, running streams, and waterfalls remind one of the western provinces. The highlight of the attraction is the 360° film, *O Canada*, showing some of the country's spectacular scenery. There is a restaurant for dining, Le Cellier, literally The

Cellar. The garden is similar to Butchart Gardens in British Columbia.

Canada '67 (film) Circle-Vision 360 film tour of Canada prepared in 1967 for Expo 67 in Montreal. See *O Canada* for the later Circle-Vision film produced for Epcot in 1982.

Canadian Bond Selling Shorts See *The Thrifty Pig, 7 Wise Dwarfs, Donald's Decision, All Together*.

Canal Boats of the World Fantasyland attraction at Disneyland, from July 17 to September 16, 1955. Became Storybook Land Canal Boats. The attraction became much more popular after the addition of the Storybook Land scenes. At one time, it was thought that Big Rock Candy Mountain would be built here, and the boats would enter the mountain and come upon Dorothy having a party with her friends from Oz.

Candido, Candy (1913–1999) Candido voiced the Indian Chief in *Peter Pan*, goons in *Sleeping Beauty*, and Fidget in *The Great Mouse Detective*.

Candle on the Water Song from *Pete's Dragon*, written by Al Kasha and Joel Hirschhorn. Nominated for an Academy Award.

Candlelight Procession A Christmastime tradition, beginning at Disneyland in 1958 with a concept developed by Dr. Charles C. Hirt of the University of Southern Califorina School of Music. A guest narrator each year, with personalities including Dennis Morgan (the first year), Cary Grant, Gregory Peck, John Wayne, Rock Hudson, Dean Jones, Jimmy Stewart, Howard Keel, Elliott Gould, and James Earl Jones, narrates the Christmas story as massed choirs holding candles parade down Main Street U.S.A., to fill the area in front of the train station. The centerpiece is a huge Christmas tree made of risers on which gathers a choir decked out in bright green robes. A full orchestra provides the music for the inspiring presentation, usually presented on two separate nights. The Disneyland Candlelight Procession and Ceremony moved to a new home at the Fantasyland Theater in 1998, returning to Main Street in 2003. With the opening of Magic Kingdom Park at Walt Disney World in 1971, a Florida version of the Candlelight Procession began a similar tradition. The procession moved to Epcot in 1994.

Candleshoe (film) A street-tough tomboy from Los Angeles poses as the long-lost heiress to a stately English manor called Candleshoe in this tale of larceny, adventure, and comedy. A series of cryptic clues leads 14-year-old Casey Brown on a wild and dangerous search for a long-lost treasure. In a rousing finale, Casey and a group of lovable characters from Candleshoe outduel a greedy con man and his rowdies for the treasure and Candleshoe as well. Initial release in L.A. on December 16, 1977, in order to qualify for Academy Award consideration (it did not receive any nominations); general release on February 10, 1978. Directed by Norman Tokar. 101 min. Stars David Niven (Priory), Helen Hayes (Lady St. Edmund), Jodie Foster (Casey), Leo McKern (Bundage), Veronica Quilligan (Cluny), Ian Sharrock (Peter), Sarah Tamakuni (Anna), David Samuels (Bobby), John Alderson (Jenkins), Mildred Shay (Mrs. McCress), Michael Balfour (Mr. McCress), Vivian Pickles (Grimsworthy). The film was based on the book *Christmas at Candleshoe* by Michael Innes. Look for David Niven in four roles—the loyal butler Priory, Scots gardener Gipping, Irish chauffeur John Henry, and retired cavalry officer Colonel Dennis. The Tudor mansion used in the film as Candleshoe is a stately house north of London, England, in Warwickshire called Compton Wynyates, which has been in the Compton family since the thirteenth century, and was often visited by Henry VIII. Filming also took place in downtown Los Angeles, Kidderminster, on the Severn Valley Railway, Hambleden village near Buckinghamshire, and Pinewood Studios in London, where all the interiors were filmed. Released on video in 1981, 1985, and 1992.

Candy, John (1950–1994) Actor/comedian, appeared in *Splash* (Freddie Bauer), *Cool Runnings* (Irv), and as the voice of Wilbur in *The Rescuers Down Under*.

Candy Palace Shop on Main Street at Disneyland; opened July 22, 1955. Also known as Candyland. The large front window allows passersby to view, and perhaps lick their lips a bit, as the confectioners make fudge or dip strawberries in chocolate. The Walt Disney World shop is the Main Street Confectionery. At Disneyland Paris the shop is known as the Boardwalk Candy Palace, hosted by Nestlé.

Canine Caddy (film) Pluto cartoon; released on May 30, 1941. Directed by Clyde Geronimi. Pluto gets into trouble with a gopher while caddying for Mickey, and the tunnels they make during the chase wreck the golf course.

Canine Casanova (film) Pluto cartoon; released on July 27, 1945. Directed by Charles Nichols. Pluto falls in love with a female dachshund whom he must rescue from the pound, only to find a family of puppies at her home.

Canine Patrol (film) Pluto cartoon; released on December 7, 1945. Directed by Charles Nichols. While patrolling the beach, Pluto runs into a baby turtle who he will not allow to go into the water because of a "No Swimming" sign. But, when Pluto inadvertently falls in quicksand, the turtle saves him and the two become friends.

Cannibal Capers (film) Silly Symphony cartoon; released on March 20, 1930. Directed by Burt Gillett. A jungle tribe's riotous musical celebration is brought to an end by the inopportune appearance of a fierce lion.

Cannon, Dyan Actress; appeared in *That Darn Cat* (remake, Mrs. Flint), and on television in *Rock 'n' Roll Mom* (Annie Hackett) and *The Beverly Hills Family Robinson* (Marsha Robinson).

Can't Buy Me Love (film) High school senior Ronald Miller longs to be popular and comes up with a unique plan—he hires the most popular cheerleader in school, Cindy Mancini, to be his girlfriend. Ronald is transformed almost overnight from nerd to the most popular guy on campus, but he does not notice when Cindy develops a real affection for him. Released on August 14, 1987. Directed by Steve Rash. A Touchstone film. 94 min. Stars Patrick Dempsey (Ronald Miller), Amanda Peterson (Cindy Mancini), Dennis Dugan (David Miller), Courtney Gains (Kenneth Wurman). Filmed entirely in Tucson, Arizona, with Tucson High School becoming the school in the movie. Hundreds of the students there got a chance to show off their acting talents as extras. Released on video in 1988.

Cantina de San Angel Fast-food eatery facing the Mexico pavilion in World Showcase at Epcot; opened on October 1, 1982.

Canvas Back Duck (film) Donald Duck cartoon; released on December 25, 1953. Directed by Jack Hannah. At a carnival, Donald shows his strength on the various "strength machines," in order to make his nephews proud. When a wimpy boy tells the nephews that his father can beat Donald, Donald doesn't hesitate to agree to fight, only to discover the father is the hulking Peewee Pete. They fight in the ring, and Donald manages to win.

Cape May Cafe Restaurant in the Beach Club Resort at Walt Disney World. There is a character breakfast in the morning, and a clambake is offered in the evening.

Capelli, Gaudenzio He spent a 33-year career supervising Disney publications in Italy; he was honored with a European Disney Legends award in 1997.

Capers, Virginia (1925–2004) Actress; appeared in *The World's Greatest Athlete*, *The North Avenue Irregulars* (Cleo), and *What's Love Got to Do With It* (choir mistress).

Capital Cities/ABC See American Broadcasting Company.

CAPS The acronym for Computer Animation Production System, this Academy Award–winning (1992) technology, utilized during the production of Disney animated features, allows artists to assemble the animation, background, special effects, and computer-animated elements onto the final piece of film.

Captain Eo (film) 3-D musical science-fiction adventure film shown in Journey Into Imagination at Epcot; opened September 12, 1986, and ended July 6, 1994, and in Tomorrowland at Disneyland on September 18, 1986, and ending April 6, 1997. Captain Eo and his crew of mythical space creatures—Hooter, Fuzzball, the Geex, Major Domo, Minor Domo—discover a colorless planet where they are confronted by the Supreme Leader and her forces of darkness. Using the power of music, dance, and light, Eo and his crew are able to turn the black-and-white land into a magical world of color and happiness. 17 min. Shown in Tomorrowland at Tokyo Disneyland beginning March 20, 1987 and ended September 1, 1996. Also in Cinémagique in Discoveryland in Disneyland Paris, opened on April 12, 1992, and ended on August 17, 1998. Stars Michael Jackson, Anjelica Huston, Dick Shawn. George Lucas was executive producer and Francis Ford Coppola was director.

Captain Eo Backstage (television) Television show; aired on May 15, 1988. Directed by Muffett Kaufman. Behind the scenes of the making of the Michael Jackson film, edited from a Disney Channel special entitled *The Making of Captain Eo*; aired with *Justin Case* in the Disney anthology time slot.

Captain Hook Menacing leader of the pirates in Never Land in *Peter Pan*; voiced by Hans Conried. The animators actually had a difficult time deciding how to handle the hook. James M. Barrie, the author of the original story, had the hook on the right arm, but the animators anticipated problems with that in animation. They wanted Hook to be able to make gestures, to write, and to perform other actions that are simpler to do with the right hand. So they made the decision to place the hook on the left.

Captain Hook's Galley Fantasyland fast-food restaurant at Disneyland; from 1969 to August 29, 1982. Formerly Chicken of the Sea Pirate Ship and Restaurant (1955–1969). Also a restaurant in Fantasyland at Tokyo Disneyland, opened

April 15, 1983, and in Adventureland at Disneyland Paris, opened on April 12, 1992.

Captain Jack's Oyster Bar At the Downtown Disney Marketplace at Walt Disney World. Located over the water of the lagoon, this lounge is a popular spot to have a drink and sample some seafood snacks. It became Cap'n Jack's Restaurant on February 20, 2000.

Captain John Smith Character in *Pocahontas*; voiced by Mel Gibson.

Captain Ron (film) Floundering in a sea of stress, corporate executive, Martin Harvey, dreams of glamour, adventure and nonstop cruises when he inherits his uncle's yacht. But, when the family casts off, they soon discover the newly acquired craft is badly in need of an overhaul. Not knowing where to turn, the Harveys find their chances for a spontaneous adventure resurfacing when they encounter Captain Ron, a bedraggled and dreadlocked happy-go-lucky professional seafarer with dubious nautical skills. Even though the Harveys worry about Captain Ron setting a bad example for their children, a trip with him brings exciting adventures with guerrillas and pirates and a newfound respect for the bumbling sailor and his carefree nature. Released on September 18, 1992. Directed by Thom Eberhardt. A Touchstone film. 100 min. Stars Kurt Russell (Captain Ron), Martin Short (Martin Harvey), Mary Kay Place (Katherine Harvey). Much of the filming took place in and around Puerto Rico. Two identical 58-foot ketches from Florida became the before and after versions of *The Wanderer*. Released on video in 1993.

Captain's Tower Landmark at the center of the Downtown Disney Marketplace used for seasonal merchandise and special sales until April 28, 2002. It became Disney Pin Traders in July, 2002.

Captive Stallion, The (television) Television title of part one of *Comanche* (*Tonka*).

Car Toon Spin See Roger Rabbit's Car Toon Spin.

Caravan Carousel Attraction in Arabian Coast at Tokyo DisneySea; opened September 4, 2001. A two-level carousel, featuring ebony horses, camels, elephants, griffins, and even the Genie himself.

Caravan Pictures Headed by Joe Roth and Roger Birnbaum, signed an exclusive agreement with Disney in 1993 to produce at least 25 films to be distributed by Buena Vista Pictures Distribution. Their first pictures included *Angie, Angels in the Outfield, The Three Musketeers, I Love Trouble, A Low Down Dirty Shame, Houseguest, The Jerky Boys, Heavyweights.* Caravan ceased to exist in 1999, and a new company, Spyglass Entertainment, headed by Roger Birnbaum and Gary Barber, succeeded it.

Card Corner Shop sponsored by Gibson on Main Street at Disneyland from June 14, 1985 to October 1988. Gibson earlier had a Greeting Card shop at another location from July 17, 1955, to 1959.

Careers in Math & Science: A Different View (film) Educational film, released in September 1986. 19 min. Demonstrates the importance of math and science classes to a student's future.

Carefree Corner Guest registration area on Main Street at Disneyland, sponsored by INA (from 1956–1974); opened August 22, 1956, and closed in 1985. Guests could sign their names in a book from their home state. It later became Card Corner then returned to the Carefree Corner name in 1988. On November 19, 1994, the area became Main Street Photo Supply.

Careless Charlie Star of a number of the educational films made for the Coordinator of Inter-American Affairs during World War II.

Carey, Harry, Jr. Actor; appeared in *The Great Locomotive Chase* (William Bensinger), *Run, Cougar, Run* (Barney), and *Tombstone* (Marshal Fred White), and on television in *Spin and Marty, Texas John Slaughter,* and *Ride a Northbound Horse.*

Caribbean Beach Resort Hotel at Walt Disney World; opened on October 1, 1988. The first of Disney's moderate-priced hotels on the Walt Disney World property, and one of the largest hotels anywhere in Florida. Old Port Royale houses a food court, restaurant, and merchandise facilities.

Caribbean Plaza Area near Adventureland in Magic Kingdom Park at Walt Disney World. Features the Pirates of the Caribbean attraction.

Carlo, the Sierra Coyote (television) Television show; aired on February 3, 1974. Directed by James Algar. A coyote tries to escape the encroachment of man onto his territory and is befriended by the wife of a couple monitoring the environment for the government. The husband is suspicious of the coyote, but Carlo helps lead rescue dogs to him when he is lost. Stars Jana Milo, Steven S. Stewart, Hal Bokar, Dale Alexander.

Carlson, Joyce After spending a decade and a half in the Disney Ink and Paint Department, she joined WED Enterprises as a show designer, and was instrumental in designing and maintaining such attractions as "it's a small world" and Carousel of Progress. She retired in 2000 after having worked for Disney for 56 years, and was named a Disney Legend the same year.

Carnation Café Patio restaurant on Main Street at Disneyland; opened on March 21, 1997.

Carnation Ice Cream Parlor A mainstay on Main Street at Disneyland from July 17, 1955, where one can have a meal or just an ice cream confection. Carnation is one of the few opening-day participants remaining in the park. In 1997, the restaurant became Carnation Cafe, moving into its former patio.

Carnation Plaza Gardens Fast-food and entertainment area on the hub at Disneyland, opened August 18, 1956, and closed in October 1998. At one time the Disneyland bandstand was situated here.

Carney, Alan (1911–1973) Actor; appeared in *The Absent-Minded Professor* (First referee), *Son of Flubber* (Referee), *Monkeys, Go Home!* (Grocer), *The Adventures of Bullwhip Griffin* (Joe Turner), *Herbie Rides Again*, and *Blackbeard's Ghost*.

Carney, Art (1918–2003) Actor; starred on television in *Christmas in Disneyland with Art Carney*. Also appeared on The Disney Channel in the movies *The Undergrads* and *Blue Yonder*.

Carnival Time (television) Television show; aired on March 4, 1962. Directed by Hamilton S. Luske. Ludwig Von Drake hosts a look at the major carnivals held in Rio de Janeiro and New Orleans, aided by José Carioca and Donald Duck, respectively, in the two cities.

Carol & Co. (television) television series on NBC, from March 31, 1990, to August 19, 1991. Each week's show featured the ensemble cast playing different roles in comedic skits. Stars Carol Burnett, Meagen Fay, Terry Kiser, Richard Kind, Anita Barone, Peter Krause, Jeremy Piven. The show won Emmy Awards for Costume Design and for guest star Swoosie Kurtz. Continued on CBS as *The Carol Burnett Show.*

Carol Burnett Show, The (television) Television series on CBS, from November 1 to December 27, 1991. Continued *Carol & Co.* as a variety show, with Meagan Fay and Richard Kind being the only holdovers in the cast.

Carolwood Pacific Railroad Walt Disney's love for trains led him to create this 1/8 scale model railroad in his own backyard in Holmby Hills in the early 1950s. It was named for the street on which the house was located. To keep things official, he even had his wife sign over to him a right-of-way through her flower gardens. The Carolwood Pacific later inspired Disney to include a railroad system in his plans for Disneyland.

Carousel of Progress See General Electric Carousel of Progress.

Carradine, Robert Actor; appeared in *Max Keeble's Big Move* (Don) and *The Lizzie McGuire Movie* (Sam McGuire), on television in *The Liberators*, *Disney's Totally Minnie* (Maxwell Dweeb), and *Mom's Got a Date with a Vampire* (Malachi Van Helsing) and *Lizzie McGuire* (Sam McGuire) on Disney Channel.

Carroll, Leo G. (1892–1972) Actor; appeared in *The Parent Trap* (Reverend Mosby).

Carroll, Lewis (1832–1898) Author of *Alice in Wonderland.*

Carroll, Pat Actress; she voiced Ursula in *The Little Mermaid.*

Carrousel de Lancelot, Le Located in Fantasyland at Disneyland Paris, opened April 12, 1992.

Cars (film) A Disney/Pixar film; scheduled for release on June 6, 2006. Directed by John Lasseter. Voices include Paul Newman, Richard Petty, Owen Wilson (Lightning McQueen), Bonnie Hunt, Cheech Marin, George Carlin, Elaine Stritch, Dan Whitney.

Carson, Blain Actor; appeared on the *Mickey Mouse Club* on The Disney Channel, from 1991 to 1993.

Carter, Jimmy The former President jogged through Disneyland before it opened to guests one morning in May 1982. He has logged in several visits to Walt Disney World over the years.

Carthay Circle Theater Famed Hollywood theater that saw the premiere of *Snow White and the Seven Dwarfs* on December 21, 1937.

Cartoon All-Stars to the Rescue (television) Television's most popular cartoon characters helping a young girl free her brother from the grip of drugs, a special that aired simultaneously throughout North America on most television stations on April 21, 1990; released on video in association with McDonald's and the Academy of Television Arts & Sciences in June 1990.

Carvey, Dana Actor; appeared in *Tough Guys* (Richie Evans), and in Cranium Command in Wonders of Life at Epcot.

Casa de Fritos Frontierland restaurant serving Mexican food at Disneyland, opened August 11, 1955, and closed on November 28, 1999. A highlight for kids was a coin slot where you would put in a coin and the Frito Kid would deliver a small bag of Fritos to you by way of an elaborate mechanism. Became Casa Mexicana on October 1, 1982.

Casanova (film) For the first time in his life, the legendary seducer, swashbuckler, master of disguise, and wit, Casanova, is about to meet his match with an alluring Venetian beauty, Francesca, who does the one thing he never thought possible: refuse him. Through a series of clever disguises and scheming ruses, he manages to get ever closer to Francesca. But he is playing the most dangerous game he has ever encountered—one that will risk not only his life and reputation, but his only chance at true passion. Limited release on December 25, 2005. Directed by Lasse Hallström. A Touchstone Picture. Stars Heath Ledger (Giacomo Casanova), Sienna Miller (Francesca Bruni), Lena Olin (Andrea Bruni), Jeremy Irons (Bishop Pucci), Oliver Platt (Papprizzio). 111

min. Began filming August in 2004 in Venice, Italy, and was screened at the Venice Film Festival on September 2, 2005. Filmed in Super 35-Scope.

Case of Murder, A (television) Television show, the first episode of *The Further Adventures of Gallegher.*

Case of the Missing Space, The (film) Educational film where viewers solve a mystery message by deciphering scrambled words and symbols, released in September 1989. 16 min.

Case of Treason, A (television) Television show; the sixth episode of *The Swamp Fox.*

Casebusters (television) Television show; aired on May 25, 1986. A brother and sister enjoy life in their suburban neighborhood—until a mysterious crime threatens their grandfather's small security business. Together they team up to solve the crime, an investigation that leads them through some pretty hairy adventures. Stars Noah Hathaway, Virginia Keehne, Pat Hingle, Gary Riley.

Casella, Max Actor, starred in *Newsies* (Racetrack) and *Ed Wood* (Paul Marco). He provided the voice of Zini in *Dinosaur*, Tip in *The Little Mermaid II*, and was in the opening cast of *The Lion King* on Broadway as Timon.

Caselotti, Adriana (1916–1977) As a teenager, Caselotti provided the voice of Snow White. She was the first of 150 young girls tested for the role and was just 18 years old when Walt Disney selected her. The childlike quality of her voice appealed to Disney, who had been looking for someone younger. Caselotti reports, "I didn't tell anyone my age." She was named a Disney Legend in 1994.

Casey at the Bat (film) Segment of *Make Mine Music*, "A Musical Recitation" by Jerry Colonna, about the mighty but vain ballplayer who strikes out to lose the game. Re-released as a short on July 16, 1954.

Casey Bats Again (film) Special cartoon; released on June 18, 1954. Directed by Jack Kinney. Casey is dismayed while trying to have sons that can follow in their dad's footsteps, because he has only daughters. Eventually, he realizes that he has nine tomboy daughters, just enough for a baseball team. He tries to regain his former glory with his nine-daughter baseball team, which wins the championship despite Casey's interference.

Casey Jones Star of *The Brave Engineer* (1950).

Casey Jr. The little train from *Dumbo* debuted as a segment of *The Reluctant Dragon* in which sound effects are showcased.

Casey Jr. Circus Train Fantasyland attraction at Disneyland, opened July 31, 1955. Themed after the train in *Dumbo* (1941). Before Storybook Land opened in 1956, this was simply a train ride, but the new attraction gave guests something to see as they rode around the small hills at the side of Fantasyland. Because of mechanical problems, the attraction was not ready for operation on opening day; it took two weeks to work the bugs out. See Le Petit Train du Cirque for the Disneyland Paris version.

Casey's Corner Coca-Cola refreshment shop on Main Street in Disneyland Paris; opened on April 12, 1992. It is also the new name of the Coca-Cola Refreshment Corner in Magic Kingdom Park at Walt Disney World, beginning May 27, 1995.

Cassidy, Joanna Actress; appeared in *Who Framed Roger Rabbit* (Dolores) and *Where the Heart Is* (Jean), and on television in *Bar Girls* (Claudia Reese).

Cast member Disney term for employee. Disney theme park cast members are considered performers, as if they were on stage in a theater. They are putting on a show for the guests (never customers). Therefore, cast members wear costumes, not uniforms. When the Disney park cast members are in the park, they are on stage; when they return to their dressing rooms, they are backstage.

Castaway, The (film) Mickey Mouse cartoon; released on April 6, 1931. Directed by Wilfred Jackson. Mickey is shipwrecked on an island after being adrift on a raft. Mickey plays a piano that has washed ashore, until a gorilla destroys it. Mickey manages to escape from the gorilla, a lion, and an alligator. He then floats downstream on a turtle, which he stood on thinking it was a rock.

Castaway Cay Uninhabited island in the Bahamas purchased by Disney to use as a day-long recreational stopover for Disney Cruise Line ships. The 1,000-acre island was originally known as Gorda Cay, until shortly after the Disney purchase in February 1996.

Castaway Cowboy, The (film) On the island of Kauai, during the 1850s, a widow rancher, Henrietta MacAvoy, and her son, Booten, rescue Lincoln Costain from drowning. Lincoln is a Texas cowboy who had been shanghaied aboard a ship from which he elected to jump. Costain is persuaded to teach the Hawaiian farmhands how to become cowboys so that they can profit from the wild cattle on Henrietta's land. After apprehending a witch doctor, stopping a stampede, and eliminating his business/romantic competition, Costain remains on the island to keep his new cowboys in line. Released on August 7, 1974. Directed by Vincent McEveety. 91 min. Stars James Garner (Costain), Vera Miles (Henrietta), Robert Culp (Bryson), Eric Shea (Booton), Manu

Tupou (Kimo), Gregory Sierra (Marrujo), Shug Fisher (Capt. Carey), Ralph Hanalei (Hopu), Kahana (Oka). The production was filmed on the island of Kauai, with the water slide scenes shot at Kilauea Falls. The main setting—the MacAvoy farm—was designed by production designer Robert Clatworthy and built on a bluff reachable only by private road. The waterfront set was built at Mahaulepu. Released on video in 1984.

Castaway Creek Guests can ride inner tubes on the 2,100-foot-long stream that meanders through Typhoon Lagoon at Walt Disney World.

Castellaneta, Don Voice actor; various roles on *Darkwing Duck* and *Goof Troop*, voiced the Genie from *Aladdin* for the television series.

Cat from Outer Space, The (film) An off-beat physicist, his girlfriend, and an odds-playing co-worker try to help an extraterrestrial space cat, ZUNAR J5/90 DORIC FOURSEVEN, or, in earth talk, Jake, fix his ship before the Army or a power-hungry businessman causes a catastrophe by catnapping the feline. The plot thickens when the alien falls for a lovely Persian earth cat, Lucy Belle. Released on June 30, 1978. Directed by Norman Tokar. 103 min. Stars Ken Berry (Frank), Sandy Duncan (Liz), Harry Morgan (Gen. Stilton), Roddy McDowall (Stallwood), McLean Stevenson (Link), Jesse White (Earnest Ernie), Alan Young (Dr. Wenger), Hans Conreid (Dr. Heffel), Ronnie Schell (Sgt. Duffy), William Prince (Mr. Olympus). Released on video in 1983. The cat, Jake, was actually played by two Abyssinian cats—Rumple and his twin sister Amber. The Abyssinian breed was selected by the producers because they thought it looked more "alien." Ronnie Schell provided the voice for Jake. The movie was shot on the Disney Studio lot, on a soundstage, in the Roy O. Disney building, at a hangar at the Burbank airport, and on an army base built for the film on the studio's 708-acre Golden Oak Ranch.

Cat Nap Pluto (film) Pluto cartoon; released on August 13, 1948. Directed by Charles Nichols.

Pluto, tired and sleepy from being out all night, tries to sleep despite Figaro's attempts to keep him awake. Pluto's sandman enlists the help of Figaro's sandman so both Pluto and Figaro can sleep.

Cat that Looked at a King, The (film) Julie Andrews and two kids leap into a chalk painting on the sidewalk and find themselves in the kingdom of King Cole. The king thinks he knows all the facts in the world, but is bested by a cat who teaches him that he is not the cleverest man in the world, but rather a merry old soul. Produced by DisneyToon Studios. Directed by Dave Bossert (animation) and Peter Schneider (live action). Released on the *Mary Poppins* DVD on December 14, 2004. Based on an original Mary Poppins story by P. L. Travers. Stars Julie Andrews, Dylan Cash, Olivia DeLaurentis. Voices are Sarah Ferguson (The Queen), Tracey Ullman (The Cat), David Ogden Stiers (King Cole/Prime Minister). 10 min.

Catastrophe Canyon Action-packed special effects area on the Backstage Studio Tour at Disney-MGM Studios. Also at Walt Disney Studios Paris; opened March 16, 2002.

Caterpillar Reclining on a toadstool and punctuating his speech with puffs of smoke, this *Alice in Wonderland* character was voiced by Richard Haydn.

Catlett, Walter (1889–1960) Voice of J. Worthington Foulfellow in *Pinocchio*.

Cat's Nightmare, The Copyright title of *The Cat's Out*.

Cat's Out, The (film) Silly Symphony cartoon; released on July 28, 1931. Copyrighted as *The Cat's Nightmare*. Directed by Wilfred Jackson. After a cat is put out of the house, it is knocked out by a falling weather vane. It has a nightmare in which giant birds, bats, scarecrows, huge spiders, and monstrous trees scare it. The cat awakens from the nightmare and goes back into the house, only to be put outside again.

Cavalcade of Songs (television) Television show; aired on February 16, 1955. Directed by Wilfred Jackson, Peter Godfrey. Walt Disney discusses the importance of music in the movies, re-enacting with some of his current artists the story meeting that came up with "Who's Afraid of the Big Bad Wolf?" for *Three Little Pigs* and promoting the upcoming *Lady and the Tramp* by showing segments of the work in progress and looking in on the composers and singers at work on the score. Appearing are Ward Kimball, Frank Thomas, Pinto Colvig, Peggy Lee, Sonny Burke, Oliver Wallace, and the Mello Men.

Cavin Courageous young page boy hero in the *Gummi Bears* television series; voiced by Jason Marsden.

Cel The clear celluloid on which the characters were painted during the animation process. The painted celluloid, or cel, was placed over a background and photographed, becoming one frame of the animated film. There are 24 frames per second in an animated film, but most cels containing characters are often held for two frames. If there are several characters in a scene, each may be painted on a different cel. Since a typical animated short runs six to eight minutes in length, that equals 4,500 to 12,000 cels, or more, per cartoon. Cels up to 1940 were nitrate based, and quite unstable. In fact, a pile of them could constitute a fire hazard. In 1940, Disney switched to cellulose acetate, a much safer medium. Disney cels were sold as works of art by the Courvoisier Galleries from 1938 to 1946, then at Disneyland beginning in 1955. The Disney Art Program, later known as Disney Art Editions and Disney Art Classics, began in the 1970s handling the sale of production cels, as well as creating special limited-edition cels, serigraphs, and other forms of collectible art. With *The Rescuers Down Under*, cels were no longer used in the production process, being replaced by the computer.

Celebrate the Spirit! Disney's All-Star 4th of July Spectacular (television) Television special on CBS (120 min.); aired on July 4, 1992. Directed by Gary Halvorson. Entertainers perform at various locations at the Disney parks. Stars John Ritter, Kris Kross, Billy Ray Cyrus, Celine Dion.

Celebration New town on the Walt Disney World property in Florida. The downtown area and the first residential phase of this self-contained city of 20,000 opened in 1996, with the first residents moving in on June 18, 1996. Facilities include a school (kindergarten through middle school), a high school, a movie theater, and rental apartments above downtown shops. A fiber-optic information network links all businesses and residences. In 2002, the golf course was sold to a private group, and the downtown area (shops, restaurants, offices, apartments) was sold to Lexin Capital on January 21, 2004.

Celebration U.S.A. Parade Parade at Disneyland from June 21 to November 24, 1991. A tongue-in-cheek look at life in the United States, celebrating the diversity of American lifestyles and America's patriotic pride.

Celebrity Celebration Aboard the Queen Mary (television) Television special on KCAL in Los Angeles, celebrating "Voyage to 1939" at the *Queen Mary* and including information about the ship and its history; aired on April 15, 1990. 60 min. Directed by Rick Locke. Stars Wil Shriner, Melissa Manchester, Michael Feinstein.

Celebrity Sports Center Denver, Colorado, sports facility, built by a group of celebrity investors, including Walt Disney, Art Linkletter, and John Payne; opened on September 17, 1960. Walt Disney Productions purchased the Center in 1962, and used it as a training ground for cast members who would soon be operating resort facilities at Walt Disney World. The Center was sold to a group of private investors on March 29, 1979.

Celeste in the City (television) Two-hour television movie, airing on ABC Family on March 14, 2004. A small-town girl from Maine, Celeste Blodgett, moves to New York City, where she discovers her glamorous writing job is really only a fact-checker, and her living quarters are dismal and rat-infested. Enter a helpful next-door neighbor, Kyle, and her gay cousin, Dana, who gives Celeste a makeover treatment and helps her gain the confidence needed to survive in the big city. Directed by Larry Shaw. Stars Majandra Delfino (Celeste), Nicholas Brendon (Dana), Ethan Embry (Kyle), Michael Boisvert (Mitch), Deborah Gibson (Monica), Sadie LeBlanc (Amanda). From Touchstone Television.

Celtic Pride (film) Jimmy Flaherty and Mike O'Hara are die-hard Boston Celtics fans who plan their lives around the basketball schedule and Sportscenter. While they are ecstatic that Boston is leading the NBA Championship series three games to one, they also know that the Utah Jazz's flamboyant and obnoxious superstar, Lewis Scott, poses a big threat to the Celtics' date with destiny. Growing more desperate and depressed as the series evens up, they realize there is only one thing to do—kidnap Scott before the big game. When best-laid plans go awry, the threesome spend a wild night learning about the true spirit of competition and the joy of the game. Released on April 19, 1996. A Hollywood Picture in association with Caravan Pictures. Directed by Tom DeCerchio. Stars Dan Aykroyd (Jimmy Flaherty), Daniel Stern (Mike O'Hara), Damon Wayans (Lewis Scott), Gail O'Grady (Carol O'Hara). 90 min. Filmed on location in Boston, and especially at the Boston Garden, home of the Celtics. The casting directors diligently worked to put together two teams of basketball players who could look like NBA caliber players, and a training camp was set up for them at Brandeis University. Wayans himself had four months of intensive training. Released on video in 1996.

Cemetery Club, The (film) Three lifelong friends, Esther, Doris, and Lucille, suddenly find themselves middle-aged widows and discover the transition to the singles scene both difficult and a challenge to their friendships. Lucille enjoys throwing herself into the over-50 singles circuit, and brings her friends along. Doris will have none of it, preferring to remember her past and a loving marriage. Esther finds herself reluctantly falling in love again with a charming widower, Ben. Conflicts come to a climax at a wedding party for their oft-married friend Selma. Esther learns that Doris and Lucille interfered with her relationship with Ben, and she is bitterly angry. But she learns to forgive, and discovers that she has the courage to live the single life, and patch up her relationship with Ben. Initial release on February 3, 1993; general release on February 12, 1993. Directed by Bill Duke. A Touchstone film. 107 min. Stars Ellen Burstyn (Esther Moskowitz), Olympia Dukakis (Doris Silverman), Diane Ladd (Lucille Rubin), Danny Aiello (Ben Katz), Lainie Kazan (Selma), Christina Ricci (Jessica). Based on the stage play by Ivan Menchell. Filmed on location in the Jewish community in Pittsburgh. Released on video in 1993.

Centorium Store in Communicore East, later Innoventions East, at Epcot; opened on October 1, 1982. The central, and largest, merchandising facility in Future World, where guests can buy merchandise themed to all of the Future World

pavilions, as well as generic Epcot merchandise. The Centorium was remodeled and became Mouse Gear in September 1999.

Ceramic Mural, The (film) Educational film; giving a step-by-step account of the design and construction of a unique ceramic mural. Released in 16mm in September 1967.

Chaffey, Don (1917–1990) Director of *Pete's Dragon*, *The Three Lives of Thomasina*, *Ride a Wild Pony*, *Born to Run*, *Greyfriars Bobby*, *The Prince and the Pauper*, and *The Horse Without a Head*.

Chain Gang, The (film) Mickey Mouse cartoon; released on September 5, 1930. The first appearance of a character who would become Pluto. Directed by Burt Gillett. Mickey is a convict who escapes and is tracked by guards using bloodhounds. After a wild horse ride, Mickey hits a post, is thrown off a cliff, crashes through the prison roof, and falls back into his cell.

Challenge of Survival, The: Chemicals (film) Educational film; released in August 1984. The film illustrates the problems caused by chemicals used in pest control.

Challenge of Survival, The: Land (film) Educational film; released in August 1984. The film shows how conservation tillage can minimize soil erosion.

Challenge of Survival, The: Water (film) Educational film; released in August 1984. The film explains how improper irrigation can ruin soil, and drip irrigation is one method of reducing water runoff.

Challengers, The (television) Syndicated television series, from September 3, 1990, to August 30, 1991. A game show featuring a question-and-answer format based on current events. Hosted by Dick Clark.

Chandar, the Black Leopard of Ceylon (television) Two-part television show, aired on November 26 and December 3, 1972. Friendship between a Ceylonese holy man and his disciple, and a leopard. The leopard had been saved by the holy man when young, and years later he returns the favor. Stars Frederick Steyne, Esram Jayasinghe.

Chango, Guardian of the Mayan Treasure (television) Television show; aired on March 19, 1972. Attendants at a Mayan ruin befriend a baby spider monkey, who helps them in the search for a fabled treasure. Stars Alonzo Fuentes, Juan Maldonado, Alex Tinne.

Character merchandise See Merchandise.

Character Shop, The Shop in Tomorrowland at Disneyland; open from 1967 until September 15, 1986. Became Star Traders. After the Emporium, it became the largest shop for buying Disney character souvenirs.

Charles, Josh Actor; appeared in *Dead Poets Society* (Knox Overstreet) and *Crossing the Bridge* (Mort Golden), and on television in *Sports Night* (Dan Rydell).

Charley and the Angel (film) A small-town businessman, during the Great Depression, has neglected his family for his business. His guardian angel, Roy Zerney, helps him to realize the error of his ways and he becomes a public hero, basking in the warmth of his family's love and admiration, through a series of hectic events involving bootleggers and the police. Released on March 23, 1973. Directed by Vincent McEveety. 93 min. Stars Fred MacMurray (Charley Appleby), Henry Morgan (Angel), Cloris Leachman (Nettie), Kurt Russell (Ray), Kathleen Cody (Leonora), Vincent Van Patten (Willie), Scott Kolden (Rupert). This was the last of Fred MacMurray's seven films for Disney. Buddy Baker, the film's musical composer and conductor, utilized many golden tunes from the 1930s for the score, including "Three Little Words," and "You're Driving Me Crazy," as well as an original song, "Livin' One Day at a Time," written by Shane Tatum and Ed Scott. To create a 1930s setting for the film, Disney art directors and set designers found the ideal location in Pasadena, California, on a quiet residential street lined with small frame bungalows. The filmmakers hid the days' television antennas, added a few stylish touring cars, dressed the cast in costume and—presto—they had recreated the 1930s. Released on video in 1986.

Charlie Crowfoot and the Coati Mundi (television) Television show; aired on September 19, 1971. A Native American working on an archaeological dig finds an injured coatimundi, names him Cocoa, and nurses him back to health. The rancher, on whose land the Native American is digging, hates the coatis but changes his tune when Cocoa helps save his life. Stars Edward Colunga, Robert Keyworth.

Charlie the Lonesome Cougar (film) In the Cascade Range of the Pacific Northwest, a tiny orphaned cougar kitten is found and adopted by a young forester. He names the cougar Charlie, and, as Charlie grows up, he has many humorous and hair-raising adventures in the logging community. Finally, for his protection, Charlie is given his freedom in a wildlife sanctuary. Released on October 18, 1967, on a bill with *The Jungle Book*. Field producers Lloyd Beebe, Charles L. Draper, and Ford Beebe. 75 min. Stars Brian Russell (Potlatch), Ron Brown (Jess Bradley), Linda Wallace (Jess's fiancée). The film was narrated by Rex Allen. Released on video in 1985.

Chase, Chevy Actor; appeared in *Man of the House* (Jack) and in the film in the Monster Sound Show at Disney-MGM Studios at Walt Disney World.

Chase, Daveigh Actress; provided the voice of Lilo in *Lilo & Stitch* and Chihiro in *Spirited Away*, and on Disney Channel, Rose in *American Dragon: Jake Long*.

Chasez, J.C. Actor; appeared on the *Mickey Mouse Club* on The Disney Channel, beginning in 1991. He was later a member of the boy band, 'N SYNC.

Château de la Belle au Bois Dormant, Le Sleeping Beauty Castle in Fantasyland at Disneyland Paris; opened April 12, 1992. The castle is quite different in design from the castles in the other Disney parks. Its tallest tower reaches 149.2 feet above the moat, and, underneath the castle, in La Tanière du Dragon, guests finds a sleeping dragon that slowly awakens.

Cheetah (film) Teenagers Ted and Susan join their parents at a Kenyan research station. After befriending a young native boy, Morogo, they find a baby cheetah whose mother has been killed by poachers. They manage to convince their parents to let them raise the cheetah, named Duma, as a pet. When it's time for the kids to return home, Duma has to be returned to the wild. Before this can be accomplished, he is captured by a local merchant hoping to race the cat against greyhounds. Ted and Susan disobey their parents and set out to rescue Duma with Morogo's help. Released on August 18, 1989. Directed by Jeff Blyth. 83 min. Stars Keith Coogan (Ted Johnson), Lucy Deakins (Susan Johnson), Collin Mothupi (Morogo). Filmed on location in Kenya, with the cast and crew setting up a small compound consisting of 85 tents as their base of operations. Released on video in 1990.

Cheetah Girls, The (television) A Disney Channel Original Movie, premiering August 15, 2003. Four multitalented New York City teens from dissimilar homes and economic backgrounds—a cultural melting pot of Black, Italian, Dominican, Puerto Rican, and Cuban heritages—have a dream to take the world by storm with their music group. All the while, they navigate "cheeta-licious" fashion and boys (including their musical archrival), family, and parents. Directed by Oz Scott. Stars Raven (Galleria Garibaldi), Lynn Whitfield (Dorothea Garibaldi), Adrienne Bailon (Chanel), Kiely Williams (Aqua), Sabrina Bryan (Dorinda Thomas), Kyle Schmid (Derek),

Sandra Caldwell (Drinka Champagne), Vincent Corazza (Jackal Johnson). Based on the books by Deborah Gregory.

Chef Donald (film) Donald Duck cartoon; released on December 5, 1941. Directed by Jack King. Donald is inspired by a radio program to make waffles but accidentally adds rubber cement to the batter resulting in so much havoc that he charges off to the radio station to give them a piece of his mind.

Chef Mickey's Restaurant at the Downtown Disney Marketplace at Walt Disney World; opened in July 1990. Formerly The Village Restaurant. It closed on September 30, 1995, and after extensive remodeling, reopened in 1996 as

the Rainforest Cafe. Also a restaurant in the Contemporary Resort, opening December 22, 1995, and taking the place of the Contemporary Café.

Chefs de France, Les Restaurant in France in World Showcase at Epcot; opened on October 1, 1982. It is operated by a trio of the finest and most-acclaimed French chefs, Paul Bocuse,

Roger Vergé, and Gaston LeNôtre, and has the reputation of having some of the finest food at Epcot. Whether one wants escargots or a tasty soufflé, here is the place to find it.

Chemistry Matters (film) Educational film; released in September 1986. 17 min. The film addresses the chemical properties of mixtures and solutions.

Chen, John S. Member of the Disney board of directors beginning January 23, 2004.

Chernabog The devil on Bald Mountain in *Fantasia*.

Cherokee Trail, The (television) Television show; aired on November 28, 1981. Directed by Kieth Merrill. The pilot for a series, later reworked as *Five Mile Creek* on The Disney Channel. A plucky woman and her daughter run a way station on a stagecoach line, to the great displeasure of the former manager, who plots to drive them off. From the story by Louis L'Amour. Stars Cindy Pickett, Mary Larkin, Timothy Scott, David Hayward, Victor French, Richard Farnsworth, Tommy Petersen.

Cheshire Cat A mischievous character in *Alice in Wonderland*; voiced by Sterling Holloway.

Chesney, Diana Actress; voiced Mrs. Judson in *The Great Mouse Detective*.

Chester & Hester's Area in Dinoland U.S.A. at Disney's Animal Kingdom consisting of Chester & Hester's Dinosaur Treasures, a gift

shop opening April 22, 1998, and Chester & Hester's Dino-Rama! consisting of TriceraTop Spin, Primeval Whirl, and Midway games, all of which opened November 18, 2001, except for Primeval Whirl, which opened April 18, 2002.

Chester, Yesterday's Horse (television) Television show; aired on March 4, 1973. Directed by Larry Lansburgh. A Belgian draft horse in Oregon is retired, but proves he still has value when he helps save a man trapped in a burning truck. Stars Bill Williams, Barbara Hale, Russ McGubbin.

Chevalier, Maurice (1888–1972) Actor; appeared in *In Search of the Castaways* (Professor Paganel) and *Monkeys, Go Home!* (Father Sylvain), and sang the title song in *The Aristocats*. He was named a Disney Legend posthumously in 2002.

Chicago City where Walt Disney was born, on December 5, 1901, at 1249 Tripp Avenue, a home that had been built by his father, Elias. (The houses on Tripp Avenue have been renumbered, and the Disney birthplace is now 2156 Tripp, at the corner of Palmer.) Elias started out as a carpenter in the city and eventually began building houses that were designed by his wife, Flora. He also built the church the family attended. The family moved to Missouri a few years after Walt's birth, but returned in time for him to attend one year at McKinley High School before joining the Red Cross during World War I.

Chicken in the Rough (film) Chip and Dale cartoon; released on January 19, 1951. Directed

by Jack Hannah. Chip and Dale, picking acorns, come across a nest of eggs. A baby chick hatches from one of the eggs and Dale, in trying to stuff the chick back into the egg, gets involved with the rooster and ends up trapped under the hen with the rooster pacing outside.

Chicken Little (film) Special cartoon, released on December 17, 1943. Directed by Clyde Geronimi. Foxey Loxey cons the farmyard chickens and dim-witted Chicken Little into believing his cave is the only safe place when the sky is falling. Once they enter, the chickens are devoured. Originally this film was planned to have definite wartime connotations—the fox would be reading *Mein Kampf* and the graves of the chickens would have swastikas for grave markers—but it was made generic so it would have more lasting appeal.

Chicken Little (film) Computer-animated feature that presents a new twist to the classic fable of a young chicken who causes widespread panic when he mistakes a falling acorn for a piece of the sky. Chicken Little is determined to restore his reputation, but just as things are starting to go his way, a real piece of the sky lands on his head. Chicken Little and his band of misfit friends— Abby Mallard (aka Ugly Duckling), Runt of the Litter, and Fish Out of Water—attempt to save the world without sending the town into a whole new panic. Released on November 4, 2005. Directed by Mark Dindal. Voices include Zach Braff (Chicken Little), Patrick Stewart (Mr. Woolensworth), Joan Cusack (Abby Mallard), Steve Zahn (Runt of the Litter), Amy Sedaris

(Foxy Loxy), Don Knotts (Mayor Turkey Lurkey), Garry Marshall (Buck Cluck), Wallace Shawn (Principal Fetchit), Dan Molina (Fish out of Water). 81 min. The film opened in 84 theaters in a new Disney digital 3-D process.

Chicken of the Sea Pirate Ship and Restaurant In Fantasyland at Disneyland, from August 29, 1955 to 1969. It then became Captain Hook's Galley until 1982. Originally, the ship was made entirely of the wood, but with wood sitting in water for so long, it began to rot. Over the years the wood was partially replaced by concrete. So when it was decided to remove the ship for the remodeling of Fantasyland, it was not possible to save it. To partially appease some of the Disneyana buffs, the Imagineers did try to save elements of the ship, by carefully prying elaborate plasterwork off the stern of the ship and placing in a truck. But when the truck hit a bump, the plasterwork fell over and broke into a thousand pieces. The ship has been re-created at Disneyland Paris as Captain Hook's Galley.

Chicken Plantation Restaurant In Frontierland at Disneyland, sponsored by Swift, from July 17, 1955 to January 8, 1962. The popular restaurant on the shores of the Rivers of America lasted until its space was needed for the expansion of Frontierland and the building of New Orleans Square, when it was torn down. In the early days of the park, the Chicken Plantation served the best meal in the park.

Chico, the Misunderstood Coyote (television) Television show; aired on October 15, 1961. Directed by Walter Perkins. A witness to his mother's death at the hand of a man, the coyote, Chico, has learned to hate and fear him. Taken into captivity and exhibited in a small desert roadside zoo, he learns much but never loses his bitterness toward his enemy: man. Chico makes his escape and bounds off for a life of adventure in the desert where he mates with Tula. He sees an eagle grab one of his pups and worries when his mate raids a chicken coop. Realizing the dangers of man, Chico decides to take his family deeper into the desert to help his family try to win the battle for survival. Narrated by Winston Hibler.

Chief Amos Slade's dog in *The Fox and the Hound*; voiced by Pat Buttram.

Child Molestation: Breaking the Silence (film) Educational film; released in August 1984. The film offers guidelines on how to identify symptons of child sexual abuse and how to respond and report it. It also shows how to teach children to protect themselves.

Child of Glass (television) Two-hour television movie; aired on May 14, 1978. Directed by John Erman. The Ainsworths have moved into a haunted house and son Alexander discovers a ghost of a young girl who needs a riddle regarding a glass china doll solved before she can rest in peace. Alexander and a neighbor girl try to solve the mystery, but are attacked by the estate's alcoholic ex-caretaker bent on revenge. They finally manage to find the glass doll and set the ghost free. Stars Barbara Barrie, Biff McGuire, Katy Kurtzman, Steve Shaw, Anthony Zerbe, Nina Foch, Olivia Barash, Irene Tedrow. Released on video in 1987.

Child Star: The Shirley Temple Story (television) Two-hour television movie; aired on *The Wonderful World of Disney* on May 13, 2001. At the height of America's Depression, the number-one movie star was Shirley Temple, a six-year-old with ringlet curls and dimples who tap danced, sang, and captivated the entire nation. She exemplified the genuine Hollywood star, complete with bodyguard, dolls and other merchandise in her image, and cemented handprints at Grauman's Chinese Theater. Directed by Nadia Tass. Stars Ashley Rose Orr (Shirley Temple), Emily Anne Hart (teen Shirley), Connie Britton (Gertrude Temple), Colin Friels (George Temple), Hinton Battle (Bill "Bojangles" Robinson). Based on Shirley Temple Black's autobiography, *Child Star*, she served as a consultant on this film. Filmed on location in Port Melbourne, Victoria, Australia. Released on video in 2001.

Childcraft Mail order company acquired by Disney in 1988.

Children of Japan, The: Learning the New, Remembering the Old (film) Educational film; released in September 1987. 21 min. A day in the life of Japan and its culture as seen through the letters of pen pals.

Children of Mexico, The (film) Educational film in the EPCOT Educational Media Collection; released on April 20, 1989. 26 min. A Mexican girl describes her lifestyle to an American pen pal.

Children of the Soviet Union (film) Educational film; released in September 1988. 22 min. Soviet history and culture as seen through the eyes of a Leningrad student.

Chim Chim Cher-ee Song from *Mary Poppins*, written by Richard M. Sherman and Robert B. Sherman. Academy Award winner.

China Pavilion in World Showcase at Epcot; opened October 1, 1982. The focal point is a recreation of the Temple of Heaven in Beijing; inside one could view some of China's unique scenery in the 360-degree motion picture presentation of *Wonders of China*. Many a person came out of the film presentation with a deep desire to someday see the real thing on a trip to China. An updated film, *Reflections of China*, debuted on

May 22, 2003. The China pavilion was one of the few World Showcase lands from opening day that did not have its own restaurant, which was a little surprising because of the popularity of Chinese cuisine with Americans. The Nine Dragons Restaurant finally opened in 1985 and has succeeded in winning several restaurant awards.

China Plate, The (film) Silly Symphony cartoon; released on May 23, 1931. Directed by Wilfred Jackson. A painted Chinese scene on a plate comes to life with a boy fisherman saving a young girl from drowning when she tries to capture a butterfly. A Mandarin chases the boy and girl after the boy accidentally jumps on him trying to capture the butterfly. They escape when the Mandarin runs into a cave, which turns out to be a dragon's mouth. They escape from the dragon when the boy rolls a huge boulder, which the dragon swallows. The boy and girl return to his fishing boat and kiss, as the China plate again becomes just a plate.

China Shop, The (film) Silly Symphony cartoon; released on January 13, 1934. Directed by Wilfred Jackson. As a shopkeeper closes his store for the night, his china pieces come alive; two figures dance until a china satyr runs off with the girl. The boy figure manages to save her and destroy the satyr, but also damages most of the store's pieces. When the resourceful owner arrives the next morning, he sees all the damaged items and changes his sign to read "Antiques."

China Voyager Restaurant Restaurant at Tokyo Disneyland; opened on July 21, 1992.

Chip The chipmunk with the black nose (think "chocolate chip"), who with his partner, Dale, made life difficult for Donald Duck. The chipmunks appeared in 24 cartoons, three in their own series. They made their film debut, unnamed, in *Private Pluto* (1943).

Chip The enchanted young cracked cup in *Beauty and the Beast*; voiced by Michael Pierce.

Chip an' Dale (film) Donald Duck cartoon; released on November 28, 1947. Directed by Jack Hannah. When Donald attempts to chop some firewood, he destroys the home of the chipmunks, who try everything in their power to save it from being burned, and succeed. Nominated for an Academy Award.

Chip 'n' Dale's Rescue Rangers (television) Television series; premiered on The Disney Channel on March 4, 1989, then syndicated beginning September 18, 1989. The chipmunks are leaders of a secret international organization devoted to tackling unsolved mysteries and mysterious oddball crimes. Other members of the Rangers are Monterey Jack, Gadget, and Zipper, and they battle Fat Cat and his cohorts. Voices include Corey Burton (Zipper, Dale), Peter Cullen (Maps, Kirby, Muldoon), Jim Cummings (Monterey Jack, Fat Cat), Tress MacNeille (Chip, Gadget). 65 episodes.

Chip 'n' Dale's Rescue Rangers to the Rescue Syndicated television special as a preview to the animated series, first aired on September 30, 1989. 120 min.

Chip 'n' Dale's Treehouse Attraction in Mickey's Toontown at Disneyland; opened on January 24, 1993. Ladders and slides make the treehouse a popular attraction for children. At Tokyo Disneyland, it is known as Chip 'n' Dale's Tree Slide.

Chips Ahoy (film) Donald Duck cartoon; released on February 24, 1956. Directed by Jack Kinney. Chip and Dale must steal a model ship from Donald in order to gather a plentiful supply of acorns on an island far out in a river. Donald's attempts to interfere are thwarted like always by the clever chipmunks, who get their food, inadvertently with Donald's help. Filmed in Cinema-Scope.

Chips, the War Dog (television) A German Shepherd goes to war in the K-9 Corps during World War II. A misfit dog paired with a misfit soldier, the two become a real team and eventually heroes. A Disney Channel Premiere Film, first aired on March 24, 1990. Stars Brandon Douglas (Danny Stauffer), William Devane (Col. Charnley), Paxton Whitehead (Smythe), Ellie Cornell (Kathy Lloyd), Ned Vaughn (Mitch Wilson). 91 min. Directed by Ed Kaplan. Released on video in 1993.

Chirac, Jacques French Prime Minister who signed the Euro Disney protocol with Michael Eisner on March 24, 1987.

Choices (A Story About Staying in School) (film) Educational film; in the EPCOT Educational Media Collection, released in August 1988. 27 min. Two very different high school students explore goal setting versus dropping out of school.

Choose Your Tomorrow (film) A film supervised by Dave Jones for use in Horizons at Epcot. It related three return trips to Earth: "Space," "Undersea," or "Desert," among which guests could choose. The film was produced in an empty hangar at the Burbank airport.

Chouinard Art Institute See California Institute of the Arts.

Christmas at Walt Disney World (television) Television show; aired on December 10, 1978. Directed by Steve Binder. Mimes Shields and Yarnell, as a robot couple, visit the Florida park. Other performers include Pablo Cruise, Andrea McArdle, Danielle Spencer, Avery Schreiber, Phyllis Diller.

Christmas Capers (film) Sixteen-mm release title of *Toy Tinkers*; released in October 1961.

Christmas Fantasy, A Holiday parade at Disneyland beginning in 1995. It superseded the Very Merry Christmas Parade.

Christmas Fantasy on Ice See Disney's Christmas Fantasy on Ice.

Christmas in Disneyland with Art Carney (television) Television special, airing on December 6, 1976. Directed by Marty Pasetta. A grumpy grandfather is persuaded to stay at Disneyland by his grandkids, and they witness Christmas festivities and special entertainment. Also stars Sandy Duncan, Glen Campbell, Brad Savage, Terri Lynn Wood.

Christmas in Many Lands Parade The Christmas parade at Disneyland from 1957 to 1964. It was succeeded by the long-running Fantasy on Parade.

Christmas Jollities (film) Shorts program; released by RKO in 1953.

Christmas Star, The (television) Two-hour television movie; aired on December 14, 1986. Directed by Alan Shapiro. A boy, having a miserable holiday, comes upon an escaped convict who he thinks is Santa Claus. The convict is trying to save his robbery loot, which is hidden in an old department store planned for demolition, and he enlists the boy and his friends to help. Stars Edward Asner, René Auberjonois, Jim Metzler, Susan Tyrrell, Zachary Ansley, Nicholas Van Burek, Fred Gwynne, John Payne.

Christmas Tree, The (television) Two-hour television movie, aired on ABC on December 22, 1996. Richard Reilly, the head gardener for Rockefeller Center, in searching for the perfect Christmas tree for the Center, locates one at the Brush Creek convent, but there he has a run-in with Sister Anthony, the convent's gardener, who has an unusual attachment to the tree and refuses to surrender it. The Sister and Reilly eventually forge a friendship, and she gives up the tree, but Reilly has to make a special trip to persuade her to come to New York for the unveiling. Directed by Sally Field, in her directorial debut. Stars Andrew McCarthy (Richard Reilly), Julie Harris (Sister Anthony), Trini Alvarado (Beth). Inspired by Julie Salamon's novel of the same name.

Christmas Visitor, The (television) A family on a drought-stricken sheep ranch in the Australian outback of the 1890s discovers the true meaning of Christmas with the help of an old vagrant who is mistaken for Father Christmas. A Disney Channel Premiere Film, first aired on December 5, 1987. Directed by George Miller. 101 min. Stars Dee Wallace Stone (Elizabeth O'Day), John Waters (Patrick O'Day), Nadine Garner (Sarah), Andrew Ferguson (Ned). Released on video in 1987 as *Miracle Down Under*.

Christopher Robin The boy character in the Winnie the Pooh films; voiced by a succession of actors—Bruce Reitherman, Jon Walmsley, Timothy Turner, Kim Christianson, Edan Gross.

Chronicles of Narnia, The: The Lion, the Witch and the Wardrobe (film) Four Pevensie siblings—Lucy, Edmund, Susan, and Peter—in World War II England enter the world of Narnia through a magical wardrobe while playing a game of hide-and-seek in the rural country home of an elderly professor. Once there, the children discover a charming, peaceful land inhabited by talking beasts, dwarfs, fauns, centaurs, and giants that has become a world cursed to eternal winter by the evil White Witch, Jadis. Under the guidance of a noble and mystical ruler, the lion Aslan, the children fight to overcome the White Witch's powerful hold over Narnia in a spectacular, climactic battle that will free Narnia from Jadis's icy spell forever. Directed by Andrew Adamson. Released on December 9, 2005, after a world premiere at Royal Albert Hall in London on December 7. A production of Walt Disney Pictures/Walden Media. Stars Georgie Henley (Lucy), Skandar Keynes (Edmund), Anna Popplewell (Susan), William Moseley (Peter), Tilda Swinton (White Witch), James Cosmo (Father Christmas), Dawn

French (voice of Mrs. Beaver), James McAvoy (Mr. Tumnus), Rupert Everett (voice of The Fox). 140 min. From the novel by C. S. Lewis. Production began June 28, 2004, in New Zealand, the Czech Republic, and London. Filmed in Super 35 Scope.

Churchill, Frank (1901–1942) Composer, joined the Disney staff in 1930 and wrote the music for many of the short cartoons, including *Three Little Pigs*. He also wrote the songs for *Snow White and the Seven Dwarfs* and *Bambi*. He was named a Disney Legend posthumously in 2001.

Cinderella (film) Animated feature; the famous rags-to-riches tale of a beautiful girl reduced to being a servant by her jealous stepmother and stepsisters, Anastasia and Drizella. With the help of a bit of magic by her Fairy Godmother, Cinderella is given a beautiful dress and use of a magnificent coach, and is able to attend a royal ball and inadvertently fall in love with the prince. Fleeing the ball at midnight, the hour when the magic spell is due to end, she leaves behind a glass slipper that the prince and Grand Duke use to search her out. With the help of her little mice and bird friends, she is discovered and assured a happy future. Cinderella was voiced by Ilene Woods, with Eleanor Audley voicing the Stepmother and Verna Felton the Fairy Godmother. Mike Douglas is the uncredited singing voice of Prince Charming. Released on February 15, 1950. Directed by Wilfred Jackson, Hamilton Luske, and Clyde Geronimi. 74 min. Songs include "A Dream Is a Wish Your Heart Makes," "The Work Song," "So This Is Love," and "Bibbidi-Bobbidi-Boo," all by Mack David, Jerry Livingston, and Al Hoffman, with "Bibbidi-Bobbidi-Boo" nominated for the

Academy Award for Best Song. The film also received a nomination for Best Scoring of Musical Picture. During its original release, the public made the film one of the highest grossing films of the year, and Disney's most successful release since *Bambi*. Because of wartime economic problems, the Disney Studio had had to be satisfied with its "package films" such as *Make Mine Music* and *Melody Time* for several years, but by the end of the 1940s, Walt Disney was able to put together the financing for another full feature telling a single story. It was a gamble for Disney, and if it had been unsuccessful, it probably would have sounded the death knell for animation at the Studio. But its resounding success ensured that animation would continue. *Cinderella* was re-released in theaters in 1957, 1965, 1973, 1981, and 1987. Released on video in 1988 and 1995.

Cinderella (film) Laugh-O-gram film made by Walt in Kansas City in 1922. Cinderella's only friend is a cat. When Cinderella hears of the Prince's ball, the Fairy Godmother appears and turns a garbage can into a Tin Lizzie in which she goes to the ball driven by the cat.

Cinderella (television) *Rodgers & Hammerstein's Cinderella* was produced many years before on television in versions starring Julie Andrews and Lesley Ann Warren, but this new version stars Brandy (Cinderella), Whitney Houston (Fairy Godmother), Whoopi Goldberg (Queen Constantina), Victor Garber (King Maximilian), Bernadette Peters (Stepmother), Jason Alexander (Lionel), Paolo Montalban (Prince), Natalie Desselle (Minerva), Veanne Cox (Calliope). Directed by Robert Iscove. Aired on *The Wonderful World of Disney* on November 2, 1997. 120 min. Most of the film's scenes were shot on stages at Sony Pictures Studios (formerly MGM Studios) in Culver City, California. Coincidentally, the Palace set for *Cinderella* was constructed on the same soundstage where Dorothy followed the yellow brick road to Oz in the famous 1939 MGM film. For the visual design of Cinderella, designers were inspired by the style of Austrian artist, Gustav Klimt, whose curious style was a synthesis of symbolism and Art Nouveau. To enhance the original musical score, and with permission from The Rodgers and Hammerstein Organization, three songs were added to the musical—"The Sweetest Sounds," written by Rodgers for the 1962 Broadway musical *No Strings*; "Falling in Love with Love," by Rodgers and Hart for *The Boys from Syracuse*, and "There's Music in You," by Rodgers and Hammerstein for the 1953 MGM film *Main Street to Broadway*. Released on video in 1998.

Cinderella: A Lesson in Compromise (film) Educational film; released in September 1981. Trying to get more than you need or deserve only leads to trouble.

Cinderella Castle Castle at the entrance to Fantasyland in Magic Kingdom Park at Walt Disney World. Teams of designers at WED Enterprises studied famous European palaces and castles, including Fontainebleau, Versailles, and the chateaus of Chenonceau, Chambord, and Chaumont. They also turned to the original designs for the 1950 *Cinderella* film prepared by the Disney animation staff. The chief designer for the castle was Herb Ryman, who also worked on Sleeping Beauty Castle at Disneyland park. King Stefan's Banquet Hall was located upstairs inside the castle. There is also a Cinderella Castle at Tokyo Disneyland, whose exterior is a copy of the one at Walt Disney World, but the interior contains the Cinderella Castle Mystery Tour rather than a restaurant. Disney purists for years wondered why the restaurant upstairs in the castle was called King Stefan's Banquet Hall, since King Stefan was the father of Sleeping Beauty, not Cinderella; this problem was rectified in 1997 with the renaming of the restaurant as Cinderella's Royal Table. During the celebrations of the park's 25th anniversary in 1996–97, the castle was transformed into a huge Cinderella Castle Cake, with large cake decorations and over 400 gallons of pink paint.

Cinderella Castle Mystery Tour Attraction in Fantasyland at Tokyo Disneyland; opened July 11, 1986.

Cinderella II: Dreams Come True (film) An animated film released direct-to-video on February 26, 2002. Cinderella is now married to Prince Charming and getting used to living in the Royal Palace. When the prince departs on a business trip, Cinderella has to try to follow the rules of Prudence, the King's strict household adviser. With the help of her mouse friends, Cinderella realizes she needs to bring her own style to the palace. Jaq yearns to be human, and his wish is granted by the Fairy Godmother, but he soon comes the realization that being human has its drawbacks. Romance is in the air, with stepsister Anastasia falling for the town baker, and the mice trying to set Lucifer up with the pampered palace cat, Pom-Pom, so they will be too busy to chase mice. Directed by John Kafka. Voices include Jennifer Hale (Cinderella). Christopher Daniel Barnes (Prince), Tress MacNeille (Anastasia), Russi Taylor (Drizella/Fairy Godmother/Beatrice/Countess Le Grande/Daphne/Mary Mouse), Rob Paulsen (Jaq/Sir Hugh/Baker), Corey Burton (Gus), Andre Stojka (King), Susanne Blakeslee (Stepmother), Holland Taylor (Prudence). 73 min.

Cinderellabration Show created for the 20th anniversary at Tokyo Disneyland beginning January 25, 2003. A new version of the show opened in front of Cinderella Castle at Magic Kingdom Park at Walt Disney World on March 17, 2005.

Cinderella's Golden Carrousel Fantasyland attraction in Magic Kingdom Park at Walt Disney World; opened October 1, 1971. The carousel was originally built by the Philadelphia Toboggan Co. in 1917 for the Detroit Palace Garden Park, later moved to Maplewood Olympic Park in New Jersey, where the Disney designers discovered it. The carousel was completely renovated, with scenes from Cinderella painted in the panels above the horses. The horses themselves are a marvel of craftsmanship; each one is different. Also in Fantasyland at Tokyo Disneyland, opened April 15, 1983, and at Hong Kong Disneyland (known as Cinderella Carousel), where it opened September 12, 2005.

Cinderella's Royal Table New name of King Stefan's Banquet Hall in Cinderella Castle in Magic Kingdom Park at Walt Disney World, beginning April 28, 1997.

Cinemagique A magical journey through a hundred years of European and American cinema, presented in the Studio Theatre at Walt Disney Studios Paris; opened March 16, 2002.

Cinémagique featuring Captain Eo Attraction in Discoveryland in Disneyland Paris, opened on April 12, 1992. The 3-D film was shown until August 17, 1998, after which it was replaced by *Chèri, j'ai rètrèci le public (Honey, I Shrunk the Audience)*.

CinemaScope The first short cartoon filmed in the wide-screen process was *Toot, Whistle, Plunk and Boom*; the first animated feature was *Lady and the Tramp*.

Cinergi Pictures Entertainment Inc. After a multiyear distribution deal with Cinergi was canceled in April 1997, Disney acquired Cinergi's film library, most of whose films had originally been distributed by Disney.

Circarama This 360-degree motion picture process debuted at Disneyland in 1955. The process originally required eleven cameras but later needed only nine. The name of the process was later changed to Circle-Vision 360 due to complaints from the owners of the similar-sounding Cinerama. See Circle-Vision/Circarama for a list of the films.

Circarama, U.S.A. Tomorrowland attraction at Disneyland showing a 360-degree motion picture filmed with a camera invented by Disney technicians; opened on July 17, 1955, sponsored by American Motors. The first film was called *A Tour of the West*. It featured eleven 16mm projectors, and ran for 12 minutes. In 1960 the motion picture *America the Beautiful* was substituted, with the process later renamed Circle-Vision 360 in 1967, and in 1984 World Premiere Circle-Vision.

Circle D Corral The Disneyland stables, until 1980 known as the Pony Farm.

Circle of Life: an Environmental Fable (film) Film shown in the Harvest Theater in The Land at Epcot, taking the place of *Symbiosis*. It opened on January 21, 1995. Directed by Bruce Morrow and Paul Justman. The combination live and animated fable has Simba, as king of the Pride Lands, counseling Timon and Pumbaa, who are clearing the savanna for a new development, about how to respect the environment. 13 min.

Circle-Vision/Circarama Process of 360-degree photography began at Disneyland in 1955. The various films have been:

1. *Circarama U.S.A. (A Tour of the West)*, Disneyland, 1955–1959. (11 cameras, 16mm)
2. *America the Beautiful*, Brussels World's Fair, 1958. (Opened at Disneyland in 1960)
3. *Italia '61*, Turin, Italy (for Fiat), 1961. (9 cameras, 16mm, blown up to 35mm)
4. *Magic of the Rails*, Lucerne, Switzerland (for Swiss Federal Railways), 1965. (Named changed to Circle-Vision 360, 9 cameras, 35mm)
5. *America the Beautiful*, Disneyland, 1967. (reshot film)
6. *Canada '67*, Expo '67, Montreal, Quebec, Canada, 1967.
7. *Magic Carpet 'Round the World*, Walt Disney World, 1974.
8. *America the Beautiful*, Walt Disney World, 1975. (revised version)
9. *O Canada*, Epcot Center, 1982.

10. *Wonders of China*, Epcot Center, 1982.
11. *Magic Carpet 'Round the World*, Tokyo Disneyland, 1983. (revised version)
12. *American Journeys*, Disneyland, 1984.
13. *Portraits of Canada*, Expo 86, Vancouver, British Columbia, Canada (for Telecom Canada), 1986.
14. *From Time to Time*, Disneyland Paris, 1992.
15. *Reflections of China*, Epcot, 2003.

Circle-Vision 360 Attraction in Tomorrowland at the Magic Kingdom in Walt Disney World, which has shown *America the Beautiful*, *Magic Carpet 'Round the World*, and *American Journeys*. See also World Premiere Circle-Vision. It closed on January 9, 1994, to be rebuilt as The Timekeeper.

Circus Day Thursday on the 1950s *Mickey Mouse Club*.

Circus Fantasy Entertainment spectacular at Disneyland in the spring of 1986, 1987, and 1988. Disney executives thought it would be good to have a special event at Disneyland during the off-season, so Main Street and the Hub area were turned into a circus. There was a circus parade, clowns, wild animals, along with various acts of skill featuring real circus performers.

Cirque du Soleil Custom-built theater at Downtown Disney West Side at Walt Disney World opened on December 23, 1998, to showcase a new production, "La Nouba." The show, performed by over 60 artists, blends circus art

and theatrics with a dazzling array of exotic costumes, magical lighting, and original sets and music.

Cítricos Restaurant at the Grand Floridian Resort and Spa at Walt Disney World, opening November 8, 1997, which offers a blend of Florida and Mediterranean cooking and features an exhibition kitchen. It replaced Flagler's.

City Fox, The (television) Television show; aired on February 20, 1972. A young fox unexpectedly finds himself in San Francisco, where, after many misadventures, he is befriended by a boy in Chinatown. The boy helps the Humane Society take the fox back to the wilds. Directed by James Algar. With Tom Chan, Jerry Jerish.

City Hall Information area on Town Square at Disneyland; opened July 17, 1955. Originally home of the Disneyland Publicity Department, it now houses Guest Relations and Main Street Operations offices. There are also City Halls at the other Disney parks.

Civil Action, A (film) A small-time, self-possessed personal-injury attorney's greed entangles him in a case that threatens to destroy him. The Woburn, Massachusetts, case (Anderson v. W. R. Grace and Beatrice Foods), regarding alledged water contamination—which appears straightforward—instead evolves into a labyrinthine lawsuit of epic proportions where truth, if it can be found at all, resides not in the courtroom, but buried deep in a network of deceit and corruption. A Touchstone Picture. Directed by Steven Zaillian. Released on December 25, 1998, in New York and Los Angeles, and nationwide on January 8, 1999. Stars John Travolta (Jan Schlichtmann), Robert Duvall (Jerome Facher), James Gandolfini (Al Love), Dan Hedaya (John Riley), Zeljko Ivanek (Bill Crowley), John Lithgow (Judge Walter J. Skinner), William H. Macy (James Gordon), Kathleen Quinlan (Anne Anderson), Tony Shalhoub (Kevin Conway). 115 min. Paramount split the costs on this production and handled overseas distribution. Based on the bestselling book by Jonathan Harr. Exteriors were filmed in Boston and New England, but the federal courtroom set was built on a soundstage at Universal Studios. Many of the real-life people who were depicted in the film visited the sets during production, and some even appeared in cameo roles. Released on video in 1999.

Civil War Several Disney films were set in the era of the Civil War, including *The Great Locomotive Chase* in the theaters and on television *Willie and the Yank*, *Johnny Shiloh*, *Million Dollar Dixie Deliverance*, and *High Flying Spy*.

Clair de Lune The Debussy piece was originally planned to be a part of *Fantasia*, and animation of flying cranes in an ethereal swamp was filmed, but when the film proved too long, the segment was shelved. Years later, a place for it was found in *Make Mine Music*, but that film featured more contemporary music, so the song "Blue Bayou" was substituted for "Clair de Lune."

Clara Cleans Her Teeth (film) Dental training film, made by Walt Disney after he moved to Hollywood, for Dr. Thomas B. McCrum of Kansas City, in 1926. Clara has problems with her teeth and refuses to see a dentist until she has a bad nightmare. Soon her teeth are fine and she can eat snacks at school without her teeth hurting.

Clara Cluck Operatic diva chicken character, who made her debut in *Orphan's Benefit* in 1934 and went on to eight more appearances. Voiced by Florence Gill.

Clarabelle Cow Bovine cartoon character known for her oversize nostrils and two buck teeth; appeared in 17 films, mostly Mickey Mouse cartoons of the 1930s, often paired with Horace Horsecollar. She made her debut in *The Plow Boy* (1929).

Clark, Carroll (1894–1968) Longtime art director on most Disney features and television shows from *The Great Locomotive Chase* to *The Love Bug*. He was nominated for an Academy Award for *Mary Poppins* and won an Emmy for *The Mooncussers*.

Clark, Dean He voiced Berlioz in *The Aristocats*.

Clark, Les (1907–1979) Leading Disney animator, the first of the Nine Old Men to join the company (1927). He specialized in animating  Mickey Mouse, beginning with one scene in *Steamboat Willie*. In his later years, he worked on directing educational films, and retired in 1975. He was named a Disney Legend posthumously in 1989.

Clark, Steven B. Publicist with Walt Disney Feature Animation and Disney Channel from 1997 to 2001, Steven co-authored *Disney: The First 100 Years* with Dave Smith, as well as writing several Disney trivia and other games for Mattel. He joined ABC in 2002, and later The Walt Disney Company as Director, Corporate Communications.

Clark, Susan Actress; appeared in *The Apple Dumpling Gang* (Magnolia "Dusty" Clydesdale) and *The North Avenue Irregulars* (Anne).

Cleanliness Brings Health (film) Educational film produced under the auspices of the coordinator of inter-American affairs. Delivered to them on June 30, 1945. Story of the difference between two families: the "clean" family that cares for their food and home and remain happy, and the "careless" family that lives in filth and are unhealthy.

Clements, Ron Animator/director, joined Disney in the early 1970s and worked as an assistant and animator on *Winnie the Pooh and Tigger Too, The Rescuers, Pete's Dragon, The Fox and the Hound,* and *The Black Cauldron.* He directed, with John Musker, *The Little Mermaid, Aladdin, Hercules,* and *Treasure Planet.* He left Disney in 2004.

Clemmons, Larry (1906–1988) Writer/storyman, hired by Disney in 1932 and, except for the 1941 to 1955 period when he left the Studio, continued to work on the stories for the Disney animated films. His writing credits on the features began with *The Reluctant Dragon* in 1941. He retired in 1978.

Cleo Goldfish character in *Pinocchio.*

Clerks (television) Miramax Television animated series produced by Walt Disney Television Animation, which had a short two-episode run on ABC starting on May 31, 2000, and ending June 7. Based on characters from Kevin Smith's 1994 movie *Clerks,* about goldbricking employees at a quick-stop food mart and next-door video store. Voices include Brian O'Halloran (Dante Hicks), Jeff Anderson (Randall Graves), Jason Mewes (Jay), Kevin Smith (Silent Bob).

Climbing High (film) Educational release in 16mm in January 1991, 25 min. A teen is pressured by his peers to try marijuana, but, as a dedicated rock climber, he discovers that the high he gets climbing mountains is far greater than any high he could get from a drug.

Clint and Mac See *The Adventures of Clint and Mac.*

Clock Cleaners (film) Mickey Mouse cartoon; released on October 15, 1937. Directed by Ben Sharpsteen. Mickey, Donald, and Goofy attempt to clean a huge clock on a high tower. Goofy is mystified by whoever is striking the bell, and when he is accidentally struck on the head by the bell-ringing figure, he begins to stagger dazedly about, performing daring acrobatics while Mickey tries to rescue him. Meanwhile, Donald fights a

losing battle against a cantankerous mainspring he is trying to clean, with Mickey and Goofy being flung by a flexible flagpole outside into the mainspring with Donald. All three end up bounced into one of the gears of the clock and onto the floor, where parts of their bodies continue to move in unison like a pendulum.

Clock of the World Icon at entrance to the original Tomorrowland at Disneyland, from 1955 to 1966. Showed the time in the 24 different time zones around the world.

Clock Store, The (film) Silly Symphony cartoon; released on September 28, 1931. Copyrighted as *In a Clock Store.* Directed by Wilfred Jackson. As night descends on a clock store, all the clocks come to life. A wall clock hits two alarm clocks when they are not looking, and referees the resulting fight. Figures from different clocks dance together. A grandfather clock dances with a grandmother clock. Two cuckoo clock birds bump heads as they both announce the time.

Clock Watcher, The (film) Donald Duck cartoon; released on January 26, 1945. Directed by Jack King. Donald works as a department store gift wrapper, but his job is threatened because of his tardiness, laziness, and playing with the merchandise.

Clopin's Festival of Foods Quick-service food court in Fantasyland at Hong Kong Disneyland; opened September 12, 2005.

Close, Glenn Actress; appeared in the live-action *101 Dalmatians* and *102 Dalmatians* (Cruella De Vil), on television in *South Pacific* (Ensign Forbush), and provided the voice for Kala in *Tarzan*.

Close-up on the Planets (film) Educational film; released in September 1982. Computer animation and footage from NASA space missions explain how our solar system evolved and the place Earth has within the system.

Clown of the Jungle (film) Donald Duck cartoon; released on June 20, 1947. Directed by Jack

Hannah. Photographer Donald is harrassed and driven half-mad by a crazy Aracuan bird who keeps sabotaging his photography of the jungle and its animals. The bird starred earlier in *The Three Caballeros* and *Melody Time*.

Club Buzz—Lightyear's Above the Rest Restaurant in Tomorrowland at Disneyland, formerly known as Tomorrowland Terrace; opened on June 30, 2001.

Club Disney A new concept in Disney themed entertainment opened on February 21, 1997, in Thousand Oaks, California, featuring a play experience for children aged four to ten and their parents. The four themed areas were called Pal Around Playground, Curiosity Castle, Starring You Studio, and The Chat Hat. Food was available in The Club Cafe, and there was a unique retail store. Birthday parties could be planned, and there were workshops on changing topics. Club Disney was the first location-based entertainment complex from the new Disney Regional Entertainment subsidiary. After five Club Disney sites were established, the clubs were all closed on November 1, 1999, when it was decided the return on investment was insufficient.

Club Lake Villas Accommodations at Lake Buena Vista that opened in August 1980; name changed to Club Suites in 1989. Originally aimed at conventioneers attending meetings at the Walt Disney World Conference Center, each villa had two queen-size beds and a sofa bed, with a sitting area separated from the bedroom area. Became part of the Disney Institute in 1996.

Club Suites Accommodations at Lake Buena Vista, formerly known as Club Lake Villas. Beginning in February 1996, when they became part of the Disney Institute, they were known as Bungalows.

Club 33 Private membership restaurant located upstairs in New Orleans Square at Disneyland, meant for Disneyland participants and VIPs and their guests. There are some private members, but there is a long waiting list. Opened on June 15, 1967. Also at Tokyo Disneyland, opened on April 15, 1983. The *33* refers solely to the street address, on Royal St.

Coats, Claude (1913–1992) Hired by Disney in 1935 as a background painter, he worked on such films as *Snow White and the Seven Dwarfs*, *Fantasia*, *Dumbo*, *Saludos Amigos*, *Make Mine Music*, *Lady and the Tramp*, *Cinderella*, and *Peter Pan*. In 1955, he moved over to WED Enterprises, where he helped design Pirates of the

Caribbean, The Haunted Mansion, the Submarine Voyage, the Grand Canyon and Primeval World dioramas, and for Walt Disney World the Mickey Mouse Revue, Universe of Energy, Horizons, World of Motion, and several World Showcase pavilions. He was one of the few Disney cast members to receive a 50-year service award. He retired in 1989, and received the Disney Legends award in 1991.

Cobb, Charles E., Jr. Member of the Disney board of directors from 1984 to 1987.

Coburn, James (1928–2002) Actor; appeared in *Sister Act 2: Back in the Habit* (Mr. Crisp) and *Snow Dogs* (Thunder Jack), and on television in *Elfego Baca*. He provided the voice for Kerchak in *Tarzan*.

Coca-Cola Refreshment Corner Located on Main Street at Disneyland; opened July 17, 1955. Coca-Cola is one of the few remaining opening-day participants at Disneyland. Also in Magic Kingdom Park at Walt Disney World, opened on October 1, 1971, and at Tokyo Disneyland, opened on April 18, 1983. At Disneyland Paris, it is Casey's Corner, and that name was applied to the Walt Disney World Refreshment Corner on May 27, 1995.

Cocina Cucamonga Mexican Grill Fast-food restaurant at Pacific Wharf in Disney's California Adventure; opened February 8, 2001.

Cock o' the Walk (film) Silly Symphony cartoon; released on November 30, 1935. Directed by Ben Sharpsteen. A farmyard battle ensues between a hick rooster and a city slicker over the love of a beautiful lady pullet, who discovers the city rooster is married. The hick avenges her, becomes the champ, and resumes his romance with her.

Cocktail (film) Returning from his military service, young Brian Flanagan finds his hopes dashed when he tries to find a career bringing him power, excitement, and quick personal profit. He ends up as a bartender, but under the tutelage of seasoned pro Doug Coughlin, his flashy expertise and killer smile make him a star on the club circuit, soon he is swept up in a seductive world of easy money and sex in New York and Jamaica. Eventually, a spirited romance with Jordan Mooney helps bring perspective to the cocksure bartender's life. Released on July 29, 1988. Directed by Roger Donaldson. A Touchstone film. 103 min. Stars Tom Cruise (Brian Flanagan), Brian Brown (Doug Coughlin), Elisabeth Shue (Jordan Mooney). Cruise and Brown spent several weeks at a bartending school, and soon each was adept at the flashy tricks that were so impressive in the movie. Filmed on location in New York City, in Jamaica, and in Toronto. Released on video in 1989.

Cody Young boy who tries to save the eagle in *The Rescuers Down Under*; voiced by Adam Ryen.

Cody, Iron Eyes (1904–1999) Native American actor, appeared in *Westward Ho the Wagons!* (Chief Many Stars) and *Ernest Goes to Camp* (Old Indian Chief), and on television in *Along the Oregon Trail* and *The Saga of Andy Burnett*. He hosted *The First Americans* on the *Mickey Mouse Club*.

Cody, Kathleen Actress; appeared in *Snowball Express* (Chris Baxter), *Charley and the Angel* (Leonora Appleby), and *Superdad* (Wendy McCready).

Cogsworth The enchanted mantel clock in *Beauty and the Beast*; voiced by David Ogden Stiers.

Cold-blooded Penguin, The (film) Segment of *The Three Caballeros* in which Pablo Penguin cannot stand the cold weather at the South Pole, so he sets off for warmer climes. 16mm release in December 1971.

Cold Creek Manor (film) Cooper Tilson and his wife, Leah, tiring of the hustle and bustle of New York City, pack up their kids and move into a recently repossessed mansion in the sticks of New York State. Once grand and elegant, the manor at Cold Creek is now a shambles, but the family has plenty of time to renovate. Then a mysterious former resident returns and a series of terrifying incidents occur at the house, leading the Tilsons to wonder about the family that used to live in their new home and what dark secrets are hidden inside. A Touchstone Picture. Directed by Mike Figgis. Released on September 19, 2003. Stars Dennis Quaid (Cooper Tilson), Sharon Stone (Leah Tilson), Stephen Dorff (Dale Massie), Juliette Lewis (Ruby), Kristen Stewart (Kristen Tilson), Ryan Wilson (Jesse Tilson), Dana Eskelson (Sheriff Ferguson), Christopher Plummer (Mr. Massie). 119 min. Filmed in Ontario, Canada. Released on video in 2004.

Cold Storage (film) Pluto cartoon; released on February 9, 1951. Directed by Jack Kinney. Pluto and a stork battle in the dead of winter for possession of Pluto's house, confiscated by the stork, until spring arrives.

Cold Turkey (film) Pluto cartoon; released on September 21, 1951. Directed by Charles Nichols. Pluto and Milton, the cat, are persuaded by a television commercial for Lurkey Turkey to cook one of their own, but the situation quickly explodes into a fight for the bird.

Cold War (film) Goofy cartoon; released on April 27, 1951. Directed by Jack Kinney. When Goofy gets a cold, he is tormented by a virus character until his wife comes home and puts him to bed. The virus goes away, only to return two weeks later when Goofy is back at work, but sitting in a draft.

Cole, Tommy Mouseketeer from the 1950s television show. Tommy became a makeup artist in later years.

Coleman, Dabney Actor; appeared in *Where the Heart Is* (Stewart McBain), *Inspector Gadget* (Chief Quimby), and *Moonlight Mile* (Mike Mulcahey), on television in *My Date with the President's Daughter* (President Richmond) and *Courting Alex* (Jack), and as the voice of Principal Prickly in *Recess: School's Out*.

College Bowl '87 (television) Dick Cavett hosted this game show for college teams on The Disney Channel, taped at Epcot.

Collegiate All-Star Band See All-American College Band.

Collette, Toni Actress; appeared in *The Sixth Sense* (Lynn Sear), for which she received an Academy Award nomination as Best Supporting Actress, and *The Last Shot* (Emily French).

Collins, Paul He appeared in *The Marrying Man* (Butler) and *Instinct* (Tom Hanley), and voiced John in *Peter Pan*.

Collins, Phil Composer; wrote and performed the songs in *Tarzan*, and received an Oscar for "You'll Be in My Heart." He provided the voice for Lucky in *The Jungle Book 2*, and wrote six songs for *Brother Bear*. He was named a Disney Legend in 2002.

Colonel Hathi Leader of the elephants in *The Jungle Book*; voiced by J. Pat O'Malley.

Colonel Hathi's Pizza Outpost Restaurant in Adventureland at Disneyland Paris; opened in April 1994. It took the place of the Explorer's Club.

Colonna, Jerry (1903–1986) He gave the musical recitation of *Casey at the Bat* and later was the voice of the March Hare in *Alice in Wonderland*.

Colony Theater *Steamboat Willie* was released at this New York theater on November 18, 1928. It later became the Broadway Theater.

Color The first Disney cartoon made in color was *Flowers and Trees* (1932). Walt Disney had the foresight to sign an exclusive two-year agreement with Technicolor for the use of their new three-color process in cartoons, so he received a terrific head start over the other cartoon producers in Hollywood. Disney then made every Silly Symphony in color, but for a time held off switching to color for the Mickey Mouse cartoons. The first Mickey Mouse cartoon in color was *The Band Concert* (1935) and soon all succeeding cartoons would be in color. Walt Disney made almost all of his television programs in color, which enabled them to be rebroadcast in color when he switched to color broadcasting in 1962. The few features that were made in black and white—*The Shaggy Dog, The Absent-Minded Professor, Son of Flubber*—had actually been planned for television, and the intricate special-effects processes utilized were thought to be less obvious in black and white. *The Absent-Minded Professor* was the first black-and-white Disney feature to be colorized, in 1986.

Color Gallery Display from Dutch Boy Paints in Tomorrowland at Disneyland from 1955 to 1963.

Color of Friendship, The (television) A Disney Channel Original Movie, first aired on February 5, 2000. In 1977, African American Congressman Ron V. Dellums and his family welcome a South African exchange student, but, expecting a student of color, they are surprised when a white South African arrives. Their surprise is no more than the girl's, a product of the Apartheid system who views black people as second-class citizens. The situation challenges them all with valuable lessons about racism and tolerance. Directed by Kevin Hooks. Stars Carl Lumbly (Ron Dellums), Penny Johnson (Roscoe Dellums), Lindsay Haun (Mahree), Shadia Simmons (Piper Dellums), Ahmad Stoner (Daniel), Anthony Burnett (Brandy Dellums), Travis Davis (Erik Dellums). The real Erik Dellums plays the role of Oliver. Released on video in 2002.

Color of Money, The (film) Former pool hustler Fast Eddie Felson sees promise in a cocky kid, Vincent. With the help of Vincent's girlfriend, Carmen, he takes the kid under his wing to prepare him for a major Atlantic City tournament. After a falling out, Felson takes up his cue stick again and the two end up playing against each other. Released on October 17, 1986. Directed by Martin Scorsese. A Touchstone Picture. 120 min. Stars Paul Newman (Eddie), Tom Cruise (Vincent), Mary Elizabeth Mastrantonio (Carmen), Helen Shaver (Janelle), John Turturro (Julian). Academy Award winner for Best Actor for Paul Newman. The filming took place in Chicago and Atlantic City. Released on video in 1987.

Color of Night (film) Haunted by the bizarre suicide of a patient, New York psychologist Dr. Bill Capa abandons his successful practice and relocates to Los Angeles. He soon finds himself entangled in an explosive sexual relationship with a beautiful but enigmatic woman named Rose, and the investigation into the brutal murder of a friend and colleague, Dr. Bob Moore. After he is persuaded by a police detective to take over his friend's counseling sessions, he is shocked to discover that the fanatic murderer, probably one of the group, is now stalking him. Released on August 19, 1994. Directed by Richard Rush. A Hollywood Pictures film, in association with Cinergi Pictures. 123 min. Stars Bruce Willis (Bill

Capa), Jane March (Rose), Rubén Blades (Martinez), Lesley Ann Warren (Sondra), Brad Dourif (Clark), Lance Henriksen (Buck), Kevin J. O'Connor (Casey). Filmed at a variety of locations in Los Angeles, California, and at the Ren Mar Studios in New York. The director's cut was released on video in 1995.

Colors of the Wind Song from *Pocahontas* by Alan Menken and Stephen Schwartz, won an Academy Award.

Columbia Distributor of the Disney cartoons from 1930 to 1932. In 1932, Walt Disney switched to United Artists.

Columbia Harbor House Restaurant in Liberty Square in Magic Kingdom Park at Walt Disney World; opened on October 1, 1971.

Columbia Sailing Ship Frontierland attraction at Disneyland; opened on June 14, 1958. The belowdecks exhibit, featuring re-created quarters of eighteenth-century American seamen, was opened on February 22, 1964. The original *Columbia* was the first ship to circumnavigate the globe in 1787, with the Columbia River in Oregon named after it when it explored the mouth of the river. Disney designers studied historical records to make their replica as accurate as possible. It only operates for guests on very busy days, but it has recently found additional use by taking on the guise of a pirate ship as a part of Fantasmic!

Colvig, Pinto (1892–1967) Storyman at the Disney Studio in the 1930s, and the original voice of Goofy. Also supplied the voices of The Grasshopper in *The Grasshopper and the Ants*,  the Practical Pig, and Sleepy and Grumpy in *Snow White and the Seven Dwarfs*. He helped Frank Churchill compose "Who's Afraid of the Big Bad Wolf?" in 1933. He resigned in 1937 but continued recording the Goofy voice from time to time and was named a Disney Legend in 1993.

Comanche (television) Television title of *Tonka* for its airing in 1962.

Come Fly with Disney (television) Syndicated television show from 1986 about flying, featuring the cartoons *Pedro*, *Goofy's Glider*, *The Plastics Inventor*, *The Flying Gauchito*, *Test Pilot Donald*, and segments from *The Rescuers* and *Dumbo*.

Comedy Warehouse Nightclub at Pleasure Island at Walt Disney World; opened on May 1, 1989. Professional and amateur comedians delight the guests.

Comet Café Food court in Tomorrowland at Hong Kong Disneyland, featuring Shanghai-style cuisine. It opened September 12, 2005.

Comets: Time Capsules of the Solar System (film) Educational film; released in September 1981. The film discusses the role comets play in contemporary scientific research about the solar system's beginnings.

Comic books The *Mickey Mouse Magazine*, which began publication in 1935, was actually the forerunner of Disney comic books. Starting out in large format, the magazine was reduced in size in stages until finally in 1940 it had reached normal comic book size. The final issue of the *Mickey Mouse Magazine* of September 1940, was succeeded the next month by the first issue of *Walt Disney's Comics and Stories*. The original cover price was ten cents. Even earlier than the *Comics and Stories*, however, there had been a few one-shot Donald Duck comics. Following these and later one-shots, Donald Duck comics began a regular monthly publication schedule in 1952, as did the Mickey Mouse comics. Artist Carl Barks began drawing the duck comics in 1942 and soon his unique style was exciting comic readers. He later created the character of Uncle Scrooge, who began starring in his own comic series, also in 1952. The comic books were created by artists employed by Western Publishing, not the Disney Studio. Dell Publishing was the original imprint, followed by Gold Key, then Whitman. Often a Disney movie or television show would be promoted by one or more special comic books. The comics reached a peak in September 1952, when over 3 million copies of a single issue of *Walt Disney's Comics and Stories* were sold. The 1980s brought changes to Disney comic publishing as Gladstone took over their production from Western Publishing for four years beginning in 1986, to be followed by several years of the Disney Studio producing the comics themselves. Gladstone returned in 1993, with Marvel handling a few of the comic lines. Gemstone Publishing began publishing the Disney comic books in 2003.

Comic strips The Mickey Mouse comic strip, distributed by King Features Syndicate, made its debut on January 13, 1930. Original artist Ub Iwerks drew the strip for a month and then was followed for three months by Win Smith. When Smith left, Floyd Gottfredson was asked to take over the strip for a few weeks until they could find a replacement. Gottfredson continued to draw the strip for 45 years, until the day he retired. The Mickey Mouse Sunday page began on January 10, 1932, and was drawn by Manuel Gonzales for over 30 years. A Donald Duck daily strip began on February 7, 1938, drawn by Al Taliaferro, who continued until his death in 1969. Taliaferro also did the Donald Duck Sunday page. Over the years, these artists were aided by various writers and inkers. There was a Silly Symphonies Sunday page, a Sunday page devoted to current Disney film releases, an Uncle Remus Sunday page, Merry Menagerie and True-Life Adventure daily panels, an annual Christmas strip, and Scamp and Winnie the Pooh strips.

Coming On (television) Variety series on The Disney Channel, hosted by Jimmy Aleck. 24 episodes. Features talent from different colleges performing the full spectrum of contemporary entertainment, from soft rock, rock, soul, and jazz, to comedy, pantomime, and regional specialties. Interviews and video capsules of campus life are included. First aired on September 3, 1983.

Commander in Chief (television) One-hour drama series that debuted on ABC on September 27, 2005. Vice President Mackenzie Allen has three children at home, an ambitious husband at the office, and she is set to become the first female president of the United States. Even though the current and dying president has asked her to step down and let someone "more appropriate" fill his shoes in the Oval Office, Mackenzie is unwilling to be a mere footnote in history, so she decides to trust her instincts and accept the job. Stars Geena Davis (Mackenzie Allen), Donald Sutherland (Nathan Templeton), Harry J. Lennix (Jim Gardner), Ever Carradine (Kelly Ludlow), Kyle Secor (Rod Allen), Julie Ann Emery (Joan Greer), Matthew Lanter (Horace Allen), Caitlin Wachs (Rebecca Allen), Jasmine Anthony (Amy Allen). From Touchstone Television and Battle Plan Productions.

Commando Duck (film) Donald Duck cartoon; released on June 2, 1944. Directed by Jack King. Donald helps battle the Japanese during World War II. With the aid of a rubber raft, he manages to carry out his instructions to wipe out an enemy airfield by causing a flood to wash it away.

Commissary, The See ABC Commissary.

Communicore The two primary buildings, known as Communicore East and Communicore West, in Future World at Epcot, radiating out from Spaceship Earth, and containing a variety of exhibits, displays, shops, and restaurants. In July 1994, it became Innoventions.

Community Service Awards Annual program run at both Disneyland and Walt Disney World to honor local service organizations with cash awards. The program began at Disneyland in 1957, with $9,000 being distributed; for its 25th anniversary in 1982, the total amount was up to $175,000, and in 2004, the amount was $440,000. Since 1957, Disneyland has distributed over $8.6 million.

Company D Cast member store at Disneyland, opened December 2, 1988. At Walt Disney World a Company D opened in the Team Disney Building on June 4, 1991, and at Epcot on April 1, 1992. Special merchandise, such as watches, buttons, and T-shirts, is often created solely for sale to cast members through Company D, and these items are coveted by collectors when they get out on the market.

Computer Software Division of The Walt Disney Company created to produce computer games and other software utilizing the Disney characters and films. Their first products were *Tron* games for Mattel Electronics' Intellivision and Atari in 1982. In 1988 they became Disney Software, which in turn became Disney Interactive in 1994.

Computer Wore Tennis Shoes, The (film) Dexter Riley, a science student, accidentally acquires all of the knowledge stored up in a used computer recently obtained for Medfield College when he tries to replace a fuse. The information includes data about a bookie ring, and Dexter's life is threatened, but he saves the day by capturing the crooks and winning a cash contest on television for dear old Medfield. Released on December 31, 1969. Directed by Robert Butler. 91 min. Stars Kurt Russell (Dexter), Cesar Romero (A. J. Arno), Joe Flynn (Dean Higgins), William Schallert (Prof. Quigley), Alan Hewitt (Dean Collingsgood), Richard Bakalyan (Chillie). The song "The Computer Wore Tennis Shoes" was written by Robert Brunner and Bruce Belland. Technical adviser Ko Suzuki, who was working on the Walt Disney World project at the time, was called upon to design and program some of the electronic equipment that was needed, and create graphs showing the comparisons of the human mind and a computer for use in Professor Quigley's classroom lecture scene. Released on video in 1985.

Computer Wore Tennis Shoes, The (television) Two-hour television movie; a remake of the 1969 motion picture, aired on ABC on February 18, 1995. The adventures of Dexter Riley, a not-so-brilliant college student who suddenly becomes the talk of the campus when he is struck by lightning when trying to reconnect a computer terminal, and becomes the repository of an enormous body of knowledge which he can call upon at will. Stars Kirk Cameron (Dexter), Larry Miller, (Dean Valentine), Jason Bernard (Prof. Quigley), Jeff Maynard (Gozin), Anne Marie Tremko (Sarah), Andrew Woodworth (Will), Dean Jones (Dean Carlson). Directed by Peyton Reed.

Computers Are People, Too! (television) Syndicated television show about computers featuring footage from *Tron*. First aired on May 23, 1982. Directed by Denis Sanders. Stars Elaine Joyce, Joseph Campanella, Michael Iceberg.

Computers: The Friendly Invasion (film) Educational film taken from *Computers Are People, Too!;* released in September 1982. Students are introduced to computers and their promise for the future.

Computers: The Truth of the Matter (film) Educational film; released in October 1983. A positive introduction to computers.

Computers: Where They Come From and How They Work (film) Educational film; released in April 1989. 9 min. History of computers from sticks and stones through microchips.

Con Air (film) When a group of the most dangerous and notorious prisoners in the U.S. penal system are transferred to a new super–maximum security facility, parolee Cameron Poe hitches a ride on their Con Air transport flight only to find himself embroiled in a meticulously planned midair hijacking masterminded by Cyrus "The Virus" Grissom. On the ground, U.S. Marshal Vince Larkin faces impossible odds as he tries to avert the takeover and, at the same time, keep his overzealous superiors from blowing up the aircraft and its passengers. Together, Poe and Larkin must stop

Cyrus and his band of savage, hardened lifers from massacring everyone on board as the damaged plane careens toward disaster on the famed Las Vegas strip. A Touchstone Picture. Directed by Simon West. Released on June 6, 1997. Stars Nicolas Cage (Cameron Poe), John Cusack (Vince

Larkin), John Malkovich (Cyrus Grissom), Steve Buscemi (Garland Greene), Ving Rhames (Nathan Jones), Colm Meaney (Duncan Malloy), Mykelti Williamson (Baby-O), Rachel Ticotin (Sally Bishop). 115 min. CinemaScope. Filming took place at airports in Utah—at Salt Lake City, Ogden, and Wendover—and on the strip in Las Vegas, where 14 cameras were utilized to film the blowing up of the front of the soon-to-be-demolished Sands Hotel. Interiors were filmed in Los Angeles.

Conch Flats General Store At the Old Key West Resort at Walt Disney World.

Concho, the Coyote Who Wasn't (television) Television show; aired on April 10, 1966. A coyote adopted by an old Navajo, Delgado, thinks he is a sheepdog, though he is not accepted by the other dogs of the area. Delgado stars as himself.

Concourse Steak House Restaurant in the Contemporary Resort at Walt Disney World;

opened August 10, 1994, on the site of the former Concourse Grill.

Condorman (film) Woody Wilkins, a comic book artist of "Condorman" stories, occasionally tests the character's comic gadgetry himself. Woody is asked by a CIA-agent friend to deliver diplomatic papers to a Russian agent with whom he falls in love, and when she offers to defect, he bumbles through a series of exciting and comic chases in trying to save her from the KGB. First released in England on July 2, 1981; U.S. release on August 7, 1981. Directed by Charles Jarrott. 90 min. Stars Michael Crawford (Woody Wilkins), Oliver Reed (Krokov), Barbara Carerra (Natalia), James Hampton (Harry), Jean-Pierre Kalfon (Morovich), Dana Elcar (Russ), Vernon Dobtcheff (Russian agent), Robert Arden (CIA chief). Suggested by *The Game of X* by Robert Sheckley. The movie was filmed at Pinewood Studios in England as well as on location in France, Monaco, Yugoslavia, Italy, and Switzerland. First- and second-unit crews filmed simultaneously in separate locations. While the principals filmed scenes with dialogue, the second-unit crew performed high-speed chases—in racing cars on stretches of road in southern France, and with boats in the Mediterranean off St. Tropez and Nice—rigged explosions and crashes, and performed aerial work on the tram cable at the Matterhorn and off the Eiffel tower. Automobiles and boats used in the movie were a speed enthusiast's dream: seven Porsche 939 Turbo Carreras comprised the deadly pursuit squadron of the Russian KGB; two Group 5 Lemans Porsches, competition racing cars, were used by the squadron leader, Morovitch, and the "Condor Car" was portrayed by four modified Sterling racers. Woody Wilkins's comic book inventions, which include a machine gun/walking stick, a laser cannon, self-propelling jet rods to ride the cable up the Matterhorn, and his semi-aeronautic Condorman wings, were built by Academy Award–winning special-effects artist Colin Chilvers. Released on video in 1981.

Conestoga Wagons Frontierland attraction at Disneyland, from August 1955 to September

1959. Guests were transported on the trails utilized also by the stagecoaches.

Confessions of a Teenage Drama Queen (film) Teen Lola Cep finds her life turned upside down when her family moves from New York City to the "cultural wasteland" of suburban New Jersey. As she juggles making new friends at a new school while standing up to a new rival, Lola finds it hard enough just to live her life, let alone remember how important it is to live her dream. Released on February 20, 2004. Directed by Sara Silverman. Stars Lindsay Lohan (Lola), Alison Pill (Ella), Megan Fox (Carla), Glenne Headly (Karen), Carol Kane (Miss Baggoli), Eli Marienthal (Sam), Adam Garcia (Stu). 90 min. Released on video in 2004.

Confessions of an Ugly Stepsister (television) A two-hour television movie airing on *The Wonderful World of Disney* on March 10, 2002. A provocative and sumptuous retelling of the Cinderella story seen through the eyes of the ugly stepsister, Iris. Directed by Gavin Millar. Stars Stockard Channing (Margarethe), Azura Skye (Iris), Trudie Styler (Fortune Teller), Emma Poole (Ruth), Jenna Harrison (Clara), Jonathan Pryce (The Master). Produced by Alliance Atlantis in Luxembourg. In Disney's 1950 animated feature, the stepsisters were named Anastasia and Drizella.

Connery, Sean Actor; appeared in *Darby O'Gill and the Little People* (Michael McBride), *Medicine Man* (Dr. Robert Campbell) and *The Rock* (John Patrick Mason). Three years after his *Darby O'Gill* role, Connery shot to fame as James Bond in the famous series of motion pictures.

Connors, Chuck Actor; appeared in *Old Yeller* (Burn Sanderson).

Conried, Hans (1917–1982) Actor, appeared in *Davy Crockett* (Thimblerig), *The Cat from Outer Space* (Dr. Heffel), *The Shaggy D.A.* (Prof. Whatley), as the slave in the Magic Mirror in several television shows, and as the voice of Captain Hook and Mr. Darling in *Peter Pan* and Thomas Jefferson in *Ben and Me*.

Consenting Adults (film) A happily married couple, Richard and Priscilla Parker, is tantalized by the lifestyle of their new neighbors, Eddy and Kay Otis. Richard is lured into an overnight wife-swapping arrangement with Eddy. The next morning, the police discover Kay, apparently brutally murdered, with Richard's fingerprints all over the murder weapon. With the help of a sympathetic detective, Richard discovers that Kay is still alive and must race against time in order to save the life of his own wife from the real killer. Released on October 16, 1992. Directed by Alan J. Pakula. A Hollywood Picture. 99 min. Stars Kevin Kline (Richard Parker), Mary Elizabeth Mastrantonio (Priscilla Parker), Kevin Spacey (Eddy Otis). Filmed in Atlanta, Georgia, and its suburbs, and on sites near Charleston, South Carolina. Released on video in 1993.

Conservation Station Climbing aboard the Wildlife Express train at Disney's Animal Kingdom at Walt Disney World, guests are transported to Conservation Station, where they are provided with a backstage look at the park's veterinary headquarters and center for conservation programs. They can meet animal experts, learn about the behind-the-scenes operations of the park, and discover more about Disney's global commitment to wildlife, and how they can help the animals they have viewed in the park. The facility was renamed Rafiki's Planet Watch in October 2000.

Consider the Alternatives (film) Educational release in December 1992, 20 min. In a magazine format, the hosts interview real kids about the many different decisions and choices they must make, and demonstrate the five steps to decision-making.

Considine, Tim Actor, appeared on television's *Mickey Mouse Club* as Spin in *Spin and Marty* (he had originally tested for the role of Marty) and as Frank in *The Hardy Boys*. He was also in

the *Annette* serial, on television in *The Swamp Fox*, and in *The Shaggy Dog* (Buzz Miller). He narrated *The Adventures of Clint and Mac*.

Constitution, The: A History of Our Future (film) Educational film; released in September 1989. 21 min. The history and significance of the U.S. Constitution.

Consumer Products See Merchandise.

Contemporary Resort One thousand forty-six room hotel at Walt Disney World; opened on October 1, 1971. The hotel, built in cooperation with U.S. Steel, was architecturally interesting, as the A-frame was built like an egg crate. The individual rooms were built elsewhere to the point where they were almost completely furnished; then they were slid into the framework by huge cranes. The Monorail was designed to glide through the hotel, above its fourth-floor level, and the interior of the A is open from there to the top. Disney artist Mary Blair designed huge 90-foot-high mosaic murals which cover the elevator core in the center. Besides the tower building, additional garden wings are built out from it. Meant originally as a convention hotel, the large exhibit space on the ground floor eventually became the vastly popular Fiesta Fun Center (later Food and Fun Center), where kids can spend their hours playing video games, watching Disney movies, or having a hamburger. A separate convention center was added in 1991.

Contraption (television) Series on The Disney Channel, hosted by Ralph Harris, with kids age seven through twelve competing to answer questions about Disney films, using a life-size, three-dimensional game board. Debuted on April 18, 1983. 40 episodes.

Contrary Condor (film) Donald Duck cartoon; released on April 21, 1944. Directed by Jack King. Donald, an egg collector, climbing in the Andes, is almost too successful when he pretends to be a baby condor when caught trying to steal an egg by the mother condor. Donald's attempts to escape with the egg are complicated by a baby condor and the mother's flying lessons. He loses in the end, still tucked under the mother's wing, along with the egg and the baby condor.

Contrasts in Rhythm (film) Special cartoon combining *Bumble Boogie* and *Trees* from *Melody Times*; released on March 11, 1955.

Conversation With . . . , A (television) Series of specials taped at Disney-MGM Studios in Florida for The Disney Channel, and featuring discussions and audience questions for such stars as George Burns, Carol Burnett, Bob Hope, Betty White. First aired in 1989.

Conway, Tim Actor; appeared in *The World's Greatest Athlete* (Milo), *The Apple Dumpling Gang* (Amos), *Gus* (Crankcase), *The Shaggy D.A.* (Tim), and *The Apple Dumpling Gang Rides Again* (Amos), and on television in *Walt Disney World Celebrity Circus*. He was named a Disney Legend in 2004.

Coogan, Jackie (1914–1984) Actor; appeared on television in *The Kids Who Knew Too Much*.

Coogan, Keith Young actor, appeared in *Adventures in Babysitting* (Brad), *Cheetah* (Ted), and *In the Army Now* (Stoner #1). As Keith Mitchell did the voice of the young Tod in *The Fox and the Hound* and appeared on television in *Gun Shy* and *Tales of the Apple Dumpling Gang*. On The Disney Channel he was in *Spooner* (D.B. Reynolds). Coogan changed his name in honor of his grandfather, actor Jackie Coogan.

Cook, Barry After coming to Disney in 1981 as an effects animator on *Tron*, he continued working on effects for the animated features. He directed the shorts *Off His Rockers* and *Trail Mix-Up*, and the feature, *Mulan*, with Tony Bancroft.

Cook, Dick Longtime president of Buena Vista Pictures Distribution, taking over from Irving Ludwig on the latter's retirement. He started with the company as a young man driving the train and Monorail at Disneyland. In 1996 he was named chairman of Walt Disney Motion Pictures Group, and in 2002 he became chairman of Walt Disney Studios.

Cooke, John Took over as president of The Disney Channel in 1985 when the channel had 1.9 million subscribers; oversaw the growth to over 8 million in less than a decade. In September 1994, he was named to head the Disney's America project, and in January 1995 he was named executive vice president, corporate affairs for The Walt Disney Company. He left the company in 1999.

Cookie Carnival, The (film) Silly Symphony cartoon; released on May 25, 1935. Directed by Ben Sharpsteen. As a beauty contest progresses, a poor girl cookie cannot attend because of her rags. But, with the help of an ingenious boy cookie and

the careful placement of candies and whipped cream, she wins the title of Cookie Queen and selects the boy as the king of the carnival.

Cookie jars, Turnabout See Leeds China Co.

Cookie Kid, The (film) Educational film produced by the Glynn Group; released in September 1981. The girl holding the world's record for selling Girl Scout Cookies shows how effective sales techniques and setting of personal goals lead to success.

Cool Runnings (film) When three determined Jamaican sprinters fail to make the Olympics, they enlist a has-been sledding expert to mold them into a bobsled team instead, and add an expert go-cart driver to their group. Through many hardships, not the least being the fact that there is no snow in Jamaica, they make it to the Olympics and earn the admiration of the world. Released on October 1, 1993. Directed by Jon Turteltaub. 98 min. Stars Leon (Derice Bannock), Doug E. Doug (Sanka Coffie), Rawle D. Lewis (Junior Bevil), Malik Yoba (Yul Brenner), John Candy (Irv). Based on the true story of the 1988 Jamaican Olympic bobsled team. The filmmakers traveled to Jamaica for the primary filming, and shot the Winter Olympics scenes in Calgary, Alberta, Canada. Released on video in 1994.

Coordinator of Inter-American Affairs See South America.

Copper Lead hound character in *The Fox and the Hound*; voiced by Corey Feldman (young) and Kurt Russell (older).

Cora, Jim He joined Disneyland as an attraction host in 1957 and after college moved into positions of increasing responsibility in management at the park. In 1971 he assisted in the opening of Walt Disney World, in 1979 became involved with operations planning for Tokyo Disneyland, and later headed Disneyland International, the division responsible for liaisons between American and foreign Disney parks. He retired in 2001 after 43 years with Disney. He was named a Disney Legend in 2005.

Coral Isle Cafe Restaurant on the second floor overlooking the lobby area in the Great Ceremonial House of the Polynesian Village Resort at Walt Disney World; opened on October 1, 1971. It closed on July 25, 1998, to reopen November 23, 1998, as Kona Café.

Coral Reef Restaurant Located in The Living Seas at Epcot; opened January 15, 1986. Large picture windows give diners an underwater view of the sea creatures swimming by in the pavilion's huge tank. The restaurant has been vastly popular since its opening.

Corcoran, Brian Child actor; appeared in *Babes in Toyland* (Willie Winkie), and on television in *Daniel Boone, Texas John Slaughter*, and *Elfego Baca*.

Corcoran, Kevin Actor; appeared in *Swiss Family Robinson* (Franz), *Old Yeller* (Arliss Coates), *The Shaggy Dog* (Moochie Daniels), *Toby Tyler* (Toby), *Pollyanna* (Jimmy Bean), *Babes in Toyland* (Boy Blue), *Bon Voyage* (Skipper Willard), *Savage Sam* (Arliss), *A Tiger Walks* (Tom Hadley), and on television in *Adventure in Dairyland* (Moochie McCandless), the role which gave him the nickname of Moochie, *Johnny Shiloh, Moochie of Pop Warner Football, Moochie of the Little League, The Mooncussers, Daniel Boone, The Further Adventures of Spin and Marty*, and *The New Adventures of Spin and Marty*. He provided a voice for *Boys of the Western Sea*, and voiced the title character in *Goliath II*. He later served as a production assistant at the Disney Studio.

Corey, Wendell (1914–1968) Actor; appeared in *The Light in the Forest* (Wilse Owens).

Corky and White Shadow (television) Serial on the *Mickey Mouse Club* during the 1955–56 season, starring Darlene Gillespie, Buddy Ebsen, Lloyd Corrigan, Buzz Henry, Richard Powers. Directed by William Beaudine, Sr. A sheriff's daughter and her German shepherd, White Shadow, get involved with a bank robber. 18 episodes.

Corky Romano (film) Good-natured veterinarian Corky Romano receives a surprising call from his long-lost father, "Pops," an underworld crime lord who has just been indicted by the grand jury and will soon go to trial. Pops realizes that his son is the one person who could infiltrate the FBI and abscond with the evidence against him. A computer hacker, intimidated into helping, goes overboard and makes Corky appear to be a superagent, a reputation he must live up to. As Agent Pissant, he tries to fake his way through one tough assignment after another while hunting for the elusive incriminating proof of his father's illegal activities.

Directed by Rob Pritts. A Touchstone Picture. Released on October 12, 2001. Stars Chris Kattan (Corky Romano), Peter Berg (Paulie), Chris Penn (Peter), Richard Roundtree (Howard Shuster), Vinessa Shaw (Kate Russo), Matthew Glave (Brick Davis), Fred Ward (Leo Corrigan), and Peter Falk (Pops). 86 min. Released on video in 2002.

Corn Chips (film) Donald Duck cartoon; released on March 23, 1951. Directed by Jack Hannah. Donald tricks Chip and Dale into shoveling his sidewalk after they dump snow on his just-shoveled sidewalk. They retaliate by stealing Donald's bowl of popcorn. When Donald builds a fire to smoke them out of their tree, the chipmunks dump a box of kernels into the tree, resulting in popcorn exploding all over the yard. Donald is back to shoveling the popcorn as if it was snow.

Coronado Springs Resort Moderately priced convention hotel, with more than 1,900 themed rooms and suites, at Walt Disney World; opened on August 1, 1997. Features Spanish-style roofs and sand walls, patterned after buildings in the American southwest. It has the largest ballroom at Walt Disney World, at 60,214 square feet. Dining facilities include the Maya Grill and the Pepper Market Food Court. An additional exhibit hall was added in April 2005.

Corpse Had a Familiar Face, The (television) Two-hour television movie; aired on CBS on March 27, 1994. A tough crime reporter is forced to examine her own life as she investigates the disappearance of an 18-year-old girl. Suggested by the autobiographical novel by Edna Buchanan. Directed by Joyce Chopra. Stars Elizabeth Montgomery (Edna Buchanan), Dennis Farina (Harry Lindstrom), Yaphet Kotto (Martin Talbot), Audra Lindley (Jean Hirsch), Lee Horsley (Ben Nicholson). See also *Deadline for Murder: From the Files of Edna Buchanan*.

Corti, Jesse Actor; he appeared in *Gone in 60 Seconds* (Cop) and *Bringing Down the House* (Italian FBI Agent), and voiced Le Fou in *Beauty and the Beast* and Jade in *Gargoyles*.

Cosby, Bill Actor; appeared in *The Devil and Max Devlin* (Barney Satin) and *Jack* (Lawrence Woodruff).

Cosmic Capers (film) Foreign theatrical release edited from *Mars and Beyond*. First released in England in December 1979. 18 min.

Cosmic Ray's Starlight Cafe Fast-food restaurant; opened on December 9, 1994, in Tomorrowland in Magic Kingdom Park at Walt Disney World taking the place of Tomorrowland Terrace.

Cost (film) Educational film from The People on Market Street series, produced by Terry Kahn; released in September 1977. The giving of a party is used to illustrate the economic concept of cost.

Costa, Mary Actress; she voiced Princess Aurora in *Sleeping Beauty*. She was named a Disney Legend in 1999.

Costello (television) Half-hour comedy series on FOX; debuted September 8, 1998, and ended October 13, 1998. Sue Murphy lives in the garage at her parents' home, works at The Bulldog, a neighborhood pub in blue-collar South Boston, dreaming of a better life beyond getting married like the other girls, living in the all-too-familiar neighborhood, and serving drinks at the pub. Stars Sue Costello (Sue Murphy), Dan Lauria (Spud Murphy), Jenny O'Hara (Lottie Murphy), Chuck Walczak (Jimmy Murphy), Kerry O'Malley (Trish Donnelly), Josie DiVincenzo (Mary McDonough). Produced by Touchstone Television/Wind Dancer Productions.

Cottonwood Creek Ranch Critter Corral In Frontierland at Disneyland Paris; opened April 12, 1992.

Cottrell, Bill (1906–1995) President of Retlaw Enterprises, the Walt Disney family corporation, from 1964 until his retirement in 1982. He joined Disney in 1929 as a cameraman, then worked as a cutter and animation director before moving into the story department. He was a sequence director on *Snow White and the Seven Dwarfs*, and worked on story on *Pinocchio, Saludos Amigos, Victory Through Air Power, The Three Caballeros, Melody Time, Alice in Wonderland*, and *Peter Pan*. Bill went on the 1941 Disney trip to South America. In 1952, he became vice president and later president of WED Enterprises, where he helped to develop the *Zorro* television series and assisted Walt Disney in the planning and construction of Disneyland. He was the first person to receive a 50-year Disney service award, and was named a Disney Legend in 1994.

Count of Monte Cristo, The (film) Alexandre Dumas's classic story of an innocent man, Edmond Dantes, wrongly but deliberately imprisoned on the infamous island prison of Chateau D'If and his brilliant strategy for revenge against those who betrayed him. After 13 years, he escapes from prison and transforms himself into the mysterious and wealthy Count of Monte Cristo, cleverly insinuating himself into the French nobility and systematically destroying the men who manipulated and enslaved him. A Touchstone Picture from Spyglass Entertainment. Released on January 25, 2002. Directed by Kevin Reynolds. Stars Jim Caviezel (Edmond Dantes), Guy Pearce (Fernand), Richard Harris (Abbe Faria), Dagmara Dominczyk (Mercedes), Luis Guzman (Jacopo), James Frain (Villefort), Henry Cavill (Albert). 131 min. Filmed on location in Ireland and Malta. Released on video in 2002.

Countdown at the Neon Armadillo (television) Television series; syndicated from September 17 to December 12, 1993. Spotlighted country western music. See also *Best of Country '92*.

Countdown to Extinction Attraction in DinoLand U.S.A. in Disney's Animal Kingdom, sponsored by McDonald's. Guests are transported back 65 million years to experience the cataclysmic events that ended the reign of the dinosaurs. It opened on April 22, 1998, changing its name to Dinosaur! on May 1, 2001.

Country (film) A soft-spoken farmer's wife, Jewell Ivy, demonstrates surprising heroism when faced with the government's forced foreclosure of her family's farm. Her husband, Gil, is nearly destroyed by the tragic turn of events. Jewell manages to hold her family together while enlisting the aid of other farmers facing the same problems. Released on September 29, 1984, after a premiere on September 28 at the New York Film Festival. A Touchstone film. Directed by Richard Pearce. 110 min. Stars Jessica Lange (Jewell Ivy), Sam Shepherd (Gil Ivy), Wilford Brimley (Otis), Matt Clark (Tom McMullen), Therese Graham (Marlene Ivy), Levi L. Knebel (Carlisle Ivy), Jim Haynie (Arlon Brewer), Sandra Seacat (Louise Brewer), Alex Harvey (Fordyce). The film was co-produced by actress Lange. Along with screenwriter/co-producer William D. Wittliff, Lange fleshed out the basic plot of *Country* and met with farmers in the Midwest whose livelihoods had been threatened by forced foreclosures. The start of production saw cast and crew in a race against the elements to film an Iowa corn harvest. Sam Shepard took the controls of a massive gleaner-combine, which harvested the crop. Next the company moved onto the key set some 20 miles northeast of Waterloo in the farmlands of Iowa. There, a turn-of-the-century farmstead, slated to be demolished by its owner who wanted additional acreage for growing feed corn, became the Ivy farm. For three months the company worked 12-hour days capturing the reality of farm living. A secondary location was the rural hamlet of Readlyn, Iowa, with its giant grain elevators and broad main street. Winter arrived sooner than expected, and during the climactic auction sequence in which 100 local townspeople appeared, the wind chill factor steadied at 25 degrees below zero. Director Pearce could only film in five-minute segments before the Iowans had to break for the barn where red-hot butane heaters unsuccessfully attempted to warm the icy air. The harsh winter caused the production to move back to the Disney Burbank studio where interiors and the tornado sequences were filmed. The affecting piano solos were provided by George Winston. Jessica Lange was nominated for an Academy Award as Best Actress. Released on video in 1985 and 1989.

Country Address Women's fashions at the Downtown Disney Marketplace at Walt Disney World, from March 1975 until July 23, 1994. Replaced by The Art of Disney.

Country Bear Jamboree Attraction at Walt Disney World Magic Kingdom Park; opened on October 1, 1971. This was the first major park attraction to debut at Walt Disney World and then to be copied for the other Disney parks. It features 18 Audio-Animatronics bears in a tuneful country-music show. The attraction was originally designed as a show for the Mineral King ski resort which Disney had planned on building in the 1960s. It was built later as a Bear Country (later Critter Country) attraction at Disneyland,

opening on March 24, 1972. A new show, *Country Bear Christmas Special*, with new sets, decorations, and costumes, debuted in November 1984, and another, *The Country Bear Vacation Hoedown*, in February 1986. These latter two shows now run seasonally each year. The Disneyland attraction was renamed the Country Bear Playhouse on July 4, 1986, and closed on September 9, 2001, to make way for a Winnie the Pooh attraction. Also in Westernland at Tokyo Disneyland; opened on April 15, 1983.

Country Bears, The (film) Like other celebrated rock-and-roll groups, the members of the legendary group, The Country Bears, were torn apart by the perils of their own success—ego, jealousy, and a little too much honey. An eager young fan, Beary Barrington, tries to convince the bitter ex-members of the rock band— brothers Ted and Fred Bedderhead, Tennessee O'Neal, and Zeb Zoober—to put aside their differences and perform a benefit concert to save Country Bear Hall, the legendary venue where the band got its start. Directed by Peter Hastings. Released on July 26, 2002. Stars Christopher Walken (Reed Thimple), Stephen Tobolowsky (Norbert Barrington), Daryl "Chill" Miller (Officer Hamm), M.C. Gainey (Roadie), Diedrich Bader (Officer Cheets and voice of Ted), Alex Rocco (Rip Holland), Candy Ford (voice of Trixie), James Gammon (voice of Big Al), Brad Garrett (voice of Fred), Toby Huss (voice of Tennessee), Kevin Michael Richardson (voice of Henry), Stephen Root (voice of Zeb), Haley Joel Osment (voice of Beary). 88 min. Featured are musical performances or appearances by real-life rock-and-roll legends Don Henley, John Hiatt, Elton John, Queen Latifah, Willie Nelson, Bonnie Raitt, and Brian Setzer. Inspired by the attraction at the Walt Disney World. Ironically, the Country Bear Playhouse at Disneyland closed in the previous year. A full-size Country Bear Hall for the movie was constructed at the Disney Golden Oak Ranch in Newhall, California. The Animatronic bear suits were created by the Jim Henson Creature Shop. Released on video in 2002.

Country Cousin, The (film) Silly Symphony cartoon; released on October 31, 1936. Directed by Wilfred Jackson. Academy Award winner for Best Cartoon. Abner, a mouse from the rural town of Podunk goes to visit his glamorous big-city cousin, Monty. But when he accidentally gets drunk, is chased by a cat, and meets

other terrors of big city life, he quickly heads for home.

Country Coyote Goes Hollywood, A (film) Featurette; released on January 28, 1965. Directed by Winston Hibler. Chico the coyote manages to hitch a ride to Los Angeles and has all sorts of misadventures with the local residents. He is finally sent away to live in the wild, only to hitch another ride to New York. The main title sequences are done as if imprinted in the cement of Grauman's Chinese Theater in Hollywood. 37 min.

Country Estates (television) One-hour pilot for a television series; aired on July 10, 1993. The Reed family moves to a suburban dream home, and while they try to cope with the pain of one son's death, the other becomes entangled in the apparent murder of a neighbor. Directed by Donald Petrie. Stars Scott Bairstow, Tom Irwin, Michelle Kelly, Perry King, Tina Lifford, Jason London, Patrick Y. Malone, Vinessa Shaw, Barbara Williams, Bruce A. Young.

Country Manor Shop in the United Kingdom in World Showcase at Epcot; opened January 5, 1986. Formerly Biscuit Barrel.

Court, The (television) Hour-long television series on ABC debuting on March 26, 2002, and ending on April 9, 2002. Kate Nolan is the newest appointed Supreme Court justice, who must prove herself in a deeply divided Court. At the same time, an aggressive television reporter, Harlan Brandt, covers the Court in a manner often at cross-purposes to the sanctity of the institution. Stars Sally Field (Kate Nolan), Pat Hingle (Chief Justice Amos Townsend), Diahann Carroll (Angela DeSett), Nicole DeHuff (Alexis Cameron), Hill Harper (Christopher Bell), Christina Hendricks (Betsy Tyler), Josh Radnor (Dylan Hirsch) Miguel Sandoval (Roberto Martinez), Chris Sarandon (Lucas Voorhees), Craig Bierko (Harlan Brandt).

Courtesy Is Caring (film) Educational film; released in September 1987. 6 min. The role of courtesy in friendship and daily life.

Courting Alex (television) Half-hour comedy series; premiered on CBS on January 23, 2006. Bex Atwell, an attractive secretary, has simple goals: find true love, have an exciting career, and have a normal relationship with her father. But, in a world where men behave like, well . . . men, she realizes that she may be overly ambitious. Bex is determined to find out what men are all about while wondering why women even bother to try to understand them in the first place. Stars Jenna Elfman (Bex), Dabney Coleman (Jack), Brady Smith (Rob), Rhea Seehorn (Chris), Hugh Bonneville (Charles), Lauren Tom (Jan). From Touchstone Television and Paramount Network Television.

Courtland, Jerome Actor; appeared as Andy Burnett on television and in *Tonka* (Lt. Henry Nowlan). He later became a producer at the Disney Studio.

Courtyard by Marriott Hotel at Lake Buena Vista at Walt Disney World; opened on January 20, 1995, taking the place of the Howard Johnson Resort Hotel, which was remodeled and renamed. It closed on December 30, 2003, to become a Holiday Inn.

Courvoisier Galleries Art dealer Guthrie Courvoisier had the foresight to see the value of Disney cels and other artwork, and through his gallery in San Francisco, he sold Disney art, including pieces from *Snow White and the Seven Dwarfs*, *Pinocchio*, *Fantasia*, *Dumbo*, and *Bambi*, from 1938 to 1946. This artwork, which he priced from a few dollars up to perhaps fifty dollars for the most elaborate pieces with original production backgrounds, is today often worth many thousands of dollars.

Cow Dog (film) Featurette; released on November 6, 1956. Directed by Larry Lansburgh. 22 min. Tells the story of a California ranch family who, in their devotion to the raising of purebred Hereford cattle, must capture an outlaw Brahma bull. A neighboring rancher brings his three Australian herding dogs, Stub, Queen, and Shorty, to help in the roundup to apprehend the bull. They are greeted with enthusiasm because of their abil-

ity, and they eventually manage to flush out the bull. Originally released with *Secrets of Life*. Nominated for an Academy Award.

Cowboy Cookout Barbecue Restaurant in Frontierland in Disneyland Paris; opened on April 12, 1992.

Cowboy Needs a Horse, A (film) Special cartoon; released on November 6, 1956. Directed by Bill Justice. In this short featuring limited animation, a little boy dreams of such Western adventures as battling Indians, capturing a bandit, and rescuing a fair damsel. Features the song "A Cowboy Needs a Horse," by Paul Mason Howard and Billy Mills.

Cox, Brian Actor; appeared in *Iron Will* (Angus McTeague), *Rushmore* (Dr. Guggenheim), *The Rookie* (Jim Morris, Sr.), and *25th Hour* (James Brogan).

Cox, Wally (1912–1973) Actor; appeared in *The One and Only, Genuine, Original Family Band* (Mr. Wampler), *The Boatniks* (Jason), and *The Barefoot Executive* (Mertons), and on television in *The Wacky Zoo of Morgan City*.

Coyote, Peter Actor; appeared in *Outrageous Fortune* (Michael), and on The Disney Channel in *The Blue Yonder* (Max).

Coyote Ugly (film) A talented 21-year-old singer, Violet Sanford, moves to Manhattan looking for her big career break in show business. Eventually she is discovered while performing in a popular Western bar, the Coyote Ugly, in Greenwich Village, where sexy, enterprising young women tantalize customers and the media alike with their outrageous antics. Violet finds success, and a genuine fan and love-struck admirer in a young chef named Kevin. Released on August 4, 2000. A Touchstone Pictures/Jerry Bruckheimer film. Directed by David McNally. Stars Piper Perabo (Violet Sanford), Adam Garcia (Kevin), Maria

Bello (Lil), Malanie Lynskey (Gloria), Izabella Miko (Cammie), Bridget Moynahan (Rachel), Tyra Banks (Zoe), John Goodman (Bill Sanford). 101 min. Filmed in CinemaScope. Released on video in 2001.

Coyote's Lament, The (television) Television show; aired on March 5, 1961. Directed by C. August Nichols. A coyote tells about his problems with man and his dogs in this animated compilation of Disney cartoons, with songs sung by the Sons of the Pioneers. Released theatrically abroad in 1968.

Crack: The Big Lie (film) Educational film; released in February 1987. Based on actual case studies, a lesson on saying "No."

Cradle Will Rock (film) The art and theater world of 1930s New York City is in the midst of a burgeoning cultural revolution. Different stories are interwoven to show how individual courage stood in the face of censorship and artists risked their livelihood by performing in shows and painting their canvasses. Nelson Rockefeller hires Mexican artist Diego Rivera to paint the lobby of Rockefeller Center, an Italian propagandist sells da Vincis to help fund the Mussolini war effort, and a paranoid ventriloquist tries to rid his vaudeville troupe of communists. The title refers to an infamous stage production being staged by Orson Welles' Federal Theater group, closed down on the eve of opening by soldiers. Released on December 8, 1999, in New York and Los Angeles, and beginning December 25, 1999, elsewhere. Directed by Tim Robbins. A Touchstone Picture. Stars Hank Azaria (Marc Blitzstein), Ruben Blades (Diego Rivera), John Cusack (Nelson Rockefeller), Cary Elwes (John Houseman), Philip Baker Hall (Grey Mathers), Cherry Jones (Hallie Flanagan), Angus MacFadyen (Orson Welles), Bill Murray (Tommy Crickshaw), Vanessa Redgrave (Countess La Grange), Susan Sarandon (Margherita Sarfatti), John Turturro (Aldo Silvano). 134 min. Filmed in CinemaScope. Released on video in 2000.

Craig, Scott (1964–2003) Mouseketeer on the new *Mickey Mouse Club*.

Cramer, Joey Child actor; appeared in *Flight of the Navigator* (David Freeman), and on television in *I-Man*.

Crane, Bob (1928–1978) Actor; appeared in *Superdad* (Charlie McReady) and *Gus* (Pepper).

Crane Company Bathroom of Tomorrow Display in Tomorrowland at Disneyland from April 5, 1956 to August 31, 1960. While an unlikely subject for Disneyland, it was actually quite intriguing to guests, for it featured the latest ideas in bathroom design. In the forecourt area, guests could turn large wheels to adjust the height of columns of water in a fountain.

Cranium Command Attraction in Wonders of Life in Future World at Epcot; opened October 19, 1989. Guests sit in a theater that doubles as the control room for the brain of a 12-year-old boy, Bobby. The fearless leader, General Knowledge, has put a rookie, Buzzy, in charge of Bobby's brain. Looking through Bobby's eyes, guests can see him go about his daily activities and witness the havoc created among the characters who run his brain as various things happen to him. Stars George Wendt, Dana Carvey, Charles Grodin, Bobcat Goldthwait, Kevin Nealon.

Crawford, Johnny Mouseketeer from the 1950s television show.

Crawford, Michael Actor; appeared as Woody Wilkins in *Condorman*.

Crazy/Beautiful (film) Nicole Oakley, the troubled daughter of a wealthy congressman, attends public school in the upscale community of Pacific Palisades. As an act of defiance, she makes a play for the attentions of Carlos Nuñez, a straight-A student who rides the bus for two hours each morning from his East Los Angeles home, and the rebellious flirtation develops into true romance. However, Nicole's self-destructive tendencies threaten Carlos' ambitions, leading to an emotional and climactic confrontation. Directed by John Stockwell. A Touchstone Picture. Released on July 20, 2001. Stars Kirsten Dunst (Nicole Oakley), Jay Hernandez (Carlos Nuñez), Lucinda Jenney (Courtney), Taryn Manning (Maddy), Rolando Molina (Hector), Bruce Davison (Congressman Tom Oakley). 99 min. Filmed on location in Pacific Palisades, Santa Monica, and Los Angeles. Released on video in 2001.

Crazy Over Daisy (film) Donald Duck cartoon; released on March 24, 1950. Directed by Jack Hannah. When Donald attempts to get revenge on the chipmunks for wrecking his bike

on his trip to Daisy's house, she scolds him for his cruel conduct.

Crazy with the Heat (film) Donald Duck and Goofy cartoon; released on August 1, 1947. Directed by Bob Carlson. Donald and Goofy, wandering helplessly in the desert when their car runs out of gas, begin to see mirages.

Creative Film Adventures, #1 (film) Educational film, released in July 1976, which used segments of *One Day on Beetle Rock*, *The Three Caballeros*, and *Mars and Beyond* to inspire students to express their own feelings or interpretations through writing.

Creative Film Adventures, #2 (film) Educational film, released in July 1976, which used *Wynken, Blynken and Nod* and a sequence from *Perri*, along with the *Clair de Lune* sequence meant for *Fantasia*, to get children to use their imaginations.

Creeper Reptilelike henchman of the Horned King in *The Black Cauldron*; voiced by Phil Fondacaro.

Creole Cafe Restaurant in New Orleans Square at Disneyland, from 1966 to 1972. Became Cafe Orleans.

Crest Theatre Theater in Westwood Village near UCLA that had a relationship to run Disney films from 1987 to 2002. Pacific Theaters, which had bought the theater in 1985, partnered with Disney. Disney hired noted theater designer Joe Musil to create a design and work with Disney Imagineers to totally refurbish the theater. The first phase of the renovations consisted of adding a new marquee and upgrading the projection and sound system and screen, leading up to an opening of *Three Men and a Baby* in 1987. The second phase made the theater look Art Deco, with a lobby, auditorium, and restroom rehab, new carpet, and recovered seats. The renovations were completed in time for *Big Business* to open in 1988.

Crew, The (film) Four former wiseguys, Bobby Bartellemeo, Joey "Bats" Pistella, Mike "The Brick" Donatelli, and Tony "The Mouth" Donato, are now getting on in years and living at the ratty Raj Mahal senior citizen residence hotel in South Beach, Miami. Management's plans for renovations of the building to force higher rents and attract a classier clientele are squeezing the geezers out. So they hatch a seemingly simple scheme to save their retirement residence. Their caper goes awry and inadvertently entangles a paranoid drug lord who is convinced that he is about to be rubbed out by a mysterious gangland rival. Released on August 25, 2000. Directed by Michael Dinner. A Touchstone Pictures film. Stars Richard Dreyfuss (Bobby Bartellemeo), Burt Reynolds (Joey Pistella), Dan Hedaya (Mike Donatelli), Seymour Cassell (Tony Donato), Carrie-Anne Moss (Olivia Neal), Jennifer Tilly (Ferris), Lainie Kazan (Pepper Lowenstein), Miguel Sandoval (Raul Ventana), Jeremy Piven (Det. Steve Menteer). 88 min. Released on video in 2001.

Crimes of Fashion (television) An ABC Family Original Movie; aired on July 25, 2004. Brooke, a shy yet creative student at the top fashion school in the country, has her world change when the family she never knew needs her. Mob boss Dominic dies and leaves her in charge of the family business, a bumbling crime syndicate that has been trying to go legit. At the same time, the handsome new student Brooke is falling for is actually an undercover FBI agent aiming to get dirt on her to bring down the family empire. Directed by Stuart Gillard. Stars Kaley Cuoco (Brooke), Dominic Chianese (George), Megan Fox (Candace), James Kall (Bartender), Serena Lee (Page), Chuck Shamata (Sal Hugo), David Sparrow (Bruno).

Criminal Minds (television) One-hour drama series airing on CBS; debuted on September 22, 2005. An elite squad of FBI profilers analyzes the country's most twisted criminal minds, anticipating their next move before they strike again. Leading the team is Special Agent Jason Gideon, the FBI's top behavioral analyst. The experts on Gideon's team include Special Agent Dr. Reid, a classically misunderstood genius; Special Agent Aaron Hotch, a family man who is able to gain people's trust and unlock their secrets; Special Agent Derek Morgan, an expert on obsessional crimes; and Elle Greenway, an agent with a background in sexual offenses. Stars Mandy Patinkin (Jason Gideon), Thomas Gibson (Aaron Hotch), Shemar Moore (Derek Morgan), Lola Glaudini (Elle Greenway), Matthew Gubler (Dr. Reid). From Touchstone Television and Paramount Network Television.

Crimson Tide (film) When an American emergency patrol on a nuclear submarine receives an urgent but unverified message to launch a strike against rebel Russian missile sites, confusion and chaos erupt onboard between rival officers, bringing the world to the brink of nuclear disaster. Released on May 12, 1995. Directed by Tony Scott. 116 min. A Hollywood Pictures film. Stars Denzel Washington (Hunter), Gene Hackman (Ramsey), George Dzundza (Cob), Viggo Mortensen (Weps), James Gandolfini (Lt. Bobby Daugherty), Matt Craven (Zimmer). Filmed in CinemaScope. Sets for the interior of the USS *Alabama* were constructed at the Culver Studios, with the largest hydraulic gimbal ever con-

structed created to simulate the sub's movement. One scene about the flooding of the *Alabama*'s bilge bay was shot for 14 hours one night in the chilly waters of the Culver City Municipal Pool. A 44-foot square cargo container housing the sets and cast was slowly lowered into the pool while the cameras rolled. Filming took place over 15 weeks, aided by two technical advisers who were both former commanding officers of the real USS *Alabama*. Released on video in 1995.

Crisler Story, The/Prowlers of the Everglades (television) Television show; aired on February 27, 1957. Directed by James Algar. Behind the scenes of *White Wilderness* with photographer team Herb and Lois Crisler spending over a year trying to get the right footage of the annual migration of the caribou, and an airing of the True-Life Adventure featurette about the Florida Everglades. Narrated by Winston Hibler.

Crisp, Donald (1880–1974) Actor; appeared in *Pollyanna* (Mayor Carl Warren) and *Greyfriars Bobby* (James Brown).

Cristal d'Orleans Shop on Royal Street in New Orleans Square at Disneyland; opened on July 24, 1966.

Cristobalito, the Calypso Colt (television) Television show; aired on September 13, 1970. In Puerto Rico, a young stable boy, Chago, steals an injured Paso Fino colt to save him from death, and nurses him back to health with the help of friends and neighbors. Chago has to convince the horse's owner that Cristobalito is ready for the All Island Horse Championships. Stars Roberto Vigoreaux, Walter Buso.

Critter Country Land at Disneyland; opened on November 23, 1988. When Splash Mountain was under construction, it was decided to change the name of the area from Bear Country, when the Country Bear Jamboree had been its biggest draw, to Critter Country, which would encompass the bears as well as the new critters who inhabited Splash Mountain. The ambience of the land remained refreshing—tall, shady trees giving a cool forest feel to the area, with rustic buildings nestled among them.

Crockett's Tavern Food facility at Fort Wilderness Resort at Walt Disney World; opened August 18, 1986. It took the place of the Campfire Snack Bar.

Crocodile Mercantile Shop in Critter Country at Disneyland; renamed from Ursus H. Bear's Wilderness Outpost on November 23, 1988. It closed in 1995 to become Pooh Corner.

Cronkite, Walter News commentator, provided narration that was used in the Spaceship Earth attraction at Epcot from 1986 to 1994, and appeared with Robin Williams in *Back to Neverland* in the Animation Studio tour at Disney-MGM Studios.

Crosby, Bing (1903–1977) Actor/singer; narrated the *Ichabod Crane* segment of *The Adventures of Ichabod and Mr. Toad*.

Cross, Marcia Actress; appeared on television in *Desperate Housewives* (Bree Van De Kamp).

CrossGen Enterprises In November 2004, Disney announced that it had acquired the assets of CrossGen Enterprises, a Tampa-based publisher of fantasy and sci-fi comic books.

Crossing the Bridge (film) Three teenage buddies, tempted by the promise of a lot of cash, confront their values and ethics when a pal asks them to smuggle drugs across the U.S./Canada border bridge. When the boys discover the package contains heroin instead of the promised hashish, they come to realize that their actions, and the potential consequences, may well affect them for the rest of their lives. Released on September 11, 1992. Directed by Mike Bender. A Touchstone Picture. 103 min. Stars Josh Charles (Mort Golden), Jason Gedrick (Tim Reese), Stephen Baldwin (Danny Morgan), Jeffrey Tambor (Uncle Alby). The filmmakers did careful

research to set the movie in the 1970s, with primary filming taking place in Minneapolis. Released on video in 1993.

Crossroads Shopping area at Walt Disney World; opening in February 1989. Located across the main highway from the Downtown Disney Marketplace, it includes a supermarket, shops, miniature golf, and restaurants. It was sold to GE Capital Realty Group in 2001.

Crossroads of the World Shop at the beginning of Hollywood Blvd. at Disney-MGM Studios, featuring a tall tower topped by Mickey Mouse. Opened on May 1, 1989.

Crothers, Scatman (1910–1986) Actor; appeared in *The Journey of Natty Gann* (Sherman) and as the voice of Scat Cat in *The Aristocats*.

Crowe, Russell Actor; appeared in *Mystery, Alaska* (John Biebe) and *The Insider* (Jeffrey Wigand), receiving an Academy Award nomination for the latter.

Crowley, Patricia Actress; appeared in *The Biscuit Eater* (Mary Lee McNeil), and on television in *Boomerang, Dog of Many Talents; Menace on the Mountain; Return of the Big Cat; The Sky Trap;* and *Elfego Baca*.

Cruella De Vil Eccentric villainess who wanted

to make coats of Dalmatian puppy fur in *One Hundred and One Dalmatians*; voiced by Betty Lou Gerson. Cruella lived in Hell Hall. Also the title of a song, written by Mel Leven, and misspelled "Cruella de Ville."

Cruise, Tom Actor; appeared in *The Color of Money* (Vincent) and *Cocktail* (Brian Flanagan).

Cruise of the Eagle (film) People and Places featurette; released on March 19, 1959. Produced by Ben Sharpsteen. The varied and important services of the U.S. Coast Guard are glimpsed. They warn ships of dangerous shoals, keep sea lanes open with icebreakers, face gale and hurricane to accurately forecast the weather in remote areas of the Atlantic and Pacific, and perform rescue services to ships and downed aircraft. We are also told of a training program of men of the Coast Guard and their many hardships. Filmed in CinemaScope. 18 min.

Crumbs (television) Half-hour comedy series; aired on ABC beginning January 12, 2006. Estranged brothers, Mitch and Jody Crumb, reunite to deal with their mother, a recent release from a psychiatric country club who has yet to discover that her ex-husband, Billy, is about to have a baby with his new girlfriend. Central to everything is the dynamic between the two brothers: Mitch, the prodigal son, is returning home after a failed Hollywood career; Jody, the older brother, stayed in the confines of their small New England town to run the family business. The family will need to stick by one another despite their combustible relationships. Stars Fred Savage (Mitch), Eddie McClintock (Jody), Maggie Lawson (Andrea), William Devane (Billy), Jean Curtin (Suzanne). From Tollin/Robbins Prods. in association with Touchstone Television.

Crump, Rolly Imagineer; joined Disney in 1952 originally as an inbetweener and assistant animator. In 1959 he moved into show design at WED Enterprises, and was a key designer on the Disney attractions for the New York World's Fair. He left the company in 1970, but returned several times, as a project designer for Epcot and an executive designer for Innoventions, among other projects. He retired in 1996. In 2004, he was named a Disney Legend.

Crusaders, The (television) One-hour investigative advocacy television series; syndicated beginning September 10, 1993, and ending January 21, 1995. A team of award-winning journalists with reporter hosts—Mark Hyman, William La Jeunesse, Howard Thompson, and Carla Wohl—help uncover solutions to the problems reported.

Crusading Reporter (television) Television show; the second episode of *Gallegher Goes West.*

Crystal Palace Restaurant Restaurant opened on the hub at Walt Disney World on October 1, 1971. Patterned after the facility Prince Albert built to honor Queen Victoria, this landmark cafeteria-style restaurant is one of the more attractive buildings in the park. In 1996, the restaurant changed to an all-you-can-eat buffet, featuring visits by the characters from *Winnie the Pooh*. Also at Tokyo Disneyland; opened April 15, 1983.

Cub's Den Supervised children's activities at the Wilderness Lodge Resort at Walt Disney World; opened in May 1994.

Culkin, Kieran Actor; appeared in *Father of the Bride* and *Father of the Bride, Part II* as Matty Banks, and in *Go Fish* as Andy "Fish" Troutner.

Cullman, Joseph F., III (1912–2004) Member of the Disney board of directors from 1984 to 1987.

Cummings, Bob (1908–1990) Actor who appeared as one of the emcees, with Ronald Reagan and Art Linkletter, for the opening-day television show for Disneyland, July 17, 1955. He was back for the 35th-anniversary celebration in 1990.

Cummings, Jim Voice actor doing many voices for the Disney animated television shows from 1985 to date, including the title roles of Winnie the Pooh, Bonkers, and Darkwing Duck, and Pete in *Goof Troop* and Monterey Jack and Fat Cat in *Chip 'n' Dale's Rescue Rangers*. Also voiced Ed in *The Lion King*, Thompkins in *Redux Riding Hood*, and Nessus in *Hercules*.

Cuoco, Kaley Actress; appeared on *8 Simple Rules* (Bridget) and in *Toothless* (Lori), on ABC Family in *Crimes of Fashion* (Brooke), on The Disney Channel in *Alley Cats Strike!* (Elisa) and as the voice of Brandy on *Brandy & Mr. Whiskers*.

Cured Duck (film) Donald Duck cartoon; released on October 26, 1945. Directed by Jack King. Daisy disgusted with Donald's temper, forces him to take a course to cure it with the aid of an "insult" machine. He is cured and returns to Daisy, but he laughs at her hat, which causes her to go into a rage, ending in a fight.

Currie, Finlay (1878–1968) Actor; appeared in *Treasure Island* (Captain Bones), *Rob Roy* (Hamish McPherson), *Kidnapped* (Cluny MacPherson), and *The Three Lives of Thomasina* (Grandpa Stirling).

Curry, Tim Actor; appeared in *Oscar* (Dr. Poole), *Passed Away* (Boyd Pinter), *The Three Musketeers* (Cardinal Richelieu), and *Muppet Treasure Island* (Long John Silver), and provided the voice of Lord Dragaunus in *The Mighty Ducks* (animated television series). He was the voice of Taurus Bulba on *Darkwing Duck*, Forte in *Beauty and the Beast: The Enchanted Christmas*, Gen. Von Talon in *Valiant*, and was S.I.R. in Alien Encounter at Walt Disney World.

Curtis, Ken (1916–1991) Actor; he voiced Nutsy in *Robin Hood*.

Cusack, Joan Actress; appeared in *Mr. Wrong* (Inga), *Too Much* (Gloria), *Grosse Pointe Blank* (Marcella), *Cradle Will Rock* (Hazel Huffman), *High Fidelity* (Liz), *The Last Shot* (Fanny Nash–uncredited), *Raising Helen* (Jenny Portman), and provided the voices of Jessie in *Toy Story 2*, and Abby Mallard in *Chicken Little*.

Cusack, John Actor; appeared in *The Journey of Natty Gann* (Harry), *Money for Nothing* (Joey Coyle), *Grosse Pointe Blank* (Martin), *Con Air* (Vince Larkin), *Cradle Will Rock* (Nelson Rockefeller), and *High Fidelity* (Rob Gordon).

Cutters (television) Television series, aired on CBS from June 11 to July 9, 1993. The wall is removed between a barber shop and a beauty salon next door, leading to a merger that brings all sorts of trouble. Stars Robert Hayes (Joe), Margaret Whitton (Adrienne), Julia Campbell (Lynn), Ray Buktenica (Chad), Julius Cary (Troy), Robin Tunney (Deb), Dakin Matthews (Harry). Five episodes.

Cyril Proudbottom Mr. Toad's horse in *The Adventures of Ichabod and Mr. Toad*. Voiced by J. Pat O'Malley.

D

D2: The Mighty Ducks (film) After an injury sidelines his career, the aggressive lawyer-turned-coach Gordon Bombay spends his days sharpening other people's skate blades at the local sport shop. However, when he is recruited to coach Team USA at the Junior Goodwill Games in Los Angeles, Gordon is reluctantly drawn back to the rink he has come to resent. He reunites his team of misfits to train in California, but the Ducks are quickly dazzled by the West Coast lifestyle, and the lure of earning big bucks with product endorsements. The players neglect their game, and the world championship seems an impossible goal unless Gordon can turn his once plucky players back into a dream team. Released on March 25, 1994. Directed by Sam Weisman. 107 min. Stars Emilio Estevez (Gordon Bombay), Michael Tucker (Tibbles), Jan Rubes (Jan), Kathryn Erbe (Michelle Mackahy), Joshua Jackson (Charlie). Sequel to *The Mighty Ducks*. The climactic championship face-off between Team USA and the Iceland team was filmed at the new Anaheim Arena, The Arrowhead Pond, where the Disney-owned Mighty Ducks NHL team plays. Among the 24,000 extras recruited to fill the stands were many local residents and cast members from nearby Disneyland. Parts of the movie were filmed on location in Minneapolis. Released on video in 1994.

D3: The Mighty Ducks (film) Gordon Bombay and the Ducks are back in Minneapolis fresh from the victories at the Goodwill Games. They have much to celebrate when they find out they've been given scholarships to the prestigious Eden Hall Academy. Once in the hallowed halls of Eden, however, the Ducks, led by team captain Charlie Conway, lose some of their focus. They become the junior varsity of the Eden Hall Warriors, resist an aggressive new coach, and suffer indignities heaped upon them by the preppy varsity team who resent their coming to the school. Eventually the players bond with their coach and face a final test in an exciting showdown game against the varsity bullies. Released on October 4, 1996. Directed by Rob Lieberman. Stars Emilio Estevez (Gordon Bombay), Jeffrey Nordling (Orion), Joshua Jackson (Charlie), David Selby (Dean Buckley), Heidi Kling (Casey). 104 min. Doubling for the fictitious Eden Hall Academy was the College of St. Catherine, in St. Paul, Minnesota. For the film, the crew also completely refurbished the Columbia Ice Arena in Anoka County. Sequel to *The Mighty Ducks* and *D2: The Mighty Ducks*. Released on video in 1997.

Dad, Can I Borrow the Car? (film) Special cartoon featurette; released on September 30, 1970. A young man humorously traces his involvement with "wheels" from his own birth, through childhood and teenage activities, including that important question, "Dad, can I borrow the car?" Then, an even more important topic comes up—love. But this only leads to a dune buggy wedding—and the wheels roll on. Directed by Ward Kimball. 22 min. Narrated by Kurt Russell. Released on video in 1986.

Daddio (television) Half-hour comedy series, which ran on NBC from March 23 to October 13, 2000. Chris Woods has exchanged traditional domestic roles with his wife, Linda, who has a new career as a lawyer, to be their family's full-time caretaker. He gives a masculine approach to his new occupation, and receives advice, welcome and not, from his neighbors and friends. Stars Michael Chiklis (Chris Woods), Anita Barone (Linda Woods), Amy Wilson (Barb Krolak), Kevin Crowley (Rod Krolak), Suzy Nakamura (Holly Martin), Steve Ryan (Bobick), Cristina Kernan (Shannon), Martin Spanjers (Max), Mitch Holleman (Jake).

Daddy Duck (film) Donald Duck cartoon; released on April 16, 1948. Directed by Jack Hannah. When he adopts Joey, a young kangaroo, Donald finds out the hard way how difficult it is to be a parent. After a difficult bath time, Donald pretends that a bear rug has swallowed him. Joey rushes in and beats up the "bear" severely, so that by nap time, Donald needs a nap far worse than Joey does.

Dafoe, Willem Actor; appeared in *The Life Aquatic with Steve Zissou* (Klaus Daimler), and provided the voice of Gill in *Finding Nemo*.

DaGradi, Don (1911–1991) Storyman/writer who was first a writer on the shorts, then on such films as *Pinocchio, Bambi, Fantasia, Dumbo, Alice in Wonderland, Peter Pan, Lady and the Tramp,* and *Sleeping Beauty*. He co-wrote, with Bill Walsh, the scripts for *Mary Poppins; Son of Flubber; Lt. Robin Crusoe, U.S.N.; Blackbeard's Ghost;* and *Bedknobs and Broomsticks*. He received the Disney Legends award posthumously in 1991.

Dailey, Dan (1913–1978) Actor; appeared on television in *Michael O'Hara the Fourth*.

Dailey, Peter H. Member of the Disney board of directors in 1984.

Daily Press vs. City Hall, The (television) Television show; the third episode of *The Further Adventures of Gallegher*.

Dairy Bar Food facility sponsored by the American Dairy Association in Tomorrowland at Disneyland from January 21, 1956, to September 1, 1958.

Daisy Duck Donald Duck's girlfriend had her debut as Donna Duck in *Don Donald* (1937), but was first known as Daisy in *Mr. Duck Steps Out* (1940). She made 14 film appearances. Daisy had three nieces in comic book stories—April, May, and June. They first appeared in *Walt Disney's Comics & Stories* no. 149 (February 1953).

Dale The chipmunk with the red nose, who with his partner, Chip, made life difficult for Donald Duck. The chipmunks appeared in 24 cartoons, three in their own series.

Dale, Jim Actor; appeared in *Pete's Dragon* (Doc Terminus), *Hot Lead and Cold Feet* (Eli, Wild Billy, Jasper Bloodshy), *Unidentified Flying Oddball* (Sir Mordred).

Dali, Salvador (1904–1989) The surrealist artist was a friend of Walt Disney's, and he was invited to come to the Disney Studio in 1946 to work on a film project to be called *Destino*, based on a Mexican ballad. During many weeks at the Studio, he worked with Disney artists John Hench and Bob Cormack, and together they created Dali-esque concepts and story sketches of ballerinas, baseball players, bicycles, and bugs for the proposed film. Un-

fortunately, it was not completed; only 18 seconds were filmed. The way-out style would have made its success problematical as a separate short cartoon, and Walt did not see how he could fit it into his production program for the 1940s package films. Fifty-seven years later, the Disney Studio finally completed a version of the film.

Dallben The wizard, and Taran's mentor, in *The Black Cauldron*; voiced by Freddie Jones.

Daly, Rad Actor; appeared on television in *The Ghosts of Buxley Hall* and *The Kids Who Knew Too Much*.

Danbury Secret of Flexible Behavior, The (film) Educational film from The Nick Price Story of Non-Manipulative Selling series; released in February 1981. The film shows how to use flexible behavior in dealing with a customer.

Dance of the Hours, The (film) Segment of *Fantasia*; composed by Amilcare Ponchielli.

Danger Bay (television) Series on The Disney Channel; premiered on October 7, 1985. A curator-veterinarian at a Pacific Northwest aquarium lives with his family on a small island in Danger Bay. The children help their dad, and also get into their own adventures. Stars Donnelly Rhodes (Grant Roberts), Susan Walden, Christopher Crabb, Ocean Hellman. Originally a Canadian television series. 122 episodes.

Dangerous Minds (film) LouAnne Johnson teaches high school English to a group of tough, inner-city teenagers who have already accepted defeat. Her unconventional approach at instilling motivation and self-esteem in her students causes her many problems with a well-meaning but entrenched education establishment that tries to thwart her efforts at every turn. She shows that one person can make a difference. Released on August 11, 1995. A Hollywood Pictures film. Directed by John N. Smith. Stars Michelle Pfeiffer (LouAnne Johnson), George Dzundza (Hal Griffith), Robin Bartlett (Carla Nichols), Courtney Vance (George Grandey). 99 min. Based on the popular 1992 book detailing Johnson's real life experiences, *My Posse Don't Do Homework*. The film was shot at various locations around the Los Angeles area, with more than one third at the Washington Middle School in Pasadena. Some filming also took place at Burlingame High School in Northern California. Interiors were shot on a soundstage at the Warner-Hollywood Studios. Released on video in 1996.

Dangerous Minds (television) One-hour television series; premiered on ABC on September 30, 1996, and ended on July 12, 1997. The story of Louanne Johnson, an ex-Marine who comes to teach English to the bright but troubled students in a special high school program at Parkmont High School in Northern California. Totally committed to her students, Johnson is fiercely determined to support them, many of whom are confronted with seemingly insurmountable obstacles to their goals. Stars Annie Potts (Louanne Johnson), Tamala Jones (Callie Timmons), Cedrick Terrell (James Revill), K. Todd Freeman (Jerome Griffin), Jenny Gago (Amanda Bardales),

Greg Serano (Gusmaro Lopez), Maria Costa (Blanca Guerrero), LaToya Howlett (Alvina Edwards), Stanley Anderson (Bud Bartkus). Based on the 1995 feature film.

Daniel Boone: [I.] The Warrior's Path (television) Television show; aired on December 4, 1960. Directed by Lewis R. Foster. In North Carolina, Daniel Boone hears amazing tales about Kentucky and decides to move his family there, but first he has to find the Indian path that will lead him and earn enough money trapping to repay a loan. The Indians are not happy that settlers are coming, and make life difficult for them. Stars Dewey Martin, Mala Powers, Richard Banke, Eddy Waller, Anthony Caruso. Many people erroneously remember the Fess Parker–starring *Daniel Boone* series as being a Disney show, since it starred the actor who had made Davy Crockett a household name for Disney, but it was not. Parker's series, made by 20th Century Fox, aired on NBC from 1964 to 1970.

Daniel Boone: [II.] And Chase the Buffalo (television) Television show; aired on December 11, 1960. Directed by Lewis R. Foster. Boone yearns to return to Kentucky, to escape the tax collector, despite his wife's wishes. With his family remaining home, he leads a small group of farmers to Kentucky, only to be thrilled when his wife and children unexpectedly arrive to join him. Stars Dewey Martin, Mala Powers, Kevin Corcoran, Brian Corcoran, Kerry Corcoran, Whit Bissell.

Daniel Boone: [III.] The Wilderness Road (television) Television show; aired on March 12, 1961. Directed by Lewis R. Foster. Daniel and his friends have troubles with Indians on their way to Kentucky. Stars Dewey Martin, Mala Powers, Diane Jergens, William Herrin, Slim Pickens, Kevin Corcoran, Anthony Caruso.

Daniel Boone: [IV.] The Promised Land (television) Television show; aired on March 19, 1961. Directed by Lewis R. Foster. The wagon train on the way to Kentucky has to lighten the loads to get across the mountains and battle Indi-ans. Stars Dewey Martin, Mala Powers, Diane Jergens, William Herrin, Kevin Corcoran.

Daniels, Jeff Actor; appeared in *Arachnophobia* (Ross Jennings), *101 Dalmatians* (Roger), and *My Favorite Martian* (Tim O'Hara).

Daniels, Lisa Actress; she voiced Perdita in *One Hundred and One Dalmatians.*

Daniels, William Actor; appeared on television in *Boy Meets World* (Mr. Feeny).

Danner, Braden Actor; appeared on the *Mickey Mouse Club* on The Disney Channel in 1989.

Danner, Tasha Actor; appeared on the *Mickey Mouse Club* on The Disney Channel, from 1991 to 1993.

Danny Little black lamb in *So Dear to My Heart.*

Danny (television) Syndicated television talk show featuring Danny Bonaduce, beginning on September 11, 1995, and ending February 2, 1996.

Danny, the Champion of the World (television) A widowed gas station attendant and his son, who live in a gypsy caravan behind the station, team up against a rich land baron to save their town. A Disney Channel Premiere Film; first aired on April 29, 1989. Directed by Gavin Millar. Based on the novel by Roald Dahl. Stars Jeremy Irons (William Smith), Sam Irons (Danny Smith), Cyril Cusack (Doc Spencer). 99 min. Not only is Jeremy Irons Sam's father, but Cyril Cusack is his grandfather (on his mother's side).

Dano, Royal (1922–1994) Character actor; provided the voice for Mr. Lincoln in Great Moments with Mr. Lincoln at Disneyland, and appeared in *Savage Sam* (Pack Underwood), *Something Wicked This Way Comes* (Tom Fury), and *Spaced Invaders* (Wrenchmuller).

Danson, Ted Actor; appeared as Jack in *Three Men and a Baby* and *Three Men and a Little Lady*, and in *Mumford* (Jeremy Brockett).

Danube, The (film) People and Places featurette; released on April 27, 1960. Produced by Ben Sharpsteen. The people who live along the Danube are studied along with their traditions, in which they take great pride. Both old and new customs and festivals are shown. The film ends with a visit to the most famous of all the Danube cities—Vienna. Filmed in CinemaScope. 28 min.

Danza, Tony Actor; appeared in *Angels in the Outfield* (Mel Clark), and on television in *Disney Goes to the Oscars*, *Disneyland's 35th Anniversary Celebration*, *The Garbage Picking Field Goal Kicking Philadelphia Phenomenon* (Barney Gorman), and *Noah* (Norman Waters). He also starred in the 2004 syndicated *The Tony Danza Show*.

Dapper Dans, The Barbershop quartet that performs on Main Street, U.S.A., at Disneyland and Magic Kingdom Park at Walt Disney World.

Darby O'Gill and the Little People (film) Darby O'Gill, used to spinning fairy tales instead of tending his job as caretaker of Lord Fitzpatrick's estate in South Ireland, is about to be replaced by young Michael McBride of Dublin. Fearful of his daughter Katie's reaction and unwilling to give up his own standing in the community, he attempts to act as matchmaker to Michael and Katie to ensure their future. To help his plans, he captures his old friend King Brian of the leprechauns, who must grant Darby three wishes. King Brian is almost successful in furthering a romance when meddlesome Pony Sugrue, a jealous townsman, tells Katie of Michael's new job. In a rage, she renounces Michael and runs off after a runaway horse, only to fall and hit her head on some rocks. Near death, she is saved only when Darby diverts the dreaded Costa Bower, the Death Coach, by making his third wish to be taken instead. Inside the coach King Brian tricks Darby into making a fourth wish, which cancels out the previous ones, and sends Darby back to earth. Michael and Katie are married, and Darby is once again free to tell his tales of his little friends, the leprechauns. World premiere in Dublin, Ireland, on June 24, 1959; U.S. release on June 26, 1959. Directed by Robert Stevenson. 90 min. Based on H. T. Kavanagh's *Darby O'Gill* stories, the film stars Albert Sharpe in the title role, with co-stars Janet Munro (Katie O'Gill), Jimmy O'Dea (King Brian), Sean Connery (Michael McBride), Estelle Winwood (Sheelah), Kieron Moore (Pony Sugrue), Walter Fitzgerald (Lord Fitzpatrick). With this film Janet Munro was signed to a Studio contract, but for Connery it would be three years before stardom would come with the James Bond series. The movie was director Stevenson's first major production, and on the strength of this assignment, he went on to direct many of the Studio's biggest hits in the 1960s. The film's production at the Studio began in the mid-1940s when Walt Disney discovered the stories, and in 1946 he sent artists to Ireland for background material, following himself soon afterward. He had a fondness for the country because his ancestors had come from there. The songs "The Wishing Song" and "Pretty Irish Girl" were written by Oliver Wallace and Lawrence E. Watkin. With the aid of lavish matte shots, the film was shot entirely in California. To film the forced perspective of the leprechauns' throne room, there was a need for huge sets, lit by many banks of lights, necessitating the building of an entire new soundstage at the Disney Studio. Special effects masters Peter Ellenshaw, Eustace Lycett, and Joshua Meador concocted the magic of the leprechauns and their appeal was undeniable. Leprechaun means "little body" in Gaelic, and according to legend they are 21 inches tall, usually dressed in grass green, 5,000 years old, and immeasurably wealthy. Walt Disney dedicated the film, in the opening credits, to these very believable Little People: "My thanks to King Brian of Knocknasheega and his leprechauns whose gracious cooperation made this picture possible." The movie features one of the scariest scenes ever to appear in a Disney movie—the wail of the hideous Banshee and the arrival of the dreaded Costa Bower. A television show to promote the film, *I Captured the King of the Leprechauns*, starred Walt Disney and Pat O'Brien. The motion picture was reissued in 1969 and 1977. Released on video in 1981 and 1992.

D.A.R.E. to Be Aware: Angela's Story (film) Educational release in January 1993. 10 min. A girl risks losing her boyfriend when she refuses to do drugs, but he respects her for her decision.

D.A.R.E. to Be Aware: Lauren's Story (film) Educational release in December 1993. 14 min. A teen is angry with her parents, but her counselor suggests she try dealing differently with her anger than her usual retreat to her room to smoke a joint. She should listen to others' points of view and calmly state her own.

D.A.R.E. to Be Aware: Matt's Story (film) Educational release in November 1992. 11 min. A teen is booked for drunk driving at the police station, and though he argues he was not drunk, the policeman tells him about the alcohol content of beer and explains the consequences of his actions—he hit a car, badly injuring a little boy.

D.A.R.E. to Be Aware: Michael's Story (film) Educational release in November 1992. 12 min. Two boys are in trouble, owing $800 to a local drug dealer, so they turn to theft.

D.A.R.E. to Be Aware: Steve's Story (film) Educational release in December 1993. 10 min. Rachel throws a party at her home, but her boyfriend, Steve, gets drunk on beer and becomes violent.

D.A.R.E. to Care: A Program for Parents (film) Educational release in 16mm in April 1991. 18 min. A video version at 27 min. was released in October 1992. Narrated by Edward James Olmos. Today's parents face a very difficult challenge—finding a way to keep their kids safe from drugs.

D.A.R.E. to Say "No" (film) Educational film; in the EPCOT Educational Media Collection, released in September 1988. 16 min. Drug Abuse Resistance Education (D.A.R.E.) presents reasons why kids should resist peer pressure and refuse drugs.

Dark Water (film) Dahlia Williams is starting a new life: newly separated, with a new job and a new apartment on Roosevelt Island in New York, she is determined to put her relationship with her estranged husband behind her and devote herself to raising her daughter, Ceci. As the strained separation disintegrates into a bitter custody battle, her situation takes a turn for the worse. Her new Apartment 9F—dilapidated, cramped, and worn—seems to take on a life of its own. Mysterious noises, persistent leaks of dark water, and strange happenings cause her imagination to run wild, sending her on a puzzling and mystifying pursuit to find out who is behind the endless mind games. As Dahlia frantically searches for the links between the riddles, the dark water seems to close around her. Directed by Walter Salles. A Touchstone Picture. Released on July 8, 2005. Stars Jennifer Connelly (Dahlia Williams), John C. Reilly (Mr. Murray), Pete Postlethwaite (Veeck), Dougray Scott (Kyle), Tim Roth (Jeff Platzer), Ariel Gade (Ceci), Camryn Manheim (Teacher), Perla Haney-Jardine (Young Dahlia). Shelley Duvall makes an uncredited appearance. 105 min. Filmed in CinemaScope. Based on the novel *Honogurai Mizuno Soko Kara*, by Koji Suzuki, and the Hideo Nakata film, *Dark Water*. Released on DVD in 2005.

Darkwing Duck (television) Animated television series; premiered on The Disney Channel on April 6, 1991, then aired on ABC and in syndication beginning September 7, 1991. The ABC run ended on September 11, 1993, and the syndication run on September 1, 1995. It returned to syndication from September 2, 1996 to August 29, 1997. When average citizen Drake Mallard dons a mask, hat, and cape, he becomes the swashbuckling crimebuster Darkwing Duck. With the help of his loyal but often clueless sidekick, Launchpad McQuack, he patrols the city of St. Canard. When he adopts his orphan niece, Gosalyn, who wants to help out with the crimebusting, his life changes drastically. Voices include Jim Cummings (Darkwing Duck and Jim Muddlefoot), Christine Cavanaugh (Gosalyn Mallard), Terry McGovern (Launchpad), Katie Leigh (Honker Muddlefoot). 91 episodes.

Darkwing Duck Premiere, The; Back to School with the Mickey Mouse Club (film) Syndicated television special; aired on September 8, 1991. The new animated television series and the return of the *Mickey Mouse Club* are both celebrated. The *Mickey Mouse Club* cast members perform several skits and songs.

Darling The family name in *Peter Pan*, with George and Mary being the parents, and Wendy, John, and Michael the children. George and Mary are voiced by Hans Conried and Heather Angel. Also the name of the wife in *Lady and the Tramp*.

Darro, Frankie (1917–1976) Actor; the voice of Lampwick in *Pinocchio*.

Darrow, Henry Actor; starred as Zorro in the television series *Zorro and Son*.

Darwell, Jane (1880–1967) Actress; she was 84 years old when she appeared as the Bird Woman in *Mary Poppins*. She had won an Oscar over two decades earlier for Best Supporting Actress in *The Grapes of Wrath*. She was living at the Motion Picture Country Home and Walt persuaded her to come out of retirement to play the role.

Date Nite Friday and Saturday evening event at Disneyland during the summer beginning in 1957.

Dateline Disneyland (television) Opening day live television special for Disneyland; airing on ABC at 4:30 P.M. Pacific time on Sunday afternoon, July 17, 1955, and being hosted by Art Linkletter, Bob Cummings, and Ronald Reagan. Directed by Stuart Phelps and John Rich. Because of the nationwide anticipation of the opening of Disneyland, fostered by Walt himself on his pre-opening reports on television, this special had a huge audience, estimated at 90 million viewers. The show was the largest live production ever attempted, utilizing 24 cameras and a staff of hundreds, and it went off with relatively few miscues.

Davalos, Elyssa Actress; appeared in *The Apple Dumpling Gang Rides Again* (Millie Gaskill) and *Herbie Goes Bananas* (Melissa).

Dave the Barbarian (television) Animated series on Disney Channel, premiering on January 23, 2004. In the Middle Ages, Dave and his offbeat family, including his primping older sister Candy and fierce younger sister Fang, protect themselves and their kingdom from a world of odd foes. Complicating matters is brawny Dave's nonbarbarian demeanor—he prefers the finer things in life, like origami, bird-watching, and gourmet cooking. With a combination of Dave's brute strength and his fine art skills, villains do not stand a chance. Voices include Danny Cooksey (Dave), Estelle Harris (Lula the magic sword), Tress MacNeille (Fang), Erica Luttrell (Candy), Kevin Michael Richardson (Uncle Oswidge), Frank Welker (Faffy), Jeff Bennett (narrator), Paul Rugg (The Dark Lord Chuckles, the Silly Piggy). 21 episodes.

Davidovich, Lolita Actress; appeared in *Adventures in Babysitting* (as Lolita David, Sue Ann) *Blaze* (Blaze Starr), *Jungle 2 Jungle* (Charlotte), *Play It to the Bone* (Grace Pasic), and *Mystery, Alaska* (Mary Jane Pitcher).

Davidson, John Actor; appeared in *The Happiest Millionaire* (Angie Duke) and *The One and Only, Genuine, Original Family Band* (Joe Carder).

Davis, Alice She joined Disney in 1959, designing a costume for a live-action model for *Sleeping Beauty*, and went on to design costumes for *Toby Tyler*. Her primary work was the researching, designing, and dressing of the animated figures in the "it's a small world" and Pirates of the Caribbean attractions. She was the wife of Disney Legend Marc Davis (married in 1956). Alice was named a Disney Legend in 2004.

Davis, Bette (1908–1989) Actress; appeared in *The Watcher in the Woods* (Mrs. Aylwood) and *Return from Witch Mountain* (Letha).

Davis, Geena Actress; appeared in the title role in *Angie* and on television in *The Geena Davis Show* (Teddie) and *Commander in Chief* (Mackenzie Allen).

Davis, Lisa Actress; provided the voice of Anita Radcliff in *One Hundred and One Dalmatians*.

Davis, Marc (1913–2000) Animator/designer; known as one of Disney's "Nine Old Men," he began his career at the Studio in December

1935, working on *Snow White and the Seven Dwarfs*. He developed such memorable characters as young Bambi and Thumper, and gained a reputation for animating such distinctive female characters as Cinderella, Tinker Bell, and Cruella De Vil, among others. In addition, he played an active role in the planning of Disneyland and all four of Disney's 1964–1965 New York World's Fair attractions. He developed story and character concepts for many Disneyland attractions, including Pirates of the Caribbean, the Haunted Mansion, "it's a small world," and later consulted on attractions for Epcot and Tokyo Disneyland after his retirement in 1978. He was honored with the Disney Legends award in 1989.

Davis, Marvin (1910–1998) Designer; joined WED Enterprises in 1953 to help in the conceptualization and architectural design of Disneyland. He was later an art director on such films as *Zorro*, *The Swamp Fox*, *Moon Pilot*, *Babes in Toyland*, and *Big Red*, and in 1964 won an Emmy for the art direction and scenic design for *Walt Disney's Wonderful World of Color*. In 1965, he returned to WED to work as a project designer on the concept for Walt Disney World. In addition to the master plan for the resort, he concentrated on the design of the hotels. He retired in 1975, and was named a Disney Legend in 1994.

Davis, Ossie (1917–2005) Actor; appeared in *We'll Take Manhattan* (man in subway), *The Ernest Green Story* (grandfather), and provided the voice of Yar in *Dinosaur*.

Davis, Virginia Child actress who Walt Disney brought from Kansas City to act as Alice in his

Alice Comedies in 1923. She was in the first 13 films in the series. She was honored as a Disney Legend in 1998.

Davy Crockett (television) The most well-known of all the Disney television shows. The shows won an Emmy Award for Best Action or Adventure Series in 1956. They started a national craze and raised Fess Parker to stardom. Because of their fame, many people erroneously believe that it was a lengthy series. In fact, there were only three shows the first season (1954–55) of the Disney television series, ending with Davy's death at the Alamo. By then, however, the series had become so popular that Walt Disney realized too late his mistake in killing off his hero at the end of the third show. So, he made two additional shows the next year based on legends of Davy Crockett. Thus, there were only five hour-long episodes starring Fess Parker. The shows were combined to make two theatrical features. The Davy Crockett craze started a run on coonskins, both real and artificial, as kids across America yearned to dress like their frontier hero with the telltale cap. "The Ballad of Davy Crockett" rushed to the top of the Hit Parade, and remained there for 16 weeks. In all, the nationwide Crockett frenzy helped Disney licensees sell $300 million worth of merchandise. Fess Parker was never able to match the success of his Davy Crockett role, though he did don frontier garb again and star in a popular *Daniel Boone* series for NBC in the 1960s. Five more Davy Crockett episodes were made by Disney in 1988–89, starring Tim Dunigan as Davy and Gary Grubbs as George Russel. These shows were entitled *Rainbow in the Thunder* (2 hours, 11/20/88), *A Natural Man* (12/18/88), *Guardian Spirit* (1/13/89), *A Letter to Polly* (6/11/89), and *Warrior's Farewell* (6/18/89). The new series tried but failed to rekindle the enthusiasm of audiences which Fess Parker's episodes had seen almost four decades earlier.

Davy Crockett: A Letter to Polly (television) Missing his family, Davy tries to take a letter to a peddler who can deliver it to them, but on the way happens upon a cabin where the family has all been slaughtered during an Indian attack, except for a boy, Aaron, who is so scared he can no longer speak. Davy takes Aaron with him, and tries to calm his fears. Aaron finally speaks in order to save Davy. Directed by Harry Falk. Stars Tim Dunigan (Davy), Aeryk Egan (Aaron), Garry Chalk (Major Benteen). Aired on June 11, 1989.

Davy Crockett: A Natural Man (television) In searching the woods for a grizzly bear that has injured George, Davy finds his long-lost uncle, Jimmy Crockett. Jimmy has a son by a Creek Indian maiden, Eyes Like Sky, who grew up to hate his father and all white men. Jimmy also harbors a secret about a rumored cache of gold. Directed by Charles Braverman. Stars Tim Dunigan (Davy), Barry Corbin (Jimmy), Rodger Gibson (Eyes Like Sky). Aired on December 18, 1988.

Davy Crockett and the River Pirates (television) Television show; aired on December 14, 1955. Episode 5. Directed by Norman Foster. Some Indian friends of Davy's have been falsely accused of raiding boat traffic on the Ohio River. With the help of George Russel and Mike Fink, Davy discovers a group of pirates masquerading as Indians, and manages to capture them. Stars Fess Parker (Davy Crockett), Buddy Ebsen (George Russel), Jeff York (Mike Fink), Kenneth Tobey (Jocko), Clem Bevans (Cap'n Cobb), Walter Catlett (Colonel Plug).

Davy Crockett and the River Pirates (film) Theatrical release of the fourth and fifth Crockett television episodes. Released July 18, 1956. Directed by Norman Foster. 81 min. Stars Fess Parker (Davy Crockett), Buddy Ebsen (George Russel), Jeff York (Mike Fink), Kenneth Tobey (Jocko), Clem Bevans (Cap'n Cobb), Walter Catlett (Colonel Plug). Released on video in 1981, 1985, and 1994.

Davy Crockett Arcade Frontierland shop at Disneyland; opened July 17, 1955, and became Davy Crockett Frontier Arcade in 1985.

Davy Crockett at the Alamo (television) Television show; aired on February 23, 1955. Episode 3. Davy heads West to Texas to help fight against the invading Mexican Army led by General Santa Anna, and has to fight his way into the Alamo, only to find that the situation there is hopeless. The stalwart defenders are eventually vanquished. Directed by Norman Foster. Stars Fess Parker (Davy Crockett), Buddy Ebsen (George Russel), Hans Conried (Thimblerig), Kenneth Tobey (James Bowie), Don Megowan (Col. Billy Travis), Nick Cravat (Bustedluck).

Davy Crockett Frontier Arcade Frontierland shop at Disneyland; name change in 1985 from Davy Crockett Arcade. Became Davy Crockett's Pioneer Mercantile in 1987. The shop sells Western-themed products.

Davy Crockett Goes to Congress (television) Television show; aired on January 26, 1955. Episode 2. Directed by Norman Foster. Davy tangles with Big Foot Mason when he tries to settle in Tennessee, and in winning the battle, is asked by the townsfolk to run for office. He declines until his wife's death changes matters and he is soon elected to Congress. His homespun ways are refreshing on Capitol Hill, but Davy soon learns that he is not cut out for politics. Stars Fess Parker (Davy Crockett), Basil Ruysdael (Andrew Jackson), William Bakewell (Tobias Norton), Mike Mazurki (Bigfoot Mason), Helene Stanley (Polly Crockett).

Davy Crockett: Guardian Spirit (television) Davy and George are sent to find a Creek meeting place, but happen upon an Indian boy undertaking a coming of age ritual. In killing a wolf coming to attack the boy, Davy unwittingly shames him with his tribe. In order to get the tribe to take the boy back, Davy feigns blindness. Directed by Harry Falk. Stars Tim Dunigan (Davy), Garry Grubbs (George), Garry Chalk (Major Benteen), Evan Adams (boy). Aired on January 13, 1989.

Davy Crockett—Indian Fighter (television) Television show; aired on December 15, 1954.

Directed by Norman Foster. The first episode of the Davy Crockett trilogy about the American folk hero. Davy is tired of the continuing war between the Indians and the settlers, so he helps the army in putting an end to it. In saving the life of an Indian leader, he is shown to have compassion, and he helps push for the signing of a peace treaty. Stars Fess Parker, Buddy Ebsen, Basil Ruysdael, William Bakewell, Helene Stanley. This episode, along with the two that followed, were combined to become the theatrical feature *Davy Crockett, King of the Wild Frontier.*

Davy Crockett, King of the Wild Frontier

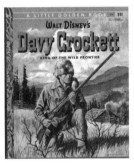

(film) Feature film combining the first three television episodes; released on May 25, 1955. 93 min. Stars Fess Parker, Buddy Ebsen. Released on video in 1980, 1985, and 1993.

Davy Crockett Museum

For about a year after the park opened in 1955, Disneyland had a Davy Crockett Museum in the Davy Crockett Arcade in Frontierland. There was an Alamo exhibit including life-size wax figures of Fess Parker and Buddy Ebsen, and a historical firearm display provided by the National Rifle Association. When the museum closed, the wax figures were moved to Fort Wilderness on Tom Sawyer Island, where they remained for several decades.

Davy Crockett: Rainbow in the Thunder

(television) In this first of a new series of Davy Crockett films, which aired as a two-hour movie on November 20, 1988, Davy is a member of a band of Tennessee volunteers called upon to crush a Creek uprising. He sympathizes with the Indians, but has to rescue a young settler, Ory Palmer, from them. He refuses to support an Indian Affairs bill that President Jackson is proposing. Directed by Ian Thomas. Stars Tim Dunigan (Davy), Gary Grubbs (George), Samantha Eggar (Ory), David Hemmings (Jackson).

Davy Crockett Ranch Campground at Euro Disney, originally known as Camp Davy Crockett. The name change occurred in May 1993.

Davy Crockett: Warrior's Farewell (television) During the Creek uprising, the soldiers are intimidated by the appearance of a medicine man who seems to have caused an earthquake. A new civilian in camp, Callahan, who is wanting to test a powerful new rifle, attempts to kill the unarmed medicine man, but Davy saves him. This incident helps bring peace, and the Tennessee volunteers can head home to their families. Directed by James J. Quinn. Stars Tim Dunigan (Davy), Ken Swofford (Callahan), Clem Fox (medicine man). Aired on June 18, 1989.

Davy Crockett's Explorer Canoes Critter Country attraction at Disneyland; opened on May 19, 1971. Formerly Indian War Canoes in Frontierland; the loading dock has had to be moved several times as progress changed the layout along the Rivers of America. The only Disneyland attraction where guests have to work—their paddling is the only means of locomotion of the 35-foot-long canoes, as they circle Tom Sawyer Island. Also a Frontierland attraction, in Magic Kingdom Park at Walt Disney World; opened October 1, 1971. Also in Westernland at Tokyo Disneyland; opened on April 15, 1983. See Indian Canoes for the Disneyland Paris version.

Davy Crockett's Keelboat Race (television) Television show; aired on November 16, 1955. Episode 4. Directed by Norman Foster. After a season of trapping, Davy and Georgie desire to take their furs downriver to New Orleans in their keelboat, the *Bertha Mae*, but are thwarted by Mike Fink. A challenge race pits the two against each other, with the furs the prize (against Fink eating his  hat). Despite unfair maneuvers by Fink on the *Gullywhumper*, Davy wins. Stars Fess Parker,

Buddy Ebsen, Jeff York, Kenneth Tobey, Clem Bevans. This show and *Davy Crockett and the River Pirates* were combined and released as the feature *Davy Crockett and the River Pirates*. The two keelboats ended up as an attraction at Disneyland.

Davy Crockett's Pioneer Mercantile Frontierland shop in Disneyland; name change from Davy Crockett Frontier Arcade in 1987.

Dawn of Better Living, The (film) Educational film about the development of home lighting from log cabin to present day, and with each change a better lighting system; made for Westinghouse Electric Co., delivered to them on May 28, 1945.

Day, Dennis Mouseketeer from the 1950s television show.

Day, Dennis (1917–1988) Singer; sang the songs in *Johnny Appleseed*, as well as voicing several of the characters.

Day at Disneyland, A (film) Video souvenir of a visit to Disneyland, released in June 1982.

Day at the Magic Kingdom, A (film) Video souvenir of a visit to Magic Kingdom Park at Walt Disney World; released in 1991. 30 min.

Day in Nature's Community, A (television) Educational film taken from the television show *One Day on Beetle Rock*, released in October 1975. A study of survival and ecological relationships among mountain animals in the Sierra Nevada.

Day in the Life of Donald Duck, A (television) Television show; aired on February 1, 1956. Directed by Jack Hannah. Walt Disney and the Mouseketeers help tell about a typical day in Don-

ald's life. Stars also Clarence Nash, Jimmie Dodd, Roy Williams.

Day-o (television) Television movie on NBC (2 hours) on May 3, 1992. Directed by Michael Schultz. Grace has an imaginary friend, who only she can see, who helps her learn self-pride, both as a child and as an adult. Stars Delta Burke, Elijah Wood, Carlin Glynn, Charles Shaughnessy, Ashley Peldon.

Deacon, Richard (1923–1984) Actor; appeared in *That Darn Cat!* (drive-in manager), *The Gnome-Mobile* (Ralph Yarby), *Blackbeard's Ghost* (Dean Wheaton), and *The One and Only, Genuine Original Family Band* (Charlie Wrenn), and on television in the *Annette* serial on the *Mickey Mouse Club*.

Deacon Street Deer, The (television) Television show; aired on May 18, 1986. Directed by Jackie Cooper. A young deer is stranded in the big city, where he is helped by a boy who guards him against a neighborhood gang. A local street vendor helps the boy take the animal back to the forest. Stars Bumper Robinson, Eve Glazier, Mario Lopez, Sean De Veritch, Richard Mulligan.

Deacon, the High Noon Dog (television) Television show; aired on March 16, 1975. Directed by Norman Wright. A mongrel dog goes searching for his young master, Jamie, and finds itself stranded in the desert. His adventures include the chasing of a cat into the OK Corral in Tombstone, which inadvertently starts the famous battle. Eventually, Deacon is reunited with his master. Stars Frank Keith, Paul Szemenyei.

Dead Poets Society (film) John Keating, a dedicated English teacher, returns to his alma mater, a stuffy Eastern boys' prep school. The administration frowns upon his teaching methods, which encourage the students not to learn by rote, but to think and feel for themselves. He awakens such passion in one group of students that they revive the "Dead Poets Society," a secret club to which he once belonged. The "Dead Poets" meet at midnight in a cave to recite and even compose poetry. Ultimately their quest for self-knowledge leads to tragedy, as one student, whose dreams of becoming an actor are smashed by his tyrannical father, chooses to die rather than continue to pretend he is something that he is not. Keating's career as a teacher is finished, but his spirit and his passion will live on in the students whose thoughts and minds he has helped to shape. Initial release on June 2, 1989; general release on June 9, 1989. Directed by Peter Weir. Academy Award winner for Best Screenplay (Tom Schulman). A Touchstone film. 129 min. Stars Robin Williams (John Keating), Robert Sean Leonard (Neil Perry), Ethan Hawke (Todd Anderson), Josh Charles (Knox Overstreet). Filmed at St. Andrew's School in Middletown, Delaware, primarily over the Thanksgiving and Christmas holidays so as not to disrupt the school's academic schedule. Released on video in 1990.

Dead Presidents (film) Young African American buddies, returned from the war in Vietnam, find things changed at home. Their neighborhood is disintegrating, ravaged by drugs and chronic poverty. To try to save themselves, they turn to acquiring dead presidents—cold, hard cash—by any means necessary, even if they end up paying with their lives. General release on October 6, 1995, with a limited release on October 4. A Hollywood Pictures film. Directed by Albert and Allen Hughes. Filmed in Cinema-Scope. 121 min. Stars Larenz Tate (Anthony Curtis), Chris Tucker (Skip), Freddy Rodriguez (Jose), Bokeem Woodbine (Cleon), Keith David (Kirby), Rose Jackson (Juanita Benson), N'Bushe Wright (Delilah Benson). Filmed primarily in New York City. Released on video in 1996.

Deadline for Murder: From the Files of Edna Buchanan (television) Two-hour television movie; aired on CBS on May 9, 1995. A crime reporter for the *Miami Herald*, Edna Buchanan, is on the beat to find out who killed alleged mobster Johnny Cresta, who had been attempting to bring legalized gambling to town. Directed by Joyce Chopra. Stars Elizabeth Montgomery (Edna Buchanan), Dean Stockwell (Aaron Bliss), Yaphet Kotto (Marty Talbot), Audra Lindley (Jean Buchanan). Montgomery reprised the role she had played in the previous season's television movie *The Corpse Had a Familiar Face*.

Dean, Loren Actor; appeared in the title role in *Billy Bathgate*, and in *Enemy of the State* (Hicks) and *Mumford* (Dr. Mumford).

Death: How Can You Live with It? (film) Educational film using sequences from *Napoleon and Samantha*. In the Questions!/Answers? series, released in 1976. A boy learns to accept the death of his grandfather.

Debt (television) Half-hour television series on Lifetime, debuting on June 3, 1996, and ending on July 3, 1998. A game show in which contestants had a chance to pay off their credit cards and other loans by answering questions. Hosted by Wink Martindale.

DeCarlo, Yvonne Actress; appeared in *Oscar* (Aunt Rosa), and on television in *The Barefoot Executive* (Norma).

Deceived (film) After six happily married years, Adrienne Saunders thinks she has it all. But after a bizarre tragedy in which her husband, Jack, is apparently killed, she is faced with a series of perplexing mysteries about the man she loved and thought she knew. She discovers a web of deceit along with some shocking truths. Evidence of murder, art forgery, and theft threaten her own life and that of her daughter. Released on September 27, 1991. Directed by Damian Harris. A Touchstone Picture. 108 min. Stars Goldie Hawn (Adrienne Saunders), John Heard (Jack). Filmed primarily in Toronto, with some exterior locations in New York City. Released on video in 1992.

Deceptive Detective, The (television) Television show; episode two of *Michael O'Hara IV*.

Decimals: What's the Point? (film) Educational film; released in September 1985. The look and sound of a music video are used to illustrate the basics of the decimal system.

Decision-Making: Critical Thought in Action (film) Educational film; released in September 1983. A series of everyday situations are used to take students through the problem-solving process.

Dee, Nita Mouseketeer on the new *Mickey Mouse Club*. Her real name was Benita Di Giampaolo.

Deep Rising (film) Somewhere in the South China Sea, horrific, lethal, and unstoppable creatures have emerged from the bottomless depths and attacked the world's most lavish luxury cruise ship, the *Argonautica*, on its maiden voyage. With indescribable strength and deadly precision, these inhuman forces have transformed the vessel into a horrific death trap. For the few remaining on the ship who have escaped, at least for the moment, plus the ill-fated smuggler John Finnegan and a bunch of mercenaries, who dock their crippled vessel, the *Saipan*, against the *Argonautica*, a living nightmare awaits. In the middle of nowhere, escape seems impossible. A Hollywood Pictures film in association with Cinergi Productions. Released on January 30, 1998. Directed by Stephen Sommers. 106 min. Stars Treat Williams (John Finnegan), Famke Janssen (Trillian), Anthony Heald (Canton), Kevin J. O'Connor (Pantucci), Wes Studi (Hanover), Derrick O'Connor (Capt. Atherton). Filmed in CinemaScope. Filming took place in and around Vancouver, British Columbia, with much of the production taking place at Versatile Shipyards, a historic ship assembly plant there.

Deer Family, The (film) Educational film; released in August 1968. Tells of the habits of the horned and antlered animals—deer, moose, antelope, caribou.

Defense Against Invasion (film) Educational film showing the human body's ability to counteract germs through vaccination. The human body is compared to a city, and the film shows how the city (or body) would react should it be invaded by germs. The city or body could die if it does not avail itself of the protection that science can provide. Produced under the auspices of the Coordinator of Inter-American Affairs. Delivered on August 11, 1943. Directed by Jack King.

DeGeneres, Ellen Actress; starred in the television series *Laurie Hill, These Friends of Mine*, and *Ellen*, and in the feature film *Mr. Wrong* (Martha). In 1997 she made headlines when she came out as a lesbian, followed by her character on the show *Ellen* doing the same on April 30. She provided the voice of Dory in *Finding Nemo*.

Deja, Andreas Animator; began his Disney career in 1980 doing conceptual drawing for *The Black Cauldron*. He helped animate Mickey Mouse in *The Prince and the Pauper*, and served as supervising animator on Gaston (*Beauty and the Beast*), Jafar (*Aladdin*), Scar (*The Lion King*), Hercules (*Hercules*), Lilo (*Lilo & Stitch*), and Slim (*Home on the Range*).

Déjà Vu (film) Directed by Tony Scott. A Touchstone/Jerry Bruckheimer picture. Stars Denzel Washington. Filming is planned to begin in Louisiana in early 2006.

Delaware The Walt Disney Company was reincorporated in Delaware on February 11, 1987.

de Leonardis, Roberto (1913–1984) He was involved with the release of Disney films in Italy for four decades. He was presented posthumously with a European Disney Legends Award in 1997.

Delivery Boy, The (film) Mickey Mouse cartoon; released on June 13, 1931. Mickey is delivering a wagon full of musical instruments when he stops to sing and dance with Minnie. Mickey accidentally hits a hornets' nest that lands on the mule pulling the wagon, upsetting it and causing the instruments to scatter everywhere. All the barnyard animals join in playing the instruments until Pluto chews on a stick of dynamite he has taken from a local demolition site. After the explosion, Mickey and Minnie continue to play on the damaged instruments. Directed by Burt Gillett.

Delizie Italiane Shop selling cookies, chocolates, and candies in Italy in World Showcase at Epcot; presented by Perugina. Opened November 23, 1989. Took the place of Arcata d'Antigiani.

DeLoach, Nikki Actress; appeared on the *Mickey Mouse Club* on The Disney Channel, beginning in 1993.

Delta Dreamflight Tomorrowland attraction in Magic Kingdom Park at Walt Disney World, opened on June 26, 1989, replacing If You Could Fly. When Delta took over the sponsorship of the attraction from Eastern, they changed the name of If You Had Wings to If You Could Fly, but continued to operate it until Delta Dreamflight could be designed and constructed to take its place. A lighthearted look at the story of aviation. Delta discontinued sponsorship on January 1, 1996, and the attraction was renamed Take Flight. It closed on January 5, 1998, and reopened in October 1998 as Buzz Lightyear's Space Ranger Spin.

DeLuise, Dom Actor; he voiced Fagin in *Oliver & Company*.

Demand (film) Educational film from The People on Market Street series, produced by Terry Kahn; released in September 1977. Demand is demonstrated by use of pricing in a gas station.

Demarest, William (1892–1983) Actor; appeared in *Son of Flubber* (Mr. Hummel) and *That Darn Cat!* (Mr. MacDougal).

Demetral, Chris Young actor; appeared in *Blank Check* (Damian Waters), and on television in *Disneyland's 35th Anniversary Celebration* and as a guest star on *Blossom*.

Democracy—Equality or Privilege? (film) Educational film in the History Alive! series, produced by Turnley Walker; released in 1972. Covers the disagreements between Thomas Jefferson and Alexander Hamilton in the 1790s on how our new government should be conducted.

De Mornay, Rebecca Actress; appeared in *The Hand That Rocks the Cradle* (Peyton), *Guilty as Sin* (Jennifer Haines), and *The Three Musketeers* (Milady De Winter).

Dempsey, Patrick Actor; appeared in *Can't Buy Me Love* (Ronald Miller), *Run* (Charlie Farrow), and *Sweet Home Alabama* (Andrew), and on television in *A Fighting Choice* and *Grey's Anatomy* (Derek Shepherd).

Dennehy, Brian Actor; appeared in *Never Cry Wolf* (Rosie) and *Return to Snowy River* (Harrison).

Denver, John (1943–1997) Actor/singer; appeared on television in *The Leftovers*. He composed his popular "Sweet Surrender" for *The Bears and I*.

Depardieu, Gérard French actor; appeared in *Green Card* (George), *My Father the Hero* (Andre), and *102 Dalmatians* (Jean Pierre Le Pelt).

Depp, Johnny Actor; starred in *Ed Wood* in the title role, and in the *Pirates of the Caribbean* trilogy of films (Captain Jack Sparrow).

Der Bücherwurm Shop in Germany in World Showcase at Epcot; opened on October 1, 1982. The building is based upon the Kaufhaus, a merchants' hall in the town of Freiburg, Germany. The shop sells prints and books about Germany.

Der Fuehrer's Face (film) Donald Duck cartoon; released on January 1, 1943. Directed by

Jack Kinney. Donald has a nightmare that he is living in Nazi Germany, envisioning bayonet discipline, starvation, hard work on the munitions assembly line, and "heiling Hitler." He awakens to find himself in the shadow of a Statue of Liberty and glad to be a U.S. citizen. Originally to be titled *Donald Duck in Nutziland*, but the success of the "Der Fuehrer's Face" song by Oliver Wallace caused it to be changed. One of the more famous renditions of the song was by Spike Jones. Academy Award winner for Best Cartoon.

Der Teddybär Shop in Germany in World Showcase at Epcot; opened on October 1, 1982. Sells a variety of toys.

Deserter, The (television) Television show; episode one of *Willie and the Yank.*

de Seversky, Alexander (1894–1974) Author of *Victory Through Air Power*, who appeared as himself in the Disney film of the same title which Walt Disney made from his book.

Desperado from Tombstone (television) Television show; episode 9 of *Texas John Slaughter.*

Desperate Housewives (television) Hour-long comedy/drama series on ABC; premiered on October 3, 2004. After her death, Mary Alice Scott is now looking down into the lives of her family, friends, and neighbors. From her unique vantage point, Mary Alice sees more now than she ever did alive, and she comments on all the delicious and dark secrets that hide behind every neighbor's closed door in a seemingly perfect American suburb. Stars Sheryl Lee (Mary Alice Scott), Mark Moses (Paul Young), Cody Kasch (Zach Young), Teri Hatcher (Susan Mayer), Andrea Bowen (Jenna Mayer), Marcia Cross (Bree Van De Kamp), Michael Reilly Burke (Rex Van De Kamp), Felicity Huffman (Lynette Scavo), Eva Longoria (Gabrielle Solis), Ricardo Chavira (Carlos Solis), James Denton (Mike Delfino), Kyle Searles (John), Nicolette Sheridan (Edie Britt), Jesse Metcalfe (John Rowland). From Touchstone Television.

Destination: Careers (film) Educational film; released in September 1984. Relates skills and interests to various job families and introduces job possibilities of the future.

Destination: Communications (film) Educational film; released in September 1984. A history of the development of communication and a demonstration of how technology has broadened our ability to communicate.

Destination: Excellence (film) Educational film; released in September 1984. Helps teachers motivate students to extend their talents and abilities to their highest potential, through examples of a variety of professionals who are tops in their fields.

Destination: Science (film) Educational film; released in September 1984. An exploration of the world of science beyond the laboratory—how major discoveries came about as the result of scientific inquiry.

Destino (film) Walt Disney and Salvador Dali collaborated on this surrealistic film in 1946, but for a number of reasons it was not completed. Decades later, Roy E. Disney took up the cause, and the film was finally completed in 2003. It premiered at the Annecy International Animated Film Festival in France on June 2, 2003, and theatrically in Los Angeles and New York on December 19, 2003. Directed by Dominique Monfery. The story is by Salvador Dali and John Hench, and the film features the song "Destino," written by Armando Dominguez and performed by Dora Luz. The film received an Academy

Award nomination for Best Animated Short. See also Salvador Dali.

Deuce Bigalow: Male Gigolo (film) Deuce is a naïve, down-on-his-luck guy who cleans fish tanks for a living. His life changes while fish-sitting for Antoine Laconte, a debonair, world-class male escort. He gets comfortable in Antoine's apartment, where his only rules are: don't answer the phone and don't drive the Porsche. After a chain of events that virtually destroys the apartment and needing money to pay for the damages, Deuce mistakenly answers the business phone and becomes Deuce Bigalow: male gigolo, entering a world beyond his wildest dreams. Released on December 10, 1999. Directed by Mike Mitchell. A Touchstone Picture. Stars Rob Schneider (Deuce), Arija Bareikis (Kate), William Forsythe (Detective Fowler), Eddie Griffin (T.J. Hicks), Oded Fehr (Antoine). 88 min. Filmed on location in the Los Angeles area. Living Color designed the custom-made aquarium for Antoine's apartment; it was a 300-gallon octagon with exact replicas of coral reef sculptures, displaying a wide range of marine life from all over the world. Released on video in 2000. A 2005 sequel, *Deuce Bigalow: European Gigolo*, was made by Columbia.

Devil and Max Devlin, The (film) To save his soul, minor league sinner Max Devlin makes a deal with the devil's right-hand man, Barney: within two months he must convince three innocent people to sell their souls. Max makes his victims' dreams come true, and tricks them into signing a "contract." At the last moment, Max learns that Barney lied, and he risks eternal damnation by burning the contracts and saving the others. Released on February 6, 1981. Directed by Steven Hilliard Stern. 95 min. Stars Elliott Gould (Max Devlin), Bill Cosby (Barney), Susan Anspach (Penny), Adam Rich (Toby), Julie Budd (Stella), Sonny Shroyer (Big Billy Hunniker), David Knell (Nerve Nordlinger). The film features the songs "Roses and Rainbows" by Marvin Hamlisch and Carole Bayer Sager and "Any Fool Could See" by Marvin Hamlisch and Allee Willis. Location shooting was done at Universal Studios,

utilizing the Universal Studios Tour and Amphitheatre. In addition, the Troubadour, the Music Center, the Pasadena Civic Auditorium, Indian Dunes, and Venice Beach were used around the Los Angeles area. Disney makeup man Bob Schiffer was responsible for Bill Cosby's convincing devilish look. He provided Cosby with a red iridescent wig, with ears and horns sewn into the base, and a heavy mauve makeup coloring as a base for his face, on top of which he used a special red water-soluble makeup from Germany. The elaborate Hell set was constructed of huge plaster stalagmites and stalactites with menacing bursts of flame provided by 20 butane furnaces. When the smoke cleared after four days of filming in "Hell," the special-effects department had consumed 150 gallons of butane fuel, not to mention the 36,000 pounds of dry ice used to provide the eerie low-lying smoke effect. Released on video in 1981.

Devine, Andy (1905–1997) Actor; appeared on television in *Ride a Northbound Horse* and *Smoke*, and provided the voice of Friar Tuck in *Robin Hood*.

DeVito, Danny Actor; appeared in *Ruthless People* (Sam Stone), *Tin Men* (Ernest Tilley), and *Renaissance Man* (Bill Rago), and provided the voice of Phil in *Hercules*.

Dewey One of Donald Duck's three nephews.

Dewhurst, Colleen (1926–1991) Actress; appeared on television in *Bigfoot* (Gladys), and in *Lantern Hill* and *Anne of Avonlea* on The Disney Channel.

deWilde, Brandon (1942–1972) Actor; appeared in *Those Calloways* (Bucky), and on television in *The Tenderfoot*.

Diamond, Eileen Mouseketeer from the 1950s television show.

Diamond Horseshoe Revue Frontierland attraction in Magic Kingdom Park at Walt Disney World; opened October 1, 1971. The original show ran until it was changed on October 1, 1986, after which time it became the Diamond Horseshoe Jamboree. Beginning April 7, 1995, reservations were no longer required and the show was

extensively changed, returning to its original name. Guests could walk in at any time during the show, purchase counter-service food, and watch the entertainment. It ended February 1, 2003, and Goofy's Country Dancin' Jamboree began July 1, 2003. Also in Westernland at Tokyo Disneyland; opened on April 15, 1983. These attractions are based on the original Golden Horseshoe Revue, which opened at Disneyland in 1955.

Diamond Is a Boy's Best Friend, A (television) Television show; episode 1 of *Moochie of the Little League*.

Diamonds on Wheels (television) Three-part television show; aired on March 10, 17, and 24, 1974. Directed by Jerome Courtland. Teenagers battle jewel thieves in England, when one of them acquires a car seat, in which the jewels had been hidden, from a junkyard to use in his racing car. The thieves follow the boys during the Hampshire Rally, an endurance race, but with the help of the police, are outwitted. Stars Patrick Allen, Peter Firth, George Sewell, Spencer Banks, Cynthia Lund. The director, Jerome Courtland, earlier starred as Andy Burnett for Disney. Originally released theatrically in England in August 1973.

Diana Goddess of the moon in the *Pastoral* segment of *Fantasia*.

Dick Tracy (film) Legendary police detective Dick Tracy is the only man tough enough to take on gangster boss Big Boy Caprice and his band of menacing mobsters. Dedicated to his work but at the same time devoted to his loyal girlfriend, Tess Trueheart, Tracy finds himself torn between love and duty. His relentless crusade against crime becomes even more difficult when he gets saddled with an engaging orphan and meets seductive and sultry Breathless Mahoney, a torch singer determined to get the best of Tracy. A faceless character, the Blank, threatens both Tracy and Big Boy, and it takes all of Tracy's skills to save the city. Released on June 15, 1990. Directed by Warren Beatty. A Touchstone film. 105 min. Stars Warren Beatty (Dick Tracy), Charlie Korsmo (Kid), Madonna (Breathless Mahoney), Al Pacino (Big Boy Caprice), Glenne Headly (Tess Trueheart), Mandy Patinkin (88 Keys), Paul Sorvino (Lips Manlis), Dustin Hoffman (Mumbles), Dick Van Dyke (D.A. Fletcher), James Caan (Spaldoni). Based on the comic strip by Chester Gould. The unique and unusual faces for the gangster characters was created by makeup and prosthetics wizards John Caglione, Jr., and Doug Drexler. Some actors needed to endure up to four hours in the makeup room getting ready for the camera. Dick Tracy's fantasy world was created on the backlot at the Warner Bros. Studio. The film won Academy Awards for Best Makeup (John Caglione, Jr., Doug Drexler), Best Art Direction/Set Decoration (Richard Sylbert, Rick Simpson), and Best Song ("Sooner or Later [I Always Get My Man]" by Stephen Sondheim). Released on video in 1990. The movie led to a shop, Dick Tracy, at Pleasure Island at Walt Disney World during part of 1990.

Dick Tracy: Behind the Badge . . . Behind the Scenes (television) Syndicated television special about the making of the Touchstone film; first aired on June 13, 1990. 30 min. Directed by Gayle Hollenbaugh.

Dick Tracy Starring in Diamond Double-Cross Show at Disney-MGM Studios from May 21, 1990, to February 16, 1991; also at Videopolis at Disneyland from June 15 to December 31, 1990. The successful release of the film *Dick Tracy* led to this popular stage show.

Diesel, Vin Actor; appeared in *The Pacifier* (Shane Wolf).

Dillon, Matt Actor; appeared in the title role in *Tex*.

Dinah Seductive dachshund who captivated Pluto, appearing in five cartoons with him, beginning with *The Sleepwalker* (1942).

Dinah Alice's kitten in *Alice in Wonderland*.

Dinky and Boomer Sparrow and woodpecker friends of Tod in *The Fox and the Hound*; voiced by Dick Bakalyan and Paul Winchell.

DinoLand U.S.A. Area in Disney's Animal Kingdom at Walt Disney World, presented by McDonald's. Guests enter what looks like a quirky roadside attraction, featuring the Boneyard playground, a rambling open-air dig site filled with fossils that kids can play on. Dinosaur! is an attraction showing guests dinosaurs facing extinction from a giant asteroid that is hurtling toward Earth. On Cretaceous Trail, they can walk through the past, amid a lush variety of cycads, palms, and ferns, and some other surprising survivors of the age of the dinosaurs. There is also the Theater in the Wild, a 1,500-seat amphitheater. In 2001–2002, an additional area, Dino-Rama, opened next to Chester & Hester's Dinosaur Treasures gift shop, featuring Primeval Whirl, TriceroTop Spin, and midway games.

Dinosaur (film) During the Cretaceous period, 65 million years ago, a three-ton iguanodon named Aladar is raised by a clan of lemurs and eventually reunited with his own kind. With flam-

ing meteors devastating the landscape and water in diminishing supply, the dinosaurs find themselves in a race against time to reach the safety of their nesting grounds. When Aladar comes to the aid of a group of misfits unable to keep up with the breakneck pace of the herd, he makes an enemy of Kron, the stone-hearted leader. Faced with such perils as treacherous rock slides and attacking carnotaurs, Aladar and his friends must overcome tremendous obstacles before they can settle into a new life in a beautiful valley. Directed by Ralph Zondag and Eric Leighton. Released on May 19, 2000. Voices include Ossie Davis (Yar), Della Reese (Eema), Joan Plowright (Baylene), D.B. Sweeney (Aladar), Alfre Woodard (Plio), Samuel E. Wright (Kron), Julianna Margulies (Neera), Hayden Panettiere (Suri), Peter Siragusa (Bruton), Max Casella (Zini). 82 min. Musical score is by James Newton Howard. The film breaks new ground by combining state-of-the-art computer character animation with digitally enhanced live-action backgrounds. While previous features using computer animation—*Toy Story*, *Toy Story 2*, and *A Bug's Life*—were produced by Pixar in association with the Disney Studio, this film was the first to be produced in-house. The Countdown to Extinction attraction at Disney's Animal Kingdom was renamed Dinosaur! to tie in with the film. Released on video in 2001.

Dinosaur New name, in May 2001, of Countdown to Extinction at Disney's Animal Kingdom.

Dinosaur Gertie's Ice Cream of Extinction Shop opened at Disney-MGM Studios on May 1, 1989. Gertie the Dinosaur was one of the first animated film characters, created by Winsor McCay in the early years of the twentieth century. The Disney Imagineers decided to honor McCay

with this dinosaur-shaped ice cream shop. Observant guests can even notice dinosaur-shaped footprints in the concrete walkway leading to the shop.

Dinosaur . . . Secret of the Lost Legend (television) Edited version of the feature *Baby*, which aired on television on January 8, 1989.

Dinosaurs (television) Television series; airing on ABC from April 26, 1991 to July 20, 1994. Jim Henson Associates created the characters in this series covering the life of a prehistoric family, the Sinclairs, in a contemporary setting. Voices were provided by Stuart Pankin (Earl Sinclair), Jessica Walter (Fran Sinclair), Jason Willinger (Robbie), Sally Struthers (Charlene), John Kennedy (Baby), Sam McMurray (Roy Hess), Sherman Hemsley (B.P. Richfield), Florence Stanley (Ethyl), Chris Meloni (Spike). The show won an Emmy Award for Art Direction in 1991.

Dinosaurs Live Parade at Disney-MGM Studios from September 26, 1991 to August 29, 1992.

Dinotopia (television) Six-hour miniseries from Hallmark Entertainment; aired on *The Wonderful World of Disney* May 12–14, 2002. Epic story of a lost continent where dinosaurs and humans live together in an almost-utopian world. Directed by Marco Brambilla. Stars David Thewlis (Cyrus Crabb), Katie Carr (Marion), Jim Carter (Mayor Waldo), Alice Krige (Rosemary), Tyron Leitso

(Karl), Wentworth Miller (David). Based on the books by James Gurney. The largest production ever filmed at Pinewood Studios in London. A production of Hallmark Entertainment.

Dinotopia (television) The miniseries continued as a weekly television series on ABC, premiering on November 28, 2002, and ending December 26, 2002. New cast members were Erik von Detten (Karl Scott), Shiloh Strong (David Scott), Michael Brandon (Frank Scott), Georgina Rylance (Marion), Jonathan Hyde (Mayor Waldo), Sophie Ward (Rosemary), Lisa Zane (Le Sage). Omid Djalili provided the voice of Zipeau. Shiloh Strong is the older brother of Rider Strong, who played Shawn on *Boy Meets World*. The series was filmed in Budapest.

Discover Magazine covering the world of science acquired by The Walt Disney Company on September 13, 1991. Disney announced the sale of the magazine in September 2005.

Discover Quest (film) Series of three educational productions, based on *Discover* magazine articles, released on laser disc in December 1994. The titles are *Explorations in Earth Science*, *Explorations in Life Science*, and *Explorations in Physical Science*.

Discovery Arcade Located behind the Main Street shops at Disneyland Paris, on the Discoveryland side of the street.

Discovery Day Thursday on the new *Mickey Mouse Club*.

Discovery Island Nature preserve at Walt Disney World; opened on April 8, 1974 as Treasure Island; name changed in 1977. It closed on April 8, 1999. An 11.5-acre island paradise, Discovery Island was home to many exotic birds and animals. Originally the island was themed to the Disney film *Treasure Island*, and a wrecked ship from that incarnation could still be seen on the shore. One of the largest walk-through aviaries in the world was featured, and guests might come upon giant tortoises. Since the area was a wildlife sanctuary, Disney curators helped the government try to save the species of Florida dusky sparrows by beginning a breeding program, but the last pure dusky sparrow passed away of old age on the island.

Disney, Diane M. Older daughter of Walt and Lillian Disney; born on December 18, 1933. With Pete Martin, she wrote a biography of her father in 1956. She married Ronald W. Miller, who later served as president of Walt Disney Productions, and they had seven children. She inspired the CD-ROM *Walt Disney: An Intimate History of the Man and His Magic* and the documentary *Walt: The Man Behind the Myth*.

Disney, Edna Francis Wife of Roy O. Disney. She was born in 1890 and met Roy in Kansas City. They married in 1925 in uncle Robert Disney's home. The couple had one son, Roy E. Disney. Edna passed away in 1984 at the age of 94. She was named a Disney Legend posthumously in 2003.

Disney, Elias Father of Walt Disney, born in Bluevale, Ontario, Canada, on February 6, 1859, the son of Irish immigrants. While still in his teens, he moved with his family to the United States, where they settled in Ellis, Kansas. A few years later, when a neighbor family named Call moved to Florida, Elias went with them and soon  married the daughter, Flora. Elias and Flora had bad luck growing oranges and running a hotel in Florida, so they moved to Chicago, where Elias became a building contractor. After trying farming in Marceline, Missouri, running a newspaper delivery business in Kansas City, and working in a jelly factory in Chicago, Elias and Flora moved to Portland, Oregon, where their daughter was living. After the success of their sons, Walt and Roy, they moved to North Hollywood to be near them in the late 1930s. Elias died on September 13, 1941.

Disney, Flora Walt Disney's mother, born Flora Call in Steuben, Ohio, on April 22, 1868. Her mother's family was of German ancestry. Flora died on November 26, 1938.

Disney, Herbert A. Eldest brother of Walt Disney, born in Florida on December 8, 1888, and died on January 29, 1961. He was a mailman.

Disney, Lillian Bounds Wife of Walt Disney. She was born in Idaho in 1899 and came to work for Walt as a secretary shortly after he founded the Disney company. He married her in 1925, and they had two children, Diane and Sharon. After Walt's death, she married John L. Truyens in 1969 but survived him on his death, in 1981. In 1987, she announced a $50 million gift to build a symphonic hall for the Los Angeles Philharmonic Orchestra, perhaps the largest ever gift by an individual to a cultural organization. She died on December 16, 1997, and was named a Disney Legend posthumously in 2003.

Disney, Ray Walt Disney's older brother, who had been in the insurance business. He was born on December 30, 1890, and died on May 24, 1989, at the age of 98.

Disney, Roy Edward Son of Roy O. Disney and nephew of Walt Disney; born in 1930. Roy began working for the company in 1954 as an assistant film editor on the True-Life Adventure films. He helped write narration for animal-related television shows from 1957 to 1971, and also directed (1973 to 1978) and produced (1968 to 1977) many of the same type of shows. He was first elected to the board of directors in 1967. He left the company for a few years, but returned in 1984 as vice chairman of the board, and head of the animation department. He was named a Disney Legend in 1998. He resigned on November 30, 2003. He was named director emeritus and a consultant on July 8, 2005.

Disney, Roy Oliver Older brother of Walt Disney, who founded the Disney company in partnership with Walt in 1923. Born June 24, 1893; died December 20, 1971. Served as president of Walt

Disney Productions from 1945 to 1968 and chairman of the board from 1964 until 1971. Roy was recuperating in Los Angeles from tuberculosis in 1923 when Walt persuaded him to join in the new venture making animated cartoons. Roy was the financial genius of the two brothers; Walt was the creative genius, and the two of them made a great pair. Modest and unassuming, Roy generally stayed in the background, finding the money for Walt's projects. It was Roy who managed the growth of licensing Disney consumer products. Roy was instrumental in deciding to break with outside distributors and form Buena Vista Distribution Company in 1953. But it was only after Walt's death in 1966 that Roy took a major public leadership position in the company and supervised the building of Walt Disney World. Through his financial acumen, that $400 million project opened in 1971 with the company having no outstanding debt. Roy was at Walt Disney World for the grand opening in October, and died two months later. In 1976, a new office building at the Disney Studio was named the Roy O. Disney Building in honor of the company's co-founder.

Disney, Ruth F. Walt Disney's sister, the youngest in the family, born in Chicago on December 6, 1903. Ruth eventually moved to Portland, Oregon, where she married Theodore Beecher. Ruth was a connoisseur of organ music, purchasing and outfitting an old theater organ at her home. She died on April 7, 1995.

Disney, Sharon M. Second daughter of Walt and Lillian Disney, born on December 31, 1936. She married first Robert B. Brown, who died shortly after Walt, and later William Lund. She had three children. She was one of the founders of Retlaw Enterprises. Sharon was elected to the board of directors of The Walt Disney Company in 1984, and passed away on February 16, 1993.

Disney, Walter Elias Founder of the Disney empire, Walt Disney was born on December 5, 1901, in Chicago, Illinois, son of Elias and Flora Call Disney. Elias decided a few years later to move his family to a farm at Marceline, Missouri,

and it was here that the young Walt grew up and got his first love for animals and the rural life, which would be so evident in his films. The family moved to Kansas City in 1911, and Walt delivered newspapers for his father, who had purchased a newspaper distribution business. Walt attended Benton School, and occasionally surprised his teachers with his talent for drawing and acting. When the family moved back to Chicago, Walt attended one year of McKinley High School. The end of World War I saw Walt serving briefly in France as an ambulance driver, but then he returned to Kansas City and attempted to put his art talents to use. After a stint with the Kansas City Film Ad Company, he started his own company, Laugh-O-gram Films, and, with some of his talented friends, made his first animated cartoons. When that business failed, Walt moved to California, and there, with his brother Roy, he started the Disney company in 1923. The company first made a series of Alice Comedies, then a year's worth of Oswald the Lucky Rabbit cartoons, but in 1928, Walt made history by creating, with the help of his trusted colleague, Ub Iwerks, the character of Mickey Mouse. The Mickey Mouse cartoons were immediately popular and ensured the success of the company. A series of Silly Symphony cartoons was added, and soon the Disney artists began work on their first animated feature film, *Snow White and the Seven Dwarfs*. That 1937 film was a huge success, becoming the highest grossing film of all time, until it was surpassed by *Gone With the Wind*. Walt had never been able to make much money with the short cartoons, but the feature films were another story. With the profits from *Snow White*, he was able to build a new studio in Burbank. Other animated features followed, until World War II caused the Disney Studio to retrench. Much of the company's effort went into making training and propaganda films for the military. The end of the war brought peace, but prosperity took a while to arrive at Disney's doors. He bided his time with a group of package films, feature length, but containing a series of two or more short films loosely tied together. *Cinderella* and the move into live-action films with *Treasure*

Island in 1950 marked a return to financial success. A series of popular True-Life Adventure nature films and a move onto television with a regular weekly program gained the Disney Studio added recognition, but it was the building of Disneyland, the first real theme park, in 1955 that finally made the Disney company financially secure. The added cash flow from the park, along with infusions of cash from merchandise licensing, enabled Walt Disney to attempt new projects. Just before his death on December 15, 1966, Walt was busy planning his Experimental Prototype Community of Tomorrow (EPCOT), which he felt would help solve some of the country's urban problems. Walt Disney married Lillian Bounds in 1925, and they had two daughters, Diane and Sharon. Disney was a genius in knowing what the public wanted in the way of family entertainment and he was willing to take chances to create that entertainment. He was an innovator; he was not a follower. When he heard of a new process or concept that interested him, he embraced it totally, often to the dismay of his financial advisers, but time and time again, Walt was proved right. He had his finger on the pulse of America, and a look at his "firsts" helps to show how successful he had been—the first synchronized sound cartoon, the first use of the

storyboard, the first full-color cartoon, the first animated feature film, the first stereophonic theater installations with Fantasound, the first popular nature series, the first major movie producer to go onto television, the first CinemaScope cartoon, the first 3-D cartoon, the first use of the Xerox process to facilitate the animation process, the first stereophonic television broadcast, the first theme park. With each of these, Walt took a chance, and with each he proved that he knew what he was doing. All of these elements became standard in the entertainment industry. Walt Disney left a lasting legacy, one which The Walt Disney Company continues to expand upon today.

Disney•ABC Cable Networks Group

Manages The Walt Disney Company's interest in global television businesses, including 24 wholly-owned international Disney Channels and the company's majority interest in the international Jetix (formerly Fox Kids) channels, plus Disney- and Jetix-branded programming (formerly known as Fox Kids programming) around the world. In addition, the group manages Disney's equity interest in the cable groups Lifetime Entertainment Services, A&E Television Networks, and E! Networks.

Disney•ABC Television Group

Formed in 2004, Disney•ABC Television Group is home to The Walt Disney Company's worldwide (non-sports) media networks and encompasses the ABC-TV network, Disney Channel Worldwide, ABC Family, Jetix (formerly Fox Kids), SOAPnet, Toon Disney, Touchstone Television, Walt Disney Television Animation, Buena Vista Television, and Buena Vista International Television.

Disney Afternoon, The

Two-hour package of animated television series; beginning September 10, 1990. The contents varied from year to year, as follows:

1990–91: *Duck Tales, The Adventures of the Gummi Bears, Chip 'n' Dale's Rescue Rangers, Tale Spin.*

1991–92: *Duck Tales, Chip 'n' Dale's Rescue Rangers, Tale Spin, Darkwing Duck.*

1992–93: *Chip 'n' Dale's Rescue Rangers, Tale Spin, Darkwing Duck, Goof Troop.*

1993–94: *Tale Spin, Darkwing Duck, Goof Troop, Bonkers.*

1994–95: *Darkwing Duck, Goof Troop, Bonkers, Aladdin.*

1995–96: *Goof Troop, Bonkers, Aladdin, Gargoyles.*

1996–97: *Darkwing Duck, Gargoyles, Aladdin, Quack Pack.*

Beginning with the 1994–95 season, additional programs played as part of The Disney Afternoon on selected days—*Gargoyles* and *The Shnookums and Meat Funny Cartoon Show*. In 1995–96 *The Lion King's Timon & Pumbaa* was added, along with *Mighty Ducks* the following year. The Disney Afternoon came to an end at the conclusion of the 1996–97 season.

Disney Afternoon Avenue Special Fantasyland promotion at Disneyland from March 15 to November 10, 1991. Featured Baloo's Dressing Room. The area in front of "it's a small world" was decorated with building fronts modeled after those on the Disney animated television shows, and costumed characters interacted with guests. The adjacent Fantasyland Autopia and Motor Boat Cruise were also themed to Disney Afternoon for the promotion.

Disney Afternoon Live! at Disneyland (television) Television special (60 min.) on KCAL, Los Angeles, airing on September 14, 1991. Includes a look at Walt Disney Imagineering and how they design a new attraction, followed by the opening of Splash Mountain, and a segment on some of Disneyland's more unusual jobs (scuba diver, harness maker, pyrotechnician, etc.). Carl Bell is host.

Disney & Co. Shop on Main Street in Disneyland Paris; opened on April 12, 1992.

Disney Animation Attraction in Hollywood Pictures Backlot at Disney's California Adventure; opened February 8, 2001. Inside, guests can decide between several venues: Animation Academy, Sorcerer's Workshop (with Magic Mirror Realm, The Beast's Library, and Ursula's Grotto), The Art of Animation, or Turtle Talk with Crush. A similar attraction at Walt Disney Studios Paris, named L'Art de l'Animation Disney, opened on March 16, 2002.

Disney Animation: The Illusion of Life (television) Television show; aired on April 26, 1981. Directed by William Reid. Hayley Mills returns to the Disney Studio to see how *The Fox and the Hound* is being made, tied to Frank Thomas and Ollie Johnston's book from which the show was titled. Hayley visits the Archives, learns how models are made for the animators, and is shown the value of the selection of the right actors to provide the voices. She attends a recording session with Pearl Bailey.

Disney Art Editions See Cel.

Disney Brothers Cartoon Studio Original name of the Disney company when it was formed as a partnership between Walt and Roy Disney in 1923.

Disney Catalog, The Mail-order catalog; began in 1984 as the *Disney Family Gift Catalog* and later titled simply *Disney*. Features Disney merchandise exclusively.

Disney Channel, The Cable television network; began broadcasting on April 18, 1983, with 18 hours of programming a day. On December 7, 1986, The Disney Channel went to a full 24 hours. The Channel became one of the fastest-growing pay cable services, reaching over 35 million subscribers after a little over a decade on  the air. It was originated under the leadership of Jim Jimirro and continued by John Cooke and Anne Sweeney. The Channel features a mixture of Disney films, original programming, and family entertainment purchased from other producers. Many Disney films have had their world television premieres on the Channel. Until 1997, the Channel published *The Disney Channel Magazine*, featuring articles, columns, and program notes. In 1993, the Channel began a transition from premium to basic cable service, eventually expanding its reach to over 80 million homes. Gradually starting in the mid-1990s, the Channel instigated a new programming strategy that emphasizes 9- to 14-year-olds, the "tween" years, through original series and movies. Beginning in March 1995 in Taiwan, a number of international channels were launched in such countries as Australia, Italy,

Brazil, and the Philippines, totalling 24 of them by 2005. The Disney Channel officially dropped "The" from its name in 1997 to become Disney Channel.

Disney Channel Original Movies New designation for films previously known as Disney Channel Premiere Films. Titles are:

1. *Northern Lights* — 8-23-97
2. *Under Wraps* — 10-25-97
3. *You Lucky Dog* — 6-27-98
4. *Brink* — 8-29-98
5. *Halloweentown* — 10-17-98
6. *Zenon: Girl of the 21st Century* — 1-23-99
7. *Can of Worms* — 4-10-99
8. *The Thirteenth Year* — 5-15-99
9. *Smart House* — 6-26-99
10. *Johnny Tsunami* — 7-24-99
11. *Genius* — 8-21-99
12. *P.U.N.K.S.* — 9-4-99
13. *Don't Look Under the Bed* — 10-9-99
14. *Horse Sense* — 11-20-99
15. *Up, Up and Away* — 1-22-00
16. *The Color of Friendship* — 2-5-00
17. *Alley Cats Strike!* — 3-18-00
18. *Rip Girls* — 4-22-00
19. *Miracle in Lane Two* — 5-13-00
20. *Stepsister from Planet Weird* — 6-17-00
21. *Ready to Run* — 7-14-00
22. *Quints* — 8-18-00
23. *The Other Me* — 9-8-00
24. *Mom's Got a Date with a Vampire* — 10-13-00
25. *Phantom of the Megaplex* — 11-10-00
26. *The Ultimate Christmas Present* — 12-1-00
27. *Zenon: The Zequel* — 1-12-01
28. *Motocrossed* — 2-2-01
29. *The Luck of the Irish* — 3-9-01
30. *Hounded* — 4-13-01
31. *Jett Jackson: The Movie* — 6-8-01
32. *The Jennie Project* — 7-13-01
33. *Jumping Ship* — 8-17-01
34. *The Poof Point* — 9-14-01
35. *Halloweentown II: Kalabar's Revenge* — 10-12-01
36. *'Twas the Night* — 12-7-01
37. *Double Teamed* — 1-18-02
38. *Cadet Kelly* — 3-8-02
39. *Tru Confessions* — 4-5-02
40. *Get a Clue* — 6-28-02
41. *Gotta Kick It Up* — 7-26-02
42. *A Ring of Endless Light* — 8-23-02
43. *The Scream Team* — 10-4-02
44. *You Wish!* — 1-10-03
45. *Right on Track* — 3-21-03
46. *The Even Stevens Movie* — 6-13-03
47. *Eddie's Million Dollar Cook-Off* — 7-18-03
48. *The Cheetah Girls* — 8-15-03
49. *Full-Court Miracle* — 11-21-03
50. *Pixel Perfect* — 1-16-04
51. *Going to the Mat* — 3-19-04
52. *Zenon: Z3* — 6-11-04
53. *Stuck in the Suburbs* — 7-16-04
54. *Tiger Cruise* — 8-6-04
55. *Halloweentown High* — 10-8-04
56. *Now You See It* — 1-14-05
57. *Buffalo Dreams* — 3-11-05
58. *Disney's Kim Possible Movie: So the Drama* — 4-8-05
59. *Go Figure* — 6-10-05
60. *Life Is Ruff* — 7-15-05
61. *Twitches* — 10-14-05
62. *High School Musical* — 1-20-06

Disney Channel Premiere Films Beginning in 1983, The Disney Channel has commissioned a number of made-for-cable motion pictures for airing on the Channel. In 1997, they ceased using the "Premiere Films" designation. Chronologically, the film titles have been:

1. *Tiger Town* — 10-9-83
2. *Gone Are the Dayes* — 5-6-84
3. *Love Leads the Way* — 10-7-84
4. *Black Arrow* — 1-6-85
5. *Lots of Luck* — 2-3-85
6. *The Undergrads* — 5-5-85
7. *The Blue Yonder* — 11-17-85

8.	*The Parent Trap II*	7-26-86
9.	*Spot Marks the X*	10-18-86
10.	*Down the Long Hills*	11-15-86
11.	*Strange Companions*	2-28-87
12.	*Anne of Avonlea:*	5-19-87
	The Continuing Story	
	of Anne of Green Gables	
13.	*Not Quite Human*	6-19-87
14.	*The Christmas Visitor*	12-5-87
15.	*Save the Dog*	3-19-88
16.	*Night Train to Kathmandu*	6-5-88
17.	*Ollie Hopnoodle's Haven*	8-6-88
	of Bliss	
18.	*A Friendship in Vienna*	8-27-88
19.	*Good Old Boy*	11-11-88
20.	*Goodbye, Miss 4th Of July*	12-3-88
21.	*Danny, The Champion*	4-29-89
	of the World	
22.	*Looking for Miracles*	6-3-89
23.	*Great Expectations*	7-9-89
24.	*Not Quite Human II*	9-23-89
25.	*Spooner*	12-2-89
26.	*Lantern Hill*	1-27-90
27.	*Chips, the War Dog*	3-24-90
28.	*Mother Goose Rock 'n'*	5-19-90
	Rhyme	
29.	*Back Home*	6-7-90
30.	*The Little Kidnappers*	8-17-90
31.	*Back to Hannibal:*	10-21-90
	The Return of Tom Sawyer	
	and Huckleberry Finn	
32.	*Bejewelled*	1-20-91
33.	*Perfect Harmony*	3-31-91
34.	*Mark Twain and Me*	11-22-91
35.	*Still Not Quite Human*	5-31-92
36.	*The Ernest Green Story*	1-17-93
37.	*Spies*	3-7-93
38.	*Heidi*	7-18-93
39.	*On Promised Land*	4-17-94
40.	*The Whipping Boy*	7-31-94
41.	*The Old Curiosity Shop*	3-19-95
42.	*The Four Diamonds*	8-12-95
43.	*The Little Riders*	3-24-96
44.	*Nightjohn*	6-1-96
45.	*Northern Lights*	8-23-97

See also Disney Channel Original Movies for later films.

Disney Channel Worldwide Representing the portfolio of kids' channels in the United States, Europe, the Middle East, Asia Pacific, and Latin America, Disney Channel Worldwide's global roster of media networks includes 24 Disney Channels, five Playhouse Disney Channels, and three Toon Disney Channels. The group also distributes approximately 100 Disney-branded blocks of programming in more than 70 countries, reaching over 600 million television viewers.

Disney Christmas Gift, A (television) Television show; aired on December 4, 1982. A holiday salute beginning and ending at Disneyland, with animated segments. Old Christmas cards and toys from the Walt Disney Archives are used as connecting footage.

Disney Christmas Gift, A (television) Television special broadcast on CBS on December 20, 1983 (different show than the series episode).

Disney Classics Theater Opened at Disney-MGM Studios on May 1, 1989.

Disney Clothiers Shop on Main Street at Disneyland; opened on March 23, 1985. Took the place of the former Hallmark card shop. Also in Magic Kingdom Park at Walt Disney World; opened on February 24, 1985. Also in Disneyland Paris; opened on April 12, 1992.

Disney Club, The Membership club launched on November 14, 2000, offering discounts on food and beverage, theme park tickets, guided tours, and merchandise. It replaced the Magic Kingdom Club. The club disbanded December 31, 2003, in favor of a Disney-branded Visa card.

Disney College Program An internship program begun as the Magic Kingdom College Program, featuring a work and learning experience, at Walt Disney World in 1980, with name changes to the Walt Disney World College Program in 1984 and the Disney Theme Parks & Resorts College Program in 2005. Recruiters visit college campuses each spring and fall to inform prospective students about the program, answer questions, and even do on-the-spot interviews. The first students were housed at the Hidden Valley Trailer Park (later known as Snow White Village Campground). An international program, the World Showcase Fellowship Program, began with the opening of Epcot in 1982. Advanced internships, with focused learning, based on specific areas of study, began in 1992. Housing complexes for the students were added, beginning with Vista Way Apartments in April 1988, The Commons in January 1998, and Chatham Square in June 2000. College Programs have also operated at Disneyland (beginning in 1989), at Disneyland Paris (beginning in 1992), and at Walt Disney Imagineering. The learning component of the program changed through the years from business seminars to college-level courses that the American Council on Education has approved for college credit.

Disney Cruise Line After successful Disney cruises licensed to other cruise operators, Disney decided to get into the cruise business itself. The first cruise ship, *Disney Magic*, set out on its maiden voyage July 30, 1998, from its home port, Port Canaveral, Florida. The second ship, *Disney Wonder*, had its maiden voyage on August 15, 1999. In February 1996, Disney announced the

 purchase of Gorda Cay, five months later renamed Disney's Castaway Cay, a 1,000-acre uninhabited island in the Bahamas, which serves as a daylong stop for cruise passengers on the two ships.

Disney Development Co. Disney subsidiary, formed in September 1984, responsible for master planning, development, and asset management of the company's non-theme park real estate assets, including hotels, company office buildings, and the town of Celebration. It merged with Walt Disney Imagineering in May 1996.

Disney Dollars Currency offered at the Disney parks beginning May 5, 1987, with equivalent value to U.S. currency. Mickey Mouse appeared on the $1 bill and Goofy on the $5 bill. A $10 bill featuring Minnie Mouse was added on November 20, 1989, and a $50 bill featuring Mickey Mouse was added on July 17, 2005, for the 50th anniversary of Disneyland.

Disney Educational Productions Formerly the Walt Disney Educational Materials Co. and Walt Disney Educational Media Co., involved in the production of educational films, video cassettes, videodiscs, DVDs, and other products for schools.

Disney Fair Live stage show, exhibits, games, and shops under a tent created to appear at state fairs nationwide, first appearing at the Washington State Fair in Puyallup, September 6–22, 1996, then later in Arizona. Instead of continuing with state fairs, the show was reworked as DisneyFest with plans for overseas productions. It began its first run in Singapore on October 30, 1997.

Disney Family Album (television) Series on The Disney Channel, premiering June 9, 1984, which featured individual shows on people who have made Disney so successful. Included were shows on the Disneyland Designers, Ward Kimball, Ollie Johnston, Annette Funicello, Jim Macdonald, Ken Anderson, Peter and Harrison Ellenshaw, Eric Larson, Richard M. Sherman and Robert B. Sherman, Clarence Nash, Milt Kahl. 20 episodes.

Disney Foundation Established in 1951 as a nonprofit corporation dedicated exclusively to the support of charitable and educational activities. Contributions to the Foundation come from The Walt Disney Company. In addition to the active support of numerous health, community, educational, and youth organizations in California,

Florida, and New York, the Foundation from time to time sponsors its own activities, such as a College Scholarship Program for the children of Disney employees.

Disney Gallery, The Display of Disneyland-related artwork, designs, and models, above Pirates of the Caribbean at Disneyland; opened on July 11, 1987. This area had originally been planned as an apartment for Walt and Roy Disney, and in fact if you study the wrought-iron railings on the balcony, you can see the initials of RD and WD. After Walt's death, Roy decided not to build the apartment. Instead, the area was later used as a VIP lounge by INA, one of the Disneyland participants, and as offices for those planning Tokyo Disneyland. When trying to decide how to help the traffic flow in front of Pirates of the Caribbean, Disney Imagineer Tony Baxter redesigned the queue area, but he also had the idea of building curved staircases up to the second floor and opening the area up to guests. The Imagineers had long wanted a place where they could display some of their concept art for the park. The artwork in the Gallery is changed from time to time, and lithographs and other limited-edition pieces are sold there. Regular signings of books and prints help draw guests to the Gallery. A Disney Gallery also opened above World Bazaar at Tokyo Disneyland on April 15, 1993.

Disney Goes to the Oscars (television) Television show; aired on March 23, 1986. Directed by Andrew Solt. Covers some of the Disney Academy Award–winning films, with Tony Danza.

Disney Halloween, A (television) Television show; aired on October 24, 1981. The Magic Mirror helps look at some of the legends surrounding Halloween, featuring segments from Disney cartoons and animated features.

Disney Inn, The Golf hotel at Walt Disney World, formerly The Golf Resort. The name was changed in 1986. The hotel was popular not only for golfers, but by other guests because its more secluded location, not on the Monorail line, made it seem quieter and more restful. Leased by the government in 1994 for military personnel and renamed Shades of Green.

Disney Institute, The Participatory vacation experience opened at Walt Disney World on February 9, 1996. Guests chose from a wide selection of interactive programs (more than 60) in the areas of Entertainment Arts, Performing Arts, Story Arts, Design Arts, Culinary Arts, Lifestyles, Gardening & the Great Outdoors, and Sports and Fitness. The facilities were located at the Disney Village and included Seasons Dining Room, a store (Dabblers), studios for animation, design arts, culinary arts, radio and TV, a 400-seat cinema, a 225-seat amphitheater, and a large 38,000-square-foot sports and fitness center and spa. The former Village Resort accommodations became part of the Disney Institute—Bungalows (formerly Club Suites), Townhouses (formerly Vacation Villas), Treehouse Villas, Fairway Villas, and Grand Vista Homes. In the summer of 2000 the Institute no longer offered programs to individual tourists, but rather focused on programs that catered to groups and corporate retreats, a shift that had begun in late 1996. The last guests stayed at the Disney Institute on February 11, 2002. In 2004, the Institute was replaced by the Saratoga Springs Resort and Spa, part of the Disney Vacation Club.

Disney Interactive Division formed in 1994 to develop, market, and distribute cartridge games and CD-ROM software; it took the place of Disney Software. It became part of Buena Vista Games in 2003.

Disney Internet Group Formed in 2000 as the umbrella organization for GO.com, ESPN.com, ABCNews.com, Disney.com, and similar businesses.

Disney Legends Beginning in 1987, The Walt Disney Company has honored individuals who have made major contributions to the company over the years, by placing bronze emblems in the sidewalk in front of the Studio theater and having the honorees put their signatures and handprints in the cement. Some individuals have been honored posthumously. There was no ceremony in 1988. A new area for the Disney Legends was dedicated on October 16, 1998, in front of the Team Disney Building. Handprints and signatures were put on brass plaques on the pillars surrounding Disney Legends Plaza, with the new ones being added each year. The Disney Legends are as follows:

1987 Fred MacMurray.

1989 Ub Iwerks, Les Clark, Marc Davis, Ollie Johnston, Milt Kahl, Ward Kimball, Eric Larson, John Lounsbery, Wolfgang Reitherman, Frank Thomas.

1990 Roger Broggie, Joseph Fowler, John Hench, Richard Irvine, Herb Ryman, Richard M. Sherman, Robert B. Sherman.

1991 Ken Anderson, Julie Andrews, Carl Barks, Mary Blair, Claude Coats, Don DaGradi, Sterling Holloway, Fess Parker, Bill Walsh.

1992 Jimmie Dodd, Bill Evans, Annette Funicello, Joe Grant, Jack Hannah, Winston Hibler, Ken O'Connor, Roy Williams.

1993 Pinto Colvig, Buddy Ebsen, Peter Ellenshaw, Blaine Gibson, Harper Goff, Irving Ludwig, Jimmy Macdonald, Clarence Nash, Donn Tatum, Card Walker.

1994 Adriana Caselotti, Bill Cottrell, Marvin Davis, Van France, David Hand, Jack Lindquist, Bill Martin, Paul Smith, Frank Wells.

1995 Wally Boag, Fulton Burley, Dean Jones, Angela Lansbury, Edward Meck, Fred Moore, Thurl Ravenscroft, Wathel Rogers, Betty Taylor.

1996 Bob Allen, Rex Allen, X. Atencio, Betty Lou Gerson, Bill Justice, Bob Matheison, Sam McKim, Bob Moore, Bill Peet, Joe Potter.

In 1997, a special Disney Legends ceremony was held at Disneyland Paris to honor European Disney Legends (primarily individuals who had been instrumental in Disney film distribution and merchandise licensing in Europe through the years): Lucien Adès, Angel Angelopoulos, Antonio Bertini, Armand Bigle, Poul Brahe Pedersen, Gaudenzio Capelli, Roberto de Leonardis, Cyril Edgar, Wally Feignoux, Didier Fouret, Mario Gentilini, Cyril James, Horst Koblischek, Gunnar Mansson, Arnoldo Mondadori, Armand Palivoda, André Vanneste, Paul Winkler.

1998 James Algar, Buddy Baker, Kathryn Beaumont, Virginia Davis, Roy E. Disney, Don Escen, Wilfred Jackson, Glynis Johns, Kay Kamen, Paul Kenworthy, Larry Lansburgh, Hayley Mills, Al and Elma Milotte, Norman "Stormy" Palmer, Lloyd Richardson, Kurt Russell, Ben Sharpsteen, Vladimir "Bill" Tytla, Dick Van Dyke. A Legends ceremony in Japan in 1998 honored Masatomo Takahashi and Matsuo Yokoyama.

1999 Tim Allen, Mary Costa, Norman Ferguson, William Garity, Yale Gracey, Al Konetzni, Hamilton Luske, Dick Nunis, Charlie Ridgway.

2000 Grace Bailey, Harriet Burns, Joyce Carlson, Ron Dominguez, Cliff Edwards, Becky Fallberg, Dick Jones, Dodie Roberts, Retta Scott, Ruthie Tompson.

2001 (ceremony held at Walt Disney World) Howard Ashman, Bob Broughton, George Bruns, Frank Churchill, Leigh Harline, Fred Joerger, Alan Menken, Marty Sklar, Ned Washington, Tyrus Wong. Special commendation to Bob Thomas.

2002 (ceremony held in France) Ken Annakin, Hugh Attwooll, Maurice Chevalier, Phil Collins, John Mills, Robert Newton, Tim Rice, Robert Stevenson, Richard Todd, David Tomlinson.

2003 Neil Beckett, Tutti Camarata, Edna Disney, Lillian Disney, Orlando Ferrante, Richard Fleischer, Floyd Gottfredson, Buddy Hackett, Harrison Price, Al Taliaferro, Ilene Woods.

2004 Bill Anderson, Tim Conway, Rolly Crump, Alice Davis, Karen Dotrice, Matthew Garber, Leonard Goldenson, Bob Gurr, Ralph Kent, Irwin Kostal, Mel Shaw.

2005 (ceremony held at Disneyland) Chuck Abbott, Milt Albright, Hideo Amemiya, Hideo "Indian" Aramaki, Charles "Chuck" Boyajian, Charles Boyer, Randy Bright, Jim Cora, Bob Jani, Mary Jones, Art Linkletter, Mary Anne Mang, Steve Martin, Tom Nabbe, Jack Olsen, Cicely Rigdon, Bill Sullivan, Jack Wagner, Vesey Walker.

Disney Live! Winnie the Pooh First of a planned series of touring family stage productions featuring Disney characters and stories. The

Hundred Acre Wood and its inhabitants are brought to the stage in an interactive and three-dimensional production. It premiered in Christchurch, New Zealand, on June 16, 2004, and had its United States bow on July 29, 2005, in Fort Lauderdale, Florida. Produced by Feld Entertainment, Inc.

Disney Magazine Colorfully illustrated quarterly news magazine about everything going on in the Disney world, sold on newsstands and by subscription, beginning summer 1996 and ending in summer 2005. The magazine evolved from *Disney News*, published by the Magic Kingdom Club starting in 1965, and contained articles about new park attractions, tips on culinary experiences, travel suggestions, question-and-answer columns, announcements of new Disney books, and other topics of interest to the Disney enthusiast.

Disney Magic First ship in the Disney Cruise Line's fleet. It is 83,000 tons and features 875 cabins, four restaurants (Parrot Cay, Animator's Palate, Lumiere's, Palo) and a buffet (Topsider), two theaters, three swimming pools, and many other amenities. It had its maiden voyage on July 30, 1998, beginning three- and four-day cruises to the Caribbean (and Disney's Castaway Cay island) from Port Canaveral, Florida. The *Magic* switched to seven-day cruises (including stops at St. Maarten and St. Thomas/St. John) on August 12, 2000, and began alternate itineraries to Key West, Grand Cayman, and Cozumel on May 11, 2002. From May 28 to August 20, 2005, the ship sailed out of Los Angeles to the Mexican ports of Puerto Vallarta, Mazatlán, and Cabo San Lucas.

Disney-MGM Studios Park opened at Walt Disney World on May 1, 1989. Originally called Disney-MGM Studios Theme Park. An operating movie studio, the first filming was done there on February 2, 1988 (the television movie *Splash Too*). Walt Disney had originally envisioned a studio tour as part of the Disney Studio in California, but little land was available and disruptions would interrupt filming. The idea was revived in the 1980s when Disney executives decided that a third gated attraction on the Walt Disney World

property would enhance the guests' vacation experience. The guest enters the park on Hollywood Blvd., where there are shops designed after actual architecture of buildings in the original Hollywood area in California. The focal point at the end of the boulevard is a detailed reproduction of the facade of Grauman's Chinese Theater, housing the Great Movie Ride. Guests can choose to begin their visit by heading down Sunset Blvd. to The Twilight Zone Tower of Terror, or taking a backstage tour, or walking through various outdoor sets, experiencing the Indiana Jones Epic Stunt Spectacular, or many other attractions. Dining possibilities range from fast food to the Hollywood Brown Derby.

Disney-MGM Studios Theme Park Grand Opening, The (television) Two-hour television show; aired on April 30, 1989, the evening before the public opening of the park. Directed by Jeff Margolis. With Harry Anderson, George Burns, Walter Cronkite, John Forsythe, Estelle Getty, Kate Jackson, Rue McClanahan, Ann Miller, Yves Montand, Willie Nelson, Tony Randall, John Ritter, Mickey Rooney, and many others. There are even cameos by Jane Fonda, Jimmy Stewart, Margaret Thatcher, Ronald Reagan, and Lech Walesa. The stars visit the various attractions at the park during the show, which concludes with a spectacular "Hooray for Hollywood" production number. The show won an Emmy Award for choreographer Walter Painter.

Disney on Ice See World on Ice.

Disney on Parade Arena show that debuted in Chicago on December 25, 1969. The costumed Disney characters put on lavish production numbers. The show was superseded by World on Ice.

Disney on Parade (television) Television show; aired on December 19, 1971. Directed by Stan Harris. A videotaped version of the first tour of the arena show, taped in Adelaide, South Australia.

Disney Online Disney Online was founded as a part of Disney Interactive in 1995 to develop

The Walt Disney Company's presence in the online world. The first offering, Disney.com, a World Wide Web site, went online February 21, 1996. Disney.com (www.disney.com) offers information and entertainment designed to showcase Disney's products and services, from movies and books to merchandise and theme parks. Disney's Daily Blast was added as an offering for kids in 1997. Students and investors can find annual reports and financial information at www.disney.com/investors/.

Disney Outfitters Shop on Discovery Island at Disney's Animal Kingdom; opened April 22, 1998. It changed its name to Wonders of the Wild from 1999 to 2001, then reverted to Disney Outfitters.

Disney Regional Entertainment Division of Disney formed in 1996 to create entertainment areas such as sports complexes, interactive entertainment, and family play centers for urban and suburban locations around the world. Their first experiment was Club Disney, which opened in Thousand Oaks, California in February 1997, followed by DisneyQuest, the first of which opened June 19, 1998.

Disney Software See Computer Software.

Disney Sound Walt Disney Records' new (2004) imprint designed to create original music for the entire family. Its first release, on February 15, 2005, was *Here Come the ABCs* from the alternative rock group They Might Be Giants, on DVD and CD.

Disney Store, The The first Disney Store, selling Disney merchandise exclusively, opened in the Glendale Galleria in California on March 28, 1987. With the exception of a store in the Orlando Airport operated by Walt Disney World, Disney had not tried retail outlets outside the parks. Michael Eisner and Frank Wells decided that Disney was missing a bet by not doing so. The Disney Store concept turned out to be highly successful, and was widely copied. All of the Disney Stores were owned and operated by The Walt Disney Company, and featured cast members who were trained as rigorously as those in the parks to be friendly and helpful. As the number of stores grew, more and more merchandise was being designed and manufactured for their exclusive sale. By 1997, there were more than 600 stores in the United States and ten other countries, with a peak in 1999 of 747 stores. The company then began closing less profitable stores, and the Japanese Disney Stores were sold to the Oriental Land Co., which owns the Tokyo Disneyland Resort, in 2001. By October 2003, the total was down to 481 stores. On November 23, 2004, the 313 remaining North American Disney Stores were sold to Children's Place. Disney retained ownership of 105 European stores.

Disney Storybook, A (television) Two-part television show; aired on November 14 and 21, 1981. Features *Mickey and the Beanstalk*, *Dumbo*, and *Working for Peanuts.*

Disney Studio See Studio.

Disney Studio 1 Guests entering this huge soundstage at Walt Disney Studios Paris find themselves on an elaborate Hollywood Blvd. set, complete with hundreds of movie props. They can dine at Restaurant en Coulisse, a 670-seat counter-service restaurant, featuring a stunning view over Hollywood Blvd., and shop at Les Légendes d'Hollywood. Opened on March 16, 2002.

Disney Studio Showcase (television) Show on The Disney Channel; beginning April 19, 1983, with such topics as behind-the-scenes looks at the Walt Disney Studios, award-winning commercials, a science fiction view of the future, a look at toy-making, and a stylized version of *Hansel and Gretel.*

Disney Sunday Movie, The (television) Television series; aired on ABC from February 2, 1986, to September 11, 1988.

Disney Traders Shop in World Showcase Plaza at Epcot; opened on April 9, 1987.

Disney University Company department created in 1962 at Disneyland to prepare new cast members for their roles by communicating a basic understanding of the Disney traditions and philosophies, to provide advanced training classes, and to handle cast communications and cast activities. The University evolved out of a training department, which had been established in the spring of 1955 by Van France, and a cast activities group known as the Disneyland Recreation Club started that same year. It was originally known as the University of Disneyland, but when Walt Disney World needed a similar department in 1971, the name Disney University was chosen. A third Disney University was established at the Disney Studio in Burbank in 1977. Additional branches later opened at Tokyo Disneyland and Disneyland Paris.

Disney Vacation, A (television) Television show; aired on May 1, 1982. An animated look at vacations in Disney films.

Disney Vacation Club See Vacation Club.

Disney Valentine, A (television) Television show; aired on February 13, 1982. Clips from Disney cartoons take a look at romance.

Disney Village New name, in 1996, for Festival Disney at Disneyland Paris.

Disney Village Clubhouse New name of Buena Vista Club, which was open from 1974 to 1994. It was extensively remodeled and rebuilt to become the main building for the Disney Institute.

Disney Village Marketplace See Downtown Disney Marketplace.

Disney Villains Fantasyland shop at Disneyland, opened July 16, 1991. Formerly Merlin's Magic Shop (1955–1983), Mickey's Christmas Chalet (1983–1987), Briar Rose Cottage (1987–1991). The shop closed on May 30, 1996, to reopen on June 13 as the Sanctuary of Quasimodo, selling merchandise from *The Hunchback*

of Notre Dame, until February 9, 1997. For a year it was the Knights Shop, then reverted to a villain shop as Villain's Lair from 1998 to 2004. There was also a Villains shop at Disney-MGM Studios from 1991 to 1996. It took merchandisers many years to appreciate the appeal of the Disney villains, but now there are several lines of specially produced items and guests enjoy wearing T-shirts emblazoned with their favorite bad guy or girl.

Disney Wilderness Preserve, The Disney agreed to purchase and preserve 12,000 acres of the Walker Ranch in south Osceola County in 1992 in exchange for the right to develop up to 550 acres of wetlands on the Walt Disney World property, primarily including the town site of Celebration. Disney in turn donated the land to the Nature Conservancy in 1993, and efforts began to return the drained ranchlands to their original habitat. The area opened to the public on November 1, 1999, with a Conservation Learning Center and self-guided nature trails.

Disney Wildlife Conservation Fund Established by Walt Disney Attractions in 1995 to promote and enable global wildlife conservation through relationships with scientists, educators, and organizations committed to preserving the earth's biodiversity. Annual cash awards are distributed to nonprofit organizations to protect and study endangered and threatened animals and their habitats.

Disney Wonder Disney Cruise Line's second ship, which had its maiden voyage on August 15, 1999. The Wonder was christened on October 1 by a laser-projected Tinker Bell. The ship is very similar to its sister ship, the *Disney Magic*, though its interior styling is more Art Moderne than the Art Deco of the former ship. Triton's restaurant takes the place of Lumiere's. The two ships alternated on the short cruises to Castaway Cay and Nassau in the Bahamas until August 2000, when the *Magic* switched to seven-day cruises and the *Wonder* added a stop in Freeport to its four-day cruises. Later, the *Wonder*'s itinerary reverted to Nassau and Castaway Cay, and occasionally Key West.

Disney World Is Your World Show on the Tomorrowland Stage in Magic Kingdom Park at Walt Disney World, beginning October 2, 1981. Featured the Kids of the Kingdom.

Disneyana Term that refers to the collecting of Disney memorabilia. The first major auction featuring Disneyana was held at Sotheby's in Los Angeles on May 14, 1972. Cecil Munsey wrote his book *Disneyana; Walt Disney Collectibles* in 1974.

Disneyana Convention After witnessing the growth and popularity of Disneyana gatherings hosted by the Mouse Club and the NFFC, The Walt Disney Company through its Walt Disney Attractions Merchandise division decided to host its own. The first Disneyana Convention was held in the Contemporary Resort Convention Center at Walt Disney World from September 24 to 27, 1992, and featured sales of Disney memorabilia, convention logo merchandise, and special limited-edition collectibles, along with speakers, an auction, tours, meals, and gala entertainment events. The 750 conventioneers were thrilled by an event of the magnitude and scope that only Disney itself could produce. A second Disneyana Convention, doubled in size, followed in 1993 at Disneyland, with a return to Walt Disney World for the third Convention in 1994. 1995 saw two Disneyana Conventions, one at each park. The 1996 through 2000 conventions were held at Walt Disney World, the 2001 one at the Disneyland Resort, and the final convention, in 2002, at Epcot.

Disneyana Shop Opened on January 9, 1976, on Main Street at Disneyland; moved across the street to former jewelry shop location on May 30, 1986. For the first few years, the shop sold old Disneyana merchandise, but it became too difficult to find this rare material to stock the shop, and it was feared that the extensive Disney purchases were creating their own artificial market prices for the material. Eventually, the shop turned instead to limited editions and current collectible merchandise. A Disneyana Shop also opened on April 15, 1983, in Fantasyland at Walt Disney World, later moving to Main Street, and

closing on October 1, 1996. Also in Disneyland Paris; opened on April 12, 1992.

DisneyFest See Disney Fair.

DisneyHand Worldwide outreach for The Walt Disney Company, dedicated to making the dreams of families and children a reality through public service initiatives, community outreach, and volunteerism in areas of learning, compassion, the arts, and the environment.

DisneyHand Teacher Awards See American Teacher Awards.

Disneykins See Louis Marx and Co.

Disneyland The first Disney park, representing an investment of $17 million, opened in Anaheim, California, on July 17, 1955, to an invited audience, and to the public the next day. Walt Disney had enjoyed taking his two daughters to carnivals, zoos, and small amusement parks when they were young, but he found that he was sitting on the bench eating popcorn while they rode the merry-go-round and they had all the fun. He wondered why a place could not be built where parents and kids could go have fun together. Eventually he put some designers on his own personal payroll and began coming up with some concepts. He first thought of building his park on a strip of land across Riverside Drive from the Disney Studio in Burbank, but when that space proved too small to hold all of his ideas, he hired the Stanford Research Institute to survey the possibilities for a site. SRI came up with the site in Anaheim, which was covered with orange groves and made up of parcels owned by 17 different people. By borrowing on his life insurance, selling his vacation home, and getting money from several companies, Walt was able to purchase an initial 160 acres and build Disneyland. It opened with an elaborate live television special, but people were already primed to see it. Walt had used episodes of the weekly evening television show to present tantalizing glimpses of what the park would be like. After its opening, guests flocked to see what Walt had built. The first guests through the turnstyles were Christine Vess and her cousin Michael Schwartner, ages 5 and 7. The fame of Disneyland spread, and soon it was on the must-see lists for not only Americans but foreign tourists as well. To keep people coming, Walt realized that he had to keep improving Disneyland. At the opening, he said, "Disneyland will never be completed. It will continue to grow as long as there is imagination left in the world." Over five decades now, Disneyland has continued to grow. New attractions have been added, sometimes carving out new space and sometimes replacing attractions that had become dated or inefficient. Parades, celebrity guests, celebrations, and other events provide incentives for the local populace to make return visits. As soon as Disneyland became a success, people throughout the world wanted Walt Disney to build a Disneyland in their town, but he bided his time until he had the park running smoothly. Only then did he start to listen to some of the entreaties, and his planning eventually led to his announcement of the Walt Disney World project in Florida shortly before his death. Disneyland was the first of its kind. Other parks have copied Disneyland since, but there will never be another like it. It is unique and continues to set the standard that all others have to follow.

On opening day, these were the attractions:

1. King Arthur Carrousel
2. Peter Pan's Flight
3. Mad Tea Party
4. Mr. Toad's Wild Ride
5. Canal Boats of the World
6. Snow White's Adventures
7. Autopia
8. Space Station X-1
9. Santa Fe and Disneyland Railroad
10. Circarama
11. Horse-drawn Streetcars
12. Fire Wagon
13. Main Street Cinema
14. Surreys
15. Jungle Cruise
16. Stage Coach
17. Mule Pack
18. *Mark Twain* Riverboat
19. Penny Arcade
20. Golden Horseshoe Revue

Disneyland has welcomed millions of guests through the years, with the following being the special record-breaking ones:

1,000,000th guest, September 8, 1955: Elsa Marquez

10,000,000th guest, December 31, 1957: Leigh Woolfenden

25,000,000th guest, April 19, 1961: Dr. Glenn C. Franklin

50,000,000th guest, August 12, 1965: Mary Adams

100,000,000th guest, June 17, 1971: Valerie Suldo

200,000,000th guest, January 8, 1981: Gert Schelvis

250,000,000th guest, August 24, 1985: Brooks Charles Arthur Burr

300,000,000th guest, September 1, 1989: Claudine Masson

400,000,000th guest, July 5, 1997: Minnie Pepito

450,000,000th guest, March 15, 2001: Mark Ramirez

500,000,000th guest, January 8, 2004: Bill Trow

Disneyland (television) Television series; on ABC, from October 27, 1954, to September 3, 1958, on Wednesday nights. It won the Emmy as Best Variety Series during its first season, and another award for Walt Disney as Best Producer of a Filmed Series the following year.

Disneyland After Dark (television) Television show; aired on April 15, 1962. Directed by Hamilton Luske, William Beaudine. Walt Disney takes the audience for a tour of Disneyland "when the lights go on." He features a look at nighttime entertainment, with Louis Armstrong, Kid Ory, Johnny St. Cyr, Bobby Rydell, Annette Funicello, Bobby Burgess. Monette Moore, and the Osmond Brothers (in their network television premiere). A colorful fireworks display and audience participation songs at Plaza Gardens wind up the visit to the park at night. Released theatrically abroad.

Disneyland-Alweg Monorail System See Monorail.

Disneyland Around the Seasons (television) Television show; aired on December 18, 1966. Directed by Hamilton S. Luske. The openings of "is a small world" and New Orleans Square are shown, with Walt providing information on the planning of Great Moments with Mr. Lincoln, Pirates of the Caribbean, and the Primeval World diorama, followed by a performance of Christmas Fantasy on Parade. The show served as a tribute to Walt Disney, airing three days after his death.

Disneyland Band When Walt Disney wanted a band for opening day at the park, he asked British bandmaster Vesey Walker to assemble one. The band was hired only for a two-week engagement, but it became so popular that it was held over and still performs at the park today. The band ranges from about 15 to 20 members, and has been directed by Walker, James Christensen, Jim Barngrover, Stanford Freese, and Art Dragon. In July 1982, the band celebrated its 50,000th performance. The band performs in parades, and gives concerts in various areas around the park, with a repertoire that includes marches, polkas, jazz, and waltzes, with perhaps the most-requested tune being the "Mickey Mouse March." The band has also performed in Band Concert Series for young people throughout Orange County.

Disneyland Blast to the Past (television) Syndicated television special; aired on KHJ-TV in Los Angeles on May 20, 1989. Directed by C. F. Bien, and starring Jon "Bowzer" Bauman, Brian Beirne, Little Anthony. 60 min.

Disneyland '59 (television) Live 90-minute television special sponsored by Kodak, introducing the Submarine Voyage, Matterhorn, Monorail, Motor Boat Cruise, and an enlarged Autopia. Aired on June 15, 1959.

Disneyland—from the Pirates of the Caribbean to the World of Tomorrow (television) Television show; aired on January 21, 1968. Directed by Hamilton S. Luske. The audience visits WED Enterprises and sees how Disneyland attractions are created, including Pirates and the new Tomorrowland. Disneyland ambassador Marcia Miner acts as hostess.

Disneyland Goes to the World's Fair (television) Television show; aired on May 17, 1964. Directed by Hamilton S. Luske. A look at the history of world's fairs, followed by a preview of Disney attractions at the 1964–1965 New York World's Fair. Walt explains Audio-Animatronics, the new Disney process that helps bring inanimate objects to life.

Disneyland Hotel When Walt Disney built Disneyland in 1955, he did not have enough money to build a hotel too, but he reasoned that such a hotel would be very successful next to the park. So, he persuaded his friend Jack Wrather to build the hotel on Disney land just across West Street from the park. The Wrather Corporation expanded their hotel through the years, until it eventually had three towers (Bonita, Marina, and Sierra), but after Walt Disney's death, the Disney company began making overtures to purchase the hotel. For one thing, it was awkward having the Disney name on something that the Disney company did not own. In 1988, Disney purchased the entire Wrather Corporation, acquiring not only the Disneyland Hotel, but the lease to operate the *Queen Mary* in Long Beach. The hotel has the advantage of being attached to Disneyland by the Monorail. Guests embarking at the hotel are whisked directly into the station in Tomorrowland inside the park. This monorail line connecting the hotel to Disneyland was the first time a monorail had been built over a city street. The hotel has a large convention space, outdoor activities, including three swimming pools, and a selection of restaurants from Goofy's Kitchen and Hook's Pointe to the upscale Granville's.

Disneyland Hotel Themed hotel over the entrance to Disneyland Paris; opened on April 12, 1992. It has a Victorian theme.

Disneyland Is Your Land Show at Disneyland beginning March 23, 1985. Featured the Kids of the Kingdom. An earlier version of the stage show was performed during the 25th anniversary celebrations in 1980.

Disneyland Pacific Hotel The Walt Disney Company purchased this 502-room hotel located next door to the Disneyland Hotel, built in 1984 and formerly known as the Emerald and the Pan Pacific, from a Japanese company in December 1995. Walkways and a park between the two hotels were finished on March 22, 1996, completing the integration of the two facilities. Featured restaurants are Yamabuki and Disney's PCH Grill. It was renamed Disney's Paradise Pier Hotel in October 2000.

Disneyland Paris First Disney resort in Europe, opening, with the original name of Euro Disney (the park itself was known as Euro Disneyland), on April 12, 1992. (The Disneyland Paris name became official on October 1, 1994.) Disney park planners had begun searching for a suitable European site for a park in the early 1980s. Eventually, two sites were selected as being ideal—one near Barcelona, Spain, and one near Paris, France. After years of studies and negotiations, the decision was made by Michael Eisner and Frank Wells to locate the park in France, at Marne-la-Vallée. After several years of construction, the park, a Festival Disney (later Disney Village) area for nighttime entertainment, and a group of themed hotels, opened in 1992. The park has a basic layout similar to Disneyland, with the major change being a substitution of Discoveryland for Tomorrowland. The park was said by many to be the most beautiful of all the Disney parks, and it certainly had the latest tech-

nology in the attractions and the latest ideas in planning and architecture. Disneyland Paris proceeded to attract almost 11 million visitors during its first year, making it the most popular tourist attraction in Europe. But because of unsatisfactory economic conditions and because of the need to pay huge interest payments on the debt needed for construction, Disneyland Paris lost money in its first years. With a financial reorganization in 1994, the park's management hoped for an eventual turnaround and they were confident that the park would eventually be a financial as well as a critical success. Profits were reported in 1995. A decade later, even though very popular with guests, the park still was having financial problems, necessitating concessions from banks holding its debt. The 100 millionth visitor (Stefan Seyffardt and family) was welcomed on January 10, 2001. With the addition of Walt Disney Studios park in 2002, the resort name changed to Disneyland Resort Paris.

Disneyland Presents a Preview of Coming Attractions Display on Main Street from 1973 until July 22, 1989. The location was the original Wurlitzer shop. It took the place of the Legacy of Walt Disney when many of the awards in that exhibit were moved into the Walt Disney Story. Models, artists' renderings, and designs of attractions being planned were displayed. Became Disneyland Showcase.

Disneyland Presents Tales of Toontown (television) Syndicated television special (60 min.); aired on July 10, 1993. In searching for a mischievous culprit who is mysteriously causing everything to go wacky in Toontown, Goofy enlists his human friend Spence Dempsey to discover the cause of all the crazy goings-on. Directed by Bruce Stuart Greenberg.

Disneyland Railroad Disneyland attraction that encircles the park; originally the Santa Fe and Disneyland Railroad (1955–1974), changed to the new name on October 1, 1974. The original two locomotives, the *E. P. Ripley* and the *C. K. Holliday* were constructed at the Disney Studio and are named for pioneers of the Santa Fe Railroad. Because of the popularity of the trains, there was a need for more locomotives, so a third one was added in 1958, the *Fred G. Gurley*, named after the then-chairman of the railroad. Rather than build the new locomotive from scratch, the Disney designers found an old Baldwin locomotive built in 1894, which had been used to haul sugar-cane in Louisiana. It was completely rebuilt for service at Disneyland. A fourth locomotive was located the following year and named for the man who was president of the railroad, *Ernest S. Marsh*. It was a somewhat newer model, built in 1925 and used in New England at a lumber mill. All trains are now open air, to afford the best views of the Disneyland scenery and the two dioramas (Grand Canyon and Primeval World) through

which the trains pass. Originally, there was an enclosed passenger train, but the windows were too small to enable all guests to see the sights. The old passenger train was stored for many years in the back of the Disneyland roundhouse. There was also once a freight train, where guests rode like cattle in cattle cars; the novelty of that wore off quickly. Original stations were on Main Street and in Frontierland; a Fantasyland station was added in 1956 and a Tomorrowland station in 1958. The Fantasyland station became the Videopolis station in 1988 and the Toontown station in 1992. Walt Disney was so fascinated with trains, he built a ⅛-scale Carolwood Pacific Railroad in the backyard of his Holmby Hills home.

He was adamant that a train be a major part of the Disneyland experience. Many guests use it to get an overall view of the park before they venture out to the other attractions. During the years that Disneyland used tickets for the attractions, the railroad ticket was a long strip with coupons to be punched by the conductor, similar to those used in real railroads of the period.

Disneyland Resort General name for the Disney facilities in Anaheim, California, including Disneyland Park, Disney's California Adventure, Disneyland Hotel, Grand Californian Hotel, Paradise Pier Hotel, and Downtown Disney.

Disneyland Showcase Shop on Main Street at Disneyland; opened October 27, 1989. The shop fills the space that was originally the Wurlitzer shop.

Disneyland Showtime (television) Television show; aired on March 22, 1970. Directed by Gordon Wiles. Performers visit Disneyland for the opening of The Haunted Mansion. When Donny Osmond gets lost, everyone goes searching, which gives the opportunity for a tour of the park. Kurt Russell narrates a look at the work that went into making The Haunted Mansion. Stars the Osmond Brothers, Kurt Russell, E. J. Peaker.

Disneyland '61/Olympic Elk (television) Television show; aired on May 28, 1961. Directed by Hamilton S. Luske. Features an enlarged version of the theatrical featurette *Gala Day at Disneyland*, with Walt Disney talking about the new Nature's Wonderland and an upcoming expansion of the Monorail. The show concludes with the True-Life Adventure featurette *The Olympic Elk*.

Disneyland Story, The (television) Opening show of the *Disneyland* television series; aired on ABC on October 27, 1954. Directed by Robert Florey. Walt Disney leads a tour of the Studio and shows a model of the under-construction Disneyland park, then previews the shows that will be on during the upcoming season, followed by a look at Mickey's career. Also known as *What is Disneyland?*

Disneyland Tenth Anniversary Show, The (television) Television show; aired on January 3, 1965. Directed by Hamilton S. Luske. The young lady who was to be the first of a long line of Disneyland ambassadors, Julie Reihm, then called "Miss Disneyland," joins Walt to look at some of the new attractions coming to the park, including Pirates of the Caribbean and The Haunted Mansion. Then there is a party at Disneyland for the Tencennial. Celebrities at the park include Hayley Mills, John Mills, Louis Armstrong, and the Firehouse Five Plus Two.

Disneyland: The First 50 Magical Years Attraction that opened in the Opera House at Disneyland on May 5, 2005, to celebrate the 50th anniversary of the park. There are displays of design artwork and models, ticket books and name tags, a large, new scale model of Disneyland as it appeared on opening day, and a 17-minute humorous film look at the 50 years with Steve Martin (who as a young man worked at Disneyland in the Magic Shop) and Donald Duck.

Disneyland the Park/Pecos Bill (television) Television show; aired on April 3, 1957. Directed by Hamilton S. Luske, Clyde Geronimi. Walt Disney leads a tour by helicopter to Disneyland, with aerial views and visits to several of the attractions. The Mouseketeers are glimpsed on a visit there. The show concludes with *Pecos Bill*.

Disneyland, U.S.A. (film) People and Places featurette; released on December 20, 1956. Directed by Hamilton Luske. Filmed in CinemaScope. 42 min. After an aerial view of Disneyland and a visit to the Disneyland Hotel, it is on through the entrance gates of the park for a tour of each of the four lands, as well as Main Street, U.S.A., and glimpses of annual parades and holiday festivities.

Disneyland's All-Star Comedy Circus (television) Television show; aired on December 11, 1988. Directed by Stan Harris. Several NBC series stars perform at Disneyland and introduce various circus acts. Stars Rue McClanahan, Christopher Daniel Barnes, Kim Fields, Danny Ponce.

Disneyland's Summer Vacation Party (television) Two-hour NBC television special featuring contemporary recording artists; aired on May 23, 1986. Directed by Marty Pasetta. Stars Mindy Cohn, Kim Fields, Scott Valentine, and Malcolm-Jamal Warner, who host a long list of entertainers.

Disneyland's 30th Anniversary Celebration (television) Two-hour television special on NBC; aired on February 18, 1985. Directed by Marty Pasetta. Stars John Forsythe, Drew Barrymore, and a host of entertainers.

Disneyland's 35th Anniversary Celebration (television) Television show; aired on February 4, 1990. Directed by John Landis. Stars Tony Danza, Charles Fleischer, Jim Varney, the Muppets, Chris Demetral. Returning for the rededication are the three original television hosts—Art Linkletter, Bob Cummings, and Ronald Reagan, and the first two kids to enter the park on opening day—Christine Vess and Michael Schwartner.

Disneyland's 25th Anniversary See *Kraft Salutes: Disneyland's 25th Anniversary*.

DisneyQuest High-tech indoor recreation site designed for families and children to spend two to three hours playing computer-based, virtual-reality, and Internet games, opening at Downtown Disney West Side at Walt Disney World on June 19, 1998.

Disney's The word *Disney's* is part of the official name of all of the Walt Disney World Resorts, but in this book, the resorts are listed under their individual names, for example, Contemporary Resort, rather than Disney's Contemporary Resort. The word *Disney's* has also been omitted from some film titles.

Disney's Adventures in Wonderland (television) Television series, starring Elisabeth Harnois (Alice), John Robert Hoffman (Mad Hatter), Armelia McQueen (Red Queen), Reece Holland (March Hare). The series builds on Lewis Carroll's literary richness and linguistic fun in a contemporary setting. Alice visits her wild and zany friends by stepping through her looking glass into a world of music, fantasy, and fun. Premiered on The Disney Channel on March 23, 1992, and was syndicated beginning September 6, 1993, and ended September 10, 1995. The show won an Emmy Award for Hairdressing in 1992, and two more for Writing and Makeup in 1994.

Disney's Adventures of the Gummi Bears (television) Television series; aired on NBC from September 14, 1985 to September 2, 1989, and on ABC from September 9, 1989 until September 8, 1990. Syndicated in 1990–91. Gummi Bears are the mythical, medieval residents of Gummi Glen, who fight ogres led by the evil Duke Igthorn, to preserve their homes. Gummiberry juice can give them the ability to bounce out of danger. The Gummis are Zummi, Gruffi, Grammi, Tummi, Cubbi, and Sunni, who are aided by the Princess Calla and her humble page, Cavin. Voices include Paul Winchell (Zummi), June Foray (Grammi), Noelle North (Cubbi, Calla), Katie Leigh (Sunni), Lorenzo Music (Tummi), Jason Marsden/R.J. Williams (Cavin), Michael Rye (Duke Igthorn). Bill Scott voiced Gruffi until his death, and Corey Burton then took over. 65 episodes.

Disney's Aladdin For the television series, see *Aladdin*.

Disney's All-American Sports Nuts (television) Television special; aired on NBC on October 16, 1988. Clips from Disney films are combined with real sports footage. Directed by Chep Dobrin. Stars David Leisure, John Matuszak, Susan Ruttan, Martin Mull, Brian Boitano, Bruce Jenner.

Disney's All-Star 4th of July Spectacular See *Celebrate the Spirit!*

Disney's All-Star Mother's Day Album (television) Television special on CBS on May 9, 1984. Includes clips of cartoons about mothers.

Disney's All-Star Valentine Party (television) Television special on CBS; aired on February 14, 1984. Disney cartoons on the subject of love.

Disney's America History-themed park announced in 1993 to be built in Prince William County near Haymarket, Virginia. Guests would be able to experience distinct periods in American history. The park would bring history to life, examining the conflicts and successes that have marked the nation's passage from colony to world power. While state officials and local residents were generally in favor of the project, there was intense opposition from a group of historians and environmentalists who complained about it being too near the Manassas Civil War battlefield. On September 28, 1994, Disney announced that a different site would be sought, but no further work has been done on the project.

Disney's Animal Kingdom See Animal Kingdom, Disney's.

Disney's Animal Kingdom: The First Adventure (television) One-hour television special; aired on April 26, 1998, on *The Wonderful World of Disney*, giving viewers a first look at the new animal park, which officially opened four days earlier. Directed by David Straiton and Joan Tosoni. Stars Tia, Tamara, Tahj, and Tavior Mowry, Will Friedle, Danielle Fishel, Paul Rodriguez, Dr. Jan Goodall, with music by George Clinton, Lebo M, and Ladysmith.

Disney's Animated Alphabet (film) Educational film; released in August 1988. 13 min. Letters of the alphabet come to life to teach the ABCs to young children.

Disney's California Adventure See California Adventure.

Disney's Captain Eo Grand Opening (television) Hour-long television special on NBC; aired on September 20, 1986. Directed by Marty Pasetta. Patrick Duffy hosts a look at the new 3-D film at Disneyland. Stars Justine Bateman, Belinda Carlisle, The Moody Blues.

Disney's Champions on Ice (television) Television special on ABC; aired on March 9, 1996. Videotaped on location at Sun Valley, Idaho. Directed by Paul Miller. Features Scott Hamilton, Nicole Bobek, Surya Bonaly, Ekaterina Gordeeva, Sergei Grinkov, Elvis Stojko.

Disney's Christmas Fantasy on Ice (television) Television special (60 min.) on CBS; first aired first on December 19, 1992. Directed by Paul Miller.

Disney's Christmas on Ice (television) Television special on CBS (60 min.); aired on December 21, 1990. Directed by Don Ohlmeyer. In Squaw Valley, Disney characters perform with ice skating stars. Stars Peggy Fleming, Tai Babilonia, Randy Gardner, Gary Beacom, Judy Blumberg, Scott Hamilton, The Party, Katarina Witt.

Disney's Countdown (film) Educational film about having fun counting numbers forward and backward, released in November 1988. 12 min.

Disney's Countdown to Kid's Day (television) Television special on NBC (60 min.); aired on November 21, 1993. A lineup of singers, comedians, and television performers—including Gloria Estefan, Celine Dion, Joey Lawrence, and Sinbad—gather at the four worldwide Disney parks to salute children with special entertainment and focus on real-life issues facing the world's youth.

Disney's Doug See *Brand Spanking New Doug* and *Doug's 1st Movie*.

Disney's Doug Live Attraction at the Disney-MGM Studios, replacing SuperStar Television, being a live show featuring the Doug characters. It opened on March 15, 1999, and closed May 12, 2001.

Disney's DTV Doggone Valentine (television) Television special; aired on NBC on February 13, 1987. 60 min. Directed by Andrew Solt.

Ludwig Von Drake, Jiminy Cricket, and Mickey Mouse host a show featuring popular songs showcased with Disney animation in MTV style.

Disney's DTV Monster Hits (television) Hour-long television special on NBC; aired on November 27, 1987. Directed by Andrew Solt. More popular songs, with a Halloween twist, set to Disney animation, hosted by the slave in the Magic Mirror. Stars Jeffrey Jones as the slave.

Disney's DTV Romancin' (television) New title for *Disney's DTV Valentine*; aired on NBC on September 7, 1986. 60 min.

Disney's DTV Valentine (television) One-hour television special on NBC; aired on February 14, 1986. Directed by Andrew Solt. Romantic songs set to Disney animation. A September 7 rerun was titled *Disney's DTV Romancin'*.

Disney's Fillmore See *Fillmore*

Disney's Fluppy Dogs (television) Television special on ABC about five magical, talking Fluppy dogs who enter the lives of a 10-year-old boy and his snobbish neighbor; aired on November 27, 1986. 60 min. Directed by Fred Wolf.

Disney's Golden Anniversary of Snow White and the Seven Dwarfs (television) Television special on NBC; aired on May 22, 1987. Directed by Louis J. Horvitz. A look at the history of the landmark animated film, with Dick Van Dyke, Jane Curtin, Sherman Hemsley, and Linda Ronstadt.

Disney's Great American Celebration (television) Television special on CBS (120 min.); airing on July 4, 1991. Directed by Michael Dimich. Entertainers at both Disneyland and Walt Disney World celebrate the holiday. Stars Robert Guillaume, Barbara Mandrell, Sheena Easton, Tim Allen, The Party, Steven Banks.

Disney's Great Ice Odyssey Title of the second Disney ice show; premiered on July 20, 1982. The original show was Disney's World on Ice.

Disney's Greatest Dog Stars (television) Television show; aired on November 28, 1976. Dean Jones hosts a look at famous Disney dog stars, leading up to a preview of *The Shaggy D.A.* A 1980 rerun substituted a segment on *The Fox and the Hound* for the segment on *The Shaggy D.A.*

Disney's Greatest Hits on Ice (television) Television special on CBS; aired on November 25, 1994. The world's most celebrated skaters, including Ekatarina Gordeeva, Sergei Grinkov, Scott Hamilton, and Nancy Kerrigan perform to the best-loved Disney songs and melodies. The show was taped on a soundstage at Paramount Studios, where an ice rink was built specially for the production. The set included a reproduction of the Team Disney Building and the fan-shaped gate at the Disney Studios. Directed by Steve Binder.

Disney's Greatest Villains (television) Television show; aired on May 15, 1977. The Magic Mirror is used to point out that every hero needs a villain, using clips from Disney cartoons and animated features.

Disney's Halloween Treat (television) Television show; aired on October 30, 1982. Cartoons cover the Halloween theme.

Disney's Haunted Halloween (film) Educational film with Goofy about the origins of Halloween traditions; released in September 1983.

Disney's Hercules For the television series, see *Hercules.*

Disney's Living Seas (television) One-hour television special on NBC celebrating the opening of the Living Seas at Epcot; aired on January 24, 1986. Directed by Ken Ehrlich. Stars John Ritter, Laura Branigan, Simon Le Bon, Olivia Newton-John.

Disney's Magic in the Magic Kingdom (television) Television special on NBC featuring magic tricks and illusions at Disneyland, including the disappearance of Sleeping Beauty Castle; aired on February 12, 1988. 60 min. Directed by

Gary Halvorson. Stars George Burns, Harry Anderson, Gloria Estefan, Morgan Fairchild, Siegfried & Roy.

Disney's Mickey MouseWorks See *Mickey MouseWorks.*

Disney's Most Unlikely Heroes (television) Half-hour television special; aired on ABC on June 18, 1996. Directed by Dan Boothe. Movie and television stars select their favorite Disney heroes, with a behind-the-scenes look at the making of *The Hunchback of Notre Dame.*

Disney's Nancy Kerrigan Special: Dreams on Ice (television) One-hour television special on CBS; aired on February 15, 1995. Nancy Kerrigan performs different roles in this show taped at Lake Placid, New York, and at Disney-MGM Studios. Also starring are Scott Hamilton, Paul Wylie, Gordeeva and Grinkov, and Paul Martini among others. Directed by Paul Miller.

Disney's One Too (television) Two-hour block of cartoons; debuted on UPN on September 6, 1999, airing Sunday through Friday, and in syndication until September 1, 2002. The series featured *Sabrina, the Animated Series; Disney's Doug; Disney's Recess*; and *Disney's Hercules.*

Disney's Oscar Winners (television) Television show; aired on April 13, 1980. Directed by William Reid. Covers some of the Disney Academy Award–winning films. Narrated by John Forsythe.

Disney's PB&J Otter See *PB&J Otter.*

Disney's Pocahontas: The Musical Tradition Continues (television) Half-hour television special on ABC; aired on June 20, 1995. Directed by John Jopson. Alan Menken takes the viewer on a musical history tour of his contributions to recent Disney animated films. Features Regina Belle, Peabo Bryson, Celine Dion, Jon Secada, Shanice, Venessa Williams.

Disney's Sing Me a Story: with Belle (television) Syndicated television series, beginning on September 9, 1995. Belle invites a group of small children into her enchanting Book and Music Shop for a half hour of stories and songs promoting a special theme, utilizing Disney's classic cartoons. Stars Lynsey McLeod (Belle), Tim Goodwin (Brioche).

Disney's Sports Special (television) Syndicated television look at Disney animated sport segments from 1986.

Disney's Tale Spin: Plunder & Lightning (television) Syndicated television special; aired on September 7, 1990, to introduce the new series.

Disney's The Kid (film) Russ Duritz finds his life as a successful "image consultant" turned upside down when he magically meets Rusty, himself as an 8-year-old child. Rusty is a sweet but slightly geeky, pudgy little kid who is not at all happy with who he turns out to be—a 40-year-old loser without a wife or a dog. Ironically, the kid helps Russ to learn about himself and remember his dreams, in order to become the grown-up he wants to be. Released on July 7, 2000. Directed by Jon Turteltaub. Stars Bruce Willis (Russ), Emily Mortimer (Amy), Spencer Breslin (Rusty), Lily Tomlin (Janet), Chi McBride (Kenny), Jean Smart (Deirdre). 104 min. Official title is *Disney's The Kid* because of title rights held by the Charlie Chaplin estate and to emphasize that this is a family film. Released on video in 2001.

Disney's The Little Mermaid (television) Animated television series; aired on CBS beginning September 12, 1992, and ending September 2, 1995.

Disney's Timon and Pumbaa in Stand by Me (film) Cartoon released on December 22, 1995, with *Tom and Huck*. A frantic music video based on the popular song. Directed by Steve Moore. 3 min. Voices by Kevin Schoen (Timon), Ernie Sabella (Pumbaa).

Disney's Totally Minnie (television) Television special on NBC in which a clumsy nerd

learns to be cool with help from Minnie, animation clips, and an all-new music video with Minnie and Elton John. Aired on March 25, 1988. 60 min. Directed by Scot Garen. Stars Suzanne Somers, Robert Carradine.

Disney's Wide World of Sports See Wide World of Sports.

Disney's Wonderful World (television) Title of Disney's long-running television series on NBC, from September 9, 1979 to September 13, 1981.

Disney's Wonderful World of Winter (film) Educational film with Goofy and Stanley the Snowman teaching students about the holidays and customs of winter; released in September 1983.

Disney's World on Ice See World on Ice.

Disney's Wuzzles (television) Television series on CBS; aired from September 14, 1985 to September 6, 1986, and on ABC from September 13, 1986 until May 16, 1987.

DisneySea Project planned by Disney designers for Long Beach, California, for the area around the *Queen Mary*. It would have consisted of a nautical-themed park, along with hotels, cruise ship docks, and other facilities. Disney eventually dropped its plans due to the numerous coastal regulatory agency standards and the expected cost of the project, Disney eventually dropped its plans. See also Tokyo DisneySea.

DisneySea AquaSphere Located at the front of Tokyo DisneySea, the AquaSphere symbolizes Earth, the "water planet," and sets the stage for the ocean-themed adventures awaiting beyond the entrance.

DisneySea Electric Railway Attraction in Port Discovery at Tokyo DisneySea; opened September 4, 2001.

DisneySea Transit Steamer Line Attraction at Tokyo DisneySea; opened September 4,

2001. Guests are ferried from Mediterranean Harbor to Lost River Delta.

DisneyToon Studios Division of Disney Feature Animation that produces video/DVD and theatrical sequels to animated features, and new stories featuring characters such as Mickey Mouse and Winnie the Pooh. It was formerly a part of Walt Disney Television Animation until 2003, when it received the DisneyToon Studios name. DisneyToon Studios Australia operated from 1988 to 2006.

Disorganized Crime (film) In a small town in Montana, cunning criminal Frank Salazar has planned the perfect bank robbery and sent invitations to four heist experts for help, only to be arrested by two New Jersey cops who had been following him. The four strangers soon arrive and find themselves in a quandary—what were they gathered to do? How are they to do it? The four dislike each other, but strive to work together, even without a leader, for what they hope will be a major payoff. Meanwhile Salazar escapes, and the cops are confounded by his actions as well as those of the bank robbers. There are miscues by both sides as they bungle their operations. Released on April 14, 1989. Directed by Jim Kouf. A Touchstone film. 101 min. Stars Hoyt Axton (Sheriff Henault), Corbin Bernsen (Frank Salazar), Rubén Blades (Carlos Barrios), Fred Gwynne (Max Green), Ed O'Neill (George Denver), Lou Diamond Phillips (Ray Forgy), Daniel Roebuck (Bill Lonigan), William Russ (Nick Bartowski). Filmed on location around Hamilton, Montana. Released on video in 1989.

Distinguished Gentleman, The (film) When Florida congressman Jeff Johnson dies, small-time con artist Thomas Jefferson Johnson scams his own name onto the ballot. Launching a campaign based on pure name recognition, he pulls off his biggest hustle yet when he manages to get elected. He quickly finds to his delight that he is raking in sums he never dreamed of without doing anything illegal. But when Thomas becomes aware of the effect of Congress's greed and chicanery on the general public, and the plight of a little girl in particular, he decides to turn the tables on Washington's business as usual, and shakes the establishment to its foundations. Released on December 4, 1992. Directed by Jonathan Lynn. A Hollywood Picture. 112 min. Stars Eddie Murphy (Thomas Jefferson Johnson), Lane Smith (Dick Dodge), Sheryl Lee Ralph (Miss Loretta), Joe Don Baker (Olaf Andersen), Victoria Rowell (Celia Kirby), Grant Shaud (Arthur Reinhardt), Kevin McCarthy (Terry Corrigan). While much of the filming took place in Washington, D.C., restrictions on filming around the Capitol necessitated a search for a substitute, and it was the State Capitol building in Harrisburg, Pennsylvania, that doubled for the U.S. Capitol. Additional filming took place in Baltimore, Maryland. Released on video in 1993.

Dixie Landings Resort Hotel at Walt Disney World; opened on February 2, 1992. A moderate-priced hotel, themed after the Old South, it has 2,048 rooms. The registration desk, restaurants, and souvenir shop are in Colonel's Cotton Mill, a building that resembles a steamship. The swimming pool is located on Ol' Man Island among the guest room buildings. One can dine at Boatwright's Dining Hall or in a food court, or buy souvenirs at Fulton's General Store. It was combined with the Port Orleans Resort on April 1, 2001, under the Port Orleans name as the Riverside area.

Dixieland at Disneyland Entertainment event first held on October 1, 1960. It was a popular annual event for several years, often featuring big-name entertainers such as Louis

Armstrong performing on rafts on the Rivers of America and at other locations around the park.

Do Dragons Dream? (film) Educational film in which Figment introduces children to their imaginations, in the EPCOT Educational Media Collection: Language Arts Through Imagination series; released in September 1988. 15 min.

D.O.A. (film) College professor Dexter Cornwell discovers he has been poisoned by a fatal, slow-acting toxin, and he has only 24 hours to unravel the mystery of his imminent demise. Enlisting the aid of Sydney Fuller, a naive student who has a crush on him, he soon becomes enmeshed in a series of murders as he attempts to find out who killed him—and why. Released on March 18, 1988. Directed by Rocky Morton and Annabel Jankel. A Touchstone Picture. 100 min. Stars Dennis Quaid (Dexter Cornell), Meg Ryan (Sydney Fuller), Daniel Stern (Hal Petersham), Charlotte Rampling (Mrs. Fitzwaring). Filmed on location in and around Austin, Texas. Released on video in 1988 and 1990.

Doc Self-appointed leader of the Seven Dwarfs; voiced by Roy Atwell.

Doctor, The (film) A successful surgeon, Dr. Jack MacKee, lacks one vital trait—true compassion for the patients under his care. Suddenly faced with throat cancer, he becomes an ordinary patient in his own hospital, and finds he has to deal with the red tape and dehumanizing conditions experienced by everyone else. Unable to relate to his wife and young son, he meets June, a fellow patient with extraordinary strength and

spirit, who is the catalyst for his own recovery as well as the realization that a healer must be able to attend to the spirit as well as the body. Initial release on July 24, 1991, in four cities; general release on August 2, 1991. Directed by Randa Haines. A Touchstone Picture. 123 min. Stars William Hurt (Jack), Christine Lahti (Anne), Elizabeth Perkins (June), Mandy Patinkin (Murray). Based on the book *A Taste of My Own Medicine* by Dr. Ed Rosenbaum. Released on video in 1992.

Dr. Dawson Basil's cohort in *The Great Mouse Detective*, with the full name of Dr. David Q. Dawson; voiced by Val Bettin.

Dr. Syn, Alias the Scarecrow (film) Theatrical version of the *Scarecrow of Romney Marsh* television episodes. Released first in England in December 1963; U.S. theatrical release on November 21, 1975. 98 min./75 min. Stars Patrick McGoohan. Released on video in 1986.

Dodd, Dickie Mouseketeer from the 1950s television show.

Dodd, Jimmie (1910–1964) The adult Mouseketeer from the 1950s television show. He was highly admired by all of the Mouseketeers, not to mention the viewers of the show. He wrote more than 30 of the *Mickey Mouse Club* songs, including the "Mickey Mouse Club March." He was named a Disney Legend in 1992.

Dodger Mongrel dog in *Oliver & Company*; voiced by Billy Joel.

Dodo Master of ceremonies of the Great Caucus Race in *Alice in Wonderland*; voiced by Bill Thompson.

Doerges, Norm He began with Disney as pool manager at the Celebrity Sports Center in Denver in 1967, then moved to Walt Disney World, where he worked up to vice president in charge of Epcot. He moved to Disneyland in 1990, becoming executive vice president there in 1994. He left the company in 1997.

Dog of Destiny (television) Television show; part 2 of *Atta Girl, Kelly!*

Dog Watch (film) Pluto cartoon; released on March 16, 1945. Directed by Charles Nichols. Pluto is a Navy dog, guarding a ship. He ends up in the brig after being blamed when a wharf rat steals the captain's food. He gets some revenge when he shakes the rope the rat is on, causing the rat and food to fall into the water.

Dognapper, The (film) Mickey Mouse cartoon; released on November 17, 1934. Directed by Dave Hand. Minnie's Pekinese is captured by Pete, and Mickey and Donald come to the rescue, discovering Pete's lair in a deserted sawmill.

Doli Hot-tempered member of the Fair Folk in *The Black Cauldron*; voiced by John Byner.

Dolores Elephant character needing a bath by Goofy in *The Big Wash* (1948). Also appeared in *Working for Peanuts*.

Dominguez, Ron He worked up from an opening day ticket taker and later a ride operator at Disneyland to executive vice president before his retirement in 1994. He had the distinction of having been born on the Disneyland property; his family was one of the 17 families that sold their land to Walt Disney in 1954. He was named a Disney Legend in 2004.

Don Defore's Silver Banjo Frontierland food facility at Disneyland; from June 15, 1957, to September 1961. Don Defore, an actor who was perhaps best known for his television portrayal of the neighbor Thorny on *The Ozzie and Harriet Show*, was a friend of Walt Disney.

Don Donald (film) Mickey Mouse cartoon; released on January 9, 1937. While released as a Mickey cartoon, Mickey does not appear; Donald Duck is the star, joined by Donna Duck (who later became known as Daisy). Directed by Ben Sharpsteen. In this south-of-the-border adventure, Donald, the troubador, will go to any lengths, including trading his burro for a car, to please the tempestuous Donna.

Don Karnage Air pirate character on *Tale Spin*; voiced by Jim Cummings.

Donald and Jose, Olé! (television) Television show; aired on January 23, 1982. 90 min. A compilation of cartoons about Latin America, including segments from *The Three Caballeros* and *Saludos Amigos*.

Donald and Pluto (film) Mickey Mouse cartoon; released on September 12, 1936. Directed by Ben Sharpsteen. While released as a Mickey cartoon, Mickey does not appear; Donald Duck is actually the star. Donald attempts to do his own home plumbing until Pluto swallows a magnet and threatens to destroy all of his work.

Donald and the Wheel (film) Donald Duck cartoon featurette; released on June 21, 1961.

Directed by Hamilton Luske. Two "Spirits of Invention" go back in time to discover the inventor of the wheel. Caveduck Donald is selected as the inventor and is shown the evolution and usefulness of the wheel over the centuries. The first stone wheel develops for use on everything from chariots to sports cars. But Donald decides he wants nothing to do with the hassles of modern life, so he returns to pulling his cart without wheels. The spirits decide they picked the wrong person. 18 min. An updated version was released as an educational film in September 1990.

Donald Applecore (film) Donald Duck cartoon; released on Janaury 18, 1952. Directed by Jack Hannah. Donald's battle with Chip and Dale over their eating his apples escalates until Donald bombs them with atomic pellets. One of his hens eats a pellet, laying an egg bomb. It explodes while Donald is holding it, creating a hole that sends him all the way to China.

Donald Duck One of the most popular of the Disney cartoon charac- ters, he made his debut in the Silly Symphony *The Wise Little Hen* on June 9, 1934. His fiery temper endeared him to audiences, and in the 1940s he took over for Mickey Mouse in the number of cartoons reaching the theaters.  Eventually, there were 128 Donald Duck car- toons, but he also appeared in a number of others with Mickey Mouse, Goofy, and Pluto. His middle name, shown in a wartime cartoon, was Fauntleroy. The original voice of Donald was Clarence "Ducky" Nash, who was succeeded after 50 years by Disney animator Tony Anselmo. A daily Donald Duck newspaper comic strip began on February 7, 1938.

Following is a list of the 128 Donald Duck cartoons:

1.	*Donald and Pluto*	1936*
2.	*Don Donald*	1937*
3.	*Modern Inventions*	1937*
4.	*Donald's Ostrich*	1937
5.	*Self Control*	1938
6.	*Donald's Better Self*	1938
7.	*Donald's Nephews*	1938
8.	*Polar Trappers*	1938
9.	*Good Scouts*	1938
10.	*The Fox Hunt*	1938
11.	*Donald's Golf Game*	1938
12.	*Donald's Lucky Day*	1939
13.	*Hockey Champ*	1939
14.	*Donald's Cousin Gus*	1939
15.	*Beach Picnic*	1939
16.	*Sea Scouts*	1939
17.	*Donald's Penguin*	1939
18.	*The Autograph Hound*	1939
19.	*Officer Duck*	1939
20.	*The Riveter*	1940
21.	*Donald's Dog Laundry*	1940
22.	*Billposters*	1940
23.	*Mr. Duck Steps Out*	1940
24.	*Put-put Troubles*	1940
25.	*Donald's Vacation*	1940
26.	*Window Cleaners*	1940
27.	*Fire Chief*	1940
28.	*Timber*	1941
29.	*Golden Eggs*	1941
30.	*A Good Time for a Dime*	1941
31.	*Early to Bed*	1941
32.	*Truant Officer Donald*	1941
33.	*Old Mac Donald Duck*	1941
34.	*Donald's Camera*	1941
35.	*Chef Donald*	1941

*Originally released as Mickey Mouse cartoons but Mickey does not appear.

36.	The Village Smithy	1942
37.	Donald's Snow Fight	1942
38.	Donald Gets Drafted	1942
39.	Donald's Garden	1942
40.	Donald's Gold Mine	1942
41.	The Vanishing Private	1942
42.	Sky Trooper	1942
43.	Bellboy Donald	1942
44.	Der Fuehrer's Face	1943
45.	Donald's Tire Trouble	1943
46.	Flying Jalopy	1943
47.	Fall Out—Fall In	1943
48.	The Old Army Game	1943
49.	Home Defense	1943
50.	Trombone Trouble	1944
51.	Donald Duck and the Gorilla	1944
52.	Contrary Condor	1944
53.	Commando Duck	1944
54.	The Plastics Inventor	1944
55.	Donald's Off Day	1944
56.	The Clock Watcher	1945
57.	The Eyes Have It	1945
58.	Donald's Crime	1945
59.	Duck Pimples	1945
60.	No Sail	1945
61.	Cured Duck	1945
62.	Old Sequoia	1945
63.	Donald's Double Trouble	1946
64.	Wet Paint	1946
65.	Dumb Bell of the Yukon	1946
66.	Lighthouse Keeping	1946
67.	Frank Duck Brings 'em Back Alive	1946
68.	Straight Shooters	1947
69.	Sleepy Time Donald	1947
70.	Clown of the Jungle	1947
71.	Donald's Dilemma	1947
72.	Crazy with the Heat	1947
73.	Bootle Beetle	1947
74.	Wide Open Spaces	1947
75.	Chip an' Dale	1947
76.	Drip Dippy Donald	1948
77.	Daddy Duck	1948
78.	Donald's Dream Voice	1948
79.	The Trial of Donald Duck	1948
80.	Inferior Decorator	1948
81.	Soup's On	1948
82.	Three for Breakfast	1948
83.	Tea for Two Hundred	1948
84.	Donald's Happy Birthday	1949
85.	Sea Salts	1949
86.	Winter Storage	1949
87.	Honey Harvester	1949
88.	All in a Nutshell	1949
89.	The Greener Yard	1949
90.	Slide, Donald, Slide	1949
91.	Toy Tinkers	1949
92.	Lion Around	1950
93.	Crazy Over Daisy	1950
94.	Trailer Horn	1950
95.	Hook, Lion and Sinker	1950
96.	Bee at the Beach	1950
97.	Out on a Limb	1950
98.	Dude Duck	1951
99.	Corn Chips	1951
100.	Test Pilot Donald	1951
101.	Lucky Number	1951
102.	Out of Scale	1951
103.	Bee on Guard	1951
104.	Donald Applecore	1952
105.	Let's Stick Together	1952
106.	Uncle Donald's Ants	1952
107.	Trick or Treat	1952
108.	Don's Fountain of Youth	1953
109.	The New Neighbor	1953
110.	Rugged Bear	1953
111.	Working for Peanuts	1953
112.	Canvas Back Duck	1953
113.	Spare the Rod	1954
114.	Donald's Diary	1954
115.	Dragon Around	1954
116.	Grin and Bear It	1954
117.	Grand Canyonscope	1954
118.	Flying Squirrel	1954
119.	No Hunting	1955
120.	Bearly Asleep	1955
121.	Beezy Bear	1955
122.	Up a Tree	1955
123.	Chips Ahoy	1956
124.	How to Have an Accident in the Home	1956
125.	Donald in Mathmagic Land	1959
126.	How to Have an Accident at Work	1959
127.	Donald and the Wheel	1961
128.	The Litterbug	1961

Donald Duck and the Gorilla (film) Donald Duck cartoon; released on March 31, 1944. Directed by Jack King. Donald and his nephews try to scare each other when they hear on the radio that a gorilla has escaped from the zoo, but when the gorilla, Ajax, shows up, they unite to defeat the creature with a tear gas bomb.

Donald Duck Cola See General Beverages, Inc.

Donald Duck Presents (television) Series on The Disney Channel featuring Disney cartoons. 125 episodes were produced. Began on September 1, 1983.

Donald Duck Quacks Up See *Kids Is Kids.*

Donald Duck Story, The (television) Television show; aired on November 17, 1954. Directed by Jack Hannah, Robert Florey. Walt tells a fictional story about Donald's career, encompassing a number of Donald Duck cartoons.

Donald Duck's 50th Birthday (television) Television special on CBS; aired on November 13, 1984. Directed by Andrew Solt. Host Dick Van Dyke takes a look at the famous Duck, with many of his celebrity friends helping out.

Donald Gets Drafted (film) Donald Duck cartoon; released on May 1, 1942. The first Disney war-themed cartoon released during World War II. Directed by Jack King. Donald learns to rue his Army induction order when his sadistic sergeant, Pete, drills him and teaches him discipline.

Donald in Mathmagic Land (film) Donald Duck featurette; released on June 26, 1959. Directed by Hamilton Luske. Donald Duck explores Mathmagic Land—a fantasy land composed of such things as square root trees and a stream running with numbers. The Spirit of Adventure teaches him the many uses of mathematics in art, architecture, and Nature as well as chess and sports such as football. Donald is introduced to the circle and the triangle, which have been the basis for many great inventions such as the telescope and airplane, and he is

shown that mathematical thinking opens the doors to the future. This thoughtful, Academy Award–nominated short ends with Galileo's quotation: "Mathematics is the alphabet in which God wrote the universe." 28 min. Made with the collaboration of such people as Disney artists John Hench and Art Riley, voice talent Paul Frees, and scientific expert Heinz Haber, who had

worked on the Disney space shows. Originally released on a bill with *Darby O'Gill and the Little People.* Two years later it had the honor of being introduced by Ludwig Von Drake and shown on the first program of *Walt Disney's Wonderful World of Color.* The film was made available to schools and became one of the most popular educational films ever made by Disney. As Walt Disney explained, "The cartoon is a good medium to stimulate interest. We have recently explained mathematics in a film and in that way excited public interest in this very important subject." Released on video in 1988.

Donald Loves Daisy (television) Syndicated television show about romance, featuring clips from Disney cartoons.

Donald Takes a Holiday (television) Syndicated television show from 1987, incorporating a number of cartoons about vacationing.

Donald's Award (television) Television show; aired on March 27, 1957. Directed by Jack Hannah. Walt offers Donald a reward if he can remain on his best behavior for a week, and he sends Jiminy Cricket to check up on him. Segments from Donald Duck cartoons emphasize his temper.

Donald's Better Self (film) Donald Duck cartoon; released on March 11, 1938. Directed by Jack King. Donald is reluctant to go to school, but is persuaded to do so by his angelic Better Self, who has to defeat his devilish Evil Self, who is continually leading Donald astray.

Donald's Camera (film) Donald Duck cartoon; released on October 24, 1941. Directed by Dick Lundy. Donald considers gun hunting to be wrong and hunts wildlife only with a camera. But, when a woodpecker becomes a pest and smashes Donald's camera, he goes after it with an arsenal of weapons.

Donald's Cousin Gus (film) Donald Duck cartoon; released on May 19, 1939. Directed by Jack King. Donald's goose cousin, Gus, comes to visit and practically eats him out of house and home. When Donald's attempts to get rid of Gus are unsuccessful, he gives up in disgust.

Donald's Crime (film) Donald Duck cartoon; released on June 29, 1945. Directed by Jack King. Donald, broke, steals from his nephews' piggy bank for a date with Daisy, but his conscience gets the best of him and he gets a job to pay them back. Nominated for an Academy Award.

Donald's Decision (film) Shows the advisability and necessity of purchasing Canadian War Bonds. Made for the National Film Board of Canada. Delivered to them on January 11, 1942. Donald wrestles with his good self and bad self to make up his mind about buying war bonds. The film reused animation from *Donald's Better Self* and *Self Control*.

Donald's Diary (film) Donald Duck cartoon; released on March 5, 1954. Directed by Jack Kinney. The narrator tells of Donald's romance with Daisy through use of Donald's diary. Daisy has almost snared him into marriage when he has a

nightmarish vision of what their married life would be like. He decides to run away, and we see him writing in his diary in the French Foreign Legion.

Donald's Dilemma (film) Donald Duck cartoon; released on July 11, 1947. Directed by Jack King. Daisy panics when a flowerpot falling on Donald's head gives him a magnificent singing voice and takes away his memory of her. A helpful psychiatrist tells her to drop another flowerpot on him for a cure, and it works.

Donald's Dog Laundry (film) Donald Duck cartoon; released on April 5, 1940. Directed by Jack King. With his squeaker toy cat, Donald attempts to entice Pluto to try his mechanical dog washer, but is unexpectedly caught himself, scrubbed, and hung on the line to dry.

Donald's Double Trouble (film) Donald Duck cartoon; released on June 28, 1946. Directed by Jack King. Donald meets his double and decides to use him to try to win back Daisy's love. But the trick backfires when the double, with a Ronald Colman voice, falls in love with Daisy himself.

Donald's Dream Voice (film) Donald Duck cartoon; released on May 21, 1948. Directed by Jack King. Donald, discouraged as a salesman because of his voice, buys miraculous voice pills that improve his vocal range, but he quickly loses the pills, and despite a long search, accidentally drops the last in the mouth of a cow.

Donald's Dynamite: Opera Box (film) When Donald attends the opera with Daisy, he finds a bomb in her purse and tries, unsuccessfully, to defuse it. Directed by William Speers. Released on March 26, 1999, with *Doug's 1st Movie. 2 min.* From the *Mickey MouseWorks* television series.

Donald's Fire Drill (film) Educational release in 16mm in August 1991. 15 min. Two kids are contestants on a game show, co-hosted by Trevor Townsend and Donald Duck, and they try to beat the clock by answering questions on fire safety information.

Donald's Fire Survival Plan (film) Educational film showing how the loss of homes and lives by fire may be prevented with a bit of thought beforehand. Released on 16mm in May 1966. An updated version, containing new footage and prevention tactics, was released in August 1984.

Donald's Garden (film) Donald Duck cartoon; released on June 12, 1942. Directed by Dick Lundy. Donald has all sorts of troubles in his garden with the watering can and pump, and a gopher that eats his prize watermelons.

Donald's Gold Mine (film) Donald Duck cartoon; released on July 24, 1942. Directed by Dick Lundy. Gold miner Donald's conflicts with his donkey result in a gold strike, but Donald gets tangled in his own gold mining equipment and ends up looking like one of the bars of gold.

Donald's Golf Game (film) Donald Duck cartoon; released on November 4, 1938. Directed by Jack King. Donald's exhibition of his golfing ability to his nephews is defeated by their constant tricks, including sneezes, trick clubs, and a grasshopper trapped inside a golf ball.

Donald's Happy Birthday (film) Donald Duck cartoon; released on February 11, 1949. Directed by Jack Hannah. The nephews earn

money to buy cigars for Donald's birthday, but Donald thinks they bought the cigars for themselves and forces them to smoke them all. He then discovers the birthday card in the bottom of the box.

Donald's Lucky Day (film) Donald Duck cartoon; released on January 13, 1939. Directed by Jack King. Bicycle messenger boy Donald has a series of mishaps on Friday the 13th. He continually tries to avoid an "unlucky" black cat. The cat turns lucky when it knocks a bomb, which Donald is unknowingly delivering, off a pier and into the water as it explodes, showering Donald and the cat with fish.

Donald's Nephews (film) Donald Duck cartoon; released on April 15, 1938. Directed by Jack King. First film appearance of Huey, Dewey, and Louie, who are sent to visit their uncle by his sister, Dumbella. Donald attempts to practice child psychology, but it is all for naught as the nephews ruin his house and play all manner of tricks on him.

Donald's Off Day (film) Donald Duck cartoon; released on December 8, 1944. The first cartoon directed by Jack Hannah. Donald is not able to go out for Sunday golf when his nephews and a book he has been reading convince him that he is not well. When he realizes the joke, he attempts to go out again but a steady downpour sends him back inside.

Donald's Ostrich (film) Donald Duck cartoon; released on December 10, 1937. Directed by Jack King. When an ostrich named Hortense

gets free of her shipping crate and swallows everything in sight, including a radio, train station agent Donald is in for a hilarious day.

Donald's Penguin (film) Donald Duck cartoon; released on August 11, 1939. Directed by Jack King. Donald gets a baby penguin as a gift, and it causes so much trouble he nearly shoots it, causing it to disappear. Remorseful, Donald is overjoyed to see the penguin return and they hug affectionately.

Donald's Silver Anniversary (television) Television show; aired on November 13, 1960. Directed by Hamilton S. Luske. Walt uses various cartoons to reminisce about Donald's career, and he creates a special award, the Duckster, to commemorate it.

Donald's Snow Fight (film) Donald Duck cartoon; released on April 10, 1942. Directed by Jack King. When Donald destroys his nephews' snowman, the snow fight escalates with Donald's snow ship attacking the nephews' snow fort. The nephews win the fight and do a victory dance above a frozen geyser holding Donald after they've melted his ship with hot coals shot by arrows.

Donald's Tire Trouble (film) Donald Duck cartoon; released on January 29, 1943. Directed by Dick Lundy. Donald, driving in the country, is frustrated in his attempts to fix a flat tire. The jack breaks, the radiator explodes, then the remaining three tires go flat. Donald gives up in disgust and drives on with the flats. The film features references to the rubber shortage during World War II.

Donald's Vacation (film) Donald Duck cartoon; released on August 9, 1940. Directed by Jack King. Donald sets up camp in the great outdoors to find peace and relaxation, only to tangle with his folding equipment, chipmunks who steal his food, and a hungry bear.

Donald's Valentine Day Salute (television) Television show; aired on February 10, 1980. Cartoons and clips about romance.

Donald's Weekend (television) Television show; aired on January 15, 1958. Directed by Jack Hannah. Cartoons tied around the theme of a typical weekend with Donald Duck.

Donovan, Tate Actor; appeared in *The Pacifier* (Howard Plummer), and provided the voice of the title character in *Hercules*.

Donovan's Kid (television) Two-part television show; aired on January 7 and 14, 1979. Directed by Bernard McEveety. At the turn of the century, a con-man, Timothy Donovan, returns to San Francisco to see his wife and daughter (who he had thought was a son). He tries to free them from the domination of his wife's uncle. Stars Darren McGavin, Mickey Rooney, Shelley Fabares, Katy Kurtzman, Murray Hamilton, Michael Conrad, Ross Martin.

Don's Fountain of Youth (film) Donald Duck cartoon; released on May 30, 1953. Directed by Jack Hannah. On his travels with his nephews, Donald tricks them into believing he has been magically transformed into a baby and then an egg by a "Fountain of Youth" until an encounter

with a mother alligator and her babies spoils Donald's fun.

Don't Look Under the Bed (film) A Disney Channel Original Movie, first airing on October 9, 1999. Fourteen-year-old Frances McCausland has always approached life with logic and reason, but that changes when someone starts playing destructive pranks in her community, and all evidence points to Frances as the culprit. Frances discovers she is being framed by a mischievous Boogeyman who lives under her bed. With the help of Larry Houdini, her brother's imaginary friend, she learns to rely on her imagination to defeat the Boogeyman. Directed by Kenneth Johnson. Stars Erin Chambers (Frances McCausland), Eric Hodges II (Larry Houdini), Jake Sakson (Darwin McCausland), Robin Riker (Karen McCausland), Steve Valentine (the Boogeyman).

Door Knob One of the stranger Disney characters, in *Alice in Wonderland*; voiced by Joseph Kearns.

Dopey Youngest of the Seven Dwarfs, who did not speak.

Dorsey, Don Audio engineer, synthesist, and designer of shows and parades at Disneyland who, after part-time work as synthesist/arranger on America on Parade in 1975, arranged and performed the music for the updated Main Street Electrical Parade in 1977 and guided the development of the park's parade-control audio computer system in 1980. Beginning in 1983, he created and directed nighttime fireworks spectaculars for Walt Disney World, including Laserphonic Fantasy, IllumiNations, and Sorcery in the Sky. He also designed the sound effects for Fantasmic! at Disneyland.

Dory Regal Blue Tang fish in *Finding Nemo*; voiced by Ellen DeGeneres.

Dotrice, Karen Child actress; appeared in *The Three Lives of Thomasina* (Mary MacDhui), *Mary Poppins* (Jane Banks), and *The Gnome-Mobile* (Elizabeth). She was named a Disney Legend in 2004.

Double Agent (television) Two-hour television movie; aired on March 29, 1987. Directed by Mike Vejar. A veterinarian reluctantly takes his brother's place as a secret agent to complete a mission. He is assigned a bumbling helper, and surprisingly manages to outwit the mysterious Scorpion. Stars Michael McKean, John Putch, Susan Walden, Christopher Burton, Lloyd Bochner, Alexa Hamilton.

Double Dribble (film) Goofy cartoon; released on December 20, 1946. Directed by Jack Hannah. A basketball game of Goofy look-alikes (P.U. vs. U.U.) in which the players play furiously, often breaking the rules of the game. All of the players are named after Disney artists.

Double Switch (television) Two-hour television movie; aired on January 24, 1987. Directed by David Greenwalt. A shy teen, who is the exact double of a rock star, switches places with him so the rock star can spend some time with a "real family." Each has problems trying to adapt to his new life, so they decide to switch back again and begin to appreciate their own families. Stars George Newbern, Elisabeth Shue, Michael Des Barres, Peter Van Norden.

Double Take (film) Successful New York investment banker, Daryl Chase, is framed for laundering money for a Mexican drug cartel. Wanted by the FBI, he makes a run for the border to find the one man who can clear his name, followed all along the way by Freddy Tiffany, an untrustworthy low-life petty thief. Taking Freddy's identity in order to make his way in the underworld, Daryl, to his horror, discovers that Freddy is even more wanted than he is. Directed by George Gallo. A Touchstone picture. Released on January 12, 2001. Stars Orlando Jones (Daryl Chase), Eddie Griffin (Freddy Tiffany), Edward Herrmann (Charles Allsworth), Gary Grubbs

(T.J. McCready), Daniel Roebuck (Norville). 88 min. Loosely based on the 1957 feature *Across the Bridge*, which in turn was based on a Graham Greene novella. Filmed in CinemaScope. Released on video in 2001.

Double Teamed (television) A Disney Channel Original Movie, first aired on January 18, 2002. Inspired by the true story of WNBA players Heidi and Heather Burge, also known as the world's "tallest twins." From their humble high school beginnings to the spotlight of professional women's basketball, the lives and differing goals of the two girls are profiled. Directed by Duwayne Dunham. Stars Poppi Monroe (Heather Burge), Annie McElwain (Heidi Burge), Mackenzie Phillips (Mary Burge), Nicky Searcy (Larry Burge), Teal Redmann (Nicky Williams), Chris Olivero (Galen Alderman).

Doubletree Guest Suite Resort Hotel at Lake Buena Vista at Walt Disney World; opened on February 23, 1995, taking the place of the Guest Quarters Suite Hotel, which was remodeled and renamed.

Doug, Doug E. Actor; appeared in *Cool Runnings* (Sanka Coffee), *Operation Dumbo Drop* (H.A.), and *That Darn Cat* (Zeke Kelso), and on the television series *Where I Live*.

Douglas, Kirk Actor; appeared in *20,000 Leagues Under the Sea* (Ned Land) and *Tough Guys* (Archie Long). He had an uncredited cameo role in *Oscar* (Papa Provolone).

Douglas, Michael Actor; appeared in *Napoleon and Samantha* (Danny).

Douglas, Mike Provided the uncredited singing voice for Prince Charming in *Cinderella*.

Doug's 1st Movie (film) Doug Funnie, an imaginative and quirky 12½-year-old, finds himself caught between saving an endangered "monster" of Lucky Duck Lake and a burning desire to take his secret crush, Patti Mayonnaise, to the school dance. Not only does he discover the mythical monster is real, and subject to an elaborate cover-up by one of Bluffington's leading citizens, but a slick upperclassman is trying to have Patti for himself. Directed by Maurice Joyce. Produced by Jumbo Pictures in association with Walt Disney Pictures. Released on March 26, 1999. Voices include Tom McHugh (Doug Funnie, Lincoln), Fred Newman (Skeeter Valentine, Mr. Dink, Porkchop, Herman Melville, Ned), Constance Shulman (Patti Mayonnaise). 77 min. Doug was originally created by Jim Jinkins for a Nickelodeon cable series. Released on video in 1999. See *Brand Spanking New Doug* for the television series.

Dow Jones Industrial Average The Walt Disney Company joined the prestigious list on May 6, 1991.

Down and Out in Beverly Hills (film) When Jerry, a down-and-out bum, tries to drown himself in a Beverly Hills swimming pool, the wealthy homeowner, Dave Whiteman, rescues him and invites him into the house to live. Jerry turns the lives of the Whiteman family completely upside down, and in doing so changes their perception of the world around them. They find they need Jerry and his unconventional attitudes as much as he needs them. Released on January 31, 1986. Directed by Paul Mazursky. A Touchstone film. 103 min. The first R rated film from the Disney Studios. Stars Nick Nolte (Jerry Baskin), Bette Midler (Barbara Whiteman), Richard Dreyfuss (Dave Whiteman), Little Richard (Orvis Goodnight), Tracy Nelson (Jenny Whiteman), Elizabeth Peña (Carmen), Evan Richards (Max Whiteman), Donald F. Muhich (Dr. Von Zimmer). For the role of the lovable Matisse, the Whiteman family's emotionally disturbed dog, a pair of look-alike Scottish Border collies were used: Davey did all the action, while Mike did the interrelational scenes. In the brief role as Sadie Whiteman, mother to Richard Dreyfuss' character, Dreyfuss' own mother, Geraldine Dreyfuss, was used. The majority of the film was shot on studio soundstages. The back of the Whiteman house as well as the swimming pool and a fully landscaped yard were constructed on the Disney backlot. Daytime shots involving the front of the house were shot at an actual location in Beverly Hills, and because of various permit restrictions, night work in front of the house had to be shot at the Columbia Ranch where a duplicate facade of the Beverly Hills house was built. There was location work at the Rodeo Collection on Rodeo Drive, the Union Rescue Mission in downtown Los Angeles, the Los Angeles International Airport, Venice Beach, the old Cyrano's restaurant on the Sunset Strip, and numerous locations in and around Beverly Hills. Released on video in 1986.

Down and Out in Beverly Hills (television) Television series on the new Fox network, from July 25 to September 12, 1987, after a preview on April 26. Further adventures of the Whiteman family and their domestic upheaval when a vagrant becomes a boarder. Stars Hector Elizondo (Dave Whiteman), Tim Thomerson (Jerry Baskin), Anita Morris (Barbara Whiteman), Evan Richards (Max Whiteman), April Ovitz (Carmen). Only Evan Richards and Mike the dog (Matisse) repeated from the feature film.

Down and Out with Donald Duck (television) Television show; aired on March 25, 1987. Directed by Scot Garen. Donald's life traced in *60 Minutes* style, utilizing footage from a number of cartoons.

Down the Long Hills (television) A young boy and girl, survivors of an Indian raid, struggle to meet their rescuers, as the boy's father carries out a desperate search for them. A Disney Channel Premiere Film; first aired on November 15, 1986. Directed by Burt Kennedy. Based on the story by Louis L'Amour. 89 min. Stars Bruce Boxleitner (Scott Collins), Thomas Wilson Brown (Hardy Collins), Lisa MacFarlane (Betty Sue Powell), Jack Elam (Squires).

Downtown Disney Name given in 1996 to the entertainment-shopping-dining district at Walt Disney World encompassing Disney Village Marketplace (renamed Downtown Disney Marketplace), Pleasure Island, and a new 66-acre area called Downtown Disney West Side, opened September 15, 1997, which includes Cirque du Soleil, Bongos Cuban Cafe, Wolfgang Puck Cafe, House of Blues, Virgin Megastore, DisneyQuest, and a number of other businesses. A California version of Downtown Disney, situated between Disneyland Park, Disney's California Adventure, and the Disneyland Hotel, opened on January 12, 2001.

Downtown Disney Marketplace New name (1997) for Disney Village Marketplace, which had opened in March 1975 as Lake Buena Vista Village, became Walt Disney World Village in 1977, and then Disney Village Marketplace in 1989. A variety of shops are clustered along the shore of the Buena Vista Lagoon next to Pleasure Island, about five miles from Magic Kingdom Park. The centerpiece was the Captain's Tower, under which seasonal merchandise displays were featured. On September 7, 1997, the Village Marketplace became part of the Downtown Disney complex and was renamed Downtown Disney Marketplace.

Dragon Around (film) Donald Duck cartoon; released on July 16, 1954. Directed by Jack Hannah. As a steam-shovel operator, Donald is clearing an excavation site when he runs into Chip and Dale, who imagine the machine is a dragon threatening their home. By getting into the tool chest, they unbolt the steam shovel, which falls apart, thus enabling them to vanquish the dragon.

Dragonslayer (film) A joint Disney/Paramount production. Directed by Matthew Robbins. After his master's untimely demise, a sorcerer's apprentice takes up his teacher's final duty—the destruction of the world's last dragon. Disney's share of the production was the creation of some of the special effects, including the ferocious dragon, Vermithrax Pejorative. Stars Peter McNicol, Caitlin Clarke, Ralph Richardson. 110 min. Filmed at Pinewood Studios, London, and on location on the Isle of Skye, Scotland, and in Snowdonia National Park, North Wales. Paramount released the film in the U.S. in June 1981, and Disney released it abroad.

Drake Mallard Alter ego of Darkwing Duck.

Drawing Conclusions (film) Educational release in 16mm in August 1991, 19 min. A high school girl's mother and friends discourage her artistic talent, but she wants to enter a drawing contest at school.

Dream Called EPCOT, A (film) Promo film shown at the EPCOT Preview Center at Walt Disney World; first shown on June 1, 1981.

Dream Called Walt Disney World, A (film) Video souvenir of a visit to Walt Disney World; released in June 1981 and later shown on television.

Dream Is a Wish Your Heart Makes, A Song from *Cinderella*, written by Mack David, Al Hoffman, and Jerry Livingston.

Dream Is a Wish Your Heart Makes, A: The Annette Funicello Story (television) Two-hour television movie on CBS, airing on October 22, 1995. Annette narrates the film about her life, which was not made by Disney. Stars Eva Larue (Annette, 1958 on), Linda Lavin (Virginia Funicello), Frank Crudelle (Joe Funicello), Len Cariou (Walt Disney).

Dream Is Alive, The: 20th Anniversary Celebration at Walt Disney World (television) Television special (60 min.); aired on CBS on October 25, 1991. Directed by Dwight Hemion. Michael Eisner is searching for the perfect host, but no one will agree to take the job. Stars include Carol Burnett, Garth Brooks, Angela Lansbury, Tim Allen, Steve Martin, Goldie Hawn.

Dream on Silly Dreamer (film) Non-Disney documentary made by two ex-Disney animators, Tony West and Dan Lund, chronicling the shift from 2-D to computer-generated films and the closing of Disney's Feature Animation studio in Florida, including original animation and interviews with dozens of artists. Debuted at the Animex International Festival in England on January 31, 2005.

Dream Quest Images Visual-effects company acquired by Disney in May 1996. The company used live-action photography, models, and motion-control cameras, as well as the latest in digital-effects technology to enhance motion pictures. Prior to the purchase, Dream Quest had won Academy Awards for special effects in *The Abyss* and *Total Recall*. Dream Quest took over the visual-effects chores formerly performed by a department at the Disney Studios. It was merged with Disney's in-house feature animation computer graphics unit in October 1999 and renamed the Secret Lab. In 2001, the Secret Lab name was retired and the personnel were reassigned.

Dreamfinder Jolly redhead who hosted, with his dragon pal, Figment, in the Journey into Imagination attraction at Epcot from 1983 to 1998. Ron Schneider provided his voice.

Dreamfinder's School of Drama Guests in the Image Works, Journey Into Imagination, Epcot, could interact in Chroma-key video playlets entitled *Daring Deputies and the Return of Sagebrush Sam*, *Acrobatic Astronauts in Galactic Getaway*, and *Enchanted Travelers—Wily Wizard and the Cranky King*.

Dreamflight See Delta Dreamflight.

Dreyer, John Vice president and later senior vice president of corporate communications for The Walt Disney Company from 1992 to 2001. He had begun his Disney career as a publicist at Walt Disney World in 1977, moving up to press and publicity manager in 1988.

Dreyfuss, Richard Actor; appeared in *Down and Out in Beverly Hills* (Dave Whiteman), *Tin Men* (Bill Babowsky), *Stakeout* (Chris Lecce), *What About Bob?* (Dr. Leo Marvin), *Another Stakeout* (Chris Lecce), *Mr. Holland's Opus* (Glenn Holland), *Krippendorf's Tribe* (James Krippendorf), and *The Crew* (Bobby Bartellemeo). He provided the voice of the centipede in *James and the Giant Peach*. On television he appeared in *Oliver Twist* (Fagin).

Drip Dippy Donald (film) Donald Duck cartoon; released on March 5, 1948. Directed by Jack King. In his effort to sleep, Donald is disturbed first by a window shade and then by a dripping faucet. After fighting all night with the leak, Donald goes cuckoo when the water company calls saying they are shutting off his water because he hasn't paid his water bill.

Driscoll, Bobby (1937–1968) Child actor; born March 3, 1937, appeared in *Song of the South* (Johnny), *Melody Time*, *So Dear to My Heart* (Jeremiah Kincaid), *Treasure Island* (Jim Hawkins), and as the voice of Peter Pan and Goofy Jr. in 1950s cartoons. He received a special juvenile Academy Award in the year he made *So Dear to My Heart* and the non-Disney *The Window*. He appeared in the television specials *One Hour in Wonderland* and the *Walt Disney Christmas Show*. He had a troubled life after he outgrew children's roles, and died of a drug overdose, a pauper and unknown, at the age of 31, in New York City.

Driver, Minnie Actress; appeared in *Grosse Pointe Blank* (Debi Newberry), *High Heels and Low Lifes* (Shannon), *Hope Springs* (Vera), and provided the voice of Jane in *Tarzan*.

Drizella One of Cinderella's evil stepsisters; voiced by Rhoda Williams.

Dru, Joanne (1923–1996) Actress; appeared in *The Light in the Forest* (Milly Elder).

Drury, James Actor; appeared in *Toby Tyler* (Jim Weaver), *Pollyanna* (George Dodds), and *Ten Who Dared* (Walter Powell), and on television in *Elfego Baca*.

DTV (television) Series of music videos on The Disney Channel, where segments of Disney cartoons served as backup for popular songs; premiered on May 5, 1984. Also released on several video collections in 1984–85.

Dubin, Gary He voiced Toulouse in *The Aristocats*.

Duchess Regal mother cat in *The Aristocats*; voiced by Eva Gabor.

Duchovny, David Actor; appeared in *Playing God* (Dr. Eugene Sands).

Duck Flies Coop (television) Television show; aired on February 13, 1959. Directed by Jack Hannah. The temperamental duck vows not to return to the Studio, and leaves on a vacation. But all does not go well, so he is ready to return when Walt Disney calls. The show uses clips from a number of Donald Duck cartoons.

Duck for Hire (television) Television show; aired on October 23, 1957. Directed by Jack Hannah. Donald decides to quit show business, but a number of disasters (clips from several Donald Duck cartoons) persuade him to return.

Duck Hunt, The (film) Mickey Mouse cartoon; released on January 28, 1932. Directed by Burt Gillett. Mickey and Pluto find duck hunting not all they expected it to be when they are turned upon by a group of angry ducks and end up being dropped by them into suits of underwear on the line.

Duck One Name given to a special PSA charter airplane used for a cross-country celebration for Donald Duck's 50th birthday in 1984. Traveling with Donald Duck was Clarence Nash, who provided his famous voice.

Duck Pimples (film) Donald Duck cartoon; released on August 10, 1945. Directed by Jack Kinney. The character of the murder mystery Donald is reading comes to life and it is only with the intervention of the author, who proves the cop is the thief, that Donald's life is saved and the character can return to the book.

Ducking Disaster with Donald and His Friends See *Man Is His Own Worst Enemy.*

Duckster Award consisting of a bronze-colored figure of Donald Duck, used to honor those who have been of service to The Walt Disney Company. It was created in 1960 for the television show *Donald's Silver Anniversary*. The Mickey Mouse equivalent is known as the Mousecar.

Ducktales (television) Animated television series; syndicated from September 21, 1987, until September 5, 1992. It was introduced by a two-hour syndicated special on September 18, 1987. On April 19, 1997, it returned to the air on ABC, until August 30, 1997. On September 1, 1997, it began a new syndication run. The theme song was written by Mark Mueller. The show featured Scrooge McDuck and the nephews, Huey, Dewey, and Louie. Scrooge's innate sense for making or finding money leads him to outrageous adventures, accompanied by his grandnephews. Helping, though sometimes hindering, are Webbigail Vanderquack ("Webby"), Gyro Gearloose, Mrs. Beakley, Doofus, and Gladstone Gander. The Beagle Boys, Magica de Spell, and Flintheart Glomgold, on the other hand, are out to destroy the McDuck empire. For the series, the nephews were given unique colors to wear for the first time: red for Huey, blue for Dewey, and green for Louie. Voices include Alan Young (Scrooge), Russi Taylor (nephews, Webby), Terence McGovern (Launchpad). 100 episodes.

Ducktales Movie Special (television) Syndicated television special, previewing *Ducktales: the Movie, Treasure of the Lost Lamp*; first aired on August 1, 1990. 30 min. Hosted by Tracey Gold and Kadeem Hardison. Directed by Adam Small and Barbara Williams.

Ducktales: the Movie, Treasure of the Lost Lamp (film) Scrooge McDuck travels to the far ends of the earth in search of the elusive buried treasure of legendary thief, Collie Baba. With his companions Huey, Dewey, and Louie, Webby, and Launchpad McQuack, Scrooge discovers not only the treasure but also that there's a mysterious madman named Merlock who is out to stop him. The travelers have to return home empty-handed except for an old lamp. The kids find it is a magic lamp and discover a genie inside, who grants their wishes. When Merlock and his henchman, Dijon, return, it takes all of Scrooge's ingenuity to thwart them. Released on August 3, 1990, as a Disney Movietoon. Directed by Bob Hathcock. 74 min. Voices include Alan Young (Scrooge), Terence McGovern (Launchpad), Russi Taylor (nephews, Webby). A true international production, with the story work and planning done in the United States, the animation done in England and France, and the cels painted in China. Released on video in 1991.

Ducktales: Time Is Money (television) Syndicated television special; aired on November 25, 1988. Directed by Bob Hathcock, James T. Walker, Terrence Harrison, James Mitchell.

Ducktales Valentine!, A (television) Television show; aired on February 11, 1990. Directed by Mircea Manita. Scrooge McDuck goes searching for the lost temple of Aphroducky, the ancient goddess of love. Also, a lecture by Ludwig Von Drake on love, utilizing three cartoons.

Dude Duck (film) Donald Duck cartoon; released on March 2, 1951. Directed by Jack Hannah. Donald, on vacation at a dude ranch, cannot wait to ride a horse. Unfortunately, the only horse available is completely unwilling to cooperate. Donald ends up on a bull's back riding out into the desert with the horse laughing wildly.

Duets (film) Six strangers from all walks of life have one thing in common—a passion for karaoke. In this road-trip comedy, three pairs of people converge on the $5,000 Grand Prize Karaoke Contest in Omaha, Nebraska, searching to find something they don't have in their lives. Released on September 15, 2000. A Hollywood Picture, in association with Seven Arts Pictures and Beacon Pictures. Directed by Bruce Paltrow. Stars Maria Bello (Suzi Loomis), André Braugher (Reggie Kane), Paul Giamatti (Todd Woods), Huey Lewis (Ricky Dean), Gwyneth Paltrow (Liv), Scott Speedman (Billy Hannon), Angie Dickinson (Blair). 112 min. Gwyneth Paltrow is the daughter of director Bruce Paltrow. Filmed in the Las Vegas area, and around Vancouver, British Columbia. Released on video in 2001.

Duff, Hilary Actress; appeared on television in *Lizzie McGuire* (Lizzie) and *Cadet Kelly* (Kelly Collins), and in *The Lizzie McGuire Movie*. She also became a best-selling recording artist for Hollywood Records.

Duffy, Patrick Actor; appeared in *Perfect Game* (Bobby Geiser) and on television in *14 Going on 30*. He also hosted *Disney's Captain Eo Grand Opening* and did the voice of Harold Hatchback on *Goof Troop*.

Dugan, Dennis Actor; appeared in *Unidentified Flying Oddball* (Tom Trimble) and *Can't Buy Me Love* (David Miller), and years later directed the television remake of *The Shaggy Dog*.

Duggan, Andrew Actor; appeared in *The Bears and I* (Commissioner Gaines), and on television in *Fire on Kelly Mountain* and *The Saga of Andy Burnett*.

Dukakis, Olympia Actress; appeared in *The Cemetery Club* (Doris Silverman), *I Love Trouble* (Jeannie), *Mr. Holland's Opus* (Principal Jacobs), *Jane Austen's Mafia!* (Sophia), and on television in *Ladies and the Champ* (Sarah Stevenson).

Duke, The (film) Direct-to-video release by Buena Vista Home Entertainment on April 18, 2000, of a Keystone Pictures film (original release in Iceland on October 30, 1999). Hubert, a bloodhound, inherits the estate of the Duke of Dingwall, including royal jewels and the title of Duke, but a disinherited nephew comes up with a plot to seize control. Directed by Philip Spink. Courtnee Draper (Charlotte), James Doohan (Clive Chives), Oliver Muirhead (Cecil Cavendish). 88 min.

Duke Igthorn The menace of the Gummi Bears; voiced by Michael Rye.

Dumb Bell of the Yukon (film) Donald Duck cartoon; released on August 30, 1946. Directed by Jack King. Arctic trapper Donald kidnaps a cub from a sleeping mother bear to get a fur coat for Daisy. Just as the mother bear is about to

attack Donald, a jar of honey falls on his head. Both bears end up licking the honey off Donald.

Dumbella Sister of Donald Duck and mother of Huey, Dewey, and Louie, according to the cartoon *Donald's Nephews* (1938).

Dumbo (film) A baby circus elephant is born with huge ears, and named Dumbo. He and his mother suffer humiliation from the other elephants and from the kids visiting the circus. But humiliation turns to triumph as Dumbo is surprised to discover through the help of his faithful mouse friend, Timothy, that he can use the oversized ears to fly. Released on October 23, 1941. Directed by

Ben Sharpsteen. From a story by Helen Aberson and Harold Pearl. 64 min. Voices include Edward Brophy (Timothy), Sterling Holloway (stork), and Cliff Edwards (Jim Crow). Among the songs are "Baby Mine," "Pink Elephants on Parade," and "When I See an Elephant Fly." The film won an Oscar for Best Scoring of a Motion Picture (Frank Churchill and Oliver Wallace), and was nominated for Best Song ("Baby Mine"). From the time that Walt first read the galleys for the story, he knew it would make a fine film. Coming after two expensive movies (*Fantasia* and *Pinocchio*) the previous year, *Dumbo* was made for only $812,000, partly because it was able to move very quickly through the animation department due to its succinct story and clear-cut characters, and it made a welcome profit for the Studio. *Dumbo* had been scheduled for the cover of *Time* magazine at the time of its general release in December 1941, but a much more momentous event occurred— Pearl Harbor—and poor Dumbo was supplanted by Japanese General Yamamoto. The movie was re-released in theaters in 1949, 1959, 1972, and 1976. It was shown on the Disney television series in 1955; it was released on video in 1981.

Dumbo: A Lesson in Being Prepared (film) Educational film; released in September 1981. One should not be over-eager and try things before one is prepared.

Dumbo Flying Elephants Fantasyland attraction at Disneyland; opened August 16, 1955. Riders fly in Dumbo-shaped vehicles, and are able to control the up-and-down movement by way of a lever. Totally remodeled in 1990 when new Dumbos and a new ride mechanism, which had been prepared for shipment to Euro Disneyland, were found not to be needed in France as early as expected. The attraction was installed at Disney-

land instead and another new one was built for France. Also, a Fantasyland attraction in Magic Kingdom Park at Walt Disney World; opened October 1, 1971, and remodeled in 1993. A Tokyo Disneyland version opened April 15, 1983, one at Disneyland Paris on April 12, 1992, and one at Hong Kong Disneyland on September 12, 2005.

Dumbo's Circus (television) Series on The Disney Channel, using "puppetronics." The

adventures of Dumbo and his pals. 120 episodes. Premiered on May 6, 1985.

Dumbo's Circus Parade Parade ran in Magic Kingdom Park at Walt Disney World from January 2 to December 21, 1979.

Duncan, Sandy Actress; appeared in *Million Dollar Duck* (Katie Dooley)—her movie debut, *The Cat From Outer Space* (Liz), and as the voice of Vixey in *The Fox and the Hound*. She headlined the television special, *Sandy in Disneyland*. Duncan came to Disney's notice while appearing in an inventive television commercial for a Los Angeles bank.

Durning, Charles Actor; appeared in *Tough Guys* (Deke Yablonski), *Dick Tracy* (Chief Brandon), *V. I. Warshawski* (Lt. Mallory), *O Brother, Where Art Thou?* (Pappy O'Daniel), and *Mr. St. Nick* (Nicholas XX).

Duvall, Robert Actor; appeared in *Newsies* (Joseph Pulitzer), *The Scarlet Letter* (Roger Chillingworth), *Phenomenon* (Doc), *Gone in 60 Seconds* (Otto Halliwell), and *A Civil Action* (Jerome Facher).

DVD The first Disney films were released on DVD on December 2, 1997. By the early 2000s, the process was rapidly gaining on and eventually surpassing VHS in popularity. One highlight of the DVDs has been the wealth of bonus material that has been added to enhance the enjoyment of the movie.

Dzundza, George Actor; appeared in *Dangerous Minds* (Hal Griffith), *Crimson Tide* (Cob), *That Darn Cat* (Boetticher), *Instinct* (John Murray), and on television in *2½ Dads*.

E

E! Entertainment In January 1997, Disney and Comcast Corporation joined together to purchase the majority of the stock of the entertainment industry-themed cable channel, E!

E ticket The coveted coupon, first offered in 1959, for the most exciting Disneyland attractions in the Disneyland ticket book. The term "an E ticket ride" entered American slang meaning the ultimate in thrills. Astronaut Sally Ride described her first excursion into space as a "real E ticket ride." The ticket books were originally introduced in October 1955, containing only A, B, and C tickets. The D ticket was added in 1956, and the E ticket three years later. The ticket books were replaced by passports, good for admission and unlimited use of park attractions, in June 1982.

Eagle Pines Golf course at Bonnet Creek Golf Club at Walt Disney World; opened in 1992. Designed by Pete Dye.

Eagle Pines & Osprey Ridge Golf Club Club that had originally opened at Walt Disney World on January 23, 1992, as the Bonnet Creek Golf Club; the name changed in April 2005.

Ear Force One Hot-air balloon designed in the shape of Mickey Mouse. Made its debut in 1987.

Earle, Eyvind (1916–2000) Background artist and color stylist; joined Disney in 1951, working on *For Whom the Bulls Toil; Toot, Whistle, Plunk and Boom; Pigs Is Pigs; Working for Peanuts; Peter Pan;* and *Lady and the Tramp*, but it is his distinctive styling for *Sleeping Beauty* that has brought him fame.

Early to Bed (film) Donald Duck cartoon; released on July 11, 1941. Directed by Jack King. Donald spends the night unable to sleep because of a ticking alarm clock and a fold-away bed that keeps trapping him when it folds up.

Earth*Star Voyager (television) Four-hour television movie, aired in two parts on January 17 and 24, 1988. Directed by James Goldstone. A select group of young cadets in the twenty-first century is sent off on a spaceship to find a new home for humanity when Earth is deteriorating. Along the way, they happen on an old failed world's fair, Expo Tomorrow, where they learn that their foe is the Outlaw Technology Zone, or OTZ, a band of criminals. Stars Duncan Regehr, Brian McNamara, Julia Montgomery, Jason Michas. Some of the filming took place at the closed site of Expo '86 in Vancouver, British Columbia, Canada.

Earth Station Information and guest services area under Spaceship Earth at Epcot, opened

October 1, 1982, and closed in 1994. Guests exited the Spaceship Earth attraction here, underneath the geodesic globe, which is the symbol of Epcot, and the WorldKey Information Service monitors were used to make reservations at Epcot restaurants. It was remodeled into Global Neighborhood, an interactive area sponsored by AT&T.

Earthquakes (film) Educational film; released in September 1986. 15 min. The hows and whys of natural earth movements, including earthquake safety tips.

Easier Said (film) Direct-to-video release by Touchstone Home Video on January 16, 2001, of a Twenty-Three Frames film from 1999. Things aren't working out for Jack, so he decides to leave the big city and pursue his life's ambition to write the "great American novel." He moves to a small Colorado town, only to find romantic chaos following him. Directed by H. Todd Von Mende. Stars Bo Clancey (Jack), Tricia Gregory (Eldora), Alex McLeod (Anna Sophia), Albie Parisella (Ciro), Walter Rheinfrank (Addison).

East, Jeff Actor; appeared on television in *The Flight of the Grey Wolf* (Russ Hanson), *Return of the Big Cat* (Josh McClaren), and *The Ghost of Cypress Swamp* (Lonny Bascombe).

Ebert & Roeper and the Movies (television) After the death of Gene Siskel, Roger Ebert continued the *Siskel & Ebert* show, using guest critics, with a title of *Roger Ebert & the Movies* during the 1999–2000 season. Starting August 28, 2000, Richard Roeper, a *Chicago Sun-Times* syndicated columnist, joined the show, which was then renamed, as a regular.

Ebsen, Buddy (1908–2003) Actor/dancer; appeared in *Davy Crockett* (George Russel) and *The One and Only, Genuine, Original Family Band* (Calvin Bower), and on television in *Corky and White Shadow* on the *Mickey Mouse Club*. He danced on film for Walt and his technicians to study for the original Project Little Man that became Audio-Animatronics.

Echo Lake Lake at Disney-MGM Studios.

Economics By Choice (film) Educational film; released in September 1985. The film illustrates basic economics concepts for children through situations that relate to their own lives.

Ed Wood (film) Edward D. Wood, Jr., an eccentric actor/writer/director, has only one thing going for him—an optimistic spirit that remains indomitable despite his obviously misguided career choices. Wood tries to make it in Hollywood, but earns the reputation of the "worst director of all time." He has a fetish for wearing women's clothes, and he gathers around him a bizarre band of characters, including the down-and-out screen legend Bela Lugosi, television horror queen Vampira, hulking Swedish wrestler Tor Johnson, psychic Criswell, and highbrow transvestite Bunny Breckinridge. Wood creates ineptly made, offbeat, low-budget independent films that somehow turn out to be cultish classics and turn their director into a legend. Limited release in Los Angeles and New York on September 28, 1994; general release on October 7, 1994. Directed by Tim Burton. A Touchstone film. Stars Johnny Depp (Ed Wood), Martin Landau (Bela Lugosi), Sarah Jessica Parker (Dolores Fuller), Patricia Arquette (Kathy O'Hara), Jeffrey Jones (Criswell), Bill Murray (Bunny Breckenridge). Based on a true story. Filmed in Los Angeles and its environs in black and white. 127 min. Martin Landau received an Academy Award for Supporting Actor for his portrayal of Bela Lugosi, and the film also won one for Makeup.

Eddie (film) Wild Bill Evert, a promotion-minded eccentric, takes over a losing NBA franchise, the New York Knicks, and happens to overhear the advice of die-hard fan Edwina "Eddie" Franklin, who yells her opinions from the stands. When Coach Bailey is canned, Eddie, as part of a publicity stunt, becomes the new coach whom no one takes seriously. Standing on the sidelines watching her team lose one game after another, Eddie begins to show herself as a real motivator, with her infectious spirit pushing the team to win and helping to convince Wild Bill to keep them in New York. A Hollywood Picture. Directed by Steve Rash. Released on May 31, 1996. Stars Whoopi Goldberg (Eddie), Frank Langella (Wild Bill Burgess), Dennis Farina (Coach John Bailey), Richard Jenkins (Zimmer), Lisa Ann Walter (Claudine), joined by many professional basketball stars. 100 min. While the character of Eddie was originally written as a male bank teller, and the team was originally the Clippers, Whoopi Goldberg's interest in the project changed everything. The motion picture was filmed in North Carolina, utilizing facilities at the Charlotte Coliseum and Winston-Salem's Lawrence Joel Veteran's Memorial Coliseum. Released on video in 1997.

Eddie's Million Dollar Cook-Off (television) A Disney Channel Original Movie, debuting on July 18, 2003. Fourteen-year-old baseball prodigy Eddie Ogden finds cooking fascinating, to the consternation of his friends and his father, who happens to be the baseball coach. He enters a major cooking contest, which turns out to be on the same day at the baseball playoffs. Eddie has to decide if he can fulfill his obligation to his team, and still be true to himself. Directed by Paul Hoen. Stars Taylor Ball (Eddie Ogden), Orlando Brown (Frankie), Reiley McClendon (DB), Rose McIver (Hannah), Mark L. Taylor (Hank Ogden), Susan Brady (Sarah). Celebrity chef Bobby Flay makes his film debut playing himself. From Solo Productions in association with Disney Channel.

Eden, Barbara Actress; appeared on television in *Brand New Life*.

Edgar Supercilious butler in *The Aristocats*; voiced by Roddy Maude-Roxby.

Edgar, Cyril (1907–1987) He was in charge of the distribution of Disney films in the United Kingdom for more than 20 years. He was presented posthumously with a European Disney Legends Award in 1997.

Edison Twins, The (television) Series on The Disney Channel, starring Andrew Sabiston (Tom Edison), Marnie McPhail (Ann Edison), Sunny Besen-Thrasher (Paul), Judith Norman, Robert Desrosiers. The 16-year-old twins use science to help them solve mysteries. Each episode ended with an animated explanation for the scientific principles used in that particular show; first aired on March 3, 1984. 78 episodes.

Edouarde, Carl (1875–1932) Orchestra conductor; retained by Walt Disney in New York City to record the music for *Steamboat Willie*, which became the first synchonized sound track for a cartoon.

Education for Death (film) Special cartoon; released on January 15, 1943. Directed by Clyde Geronimi. Offscreen narration tells the story of little Hans, a German child being taught Nazi principles of hate and cruelty in school, who grows up to become a soldier. The picture fades out with soldiers' swords and helmets resembling grave markers, showing their education for death is complete.

Educational films The first Disney educational film was *Tommy Tucker's Tooth*, which Walt Disney prepared for a local dentist in Kansas City in 1922. When World War II arrived, he realized that animation could help in training, by showing things that could not be shown in live action, so he made *Four Methods of Flush Riveting* as a sample (for Lockheed Aircraft Company), and soon was making dozens of films for the U.S. Government. These films did not feature the Disney characters, but instead utilized graphics, stop-motion, limited animation, and diagrams to get across a point. After the war, the techniques he learned on the war films came in handy as he continued to produce films, such as *The ABC of Hand Tools* and *Bathing Time for Baby*, under contract for various companies. *How to Catch a Cold* and *The Story of Menstruation*, produced during this period, became widely used in schools. Soon thereafter, however, Walt decided to get out of the educational film business. He reasoned that his business was entertainment, not education. With the advent of television and changes in education in the 1950s, however, he saw that there were ways in which he could teach, but still entertain. One of the finest examples was *Donald in Mathmagic Land*. After Walt's death, the company moved even deeper into educational productions, incorporating a subsidiary, the Walt Disney Educational Materials Company (later Walt Disney Educational Media Company), in 1969 and embarking on a prolific program of film strips, films, study prints, and other materials for schools. Many of these materials would win awards from educational organizations. In the 1990s, the education arm was renamed Disney Educational Productions.

Edwards, Cliff (1895–1971) Performer, known as Ukulele Ike, who provided the voice for Jiminy Cricket in *Pinocchio* and *Fun and Fancy Free* and in later television cartoons. He also did voices for crows in *Dumbo*.

Eega Beeva Character that made his first appearance in the daily Mickey Mouse comic strip of September 26, 1947. He looked somewhat beetlelike and was considered a "little man of the future."

Eeyore Donkey character in the Winnie the Pooh films; voiced by Ralph Wright.

Egan, Richard (1923–1987) Actor; appeared in *Pollyanna* (Dr. Edmund Chilton).

Egan, Susan Actress; starred as Belle on Broadway in *Beauty and the Beast*, provided the voices of Megara in *Hercules* and Lin in *Spirited Away*, and the singing voice of Angel in *Lady and the Tramp II: Scamp's Adventure*. Appeared on Disney Channel in *Gotta Kick It Up* (Heather Bartlett).

Egyptian Melodies (film) Silly Symphony cartoon; released on August 27, 1931. Directed by Wilfred Jackson. In a spider's misadventures with the Sphinx and the pyramids, hieroglyphics entertain until mummies are disturbed and frighten him away.

8mm A number of segments from Disney animated classics, short cartoons, live action/animal adventures, and Disneyland and Walt Disney World films, were released on 8mm and Super 8mm film for home use. There were also some sound Super 8mm versions. Earlier, 8mm shortened versions of Disney theatrical cartoons were released by Hollywood Film Enterprises.

8 Simple Rules for Dating My Teenage Daughter (television) Half-hour television series on ABC, premiering on September 17, 2002, and ending on August 19, 2005. Family comedy about a loving, rational dad who suddenly discovers that his two darling daughters have unexpectedly become hormonally charged, incomprehensible teenagers. Stars John Ritter (Paul Hennessy), Katey Sagal (Cate Hennessy), Kaley Cuoco (Bridget), Amy Davidson (Kerry), Martin Spanjers (Rory). From Touchstone Television. Based on the book by W. Bruce Cameron. After John Ritter's unexpected death during production of the fourth episode of the 2003–04 season, James Garner joined the cast as Cate's father, Jim (Suzanne Pleshette played her mother, Laura, briefly) and the series title was shortened to *8 Simple Rules* with the seventh episode. David Spade also joined the cast as C.J., Cate's wayward nephew.

8TRAX Club at Pleasure Island at Walt Disney World; opened December 31, 1992. Formerly Cage.

88 Minutes (film) Directed by Jon Avnet. From Touchstone Pictures/Millennium Films/Emmett/

Furla Films. Stars Al Pacino, Alicia Witt, Leelee Sobieski, Benjamin McKenzie. Began filming in Vancouver in October 2005.

Eight Below (film) Released on February 17, 2006. Filmed in Super 35 Scope.

Eiler, Barbara Actress; appeared on television in *Bristle Face* (Poor Woman), *For the Love of Willadean* (Mrs. Mason), and *The Swamp Fox* (Mary Videaux).

Eilonwy Taran's girl-friend in *The Black Cauldron*; voiced by Susan Sheridan.

Einstein Slow-moving Great Dane in *Oliver & Company*; voiced by Richard Mulligan.

Eisenhower, Dwight D. Former President Eisenhower and his wife visited Disneyland in December 1961.

Eisenmann, Ike Actor; appeared as Tony in *Escape to Witch Mountain* and *Return from Witch Mountain*, and on television in *Kit Carson and the Mountain Men*, *Shadow of Fear*, *The Sky's the Limit*, and *The Secret of the Pond.*

Eisner, Michael D. He has served as chairman of the board and chief executive officer of The Walt Disney Company since September 22, 1984. Additionally, he assumed the presidency on April 4, 1994, for a year and a half, after the death of Frank Wells. He was born on March 7, 1942, in

Mount Kisco, New York, and attended the Lawrenceville School and Denison University, where he received a B.A. in English literature and theater. He was a senior vice president at ABC Entertainment and president and chief operating officer of Paramount Pictures Corp. before coming to Disney. He is married to the former Jane Breckenridge, and they have three sons. He stepped down from the chairman post on March 3, 2004, and retired from the company on October 2, 2005.

El Bandido (television) Television show about Zorro. See *Zorro.*

El Capitan Movie theater in Hollywood remodeled by Disney in conjunction with its owner, Pacific Theaters; many Disney films have since premiered at the theater, occasionally with a special stage show. The first film to play at the restored theater was *The Rocketeer* in 1991.

El Gaucho Goofy (film) Segment of *Saludos Amigos*, with Goofy as an American cowboy becoming an Argentinian gaucho; re-released as a short on June 10, 1955.

El Río del Tiempo Attraction in Mexico in World Showcase at Epcot, opened on October 1, 1982. Translated as The River of Time, the attraction features boats on which guests travel for an eight-minute glimpse of Mexican history and culture, all to the sounds of a catchy theme song, which repeats throughout the attraction.

El Terrible Toreador (film) The second Silly Symphony cartoon; released in 1929. Directed by Walt Disney. This cartoon features a burlesque of bullfight drama.

Elaborate Lives: The Legend of Aida See Aida.

Elam, Jack (1920–2003) Actor; appeared in *Never a Dull Moment* (Ace Williams), *The Wild Country* (Thompson), *Hot Lead and Cold Feet* (Rattlesnake), and *The Apple Dumpling Gang Rides Again* (Big Mac), and on television in *Zorro* (Gomez) and *Ride a Northbound Horse*. He also appeared on The Disney Channel in *Down the Long Hills* (Squires).

Elcar, Dana (1927–2005) Actor; appeared in *The Last Flight of Noah's Ark* (Benchley) and *Condorman* (Russ), and on television in *Herbie, the Love Bug* (Warden) and *Small and Frye* (Problems).

Electric Umbrella Fast-food facility in Innoventions East at Epcot; opened June 24, 1994. Formerly Stargate.

Electrical Water Pageant On Bay Lake and the Seven Seas Lagoon at Walt Disney World, beginning October 26, 1971. First known as Electrical Pageant, it consists of a string of floating structures, 1,000 feet long, covered with tiny lights that blink on and off to represent dragons and other creatures. With a synthesizer sound track, the pageant is pulled through the waterways each evening around 9 o'clock. This pageant was the forerunner of the Main Street

Electrical Parade, which began at Disneyland in 1972.

Electronic Forum (Epcot Poll) Attraction in Communicore East at Epcot, from December 23, 1982 to March 16, 1991. The pre-show area then became the World News Center. The poll was taken when guests were ushered into a theater and shown short films, usually on current affairs. Then opinions were solicited, with the guests pressing buttons on the armrests of their seats, and the results being tabulated instantaneously. For several years, compiled results of the Epcot Poll were distributed to newspapers throughout the country.

Elephanchine Elephant dancer in the *Dance of the Hours* segment of *Fantasia*.

Elephant Journey (television) Follows a herd of elephants on their epic annual migration through northwestern Namibia, traversing routes that the enormous pachyderms have followed instinctively for centuries. Produced by Adrian Warren. Aired in syndication beginning May 8, 2000, as a New True Life Adventure. 45 min.

Elephants and Hippos in Africa (film) Portion of *The African Lion*; released on 16mm for schools in May 1969. Shows the daily life of elephants and hippos.

Elfego Baca (Episode 1): The Nine Lives of Elfego Baca (television) Television show; aired on October 3, 1958. Directed by Norman Foster. Tales of a gunman who became a lawyer in the Old West. In this first episode, Elfego is deputized to catch a rampaging cowboy, but this leads to problems with other cowboys in the area. Finally Elfego is named sheriff of Socorro. Stars Robert Loggia, Robert F. Simon, Lisa Montell, Nestor Paiva.

Elfego Baca (Episode 2): Four Down and Five Lives to Go (television) Television show; aired on October 17, 1958. Directed by Norman Foster. Elfego is so feared by the bad guys that when he becomes sheriff and asks them all to turn themselves in, they almost all do so. Later he is badly injured trying to catch a murderer, and he realizes that being sheriff is not what he is cut out to do; instead he decides to study law. Stars Robert Loggia, Robert F. Simon, Lisa Montell, Nestor Paiva.

Elfego Baca (Episode 3): Lawman or Gunman (television) Television show; aired on November 28, 1958. Directed by Christian Nyby. Elfego tries to defend a rancher friend whose land is in danger of being stolen by a crooked judge. He is able to overcome numerous roadblocks, including capture by the crooks, and escapes just in time to reach the trial and prove his friend the rightful owner of the land. Stars Robert Loggia, James Dunn, Ramon Novarro, Skip Homeier, Valerie Allen, Carl Benton Reid.

Elfego Baca (Episode 4): Law and Order, Incorporated (television) Television show; aired on December 12, 1958. Directed by Christian Nyby. As a new partner in his law firm, Elfego must try to save the land of a friend whose deeds have been stolen from the archives in Santa Fe. The local banker seems to be one of the crooks. Stars Robert Loggia, James Dunn, Ramon Novarro, Skip Homeier, Raymond Bailey, Valerie Allen.

Elfego Baca (Episode 5): Attorney at Law (television) Television show; aired on February 6, 1959. Directed by Christian Nyby. Elfego becomes a lawyer, and with his first case, he is to defend an accused thief. He discovers the man is being framed, eventually discovering that the real thief is the local deputy. Stars Robert Loggia, James Dunn, Lynn Bari, Kenneth Tobey, James Drury, Annette Funicello.

Elfego Baca (Episode 6): The Griswold Murder (television) Television show; aired on February 20, 1959. Directed by Christian Nyby. Elfego defends a rancher who has been unjustly accused of murder. It is up to Elfego to track down the real murderer, and in doing so, he wins his first case in Santa Fe. Stars Robert Loggia,

James Dunn, Jay C. Flippen, Patrick Knowles, Audrey Dalton, Annette Funicello.

Elfego Baca (Episode 7): Move Along Mustangers (television) Television show; aired on November 13, 1959. Directed by George Sherman. Elfego is asked to help a religious sect, the Mustangers, who wants to settle in the area but is being harassed by the local ranchers. When the son of a rancher is captured, the sheriff resigns rather than jail him, and Elfego has to become the law in the town. Stars Robert Loggia, Brian Keith, Arthur Hunnicutt, Beverly Garland, Barry Kelley, Roger Perry, William Schallert, James Coburn.

Elfego Baca (Episode 8): Mustang Man, Mustang Maid (television) Television show; aired on November 20, 1959. Directed by George Sherman. Elfego continues to help the Mustangers who are being persecuted by the townsfolk who arrange a boycott against them. After the cattlemen cause a stampede through the Mustangers' crops, Elfego captures one of the raiders and again discovers it is the son of the rancher. Eventually Elfego manages to capture the ringleaders and peace comes to the area. Stars Robert Loggia, Brian Keith, Arthur Hunnicutt, Beverly Garland, Barry Kelley, Roger Perry, James Coburn, William Schallert.

Elfego Baca (Episode 9): Friendly Enemies at Law (television) Television show; aired on March 18, 1960. Directed by William Beaudine. Lawyer Elfego is called upon to accuse a powerful rancher who is suspected of receiving stolen cattle. Elfego finds roadblocks every way he turns, but finally he discovers that the rancher's foreman is the culprit. Stars Robert Loggia, John Kerr, Patricia Crowley, Barton MacLane, Robert Lowery.

Elfego Baca (Episode 10): Gus Tomlin Is Dead (television) Television show; aired on March 25, 1960. Directed by William Beaudine. Elfego travels to Granite searching for Gus Tomlin, a murderer thought long dead. He discovers that Tomlin is still living, but is being protected by the town because he saved it from a typhoid epidemic. Elfego decides to help the town protect the now honest man. Stars Robert Loggia, Alan Hale, Jr., Coleen Gray, Brian Corcoran.

Elfman, Jenna Actress; appeared in *Krippendorf's Tribe* (Veronica Micelli), *Grosse Pointe Blank* (Tanya), and *Keeping the Faith* (Anna Reilly), and on television in *Courting Alex* (Bex Atwell). She is best known for her role as Dharma in the ABC comedy series *Dharma and Greg*.

Elgin National Industries, Inc. See Bradley Time.

Elizondo, Hector Actor; appeared in *Pretty Woman* (hotel manager), *Taking Care of Business* (warden), *The Other Sister* (Ernie), *Runaway Bride* (Fisher), *The Princess Diaries* and *The Princess Diaries 2* (Joe), *Raising Helen* (Mickey Massey), on television in *Miracles* (Father Bellamy). He provided the voice of Zafiro in *Gargoyles*.

Ellen (television) Television series; debuted on March 9, 1994, as *These Friends of Mine*, but changed its title in the summer of 1994. It ended on July 29, 1998. A single woman living in Los Angeles and her kindhearted but clumsy handling of people and matters that come careening into her life. Stars Ellen DeGeneres (Ellen Morgan), Joely Fisher (Paige Clark), David Anthony Higgins (Joe Farrell), Arye Gross (Adam Green). Joining the regular cast in the Fall of 1995 were Clea Lewis (Audrey) and Jeremy Piven (Spence). The show made headlines and stirred up controversy when the lead character, Ellen Morgan, came out as a lesbian on April 30, 1997, after actress Ellen DeGeneres had earlier done the same.

Ellen Burstyn Show, The (television) Television series; aired on ABC from September 20 to November 15, 1986, and from August 8, 1987 to September 12, 1987. Professor Ellen Brewer teaches literature at a college in Baltimore. She is divorced and trying to live in a house with her mother, her opinionated daughter, and her daughter's young son. Stars Ellen Burstyn (Ellen Brewer), Elaine Stritch (Sydney), Megan Mullally (Molly), Barry Sobel (Tom Hines), Jesse Tendler (Nick), Winifred Freedman (Carrie).

Ellen's Energy Adventure Ellen DeGeneres stars in a film and Audio-Animatronics show in the Universe of Energy at Epcot beginning September 15, 1996.

Ellenshaw, Harrison Son of Peter Ellenshaw, he came to Disney in 1970 as an apprentice matte artist on *Bedknobs and Broomsticks*. After several years at other studios, he returned in 1990 as vice president of visual effects. He left the company in 1996 and later became a painter of fine art.

Ellenshaw, Peter Selected by Walt Disney in England to paint the mattes for *Treasure Island* and the other Disney films made there in the early 1950s. He later came to the States to work on *20,000 Leagues Under the Sea*, *Darby O'Gill and the Little People*, and other films. He painted one of the original layouts for Disneyland on a 4x8 foot storyboard, which is on display in the Disney Gallery at Tokyo Disneyland. He received an Oscar for Special Visual Effects in *Mary Poppins*. Later, he served as production designer on *Island at the Top of the World* and *The Black Hole*. He was named a Disney Legend in 1993.

Elliott Green dragon in *Pete's Dragon*; voiced by Charlie Callas.

Elliott, Chris Actor; appeared in *Cabin Boy* (Nathanial Mayweather), and on television in *The Barefoot Executive* (Jase Wallenberg).

Elmer Elephant (film) Silly Symphony cartoon; released on March 28, 1936. Directed by Wilfred Jackson. Poor Elmer is teased for having a trunk until a fire threatens Tillie Tiger and only he can rescue her. Elmer was  one of the first Disney characters since the

Three Little Pigs to appear on some merchandise items.

Eloise at Christmastime (television) Two-hour television movie; aired on *The Wonderful World of Disney* on November 22, 2003. New York's Plaza Hotel is deep in preparations for a Christmas Eve wedding of the owner's daughter, and Eloise decides to "help" with the arrangements. She goes head-to-head with event coordinator Prunella Stickler and even plays matchmaker when she has suspicions about the groom. The wedding isn't the only thing in which Eloise gets involved—as usual she interferes with the lives of all her friends at the hotel, and tries to deliver each the best Christmas present imaginable. Directed by Kevin Lima. Stars Julie Andrews (Nanny), Sofia Vassilieva (Eloise), Jeffrey Tambor (Mr. Salomone), Christine Baranski (Prunella Stickler), Debra Monk (Maggie), Gavin Creel (Bill). Produced by Hand Made Films in association with Di Novi Pictures. This movie was filmed at the same time as *Eloise at the Plaza*, which aired seven months earlier. Released on video in 2004.

Eloise at the Plaza (television) Eloise is a precocious but lovable six-year-old resident of New York's Plaza Hotel, who roams the landmark in search of adventure. Along with her pug dog and turtle, Eloise is always causing mischief and mayhem, often dragging along her beleaguered Nanny. As the Plaza prepares for a debutante ball and the stately visit of a prince, Eloise is determined to get an invitation to the ball with the royal prince as her escort. She befriends a sad boy, Leon, whisking him away for a day of sightseeing, unaware that he is actually the prince. Aired on *The Wonderful World of Disney* on April 27, 2003. Directed by Kevin Lima. Stars Julie Andrews (Nanny), Sofia Vassilieva (Eloise), Jeffrey Tambor (Mr. Salomone), Christine Baranski (Prunella Stickler), Debra Monk (Maggie), Kintaro Akiyama (Leon). Based on the popular Eloise books by Kay Thompson, illustrated by Hilary Knight (who makes a cameo appearance as himself). Produced by Hand Made Films, in association with Di Novi Pictures. Released on video in 2003.

Elrod, Tom He joined Walt Disney World in the Marketing Division in 1973; was president of Marketing and Entertainment for Walt Disney Attractions from 1992 until he left the company in 1997.

Embry, Ethan See Ethan Randall.

Emerald Cove (television) Serial on the *Mickey Mouse Club* on The Disney Channel, first airing on June 26, 1993. Kids at the beach for the summer, dealing with teen issues of the day. Stars Tony Lucca (Jeff Chambers), Marc Worden (Will Jenkins), Ricky Luna (Ricky), Matt Morris (Matt), Rhona Bennett (Nicole), J.C. Chasez (Wipeout), Jennifer McGill (Melody). Compiled episodes were shown as a stand-alone series beginning September 8, 1993.

Emerson, Douglas Actor; appeared on television in *The Leftovers* and the *Herbie, the Love Bug* limited series, and on The Disney Channel in *Good Old Boy*.

Emhardt, Robert (1914–1994) Character actor; appeared in *Rascal* (constable), and on television in *Kilroy* and *The Mooncussers*.

Emil and the Detectives (film) Emil, on his first trip to Berlin, carries money to his grandmother, a mission of great responsibility, but a pickpocket cannot resist robbing the boy while he is napping on the bus. Awakening in time, Emil follows the crook and with the aid of a group of resourceful boys his age (the Detectives) comes upon a rendezvous with two master thieves who are engaged in a plan to rob the Bank of Berlin. Because of the pickpocket's inability to resist petty theft, he causes the collapse of the big job they might have gotten away with had it not been for Emil and the Detectives. Released on December 18, 1964. Directed by Peter Tewksbury. 99 min. Stars Walter Slezak (Baron), Bryan Russell (Emil), Roger Mobley (Gustav), Heinz Schubert (Grundeis), Peter Erlich (Muller), Cindy Cassell (Pony), Elsa Wagner (Nana), Wolfgang Volz (Stucke). The film was made on location in Germany, and was based on a book by

Erich Kastner. Released on video in 1987. Serialized on the new *Mickey Mouse Club* as *The Three Skrinks*.

Emmy Awards Disney individuals and television programs have been honored by the Academy of Television Arts and Sciences with many Emmy Awards over the years. The list of awards is as follows:

1955

Walt Disney Studio for *Disneyland*: Best Variety Series, 1954

Walt Disney Studio for *Operation Undersea* on *Disneyland*: Best Individual Show, 1954

Walt Disney Studio (Grant Smith and Lynn Harrison) for *Operation Undersea* on *Disneyland*: Best Television Film Editing, 1954

1956

Walt Disney for *Disneyland*: Best Producer of Filmed Series, 1955

Walt Disney Studios for the *Davy Crockett* series on *Disneyland*: Best Action or Adventure Series, 1955

1964

Walt Disney's Wonderful World of Color for "outstanding program achievements in the field of children's programming"

Carroll Clark and Marvin Aubrey Davis for "outstanding achievement in Art Direction and Scenic Design": *Walt Disney's Wonderful World of Color*

1986

The Golden Girls for Outstanding Comedy Series (9/21/86)

Betty White for Outstanding Lead Actress in a Comedy Series (*The Golden Girls*) (9/21/86)

Barry Fanaro, Mort Nathan for Outstanding Writing in a Comedy Series (*The Golden Girls*) (9/21/86)

Gerry Bucci, Randy Baer, Dale Carlson, Steve Jones, Donna J. Quante, and Victor Bagdadi for Outstanding Technical Direction/Electronic Camerawork/Video Control (*The Golden Girls*) (9/21/86)

Carl Gibson (lighting director) for Lighting Direction: *Kids Incorporated*, The Disney Channel

1987

The Golden Girls for Outstanding Comedy Series (9/20/87)

Rue McClanahan for Outstanding Lead Actress in a Comedy Series (*The Golden Girls*) (9/20/87)

Terry Hughes for Outstanding Directing in a Comedy Series (*The Golden Girls*) (9/20/87)

1988

Beatrice Arthur for Lead Actress in a Comedy Series (*The Golden Girls*) (8/28/88)

Estelle Getty for Supporting Actress in a Comedy Series (*The Golden Girls*) (8/28/88)

O. Tamburri, Jack Chisholm, Stephen A. Jones, Ritch Kenney, Ken Tamburri, Robert G. Kaufmann for Technical Direction/Electronic Camerawork/Video Control for Series: Old Friends episode of *The Golden Girls* (8/28/88)

1989

Walt Disney Television Animation for *The New Adventures of Winnie the Pooh*; Best Animated Program, Daytime. Presented to Karl Geurs, Producer/Director and Mark Zaslove, Story Editor/Writer (6/29/89)

Richard Mulligan for Lead Actor in a Comedy Series (*Empty Nest*) (9/17/89)

Walter Painter for Choreography: *Disney-MGM Studios Theme Park Grand Opening* (9/17/89)

Carl Gibson (lighting director) for Lighting Direction: *Kids Incorporated*, The Disney Channel

1990

Walt Disney Television Animation for *The New Adventures of Winnie the Pooh*: Best Animated Program, Daytime (6/23/90)

Greg Spottiswood for Outstanding Performer in a Children's Special: *Looking for Miracles* (6/23/90)

Charles King, Rick Hinson, Richard Harrison [Walt Disney Television Animation] for Film Sound Editing: *Ducktales* (6/23/90)

George Burns for Individual Achievement—Informational Programming/Performance: *A*

Conversation With George Burns, The Disney Channel (9/15/90)

Swoosie Kurtz for Guest Actress in a Comedy Series: *Carol & Company* (9/15/90)

Pat Field for Costume Design—Variety or Music Program: *Mother Goose Rock 'N' Rhyme*, The Disney Channel (9/15/90)

NBC, producers Ted Field, Robert W. Cort, Patricia Clifford, Kate Wright, Richard L. O'Connor, Chet Walker for Children's Program: *A Mother's Courage: The Mary Thomas Story*, *The Magical World of Disney* (9/15/90)

1991

Brian Henson, Michael Kerrigan for Directing in a Children's Series: *Jim Henson's Mother Goose Stories*, The Disney Channel (6/22/91)

Jacqueline Mills, Jill Thraves for Achievement in costume design: *Jim Henson's Mother Goose Stories*, The Disney Channel (6/22/91)

Michael Scott, Michael MacMillan (Executive producers), Seaton McLean, Joan Scott (Producers) for Best Children's Special (daytime): *Lost in the Barrens*, The Disney Channel (6/27/91)

John C. Mula (Production Designer), Kevin Pfeiffer (Art Director), Brian Savegar (Set Decorator) for Art Direction, series: *Dinosaurs: The Mating Dance*, ABC (8/25/91)

Ret Turner (Costume Designer) and Bob Mackie (Costume Designer for Carol Burnett) for Costume Design, variety or music program: *Carol & Company: That Little Extra Something*, NBC (8/25/91)

David Gumpel and Girish Bhargava for Editing, miniseries or special (multi-camera production): *The Muppets Celebrate Jim Henson*, CBS (8/25/91)

Ian Fraser, Bill Byers, Chris Boardman, J. Hill for Music Direction: *The Walt Disney Company Presents the American Teacher Awards*, The Disney Channel (8/25/91)

1992

Kirk Bergstrom (exec. producer), Kit Thomas (prod.), Krystyne Haje (host) for Special Class Program: *Spaceship Earth: Our Global Environment*, The Disney Channel (6/20/92)

Kerry Millerick, Julie Engleman, Neal Rogin for Writing, Special Class: *Spaceship Earth: Our Global Environment*, The Disney Channel (6/20/92)

David Cobham for Directing a Children's Special: *Woof!*, The Disney Channel (6/20/92)

Richard Sabre (hair designer), Tish Simpson (hairstylist) for Hairstyling: *Disney's Adventures in Wonderland*, The Disney Channel (6/20/92)

Eli Adler, Lex Fletcher (directors of photography) for Cinematography: *Scenic Wonders of America*, The Disney Channel (6/20/92)

Carl Gibson for Lighting Direction: *Kids Incorporated*, The Disney Channel (6/20/92)

Rock Demers (producer), Daniel Louis (line producer), Claude Nedjar (co-producer) for Children's Special: *Vincent and Me*, The Disney Channel (6/23/92)

Christopher Lloyd (guest) for Lead Actor in a Drama Series: *Avonlea*, The Disney Channel (8/30/92)

Geoffrey Cowan, Julian Fowles (executive producers), Daniel Petrie (producer) for Children's Program: *Mark Twain and Me*, The Disney Channel (8/30/92)

Kenneth Tamburri (technical director), Ritch Kenney, Stephen A. Jones, Dave Heckman, Chester Jackson (camera operators), Randy Johnson, Richard Steiner, John O'Brien (video control) for Technical Direction/Camera/Video for Series: *The Golden Girls* ("One Flew Out of the Cuckoo's Nest" parts 1 and 2), NBC (8/30/92)

Donald Morgan (director of photography) for Lighting Direction (Electronic) for Comedy Series: *Home Improvement* ("Luck Be a Taylor Tonight"), ABC (8/30/92)

Kevin Haney (makeup for Jason Robards), Donald Mowat (makeup) for Makeup for Miniseries or a Special: *Mark Twain and Me*, The Disney Channel (8/30/92)

1993

Children's Program (tie): *Avonlea*, The Disney Channel (9/19/93)

Gregg Rubin, Randy Ezratty, John Alberts for Sound Mixing, Variety or Music Series or Special: *Harry Connick, Jr.: The New York Big Band Concert*, The Disney Channel (9/19/93)

Donald A. Morgan for Lighting Direction (Electronic), Comedy Series: *Home Improvement*, ABC (9/19/93)

Kim Thomas, James R. Conner, Edward J. Murphy (executive producers), Chris Valentini (producer) for Special Class Program: *Great Wonders of the World: Wonders of Nature*, The Disney Channel

Laszlo Pal (director) for Directing in a Children's Special: *Journey to Spirit Island*, The Disney Channel

Victoria Costello (writer) for Writing—Special Class: *This Island Earth*, The Disney Channel

Eli Adler, David Breashears, Don Briggs, Tony Clark, Lex Fletcher (directors of photography) for Single Camera Photography: *Great Wonders of the World: Wonders of Nature*, The Disney Channel

"This Island Earth," Kenny Loggins (composer & lyricist) for Original Song: *This Island Earth*, The Disney Channel

Bill Campbell, Doug Enderle (costume designers) for Costume Design: *Walt Disney World Very Merry Christmas Parade*, ABC

1994

Daryl Busby, Tom J. Astle (head writers) for Writing in a Children's Series: *Disney's Adventures in Wonderland*, The Disney Channel (5/21/94)

Ron Wild, Karen Stephens (makeup artists) for Makeup: *Disney's Adventures in Wonderland*, The Disney Channel (5/21/94)

1995

Bob Carruthers for Special Class Writing: *Dinosaurs: Myths & Reality*, The Disney Channel (5/13/95)

Mark Watters (supervising composer), John Given, Harvey Cohen, Carl Johnson, Thom Sharp (composers) for Music Direction and Composition: *Disney's Aladdin*, syn./CBS (5/13/95)

John O. Robinson III, Michael Geisler (supervising sound editors), Marc S. Perlman, William Griggs (supervising music editors), Melissa Gentry-Ellis, Ray Leonard, Phyllis Ginter, Michael Gollom, Timothy J. Borquez, Thomas

Jaeger, Charles Rychwalski, Gregory A. Laplante, Kenneth D. Young, Jenifer Mertins (sound editors), Robert Duran, William Koepnick, James C. Hodson (sound effects editors) for Film Sound Editing: *Disney's Aladdin*, syn./CBS (5/13/95)

Timothy J. Borquez, James C. Hodson (supervising re-recording mixers), Timothy Garrity, William Koepnick, Melissa Gentry-Ellis (re-recording mixers), Deborah Adair (production mixer) for Film Sound Mixing: *Disney's Aladdin*, syn./CBS (5/13/95)

Lois de Armond for Costume Design: *Adventures in Wonderland*, The Disney Channel (5/13/95)

Madeleine Stewart (costume designer) for Costume Design for a Series: *Avonlea* ["Strictly Melodrama" episode], The Disney Channel (9/10/95)

Donald A. Morgan (lighting director) for Lighting Direction (Electronic) for a Comedy Series: *Home Improvement* ["My Dinner with Wilson" episode], ABC (9/10/95)

1996

Nathan Lane for Performer in an Animated Program: *The Lion King's Timon and Pumbaa*, CBS/syn. (5/22/96)

David Grossman, Gary Halvorson, Shelley R. Jensen (directors) for Directing in a Children's Series: *Adventures in Wonderland*, The Disney Channel (5/22/96)

Erren Gottlieb, Bill Nye, James McKenna, Scott Schaefer, Adam Gross, Seth Gross (writers) for Writing in a Children's Series: *Bill Nye the Science Guy*, syn. (5/22/96)

Ron Wild (makeup designer), Karen Stephens (key makeup) for Makeup: *Adventures in Wonderland*, The Disney Channel (5/22/96)

Jim Wilson, Tom McGurk, Mike McAuliff (sound designer/editors), Dave Howe, Ella Bracket (sound editors) for Sound Editing: *Bill Nye the Science Guy* (5/22/96)

Michael E. Jiron, Allen L. Stone (re-recording mixers) for Sound Mixing—Special Class: *Disney's Aladdin*, CBS/syn. (5/22/96)

Donald A. Morgan (lighting director) for Lighting Direction (Electronic) for a Comedy Series: *Home Improvement*, ABC (9/8/96)

1997

Darrell Suto, Michael Gross, Erren Gottlieb, James McKenna (directors) for Directing in a Children's Program: *Bill Nye the Science Guy*, PBS/syn. (5/17/97)

Kit Boss, Erren Gottlieb, Michael Gross, James McKenna, Bill Nye, Ias Saunders, Scott Schaefer, Darrell Suto, William Sleeth (writers) for Writing in a Children's Series: *Bill Nye the Science Guy*, PBS/syn. (5/17/97)

Kexx Singleton (color director) for Individual Achievement in Animation: *The Lion King's Timon & Pumbaa* (*Beethoven's Whiff*), CBS/syn. (5/17/97)

Darrell Suto, Michael Gross (senior editors), Felicity Oram, John Reul (editors) for Single Camera Editing: *Bill Nye the Science Guy*, PBS/syn. (5/17/97)

Thomas McGurk, Michael McAuliffe, Dave Howe (sound editors) for Sound Editing: *Bill Nye the Science Guy*, PBS/syn. (5/17/97)

Paca Thomas (supervising sound effects editor), Melissa Gentry-Ellis (sound editor), Marc Perlman (supervising music editor), Kris Daly, Phyllis Ginter, Paul Holzborn (sound editors), William B. Griggs (supervising sound editor), Nicholas Carr (supervising music editor), Jeff Hutchins, Ken D. Young, Bill Kean, David Lynch, Otis Van Osten (sound effects editors), Jennifer E. Mertens, Eric Hertsgaard (sound editors) for Sound Editing—Special Class: *The Mighty Ducks*, ABC (5/17/97)

James C. Hodson, Melissa Gentry-Ellis, Michael Beiriger, Daniel Hiland, Joseph Citarella, Allen L. Stone, Michael Jiron (re-recording mixers), Deb Adair (production mixer) for Sound Mixing—Special Class: *The Lion King's Timon & Pumbaa*, CBS/syn. (5/17/97)

1998

Bill Nye for Outstanding Performer in a Children's Series: *Bill Nye the Science Guy*, syn. (5/15/98)

Dennis Rosenblatt (director) for Directing in a Game/Audience Participation Show: *Win Ben Stein's Money*, Comedy Central (5/15/98)

Carlyle Kyzer, Greg Poschman, Krysia Carter-Giez (directors) for Directing in a Children's Special: *Letters From Africa*, Disney Channel (5/15/98)

Gary Halvorson, Alan Carter (directors) for Special Class Directing: *A Magical Walt Disney World Christmas*, ABC (5/15/98)

Erren Gottlieb, James McKenna, Bill Nye, Michael Gross, Darrell Suto, Scott Schaefer, Kit Boss, Lynne Brunell, Michael Pelleschi, Ian Saunders, Simon Griffith (writers) for Writing in a Children's Series: *Bill Nye the Science Guy*, syn. (5/15/98)

Doug Armstrong, Jonathan Barry, Lou Dimaggio, Carla Kaufman (writers) for Special Class Writing: *Win Ben Stein's Money*, Comedy Central (5/15/98)

Felicity Oram, John Ruel, Darrell Suto, Michael Gross (editors) for Single Camera Editing: *Bill Nye the Science Guy*, syn. (5/15/98)

Dave Howe, Thomas McGurk, Mike McAuliffe (sound editors) for Sound Editing: *Bill Nye the Science Guy*, syn. (5/15/98)

Dave Howe, Thomas McGurk, Mike McAuliffe (re-recording mixers), Bob O'Hern, Resti Bagcal, Marion Smith (production mixers) for Sound Mixing: *Bill Nye the Science Guy*, syn. (5/15/98)

Craig Kemplin (storyboard artist) for Outstanding Individual Achievement in Animation: *Disney's 101 Dalmatians: The Series*, ABC (5/15/98)

Emma Thompson for Guest Actress in a Comedy Series: *Ellen*, ABC (8/29/98)

Jim Henson Co. for Children's Program: *Muppets Tonight*, Disney Channel (8/29/98)

Randy Ser (production designer), Edward L. Rubin (art director), and Julie Kaye Fanton (set decorator) for Art Direction for a Variety of Music Program: *Rodgers & Hammerstein's Cinderella* [*Wonderful World of Disney*], ABC (8/29/98)

Donald A. Morgan (director of photography) for Lighting Direction (Electronic) for a Comedy Series: *Home Improvement* ["A Night to Dismember" episode], ABC (8/29/98)

Kasumi Mihori, Billy Pittard, Ed Sullivan (title designers) for Main Title Design: *The Wonderful World of Disney*, ABC (8/29/98)

1999

Michael Gross, Darrell Suto for Directing in a Children's Series: *Bill Nye the Science Guy*, syn. (5/15/99)

Doug Armstrong, Jonathan Barry, Jonathan Bourne, Henriette Mantel (writers) for Special Class Writing: *Win Ben Stein's Money*, Comedy Central (5/15/99)

Felicity Oram, John Reul, Michael Gross, Darrell Duto (editors) for Single Camera Editing: *Bill Nye the Science Guy*, syn. (5/15/99)

Dave Howe, Thomas McGurk, Michael McAuliffe (sound editors) for Sound Editing: *Bill Nye the Science Guy*, syn. (5/15/99)

Erren Gottleib, James McKenna, Elizabeth Brock (executive producers), Jamie Hammond, Hamilton Mcculloch (coordinating producers), Bill Nye (producer) for Children's Series: *Bill Nye the Science Guy*, syn. (5/21/99)

Andrew J. Golder, Al Burton, Byron Glore (executive producers), Terrence McDonnell (producer) for Game/Audience Participation Show: *Win Ben Stein's Money*, Comedy Central (5/21/99)

Ben Stein & Jimmy Kimmel (co-hosts) for Game Show Host: *Win Ben Stein's Money*, Comedy Central (5/21/99)

Ja'Net DuBois for [voice-over performance in animation]: *The PJs*, Fox (8/4/99)

Robert Primes (director of photography) for Cinematography for a Series: *Felicity* ["Todd Mulcahy, Part II" episode] WB (8/28/99)

Janet Ashikaga (editor) for Multicamera Picture Editing for a Series: *Sports Night* ["Small Town" episode] ABC (8/28/99)

Donald A. Morgan (director of photography) for Lighting Direction (Electronic) for a Comedy Series: *Home Improvement* ["Mark's Big Break" episode], ABC (8/28/99)

William Joyce (production designer) for Outstanding Achievement in Animation: *Rolie Polie Olie*, Disney Channel (5/15/99)

2000

James McKenna, Erren Gottleib, Elizabeth Brock (executive producers), Jamie Hammond (coordinating producer), Bill Nye (science producer) for Children's Series: *Bill Nye the Science Guy*, syn. (5/13/00)

William Joyce, Michael Hirsh, Patrick Loubert, Clive Smith, Fabrice Giger (executive producers), Stephen Hodgins (supervising producer), Scott Dyer, Guillaume Hellouin, Pam Lehn, Corrine Kouper, Eric Flaherty, Christophe Archimbault (producers), Mike Fallows (supervising director), Ron Pitts (director), Nadine Van Der Velde, Ben Joseph, Scott Kraft, Pete Sauder, Nicola Barton (writers) for Special Class Animated Program: *Rolie Polie Olie*, Disney Channel (5/13/00)

Bill Nye, Michael Gross, Darrell Suto, Ian G. Saunders, Michael Palleschi, Lynn Brunelle, Mike Greene for Writing in a Children's Series: *Bill Nye the Science Guy*, syn. (5/13/00)

Teresa Strasser, Jonathan Barry, Bob Stone, Gary Stuart Kaplan, Susan Flanagan for Special Class Writing: *Win Ben Stein's Money*, Comedy Central (5/13/00)

Mark Gentile for Directing in a Game/Audience Participation Show: *Who Wants to Be a Millionaire*, ABC (5/13/00)

James Woods for Performer in an Animated Program: *Disney's Hercules*, ABC (5/13/00)

Dave Howe, Mike McAuliffe, Tom McGurk for Sound Editing: *Bill Nye the Science Guy*, syn. (5/13/00)

Peter Hefter (production mixer), John Alberts (re-recording mixer) for Sound Mixing (tie): *Bear in the Big Blue House*, Disney Channel (5/13/00)

Dave Howe, Mike McAuliffe, Tom McGurk (rerecording mixers), Myron Partman, Resti Bagcal (production mixers) for Sound Mixing (tie): *Bill Nye the Science Guy*, syn. (5/13/00)

R. William A. Thiederman, Dean Okrand, Michael Brooks (re-recording mixers), Clancy Livingston (production mixer) for Sound Mixing (tie): *Honey I Shrunk the Kids: The TV Show*, syn. (5/13/00)

Mike Moon (art director) and Chris Roszak (key background painter) for Individual Achievement in Animation: *Disney's Mickey Mouse-Works*, ABC (5/13/00)

Michael Davies, Paul Smith (executive producers), Vincent Rubino (producer), Ann Miller (supervising producer), Terrence McDonnell (senior producer), Nikki Webber (coordinating producer) for Game/Audience Participation Show: *Who Wants to Be a Millionaire*, ABC (5/19/00)

Alan Sacks (executive producer), Christopher Morgan, Kevin Hooks (producers) for Children's Program: *The Color of Friendship*, Disney Channel (8/26/00)

Rob Marshall (choreographer) for Choreography: *Annie*, ABC (8/26/00)

Peter Smokler (director of photography) for Cinematography for a Multicamera Series: *Sports Night* ["Cut Man" episode], ABC (8/26/00)

Paul Bogaev (music director) for Music Direction: *Annie*, ABC (8/26/00)

Nelson Lowry (art director) for Individual Achievement in Animation: *The PJs* ["How the Super Stoled Christmas" episode], WB (8/26/00)

2001

Nathan Lane for Performer in an Animated Program: *Disney's Teacher's Pet*, ABC (5/18/01)

Michael Davies, Paul Smith (executive producers), Leslie Fuller (producer), Ann Miller, Wendy Roth, Tiffany Trigg (supervising producers), Leigh Hampton (senior producer), Nikki Webber (coordinating producer) for Game/Audience Participation Show: *Who Wants to Be a Millionaire*, ABC (5/18/01)

Regis Philbin for Game Show Host: *Who Wants to Be a Millionaire*, ABC (5/18/01)

Regis Philbin for Talk Show Host: *Live with Regis*, syn. (5/18/01)

Mark Watters for Outstanding Music (News & Documentary Emmy): *Alaska: Dances of the Caribou*, syn. (5/18/01)

Ja'Net DuBois for [voice-over performance in animation]: *The PJs*, Fox (9/8/01)

James Newton Howard (composer) for Main Title Theme Music: *Gideon's Crossing*, ABC (9/8/01)

2002

Charles Shaughnessy for Performer in an Animated Program: *Disney's Stanley*, Disney Channel (5/11/02)

Gary Baseman, Bill & Cheri Steinkellner (executive producers), Jess Winfield (co-executive producer), Nancy Lee Myatt (producer), Timothy Bjorklund, Don MacKinnon, Alfred Gimeno, Jamie Thomason, Julie Morgavi (directors), David Maples, Billiam Coronel (writers) for Special Class Animated Program: *Disney's Teacher's Pet*, ABC (5/11/02)

Dennis Rosenblatt (director) for Directing in a Game/Audience Participation Show: *Win Ben Stein's Money*, Comedy Central (5/11/02)

Mitchell Kriegman, Dean Gordon (directors) for Directing in a Children's Series: *The Book of Pooh*, Disney Channel (5/11/02)

Andy Heyward, Michael Maliani, Robby London, Saul Cooper, Pancho Kohner (executive producers), Judy Rothman Rofe (supervising producer), Judy Reilly, Stephanie Louise Vallance, Marsha Goodman Einstein, Paul F. Quinn (directors) for Children's Animated Program: *Madeline*, Disney Channel (5/17/02)

Scott Chambliss (production designer), Cece Destefano (art director), Karen Manthey (set decorator) for Art Direction, Single-Camera Series: *Alias* ["Truth Be Told" episode], ABC (9/14/02)

Michael Bonvillain (director of photography) for Cinematography, Single-Camera Series: *Alias* ["Truth Be Told" episode], ABC (9/14/02)

2003

Gary Baseman, Bill Steinkellner, Cheri Steinkellner (executive producers), Jess Winfield, (co-executive producer), Don Mackinnon, Ennio Torresan, Jr., Alfred Gimeno, Julie Morgavi (directors), David Maples, Billiam Coronel (writers) for Special Class Animated Program: *Disney's Teacher's Pet*, ABC (5/10/03)

Gary Baseman, production designer for Individual Achievement in Animation: *Disney's Teacher's Pet*, ABC (5/10/03)

Brian Chapman (tie) for Directing in a Talk Show: *Live with Regis and Kelly*, syn. (5/10/03)

Liz Plonka (tie) for Directing in a Talk Show: *The Wayne Brady Show*, syn. (5/10/03)

Mitchell Kriegman, Dean Gordon for Directing in a Children's Series: *Bear in the Big Blue House*, Disney Channel (5/10/03)

Peter Baird, production mixer for Live & Direct to Tape Sound Mixing: *The Wayne Brady Show*, syn. (5/10/03)

Shia LeBeouf for Performer in a Children's Series: *Even Stevens*, Disney Channel (5/16/03)

Wayne Brady for Talk Show Host: *The Wayne Brady Show*, syn. (5/16/03)

Bernie Brillstein, Robert Morton (executive producers), Krysia Plonka, John Redmann (supervising producers), KP Anderson (coordinating producer), Danny Breen, Wendy Miller, Lee Farber, Erin Irwin, Maria Notaras, Shane Farley, Josh Gilbert, Michael Carnes (producers): *The Wayne Brady Show*, syn. (5/16/03)

Angela Nogaro, Kaori Turner (makeup artists), Diana Brown (key makeup) for Makeup for a Series, Non-Prosthetic: *Alias* ["The Counteragent" episode], ABC (9/13/03)

Bruce Broughton for Music Composition for a Miniseries, Movie or a Special—Dramatic Underscore: *Eloise at the Plaza* [*Wonderful World of Disney*], ABC (9/13/03)

Jeff Beal for Main Title Theme Music: *Monk*, USA (9/13/03)

Jeff Habberstad, stunt coordinator for Stunt Coordination: *Alias* ["The Telling" episode], ABC (9/13/03)

Tony Shalhoub for Actor in a Comedy Series: *Monk*, USA (9/21/03)

The Amazing Race for Reality-Competition Program, CBS (9/21/03)

2004

Matthew Cohen for Directing in a Game/Audience Participation Show: *Who Wants to Be a Millionaire*, syn. (5/15/04)

Diane D'Agostino for Hairstyling: *Live with Regis and Kelly*, syn. (5/15/04)

Michelle Champagne for Makeup: *Live with Regis and Kelly*, syn. (5/15/04)

Bob Stone, Phil Andres, Patricia Cotter, Gary Stuart Kaplan Gary Lucy, Vince Waldron for Special Class Writing: *Win Ben Stein's Money*, Comedy Central (5/15/04)

Wayne Brady for Talk Show Host: *The Wayne Brady Show*, syn. (5/21/04)

John Turturro for Guest Actor in a Comedy Series: *Monk*, USA (9/12/04)

Bruce Finn for Cinematography for a Multi-Camera Series: *8 Simple Rules* ["Goodbye" episode], ABC (9/12/04)

Bruce Broughton for Music Composition for a Miniseries, Movie or Special-Dramatic Underscore: *Eloise at Christmastime*, ABC (9/12/04)

Randy Newman for Main Title Theme Music: *Monk*, USA (9/12/04)

The Amazing Race for Reality-Competition Program, CBS (9/19/04)

2005

Rossen Varbanov for Individual Achievement in Animation: *Brandy & Mr. Whiskers*, Disney Channel (5/14/05)

William Joyce, Michael Hirsh, Scott Dyer, Corinne Kouper, executive producers; Guillaume Hellouin, Pamela Lehn, supervising producers; Susie Grondin, Eric Flaherty, Christophe Archambault, producers; Mike Fallows, supervising director; Ron Pitts, Bill Giggie, directors; Nadine Van Der Velde, Steve Sullivan, Alice Prodanau, Robin Stein, writers for Special Class Animated Program: *Rolie Polie Olie*, Disney Channel (5/14/05)

Matthew Cohen for Directing a Game/Audience Participation Show: *Who Wants to Be a Millionaire*, syn. (5/14/05)

Diane D'Agostino for Hairstyling: *Live with Regis & Kelly*, syn. (5/14/05)

Michelle Champagne for Makeup: *Live with Regis & Kelly*, syn. (5/14/05)

Melissa Ellis & Fil Brown, rerecording mixers for Sound Mixing, Live Action and Animation: *Kim Possible*, Disney Channel (5/14/05)

Meredith Vieira for Game Show Host: *Who Wants to Be a Millionaire*, syn. (5/20/05)

Felicity Huffman for Lead Actress in a Comedy Series: *Desperate Housewives* (9/18/05)

Charles McDougall for Directing for a Comedy Series: *Desperate Housewives* ("Pilot") (9/18/05)

Scott Genkinger & Junie Lowry-Johnson for Casting for a Comedy Series: *Desperate Housewives* (9/11/05)

Michael Berenbaum for Single-Camera Picture Editing for a Comedy Series: *Desperate Housewives* ("Pilot") (9/11/05)

Danny Elfman for Main Title Theme Music: *Desperate Housewives* (9/11/05)

Kathryn Joosten for Guest Actress in a Comedy Series: *Desperate Housewives* (9/11/05)

J.J. Abrams, Damon Lindelof, Bryan Burk, Carlton Cuse, Jack Bender, David Fury, Jesse Alexander, Javier Grillo-Marxuah, Jean Higgins, Sarah Caplan, Leonard Dick for Drama Series: *Lost* (9/18/05)

J.J. Abrams for Directing for a Drama Series: *Lost* ("Pilot") (9/18/05)

April Webster, Mandy Sherman, Alyssa Weisberg, Veronica Collins Rooney for Casting for a Drama Series: *Lost* (9/11/05)

Mary Jo Markey for Single-Camera Picture Editing for a Drama Series: *Lost* (9/11/05)

Michael Giacchino, composer, for Music Composition for a Series (Dramatic Underscore): *Lost* ("Pilot") (9/11/05)

Kevin Blank, Mitch Suskin, visual effects supervisors; Archie Ahuna, special effects supervisor; Jonathan Spencer Levy, Benoit "Ben" Girard, Laurent M. Abecassis, CGI supervisors; Kevin Kutchaver, Bob Lloyd, visual-effects compositors for Special Visual Effects for a Series: *Lost* ("Pilot") (9/11/05)

The Amazing Race for Reality-Competition Program (9/18/05)

Tony Shalhoub for Actor in a Comedy Series: *Monk* (9/18/05)

John F. Michel for Multicamera Picture Editing for a Series: *Scrubs* ("My Life in Four Cameras") (9/11/05)

Matt Deitrich, Mike Bolanowski, Heeyeon Chang, Chris Dalzell, Evan Finn, Danny Flynn, Michael "Mighty" Friedman, Eric Goldfarb, Julian Gomez, Andy Kozar, Paul Neilsen, Jacob Parsons, Jeff Runyan, Eric Wilson for Picture Editing for Nonfiction Programming: *The Amazing Race* ("We're Moving up the Food Chain") (9/11/05)

Emperor Penguins, The (film) Live-action short; released on October 13, 1955. Directed by Maris Marret. Documents the life and habits of the largest of all penguins, filmed during a French Antarctic expedition led by Paul Emile Victor. 11 min.

Emperor's New Groove, The (film) In a mythical mountain kingdom, arrogant young Emperor Kuzco is transformed into a llama by his power-hungry adviser—the devious diva Yzma. Stranded in the jungle, Kuzco's only chance to get back home and reclaim the high life rests with a good-hearted peasant named Pacha. Kuzco's "perfect world" becomes a perfect mess as this most unlikely duo must deal with hair-raising dangers, wild comic predicaments, and, most horrifying of all, each other as they race to return Kuzco to the throne before Yzma (aided by her muscle-bound manservant, Kronk) tracks them down and finishes them off. Ultimately, Kuzco's budding friendship with Pacha teaches this royal pain to see his world in a different way. Released on December 15, 2000. Directed by Mark Dindal. Voices include David Spade (Kuzco), John Goodman (Pacha), Eartha Kitt (Yzma), Patrick Warburton (Kronk), Wendie Malick (Chicha). 78 min. With a score by John Debney and songs by Sting and David Hartley. Work started on a project with a very different version of the story, and the title *Kingdom of the Sun*, in 1994. In 1998, the story was completely revamped, maintaining only two of the main comedic characters and a few elements from the original treatment. The song "My Funny Friend and Me" was nominated for an Academy Award. A documentary about problems encountered during the making of the film, *The Sweatbox*, was made by Sting's wife, Trudie Styler. Released on video in May 2001. There was a direct-to-video sequel, *Kronk's New Groove*, in 2005.

Empire (television) An epic six-hour miniseries, airing on ABC beginning June 28, 2005, and ending July 26, 2005. In 44 B.C., Julius Caesar returns from triumphs in Spain to a neglected republic and a corrupt senate drunk with power. Though he's hailed as a hero by the masses, the senate is wary of Caesar's plans that might place him in a position of ultimate power. Brutus and Cassius plot against Caesar, who is protected by

Tyrannus, Rome's finest warrior. The senate manages to separate Tyrannus from Caesar by kidnapping his son—a diversion to get Tyrannus out of the way while Brutus assassinates the great conqueror. As he is drawing his last breath, Caesar makes Tyrannus swear to protect his successor, Octavius, his 18-year-old nephew. Tyrannus and Octavius are forced into exile, where they are joined by Agrippa, a young soldier, and Camane, a vestal virgin. Together they strive to help Octavius fulfill his destiny and become emperor. Directed by John Gray and Greg Yaitanes. Stars include Jonathan Cake (Tyrannus), Santiago Cabrera (Octavius), Emily Brunt (Camane), Chris Egan (Agrippa), Vincent Regan (Mark Antony), Colm Feore (Julius Caesar), Trudie Styler (Servilia), James Frain (Brutus). Filmed on location in south central Italy and at Cinecitta Studios. From Storyline Entertainment and Touchstone Television.

Emporium The largest store on Main Street at Disneyland; opened July 17, 1955. It serves as the primary place for Disneyland to showcase its souvenir merchandise, and, located right at the end of Main Street as one is leaving the park, it is ideal for those last-minute purchases. A highlight at the Emporium are its windows. Facing Main

Street, they are usually filled with elaborate dioramas telling the story of the latest Disney animated film release. Also in Magic Kingdom Park at Walt Disney World; opened October 1, 1971. Also in World Bazaar in Tokyo Disneyland; opened on April 15, 1983. At Disneyland Paris; opened on April 12, 1992. At Hong Kong Disneyland; opened September 12, 2005.

Empress Lilly Riverboat moored at Pleasure Island at Walt Disney World containing three restaurants—the Fisherman's Deck, the Steerman's Quarters, and the Empress Room; opened on May 1, 1977. Named after Walt Disney's wife, Lilly Disney. Until the opening of Victoria and Albert's at the Grand Floridian, the Empress Room provided the most elegant dining experience on the Walt Disney World property. The culinary delights are prepared by top chefs. The riverboat was originally considered part of the Disney Village Marketplace, but Pleasure Island was built immediately adjacent to it in 1989, so it became part of the new area. The boat closed as a Disney operation on April 22, 1995, and reopened as Fulton's Crab House on March 10, 1996.

Empty Nest (television) Television series on NBC, beginning October 8, 1988, and ending July 8, 1995. The contemporary problems and joys in the relationship between a widowed pediatrician father and his daughter living under the same roof with a huge dog. Starred Richard Mulligan (Dr. Harry Weston), Dinah Manoff (Carol Weston), David Leisure (Charley Dietz), Park Overall (Laverne Todd), Estelle Getty (Sophia Petrillo), Marsha Warfield (Dr. Maxine Douglas). Kristy McNichol played a second daughter, Barbara, a policewoman, in the first five seasons. Dreyfuss the dog was played by Bear, a combination St. Bernard/golden retriever. Richard Mulligan won the Emmy Award for Lead Actor in a Comedy Series in 1989.

Empty Socks (film) Oswald the Lucky Rabbit cartoon; released on December 12, 1927.

Enchanted Book Shoppe, The *Beauty and the Beast* show at Plaza Gardens at Disneyland from November 28, 1991 to April 26, 1992. It was superseded by the more sophisticated *Beauty and the Beast* stage show presented at Videopolis.

Enchanted Tiki Room Adventureland attraction at Disneyland; opened on June 23, 1963. The first attraction to feature sophisticated Audio-Animatronics figures. The term Audio-Animatronics had been utilized earlier in describing the movable figures populating Nature's Wonderland, but the process was greatly changed, enabling press releases to call the Enchanted Tiki Room the first to use Audio-Animatronics. The four parrot hosts of the show are named Fritz, Michael, Pierre, and José. They introduce a lively 17-minute musical presentation by more than 200 birds, flowers, and tikis. The audience is invited to join in with "Let's All Sing Like the Birdies Sing." It had originally been planned to have the Tiki Room as a restaurant, but that would have greatly limited capacity. Sponsored from 1964 to 1973 by United Airlines, and from January 1976 on by Dole Pineapple. Also in Adventureland at Tokyo Disneyland; opened April 15, 1983. The similar attraction in Magic Kingdom Park at Walt Disney World was known as the Tropical Serenade, located in the Sunshine Pavilion. The Florida attraction's show was exten-

sively renovated, reopening in the spring of 1998 as The Enchanted Tiki Room—Under New Management starring Iago from *Aladdin* and Zazu from *The Lion King*. The Tokyo Disneyland version had a revised show, called The Enchanted Tiki Room: Now Playing Get the Fever! in 1999.

Encino Man (film) Two high school outcasts, Dave Morgan and his best friend Stoney, uncover a frozen caveman while excavating a backyard swimming pool. They hope their accidental discovery will bring them fame and fortune, not to mention a newfound social status on campus. When the caveman accidentally thaws out and comes to life, they quickly concoct a scheme to disguise him as a foreign exchange student so no suspicions would be aroused. Link, as he is

called, soon learns to speak, dress, and act like a typical valley boy, becoming the most popular kid in school, frustrating Dave and Stoney's goals. As Link learns more about the twentieth century, he begins to realize that he does not fit in. But an earthquake suddenly hits, unearthing a frozen cavewoman, Link's link to his own past. Released on May 22, 1992. Directed by Les Mayfield. A Hollywood Picture. 88 min. Stars Sean Astin (Dave Morgan), Brendan Fraser (Link), Pauly Shore (Stoney Brown), Megan Ward (Robyn Sweeney), Mariette Hartley (Mrs. Morgan), Richard Masur (Mr. Morgan). Filmed in California's San Fernando Valley. Released on video in 1992.

Encino Woman (television) Two-hour television movie; aired on ABC on April 20, 1996. A beautiful prehistoric woman, to be known as Lucy, awakens from her million-year slumber to encounter an advertising executive, David Horsenfelt, who promotes her to his agency as the "primal" woman they have been searching for to advertise a new perfume, meanwhile falling in love with her. Stars Katherine Kousi (Lucy), Corey Parker (David), Jay Thomas (Marvin Beckler), John Kassir (Jean Michel). A television sequel to the theatrical film *Encino Man*. Directed and co-written by Shawn Schepps, who had written the script for the theatrical film.

End of the Trail (television) Television show; episode 13 of *Texas John Slaughter*.

Endurance (film) The story of distance runner Haile Gebrselassie from Ethiopia, and how he eventually won the 10,000-meter race at the Atlanta Olympics in 1996. A Walt Disney Pictures presentation of a La Junta Production in association with Film Four and Helkon Media Film Veritrieb. Directed by Leslie Woodhead. (The race sequence at the Atlanta Olympics directed by Bud Greenspan.) Limited release in New York and Los Angeles on May 14, 1999. CinemaScope. 83 min. The film combines elements of cinema vérité, traditional documentary filmmaking, sports coverage, docudrama, and feature film devices, backed by a score drawn from East African musical traditions. Released on video in 2000.

Enemy of the State (film) A chance encounter with an old friend destroys Robert Dean's fast-track career and happy home life when he is framed for a murder by a corrupt intelligence official. As an administrator within the National Security Agency, Thomas Brian Reynolds sees his role as being the ultimate guardian of the United States, and when stakes are high, he believes he must bend the rules to protect her secrets. He thus appropriates the vast resources of his department to commit the perfect crime and conceal a political cover-up of the murder of a congressman by government agents. Dean's only hope to reclaim his life and prove his innocence is a man he's never met, a mysterious underground information broker and ex-intelligence operative known only as Brill. A Don Simpson/Jerry Bruckheimer Production in association with Touchstone Pictures. Directed by Tony Scott. Released on November 20, 1998. Stars Will Smith (Robert Dean), Jon Voight (Thomas Brian Reynolds), Gene Hackman (Brill), Regina King (Carla Dean), Loren Dean (Hicks), Jake Busey (Krug), Barry Pepper (David Platt), Jason Lee (Daniel Zavitz), Gabriel Byrne (NSA agent), Lisa Bonet (Rachel Banks). 132 min. CinemaScope. Filming took place around Baltimore and Washington, D.C., and in Los Angeles. For a tunnel sequence, several cars had to be cut in pieces, lowered through a manhole, then rebuilt 20 feet underground. Released on video in 1999.

Energy Creation Story (film) Animated story of the creation of fossil fuels, for Theater I of the Universe of Energy, Epcot; opened on October 1, 1982.

Energy Exchange Display in Communicore East at Epcot sponsored by Exxon, from October 1, 1982 to January 31, 1994. Computers helped tell about elements of the energy story.

Energy in Physics (film) Educational film; released in August 1984. The fundamental law of physics, the Law of Conservation of Energy, is introduced to students.

Energy Savers, The (film) Educational film with Donald Duck, Mickey Mouse, and Goofy helping teach good energy conservation habits; released in September 1982.

Energy, You Make the World Go 'Round (film) Kinetic, multi-image pre-show for the Universe of Energy at Epcot; opened on October 1, 1982.

Engine-Ears Toys Shop at Golden Gateway at Disney's California Adventure; opened February 8, 2001.

Englander, Otto (1906–1969) Storyman on animated films for 22 years; he was story director on *Dumbo*.

English, Liz She voiced Marie in *The Aristocats*.

Enjoy It! Song from *In Search of the Castaways*, written by Richard M. Sherman and Robert B. Sherman, and sung by Maurice Chevalier.

Entropy (film) Jake, a young filmmaker, begins to direct his first film, a documentary about the rock band U2, but runs up against cast, budget, and production problems with it and at the same time sees his personal life unraveling. A Touchstone release on video on February 15, 2000, of an independent film from Tribeca Productions, originally shown on April 15, 1999, at the Los Angeles Independent Film Festival. Directed by Phil Joanou. Stars Stephen Dorff (Jake Walsh), Judith Godreche (Stella), Kelly MacDonald (Pia), Hector Elizondo (the Chairman). 104 min.

Environmental Sanitation (film) Educational film about the growth of a city and the need to build proper water and sanitation systems for a growing populace. Produced under the auspices of the Coordinator of Inter-American Affairs. Delivered on April 3, 1946.

EPCOT Acronym coined by Walt Disney in 1966 meaning Experimental Prototype Community of Tomorrow. The park was called EPCOT Center when it opened on October 1, 1982. It was a major undertaking for Disney, costing in the neighborhood of $1 billion. Toward the end of his life, Walt Disney became interested in the problems of cities. He had read books on the subject and thought it would be great if he could do something to help. With the huge number of acres that he was accumulating in Florida, an ideal place was available. He made a film in October 1966, meant for the people of Florida, which explained what some of his ideas were. He wanted to build a place where people could live in an environment like no other. The central core would be the commercial center. Radiating out from it would be strips of residences, with vast green spaces in between for recreation, schools, and similar facilities. Supply trucks and other traffic would use underground tunnels. Unfortunately, Walt died before he could refine his ideas. Nothing definite had been planned. Roy O. Disney, taking over for his brother, rationalized that since the company knew how to build a Magic Kingdom, they should start with that, to get some cash flow started, and then they could consider Walt's final dream of an experimental community. The Walt Disney World Magic Kingdom did open successfully in 1971, and the Disney executives never forgot Walt's ideas for EPCOT, even though Roy Disney also passed away. In 1975, Card Walker, president of Walt Disney Productions, announced that the company would proceed with EPCOT. But Walker and his advisers determined that Walt's ideas for an idealistic city were unrealistic; one could not expect people to live under a microscope, as it were. It could not be both a showplace and a place to live. Instead, the Disney Imagineers got busy and soon had their proposals ready for a park consisting of two areas—Future World and World Showcase. When it was ready to open in 1982, they decided to call it EPCOT Center, reasoning that the whole Walt Disney World property was part of Walt's grand idea, and this was only the Center of it. It was a little difficult marketing a name like EPCOT, which no longer had its original meaning, but over the first decade of the park's history, people forgot that it was an acronym and it became its own word. Thus *Center* was dropped

from the name in December 1993, the letters were lowercased, and Epcot came into its own.

EPCOT (film) Walt Disney's final film, in which he tells Florida residents the plans for Walt Disney World and EPCOT. Filmed in late 1966 and released in 1967 for showing in Florida.

EPCOT Advanced Information System (film) Educational film about the development of the WorldKey Information System from concept to completion; released in August 1984.

EPCOT America! America! (television) Show on The Disney Channel, beginning April 21, 1983, originating from Epcot and featuring filmed segments of all that is best in America.

EPCOT Building Code Passed by the Reedy Creek Improvement District in 1970 to enable the construction of Walt Disney World. It was written in such a way that it required strict compliance with current building regulations included in the building codes from other governmental bodies, but it also enabled the building of castles and other structures that were not addressed in most building codes.

EPCOT Center See EPCOT.

EPCOT Center: A Souvenir Program (film) Video souvenir; released in January 1984.

EPCOT Center: The Opening Celebration (television) Television show; aired on October 23, 1982. Directed by Dwight Hemion. Rainy weather fails to dampen the enthusiasm as EPCOT Center is opened. Danny Kaye is the host, looking at the history of the project from Walt's first announcement through construction. Celebrity guests help Kaye look around the park and visit several of the attractions. With Drew Barrymore, Roy Clark, Marie Osmond, Eric Severeid, the West Point Glee Club. For the opening, Disney put together the All-American Marching Band, consisting of top school musicians from all over the country.

EPCOT Computer Central Display of the actual computers which run Epcot in Communicore East, sponsored by Sperry, from October 1, 1982 to January 30, 1994. Featured Astuter Computer Revue (later Backstage Magic).

Epcot Discovery Center Information area at Epcot; opened on July 1, 1994, and closed in October 1996. Formerly Epcot Outreach and Epcot Teacher's Center. This was an area where guests could ask their questions about any of the subjects covered at Epcot or throughout the Walt Disney World Resort. The hosts and hostesses could access their detailed computer programs or consult their library for the answers. In addition, a variety of take-home informational resources were available.

EPCOT Earth Station Film, The (film) An educational look at the wonders of EPCOT Center at Walt Disney World. This film was created for showing on giant screens within Earth Station, the information center neighboring Spaceship Earth.

EPCOT Magazine (television) Series on The Disney Channel, hosted by Michael Young, with each show including several different segments on topical news and entertainment, ranging from food and fashion to travel and family relationships. A two-part episode in 1984 visited the Walt Disney Archives. The show debuted on April 18, 1983.

Epcot Outreach Information area in Communicore West, from May 26, 1983 to July 1, 1994, including Epcot Teacher's Center. It moved its location and became Epcot Discovery Center.

Epcot Poll See Electronic Forum.

Epcot Resorts At Walt Disney World; consists of the Caribbean Beach, Yacht Club, Beach Club, BoardWalk, Port Orleans, Swan, and Dolphin.

EPCOT 77 (film) Sixteen mm promotional film describing World Showcase and Future World, being built at EPCOT Center.

Ernest Goes to Camp (film) Ernest P. Worrell, working as a handyman at a boys' summer camp, aspires to be a counselor and is "rewarded" by being put in charge of a group of juvenile delinquents. After initial problems, highlighted by slapstick humor, Ernest and the boys gain some mutual respect and help save the camp from developers. Released on May 22, 1987. Directed by John R. Cherry III. A Touchstone Picture. 92 min. Stars Jim Varney (Ernest P. Worrell), Victoria Racimo (Nurse St. Cloud), John Vernon (Sherman Krader), Iron Eyes Cody (Old Indian Chief). Filmed in Nashville, Tennessee. Released on video in 1987.

Ernest Goes to Jail (film) When lovable but inept Ernest P. Worrell becomes a juror on a murder trial, the scheming defendant notices that Ernest is a dead ringer for jailed crime boss Felix Nash. A plot is quickly hatched to switch the two look-alikes and soon Ernest finds himself in jail while his notorious double sneaks away to freedom, taking over Ernest's job as a night janitor in a bank. Released on April 6, 1990. Directed by John Cherry. A Touchstone Picture. 82 min. Stars Jim Varney (Ernest P. Worrell/Felix Nash/Auntie Nelda), Gailard Sartain (Chuck). Filmed in Nashville, Tennessee. Released on video in 1990.

Ernest Goes to Splash Mountain (television) Television special; first aired on The Disney Channel on July 7, 1989, then in syndication beginning August 19, 1989. 30 min. Ernest P. Worrell goes to Disneyland to test the new attraction before it opens to the public. Stars Jim Varney (Ernest P. Worrell), Danny Breen, Sheryl Bernstein.

Ernest Green Story, The (television) Disney Channel Premiere Film; first aired on January 17, 1993. Directed by Eric Laneuville. The story of one of the nine students who, in 1957, were the first African Americans to attend the previously all-white Central High School in Little Rock, Arkansas. Ernest Green overcomes prejudice and threats of violence to pursue his dreams of education. Stars Morris Chestnut (Ernest Green), Ossie

Davis, C.C.H. Pounder. President-elect Bill Clinton and his longtime friend Ernest Green attended a special showing of the film at the Little Rock Central High School before its premiere on The Disney Channel.

Ernest Saves Christmas (film) Santa Claus travels to Orlando to find a successor, a sometime actor and puppeteer, Joe. On the way to find Joe, Santa meets bumbling cab driver, Ernest, and by mistake leaves his sack in the cab. Ernest and a runaway girl, Pamela, try to help Santa. Pamela, who had attempted to steal the sack, returns it, and Ernest, after many mishaps, manages to deliver Santa's sleigh and reindeer from the airport, just in time for Joe to take over on Christmas Eve. Released on November 11, 1988. Directed by John Cherry. A Touchstone Picture. 90 min. Stars Jim Varney (Ernest P. Worrell), Douglas Seale (Santa), Oliver Clark (Joe Carruthers), Noëlle Parker (Pamela Trenton/Harmony Star). Filmed at Disney-MGM Studios and on location in Orlando, Florida, and Nashville, Tennessee. Released on video in 1989.

Ernest Scared Stupid (film) After accidentally using a magic spell to revive a slimy troll, Trantor, who was condemned centuries before by a Worrell ancestor, bumbling Ernest P. Worrell enlists the aid of Old Lady Hackmore, the town eccentric, to dispose of the creature, break the curse, and make the town safe for children once again. Released on October 11, 1991. Directed by John Cherry. A Touchstone Picture. 92 min. Stars Jim Varney (Ernest P. Worrell), Eartha Kitt (Old Lady Hackmore), Jonas Moscartolo (Trantor). Filmed in Nashville, Tennessee, and its vicinity. Released on video in 1992. For a later direct-to-video Ernest movie, see *Slam Dunk Ernest.* Two other Ernest video releases were from Monarch, not Disney—*Ernest Rides Again* (1993) and *Ernest Goes to School* (1994), the former having had a limited theatrical run.

Erwin, Stuart (1903–1967) Actor; appeared in *Son of Flubber* (Coach Wilson) and *The Misadventures of Merlin Jones* (Capt. Loomis), and on television in *Moochie of the Little League.*

Escapade in Florence (television) Two-part television show; aired on September 30 and October 7, 1962. Directed by Steve Previn. Two teens get involved in intrigue in Florence, Italy, when Tommy Carpenter is given the wrong painting in an art store. A group of criminals try to get it back, causing Tommy to wonder what is so valuable about it. It turns out an art forger is copying valuable paintings and substituting the copy for the original. Tommy and his friend, Annette Aliotto, manage to solve the plot and turn the art thieves into the police. Stars Tommy Kirk, Annette Funicello, Nino Castelnuovo, Ivan Desny.

Escape from the Dark (film) Foreign theatrical title of *The Littlest Horse Thieves.*

Escape to Nowhere (television) Television show; part 2 of *Andrews' Raiders.*

Escape to Paradise/Water Birds (television) Television show; aired on December 18, 1960. A behind-the-scenes show on the filming of *Swiss Family Robinson* on the West Indian island of Tobago, followed by the True-Life Adventure *Water Birds.* Stars John Mills, Dorothy McGuire, James MacArthur, Janet Munro, Sessue Hayakawa, Tommy Kirk, Kevin Corcoran.

Escape to Witch Mountain (film) Tony Malone, 13, and his sister Tia, 11, orphaned by the loss of their foster parents, live in a children's home. But their incredible psychic powers attract rich and powerful Aristotle Bolt, who has his assistant, Lucas Deranian, adopt them as wards to exploit them. Terrified, they escape with the aid of a new friend, Jason O'Day, in his camper. Jason agrees to help them find Stony Creek, a town on a cryptic map in Tia's possession. Pursued by Bolt, Deranian, and the police, the youngsters are jailed but once again escape. As time runs out, the children remember they are castaways from another planet and are soon led by one of their own kind, Uncle Bene, to a flying saucer which blasts off for the sanctuary of Witch Mountain, leaving their captors below far behind. Released on March 21, 1975. Directed by John

Hough. 97 min. Stars Eddie Albert (Jason), Ray Milland (Bolt), Donald Pleasence (Deranian), Ike Eisenmann (Tony), Kim Richards (Tia), Walter Barnes (Sheriff Purdy), Reta Shaw (Mrs. Grindley), Denver Pyle (Uncle Bene). Based on the book by Alexander Key. The music score was by Johnny Mandel. The film was shot around Monterey and Palo Alto, California, including a Victorian mansion at Menlo Park for the Pine Woods orphanage. Aristotle Bolt's kingly abode Xanthus was filmed in a $3 million replica of a Byzantine castle built by Templeton Crocker between 1926 and 1934 from lava rock from Mt. Vesuvius and materials gathered all over Europe. The castle overlooks the beach at Pebble Beach. Other location scenes were shot at Carmel Valley, Big Sur, and the town of Felton in the Santa Cruz Mountains. The many special effects in the film were created by Art Cruickshank. Released on video in 1980, 1985, and 1993.

Escape to Witch Mountain (television) Two-hour television movie based on the 1975 feature film; aired on ABC on April 29, 1995. A compelling mystery about two twins with supernatural powers who are separated as babies and find their way back to each other and to their "real home." Directed by Peter Rader. Stars Robert Vaughn (Edward Bolt), Elisabeth Moss (Anna), Erik von Detten (Danny), Lynne Moody (Lindsay Brown), Perrey Reeves (Zoe Moon), Lauren Tom (Claudia Ford), Henry Gibson (Prof. Ravetch), Kevin Tighe (Sheriff), Brad Dourif (Luther/Bruno).

Escen, Don Longtime Disney Company financial leader, retiring in 1984 as Treasurer. He was named a Disney Legend in 1998.

Esmeralda Character in *The Hunchback of Notre Dame*, with her singing voice by Heidi Mollenhauer and speaking voice by Demi Moore.

Espace Euro Disney Preview center for Euro Disney; opened on December 5, 1990.

Espinosa, Mary Mouseketeer from the 1950s television show.

ESPN With the purchase of Capital Cities/ABC, Disney acquired 80 percent ownership of the ESPN and ESPN2 cable networks. ESPN, the worldwide leader in sports, was launched in 1979, and its sister network, ESPN2, came along in 1993. In 1997, a new division of The Disney Store was created, named ESPN—The Store, to offer sports merchandise in malls, with the first store opening in the Glendale Galleria in California on September 16. *ESPN Magazine* debuted March 23, 1998.

ESPN Zone Sports-themed dining and entertainment complex opened in Baltimore, Maryland, on July 12, 1998, the first of a number that were later opened in such cities around the country as Chicago, New York, Atlanta, Washington, Anaheim, Las Vegas, and Denver. A similar facility, the ESPN Club, had opened at the Board-Walk Resort at Walt Disney World on July 1, 1996.

ESPN's Ultimate X (film) The highlights and dramatic stories behind the 2001 Summer X Games, covering skateboarding, biking, moto X, and street luge competitions, and the athletes who compete. Directed by Bruce Hendricks. A Touchstone Picture. Released on May 10, 2002. A documentary released in 70mm for exclusive showing in IMAX and large-format theaters worldwide. 39 min.

Estevez, Emilio Actor; appeared in *Tex* (Johnny Collins), *Stakeout* and *Another Stakeout* (Bill Reimers), *The Mighty Ducks*, *D2: The Mighty Ducks* (Gordon Bombay), and *The War at Home* (Jeremy Collier).

Esther Emu star of *Mickey Down Under* (1948).

Estrin, Judith Member of the Disney board of directors beginning June 24, 1998.

Eternal Sea, The Two-hundred-degree film attraction in Tomorrowland at Tokyo Disneyland, from April 15, 1983 to September 16, 1984. Superseded by *Magic Journeys* and then *Captain Eo*.

Ethics in the Computer Age (film) Educational film presenting two mini-dramas about software piracy and computer hacking; released in August 1984.

Euro Disney See Disneyland Paris.

Euro Disney: When the Dream Becomes Reality (Euro Disney: Quand l'imaginaire devient realité) (film) Preview film shown at Espace Euro Disney in France; premiered on December 5, 1990. 13 min.

Euro Disneyland See Disneyland Paris.

Euro Disneyland Railroad Opened April 12, 1992. Main Street, Frontierland, and Fantasyland stations opened on April 12, 1992; Discoveryland station opened on June 24, 1993.

Eurospain Shop sponsored by Arribas Brothers in the Downtown Disney Marketplace at Walt Disney World, featuring handcrafted gifts and decorative articles from European artists.

Ceramics Shaw, Evan K. Company also known as American Pottery. They created some of the most handsome and collectible Disney ceramic figurines from 1943 to 1955. Prices are high on the collector market, especially if the figurines have their original gold label.

Evans, Monica She voiced Abigail Gabble (*The Aristocats*) and Maid Marian (*Robin Hood*).

Evans, Morgan ("Bill") (1910–2002) With his brother, Jack, he designed the landscaping for Walt Disney's home in the early 1950s. Walt then selected him to continue the same work for Disneyland. He became director of landscape design for WED Enterprises and worked on all of the Disney parks, even consulting after his retirement. He was named a Disney Legend in 1992.

Even Stevens (television) Comedy series on Disney Channel, premiering June 17, 2000, featuring the misadventures of Louis Stevens, a typical 13-year-old middle school kid and his overachieving sister, Ren. There is constant sibling rivalry as Ren tries to live down the embarrassment of being related to the class clown, while Louis strives to live outside the shadow of his supersuccessful sister. Stars Shia La Beouf (Louis), Christy Carlson Romano (Ren), Nick Spano (Donnie), Donna Pescow (Eileen), Tom Virtue (Steve).

Even Stevens Movie, The (television) A Disney Channel Original Movie; premiered on June 13, 2003. The Stevens family wins an all-expense-paid trip to an exclusive island hideaway. What the family doesn't know is that their week in paradise has been set up by a new "extreme reality" television series and the producer's quest for blockbuster ratings threatens to turn their dream vacation into a nightmare. Eventually the Stevens discover that they have been had and set out to even the score. Directed by Sean McNamara. Stars Shia LaBeouf (Louis Stevens), Christy Carlson Romano (Ren Stevens), Nick Spano (Donnie Stevens), Tom Virtue (Steve Stevens), Donna Pescow (Eileen Stevens), Steven Anthony Lawrence ("Beans" Aranguren), AJ Trauth (Alan Twitty). The first original movie on Disney Channel inspired by an original comedy series.

Everglades, The: Home of the Living Dinosaurs (television) A look at the animal characters found in Florida's Everglades, with an intimate look at the fascinating life stories of its mysterious native crocodiles and alligators. Produced by Pete Zuccarini. Aired in syndication beginning November 20, 2000, as a New True Life Adventure.

Everhart, Rex (1920-2000) Actor; he voiced Maurice in *Beauty and the Beast*.

Everything You Wanted to Know About Puberty . . . for Boys (film) Educational release in 16mm in August 1991. 16 min. Two boys have questions about recent physical changes but are too embarrassed to ask an older brother to borrow a book on the subject.

Everything You Wanted to Know About Puberty . . . for Girls (film) Educational release in 16mm in August 1991. 13 min. While staying at a friend's house, a girl has her first period, and the friend's older sister shares her knowledge and experience with the girls.

Evinrude Dragonfly character in *The Rescuers*. His sounds were provided by Jim Macdonald.

Evita (film) The musical story of Argentina's controversial and charismatic Eva Perón, a girl who rose from poverty to become one of the most powerful women in the world as the wife of Juan Perón, changing her country's history through sheer determination and a conviction that all Argentineans should prosper. Attracting attention like no other woman before or since, she hypnotized a nation of 18 million people for seven years before her untimely death at the age of 33 in 1952. Directed by Alan Parker. A Cinergi production released by Hollywood Pictures. Released on December 25, 1996, in New York and Los Angeles; wider release on January 1 and general release on January 10, 1997. (The film had an earlier opening on December 20 in London.) Stars Madonna (Eva Perón), Antonio Banderas (Ché), Jonathan Pryce (Juan Perón). 135 min. Filmed in CinemaScope, in Argentina, Budapest (which more accurately replicated Buenos Aires of the 1930s and 1940s), and the U.K. It took much backstage persuasion, including entreaties by Madonna herself to the president of Argentina, to obtain last-minute permission to shoot on the balcony of the Casa Rosada, the official government house. Madonna was fitted for more than 80 costumes for the production. The film was based on a stage musical by Andrew Lloyd Webber and Tim Rice, which originated in a concept album released in 1976 while

still unproduced on the stage; it opened on the stage in London in 1978 to great acclaim. The song "You Must Love Me," written specifically for the film by Webber and Rice, won the Academy Award for Best Song for 1996. Released on video in 1997.

Ev'rybody Wants to Be a Cat Song from *The Aristocats*, written by Floyd Huddleston and Al Rinker.

Ewok Village Opened at Disney-MGM Studios on August 24, 1989, at the entrance to the Star Tours attraction.

Exile (television) Two-hour television movie; aired on January 14, 1990. Directed by David Greenwalt. A group of students becomes marooned on an island when their plane is forced to land. The pilot takes the plane to get help, but he crashes. With no adults around, the kids have to manage by themselves. The pilot turns up alive, but he desperately steals their supplies and terrorizes the girls. Stars Christopher David Barnes, Corey Feldman, Mike Preston, Michael Stoyanov, Chris Furrh, Kate Benton, Alice Carter, Gino DeMauro, Stacy Galina, Christian Jacobs, Kiersten Warren.

Expectations: A Story About Stress (film) Educational film; released in September 1985. Helps pre-adolescents recognize and deal with stress.

Expedition Everest Thrill attraction opening at Disney's Animal Kingdom on April 7, 2006. At just under 200 feet, the mountain will be the tallest mountain in Florida. Guests take a perilous journey aboard a runaway train through the Himalayan mountains, traveling in 34-passenger vehicles patterned after an aging, steam-engine tea train. Adventurous riders push deep into the lair of the feared Yeti, guardian of the forbidden mountain, and encounter torn tracks, which cause them to spiral backward into an ice cavern, and dart in and out of the mountain at high speeds.

Explorer's Club Restaurant in Adventureland at Disneyland Paris; opened on April 12, 1992. It closed in March 1994, reopening a month later as Colonel Hathi's Pizza Outpost.

Expo Robotics Robot demonstration in Communicore West at Epcot, from February 13, 1988 to October 3, 1993. The intricate movements of the robotic arms amazingly performed various programmed tricks. Some robots were set up to draw a picture of a guest's face, taken from a video monitor. This was an expansion of the popular Bird and the Robot presentation in Transcenter in the World of Motion.

ExtraTERRORestrial Alien Encounter, The Attraction in Tomorrowland in Magic Kingdom Park at Walt Disney World, from Disney and George Lucas, opened on June 20, 1995. Housed in the Tomorrowland Interplanetary Convention Center was the laboratory of X-S Tech, a corporation from a distant planet intent on demonstrating its interplanetary teleportation apparatus. But the demonstration was marred by difficulties and an alien creature was accidentally teleported into the laboratory. Took the place of Mission to Mars. The attraction closed October 11, 2003 and reopened November 16, 2004, as Stitch's Great Escape!

Extremely Goofy Movie, An (film) Direct-to-video release on February 29, 2000. Goofy enrolls in college with his son Max, but brings his 1970s ideas on college with him. When he teams up with a like-minded school librarian, the disco lights and mood rings swing back to action on campus. At the College X Games competition, Max is the hot new talent until Goofy joins in and shows the kids a whole new way to skateboard. Directed by Douglas McCarthy. Voices include Bill Farmer (Goofy), Jason Marsden (Max), Pauly Shore (Bobby), Vicki Lewis (Beret Girl), Bebe Neuwirth (Sylvia).

Eyes Have It, The (film) Donald Duck cartoon; released on March 30, 1945. Directed by Jack Hannah. Donald experiments with his power of hypnotism to change Pluto into a mouse, turtle, chicken, and finally a lion, which chases Donald about until a fall regains Pluto's senses.

Eyes in Outer Space (film) Featurette; released on June 18, 1959. Directed by Ward Kimball. Winner of the 1960 Thomas Edison Foundation Award, this featurette explores satellites' future ability to forecast the weather. 26 min. Later shown on *Walt Disney's Wonderful World of Color* in 1962 as part of the episode "Spy in the Sky."

Eyewitness to History: The Events (film) Educational film; released in September 1978. Famous events from history are shown through newsreel footage.

Eyewitness to History: The Life Styles (film) Educational film; released in September 1978. A glimpse at life in our century, from newsreel accounts.

Eyewitness to History: The People (film) Educational film; released in September 1978. Newsreel cameramen capture mini-portraits of famous people from history.

F

Fa Zhou Mulan's father in *Mulan*; voiced by Soon-Tek Oh.

Fabray, Nanette Actress; appeared in *Amy* (Malvina). Fabray found it easy to relate to the young boys and girls recruited from the California School for the Deaf in Riverside to act in the film; she herself suffered from a hearing loss that stemmed from a hereditary disease. She underwent several operations spanning two decades to have her hearing restored.

Facts of Life Reunion, The (television) Aired on *The Wonderful World of Disney* on November 18, 2001. A reunion of the stars from the 1979–1988 sitcom finds Natalie's *two* boyfriends arriving for Thanksgiving dinner, so Blair, Tootie, and Mrs. Garrett have to attempt to keep the peace. Stars Lisa Whelchel (Blair), Kim Fields (Tootie), Mindy Cohn (Natalie), Charlotte Rae (Mrs. Garrett).

Fagin Master of the gang of dog thieves in *Oliver & Company*; voiced by Dom DeLuise.

Fain, Sammy (1902–1989) Composer; wrote songs for *Alice in Wonderland*, *Peter Pan*, and *Sleeping Beauty*, and nominated for an Academy Award with Carol Connors and Ayn Robbins for "Someone's Waiting for You" from *The Rescuers*.

Fair Folk Fairylike characters who help Taran find the cauldron in *The Black Cauldron*.

Fairest of Them All, The (television) Syndicated television special for the re-release of *Snow White and the Seven Dwarfs*; aired on May 23, 1983. Directed by Cardon Walker. Dick Van Patten hosts and introduces many of the artists who worked on the film, and Adriana Caselotti and Harry Stockwell, the voices of Snow White and the Prince, are reunited. The director, Cardon Walker, is the son of Disney executive E. Cardon Walker.

Fairway Villas Two-bedroom accommodations at Lake Buena Vista, at Walt Disney World; opened in 1978 and closed in 2002. Became part of The Disney Institute in 1996.

Fairy Godmother She enables Cinderella to attend the ball; voiced by Verna Felton.

Fairy Tale Wedding Pavilion On an island by the Seven Seas Lagoon near the Grand Floridian Beach Resort at Walt Disney World, this glass-enclosed pavilion evokes images of a Victorian summer house. It is nondenominational and perfect for wedding parties from 2 to 250. Opened July 15, 1995.

Faline Bambi's girlfriend; voiced by Cammie King and Ann Gillis.

Falk, Peter Actor; starred in *Roommates* (Rocky Holeczek) and *Corky Romano* (Pops).

Fall Out—Fall In (film) Donald Duck cartoon; released on April 23, 1943. Directed by Jack King. Donald experiences the trials and tribulations of Army life: marching through summer sun and rain day after day and setting up camp in the evening, which takes Donald so long it is sunrise before he is finished.

Fall Varieties (film) Cartoon compilation; released by RKO in 1953.

Fallberg, Becky Longtime head of the Ink and Paint Department at the Disney Studio. She began at Disney in 1942, and became manager of the department in 1975. She retired in 1986. She was named a Disney Legend in 2000.

Fallberg, Carl (1915–1996) He went to Disney in 1935 as an assistant director on cartoons, and later became a storyman and writer of comic book stories. It was he who was given the assignment of scouting out Hollywood costume shops to find a pointed sorcerer's hat for the live-action model to wear for *Fantasia*.

Family, The (television) Reality series on ABC; debuted on March 4, 2003 and ended on September 10, 2003. Ten members of an extended blue-collar, Italian-American family are moved to a luxurious Palm Beach mansion where they compete for $1 million, with the mansion's staff doubling as a board of trustees to vote one person off at every episode's end. Hosted by George Hamilton. Produced by Buena Vista Productions. 9 episodes.

Family Band, The (television) Television title of the feature *The One and Only, Genuine, Original Family Band*. See under that entry.

Family PC Magazine published by Disney beginning August 15, 1994, and ending with the issue for January 1998.

Family Planning (film) Educational film; produced in association with the Population Council; released in December 1967. The film explains that the ultimate goal of family life is the enrichment not the restriction of life.

Famous Jett Jackson, The (television) Half-hour series on Disney Channel, debuting October 25, 1998, and airing through 2001. Jett Jackson, a 13-year-old television star, longs to have a normal life, so he leaves Hollywood and his television-star mother behind to go live with his father, the town sheriff in Wilsted, North Carolina, where he was born. But Jett's friends and fans will not let him live the simple life, for they expect him to live up to the image of Silverstone, the heroic private investigator he plays on television. Stars Lee Thompson Young (Jett), Ryan Sommers Baum (J.B. Halliburton), Kerry Duff (Kayla West), Gordon Greene (Wood Jackson), Montrose Hagins (Coretta Jackson).

Fanelli Boys, The (television) Television series; aired on NBC from September 8, 1990 to February 16, 1991. Four grown brothers from a boisterous Italian family in Brooklyn move back in with their strong-willed, widowed mother when their lives go awry. Stars Joe Pantoliano (Dominic), Ann Guilbert (Theresa), Christopher Meloni (Frank), Ned Eisenberg (Anthony), Andy Hirsch (Ronnie), Richard Libertini (Father Angelo).

Fantasia (film) One of the most highly regarded of the Disney classics, a symphonic concert with Leopold Stokowski and the Philadelphia Orchestra, embellished by Disney animation. Directed by Samuel Armstrong, James Algar, Bill Roberts, Paul Satterfield, Hamilton Luske, Jim Handley, Ford Beebe, T. Hee, Norm Ferguson, and Wilfred Jackson. Narrated by Deems Taylor. Includes eight sequences: *Toccata and Fugue in D Minor* (Bach), *The Nutcracker Suite* (Tchaikovsky), *The Sorcerer's Apprentice* (Dukas), *Rite of Spring* (Stravinski), *Pastoral*

(Beethoven), *Dance of the Hours* (Ponchielli), *Night on Bald Mountain* (Moussorgsky), and *Ave Maria* (Schubert). Premiered on November 13, 1940, at the Broadway Theater in New York. The film was presented in Fantasound, an early stereo system, devised at the Disney Studio, but which required theaters to be specially equipped. Because of the expense, the film originally opened in only 14 theaters. The stereo sound enhanced the effect of the movie and won special certificates for Walt Disney, technicians William Garity and John N.A. Hawkins and RCA, and for Leopold Stokowski and his associates (for unique achievement in the creation of a new form of visualized music) at the 1941 Academy Awards. 125 min. New interest in the film in the 1970s led to a new sound track in 1982, with the orchestra conducted by Irwin Kostal, narration by Hugh Douglas, and a recording in digital stereo, but its full-length restoration in 1990 brought back the original sound track, while trying to duplicate some of the effects of the Fantasound presentation. The film was re-released theatrically in 1946, 1956, 1963, 1969, 1977, 1982, 1985, and 1990. Released on video in 1991. Corey Burton replaced Deems Taylor on the DVD. *Fantasia* has taken its place as one of the great cinematic classics of all time. It took 60 years, but in line with Walt Disney's plan to add new segments regularly to the film, *Fantasia/2000* retained *The Sorcerer's Apprentice* but added eight new sequences.

Fantasia Gardens Topiary water garden at Disneyland, replacing the Motor Boat Cruise in January 1993.

Fantasia Gardens Miniature Golf and Garden Pavilion Two 18-hole miniature golf courses, a putting course, and a covered 22,000-square-foot outdoor meeting facility, opened on May 20, 1996, adjacent to the Swan and Dolphin hotels at Walt Disney World.

Fantasia/2000 (film) A new generation of Disney animators showcase their talents as they visually interpret classical compositions. *Symphony No. 5* by Ludwig van Beethoven features abstract visions of color, shape, and light; Dmitri

Shostakovich's *Piano Concerto No. 2, Allegro, Opus 102* tells the Hans Christian Andersen fable of *The Steadfast Tin Soldier*, Ottorino Respighi's *Pines of Rome* tells the story of a pod of whales who can fly; Camille Saint-Saëns's *Carnival of the Animals, Finale* shows what can happen when you give a yo-yo to a flock of flamingos; Sir Edward Elgar's *Pomp and Circumstance, Marches 1, 2, 3, and 4* stars Donald Duck as an assistant on Noah's ark; George Gershwin's *Rhapsody in Blue* presents a stylized look at life in Manhattan during the Jazz Age; and Igor Stravinsky's *Firebird Suite (1919 version)* tells a tale of death and rebirth as a young sprite triumphantly awakens a ravaged forest. These new pieces are combined with one selection (*The Sorcerer's Apprentice*) from the 1940 classic. Premiered at Carnegie Hall in New York on December 15, 1999, had a New Year's Eve gala at the Pasadena Civic Auditorium, then opened in Imax theaters worldwide on January 1, 2000, for four months, with a general release on June 16. Supervising Director: Hendel Butoy. Segment Directors: Hendel Butoy, Francis Glebás, Eric Goldberg, Paul and Gaëtan Brizzi, Pixote Hunt, James Algar. Host sequences director: Don Hahn. The Chicago Symphony Orchestra, conducted by James Levine, provides the sound track. This film was a longtime pet project of Roy E. Disney, receiving his personal supervision. 74 min. Released on video in November 2000.

Fantasmic! Evening water show presented on the south end of Tom Sawyer Island at Disneyland, beginning May 13, 1992. Mickey Mouse appears and uses his magical powers to bring beloved characters to life in his imagination—until such classic Disney villains as Ursula and Maleficent threaten Mickey's fantasy world. To prepare for Fantasmic! the Rivers of America had to be drained to enable the installation of various mechanisms, and the mill and part of the south end of Tom Sawyer Island were removed so the rustic stage setting for the show could be built. (The mill was rebuilt in a new location.) Utilizing projections of film clips on three giant screens of mist, music, the *Mark Twain* and the *Columbia*, various rafts, mechanical figures, fire effects, and

50 Disneyland cast members in costume, the elaborate show was immediately more popular than had been expected. The audience, which has to line the shores of the Rivers of America, created initial major traffic jams on that side of Disneyland each evening. Guests would often stake out their places hours ahead of the show. To help solve some of the problems, the shore area was terraced to give more guests an unimpeded view. A new version of Fantasmic! opened in a new Hollywood Hills amphitheater at the Disney-MGM Studios at Walt Disney World on October 15, 1998.

Fantasound Innovative stereophonic sound system created for *Fantasia*.

Fantasy Faire Covered area, also known as Fantasyland Pavilion after January 1995, originally used for outdoor stage shows in Fantasyland in Magic Kingdom Park at Walt Disney World, and later for additional seating for the Pinocchio Village Haus. It closed in 1996.

Fantasy Gardens Area at Hong Kong Disneyland where guests can meet and greet Disney characters in five little garden buildings in a park-like setting; opened September 12, 2005.

Fantasy in the Sky Fireworks show at Disneyland that debuted in 1956. The fireworks are timed to coincide with the musical sound track being played throughout Disneyland. Tinker Bell began her nightly flights from the top of the Matterhorn and above Sleeping Beauty Castle in 1961 as part of the show. The Disneyland show was changed to *Believe . . . There's Magic in the Stars* for the park's 45th anniversary in February 2000. Walt Disney World Magic Kingdom Park had a Fantasy in the Sky fireworks show since 1971; it was changed to *Wishes: A Magical Gathering of Disney Dreams* in October 2003.

Fantasy on Parade Christmas parade at Disneyland, from 1965 to 1976 and 1980 to 1985. A long-running and much-awaited Disneyland holiday tradition, featuring over 350 performers. Superseded by the Very Merry Christmas Parade.

Fantasy on Skis (television) Television show; aired on February 4, 1962. Directed by Fred Iselin. A nine-year-old girl in Aspen dreams of winning a ski race and works hard to earn the money for new skis. She is almost killed in an avalanche, but is saved by her St. Bernard, Bruno, and she recovers in time for the race. A shortened, 28 min., version of the show was released theatrically on December 20, 1975, with *Snowball Express*.

Fantasyland One of the original lands of Disneyland, and called by Walt Disney the happiest land of all. The attractions are based on the classic Disney animated tales, so they evoke pleasant memories in the minds of many a guest. Fantasyland was built to look somewhat like a medieval fair, with banners and flags decorating the entrances to the attractions. The Snow White, Peter Pan, and Mr. Toad attractions were the park's original "dark rides," where participants sat in a vehicle and were moved through black-light illuminated scenes telling the stories of the films. One enters Fantasyland over a drawbridge and through Sleeping Beauty Castle. The attractions are seemingly in the Castle's courtyard. In the center is the majestic King Arthur Carrousel. A totally new Fantasyland opened at Disneyland on May 25, 1983. The attractions were all completely remodeled, with facades now themed to the locale and era of the films. Thus, the Mr. Toad attraction is now in Toad Hall, as opposed to a medieval circus tent. There are Fantasyland areas in all five of the Disney Magic Kingdoms.

Fantasyland Autopia Attraction at Disneyland; opened January 1, 1959, and closed September 7, 1999. Became Rescue Rangers Raceway from March to November 1991. This attraction was added to take some of the pressure off the Tomorrowland Autopia, which always had a long line. Its main difference was that you saw different scenery on your ride. The attraction was later combined as part of Tomorrowland Autopia in 2000.

Fantasyland, New See *Believe You Can . . . and You Can!*

Fantasyland Theater Theater at Disneyland that showed Disney cartoons, formerly Mickey Mouse Club Theater (1955–64); closed December 20, 1981, so that Pinocchio's Daring Journey could be built in its place. During the opening-day television show, the Mouseketeers streamed out of the theater at one point and were introduced to the television audience for the first time. This was several months before the *Mickey Mouse Club* television show went on the air. One fondly remembered highlight at the theater was the *3D Jamboree*, which played there beginning in June 1956 for several years. Besides two 3-D cartoons, it included specially filmed 3-D footage of the Mouseketeers. The name Fantasyland Theater was reused beginning June 23, 1995, for the former Videopolis.

Fantillusion Nighttime illuminated parade, which succeeded the Electrical Parade at Tokyo Disneyland, beginning July 21, 1995, and ending May 15, 2001. It was also presented at Disneyland Paris, beginning July 5, 2003.

Fantini, T.J. Actor; appeared on the *Mickey Mouse Club* on The Disney Channel, beginning in 1993.

Far Off Place, A (film) When an attack by an elephant poacher on her African home leaves a teenage girl, Nonnie Parker, and her visiting friend, Harry Winslow, orphaned, the two teenagers set off to find the one man who can help them—Colonel Mopani Theron, who leads an antipoaching squad. With the help of a native Bushman, Xhabbo, they set out on a 1,000-mile trek across the Kalahari desert. Many dangers await them there, not the least being the hostile climate, but by sheer determination and courage they reach safety and are able to get their revenge on the poachers. Released on March 12, 1993. Directed by Mikael Salomon. 107 min. Stars Reese Witherspoon (Nonnie Parker), Ethan Randall (Harry Winslow), Jack Thompson (John Ricketts), Maximilian Schell (Col. Mopani Theron), Sarel Bok (Xhabbo). Filmed in Zimbabwe and the Namib desert. Released on video in 1993.

Faraway Places—High, Hot and Wet (television) Television show; aired on January 1, 1958. Herbert and Trudie Knapp take photo assignments in the Andes mountain range in Peru, on the Fiji Islands, and in Siam. The People and Places featurette *Siam* is shown. Narrated by Winston Hibler.

Farmer, Bill Voice actor, the current voice of Goofy.

Farmers Market Food court area in The Land at Epcot, from October 1, 1982 to October 25, 1993. Became Sunshine Season Food Fair in 1993.

Farmyard Symphony (film) Silly Symphony cartoon; released on October 14, 1938. The first cartoon directed by Jack Cutting. A farmyard musical set to familiar classical themes, including Franz Liszt's *Hungarian Rhapsody*, is led by a rooster and pullet with all the other animals participating.

Farnsworth, Richard (1920–2000) Actor; appeared in *The Straight Story* (Alvin Straight), for which he received an Academy Award nomination for Best Actor, as well as on television in *The Cherokee Trail* (Ridge Fenton), *High-Flying Spy* (Farmer), and on the Disney Channel in *Good Old Boy* (Grandpa Percy).

Farrow, Mia Actress; appeared in *New York Stories* (Lisa), *Miami Rhapsody* (Nina), and on television in *Miracle at Midnight* (Doris Koster). She provided the voice of Doris in *Redux Riding Hood*.

FastPass An innovation at the Disney parks, whereby guests can pick up a pass that designates

a specific time for them to return and board an attraction without waiting in lengthy queues. After initial tests, the pass was first introduced for the most popular Animal Kingdom attractions in July 1999, and soon was used at major attractions in the other Walt Disney World parks. It was first offered at Disneyland Paris at Indiana Jones et le Temple de Péril on October 2, 1999, and at Disneyland at "it's a small world" on November 19, 1999.

Fat Cat Villain character in *Chip 'n' Dale's Rescue Rangers*; voiced by Jim Cummings.

Father Hood (film) Jack Charles is a small-time hood who plans to travel cross-country to New Orleans to participate in a criminal heist that will set him up for life, but his daughter, Kelly, shows up and his plans are endangered. Kelly and her little brother Eddie had long ago been abandoned to foster care, and the abuse they received there warranted Kelly's escape. Jack reluctantly rescues Eddie too and plans to leave them with their grandmother, Rita. But Rita has her own life of gambling to live, and tells Jack to own up to his responsibilities as a father. As the trio makes its way across the country, pursued by the police and the FBI, Jack learns what it takes to raise children. By the time they reach New Orleans, he is ready to sacrifice his criminal activity for his children's welfare. Released on August 27, 1993. Directed by Darrell James Roodt. A Hollywood Picture. 95 min. Stars Patrick Swayze (Jack Charles), Halle Berry (Kathleen Mercer), Diane Ladd (Rita), Sabrina Lloyd (Kelly Charles), Brian Bonsall (Eddie Charles). Filmed in Texas, Louisiana, Arizona, and California. Released on video in 1994.

Father Noah's Ark (film) Silly Symphony cartoon; released on April 8, 1933. Directed by Wilfred Jackson. The first Disney version of the Biblical tale of Noah, his ark, and its inhabitants, along with their efforts to weather the great flood. There is also a 1959 stop-motion version (*Noah's Ark*).

Father of the Bride (film) After 22 years of being a father to his little girl, Annie, George Banks finds it hard to cope with the fact that she is grown up and ready to marry. He is unable to warm up to his future son-in-law, Bryan MacKenzie, and grumbles every step of the way as their wedding is planned. A flamboyant wedding adviser named Franck only makes matters worse. Eventually the wedding is held and George accepts the new couple. Released on December 20, 1991. Directed by Charles Shyer. A Touchstone Pictures. 105 min. Stars Steve Martin (George Banks), Diane Keaton (Nina Banks), Kimberly Williams (Annie Banks), Martin Short (Franck Eggelhoffer), George Newbern (Bryan MacKenzie). Based on the novel by Edward Streeter; a remake of an MGM motion picture from 1950 that had starred Spencer Tracy, Elizabeth Taylor, and Joan Bennett. The house exterior was filmed in Pasadena, California, with the wedding scene filmed in the Trinity Baptist Church in Santa Monica. The character name of George Banks is coincidentally the same as that of the father in *Mary Poppins*. Released on video in 1992.

Father of the Bride, Part II (film) After George Banks has finally recovered from his daughter's wedding, he receives a double shock. First his daughter announces that he is going to be a grandfather, and then his own wife announces that she also is pregnant. George feels that he is much too young to be a grandfather, and way too old to be a father again. Coming along to coordinate a double baby shower is Franck Eggelhoffer, who had arranged the daughter's wedding. Directed by Charles Shyer. A Touchstone Picture. Released on December 8, 1995. Stars Steve Martin (George), Diane Keaton (Nina), Kimberly Williams (Annie), George Newbern (Bryan), Kieran Culkin (Matty), Martin Short (Franck). 106 min. Sequel to the 1991 film *Father of the Bride*. The production filmed at an Eastern Colonial–style house in Pasadena, California. Released on video in 1996.

Fathers Are People (film) Goofy cartoon; released on October 21, 1951. Directed by Jack Kinney. Goofy experiences the trials and tribulations of fatherhood, with Junior always coming out ahead in each situation.

Father's Day Off (film) Goofy cartoon; released on March 28, 1953. Directed by Jack Kinney. Goofy takes over the household chores when his wife goes out but he gets so completely confused that the house is a shambles and on fire when she returns.

Father's Lion (film) Goofy cartoon; released on January 4, 1952. Directed by Jack Kinney. Goofy and his son go on a camping trip, and in the midst of Goofy's tall tales about himself as a great adventurer, they encounter a mountain lion.

Father's Week End (film) Goofy cartoon; released on June 20, 1953. Directed by Jack Kinney. Goofy runs his life by the clock all week and relaxes on Sunday, but he has such a frantic day with his son at the beach that he is delighted to go back to work to rest up from his day of rest.

Fauna Good fairy in *Sleeping Beauty* who wore green; voiced by Barbara Jo Allen.

Faylen, Frank (1907–1985) Actor; appeared in *The Reluctant Dragon* (orchestra leader) and *The Monkey's Uncle* (Mr. Dearborne).

Feast of July (film) Bella Ford is a young woman setting forth in winter on an arduous journey to locate Arch Wilson, the lover who abandoned her. Suffering a grave personal misfortune along the way, she finds shelter in the home of the Wainwright family whose three sons, Jedd, Con, and Matty, eventually battle among each other for the affections of their enchanting and mysterious guest. After much courtship, Bella agrees to marry the middle son, Con, but tragedy strikes again when the man for whom she has been searching reappears, triggering a series of dramatic events that will forever change the lives of all concerned. Directed by Christopher Menaul. Touchstone Pictures presents a Merchant Ivory Production in association with Peregrine Productions. Limited release in New York, Los Angeles, and Montreal on October 13, 1995; wider release on October 20. Stars Embeth Davidtz (Bella Ford), Greg Wise (Arch Wilson), James Purefoy (Jedd Wainwright), Kenneth Anderson (Matty Wainwright), Ben Chaplin (Con Wainwright), Tom Bell (Ben Wainwright), Gemma Jones (Mrs. Wainwright). Filmed in CinemaScope. 118 min. With the story set in Victorian England, the producers had to search throughout the country for appropriate settings before settling on Brecon in Wales, Ironbridge and Dudley's Black Country Museum in the Midlands, and Porlock Weir in Devon. Released on video in 1996.

Feather Farm, The (television) Television show; aired on October 26, 1969. Ostrich raising in 1915 is not as easy as it seems, as a Boston matron and her niece sadly discover. They almost lose their investment as the ostriches run away, but the hired men finally find them. Stars Nick Nolte, Mel Weiser, Christine Coates, Shirley Fabricant. Narrated by Rex Allen.

Feather in His Collar, A (film) Commercial starring Pluto made for the Community Chests of America; delivered on August 7, 1946. Pluto is awarded a Red Feather for giving his life savings of bones to a Community Chest campaign.

Feature Animation The new name given to the Disney animation department in the 1980s to differentiate it from Television Animation. Walt Disney Feature Animation creates the Disney animated feature films, and is headquartered at the Disney Studio in Burbank, based in a new building occupied in late 1994. A division of Feature Animation opened at Disney-MGM Studios at Walt Disney World in 1989 and closed in 2004. A Feature Animation Studio opened in France in 1994, taking over Brizzi Films, which had worked on Disney television projects since 1989. It closed in 2003. There was a Disney animation studio in Tokyo, Japan, working primarily on television and video productions, from 1989 to 2004.

Feature film A full-length film, live-action or animated, normally over sixty minutes in length. *Snow White and the Seven Dwarfs* was the first Disney feature, in 1937. One exception to the general rule of length is *Saludos Amigos*, which at 42 minutes is still considered one of the Disney

Animated Classic Features. The complete list is as follows:

1. 1937 *Snow White and the Seven Dwarfs* (G)
2. 1940 *Pinocchio* (G)
3. 1940 *Fantasia* (G)
4. 1941 *The Reluctant Dragon*
5. 1941 *Dumbo* (G)
6. 1942 *Bambi* (G)
7. 1943 *Saludos Amigos*
8. 1943 *Victory Through Air Power*
9. 1945 *The Three Caballeros* (G)
10. 1946 *Make Mine Music*
11. 1946 *Song of the South* (G)
12. 1947 *Fun and Fancy Free*
13. 1948 *Melody Time*
14. 1949 *So Dear to My Heart* (G)
15. 1949 *The Adventures of Ichabod and Mr. Toad* (G)
16. 1950 *Cinderella* (G)
17. 1950 *Treasure Island* (PG)
18. 1951 *Alice in Wonderland* (G)
19. 1952 *The Story of Robin Hood and His Merrie Men* (PG)
20. 1953 *Peter Pan* (G)
21. 1953 *The Sword and the Rose* (PG)
22. 1953 *The Living Desert*
23. 1954 *Rob Roy, the Highland Rogue*
24. 1954 *The Vanishing Prairie*
25. 1954 *20,000 Leagues Under the Sea* (G)
26. 1955 *Davy Crockett, King of the Wild Frontier* (PG)
27. 1955 *Lady and the Tramp* (G)
28. 1955 *The African Lion*
29. 1955 *The Littlest Outlaw*
30. 1956 *The Great Locomotive Chase*
31. 1956 *Davy Crockett and the River Pirates*
32. 1956 *Secrets of Life*
33. 1956 *Westward Ho the Wagons!*
34. 1957 *Johnny Tremain*
35. 1957 *Perri* (G)
36. 1957 *Old Yeller* (G)
37. 1958 *The Light in the Forest*
38. 1958 *White Wilderness*
39. 1958 *Tonka*
40. 1959 *Sleeping Beauty* (G)
41. 1959 *The Shaggy Dog* (G)
42. 1959 *Darby O'Gill and the Little People* (G)
43. 1959 *Third Man on the Mountain* (G)
44. 1960 *Toby Tyler, or Ten Weeks with a Circus* (G)
45. 1960 *Kidnapped*
46. 1960 *Pollyanna* (G)
47. 1960 *The Sign of Zorro*
48. 1960 *Jungle Cat*
49. 1960 *Ten Who Dared*
50. 1960 *Swiss Family Robinson* (G)
51. 1961 *One Hundred and One Dalmatians* (G)
52. 1961 *The Absent-Minded Professor* (G)
53. 1961 *The Parent Trap*
54. 1961 *Nikki, Wild Dog of the North* (G)
55. 1961 *Greyfriars Bobby*
56. 1961 *Babes in Toyland*
57. 1962 *Moon Pilot*
58. 1962 *Bon Voyage*
59. 1962 *Big Red*
60. 1962 *Almost Angels*
61. 1962 *The Legend of Lobo* (G)
62. 1962 *In Search of the Castaways* (G)
63. 1963 *Son of Flubber* (G)
64. 1963 *Miracle of the White Stallions*
65. 1963 *Savage Sam*
66. 1963 *Summer Magic*
67. 1963 *The Incredible Journey* (G)
68. 1963 *The Sword in the Stone* (G)
69. 1963 *The Three Lives of Thomasina* (PG)
70. 1964 *The Misadventures of Merlin Jones* (G)
71. 1964 *A Tiger Walks*
72. 1964 *The Moon-Spinners* (PG)
73. 1964 *Mary Poppins* (G)
74. 1964 *Emil and the Detectives*
75. 1965 *Those Calloways* (PG)
76. 1965 *The Monkey's Uncle*
77. 1965 *That Darn Cat!* (G)
78. 1966 *The Ugly Dachshund*
79. 1966 *Lt. Robin Crusoe U.S.N.* (G)
80. 1966 *The Fighting Prince of Donegal*
81. 1966 *Follow Me, Boys!* (G)
82. 1967 *Monkeys, Go Home!*
83. 1967 *The Adventures of Bullwhip Griffin*
84. 1967 *The Happiest Millionaire* (G)

85. 1967 *The Gnome-Mobile* (G)
86. 1967 *The Jungle Book* (G)
87. 1967 *Charlie, The Lonesome Cougar*
88. 1968 *Blackbeard's Ghost* (G)
89. 1968 *The One and Only, Genuine, Original Family Band*
90. 1968 *Never a Dull Moment* (G)
91. 1968 *The Horse in the Gray Flannel Suit*
92. 1969 *The Love Bug* (G)
93. 1969 *Smith!*
94. 1969 *Rascal*
95. 1969 *The Computer Wore Tennis Shoes*
96. 1970 *King of the Grizzlies* (G)
97. 1970 *The Boatniks* (G)
98. 1970 *The Aristocats* (G)
99. 1971 *The Wild Country* (G)
100. 1971 *The Barefoot Executive* (G)
101. 1971 *Scandalous John* (G)
102. 1971 *The Million Dollar Duck* (G)
103. 1971 *Bedknobs and Broomsticks* (G)
104. 1972 *The Biscuit Eater* (G)
105. 1972 *Napoleon and Samantha* (G)
106. 1972 *Now You See Him, Now You Don't* (G)
107. 1972 *Run, Cougar, Run* (G)
108. 1972 *Snowball Express* (G)
109. 1973 *The World's Greatest Athlete* (G)
110. 1973 *Charley and the Angel* (G)
111. 1973 *One Little Indian* (G)
112. 1973 *Robin Hood* (G)
113. 1973 *Superdad* (G)
114. 1974 *Herbie Rides Again* (G)
115. 1974 *The Bears and I* (G)
116. 1974 *The Castaway Cowboy* (G)
117. 1974 *The Island at the Top of the World* (G)
118. 1975 *The Strongest Man in the World* (G)
119. 1975 *Escape to Witch Mountain* (G)
120. 1975 *The Apple Dumpling Gang* (G)
121. 1975 *One of Our Dinosaurs Is Missing* (G)
122. 1975 *The Best of Walt Disney's True-Life Adventures* (G)
123. 1976 *Ride a Wild Pony* (G)
124. 1976 *No Deposit, No Return* (G)
125. 1976 *Gus* (G)
126. 1976 *Treasure of Matecumbe* (G)
127. 1976 *The Shaggy D.A.* (G)
128. 1977 *Freaky Friday* (G)
129. 1977 *The Littlest Horse Thieves* (G)
130. 1977 *The Many Adventures of Winnie the Pooh* (G)
131. 1977 *The Rescuers* (G)
132. 1977 *Herbie Goes to Monte Carlo* (G)
133. 1977 *Pete's Dragon* (G)
134. 1978 *Candleshoe* (G)
135. 1978 *Return from Witch Mountain* (G)
136. 1978 *The Cat from Outer Space* (G)
137. 1978 *Hot Lead and Cold Feet* (G)
138. 1979 *The North Avenue Irregulars* (G)
139. 1979 *The Apple Dumpling Gang Rides Again* (G)
140. 1979 *Unidentified Flying Oddball* (G)
141. 1979 *The Black Hole* (PG)
142. 1980 *Midnight Madness* (PG)
143. 1980 *The Last Flight of Noah's Ark* (G)
144. 1980 *Herbie Goes Bananas* (G)
145. 1981 *The Devil and Max Devlin* (PG)
146. 1981 *Amy* (G)
147. 1981 *The Fox and the Hound* (G)
148. 1981 *Condorman* (PG)
149. 1981 *The Watcher in the Woods* (PG)
150. 1982 *Night Crossing* (PG)
151. 1982 *Tron* (PG)
152. 1982 *Tex* (PG)
153. 1983 *Trenchcoat* (PG)
154. 1983 *Something Wicked This Way Comes* (PG)
155. 1983 *Never Cry Wolf* (PG)
156. 1984 *Splash* (Touchstone) (PG)
157. 1984 *Tiger Town* (G)
158. 1984 *Country* (Touchstone) (PG)
159. 1985 *Baby . . . Secret of the Lost Legend* (Touchstone) (PG)
160. 1985 *Return to Oz* (PG)
161. 1985 *The Black Cauldron* (PG)
162. 1985 *My Science Project* (Touchstone) (PG)
163. 1985 *The Journey of Natty Gann* (PG)
164. 1985 *One Magic Christmas* (G)
165. 1986 *Down and Out in Beverly Hills* (Touchstone) (R)
166. 1986 *Off Beat* (Touchstone) (R)
167. 1986 *Ruthless People* (Touchstone) (R)
168. 1986 *The Great Mouse Detective* (G)
169. 1986 *Flight of the Navigator* (PG)
170. 1986 *Tough Guys* (Touchstone) (PG)

171. 1986 *The Color of Money* (Touchstone) (R)
172. 1987 *Outrageous Fortune* (Touchstone) (R)
173. 1987 *Tin Men* (Touchstone) (R)
174. 1987 *Ernest Goes to Camp* (Touchstone) (PG)
175. 1987 *Benji the Hunted* (G)
176. 1987 *Adventures in Babysitting* (Touchstone) (PG-13)
177. 1987 *Stakeout* (Touchstone) (R)
178. 1987 *Can't Buy Me Love* (Touchstone) (PG-13)
179. 1987 *Hello Again* (Touchstone) (PG)
180. 1987 *Three Men and a Baby* (Touchstone) (PG)
181. 1987 *Good Morning, Vietnam* (Touchstone) (R)
182. 1988 *Shoot to Kill* (Touchstone) (R)
183. 1988 *D.O.A.* (Touchstone) (R)
184. 1988 *Return to Snowy River* (PG)
185. 1988 *Big Business* (Touchstone) (PG)
186. 1988 *Who Framed Roger Rabbit* (Touchstone) (PG)
187. 1988 *Cocktail* (Touchstone) (R)
188. 1988 *The Rescue* (Touchstone) (PG)
189. 1988 *Heartbreak Hotel* (Touchstone) (PG-13)
190. 1988 *The Good Mother* (Touchstone) (R)
191. 1988 *Ernest Saves Christmas* (Touchstone) (PG)
192. 1988 *Oliver & Company* (G)
193. 1988 *Beaches* (Touchstone) (PG-13)
194. 1989 *Three Fugitives* (Touchstone) (PG-13)
195. 1989 *New York Stories* (Touchstone) (PG)
196. 1989 *Disorganized Crime* (Touchstone) (R)
197. 1989 *Dead Poets Society* (Touchstone) (PG)
198. 1989 *Honey, I Shrunk the Kids* (PG)
199. 1989 *Turner & Hooch* (Touchstone) (PG)
200. 1989 *Cheetah* (G)
201. 1989 *An Innocent Man* (Touchstone) (R)
202. 1989 *Gross Anatomy* (Touchstone) (PG-13)
203. 1989 *The Little Mermaid* (G)
204. 1989 *Blaze* (Touchstone) (R)
205. 1990 *Stella* (Touchstone) (PG-13)
206. 1990 *Where the Heart Is* (Touchstone) (R)
207. 1990 *Pretty Woman* (Touchstone) (R)
208. 1990 *Ernest Goes to Jail* (Touchstone) (PG)
209. 1990 *Spaced Invaders* (Touchstone) (PG)
210. 1990 *Fire Birds* (Touchstone) (PG-13)
211. 1990 *Dick Tracy* (Touchstone) (PG)
212. 1990 *Betsy's Wedding* (Touchstone) (R)
213. 1990 *Arachnophobia* (Hollywood Pictures) (PG-13)
214. 1990 *Ducktales: the Movie, Treasure of the Lost Lamp* (Disney Movietoons) (G)
215. 1990 *Taking Care of Business* (Hollywood Pictures) (R)
216. 1990 *Mr. Destiny* (Touchstone) (PG-13)
217. 1990 *The Rescuers Down Under* (G)
218. 1990 *Three Men and a Little Lady* (Touchstone) (PG)
219. 1990 *Green Card* (Touchstone) (PG-13)
220. 1991 *White Fang* (PG)
221. 1991 *Run* (Hollywood Pictures) (R)
222. 1991 *Scenes from a Mall* (Touchstone) (R)
223. 1991 *Shipwrecked* (PG)
224. 1991 *The Marrying Man* (Hollywood Pictures) (R)
225. 1991 *Oscar* (Touchstone) (PG)
226. 1991 *One Good Cop* (Hollywood Pictures) (R)
227. 1991 *What About Bob?* (Touchstone) (PG)
228. 1991 *Wild Hearts Can't Be Broken* (G)
229. 1991 *The Rocketeer* (PG)
230. 1991 *The Doctor* (Touchstone) (PG-13)
231. 1991 *V. I. Warshawski* (Hollywood Pictures) (R)
232. 1991 *True Identity* (Touchstone) (R)
233. 1991 *Paradise* (Touchstone) (PG-13)
234. 1991 *Deceived* (Touchstone) (PG-13)
235. 1991 *Ernest Scared Stupid* (Touchstone) (PG)
236. 1991 *Billy Bathgate* (Touchstone) (R)
237. 1991 *Beauty and the Beast* (G)

238. 1991 *Father of the Bride*
(Touchstone) (PG)

239. 1992 *The Hand That Rocks the Cradle*
(Hollywood Pictures) (R)

240. 1992 *Medicine Man* (Hollywood
Pictures) (PG-13)

241. 1992 *Blame It on the Bellboy*
(Hollywood Pictures) (PG-13)

242. 1992 *Noises Off* (Touchstone) (PG-13)

243. 1992 *Straight Talk* (Hollywood
Pictures) (PG)

244. 1992 *Newsies* (PG)

245. 1992 *Passed Away* (Hollywood
Pictures) (PG-13)

246. 1992 *Encino Man* (Hollywood
Pictures) (PG)

247. 1992 *Sister Act* (Touchstone) (PG)

248. 1992 *Honey, I Blew Up the Kid* (PG)

249. 1992 *A Stranger Among Us* (Hollywood
Pictures) (PG-13)

250. 1992 *Ninjas* (Touchstone) (PG)

251. 1992 *The Gun in Betty Lou's Handbag*
(Touchstone) (PG-13)

252. 1992 *Crossing the Bridge*
(Touchstone) (R)

253. 1992 *Sarafina!* (Hollywood
Pictures) (PG-13)

254. 1992 *Captain Ron* (Touchstone) (PG-13)

255. 1992 *The Mighty Ducks* (PG)

256. 1992 *Consenting Adults* (Hollywood
Pictures) (R)

257. 1992 *Aladdin* (G)

258. 1992 *The Distinguished Gentleman*
(Hollywood Pictures) (R)

259. 1992 *The Muppet Christmas Carol* (G)

260. 1993 *Alive* (Touchstone) (R)

261. 1993 *Aspen Extreme* (Hollywood
Pictures) (PG-13)

262. 1993 *The Cemetery Club*
(Touchstone) (PG-13)

263. 1993 *Homeward Bound:
The Incredible Journey* (G)

264. 1993 *Swing Kids* (Hollywood
Pictures) (PG-13)

265. 1993 *A Far Off Place* (PG)

266. 1993 *Born Yesterday* (Hollywood
Pictures) (PG)

267. 1993 *Adventures of Huck Finn* (PG)

268. 1993 *Indian Summer*
(Touchstone) (PG-13)

269. 1993 *Bound by Honor* (Hollywood
Pictures) (R)

270. 1993 *Super Mario Bros.* (Hollywood
Pictures) (PG)

271. 1993 *Guilty as Sin* (Hollywood
Pictures) (R)

272. 1993 *Life with Mikey* (Touchstone) (PG)

273. 1993 *What's Love Got to Do with It*
(Touchstone) (R)

274. 1993 *Son-In-Law* (Hollywood Pictures)
(PG-13)

275. 1993 *Hocus Pocus* (PG)

276. 1993 *Another Stakeout*
(Touchstone) (PG-13)

277. 1993 *My Boyfriend's Back*
(Touchstone) (PG-13)

278. 1993 *Father Hood* (Hollywood
Pictures) (PG-13)

279. 1993 *The Joy Luck Club* (Hollywood
Pictures) (R)

280. 1993 *Money for Nothing* (Hollywood
Pictures) (R)

281. 1993 *The Program* (Touchstone) (R)

282. 1993 *Cool Runnings* (PG)

283. 1993 *Tim Burton's The Nightmare
Before Christmas* (Touchstone) (PG)

284. 1993 *The Three Musketeers* (PG)

285. 1993 *Sister Act 2: Back in the Habit*
(Touchstone) (PG)

286. 1993 *Tombstone* (Hollywood
Pictures) (R)

287. 1994 *Cabin Boy* (Touchstone) (PG-13)

288. 1994 *The Air Up There* (Hollywood
Pictures) (PG)

289. 1994 *Iron Will* (PG)

290. 1994 *My Father the Hero*
(Touchstone) (PG)

291. 1994 *Blank Check* (PG)

292. 1994 *Angie* (Hollywood Pictures) (R)

293. 1994 *The Ref* (Touchstone) (R)

294. 1994 *D2: The Mighty Ducks* (PG)

295. 1994 *Holy Matrimony* (Hollywood
Pictures) (PG-13)

296. 1994 *White Fang 2: The Myth of the
White Wolf* (PG)

297. 1994 *The Inkwell* (Touchstone) (R)

298. 1994 *When a Man Loves a Woman* (Touchstone) (R)
299. 1994 *Renaissance Man* (Touchstone) (PG-13)
300. 1994 *The Lion King* (G)
301. 1994 *I Love Trouble* (Touchstone) (PG)
302. 1994 *Angels in the Outfield* (PG)
303. 1994 *In the Army Now* (Hollywood Pictures) (PG)
304. 1994 *Color of Night* (Hollywood Pictures) (R)
305. 1994 *It's Pat* (Touchstone) (PG-13)
306. 1994 *Camp Nowhere* (Hollywood Pictures) (PG)
307. 1994 *A Simple Twist of Fate* (Touchstone) (PG-13)
308. 1994 *Quiz Show* (Hollywood) (PG-13)
309. 1994 *Terminal Velocity* (Hollywood Pictures) (PG-13)
310. 1994 *Ed Wood* (Touchstone) (R)
311. 1994 *Robert A. Heinlein's The Puppet Masters* (Hollywood Pictures) (R)
312. 1994 *Squanto: A Warrior's Tale* (PG)
313. 1994 *The Santa Clause* (PG)
314. 1994 *A Low Down Dirty Shame* (Hollywood Pictures) (R)
315. 1994 *Rudyard Kipling's The Jungle Book* (PG)
316. 1995 *Houseguest* (Hollywood Pictures) (PG)
317. 1995 *Bad Company* (Touchstone) (R)
318. 1995 *Miami Rhapsody* (Hollywood Pictures) (PG-13)
319. 1995 *The Jerky Boys* (Touchstone) (R)
320. 1995 *Heavyweights* (PG)
321. 1995 *Man of the House* (PG)
322. 1995 *Roommates* (Hollywood Pictures) (PG)
323. 1995 *Tall Tale* (PG)
324. 1995 *Funny Bones* (Hollywood Pictures) (R)
325. 1995 *Jefferson in Paris* (Touchstone) (PG-13)
326. 1995 *A Goofy Movie* (G)
327. 1995 *While You Were Sleeping* (Hollywood Pictures) (PG)
328. 1995 *A Pyromaniac's Love Story* (Hollywood Pictures) (PG)

329. 1995 *Crimson Tide* (Hollywood Pictures) (R)
330. 1995 *Mad Love* (Touchstone) (PG-13)
331. 1995 *Pocahontas* (G)
332. 1995 *Judge Dredd* (Hollywood Pictures) (R)
333. 1995 *Operation Dumbo Drop* (PG)
334. 1995 *Dangerous Minds* (Hollywood Pictures) (R)
335. 1995 *A Kid in King Arthur's Court* (PG)
336. 1995 *The Tie that Binds* (Hollywood Pictures) (R)
337. 1995 *Unstrung Heroes* (Hollywood Pictures) (PG)
338. 1995 *The Big Green* (PG)
339. 1995 *Dead Presidents* (Hollywood Pictures) (R)
340. 1995 *Feast of July* (Touchstone) (R)
341. 1995 *The Scarlet Letter* (Hollywood Pictures) (R)
342. 1995 *Frank and Ollie* (PG)
343. 1995 *Powder* (Hollywood Pictures) (PG-13)
344. 1995 *Toy Story* (G)
345. 1995 *Father of the Bride, Part II* (Touchstone) (PG)
346. 1995 *Nixon* (Hollywood Pictures) (R)
347. 1995 *Tom and Huck* (PG)
348. 1996 *Mr. Holland's Opus* (Hollywood Pictures) (PG)
349. 1996 *White Squall* (Hollywood Pictures) (PG-13)
350. 1996 *Mr. Wrong* (Touchstone) (PG-13)
351. 1996 *Muppet Treasure Island* (G)
352. 1996 *Before and After* (Hollywood Pictures) (PG-13)
353. 1996 *Up Close and Personal* (Touchstone) (PG-13)
354. 1996 *Homeward Bound II: Lost in San Francisco* (G)
355. 1996 *Two Much* (Touchstone) (PG-13)
356. 1996 *Little Indian, Big City* (Touchstone) (PG)
357. 1996 *James and the Giant Peach* (PG)
358. 1996 *Celtic Pride* (Hollywood Pictures) (PG-13)
359. 1996 *Last Dance* (Touchstone) (R)
360. 1996 *Boys* (Touchstone) (PG-13)

361. 1996 *Spy Hard* (Hollywood Pictures) (PG-13)
362. 1996 *Eddie* (Hollywood Pictures) (PG-13)
363. 1996 *The Rock* (Hollywood Pictures) (R)
364. 1996 *The Hunchback of Notre Dame* (G)
365. 1996 *Phenomenon* (Touchstone) (PG)
366. 1996 *Kazaam* (Touchstone) (PG)
367. 1996 *Jack* (Hollywood Pictures) (PG-13)
368. 1966 *First Kid* (PG)
369. 1966 *The Rich Man's Wife* (Hollywood Pictures) (R)
370. 1996 *D3: The Mighty Ducks* (PG)
371. 1996 *The Associate* (Hollywood Pictures) (PG-13)
372. 1996 *Ransom* (Touchstone) (R)
373. 1996 *The War at Home* (Touchstone) (R)
374. 1996 *101 Dalmatians* [live action](G)
375. 1996 *The Preacher's Wife* (Touchstone) (PG)
376. 1997 *Evita* (Hollywood Pictures) (PG)
377. 1997 *Metro* (Touchstone) (R)
378. 1997 *Prefontaine* (Hollywood Pictures) (PG-13)
379. 1997 *Shadow Conspiracy* (Hollywood Pictures) (R)
380. 1997 *That Darn Cat* [remake](PG)
381. 1997 *Jungle 2 Jungle* (PG)
382. 1997 *The Sixth Man* (Touchstone) (PG-13)
383. 1997 *Grosse Pointe Blank* (Hollywood Pictures) (R)
384. 1997 *Romy and Michele's High School Reunion* (Touchstone) (R)
385. 1997 *Gone Fishin'* (Hollywood Pictures) (PG)
386. 1997 *Con Air* (Touchstone) (R)
387. 1997 *Hercules* (G)
388. 1997 *George of the Jungle* (PG)
389. 1997 *Nothing to Lose* (Touchstone) (R)
390. 1997 *Air Bud* (PG)
391. 1997 *G.I. Jane* (Hollywood Pictures) (R)
392. 1997 *A Thousand Acres* (Touchstone) (R)
393. 1997 *Washington Square* (Hollywood Pictures) (PG)
394. 1997 *RocketMan* (PG)
395. 1997 *Playing God* (Touchstone) (R)
396. 1997 *Flubber* (PG)

397. 1997 *An American Werewolf in Paris* (Hollywood Pictures) (R)
398. 1997 *Mr. Magoo* (PG)
399. 1998 *Kundun* (Touchstone) (PG-13)
400. 1998 *Deep Rising* (Hollywood Pictures) (R)
401. 1998 *Krippendorf's Tribe* (Touchstone) (PG-13)
402. 1998 *An Alan Smithee Film: Burn, Hollywood, Burn* (Hollywood Pictures) (R)
403. 1998 *Meet the Deedles* (PG)
404. 1998 *He Got Game* (Touchstone) (R)
405. 1998 *The Horse Whisperer* (Touchstone) (PG-13)
406. 1998 *Six Days, Seven Nights* (Touchstone) (PG-13)
407. 1998 *Mulan* (G)
408. 1998 *Armageddon* (Touchstone) (PG-13)
409. 1998 *Jane Austen's Mafia!* (Touchstone) (PG-13)
410. 1998 *The Parent Trap* (PG)
411. 1998 *Firelight* (Hollywood Pictures) (R)
412. 1998 *Simon Birch* (Hollywood Pictures) (PG)
413. 1998 *Holy Man* (Touchstone) (PG)
414. 1998 *Beloved* (Touchstone) (R)
415. 1998 *The Waterboy* (Touchstone) (PG-13)
416. 1998 *I'll Be Home for Christmas* (PG)
417. 1998 *Enemy of the State* (Touchstone) (R)
418. 1998 *a bug's life* (G)
419. 1998 *Mighty Joe Young* (PG)
420. 1999 *A Civil Action* (Touchstone) (PG-13)
421. 1999 *Rushmore* (Touchstone) (R)
422. 1999 *My Favorite Martian* (PG)
423. 1999 *The Other Sister* (Touchstone) (PG-13)
424. 1999 *Doug's 1st Movie* (G)
425. 1999 *10 Things I Hate About You* (Touchstone) (PG-13)
426. 1999 *Endurance* (G)
427. 1999 *Instinct* (Touchstone) (R)
428. 1999 *Tarzan* (G)
429. 1999 *Summer of Sam* (Touchstone) (R)
430. 1999 *Inspector Gadget* (PG)
431. 1999 *The Sixth Sense* (Hollywood) (PG-13)

432. 1999 *The 13th Warrior* (Touchstone) (R)
433. 1999 *Breakfast of Champions* (Hollywood) (R)
434. 1999 *Mumford* (Touchstone) (R)
435. 1999 *Mystery Alaska* (Hollywood) (R)
436. 1999 *The Hand Behind the Mouse: The Ub Iwerks Story* (G)
437. 1999 *The Straight Story* (G)
438. 1999 *The Insider* (Touchstone) (R)
439. 1999 *Toy Story 2* (G)
440. 1999 *Deuce Bigalow: Male Gigolo* (Touchstone) (R)
441. 1999 *Cradle Will Rock* (Touchstone) (R)
442. 1999 *Bicentennial Man* (Touchstone) (PG)
443. 2000 *Fantasia/2000* (G)
444. 2000 *Play It to the Bone* (Touchstone) (R)
445. 2000 *Gun Shy* (Hollywood) (R)
446. 2000 *The Tigger Movie* (G)
447. 2000 *Mission to Mars* (Touchstone) (PG)
448. 2000 *Whispers* (G)
449. 2000 *High Fidelity* (Touchstone) (R)
450. 2000 *Keeping the Faith* (Touchstone) (PG-13)
451. 2000 *Dinosaur* (PG)
452. 2000 *Shanghai Noon* (Touchstone) (PG-13)
453. 2000 *Gone in 60 Seconds* (Touchstone) (PG-13)
454. 2000 *Disney's The Kid* (PG)
455. 2000 *Coyote Ugly* (Touchstone) (PG-13)
456. 2000 *The Crew* (Touchstone) (PG-13)
457. 2000 *Duets* (Hollywood) (R)
458. 2000 *Remember the Titans* (PG)
459. 2000 *Playing Mona Lisa* (no label) (R)
460. 2000 *Unbreakable* (Touchstone) (PG-13)
461. 2000 *102 Dalmatians* (G)
462. 2000 *The Emperor's New Groove* (G)
463. 2000 *O Brother, Where Art Thou?* (Touchstone) (PG-13)
464. 2001 *Double Take* (Touchstone) (PG-13)
465. 2001 *Recess: School's Out* (G)
466. 2001 *Just Visiting* (Hollywood) (PG-13)
467. 2001 *Pearl Harbor* (Touchstone) (PG-13)
468. 2001 *Atlantis: The Lost Empire* (PG)
469. 2001 *crazy/beautiful* (Touchstone) (PG-13)
470. 2001 *The Princess Diaries* (G)
471. 2001 *Bubble Boy* (Touchstone) (PG-13)
472. 2001 *New Port South* (Touchstone) (PG-13)
473. 2001 *Max Keeble's Big Move* (PG)
474. 2001 *Corky Romano* (Touchstone) (PG-13)
475. 2001 *High Heels and Low Lifes* (Touchstone) (R)
476. 2001 *Monsters, Inc.* (G)
477. 2001 *Out Cold* (Touchstone) (PG-13)
478. 2001 *The Royal Tenenbaums* (Touchstone) (R)
479. 2002 *Snow Dogs* (PG)
480. 2002 *The Count of Monte Cristo* (Touchstone) (PG-13)
481. 2002 *Return to Never Land* (G)
482. 2002 *Sorority Boys* (Touchstone) (R)
483. 2002 *The Rookie* (G)
484. 2002 *Big Trouble* (Touchstone) (PG-13)
485. 2002 *Frank McKlusky, C. I.* (Touchstone) (PG-13)
486. 2002 *ESPN's Ultimate X* (Touchstone) (PG)
487. 2002 *Bad Company* (Touchstone) (PG-13)
488. 2002 *Lilo & Stitch* (PG)
489. 2002 *Reign of Fire* (Touchstone) (PG-13)
490. 2002 *The Country Bears* (G)
491. 2002 *Signs* (Touchstone) (PG-13)
492. 2002 *Spirited Away* (Walt Disney Studios) (PG-13)
493. 2002 *Moonlight Mile* (Touchstone) (PG-13)
494. 2002 *Sweet Home Alabama* (Touchstone) (PG-13)
495. 2002 *Tuck Everlasting* (PG)
496. 2002 *Santa Clause 2* (G)
497. 2002 *Treasure Planet* (PG)
498. 2002 *The Hot Chick* (Touchstone) (PG-13)
499. 2002 *25th Hour* (Touchstone) (R)
500. 2003 *The Recruit* (Touchstone) (PG-13)
501. 2003 *Shanghai Knights* (Touchstone) (PG-13)
502. 2003 *The Jungle Book 2* (G)
503. 2003 *Bringing Down the House* (Touchstone) (PG-13)
504. 2003 *Piglet's Big Movie* (G)
505. 2003 *Ghosts of the Abyss* (G)

506. 2003 *Holes* (PG)
507. 2003 *The Lizzie McGuire Movie* (PG)
508. 2003 *Finding Nemo* (G)
509. 2003 *Pirates of the Caribbean: The Curse of the Black Pearl* (PG-13)
510. 2003 *Freaky Friday* (PG)
511. 2003 *Open Range* (Touchstone) (R)
512. 2003 *Cold Creek Manor* (Touchstone) (R)
513. 2003 *Under the Tuscan Sun* (Touchstone) (PG-13)
514. 2003 *Veronica Guerin* (Touchstone) (R)
515. 2003 *Brother Bear* (G)
516. 2003 *The Haunted Mansion* (PG)
517. 2003 *Calendar Girls* (Touchstone) (PG-13)
518. 2003 *The Young Black Stallion* (G)
519. 2004 *Teacher's Pet* (PG)
520. 2004 *Miracle* (PG)
521. 2004 *Confessions of a Teenage Drama Queen* (PG)
522. 2004 *Hidalgo* (Touchstone) (PG-13)
523. 2004 *The Ladykillers* (Touchstone) (R)
524. 2004 *Home on the Range* (PG)
525. 2004 *The Alamo* (Touchstone) (PG-13)
526. 2004 *Sacred Planet* (G)
527. 2004 *Raising Helen* (Touchstone) (PG-13)
528. 2004 *Around the World in 80 Days* (PG)
529. 2004 *America's Heart & Soul* (PG)
530. 2004 *King Arthur* (Touchstone) (PG-13)
531. 2004 *The Village* (Touchstone) (PG-13)
532. 2004 *The Princess Diaries 2: Royal Engagement* (G)
533. 2004 *Mr. 3000* (Touchstone) (PG-13)
534. 2004 *The Last Shot* (Touchstone) (R)
535. 2004 *Ladder 49* (Touchstone) (PG-13)
536. 2004 *The Incredibles* (PG)
537. 2004 *National Treasure* (PG)
538. 2004 *The Life Aquatic with Steve Zissou* (Touchstone) (R)
539. 2005 *Aliens of the Deep* (G)
540. 2005 *Pooh's Heffalump Movie* (G)
541. 2005 *The Pacifier* (PG)
542. 2005 *Ice Princess* (G)
543. 2005 *A Lot Like Love* (Touchstone) (PG-13)
544. 2005 *The Hitchhiker's Guide to the Galaxy* (Touchstone) (PG)
545. 2005 *Howl's Moving Castle* (PG)
546. 2005 *Herbie: Fully Loaded* (G)
547. 2005 *Dark Water* (Touchstone) (PG-13)
548. 2005 *Sky High* (PG)
549. 2005 *Valiant* (G)
550. 2005 *Flightplan* (Touchstone) (PG-13)
551. 2005 *The Greatest Game Ever Played* (PG)
552. 2005 *Shopgirl* (Touchstone) (R)
553. 2005 *Chicken Little* (G)
554. 2005 *The Chronicles of Narnia: The Lion, the Witch and the Wardrobe*
555. 2005 *Casanova* (Touchstone) (R)
556. 2006 *Glory Road* (PG)
557. 2006 *Annapolis* (Touchstone) (PG-13)
558. 2006 *Roving Mars* (G)
559. 2006 *Eight Below* (PG)

Featurette Term used at Disney to refer to a film that is longer than a short (10 minutes) but shorter than a feature (60 minutes).

Feignoux, Wally (1906–1981) He was instrumental in handling Disney film releases in Europe, from 1936 to 1971, and was presented posthumously with a European Disney Legends award in 1997.

Feldman, Corey Actor; provided the voice of the young Copper in *The Fox and the Hound*, and appeared on television in *Exile*, provided the voice of SPRX-77 on *Super Robot Monkey Team Hyperforce Go!*

Feldman, Mindy Mouseketeer on the new *Mickey Mouse Club*.

Felicia Fat feline friend of Ratigan's in *The Great Mouse Detective*.

Felicity (television) One-hour coming-of-age dramatic television series, debuting on the WB Network on September 29, 1998, and ending on May 22, 2002. The life of recent high school graduate Felicity Porter is turned upside down when she suddenly changes her very well-laid-out college plans and moves instead to New York City to attend school. Her defied parents refuse to support her, but she feels she must take charge of her life's plan by striking out on her own for the first time. Stars Keri Russell (Felicity Porter), Scott Speedman (Ben Covington), Amy Jo Johnson (Julie Emrick), Tangi Miller (Elena Tyler), Scott Foley (Noel Crane). In the 1999 season, Felicity becomes a Resident Adviser, with added regular cast members Greg Grunberg (Sean Blumberg) and Amanda Foreman (Meghan Rotundi). The complete first season was released on DVD in 2002.

Feliz Navidad (film) Segment from *The Three Caballeros*; released on 16mm in October 1974. Christmas in Mexico, with Las Posadas, featuring Donald Duck, José Carioca, and Panchito.

Felton, Verna (1890–1966) Popular Disney voice actress, doing elephants (*Dumbo* and *The Jungle Book*), the Fairy Godmother (*Cinderella*), the Queen of Hearts (*Alice in Wonderland*), Aunt Sarah (*Lady and the Tramp*), and Flora (*Sleeping Beauty*).

Ferdinand the Bull (film) Special cartoon; released on November 25, 1938. The first cartoon directed by Dick Rickard. Based on the story by Munro Leaf and the illustrations by Robert Lawson, it is about a ferocious-looking but quiet bull who wants only to sit and smell the flowers. He is mistaken for a feisty animal by a matador when he snorts and charges after being stung by a bee. The matador takes him to the arena in the city, only to see him revert to his peaceful demeanor and refuse to fight. Ferdinand is happily sent back to his flowers. Academy Award winner for Best Cartoon. Several of the characters at the bullfight are caricatures of Disney personnel, including Walt Disney himself as the matador. Animator Milt Kahl took on a slight extra chore by providing the voice of Ferdinand's mother, while Walt Disney added Ferdinand's few words.

Ferdinand the Bull and Mickey (television) Television show; aired on January 18, 1983. Reluctant and actual heroes are spotlighted in various animation clips.

Ferdy Sometimes spelled Ferdie; a nephew of Mickey Mouse; appeared only in one cartoon, *Mickey's Steam Roller* (1934), with his brother Morty. Morty and Ferdy first appeared in the Mickey Mouse comic strip on September 18, 1932.

Fergi Diversifies (film) Educational film about a corporation's growth, stock sales, mergers, and acquisitions, produced by Dave Bell; released in September 1977.

Fergi Goes Inc. (film) Educational film about the growth of a small business and its eventual incorporation, produced by Dave Bell; released in September 1977. See also: *If the Fergi Fits, Wear It*.

Fergi Meets the Challenge (film) Educational film about how to cope with successes and failures in an expanding company, produced by Dave Bell; released in September 1978.

Ferguson, Norm (1902–1957) Animator and director; started at Disney in 1929 and remained until 1953. He animated on dozens of short cartoons and served as a directing animator on most Disney features from *Snow White and the Seven Dwarfs* to *Peter Pan*. He was responsible for the

witch in *Snow White* and the Fox and Cat in *Pinocchio*, and was known for his animation of Pluto. ASIFA, the animated film society, presented him posthumously the Winsor McCay award, their highest honor, in 1987. He was named a Disney Legend in 1999.

Ferrante, Orlando Imagineer who joined the Disney staff in 1962. Beginning with the

Enchanted Tiki Room, he was involved with the installation of many Disneyland and Walt Disney World attractions. In 1966 he set up a department named PICO (Project Installation and Coordinating Office), and six years later moved into Imagineering administration. He retired in 2002 after helping with engineering, production, and installation at Disneyland Paris, Disney Cruise Line, and Tokyo DisneySea. He was named a Disney Legend in 2003.

Festival Disney Area outside the gates of Disneyland Paris consisting of nightclubs, restaurants, and shops, primarily for evening entertainment. Includes Buffalo Bill's Wild West Show. Designed by architect Frank Gehry. The area name was changed to Disney Village in 1996.

Festival of Folk Heroes (film) Sixteen mm release of *Pecos Bill*, *Johnny Appleseed*, *Paul Bunyan*, *The Saga of Windwagon Smith*, and *Casey at the Bat*; released in April 1971.

Festival of Foods The Big Thunder Barbecue at Disneyland was re-themed on June 21, 1996, to tie in with the *Hunchback of Notre Dame* outdoor show.

Festival of the Lion King Show in the Lion King Theater in Camp Minnie-Mickey at Disney's Animal Kingdom; opened April 22, 1998. The formerly roofed, but otherwise open-air, theater was enclosed in 2003. The show used float units from The Lion King Celebration from Disneyland. Also at Hong Kong Disneyland; opened September 12, 2005.

Fethry Duck Beatnik-type duck who reads too many "how-to-do-it" books and then gets Donald involved in his harebrained schemes. He was created around 1963 by Dick Kinney for foreign comic books.

Fflewddur Fflam Wandering minstrel in *The Black Cauldron*; voiced by Nigel Hawthorne.

Fiddling Around (film) Copyright title of *Just Mickey*.

Fidget Ratigan's creepy henchman in *The Great Mouse Detective*; voiced by Candy Candido.

Fiedler, John (1925–2005) Character actor, appeared in *Rascal* (Cy Jenkins), *The Shaggy D.A.* (Howie Clemmings), *Midnight Madness* (Mr. Thorpe), on television in *The Mystery in Dracula's Castle* and *The Whiz Kid and the Mystery at Riverton*, and as the voices of Piglet in *Winnie the Pooh*, the owl in *The Rescuers*, the church mouse in *Robin Hood*, and the porcupine in *The Fox and the Hound*.

Field, Sally Actress; provided the voice of Sassy in *Homeward Bound: The Incredible Journey* and appeared on television as Justice Kate Nolan in *The Court*.

Fields, Albert Actor; appeared on the *Mickey Mouse Club* on The Disney Channel, beginning in 1989, and was a member of The Party.

Fields, Bonnie Lynn Mouseketeer from the 1950s television show.

Fiesta Fun Center Game area in the Contemporary Resort at Walt Disney World. This large area was originally built as convention exhibit space, but the demand for more facilities for evening entertainment for guests necessitated the building of the Fiesta Fun Center. Its video games, air hockey, and other amusements seem to be always popular. A theater in one corner of the

room has featured screenings of Disney films, and there is a snack bar. Later known as Food and Fun Center.

Fifi Mischievous little brown dog with black ears who often played Pluto's girlfriend; she appeared in five cartoons, beginning with *Puppy Love* (1933).

Fifth Freedom Mural Artwork at the exit of Great Moments with Mr. Lincoln at Disneyland. In its 53-foot length it attempts to depict some of the people who rose to greatness through the fifth freedom, that of free enterprise, including Walt Disney himself.

50s Prime Time Cafe Restaurant at Disney-MGM Studios at Walt Disney World; opened on May 1, 1989. Guests sit around breakfast room Formica-topped tables, with a television set playing clips from 1950s situation comedies, as "Mom" serves the wholesome fare. Memorabilia from the fifties fills the shelves.

Fifty Happy Years (television) Television show; aired on January 21, 1973. A fiftieth-anniversary salute to the Disney company, featuring a history of the Disney Studio and film clips from the 1920s up to *Robin Hood*. Narrated by Danny Dark.

Figaro Endearing kitten co-star of *Pinocchio*, who went on to have his own short series of cartoons making a total of seven additional appearances.

Figaro and Cleo (film) Figaro cartoon; released on October 15, 1943. Directed by Jack Kinney. Figaro, the cat, tries various methods to catch Cleo, the goldfish, but is scolded for his efforts. When Cleo's bowl accidentally falls on Figaro's head, his owner momentarily thinks he has drowned, and pampers him. Figaro and Cleo eventually become friends.

Figaro and Frankie (film) Figaro cartoon; released on May 30, 1947. Directed by Charles Nichols. Though Frankie, the canary, becomes quite an annoyance with his singing and birdseed shooting, Figaro must save him from the jaws of Butch, the bulldog.

Fight, The (film) Educational film about how to solve problems peaceably, from the What Should I Do? series; released in August 1969.

Fighting Choice, A (television) Two-hour television movie; aired on April 13, 1986. Directed by Ferdinand Fairfax. A teenager, Kellin Taylor, suffering from epilepsy, which seems to be getting worse, wants a serious brain operation, but his parents are afraid of the possible consequences. Kellin has to go to court to get his parents to agree. Stars Beau Bridges, Karen Valentine, Patrick Dempsey, Lawrence Pressman, Frances Lee McCain, Danielle Von Zerneck.

Fighting Prince of Donegal, The (film) In the time of Queen Elizabeth I, the English fear that Spain will attack through Ireland, so English troops occupy the Irish countryside. It is a gallant young man, Hugh O'Donnell, the prince of Donegal, who leads resistance against them. Hugh has many exciting adventures while he is uniting the clans of Ireland. He is captured and imprisoned—twice. But he escapes again to lead and win the final battle against the English, and to rescue Kathleen, his lady love. Released on October 1, 1966. Directed by Michael O'Herlihy. 110 min. Stars Peter McEnery (Hugh O'Donnell), Susan Hampshire (Kathleen Mac-Sweeney), Tom Adams (Henry O'Neill), Gordon Jackson (Capt. Leeds), Andrew Keir (Lord Mac-Sweeney), Donal McCann (Sean O'Toole), Maurice Roeves (Martin), Richard Leech (O'Neill). This was the first live-action theatrical swashbuckler Disney had made since *Kidnapped*, in 1960, and it sparkles with the exuberant talents of its two leads and the guidance of first-time theatrical director O'Herlihy. A fictional story, but based on authentic exploits of the real Prince of Donegal, Red Hugh, as told in a book by Robert T. Reilly. Released on video in 1986.

Figment Small purple dragon who hosted the Journey into Imagination at Epcot along with Dreamfinder from 1983 to 1998. He returned in 2002 with a new show, Journey Into Imagination with Figment.

Fillmore, Disney's (television) Animated television series; premiered as part of ABC Kids on September 14, 2002. Middle school safety patrol officer Cornelius Fillmore is a former delinquent who has turned his life around, and he is making up for his shady past by helping others. Voices include Orlando Brown (Cornelius Fillmore). 26 episodes.

Filming Nature's Mysteries (film) Educational film taken primarily from the television show *Searching for Nature's Mysteries*; released in July 1976. Shows how filmmakers capture the miracles of nature, with microphotography, time-lapse, stop-action, and underwater photography.

Finch, Peter (1916–1977) Actor; appeared in *The Story of Robin Hood* (Sheriff of Nottingham) and *Kidnapped* (Alan Breck Stewart).

Finding Nemo (film) A Disney-Pixar production. Nemo, a 6-year-old clownfish, is tragically stolen away from the safety of his undersea home at the Great Barrier Reef, ending up in a dentist's office fish tank overlooking Sydney harbor. His timid father, Marlin, launches a search to find and rescue him, accompanied by a good samaritan, a Regal Blue Tang fish named Dory. Meanwhile, Nemo is hatching a few daring plans of his own to return safely home. Directed by Andrew Stanton. Released on May 30, 2003. Voices include Alexander Gould (Nemo), Albert Brooks (Father), Ellen DeGeneres (Dory), Willem Dafoe (Gill), Brad Garrett (Bloat), Austin Pendleton (Gurgle), Vicki Lewis (Deb/Flo), Geoffrey Rush (Nigel), Allison Janney (Peach), John Ratzenberger (Moonfish), Barry Humphries (Bruce). 100 min. All the animation was done at the Pixar Animation Studios in Emeryville, California. Released with Pixar's 4-minute short *Knick Knack*. The film set a Disney record for an opening weekend, with a gross of $70.2 million, eventually becoming the highest grossing animated film of all time, with over $339 million, and the box office champ for

2003. It won the Academy Award for Best Animated Feature, as well as three other nominations (Original Screenplay, Original Score, and Sound Editing). Released on video in 2003.

Fire Birds (film) Jake Preston and Billie Lee Guthrie are pilots in an elite Army helicopter task force, flying the high-tech Apache helicopter, the Army's most advanced flying fighting machine. Just how far the choppers and their crew can go is put to the test when the Apache task force is assigned to complete a secret mission in Latin America. Infiltrating hostile territory to do combat with an international enemy, the seemingly fearless flyers soon discover they are fighting a desperate war both on the ground and in the sky. Released on May 25, 1990. Directed by David Green. A Touchstone film. 86 min. Stars Nicolas Cage (Jake Preston), Tommy Lee Jones (Brad Little), Sean Young (Billie Lee Guthrie), Bryan Kestner (Breaker). Featured the Apache helicopter, also known as the AH-64A, a $10 million high-tech attack helicopter with a 1,700-horsepower engine. Filmed on location in Texas and Arizona. Released on video in 1990.

Fire Called Jeremiah, A (television) Television show; aired on December 3, 1961. Produced by James Algar. This is the story of the "smoke jumpers," specially trained by the Forest Service to reach forest fires when they are in the inaccessible areas of our National Forests. Scanning their assigned areas from patrolling planes and lookout towers they are able to set in motion the operation that converges on the hot spots before they grow into disastrous fire storms that destroy vital watersheds. In one such incident, a small blaze spotted from a fire lookout tower grows ominously and soon turns into a conflagration. The fire changes course and threatens the fire tower itself, and the female lookout has to be rescued by helicopter. Stars (all playing themselves) Cliff Blake, Carole Stockner, Roy Carpenter. Released theatrically abroad.

Fire Chief (film) Donald Duck cartoon; released on December 13, 1940. Directed by Jack King. Fire Chief Donald accidentally sets fire to his own station house. By not listening to his nephews, he attaches the water hose to the gasoline supply, and totally incinerates the fire house, fire truck, and even his fire helmet.

Fire Fighters, The (film) Mickey Mouse cartoon; released on June 25, 1930. Directed by Burt Gillett. Fire Chief Mickey saves Minnie from her burning house after a series of episodes involving the fire house and answering the alarm.

Fire on Kelly Mountain (television) Television show; aired on September 30, 1973. Directed by Robert Clouse. A forest service fire lookout gets his wish when he wants to fight fires, for he is sent to check out a blaze, but the fire he finds almost gets the best of him. He also has problems with an enraged bear that has been spooked by the fire. Stars Andrew Duggan, Larry Wilcox, Anne Lockhart, Noam Pitlik, Ted Hartley.

Fire Station On Town Square at Disneyland from opening day. A fire wagon and other fire-fighting memorabilia are displayed. Walt Disney had a small apartment upstairs where he could relax and entertain friends and family members while on visits to the park. It consisted of a large sitting room, with built-in sofas that could be pulled out as beds, a small dressing room, and a bathroom. Many of the furnishings were antiques that had been personally selected by Mrs. Disney. An alcove contained a small sink and a refrigerator. At one time the fire pole from the fire station extended on up into the apartment, but it was blocked off after someone climbed up the pole into the apartment. The apartment has been maintained up to the present, and is occasionally used by Disney executives. There are also fire sta-

tions on Town Square in Magic Kingdom Park at Walt Disney World, at Disneyland Paris, and at Hong Kong Disneyland.

Fire Station, The (film) Educational film in which Mickey tours a fire station, in the Mickey's Field Trips series; released in September 1987. 12 min.

Fire Truck Main Street vehicle at Disneyland, began on August 16, 1958. Also in Magic Kingdom Park at Walt Disney World, opening October 1, 1971; in World Bazaar at Tokyo Disneyland, opening April 15, 1983; and on Main Street at Disneyland Paris, opening April 12, 1992.

Fire-Wagon Horse-drawn Main Street vehicle at Disneyland; began July 17, 1955, and operated until 1960. It is now on display in the fire station on Town Square.

Firehouse Five Plus Two Dixieland jazz group composed of Disney Studio personnel that evolved from bands created to play in camp shows during World War II. Led by Ward Kimball, the

group appeared on television in *At Home with Donald Duck*, *The Disneyland Tenth Anniversary Show*, and the *Mickey Mouse Club (Fun with Music Day)*. Other members included George Probert, Frank Thomas, Harper Goff, and Eddie Forrest. The group was caricatured in the Goofy cartoon *How to Dance*. They had a catalog of a number of phonograph records on the Good Time Jazz label. The group was disbanded in 1971.

Firelight (film) Beautiful but poor Swiss governess Elisabeth meets secretly in 1837 with an

English landowner, Charles Godwin, to conceive a child in exchange for money. Seven years later, the two are drawn together again when Elisabeth joins Charles' forlorn household, Selcombe Place in the Sussex countryside, as governess to Louisa. Sworn to secrecy, Elisabeth must now hide her passionate feelings for the man she loves, and the child she brought into the world. A Hollywood Pictures film. Released on a limited basis on September 4, 1998. Directed by William Nicholson. Stars Sophie Marceau (Elisabeth), Stephen Dillane (Charles Godwin), Dominique Belcourt (Louisa), Kevin Anderson (John Taylor), Lia Williams (Constance), Joss Ackland (Lord Clare). CinemaScope. 104 min. Firle Place in the south of England became Selcombe Place, and the surrounding farmlands and village church became primary locations for the film. Released on video in 1999.

First Aiders (film) Pluto cartoon; released on September 22, 1944. Directed by Charles Nichols. Minnie practices first aid on Pluto, but, being heckled by a kitten, he gives chase which results in both falling downstairs. Minnie rushes to their aid and encourages Pluto and the kitten to make up.

First Americans, The (television) Serial on the *Mickey Mouse Club* during the 1956–57 season, hosted by Tony Nakina and Iron Eyes Cody. Tells stories about the American Indians. 4 episodes.

First Kid (film) Sam Simms is a Secret Service agent whose sense of style keeps him off the elite force assigned to protect "The Eagle," the president of the United States. When the president's teenage son, Luke, makes the nightly news mooning a mall opening crowd, Simms is assigned to look after "The Prince." Going through adolescence in the White House is not easy, but Simms helps Luke through many of his youthful skirmishes and together they even foil a threat to the first family's security. A Hollywood picture in association with Caravan Pictures. Released on August 30, 1996. Directed by David Mickey Evans. Stars Sinbad (Simms), Robert Guillaume (Wilkes), Timothy Busfield (Woods), Brock Pierce (Luke),

James Naughton (President Davenport), Art LaFleur (Morton), Linda Eichhorn (Linda Davenport), Bill Cobbs (Speed), Zachery Ty Bryan (Rob). 101 min. Most of the film was shot in and around Richmond, Virginia, including St. Catherine's private school, though exteriors of the landmarks such as the Washington Monument, the Mall, and the Treasury Building were shot in Washington, D.C. Special sets had to be constructed of the Executive Residence and the Oval Office, since filming at the White House was not possible. Retired assistant director of the Secret Service Bob Snow served as technical adviser. Released on video in 1997.

Firth, Peter Actor; appeared in *Mighty Joe Young* (Garth) and *Pearl Harbor* (Captain of West Virginia), on television in *Diamonds on Wheels*, and provided the voice of Red in *The Rescuers Down Under*.

Fischinger, Oskar (1900–1967) Experimental animator, at the Disney Studio in 1938 and 1939, during which time he contributed to the *Toccata and Fugue* segment of *Fantasia*.

Fishburne, Laurence Actor; appeared in *What's Love Got to Do With It* (Ike Turner) and *Bad Company* (Nelson Crowe).

Fishin' Around (film) Mickey Mouse cartoon; released on September 25, 1931. Directed by Burt Gillett. In one of his most mischievous adventures, Mickey, along with Pluto, fishes in a forbidden area and becomes frustrated with the taunting fish until the sheriff chases them away.

Fit to Be You: Flexibility and Body Composition (film) Educational film; released in September 1980. The film explains the relationship of body mass to body fat and stresses the importance of exercise.

Fit to Be You: Heart-Lungs (film) Educational film; released in September 1980. Shows the function of the heart and lungs, and how they perform more effectively if one follows planned, continuous exercise programs.

Fit to Be You: Muscles (film) Educational film; released in September 1980. Shows students the importance of developing the strength and endurance of their muscles.

Fitness and Me (film) Series of three educational films; released in March 1984: *How to Exercise, What Is Fitness Exercise, Why Exercise?*

Fitness for Living (film) Series of three educational films; released in September 1982: *What Is Physical Fitness, How to Get Fit, Measuring Up.*

Fitness Fun with Goofy (film) Educational release in 16mm in March 1991. 19 min. Sport Goofy takes the class through a complete workout that includes both warm-up and cool-down exercises, illustrating them with clips from Disney films.

Fittings & Fairings, Clothes & Notions Shop in the Yacht Club Resort at Walt Disney World; opened on November 5, 1990. Merchandise is themed to the nautical feel of the hotel.

Fitzpatrick, Robert President of Euro Disney from 1987 to 1993. Formerly president of the California Institute of the Arts.

Five Mile Creek (television) Series on The Disney Channel, based on a book by Louis L'Amour. An isolated coach stop run by two women on a stage line between the harbor town of Port Nelson and the mining camp of Wilga in Australia at the time of the 1860s gold rush is the setting for this adventure series. Debuted on November 4, 1983. Stars Louise Caire Clark, Rod Mullinar, Jay Kerr, Liz Burch, Michael Caton, Priscilla Weems. Filmed on location 40 miles north of Sydney, Australia. 39 episodes. The pilot for *Five Mile Creek* aired on the Disney CBS series on November 28, 1981, as *The Cherokee Trail*. That film was set at Cherokee Station, in the heart of the Colorado wilderness. When producer Doug Netter got the go-ahead for a series, he transplanted the locale to Australia. Over 500 hours of in-depth research insured accuracy in all phases of the production, from the choice of locations to the construction of the stagecoaches and sets, to the dialogue of the characters.

Fjording Shop in Norway in World Showcase at Epcot; opened on May 6, 1988.

Flagler's Restaurant on the second floor in the Grand Floridian Beach Resort at Walt Disney World; opened on June 28, 1988. Featured Italian and continental cuisine. It closed on July 6, 1997, to become Cítricos on November 8.

Flame Tree Barbecue Fast-food restaurant on Discovery Island at Disney's Animal Kingdom; opened on April 22, 1998.

Flannery Stationmaster in *Pigs Is Pigs* (1954).

Flash (television) Two-hour made-for-television movie; aired on *The Wonderful World of Disney* on December 21, 1997. The prized possession of teenaged Connor is his two-year-old horse, Flash. When hard times force his father to join the merchant marine and go off to sea, and Connor's grandmother dies, Flash must be sold. Working as a stable boy, Connor sees firsthand how the new owner abuses and mistreats his beloved horse. Connor decides to rescue Flash, and together they begin a perilous ride across the country in search of Connor's father. Directed by Simon Wincer. Stars Lucas Black (Connor), Brian Kerwin (David Strong), Shawn Toovey (Tad Rutherford), Tom Nowicki (Alfred Rutherford), Ellen Burstyn (Laura Strong).

Flash Forward (television) Television series on The Disney Channel, beginning January 5, 1997, after a ten-episode marathon on New Year's Day. Becca Fisher and Tucker James are lifelong friends. They have the same birthday, they were raised next door to one another, and they shared many of the same experiences. But when they hit the teen years, they find themselves coping with a landslide of changes that occur within and around them. Stars Jewel Staite (Becca), Ben Foster (Tucker), Theodore Borders (Miles Vaughn), Asia Vieira (Chris).

Flash, the Teenage Otter (television) Television show; aired on April 30, 1961. Directed by Hank Schloss. An otter battles nature and humans, trying to live in a safe environment. Narrated by Winston Hibler.

Fleischer, Charles Actor/comedian; provided the voice of Roger Rabbit (as well as Benny the Cab, Greasy, and Psycho) in *Who Framed Roger Rabbit*, and appeared in *Gross Anatomy* (lecturing professor), *Dick Tracy* (reporter), and *Straight Talk* (Tony), and on television in *Disneyland's 35th Anniversary Celebration* and *Mickey's 60th Birthday*. On Disney Channel he was in *Genius* (Dr. Krickstein).

Fleischer, Richard Son of animation pioneer Max Fleischer, he was selected by Walt Disney to direct *20,000 Leagues Under the Sea*. He was named a Disney Legend in 2003.

Flight! (film) Educational film; released in September 1985. An innovative discussion of the principles of aerodynamics.

Flight Circle Tomorrowland area at Disneyland, from 1955 to 1966. Also known as Thimble Drome Flight Circle. Model airplanes were demonstrated here to the enjoyment of kids, but the noise was awesome. At one time, a spaceman in an experimental rocket pack would take off from here and fly around Tomorrowland.

Flight of the Grey Wolf, The (television) Two-part television show; aired on March 14 and 21, 1976. Directed by Frank Zuniga. A pet wolf leads to problems for a teenager, Russ Hanson, when the local populace fears it has attacked a girl. Russ realizes the wolf must be returned to the wild, and he tries to teach it how to survive on its own, but only after it meets a female wolf does it start acting like a wolf. Stars Jeff East, Bill Williams, Barbara Hale, William Bryant, Eric Server, Judson Pratt.

Flight of the Navigator (film) A boy goes out into the woods one evening, has a fall, and when he gets up and returns to his house, he discovers his family no longer lives there. It is eight years later and

everyone has aged except the boy. Eventually it turns out that he had been on a spaceship, helping an alien to navigate it. Released on July 30, 1986. Directed by Randal Kleiser. 89 min. Stars Joey Cramer (David Freeman), Cliff De Young (Bill Freeman), Sarah Jessica Parker (Carolyn McAdams). Filmed on location in Broward County, Florida, with some filming also taking place in Norway. Released on video in 1987 and 1993.

Flight of the White Stallions (television) Television title of *The Miracle of the White Stallions*.

Flight to the Moon Tomorrowland attraction at Disneyland, sponsored by McDonnell-Douglas, from August 12, 1967 to January 5, 1975. Followed Rocket to the Moon and preceded Mission to Mars. Also a Tomorrowland attraction in Magic Kingdom Park at Walt Disney World, from December 24, 1971 until April 15, 1975. That attraction also became Mission to Mars.

Flightplan (film) Flying at 40,000 feet in a cavernous aircraft, Kyle Pratt faces every mother's worst nightmare when her 6-year-old daughter, Julia, vanishes without a trace midflight from Berlin to New York. Already emotionally devastated by the unexpected death of her husband, Kyle desperately struggles to prove her sanity to the disbelieving flight crew and passengers while facing the very real possibility that she may be losing her mind. While neither Captain Rich nor Air Marshal Gene Carson wants to doubt the bereaved widow, all evidence indicates that her daughter was never on board resulting in paranoia and doubt among the passengers and crew of the plane. Finding herself desperately alone, Kyle can only rely on her own wits to solve the mystery and save her daughter. A Touchstone Picture, with Imagine Entertainment. Directed by Robert Schwentke. Released on September 23, 2005. Stars Jodie Foster (Kyle Pratt), Peter Sarsgaard (Gene Carson), Sean Bean (Captain Rich), Erika Christensen (Fiona), Marlene Lawston (Julia), Kate Beahan (Stephanie), Michael Irby (Obaid), Brent Sexton (Elias), Judith Scott (Estella). 98 min. Filmed in Super 35 Scope. The fictional plane, Alto Air's E-474 Jumbo Jet, seating more than 700 passengers, was conceived by Brian Grazer and Robert Schwentke.

Flights of Fantasy Parade At Disneyland from June 18 to September 10, 1983. Featured huge inflatable characters.

Flik Lead character, a worker ant, in *a bug's life*; voiced by Dave Foley.

Flintheart Glomgold Second-richest duck in the world, after Uncle Scrooge, and thus his long-time rival, in the comics and *Ducktales*. He was created by Carl Barks and made his debut in *Uncle Scrooge* no. 15 in 1956.

Flora Good fairy in *Sleeping Beauty* who wore reds; voiced by Verna Felton.

Florez, Angel Mouseketeer on the new *Mickey Mouse Club*. He also appeared in later years as a parade performer at Disneyland.

Florida's Disney Decade (television) Television special shown in Florida about the 10-year history of Walt Disney World; aired on October 1, 1981, simultaneously on all three Orlando television stations. Many Disney executives and Florida businessmen and politicians are interviewed about their roles in bringing Walt Disney World to Florida. Narrated by Gene Burne.

Flotsam and Jetsam Two slithery eels who act as Ursula's henchmen in *The Little Mermaid*.

Flounder Fish friend of Ariel in *The Little Mermaid*; voiced by Jason Marin. Edan Gross provided the voice in the television series.

Flounder's Flying Fish Coaster Attraction in Mermaid Lagoon at Tokyo DisneySea, opening on September 4, 2001. Guests ride cartoony flying fish, linking the undersea world of *The Little Mermaid* and the human world above the waves.

Flower Skunk friend of Bambi; voiced by Stanley Alexander as a youngster and Sterling Holloway as an adult.

Flowers and Trees (film) Silly Symphony cartoon; released on July 30, 1932. Directed by Burt Gillett. The 29th Silly Symphony is indeed a landmark in Disney animation. Originally begun as a black-and-white cartoon, the work was scrapped at great cost, and the cartoon was made in color at Walt Disney's insistence, for he believed color could greatly enhance animation. He signed a two-year agreement with Technicolor giving him sole rights to the process for animated shorts, and a great head start over all of the other cartoon producers in Hollywood. Very soon all the Disney cartoons would be in color. Disney's faith in the process not only enhanced the quality of his films, but helped make Technicolor a respected standard in the film industry. The story of the cartoon concerns two trees in love who are threatened by a jealous old stump that attempts to burn the forest

down in order to destroy them. But he only succeeds in reducing himself to ash. The forest revives and celebrates the wedding. Academy Award winner for Best Cartoon. The film was re-released in two Academy Award specials in 1937 and 1967, and as part of *Milestones in Animation* (1973).

Flubber Magical substance invented by Professor Ned Brainard in *The Absent-Minded Professor*. Disney gave away its formula for making Flubber in the film's publicity: "To one pound of salt water taffy add one heaping tablespoon polyurethane foam, one cake crumbled yeast. Mix until smooth, allow to rise. Then pour into saucepan over one cup cracked rice mixed with one cup of water. Add topping of molasses. Boil until it lifts lid and says 'Qurlp.'" At the time of the film's release in 1961, Hassenfeld Brothers (Hasbro) made a pliable plastic-like material that they merchandised as "Flubber." It sold for $1 and was advertised as "Every bubble a bounce."

Flubber (film) Professor Phillip Brainard is a man so lost in thought that he appears, at times, not to pay attention. He's even forgotten two dates to marry his sweetheart, Sara. But the guy has a lot on his mind. He is working with his high-voltage,

over-amorous flying robot assistant, Weebo, on an idea for a substance that is not only a revolutionary source of energy, but may well be the salvation of his financially troubled Medfield College, where his beloved Sara is the president. But it all comes together late on the afternoon of his third attempt at a wedding when the professor creates a miraculous goo that when applied to any object—cars, bowling balls . . . even people—enables them to fly through the air at miraculous speeds. The stuff, called Flubber, defies gravity and looks like rubber. Chester Hoenicker, a corrupt businessman who at first wants only to punish Brainard for giving his son a failing grade, learns about the existence of the substance, and sends goons to steal it from the professor's lab. Directed by Les Mayfield. Stars Robin Williams (Phillip Brainard), Marcia Gay Harden (Sara), Christopher McDonald (Wilson Croft), Raymond Barry (Chester Hoenicker), Wil Wheaton (Bennett Hoenicker). The voice of Weebo is provided by Jodi Benson. 94 min. An updated version of the 1961 Disney feature The Absent-Minded Professor. Many of the special effects were produced in the huge Building Three at the Treasure Island Naval Base off San Francisco. With 90,000 square feet of space, the producers were able to create the professor's basement laboratory, the interior of the team's locker room, and a 2,500-seat basketball stadium, all under one roof, at one time. Differing from the original film, the substance Flubber is given a personality of its own. Michievous and uncontrollable, it creates havoc everywhere.

Fluppy Dogs See *Disney's Fluppy Dogs*.

Fly 'n' Buy Shop at Condor Flats in Disney's California Adventure; opened February 8, 2001.

Fly with Von Drake (television) Television show; aired on October 13, 1963. Directed by Hamilton S. Luske. The professor, Ludwig Von Drake, describes the history of flight, with segments from previous animated television shows and *Victory Through Air Power*.

Flying Carpets Over Agrabah (Les Tapis Volants) Attraction at Walt Disney Studios

Paris where the Genie invites guests to ride in flying carpets; opened on March 16, 2002.

Flying Fish Café Elegant seafood restaurant at the BoardWalk Resort at Walt Disney World; opened on October 3, 1996.

Flying Gauchito, The (film) Segment of *The Three Caballeros* in which a little boy trains a flying donkey for racing. Re-released as a short on July 15, 1955.

Flying Jalopy (film) Donald Duck cartoon; released on March 12, 1943. Directed by Dick Lundy. Donald buys a rattletrap plane from Ben Buzzard, who makes Donald's insurance out to himself and then proceeds to try to wreck the plane.

Flying Mouse, The (film) Silly Symphony cartoon; released on July 14, 1934. Directed by Dave Hand. A mouse is granted his wish to fly by a butterfly fairy he saved from a spider's web. He soon regrets his decision when everyone takes him for a bat. Luckily, the fairy appears to change him back and he returns happily home. Features the popular song "You're Nothin' but a Nothin'," which was released on sheet music.

Flying Saucers Tomorrowland attraction at Disneyland, from August 6, 1961 to September 5, 1966. Individually controlled vehicles floated on a cushion of air, but the technology was not per-fected and the attraction was constantly breaking down. It was one of the worst maintenance headaches at Disneyland, as the technicians continually tried to keep it operating. Eventually, they gave up.

Flying Squirrel, The (film) Donald Duck cartoon; released on November 12, 1954. Directed by Jack Hannah. Donald promises a peanut to a flying squirrel if it will hang his peanut sign in a nearby tree. But when the peanut turns out to be rotten, the squirrel gets his just revenge.

Flynn, Joe (1924–1974) Actor and Disney regular, appeared in *Son of Flubber* (announcer in television commercial), *The Love Bug* (Havershaw), *The Computer Wore Tennis Shoes* (Dean Higgins), *The Barefoot Executive* (Francis X. Wilbanks), *Million Dollar Duck* (Finley Hooper), *Now You See Him, Now You Don't* (Dean Higgins), *Superdad* (Cyrus Hershberger), *The Strongest Man in the World* (Dean Higgins), on television in *My Dog, the Thief* and *The Wacky Zoo of Morgan City*. He also provided the voice of Mr. Snoops in *The Rescuers*.

Follow Me, Boys! (film) Dissatisfied with his life as a saxophonist in a traveling jazz band, Lemuel Siddons impulsively settles down in the small Illinois town of Hickory (population 4,951), not realizing that he will remain there the rest of his days. This heartwarming and humorous story tells how Lem becomes the local scoutmaster, and how he courts and marries the lovely Vida. But, mostly, it is the story of a man who sacrifices his own personal goals to devote himself to several generations of boys, teaching them enduring values through scouting. And, for Lem, this brings the love, respect, and recognition he so richly deserves. Released on December 1, 1966. Directed by Norman Tokar. 131 min. Stars Fred MacMurray (Lemuel Siddons), Vera Miles (Vida Downey), Kurt Russell (Whitey), Lillian Gish (Hetty Seibert), Charlie Ruggles (John Everett Hughes), Elliott Reid (Ralph Hastings), Ken Murray (Melody Murphy), Sean McClory (Edward White, Sr.). This was the first big film role for Kurt Russell. The film was a popular Christmastime hit, playing Radio City Music Hall. Based on the book

God and My Country by Mackinlay Kantor, the movie also featured one-time Disney starlet Luana Patten in a key role, as Nora White. A tremendous assemblage of vintage cars added to the nostalgic feel of the film; included were a 1915 Baker Electric, a 1927 Lincoln touring car, a fleet of 1929 Fords and Chevrolets, and three plush Cadillacs of 1940, 1946, and 1950 vintage. The film was re-released in 1976, but was edited from the original 131-minute version to 107 minutes. Released on video in 1984.

Follow Us . . . to Walt Disney World (film) Documentary featurette; released first in England on July 11, 1985. 16 min.

Follow Your Heart (television) Television show; part 1 of *The Horsemasters.*

Fondacaro, Phil He voiced Creeper in *The Black Cauldron.*

Fonte, Allison Mouseketeer on the new *Mickey Mouse Club.*

Food for Feudin' (film) Pluto cartoon; released on August 11, 1950. Directed by Charles Nichols. The chipmunks and Pluto battle over possession of a supply of nuts.

Food Rocks Peppy Audio-Animatronics show in The Land at Epcot, beginning March 26, 1994, and closing January 3, 2004. Superseded Kitchen Kabaret. The only figure remaining from the previous show is the milk carton. The theme of the show is nutrition, and the title spoofs rock concerts that are fund-raisers, such as World Aid, Farm Aid.

Food Will Win the War (film) Educational film made for the U.S. Department of Agriculture. Delivered to them on July 21, 1942. Amazing and interesting comparisons regarding the vast food resources of the United States are detailed in animation.

Foods and Fun: A Nutrition Adventure (film) Educational film starring the Orange Bird; released in September 1980. The importance of good nutrition and proper exercise, told through animation.

Football Now and Then (film) Special cartoon; released on October 2, 1953. Directed by Jack Kinney. A boy and his grandfather argue the merits of football past and present while watching two teams, Bygone U and Present State, on television. Though the game ends in a tie, Grandfather is more impressed with a commercial and goes out to buy the advertised dishwasher.

Footloose Fox (film) Featurette; released on June 7, 1979. A young fox and an apartment-hunting badger become roommates and fast friends while sharing a den. One day, the fox, leading a wolf pack away from the badger, ends up far from home. After a winter storm, the fox finds a female counterpart and they return to the fox's den. Knowing that three's company, the badger goes apartment-hunting once again. 30 min. Directed by Jack Speirs.

Footloose Goose, The (television) Television show; aired on March 9, 1975. Directed by James Algar. A gander in Minnesota is injured and blown far away from his home by a tornado, so after he recovers in a bird sanctuary in Canada, he returns to Minnesota and searches for his mate. Stars Brett Hadley, Paul Preston, Judy Bement.

For the Love of Willadean (film) Two-part television show; aired on March 8 and 15, 1964. Directed by Byron Paul. The two parts were titled *A Taste of Melon* and *Treasure in the Haunted House.* A new boy, Harley, joins a club but shows an interest in the leader's girlfriend. The two club members trick Harley into stealing a prize watermelon to the dismay of the furious farmer, and later dare him to enter a supposedly haunted house. In the house they uncover a bag of money stolen in a bank robbery. Stars Ed Wynn, Michael McGreevey, Billy Mumy, Roger Mobley, Terry Burnham, John Anderson, Barbara Eiler.

For Whom the Bulls Toil (film) Goofy cartoon; released on May 9, 1953. Directed by Jack

Kinney. Goofy, on a tour of Mexico, is mistaken for a great matador and is rushed into the bullring where, after a mad, crazy chase, he eventually does subdue the bull.

Foray, June Voice actress; Witch Hazel in *Trick or Treat*, Magica de Spell on *Ducktales*, and Grammi Gummi on *Disney's Adventures of the Gummi Bears*, among many other roles. She provided the voice of Grandmother Fa in *Mulan*, and Grandma in *Redux Riding Hood*. She is known for doing the voices of Natasha and Rocky on *The Bullwinkle Show*.

Ford, Glenn Actor; appeared in *Smith*, and on television in *My Town*.

Ford, Harrison Actor; appeared in *Six Days, Seven Nights* (Quinn Harris).

Forrest, Steve Actor; appeared in *Rascal* (Willard North) and *The Wild Country* (Jim Tanner), and narrated *Wild Geese Calling* and *The Owl that Didn't Give a Hoot* on television.

Fort Langhorne See Fort Sam Clemens.

Fort Sam Clemens Located on Tom Sawyer Island in Magic Kingdom Park at Walt Disney World. The name changed to Fort Langhorne (Clemens' middle name) in 1996.

Fort Wilderness Located on Tom Sawyer Island at Disneyland.

Fort Wilderness Railway A train trip that operated from 1973 to 1977 at the Fort Wilderness Resort at Walt Disney World.

Fort Wilderness Resort Campground, with campsites and trailers, in a 640-acre forest setting of pines and cypress at Walt Disney World; opened on November 19, 1971. It has been expanded through the years, with additional facilities at Pioneer Hall, where the Hoop-Dee-Doo Musical Revue is performed. Recreation includes horseback riding, jogging, bicycling, and fishing or swimming in Bay Lake.

Fortress Explorations Attraction at Explorers' Landing in Tokyo DisneySea; opened on September 4, 2001. Offers hands-on activities and exhibits.

Fortuosity Song from *The Happiest Millionaire*, sung by Tommy Steele, written by Richard M. Sherman and Robert B. Sherman.

40 Pounds of Trouble (film) Motion picture made by Universal in 1962, starring Tony Curtis and Suzanne Pleshette, notable for a lengthy chase scene that takes place inside Disneyland. This was the first non-Disney motion picture to use Disneyland as a setting.

40 Years of Adventure (television) Syndicated one-hour television special hosted by Wil Shriner, commemorating the 40th anniversary of Disneyland and the opening of the Indiana Jones Adventure. Included are interviews with celebrities on hand for the opening. Directed by Melanie Steensland. Aired on KCAL on March 4, 1995.

Foster, Ben Actor; appeared in *Big Trouble* (Matt Arnold) and as a co-star of *Flash Forward* on Disney Channel.

Foster, Jodie Actress; appeared in *Napoleon and Samantha* (Samantha), *One Little Indian* (Martha Melver), *Freaky Friday* (Annabel Andrews), *Candleshoe* (Casey), *Flightplan* (Kyle Pratt), and on television in *Menace on the Mountain*.

Foster, Lewis R. (1899–1974) Director of *Swamp Fox* and *Zorro* films.

Foster, Norman (1900–1976) Director of *Davy Crockett* and *Zorro* films.

Foul Hunting (film) Goofy cartoon; released on October 31, 1947. Directed by Jack Hannah.

Goofy's duck hunting is not going well when he encounters a duck that imitates the decoy and gets his gun soaked. He ends up eating the decoy.

Fountainview Espresso & Bakery Dessert and espresso area formerly part of Sunrise Terrace, in Innoventions West at Epcot; opened on November 9, 1993.

4 Artists Paint 1 Tree (film) Sixteen-mm release title of a part of the television show *An Adventure in Art*; released in May 1964. Four Disney artists were asked to paint the same tree, and their differing styles created widely varying results. They explain their approach and interpretation.

Four Corners Food Faire Located in Fantasyland at Tokyo Disneyland; opened on April 15, 1983. Name changed to Small World Restaurant in March 1987.

Four Diamonds, The (television) A Disney Channel Premiere Film; first aired on August 12, 1995. Young cancer patient Chris Millard escaped into his imagination by writing *The Four Diamonds*. In the tale, he cast members of his family in various roles, including himself as Sir Millard, and his doctor, Dr. Burke, as Raptenahad, the evil sorceress. Taken prisoner by Raptenahad, Sir Millard must win his freedom by carrying out a quest demanded by the sorceress: he must obtain for her the four diamonds of courage, honesty, wisdom, and strength. Directed by Peter Werner. Stars Thomas Guiry (Chris), Christine Lahti (Dr. Burke), Kevin Dunn (Charles Millard), Jayne Brook (Irma Millard), Sarah Rose Karr (Stacie), Michael Bacall (Tony Falco).

Four Down and Five Lives to Go (television) Television show; episode 2 of *Elfego Baca*.

Four Fabulous Characters (television) Television show; aired on September 18, 1957. Directed by Hamilton S. Luske. Walt introduces the folk heroes Casey Jones, the Martins and the Coys, Casey at the Bat, and Johnny Appleseed.

Four Methods of Flush Riveting (film) Training film produced for Lockheed Aircraft Corp. and then distributed by the National Film Board of Canada. Delivered on July 14, 1942. This was Walt's "pilot" film to show how animation could be used effectively in training films.

Four Musicians of Bremen, The (film) Laugh-O-gram film made by Walt in Kansas City in 1922. A cat, dog, donkey, and rooster try to catch some fish by serenading them with music. Later they have a run-in with a house full of robbers and exchange cannon fire.

Four Tales on a Mouse (television) Television show; aired on April 16, 1958. Directed by Hamilton S. Luske. Tells how Mickey helped other Disney performers with their careers by using a series of cartoons.

Fouret, Didier (1927–1989) He handled Disney publications at the Hachette publishing company in France, beginning in 1950, and was presented posthumously with a European Disney Legends award in 1997.

14 Going on 30 (television) Two-part television show; aired on March 6 and 13, 1988. Directed by Paul Schneider. A young teenage student, Danny, has a crush on a teacher, and, unlike most of his peers, is able to do something about it when he tests a machine, invented by his cousin, that greatly accelerates growth. But, after the test, the machine is destroyed and Danny has to remain an adult. He masquerades as the new principal in the school, changing rules to the delight of the kids. Finally the machine is fixed, leading to a surprise ending. Stars Steve Eckholdt, Adam Carl, Gabey Olds, Daphne Ashbrook, Irene

Tedrow, Patrick Duffy, Harry Morgan, Loretta Swit, Alan Thicke, Dick Van Patten.

Fourth Anniversary Show, The (television) Television show; aired on September 11, 1957. Directed by Sidney Miller. Celebrating four years on television, Walt Disney first describes his 1938 meeting with Serge Prokofieff, and shows the resulting film, *Peter and the Wolf*. Then he joins the Mouseketeers to tell about plans for future shows, introducing Jerome Courtland (Andy Burnett) and Guy Williams (Zorro). The Mouseketeers then surprise Walt with two musical sequences from a movie they hope he will let them star in, *The Rainbow Road to Oz*. He agrees, and they celebrate. Stars Fess Parker and the Mouseketeers. *The Rainbow Road to Oz* was never made, so these are the only two sequences that were ever filmed. Instead, in 1985 Disney made *Return to Oz*, with a totally different plot line and no longer a musical.

4th of July Firecrackers (film) Shorts program; released by RKO in 1953.

Fowler, Joseph ("Joe") (1894–1993) Ex-Navy admiral, chosen in 1954 by Walt Disney to build Disneyland. He remained to be in charge of construction of Walt Disney World also. He retired in 1972, and received the Disney Legends award in 1990.

Fowler's Harbor Dry dock area of Frontierland at Disneyland, where the *Columbia* is usually moored. It was named in honor of Rear Admiral Joseph Fowler.

Fox, Michael J. Actor; appeared in his film debut in *Midnight Madness* (Scott) and later in *Life With Mikey* (Michael Chapman). He provided the voice of Chance in *Homeward Bound: The Incredible Journey* and *Homeward Bound: Lost in San Francisco*, and Milo Thatch in *Atlantis: The Lost Empire*.

Fox and the Hound, The (film) The animated story of two friends who didn't know they were supposed to be enemies. Tod, an orphaned baby fox, raised by Widow Tweed, is best friends with

Copper, a young hunting dog. When they grow up, Copper learns to hunt and discovers he must pursue his friend. Tod is taken to a game preserve for safety, and there he falls in love with Vixey, a beautiful female fox. Copper and his master hunt Tod in the preserve, but when the chips are down, Tod and Copper realize that their friendship overcomes all. Released on July 10, 1981. Directed by Art Stevens, Ted Berman, and Richard Rich. 83 min. Featuring the voices of Mickey Rooney (older Tod), Keith Mitchell (young Tod), Kurt Russell (older Copper), Corey Feldman (young Copper), Pearl Bailey (Big Mama), Pat Buttram (Chief), Sandy Duncan (Vixey), Dick Bakalyan (Dinky), Paul Winchell (Boomer), Jack Albertson (Amos Slade), and Jeanette Nolan (Widow Tweed), the film is based on a story by Daniel P. Mannix. The feature film marked the premier effort of a new generation of Disney animators who would, in a few years create *The Little Mermaid* and *Beauty and the Beast*. With the exception of some early scenes and character development done by veteran animators Frank Thomas, Ollie Johnston, and Cliff Nordberg, this film represented the combined talent and imagination of a new team. Production on *The Fox and the Hound* began in the spring of 1977, but it was delayed by the defection from the animation department of Don Bluth, Gary Goldman, John Pomeroy, and an additional group of animators who were unhappy at the Disney Studio and eager to set up their own studio and produce movies that they felt were more in line with the style and quality of movies that Disney used to make in its golden years. By the time *The Fox and the Hound* was finished, four years later, it would require

approximately 360,000 drawings, 110,000 painted cels, 1,100 painted backgrounds, and a total of 180 people, including 24 animators. As in all Disney animated outings, music served to accentuate the action, highlight the humor, and, in general, enhance the story. The movie features the songs "Best of Friends," by Richard O. Johnston, son of animator Ollie Johnston, and Stan Fidel; "Lack of Education," "A Huntin' Man," and "Appreciate The Lady" by Jim Stafford; and "Goodbye May Seem Forever" by Richard Rich and Jeffrey Patch. The film was an enormous box office success. The film was re-released theatrically in 1988. Released on video in 1994.

Fox and the Hound, The: A Lesson in Being Careful (film) Educational film; released in September 1981. The important lesson that warnings should not be ignored is stressed in this film.

Fox Chase, The (film) Oswald the Lucky Rabbit cartoon; released on June 25, 1928.

Fox Family Worldwide Disney completed the acquisition on October 24, 2001, of Fox Family Worldwide, including the Fox Family Channel in the United States and Fox Kids channels worldwide, for $5.2 billion. The channel was renamed the ABC Family Channel. Fox Kids was rebranded as Jetix in 2004.

Fox Hunt, The (film) Silly Symphony cartoon; released on October 20, 1931. Directed by Wilfred Jackson. As a gag-filled fox hunt winds down, which includes misadventures with a porcupine, the hunters unfortunately catch a skunk instead of a fox, and flee. The skunk and the fox shake hands. The film was remade in color as a Donald Duck and Goofy cartoon, released on July 29, 1938. Directed by Ben Sharpsteen. In this later film, Donald is the Master of the Hounds and Goofy one of the riders. Just when it looks as if Donald will capture the fox, a skunk turns up to chase them all away.

France Pavilion in World Showcase at Epcot; opened October 1, 1982. The focal point at the rear of the pavilion is a 74-foot scaled-down replica of the Eiffel Tower, and the featured attraction is the presentation in the Palais de Cinema of *Impressions de France*, a travel film enhanced by stereophonic recordings of music by the great French classical composers. Repeat visitors to Epcot often count this film as one must-see return engagement.

France, Van (1912–1999) Starting work with Disneyland in March 1955, he created the Disney University where he taught new concepts in guest service, and years later, after his retirement in 1978, headed the Disneyland Alumni Club. He wrote his reminiscences in *Window on Main Street*. He was named a Disney Legend in 1994.

Francis The oh-so-proper bulldog in *Oliver & Company*; voiced by Roscoe Lee Browne.

Francis, Edna Maiden name of Roy O. Disney's wife. They were married in Hollywood at the home of Robert S. Disney, Roy's uncle, on April 11, 1925. Edna died in 1984.

Frank Dim-witted frill-necked lizard in *The Rescuers Down Under*; voiced by Wayne Robson.

Frank, Richard Formerly with Paramount Pictures, he joined Disney as president of the Walt Disney Studios in 1985. In 1994, on the resignation of Jeffrey Katzenberg, he was named chairman of Walt Disney Television and Telecommunications. He has also served as president of the Academy of Television Arts and Sciences. He resigned from the company in 1995.

Frank and Ollie (film) Documentary feature film about the lives and careers of legendary Disney animators, Frank Thomas and Ollie Johnston, made by Thomas's son, Ted Thomas. Premiered as a Disney film at the Cleveland Film Festival on April 7, 1995, after a January 22, 1995, preview at the Sundance Festival. First theatrical release was October 20, 1995, in Los Angeles for Academy Award consideration. 89 min. Released on video in 1998.

Frank Clell's in Town (television) Television show; episode 16 of *Texas John Slaughter*.

Frank Duck Brings 'em Back Alive (film) Donald Duck and Goofy cartoon; released on November 11, 1946. Directed by Jack Hannah. Donald loses his sanity in trying to capture "wild man of the jungle" Goofy.

Frank McKlusky, C.I. (film) An insurance claims investigator, Frank McKlusky, traumatized by his father having been left in a coma because of a horribly conceived motorcycle stunt, has developed an unhealthy aversion to any kind of risk—he lives with his parents, wears a helmet everywhere he goes, and lives his life strictly by the rules. He lets his partner do all the dirty work, but when his partner is killed in the line of duty, Frank is forced to come out from under his helmet to crack the case. Directed by Arlene Sanford. A Touchstone Picture. Limited theatrical release on April 26, 2002, only in ten Florida cities. Stars Dave Sheridan (Frank McKlusky), Randy Quaid (Madman McKlusky), Enrico Colantoni (Scout Bayou), Kevin Pollak (Ronnie Rosengold), Orson Bean (Gafty), Andy Richter (Herb), Cameron Richardson (Sharon), Dolly Parton (Edith McKlusky). 83 min. Released on video in 2002.

Frankenweenie (film) Featurette, released in Los Angeles on December 14, 1984, and again on March 6, 1992 (with *Blame It on the Bellboy*). An homage to the great horror films of the 1930s. After young Victor Frankenstein's dog, Sparky, is killed by a car, his parents become concerned when their son accumulates a collection of electrical junk in their attic. Using techniques of his legendary namesake, Victor's secret purpose is to bring his beloved pet back to life. The result of

the experiment causes panic in the neighborhood. 30 min. Directed by Tim Burton. Stars Barret Oliver, Shelley Duvall, Daniel Stern, Paul Bartel. The filmmakers managed to find and use some of the same laboratory equipment that had been used in the original *Frankenstein* film many years earlier. Shown on The Disney Channel and released on video in 1992.

Frankie Canary who appeared with Figaro in *Figaro and Frankie* (1947).

Freaky Friday (film) A harried mother thinks her 13-year-old daughter's life is a bed of roses. The daughter is similarly envious of her mother. Each wishes she could trade places with the other, and miraculously, one freaky Friday they exchange bodies. While Mom is experiencing the hilarious horrors of junior high school, the teenager is finding out what it's like to be an overburdened wife and mother. Both are glad to see the end of *that* day. Released initially in L.A. on December 17, 1976; general release on January 21, 1977. Directed by Gary Nelson. 98 min. Stars Jodie Foster (Annabel), Barbara Harris (Ellen), John Astin (Bill), Patsy Kelly (Mrs. Schmauss), Dick Van Patten (Harold), Vicki Schreck (Virginia), Sorrell Booke (Mr. Dilk), Ruth Buzzi (opposing coach), Kaye Ballard (Coach Betsy). Based on the book by Mary Rodgers. The song "I'd Like to Be You For a Day" was written by Al Kasha and Joel Hirschhorn. Los Angeles locations were used for the major part of the film, though the dedication at the marina was shot at San Diego's beautiful Mission Bay. Released on video in 1982 and 1992.

Freaky Friday (television) Two-hour television movie, a remake of the 1977 theatrical feature; aired on ABC on May 6, 1995. Thirteen-year-old

Annabelle Andrews and her mother, Ellen, magically trade places on a fateful Friday the 13th, and each then experiences firsthand the day-to-day difficulties that the other goes through, creating a new sense of empathy in each case. However, because of their different perspectives, they are sometimes able to handle the other's problems and decisions more forthrightly. Directed by Melanie Mayron. Stars Shelley Long (Ellen Andrews), Gaby Hoffman (Annabelle Andrews), Catlin Adams (Mrs. Barab), Sandra Bernhard (Frieda Debny), Eileen Brennan (Principal Handel), Alan Rosenberg (Bill Davidson). Most of the location filming for the film took place in Pasadena, California, doubling for Short Hills, New Jersey, where the story is set.

Freaky Friday (film) Dr. Tess Coleman and her 15-year-old daughter, Anna, are not getting along. They don't see eye to eye on clothes, hair, music, and certainly not in each other's taste in men. One Thursday evening, their disagreements reach a fever pitch. Anna is incensed that her mother doesn't support her musical aspirations, and Tess, a widow about to remarry, cannot see why Anna won't give her fiancé a break. Everything soon changes when two identical Chinese fortune cookies cause a little mystic mayhem. On the next morning, their Friday gets freaky when Tess and Anna find themselves inside each other's body, eventually gaining a little newfound respect for the other's point of view. But with Tess's wedding coming up on Saturday, the two have to find a way to switch back (and fast). Released on August 6, 2003. Directed by Mark Waters. Stars Jamie Lee Curtis (Tess Coleman), Lindsay Lohan (Anna), Harold Gould (Grandpa), Chad Michael Murray (Jake), Christina Vidal (Maddie), Mark Harmon (Ryan), Stephen Tobolowsky (Mr. Bates), Haley Hudson (Peg). Marc McClure, who played Boris in the original film, returns in a cameo. 97 min. Based on Mary Rodgers' classic novel, it is a remake of the 1977 film and 1995 television movie. The film made use of Southern California locations, including Palisades High School.

Freberg, Stan Actor; the voice of the Beaver in *Lady and the Tramp*; narrated *The Wuzzles*.

Freeman, Jonathan Actor; appeared in *The Associate* (hockey game executive) and provided the voice of Jafar in *Aladdin*.

Frees, Paul (1920–1986) Voice actor; did Ludwig Von Drake for the television shows, along with voices for The Haunted Mansion and Pirates of the Caribbean attractions at the parks.

Freewayphobia No. 1 (film) Goofy cartoon; released on February 13, 1965. Goofy, essaying the roles of Driverius Timidicus, Motoramus Fidgitus, and Mr. Neglecterus Maximus, graphically enacts the perils timid and neglectful motorists can and do encounter on the nation's freeways. Pointing out that lane changes can often be a direct route to death, Goofy reminds his audience to maintain a proper distance from vehicles in front of them. Directed by Les Clark. 16 min. For No. 2 see *Goofy's Freeway Trouble*.

Freight Train Disneyland train which operated from opening day for a few years. Guests rode in closed cattle cars, looking out through the slats. The train later had its cars converted into open viewing cars and still operates today, known as "Holiday Red."

French Market Buffeteria restaurant in New Orleans Square at Disneyland serving Creole cuisine; opened in 1966. The seating on the open-air terrace is perfect for watching the passersby and even glimpsing Fantasmic! in the evening. A small stage occasionally features performers playing Dixieland jazz.

Friar Tuck Badger holy man in *Robin Hood*; voiced by Andy Devine.

Friday Talent Roundup Day on the 1950s *Mickey Mouse Club*. Showtime Day on the new *Mickey Mouse Club*.

Friedle, Will Actor; appeared on television in *Boy Meets World* (Eric Matthews), *Go Fish* (Pete Troutner), *My Date with the President's Daughter* (Duncan Fletcher), *Walt Disney World's 25th Anniversary Party*, *Disney's Animal Kingdom: The First Adventure*, and *H-E-Double Hockey Sticks* (Griffelkin). He provides the voice of Ron Stoppable on *Kim Possible*.

Friend Like Me Song from *Aladdin*, sung by Robin Williams, written by Howard Ashman and Alan Menken. Nominated for an Academy Award for Best Song.

Friendly Enemies at Law (television) Television show; episode 9 of *Elfego Baca*.

Friendship in Vienna, A (film) Two girls—one Jewish, one with Nazi sympathizer parents—test their friendship in prewar Austria. A Disney Channel Premiere Film, first aired on August 27, 1988. 99 min. Directed by Arthur Allan Seidelman. Stars Ed Asner (Opah Oskar), Jane Alexander (Hannah Dornenwald), Stephen Macht (Franz Dornenwald), Jenny Lewis (Inge Dornenwald), Kamie Harper (Lise Mueller). Filmed entirely on location in Budapest, marking the first time The Disney Channel went behind the Iron Curtain to produce a film.

FriendShips Ferries that ply the World Showcase Lagoon at Epcot, delivering guests from one side to the other. Began operation on October 1, 1982.

Frolicking Fish (film) Silly Symphony cartoon; released on June 21, 1930. Directed by Burt Gillett. In an underwater musical, fish ride sea horses, lobsters and starfish play the harp and dance, and a villainous octopus has an anchor dropped on its head for trying to capture a bubble-dancing fish.

From Aesop to Hans Christian Andersen (television) Television show; aired on March 2, 1955. Directed by Clyde Geronimi. Walt Disney describes the age-old art of storytelling by offering cartoon versions of two of Aesop's fables, then de la Fontaine's classic story of the Country Mouse and his cousin the City Mouse, followed by tales from the Brothers Grimm, and finally Andersen's *The Ugly Duckling*.

From All of Us to All of You (television) Television show; aired first on December 19, 1958, then in eight later Christmas seasons. Directed by Jack Hannah. The holiday show, featuring Christmas cartoons, was changed for later runs, often by adding a segment on the latest animated feature.

From Ticonderoga to Disneyland (television) Television show; part 2 of *Moochie of Pop Warner Football*.

From Time to Time (film) Circle-Vision film, created for Visionarium at Disneyland Paris; opened on April 12, 1992. Audio-Animatronics characters 9-Eye and Timekeeper interact with the film, which presents a time travel journey through Europe, including scenes of eight countries. Presented by Renault. Opened in revised form (American scenes were added) in the Transportarium in Magic Kingdom Park at Walt Disney World on November 21, 1994.

Frontier Shooting Gallery Frontierland attraction in Magic Kingdom Park at Walt Disney World; opened October 1, 1971. Became Frontierland Shootin' Arcade. One of the more elaborate shooting galleries in the world.

Frontier Trading Post Frontierland shop at Disneyland; opened on July 17, 1955. Became Westward Ho Trading Co. in 1987. Also at Walt Disney World, beginning in 1971. Sells Western-themed gifts and souvenirs.

Frontierland One of the original lands of Disneyland. Walt Disney was always interested in the country's Western and Mexican heritages, and he was determined to give his Disneyland guests a feel for the real West. That meant mules and horses to add to the ambience, but that also meant trouble. Mules were ornery and occasionally bit the guests or refused to move. Horses pulling the stagecoaches and wagons would get spooked by the whistles of the trains as they passed nearby. Finally, with great regret, Walt agreed that the live animals had to go from Frontierland. Frontierland is also in Magic Kingdom Park at Walt Disney World and at Disneyland Paris. In Tokyo Disneyland, it is known as Westernland.

Frontierland Shootin' Arcade Frontierland gallery at Disneyland, opened on March 29, 1985, taking the place of the former Shooting Gallery. The attraction was completely rebuilt, becoming entirely electronic. The rifles fire infrared beams which, if on target, trigger humorous reactions. This is one of the few attractions in the park that is not included in the price of admission—others are the Main Street Penny Arcade and the Starcade. It was later known as Frontierland Shootin' Exposition. Also an attraction in Magic Kingdom Park at Walt Disney World, opened September 24, 1984, taking the place of the former Frontier Shooting Gallery.

Frou-Frou Horse in *The Aristocats*; voiced by Nancy Kulp.

Fuente del Oro Restaurante In Frontierland in Disneyland Paris; opened on April 12, 1992. A cantina with Tex-Mex specialties.

Full-Court Miracle (television) A Disney Channel Original Movie, premiering on November 21, 2003. Alex Schlotsky, team captain for the Philadelphia Hebrew Academy Lions basketball team, dreams of a pro basketball career. When he meets Lamont Carr, who is pursuing a pickup by the NBA, Alex persuades him to coach some seemingly hapless kids into champions. Although their minds are often on basketball, the boys are also studying the miraculous Chanukah story of Judah and the Maccabees. They soon find similarities between Lamont and Judah and become convinced that Lamont is an incarnation of the Jewish hero. Directed by Stuart Gillard. Stars Alex D. Linz (Alex Schlotsky), Richard T. Jones (Lamont Carr), R. H. Thomson (Rabbi Lewis),

Linda Kash (Cynthia Schlotsky), Jason Blicker (Marshall Schlotsky), Sheila McCarthy (Mrs. Klein), Cassie Steele (Julie), Jase Blankfort (Stick Goldstein), David Sazant (Joker Levy), Eric Knudsen (TJ Murphy), Sean Marquette (Big Ben Schwartz). Working title was *Lamont's Maccabees*. Based on a true story. The real Lamont Carr served as consultant and coached the young actors in basketball scenes.

Fulton's Crab House Restaurant on the former *Empress Lilly* riverboat at Pleasure Island at Walt Disney World, operated by Chicago-based Levy Restaurants. The 700-seat crab house opened on March 10, 1996.

Fulton's General Store In the Dixie Landings Resort at Walt Disney World; opened in February 1992. Merchandise is themed to the Old South feel of the hotel.

Fun and Fancy Free (film) Jiminy Cricket begins the film by playing a Dinah Shore record that tells the tale of *Bongo* to cheer up a desolate-looking doll and bear. Bongo, a circus bear, meets and falls in love with a girl bear named Lulubelle. But first he must confront a bear rival, Lumpjaw, whose looks match his name, before he wins her. When the story is completed, Jiminy finds he has been invited to ventriloquist Edgar Bergen's house, where he is entertaining starlet Luana Patten, Charlie McCarthy, and Mortimer Snerd. Bergen tells the story of *Mickey and the Beanstalk*, in which Mickey and his friends Donald and Goofy climb a beanstalk to rescue the lovely singing harp from a giant to restore happiness to their Happy Valley. As Bergen finishes the story, the giant appears, lifting the roof, in search of Mickey Mouse, then goes on down the hill toward Hollywood. Released on September 27, 1947. Directed by William Morgan with animation sequences directed by Jack Kinney, Bill Roberts, and Hamilton Luske. 73 min. Songs include "Fun and Fancy Free," "My, What a Happy Day," "Fe Fi Fo Fum," and "My Favorite Dream." The opening song by Jiminy, "I'm a Happy Go Lucky Fellow," was originally written and recorded for *Pinocchio*. Billy Gilbert did the voice of the giant.

Jim Macdonald began doing the voice of Mickey Mouse in this film when Walt Disney became too busy. In the 1960s, Disney animated new introductory material of Ludwig Von Drake and his pet, Herman, to replace Edgar Bergen when the *Beanstalk* segment was run on Disney's television show. Released on video in 1982.

Fun to Be Fit (film) Series of three educational films: *Why Be Physically Fit, Getting Physically Fit, Physical Fitness*; released in March 1983.

Fun With Mr. Future (film) Special cartoon; released only in Los Angeles on October 27, 1982, for Academy Award consideration. Mr. Future, an Audio-Animatronics "talking head" gives us a glimpse of what life will be like tomorrow—and what we thought it would be like today. A new animated sequence depicting a typical day in the life of a "future" family is used along with live-action footage taken from previously released films.

Fun with Music Day Monday on the 1950s *Mickey Mouse Club.*

Funicello, Annette Actress; besides her *Mickey Mouse Club* work as a Mouseketeer, and on the *Adventure in Dairyland, Annette,* and *Spin and Marty* serials, she appeared in *The Shaggy Dog* (Allison D'Allessio), *Babes in Toyland* (Mary Contrary), and as Jennifer in *The Misadventures of Merlin Jones* and *The Monkey's Uncle.* She appeared on television in *Backstage Party, Disneyland After Dark, Elfego Baca, Escapade in Florence, The Horsemasters, The Golden Horseshoe Revue, Zorro,* and *The Best of Disney: 50 Years of Disney Magic,* and in *Lots of Luck* on The Disney Channel. Annette also became a recording star, singing a number of songs on the Disney record labels. Walt Disney discovered Annette when he saw her while attending an amateur program at the Starlight Bowl in Burbank, where she was performing a number entitled "Ballet vs. Jive." She was named a Disney Legend in 1992. A non-Disney film about her life, *A Dream Is a Wish Your Heart Makes,* aired on CBS in 1995.

Funny Bones (film) A young comedian, Tommy Fawkes, trying to succeed but living in the shadow of his famous father, George, flees to Blackpool, England, where he spent the first six years of his life and where he hopes to find the perfect physical comedy act. While auditioning acts there, he discovers dark secrets about his father's past, most importantly that he has a half brother. Directed by Peter Chelsom. A Hollywood Pictures film. Released on March 24, 1995, exclusively in New York City. 128 min. Stars Oliver Platt (Tommy Fawkes), Lee Evans (Jack), Richard Griffiths (Jim Minty), Oliver Reed (Dolly Hopkins), George Carl (Thomas Parker), Leslie Caron (Katie), Jerry Lewis (George Fawkes). The film was shot on location in Blackpool, in Las Vegas, and at Ealing Studios in West London. Released on video in 1995.

Funny Little Bunnies (film) Silly Symphony cartoon; released on March 24, 1934. Directed by Wilfred Jackson. At rainbow's end lies the magic land of the Easter bunnies, preparing Easter eggs

and candies. Birds and animals help in the creation of painted eggs, using such oddities as plaid and polka-dot paint, and chocolate bunnies. The only Easter-themed Disney cartoon, this was the first film on which later director Wolfgang Reitherman animated.

Funny, You Don't Look 200 (television) Television special on ABC celebrating the bicentennial of the U.S. Constitution, including new animation done by Disney; aired on October 12, 1987. Hosted by Richard Dreyfuss, with a cast of dozens of celebrities. Directed by Jim Yukich.

Further Adventures of Gallegher, The: A Case of Murder (television) Television show; aired on September 26, 1965. Episode 1. Directed by Jeffrey Hayden. The aspiring newspaper reporter, Gallegher, gets involved in a murder of a traveling actor, and must help his reporter friend, Brownie, who is blamed. Stars Roger Mobley, Edmond O'Brien, Harvey Korman, Victoria Shaw, Peter Wyngarde.

Further Adventures of Gallegher, The: The Big Swindle (television) Television show; aired on October 3, 1965. Episode 2. Directed by Jeffrey Hayden. The young copyboy helps the town's first female newspaper reporter, who is writing a series on confidence men. The swindlers are caught up in a sting, but they catch on and the reporter and Gallegher have to subdue them in order to escape and write their article. Stars Roger Mobley (Gallegher), Edmond O'Brien, Anne Francis, Harvey Korman.

Further Adventures of Gallegher, The: The Daily Press vs. City Hall (television) Television show; aired on October 10, 1965. Episode 3. Directed by Jeffrey Hayden. Gallegher teams with a female reporter, Adeline Jones, for an exposé on graft and corruption in city government, after a gas explosion implicates the mayor, who awarded a contract that resulted in faulty pipes. The mayor's friend whose company installed the pipes is naturally enraged, and he tries to put the paper out of business. Stars Edmond O'Brien, Anne Francis, Roger Mobley, Harvey Korman, Parley Baer, James Westerfield, Edward Platt.

Further Adventures of Spin and Marty, The (television) Serial on the *Mickey Mouse Club* during the 1956–57 season. Directed by William Beaudine, Sr. The boys return to camp and Marty now is friendly with the others. The boys plan for a big dance, with girls from a neighboring camp, and a swimming meet. Stars Tim Considine, David Stollery, Annette Funicello, B. G. Norman, Brand Stirling, Roger Broaddus, Kevin Corcoran, Melinda Plowman, Roy Barcroft, Harry Carey, Jr., Lennie Geer, J. Pat O'Malley, Sammee Tong. Sammy Ogg. 23 episodes.

Further Report on Disneyland, A/A Tribute to Mickey Mouse (television) Television show; aired on July 13, 1955. Cartoon sequences directed by Wilfred Jackson. A preview of Disneyland, just four days before its opening, with Winston Hibler hosting a look at how the attractions were designed and built. Stop-motion photography is used to show a speeded-up version of the construction as the deadline approaches. The Mickey Mouse segment was originally shown with *The Disneyland Story*. The show is also known as *A Pre-Opening Report from Disneyland.*

Future Work (film) Educational film about new careers available in the high-tech workplace; released in September 1983.

Future World Major section of Epcot at Walt Disney World, the first area seen by guests as they enter the main entrance. Extensive pavilions, sponsored by major corporations, celebrate the past and look to what we might find in the future. Pavilions are Spaceship Earth, The Living Seas, The Land, Journey into Imagination, World of Motion, Horizons, Universe of Energy, and Wonders of Life, all surrounding Innoventions (formerly Communicore). Guests pass through Future World on the way to World Showcase.

FutureCom Display in Communicore West sponsored by Bell, from October 1, 1982 to January 31, 1994. Showed how people gather information, including some of the latest technological advances.

Fuzzbucket (television) Television show; aired on May 18, 1986. An invisible, furry creature befriends a boy who is insecure about the starting of junior high school and his parents' arguing. Causing trouble and havoc everywhere he goes, Fuzzbucket helps the boy overcome both school and family problems. Directed by Mick Garris. Stars Chris Hebert, Phil Fondacaro, Joe Regalbuto, Wendy Phillips, Robin Lively, John Vernon. This was the first half of a program with *The Deacon Street Deer*.

G

Gabble Sisters, The Amelia and Abigail are the two English spinster geese in *The Aristocats*; voiced by Carole Shelley and Monica Evans.

Gabor, Eva (1921–1995) Actress, she voiced Duchess in *The Aristocats* and Bianca in *The Rescuers* and *The Rescuers Down Under*.

Gadget An inventive female mouse character in *Chip 'n' Dale's Rescue Rangers*. Voiced by Tress MacNeille.

Gadget's Go-Coaster Attraction opened in Mickey's Toontown at Disneyland on January 24, 1993. A short but fun roller-coaster ride themed around the inventive female mouse character in *Chip 'n' Dale's Rescue Rangers*. Also at Tokyo Disneyland; opened April 15, 1996.

Gag Factory/Five and Dime Shop in Mickey's Toontown at Disneyland; opened January 24,

1993. Also at Tokyo Disneyland; opened April 15, 1996.

Gala Day at Disneyland (film) Documentary featurette; released on January 21, 1960. Produced by Hamilton Luske. The gala dedication ceremonies at the opening of three new major attractions at Disneyland—Matterhorn Bobsleds, Submarine Voyage, and the new Monorail—include a parade down Main Street with appearances by Walt and Roy Disney and members of their families, along with Vice President Richard Nixon and family, and numerous film stars. The celebrations end at night with a fireworks display. 27 min.

Gallegher (television) Three-part television show; aired on January 24, 31, and February 7, 1965. Directed by Byron Paul. An energetic newspaper copyboy in 1889 wants to become a reporter, and he is soon more deeply involved in his stories than he had expected. When he discovers a bank robbery, he helps the reporter, Brownie, to apprehend the four-fingered culprit. Later he helps the police chief who has been framed, and tries to convince the authorities that he has discovered a wanted felon in town. Stars Roger Mobley (Gallegher), Edmond O'Brien (Jefferson Crowley), Jack Warden (Lt. Fergus), Ray Teal (Snead), Robert Middleton (Dutch

Mac), Harvey Korman (Brownie), Philip Ober (Hade), Bryan Russell (Jimmy). Based on a book by Richard Harding Davis. See also *The Further Adventures of Gallegher*, *Gallegher Goes West*, and *The Mystery of Edward Sims*.

Gallegher Goes West: Crusading Reporter (television) Television show; aired on October 30, 1966. Episode 2. Directed by Joseph Sargent. Gallegher and his colleagues work for the recall of the corrupt mayor of Brimstone, even though the mayor tries to stop them by force. Stars Dennis Weaver, John McIntire, Roger Mobley, Ray Teal, Jeanette Nolan, Larry D. Mann, Peter Graves.

Gallegher Goes West: Showdown with the Sundown Kid (television) Television show; aired on October 23, 1966. Part 1. Directed by Joseph Sargent. Gallegher befriends a man on the stagecoach while heading west, only to discover he is a famous outlaw, the Sundown Kid. The sheriff is crooked, too, so it is difficult for Gallegher and his friend, Detective Snead, to capture the Sundown Kid. Stars Dennis Weaver, John McIntire, Roger Mobley, James Gregory, Ray Teal, Jeanette Nolan, Peter Graves.

Gallegher Goes West: Tragedy on the Trail (television) Television show; aired on January 29, 1967. Episode 3. Directed by James Sheldon. Gallegher buys and trains a horse, then is surprised when a local rancher is accused of murder. The boy is sure it is a frame-up, and he tries to help out. Stars Roger Mobley, John McIntire, Beverly Garland, Harry Townes, Ron Hayes, Jeanette Nolan, Bill Williams.

Gallegher Goes West: Trial by Terror (television) Television show; aired on February 5, 1967. Episode 4. Directed by James Sheldon. Gallegher continues to help the rancher who has been framed for murder, and after he finds an incriminating watch, he is able to reach the trial just in time to save the day. Stars John McIntire, Roger Mobley, Beverly Garland, Harry Townes, Ron Hayes, Jeanette Nolan, Bill Williams, Ray Teal, Darlene Carr.

Gallopin' Gaucho, The (film) The second Mickey Mouse cartoon produced. Made as a silent cartoon, but released in 1928 after sound was added. In a parody of Douglas Fairbanks swashbucklers, Mickey falls in love with Minnie in a South American cantina, and then rescues her from unwanted suitor, Pete, after a violent swordfight. Directed by Walt Disney.

Game, The (film) Educational film about how to follow rules and not demand special treatment, from the What Should I Do? series, released in December 1969.

Garay, Joaquin He voiced Panchito, the rooster in *The Three Caballeros*. Thirty-five years later, his son Joaquin Garay III carried on a family tradition by appearing as Paco in *Herbie Goes Bananas*.

Garbage Picking Field Goal Kicking Philadelphia Phenomenon, The (television) Two-hour television movie; aired on *The Wonderful World of Disney* on February 15, 1998. Barney Gorman, a Philadelphia garbage man, finds that his kicking abilities get him a once-in-a-lifetime opportunity to be a placekicker for the Philadelphia Eagles. After a grueling training period, he wins a game for the Eagles with his first professional kick. But, eventually, he finds that happiness can still come from his old garbage route. Directed by Tim Kelleher. Stars Tony Danza (Barney Gorman), Jessica Tuck (Marie Gorman), Art LaFleur (Gus Rogenheimer), Jaime Cardriche (Bubba), Julie Stewart (Wendy Fox), Gil Filar (Danny Gorman), Al Ruscio (Pop Gorman), Ray Wise (Randolph Pratt). The producers used locations in Toronto to double for Philadelphia. The real-life owner of the Eagles, Jeff Lurie, has a small role as a friend of Barney's.

Garber, Matthew (1956–1977) Child actor, appeared in *The Three Lives of Thomasina* (Geordie), *Mary Poppins* (Michael Banks), and *The Gnome-Mobile* (Rodney). He was named a Disney Legend in 2004.

Garber, Victor Actor; appeared in *Life With Mikey* (Brian Spiro) and *Tuck Everlasting* (Father

Foster), and on television in *Rodgers and Hammerstein's Cinderella* (king), *Annie* (Daddy Oliver Warbucks), *Meredith Willson's The Music Man* (Mayor Shinn), and *Alias* (Jack Bristow).

Garden Gallery Restaurant in the former Disney Inn at Walt Disney World, until the hotel became Shades of Green, the military's R&R establishment.

Garden Grill Restaurant Restaurant in The Land at Epcot; opened on November 15, 1993. Formerly known as the Good Turn Restaurant and the Land Grille Room.

Gargoyles (television) Animated television series; premiered October 24, 1994, in syndication and ended August 29, 1997. A mysterious medieval race, stone by day and alive by night, turn up in New York where they emerge from their stone slumber to protect Manhattan from modern-day barbarians. The voice cast includes Keith David (Goliath), Edward Asner (Hudson), Salli Richardson (Elisa Maza), Jonathan Frakes (David Xanatos), Marina Sirtis (Demona), Bill Fagerbakke (Broadway). 65 episodes.

Gargoyles: The Goliath Chronicles (television) Animated television series, debuting on ABC on September 7, 1996, and ending on April 12, 1997. In this spin-off from the *Gargoyles* series, Goliath and his small clan of Gargoyle warriors must now contend with a growing anti-gargoyle faction called the Quarrymen. Organized and bitterly hostile, the Quarrymen will stop at nothing until the Gargoyles are captured. Voices include Keith David (Goliath), Edward Asner (Hudson), Bill Fagerbakke (Broadway), Marina Sirtis (Demona), Jonathan Frakes (David Xanatos), Salli Richardson (Elisa Maza). 13 episodes.

Gargoyles the Movie: The Heroes Awaken (film) Video release in February 1995. 80 min.

Garity, William (1899–1971) After helping record the sound for *Steamboat Willie*, sound engineer Bill Garity joined the Disney Studio the next year, where he helped Walt Disney make his cartoons the most technically advanced in the industry. Bill's team created the multiplane camera and invented Fantasound for *Fantasia*, while supervising the construction of the new Disney Studio in Burbank. He left Disney in 1942. Bill was named a Disney Legend posthumously in 1999.

Garland, Beverly Actress; appeared on television in *Elfego Baca*, *Texas John Slaughter*, and *Gallegher Goes West*.

Garner, James Actor; appeared in *One Little Indian* (Clint Keyes), *The Castaway Cowboy* (Costain), and *The Distinguished Gentleman* (Jeff Johnson). He provided the voice of Commander Rourke in *Atlantis*, and appeared in *8 Simple Rules* (Jim Hennessy).

Garner (Wall), Marcellite (1910–1993) Member of the Ink and Paint Department at the Disney Studio in the 1930s; the first voice of Minnie Mouse.

Garson, Greer (1904–1996) Actress; appeared in *The Happiest Millionaire* (Mrs. Drexel Biddle).

Gaskill, Andy Animator; joined Disney first in 1973. He is credited with the art direction for *The Lion King*, *Hercules*, and *Treasure Planet*.

Gasparilla Grill & Games Fast-food and game arcade at the Grand Floridian Resort & Spa at Walt Disney World.

Gaston Oafish hunk who courts Belle in *Beauty and the Beast*; voiced by Richard White, and animated by Andreas Deja.

Gay, Margie (1919–2003) Child actress who acted in the largest number of the Alice Comedies as Alice. Her real name was Marjorie Teresa Gossett.

Gaynor's Nightmare Cartoon sequence animated at Disney, which was inserted in the 20th Century Fox film *Servant's Entrance* (1934).

Geena Davis Show, The (television) Half-hour television series on ABC, premiering October 10, 2000, and ending July 12, 2001. Teddie Cochran is a successful New York career woman who meets the man of her dreams, Max Ryan, only to learn he comes with an instant family and a home in the suburbs. Stars Geena Davis (Teddie), Peter Horton (Max), Mimi Rogers (Hillary), Kim Coles (Judy), Harland Williams (Alan), John Francis Daley (Carter), Makenzie Vega (Eliza), Esther Scott (Gladys).

Geer, Will (1902–1978) Actor; appeared in *Napoleon and Samantha* (grandfather).

Gehry, Frank Architect; designed Festival Disney (later Disney Village) at Disneyland Paris, and the Walt Disney Concert Hall for downtown Los Angeles.

General Beverages, Inc. Chattanooga-based soft drink manufacturer that produced Donald Duck beverages from 1952 to 1955, and sold them throughout the country. The Donald Duck cola bottles often turn up at flea markets and are popular with bottle collectors as well as Disney collectors.

General Electric Carousel of Progress Attraction at the 1964–65 New York World's Fair, later moved to Tomorrowland at Disneyland, where it opened July 2, 1967. Closed September 9, 1973, and moved to Walt Disney World. America Sings, then moved into the carousel theater at Disneyland. At Disneyland, the attraction was tied to the theme song "There's a Great Big Beautiful Tomorrow," which echoed General Electric's then current philosophy. The attraction featured the increased importance of electricity in the home through four different scenes of an Audio-Animatronics family. When the attraction moved to Walt Disney World, where it opened on January 15, 1975, the theme song changed to "The Best Time of Your Life," reflecting General Electric's changed philosophy. General Electric ended sponsorship in 1985, but the attraction continues to operate, and to satisfy nostalgia

buffs, the song "There's a Great Big Beautiful Tomorrow" was returned during a 1993 rehab, which also saw a theming of the four tableaux to various holidays. It was renamed Walt Disney's Carousel of Progress in 1994.

Genest, Emile (1921–2003) Actor; appeared in *Nikki, Wild Dog of the North* (Jacques LeBeau), *Big Red* (Emile Fornet), and *The Incredible Journey* (John Longridge), and on television in *Kit Carson and the Mountain Men*.

Genie Wisecracking, all-powerful force in *Aladdin*; voiced by Robin Williams. In the television series and in *Return of Jafar*, he was voiced by Dan Castellaneta.

Genius (television) A Disney Channel Original Movie; premiered on August 21, 1999. Charlie, a supersmart 13-year-old, ends up feeling a little out of place when he chooses to attend Northern University to study physics under his favorite professor, Dr. Krickstein. Charlie finds it difficult to fit in until he creates an alter ego, "Chaz," a "cool kid," and simultaneously attends a local junior high so he can be near the girl of his dreams. At first he is able to juggle his double life, but it isn't long before both worlds collide. Directed by Rod Daniel. Stars Trevor Morgan (Charlie Boyle), Emmy Rossum (Claire Addison), Charles Fleischer (Dr. Krickstein), Peter Keleghan (Dean Wallace).

Gentilini, Mario (1909–1988) He was in charge of *Topolino* magazine at the Mondadori publishing company in Italy for many years; presented posthumously with a European Disney Legends award in 1997.

Gentleman's Gentleman, A (film) Pluto cartoon; released on March 28, 1941. Directed by Clyde Geronimi. Pluto, sent for the Sunday paper by Mickey, loses the dime in a grate, but recovers it with gum on his tail and despite other tribulations finally presents the paper to Mickey all covered with mud.

George, Chief Dan (1899–1981) Native American actor; appeared in *Smith* (Ol' Antoine) and *The Bears and I* (Chief Peter A-Tas-Ka-Nay).

George, Gil [Hazel] (1904–1996) Lyricist on a number of Disney songs in the 1950s, including the title songs for *Old Yeller*, *Tonka*, and *The Light in the Forest*. Gil George was the pseudonym of Hazel George, the Disney Studio nurse.

George of the Jungle (film) Based on the well-known animated 1960s television series, this live-action film features the klutzy George, who grows up as a Tarzan-like character after surviving a jungle plane crash and being raised by gorillas. He rescues a beautiful wayward traveler named Ursula when a lion attacks her while she is on safari. While Ursula warms to George and his fantasy jungle world—complete with a talking ape, named Ape, and an elephant who thinks it is a dog—Ursula's irksome fiancé, Lyle, plots to regain his lady love and destroy the balance of nature in George's rain forest kingdom. When George is injured, Ursula brings him back to her world, specifically San Francisco, where he naturally has a difficult time adjusting and longs to return to his jungle home. Directed by Sam Weisman. Released on July 16, 1997. Stars Brendan Fraser (George), Leslie Mann (Ursula Stanhope), Thomas Haden Church (Lyle Van de Groot). 92 min. The elephant, Shep, is played by Tai, the 28-year-old veteran of such films as *Rudyard Kipling's The Jungle Book* and *Operation Dumbo Drop*, with his dog-like movements added by Dream Quest Images through computer-generated enhancements. Ape and the other gorillas were the result of teaming live actors with a sophisticated radio telemetry system devised by the Jim Henson Creature Shop. Inspired by the wit, style, and humor of Jay Ward, who produced the animated series for four years, the film's producers even retained the series' catchy and now classic theme song. While San Francisco and Hawaii provided outdoor locations, parts of the jungle were also built indoors, utilizing the former Hughes Aircraft hangar in Playa del Rey, California, the same place where Howard Hughes built his Spruce Goose. Released on video in 1997.

George of the Jungle II (film) A sequel to the 1997 film. George's scheming mother-in-law, Beatrice Stanhope, teams with Ursula's ex-fiancé Lyle to hypnotize Ursula into leaving George, so they can turn the jungle to mulch. George and his animal pals must travel to Las Vegas to rescue Ursula before returning to the jungle to stop the bulldozers. Directed by David Grossman. Released direct-to-video on October 21, 2003. Stars Christopher Showerman (George), Thomas Haden Church (Lyle Van de Groot), Julie Benz (Ursula), Christina Pickles (Beatrice Stanhope), Kelly Miller (Betsy), Angus T. Jones (George Jr.), John Cleese (Ape). Based on characters created by Jay Ward. Filmed on location in Queensland, Australia.

George Wendt Show, The (television) Half-hour television series focusing on the relationship between two brothers, George and Dan

Coleman, who own a garage in Madison, Wisconsin, and who also produce a local call-in radio show, dispensing their sage wisdom to the mechanically challenged. Debuted on CBS on March 8, 1995, and ended April 12, 1995. Stars George Wendt (George), Pat Finn (Dan), Mark Christopher Lawrence (Fletcher), Kate Hodge (Libby), Brian Doyle-Murray (Finnie).

Georgette Prissy poodle in *Oliver & Company*; voiced by Bette Midler.

Geppetto Kindly wood-carver who made Pinocchio; voiced by Christian Rub.

Geppetto (television) A two-hour musical for *The Wonderful World of Disney*; airing on May 7, 2000. In Villagio, the lonely toy maker, Geppetto, yearns for a son. The Blue Fairy grants him his wish by bringing Pinocchio to life, but Geppetto's unrealistic expectations for his son cause the boy to run away and join Stomboli's traveling puppet show. The Blue Fairy helps Geppetto in his search for Pinocchio, and Geppetto is horrified to visit Idyllia—where Prof. Buonragazzo has a machine that can create the perfect child—and Pleasure Island. Eventually, Pinocchio and Geppetto are reunited. Stars Drew Carey (Geppetto), Julia Louis-Dreyfus (Blue Fairy), Brent Spiner (Stromboli), Rene Auberjonois (Buonragazzo), Seth Adkins (Pinocchio), Usher Raymond (Ring Leader). There is new music by Stephen Schwartz and reuse of one song ("I've Got No Strings") from the 1940 animated feature. Released on video in 2000.

Gere, Richard Actor; appeared in *Pretty Woman* (Edward Lewis) and *Runaway Bride* (Ike Graham).

Germany Pavilion in World Showcase at Epcot; opened October 1, 1982, patterned after towns such as the picturesque, walled Rothenberg. A statue honoring St. George, the patron saint of soldiers, is in the center of the square, and a glockenspiel chimes tunes themed to the pavilion.

Geronimi, Clyde ("Gerry") (1901–1989) He was hired at Disney in 1931 as an animator on the short cartoons, promoted to director in 1939 and directed the Academy Award winners *The Ugly Duckling* and *Lend a Paw*. He was a sequence director on the features from *Victory Through Air Power* to *One Hundred and One Dalmatians*, and Supervising Director on *Sleeping Beauty*. He also directed many of the early television shows. He retired in 1959.

Geronimo's Revenge (film) John Slaughter has been desperately trying to stop Geronimo from violating the rather delicate and nervous peace that has been established with Natchez, the chief of the Apache tribe, who desires a continued peace rather than fruitless bloodshed. The impetuous Geronimo stages increasingly damaging and ferocious raids and escapes below the border. Knowing that he will return, Gen. Nelson A. Miles has sought out Slaughter as the only one who would know how to deal with this dangerous threat. Because of what has happened, Slaughter leaves his ranch and family and plans the strategy that eventually lures Geronimo into a trap that brings to an end his days as a raider. Foreign theatrical compilation of *Texas John Slaughter* television episodes. First released in England in May 1964. Directed by James Neilson and Harry Keller. 77 min. Stars Tom Tryon, Darryl Hickman. Released on video in 1986. Also the title of episode 12 of the *Texas John Slaughter* television series.

Gerson, Betty Lou (1914–1999) She voiced Cruella De Vil in *One Hundred and One Dalmatians*, and narrated *Cinderella*. She was named a Disney Legend in 1996.

Get a Clue (television) A Disney Channel Original Movie; first aired on June 28, 2002. Thirteen-year-old Lexy is a fashion queen and budding journalist for the newspaper at Millington, the prep school she attends in Manhattan. After the disappearance of her English teacher, Mr. Walker, she, her street-smart editor Jack, and her pals find themselves embroiled in a scheme bigger than they ever could have imagined. They use their investigative skills to rescue Mr. Walker from Meaney's malicious mischief. Directed by Maggie Greenwald. Stars Lindsay Lohan (Alexandra "Lexy" Gold), Bug Hall (Jack Downey), Brenda Song (Jennifer Hervey), Ali Mukaddam (Gabe Nelson), Ian Gomez (Mr. Walker), Amanda Plummer (Miss Dawson), Charles Shaughnessy (Meaney). 83 min.

Get it Right: Following Directions with Goofy (film) Educational film; released in September 1982. Goofy helps illustrate why directions—visual, spoken, and written—are so important.

Get Rich Quick (film) Goofy cartoon; released on August 31, 1951. Directed by Jack Kinney.

Again playing Everyman, Goofy wins money at poker and though his wife is initially angry with his gambling, she forgives him when she sees the amount of cash he has won, causing Goofy to say, "Easy come, easy go!"

Get the Message (film) Educational film explaining the importance of communication to mankind and tracing the development of communication techniques; released in December 1971.

Getting Physically Fit (film) Educational film, from the Fun to Be Fit series; released in March 1983. Students learn how to achieve fitness through a carefully planned program.

Getty, Balthazar Actor; appeared in *Judge Dredd* (Olmeyer), *White Squall* (Tod Johnston), and *Ladder 49* (Ray Gauquin).

Getty, Estelle Actress; appeared on television in *The Golden Girls* and *The Golden Palace*, and eventually on *Empty Nest*, all as Sophia Petrillo. She won the Emmy Award as Outstanding Supporting Actress in a Comedy Series in 1988.

Ghost of Cypress Swamp, The (television) Two-hour television movie; aired on March 13, 1977. Directed by Vincent McEveety. A teen, Lonny Bascombe, and his dad hunt a black panther that has been terrorizing local farms, but it eludes them. Lonny is captured by and then befriends an escaped fugitive living in the swamp, as both help each other survive. The boy promises to keep the hermit's secret, and finally is able to kill the marauding panther. Stars Vic Morrow, Jeff East, Tom Simcox, Jacqueline Scott, Noah Beery, Louise Latham, Shug Fisher, Cindy Eilbacher.

Ghost Whisperer, The (television) One-hour television series; airing on CBS beginning September 23, 2005. Melinda Gordon has a gift of being able to see, and talk to, spirits. These are earthbound ghosts who have yet to cross over to the other side, who seek Melinda's help in communicating with the living. Although Melinda sometimes embraces her abilities as a blessing and other times sees them as a curse, she always helps her clients—alive or dead—find emotional closure. Stars Jennifer Love Hewitt (Melinda Gordon), David Conrad (Jim Clancy), Aisha Tyler (Andrea Moreno). From Sander/Moses Prods. In association with Touchstone Television and Paramount Television.

Ghosts of Buxley Hall, The (television) Two-part television show; aired on December 21, 1980, and January 4, 1981. Directed by Bruce Bilson. Girls come to a private boys' military academy to the horror of the boys and the ghosts of the academy's founders, who come out to help rid the academy of the females. There is a plot afoot to tear down the school, unless the guardian of one of the cadets comes through with a promised donation. Stars Victor French, Louise Latham, Rad Daly, Monte Markham, Ruta Lee, Vito Scotti, Don Porter, Christian Juttner, Tricia Cast, John Myhers.

Ghosts of the Abyss (film) Cameras make an expedition below the surface of the ocean to the final resting place of the *Titanic*. Using state-of-the-art technology developed expressly for this expedition, the filmmakers are able to explore virtually all of the wreckage, inside and out, as never before. Directed by James Cameron. Produced in association with Walden Media. Released on April 11, 2003. With Bill Paxton. 60 min. Simultaneous release in 3-D in regular and large format/IMAX theaters. James Cameron is best known for directing the award-winning *Titanic* (1997), in which Bill Paxton was one of the actors. Released on DVD in 2004.

Giantland (film) Mickey Mouse cartoon; released on November 25, 1933. Directed by Burt Gillett. Mickey tells his nephews a loose version of "Jack and the Beanstalk" in which he climbs the beanstalk and meets a formidable giant. Mickey only manages to escape with the aid of pepper and burning the beanstalk, which sends the giant hurtling toward the ground and on through to China. A forerunner to the *Mickey and the Beanstalk* segment of *Fun and Fancy Free.*

Gibson See Card Corner.

Gibson, Blaine Artist and sculptor; joined Disney in 1939 as an inbetweener and assistant animator, working on the features through *One Hundred and One Dalmatians*. In 1954 he began working on projects at WED Enterprises in his spare time, and went over there permanently in 1961. He headed the sculpture department, responsible for most of the heads of the Audio-Animatronics characters, from pirates to the presidents. His statue of Walt and Mickey graces the

hub at Disneyland. He retired in 1983, and was made a Disney Legend in 1993.

Gibson, Mel Actor; voiced Capt. John Smith in *Pocahontas*, and appeared in *Ransom* (Tom Mullen) and *Signs* (Graham Hess).

Gibson Girl Ice Cream Parlour, The Located on Main Street in Disneyland Paris; opened on April 12, 1992. Also opened on Main Street at Disneyland in 1997 (using the American spelling of Parlor), taking the place of the former Carnation Ice Cream Parlor, but one door down the street in space formerly occupied by Blue Ribbon Bakery.

Gideon's Crossing (television) One-hour television drama; aired on ABC from October 18, 2000 to April 9, 2001. As chief of experimental medicine at a prestigious Boston teaching hospital, Benjamin Gideon, an unorthodox doctor who explores the brave new world of cutting-edge medicine, ventures into the even-trickier terrain of his patients' lives. Stars Andre Braugher (Ben Gideon), Rubén Blades (Max Cabranes), Russell Hornsby (Aaron Boies), Hamish Linklater (Bruce

Cherry), Eric Lane (Wyatt Cooper), Rhoda Mitra (Ollie Klein).

Gift Card On November 8, 2004, the Disneyland Resort began selling a gift card at merchandise locations throughout the resort. The cards can be purchased in any amount from $5 to $1,500. This was the first gift card offered in a Disney park.

Gift of Time, A: Pediatric AIDS (film) Educational film discussing drug treatments and other aspects, in the EPCOT Educational Media Collection; released in October 1989. 18 min.

Gift-Giver Extraordinaire Machine Promotion at Disneyland for its 30th anniversary in 1985. During that year, every 30th guest coming to the park received a prize on entering the front gate; for the more elaborate prizes, up to and including a new car, selected winners would get to spin the Gift-Giver Machine located in the Hub.

G.I. Jane (film) Navy intelligence officer Lt. Jordon O'Neil sets a historic precedence when she is recruited as a test case to be the first woman allowed to train for the highly covert operations unit known as the Navy SEALs. Selected for her courage, skills, and levelheadedness, O'Neil is determined to succeed in the most demanding, most merciless, and most honored fighting force in the world, in which 60 percent of her male counterparts will fail. Under the relentless command of Master Chief John Urgayle, O'Neil is put through weeks of physical and emotional hell, and is not expected to succeed. Indeed, military and high-ranking government officials—including her sponsor, Senator Lillian DeHaven—are *counting* on her to fail. However, to their dismay and perplexity, O'Neil perseveres. When the recruits' final training exercise is diverted to aid in extricating American troops in Libya, Urgayle is critically wounded, and O'Neil must gather all her leadership experience and courage to save him and the mission—even at the cost of risking her own life. A Hollywood Picture, in association with Scott Free Productions and Largo Enter-

tainment. Directed by Ridley Scott. Released on August 22, 1997. 125 min. Filmed in CinemaScope. Stars Demi Moore (Jordan O'Neil), Viggo Mortensen (John Urgayle), Anne Bancroft (Lillian DeHaven), Jason Beghe (Royce). Casting directors began a search for actors and extras who were in perfect physical shape, and were lucky in finding many who had military backgrounds. For the training base, the filmmakers selected Camp Blanding, a 30,000-acre National Guard training site in northern Florida. Other filming took place in Jacksonville's Huguenot Park, at Hunting Island State Park near Beaufort, South Carolina, and in Washington, D.C., and neighboring Virginia and Maryland.

Gilbert, Billy (1893–1971) He voiced Sneezy in *Snow White and the Seven Dwarfs* and Willie the Giant in *Mickey and the Beanstalk.*

Gilbert, Ray (1912–1976) Lyricist; wrote the words for a number of Disney songs in the 1940s including "Zip-A-Dee-Doo-Dah," "You Belong to My Heart," and "Baia."

Gilkyson, Terry (1916–1999) Composer who contributed memorable songs to *Swiss Family Robinson* ("My Heart Was an Island"), *The Three Lives of Thomasina* ("Thomasina"), *Savage Sam* (title song), *The Moon-Spinners* (title song), *The Scarecrow of Romney Marsh* (title song), *The Jungle Book* ("The Bare Necessities"), *My Dog, the Thief* (title song), and *The Aristocats* ("Thomas O'Malley")

Gill, Florence (1877–1965) She voiced Clara Cluck and the Wise Little Hen.

Gillespie, Darlene Mouseketeer from the 1950s television show.

Gillett, Burton (1891–1971) Director; he started at Disney in 1929 and remained until 1934, returning for a year in 1936. He directed 48 Disney cartoons, including *The Chain Gang, The Picnic, The Birthday Party, The Moose Hunt, Blue Rhythm, Flowers and Trees, King Neptune, Mickey's Good Deed, Three Little Pigs, Mickey's*

Gala Premiere, Orphans' Benefit, and *Lonesome Ghosts*.

Gipson, Fred (1908–1973) Author of the book, *Old Yeller*, on which the Disney movie was based.

Girl Who Spelled Freedom, The (television) Two-hour television movie; aired on February 23, 1986. Directed by Simon Wincer. A Cambodian refugee living with an American family has problems adjusting to her new life, but she excels at school and within a few years is accomplished enough to enter and win a spelling bee. Stars Wayne Rogers, Mary Kay Place, Jade Chinn.

Give a Little Whistle Song from *Pinocchio*, written by Ned Washington and Leigh Harline.

Givot, George (1903–1984) He voiced Tony, the proprietor of the spaghetti restaurant, in *Lady and the Tramp*.

Gladstone Gander Comic book character with an abrasive personality; never appeared in films. Created by Carl Barks, he debuted in *Walt Disney's Comics and Stories* no. 88 in January 1948. He was a cousin of Donald Duck, and extremely lucky. He was also a loafer and a chiseler. Gladstone has appeared on television, in *Ducktales*.

Glas und Porzellan Shop selling Hummel and Goebel collectibles in Germany in World Showcase at Epcot, presented by W. Goebel Porzellanfabrik; opened October 1, 1982.

Glass Fantasies Shop on Main Street in Disneyland Paris; opened on April 12, 1992.

Global Van Lines Company operated a locker area on Town Square at Disneyland from May 1963 to 1979. The area was formerly sponsored by Bekins, and later by National Car Rentals.

Glory Road (film) Directed by James Gartner. Stars Josh Lucas, Derek Luke, Austin Nichols, Evan Jones, Mehcad Brooks, Emily Deschanel, Sam Jones III, Schin A.S. Kerr, Alphonso McAuley, Damaine Radcliff, Al Shearer, Tatyana

Ali. Began filming on August 2, 2004, in New Orleans and El Paso. Released on January 13, 2006. Filmed in Super 35 Scope.

Glover, Danny Actor; appeared in *Angels in the Outfield* (George Knox), *Operation Dumbo Drop* (Sam Cahill), *Gone Fishin'* (Gus Green), *Beloved* (Paul D.), and *The Royal Tenenbaums* (Henry Sherman).

Glover, William He voiced Winston in *Oliver & Company*, and appeared on television in *Meet the Munceys* (Edmund Haddy).

Gnome-Mobile, The (film) In the redwood forests of California, a multimillionaire lumberman and his two young grandchildren encounter two gnomes, old Knobby and young Jasper. Supposedly, they're the last of their kind, but everyone sets off on a trip in a Gnome-Mobile (an old Rolls Royce) to find the rest of the gnomes. After a series of adventures and mishaps, they do, and the lumberman deeds the forest to the gnomes for eternity. Released on July 12, 1967. Directed by Robert Stevenson. 85 min. Stars Walter Brennan (Knobby/D.J. Mulrooney), Matthew Garber (Rodney), and Karen Dotrice (Elizabeth) (both advertised as "the *Mary Poppins* kids" in the credits), Richard Deacon (Ralph Yarby), Tom Lowell (Jasper), Sean McClory (Horatio Quaxton), Ed Wynn (Rufus), Jerome Cowan (Dr. Ramsey). Based on a book by Upton Sinclair, who was inspired to write the story while on his first car trip visiting the redwood forests along the Pacific Coast. The title song was written by Richard M. Sherman and Robert B. Sherman. Walter Brennan was used to dual advantage as crochety old Knobby and as the wealthy grandfather, D. J. Mulrooney. The wondrous special effects were accomplished by Eustace Lycett and Robert A. Mattey. Released on video in 1985.

Go Figure (television) A Disney Channel Original Movie, premiering on June 10, 2005. Fourteen-year-old Katelin Kingsford dreams of being an Olympic figure-skating champion. In order to train with a renowned coach, she is forced to join the Buckston Academy girls' hockey team. To her surprise, she discovers true friendship and team-work for the first time and gains a new appreciation of the meaning of family. Directed by Francine McDougall. Stars Jordan Hinson (Katelin Kingsford), Whitney Sloan (Hollywood Henderson), Amy Halloran (Ronnie), Tania Gunadi (Mojo), Jake Abel (Spencer), Cristine Rose (Natasha Goberman), Ryan Malgarini (Bradley Kingsford), Curt Dousett (Ed Kingsford), Sabrina Speer (Shelby), Paul Kiernan (Coach Reynolds). Skating star Kristi Yamaguchi appears as herself. Filmed in Salt Lake City, Utah.

Go Fish (television) Half-hour television series; beginning on ABC on June 19, 2001, and ending July 3. High-school freshman, Andy Troutner, plots to become popular and win the affections of the beautiful Jess Riley, while his older brother, Pete, joins the teaching staff, hoping to inspire students with his boundless enthusiasm. Stars Kieran Culkin (Andy), Will Friedle (Pete), Katherine Ellis (Jess), Kyle Sabihy (Henry Krakowski), Taylor Handley (Hazard).

GO Network Internet portal site created by Disney and Infoseek; launched on January 12, 1999. The network offered such services as news, stock quotes, chat rooms, search engines, e-mail, and weather, with the ability to personalize certain areas. On November 17, 1999, Disney stockholders approved a spin-off of GO.com and the purchase of Infoseek with that company merging with Disney's Buena Vista Internet Group as a separate Disney entity. The new GO.com's shares began trading on the New York Stock Exchange the next day. This tracking stock in 2000 changed its name to Disney Internet Group. On March 1, 2001, the company converted the stock to Disney Common Stock and closed the GO.com portal business.

Go West, Young Dog (television) Television show; aired on February 20, 1977. Directed by William Stierwalt. Dorsey is a dog in the 1880s who carries the mail, and gets mixed up with crooked gold miners. Stars Frank Keith, Charles Granata, Dennis Dillon.

Godboldo, Dale Actor; appeared on the *Mickey Mouse Club* on The Disney Channel, beginning in 1991.

Goddess of Spring, The (film) Silly Symphony cartoon; released on November 3, 1934. Directed by Wilfred Jackson. One of Disney's early attempts at human animation. The goddess Persephone is captured by the devil as his bride and sent to the underworld, with the agreement to return to earth six months each year. While the animation of the goddess was unrealistic, it did give the animators some early practice for eventually animating another young lady, Snow White.

Goff, Harper (1912–1993) Artist and production designer; at Disney as a storyman for *20,000 Leagues Under the Sea*, for which he designed the *Nautilus*. He later worked at WED Enterprises on the designs for Main Street and the Jungle Cruise at Disneyland, and created the layout for World Showcase. He was a member of the Firehouse Five Plus Two, playing the banjo. He died in 1993, the same year he was named a Disney Legend.

Going Bonkers (television) Syndicated two-hour television special, aired first on September 3, 1993. Directed by Robert Taylor. Introducing the *Bonkers* television series, this special presents an introduction to the character of Bonkers D. Bobcat, showing his transition from Toon television star to Toon cop. The second half of the show turns to Donald Duck with the show, *Down and Out with Donald Duck*.

Going to the Mat (television) Disney Channel Original Movie; premiering on March 19, 2004. When Jace Newfield's family moves from New York to the Midwest, the accomplished, but blind, drummer must find a way—besides music—to fit in at his new school. In addition to experiencing the cultural differences, Jace must learn his way around a new house and school while struggling to maintain his independence. Soon, he takes up wrestling, the only sport in which the blind compete on an equal footing with the sighted. With the help of his wrestling coach, Mr. Rice, and his music teacher, Mr. Wyatt, who is also blind, Jace strives to master his wrestling skills and follow his instincts to bring his team to the championships as he discovers the importance of self-acceptance. Directed by Stuart Gillard. Stars Andrew Lawrence (Jace Newfield), Khleo Thomas (Vince Shu), Billy Aaron Brown (John Lambrix), Brenda Strong (Patty Newfield), D.B. Sweeney (Coach Rice), Brett Yoder (Mike Mallon), T.J. Lowther (Luke Nolan), Alessandra Toreson (Mary Beth Rice), Tim Whitaker (Boomer Cleason), Brian Wimmer (Tom Newfield), Danny Henze (T-Rex Turner), Wayne Brady (Mr. Wyatt).

Gold, Stanley P. Member of the Disney board of directors in 1984 and again from 1987 to 2003. He is an officer in Roy E. Disney's company, Shamrock.

Goldberg, Whoopi Actress; appeared in *Sarafina* (Mary Masembuko), *The Associate* (Laurel Ayres), *Eddie* (title role), as Deloris in *Sister Act* and *Sister Act 2: Back in the Habit*, *An Alan Smithee Film: Burn Hollywood Burn* (as herself) and as the voice of Shenzi the hyena in *The Lion King*. On television, she appeared in *Rodgers & Hammerstein's Cinderella* (Queen Constantina), *A Knight in Camelot* (Vivien Morgan) and *Captain EO Backstage* (narrator). She appears as the narrator (Calafia) in *Golden Dreams* at Disney's California Adventure.

Goldblum, Jeff Actor; appeared in *Powder* (Donald Ripley), *Holy Man* (Ricky Hayman), and *The Life Aquatic with Steve Zissou* (Alistair Hennessey).

Golden Anniversary of Snow White and the Seven Dwarfs See *Disney's Golden Anniversary of Snow White and the Seven Dwarfs*.

Golden Bear Lodge See Hungry Bear Restaurant.

Golden Dog, The (television) Television show; aired on January 2, 1977. Directed by William

Stierwalt and Fred R. Krug. A ghost tries to help his two former gold-mining partners get along with each other. His first plot backfires as the two practically tear the town apart looking for suspected gold, but later he strands them in the desert, and they have to help each other, deciding that friendship is more important than gold. Stars Paul Brinegar, Alan Napier.

Golden Dream Song from the American Adventure in World Showcase at Epcot; written by Randy Bright and Robert Moline.

Golden Dreams (film) Film attraction at Disney's California Adventure that chronicles the hopes, dreams, and hard work of the pioneers who shaped what is California today. Calafia as narrator covers the Gold Rush, the immigrant experience, and the glittering beginnings of Hollywood. Opened on February 8, 2001. Directed by Agnieszka Holland. Stars Whoopi Goldberg (Calafia). 21 min.

Golden Eggs (film) Donald Duck cartoon; released on March 7, 1941. Directed by Wilfred Jackson. Donald Duck unsuccessfully disguises himself as a chicken to recover a basket of eggs protected by a rooster.

Golden Girls, The (television) Television series on NBC; aired from September 14, 1985, until September 12, 1992. Three aging, active, and independent women share a house in Miami with the feisty mother of one of them, supporting each other but also occasionally getting on each other's nerves. Stars Rue McClanahan (Blanche Devereaux), Betty White (Rose Nyland), Bea Arthur

(Dorothy Zbornak), and Estelle Getty (Sophia Petrillo). The cast and crew won 11 Emmy Awards from 1986 to 1992. A spin-off show was called *The Golden Palace*.

Golden Horseshoe Revue Frontierland show at Disneyland; opened on July 17, 1955, and was the longest-running show ever when it ended on October 12, 1986. It was sponsored by Pepsi-Cola from 1955 to September 30, 1982, and by Eastman Kodak from October 1, 1982 to April 30, 1984. A new show, the Golden Horseshoe Jamboree, opened on November 1, 1986, and closed on December 18, 1994. Wonder Bread took over the sponsorship in 1990. The first stars were Donald Novis, the "silver-toned tenor," Judy Marsh, and comedian Wally Boag. Betty Taylor had a long run as Slue Foot Sue, and Fulton Burley took the tenor role. The new show featured talented singers and dancers, including those portraying Lily Langtree and Sam, the owner of the saloon. A mainstay since the beginning was the can-can number. Walt used to enjoy the show, and he had his favorite box right next to the stage. The corny jokes and enduring songs continued to endear the show to guests throughout its long run.

Golden Horseshoe Revue, The (television) Television show; aired on September 23, 1962. Directed by Ron Miller. Walt celebrates the 10,000th performance of the Disneyland park show, with its stars Betty Taylor and Wally Boag, augmented by Annette Funicello, Gene Sheldon, and Ed Wynn.

Golden Oak Ranch Located in Placerita Canyon, about 25 miles north of the Disney Studio in Burbank, this 708-acre ranch was purchased by Disney on March 11, 1959, to serve as a film location. Walt had become familiar with the

area while using it as a location for the Spin and Marty serials. Over the years, parts of films such as *Toby Tyler; Follow Me, Boys!; The Parent Trap; The Apple Dumpling Gang*; and *The Horse in the Gray Flannel Suit* were filmed there. A meandering stream with a covered bridge has been featured in many films. Other studios use the ranch also, and it has been featured in *Mame, Roots, The Waltons, Back to the Future, Dynasty*, and *Little House on the Prairie*. With 20th Century Fox and Paramount selling their large ranches in recent years, the Golden Oak Ranch has become practically the sole surviving movie ranch.

Golden Opportunity (film) Promotional film, introduced by Walt Disney, prepared for Californians for Beaches and Parks to aid in their campaign for a ballot proposition in a state election in 1964. Walt explains that, with increasing population in California, more state beaches and parks are needed. 13 min.

Golden Palace, The (television) Television series; aired on CBS from September 18, 1992 to August 6, 1993. Spin-off of *The Golden Girls*. Two of the women from the previous show run a Miami hotel. Stars Rue McClanahan, Betty White, Estelle Getty, Cheech Marin, Don Cheadle.

Golden Press Division of Western Publishing Co.; began publishing Little Golden Books and Big Golden Books featuring the Disney characters in 1948, and later added many other series. Some of the Golden Book titles went through dozens of printings, with millions of copies in circulation. Golden Books was acquired by Random House in August 2001.

Golden Touch, The (film) Silly Symphony cartoon; released on March 22, 1935. Directed by Walt Disney himself, a task he thought would be easy but which he never again repeated. Greedy King Midas wants to amass more treasure, so a magical dwarf grants him the power to turn anything

he touches to gold. To his horror, he can no longer eat, for even his food turns to gold. Finally, in exchange for a hamburger, the king gives up the golden touch and all his worldly possessions.

Golden Vine Winery Area in Golden State at Disney's California Adventure; opened on February 8, 2001. Originally presented by the Robert Mondavi Family; Disney took over the operation on October 1, 2001. The Vineyard Room and Golden Vine Terrace opened on February 8, 2001. The Wine Country Trattoria, taking the place of the Wine Country Market, opened on December 14, 2001.

Golden Zephyr Attraction at Paradise Pier at Disney's California Adventure; opened February 8, 2001. This swing ride brings back visions of a retro-future with zeppelin-shaped 12-passenger stainless steel spaceships, suspended by cable from a rotating 85-foot tower.

Goldenson, Leonard H. (1905–1999) Founder and former chairman of the board of ABC, Inc., Goldenson started with the organization in 1953 when he helped arrange the merger of United Paramount Theaters with the fledgling ABC (a failing collection of five television stations). He took a chance in 1954 by contracting for the first Disney television series, *Disneyland*, and investing in the park Walt was building in Anaheim. In 1985, he merged ABC with Cap Cities. He was named a Disney Legend posthumously in 2004.

Goldie Locks and the Three Bears (film) Laugh-O-gram film made by Walt in Kansas City in 1922.

Goldrush: A Real Life Alaskan Adventure (television) A two-hour movie on *The Wonderful World of Disney*; aired on March 8, 1998. A spirited young woman, known as Fizzy, challenges both the social conventions of her time and nature's harshest elements when she seeks her fortune in the turn-of-the-century Alaskan Gold Rush. Directed by John Power. Stars Alyssa Milano (Frances Ella Fitz), W. Morgan Sheppard (Whiskers), Stan Cahill (Ed Hawkins), Peter Fleming (Barry Keown), Tom Scholte (Monty Marks), Bruce Campbell (Pierce Thomas Madison). Released on video in 1999.

Goldwyn, Tony Actor; appeared in *Nixon* (Harold Nixon) and provided the voice of the title character in *Tarzan*.

Golf Resort, The Golf hotel at Walt Disney World; opened in 1973, became The Disney Inn in 1986. See Disney Inn.

Goliath II (film) Special cartoon; released on January 21, 1960. Directed by Wolfgang Reitherman. Golaith II, at eight, is still only five inches tall—to the shame of his father, Goliath I, giant of the jungle and king of the elephants. Little Goliath runs away and though he is rescued by his mother from Raja, the tiger, he is now marked a rogue. But when a mouse attacks the herd, frightening them all away, Goliath redeems himself by battling and defeating the mouse. Written by Disney storyman Bill Peet, with Kevin Corcoran voicing Goliath II, the film also boasts the distinction of being the first Disney film to be fully animated using the new Xerox process for transferring the pencil drawings to cels (a few scenes of *Sleeping Beauty* had previously used the

technique). It is also notable for being one of the few Disney films in which a mouse is the villain.

Gone Are the Dayes (television) The second Disney Channel Premiere Film, about a family that witnesses a gangland shooting and has a hard time staying hidden before the trial. A veteran government relocation agent, Charlie Mitchell, is determined to hide and protect them, while the mobsters are just as determined to get them. Aired first on May 6, 1984. Directed by Gabrielle Beaumont. Stars Harvey Korman (Charlie Mitchell), Robert Hogan, Susan Anspach, David Glasser, Sharee Gregory. Released on video in 1984.

Gone Fishin' (film) It is the weekend and best friends Gus and Joe have decided to leave the wives and their problems at home and go fishing, having won a grand-prize vacation to the Florida Everglades from *Bait & Tackle* magazine by writing an essay on "How Come We Fish." But the duo never gets close enough to the water to bait their hooks because they stumble into a wild adventure. They run into a con artist, Dekker Massey, who speeds off in their '68 Plymouth Barracuda, leaving them with their fishing boat and trailer. When two beautiful women, Rita and Angie, arrive in hot pursuit of Dekker, Gus and Joe hitch a ride, becoming entangled in the chase and, despite constantly leaving disaster in their wake, prove they are ingenious and daring while on the trail of a dangerous criminal. They return home as heroes. A Hollywood Picture, in association with Caravan Pictures. Directed by Christopher Cain. Released on May 30, 1997. Stars Joe Pesci (Joe Waters), Danny Glover (Gus Green), Rosanna Arquette (Rita), Lynn Whitfield (Angie), Nick Brimble (Dekker Massey). 94 min. Location filming took place in the Everglades and nearby towns, including the charming, weathered atmosphere of Everglades City, a sleepy community of 700. Released on video in 1997.

Gone Hollywood Shop in Hollywood Pictures Backlot at Disney's California Adventure; opened February 8, 2001.

Gone in 60 Seconds (film) Automobile aficionado Randall "Memphis" Raines is a car thief of legendary proportion. No fancy lock or alarm could stop him; your car would be there, and then suddenly gone in 60 seconds. For years Memphis eluded the law while boosting every make and model imaginable. When the heat became too intense, he abandoned his life of crime and left everything and everyone he loved to find a different life. Now, when his kid brother tries to follow in his footsteps, only to become dangerously embroiled in a high-stakes caper, Memphis is sucked back into his old ways in order to save his brother's life. Released on June 9, 2000. A Touchstone Pictures/Jerry Bruckheimer Films production. Directed by Dominic Sena. Stars Nicolas Cage (Memphis Raines), Angelina Jolie (Sway Wayland), Giovanni Ribisi (Kip Raines), Delroy Lindo (Roland Castelbeck), Will Patton (Atley Jackson), Christopher Eccleston (Raymond Calitri), Chi McBride (Kenny), Robert Duvall (Otto Halliwell). 118 min. Based on a 1974 film of the same title from writer-producer-director H. B. ("Toby") Halicki. Filmed in CinemaScope. Released on video in 2000.

Gonzales, Manuel (1913–1993) Comic strip artist; began with Disney in 1936 as an artist in the publicity and comic strip departments. From 1938 until his retirement in 1981, he penciled and inked the Mickey Mouse Sunday page for newspapers.

Good and Evil (television) Television series; aired on ABC from September 25 to October 31, 1991. The lives of two sisters, one, Genny, is good, a doctor in microbiology, and the other, Denise, is evil, vice president of marketing for their mother's cosmetic company. Stars Seth Green (David), Teri Garr (Denise), Margaret Whitton (Genny), Mark Blankfield (George), Lane Davies (Dr. Eric Haan), Mary Gillis (Mary).

Good Housekeeping In the 1930s and early 1940s, *Good Housekeeping* magazine had a monthly page of Disney illustrations, usually tied to a recent cartoon or animated feature release.

Good Life, The (television) Television series; debuting on NBC on January 3 and ending April

12, 1994. A hardworking, middle-class family man, trying to strike a bargain between work and domestic life, discovers that it is harder than it seems to snare a slice of "the good life." Stars John Caponera (John Bowman), Eve Gordon (Maureen Bowman), Drew Carey (Drew Clark), Jake Patellis (Paul Bowman), Shay Astar (Melissa Bowman), Justin Berfield (Bob Bowman), Monty Hoffman (Tommy Bartlett).

Good Morning Mickey! (television) Original program on The Disney Channel; beginning on April 18, 1983, highlighting classic cartoons of the entire Disney gang.

Good Morning, Miss Bliss (television) Series on The Disney Channel; starring Hayley Mills, Dennis Haskins, Joan Ryan, Max Battimo, Dustin Diamond, Mark-Paul Gosselaar, Heather Hopper, Lark Voorhies. An eighth-grade teacher tries to make her class appreciate her lessons. Began on November 30, 1988. After only five episodes, The Disney Channel canceled the series, and it then continued on NBC with a change of title as the long-running *Saved by the Bell*, though without Hayley Mills.

Good Morning, Vietnam (film) When airman disc jockey Adrian Cronauer takes up his post on Armed Forces Radio in Saigon in 1965, he abandons the approved playlist for rock and roll and adds irreverent remarks. His superiors are horrified, but the men love him as he accomplishes his mission of boosting morale. As he gets to know the people of Saigon—Americans and Vietnamese alike—he becomes increasingly frustrated by the military's censorship of the news. After he broadcasts an "unofficial" report and is cut off the air, his commander deliberately sends him into danger, but a young Vietnamese boy helps rescue him. The boy turns out to be a Vietcong rebel, and Cronauer is sent home for having unwittingly fraternized with the "enemy." Still, his broadcasts paved the way for changes on Armed Forces Radio. Premiered on December 23, 1987; general release on January 15, 1988. Directed by Barry Levinson. A Touchstone Picture. 121 min. Stars Robin Williams (Adrian Cronauer), Forest Whitaker (Edward Garlick), Tung Thanh Tran (Tuan), Chintara Sukapatana (Trinh), Bruno Kirby (Lt. Steven Hauk), Robert Wuhl (Marty Lee Dreiwitz), J.T. Walsh (Sgt. Major Dickerson). The film is loosely based on the real-life experiences of a disc-jockey who had a popular rock-and-roll show on Armed Forces Radio. It was shot primarily in Bangkok, where many local citizens were introduced to the rigors of moviemaking for the first time. For the final week, the unit moved to Phuket, a lush tropical island located at the southern tip of Thailand, where a Vietnamese village was constructed. Released on video in 1988.

Good Mother, The (film) After weathering an unexciting marriage, single parent Anna Dunlap is totally wrapped up in her daughter, Molly, who is her whole life. When an unconventional Irish sculptor, Leo Cutter, enters Anna's life, she falls passionately in love. However, their openness and permissiveness cause her ex-husband to turn against her, and he files a custody suit for Molly. In trying to retain custody, on her lawyer's recommendation, she reluctantly sacrifices Leo, all to no avail. Eventually she must pick up her life, and begin anew with only weekend and vacation visits from Molly. Released on November 4, 1988. Directed by Leonard Nimoy. A Touchstone Picture. 104 min. Stars Diane Keaton (Anna Dunlap), Liam Neeson (Leo Cutter), Jason Robards (Muth), Ralph Bellamy (Grandfather). Based on the novel by Sue Miller. Filmed in Boston and Toronto, and at Whitefish Lake in Southern Ontario. Released on video in 1989.

Good Old Boy (television) A 12-year-old boy discovers racial injustice and learns some hard lessons in a small Mississippi town during World War II. A Disney Channel Premiere Film; first aired on November 11, 1988. Directed by Tom G. Robertson. Based on the novel by Willie Morris. Stars Ryan Francis (Willie), Douglas Emerson (Spit), Kevin Josephs (Henjie), Gennie James (Rivers Applewhite), Ben Wylie (Billy), Richard Farnsworth (Grandpa Percy), Maureen O'Sullivan (Aunt Sue). 101 min. Filmed in and around Natchez, Mississippi.

Good Scouts (film) Donald Duck cartoon; released on July 8, 1938. Directed by Jack King. Donald takes his nephews on a scouting expedition filled with many outdoor adventures including a disagreeable bear and the geyser, Old Faithful.

Good Time for a Dime, A (film) Donald Duck cartoon; released on May 9, 1941. Directed by Dick Lundy. Donald has problems in a penny arcade, being frustrated in his efforts to win money from a claw machine and in his encounter with a wild mechanical airplane.

Good Turn Restaurant, The Restaurant in The Land at Epcot, from October 1, 1982 to May 1986. Became The Land Grille Room and later the Garden Grill Restaurant. The restaurant slowly rotates while one eats, providing views into settings on the nearby boat ride attraction originally known as Listen to the Land and later as Living with the Land. The Good Turn served some of the best breakfasts at Walt Disney World.

Goodbye, Miss 4th of July (television) In 1917 West Virginia, a Greek girl battles the forces of racism, and her family is able to overcome prejudice and change the town in the process. A Disney Channel Premiere Film. Directed by George Miller. Aired on December 3, 1988. Stars Roxana Zal (Niki Janus), Chris Sarandon (George Janus), Chantal Contouri (mother), Louis Gossett, Jr. (Big John). 89 min. Released on video in 1993.

Gooding, Cuba, Jr. Actor; appeared in *Instinct* (Theo Calder), *Pearl Harbor* (Doris "Dorrie" Miller), and *Snow Dogs* (Ted), and on television in *The Oldest Rookie* (street kid leader). He provided the voice of Buck in *Home on the Range*.

Goodman, Benny (1909–1986) Bandleader who was the first big-name star to appear at Disneyland for more than one performance when he headlined a three-night engagement during Date Nite in May 1961. He and his orchestra had earlier performed on "All the Cats Join In" and "After You've Gone" for *Make Mine Music*.

Goodman, John Actor; appeared in *Stella* (Ed Munn), *Arachnophobia* (Delbert McClintock), *Born Yesterday* (Harry Brock), *Bringing Out the Dead* (Larry), *Coyote Ugly* (Bill), and *O Brother, Where Art Thou?* (Big Dan Teague), and he provided the voices of Pacha in *The Emperor's New Groove*, James P. Sullivan in *Monsters, Inc.*, and Baloo in *The Jungle Book 2*.

Goof Troop (television) Animated television series; premiered on April 20, 1992, on The Disney Channel. Syndicated beginning September 7, 1992, and ending August 30, 1996, and shown on ABC beginning September 12, 1992, and ending September 11, 1993. There was a two-hour syndicated television special that aired on September 6, 1992, previewing the series with an episode entitled *Forever Goof*, and including a *Goof Troop* music video and an edited version of *The Goofy Success Story*. The Goof, a single-parent family man, struggles to raise his son in suburbia. His son, Max, however, wants to be different than his old man—in other words, cool. The results are misunderstandings and misadventures, complicated by their next-door neighbor Pete. He's a snarling used-car salesman with a big ego and temper to match. Voices include Bill Farmer (Goofy), Dana Hill (Max), Jim Cummings (Pete), April Winchell (Peg), Nancy Cartwright (Pistol), Rob Paulsen (P.J.), Frank Welker (Waffles/Chainsaw). 78 episodes.

Goof Troop Christmas, A (television) Syndicated television special; aired first in December 1992, and was repeated the following Christmas season (each having a different group of cartoons for the second half of the show). Pete takes his family to Colorado to avoid the hectic season, but he cannot escape Goofy, a hungry bear, or the destruction of their cabin.

Goofing Around with Donald Duck See *A Square Peg in a Round Hole*.

Goofy Good-natured but stupid, the cartoon character made his first appearance, somewhat disguised, as a member of the audience in *Mickey's Revue* (1932). What distinguished Goofy from those sitting around him was not so much his appearance but his raucous laugh. That laugh, supplied by Disney storyman, musician, and former circus clown, Pinto Colvig, created such an impression on Walt Disney and his staff that the character soon began to be featured in other cartoons. Before long, Goofy was part of the gang that included Mickey, Minnie, Pluto, Clarabelle Cow, and Horace Horsecollar. This new character was first given a name, Dippy Dawg, in the newspaper comic strips. A 1938 book indicated the first change to Dippy's name, *The Story of Dippy the Goof*, and by 1939 the final change was made with the release of the cartoon *Goofy and Wilbur*. Goofy was created as a human character, as opposed tso Pluto, so he walked upright and had a speaking voice (first supplied by Colvig, and later by George Johnson, Bob Jackman, and Bill Farmer). There were 48 Goofy cartoons (primarily in the 1940s and 1950s), but he also appeared in many cartoons with Mickey Mouse and Donald Duck. He was best known for his series of "How to" cartoons, where he bumbled through the explanations. In the 1950s, he appeared in several cartoons as Mr. Geef, with a wife and son. The 1990s television series *Goof Troop* reintroduced Goofy and son, but by this time the son was Max, quite different from his earlier incarnation, and the wife was no longer on the scene.

The 48 Goofy cartoons are as follows:

1.	*Goofy and Wilbur*	1939
2.	*Goofy's Glider*	1940
3.	*Baggage Buster*	1941
4.	*The Art of Skiing*	1941
5.	*The Art of Self Defense*	1941
6.	*How to Play Baseball*	1942
7.	*The Olympic Champ*	1942
8.	*How to Swim*	1942
9.	*How to Fish*	1942
10.	*Victory Vehicles*	1943
11.	*How to Be a Sailor*	1944
12.	*How to Play Golf*	1944
13.	*How to Play Football*	1944
14.	*Tiger Trouble*	1945
15.	*African Diary*	1945
16.	*Californy 'er Bust*	1945
17.	*Hockey Homicide*	1945
18.	*Knight for a Day*	1946
19.	*Double Dribble*	1946
20.	*Foul Hunting*	1947
21.	*They're Off*	1948
22.	*The Big Wash*	1948
23.	*Tennis Racquet*	1949
24.	*Goofy Gymnastics*	1949
25.	*Motor Mania*	1950
26.	*Hold That Pose*	1950
27.	*Lion Down*	1951
28.	*Home Made Home*	1951
29.	*Cold War*	1951
30.	*Tomorrow We Diet*	1951
31.	*Get Rich Quick*	1951
32.	*Fathers Are People*	1951
33.	*No Smoking*	1951
34.	*Father's Lion*	1952
35.	*Hello, Aloha*	1952
36.	*Man's Best Friend*	1952
37.	*Two-Gun Goofy*	1952
38.	*Teachers Are People*	1952
39	*Two Weeks Vacation*	1952
40.	*How to Be a Detective*	1952
41.	*Father's Day Off*	1953
42.	*For Whom the Bulls Toil*	1953
43.	*Father's Week End*	1953
44.	*How to Dance*	1953
45.	*How to Sleep*	1953
46.	*Aquamania*	1961
47.	*Freewayphobia No. 1*	1965
48.	*Goofy's Freeway Troubles*	1965

Goofy Adventure Story, The Alternate title for *The Adventure Story*.

Goofy and Wilbur (film) Goofy cartoon; released on March 17, 1939. Directed by Dick Huemer. Goofy and his pet grasshopper, Wilbur, are fishing partners with Wilbur attracting fish for Goofy to catch. In trying to avoid being eaten by a fish, Wilbur is swallowed by a frog. Goofy gives chase, but the frog is swallowed by a stork. Goofy is sad when the stork gets away from him at the nest, but he finds Wilbur in the stork's egg.

Goofy Gymnastics (film) Goofy cartoon; released on September 23, 1949. Directed by Jack

Kinney. Goofy gives a muscle-building course a try but is soon entangled with the various apparatus that results in crashing out a window and having the body of a strong man from a chart superimposed over his. The deadpan narration was by John McLeish.

Goofy Look at Valentine's Day, A (film) Educational film; released in September 1983. Goofy learns the significance of Valentine's Day and how people have expressed their love through the years on the holiday.

Goofy Movie, A (film) Goofy takes his son Max on a fishing trip in an effort to bridge the generation gap and spend some quality time bonding with his son, even though Max would rather be spending time with his girlfriend, Roxanne. Rather than explaining to Roxanne the real reason for his trip, Max uses a little deception, which results in all sorts of complications. Goofy and Max head for Lake Destiny, and along the way have an encounter with Bigfoot and visit the delapidated Lester's Possum Park. Released on April 7, 1995. Directed by Kevin Lima. 77 min.

Voices include Bill Farmer (Goofy), Jason Marsden (Max), Aaron Lohr (Max singing), Kellie Martin (Roxanne), Jenna Von Oy (Stacey), Jim Cummings (Pete), Rob Paulsen (P.J.), Wallace Shawn (Principal Mazur), Joey Lawrence (Chad), Julie Brown (Lisa), Frank Welker (Bigfoot). The film was animated primarily at a new Disney studio in France, after character design, art direction, and storyboarding had been completed in Burbank. Released on video in 1995.

Goofy Over Dental Health (film) Educational release in 16mm in January 1991. 13 min. A

laserdisc version at 22 minutes was released in February 1993. A kid neglects brushing his teeth, but that night Goofy leaves a magical toothbrush under his pillow and he is transported to a dental office where he learns how to have healthy teeth.

Goofy Over Health (film) Educational release in 16mm in January 1991. 11 min. A video version at 19 minutes was released in March 1993. By reading Goofy's health journal, an 8-year-old learns that she has been suffering from fatigue caused by poor health habits; Goofy teaches her the keys to good health and fitness.

Goofy Sports Story, The (television) Television show; aired on March 21, 1956. Directed by Wolfgang Reitherman. Walt introduces a history of the Olympic Games followed by a series of Goofy sport cartoons.

Goofy Success Story, The (television) Television show; aired on December 7, 1955. Directed by Jack Kinney. A look at Goofy's rise to stardom, leading into several of his cartoons—*Moving Day*, *Moose Hunters*, *How to Ride a Horse*, and *Motor Mania*. Released theatrically abroad.

Goofy Takes a Holiday Alternate title of *Holiday for Henpecked Husbands*.

Goofy's Bounce House Attraction opened in Mickey's Toontown at Disneyland on January 24, 1993. This is one attraction where the kids can lord it over the adults; if you are above a certain height, you cannot enter. Kids remove their shoes, and leap into the house with its almost balloon-like furniture, walls, and floor. Also at Tokyo Disneyland; opened on April 13, 1996.

Goofy's Cavalcade of Sports (television) Television show; aired on October 17, 1956. Directed by Wolfgang Reitherman. Goofy attempts to participate in a number of sports, as seen in several of his cartoons.

Goofy's Extreme Sports: Paracycling (film) Goofy defies the laws of physics and common sense when he bicycles off a cliff, engages in aerial acrobatics, and ungracefully parachutes to the ground. Directed by Tony Craig. 2 min. From the *Mickey MouseWorks* television series. Released with *Mighty Joe Young* on December 25, 1998.

Goofy's Extreme Sports: Skating the Half Pipe (film) Goofy demonstrates the beautiful, yet dangerous, sport of stunt skating—complete with all safety precautions. But once he gets rolling, he has trouble putting on the brakes. Directed by Bob Zamboni. 2 min. From the *Mickey MouseWorks* television series. Released with *I'll Be Home for Christmas* on November 13, 1998.

Goofy's Field Trips (film) Series of three educational films: *Ships*, *Trains*, *Planes*; released in August 1989.

Goofy's Freeway Troubles (film) Goofy cartoon; released on September 22, 1965. Directed by Les Clark. Goofy, appearing as Stupidus Ultimas, illustrates what can happen when a careless motorist ignores the state of his tires and the mechanical condition of his vehicle. Showing his audience tires blowing out and wheels coming free, Goofy clearly warns of alcohol and driving being a dangerous combination. Dangerous, too, Goofy concludes, is staying at the wheel while fatigued. 13 min.

Goofy's Glider (film) Goofy cartoon; released on November 22, 1940. Directed by Jack Kinney.

Goofy tries to demonstrate glider flying, but is unsuccessful in trying to launch himself whether using foot power, a bicycle, a slingshot, or skates. Finally, a cannon does the job, shooting him into orbit.

Goofy's Hygiene Game (film) Educational film; released in August 1987. It presents lessons on cleanliness habits such as bathing, grooming, dental care, and others.

Goofy's Office Safety Championship (film) Educational film; released on April 30, 1990. 12 min. Office workplace hazards turn into an athletic competition.

Goofy's Plant Safety Championship (film) Educational film; released on April 30, 1990. 13 min. Plant workplace hazards become an athletic competition.

Goofy's Salute to Father Alternate title of *A Salute to Father*.

Gopher Character Walt Disney created to add to the *Winnie the Pooh* stories; voiced by Howard Morris.

Gordon, Bruce Designer; joined WED Enterprises in 1979 as a production designer, and worked on the Journey into Imagination attraction and new Fantasyland at Disneyland. He was show producer of Splash Mountain at Disneyland. As an unofficial historian at Walt Disney Imagineering, he, along with David Mumford, has made many appearances as a popular speaker at Disneyana conventions, and has written several Disney books. He was at WDI for twenty-five years.

Gordon-Levitt, Joseph Actor; appeared in *Plymouth* (Simon), *Angels in the Outfield* (Roger), *Holy Matrimony* (Zeke), *10 Things I Hate About You* (Cameron James), and provided the voice of Jim Hawkins in *Treasure Planet*.

Gordy (film) In a world where pigs can talk, and be heard by two children who are "pure of heart," Gordy sets off to find his family. Gordy and the children try to teach the adult world the meaning of friendship and the value of family. Directed by Mark Lewis. Stars Doug Stone, Tom Lester. 90 min. Originally released theatrically in May 1995 as a Miramax film. Released in 1995 on video by Walt Disney Home Video under the label "Disney Presents."

Gorilla Falls Exploration Trail See Pangani Forest Exploration Trail.

Gorilla Mystery, The (film) Mickey Mouse cartoon; released on October 10, 1930. Directed by Burt Gillett. When a gorilla escapes from the zoo and threatens Minnie, Mickey races over to save his sweetheart.

Gosalyn Mallard Drake Mallard's daughter on *Darkwing Duck*; voiced by Christine Cavanaugh.

Gosling, Ryan Actor; appeared on the *Mickey Mouse Club* on The Disney Channel, beginning in 1993, and in *Remember the Titans* (Alan Bosley).

Gotta Kick It Up (television) A Disney Channel Original Movie, premiering on July 26, 2002. An ex–dot com executive takes a handful of Latina schoolgirls and motivates them to find their potential and overcome societal obstacles. With her guidance the girls work hard to beat the

odds, becoming a championship dance team. Directed by Ramon Menendez. Stars: Susan Egan (Heather), Camile Guaty (Daisy), America Ferrera (Yolanda), Sabrina Wiener (Esmeralda), Jhoanna Flores (Alyssa), Suilma Rodriguez (Marisol), Miguel Sandoval (Zavala).

Gottfredson, Floyd (1905–1986) Comic strip artist; hired by Disney in 1929 as an animation inbetweener, but Walt Disney asked him if he would take over the Mickey Mouse comic strip for a couple of weeks when the previous artist, Win Smith, left the Studio. Floyd's first strip was for May 5, 1930, and he stayed more than a couple of weeks—he continued doing the strip until his retirement in 1975. Besides drawing the Mickey daily strip, he also wrote it from 1930 to 1932, drew the Sunday page from 1932 to 1938, and served as head of the Comic Strip Department from 1930 to 1946. He was named a Disney Legend posthumously in 2003.

Gottfried, Gilbert Actor/comedian; voice of Iago in *Aladdin* and on the *Aladdin* television series, also at The Enchanted Tiki Room—Under New Management.

Gould, Elliott Actor; appeared in *The Last Flight of Noah's Ark* (Noah Dugan), *The Devil and Max Devlin* (Max Devlin), and *Playing Mona Lisa* (Bernie Goldstein).

Goulet, Robert Actor; appeared in *Mr. Wrong* (Dick Braxton) and on television in *Acting Sheriff.*

Governor Ratcliffe Character in *Pocahontas*; voiced by David Ogden Stiers.

Grabowski, Norman Actor; appeared in *Son of Flubber* (football player), *The Misadventures of Merlin Jones* and *The Monkey's Uncle* (Norman), *The Gnome-Mobile* (nurse), *The Happiest Millionaire* (Joe Turner), *Blackbeard's Ghost*, and *The Horse in the Gray Flannel Suit* (truck driver).

Grace Cow character in *Home on the Range*; voiced by Jennifer Tilly.

Gracey, Yale (1910–1983) Special effects expert; joined Disney in 1939 as a layout artist on *Pinocchio* and *Fantasia*. He moved to WED Enterprises in 1961, where he created special effects and lighting for The Haunted Mansion and Pirates of the Caribbean, among other attractions. He retired in 1975, and was named a Disney Legend posthumously in 1999.

Grad Nites Annual all-night parties for high school graduates, first held at Disneyland on June 15, 1961. The first Grad Nite drew 8,500 students, the largest high school graduation party ever held in the U.S. Within the first decade that number would approach 100,000, and by the end of the second decade 135,000. Today, Grad Nite stretches over a number of nights. Schools come from near and far, with the students adhering to a strict dress code (dressy for Grad Nite). In 2005, Honda signed a ten-year sponsorship deal for the Grad Nites at Disneyland. Grad Nites are also held at Walt Disney World.

Grady, Don See Don Agrati.

Graham, Don (1903–1976) Art instructor at the Chouinard Art Institute in the 1930s; helped organize art classes for the artists at Disney in 1932.

Grain That Built a Hemisphere, The (film) Educational film telling the story of corn, including its genealogy and discovery by the Native Americans, how it has been developed in modern usage, and how its culture has spread over the earth and influenced the economic structure of the world. Produced under the auspices of the Coordinator of Inter-American Affairs. Delivered on January 4, 1943. Directed by Bill Roberts. Nominated for an Academy Award for Best Documentary.

Gramatky, Hardie (1907–1979) Artist and storyman; he joined Disney in 1930 and worked in animation for six years. He wrote the story *Little Toot*, which was made into a Disney cartoon.

Grammer, Kelsey Actor; provided voices in *Runaway Brain* (Dr. Frankenollie), *Toy Story 2* (Prospector), *The Hand Behind the Mouse* (narrator), and *Teacher's Pet* (Dr. Krank). Appeared on television in *Mr. St. Nick* (Nick St. Nicholas), and in *Disneyland's 35th Anniversary Celebration* and *Mickey's 60th Birthday*.

Grand Californian Hotel The first Disney resort to be located inside a theme park, Disney's California Adventure, the Grand Californian celebrates the turn-of-the-century romantic Craftsman movement of California. The design captures the artistic exploration of California's coastline, with its Monterey pines and redwood forests, layered with the memories of the arroyo craftsmen, the mission pioneers, the Plein Air school of painters, and daring architecture. There are 712 standard rooms, 34 Artisan suites, two vice presidential, and two presidential suites, along with a convention center featuring a large ballroom. Restaurants are the Napa Rose, Storyteller's Café, and White Water Snacks. The hotel welcomed its first paying guests on January 2, 2001, with the first event held in the hotel's ballroom earlier on December 1, 2000. Grand opening was on February 8, 2001.

Grand Canyon (film) CinemaScope featurette; released initially on December 17, 1958; general release on January 29, 1959, with *Sleeping Beauty*. Directed by James Algar. The ever-changing moods of the canyon and its wildlife are portrayed with the background music of the "Grand Canyon Suite" by Ferde Grofé. Academy Award–winner for Best Live-Action Short Subject. 29 min. The production of this popular film inspired the diorama simulation of the canyon on the Disneyland Railroad route.

Grand Canyon Diorama Dimensional views of the Grand Canyon, added to the Santa Fe and Disneyland Railroad on March 31, 1958. To the sounds of Ferde Grofé's "Grand Canyon Suite," guests view scenery from the South Rim of the Grand Canyon in a realistic diorama, as they slowly ride by in the train. The diorama is 306 feet in length, and features many varieties of animals among the quaking aspens and pine trees. It was billed as the Longest Diorama in the World. Also on the Disneyland Paris Railroad.

Grand Canyonscope (film) Donald Duck cartoon; released on December 23, 1954. Directed by Charles Nichols. Filmed in CinemaScope. Donald proves to be a meddlesome tourist to Ranger J. Audubon Woodlore, getting the two of them involved with an angry mountain lion who chases them all about the canyon, ultimately destroying the national monument.

Grand Circuit Raceway Attraction in Tomorrowland at Tokyo Disneyland; opened April 15, 1983.

Grand Floridian Cafe Restaurant in the Grand Floridian Resort & Spa at Walt Disney World; opened on June 28, 1988.

Grand Floridian Resort & Spa Hotel at Walt Disney World; opened on June 28, 1988. This is one of the more elegant hostelries in Florida with its 800-plus rooms, each with ceiling fans and Victorian decor. The five-story lobby is a

wonder to behold, with its stained-glass domes and shimmering chandeliers. In the center, a musician may be playing at a grand piano, or a small orchestra may be entertaining from the balcony. A choice of a grand staircase or an open-cage elevator leads upward to shops and restaurants. The most exclusive of the Walt Disney World dining rooms is located here, Victoria and Albert's. An adjacent 27,037-square-foot convention center opened in 1992. In 1997, the name was changed from the original Grand Floridian Beach Resort.

Grand Opening of Euro Disney, The (television) Television special; aired on CBS (120 min.) on April 11, 1992. Directed by Don Mischer. Simulcast across Europe in five languages, the show was broadcast later the same day in the United States. Top entertainers from around the world were featured along with the opening ceremonies, information on the building of Euro Disney, and an inside glimpse of some of its attractions. The shows were personalized for each country—for the United States the hosts were Melanie Griffith and Don Johnson.

Grand Opening of Walt Disney World (television) Television special; aired on October 29, 1971. Directed by Robert Scheerer. Stars Julie Andrews, Glen Campbell, Buddy Hackett, Jonathan Winters, Bob Hope. For the opening parade, Meredith Willson leads a marching band of 1,076 musicians.

Grand Prix Raceway Tomorrowland attraction in Magic Kingdom Park at Walt Disney World; opened on October 1, 1971. Patterned after Autopia at Disneyland, this attraction enables drivers young and old to race (at about seven miles per hour) around a 2,260-foot-long track. The track was moved slightly and shortened somewhat to accommodate construction of Mickey's Birthdayland (later Mickey's Starland and Mickey's Toontown Fair). Presented by Goodyear. In September 1996 the name was changed to Tomorrowland Speedway, and in 1999 to Tomorrowland Indy Speedway.

Grandma Duck's Farm Petting farm originally featuring Minnie Moo, a cow with Mickey Mouse–shaped markings, in Mickey's Toontown Fair at Magic Kingdom Park at Walt Disney World; open from June 18, 1988 to March 11, 1996. Presented by Friskies. Grandma Duck was a popular character in the comic books.

Grandma Sara's Kitchen Restaurant in Critter Country at Tokyo Disneyland; opened on October 1, 1992.

Grandpa Duck Donald's grandfather, who appeared in *No Hunting* (1955).

Granny's Cabin See Miniatures.

Grant, Joe (1908–2005) Character designer and storyman; at Disney from 1937 to 1949. He headed the character model department in the 1940s and was responsible for okaying all model sheets. He worked on such classics as *Snow White and the Seven Dwarfs, Fantasia, Saludos Amigos, Make Mine Music,* and *Alice in Wonderland.* He returned decades later to receive credit for visual development on *Beauty and the Beast* and was a story adviser on *Pocahontas, The Hunchback of Notre Dame, Hercules, Mulan, Tarzan, Fantasia/2000, Treasure Planet,* and *Home on the Range.* He was named a Disney Legend in 1992.

Grasshopper and the Ants (film) Silly Symphony cartoon; released on February 10, 1934. Directed by Wilfred Jackson. When a lazy grasshopper prefers to sing and dance rather than

forage like his friends the ants, he learns to regret it when winter approaches. The ants save his life and in return he entertains them with his music. Introduced the song "The World Owes Me a Living," sung by Pinto Colvig, who voiced the grasshopper (and also Goofy). The song was published on sheet music.

Graves, Michael Architect; designed the Team Disney Building at the Disney Studio in Burbank, a building noted for huge statues of the Seven Dwarfs holding up the roof. He also designed the Swan and Dolphin Hotels at Walt Disney World and the Hotel New York at Disneyland Paris, as well as some merchandise items.

Graves, Peter Actor; appeared on television in *Gallegher Goes West* and narrated *Race for Survival.*

Graveyard of Ships (television) Television show; part 1 of *The Mooncussers.*

Great Cat Family, The (television) Television show; aired on September 19, 1956. Directed by Clyde Geronimi. Tells the history of cats from the days of the Egyptians to the present, and shows how they have been used in Disney films.

Great Expectations (television) Adaptation of Charles Dickens's classic, airing in three parts as a Disney Channel Premiere Film. Set in the Victorian era, the story follows the fortunes of Pip from his meeting with a convict, Magwitch, to his early adulthood. Thanks to a mysterious benefactor, Pip becomes a young man with "great expectations"—a gentleman who will one day inherit a fortune. In his rise in society, Pip must constantly confront hard lessons about himself, his values, and his own expectations. First aired beginning on July 9, 1989. Directed by Kevin Connor. Stars John Rhys-Davies (Joe Gargery), Jean Simmons (Miss Havisham), Anthony Hopkins (Abel Magwitch), Martin Harvey (young Pip), Anthony Calf (older Pip), Kim Thomson (Estella), Ray McAnally (Mr. Jaggers). 308 min. Released on video in 1990.

Great Guns (film) Oswald the Lucky Rabbit cartoon; released on October 17, 1927.

Great Ice Odyssey See World on Ice.

Great Locomotive Chase, The (film) On April 22, 1862, a party of 22 Union spies stole a train from right under the noses of 4,000 Confederate troops near Atlanta, Georgia, and began a race that might have brought an early end to the Civil War had it succeeded. Intrepid Confederates, led by the train's conductor, William A. Fuller, commandeered rolling stock for the chase, and persevered long enough to recapture the train. Union leader James J. Andrews and many of his men were hanged in the South, but those who survived and made their way home were given Congressional Medals of Honor by the secretary of war. Released June 8, 1956. Directed by Francis D. Lyon. 87 min. Stars Fess Parker (James J. Andrews), Jeffrey Hunter (William A. Fuller), Jeff York (William Campbell), Kenneth Tobey (Anthony Murphy). Because of Walt Disney's love of trains, he was especially enthused about this film, and he managed to secure aid from the Baltimore and Ohio Railroad Museum to obtain an authentic locomotive. From the B&O he borrowed the *William Mason*, which doubled for the *General*. The *Inyo*, playing the *Texas*, was borrowed from Paramount Pictures. While the two original locomotives were still in existence, they were museum objects and not available for filming. (Both can be visited in Atlanta-area museums today.) A section of track near Clayton, Georgia, was utilized for the production. The technical adviser, Wilbur Kurtz, who had performed similar chores on *Gone With the Wind*, happened to be a descendant of one of the Confederates who participated in the chase. The film aired on television in two parts in 1961 as *Andrews' Raiders*. See also *Behind the Scenes with Fess Parker*. Released on video in 1983.

Great Moments in Disney Animation (television) Television show; aired on January 18, 1987. Directed by Andrew Solt. Carol Burnett hosts this look at some of the finer moments of Disney animation.

Great Moments with Mr. Lincoln Main Street attraction at Disneyland, opened on July 18, 1965, featuring an Audio-Animatronics Abraham Lincoln reciting excerpts from several of his speeches. Succeeded the State of Illinois attraction at the New York World's Fair (1964–1965). Closed on January 1, 1973, so the Walt Disney Story could take its place, but returned due to popular demand as The Walt Disney Story Featuring Great Moments with Mr. Lincoln on June 12, 1975. The Lincoln figure was reprogrammed in 1984 utilizing new technology used for artificial human limbs pioneered at the University of Utah. Actor Royal Dano was the voice of Lincoln; he occasionally portrayed Lincoln in films, since he happened to bear an uncanny resemblance to the sixteenth president. The show went through a major rehab in 2001, adding a story line about a visit to Matthew Brady's photography studio and changing Lincoln's speech to the Gettysburg Address. A special audio effect uses binaural sound delivered through headphones. The actor now providing Mr. Lincoln's voice is Warren Burton. In 2005, the show closed so the area could become a Disneyland 50th anniversary display.

Great Mouse Detective, The (film) Animated adventures of a mouse, Basil of Baker Street, who is called upon to search for a toy maker, Flaversham, who has been kidnapped to make a robot replica of the queen for the evil Ratigan. Basil, aided by the intrepid Dr. Dawson, helps the toy maker's daughter, Olivia, search for her father. They foil Ratigan's plot and eventually save the queen. Released on July 2, 1986. Directed by John Musker, Ron Clements, Dave Michener, Burny Mattinson. 74 min. Featured voice actors were Vincent Price (Ratigan), Barrie Ingham (Basil), Val Bettin (Dr. Dawson), Candy Candido (Fidget), Diana Chesney (Mrs. Judson), Alan Young (Hiram Flaversham). The score was written by composer Henry Mancini, who also collaborated on two of the three featured songs with lyricists Larry Grossman and Ellen Fitzhugh; the third song, "Let Me Be Good to You," was written and performed by Melissa Manchester. Based on Eve Titus's book, *Basil of Baker Street*. After a four-year period of story development, animation

took just over one year to complete. This remarkably short production span was possible due to new efficiencies in the production process (such as video tests and computer-assisted layouts and graphics), and an increased emphasis on story development prior to the start of production. A total of 125 artists were involved in making the film. An innovative application of computer technology can be seen in the climactic scene where Basil faces Ratigan in a final confrontation inside the turning and thrashing gear works of Big Ben. The 54 moving gears, winches, ratchets, beams, and pulleys were literally drawn by the computer, and created a unique background for the characters that had been animated in the usual way. The film was re-released in theaters in 1992 under the title *The Adventures of the Great Mouse Detective*. Released on video in 1992 and 1999.

Great Movie Ride, The Attraction opened at Disney-MGM Studios on May 1, 1989. The tour takes guests into the midst of some of the greatest movies ever made, including *Casablanca*, *The Wizard of Oz*, *Alien*, *Mary Poppins*, *Singin' in the Rain*, *Fantasia*, *Tarzan*.

Great Quake Hazard Hunt, The (film) Educational video with Chip and Dale showing children how earthquakes happen and how to prepare for them at home and at school, produced by KCAL-TV and KFWB News Radio. Released on October 18, 1990.

Great Search, The (film) Educational film about humankind's search for power and energy, stressing his responsibility to develop new power potentials that will not upset the ecological balance; released in July 1972.

Greatest Game Ever Played, The (film) In 1913, when golf was a rich man's sport, dominated by English and Scottish athletes, a 20-year-old amateur player and former caddy, Francis Ouimet, against all odds, becomes the first American, and amateur, to win the U.S. Open. Caught between a world of hardship and a beckoning life of privilege, Francis needs to prove his unfailing will and ability to make it to the tournament. There, flanked by his ten-year-old caddy, Eddie, he defeats his idol, the defending British champion Harry Vardon. Directed by Bill Paxton. Released on September 30, 2005. Stars Shia LaBeouf (Francis Ouimet), Stephen Dillane (Henry Vardon), Elias Koteas (Arthur Ouimet), Peter Firth (Lord Northcliffe), Stephen Marcus (Ted Ray), Peyton List (Sarah Wallis), Josh Flitter (Eddie Lowery), Luke Askew (Alec Campbell), Michael Weaver (John McDermott), Marnie McPhail (Mary Ouimet), George Asprey (Wilfred Reid), Max Kasch (Freddie Wallis), Matthew Knight (Young Francis Ouimet), Luke Kirby (Frank Hoyt). 120 min. Filming took place in Montreal. Based on the book of the same title by Mark Frost.

Green, Judson He joined Walt Disney World in 1981 as management audit manager. In 1987 he was named senior vice president and CFO for Euro Disneyland, and in 1989 he became senior vice president and CFO for The Walt Disney Company. He was named president of Walt Disney Attractions in 1991 and chairman in 1998. He served until April 2000.

Green Card (film) A mutual friend arranges a marriage of convenience for Frenchman George Faure and Brontë Parrish, a native New Yorker. George needs a green card in order to remain in the United States, while Brontë, a horticulturist, has found the perfect apartment with a greenhouse, but it is only available to a married couple. After a swift legal ceremony, each getting what they want, they part with the intention of never seeing each other again. However, a government investigation brings them back together again, and despite initial irritation and incompatibility, the two begin to make some interesting discoveries about themselves and the nature of romance. Initial release in Los Angeles on December 23, 1990;

general release on January 11, 1991. Directed by Peter Weir. A Touchstone Picture. 107 min. Stars Gérard Depardieu (George), Andie MacDowell (Brontë), Bebe Neuwirth (Lauren). Filmed in New York City as an Australian-French co-production. Released on video in 1991.

Green Thumb Emporium, The Shop in The Land at Epcot; opened on November 10, 1993, and closed on April 25, 2004. Formerly Broccoli & Co.

Greener Yard, The (film) Donald Duck cartoon; released on October 14, 1949. Directed by Jack Hannah. When his son is unhappy with only beans to eat, Bootle Beetle tells him a story about the trouble he had with next-door neighbor Donald Duck in trying to get better food. When his son agrees that beans aren't so bad after all, Bootle Beetle risks going next door to bring back some watermelon for dessert.

Greenhouse Tours Guided walking tour in The Land at Epcot; beginning on December 10, 1993. Superseded Tomorrow's Harvest tours. Guides who are usually agricultural graduate students take small groups behind the scenes in the attraction, explaining hydroponics, aquaculture, drip irrigation, and other agricultural concepts, and are available to answer questions one might have posed while riding Living with the Land. The name changed to Behind the Seeds Tour in September 1996.

Greetings from California: Everything Under the Sun Shop at Golden Gateway at Disney's California Adventure; opened on February 8, 2001.

Gregory, Natalie She appeared as Annie in Cranium Command, Kathy in *Spot Marks the X*, and voiced Jenny Foxworth in *Oliver & Company*.

Gremlins, The Small, mischievous characters in stories told by Royal Air Force Lieutenant Roald Dahl. Walt Disney planned to make a movie about them, but it was never done. The only outcome of the project was a book published by Random House in 1943, several limited-edition dolls, and a few insignias created for military units.

Greta, the Misfit Greyhound (television) Television show; aired on February 3, 1963. Directed by Larry Lansburgh. A racing greyhound is deserted and has to learn to live on her own. Finally she is taken in by a shepherd, and helps him by using her speed to chase away coyotes threatening the flock and to track down a prowling bear. Stars Tacolo Chacartegui. Narrated by Rex Allen.

Greyfriars Bobby (film) When old Jock, a shepherd, is dismissed from service because of age, the little Skye terrier, Bobby, his constant companion, goes with him. And when old Jock dies of exposure a few days later, it is Bobby who travels unseen under the coffin as his friend is taken to be buried in Greyfriars Kirkyard, and keeps vigil over the grave. Nothing the caretaker, James Brown, can do prevents the little dog from getting back into the kirkyard, and eventually he stops trying as Bobby wins his heart, as well as the hearts of the poor children in the tenements nearby. The day comes when Bobby is picked up for lack of a dog license. Mr. and Mrs. Brown and a band of children come to pay the fine, telling the Lord Provost Bobby's story. He not only gives Bobby a license with his own hands, he also grants him the Freedom of the City, an honor bestowed only on the brave and faithful. Released on July 17, 1961. Directed by Don Chaffey. Based on a true story, as told by Eleanor Atkinson. 91 min. Stars Donald Crisp (James Brown), Laurence Naismith (Mr. Traill), Alex MacKenzie (Old Jock), Kay Walsh (Mrs. Brown). Filmed on location in Scotland. The film received favorable reviews, but the Scottish accents were hard on Americans' ears, so the film very soon appeared on *Walt Disney's Wonderful World of Color* for a television airing in 1964. Today a visitor to Edinburgh is often surprised to see a statue near the entrance to Greyfriars Kirkyard honoring the devoted Greyfriars Bobby. Released on video in 1986.

Grey's Anatomy (television) Hour-long drama program; premiered on ABC on March 27, 2005.

Grace Hospital has the toughest surgical residency program west of Harvard, a brutal training ground for the newest medical recruits. Meredith, Izzie, Christina, and George are the latest aspiring surgeons, trying to make it through seven years of the finest hell Grace has to offer. Along the way, they have to deal with impossible bosses, lack of sleep, sick parents, one-night stands, and housing crises, with only each other to rely upon. Stars Ellen Pompeo (Meredith Grey), Patrick Dempsey (Derek Shepherd), James Pickens, Jr. (Richard Webber), T.R. Knight (George O'Malley), Sandra Oh (Christina Yang), Katherine Heigl (Isobel "Izzie" Stevens), Chandra Wilson (Miranda Bailey), Isaiah Washington (Preston Burke). From Touchstone Television.

Griffith, Andy Actor; appeared in *Spy Hard* (General Rancor).

Griffith, Don (1918–1987) Layout artist; worked on layouts for animated features from *Victory Through Air Power* through *The Black Cauldron*. He retired in 1984.

Griffith, Melanie Actress, appeared in *Paradise* (Lily Reed), *A Stranger Among Us* (Emily Eden), *Born Yesterday* (Billie Dawn), *Two Much* (Betty), and on television as a host of *The Grand Opening of Euro Disney*.

Grimes, Gary Actor; appeared in *Gus* (Andy Petrovic).

Grimm Brothers Authors of *Snow White and the Seven Dwarfs*.

Grimsby Prince Eric's retainer in *The Little Mermaid*; voiced by Ben Wright, who died just before the film was released.

Grin and Bear It (film) Donald Duck cartoon; released on August 13, 1954. Directed by Jack Hannah. Ranger J. Audubon Woodlore, in his first appearance, tries to get the bears to behave during tourist season at Brownstone National Park. Each of the other bears selects their own tourists, from which they get plenty of food, but

Humphrey, with stingy Donald Duck as his tourist, gets nothing to eat. Humphrey tries to trick Donald out of his ham and picnic basket by making Donald think he has run over the bear with his car. In the resulting melee, food gets scattered all over the highway, and the ranger gives

both Donald and Humphrey pointed sticks to use to pick it up. He tries surreptitiously to keep the ham for himself, but Donald and Humphrey foil his plan.

Griswold Murder, The (television) Television show; episode 6 of *Elfego Baca*.

Grizzly River Run Attraction, appropriately nicknamed "Grr," at Disney's California Adventure; opened on February 8, 2001. Up a clattering 300-foot-long gold ore conveyor, eight-passenger rafts are lifted into swirling rapids 45 feet above the valley along one side of the 110-foot high Grizzly Peak, the icon for the park. More than 130,000 gallons of water a minute roar down the river flume, carrying guests on a wild and thrilling, and, yes, wet journey.

Grocery Boy, The (film) Mickey Mouse cartoon; released on February 11, 1932. Directed by Wilfred Jackson. Mickey is overjoyed to deliver Minnie's groceries to her and help prepare dinner. But the mood is spoiled when Pluto takes off with the turkey and in the resulting chase Mickey gets covered with chocolate cake.

Grodin, Charles Actor; appeared in *Taking Care of Business* (Spencer), and on television in *The Muppets at Walt Disney World*. He also appears in Cranium Command in Wonders of Life at Epcot.

Gross, Edan Actor; appeared on television in *We'll Take Manhattan* and the series *Walter and Emily*, and did the voices of Flounder and Christopher Robin on television.

Gross Anatomy (film) First-year med student Joe Slovak approaches the usually dreaded gross anatomy class—the systematic dissection of the human body—with his usual cocky manner. But he meets his match in Dr. Rachel Woodruff, the uncompromising instructor, who recognizes Joe's natural gift for medicine under his outspoken rebelliousness, and begins a tough campaign to discover whether her class clown really has what it takes to become a doctor. The test of wills ultimately becomes a touching and revealing experience for both student and teacher. Released on October 20, 1989. Directed by Thom Eberhardt. A Touchstone Picture. 107 min. Stars Matthew Modine (Joe Slovak), Daphne Zuniga (Lori Rohrbach), Christine Lahti (Rachel Woodruff). Filmed at various Southern California locations, including the defunct Queen of the Angels hospital and the University of Southern California. For the anatomy lab scenes shot on a Disney Studio soundstage, 16 realistic-looking cadavers had to be created. Released on video in 1990.

Grosse Pointe Blank (film) A hitman, Martin, specializes in assassinations in this comedy, but he has begun to have an identity crisis, realizing that his life lacks meaning. Therefore, in his twisted search to find "fulfillment and truth," he decides to return home to Grosse Pointe, Michigan, for his ten-year high school reunion, where he plans to reunite with Debi, the girl he left behind, as well as doing "one last hit." However, his archrival, Grocer, shows up with plans to hit Martin instead. Directed by George Armitage. A Hollywood Pictures film in association with Caravan Pictures; released on April 11, 1997. Stars John Cusack (Martin), Minnie Driver (Debi), Dan Aykroyd (Grocer), Alan Arkin (Dr. Oatman). 107 min. Filming took place around

Los Angeles, with the communities of Monrovia, Duarte, and Pasadena substituting for Grosse Pointe. Released on video in 1997.

Grosvenor Resort Hotel at Lake Buena Vista, at the Walt Disney World Resort, formerly Americana's Dutch Resort.

Growing up with Winnie the Pooh (film) A new series of DVDs and videos from Walt Disney Home Entertainment, giving preschoolers the social skills they need to get a head start to successful learning. The first two films in the series, released on February 8, 2005, were *A Great Day of Discovery* and *Friends Forever*.

Grumpy One of the Seven Dwarfs; voiced by Pinto Colvig.

Guardian, The (film) Directed by Andrew Davis. Stars Kevin Costner, Ashton Kutcher. Shooting began in December 2005 in Shreveport and nearby cities for a proposed 2006 release.

Guatemalan Weavers Adventureland shop at Disneyland from 1956 to February 23, 1986. Became Safari Outpost.

Guest Disney term for visitor at the Disney parks.

Guest Quarters Suite Resort Hotel in Lake Buena Vista at Walt Disney World, formerly Pickett Suite Resort Hotel. It became the Doubletree Guest Suite Resort in 1995.

Guest Star Day Tuesday on the 1950s *Mickey Mouse Club*.

Guillaume, Robert Actor; appeared on television in *Disney's Great American Celebration*, and provided the voice of Rafiki in *The Lion King*. He starred in the television series *Pacific Station* and *Sports Night*, and appeared in *First Kid* (Wilkes) and *Spy Hard* (Steve Bishop).

Guilty as Sin (film) Jennifer Haines is a hot-shot criminal defense attorney renowned for her ability to get anybody acquitted. She is challenged to defend a playboy, David Greenhill, charged with murdering his wife, but finds him more complex and dangerous than she ever imagined. To her horror, she discovers that he is twisting the law, and using his own disarming charm to continue his deadly schemes—with Jennifer as an accomplice. After he is successfully acquitted, Jennifer must decide to put her life and career on the line and destroy him. Released on June 4, 1993. Directed by Sidney Lumet. A Hollywood Picture. 107 min. Stars Rebecca DeMornay (Jennifer Haines), Don Johnson (David Greenhill), Stephen Lang (Phil Garson), Jack Warden (Moe). Filmed on location in Toronto. Released on video in 1993.

Gulager, Clu Actor; appeared on television in *The Mystery in Dracula's Castle*.

Gulf Coast Room Restaurant in the Contemporary Resort at Walt Disney World, from 1971 until May 28, 1988.

Gulliver Mickey (film) Mickey Mouse cartoon; released on May 19, 1934. Directed by Burt Gillett. In telling the story to his nephews, Mickey is Gulliver, who is bound on shore by the Lilliputians.

He escapes out to sea only to be attacked by the Lilliputians' small navy. But, when he saves the town from a huge spider, Mickey becomes the hero of the day.

Gullywhumper Mike Fink's keelboat in *Davy Crockett's Keel Boat Race*, also one of the Mike Fink Keel Boats at Disneyland and in Magic Kingdom Park at Walt Disney World.

Gummi Bears See *Disney's Adventures of the Gummi Bears*.

Gummi Bears: a New Beginning, The (film) Foreign theatrical release of the television cartoon, first in England on July 18, 1986. A young page, Cavin, discovers the existence of supposedly mythical Gummi Bears, and with the aid of their magic Gummiberry juice, they help him foil the evil Duke Igthorn's plan to destroy Dunwyn Castle.

Gummi Bears: Faster Than a Speeding Tummi, The (film) Foreign theatrical release of the television cartoon, first in England on April 10, 1987. When Tummi is too slow cleaning up a mess of purple bubbles he caused, he tricks Zummi into zapping him with a "speed spell" that goes awry. However, he is able to use the speed to rescue his friends from Igthorn.

Gun in Betty Lou's Handbag, The (film) A pretty but shy librarian, Betty Lou Perkins, is bored with her small-town life. Alex, her police detective husband, ignores her, and her job has become routine and uninteresting. The town is shaken into life by the discovery of a murder victim. When Betty Lou stumbles upon the murder weapon, she decides to confess to the crime hoping her bold action will grab everyone's attention. Along comes mobster Billy Beaudeen who is both intrigued and threatened by the sudden appearance of the new "hit-woman" on the scene. Betty Lou uses her newly gained self-confidence and notoriety to uncover the truth about the murder and, at the same time, to show her husband that she refuses to be taken for granted. Released on August 21, 1992. Directed by Allan Moyle. A

Touchstone Picture. 90 min. Stars Penelope Ann Miller (Betty Lou Perkins), Eric Thal (Alex), Alfre Woodard (Ann), William Forsythe (Beaudeen), Cathy Moriarty (Reba). Filmed in Oxford, Mississippi. Released on video in 1993.

Gun Shy (film) Charlie Cutter is a legendary DEA undercover agent who has a traumatic memory of his latest bust. Even though he loathes his job and wants out, he has carefully planned an operation for the arrest of Cheemo, a drug lord. The bust goes bad and Charlie is forced to watch helplessly as bloody carnage rips everything apart. He lives to tell the tale, but the memory will not leave him alone. Fear has now taken over his life. He seeks psychiatric help and finds himself relying on the support of an unstable therapy group, and nurse Judy, just to get through his work. A Hollywood Picture. Directed by Eric Blakeney. Limited release on February 4, 2000. Stars Liam Neeson (Charlie Cutter), Oliver Platt (Fulvio Nesstra), Sandra Bullock (Judy Tipp), Jose Zuniga (Fidel Vaillar), Richard Schiff (Elliott), Andy Lauer (Jason Kent), Taylor Negron (Cheemo). 102 min. Sandra Bullock also served as producer. Filmed on location in New York (and at Los Angeles locations doubling as New York). Released on video in 2000.

Gun Shy (television) Limited television series of six episodes; aired on CBS from March 25 to April 19, 1983. Based on *The Apple Dumpling Gang*, about two orphans in Quake City who have become wards of a professional gambler. Stars Barry Van Dyke, Tim Thomerson, Keith Mitchell, Adam Rich, Bridgette Andersen, Henry Jones, Geoffrey Lewis, Janis Paige, Pat McCormick.

Gund Manufacturing Co. Licensee for Disney plush characters from 1947 to 1971. Many of their dolls are recognizable by their molded plastic faces. For the first two Disneyana Conventions in 1992 and 1993, Gund manufactured reproductions of their earliest Mickey Mouse and Minnie Mouse dolls.

Gunfight at Sandoval (film) Foreign theatrical compilation of *Texas John Slaughter* episodes.

First released in Germany in December 1961. 92 min. Stars Tom Tryon. Released on video in 1987.

Gunpowder Brom Bones's scary horse in *The Adventures of Ichabod and Mr. Toad.*

Guns in the Heather (film) Foreign theatrical compilation of television episodes of *The Secret of Boyne Castle*. Also known as *Spybusters*. First released in England in July 1969. 89 min.

Gurgi Nondescript furry creature who joins Taran on his quest in *The Black Cauldron;* voiced by John Byner.

Gurgi's Munchies and Crunchies Fast-food facility in Fantasyland in Magic Kingdom Park at Walt Disney World, from October 26, 1986 to February 13, 1993. Formerly Lancer's Inn; became Lumiere's Kitchen.

Gurr, Bob Imagineer who specialized in vehicle design, first being retained by Disney in 1954 to consult on the design of the Autopia cars. At WED Enterprises, he worked on designs for such attractions as the Monorail, Matterhorn Bobsleds, Flying Saucers, and the antique cars and double-decker buses utilized on Main Street, U.S.A. He retired in 1981. He was named a Disney Legend in 2004.

Gus (film) The inept California Atoms, floundering in the cellar of the National Football League, welcome the team's newest member—a mule capable of placekicking a football 100 yards with deadly accuracy. The endearing animal turns the League upside down, eludes kidnappers, masterminds the romance of the shy young man who owns him, and single-handedly (single-hoofedly?) turns the hapless Atoms into a championship team. Released on July 7, 1976. Directed by Vincent McEveety. 97 min. Stars Ed Asner (Hank Cooper), Don Knotts (Coach), Gary Grimes (Andy), Tim Conway (Crankcase), Liberty Williams (Debbie), Dick Van Patten (Cal), Ronnie Schell (Joe Barnsdale), Bob Crane (Pepper), Tom Bosley (Spinner), Dick Butkus (Rob Cargil), and special guest stars Johnny Unitas, Dick

Enberg, George Putnam, Stu Nahan. The film was based on the book by Ted Key. Football scenes were filmed at the Los Angeles Coliseum, the Sports Arena, and on a portable field of sod covering a parking lot at the Disney Studio in Burbank. Backgrounds were filmed at many professional games. The fabled Animation Building on the lot was even used—as a hospital. Executive producer Ron Miller had personal background experience for this film—he used to play professionally and spent a year as a tight end with the Los Angeles Rams. A special acknowledgment is made in the credits to the National Football League for their assistance in the football sequences. Released on video in 1981 and 1985.

Gus Chubby mouse friend of Cinderella; voiced by Jim Macdonald.

Gus Goose Gluttonous title star of *Donald's Cousin Gus* (1939).

Gus Tomlin is Dead (television) Television show; episode 10 of *Elfego Baca*.

Guttenberg, Steve Actor; appeared as Michael in *Three Men and a Baby* and *Three Men and a Little Lady*, and in *The Big Green* (Tom Palmer). On television he appeared in *Tower of Terror* (Buzzy Crocker).

Gwynne, Fred (1926–1993) Actor; appeared in *Off Beat* (commissioner) and *Disorganized Crime* (Max Green), and on television in *The Christmas Star*.

Gyllenhaal, Jake Actor; starred in *Bubble Boy* (Jimmy Livingston) and *Moonlight Mile* (Joe Nast).

Gyro Gearloose Cartoon character created by artist Carl Barks, he debuted in *Walt Disney's Comics and Stories* no. 140 in May 1952. His assistant, a lightbulb called Helper, made his debut in 1956. He was a fabulous inventor of weird and wonderful things. Gyro appeared on television in *Ducktales*.

H

Haber, Heinz (1913–1990) Scientist; acted as adviser on Disney space-themed television shows in the 1950s, personally appearing occasionally on screen. He collaborated on *Donald in Mathmagic Land* and wrote the book, *Our Friend the Atom*.

Hackett, Buddy (1924–2003) Actor; appeared in *The Love Bug* (Tennessee Steinmetz), and provided the voice of Scuttle in *The Little Mermaid*. He was named a Disney Legend posthumously in 2003.

Hackman, Gene Actor; appeared in *Crimson Tide* (Ramsey), *Enemy of the State* (Brill), and *The Royal Tenenbaums* (Royal Tenenbaum).

Hacksaw (television) Two-part television show; aired on September 26 and October 3, 1971. Directed by Larry Lansburgh. A girl, on vacation in the Canadian Rockies, tries to capture a wild stallion, whose great strength leads to a pulling contest at the Calgary Stampede. Stars Tab Hunter, Susan Bracken, Victor Millan, Ray Teal, Russ McCubbin, George Barrows.

Hades The scheming god of the Underworld in *Hercules*; voiced by James Woods.

Hagen-Renaker Potteries Licensee of Disney ceramic figurines from 1955 to 1961. Their figurines, primarily small in size, were popular souvenirs at Disneyland, but today command high prices. The intricate craftsmanship on the small figurines is remarkable. Some of their more popular sets are of characters from *Lady and the Tramp*, *Snow White and the Seven Dwarfs*, and *Sleeping Beauty*. They also did *Fantasia* figurines for sale in the Disney parks in the 1980s.

Hahn, Don He began working for Disney in 1976, first on *Pete's Dragon*. He worked as associate producer on the animated sequences in *Who Framed Roger Rabbit*, and later produced *Beauty and the*  *Beast*, *The Lion King*, *The Hunchback of Notre Dame*, and *Atlantis: The Lost Empire*, and was executive producer on *The Emperor's New Groove*. He was also a producer on the live-action *The Haunted Mansion*.

Hakuna Matata Restaurant in Adventureland at Disneyland Paris, named after the song sung by Timon and Pumbaa in *The Lion King*, which took the place of Aux Epices Enchantèes in May 1995.

Hale, Barbara Actress; appeared on television in *Chester, Yesterday's Horse; The Young Runaways*; and *The Flight of the Grey Wolf.*

Hale, Tiffini Actress; appeared on the *Mickey Mouse Club* on The Disney Channel beginning in 1989, and was a member of The Party.

Hall, Bug Actor; appeared in *The Big Green* (Newt Shaw), on video in *Honey, We Shrunk Ourselves* (Adam), and on television in *Safety Patrol* (Scout Bozell) and *Get a Clue* (Jack Downey). He provided the voice of a little boy in *Hercules*.

Hall, David (1905–1964) Storyman; worked at Disney from 1939 to 1940, and during that time produced hundreds of detailed story sketches and paintings for *Alice in Wonderland* (with a few also on *Peter Pan*). The concepts for these films changed during the many years before they were made, but Hall's sketches stand out as wonderful works of art. A book containing his *Alice* sketches, *Alice's Adventures in Wonderland*, was published in 1986.

Hall, Huntz (1919–1999) Actor; appeared in *Herbie Rides Again* (Judge), and on television in *The Sky's the Limit.*

Hall Brothers Company later known as Hallmark Cards, Inc. Joyce Hall of Kansas City was a friend of Walt Disney's, and he received the license to produce greeting cards featuring the Disney characters beginning in 1931. Gibson took over the national license after Disneyland opened, but Hallmark was back as a licensee beginning in the 1970s.

CHEER UP! It might be worse!

Hall of Aluminum Fame Sponsored by Kaiser Aluminum in Tomorrowland at Disneyland from 1955 until July 1960. Told the history of the metal and the men who developed the processes for its mass production, and described the methods used. A major icon was a huge aluminum pig.

Hall of Presidents, The Liberty Square attraction in Magic Kingdom Park at Walt Disney World, opening October 1, 1971. At one time this show had been proposed for Disneyland, under the title of One Nation Under God. A pre-show film discusses how the Constitution was drafted and how it has had increased significance at various periods of American history from the eighteenth century to the present. The motion picture was shot on 70mm film, using a special system invented by Ub Iwerks to scan the specially produced paintings (some of which are on display in the waiting area), and it is projected on a huge screen. Then the screen parts and all the presidents are on stage, represented by Audio-Animatronics figures. Originally, they were all introduced by the narrator, then George Washington sat down and Abraham Lincoln spoke his remarks. Royal Dano speaks for Lincoln. The presidents elected after 1971 were added within a year or so of their elections. When Bill Clinton was added in 1993, the pre-show film and Lincoln speech were shortened, and Clinton made a few remarks. The Clinton speech was actually recorded by the president in the White House. The same was done when George W. Bush became president. For the presidents, detailed research was done by the Disney designers, to provide not only images that the sculptors could follow in creating the figures themselves, but information on hairstyles, costumes, fabrics, and jewelry. Everything was then reproduced as authentically as possible.

Hallmark Card shop on Main Street at Disneyland from June 15, 1960 to 1985. The shop was previously sponsored by Gibson Cards. Also in Magic Kingdom Park at Walt Disney World from 1974 until 1985. Hallmark was a longtime Disney merchandise licensee. See also Hall Brothers.

Halloween Hall of Fame (television) Television show; aired on October 30, 1977. Directed by Arthur J. Vitarelli. A Disney Studio watchman finds a room of props, including a jack o'lantern that comes to life. Several cartoons are used to tell "the real story of Halloween." Stars Jonathan Winters. Director Art Vitarelli was primarily a second unit director at the Disney Studio, unsung for his directing many fantastic special effects scenes in films of the period, at a time when Disney was famed for its effects.

Halloween Hilarities (film) Shorts program; released by RKO in 1953.

Halloween Surprises (film) Educational film with Mickey's clubhouse members learning about Halloween safety rules, in the Mickey's Safety Club series, released in September 1989. 13 min.

Halloweentown (television) Aggie Cromwell, an eccentric and high-spirited witch, travels from her spooky and wonderful hometown, Halloweentown, to the mortal world to enlist the help of her daughter, Gwen, and her grandchildren in her mission to save Halloweentown from the sinister forces of evil which threaten to take it over. A Disney Channel Original Film; first airing on October 17, 1998. Directed by Duwayne Dunham. Stars Debbie Reynolds (Aggie Cromwell), Judith Hoag (Gwen Piper), Robin Thomas (Kalabar), Kimberly J. Brown (Marnie Piper), Joey Zimmerman (Dylan Piper), Emily Roeske (Sophie Piper), Phillip Van Dyke (Luke).

Halloweentown High (television) A Disney Channel Original Film; first airing on October 8, 2004. With the portal opened, much to the chagrin of some in Halloweentown, Marnie sets up an exchange program bringing a group of Halloweentown students to attend her human high school. She inadvertently bets the Cromwell family magic that no harm will come to them. When strange things start happening, Marnie and her family must protect the students from the legendary Knights of the Iron Dagger, and at the same time, save their own powers. Directed by Mark A.Z. Dippé. Stars Debbie Reynolds (Aggie Cromwell), Kimberley J. Brown (Marnie), Judith Hoag (Gwen), Joey Zimmerman (Dylan), Clifton Davis

(Principal Flannigan), Finn Wittrock (Cody), Michael Flynn (Dalloway), Emily Roeske (Sophie).

Halloweentown II: Kalabar's Revenge (television) A Disney Channel Original Film; premiering on October 12, 2001. The place where witches, ghosts, and goblins live for 365 days a year is threatened by warlock Kal, who has cast a spell. Halloweentown turns gray and its inhabitants become human caricatures. Kal also has plans for everyone in the mortal world to become the costume they are wearing at midnight on Halloween. Aggie and her granddaughter, Marnie, must use their skills to vanquish the young and charismatic villain. Directed by Mary Lambert. Stars Debbie Reynolds (Aggie Cromwell), Kimberly J. Brown (Marnie), Judith Hoag (Gwen), Daniel Kountz (Kal), Peter Wingfield (Alex), Joey Zimmerman (Dylan), Emily Roeske (Sophie), Phillip Van Dyke (Luke).

Hamad and the Pirates (television) Two-part television show; aired on March 7 and 14, 1971. An orphaned pearl diver, Hamad, who lives in the Persian Gulf, is captured by pirates that have been stealing artifacts. When the Royal Navy approaches, the pirates throw their treasure overboard, and Hamad, who escapes, tries to find it while diving with a friend. The pirates return too soon, but Hamad helps foil them and save the treasure for the Bahrain museum. Narrated by Michael Ansara. Stars Khalik Marshad, Abdullah Masoud, Khalifah Shaheen.

Hampshire, Susan Actress; appeared in *The Three Lives of Thomasina* (Lori MacGregor) and *The Fighting Prince of Donegal* (Kathleen MacSweeney).

Hampton, Chase Actor; appeared on the *Mickey Mouse Club* on The Disney Channel, beginning in 1989, and was a member of The Party.

Hand, Dave (1900–1986) Animator/director; joined Disney in 1930 where he began as an animator on the short cartoons for three years before becoming a director. He is credited with directing

70 shorts and three features, including *Building a Building*, *The Mad Doctor*, *Old King Cole*, *Flowers and Trees*, *The Flying Mouse*, *Who Killed Cock Robin?*, *Three Orphan Kittens*, *Thru the Mirror*, *Alpine Climbers*, *Little Hiawatha*, *Snow White and the Seven Dwarfs*, *Bambi*, and *Victory Through Air Power*. Hand left Disney in 1944 to set up an animation studio in England. He was named a Disney Legend posthumously in 1994.

Hand Behind the Mouse, The: The Ub Iwerks Story (film) Documentary film about animation pioneer and early Walt Disney collaborator, Ub Iwerks, written, produced, and directed by his granddaughter, Leslie Iwerks. Released in Los Angeles for one week for Academy Award qualification on October 8, 1999. 92 min. Released on video in 2001.

Hand That Rocks the Cradle, The (film) A seemingly sweet woman named Peyton becomes a live-in nanny for warmhearted Claire, but the nanny has actually ingratiated herself into the family in order to plot vengeance for her husband's suicide, which she blames on Claire. Released on January 10, 1992. Directed by Curtis Hanson. A Hollywood Picture. 110 min. Stars Rebecca DeMornay (Peyton), Annabella Sciorra (Claire), Matt McCoy (Michael), Ernie Hudson (Solomon). The home used for the filming was found in Tacoma, Washington; other scenes were shot in the Seattle area. Released on video in 1992.

Handley, Taylor Actor; appeared in *Phantom of the Megaplex* (Pete Riley) on Disney Channel, and as a regular on the television series *Go Fish* (Hazard).

Hang Your Hat on the Wind (film) Featurette; directed by Larry Lansburgh. A handsome thoroughbred yearling accidentally escapes from a cross-country van in the desert, and is found and loved by a young Mexican boy. He hides the horse from searchers, but eventually mends his ways and tries to return the animal. However, two hoodlums steal the horse. The boy leads a sheriff to the rescue, and receives an apt reward. Released on June 11, 1969, on a bill with *Rascal*. 48 min. Stars Ric Natoli, Judson Platt, Angel Tompkins, Edward Faulkner.

Hanks, Tom Actor; appeared in *Splash* (Allen Bauer), *Turner & Hooch* (Scott Turner), and *The Ladykillers* (Prof. Goldthwait Higginson Dorr). He provided the voice for Woody in *Toy Story* and *Toy Story 2*.

Hannah, Daryl Actress; appeared as Madison in *Splash*. and in *The Tie That Binds* (Leann Netherwood), *Two Much* (Liz), and *My Favorite Martian* (Lizzie).

Hannah, Jack (1913–1994) Animator/director; joined Disney's animation staff in 1933 working as an inbetweener and clean-up artist on many early Mickey, Donald, and Silly Symphony cartoons. He was a key animator on the Academy Award–winning film, *The Old Mill*. He directed over 75 shorts, eight of which were nominated for Academy Awards. After he retired in 1959, he spent a number of years creating and then heading the character animation program at the California Institute of the Arts. He was honored with the Disney Legends Award in 1992.

Hans The example of a brainwashed German youth during World War II, in *Education for Death* (1943).

Hans Brinker or the Silver Skates (television) Two-part television show; aired on January 7 and 14, 1962. Directed by Norman Foster. Hans's father is injured and all the family's money saved for Hans's education must go for medical bills. Hans dabbles in art, and hopes to sell some of his paintings, but then there are more problems with the father. Hans hears of an annual skating race, and he is determined to win it for the prize money and help his family. Hans aborts the race to save a fellow racer, who happens to be the mayor's son, and the mayor agrees to pay for the needed surgery. Stars Rony Zeander, Carin Rossby, Gunilla Jelf, Erik Strandmark, Inga Landgre.

Hans Christian Andersen's The Ugly Duckling (film) Educational film; released in

September 1986, 13 min. Walt Disney introduces an animated biography of Andersen, followed by the Silly Symphony. Retitled in 1987 as *An Introduction to Hans Christian Andersen.*

Hansel and Gretel Story adapted in the Silly Symphony cartoon, *Babes in the Woods.*

Happiest Celebration on Earth In salute to the 50th anniversary of Disneyland, Disney theme parks around the world united in 2005 to bring guests never-before-seen attractions, entertainment, and activities. Featured additions at Disneyland included a new parade and a new fireworks extravaganza, Walt Disney's Parade of Dreams and Remember . . . Dreams Come True; a new attraction, Buzz Lightyear Astro Blasters; the relaunch of Space Mountain; and a royal makeover for Sleeping Beauty Castle. The Opera House hosted Disneyland: The First 50 Magical Years, an attraction tracing the history of the park. Disney's California Adventure held a Block Party Bash, a street celebration featuring Disney/Pixar's most memorable characters. At Walt Disney World Resort, Soarin', a popular attraction in Disney's California Adventure, debuted at Epcot; Tokyo Disneyland's "Cinderellabration" premiered at Magic Kingdom Park; Lights, Motors, Action! Extreme Stunt Show, a popular attraction at Walt Disney Studios Paris, opened to guests at Disney-MGM Studios; and Expedition Everest, a new thrill attraction, opened its icy slopes to guests at Disney's Animal Kingdom. Special events also happened at Tokyo Disney Resort and Disneyland Resort Paris.

Happiest Millionaire, The (film) In words and music, this is the story of "the happiest millionaire," nonconformist Anthony J. Drexel Biddle, and his unusual Philadephia family, seen through the eyes of their new-to-the-U.S. Irish butler. The year is 1916, and in the busy household on Rittenhouse Square each of the family members has hopes and dreams. For Mr. Biddle it is strengthening the "Biddle Bible Class," campaigning for military preparedness, and caring for his prized alligators. For daughter Cordelia Biddle, it is first love with the wealthy Angie Duke,

who is infatuated with the automobile. For Mrs. Biddle it is keeping order in the family despite frozen alligators, a wedding, confrontations with the Duke family, World War I, and comforting her husband when the children have left home. Premiered in Hollywood on June 23, 1967. Directed by Norman Tokar. 159 min. (164 min. with overtures) for the original roadshow version; 144 min. for the stereo general release; 141 min. for the mono general release. Stars Fred MacMurray (Anthony J. Drexel Biddle), Tommy Steele (John Lawless), Lesley Ann Warren (Cordelia Drexel Biddle), John Davidson (Angie Duke), Greer Garson (as Mrs. Biddle in her last feature film role), Geraldine Page (Mrs. Duke), Gladys Cooper (Aunt Mary), Hermione Baddeley (Mrs. Worth), Paul Peterson (Tony), Eddie Hodges (Liv), and Joyce Bulifant (Rosemary). This was the Disney Studio's most lavish and starry musical production since *Mary Poppins.* The Sherman brothers, Richard and Robert, wrote twelve songs, including "I'll Always Be Irish," "Detroit," "Fortuosity," "Watch Your Footwork," "Valentine Candy," "There Are Those," "Let's Have A Drink On It," and "Strengthen The Dwelling." The film was heavily edited during its release due to the Studio's disappointment that the film did not equal *Mary Poppins*'s success. Cut footage from the original 159 min. roadshow version and the stereophonic sound track were restored and a heretofore unseen musical number, "It Won't Be Long 'Til Christmas," sung by Greer Garson and Fred MacMurray, was added for a Disney Channel airing in November 1984, though some dialogue preceding the song was still missing. The film has many highlights, from Tommy Steele's, Fred MacMurray's, and Greer Garson's portrayals, to a pair of mischievous alligators who dance with Steele. Some exhilarating dance numbers, including a riotous barroom sequence, were staged by Marc Breaux and Dee Dee Wood. The film's origins date back to the published true story of the Biddles, written by Cordelia Drexel Biddle and Kyle Crichton, which was subsequently made into a successful Broadway comedy. A J Carothers adapted the screenplay when Walt Disney enlisted the Sherman brothers to make it into a musical event. There were other contenders for the role of Mr. Biddle, including Rex Harrison (who was favored by the Sherman brothers), Burt Lancaster, and Brian Keith, but Walt Disney chose his favorite, Fred MacMurray, whom he had wanted from the beginning. Released on video in 1984.

Happy One of the Seven Dwarfs; voiced by Otis Harlan.

Happy Birthday Donald Duck (television) Rerun title of *At Home with Donald Duck*.

Harambe Disney designers and native craftsmen created an African jungle town, featuring the Kilimanjaro Safaris, along with shops and restaurants, in Disney's Animal Kingdom. Harambe means "come together" in Swahili.

Harbor Blvd. Anaheim street on which Disneyland is located. It is a major thoroughfare, beginning at the Pacific Ocean, some miles from Disneyland.

Hard Time on Planet Earth (television) Television series on CBS; aired March 1 to July 5, 1989. An alien warrior from the planet Andarius is sent to earth, transformed into human form, kept under surveillance by a "correctional unit" named Control, and forced to perform a series of good deeds before he can return home. Stars Martin Kove (Jesse), Danny Mann (voice of Control).

Hardball (television) Television series; debuting on September 4, 1994 on Fox, and airing until October 23, 1994. About the trials and triumphs of the Pioneers, a fictitious American League baseball team. Stars Bruce Greenwood (Dave Logan), Mike Starr (Mike Widmer), Dann Florek (Ernest "Happy" Talbot), Alexandra Wentworth (Lee Emory), Rose Marie (Mitzi Balzer).

Hardy Boys, The: The Mystery of Ghost Farm (television) Serial on the *Mickey Mouse Club* during the 1957–1958 season. Directed by Robert Springsteen. Joe discovers a haunted farm, and Frank helps him investigate. Stars Tim Considine (Frank), Tommy Kirk (Joe), Carole Ann Campbell, Sarah Selby, Russ Conway, John Baer, Hugh Sanders, Bob Amsberry, Andy Clyde. 15 episodes.

Hardy Boys, The: The Mystery of the Applegate Treasure (television) Serial on the *Mickey Mouse Club* during the 1956–1957 season. Directed by Charles Haas. Frank and Joe Hardy, sons of a famous detective, try to solve a mystery about a lost treasure themselves. Based on the books by Franklin W. Dixon. Stars Tim Considine, Tommy Kirk, Carole Ann Campbell, Donald MacDonald, Florenz Ames, Russ Conway, Sarah Selby. 20 episodes.

Harem Scarem (film) Oswald the Lucky Rabbit cartoon; released on January 9, 1928.

Harlan, Otis (1865–1940) Voice of Happy in *Snow White and the Seven Dwarfs*.

Harline, Leigh (1907–1969) Composer at Disney from 1932 to 1941, he wrote songs for short subjects and features, including the underscoring on *Snow White and the Seven Dwarfs* and *Pinocchio* with Paul Smith, and the music for several *Pinocchio* songs. He died in 1969, and was named a Disney Legend posthumously in 2001. His name is pronounced Lee Har-LEEN.

Harman, Hugh (1903–1982) One of Walt Disney's first employees, originally at Laugh-O-gram Films in Kansas City, and then in Hollywood. He worked on the Alice Comedies and left in 1928 to partner with another early Disney employee, Rudolf Ising.

Harman-Ising Cartoon production organization, headed by Hugh Harman and Rudy Ising, who had worked for Walt Disney in Kansas City. Disney hired them to produce the cartoon *Merbabies* (1938) for him.

Harmony Barber Shop Located on Main Street in Magic Kingdom Park at Walt Disney World; opened in 1971. Also in Disneyland Paris; opened on April 12, 1992. In a nostalgic setting, many guests decide to have a quick trim.

Harnois, Elisabeth Actress; appeared in *One Magic Christmas* (Abbie Grainger), and on television as Alice in *Disney's Adventures in Wonderland* and in *My Date with the President's Daughter* (Hallie Richmond).

Harold and His Amazing Green Plants (film) Educational film; released in August 1984. A basic botany lesson for the youngest audience about Harold and his unusual "pet" plant.

Harriet, Judy Mouseketeer from the 1950s television show.

Harrington Bay Clothiers Men's fashions at the Downtown Disney Marketplace at Walt Disney World; opened March 23, 1992, and closed July 15, 2001.

Harrington's Fine China & Porcelains Shop on Main Street in Disneyland Paris; opened on April 12, 1992.

Harris, Barbara Actress; appeared in *Freaky Friday* (Ellen Andrews), *The North Avenue Irregulars* (Vickie), and *Grosse Pointe Blank* (Mary Blank).

Harris, Phil (1906–1995) Voiced Baloo (*The Jungle Book*), Thomas O'Malley (*The Aristocats*), and Little John (*Robin Hood*).

Harriss, Cynthia After starting out with Disney in the Disney Stores in 1992, Harriss moved to Disneyland in 1997 as head of park operations and merchandise. She was promoted to Executive Vice President of Disneyland Resort in December 1998, and to President in December 1999. She served until October 2003.

Harry (television) Television series; aired from March 4 to 25, 1987. Harry Porschak runs the supply room at County General Hospital, and he is not above making questionable deals to keep his operation running smoothly. This alienates some of his superiors, but endears him to many of his fellow workers. Stars Alan Arkin (Harry), Thom Bray (Lawrence), Matt Craven (Bobby), Barbara Dana (Sandy), Kurt Knudson (Richard).

Hartman, David Actor; appeared as Professor Ivarsson in *Island at the Top of the World.*

Harvest Theatre In The Land at Epcot, showing the film *Symbiosis* beginning on October 1, 1982. The film was shot in 70mm and projected on a large screen. It looked at how man's technology could exist without destroying the environment. A new film premiered in 1995, *Circle of Life: an Environmental Fable.*

Haskin, Byron (1899–1984) Director; helmed *Treasure Island* for Disney.

Hatcher, Teri Actress; appeared in *Straight Talk* (Janice) and on television in *Desperate Housewives* (Susan Mayer).

Hathaway, Ann Actress; appeared as Mia Thermopolis in *The Princess Diaries* and *The Princess Diaries 2: The Royal Engagement.*

Haunted House, The (film) Mickey Mouse cartoon; released in 1929. Directed by Walt Disney. When Mickey retreats from a storm into a haunted house, the skeleton inhabitants, including a Grim Reaper skeleton, force him to play the organ for them. Finally, he escapes through a window.

Haunted Mansion, The New Orleans Square attraction at Disneyland, supposedly the home of 999 ghosts with "always room for one more"; opened on August 9, 1969. The mansion had actually been built in 1962–1963 but work on the interior was first halted by the 1964–1965 New York World's Fair. Then Disney designers could not decide on what to put inside, so guests were simply tantalized by a promise of an attraction to come. At one time, it was thought that there would be a walk-through attraction, but it was realized that there would be traffic flow problems. The advent of the Omnimover—here, "Doom Buggies"—provided the solution. From the outside the Mansion looks elegant; some designers wanted it to look ominous and scary, in a state of disrepair, but Walt Disney said that he'd keep up the outside and let the ghosts take care of the interior. Within the house, guests hear narration by Paul Frees as they ride past a number of spooky exhibits and special effects that defy explanation. In Liberty Square at Magic Kingdom Park at Walt Disney World, opened October 1, 1971. Also in Fantasyland at Tokyo Disneyland, opened on April 15, 1983. See also Phantom Manor for the Disneyland Paris version. The only major attraction in four different lands in the four Disney parks. The Haunted Mansion at Disneyland was changed to a holiday theme of *Tim Burton's The Nightmare Before Christmas*, beginning October 5, 2001, and repeated in later holiday seasons. A Japanese version, The Haunted Mansion "Holiday Nightmare" began at Tokyo Disneyland on September 15, 2004.

Haunted Mansion, The (film) Workaholic real estate agent Jim Evers and his wife and business partner, Sara, drag their family up to the big, creepy Gracey mansion, located on a remote Louisiana bayou, when Jim gets a call that owner Edward Gracey wants to sell. Jim senses the biggest deal of his career, hoping to rebuild the mansion into a lavish new condo development. When the Evers family gets there, however, they are stranded by a torrential thunderstorm and quickly find that they are not alone—not when 999 grim, grinning ghosts come out to socialize. With all these happy haunts that won't leave until their unfinished business has been completed, it is up to Jim to break the curse, while at the same time, he discovers how much his family needs him. Directed by Rob Minkoff. Released on November 26, 2003. Stars Eddie Murphy (Jim Evers), Terence Stamp (Ramsley), Nathaniel Parker (Master Gracey), Marsha Thomason (Sara Evers), Jennifer Tilly (Madame Leota), Wallace Shawn (Ezra), Dina Waters (Emma), Marc John Jefferies (Michael), Aree Davis (Megan). 88 min. Filmed in Super 35-Scope. The film features special effects and makeup design by Academy Award–winner Rick Baker. Released on video in 2004.

Havoc, June Actress; appeared on television in *The Boy Who Stole the Elephant*.

Hawaiian Holiday (film) Mickey Mouse cartoon; released on September 24, 1937. Directed by Ben Sharpsteen. On a sunny beach, Minnie does the hula, accompanied by Mickey, Donald, and  Goofy. Pluto makes an enemy out of a starfish while Goofy attempts to surf despite some troubles with the waves.

Hawk, Alonzo Villain role played by actor Keenan Wynn in *The Absent Minded Professor*, *Son of Flubber*, and *Herbie Rides Again*, all films written and produced by Bill Walsh.

Hawke, Ethan Actor; appeared in *Dead Poets Society* (Todd Anderson), *White Fang* (Jack), and *Alive* (Nando Parrado).

Hawley, Philip M. Member of the Disney board of directors from 1975 to 1985.

Hawn, Goldie Actress; appeared in *The One and Only*, *Genuine*, *Original Family Band* (giggly girl), and *Deceived* (Adrienne), and on television in *The Dream Is Alive*.

Hawthorne, Nigel (1929–2001) Voiced Fflewddur Fflam in *The Black Cauldron* and Prof. Porter in *Tarzan*.

Hayakawa, Sessue (1889–1973) Actor; appeared in *Swiss Family Robinson* (pirate chief).

Haydn, Richard (1905–1985) Actor; appeared in *The Adventures of Bullwhip Griffin* (Quentin Bartlett) and provided the voice of the Caterpillar in *Alice in Wonderland*.

Hayes, Helen (1900–1993) Actress; starred in *Herbie Rides Again* (Mrs. Steinmetz), *One of Our Dinosaurs Is Missing* (Hettie), and *Candleshoe* (Lady St. Edmund). Appeared in a cameo as a tourist in *Third Man on the Mountain*, starring her son, James MacArthur.

Hays, Robert Actor; appeared in *Trenchcoat* (Terry Leonard), *Homeward Bound: The Incredible Journey* (Bob), and *Homeward Bound II: Lost in San Francisco* (Bob).

Hayward, Lillie (1891–1927) Screenwriter; wrote scripts for *Tonka*, *The Shaggy Dog*, and *Toby Tyler*, the latter two with Bill Walsh. Also worked on the *Mickey Mouse Club*.

He Got Game (film) The Governor, a big supporter of his alma mater, Big State, temporarily paroles Jake Shuttlesworth from prison after over six years behind bars and gives him a chance of a commuted sentence, if he can accomplish one task. Jake's estranged son, Jesus, is the #1 basketball player in America, and the Governor wants him to turn down the large number of offers he has received and play for Big State. With a deadline for Jesus only a week away, his father unexpectedly returns home and must somehow reconcile with his son and induce him to accept Big State's offer. During the often explosive ensuing days, father and son reach a surprising turning point in their lives as they grow to understand and find respect for each other. Directed by Spike Lee. A Touchstone Picture. Released on May 1, 1998. Stars Denzel Washington (Jake Shuttlesworth), Ray Allen (Jesus), Milla Jovovich (Dakota Burns), Hill Harper (Coleman "Booger" Sykes), Bill Nunn (Uncle Bubba), Jim Brown (Spivey). 136 min. Having never acted before, Milwaukee Bucks star player Ray Allen, chosen for the role of Jesus, took eight weeks of acting lessons before the start of production. Filmed on location primarily in and around Coney Island, New York. Released on video in 1998.

Headless Horseman Apparition that chases Ichabod Crane in *The Adventures of Ichabod and Mr. Toad.*

Headly, Glenne Actress; appeared in *Dick Tracy* (Tess Truehart), *Mr. Holland's Opus* (Iris Holland), *Breakfast of Champions* (Francine Petko), *Confessions of a Teenage Drama Queen* (Karen), and on television did the voice of Miss Sansome in *Recess*.

Heard, John Actor; appeared in *Beaches* (John Pierce), *Deceived* (Jack), and *Before and After* (Wendell Bye).

Health for the Americas Series of educational films made for the South American market at the request of the Coordinator of Inter-American Affairs from 1943 to 1946.

Heart and Lungs Play Ball, The (film) Educational film, in the Wonders of Life series, released on January 26, 1990. 11 min. The film shows how the heart and lungs work together delivering oxygen and blood to the body parts of a football player.

Heartbreak Hotel (film) Aspiring rock 'n' roller, Johnny Wolfe, loves his mother but realizes the only person who can bring her out of the doldrums is her idol, Elvis Presley. Johnny arranges to kidnap Elvis after a nearby concert, and accuses him of abandoning rock 'n' roll. The idealistic youth's questioning of the celebrity's values causes Elvis to remain in the small town for a few days, and not only help Johnny's mother, but reassess his own place in the music world and the type of person he has become in recent years. Released on September 30, 1988. Directed by Chris Columbus. A Touchstone film. 101 min. Stars David Keith (Elvis Presley), Tuesday Weld (Marie Wolfe), Charlie Schlatter (Johnny Wolfe). Filmed entirely on location in Austin and Taylor, Texas. When the call went out for 3,000 extras for a concert scene, the filmmakers were amazed that they all were able to come in 1970s outfits. Producer Lynda Obst remarked, "I could never have gotten these costumes in Los Angeles. What was most amazing is that people didn't rent these outfits, they simply went into their closets and pulled out what they still had on the shelf." Released on video in 1989.

Heath, D. C., and Co. Publisher of a series of popular school readers featuring the Disney characters, beginning in 1939. For collectors, the scarcest title is *Dumbo*, as a much smaller number of copies of that title was published.

Heavyweights (film) An overweight teen, Gerry, and his friends at Camp Hope are forced to spend their vacation with an out-of-control fitness freak and prepare for the end-of-summer Apache Games with their muscle-bound rivals from Camp MVP. Eventually the overweight campers oust their leader, implement sensible diet and training programs of their own, and use their smarts to outwit the Camp MVPers. Released on February 17, 1995. 98 min. Directed by Steven Brill. In association with Caravan Pictures. Stars Tom McGowan (Pat), Aaron Schwartz (Gerry), Shaun Weiss (Josh), Tom Hodges (Lars), Leah Lail (Julie), Paul Feig (Tim), Jeffrey Tambor (Maury Garner), Jerry Stiller (Harvey Bushkin),

Anne Meara (Alice Bushkin). Released on video in 1995.

Heche, Anne Actress; appeared in *The Adventures of Huck Finn* (Mary Jane Wilks) and *Six Days, Seven Nights* (Robin Monroe), and provided the voice of the waitress on *Higglytown Heroes*.

Hector the Stowaway Dog See *The Ballad of Hector the Stowaway Dog*.

H-E-Double Hockey Sticks (television) Two-hour television movie airing on *The Wonderful World of Disney* on October 3, 1999. An underachieving devil-in-training, Griffelkin, is sent to the surface to earn his horns by stealing the soul of Dave Heinrich, a hotshot hockey player with his eye on the Stanley Cup. Griffelkin eventually questions his mission's objective and angers Ms. B, head of the Beelzebub Vocational Institute where he has been studying. Directed by Randall Miller. Stars Will Friedle (Griffelkin), Matthew Lawrence (Dave Heinrich), Gabrielle Union (Gabby), Shawn Pyfrom (Louis), Tara Spencer-Nairn (Anne), Rhea Perlman (Ms. B). Based on the opera, *Griffelkin*, by Lucas Foss and Alastair Reid.

Hee, T. (1911–1988) Yes, this was a real person. People for years have chuckled over his name in the credits for many of the Disney cartoons. T(hornton) Hee worked at the Disney Studio on and off for three decades, beginning in 1938, as director, caricaturist, stylist, and storyman. He co-directed the *Dance of the Hours* segment of *Fantasia*, directed the Honest John and Gideon sequence in *Pinocchio*, worked on story on *Victory Through Air Power* and *Make Mine Music*, and created the titles for *The Reluctant Dragon* and *The Shaggy Dog*. He left Disney in 1946, but returned from 1958 through 1961, and in 1964 worked for WED Enterprises on the New York World's Fair projects. He also served as an animation instructor and was a renowned caricaturist.

Heffalump Character who appears in *Pooh's Heffalump Movie*; voiced by Kyle Stanger. His full name is Heffridge Trumpler Brompet Heffalump III, nicknamed Lumpy.

Heffalumps and Woozles Pooh's nightmare characters in *Winnie the Pooh and the Blustery Day* (1968). See also *Pooh's Heffalump Movie.*

Heidi (television) A Disney Channel Premiere Film; first aired on July 18, 1993. The story of a young orphan who struggles to win her stern grandfather's love, and who then must struggle to stay with him in their beloved mountains. Stars Jason Robards (grandfather), Noley Thornton (Heidi), Jane Seymour (Fraulein Rottenmeier), Patricia Neal (grandmother), Lexi Randall (Klara). Filmed on location near Salzberg and in the Austrian Alps. 193 min. Directed by Michael Rhodes.

Heigh-Ho Song from *Snow White and the Seven Dwarfs*, written by Larry Morey and Frank Churchill.

Hell's Bells (film) Silly Symphony cartoon; released on October 30, 1929. The first cartoon directed by Ub Iwerks. In this burlesque of the satanic underworld, Satan and his creatures cavort.

Hello Again (film) Lucy Chadman is a klutz. She has a hard time fitting in with her doctor-husband's social circle. One day she chokes to death on a Korean chicken ball. Her sister Zelda, who runs a shop devoted to mysticism and the occult, manages one year later to work a spell that brings Lucy back to life. Lucy finds her husband has married her former best friend, and she must make a new life for herself. An instant celebrity for "coming back from the dead," Lucy finds true love with the emergency room doctor who tried to save her life. Released on November 6, 1987. Directed by Frank Perry. A Touchstone film. 96 min. Stars Shelley Long (Lucy Chadman), Judith Ivey (Zelda), Gabriel Byrne (Kevin Scanlon), Corbin Bernsen (Jason Chadman), Sela Ward (Kim Lacey). Filmed at various New York locations, including the Mount Sinai Hospital. Released on video in 1988.

Hello Aloha (film) Goofy cartoon; released on February 29, 1952. Directed by Jack Kinney. Goofy, as Mr. Geef, decides to move to the islands and enjoy the carefree life there. As the guest of honor at a luau, he is suddenly thrown into a nearby volcano to appease the fire goddess, but he manages to save himself.

Help Wanted: Kids (television) Two-hour television movie; aired on February 2, 1986. Directed by David Greenwalt. A couple moves from New York City to Arizona for a new job only to discover the husband's boss wants his employees to all have children, so the couple decides to rent some. Two neighborhood youngsters fit the bill, but they see that they can succeed with a little blackmail. Meanwhile, the couple is busy trying to keep their deception secret from nosy neighbors. It turns out the kids are orphans, and soon the four start acting like a real family. Stars Cindy Williams, Bill Hudson, Chad Allen, Hillary Wolf, John Dehner, Joel Brooks. Led to a Disney Channel series, *Just Like Family.*

Hen Wen Oracular pig seized by the Horned King in *The Black Cauldron.*

Hench, John (1908–2004) Artist/designer; started in the Disney Story Department in 1939,  later painting backgrounds for the *Nutcracker Suite* segment of *Fantasia.* He worked on *Cinderella* and *Alice in Wonderland*, and aided Salvador Dali in the aborted *Destino* project. He worked on the special effects in *20,000 Leagues Under the Sea.* In 1955, he moved to WED Enterprises to work on the Tomorrowland area at Disneyland. In 1972 he was named Executive Vice President of WED. He is known for painting the company's official portraits of Mickey Mouse for his 25th, 50th, 60th, 70th, and 75th birthdays. In 1999, at the age of 90, he passed his 60th year with the company, longer than any other person. He was named a Disney Legend in 1990.

Henn, Mark Animator; joined Disney in 1980 and animated Mickey Mouse in *Mickey's Christmas Carol* and worked on Oliver and the Artful Dodger in *Oliver & Company*. In 1989 he moved to Florida to help establish the feature animation studio there. He animated Ariel in *The Little Mermaid*, Belle in *Beauty and the Beast*, and young Simba in *The Lion King*. He was also a supervising animator on *The Rescuers Down Under*, *Aladdin*, *Mulan*, and *Home on the Range*, and an animator on *Pocahontas* and *The Emperor's New Groove*.

Henry O. Tanner: Pioneer Black American Artist (film) Educational film produced by Anthony Corso; released in September 1973. This is the story of the first African American artist to earn worldwide acclaim.

Herbie Day at Disneyland (television) Syndicated television special; aired on July 11, 1974. A contest for decorated Volkswagens at Disneyland is a promotion for the opening of *Herbie Rides Again*. Stars Bob McAllister, Bob Crane, Helen Hayes. An earlier Herbie Day had been held at Disneyland on March 23, 1969 to promote the original *The Love Bug*.

Herbie: Fully Loaded (film) The famous VW enters the world of NASCAR racing with his new owner, Maggie Peyton, a third-generation member of a legendary NASCAR family. Racing is in Maggie's blood, but she has been forbidden from pursuing her dreams by her overprotective father, Ray. Ray offers to buy Maggie a car for her college graduation, but takes her to a junkyard where a 1960s era Volkswagen beetle catches her eye. She leaves in the rusty, banged-up car, soon discovering it is no ordinary auto, but a charmed car that will literally help change the course of her life. With a little help, Herbie becomes stronger and faster than ever, and he and Maggie get the chance to realize their dreams on the NASCAR track. Released on June 22, 2005. Directed by Angela Robinson. Stars Lindsay Lohan (Maggie Peyton), Michael Keaton (Ray Peyton, Sr.), Matt Dillon (Trip Murphy), Justin Long (Kevin), Breckin Meyer (Ray Peyton, Jr.), Cheryl Hines (Sally), Jimmi Simpson (Crash), Jill Ritchie (Charisma). 101 min. Herbie's NASCAR appearance took place at the NASCAR Nextel Cup Series's Pop Secret 500, held on September 4, 2004, at the California Speedway, in Fontana. Released on DVD in 2005.

Herbie Goes Bananas (film) While Pete Stanchek and his friend, Davie Johns, are transporting a VW (Herbie) via ocean liner from Puerto Vallarta to Brazil for an auto race, their lives are complicated by a stowaway in Herbie's trunk—a loveable Mexican orphan, Paco, who's made the mistake of stealing a map of golden Incan ruins from a criminal now hot in pursuit. The ensuing chase (which grows to include the ship's captain and an unsuspecting man-hungry passenger and her niece) stretches across South America—from Panama to Peru to Brazil. Eventually, the gold is saved. Herbie emerges a hero and Paco is preparing to be Herbie's driver in the Grande Premio do Brasil auto race. Released on June 25, 1980. Directed by Vincent McEveety. 92 min. Stars Cloris Leachman (Aunt Louise), Charlie Martin Smith (D.J.), John Vernon (Prindle), Stephen W. Burns (Pete), Elyssa Davalos (Melissa), Joaquin Garay III (Paco), Harvey Korman (Capt. Blythe), Richard Jaeckel (Shepard), Alex Rocco (Quinn). The songs "Look At Me," and "I Found A Friend" were written by Frank De Vol. Much of the action of the movie was shot on location in the Mexican cities of Puerto Vallarta, Guadalajara, and Tijuana, as well as in the Panama Canal Zone. The enormous amount of special effects in the film required meticulous storyboards, the mechanical techniques department headed by Danny Lee, 26 VW bugs, and 3 Cessna Centurian airplanes. The film was reissued in 1981, and released on video in 1984.

Herbie Goes to Monte Carlo (film) Driver Jim Douglas, mechanic Wheely Applegate, and Herbie, the magical little VW, enter a spectacular road race from Paris to Monte Carlo. One of the competing cars is a beautiful powder blue Lancia named Giselle. For Herbie it is love at first sight. Jim falls for the Lancia's pretty driver, Diane.

Meanwhile, a fabulous diamond is stolen from a museum by two thieves and hidden in Herbie's gas tank. Throughout the race the thieves try to recover the gem. With Herbie's help, the thieves are caught, Herbie wins the race, and he and Jim both get their girls. Released on June 24, 1977. Directed by Vincent McEveety. 113 min. Stars Dean Jones (Jim Douglas), Don Knotts (Wheely Applegate), Julie Sommars (Diane), Jacques Marin (Inspector Bouchet), Roy Kinnear (Quincey), Bernard Fox (Max), Eric Braeden (Bruno). The film was shot on location in France en route to Monte Carlo and in Paris at the Esplanade du Trocadero, Eiffel Tower, Place de la Concorde, Place Vendôme, Place d'Iéna, Arc de Triomphe, and down the Champs-Elysées at 80 miles an hour. Released on video in 1984.

Herbie Rides Again (film) In San Francisco, the dreams of Alonzo Hawk to build a skyscraper in his name are thwarted by Grandma Steinmetz who sits stubbornly in her firehouse home on the property he needs. Hawk sends his nephew, Willoughby, to charm Mrs. Steinmetz who, along with a beautiful airline hostess boarder and the magical Volkswagen Herbie, convinces him he should stay out of the whole mess. After many chases and confrontations, Herbie emerges victorious and both Mrs. Steinmetz and Willoughby find romance. Released first in England on February 15, 1974; U.S. release on June 6, 1974. 88 min. Stars Helen Hayes (Mrs. Steinmetz), Ken Berry (Willoughby), Stefanie Powers (Nicole), John McIntire (Mr. Judson), Keenan Wynn (Alonzo Hawk), Huntz Hall (Judge), Raymond Bailey (Lawyer), Liam Dunn (Doctor). This was the first sequel to the Disney favorite, *The Love Bug*. It was filmed on location in San Francisco, in an obsolete cablecar, at the Garden Court of the Sheraton Palace Hotel, and on the Golden Gate Bridge. While the cast was quite different from the first film, the car, Herbie, remained. The car

was a 1963 Sunroof model 1200 Volkswagen. Bill Walsh, the producer and writer, explained that he got the number 53 from television. In a Disney press release he noted: "I was seeing lots of 53's on television while I was developing Herbie as a character. It was [Los Angeles Dodgers] pitcher Don Drysdale's number among other things." Released on video in 1982 and 1993.

Herbie, the Love Bug (television) Limited television series of five episodes, airing from March 17 to April 14, 1982 on CBS. Directed by Charles S. Dubin, Bill Bixby, Vincent McEveety. Jim Douglas is now running a driving school. Stars Dean Jones, Patricia Hardy, Richard Paul, Claudia Wells, Nicky Katt, Douglas Emerson, Larry Linville.

Hercules (film) Hercules, the mighty son of Zeus and Hera, is taken from his Mount Olympus home and raised on Earth. The fiery figure behind Hercules's disappearance is Hades, the hot-headed god of the Underworld who has grown tired of looking after a "bunch of deadbeats" and sees Zeus's son as an obstacle to his plans to take over Olympus. Hades sends his two dim-witted sidekicks, Pain and Panic, to abduct Hercules, though

they bungle their mission by not administering the final drop of a potent potion, which leaves the infant with godlike strength but human mortality. As Hercules grows up, he discovers the truth about his origins and sets out to prove himself a true hero (with the help of a veteran hero-training satyr named Philoctetes) so he can return to Olympus. Hades has other plans and tries to kill him by arranging a catalogue of calamities (a multiheaded Hydra, a Minotaur, a Cyclops, an army of Titans and the traitorous damsel-in-distress, Megara).

Along the way, Hercules discovers that a true hero is not measured by the size of his strength but the strength of his heart. Directed by John Musker and Ron Clements. General release on June 27, 1997, after a June 14 premiere at the New Amsterdam Theater in New York City, and a limited release beginning there the next day. Stars the voices of Danny DeVito (Phil), Tate Donovan (adult Hercules), Susan Egan (Megara), James Woods (Hades), Charlton Heston (opening narrator), Matt Frewer (Panic), Bobcat Goldthwait (Pain), Paul Shaffer (Hermes), Rip Torn (Zeus), Samantha Eggar (Hera), Joshua Keaton (teen Hercules speaking), Roger Bart (teen Hercules singing), Hal Holbrook (Amphitryon), Barbara Barrie (Alcmene). 93 min. Music, with six songs in a pastiche of styles, including gospel, is by Alan Menken with lyrics by David Zippel. Musker and Clements were attracted by the mythological aspects of the Hercules story, and decided to produce the film, along with Alice Dewey, in the fall of 1993. Over the next nine months, the two collaborated on an outline, several treatments, and eventually an initial script, aided by art director Andy Gaskill, who oversaw the visual development on the film. British artist/ political cartoonist Gerald Scarfe, with a bold, expressive linear style, was brought in to assist with character design, and he remained involved as an ongoing artistic adviser to the animators. A field trip to Greece and Turkey in the summer of 1994 gave artists a firsthand look at landscapes and ancient sites, and an opportunity to hear expert accounts of classic Greek mythology. Animation began in early 1995, and eventually a team of nearly 700 artists were involved with the project. The film features the first use in animation of the process of morphing, wherein an object is made to smoothly transform into another, utilizing computer technology. Released on video in 1998.

Hercules (television) Half-hour television series; debuting in syndication on August 31, 1998, which expands upon the Greek demigod's feats during his formative, adolescent hero-in-training years. Many of the actors reprise their voices from the feature, including Tate Donovan (Hercules) and James Woods (Hades), but added are new friends of Hercules—French Stewart (Icarus) and Sandra Bernhard (Cassandra)—and numerous guest stars. 65 episodes.

Hercules: Zero to Hero (film) Three classic stories from the television series; released on video as a feature on August 17, 1999. A more vulnerable and mortal Hercules toils to get through his school years without his mythological powers. Directed by Bob Kline. 70 min.

Hercules "Zero to Hero" Victory Parade Began at Disney-MGM Studios on June 27, 1997, saluting "the greatest hero of all time," and featuring parade commentators Ridges Philbinylus and Appollonia Airheadenese. A Hercules Victory Parade also began at Disneyland on the same day.

Here Come the Muppets Show at Disney-MGM Studios from May 25, 1990, to September 2, 1991. Replaced by Voyage of the Little Mermaid.

Heritage House Shop in Liberty Square in Magic Kingdom Park at Walt Disney World; opened in 1971. Sells memorabilia themed to American history.

Heritage Manor Gifts Shop in The American Adventure in World Showcase at Epcot; opened in 1985, selling nostalgic American gifts.

Herman's Head (television) Television series on Fox; beginning September 8, 1991, and ending June 16, 1994. Herman is a young writer who has a group of emotions—Angel, Wimp, Genius, and Animal—who battle in his brain to gain control of him. Stars William Ragsdale (Herman Brooks), Hank Azaria (Jay Nichols), Jane Sibbett (Heddy Newman), Yeardley Smith (Louise Fitzer), Molly Hagan (Angel), Rick Lawless (Wimp), Ken Hudson Campbell (Animal), Peter MacKenzie (Genius).

Hero in the Family (television) Two-hour television show; aired on September 28, 1986. Directed by Eric Fraser. A boy's astronaut father accidentally has his brain switched with that of a chimp, but when he goes home, the boy cannot find anyone to believe the story. If they cannot get the transfer reversed in a short time, it will become permanent. After some exciting escapades, the father is returned to normal, and he has a new respect for his son. Stars Christopher Collet, Cliff De Young, Annabeth Gish, Darleen Carr, Keith Dorman, M. Emmet Walsh.

Herring, Roqué Actress; appeared on the *Mickey Mouse Club* on The Disney Channel from 1989 to 1990.

Herrmann, Edward Actor; appeared in *The North Avenue Irregulars* (Michael Hill), *Big Business* (Graham Sherbourne), *Born Yesterday* (Ed Devery), *My Boyfriend's Back* (Mr. Dingle), *Double Take* (Charles Allsworth), and on television in *MDs* (Jeremiah Orbach).

Hershey, Barbara Actress; appeared in *Tin Men* (Nora Tilley), *Beaches* (Hillary Whitney Essex), *Swing Kids* (Frau Muller), and *Breakfast of Champions* (Celia Hoover).

Hervey, Jason Actor; appeared on television in *Little Spies*, *Wildside*, and *The Last Electric Knight*.

Heston, Charlton Actor; appeared in *Tombstone* (Henry Hooker), and on The Disney Channel in *The Little Kidnappers*, and provided the opening narration for *Hercules*. He also narrated *Armageddon*.

Hewitt, Alan (1915–1986) Actor; appeared in *The Absent Minded Professor* (Gen. Hotchkiss), *Son of Flubber* (prosecutor), *The Misadventures of Merlin Jones* and *The Monkey's Uncle* (Prof. Shattuck), *The Horse in the Gray Flannel Suit* (Harry Tomes), *The Computer Wore Tennis Shoes* and *Now You See Him, Now You Don't* (Dean Collingsgood), and *The Barefoot Executive* (Farnsworth).

Heymann, Tom Joined Disney in 1991 and was named president of The Disney Store in 1996. He left the company in 1999.

Hibler, Winston (1911–1976) Longtime Disney producer, associated with the nature films as a writer, and who was perhaps best known as the narrator of the True-Life Adventures. He joined Disney in 1942, scripting and directing armed-service training films during World War II. He went on to be a storyman and dialogue director on several animated features, including *Alice in Wonderland*, *Cinderella*, and *Peter Pan*. Affectionately known as Hib around the Disney lot, he

produced such films as *Perri*, *The Bears and I*, *Island at the Top of the World*, and *One Little Indian*. Hib received the Disney Legends Award posthumously in 1992.

Hickman, Darryl Actor; appeared on television in *Johnny Shiloh* and *Texas John Slaughter*.

Hickman, Dwayne Actor; appeared on television in *My Dog, the Thief*.

Hidalgo (film) The film is based on the true story of the greatest long-distance horse race ever run. Held yearly for centuries, the Ocean of Fire, a 3,000-mile survival race across the Arabian Desert, was a challenge restricted to the finest Arabian horses ever bred, the purest and noblest lines, owned by the greatest royal families. In 1890, a wealthy sheik invited an American and his horse to enter the race for the first time. Frank T. Hopkins was a cowboy and dispatch rider for the U.S. Cavalry who had once been billed as the greatest rider the West had ever known. The sheik would put this claim to the test, pitting the American cowboy and his mustang, Hidalgo, against the world's greatest Arabian horses and Bedouin riders, some of whom were determined to prevent the foreigner from finishing the race. For Frank, the Ocean of Fire becomes not only a matter of pride and honor, but a race for his very survival. Released on March 5, 2004. A Touchstone picture. Directed by Joe Johnston. Stars Viggo Mortensen (Frank T. Hopkins), Omar Sharif (Sheik Riyadh), Zuleikha Robinson (Jazira), Peter Mensah (Jaffa), Louise Lombard (Lady Anne Davenport), Said Taghmaoui (Prince Bin Al Reeh), J.K. Simmons (Buffalo Bill Cody), Adam Alexi-Malle (Aziz). 136 min. Filmed in CinemaScope. An unbilled Malcolm McDowell appears briefly as Lord Davenport. Filming took place in Morocco, Montana, South Dakota, and California. Released on video in 2004.

Hidden Mickeys Starting out as inside jokes by the Disney Imagineers in the 1980s, the subtly visible silhouette of Mickey Mouse began appearing in a few attractions in the Disney parks. Soon, park guests were having a great time trying to discover these "hidden" Mickeys, to such an extent that they were finding the common three-circle form in areas where it was simply a design fluke and never meant to be a Mickey shape.

Higglytown Heroes (television) Four adventurous kids encounter the diverse residents of colorful Higglytown, who resemble traditional Russian nesting dolls, and learn that there are everyday heroes in the world around them. Among them are a grocer, a librarian, a truck driver, a mail carrier, and a crossing guard. Animated series for preschoolers on Disney Channel; premiering on September 12, 2004. Voices include Rory Thost (Kip), Frankie Ryan Manriquez (Wayne), Taylor Masamitsu (Eubie), Edie McClurg (Fran), Liliana Mumy (Twinkle), Dee Bradley Baker (Pizza Guy). The heroes are voiced by special celebrity guest stars such as Sean Astin, Lance Bass, Tim Curry, Anne Heche, Cyndi Lauper, Susan Lucci, Katey Sagal, Sharon Stone, and Betty White.

High Fidelity (film) Rob Gordon is the owner of a semi-failing record store in Chicago where he sells old-fashioned vinyl records. He is a self-professed music junkie who spends his days at Championship Vinyl with his two employees, Dick

and Barry. Although they have an encyclopedic knowledge of pop music and are consumed with the music scene, it is of no help to Rob when his longtime girlfriend, Laura, walks out on him. Rob struggles through a sometimes comic, sometimes painful self-examination. Directed by Stephen Frears. Released on March 31, 2000. Stars John Cusack (Rob Gordon), Jack Black (Barry), Lisa Bonet (Marie DeSalle), Joelle Carter (Penny), Joan Cusack (Liz), Sara Gilbert (Anna), Iben Hjejle (Laura), Todd Louiso (Dick), Catherine Zeta-Jones (Charlie). 114 min. Based on the novel by Nick Hornby, with the setting changed from London to Chicago. Released on video in 2000.

High Flying Spy, The (television) Three-part television show; aired on October 22, 29, and November 5, 1972. Directed by Vincent McEveety. During the Civil War, Prof. Thaddeus Lowe uses a balloon to spy for the Union forces, and hires a young telegrapher to join him and send messages to the ground. His work impresses President Lincoln who founds the Aeronautic Corps, the country's first air force. Eventually, they are captured by the Confederates and try to get away by stealing hydrogen from a Southern gas factory to fill their balloon. Stars Stuart Whitman, Vincent Van Patten, Darren McGavin, Andrew Prine, Shug Fisher, Jim Davis, Jeff Corey, Robert Pine. The working title was *High Flying Lowe*.

High Heels and Low Lifes (film) London nurse, Shannon, and her best friend, American actress Frances, overhear a mobile phone conversation between gang members involved in a bank robbery, but are unable to convince the police. So, they decide, as a dare, to try to extort a little money from the gang in return for not revealing their identities. Of course, the criminals would rather kill than give up their money, so the stakes are raised as the women get further drawn into their scheme. A Touchstone Picture. Released on October 26, 2001. 86 min. Directed by Mel Smith. Stars Minnie Driver (Shannon), Mary McCormack (Frances), Kevin McNally (Mason), Mark Williams (Tremaine), Danny Dyer (Danny), Michael Gambon (Kerrigan). Released on video in 2002.

High School Musical (television) A Disney Channel Original Movie; premiered on January 20, 2006. In this contemporary musical comedy, Troy Bolton, a popular basketball star, and Gabriella Montez, a shy, academically-gifted newcomer, discover that they share a secret passion for singing. When they sign up for the lead roles in the school musical, it threatens East High's rigid social order and sends their peers into an uproar. Soon the jocks, the brainiacs, and even the drama club regulars, are hatching convoluted plots to separate the pair and keep them offstage. By defying expectations and taking a chance on their dreams, the couple inspires other students to go public with some surprising hidden talents of their own. Directed by Kenny Ortega. Stars Zac Efron (Troy Bolton), Vanessa Anne Hudgens (Gabriella Montez), Ashley Tisdale (Sharpay Evans), Lucas Gabeel (Ryan Evans), Corbin Bleu (Chad), Monique Coleman (Taylor), Chris Warren, Jr. (Zeke). Filming took place in Salt Lake City, Utah.

Highway to Trouble (television) Television show; aired on March 13, 1959. Directed by Jack Hannah. Donald tries to awaken his nephews' interest in geography through the use of several cartoons and finally taking them to Disneyland.

Higitus Figitus Song from *The Sword in the Stone*, written by Richard M. Sherman and Robert B. Sherman.

Hill, Arthur Actor, appeared on television in *Atta Girl, Kelly*, and years later on The Disney Channel in *Love Leads the Way*. Coincidentally, both films were about guide dogs for the blind.

Hill, Dana (1964–1996) Actress; she voiced Max on *Goof Troop*, Tank Muddlefoot on *Darkwing Duck*, and had an uncredited voice part in *The Hunchback of Notre Dame*. She also played Foxy Cooper in the TV movie *The Kids Who Knew Too Much*.

Hiller and Diller (television) Series which debuted on ABC on September 23, 1997, and ended March 13, 1998. Ted Hiller and Neil Diller are comedy writers who have been best friends and partners for years. In fact, Ted feels he owes his career (and his comfortable lifestyle) to Neil, so he is always there for his partner, no questions asked—a situation his family has learned to accept. Unlike his happily married friend, Neil has neurotic tendencies that drove his wife away, but not before she asked him to care for their two children, a proposition he finds frightening. Stars Kevin Nealon (Ted Hiller), Richard Lewis (Neil Diller), Jordan Baker (Jeanne Hiller), Allison Mack (Brooke Diller).

Hills Brothers Coffee House On Town Square at Disneyland from 1958 to winter 1976. The restaurant was originally Maxwell House Coffee House, and later became the American Egg House and Town Square Cafe.

Hilton Hotel in Lake Buena Vista at Walt Disney World, opened November 18, 1983.

Hilton Head Island Resort, South Carolina See Vacation Club Resort, Hilton Head Island.

Hingle, Pat Actor; appeared in *One Little Indian* (Captain Stewart), *Running Brave*, and *A Thousand Acres* (Harold Clark) and on television in *Casebusters* and *The Court* (Chief Justice Amos Townsend).

Hinton, Darby Actor; appeared in *Son of Flubber* (Second hobgoblin), and on television in *Boomerang, Dog of Many Talents*.

Hiram Flaversham Toy maker kidnapped by Ratigan in *The Great Mouse Detective*; voiced by Alan Young.

Hirohito, Emperor of Japan He visited Disneyland in October 1975, and was presented with a Mickey Mouse watch, which he proudly wore.

Hirsch, Lou He provided the adult voice of Baby Herman in *Who Framed Roger Rabbit*.

His Lordship Shop in United Kingdom in World Showcase at Epcot; opened October 1, 1982. Became Lords & Ladies. Adjoins The Toy

Soldier, selling English cottage replicas and similar items.

His Majesty King of the Beasts (television) Television show; aired on November 7, 1958. Directed by Jim Algar. Edited version of the True-Life Adventure, *The African Lion.* Narrated by Winston Hibler.

Historia de José, A (film) Portuguese Reading Film no. 1. Produced under the auspices of the Coordinator of Inter-American Affairs. Delivered to them on March 14, 1945.

History Alive! (film) Series of five educational films that teach American history through specific historical events, produced by Turnley Walker and released in 1972: *Democracy—Equality or Privilege, The Right of Dissent, States' Rights, The Right of Petition, Impeachment of a President.*

History Channel, The With the purchase of Capital Cities/ABC in 1996, Disney obtained a 37.5 percent ownership of The History Channel, which specializes in historical documentaries.

History of Aviation (film) Humorous history of aviation from the Wright Brothers to World War II, originally part of *Victory Through Air Power*; released as a 16mm educational film in December 1952.

Hitchhiker's Guide to the Galaxy (film) The Earthman Arthur Dent is having a very bad day. His house is about to be bulldozed, he discovers that his best friend is an alien, and to top things off, Planet Earth is about to be demolished to make way for a hyperspace freeway. Arthur's only chance for survival is to hitch a ride on a passing spacecraft with the help of his best friend Ford Prefect. Arthur sets out on a journey in which he finds that nothing is as it seems—for example, a towel is the most important thing in the universe. He finds the meaning of life, and discovers that everything anyone ever wanted to know can be found in one fantastically entertaining electronic book, The Hitchhiker's Guide to the Universe. A Touchstone Pictures/Spyglass

Entertainment film. Released on April 29, 2005 after an April 20 premiere in London. Directed by Garth Jennings. Stars Mos Def (Ford Prefect), Zooey Deschanel (Trillian), Martin Freeman (Arthur Dent), Sam Rockwell (Zaphod Beeblebrox), Bill Nighy (Slartibartfast), Warwick Davis (Marvin), Anna Chancellor (Questular), John Malkovich (Humma Kavula). The film is narrated by Stephen Fry, and includes the voices of Alan Rickman (Marvin) and Helen Mirren (Deep Thought). 109 min. Based on the novel by Douglas Adams, which was created after a 1978 BBC Radio 4 play. Over the years, the book and five more in the series have become more than mere best sellers; they were a cultural phenomenon in their own right with fans the world over discussing and debating them. Adams passed away shortly after finishing the second draft of the screenplay. Filmed in Super 35-Scope at Elstree Studios in England. Released on DVD in 2005.

Hoberman, David He came to Disney from ICM in 1985, working up to President of Touchstone and Walt Disney Pictures in 1988 and President of Motion Pictures for Walt Disney Studios in 1994. He resigned in early 1995 to become an independent producer.

Hockey Champ (film) Donald Duck cartoon; released on April 28, 1939. Directed by Jack King. Donald attempts to show off his professional hockey ability to his nephews, but their skill finally gets the best of him.

Hockey Homicide (film) Goofy cartoon; released on September 21, 1945. Directed by Jack Kinney. Goofy plays all the parts in a hockey game until the crowd, in their excitement, comes

out on the ice and the players can relax in the bleachers.

Hocus Pocus (film) Accidentally brought back to life in Salem on Halloween night, three witches, known as the Sanderson sisters, attempt to steal the life essence from the town's children so they can have eternal life. They are outwitted by a boy, Max Dennison, his young sister, Dani, and his girlfriend, Allison, and aided by a boy, Thackery Binx, who had been changed into a cat for trying to interfere with the witches centuries earlier. Released on July 16, 1993. Directed by Kenny Ortega. 96 min. Stars Bette Midler (Winifred), Sarah Jessica Parker (Sarah), Kathy Najimy (Mary), Omri Katz (Max), Thora Birch (Dani), Vinessa Shaw (Allison). The use of computer graphics technology enabled the cat to talk. The flying scenes were accomplished using wires on a soundstage at the Disney Studio. Besides the studio work, there was one week of location filming in Salem, Massachusetts. Released on video in 1994.

Hodges, Eddie Actor; appeared in *Summer Magic* (Gilly Carey) and *The Happiest Millionaire* (Livingston Drexel Biddle), though his role in the latter was edited out of shortened versions of the film.

Hoff, Christian Actor; appeared in *Encino Man* (Boog), and was the first actor ever to appear in a Disney film as Walt Disney (as a child)—the television movie, *Walt Disney: One Man's Dream*.

Hoffman, Dustin Actor; appeared in *Dick Tracy* (Mumbles), *Billy Bathgate* (Dutch Schultz), and *Moonlight Mile* (Ben Floss).

Hoffman, Gaby Actress; she starred in the television series, *Someone Like Me*, and in the television remake of *Freaky Friday* (Annabelle Andrews).

Hog Wild (television) Two-part television show; aired on Janury 20 and 27, 1974. Directed by Jerome Courtland. A man moves his family in the 1880s to Idaho and starts a pig ranch; an accident causes him to rely on his son to take the pigs to market. It is a race against a neighboring pig rancher since the first one to arrive gets the best prices. While the boy loses the race, he wins a wager large enough to pay for an operation for his father. Stars John Ericson, Diana Muldaur, Clay O'Brien, Nicholas Beauvy, Kim Richards, Shug Fisher, Walter Barnes, Denver Pyle.

Hold that Pose (film) Goofy cartoon; released on November 3, 1950. Directed by Jack Kinney. Goofy buys photographic equipment for his new hobby and eagerly goes out to find a subject which turns out to be a bear. But he so angers the bear with the flash apparatus that it chases him back to his apartment.

Hold Your Horsepower (film) Educational film showing the development of farm machinery, illustrating farmers' ability to produce more crops and lighten their labor, and how to care for the machinery, made for the Texas Company. Delivered to them on August 8, 1945.

Holdridge, Cheryl Mouseketeer from the 1950s television show.

Holes (film) Stanley Yelnats, is a young man coming of age, dogged by bad luck stemming from an ancient family curse. Perpetually in the wrong place at the wrong time, Stanley is unfairly sentenced to months of detention at Camp Green Lake for a crime he did not commit. There, he and his camp mates are forced by the menacing warden and her right-hand men to dig holes in order to build character. Nobody knows the real reason they are digging all these holes, but Stanley soon begins to question why the warden is so interested in anything "special" the boys find. Stanley and his camp mates must stick together and keep one step ahead of the warden and her henchmen as they plot a daring escape from the camp to solve the mystery and break the Yelnats family curse. From Walt Disney Pictures in association with Walden Media. Released on April 18, 2003.

Directed by Andrew Davis. Stars Shia LaBeouf (Stanley), Sigourney Weaver (Warden), John Voight (Mr. Sir), Tim Blake Nelson (Dr. Pendanski), Henry Winkler (Stanley's father), Eartha Kitt (Madame Zeroni), Dulé Hill (Sam), Patricia Arquette (Kissin' Kate Barlow). 117 min. Based on the award-winning book by Louis Sachar. Location filming was primarily on the Cuddeback Dry Lake and in Red Rock Canyon in the desert west of Death Valley. Released on video in 2003.

Holiday for Henpecked Husbands (television) Television show; aired on November 26, 1961. Directed by Wolfgang Reitherman. A series of Goofy cartoons cover the theme. Reruns aired as *Goofy Takes a Holiday*.

Holiday Inn Hotel at Downtown Disney at Walt Disney World, taking the place of Courtyard by Marriott on December 30, 2003.

Holiday Time at Disneyland (television) Television show; aired on December 23, 1962. Directed by Hamilton S. Luske. Festivities at Christmas time at Disneyland with Walt Disney showing viewers around the park (including the since-removed Flying Saucers attraction in Tomorrowland). Past parades for Easter and special events are highlighted before the Candlelight Procession and the Christmas parade make their way down Main Street.

Holidayland Picnic area outside the Disneyland berm that opened on June 16, 1957, and operated until 1961. Holidayland utilized the circus tent that Walt had purchased for his short-lived Mickey Mouse Club Circus. It was used for corporate picnics and other events; the guests could then enter Disneyland through a special gate.

Holliman, Earl Actor; appeared in *The Biscuit Eater* (Harve McNeil), and on television in *The Boy and the Bronc Buster* and *Smoke*.

Holloway, Sterling (1905–1992) Popular Disney voice actor; first used in *Dumbo* as the stork. He also narrated *Peter and the Wolf*, *The Pelican and the Snipe*, *The Little House*, *Goliath II*, and

The Cold-Blooded Penguin, and voiced the adult Flower (*Bambi*), the Cheshire Cat (*Alice in Wonderland*), Amos (*Ben and Me*), Kaa (*The Jungle Book*), Roquefort (*The Aristocats*), and Winnie the Pooh. Probably no other actor in Hollywood was as well known by his distinctive voice alone. He was named a Disney Legend in 1991.

Hollywood & Vine Restaurant at Disney-MGM Studios; opened on May 1, 1989. Also known as Cafeteria of the Stars.

Hollywood Boulevard Shopping street at Disney-MGM Studios. Most of the buildings are copied from originals in Hollywood, California. Special actors, known as Streetmosphere, portray cops, cabbies, movie starlets, talent agents, and excited autograph seekers. The shops sell movie memorabilia, both old and new, along with Disney

souvenirs and clothing. The shops have included Movieland Memorabilia, Crossroads of the World, Sights and Sounds, Oscar's Classic Car Souvenirs and Super Service Station, Mickey's of Hollywood, Sid Cahuenga's One-of-a-Kind, Pluto's Toy Palace, Disney & Co., Lakeside News, Cover Story, Celebrity 5 & 10, The Darkroom, Sweet Success, and L.A. Cinema Storage.

Hollywood Brown Derby, The The most elegant restaurant at Disney-MGM Studios;

opened on May 1, 1989. Replica of one of the most famous early restaurants of Hollywood, where the Cobb Salad and a delicious grapefruit cake were invented. Both are served here, along with many other tasty meals, in a teak and mahogany setting. The waiters and waitresses are all dressed in tuxedos, a sharp contrast to the attire of the normal theme park guest. On the wall are copies of the famous caricatures of Hollywood personalities that graced the wall of the original Brown Derby.

Hollywood Film Enterprises From 1932 to 1950, Hollywood Film Enterprises was licensed to sell shortened versions of Disney cartoons in 16mm and 8mm home movie versions. Most were silent and, since each cartoon was cut into several parts, the segments were given new titles. Some of the films were also in Carmel Hollywood Films and Castle Films boxes. These films turn up quite frequently today, though have little collector value.

Hollywood Hotel, Disney's Hotel at the Hong Kong Disneyland Resort, with 600 rooms; opened on September 12, 2005. There is a buffet restaurant, Chef Mickey's, and a fast-food location, Hollywood and Dine. In addition there are lounges and gift shops.

Hollywood Party, The (film) Black-and-white MGM movie from 1934 that includes a segment with Mickey Mouse and Jimmy Durante leading into a color Silly Symphony-type sequence entitled *The Hot Choc-late Soldiers*.

Hollywood Pictures Division of The Walt Disney Company that produces fare which is of more adult interest than the usual Disney film. It began operations on February 1, 1989; its first release was *Arachnophobia* (1990). The division was originally headed by Ricardo Mestres, succeeded by Michael Lynton. For a listing of films made by Hollywood Pictures, see Features. In 1996, Hollywood Pictures' role as a producing entity ended, but its label was still used for the distribution of films. David Vogel became president in 1997.

Hollywood Records Disney label; began operation on January 1, 1990. Hollywood Records develops and produces recorded mainstream music from the entire spectrum of popular styles. Their first release was the sound track from *Arachnophobia*. Recording artists have included The Party, Queen, and others.

Hollywood's Pretty Woman Stage show at Disney-MGM Studios from September 24 to November 3, 1991.

Holm, Celeste Actress; appeared in *Three Men and a Baby* (Jack's mother), and on television in *The Bluegrass Special*; *Polly*; *Polly—Comin' Home*; and *Kilroy*.

Holmes, Taylor (1872–1959) Provided the voice of King Stefan in *Sleeping Beauty*.

Holster Full of Law, A (film) Foreign theatrical compilation of *Texas John Slaughter* television episodes: *A Holster Full of Law*, *Frank Clell's in Town*, and *Trip to Tucson*. First released in Italy in July 1966. 90 min. Stars Tom Tryon. Also the title of episode 14 of *Texas John Slaughter*.

Holt, Harry (1911–2004) Animator; he joined Disney in 1936 and remained until 1956. A few years later he returned as a sculptor and art director for WED Enterprises. He retired in 1982, but beginning in mid-1987 he staffed an animator's desk, doing drawings for park guests, for several years in the Walt Disney Story exit lobby in Magic Kingdom Park at Walt Disney World.

Holy Man (film) When Ricky Hayman, a top executive at the Good Buy Shopping Network, finds his job on the line, he desperately searches for an innovative idea to boost his network's sales. A chance encounter with "G," an itinerant street guru, gives him an idea—give the charismic holy man his own television show and make shopping via the tube a truly religious experience. A Touchstone Picture in association with Caravan Pictures. Released on October 9, 1998. Directed by Stephen Herek. Stars Jeff Goldblum (Ricky Hayman), Eddie Murphy (G), Robert Loggia (McBainbridge), Kelly Preston (Kate Newell), Jon Cryer (Barry). 114 min. CinemaScope. Filming took place in Miami, Florida. Released on video in 1999.

Holy Matrimony (film) When sassy and street-wise Havana loses her criminal husband and is forced to hide out with his relatives, a whole-some, strict colony of religious disciples known as Hutterites, she finds that their archaic command-ments on chastity and hard work clash with her modern morality. The Hutterites have never met anyone remotely like the sexy Havana, and she has never spent time with people who are so uncorrupted by the influences of society. While she goes along with their rules and regulations, in order to buy time to find stolen money hidden on their property, she is aghast to discover that—because of a part of their religious law—to remain in the colony she must marry the 12-year-old brother of her former husband. Tem-porarily stuck with each other, the two square off for a comic battle of wills. Released in a limited number of cities on April 8, 1994. Directed by Leonard Nimoy. A Hollywood Pictures film. 93 min. Stars Patricia Arquette (Havana), Joseph Gordon-Levitt (Zeke), Tate Donovan (Peter), Armin Mueller-Stahl (Uncle Wilhelm), John Schuck (Markowski). Filmed in Great Falls, Montana. Released on video in 1994.

Holz, Karl He joined Walt Disney World in 1996 as vice president of Downtown Disney, moving to vice president of Epcot in 2000. In 2001 he was named senior vice president of Walt Disney World Operations. He was promoted to president of Disney Cruise Line Services in 2003. He became president of Disneyland Resort Paris in 2004, and chairman in 2005.

Home Alone 4 (television) Two-hour television movie from 20th Century Fox Television; aired on *The Wonderful World of Disney* on November 3, 2002. While young Kevin McCallister's parents are divorcing, Kevin is invited to spend Christ-mas with his dad, at the mansion of his dad's girl-friend, Natalie. The mansion is a "smart house" with everything remote controlled. While there, Kevin meets up with a robber and his girlfriend,

and resorts to his usual pranks to get rid of them. Directed by Rod Daniel. Stars Mike Weinberg (Kevin McCallister), Jason Beghe (Peter McCal-lister), Clare Carey (Kate McCallister), Erick Avari (Prescott), Joanna Going (Natalie), French Steward (Marv), Missi Pyle (Vera). Based on the previous *Home Alone* movies produced by Fox. Filmed in Cape Town, South Africa.

Home Defense (film) Donald Duck cartoon; released on November 26, 1943. Directed by Jack King. Donald falls asleep at his wartime post of aircraft spotter, and his nephews take advan-tage by frightening him with their toy plane and parachutists.

Home Improvement (television) Television series on ABC; beginning September 17, 1991, and ending September 17, 1999. The star of tele-vision's *Tool Time* show is often a bungler when he tries his home-improvement skills around the house. He is also not always terribly adept in his relationships with his wife and three boys. Stars Tim Allen, Patricia Richardson, Zachery Ty Bryan, Jonathan Taylor Thomas, Taran Noah Smith, Earl Hindman, Richard Kam. The popu-lar show frequently resided at the top of the weekly ratings, and it won Emmy Awards for Electronic Lighting Direction in 1992 and 1993. A special, *Tim Allen Presents: A User's Guide to Home Improvement*, aired May 4, 2003.

Home Made Home (film) Goofy cartoon; released on March 23, 1951. Directed by Jack Kinney. Goofy encounters many problems build-ing his own house, but is relieved when the work is done and he has company in—until the house collapses.

Home of the Future See Monsanto House of the Future.

Home on the Range (film) A greedy outlaw named Alameda Slim schemes to take possession of the Patch of Heaven dairy farm from its kindly owner, Pearl. Unwilling to stand by and see their idyllic way of life threatened, three determined cows—Mrs. Caloway, Maggie, and Grace—a karate-kicking stallion named Buck, and a colorful corral of critters join forces to save the farm. This unlikely assortment of animals braves bad guys and the rugged western landscape as they match wits with a mysterious bounty hunter named Rico in a high-stakes race to capture Slim and collect the reward money. Directed by Will Finn and John Sanford. Released on April 2, 2004. Voices include Roseanne Barr (Maggie), Judi Dench (Mrs. Caloway), Jennifer Tilly (Grace), Cuba Gooding, Jr. (Buck), Randy Quaid (Slim), Charles Dennis (Rico), Steve Buscemi (Wesley), Carole Cook (Pearl), Ann Richards (Annie). 76 min. An early version title was *Sweating Bullets*. Ann Richards was formerly the Governor of Texas. Songs by Alan Menken and Glenn Slater. Released on video in 2004.

Homeboys in Outer Space (television) Half-hour television series, beginning August 27, 1996, on UPN, and ending on May 13, 1997. In the 23rd century, spacemen Tyberious Walker and Morris Clay, two "brothers" from Earth, scour the galaxies looking for the ultimate mission that will make them their fortunes. The two have purchased a used space vehicle, the Hoopty, which comes with a special commuter, the Loquatron 2000, known affectionately as Loquatia. Stars Flex (Tyberious), Darryl M. Bell (Morris), Kevin Michael Richardson (Vashti), Rhona L. Bennett (Loquatia), Paulette Braxton (Amma), James Doohan (Pippen).

Homeier, Skip Actor; appeared on television in *The Strange Monster of Strawberry Cove*, *Johnny Shiloh*, and *Elfego Baca*.

Homeward Bound: The Incredible Journey (film) When a young family decides to make a temporary move from the country to San Francisco, they must leave their beloved pets behind until they can return. Left in the care of a family friend, the three forlorn animals—Shadow, an aged golden retriever; Chance, an American bulldog puppy; and Sassy, a Himalayan cat—set off through the wilds of the Sierras to find their owners. Conversing among themselves in human voices, the animals swim deep rivers, outwit a deadly mountain lion, and keep ahead of pursuing humans.

Their camaraderie and courage manage to see them through and discover the path that leads to home. Initial release on February 3, 1993; general release on February 12, 1993. Directed by Duwayne Dunham. 84 min. Stars Robert Hays (Bob), Kim Greist (Laura), Veronica Lauren (Hope), Kevin Chevalia (Jamie), Benj Thal (Peter). Voices of the animals by Michael J. Fox (Chance), Sally Field (Sassy), Don Ameche (Shadow). A remake of the 1963 Disney film, *The Incredible Journey*. Filmed in eastern Oregon. Released on video in 1993.

Homeward Bound II: Lost in San Francisco (film) The Seaver family has decided to take Chance, an American bulldog; Sassy, a Himalayan cat; and Shadow, a golden retriever, with them on a trip to the Canadian Rockies. When Chance escapes from his kennel at San Francisco's airport, his friends Shadow and Sassy are forced to rescue him. Being from suburbia, they find themselves unprepared for the dangers that lurk in the perilous streets of San Francisco. Eluding determined dogcatchers and outsmarting alleyway mutts Ashcan and Pete, the three friends are aided in their journey by a gang of tough-talking strays led by the charismatic Riley. It is among this pack that Chance encounters the beautiful, streetwise Delilah, with whom he falls hopelessly in love. In their struggles to return home, the three pets learn some tough lessons about life, friendship, loyalty, and love. Directed by David R. Ellis. Released on March 8, 1996. Stars Robert Hays (Bob Seaver), Kim Greist (Laura Seaver), Veronice Lauren (Hope), Kevin Chevalia (Jamie), Benj Thall (Peter). The lead dogs' voices are provided by Michael J. Fox (Chance), Sally Field (Sassy), and Ralph Waite (Shadow). 89 min. A sequel to *Homeward Bound: The Incredible Journey*. Filmed entirely on location in and around Vancouver, British Columbia, and San Francisco, California, featuring an animal cast of 40 canine and 10 feline performers. Four dogs were used to portray Chance and Shadow, though the lead roles went to dogs named Petey and Clovis; six different cats portrayed Sassy. Released on video in 1996.

Honest John See J. Worthington Foulfellow.

Honey Harvester (film) Donald Duck cartoon; released on August 5, 1949. Directed by Jack Hannah. A bee, taking honey from flowers in Donald's greenhouse and depositing it in the duck's car radiator, attempts to stop Donald from stealing the honey by attacking with the addition of a cactus spine to his stinger.

Honey, I Blew Up the Kid (film) Sequel to *Honey, I Shrunk the Kids*; Wayne Szalinski's new invention is a ray that expands molecules when they come into contact with electricity, with the unexpected experiment being his own young son, Adam. The toddler wanders in front of the ray, and before long is 112 feet tall, getting even bigger each time he encounters electricity, and heading straight for the bright lights of Las Vegas. Released on July 17, 1992. Directed by Randall Kleiser. 89 min. Stars Rick Moranis (Wayne Szalinski), Marcia Strassman (Diane Szalinski), Lloyd Bridges (Clifford Sterling), Robert Oliveri (Nick), John Shea (Charles Henderickson). For the production, the filmmakers were given permission to block off Fremont Street in Las Vegas. Also filmed in Simi Valley, California. Special effects wizards relied on both miniature sets and huge props. Released on video in 1993.

Honey, I Shrunk the Audience (film) Three-dimensional film shown in Journey into Imagination in Future World at Epcot, premiered on November 21, 1994. Guests enter the laboratory of Professor Wayne Szalinski's Imagination Institute, but the audience becomes accidental victims of the professor's famed, but flawed, shrinking machine. They must face such terrors as a giant python, a huge sneezing dog, and a humongous five-year-old child. At Tokyo Disneyland, the film, with new sequences shot specifically for the Japanese audience, debuted on April 15, 1997, as *MicroAdventure*. The attraction opened also at Disneyland on May 22, 1998, and at Disneyland Paris, as *Chérie, J'ai Rétréci le Public*, on March 28, 1999.

Honey, I Shrunk the Kids (film) Professor Wayne Szalinski is trying to perfect an electromagnetic shrinking machine, but everyone thinks he is a crackpot. When Szalinski's two kids, Amy

and Nick, along with neighbor kids, Ron and Little Russ Thompson, are accidentally zapped by the machine, they find themselves ¼-inch high. The professor unknowingly sweeps them up and throws them out with the trash, and they find it necessary to complete a major trek across the backyard, now a teeming jungle to them. As their parents search for them, the tiny kids face seemingly insurmountable obstacles and unexpected terrors as they make their way toward the house and hoped-for restoration by the machine. Released on June 23, 1989. Directed by Joe Johnston. 93 min. Stars Rick Moranis (Wayne Szalinski), Matt Frewer (Big Russ Thompson), Marcia Strassman (Diane Szalinski), Kristine Sutherland (Mae Thompson), Amy O'Neill (Amy), Robert Oliveri (Nick), Thomas Brown (Little Russ), Jared Rushton (Ron). Filmed at Churubusco Studio in Mexico City. Released on video in 1990.

Honey, I Shrunk the Kids (television) One-hour syndicated television series, debuting the week of September 22, 1997 and ending May 20, 2000. Mad scientist Wayne Szalinski comes up with inventions from time machines to shrink rays to spaceships and constantly involves his family in a series of misadventures. Wife Diane, a working mother, balances marriage, family, and her career as a top-notch lawyer, acting as the voice of reason in the midst of the outrageousness. Stars Peter Scolari (Wayne Szalinski), Barbara Alyn Woods (Diane), Hillary Tuck (Amy), Thomas Dekker (Nick). While the series was filmed in an old Army barracks in Calgary, Alberta, Canada, it is set in the fictional small town of Matheson, Colorado. 66 episodes.

Honey, I Shrunk the Kids Adventure Zone Attraction opened at Disney-MGM Studios on December 17, 1990. Also known as

Honey, I Shrunk the Kids Movie Set Adventure. Guests discover what it is like to be miniaturized as they wander in a gigantic world.

Honey, We Shrunk Ourselves (film) Wayne Szalinski is back and this time his notorious shrink machine misfires again, and it is the adults who are shrunk. Believing their parents have left them home alone for the weekend, the kids take advantage of their newfound unsupervised freedom by filling up on junk food, Rollerblading in the house, playing loud music, and throwing a party for their friends. While desperately trying to get the kids to notice them, since they are only ¾ of an inch tall, the adults are able to learn a few things about their kids. Direct-to-video release on March 18, 1997. Directed by Dean Cundey, making his directorial debut (his previous career had been as a famed cinematographer of such films as *Who Framed Roger Rabbit*, *Hook*, and *Jurassic Park*). Stars Rick Moranis (Wayne), Eve Gordon (Diane), Bug Hall (Adam), Robin Bartlett (Patty), Stuart Pankin (Gordon), Allison Mack (Jenny), Jake Richardson (Mitch). 76 min. Rated PG. The film was extremely complicated to produce, with almost 400 composite shots totaling approximately 40 minutes of screen time. Dream Quest Images, which produced the visual effects, had the advantage of new technologies that were not available when the first film in the series was made.

Hong Kong Disneyland The eleventh Disney park, which opened in Hong Kong on September 12, 2005. Phase I of the development, located on 310 acres of land on Lantau Island, is on land reclaimed from Penny's Bay. The resort includes the park and two hotels—the Hong Kong Disneyland Hotel and Disney's Hollywood Hotel—totaling 1,000 rooms. There is a Main Street, U.S.A., Fantasyland, Adventureland, and Tomorrowland. Tomorrowland is entirely themed as an intergalactic spaceport, with restaurants, shops, and attractions all carrying through the theme. Fantasyland is entered through Sleeping Beauty Castle, based on the one at Disneyland. In 1999, Disney and the Government of the Hong Kong Special Administrative Region signed a master project agreement for the development and operation of Hong Kong

Disneyland. The site is 30 minutes from downtown Hong Kong. After initial reclamation work on the land, a groundbreaking ceremony was held on January 12, 2003, and after over a year of construction, a castle-topping ceremony was held on September 23, 2004.

Hong Kong Disneyland Hotel Hotel in the Victorian style, with 400 rooms; opened on September 12, 2005. There are restaurants (Crystal Lotus, Enchanted Garden), as well as lounges, a spa, a conference center, and a gift shop.

Hong Kong Disneyland Railroad Opened on September 12, 2005, with stations in Fantasyland and Main Street, U.S.A.

Honker Muddlefoot Little boy duck; voiced by Katie Leigh, on *Darkwing Duck*, the best friend of Gosalyn Mallard.

Hook, Lion and Sinker (film) Donald Duck cartoon; released on September 1, 1950. Directed by Jack Hannah. A mountain lion and cub try various ways to steal fish from Donald, always with the same result—the cub picking Donald's buckshot out of his father's bottom.

Hooked Bear (film) Special cartoon; released on April 27, 1956. Directed by Jack Hannah. Ranger J. Audubon Woodlore attempts to keep Humphrey the bear from fishing with the human fishermen, telling him, "Now go fish like a bear!" But Humphrey keeps looking for an easier way until, before he knows it, fishing season is over and bear hunting season is on. Filmed in CinemaScope.

Hook's Pointe & Wine Cellar Restaurant at the Disneyland Hotel; opened on April 8, 1999. It took the place of the Shipyard Inn.

Hookworm (film) Educational film about the dangers of hookworm. Produced under the auspices of the Coordinator of Inter-American Affairs. Delivered to them on June 30, 1945. Careless Charlie and his family are infected with hookworm, and they learn about the proper medications and safe living conditions from a local clinic.

Hoop Dee Doo Musical Revue In Pioneer Hall at Fort Wilderness at Walt Disney World; beginning on September 5, 1974. After a meal of fried chicken, barbecued ribs, and corn on the cob, the audience joins in the rousing musical celebration of country-western entertainment. In 1983, the show opened at the Diamond Horseshoe at Tokyo Disneyland.

Hoopz Stage musical in development, about the rise of the Harlem Globetrotters basketball team in the mid–20th century.

Hop Low Cute runt in the Mushroom Dance in the *Nutcracker Suite* segment of *Fantasia*.

Hope & Faith (television) Half-hour comedy series on ABC; premiering on September 26, 2003. Stay-at-home mom, Hope, leads a busy, family-centered life with her husband, children, and live-in father. But when her Hollywood celebrity sister, Faith, is written out of the soap opera in which she stars and comes to stay with her sister's family in suburbia, Hope's sensible, down-to-earth world changes drastically. Raising three kids has never been easy for Hope, but the appearance of trendy, theatrical Faith turns parenting into crisis management. Stars Faith Ford (Hope), Kelly Ripa (Faith), Josh Stamberg (Charley), Harve Presnell (Jack), Macey Cruthird (Hayley), Brie Larson (Sydney), Slade Pearce (Justin). From Touchstone Television.

Hope Springs (film) British artist Colin Ware discovers that his fiance, Vera, the love of his life, is going to marry another man. Distraught and despondent, he gets on a plane for America and ends up in the tiny town of Hope in New England. At first, Colin is depressed, but he soon finds more than a shoulder to cry on when his innkeepers introduce him to Mandy, a beautiful nurse. All's going well and Colin has almost forgotten his old flame until Vera suddenly shows up with a surprise of her own. A Touchstone Picture. Directed by Mark Herman. Original release in England, May 9, 2003. Test screened in certain Florida cities on September 5, 2003 before a direct-to-video release on April 6, 2004. Stars Colin Firth (Colin Ware), Heather Graham (Mandy), Minnie Driver (Vera), Oliver Platt (Doug Reed), Mary Steenbergen (Joanie Fisher). 92 min. Filmed in CinemaScope. Based on the novel, *New Cardiff*, by Charles Webb; working title of the film was *New Cardiff*. Filmed in Vancouver, B.C., Canada. Released on video in 2004.

Hopkins, Anthony Actor; appeared in *Nixon* (Richard Nixon), *Instinct* (Ethan Powell), and *Bad Company* (Gaylord Oakes), and on The Disney Channel in *Great Expectations* (Abel Magwitch).

Hopper, Dennis Actor; appeared in *My Science Project* (Bob Roberts), *Super Mario Bros.* (King Koopa), and *Meet the Deedles* (Frank Slater).

Horace Horsecollar Known for the oversize collar around his neck, this horse character was a bit player primarily in the Mickey Mouse cartoons of the 1930s. He made 11 appearances, beginning with *The Plow Boy* (1929), often paired with Clarabelle Cow.

Hordern, Michael (1911–1995) Actor; appeared in *The Story of Robin Hood* (Scathelock) and on television in *The Scarecrow of Romney Marsh* (Squire).

Horizons Pavilion in Future World at Epcot, opened on October 1, 1983, sponsored by General Electric until September 30, 1993. It closed on January 9, 1999. Horizons was one of the first attractions in Future World to be devoted primarily to the future. Guests first saw how the future was visualized by people such as Jules Verne; then they witnessed living experiences in the desert, in space, and under the sea. Through aromas, visual effects, sound effects, and a short Omnimax film presentation, guests saw how life might be in the future. Finally, they could select how they wanted their experience to end by pressing appropriate buttons in their ride vehicle, the first time that this was done in a Disney attraction. Until the theme song, "There's a Great Big Beautiful Tomorrow," was returned to the Carousel of Progress in the Magic Kingdom, it could be heard by savvy guests here on a television in a 1940s setting. The attraction was totally rebuilt to become Mission: SPACE.

Horned King, The  Evil villain in *The Black Cauldron* who wants to unleash the Cauldron Born as his soldiers; voiced by John Hurt.

Horse Called Comanche, A Serialized version of *Tonka* on the new *Mickey Mouse Club*.

Horse in the Gray Flannel Suit, The (film) An executive in an ad agency comes up with a great idea; he gets his firm to buy a horse and gives it to his teenaged daughter. She'll ride it to victory in some horse shows, and the animal, named for the Allied Drug Company product, an indigestion remedy called Aspercel, will get lots of publicity. But it doesn't quite work out that way. His daughter, Helen, is only an amateur, and it is only with the love and support of her father, trainer Suzie Clemens, and her new boyfriend, Ronnie, that she can win the title of Grand Champion Open Jumper in the prestigious Washington International Horse Show. Released on December 20, 1968. Directed by Norman Tokar. 113 min. Stars Dean Jones (Frederick Bolton), Diane Baker (Suzie Clemens), Ellen Janov (Helen Bolton), Lloyd Bochner (Archer Madison), Morey Amsterdam (Charlie Blake), Kurt Russell (Ronnie Gardner), Lurene Tuttle (Aunt Martha). Based on the book, *The Year of the Horse*, by Eric Hatch. The movie was shot mostly on Disney's Golden Oak Ranch, near Newhall, California. Student riders from the Flintridge Riding Academy were used in the film. Released on video in 1986.

Horse of the West, The (television) Television show; aired on December 11, 1957. Directed by Larry Lansburgh. The story of the life of a quarter horse through her various owners. Narrated by Rex Allen. Stars Sammy Fancher, George Masek, Jimmy Williams.

Horse Sense (television) A Disney Channel Original Film; first aired on November 20, 1999. eleven-year-old Tommy visits his wealthy cousin, Michael, in Beverly Hills, but Michael ignores the kid. Michael is punished for his behavior by being sent to Tommy's ranch in Montana for the summer, and he has a miserable time trying to acclimate himself to ranch life. However, when Michael discovers that Tommy and his mother are in jeopardy of losing their property due to foreclosure, he and Tommy unite to save the ranch, and in the process he learns an important lesson about hard work, family, and love. Directed by Greg Beeman. Stars Andy Lawrence (Tommy Biggs), Joey Lawrence (Michael Woods), Susan Walters (Jules Biggs), M.C. Gainey (Twister), Leeann Hunley (Jacy Woods), Robin Thomas (Glenn Woods). In 2001, there was a sequel—*Jumping Ship*.

Horse Whisperer, The (film) fourteen-year-old Grace Maclean is physically and emotionally scarred after a terrible riding accident while astride her prized horse, Pilgrim. Her mother, Annie, a high-powered magazine editor, realizes that the fates of her daughter and the horse are inextricably linked, so she searches for a "horse whisperer," someone with a unique gift for curing troubled horses. She finds Tom Booker, a legend for this type of work, and takes both Grace and Pilgrim to Montana to seek his help. There, love blossoms between the gentle horseman and the uprooted sophisticate. Directed by Robert Redford. A Touchstone Picture. Released on May 15, 1998. Stars Robert Redford (Tom Booker), Kristin Scott Thomas (Annie), Sam Neill (Robert Maclean), Dianne Wiest (Diane Booker), Scarlett Johansson (Grace), Chris Cooper (Frank Booker), Cherry Jones (Liz Hammond). 169 min. This is the first time that Redford starred in a film he also produced and directed. Based upon the best-selling first novel by British author Nicholas Evans. Filmed in CinemaScope. After filming at various locations in New York State, the production moved to Montana where a working cattle ranch of the Engle family, located about an hour from Livingston, Montana, became the fictitious Double Divide Ranch, though a new ranch house was built. Released on video in 1998.

Horse with the Flying Tail, The (film) Featurette; released on December 21, 1960, on a bill with *Swiss Family Robinson*. Directed by Larry Lansburgh. The true story of Nautical, star jumper of the U.S. Equestrian Team. As a cow pony, this palomino is noticed by an ex-cavalry man who trains him. Near disaster overtakes the jumper when he is sold to an unscrupulous trainer. However, Bertalan de Nemethy, coach of the U.S. team, spots Nautical, buys and rejuvenates him, and ships him to Europe where he finally wins the world-famous King George V cup. Made at a 47-minute length for the television show, the film was instead deemed worthy to receive a theatrical release, and it won the Academy Award as Best Documentary Feature of 1960. It was later telecast on *Walt Disney's Wonderful World of Color* in 1963.

Horse Without a Head, The (television) Two-part television show; aired on September 29 and October 6, 1963. Directed by Don Chaffey. The two episodes were titled *The 100,000,000 Franc Train Robbery* and *The Key to the Cache*. In France, a daring mail-train robbery goes awry, and a group of kids thwart the robbers by finding a key to the hiding place of the loot, which the crooks have hidden in a "headless horse-cart" the kids enjoy riding. Stars Jean Pierre Aumont, Herbert Lom, Leo McKern, Pamela Franklin, Vincent Winter, Lee Montague, Denis Gilmore.

Horse-Drawn Streetcars Main Street vehicles at Disneyland; began on July 17, 1955. The tracks part halfway down Main Street to form double tracks so that two streetcars can pass each other. The majestic Belgian horses pulling the streetcars are the last remaining horses utilized daily in the park, and they greatly add to the atmosphere of a turn-of-the-century street. Also in Magic Kingdom Park at Walt Disney World, beginning October 1, 1971, and at Disneyland Paris, beginning April 12, 1992.

Horseless Carriages Main Street vehicles at Disneyland; began in 1956. Designed and built by Disney Imagineers based on cars of the period. Also in Magic Kingdom Park at Walt Disney World, opening October 1, 1971, and in World Bazaar at Tokyo Disneyland, opening April 15, 1983.

Horsemasters, The (television) Two-part television show; aired on October 1 and 8, 1961. Directed by William Fairchild. The two episodes were titled *Follow Your Heart* and *Tally Ho*. American students are having a difficult time at a prestigious English riding school. Dinah Wilcox is overly cautious because of memories of an accident, but Danny Grant gives her confidence. The strict, but admired, instructor fears she must sell her favorite horse because of school tradition, but the students end up taking up a collection to buy it back for her. Stars Annette Funicello, Tommy Kirk, Janet Munro, Donald Pleasence, Tony Britton, John Fraser, Jean Marsh, Millicent Martin. The Sherman brothers, Robert and Richard, wrote "The Strummin' Song," their first song for a Disney film, for this show.

Horses for Greene (television) Television show; episode 8 of *The Swamp Fox*.

Hortense Title star of *Donald's Ostrich* (1937).

Horvath, Ferdinand Huszti (1891–1973) Story sketch artist at Disney from 1934 to 1937, a very meticulous person who specialized in fine, detailed pencil sketches. Born in Budapest, he brought a European style to the Disney films. He worked on many of the Disney shorts and did preliminary work on *Snow White and the Seven Dwarfs*.

Hoskins, Bob Actor; appeared in *Who Framed Roger Rabbit* (Eddie Valiant), *Passed Away* (Johnny Scanlan), *Super Mario Bros.* (Mario Mario), and *Nixon* (J. Edgar Hoover).

Hospital, The (film) Educational film in which Mickey learns about the various parts of a hospital and the work that goes on there, in the

Mickey's Field Trips series, released in September 1987. 10 min.

Hot Chick, The (film) Jessica Spencer, the hottest, most popular girl in high school, captain of the cheerleading squad and dating the dreamy quarterback, gets a big dose of reality when she wakes up in the body of a 30-year-old man. Until she can figure out how to change herself back, she must find a way to win the Cheer Competition, go to the prom, and win her boyfriend back—all as a guy. A Touchstone Picture. Released on December 13, 2002. Directed by Tom Brady. Stars Rob Schneider (Clive), Anna Faris (April), Matthew Lawrence (Billy), Eric Christian Olsen (Jake), Robert Davi (Stan), Melora Hardin (Carol), Rachel McAdams (Jessica Spencer), Michael O'Keefe (Richie). 101 min. Released on video in 2003.

Hot Choc-late Soldiers, The (film) Color Silly Symphony–type sequence produced for the MGM film, *The Hollywood Party* (1934). The Hot Chocolate Soldiers leave home to battle the Gingerbread Men of Pastry Land, using all sorts of candies and pastries as weapons. The soldiers capture the Gingerbread Men with a "Trojan Horse" trick—a giant candy dish of a dove holding an olive branch. The soldiers return home triumphant with their prisoners, only to melt in the hot sun. Directed by Ben Sharpsteen.

Hot Dog (film) Oswald the Lucky Rabbit cartoon; released on August 20, 1928.

Hot Lead and Cold Feet (film) This rip-roaring comedy saga of the Old West involves twin brothers who compete for possession of a rickety cow town founded by their father. The look-alike siblings (one a rough and rowdy cowboy, the other a mild-mannered easterner) take part in a winner takes all, no-holds-barred endurance contest, complete with train racing, wagon hauling, river-rapid running, and mountain climbing. All this takes place while a crooked mayor tries to put an end to the competitors so he can inherit the town himself. Eventually, the brothers join forces to save the town from the mayor and his minions. Released on July 5, 1978. Directed by

Robert Butler. 90 min. Stars Jim Dale (Jasper, Eli, Wild Billy), Karen Valentine (Jenny), Don Knotts (Denver Kid), Jack Elam (Rattlesnake), Darren McGavin (Mayor Ragsdale), John Williams (Mansfield), Warren Vanders (Boss Snead), Debbie Lytton (Roxanne), Michael Sharrett (Marcus). Two songs are featured in the film: "May The Best Man Win," by Al Kasha and Joel Hirschhorn, and "Something Good Is Bound To Happen," by Buddy Baker, Arthur Alsberg, and Don Nelson. Portions of the film were shot on location in Deschutes National Forest in Oregon, from snowy Mt. Bachelor along the Cascade Range, across the Deschutes River gorge, to the black rocks of Lava Butte. Released on video in 1980 and 1985.

Hotel Cheyenne Hotel at Disneyland Resort Paris; opened on April 12, 1992. Themed to the Old West. Designed by architect Robert A. M. Stern.

Hotel New York Hotel at Disneyland Resort Paris; opened on April 12, 1992. Designed by architect Michael Graves. It features an outdoor reflecting pool that is turned into a skating rink during the winter.

Hotel Santa Fe Hotel at Disneyland Resort Paris; opened on April 12, 1992. Has a southwestern theme, with buildings resembling Native American pueblos. Designed by architect Antoine Predock.

Hound that Thought He Was a Raccoon, The (film) Featurette; released on August 10, 1960. Directed by Tom McGowan. Hound puppy, Nubbin, lost in the woods, is nursed by a female raccoon who has lost all her babies, except Weecha. Normally natural enemies, the baby hound and raccoon grow up together, first in the den, later at the farm of Nubbin's master. Weecha wants to escape the farm, and with Nubbin's intervention, is allowed to leave. Based on the story *Weecha the Raccoon* by Rutherford Montgomery. 48 min. Originally planned to fit an hour-long television slot, it finally reached television in 1964. It was cut to 28 min. for a 1975 reissue.

Hounded (television) A Disney Channel Original Movie; first aired on April 13, 2001. Thirteen-year-old Jay Martin is committed to winning a scholarship competition so he won't be sent to military school, but his rival, Ronny Van Dusen, the principal's son, spoils his plans by stealing Jay's speech. Jay's plans are thwarted again when he accidentally kidnaps his principal's obnoxious dog, Camille. Directed by Neal Israel. Stars Tahj Mowry (Jay Martin), Craig Kirkwood (Mike Martin), Shia La Beouf (Ronny Van Dusen), Ed Begley, Jr. (Ward Van Dusen), Stephen Bendik (Bill Lipka), Sara Paxton (Tracy Richburg).

House Calls (television) Syndicated half-hour series debuting on September 11, 2000 and ending in 2001. In this reality series, cameras follow psychiatrist Dr. Irvin Wolkoff into the homes of real people, as he counsels them about real problems. 88 episodes. From Buena Vista Television.

House of Magic Shop on Main Street in Magic Kingdom Park at Walt Disney World; opened on October 1, 1971, and closed March 19, 1995, to become part of the Main Street Athletic Club.

House of Mouse (television) Animated characters gather each Saturday at this "nightclub" to enjoy musical guests, cartoon shorts, and Mickey Mouse's comical introductions from the stage. There is constant backstage pandemonium as Mickey, Donald Duck, Goofy, Minnie Mouse, Daisy Duck, and Pluto attempt to ensure that "the show goes on." Premiered on ABC on January 13, 2001.

House of the Future See Monsanto House of the Future.

Houseguest (film) Enterprising Kevin Franklin's wishes and dreams turn out to be short-lived when his latest get-rich scheme fails, and he is forced to leave town in a hurry. With loan sharks and hit men after him, he heads to the airport where he meets lawyer Gary Young and convinces him that he is the childhood chum who was due in for a family visit. Masquerading as a houseguest is tricky enough, but soon Franklin is expected to be a world-famous oral surgeon, causing many complications. Released on January 6, 1995. Directed by Randy Miller. A Hollywood Picture in association with Caravan Pictures. 109 min. Stars Sinbad (Kevin Franklin), Phil Hartman (Gary Young), Kim Greist (Emily Ford), Jeffrey Jones (Ron Timmerman). Released on video in 1995.

Houston, Whitney Actress; starred in *The Preacher's Wife* (Julia) and on television in *Cinderella* (Fairy Godmother).

Houston, Texas Disney constructed a WED-Way PeopleMover at the Houston Intercontinental Airport. It opened on August 17, 1981, and was the only transportation system actually sold by Disney's Community Transportation Services division. The technology for the PeopleMover and monorails was later sold to a Canadian company, Bombardier, Inc. The visitor center at the Johnson Space Center, which opened in 1972, was designed by Walt Disney Imagineering.

How Alaska Joined the World (film) Sixteen-mm film released in June 1973, of television film. It traces Alaska's history, in animation, from its discovery to its purchase by the United States.

How Disease Travels (film) Educational film. Produced under the auspices of the Coordinator of Inter-American Affairs. Delivered to them on August 13, 1945. The animation shows how latrines can be built to prevent the spread of disease.

How Does It Feel to Be an Elephant? (film) Educational film in the EPCOT Educational Media Collection: Language Arts Through Imagination series; released in September 1988. Learning skills of comparing and contrasting, observing and interpreting.

How Does It Feel to Fly? (film) Educational film describing the world through classifying and sequencing, in the EPCOT Educational Media Collection: Language Arts Through Imagination series; released in September 1988. 14 min.

How Does Sound Sound? (film) Educational film about language and the sound around us, in the EPCOT Educational Media Collection: Language Arts Through Imagination series; released in September 1988. 13 min.

How the West Was Lost (television) Television show; aired on September 24, 1967. Directed by Hamilton S. Luske. Cartoons about the Old West, introduced by one of Donald Duck's ancestors, known as the Oldtimer, whose voice was provided by Bill Thompson.

How to Be a Detective (film) Goofy cartoon; released on December 12, 1952. Directed by Jack Kinney. Goofy is "Johnny Eyeball, Private Eye" who gets mixed up in a surreal whodunnit involving a classy dame, a cop, weasels, and the mysterious missing Al.

How to Be a Sailor (film) Goofy cartoon; released on January 28, 1944. Directed by Jack Kinney. Goofy demonstrates methods of navigation of the sea from early vessels to modern ships, and engages in a victorious battle with the Japanese fleet and The Rising Sun symbol.

How to Catch a Cold (film) Educational film, made for International Cellucotton Co. Delivered to them on August 1, 1951. About the myths and facts of the cold virus. Shows the manner in which a cold is caught and spread throughout a community, and how it should be treated. A revised version was released in September 1986.

How to Dance (film) Goofy cartoon; released on July 11, 1953. Directed by Jack Kinney. A short history of the dance, followed by Goofy trying to learn with the aid of a dummy and dancing school.

How to Exercise (film) Educational film in the Fitness and Me series; released in March 1984. Two weaklings, a knight and a dragon, are used as examples in showing the value of a shape-up plan.

How to Fish (film) Goofy cartoon; released on December 4, 1942. Directed by Jack Kinney. Goofy's demonstration of fishing is fouled up by his clumsy casting and fly fishing, and problems with his boat.

How to Get Fit (film) Educational film in the Fitness for Living series; released in September 1982. The film provides a practical guide for students in developing their own fitness plan.

How to Have an Accident at Work (film) Donald Duck cartoon; released on September 2, 1959. Directed by Charles Nichols. The bearded

duck named J. J. Fate, who had previously appeared in *How to Have an Accident in the Home*, warns of the dangers of being careless in the workplace, with Donald Duck as the example. Throwing all caution aside, Donald forgets his safety helmet, ignores signs, gets mixed up in the machinery, daydreams, and even gets in an accident in his rush to clock out.

How to Have an Accident in the Home (film) Donald Duck cartoon; released on July 8, 1956. Directed by Charles Nichols. Filmed in CinemaScope. Donald demonstrates, to his own detriment, how dangerous many household activities can be, such as lighting pipes in gas-filled rooms, climbing a littered stairway, and standing on a rocking chair. The film's narrator is J. J. Fate; voiced by Bill Thompson.

How to Play Baseball (film) Goofy cartoon; released on September 4, 1942. Directed by Jack Kinney. Goofy demonstrates the game by playing all the positions on both teams and displaying the different types of pitching, with an offscreen narrator. The film was rushed into production, and made in just 12 weeks, so as to be released to accompany Samuel Goldwyn's *The Pride of the Yankees.*

How to Play Football (film) Goofy cartoon; released on September 15, 1944. Directed by Jack Kinney. Taking all the places on both teams, Goofy demonstrates the game of football with varying results, having problems with the coach and the goal post.

How to Play Golf (film) Goofy cartoon; released on March 10, 1944. Directed by Jack

Kinney. Aided by a diagrammatical figure, Goofy demonstrates golf techniques until an angry bull chases them and wrecks the course.

How to Relax (television) Television show; aired on November 27, 1957. Directed by Wolfgang Reitherman. A series of Goofy cartoons demonstrate his desire to relax.

How to Ride a Horse (film) Goofy cartoon; released on February 24, 1950. It was earlier released as part of the feature, *The Reluctant Dragon* (1941). Goofy is not very adept at horseback riding, and the horse constantly gets the best of him.

How to Sleep (film) Goofy cartoon; released on December 25, 1953. Directed by Jack Kinney. Goofy shows the various ways humans sleep, and has no trouble falling asleep throughout the day, including at his desk at work, but when he goes home to bed at night, he cannot sleep. He tries various gadgets, but finally a scientist has to hit him over the head.

How to Swim (film) Goofy cartoon; released on October 23, 1942. Directed by Jack Kinney. In his attempt to demonstrate swimming, Goofy first has trouble undressing in the small locker room but then manages to showcase diving and swimming techniques.

Howard, Clint Actor; appeared in *The Wild Country* (Andrew), *Splash* (wedding guest), *The Rocketeer* (Monk), *The Waterboy* (Paco), and provided the voice of Roo in *Winnie the Pooh* and Baby Elephant in *The Jungle Book.*

Howard, Ron Actor; appeared in *The Wild Country* (Virgil) and on television in *Smoke* and *A Boy Called Nuthin'*, returned years later to direct the first Touchstone film, *Splash.*

Howard Johnson's Hotel in Lake Buena Vista at Walt Disney World. Became Courtyard by Marriott in 1995.

Howl's Moving Castle Animated film directed by Hayao Miyazaki, and distributed in the United States by Disney. Sophie Halter, an 18-year-old girl, seems doomed to the life of a hatmaker, but when she is cursed by the Witch of the Waste with the body of a 90-year-old woman, she goes to the moving castle of the wizard Howl, who is supposed to have eaten the souls of young girls. But

Howl himself has been cursed by the Witch, and is looking for the love of a young girl to help him break the curse. Sophie befriends Calcifer, the fire demon, who is under contract to Howl, and she helps him break the contract so Calcifer can help her return to her original shape. Limited release on June 10, 2005, in New York, Los Angeles, San Francisco, and in other selected cities; general release on June 17, 2005. Original release in Japan on November 20, 2004, after a showing in September at the Venice Film Festival. U.S. production directed by Pete Docter and Rick Dempsey. Voices include Jean Simmons (Grandma Sophie), Christian Bale (Howl), Lauren Bacall (Witch of the Waste), Blythe Danner (Madame Suliman), Emily Mortimer (Young Sophie), Josh Hutcherson (Markl), Billy Crystal (Calcifer). 119 min. Based on the book by Diana Wynne Jones.

Hudson, Ernie Actor; appeared in *The Hand that Rocks the Cradle* (Solomon) and *Mr. Magoo* (Agent Gus Anders), and on television in *10-8* (John Henry Barnes).

Huemer, Dick (1898–1979) Animation story director and comic-strip artist; he joined Disney in 1933 as an animator. In 1938–39, he directed *The Whalers* and *Goofy and Wilbur*. He was story director on *Fantasia*, and worked on story on *Dumbo*, *Saludos Amigos*, *Make Mine Music*, and *Alice in Wonderland*. He left in 1948 but returned in 1951 to work in story and television. From 1955 until his retirement in 1973, he wrote the True-Life Adventures newspaper panel for the comic strip department.

Huey One of Donald Duck's three nephews.

Huey, Dewey, and Louie Originally there was no way to tell Donald's nephews apart, because the colors on their costumes were used interchangeably. Because the stories for the *Ducktales* television series were more complicated than they were for the short Donald Duck cartoons, it was deemed necessary to distinguish between the three nephews. So, Huey was dressed in red, Dewey in blue, and Louie in green. You can remember this by noting that the brightest *hue* of the three is red (Huey), the color of water, *dew*, is blue (Dewey), and that *leaves* Louie, and leaves are green. The nephews made their debut in the Donald Duck Sunday comic page on October 17, 1937, and first appeared on film in *Donald's Nephews*.

Huffman, Felicity Actress; appeared in *Raising Helen* (Lindsay Davis) and on television in *Sports Night* (Dana Whitaker) and *Desperate Housewives* (Lynette Scavo). She won an Emmy award for Lead Actress in a Comedy Series in 2005.

Hughes, Barnard Actor; appeared in *Tron* (Dr. Walter Gibbs, Dumont) and *Sister Act 2: Back in the Habit* (Father Maurice).

Hughes, Linda Mouseketeer from the 1950s television show.

Hulce, Tom Actor; provided the acting and singing voice of Quasimodo in *The Hunchback of Notre Dame*.

Hull High (television) Musical comedy/drama television series on NBC from September 23 to December 30, 1990. There were previews on August 20 and September 15, 1990. The series took an irreverent look at the daily lives of students and teachers at a Southern California high school as they dealt with themselves and each other. Musical production numbers served to underscore the conflicts and emotions of each show. Stars Will Lyman (John Deerborn), Nancy Valen (Donna Breedlove), George Martin (Mr. Dobosh), Harold Pruett (Cody Rome), Mark Ballou (Mark), Marty Belafsky (Louis Plumb), Marshall Bell (Jim Fancher), Kristin Dattilo (DJ), Cheryl Pollack (Camilla). The musical numbers were choreographed by Kenny Ortega.

Human Body, The (film) Educational film produced under the auspices of the Coordinator of Inter-American Affairs. Delivered on August 13, 1945. Animation tells the function of muscles, bones, food digestion, blood vessels, heart, and brain, and how they react properly to make healthy bodies with proper food and fresh air.

Humphrey Friendly grizzly bear who appeared in seven cartoons, beginning with *Hold That Pose* (1950).

Humunga Kowabunga The two longest water slides, at 214 feet, at Typhoon Lagoon at Walt Disney World, sweeping guests along at 30 miles an hour.

Hunchback of Notre Dame, The (film) The tale of Quasimodo, the lonely outsider who longs to be out in the world beyond his bell tower in the Cathedral of Notre Dame in Paris. Defying the orders of his evil surrogate father, Minister of Justice Frollo, the frightened hunchback journeys into the streets of medieval Paris, where he meets and falls in love with a beautiful gypsy girl named Esmeralda. He also befriends Phoebus, Captain of the King's guards. Although heartbroken when he discovers Phoebus and Esmeralda's love for each other, Quasimodo ultimately risks everything to bring them together. Quasimodo's selfless love overcomes both his heartache and Frollo's obsessive hatred of Esmeralda. Along the way, Quasimodo finds support and friendship from the cathedral's trio of comic gargoyles: Victor, Hugo, and Laverne. Directed by Kirk Wise and Gary Trousdale. Released on June 21, 1996. With the voices of Tom Hulce (Quasimodo), Demi Moore (Esmeralda), Kevin Kline (Phoebus), Tony Jay (Frollo), Paul Kandel (Clopin), Charles Kimbrough (Victor), Jason Alexander (Hugo), Mary Wickes (Laverne), David Ogden Stiers (Archdeacon). After the passing of Mary Wickes, Jane Withers completed the role of Laverne. 91 min. From the Victor Hugo epic novel, first published in 1831. Songs by Alan Menken and Stephen Schwartz. The film had a premiere on June 19 at the Superdome in New Orleans, utilizing six enormous screens, and preceded by a parade through the French Quarter. The song "Someday" was sung over the credits by the group All-4-One, but the European version replaced them with the British band Eternal. Released on video in 1997.

Hunchback of Notre Dame, The Stage musical version of the story had its world premiere as *Der Glöckner Von Notre Dame* on June 5, 1999, at the Stella Musical Theater at Potsdamer Platz in Berlin, Germany, and closed June 16, 2002. Composers Alan Menken and Stephen Schwartz wrote nine new songs for this version, and adapted their music from the film as well.

Hunchback of Notre Dame—a Musical Adventure Stage show opened on June 21, 1996, at Disney-MGM Studios at the Backstage Theater. It closed on September 28, 2002.

Hunchback of Notre Dame Festival of Fools, The A 25-minute French comedic troupe theater-in-the-round experience at Disneyland, in the area formerly known as Big Thunder Ranch, opened June 21, 1996, and closed April 19, 1998.

Hunchback of Notre Dame II, The (film) Seven years have passed, and Quasimodo is now accepted by his fellow Parisians, especially his friends, Esmeralda and Phoebus, who have married and have a son, Zephyr. A greedy circus master, Sarousch, plots to steal a treasured bell from the bell tower, and coerces his beautiful assistant, Madellaine, to lure Quasimodo away. However, Madellaine finds she cares for Quasimodo and tries to foil the plot. When the bell is stolen anyway, Quasi blames Madellaine, but eventually realizes she can be trusted to help catch the evil Sarousch. Released direct-to-video on March 19, 2002. Directed by Bradley Raymond. The voice cast includes the stars from the original film, along with Jennifer Love Hewitt (Madellaine), Michael McKean (Sarousch), and Haley Joel Osment (Zephyr). Jane Withers, who finished the role of Laverne after the passing of Mary Wickes, returns.

Hundred and One Dalmatians See *One Hundred and One Dalmatians*.

Hungry Bear Restaurant Opened in Bear Country at Disneyland in 1972. Originally known as Golden Bear Lodge. Set among the forest trees on the shore of the Rivers of America, the restaurant's terrace offers picturesque views of the river craft sailing by. Also in Westernland at Tokyo Disneyland, opened on April 15, 1983.

Hungry Hoboes (film) Oswald the Lucky Rabbit cartoon; released on May 14, 1928.

Hunnicutt, Arthur (1911–1979) Actor; appeared in *A Tiger Walks* (Lewis), *The Adventures of Bullwhip Griffin* (Referee), and *Million Dollar Duck* (Mr. Purdham), and on television in *Elfego Baca*, *The Swamp Fox*, and *Kilroy*.

Hunt, Bonnie Actress; provided the voices of Rosie in *a bug's life* and Flint in *Monsters, Inc.*, and starred in her own television series, *Life with Bonnie* (Bonnie Molloy).

Hunt, Linda Actress; voiced Grandmother Willow in *Pocahontas*.

Hunter, Holly Actress; appeared in *Woman Wanted* (Emma), *O Brother, Where Art Thou?* (Penny), and *Moonlight Mile* (Mona Camp), and provided the voice of Helen Parr/Elastigirl in *The Incredibles*.

Hunter, Jeffrey (1926–1969) Actor; appeared in *The Great Locomotive Chase* (William A. Fuller), and on television in *Behind the Scenes with Fess Parker*.

Hunter, Tab Actor; appeared on television in *Hacksaw*.

Hunter and the Rock Star, The Alternate title of *Sultan and the Rock Star*.

Hunting Instinct, The (television) Television show; aired on October 22, 1961. Directed by Wolfgang Reitherman. Prof. Von Drake, with his assistant Herman (Bootle Beetle), teaches about hunting utilizing a series of cartoons.

Hurricane Hannah (television) Television show; aired on December 16, 1962. The story of a hurricane from its birth, told with the cooperation of the U.S. Weather Bureau National Hurricane Center in Miami. It is spotted first as an unusual cloud formation by a weather satellite, then the meteorologists follow its progress as it grows to a full-blown hurricane and threat-ens Galveston, Texas. Stars (as themselves) Gordon E. Dunn, Cmdr. Joshua Langfur, Lt. John Lincoln. Narrated by Robert P. Anderson.

Hurricane, The (film) Co-production between Buena Vista International and Beacon Pictures. A true story of an innocent man's 20-year fight for justice. Originally shown at the Toronto Film Festival on September 17, 1999. General U.S. release on January 14, 2000. Directed by Norman Jewison. Stars Denzel Washington (Rubin "Hurricane" Carter), Vicellous Reon Shannon (Lesra), Deborah Kara Ungar (Lisa), Liev Schreiber (Sam), John Hannah (Terry). 145 min. Universal distributed in the United States, with Buena Vista International handling foreign distribution.

Hurricanes A disc jockey spins the top 40 hits in this club at Disney Village at Disneyland Resort Paris.

Hurt, John Actor; appeared in *Night Crossing* (Peter Strelzyk) and provided the voices of The Horned King in *The Black Cauldron* and Mercury in *Valiant*. He narrated *The Tigger Movie*.

Hurt, William Actor; appeared in *The Doctor* (Jack), *Tuck Everlasting* (Angus Tuck), and *The Village* (Edward Walker).

Hurter, Albert (1883–1941) Sketch artist; joined Disney in 1932. He was given the freedom to come up with ideas, and he made distinctive contributions to many Disney films from *Three Little Pigs* to *Snow White and the Seven Dwarfs*. In 1953, Walt Disney wrote about him, "That impenetrable mind of his was never easily fig-ured out, but he was a most lovable character when you got to know him. His imagination was rare and unique." A book featuring a selection of his drawings was published in 1948, entitled *He Drew as He Pleased*.

Hussein, King of Jordan He visited Disneyland with Walt Disney in April 1959 and again with his wife in November 1981.

Huston, Angelica Actress; appeared in *The Royal Tenenbaums* (Etheline Tenenbaum) and *The Life Aquatic with Steve Zissou* (Eleanor Zissou), and in the Disney parks as the Witch Queen in *Captain Eo*.

Hutton, Timothy Actor; appeared in *Playing God* (Raymond Blossom), and on television in *Sultan and the Rock Star*.

Huxley, Aldous (1894–1963) Prominent author, he was retained by Walt in 1945 to write a film treatment of *Alice in Wonderland*.

Hyacinth Hippo Hippo dancer in the *Dance of the Hours* segment of *Fantasia*.

Hyperion Disney publishing company; published its first book, *Amazing Grace*, on September 26, 1991. Hyperion's catalog has been quite varied, with adult fiction, biographies, cookbooks, travel guides, and sports titles, as well as a number of Disney-themed publications. In 1999, Disney Editions took over as the imprint of the Disney-themed adult books.

Hyperion Studio The Disney brothers moved their Studio from the original Kingswell Avenue location to 2719 Hyperion in Los Angeles in January 1926, and named it The Walt Disney Studio.

Over the years, a number of buildings were constructed to house Walt Disney's growing staff. It was at the Hyperion Studio that Mickey Mouse was born and *Snow White and the Seven Dwarfs* was produced. But, with the success of *Snow White*, the Disneys needed more space to increase production and none was available at that location. So, they searched for a new site, which they found in Burbank. They moved from Hyperion to Burbank around January 1, 1940. The move was completed on May 6, 1940. A few of the Hyperion buildings had been moved to Burbank, but the remainder were sold, and 26 years later they were razed for a supermarket.

Hyperion Theater Two thousand–seat theater in the Hollywood Pictures Backlot at Disney's California Adventure. Inspired by the great movie palaces of the past, the theater features the latest in sound, lighting, and staging technology. The theater opened with the park on February 8, 2001, with its first show being a Broadway-style compilation of Disney songs entitled *Steps in Time*. This show was followed on November 22, 2001, by *The Power of Blast!* and on December 9, 2002, by *Aladdin: A Musical Spectacular*.

I Captured the King of the Leprechauns (television) Television show; aired on May 29, 1959. Directed by Robert Stevenson and Harry Keller. A behind-the-scenes look at the filming of *Darby O'Gill and the Little People*, starring Pat O'Brien and Walt Disney. Walt Disney really proves himself an actor in this show. He learns about Irish traditions and customs from O'Brien, then heads to Ireland where he meets King Brian of the Leprechauns and Darby O'Gill. He loves their stories so much, he invites them back to California to star in his movie.

I Love Trouble (film) Sabrina Peterson, a cub reporter on a Chicago newspaper, has a resourcefulness and quick wit matched only by her competitive spirit, which spells trouble for seasoned columnist-turned-novelist Peter Brackett who works for a rival paper. They try to outwit and outscoop each other when they are both sent to cover a train wreck, where they unearth evidence of corruption and murder. Running into each other everywhere they turn, they nearly get themselves killed scrambling for the ultimate front-page story. Along the way, they gain new respect, and love, for each other. Released on June 29, 1994. Directed by Charles Shyer. A Touchstone film, in association with Caravan Pictures. 123 min. Stars Julia Roberts (Sabrina Peterson), Nick Nolte (Peter Brackett), Saul Rubinek (Sam

Smotherman), Robert Loggia (Matt Greenfield), James Rebhorn (The Thin Man), Olympia Dukakis (Jeannie), Marsha Mason (Sen. Gayle Robbins), Charles Martin Smith (Rick Medwick). Filmed in Wisconsin, Chicago, Las Vegas, and Los Angeles. Released on video in 1994.

I Wan'na Be Like You Song from *The Jungle Book*; written by Richard M. Sherman and Robert B. Sherman.

Iago Jafar's loud-mouthed parrot henchman in *Aladdin*; voiced by Gilbert Gottfried.

Ice Princess (film) Casey Carlyle, a brainy bookworm, gives up a life devoted to schoolwork for a thrilling new world of ice skating. After deciding to do a report on the physics of figure skating, she gets to meet the elite skaters at her local rink. It turns out that Casey's smarts have helped her become a skating prodigy. She gets a chance to train with champion-in-the-making Gen Harwood and her famously tough coach and mother, Tina, and soon sets off on a fun, comedic, and life-changing adventure as she prepares for the big championship. At the same time, she gets her first taste of romance as she falls for Gen's teenage brother, Teddy, the rink's hunky Zamboni driver. Released on March 18, 2005. Directed by Tim Fywell. Stars Michelle Trachtenberg (Casey

Carlyle), Hayden Panettiere (Gen Harwood), Trevor Blumas (Teddy Harwood), Joan Cusack (Joan Carlyle), Kim Cattrall (Tina Harwood). Michelle Kwan and Brian Boitano have cameo roles. 98 min.

Ice shows See World on Ice.

Ichabod Crane Gangly schoolmaster hero in *The Adventures of Ichabod and Mr. Toad.*

Ida, the Offbeat Eagle (television) Television show; aired on January 10, 1965. In Idaho's Snake River Valley, a hermit nurses an injured eagle back to life, and the grateful eagle does not forget this. Eventually she is called upon to save the hermit. Stars Clifton E. Carver.

If I Didn't Have You Song from *Monsters, Inc.*, by Randy Newman. It won the Oscar as Best Song for 2001.

If I'm Lyin' . . . I'm Dyin' (A Program About Smoking) (film) Educational film; released in November 1990. 17 min. Teens learn myths about smoking, develop resistance skills, and discover the effects of smoking on the body.

If Not for You (television) Half hour television series, debuted on CBS on September 18, 1995, and ended October 9, 1995. Jessie Kent and Craig Schaeffer fall in love, but they are each engaged to other people. The series follows the trials and tribulations of their attempts to extricate themselves from their present relationships. Stars Elizabeth McGovern (Jessie), Hank Azaria (Craig), Debra Jo Rupp (Eileen), Jim Turner (Cal), Reno Wilson (Bobby).

If the Fergi Fits, Wear It (film) Educational film teaching free enterprise principles, produced by Dave Bell, released in September 1975. Young people attempt to run a T-shirt business. See also *Fergi Goes Inc., Fergi Diversifies*, and *Fergi Meets the Challenge.*

If You Could Fly Tomorrowland attraction in Magic Kingdom Park at Walt Disney World,

from June 6, 1987, until January 3, 1989, sponsored by Delta. When Delta replaced Eastern as sponsor of this attraction, they temporarily changed If You Had Wings by giving it this new name and dropping references to Eastern. As soon as they could, Disney Imagineers working with Delta came up with the totally new attraction, Delta Dreamflight, which opened in 1989.

If You Had Wings Tomorrowland attraction in Magic Kingdom Park at Walt Disney World sponsored by Eastern Airlines, from June 5, 1972, until June 1, 1987. Guests were transported past exhibits, many of them utilizing film clips, showing areas serviced by Eastern. Replaced by If You Could Fly when Delta became the sponsor, and later Delta Dreamflight.

Iger, Robert A. He became president and chief operating officer of The Walt Disney Company in January 2000. He had been chairman of the ABC Group and president of Walt Disney International, and prior to that was president of ABC. On March 13, 2005, the company announced that he would take over as CEO on October 1, 2005.

Ikspiari Shopping, dining, and entertainment area adjacent to Tokyo Disneyland; opened July 7, 2000.

Il Bel Cristallo Shop in Italy in World Showcase at Epcot; opened on October 1, 1982. Sells

fine Venetian glassware, Capodimonte florals and figurines, and gifts.

I'll Be Home for Christmas (film) Jake Wilkinson, a self-absorbed prep school student, finds himself, just days before Christmas, stranded in the middle of the California desert, wearing a Santa suit and a white beard glued to his face. Put there by the football team who thinks he double-crossed them by not providing the correct answers on a finals test, Jake has to find a way to get to New York by 6:00 P.M. on Christmas Eve, or risk forfeiting the vintage Porsche his father promised if his son comes home for the holidays. Hitchhiking his way east, Jake finds people looking to Santa for help and advice. Directed by Arlene Sanford. Released on November 13, 1998. Stars Jonathan Taylor Thomas (Jake Wilkinson), Jessica Biel (Allie), Adam La Vorgna (Eddie), Gary Cole (Harry Wilkinson), Sean O'Bryan (Max), Eve Gordon (Carolyn), Andy Lauer (Nolan Briggs). 86 min. Principal photography took place in Canmore, Alberta, Canada, and at locations around Vancouver, B.C., which doubled for several American towns Jake visits on his cross-country trek. Artificial snow had to be utilized to create a winter landscape in the spring. Additional photography took place at various locations in California, including Red Rock Canyon State Park, the desert east of Lancaster, and the campus of Mount St. Mary's College in Brentwood. Released on video in 1999.

IllumiNations Fireworks, lasers, fountains, and music show at Epcot, beginning on January 30, 1988. Superseded Laserphonic Fantasy. General Electric sponsors this nightly show, during which different pavilions of World Showcase are individually spotlighted, accompanied by music associated with that particular country. Lasers synchronized to music blast from the tops of many of the buildings across the lagoon. The climactic fireworks and triumphant symphonic music provide a thrilling end to a day at Epcot. A special new version of the show, called IllumiNations 25, was created for the 25th anniversary of Walt Disney World in 1996–97. Another version, IllumiNations 2000: Reflections of Earth, was introduced October 1, 1999, for the millennium, and it continued thereafter, dropping the "2000" from its title. General Electric ended sponsorship on December 31, 2002.

I'm Going to Disney World In 1987, following up on a suggestion by Michael Eisner's wife, Jane, Tom Elrod and his Walt Disney World marketing staff came up with the idea of asking quarterback Phil Simms on camera as he ran off the field, "Now that you've won the Super Bowl, what are you going to do next?" "I'm going to Disney World!" was the reply. Thus began a popular series of television commercials that has continued for over a decade and a half. Besides the stars of each ensuing Super Bowl, subjects have included champions from other sports, such as baseball, basketball, and the Olympics, and even included Miss America in 1988 and a group of college graduates in 1990. Almost every commercial has been filmed twice; once for Walt Disney World, and once for Disneyland.

I'm Late Song from *Alice in Wonderland*, written by Bob Hilliard and Sammy Fain.

I'm No Fool as a Pedestrian (film) Cartoon made for the *Mickey Mouse Club* and later released, in October 1956, in 16mm for schools. Jiminy Cricket relates the history of reckless driving from 3000 B.C. to the present, then explains how to walk properly and with safety, showing the problems faced by the pedestrian. He presents safety rules. An updated version was released in September 1988.

I'm No Fool Having Fun (film) Cartoon made for the *Mickey Mouse Club* and later released, in April 1957, in 16mm for schools. Jiminy Cricket stresses the importance of recreation and points out safety rules to be observed when having fun.

I'm No Fool in a Car (film) Educational video released in April 1992, 15 min. An alien falls to Earth when he unfastens the safety belt in his spaceship; on Earth he learns the importance of car safety.

I'm No Fool in an Emergency (film) Educational video release in April 1992. 13 min. A patrol officer trying to capture an alien sustains an injury, and two kids calmly handle the situation by calling the paramedics.

I'm No Fool in Unsafe Places (film) Educational release in 16mm in January 1991 (14 min.); videodisc version (28 min.) released in March 1993. Pinocchio becomes a real boy, but he must learn how to be safe in the real world, and not to play in refrigerators or at construction sites.

I'm No Fool in Unsafe Places II (film) Educational release on video in April 1992. 15 min. Two kids try to keep an alien safe and away from hazardous sites.

I'm No Fool in Water (film) Cartoon made for the *Mickey Mouse Club* and later released, in April 1957, in 16mm for schools. Jiminy Cricket summarizes the rules for water safety and shows how one should behave while swimming. Updated version released in September 1987.

I'm No Fool on Wheels (film) Educational release in 16mm in January 1991 (13 min.); videodisc version (25 min.) released in March 1993. Pinocchio's friends teach him the vital procedures and equipment that need to be used for roller skating, bicycling, and skateboarding.

I'm No Fool With a Bicycle (film) Cartoon made for the *Mickey Mouse Club* and later released, in April 1956, in 16mm for schools. A novel contest between Y-O-U and a Common Ordinary Fool that serves to point up basic bicycle safety rules. Jiminy Cricket gives a brief history of this unique transportation vehicle. An updated version was released in September 1988.

I'm No Fool With Electricity (film) Educational film, released in October 1973. Jiminy Cricket explains the basic rules of electrical safety, with information about the discovery of electricity and the uses to which man has put it. An updated version was released in September 1988.

I'm No Fool With Fire (film) Cartoon made for the *Mickey Mouse Club* and later released, in April 1956, in 16mm for schools. Jiminy Cricket shows humankind's reliance on fire through the ages and the necessity of understanding the rules pertaining to fire safety because of its potentially destructive nature. An updated version was released in September 1986.

I'm No Fool With Safety at School (film) Educational release in 16mm in January 1991 (12 min.); videodisc version (28 min.) released in March 1993. Jiminy Cricket and Pinocchio join elementary school students to learn about safety at school.

Image Works Hands-on area of Journey into Imagination at Epcot; opened October 1, 1982. Guests can experience a multitude of activities, from the Rainbow Corridor (neon tubes of all of the colors of the rainbow surround you) to the Stepping Tones (compose your own symphony by stepping on lighted spots on the floor causing various tones to sound). Image Works closed in October 1998, to reopen on October 1, 1999, as ImageWorks—The Kodak "What If?" Labs.

IMAGINATION! See *Journey Into Imagination*.

Imagine That (television) Half-hour comedy series on NBC about the life of a sketch comedy writer. Premiered on January 8, 2002, and ended January 15. Stars Hank Azaria (Josh Miller), Jayne Brook (Wendy), Joshua Malina (Kenny), Katey Sagal (Barb). Produced by Columbia TriStar Television, Seth Kurland Productions, and Touchstone Television.

Imagineers Term used by Disney to refer to the designers, engineers, architects, technicians, and others involved in creating the Disney theme park experiences. It is taken from the words *imagination* and *engineers*. At first their company was known as WED Enterprises (Walt Disney's initials), but it was changed to Walt Disney Imagineering in 1986.

I-Man (television) Two-hour television show; meant as a pilot for a possible series, aired on

April 6, 1986. Directed by Corey Allen. A cab driver, Jeffrey Wilder, is exposed to a mysterious gas that makes him invincible; the government realizes they can use him, and he reluctantly agrees. Jeffrey needs to use his powers to battle an eccentric billionaire, who has stolen a group of experimental military lasers that the government realizes are defective and could cause an atomic explosion. Stars Scott Bakula, Ellen Bry, Joey Cramer, John Bloom, Herschel Bernardi, John Anderson.

Impeachment of a President (film) Educational film in the *History Alive!* series, produced by Turnley Walker, released in 1972. Thaddeus Stevens leads the attempt to impeach President Andrew Johnson in 1868.

Impressions de France (film) Film highlighting the scenery of France against a background of music by the French classical composers, for the France pavilion, World Showcase, Epcot; opened on October 1, 1982.

In a Clock Store Copyright title of *The Clock Store*.

In a Heartbeat (television) Disney Channel original half-hour series about a volunteer EMT squad staffed by high school students. Premiered with a one-hour episode on August 26, 2000, and ended March 25, 2001. Stars Shawn Ashmore (Tyler Connell), Reagan Pasternak (Val Lanier), Danso Gordon (Hank Beecham), Christopher Ralph (Jamie Waite), Jackie Rosenbaum (Caitie Roth), Lauren Collins (Brooke Lanier). 21 episodes.

In Beaver Valley See *Beaver Valley*.

In Dutch (film) Pluto cartoon; released on May 10, 1946. Directed by Charles Nichols. Pluto and Dinah fool the villagers with a false flood alarm in Holland, but when the dike does begin to leak, it is up to Pluto to get help while Dinah plugs the leak with her paw. Because of "crying wolf," he has a difficult time.

In Justice (television) One-hour drama series; premiered on ABC on January 1, 2006. Every year, hundreds of innocent men and women are convicted of crimes they did not commit. The innocent have finally found a champion in a blustery but legendary litigator named David Swayne. Swayne is head of the Justice Project, a high-profile, non-profit organization made up of hungry young associates who fight to liberate the falsely accused and discover the identify of those really to blame. Swayne is ego driven, but he has a partner, crackerjack investigator and ex-cop Charles Conti, to keep him honest. Stars Jason O'Mara (Charles Conti), Kyle MacLachlan (David Swayne), Constance Zimmer (Brianna), Daniel Cosgrove (Jon), Larissa Gomes (Tina). From Touchstone Television.

In Search of the Castaways (film) With good reason to believe that Captain Grant, skipper of the S.S. *Brittania*, is still alive, Lord Glenarvan, owner of the Steam Navigation Company, sets out to rescue him. Aboard his ship are Grant's daughter and son as well as their companion, a Frenchman named Jacques Paganel. A series of hair-raising incidents as they travel the 37th parallel, including surviving an earthquake, flood, and attack by a giant condor, adds up to exciting adventure. In Australia, they team up with a former member of Grant's crew, Thomas Ayerton, who turns out to be a gunrunner who had set Grant adrift. Eventually, in New Zealand, the children manage to outwit him and rescue Grant. From the Jules Verne story. World premiere in London on November 14, 1962; U.S. release on December 19, 1962. Directed by Robert Stevenson. 98 min. Stars Hayley Mills (Mary Grant), Maurice Chevalier (Prof. Paganel), George Sanders (Thomas

Ayerton), Wilfred Hyde-White (Lord Glenarvan), Michael Anderson, Jr. (John Glenarvan). Young Keith Hamshire, who plays Hayley Mills's younger brother, Robert, was discovered by Disney talent agents while playing the title role in the original London production of the well-known musical *Oliver*. The film contained some of the most elaborate special effects of any Disney film to that time, with the set designers building a live volcano, part of the Andes Mountains, reproductions of the ports of Glasgow and Melbourne from the 1870s, along with a complete New Zealand Maori village. All of this was accomplished at Pinewood Studios in England. The special effects team was headed by Syd Pearson and Peter Ellenshaw. The songs, "Merci Beaucoup," "Grimpons," "Enjoy It," and "The Castaways Theme," were written by Richard M. Sherman and Robert B. Sherman. The film was re-released theatrically in 1970 and 1978 and released on video in 1984 and 1992.

In Shape with Von Drake (television) Television show; aired on March 22, 1964. Directed by Hamilton S. Luske. Prof. Von Drake expounds on sports, utilizing a series of cartoons.

In the Army Now (film) Bones Conway is not ideal Army material, but that doesn't stop him from joining up for a hitch in the Reserves in order to cash in on all the great perks, including free room and board and a steady salary for doing minimal work. He manages to bluff his way through basic training, but is then shocked to find his unit called up for service in the African desert. He ends up not only battling the rules and regulations, but also power-hungry authority figures and would-be world dictators. Released on August 12, 1994. Directed by Daniel Petrie, Jr. A Hollywood Pictures film. 92 min. Stars Pauly Shore (Bones Conway), Lori Petty (Christine Jones), David Alan Grier (Fred Ostroff), Andy Dick (Jack Kaufman), Esai Morales (Sgt. Stern). Filmed on locations in California and Arizona, and at Fort Sill, Oklahoma. Released on video in 1995.

In the Bag (film) Special cartoon; released on July 27, 1956. Directed by Jack Hannah. Filmed

in CinemaScope. The Ranger enlists the park's bears to help clean up, under threat of starvation, and in desperation all the bears shove the trash in Humphrey's sector. Humphrey stuffs it down a geyser hole, and just as he is about to be rewarded with a meal, the geyser erupts, sending garbage everywhere.

In the Land of the Desert Whales (television) Television show; part 2 of *Three Without Fear*.

In the Nick of Time (television) Television movie on NBC (two hours) on December 16, 1991. Directed by George Miller. Santa Claus has only seven days to find his replacement, or Christmas will end forever. He roams the icy streets of New York City in search of the one generous soul destined to be the next Kris Kringle. Stars Lloyd Bridges (Nick), Michael Tucker (Ben Talbot), Alison LaPlaca (Susan Roswell), Jessica DiCicco (Aimee Misch), A Martinez (Charlie Misch), Cleavon Little (Freddy).

Inbetweener Animation term for the artist who creates the drawings in between the extremes of an action drawn by the animator, assistant animator, and breakdown artist.

Incident at Hawk's Hill (film) Educational film version of part of *The Boy Who Talked to Badgers*; released in September 1979.

Inconceivable (television) One-hour drama series airing on NBC, beginning September 23, 2005. Doctors at the Family Options Fertility Clinic follow a noble quest as they help desperate couples give birth. Clinic cofounders Dr. Malcolm Bower and Rachel Lew, and their staff, are not above their own adventures involving sex, deception, and secrets, while they cope with superegos, missing frozen embryos, and impending malpractice suits. Stars Jonathan Cake (Dr. Malcolm Bower), Ming-Na (Rachel Lew), Joelle Carter (Nurse Patrice), Mary Catherine Garrison (Marissa), David Norona (Scott), Davin Alejandro (Angel). From Touchstone Television.

Incredible Journey, The (film) Story of the 200-mile trek across the wilds of Canada by three inseparable animal friends in search of their beloved owners, a family who has gone to Europe, leaving the animals with a friend. After hardship, danger, and near-fatal accidents, together with some moving encounters with friendly humans, the two dogs, Bodger and Luath, and a cat, Tao, complete their incredible journey, and have a joyful reunion with their owners, who have returned from their own journey and have come to believe their beloved pets to be dead. Released on  October 30, 1963. Directed by Fletcher Markle. 80 min. Stars Emile Genest (John Longridge), John Drainie (Prof. Jim Hunter), Tommy Tweed (Hermit), Sandra Scott (Mrs. Hunter), with the film's narration provided by Rex Allen. Based on the best seller by Sheila Burnford, the film was reissued in 1969, and remade in 1993 as *Homeward Bound: The Incredible Journey*. Released on video in 1984 and 1994.

Incredibles, The (film) Bob Parr used to be one of the world's greatest superheroes, known to all as "Mr. Incredible," saving lives and fighting evil on a daily basis. But now, 15 years later, he and his wife, Helen, a former superhero in her own right, have been forced, because of a series of unfortunate accidents and frivolous lawsuits, to take on civilian identities and retreat to the suburbs to live normal lives with their three kids. As a clock-punching insurance claims adjuster, the only thing Bob fights these days is boredom and a bulging waistline. Itching to get back into action, the sidelined superhero gets his chance when a mysterious communication summons him to the remote island of Nomanisan for a top-secret assignment. When things go seriously awry, and Bob is taken prisoner by an evil genius named Syndrome, Helen and the kids fly to the rescue to help straighten things out. The whole family has to battle Syndrome and his seemingly unstop-

pable ominous Omnidroids. From Pixar Animation Studios. Directed by Brad Bird. Released on November 5, 2004. Voices include Craig T. Nelson (Bob Parr/Mr. Incredible), Holly Hunter (Helen Parr/Elastigirl), Samuel L. Jackson (Frozone), Wallace Shawn (Gilbert Huph), Jason Lee (Buddy Pine/Syndrome), Sarah Vowell (Violet), John Ratzenberger (The Underminer), Spencer Fox (Dash), Elizabeth Peña (Mirage), Brad Bird (Edna Mode). 115 min. Filmed in CinemaScope. Released with a Pixar short, *Boundin'*. *The Incredibles* won Academy Awards for Best Animated Feature and for Best Sound Editing (Randy Thom, Michael Silvers). It was also nominated for Best Original Screenplay (Brad Bird) and Best Sound Mixing (Randy Thom, Gary A. Rizzo, Doc Kane). Released on video in 2005.

Independence Lake In the 1970s, after the loss of the Mineral King project, Disney proposed another ski resort in the Sierra Nevada Mountains near Truckee, California. The land around the lake was jointly owned by the Southern Pacific Railroad and the U.S. government. Disney tried to arrange a land swap to put together a workable parcel of land, but nothing came of the project and Disney gave up thoughts of a ski resort.

Indian Canoes Attraction in Frontierland at Disneyland Paris; opened April 12, 1992, and closed in October 1994. For the Disneyland attraction, see Davy Crockett's Explorer Canoes.

Indian Summer (film) A group of adults hoping to relive childhood memories gather for a reunion at their former childhood summer camp, Tamakwa, but each comes with his own problems. Despite the group's efforts to simply relax, the rigorous camp activities, plus two decades of memories, trigger each of them to examine where their life choices have taken them, and to wonder if, perhaps, it is possible to come of age more than once. Released on April 23, 1993. Directed by Mike Bender. A Touchstone film. 98 min. Stars Alan Arkin (Unca Lou), Matt Craven (Jamie Ross), Diane Lane (Beth Warden), Bill Paxton (Jack Belston), Elizabeth Perkins (Jennifer Morton), Kevin Pollack (Brad Berman), Vincent Spano (Matthew

Berman), Julie Warner (Kathy Berman), Kimberly Williams (Gwen Dougherty). Filmed at the actual Camp Tamakwa in Algonquin Provincial Park, Ontario, Canada. Released on video in 1993.

Indian Trading Post Shop in Frontierland; opened July 4, 1962; later in Bear Country (1972) and changed to The Briar Patch in 1988 with the change of the area to Critter Country.

Indian Village Frontierland attraction at Disneyland; open from 1955 until 1971. It moved locations in 1956 and had additions in 1962. Native American dancers would put on regular shows, encouraging audience participation.

Indian War Canoes Frontierland attraction at Disneyland; from July 4, 1956, to 1971. Moved to Bear Country and became Davy Crockett's Explorer Canoes.

Indiana Jones Adventure Adventureland attraction at Disneyland; opened on March 3, 1995. Aboard a well-worn troop transport, guests embark on what appears to be a standard archeological tour through the Temple of the Forbidden Eye, but they find surprises around every bend in this subterranean world. Bubbling lava pits, crumbling ceilings, screaming mummies, and an avalanche of creepy crawlies are just a few of the exciting adventures guests experience. This attraction is a collaboration between George Lucas and Disney.

Indiana Jones Adventure: Temple of the Crystal Skull Attraction at Tokyo Disney-Sea in the Lost River Delta area; opened on September 4, 2001, sponsored by Matsushita. Guests board jungle transports to search for the Fountain of Youth in an ancient Central American temple guarded by a supernatural and vengeful Crystal Skull.

Indiana Jones and the Temple of Peril: Backwards! Roller coaster attraction in Adventureland at Disneyland Paris; opened July 30, 1993. In order to quickly add needed capacity at the park, designers selected a stock roller-coaster

attraction, but then added theming to make it into an exciting Disney experience. Beginning April 1, 2000, the roller coaster was operated backwards.

Indiana Jones Epic Stunt Spectacular Grand opening at Disney-MGM Studios on August 25, 1989. Thrilling stunts and special effects are presented by a trained cast, aided by a few volunteers from the audience, on a gigantic movie set.

Infant Care (film) Educational film. Produced under the auspices of the Coordinator of Inter-American Affairs. Delivered on July 31, 1945. Stresses the importance of proper pre-natal care, nursing, and weaning.

Inferior Decorator (film) Donald Duck cartoon; released on August 27, 1948. Directed by Jack Hannah. Don is hanging flowered wallpaper which fools a bee. The bee gets so irritated with Donald and the fake flowers that he must call in his swarm of bees to attack.

Infoseek Corp. On November 18, 1998, Disney announced the completion of the acquisition of approximately 43 percent of the outstanding common stock of Infoseek Corp. Combining with a previous Disney acquisition of Starwave Corp., the new Internet entity developed, launched, and promoted a new portal service named GO Network (www.go.com). On November 17, 1999, stockholders approved the acquisition of the remainder of Infoseek, which became a wholly-owned subsidiary of the company.

Ingersoll-Waterbury Co. First licensee of Disney watches, beginning in 1933. See also Watches.

Ingham, Barrie Actor; he voiced Basil in *The Great Mouse Detective.*

Inkwell, The (film) The ritzy resort island of Martha's Vineyard is a vacation haven where the rich relax at the famous Inkwell Beach and where, in 1976, 16-year-old African American Drew Tate is about to spend a summer holiday with wealthy relatives. There he learns to combat his shyness, meet members of the opposite sex, and come of age. Released on April 22, 1994. Directed by Matty Rich. A Touchstone film. 112 min. Stars Larenz Tate (Drew Tate), Joe Morton (Kenny Tate), Suzzanne Douglas (Brenda Tate), Glynn Turman (Spencer Phillips). To represent the resort of Martha's Vineyard in 1976, the producers went to North Carolina, using sites in Wilmington, Fort Fisher, Rocky Point, Surf City, Southport, and Swansboro. Released on video in 1994.

Inky, the Crow (television) Television show; aired on December 7, 1969. A girl, Carol Lee, adopts a mischievous crow, but has to work hard to keep it from being shot by a farmer who hates crows. Stars Deborah Bainbridge, Margo Lungreen, Willard Granger, Rowan Pease.

Innocent Man, An (film) When two ruthless, on-the-take narcotics cops mistake Jimmie Rainwood's home for that of a local drug dealer, they break in and shoot him before they realize they've busted the wrong man. Jimmie is convicted of a crime he did not commit and is sent to prison where he learns to survive with the help of veteran con, Virgil Cane. He is paroled, a changed man no longer trusting the system, and he vows to set the record straight and settle the score with the sleazy detectives whose lies put an innocent man behind bars for three years. Released on October 6, 1989. Directed by Peter Yates. A Touchstone film. 113 min. Stars Tom Selleck (Jimmie Rainwood), F. Murray Abraham (Virgil Cane), Leila Robins (Kate Rainwood). The filmmakers selected the Cincinnati "Old Workhouse" for the interior prison scenes, and the Nevada State Penitentiary in Carson City for the exteriors. Several hundred inmates at the latter institution were utilized as extras, though the decision was made to exclude those on death row or in solitary confinement. While they were working in the prison, all of the cast and crew were required to wear oversized fluorescent orange vests to distinguish them from the prisoners. Released on video in 1990.

Innoventions New technology display area taking the place of Communicore at Epcot, opened July 1, 1994. A selection of America's top companies were invited to display some of their latest gizmos and technologies, with interactive participation by guests. The exhibits continually change to keep the area new and exciting. Walt Disney Imagineering included its own display of virtual reality prototypes. An Innoventions attraction opened at Disneyland, in the former Carousel of

Progress building, on July 3, 1998, with grand opening ceremonies on November 10.

Insects as Carriers of Disease (film) Educational film. Produced under the auspices of the Coordinator of Inter-American Affairs. Delivered on June 30, 1945. Careless Charlie learns to his horror how household pests such as flies, mosquitoes, and lice carry dangerous diseases, and that cleanliness of food, body, and living conditions can prevent them.

Inside Donald Duck (television) Television show; aired on November 5, 1961. Directed by Hamilton S. Luske. Professor Von Drake tries to diagnose Donald's problems, deciding that the cause is the opposite sex. The show includes clips from a series of Donald Duck cartoons.

Inside Out See *Walt Disney World Inside Out.*

Inside Outer Space (television) Television show; aired on February 10, 1963. Directed by Hamilton S. Luske. Ludwig Von Drake takes a look at outer space, using footage from the Disney space shows of the 1950s such as *Man in Space* and *Mars and Beyond*.

Inside the Magic: Special Effects and Production Tour See *Backstage Studio Tour*.

Insider, The (film) Jeffrey Wigand was a central witness in the lawsuits filed by Mississippi and all 49 other states against the tobacco industry, which eventually were settled for $246 billion. Wigand, former head of research and development and a corporate officer at Brown & Williamson, was a top scientist, the ultimate insider. No one like him had ever gone public before. Meanwhile, Lowell Bergman, investigative reporter and *60 Minutes* producer, arranged a legal defense team for Wigand and taped a famous Mike Wallace interview that contained devastating testimony. However, before *60 Minutes'* most newsworthy segment in years could air, Bergman lost a CBS corporate decision to kill the piece causing bitter divisions within *60 Minutes*. Wigand would find himself sued, targeted in a national smear campaign, divorced, and facing possible incarceration. Wigand, having wagered so much and now unable to deliver his testimony to the American people, and Bergman, trying to defeat the smear campaign and force CBS to air the interview, were ordinary people in extraordinary circumstances. Released on November 5, 1999. A Touchstone Picture. Directed by Michael Mann. Stars Al Pacino (Lowell Bergman), Russell Crowe (Jeffrey Wigand), Christopher Plummer (Mike Wallace), Diane Venora (Liane Vigand), Philip Baker Hall (Don Hewitt), Lindsay Crouse (Sharon Tiller), Debi Mazar (Debbie De Luca). Based on the *Vanity Fair* article, "The Man Who Knew Too Much," by Marie Brenner. 158 min. Filmed in CinemaScope. While *The Insider* is not a documentary, Mississippi's aggressive attorney general, Michael Moore, and investigator Jack Palladino do play themselves, lending a sense of reality to the drama. Filming locations ranged from Louisville, Kentucky, to San Francisco, to

Pascagoula, Mississippi, to New York, and to the Bahamas. The film received seven Academy Award nominations including Best Picture and Best Actor (Russell Crowe). Released on video in 2000.

Insignias During World War II, Walt Disney was asked by various military units to design insignias that they could put on their planes, jackets, and ships. Over 1,200 of these insignias were produced, many containing Disney characters, but occasionally, as with the Flying Tigers, the units already had a character in mind. Donald Duck was perhaps the most requested character, appearing on several hundred insignias. Mickey Mouse, being a less-warlike figure, was used only rarely, and then for such units as signal corps and chaplains corps. The drawings were prepared by several Disney artists, led by Hank Porter and Roy Williams. Walt provided these insignias to the units without charge as part of his donation to the war effort. Other animation studios in Hollywood were also called upon for insignias, and during the war, many of the Disney and non-Disney insignias were published on poster stamps for affixing in albums supplied by local newspapers.

Inspector Gadget (film) A mild-mannered security officer, John Brown, is blown to pieces by a nefarious villain, but is then rebuilt into a resourceful detective by the beautiful scientist Brenda Bradford. Fourteen thousand useful and handy devices are stored all over his body, making Inspector Gadget a virtual human Swiss army knife, and helping inspire him to become the world's top detective. When faced with the insanely wealthy and evil Sanford Scolex, the often clueless Gadget must use all his common sense and robotic parts to save not only his good name but the world as well. A Walt Disney Picture in association with Caravan Pictures. Directed by David Kellogg. Released on July 23, 1999. Stars Matthew Broderick (John Brown/ Inspector Gadget), Rupert Everett (Sanford Scolex), Joely Fisher (Brenda Bradford), Michelle Trachtenberg (Penny). 78 min. Based on the animated series produced by DIC Entertainment. Released on video in 1999.

Inspector Gadget 2 (film) Direct-to-video sequel. In idyllic Riverton, the evildoer Dr. Claw escapes from jail and plots to steal trillions of dollars worth of gold. After half-human, half-robot Inspector Gadget is taken off the case because of glitches in his machinery, he is replaced by the gorgeous and superior G2. Released on March 11, 2003. Directed by Alex Zamm. Stars French Stewart (Inspector Gadget), Elaine Hendrix (G2), Tony Martin (Dr. Claw), Bruce Spence (Baxter), Caitlin Wachs (Penny), Mark Mitchell (Chief Quimby), Sigrid Thornton (Mayor Wilson), John Batchelor (McKible), James Wardlaw (Brick). Filmed in Brisbane, Australia.

Instinct (film) A brilliant young psychiatrist, Theo Caulder, must unlock the secrets within the mind of Dr. Ethan Powell, an anthropologist who lived in the wilds for three years with a family of mountain gorillas. Dr. Powell, who has not spoken in years, has discovered a secret that could alter the future of mankind, but before his knowledge can be revealed, the psychiatrist must learn the truth behind a homicidal attack in the jungles of Rwanda of which the doctor stands accused, and for which he is now held captive in a brutal prison for the criminally insane. Directed by Jon Turtletaub. A Touchstone picture from Spyglass Entertainment. Inspired by the novel, *Ishmael*, by Daniel Quinn. Released on June 4, 1999. Stars Anthony Hopkins (Ethan Powell), Cuba Gooding, Jr. (Theo Caulder), Donald Sutherland (Ben Hillard), Maura Tierney (Lyn Powell), George Dzundza (John Murray). 126 min. CinemaScope. Jamaica substituted for Rwanda in the filming; other filming took place in Wisconsin, Orlando, and Los Angeles. Released on video in 1999.

Inter-Governmental Philatelic Corp. Producer of postage stamps for small countries all over the world, received the license to use Disney characters on stamps beginning in 1979. See also Stamps.

International Gateway Entrance into Epcot from the Yacht and Beach Club hotel area; opened on January 12, 1990. With the building of these two new hotels, as well as the Swan and Dolphin, and eventually the BoardWalk Inn, an entrance was opened into World Showcase, so that hotel guests could easily approach Epcot by foot, boat, or tram without having to go all the way around to the other side of the park.

Introduction to Aesop, An (film) Retitled educational film, originally released as *Aesop's Hare and the Tortoise.*

Introduction to Hans Christian Andersen, An (film) Retitled educational film originally released as *Hans Christian Andersen's The Ugly Duckling.*

Invincible (film) Directed by Ericson Core. Stars Mark Wahlberg, Greg Kinnear, Elizabeth Banks, Kirk Acevedo. Began filming in Philadelphia on July 27, 2005.

Irish in America, The: Long Journey Home (television) six-hour miniseries produced and directed by Thomas Lennon in collaboration with the Walt Disney Studios and WGBH Boston for PBS, aired on January 26–28, 1998. Released concurrently on video. The series chronicles the triumphant role that the Irish have played in shaping America, beginning with the potato famine and continuing to the White House. This project was close to the heart of Roy E. Disney, whose great-grandfather was one of the Irish immigrants.

Iron Will (film) In 1917, young Will Stoneman's life is turned upside down when his father is killed. Jack Stoneman had planned a bright future for his son, including sending him to college. In order to win a $10,000 prize needed to save the family from financial ruin, the courageous young man and his loyal team of sled dogs embark on a treacherous cross-country race, on a 522-mile course from Winnipeg to St. Paul. Nothing in his imagination could prepare him for the perilous trek, however, and his survival depends on the strength and courage of his faithful team of dogs, led by the stalwart Gus. Exhausted and numb from the arduous journey, Will must find the tenacity to persevere against impossible odds, while it seems the whole world is cheering him on through newspaper bulletins sent in by an enterprising reporter, Harry Kingsley, keeping up with the racers by train. Despite the harsh weather and terrain, and the threat of a dangerous opponent, Borg Guillarson, Will wins the race. Released on January 14, 1994. Directed by Charles Haid. 109 min. Stars Mackenzie Astin (Will Stoneman), Kevin Spacey (Harry Kingsley), David Ogden Stiers (J.P. Harper), George Gerdes (Borg Guillarson), John Terry (Jack Stoneman). Based on a true story. Principal photography took place in Duluth and the surrounding area in Minnesota, and the neighboring state of Wisconsin. The vintage 1913 steam engine that figures so prominently in the film was borrowed from the Lake Superior Museum of Transportation. Released on video in 1994.

Irons, Jeremy Actor; provided the voice of Scar in *The Lion King*, and appeared on The Disney Channel in *Danny, the Champion of the World* (William Smith). Beginning in 1994, he narrated the Spaceship Earth attraction at Epcot. He appeared in *Casanova* (Bishop Pucci).

Irvine, Dick (1910–1976) He worked as an art director at Disney in the 1940s, then returned in 1953 to head the team of designers, artists, architects, and engineers in planning and developing Disneyland. He headed WED Enterprises and until his retirement in 1973 continued to be in charge of planning and design for all park and World's Fair projects. He received a Disney Legends award in 1990. See also *Richard F. Irvine* Riverboat.

Ising, Rudolf (1903–1992) Friend of Walt Disney's in Kansas City who joined him in the Laugh-O-gram Films studio. At Disney's request, he left Kansas City to come to California and work at the new Walt Disney Studio on the Alice Comedies and Oswald the Lucky Rabbit cartoons. Later he joined up with Hugh Harman to produce the Harman-Ising cartoons at MGM.

Island at the Top of the World, The (film) In 1907, a wealthy Englishman, Sir Anthony, commands a giant airship as it searches the Arctic for his missing son. The only clues they have are a page from an old Hudson's Bay Company journal mentioning a hidden island "far beyond land's end where the whales go to die," and a curious map of carved whalebone. The crew discover a volcanic Nordic island, a fabled whales' graveyard, and encounter Viking warriors who are far from friendly. Sir Anthony is reunited with his son Donald whose sweetheart, Freyja, helps them escape a death decree. Recaptured after a battle with killer whales, the fugitives are finally given their freedom in exchange for an American professor remaining behind as hostage. Premiered on December 16, 1974, in England; U.S. release on December 20, 1974. Directed by Robert Stevenson. 94 min. Stars David Hartman (Prof. Ivarsson), Don-

ald Sinden (Sir Anthony Ross), Jacques Marin (Capt. Brieux), Mako (Oomiak), David Gwillim (Donald Ross), Agneta Eckemyr (Freyja), Gunnar Ohlund (The Godi), Lasse Kolstad (Erik), Niels Hinrichsen (Sigurd), Brendan Dillon (The Factor). Based on *The Lost Ones* by Ian Cameron. With music composed by Maurice Jarre and spectacular special effects by Peter Ellenshaw, Art Cruickshank, and Danny Lee, this lavish film was filmed on locations spanning the Arctic Circle from Alaska to Greenland to Norway. The large budget allowed creation of the airship *Hyperion*, a 220-foot motor-driven tapered dirigible; a complete Viking village with a temple of lava rock; 850 feet of coconut-fiber rope, handmade in Egypt, to hold up a suspension bridge; and a Viking longship to be used on location in Balestrand, Norway. The film was not a box office success, but was nominated for an Academy Award for Art Direction/Set Direction by Peter Ellenshaw, John B. Mansbridge, Walter Tyler, Al Roelofs, and Hal Gausman. Released on video in 1983 and 1994.

Island Mercantile Shop on Discovery Island at Disney's Animal Kingdom; opened April 22, 1998.

Islands of the Sea (film) Documentary featurette; released on March 16, 1960. Produced by Ben Sharpsteen. A nature film concentrating on the strange and wonderful birds, beasts, and fish found in and around the least known islands of the world. Included are the Galapagos, the Guadalupes, the Falklands, and the tiny islands and atolls of the Midway group. 28 min. Nominated for an Academy Award.

Isozaki, Arata Architect; designed the futuristic Team Disney building at Walt Disney World.

It Runs in the Family (film) Buena Vista International handled the foreign distribution and MGM the domestic distribution of this film from Further Films. Three generations of an American family, living separate lives, each in their own dysfuctional way, comes together every once in a while to laugh, to fight, to cry, and to care for each other. Directed by Frank Schepisi. U.S. release on April 25, 2003. Stars Michael Douglas (Alex Gromberg), Kirk Douglas (Mitchell Gromberg), Bernadette Peters (Rebecca), Diana Douglas (Evelyn), Cameron Douglas (Asher), Rory Culkin (Eli). Kirk Douglas is Michael's father, Diana Douglas his mother, and Cameron Douglas his son. Michael produced the film, with his brother, Joel, as co-producer.

Italia '61 (film) Circarama film prepared in 1961 for the Italia '61 Exposition in Turin, under sponsorship of Fiat; features a tour of Italy with spectacular views of the harbor at Genoa, and Mount Vesuvius. The Italian film crew was taught use of the cameras by Don Iwerks, son of Disney animator and special effects magician Ub Iwerks.

Italy Pavilion in World Showcase at Epcot; opened October 1, 1982. Disney designers carefully studied Italian architecture, and determined that their pavilion should have the look of Venice. A small island gives the impression of the canals. One can sometimes even get the feeling that he is actually in St. Mark's Square, with the Doge's Palace, statues of Neptune and St. Mark the Evangelist, and the Campanile being smaller versions of their models. In the square, a troupe of actors renowned for their broad comedy, Il Commedia di Bologna, frequently inveigles passersby to put aside their fears of embarrassment and join in the hilarious 15-minute pageants. The pavilion's attractions are its several shops selling Italian arts and crafts, and the fine Alfredo's restaurant.

It's a Small World Fantasyland attraction at Disneyland; opened on May 28, 1966, having been moved from the 1964–65 New York World's Fair. Sponsored by the Bank of America from 1966 to 1992 and by Mattel from 1992 to 1999. Richard M. Sherman and Robert B. Sherman, who won two Oscars for their music for *Mary Poppins*, were asked by Walt to come up with a simple piece that could be repeated over and over, sung in different languages, as guests passed through the attraction in boats. The resulting song became one of the best known Disney tunes of all time. Audio-Animatronics was used for 297 children and 256 toys in stylized settings representing over a hundred regions of the world. As in most of the Disney attractions, there is way too much to see in one visit; each time you go through you catch something new and different. At Disneyland, the facade is almost as impressive as the interior attraction. A huge ticking clock is the centerpiece, and every 15 minutes brings a parade of characters marching around it. Also a Fantasyland attraction in Magic Kingdom Park at Walt Disney World, opened October 1, 1971; in Fantasyland at Tokyo Disneyland, opened April 15, 1983; and in Disneyland Paris, opened April 12, 1992. Walt Disney World lacks the impressive facade, but for Tokyo and Paris it was brought back. Because skies are often overcast in northern France, designers felt that the facade needed a colorful pastel paint job rather than the classical white and gold look of the previous incarnations. After the opening of Disneyland Paris, and the general satisfaction with the new look, the facade at Disneyland was repainted to use the new color scheme. For the 1997 Christmas season, and each succeeding year, the attraction was redressed for the holidays with colored lights and decorations, both inside and out, with the Audio-Animatronics children dancing and singing "Jingle Bells" and "Deck the Halls" interwoven in counterpoint with the original song. The white and gold facade was returned to the attraction as the park prepared for its 50th anniversary celebration.

It's a Small World Toy Shoppe Fantasyland shop at Disneyland originally sponsored by Mattel; opened December 18, 1992. The shop was built at the end of the exit path from the "it's a small world" attraction after Mattel became the sponsor.

It's All Relative (television) Half-hour comedy series on ABC; debuting on October 1, 2003, and ending on April 6, 2004. Bobby and Liz get engaged, but find that their two families clash. Bobby's father owns and operates a Boston pub, and heads a close-knit Irish Catholic family. Liz attends Harvard, is Protestant, and she has two dads, a gay gallery owner and his life partner, a schoolteacher. Stars Lenny Clarke (Mace O'Neil), Harriet Sansom Harris (Audrey), Reid Scott (Bobby), Maggie Lawson (Liz), Christopher Sieber (Simon), Paige Moss (Maddy), John Benjamin Hickey (Philip). From Paramount Television and Touchstone Television.

It's Not My Fault (film) Educational release in 16mm in August 1991, 18 min. An 11-year-old boy seems to be disagreeing with everyone, but he learns to communicate his feelings and listen to those of others.

It's Pat (film) The androgynous, pudgy, and obnoxious Pat, from *Saturday Night Live*, baffles friends and neighbors alike, who cannot decide if Pat is male or female. Pat has a relationship with Chris, a kindly bartender who, with his hippie clothing and hair, is also sexually ambiguous. When handsome neighbor, Kyle, a married but uptight young man, becomes inexplicably obsessed with Pat, he comes to wonder if he is gay or straight. But basically, it's Pat who is Pat's most devoted admirer. Limited release on August 26, 1994. Directed by Adam Bernstein. A Touchstone film. 78 min. Stars Julia Sweeney (Pat), David Foley (Chris), Charles Rocket (Kyle). Julia Sweeney developed the Pat character at the Los Angeles comedy troupe known as The Groundlings. Filmed in and around Los Angeles, California. Released on video in 1995.

It's Tough to Be a Bird (film) Special live-action and cartoon featurette; released on December 10, 1969. Directed by Ward  Kimball. The story is told of the bird's contribution to mankind and his never-ending fight for survival from prehistoric times to the present. There are humorous moments throughout, and even the buzzard is honored in the epic struggle that still continues between humans and birds. This popular short received the Academy Award as Best Cartoon Short Subject of 1969. The film is hosted by M.C. Bird, voiced by Richard Bakalyan, and features many highlights, including a hilarious musical number by Ruth Buzzi entitled "When The Buzzards Return to Hinckley Ridge." 22 min. An extended version aired on television on December 13, 1970. Released on video in 1986.

It's Tough to Be A Bug (film) A multimedia production for a 450-seat theater underneath the Tree of Life at Disney's Animal Kingdom, featuring 3-D film, Audio-Animatronics, and special effects that provide an amusing look at a bug's world. Opened on April 22, 1998. The attraction, minus the tree, opened also at Disney's California Adventure on February 8, 2001.

Ivan Cat friend of Peter in *Peter and the Wolf*, represented by a clarinet.

Ives, Burl (1909–1995) Actor/singer; appeared in *So Dear to My Heart* (Uncle Hiram) and *Summer Magic* (Osh Popham).

Iwerks, Ub (1901–1971) Animator and special effects wizard. Born in Kansas City, Missouri, in 1901, of Dutch extrac-tion, he had his first major job with the Pesmen-Rubin Commercial Art Studio, where he did lettering and airbrush work. It was there that Ub met Walt Disney, another aspiring artist. Both boys were 19, and when they were laid off, decided to set up their own company to do commercial artwork. The company, established in 1920, was called the Iwerks-Disney Studio. Originally they had thought to call it Disney-Iwerks, but that sounded too much like a place that manufactured eyeglasses. The Studio only lasted a month, but then both Ub and Walt were able to get more secure jobs with the Kansas City Slide Company, later known as the Kansas City Film Ad Company. When Walt set up Laugh-O-gram Films in 1922, Ub joined him as chief animator. This company also lasted only a short time. Walt went to Hollywood to begin producing Alice Comedies and Ub joined him there in 1924. Ub's starting salary was $40 a week, higher even than Walt's, attesting to his importance. Several years later, when Walt lost the rights to Oswald the Lucky Rabbit, it was Ub who came to his salvation by helping him design a new character—Mickey Mouse. Ub animated the entire cartoon, *Plane Crazy*, all by himself. He worked at a tremendous speed. Ub was renowned for doing 700 drawings in a day; today a proficient animator turns out about 80–100 drawings a week. *The Gallopin' Gaucho* followed, then *Steamboat Willie*, the first Mickey Mouse cartoon ever released. Ub continued animating on the Mickeys and also painted the backgrounds and drew the posters. When the Silly Symphonies started, he took over direction of them. Because

of disagreements over production techniques and a desire to set up his own studio, Ub left Disney in 1930 for ten years. By the time he returned in 1940, he had decided to leave animation altogether and return to his first love, cameras and special effects. One of his first inventions at Disney was the multihead optical printer, used so successfully in the combination of live action and animation in *Melody Time* and *Song of the South*. Of tremendous importance to animation was Ub's design of the modified Xerox process, whereby pencil animation drawings could be transferred directly to cels without the more expensive hand-inking. Over the years, Ub won two Academy Awards, for designing an improved optical printer for special effects and for collaborating on the perfection of color traveling matte photography. Ub's inventions helped make the impossible possible and Disney screenwriters and art directors kept this in mind. It was primarily due to Ub that the Disney Studio moved to the forefront in special photographic effects. Disneyland and Walt Disney World occupied much of Ub's technical attention in the 1960s, including such attractions as "it's a small world," Great Moments with Mr. Lincoln, and the Circle-Vision 360 process used in *America the Beautiful*. The design of the film process for The Hall of Presidents at Walt Disney World was Ub's last project. He was honored posthumously with the Disney Legends Award in 1989. Ub's sons Don and Dave were longtime Disney employees. Ub was a quiet, unassuming man, who was devoted to his work, making his mark not only in animation but also in the field of motion picture technology. He was an animation genius, perhaps the greatest of all time, whose contributions to the art in the 1920s and 1930s helped make animation much more appealing to a wider audience. A documentary on his life, *The Hand Behind the Mouse: The Ub Iwerks Story*, was produced by his granddaughter, Leslie Iwerks, in 1999.

Iyanla (television) One-hour talk show featuring Iyanla Vanzant, premiering in syndication on August 13, 2001.

J

J. Audubon Woodlore See Ranger.

J. Thaddeus Toad The lead character in the *Wind and the Willows* half of *The Adventures of Ichabod and Mr. Toad*; voiced by Eric Blore.

J. Worthington Foulfellow Fox character in *Pinocchio*, also known as Honest John; voiced by Walter Catlett.

Jacchus Donkey ridden by Bacchus in the *Pastoral* segment of *Fantasia*.

Jack (film) Jack Powell appears to be an average, middle-aged 40-year-old man—who plays with toys and wears kids' pajamas. But Jack is only ten years old. He suffers from a rare genetic disorder that causes him to physically age four times faster than a normal person. Fearing ridicule from the outside world, Jack's parents have kept him secluded in their home, which they have stocked with every toy a young boy could want, and have had him taught by a kindly tutor, Mr. Woodruff. Toys, however, cannot take the place of the real friends Jack craves. At the urging of his tutor, his parents finally allow him to embark on the greatest adventure of his unusual life—entering the fifth grade. Slowly he gains acceptance from his much smaller classmates, especially after showing his prowess with basketball. Years later, as they graduate from high school, Jack is still a beloved part of the gang, but he is now an elderly man. A Hollywood picture. Directed by Francis Ford Coppola. Released on August 9, 1996. Stars Robin Williams (Jack Powell), Diane Lane (Karen Powell), Jennifer Lopez (Ms. Marquez), Brian Kerwin (Brian Powell), Fran Drescher (Dolores Durante), Bill Cosby (Lawrence Woodruff). 113 min. The picturesque town of Ross, California, provided some of the town sets; additional filming was done in San Francisco. Many of the interiors were built at the Mare Island Naval Base in Vallejo. Released on video in 1997.

Jack and Old Mac (film) Special cartoon; released on July 18, 1956. Directed by Bill Justice. A combination of two stories: the nursery rhyme "This Is the House that Jack Built" and a variation on the children's song "Old MacDonald Had a Farm," with "Farm" paraphrased as "Band."

Jack and the Beanstalk (film) Laugh-O-gram film made by Walt Disney in Kansas City in 1922. A later version starring Mickey Mouse, *Mickey and the Beanstalk*, appeared in the feature *Fun and Fancy Free*.

Jack-Jack's Attack (film) Animated short from Pixar which appeared first on the DVD for *The Incredibles*; released on March 15, 2005.

Jack-Jack, the baby of the superhero family, is at home with babysitter Kari while the family is away, and the toddler reveals his latent powers.

Jackman, Bob (1915–1996) He joined Disney in 1942, working in accounting. He moved to the music department in 1955 and became its manager that same year. He provided the voice of Goofy in a number of cartoons in the 1950s.

Jackson, Michael He wrote the songs for and starred in the 3-D *Captain Eo* film at the Disney parks. Jackson is an avid Disney fan, making many trips to the parks, occasionally in disguise.

Jackson, Samuel L. Actor; appeared in *Betsy's Wedding* (Taxi Dispatcher), *Unbreakable* (Elijah Price), and provided the voice of Frozone in *The Incredibles*.

Jackson, Wilfred ("Jaxon") (1906–1988) He joined Disney in 1928 and worked on *Steamboat Willie*. He served as an animator, director, and as producer-director on the *Disneyland* television show. He pioneered a method of pre-timing animation with sound, and invented the bar sheet to coordinate the animation action with the sound track. Several of the cartoons he directed were honored with Academy Awards. He also worked as a sequence director on 11 features from *Snow White and the Seven Dwarfs* to *Lady and the Tramp*. Jackson retired in 1961, and was honored posthumously as a Disney Legend in 1998.

Jackson Square Gifts and Desires Souvenir shop at the Port Orleans Resort hotel at Walt Disney World; opened on May 17, 1991.

Jaeckel, Richard (1926–1997) Actor; he appeared in *Herbie Goes Bananas* (Shepard), on television in *Kit Carson and the Mountain Men* (Ed Kern), and narrated *Adventure in Satan's Canyon*.

Jafar Evil vizier in the Sultan's palace in *Aladdin*; voiced by Jonathan Freeman.

Jake Australian kangaroo rat in *The Rescuers Down Under*; voiced by Tristan Rogers.

James, Cyril (1910–1975) He worked with merchandising and film distribution for Disney in London for his entire career, from 1938 to 1972. He was presented posthumously with a European Disney Legends Award in 1997.

James and the Giant Peach (film) Nine-year-old James Henry Trotter, a young orphan, has been sent to live with his wicked, miserly aunts Spiker and Sponge. Life is the pits for the lonely boy, who dreams of going to New York City. He finally gets his chance when he meets a mysterious hobo who presents him with a bag of magical "crocodile tongues." Accidentally spilling his precious treasure at the base of a peach tree, James is astonished to see a peach on the tree grow to an enormous size. Finding a secret entryway into the peach, he crawls inside where he meets a wondrous group of human-sized insects—including a brash centipede, a grandfatherly grasshopper, a motherly ladybug, and a dotty glowworm. When the peach breaks loose from the tree, James and his insect pals find themselves on a roll, headed for the adventure of a lifetime. Directed by Henry Selick. Released on April 12, 1996. Stars Miriam Margolyes (Sponge, Glowworm), Joanna Lumley (Spiker), Paul Terry (James), Pete Postlethwaite (old man), and the voices of Richard Dreyfuss (Centipede), Susan Sarandon (Miss Spider), Jane Leeves (Lady Bug), David Thewlis (Earthworm), Simon Callow (Grasshopper). 79 min. Based on the 1961 book by Roald Dahl. Five songs were written by Randy Newman: "My Name Is James," "That's the Life," "Eating the Peach," "We're Family," and "Good News." Newman himself is the vocalist on the last song. The fantasy scenes were filmed using stop-motion animation enhanced by computer-generated imagery and digital effects. Live-action photography took place in a large hangar at a decommissioned naval base on Treasure Island in San Francisco Bay and at nearby Hunter's Point. The animation was done at Skellington Productions in San Francisco, the same studio where *The Nightmare Before Christ-*

mas had been produced, and it utilized some of the same crew. In the underwater sequence, one can even find a cameo appearance by Jack Skellington from the earlier film. More than 50 peaches were constructed for the film, ranging in size from three-inch miniatures up to 20-foot diameter jumbos. Two granddaughters of Roald Dahl, children of his daughter, Lucy, appear briefly as extras in the film. Lucy wrote the movie scrapbook, published by Disney Press and illustrated with her own photographs. Released on video in 1996.

James P. Sullivan ("Sulley") Monster in *Monsters, Inc.*; voiced by John Goodman.

Jamie Fort Story, The (A Story About Self-Esteem) (film) Educational film about a fire victim who discovers the power of determination and a positive attitude; released in September 1988. 30 min.

Jane Character in *Tarzan*, the daughter of Professor Porter; voiced by Minnie Driver.

Jane Austen's Mafia! (film) This parody of films about organized crime begins with young Vincenzo Cortino forced to leave Sicily and swim to America, where he becomes the infamous, though clutzy, patriarch of a powerful crime family. As he ages, he realizes that he will have to hand the reins of power to one of his sons—either the psychotic Joey or the war hero Anthony. In the background are the themes of strong family loyalty, the struggle for power, and relentless treachery. Directed by Jim Abrahams. A Touchstone Picture. Released on July 24, 1998. Stars Lloyd Bridges (Vincenzo Cortino), Jay Mohr (Anthony), Olympia Dukakis (Sophia), Christina Applegate (Diane), Billy Burke (Joey). 87 min. The movie covers the years from 1912 to the present, filmed in and around Los Angeles, and in Reno, Nevada. Advertised as *Mafia*, after initial research showed most theatergoers had never heard of Jane Austen. Released on video in 1999.

Jani, Bob (1934–1989) Director of entertainment for Disneyland and Walt Disney World; he produced the grand opening dedication events for Walt Disney World in 1971, as well as America on Parade, Disney on Parade, and the Main Street Electrical Parade, among others. He left Disney in 1978 but continued to work as a consultant. He was named a Disney Legend in 2005.

Japan Pavilion in World Showcase at Epcot; opened October 1, 1982. The landscaping of Japan is one of the highlights of the pavilion. Guests can wander through pathways in some typical Japanese gardens before shopping in the gigantic, by Epcot standards, Mitsukoshi Department Store. Upstairs guests can eat in Japanese fashion, watching the cook prepare their food right at their own table. Japan is one of only a few World Showcase countries to have a museum area, the Bijutsu-Kan Gallery, where rotating displays of rare items, such as costumes, clocks, or kites, from Japan can be shown in an attractive gallery with subdued lighting levels.

Japan (film) People and Places featurette; released on April 6, 1960. Produced by Ben Sharpsteen. This is the story of colorful Japanese customs and manners of the past, and their con-

trast with present-day Japan. We see ancient farming customs, agricultural ceremonies, ancestor worship, schoolteaching, marriage customs, sports, all against the background of beautiful Japan. Filmed in CinemaScope. 28 min.

Japan Harvests the Sea (film) Sixteen mm release title of *Ama Girls*; released in September 1961.

Jaq Cunning mouse friend of Cinderella; voiced by Jim Macdonald.

Jasmine Princess with whom Aladdin falls in love; speaking voice by Linda Larkin; singing voice by Lea Salonga.

Jay, Tony Actor; provided the voice of Monsieur D'Arque in *Beauty and the Beast* and Frollo in *The Hunchback of Notre Dame*, and that of Shere Khan on television in *Tale Spin* and on film in *The Jungle Book 2*. He narrated *Treasure Planet*.

Jazz Fool, The (film) Mickey Mouse cartoon; released in 1929. Directed by Walt Disney. Mickey appears to be the toast of this musical cartoon, playing a calliope and a piano to which other animals can dance until the piano begins to chase him.

Jefferson in Paris (film) Historical drama about Thomas Jefferson's five years, 1784 to 1789, in romantic, politically-charged, pre-revolutionary Paris, where he was originally appointed by the Continental Congress to assist Benjamin Franklin as minister to the court of King Louis XVI but later took over the post when Franklin returned to America. While in Paris, Jefferson, who has recently lost his wife, enters into a love affair with a beautiful Anglo-Italian painter and musician, Maria Cosway, giving him the experience of an attachment, in the European manner to a highly sophisticated woman having advanced ideas about love and marriage. When Jefferson's daughter, Polly, arrives in Paris, accompanied by her nurse, Sally Hemings, he finds himself attracted to the slave girl. When Jefferson decides to return home, he offers Sally and her brother their freedom if they will join him—Sally is already pregnant with his child—and they consent. Released on March 31, 1995, in New York and Los Angeles; general release on April 7, 1995. Directed by James Ivory. 142 min. A Touchstone Picture. Stars Nick Nolte (Thomas Jefferson), Greta Scacchi (Maria Cosway), Lambert Wilson (Lafayette), Simon Callow (Richard Cosway), Seth Gilliam (James Hemings), James Earl Jones (Madison Hemings), Thandie Newton (Sally Hemings), Estelle Eonnet (Polly). The movie was produced by the prestigious Merchant-Ivory filmmaking team and was filmed on location in France, garnering special permission to shoot at Versailles, at the Chateau of Chantilly, and at many other historic sites in the country. Released on video in 1995.

Jennie Project, The (television) Disney Channel Original Movie; premiered on July 13, 2001. Dr. Hugo Archibald has brought home from Africa a chimpanzee named Jennie. Originally mischievous and destructive, but eventually accepted as a member of the family, Jennie, who is learning sign language, develops a close relationship with 11-year-old Andrew. But there are problems in having even a domesticated wild animal in a home situation, and the family has to figure out what to do with Jennie. Directed by Gary Nadeau. Stars Alex D. Linz (Andrew Archibald), Lance Guest (Hugo Archibald), Sheila Kelley (Lea Archibald), Sheryl Lee Ralph (Dr. Pamela Prentiss), Abigail Mavity (Sarah Archibald).

Jenny Foxworth Rich girl who finds Oliver in *Oliver & Company*; voiced by Natalie Gregory.

Jerky Boys, The (film) A pair of young men from Queens, New York, create outrageous characters with their voices when they make phone calls to the unwary, but they get in trouble both with the law and the mob. Released on February 3, 1995. Directed by James Melkonian. A Touchstone Picture in association with Caravan

Pictures. 82 min. Stars John G. Brennan (Johnny B.), Kamal Ahmed (Kamal), Alan Arkin (Lazarro), Brad Sullivan (Worzic), William Hickey (Uncle Freddy). Filmed in New York City. Released on video in 1995.

Jersey, The (television) Half-hour original series on Disney Channel; premiered on September 24, 1999. Two teens' love of sports takes on a life of its own through the fantastic powers of an old football jersey. Each time the 13-year-old cousins don the jersey, they enter a magical portal that transports them into the world of professional athletics, placing them directly into the shoes of major sports celebrities. Stars Michael Galeota (Nick Lighter), Courtnee Draper (Morgan Hudson), Jermaine Williams (Coleman Galloway), Theo Greenly (Elliot Rifkin). Sports superstars guest on each episode. Based on a January 30, 1999, Disney Channel half-hour special entitled *The Magic Jersey*. 61 episodes.

Jessica Rabbit Roger Rabbit's human female wife in *Who Framed Roger Rabbit*, with an uncredited speaking voice provided by Kathleen Turner, though she was credited in later Roger Rabbit shorts. The singing voice was provided by Amy Irving. A Jessica's shop at Pleasure Island at Walt Disney World, featuring lingerie and other items, opened on December 15, 1990, and closed in February 1993.

Jet Propulsion Educational film showing the development of airplanes, from early models to the planes of today, demonstrating the aerodynamics of jet propulsion, and breaking down of the various parts of a jet. A jet plane's characteristics are compared with those of conventional aircraft. Made for General Electric Company; delivered on April 9, 1946.

Jetix Rebranding in February 2004 of the Fox Kids channels for action-adventure programming worldwide.  It airs on ABC Family and Toon Disney in the United States, and on other Jetix channels

throughout Europe and Latin America. Disney owns 75 percent of Jetix Europe.

Jett Jackson: The Movie (television) A Disney Channel Original Movie; premiered on June 8, 2001. Jett trades places with his on-screen alter ego, Silverstone, after Jett has an accident on the set of his popular television series (*The Famous Jett Jackson*). Now Jett rather than Silverstone must defeat the evil Dr. Kragg, who is using a dimensional field device to steal the major cities of the world, while Silverstone must navigate through Jett's tumultuous teen world. Directed by Shawn Levy. Stars Lee Thompson Young (Jett Jackson), Lindy Booth (Hawk/Riley), Nigel Shawn Williams (Artemus), Ryan Sommers Baum (JB Halliburton), Kerry Duff (Kayla West), Michael Ironside (Dr. Kragg).

Jim Dear and Darling Human owners of Lady in *Lady and the Tramp*; voiced by Lee Millar and Peggy Lee.

Jim Henson's Muppet*Vision 3D Attraction at Disney-MGM Studios; opened on May 16, 1991. Sensational in-theater effects add to the impact of the 3-D film starring the Muppets. Sponsored by Kodak. It also opened in Disney's California Adventure on February 8, 2001.

Jiminy Cricket Pinocchio's conscience, who was later used to introduce educational cartoons on the Mickey Mouse Club television show; voiced by Cliff Edwards. Before Walt Disney selected Jiminy Cricket as the character's name, the phrase was used as an exclamation denoting surprise or bewilderment. According to the *Oxford English Dictionary*, the phrase has been around since 1848. In *Snow White and the Seven Dwarfs*, made over two years before *Pinocchio*, the Dwarfs exclaim, "Jiminy Crickets!" when they return to their cottage and find the lights on.

Jiminy Cricket Presents Bongo (television) Television show; aired on September 28, 1955. Directed by Hamilton S. Luske. Walt discusses the creation of "When You Wish Upon a Star," sung in *Pinocchio* by Jiminy Cricket; then Jiminy introduces *Bongo* along with *Chicken Little* and *Figaro and Cleo*.

Jiminy Cricket, P.S. (Problem Solver) (film) Educational film; released in September 1983. The film uses clips from Disney cartoons to introduce children to logic and critical thinking.

Jimirro, James P. He joined Disney in 1973 in the Walt Disney Educational Media Company, becoming its executive vice president in 1974. In 1982 he was made executive vice president telecommunications for Walt Disney Productions, and he spearheaded the establishment of The Disney Channel, serving as its first president until 1985.

Jimmy Kimmel Live (television) Hour-long late-night talk show, starring Jimmy Kimmel; premiered on ABC on January 26, 2003. The show features celebrity guests and live comedy segments, and is taped each weeknight on Hollywood Blvd. next door to the El Capitan Theatre. Produced by Jackhole Industries in association with Touchstone Television.

Jitney Main Street vehicle in Magic Kingdom Park at Walt Disney World; opened on October 1, 1971.

Jittlov, Mike Filmmaker; created the inventive stop-motion *Mouse Mania* for the *Mickey's 50* television show and appeared in *Major Effects* along with two additional films he had made.

Joanna Goanna lizard working with Percival McLeach; voiced by Frank Welker in *The Rescuers Down Under*.

Job, The (television) Half-hour comedy series on ABC; premiered on March 14, 2001, and ended on April 24, 2002. The lives and hijinks of a group of opportunistic New York City police detectives. From DreamWorks Television and Touchstone Television. Stars Denis Leary (Mike McNeil), Adam Ferrara (Tommy Manetti), Lenny Clarke (Frank Harrigan), Bill Nunn (Pip Phillips), Diane Farr (Jan Fendrich), John Ortiz (Ruben Sommariba), Julian Acosta (Al Rodriguez), Keith David (Lt. Williams).

Jock Plucky terrier friend of Lady's in *Lady and the Tramp*; voiced by Bill Thompson. Jock's real name is Heather Lad o' Glencairn.

Joe Carioca See *José Carioca*.

Joel, Billy Singer; he voiced Dodger in *Oliver & Company*.

Joerger, Fred (1913–2005) As an Imagineer from 1953 until his retirement in 1979, Fred crafted three-dimensional models for park attractions, as well as for motion pictures. He had a special knack for creating decorative rockwork out of plaster. After his retirement, he returned to Disney as field art director for the building of Epcot. He was named a Disney Legend in 2001.

Joey Baby kangaroo star of *Daddy Duck* (1948).

Johann, Dallas He was hired as a Mouseketeer for the *Mickey Mouse Club*, but was fired shortly afterward. Replaced by his brother, John Lee Johann.

Johann, John Lee Mouseketeer from the 1950s television show.

John, Elton Wrote the music for the songs in *The Lion King* with Tim Rice writing the lyrics. They won an Academy Award for "Can You Feel the Love Tonight," and provided additional material for the Broadway version of the film. He also cooperated with Rice on *Elaborate Lives: The Legend of Aida* (later *Aida*) for the stage.

John The older of Wendy's two brothers in *Peter Pan*, wearing a top hat and glasses; voiced by Paul Collins.

John Henry (film) A short cartoon telling the story of the legendary African American folk hero, who pitted his strength against that of a machine, and won the contest. The story is told from the point of view of John's wife, Polly. Directed by Mark Henn. Released in Los Angeles for Academy Award consideration on October 30, 2000. Voices include Geoffrey Jones (John Henry), Alfre Woodard (Polly speaking), Carrie Harrington (Polly singing), Tim Hodge (Mac-Tavish), David Murray (Thomas). 9 min. The cartoon was completely made by Disney's Feature Animation Studio in Florida. The Grammy Award–winning ensemble, Sounds of Blackness, provided the music. Released on video in 2002.

John Muir: Father of Our National Parks (film) Educational film produced by Anthony Corso; released in September 1973. Dramatization of Muir's struggle to preserve our scenic wonders.

Johnny Appleseed (film) Segment of *Melody Time*, with Dennis Day telling the story of the

young man who planted apple trees throughout the west. Re-released as a short on December 25, 1955. 19 min. Released for schools as *Legend of Johnny Appleseed*.

Johnny Fedora and Alice Bluebonnet (film) Segment of *Make Mine Music*, sung by the Andrews Sisters, about the romance between a boy and girl hat. Re-released as a short on May 21, 1954.

Johnny Shiloh (television) Two-part television show; aired on January 20 and 27, 1963. Directed by James Neilson. Johnny Clem becomes a drummer boy in the Civil War at the age of ten. Though he is too young to join the soldiers as they march off to battle, he sneaks after them. At Shiloh, with the Union soldiers losing, Johnny begins drumming to encourage them, and his courage under battle conditions leads to instant fame. He gets a promotion and becomes a messenger for the general. Stars Kevin Corcoran, Brian Keith, Darryl Hickman, Skip Homeier, Edward Platt, Regis Toomey, Rickie Sorensen, Eddie Hodges. Based on a true story as told in the book by James A. Rhodes and Dean Jauchius; the real Johnny Clem remained in the army and retired as a brigadier general in 1916.

Johnny Tremain (film) Johnny, through an injury to his hand in a silversmith's shop, gains new insight into himself and those around him as he is plunged into exciting events leading up to the Boston Tea Party at the outbreak of the American Revolution. Released on June 19, 1957. The first Disney feature directed by Robert Stevenson, who would go on to be one of the major Disney directors in the 1960s and 1970s. 80 min. Stars Hal Stalmaster (Johnny Tremain), Luana Patten (Cilla Lapham), Dick Beymer (Rab Silsbee), Jeff York (James Otis), Sebastian Cabot (Jonathan Lyte). Sharon Disney has a small part in the film. Features the song "The Liberty Tree" by George Bruns and Tom Blackburn. The film was originally meant as programming for the Disney television series, but when production costs mounted, Walt decided to release it as a feature film. It aired on television the following year in two parts entitled *The Boston Tea Party* and *The Shot Heard 'Round the World*. Released on video in 1983.

Johnny Tsunami (television) A Disney Channel Original Movie; first airing on July 24, 1999. Johnny Kapahaala, a teen surfing sensation, is uprooted from his Hawaii home and forced to move to a tiny ski resort town in Vermont. After getting caught in the middle of a longstanding rivalry between the local prep school skiers and the public school snowboarders, with the help of his legendary grandfather, Johnny Tsunami, he learns to use his competitive spirit and athletic abilities to unite the two. Directed by Steve Boyum. Stars Brandon Baker (Johnny Kapahaala), Cary-Hiroyuki Tagswa (Johnny Tsunami), Kirsten Storms (Emily Pritchard), Lee Thompson Young (Sam Sterling).

Johns, Glynis Actress; appeared in *The Sword and the Rose* (Mary Tudor), *Rob Roy* (Helen Mary MacGregor), *Mary Poppins* (Winifred Banks), *The Ref* (Rose), and *While You Were Sleeping* (Elsie). She was honored as a Disney Legend in 1998.

Johnson, Ben (1919–1996) Actor; appeared in *Ten Who Dared* (George Bradley), *Tex* (Cole Collins), and *Angels in the Outfield* (Hank Murphy), and on television in *Ride a Northbound Horse*.

Johnson, Don Actor; appeared in *Paradise* (Ben Reed), *Born Yesterday* (Paul Verrall), and *Guilty as Sin* (David Greenhill), and on television as a host of *The Grand Opening of Euro Disney*.

Johnson, George A. He provided the voice of Goofy in several cartoons in the 1940s.

Johnson, James A. (1917–1976) He joined Disney in 1938, became assistant secretary of the corporation in 1947, and was named secretary in 1950. He worked with Disney publications from 1950 to 1962, and became general manager (and

later president) of the Walt Disney Music Company in 1958. He retired in 1975.

Johnson Space Center Educational film in the EPCOT Educational Media Collection: Minnie's Science Field Trips series; released in September 1988. 18 min. A guided tour through the astronaut training center explaining principles of space science. (Walt Disney Imagineering designed the new visitor center at the Space Center in Houston, which opened in 1992.)

Johnston, O. B. (1901–1992) He joined Disney in 1934 in merchandising and eventually headed the character merchandise division, operating first out of New York and then Burbank, until his retirement in 1972.

Johnston, Ollie Animator; known as one of Walt's "Nine Old Men," he joined the Studio in 1935 as an inbetweener on Mickey Mouse cartoons. His work can be seen in 24 animated features beginning with *Snow White and the Seven Dwarfs*, many as directing animator. He retired in 1978. With his lifelong friend Frank Thomas he authored *Disney Animation: the Illusion of Life*, and several other  books on the subject. He was honored with the Disney Legends Award in 1989. He was profiled with Frank Thomas in the documentary *Frank and Ollie*, produced by Thomas's son.

JoJo's Circus (television) Stop-motion animated series on Playhouse Disney on Disney Channel; premiered on September 28, 2003. JoJo Tickle is a curious 6-year-old circus clown who invites preschoolers to join her in lively, imaginative movement with games and songs. Created by Jim Jinkins and David Campbell. Voices include Madeleine Martin (JoJo), Robert Smith (Goliath), Cole Caplan (Tater).

Joker, the Amiable Ocelot (television) Television show; aired on December 11, 1966. A desert loner adopts an ocelot he finds in an old car, but later realizes that it must be set free. The ocelot finds a mate, and so does the loner, falling for a young nurse who moves to the area. Stars Robert Becker, Jan McNabb. Narrated by Winston Hibler.

Jolly Trolley Attraction in Mickey's Toontown at Disneyland; opened on January 24, 1993. To get the cartoony look to the trolley, Disney Imagineers arranged its wheel sizes so it did not just glide down the tracks of Toontown, but it jiggles, lurches, and weaves. The popularity of Toontown has meant that it is sometimes difficult for the trolley to get through the masses of people. Also at Tokyo Disneyland; beginning April 15, 1996.

Jones, Dean Actor; appeared in *That Darn Cat!* (Zeke Kelso), *The Ugly Dachshund* (Mark Garrison), *Monkeys, Go Home* (Hank Dussard), *Blackbeard's Ghost* (Steve Walker), *The Horse in the Gray Flannel Suit* (Frederick Bolton), *The Love Bug* (Jim Douglas), *Million Dollar Duck* (Prof. Albert Dooley), *Snowball Express* (Johnny Baxter), *The Shaggy D.A.* (Wilby Daniels), and *Herbie Goes to Monte Carlo* (Jim Douglas), *That Darn Cat* (1997 remake, Mr. Flint), and on television in *Disney's Greatest Dog Stars, Kraft Salutes Walt Disney World's 10th Anniversary*, the 1995 remake of *The Computer Wore Tennis Shoes* (Dean Carlson), and the *Herbie, the Love Bug* limited series and the 1997 TV movie of *The Love Bug*, reprising the role of Jim Douglas. He was named a Disney Legend in 1995.

Jones, Dickie He voiced Pinocchio, and was named a Disney Legend in 2000.

Jones, Freddie He voiced Dallben in *The Black Cauldron*, and appeared in *The Count of Monte Cristo* (Col. Villefort).

Jones, James Earl Actor; appeared in *Three Fugitives* (Dugan), *True Identity* (himself), *Jefferson in Paris* (Madison Hemings), and provided the voice of Mufasa in *The Lion King*. He was a host of *Fantasia/2000*.

Jones, Shirley Actress; appeared on television in *The Adventures of Pollyanna* (Aunt Polly).

Jordan, Jim (1896–1988) He voiced Orville in *The Rescuers*.

José Carioca Also known as Joe Carioca, Donald Duck's Brazilian parrot pal, first appearing in *Saludos Amigos* (1943), voiced by José Oliveira. The name came from the Portuguese word that is used to refer to a native of Rio de Janeiro, "carioca." The character was so popular he was brought  back in *The Three Caballeros* in 1945. He also starred in a newspaper comic strip for two years.

José Come Bien (film) Portuguese Reading Film #2. Produced under the auspices of the Coordinator of Inter-American Affairs. Delivered on March 14, 1945.

Journey into Imagination Future World pavilion at Epcot; opened October 1, 1982, featuring a ride of the same title, which opened on March 5, 1983, sponsored by Eastman Kodak. The pavilion itself consists of pyramids of glass at odd angles, which, when lit from within at night, present a unique view. Outside, children and the parents are often transfixed by the leapfrog fountains, with plumes of water shooting over their heads to disappear into nearby planters. Some of

the kids find themselves getting an unexpected soaking when they leap up to try to impede the path of the water spout. Inside, Disney Imagineers given the near impossible task of trying to portray imagination nevertheless engineered a fascinating look at what the Imagineers could imagine. The jolly, redheaded Dreamfinder, with his small purple dragon pal, Figment, was the host. Also in the pavilion are the hands-on Image Works and a 3-D film. Originally, *Magic Journeys* was the featured 3-D film; it was followed by *Captain Eo* and in 1994 *Honey, I Shrunk the Audience*. The pavilion was renamed imagination! on October 1, 1999, with a totally revised ride called Journey Into Your Imagination and a revised Image Works, called ImageWorks—The Kodak "What If?" Labs. On June 1, 2002, the ride was changed to Journey Into Imagination with Figment.

Journey of Natty Gann, The (film) During the mid-1930s, the father of 14-year-old Natty has to leave Chicago suddenly to find lumbering work in Washington State. She sets off alone to follow him across the country. She hops trains, befriends a wolf and a teenage drifter, and after a series of adventures is reunited with her father. Released on September 27, 1985. Directed by Jeremy Kagan. 101 min. Stars Meredith Salenger (Natty Gann), John Cusack (Harry), Ray Wise (Sol Gann), Barry Miller (Parker), Scatman Crothers (Sherman), Lainie Kazan (Connie), Verna Bloom (Farm woman), Bruce M. Fischer (Charlie Linfield). Production designer Paul Sylbert was called upon to create a vintage Chicago street scene complete with pushcart vendors, a Hooverville consisting of 60 shacks, and an authentic period logging camp. The film's emphasis on authenticity extended to the activities of the lumber camp. Ray Wise, playing Natty's father, learned how to top trees with a big ax as it was actually done 50 years ago. For some scenes he had to climb 40-foot-high trees. The local experts recognized his talents and at the completion of shooting awarded him a handmade throwing ax and target. Salenger performed most of her own stunts. The "wolf" Natty encounters in the film was a wolf/malamute mix named "Jed," who, with the application of some water-

based makeup, looked the part. Costume designer Albert Wolsky also relied heavily on photographic research in creating the wardrobe. In all, Wolsky came up with nearly 2,000 costumes for the film, including some scenes with more than 250 extras. Hats were frequently used to disguise the 1980s-style coiffures. The film was nominated for an Academy Award for Best Costume Design. Released on video in 1986.

Journey to the Center of the Earth Attraction at Tokyo DisneySea; opened on September 4, 2001, sponsored by Dai-Ichi Mutual Life Insurance Co. Boarding fantastic subterranean vehicles developed by Captain Nemo, guests explore vast underground realms of never-before-seen beauty, mystery, and wonder, along the way encountering unexpected peril.

Journey to the Valley of the Emu, The (television) Television show; aired on January 22, 1978. Directed by Roy E. Disney. An aborigine boy in the Australian outback adopts an injured dingo. The two of them set off to find an emu, so he can bring back a feather and signify that he is a man. A snakebite necessitates an emergency airlift to a hospital, but eventually the boy is able to return to his quest. Stars Victor Palmer. Narrated by Paul Ricketts.

Joy Luck Club, The (film) The lives of three generations of Chinese women are interwoven in this story of mothers and daughters attempting to break through the barriers that often stand in the way of understanding each other. Four mothers, born in China, now Americans, have met weekly for 30 years to pay mah-jongg and have named themselves the Joy Luck Club. At the most recent meeting, June, the daughter of Suyuan, who has died, is inducted into the group. Playing with her "aunties," June learns much about them, her culture, and herself. The lives of each of the mothers in China are chronicled as well as the lives of their American daughters. June discovers her mother's secret of having abandoned twin daughters in wartime China, and she is able to realize her mother's greatest dream by going to China herself and reuniting the family. Released on September

8, 1993. Directed by Wayne Wang. A Hollywood Picture. Based on the best-selling book by Amy Tan. 139 min. Stars Kieu Chinh (Suyuan), Tsai Chin (Lindo), Lisa Lu (An Mei), France Nuyen (Ying Ying), Rosalind Chao (Rose), Lauren Tom (Lena), Tamlyn Tomita (Waverly), Ming-Na Wen (June). Filmed on location in the San Francisco area, with interiors in a former chocolate factory in Richmond, as well as a six-week location shoot in China. Released on video in 1994.

Judels, Charles (1881–1969) He voiced Stromboli and the Coachman in *Pinocchio*.

Judge Dredd (film) In the 22nd century, Mega-City One has become a haven for millions of people from the surrounding towns and rural areas destroyed by war and ecological disaster. Thrown together and confined in cramped, overcrowded, monolithic apartment buildings, with no hope of employment or a better future, they strike out at each other, rocking the city with rioting and unrest. Since regular law enforcement cannot maintain order amidst such monumental chaos, Judge Dredd is created as part of a top secret DNA experiment, the Janus Project. In his mind are all the great minds of jurisprudence, and he is a one-man police force, judge, jury, and executioner. But part of the project went askew, creating a master criminal, Rico, as evil as Judge Dredd is just. Judge Dredd has to battle both against the powers of evil and for his own soul. A Hollywood Pictures film, in association with Cinergi Productions. Directed by Danny Cannon. Released on June 30, 1995. Stars Sylvester Stallone (Judge Dredd), Armand Assante (Rico), Diane Lane (Judge Hershey), Rob Schneider (Fergie), Joan Chen (Ilsa), Jurgen Prochnow (Judge Griffin), Max Von Sydow (Judge Fargo), Balthazar Getty (Olmeyer). 96 min. Filmed in CinemaScope in Iceland and at England's Shepperton Studios. Based on the English science-fiction comic hero created by writer John Wagner and artist Carlos Ezquerra. Released on video in 1995.

Judge for Yourself (television) One-hour syndicated television series; premiered on September 12, 1994. A talk-show/courtroom combination, with the in-studio jury witnessing a discussion of a particular topic among the show's guests, then deliberating and handing down a verdict. Hosted by Bill Handel.

Julius Walt Disney's first named animated cartoon character, a cat who appeared in the Alice Comedies from 1924 to 1927.

Jumbo Pictures Animation company founded by Jim Jinkins and David Campbell in 1991, and acquired by Disney in 1996. The company produced *Brand Spanking New Doug*, later renamed *Disney's Doug*, after a series that had begun on Nickelodeon, and in 1999 produced *Doug's 1st Movie* for theaters. They also produced *101 Dalmatians: The Series* for ABC and *PB & J Otter* for Disney Channel.

Jumpin' Jellyfish Attraction at Paradise Pier at Disney's California Adventure; opened February 8, 2001. Young guests bounce up and down in a total of 12 jellyfish-shaped vessels which lurch up two 50-foot towers.

Jumping Ship (television) A Disney Channel Original Movie; premiered on August 17, 2001. Michael has big plans to show his country cousin, Tommy, a good time aboard a luxury yacht, only to discover the yacht he's chartered is actually a dilapidated fishing boat. When modern-day pirates give chase, the boys are forced to jump ship, leaving them stranded on a desert island with the boat's captain, Jake Hunter. Directed by Michael Lange. Stars Andy Lawrence (Tommy Biggs), Joey Lawrence (Michael Woods), Matt Lawrence (Jake Hunter), Susan Walters (Jules Biggs), Stephen Burleigh (Glenn Woods). A sequel to *Horse Sense*, this film was shot on the Gold Coast of Australia.

Jungle Book, The (film) A human boy, Mowgli, is raised in the jungle by wolves until it is deemed unsafe for him to stay because of Shere Khan, the tiger, who has vowed to kill the man cub. Bagheera, the panther, is selected to accompany Mowgli on his journey back to civilization, but has a difficult time because the boy does not want to leave. Meeting Baloo the bear, a lovable "jungle bum," Mowgli is even more certain he wants to stay with his friends. But after an encounter with the mad King Louie of the Apes, and pressed to return to the man village by Baloo and Bagheera, Mowgli runs away. Alone in the jungle, he meets Shere Khan, but only after the last-minute intervention of his friends does he manage to defeat the tiger. Soon after, he meets a young girl from the man village and willingly returns to civilization. Released on October 18, 1967. Directed by Wolfgang Reitherman. Rudyard Kipling's classic tale of the jungle was the last animated feature Walt Disney supervised. 78 min. Featuring the voices of Phil Harris (Baloo), Sebastian Cabot (Bagheera), Louis Prima (King Louie), George Sanders (Shere Khan), Sterling Holloway (Kaa), J. Pat O'Malley (Buzzie), and Bruce Reitherman (Mowgli), the film became

one of Disney's all-time box-office winners. Richard M. Sherman and Robert B. Sherman wrote the songs, which include "I Wanna Be Like You," "Trust in Me," "My Own Home," "That's What Friends Are For," and "Colonel Hathi's March," and Terry Gilkyson provided the Oscar-nominated "Bare Necessities." It was re-released in theaters in 1978, 1984, and 1990. Released on video in 1991 and 1997. A live-action version of the story was released in 1994.

Jungle Book, Rudyard Kipling's The (film) Mowgli, a young man raised since childhood by wild animals in the jungles of India, is eventually drawn from the jungle by his attraction to the beautiful Kitty, daughter of Major Brydon, an important English military official. Mowgli's life changes as he reenters civilization. When an avaricious military officer, Capt. Boone, forces Mowgli to reveal the jungle's hidden treasures, Mowgli has to rely on his loyal animal friends—Grey Brother (a wolf), Baloo, and Bagheera—to survive the perilous ordeal and reunite with Kitty. Released on December 25, 1994. Directed by Stephen Sommers. Filmed in CinemaScope. 111 min. Stars Jason Scott Lee (Mowgli), Cary Elwes (Boone), Lena Headey (Kitty), Sam Neill (Col. Brydon), John Cleese (Dr. Plumford). The Kipling story had been filmed as a live-action motion picture by Alexander Korda in 1942 with Sabu as Mowgli, and as an animated film by Disney in 1967. For this production, interiors were filmed at the Mehboob Studios in Bombay, India, with jungle locations in Jodhpur. Because of the problems of shipping trained animals to India, additional "jungle" sets were created in Tennessee and on Fripp Island, South Carolina. The production had the largest group of trained animals—52 tigers, leopards, wolves, bears, elephants, horses, Brahma bulls, and monkeys—that had been assembled for any film since *Doctor Doolittle*. Released on video in 1995.

Jungle Book, The: A Lesson in Accepting Change (film) Educational film; released in September 1981. How change, in friends and environment, can be faced.

Jungle Book, The: Mowgli's Story (film) Direct-to-video release on September 29, 1998, of a live-action sequel to the 1967 animated feature. The narrator, the adult Mowgli, reflects of his childhood jungle adventures, from his being raised by wolves to his friendship with Baloo. He has to learn to be cunning and brave against the jungle's most fearsome animal, the menacing and vengeful tiger, Shere Khan. Directed by Nick Marck. Stars Brandon Baker (Mowgli), and the voices of Fred Savage (narrator), Eartha Kitt (Bagheera), Bryan Doyle-Murray (Baloo). 93 min.

Jungle Book Reunion, The (television) Syndicated television special; aired on July 19, 1990. Directed by Eric Schotz. Downtown Julie Brown hosts a look at *The Jungle Book* on the occasion of its reissue, taped at Disney-MGM Studios. 30 min.

Jungle Book 2, The (film) Mowgli now lives in the man village, and he loves his new family and friends, especially his feisty little stepbrother Ranjan and his best pal Shanti, the girl who initially wooed Mowgli from the jungle. But Mowgli misses his buddy Baloo, who likewise pines for his little man cub. Baloo isn't the only one  hoping to see Mowgli again soon—Shere Khan impatiently awaits his revenge. When Mowgli sneaks away to the jungle, the chase is on to see who will find Mowgli first—his old pals, his new family, or the man-eating tiger. Released on February 14, 2003, after earlier releases on February 5 in France and February 7 in Sweden. From Disney-Toon Studios. Directed by Steve Trenbirth. Voices include John Goodman (Baloo), Haley Joel Osment (Mowgli), Mae Whitman (Shanti), Tony Jay (Shere Khan), Bob Joles (Bagheera), John Rhys-Davies (Ranjan's father), Phil Collins (Lucky), Connor Funk (Ranjan), Jim Cummings (Kaa/Colonel Hathi/M.C. Monkey). 72 min. Released on video in 2003.

Jungle Cat (film) True-Life Adventure feature; initial release on December 16, 1959; general release on August 10, 1960. Directed by James Algar. The last of the True-Life Adventure series, Winston Hibler narrates the story of the South American jaguar. After a background is given on the cat's history, the daily life of the jaguar is shown. Two jaguars mate, teach their kittens, hunt, and fight their worst enemies, the crocodile and huge boa constrictor who are after their kittens. The setting of the film is the vivid jungle and its inhabitants, with a striking finale of a sunset on the Amazon River. Animals depicted include giant anteaters, jungle otters, iguana, tapir, sloth, and monkeys. Three top naturalist-photographers spent over two years in the Amazon basin

of Brazil filming this superbly photographed documentary. 70 min. Released on video in 1986.

Jungle Cat of the Amazon (film) Segment from *Jungle Cat*; released on 16mm for schools in December 1974. Shows the jaguar hunting and teaching its cubs the laws of survival.

Jungle Cruise Adventureland attraction at Disneyland; opened on July 17, 1955. One of the most eagerly awaited attractions because of extensive publicity given by Walt Disney on pre-opening television shows. Very little else was far enough along for him to show, but the channel was dug for the Jungle Cruise, trees were being planted, and Walt was able to talk his viewers through a typical ride, and eventually drive them through in his Nash Rambler (one of the television show's sponsors). The attraction was expanded in 1962 (bathing pool of the Indian elephants), with more additions in 1964 (trapped safari, African veldt region) and 1976 (7 new scenes and 31 figures). A new two-story queue building was added in June 1994, and the channel was moved slightly to allow space for the queue area for the new Indiana Jones attraction, which opened in 1995. Also, Adventureland attraction in Magic Kingdom Park at Walt Disney World, opened October 1, 1971; in Tokyo Disneyland, opened April 15, 1983; and in Hong Kong Disneyland (known as Jungle River Cruise), opened September 12, 2005. A Jungle Cruise was not built at Disneyland Paris because after the popularity of the Disneyland attraction, a number of European parks had already copied the concept, and to build one at Disneyland Paris would not have provided anything new to European visitors.

Jungle Cubs (television) Animated television series; aired on ABC from October 5, 1996 to September 5, 1998. The characters from the 1967 feature are back—Baloo, Bagheera, Louie, Shere Khan, Kaa, and Hathi—but this time as youthful "jungle cubs." They are joined by a couple of misguided, laughable buzzards, Cecil and Arthur. The cubs find the jungle an unknown place where they experience the fun—and sometimes, sadness—of growing up. Voices include Jim Cummings (Kaa), E. G. Daily (Bagheera), Jason Marsden (Shere Khan and Prince Louie), Rob Paulsen (Hathi), Pam Segall (Baloo), Michael McKean (Cecil), David Lander (Arthur). 21 episodes.

Jungle Rhythm (film) Mickey Mouse cartoon; released in 1929. Directed by Walt Disney. With his natural musical flair, Mickey soon has some fierce animals dancing and cavorting through the jungle.

Jungle 2 Jungle (film) Successful commodities trader Michael Cromwell is engaged to marry Charlotte, but first he must finalize his divorce from his estranged wife, Dr. Patricia Cromwell. Leaving everything behind, including his hyperactive business partner, Richard, Michael travels deep into the Amazon jungle, where Patricia has been living since she left him, and gets the surprise of his life when he discovers that he has a 13-year-old son, Mimi-Siku, who has been raised among tribesmen. Michael inadvertently agrees to take Mimi to visit his own jungle—New York City. Cultures collide when the boy, who has more skill with blow darts than with social graces, comes to the most sophisticated city on the planet and wreaks havoc on his father's life. Meanwhile, Richard has bungled a coffee trade on the commodities market, and soon a group of sinister Russians is coming after Richard and Michael. Eventually, the Russians are outsmarted, and Michael and Mimi learn some unexpected lessons from each other about the important things in life. Directed by John Pasquin. Released on March 7, 1997. Stars Tim Allen (Michael Cromwell), Jobeth Williams (Dr. Patricia Cromwell), Martin Short (Richard), Sam Huntington (Mimi-Siku), Lolita Davidovich (Charlotte), David Ogden Stiers (Jovanovic). 105 min. A remake of the French film *Un indien dans la ville* released by Buena Vista in 1996 in a dubbed version as *Little Indian, Big City*. For the jungle setting, the film's producers selected a remote area near Canaima, Venezuela, experiencing all sorts of problems trying to make a film in a rain forest. In New York, sequences were filmed throughout the city, and in suburban Pound Ridge and the Playland amusement park in Rye. Released on video in 1997.

Junior Autopia Fantasyland attraction at Disneyland; opened on July 23, 1956, and closed in December 1958. A block of wood was added to the gas pedal to enable "juniors" to drive.

Junior Woodchucks A pseudo-scout organization to which Donald's nephews belonged, created by artist Carl Barks. It made its first appearance in *Walt Disney's Comics and Stories* no. 125 in 1951. There were Junior Woodchucks comic books from 1966 to 1984 (and in 1991), and even a Junior Woodchucks manual.

Jurgens, Curt (1915–1982) Actor; appeared in *Miracle of the White Stallions* (Gen. Tellheim).

Just Dogs (film) Silly Symphony cartoon; released on July 30, 1932. Directed by Burt Gillett. In an effort to befriend a large mongrel, a little puppy releases all of the dogs in the pound. When the pup finds a bone to share with his unfriendly companion, a free-for-all ensues in which the pup outwits the entire troupe of hungry dogs and finally earns the large dog's friendship.

Just Like Family (television) Series on The Disney Channel, based on the Disney television show, *Help Wanted: Kids*, about a couple who have to hire a couple of children to impress the man's boss. Stars Cindy Williams (Lisa Burke), Bill Hudson (Tom Burke), Gabriel Damon (Coop), Grace Johnston (Emily). First aired May 17, 1989.

Just Mickey (film) Mickey Mouse cartoon; released on April 21, 1930, featuring Mickey as a violinist. Copyrighted as *Fiddling Around*. Directed by Walt Disney. One of Mickey's musical adventures, in which he is an eager violinist with a full head of unruly hair who stops his playing only to talk to the movie audience.

Just Perfect (television) Serial on The Disney Channel's *Mickey Mouse Club*; aired from April 9 to May 4, 1990. Stars Christopher Daniel Barnes as Trent Beckerman, a model teenager, who happens to be left in charge of a big, slobbering 120-pound St. Bernard when his parents and grandmother go on vacation. Also stars Jennie Garth (Crystal) and Sean Patrick Flanery (Dion).

Just Visiting (film) French nobleman, Count Thibault of Malfete, with his servant André, are transported from the 12th century to modern-day Chicago, due to a wizard's flawed time-travel potion. After meeting the count's descendant, Julia Malfete, they realize that they must quickly find a way back to their own time, or Julia and all of Thibault's lineage will never exist. Thibault and André wreak havoc as they foil diabolical plots in both the 12th and 21st centuries. A Hollywood Picture. Directed by Jean-Marie Gaubert. Released on April 6, 2001. Stars Jean Reno (Thibault), Christian Clavier (André), Christina Applegate (Julia Malfete/Rosalinda), Matt Ross (Hunter), Tara Reid (Angelique), Bridgette Wilson (Amber), Malcolm McDowell (Wizard). 88 min. Location filming, in CinemaScope, was done in Chicago and England. Based on the 1993 French comedy *Les Visiteurs*. The director, along with stars Reno and Clavier, reprised their roles from that film. Released on video in 2001.

Justice, Bill Animator; began his Disney career in 1937, and received film credit as an animator on *Fantasia*, *Bambi*, *Alice in Wonderland*, *Peter Pan*, and others. He developed such memorable characters as Thumper and Chip and Dale, and directed acclaimed experimental shorts such as *Jack and Old Mac*, *Noah's Ark*, and *Symposium on Popular Songs*. In 1965, Walt Disney moved him to WED Enterprises where he programmed Audio-Animatronics figures for Great Moments

with Mr. Lincoln, Pirates of the Caribbean, The Haunted Mansion, Country Bear Jamboree, The Hall of Presidents, and others. He designed many of the character costumes for the parks, as well as floats and costumes for many Disneyland parades, including the Main Street Electrical Parade. He retired in 1979, and has written an autobiography entitled *Justice for Disney*. He was named a Disney Legend in 1996.

Justice, James Robertson (1905–1975) Actor; appeared in *The Story of Robin Hood* (Little John), *The Sword and the Rose* (Henry VIII), and *Rob Roy* (Duke of Argyll).

Justin Case (television) Television movie (90 min.); aired on May 15, 1988 (with *Captain Eo Backstage*). Directed by Blake Edwards. A ghost of a private detective helps a young lady find his murderer. After another murder, they are able to prevent a third one and catch the culprit. They are so pleased with their success that they decide to stay in the detective business together. A pilot for a series. Stars George Carlin, Molly Hagan, Timothy Stack, Kevin McClarnon, Douglas Sills, Gordon Jump, Valerie Wildman.

Justin Morgan Had a Horse (television) Two-part television show; aired on February 6 and 13, 1972. Directed by Hollingsworth Morse. Justin Morgan develops a new, versatile breed of horse, eventually known as the Morgan Horse, in the years shortly after the Revolutionary War. The horse's value is proven in a thrilling race finale. Stars Don Murray, Lana Wood, Gary Crosby, R. G. Armstrong, Whit Bissell.

Juttner, Christian Actor; appeared in *Return from Witch Mountain* (Dazzler), and on television in *The Boy Who Talked to Badgers* (Ben), *The Million Dollar Dixie Deliverance*, *The Mystery of Rustler's Cave*, *Return of the Big Cat*, and *The Ghosts of Buxley Hall*.

K

K for Kelly (television) Television show; episode 1 of *Atta Girl, Kelly!*

Kaa Hypnotic slithering snake character in *The Jungle Book*; voiced by Sterling Holloway.

Kahl, Milt (1909–1987) Animator; one of Disney's "Nine Old Men," he started at Disney in 1934, and worked on many Disney classics, usually as directing animator, including *Snow White and the Seven Dwarfs*, *Sleeping Beauty*, *The Jungle Book*, and *The Rescuers*. He was honored with the Disney Legends Award posthumously in 1989. He has been called one of the finest animators ever to work at the Disney Studio.

Kahn, Madeline Actress; appeared in *Betsy's Wedding* (Lola Hopper) and *Nixon* (Margaret Mitchell). She appeared on television in *Avonlea* (Pidgeon Plumtree), and did the voice of Gypsy in *A Bug's Life*.

Kala Gorilla who adopts and mothers *Tarzan*; voiced by Glenn Close.

Kali River Rapids Whitewater rafting adventure in the Asia section of Disney's Animal Kingdom at Walt Disney World; opened on March 1, 1999. Guests ride in 12-person rafts on the exciting Chakranadi River (meaning: river that runs in a circle).

Kamen, Kay (1892–1949) Creative salesman from Kansas City who in 1932 became the exclusive representative of the Disney character merchandising division in New York. He was honored posthumously as a Disney Legend in 1998. See Merchandise.

Kane, Brad He provided the singing voice of Aladdin.

Kanga Kangaroo character in the Winnie the Pooh films; voiced by Barbara Luddy and Julie McWhirter Dees.

Kansas City, Missouri When Elias Disney became ill in 1909 and was unable to continue operation of his Marceline, Missouri, farm, he decided to move his family to Kansas City. He purchased a newspaper distributorship, and soon his sons Walt and Roy were helping out. Walt attended Benton School, and graduated from the seventh grade in 1917. At that time, the family was living at 3028 Bellefontaine. With a neighbor kid, Walt Pfeiffer, Walt got interested in the theater, and they occasionally put on shows as "The Two Walts" at local vaudeville theaters. When Elias decided to move again, this time back to Chicago, Walt stayed the summer and got a job as a news butcher on the railroad. It was an exciting job for a teenager. After the summer season, Walt joined his family in Chicago.

Walt returned to Kansas City after his service in the Red Cross at the end of World War I. After a few minor jobs, he managed to land a position at the Kansas City Slide Company (later Kansas City Film Ad Company), a firm that made advertising slides for movie theaters. On the side, Walt borrowed one of the company's cameras and tried some simple animation, selling a few short pieces to the Newman Theater, where they were called *Newman Laugh-O-grams*. To earn some

needed money, Walt made a dental training film, *Tommy Tucker's Tooth*, for a local dentist, Dr. Thomas B. McCrum. In 1922, Walt left Film Ad to set up his own company, which he called Laugh-O-gram Films. He managed to raise the needed capital by selling stock, with the buyers including his sister, parents, and friends. When Laugh-O-gram Films folded in 1923, Walt scraped together enough money, by taking the camera into the neighborhood to photograph babies for their parents, to buy a train ticket to Hollywood and that summer he cut his ties with Missouri to head west.

Karnival Kid, The (film) First Mickey Mouse cartoon in which Mickey speaks; released in 1929. Directed by Walt Disney. Enjoying his day selling hot dogs in an amusement park, Mickey, along with his friends, serenades Minnie, who is working as a "shimmy dancer."

Kater, David Actor; appeared on the *Mickey Mouse Club* on The Disney Channel, in 1989. He later appeared in *Sister Act 2: Back in the Habit*.

Katrina Popular song from *The Adventures of Ichabod and Mr. Toad*, composed by Don Raye and Gene De Paul. A rendition by Bing Crosby became a hit, and there were other recordings by Lawrence Welk, Tex Beneke, and Kay Kyser.

Katrina Van Tassel Ichabod Crane's girlfriend in *The Adventures of Ichabod and Mr. Toad*.

Katt, William Actor; appeared in *Baby* (George Loomis).

Katz, Omri Actor; appeared in *Hocus Pocus* (Max). Also starred in the non-Disney series *Eerie, Indiana*, which was shown on The Disney Channel.

Katzenberg, Jeffrey Chairman of the Walt Disney Studios from 1984 to 1994. He was credited with helping to bring Disney to the top of the motion picture industry, supervising such box-office hits as *Down and Out in Beverly Hills*, *Pretty Woman*, *Dead Poets Society*, *Who Framed Roger Rabbit*, and *Good Morning, Vietnam*. He worked closely with animation, bringing his talents to such films as *The Little Mermaid*, *Beauty and the Beast*, *Aladdin*, and *The Lion King*. He left the company to partner with Steven Spielberg and David Geffen in a new studio enterprise, Dreamworks SKG.

Kaye, Stubby (1918–1997) Actor; appeared in *Who Framed Roger Rabbit* (Marvin Acme).

Kazaam (film) Life in the city can be pretty tough, especially for 12-year-old Max Connor, whose mother has raised him alone since her husband left when Max was two. To make things worse, Max's mother has found love again with Travis, a kindly firefighter who cannot seem to make friends with Max. Distraught by his mother's impending marriage, Max demands to meet his real father. To add to Max's complicated life, he is the object of torture by a local group of bullies and one day, while hiding in an abandoned building, he accidentally opens the door on a battered boom box, freeing a seven-foot, 3,000-year-old genie, Kazaam. While Max initially does not believe in magic, Kazaam, in trying to give the kid his three wishes, soon makes him a believer. Released on July 17, 1996. A Touchstone Picture. Directed by Paul Michael Glaser. Stars Shaquille O'Neal (Kazaam), Francis Capra (Max), Ally Walker (Alice), James Acheson (Nick). 93 min. The production filmed in Los Angeles, California. Released on video in 1996.

Kazan, Lainie Actress; appeared in *The Journey of Natty Gann* (Connie), *Beaches* (Leona Bloom), and *The Cemetery Club* (Selma). She

appeared on television in *Safety Patrol* (Mrs. Day) and *The Crew* (Pepper Lowenstein).

KCAL Television station in Los Angeles, Channel 9, acquired by Disney on December 2, 1988. Earlier known as KHJ. The TV station was sold to Young Broadcasting in 1996 per the divestiture order received when Disney purchased Cap Cities/ABC. Young formally took over operation of the station on November 23, 1996.

Keane, Glen Animator; began his career at Disney in 1974 as an animator on *The Rescuers*. He animated the fierce fight with the bear in *The Fox and the Hound*, and later brought to life as a directing animator such memorable characters as Ariel in *The Little Mermaid*, Beast in *Beauty and the Beast*, and Aladdin. He worked on story and as a supervising animator on *Pocahontas*, *Tarzan*, and *Treasure Planet*.

Kearns, Joseph (1907–1962) Voice of the Door Knob in *Alice in Wonderland*.

Keaton, Diane Actress; appeared in *The Good Mother* (Anna), *Father of the Bride* and *Father of the Bride, Part 2* (Nina Banks), and *The Other Sister* (Elizabeth Tate). On The Disney Channel she appeared in *Northern Lights* (Roberta Blumstein).

Keegan, Andrew Actor; appeared in *Camp Nowhere* (Zack Dell) and *10 Things I Hate About You* (Joey Donner), and on television in *Thunder Alley* (Jack Kelly) and *Freaky Friday* (Luke).

Keenen Ivory Wayans Show, The (television) Syndicated late-night talk show; premiered on August 4, 1997, and ended April 24, 1998. Hosted by Wayans, featuring a mixture of celebrity interviews, comedy sketches, live musical performances, and game elements.

Keeping the Faith (film) Best friends since they were kids, Rabbi Jacob Schram and Father Brian Finn are dynamic and popular young men living and working on New York's Upper West Side. When Anna Reilly, once their childhood friend and now grown into a beautiful corporate executive, suddenly returns to the city, she reenters Jake's and Brian's lives with a vengeance. Sparks fly and an unusual and complicated love triangle ensues. A Touchstone Pictures/Spyglass Entertainment production. Released on April 14, 2000. Directed by Edward Norton. Stars Edward Norton (Brian Finn), Jenna Elfman (Anna Reilly), Ben Stiller (Jacob Schram), Anne Bancroft (Ruth Schram), Eli Wallach (Rabbi Lewis), Milos Forman (Father Havel), Holland Taylor (Bonnie Rose), Ron Rifkin (Larry Friedman). 129 min. Filming in New York City, the producers selected for the locations where the two lead actors worked, B'nai Jeshurun on West 88th and the Church of the Ascension on West 107th. Released on video in 2000.

Keith, Brian (1921–1997) Actor; appeared in *Ten Who Dared* (Bill Dunn), *The Parent Trap* (Mitch Evers), *Moon Pilot* (Maj. Gen. John Vanneman), *Savage Sam* (Uncle Beck), *A Tiger Walks* (Pete Williams), *Those Calloways* (Cam Calloway), and *Scandalous John* (John McCanless), and on television in *The B.R.A.T. Patrol*, *Elfego Baca*, *Johnny Shiloh*, *The Tenderfoot*, *Bristle Face*, and the series *Walter and Emily*.

Kellaway, Cecil (1891–1973) Actor; appeared in *The Shaggy Dog* (Prof. Plumcutt) and *The Adventures of Bullwhip Griffin* (Mr. Pemberton), and on television in *The Wacky Zoo of Morgan City*.

Keller's Jungle Killers After the demise of the Mickey Mouse Club Circus at Disneyland, George Keller remained for several months with a show featuring his wild animals. At Disneyland from February 19 to September 7, 1956.

Kelly, Moira Actress; appeared in *Billy Bathgate* (Rebecca) and *The Tie That Binds* (Dana Clifton), and provided the voice for the adult Nala in *The Lion King*.

Kelly, Patsy (1910–1981) Actress; appeared in *Freaky Friday* (Mrs. Schmauss) and *The North Avenue Irregulars* (Patsy).

Kelly, Walt (1913–1973) He started at Disney in 1936 and remained until 1941. He specialized in animation of Mickey Mouse, notably on *The Nifty Nineties*. He started as a story man, did some animation on the *Pastoral* sequence of *Fantasia*, working usually with Ward Kimball. He animated on *The Reluctant Dragon* and *Dumbo*, then left to go into comic book work on his own, where he created the character of Pogo.

Kenai Originally human, then bear character in *Brother Bear*; voiced by Joaquin Phoenix.

Ken-L-Land Pet boarding facility outside the Disneyland main gate; opened on January 18, 1958. Walt felt that it was important that travelers visiting Disneyland have a place where they could board their pets for the day rather than leave them in their hot cars. Hosted by Ken-L-Ration (Quaker Oats Co.) until 1967. Later called Kennel Club and Pet Care Kennel.

Kennel Club Pet boarding facility at Disneyland, renamed from Ken-L-Land in 1968 when Kal Kan took over as sponsor. They remained until 1977. Gaines was the sponsor from 1986 to 1991, when it was known as Pet Care Kennel. Friskies took over in 1993, returning to the Kennel Club name. There are also kennels at Magic Kingdom Park and Epcot at Walt Disney World.

Kent, Ralph Artist; joined Disneyland as a production artist in 1963, working on projects not only for the park but also for the New York World's Fair and Celebrity Sports Center. He moved to Walt Disney World in 1971, working in the Merchandise Art department, and later as a director of Walt Disney Imagineering East. In 1990 he joined the Disney Design group as Corporate Trainer, passing on his valuable knowledge to newly hired artists, before retiring in 2004, the same year he was named a Disney Legend.

Kentucky Gunslick (television) Television show; episode 11 of *Texas John Slaughter*.

Kenworthy, Paul Nature photographer whose work helped ensure the success of *The Living*

Desert, The Vanishing Prairie, and *Perri*. He was named a Disney Legend in 1998.

Kern, Bonnie Lee Mouseketeer from the 1950s television show.

Kerrigan, Nancy See *Disney's Nancy Kerrigan Special: Dreams on Ice*.

Kerry, Margaret Actress who was the model for Tinker Bell.

Ketchakiddie Creek Special water area for youngsters at Typhoon Lagoon at Walt Disney World.

Kevin Hill (television) Hour-long drama; debuted on UPN on September 29, 2004, and ended June 8, 2005. Kevin Hill, a 28-year-old self-made, hotshot attorney in New York City, has the ultimate bachelor life—a high-powered job, plenty of pretty ladies, and enough money to buy whatever he wants. But his whole life turns upside down when he's left to raise the ten-month-old daughter of his cousin, who unexpectedly died. After figuring out how to deal with bottles, diapers, and his new no-nonsense gay nanny, Kevin quits his workaholic law firm for a flex-time, boutique law office, Grey & Associates, owned and completely staffed by women. Stars Taye Diggs (Kevin Hill), Jon Seda (Dame Butler), Patrick Breen (George Weiss), Christina Hendricks (Nicolette Raye), Kate Levering (Veronica Carter), Michael Michele (Jessie Grey). From Touchstone Television.

Key to the Cache, The (television) Television show; part 2 of *The Horse Without a Head*.

Key West Seafood Restaurant in Disney Village at Disneyland Paris; opened on April 12, 1992.

KHJ Los Angeles television station, Channel 9, acquired by Disney on December 2, 1988; call letters changed to KCAL a year later.

Khrushchev, Nikita Soviet chairman who raised a fuss when the State Department did not let him visit Disneyland in September 1959. Walt was all ready to receive him, and in fact, Mrs. Disney, who was not impressed by many of the celebrities who visited Disneyland, really wanted to meet Khrushchev.

Kid, The See *Disney's The Kid*.

Kid in King Arthur's Court, A (film) An earthquake occurs during a Little League game in Southern California, and 14-year-old Calvin Fuller, playing for a team known as the Knights, falls through a crack in the earth and is inexplicably thrust back in time to the mythical medieval kingdom of Camelot and the court of the legendary King Arthur. Calvin discovers that he has been summoned to the 12th century by Merlin to help restore Arthur's fading glory, and to prevent the realm from falling into the clutches of the sinister Lord Belasco. Calvin must find the courage to face Belasco and prove to himself that he has what it takes to be a worthy knight. Directed by Michael Gottlieb. A Walt Disney Picture in association with Tapestry Films and Trimark Pictures. Released on August 11, 1995. 90 min. Stars Thomas Ian Nicholas (Calvin Fuller), Joss Ackland (King Arthur), Ron Moody (Merlin), Art Malik (Lord Belasco). Kate Winslet, before becoming famous for her role in *Titanic*, played the role of Princess Sarah. To gain an authentic look, the producers decided to film in and around Budapest, Hungary. There they found a medieval castle and village set being used by a BBC television series that was on hiatus for the season. With a little redressing and redesigning, the set was just right. The production was truly international, for a final scene was filmed in England, the music was scored in Prague, and the final sound mix was done in Australia. An interesting bit of trivia—Ron Moody, who plays Merlin, played the same role for Disney 16 years earlier in *Unidentified Flying Oddball*. Released on video in 1996. A sequel, *A Kid in Aladdin's Palace* (1997), with Thomas Ian Nicholas reprising his role as Calvin Fuller, was made as a direct-to-video film by Trimark, and had its world television premiere on Disney Channel in March 1999.

Kidder, Margot Actress; appeared in *Trenchcoat* (Mickey Raymond).

Kidnapped (film) Young David Balfour attempts to regain his rightful inheritance, the house, and lands of Shaws in Scotland, and in doing so is nearly killed and then kidnapped due to his treacherous Uncle Ebenezer. But the doughty Scottish laird, Alan Breck Stewart, takes a hand and after a shipwreck, hairbreadth escapes, and a chase the length of the Highlands, David, with Alan's help, confronts his uncle and recovers his estate. Released February 24, 1960. Directed by Robert Stevenson. Although publicists tried to prove otherwise, the director insisted there was no relation between him and the Robert Louis Stevenson who wrote this classic adventure story. 94 min. Stars James MacArthur (David Balfour), Peter Finch (Alan Breck Stewart), Bernard Lee (Capt. Hoseason), Niall MacGinnis (Shaun), John Laurie (Uncle Ebenezer), Finlay Currie (Cluny MacPherson), and the then unknown Peter O'Toole (Robin Og MacGregor). Released on video in 1983 and 1992.

Kids Is Kids (television) Television show; aired on December 10, 1961. Directed by Hamilton S. Luske. Reruns were titled *Donald Duck Quacks Up*, and an edited version was shown as *Mickey and Donald Kidding Around*. Prof. Von Drake covers child psychology with a series of cartoons, trying to give Donald some advice on raising his nephews.

Kids of the Kingdom Group of talented and energetic young singers and dancers who perform at the Disney parks; begun at Disneyland in the summer of 1974.

Kids Who Knew Too Much, The (television) Two-hour television movie; aired on March 9, 1980. Directed by Robert Clouse. A dying man leaves a note in a kid's toy speedboat; the boy and his friends help a lady reporter solve the case and save the life of a visiting Russian premier. Stars Sharon Gless, Larry Cedar, Rad Daly, Dana Hill, Christopher Holloway, Lloyd Haynes, Jared Martin, Kevin King Cooper, Jackie Coogan. Roger

Mobley, who had starred as Gallegher 15 years earlier, returned to play a small role as a policeman.

Kilimanjaro Safaris Attraction at Disney's Animal Kingdom at Walt Disney World. Guests board open-sided safari vehicles at the modern-day town of Harambe for an exciting exploration of more than 100 acres of savanna, forest, rivers, and rocky hills. There are up-close encounters with great herds of animals roaming the land, and there is even some adventure as the safari vehicle surprises a band of elephant poachers and gives chase. The vehicles seat 32 guests and are environmentally safe with propane-fueled engines.

Killer Mountain, The (television) Television show; part 2 of *Banner in the Sky*.

Killers from Kansas (television) Television show; episode 3 of *Texas John Slaughter*.

Killers of the High Country (television) Television show; aired on October 16, 1959. Mountain lions and their struggle to live alongside humans in the Rocky Mountains. Directed by Tom McGowan.

Kilmer, Val Actor; appeared in *Tombstone* (Doc Holliday).

Kilroy (television) Four-part television show; aired on March 14, 21, 28, and April 4, 1965. Directed by Robert Butler. Oscar Kilroy, discharged from the Marines, visits a small town and decides to stay; his ability to involve himself in other people's problems leads to some unusual results. Stars Warren Berlinger, Celeste Holm, Allyn Joslyn, Bryan Russell, Robert Emhardt, Philip Abbott, Arthur Hunnicutt.

Kim Possible (television) Animated series on Disney Channel; premiered on June 7, 2002. Teenager Kim Possible balances her personal life (including school, boys, and shopping) with her duties going on missions to save the world from evil villains. Voices include Christy Carlson Romano (Kim), Will Friedle (Ron Stoppable), Nancy Cartwright (Rufus), Kirsten Storms (Bon-Bon Rockweiler), Rider Strong (Brick). 65 episodes.

Kim Possible: A Sitch in Time (television) Animated special premiering on Disney Channel on November 28, 2003. The fate of the future, humanity, and planet earth rests in Kim's hands when notorious supervillains exploit time travel to tamper with the past and the future. Kim goes back in time to thwart them, only to have her opponents strike when she is most vulnerable. When she traverses to the future, Kim must team with her now grown friends to restore the time-space continuum. Directed by Steve Loter. Voices include Christy Carlson Romano (Kim), Will Friedle (Ron), Nancy Cartwright (Rufus), Tahj Mowry (Wade). 65 min.

Kim Possible Movie, Disney's: So the Drama (television) A Disney Channel Original Movie; aired on April 8, 2005. Kim is swept off her feet by the new guy at school, Erik, who asks her to go to the junior prom, an invitation that makes Kim's best friend, Ron Stoppable, jealous. The omnipresent evil villain, Dr. Drakken, kidnaps Kim's rocket scientist dad, and now it's up to Ron to put his jealousy aside, track down a love-struck Kim, and together rescue her dad—all before the big school dance. Directed by Steve

Loter. 66 min. Voices include Christy Carlson Romano (Kim Possible), Will Friedle (Ron Stoppable), Ricky Ullman (Erik), John DiMaggio (Drakken), Nancy Cartwright (Rufus), Tahj Mowry (Wade), Kirsten Storms (Bonnie Rockwaller), Raven (Monique), Gary Cole (Dad), Jean Smart (Mom), Rider Strong (Brick).

Kim Possible: The Secret Files (film) Direct-to-video movie released on September 2, 2003, consisting of episodes from the television series (including one never-aired episode). A computer-generated Rufus (the naked mole rat) serves as host. Directed by Chris Bailey and David Block. Voices include Christy Carlson Romano (Kim), Will Friedle (Ron), Nancy Cartwright (Rufus), Tahj Mowry (Wade). 71 min.

Kimball, Ward (1914–2002) Animator; began his Disney career in 1934, known as one of Walt's "Nine Old Men." He animated on such Disney classics as *Pinocchio* (on which he was noted for his creation of Jiminy Cricket), *Dumbo*, *The Three Caballeros*, and directed the Academy Award-winning shorts *Toot, Whistle, Plunk and Boom* and *It's Tough to Be a Bird*. He also produced episodes for the television series *Disneyland*, most notably the shows on the subject of Man in Space, and consulted on World of Motion for Epcot. Ward was a train enthusiast, whose love of the hobby helped get Walt himself interested. He was honored with the Disney Legends award in 1989.

Kindercare Center Child-care facility at Walt Disney World; opened on May 25, 1981. A second center opened on August 27, 1984. Kindercare's

contract expired in 2004, and Central Florida YMCA took over the operation of child-care centers on resort property.

King, Jack (1895–1958) Animator/director; worked at Disney from 1929 to 1933 and from 1936 to 1946. He directed the early Donald Duck cartoons before Jack Hannah took over. He was a sequence director on such features as *Pinocchio*, *Saludos Amigos*, *Dumbo*, *The Three Caballeros*, *Make Mine Music*, *Melody Time*, and *The Adventures of Ichabod and Mr. Toad*.

King Arthur (film) A reluctant leader, Arthur wishes only to leave Britain and return to the peace and stability of Rome. Before he can, one final mission leads him and his Knights of the Round Table—Lancelot, Galahad, Bors, Tristan, and Gawain—to the conclusion that when Rome is gone, Britain will need a leader to fill the vacuum. Under the guidance of Merlin, a former enemy, and with the beautiful Guinevere by his side, Arthur will have to find the strength within himself to change the course of history and lead Britain into a new age. A story of chivalry, bravery, and one man's destiny, being a fresh look at the origins of the legendary hero. A Jerry Bruckheimer Films/Touchstone Picture. Released on July 7, 2004, after a June 28 world premiere at the Ziegfeld Theater in New York. Directed by Antoine Fuqua. Stars Clive Owen (Arthur), Keira Knightley (Guinevere), Ioan Gruffudd (Lancelot), Steven Dillane (Merlin), Ray Winstone (Bors), Til Schweiger (Cynric), Stellan Skarsgård (Cerdic), Hugh Dancy (Galahad), Mads Mikkelsen (Tristan), Ray Stevenson (Dagonet), Ken Stott (Marius Honorius). 126 min. Filmed in Ireland, in CinemaScope. Released on video in 2004.

King Arthur Carrousel Fantasyland attraction at Disneyland; opened on July 17, 1955; it was moved to a new location in 1982–83. Walt Disney bought an old 1922 Dentzel carousel from a Toronto amusement park, supplementing it with Murphy horses from another at Coney Island. He wanted all horses, so assorted other animals on the purchased carousels were put into storage. He also wanted all of his horses to be leaping, so legs of standing horses were broken and reset into the proper configurations. Each horse is different, both in carving and in paint configuration. There are a total of 68 horses, 17 rows of four abreast, and one bench for wheelchair guests. Hand-painted scenes from *Sleeping Beauty* grace the interior. During the reconstruction of Fantasyland in 1982–83, the carousel was moved back several feet, to open up the castle courtyard somewhat and give guests a better view of the impressive carousel as they cross the drawbridge and enter the castle.

King David World premiere concert event, opening May 18, 1997 (after three previews), for six performances, as the inaugural production at the restored New Amsterdam Theater in New York City. The musical by Alan Menken and Tim Rice retells the Old Testament story of the shepherd boy, David, who rises from his humble roots to become King of Israel. Directed by Mike Ockrent. Stars Marcus Lovett (David), Roger Bart (Jonathan), Stephen Bogardus (Joab), Judy Kuhn (Michal), Alice Ripley (Bathsheba), Peter Samuel (Samuel), Martin Vidnovic (Saul).

King Eidilleg King of the Fair Folk in *The Black Cauldron*; voiced by Arthur Malet.

King Hubert Father of Prince Phillip in *Sleeping Beauty*; voiced by Bill Thompson.

King Leonidas Ruler of Naboombu in *Bedknobs and Broomsticks*; voiced by Lennie Weinrib.

King Louie Scatting king of the monkey characters in *The Jungle Book*; voiced by Louis Prima.

King Neptune (film) Silly Symphony cartoon; released on September 10, 1932. Directed by Burt Gillett. When pirates cruelly capture a mermaid, the underwater denizens come to the rescue, alerting King Neptune who stirs up a storm at sea, sinking the pirates and rescuing the mermaid who has discovered the pirates' treasure.

King of the Grizzlies (film) Ernest Thompson Seton, the well-known American artist and author, tells the story of Wahb, a mighty grizzly who roamed the Greybull country of the old West. A Cree Indian, Moki, befriends Wahb as a cub, and, in later years, the Indian and the bear have many strange encounters, but always recognize each other as "brothers." Released on February 11, 1970. Directed by Ron Kelly. 93 min. Stars John Yesno (Moki), Chris Wiggins (Colonel), Hugh Webster (Shorty), Jan Van Evera (Slim). Based on *The Biography of a Grizzly*, by Ernest Thompson Seton, the film is narrated by Winston Hibler, who also produced. Lloyd Beebe, long involved with many of the Disney's nature films, supervised the film as field producer. The star of the film, Big Ted, the grizzly, was a 7-year-old, 10-foot tall, 1,300-pound bear who completed many of his scenes for the reward of his favorite food, marshmallows. Much of the filming was done over a two-year period on location in the Canadian Rockies of Alberta and British Columbia, including Moraine Lake, within Banff National Park, Yoho National Park, and the Kananaskis River and forest. Released on video in 1986.

King Stefan Father of Sleeping Beauty; voiced by Taylor Holmes.

King Stefan's Banquet Hall Restaurant upstairs in Cinderella Castle in Magic Kingdom Park at Walt Disney World; opened on October 1, 1971. Disney designers have not been able to explain why Cinderella Castle contains King Stefan's Banquet Hall, since King Stefan is one of the kings in *Sleeping Beauty*. Controversy aside, the restaurant is one of the park's most charming. Originally, there were 13th-century costumes of brown and orange tights and tunics for the young men, and medieval headdresses and gowns with overskirts for the young ladies. When the park first opened, diners were frequently serenaded by madrigal singers. Renamed Cinderella's Royal Table, beginning April 28, 1997.

King Triton Father of Ariel and the ruler of the seas in *The Little Mermaid*; voiced by Kenneth Mars.

King Triton's Carousel Attraction at Paradise Pier at Disney's California Adventure; opened on February 8, 2001. Guests ride on 56 California sea critters—dolphins, sea lions, whales, sea horses, otters, and flying fish.

Kingdom Films Partnership formed in 2005 to raise financing for Disney films, with *Flightplan* being the first film released. Kingdom Films raised $135 million in equity and $370 million in debt, and it was to provide 40 percent of production and distribution costs and receive 40 percent of the profit from box office and video sales for about 32 films over the following four years. It followed a previous film-financing venture, Mariner Film Partners, which raised $200 million in 1996.

Kingdom of Dreams and Magic—Tokyo Disneyland (film) Documentary featurette; released in Japan on July 23, 1983. 24 min. After the opening of Tokyo Disneyland in 1983, and due to the success of previous short films relating

Signs (2002)

Rock 'N Roller Coaster at Disney-MGM Studios

King Triton's Carousel at Disney's California Adventure

Grizzly River Run at Disney's California Adventure

Soarin' Over California at Disney's California Adventure

Cinderella II (2002)

Piglet's Big Movie (2003)

101 Dalmations II: Patch's London Adventure (2003)

The Emperor's New Groove (2000)

The Little Mermaid II: Return to the Sea (2000)

Lilo & Stitch (2002)

Pirates of the Caribbean: The Curse of the Black Pearl (2003)

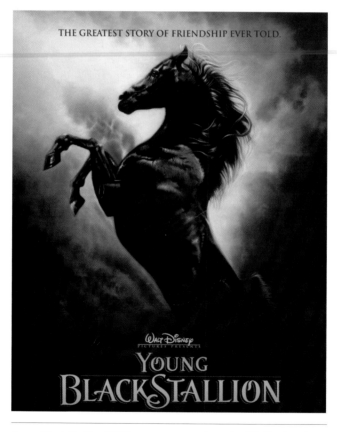

Young Black Stallion (2003)

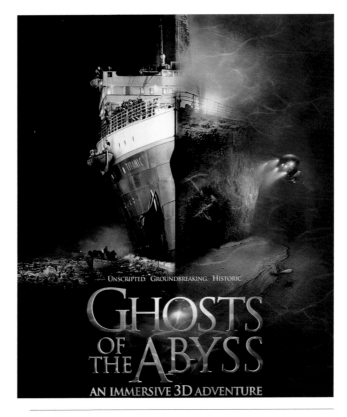

Ghosts of the Abyss (2003)

Pearl Harbor (2001)

Treasure Planet (2002)

Mission: SPACE at Epcot

Stitch's Great Escape! at Magic Kingdom Park

Golden Dreams at Disney's California Adventure

Lights, Motors, Action! Extreme Stunt Show at Disney-MGM Studios

The Incredibles (2004)

Monsters, Inc. (2001)

Finding Nemo (2003)

Chicken Little (2005)

Sun Wheel at Disney's California Adventure

a bug's land at Disney's California Adventure

House of Mouse—television show (2001)

Fantasia/2000 (2000)

Return to Never Land (2002)

Dinosaur at Disney's Animal Kingdom Park

Primeval Whirl at Disney's Animal Kingdom Park

Playhouse Disney—Live on Stage! at Disney-MGM Studios

Turtle Talk with Crush! at Epcot

TriceraTop Spin at Disney's Animal Kingdom Park

Kim Possible—television show (2002)

Lizzie McGuire—television show (2001)

Be careful what you wish for.

DISNEY'S
TEACHER'S PET

A musical tail about one dog's dream of becoming a boy

Teacher's Pet—television show (2000)

Stanley—television show (2001)

W.I.T.C.H.—Disney Publishing Worldwide (2001)

the pleasures of earlier Disney parks, this promotional film was created to document the new facility.

Kingswell Avenue Site of the first Disney Studio in Hollywood. When Walt received a contract to produce a series of Alice Comedies, he was living with his Uncle Robert on Kingswell, near Commonwealth, in Hollywood. A couple of blocks down the same street, he found a real estate firm at 4651 Kingswell that was not using the back half of their office, so he made arrangements to rent it and moved in during October 1923. Soon, however, after a little money had come in, he was able to rent the next-door store at 4649 Kingswell, and the Disney Brothers Cartoon Studio had its own first real location. The Disneys moved to a new studio on Hyperion Avenue in 1926.

Kinnear, Roy Actor; appeared in *One of Our Dinosaurs Is Missing* (Supt. Grubbs) and *Herbie Goes to Monte Carlo* (Quincey).

Kinney, Jack (1909–1992) Animator/director; joined Disney in 1931, working first as an animator on the shorts. He was a sequence director on such films as *Pinocchio* and *Dumbo*, and directed *Der Fuehrer's Face*. He first directed Goofy in *Goofy's Glider* and soon became established as the director of the Goofy cartoons. He left Disney in 1959 to form his own animation company, and in 1988 he wrote the book *Walt Disney and Assorted Other Characters*.

Kirby, Bruno Actor; appeared in *Superdad* (Stanley Schlimmer), *Tin Men* (Mouse), and *Good Morning, Vietnam* (Lt. Steven Hauk).

Kirk, Tommy Actor; appeared in *Swiss Family Robinson* (Ernst), *Old Yeller* (Travis Coates), *The Shaggy Dog* (Wilby Daniels), *The Absent-Minded Professor* (Biff Hawk), *Babes in Toyland* (Grumio), *Moon Pilot* (Walter Talbot), *Bon Voyage* (Elliott Willard), *Son of Flubber* (Biff Hawk), *The Misadventures of Merlin Jones* and *The Monkey's Uncle* (Merlin Jones), and on television on *The Hardy Boys* (Joe) on the *Mickey Mouse Club*, on which he also provided a voice for *Boys of the Western Sea*. Appeared also on television in *Escapade in Florence* and *The Horsemasters*.

Kiss the Girl Song from *The Little Mermaid*, written by Howard Ashman and Alan Menken. Nominated for an Academy Award.

Kissimmee Neighboring town to Walt Disney World in Florida.

Kit Carson and the Mountain Men (television) Two-part television show; aired on January 9 and 16, 1977. Directed by Vincent McEveety. Kit Carson joins Fremont's survey party, where he is idolized by the General's young brother-in-law; both get caught up in intrigue by those trying to sabotage the expedition. Stars Christopher Connelly, Robert Reed, Ike Eisenmann, Gary Lockwood, Emile Genest, Richard Jaeckel, Val de Vargas.

Kit Cloudkicker Bear cub star of *TaleSpin*, voiced by R. J. Williams.

Kitchen Kabaret Audio-Animatronics show in The Land at Epcot; from October 1, 1982 until January 3, 1994. The show taught nutrition in an entertaining way by having representatives of all of the food groups sing about their value. The characters were led by Bonnie Appetit, and included Mr. Hamm and Mr. Eggz, the Cereal Sisters, and the Colander Combo. There were corny lyrics to such songs as "Veggie Veggie Fruit Fruit." The show was superseded by Food Rocks.

Kitt, Eartha Actress; appeared in *Ernest Scared Stupid* (Old Lady Hackmore) and *Holes* (Madame Zeroni), and provided the voice of Yzma in *The Emperor's New Groove* and Bagheera in *The Jungle Book: Mowgli's Story*.

Kline, Kevin Actor; appeared in *Consenting Adults* (Richard Parker), and voiced Phoebus in *The Hunchback of Notre Dame*.

Klondike Kid, The (film) Mickey Mouse cartoon; released on November 12, 1932. Directed by Wilfred Jackson. Mickey, a piano player in a

Klondike saloon, finds Minnie outside cold and starving. Peg Leg Pierre takes off with her and Mickey goes after him, saving her just as Pierre is run over a cliff by his own runaway log cabin.

Knell, David Actor; appeared in *The Devil and Max Devlin* (Nerve Nordlinger), *Splash* (Claude), and *Turner & Hooch* (Ernie).

Knife & Gun Club, The (television) Unsold pilot for a television series about life and death in an emergency room at an inner-city hospital; aired on ABC on July 30, 1990. 60 min. Directed by Eric Laueuville. Stars Dorian Harewood, Perry King, Daniel Jenkins, Cynthia Bain.

Knight for a Day, A (film) Goofy cartoon; released on March 8, 1946. Directed by Jack Hannah. In a jousting tournament, a squire accidentally is put in a knight's place and beats all the contestants, winning the hand of Princess Esmerelda. Goofy plays all the parts.

Knight in Camelot, A (television) Two-hour television movie; aired on November 8, 1998, on *The Wonderful World of Disney*. Computer researcher Vivien Morgan finds herself transported back in time to 589 A.D. at the court of King Arthur. Convincing everyone she has magical powers, she sets about introducing 20th-century "improvements" at Camelot with the aid of Clarence, a quick-witted young page of the court. But perhaps Camelot is not ready for Vivien's "progress." She soon has rivals, including the crafty Merlin. Directed by Roger Young. Stars Whoopi Goldberg (Vivien), Michael York (King Arthur), Simon Fenton (Clarence), Paloma Baeza (Sandy), James Coombes (Sir Lancelot), Robert Addie (Sir Sagramour), Ian Richardson (Merlin), Amanda Donohoe (Queen Guinevere). Filming took place in England and at MaFilm Studios near Budapest, Hungary. Released on video in 1999.

Knightley, Keira Actress; starred in the *Pirates of the Caribbean* trilogy (Elizabeth Swann) and *King Arthur* (Guinevere), and on television in *Princess of Thieves* (Gwyn).

Knotts, Don Actor; appeared in *The Apple Dumpling Gang* (Theodore Ogelvie), *No Deposit, No Return* (Bert), *Gus* (Coach Venner), *Herbie Goes to Monte Carlo* (Wheely Applegate), *Hot Lead and Cold Feet* (Denver Kid), *The Apple Dumpling Gang Rides Again* (Theodore), and on Disney Channel in *Quints* (Governor Healy). He provided the voice of Mayor Turkey Lurkey in *Chicken Little*.

Koblischek, Horst (1926–2002) He led Disney merchandising in Germany from 1958 until his retirement in 1993, and was presented a European Disney Legends award in 1997.

Kodak Presents Disneyland '59 See Disneyland '59.

Kona Café Restaurant in the Polynesian Resort at Walt Disney World, taking the place of the Coral Isle Café; opened on November 23, 1998.

Konetzni, Al He joined Disney's Consumer Products Division in New York in 1953 as an artist and idea man, and for three decades he was responsible for developing and designing hundreds of different products featuring Disney characters. Among his best-known products are a Disney character lunch box in the shape of a school bus made by Aladdin, and the Pez Mickey and Donald candy dispensers. He retired in 1981 and was named a Disney Legend in 1999.

Korman, Harvey Actor; appeared in *Son of Flubber* (husband in television commercial) and *Herbie Goes Bananas* (Capt. Blythe), and on television on the *Gallegher* series and in *The Nutt*

House. He also starred on The Disney Channel in *Gone Are the Dayes*.

Korsmo, Charlie Child actor; appeared in *Dick Tracy* (Kid), *What About Bob?* (Siggy Martin), and *The Doctor* (Nicky).

Kostal, Irwin (1911–1994) Musical director, worked on the score and background music for *Mary Poppins*, *Bedknobs and Broomsticks*, and *Pete's Dragon*, and for all three received Academy Award nominations. He was also called upon to create a new digitally recorded sound track for *Fantasia* in 1982, an assignment that he felt was the most challenging of his career. He was named a Disney Legend in 2004.

Kraft Salutes Disneyland's 25th Anniversary (television) Television special hosted by Danny Kaye, along with many other celebrities in cameo appearances; aired on March 6, 1980. Michael Jackson and the Osmonds perform. Directed by Dwight Hemion.

Kraft Salutes Walt Disney World's 10th Anniversary (television) Television special on CBS; aired on January 21, 1982. Directed by Dwight Hemion. The Lane family, played by Dean Jones, Michelle Lee, Eileen Brennan, Dana Plato, and Ricky Schroder, visit Walt Disney World.

Krag, the Kootenay Ram (television) A bighorn ram struggles to survive in the wilderness of the Rocky Mountains. Prepared for the American television show, but did not air. First aired in Canada on November 27, 1983. Later shown on The Disney Channel. Directed by Frank Zuniga.

Kringla Bakeri og Kafe Fast-food restaurant in Norway in World Showcase at Epcot; opened on May 6, 1988.

Krippendorf's Tribe (film) Anthropologist James Krippendorf, a single father trying to raise three kids, has for two years been living off a Proxmire Foundation grant to study an "undiscovered" tribe in New Guinea. Unfortunately, there is no tribe and the grant money has been spent on his kids. When he must prove the tribe exists by documenting it on film, he begs his dysfunctional family to pose as the fictional "Krippendorf's Tribe." He names the tribe the Shelmikedmu, after his kids—Shelly, Mickey, and Edmund—and turns his backyard into a jungle, hoping to match film he had shot of a New Guinea tribe. Doubts are raised about the "discovery" by anthropologist Veronica Micelli and anthropology department head Ruth Allen. A Touchstone Picture. Released on February 27, 1998. 94 min. Directed by Todd Holland. Stars Richard Dreyfuss (James Krippendorf), Jenna Elfman (Veronica Micelli), Natasha Lyonne (Shelly), Gregory Smith (Mickey), Carl Michael Lindner (Edmund), Stephen Root (Gerald Adams), Elaine Stritch (Irene Harding), Tom Poston (Gordon Harding), Lily Tomlin (Ruth Allen), David Ogden Stiers (Henry Spivey). Based on the novel of the same title by Larry Parkin. The tribal villages were created at the Kualoa Ranch on the island of Oahu in Hawaii. Video release in 1998.

Krisel, Gary Head of Walt Disney Television Animation from 1984 to 1995 (vice president 1984–1990, president thereafter), he had originally started with the company in marketing at Disneyland in 1972. Later he joined the Walt Disney Music Company, and served as its president from 1981–1986. He resigned in 1995.

Kronk's New Groove (film) Direct-to-video animated film; released on December 13, 2005. Kronk is content as head chef at Mudka's Meat Hut, where he is surrounded by his friends Pacha and Chica, and visited on occasion by Emperor Kuzco. However, word arrives of an impending disaster—Kronk's blustery, hard-to-please father, Papi, is coming for a visit. Kronk is terrified because he has been leading his father to believe that his life is more than it is. The evil Yzma meanwhile has conned Kronk into helping her with a dastardly scheme. With Papi still on his way, Kronk's friends come to the rescue. Our soft-hearted hero learns that he is rich and successful because he has true friends, and that to be happy, one must be "true to your groove." Directed by Elliot M. Bour and Saul Andrew Blinkoff. Voices include Patrick Warburton (Kronk), Eartha Kitt (Yzma), Tracey Ullman (Birdwell), John Mahoney (Papi), David Spade (Kuzco), John Fiedler (Rudy), John Goodman (Pacha), Wendie Malick (Chica).

Krumholtz, David Actor; appeared in *Life with Mikey* (Barry Corman), *The Santa Clause* and *The Santa Clause 2* (Bernard), *10 Things I Hate About You* (Michael Eckman), and on the television series *Monty*.

Kulp, Nancy (1921–1991) Actress; appeared in *The Parent Trap* (Mrs. Grunecker), *Moon Pilot* (nutritionist), and provided the voice of Frou-Frou in *The Aristocats*.

Kundun (film) In 1937 a two-and-a-half-year-old boy, Tenzin Gyatso, from a simple family in rural Tibet was recognized as the 14th reincarnation of the Buddha of love and compassion, and destined to become the spiritual and political leader of his country. Told through the eyes of the Dalai Lama, the movie chronicles his early life, from childhood through the Chinese invasion in 1950 and his journey into exile in 1959. A Touchstone Picture. Released exclusively in New York and Los Angeles on December 25, 1997, and expanded to more theaters on January 16, 1998. Directed by Martin Scorsese. Stars Tenzin Thuthob Tsarong (Dalai Lama as adult), Gyurme Tethong (Dalai Lama age 12), Tenzin Chodon Gyalpo (mother). 135 min. Filmed in CinemaScope. Screenwriter Melissa Mathison based her script on research plus 15 interviews with the Dalai Lama himself.

The title of the film means "great compassionate teacher." Actors for the film were found among Tibetans living in India, the United States, and Canada; while none were professional actors, several were members of the Tibetan Institute of Performing Arts. Since it was not possible to film in Tibet or India, the home of the exiled Tibetan government, the company decided to film in Morocco, which has a high desert and mountains as needed to approximate Tibet. Production base was at the Atlas Studios outside of Ouarzazate. The release of the film caused political repercussions because the Chinese government was not pleased with it and several other Hollywood films that they felt aided an independence movement and glorified the Tibetans whose homeland, the Chinese insist, has always been part of China. Video release in 1998.

Kuri, Emile (1907–2000) He joined Disney in 1952 as head decorator. He worked on *20,000 Leagues Under the Sea*, winning an Oscar. He supervised the set decoration on such films as *The Absent-Minded Professor, Mary Poppins, Bedknobs and Broomsticks*, and *Million Dollar Duck*, and helped decorate company executive offices and interior and exterior settings at Disneyland and Walt Disney World.

Kurtz, Swoosie Actress; won an Emmy Award for a guest appearance on *Carol & Company* in 1990, and appeared in *Bubble Boy* (Mrs. Livingston).

Kurtzman, Katy Actress; appeared on television in *Child of Glass* and *Donovan's Kid.*

Kuzco Emperor and llama character in *The Emperor's New Groove*; voiced by David Spade.

L

L.A. Bar and Grill Restaurant in Disney Village at Disneyland Paris; opened on April 12, 1992.

La Boutique des Provinces Shop in Canada in World Showcase at Epcot; opened on September 24, 1986. Decorative gifts, jewelry, and fashion accessories are offered from French Canada.

La Maison du Vin Shop in France in World Showcase at Epcot; opened on October 1, 1982. Taste a few wines as you visit France. Presented by Barton & Guestier.

La Piñata (film) Segment of *The Three Caballeros* in which Donald Duck learns of "Las Posadas."

LaBeouf, Shia Actor; appeared in *Holes* (Stanley Yelnats) and *The Greatest Game Ever Played* (Francis Ouimet), and on Disney Channel in *Even Stevens* (Louis Stevens), *Tru Confessions* (Eddie Walker), *Hounded* (Ronny Van Dusen), and *The Even Stevens Movie*. He won a Daytime Emmy in 2003 for Performer in a Children's Series.

Lacroix, André Joined the company as chairman of Euro Disney on July 1, 2003. He was formerly head of the international arm of Burger King Corp. He left Disney in 2005.

Ladd, Alan (1913–1964) Actor who appears and tells the *Baby Weems* story in *The Reluctant Dragon*.

Ladd, Diane Actress; appeared in *Something Wicked This Way Comes* (Mrs. Nightshade), *The Cemetery Club* (Lucille Rubin), and *Father Hood* (Rita).

Ladder 49 (film) A devoted firefighter, Jack Morrison, is trapped in a major warehouse blaze, and while wondering if he will be rescued, he reflects back on his life. He remembers back to his first day with the Baltimore Fire Department and recalls his initiation into the close-knit, prank-filled, courage-fed band of brothers at the firehouse, and the discovery of his own deeply held compulsion to save lives. Pushed to the limits of loyalty and courage, Jack holds tight to indelible memories as he waits for his own rescue. Outside, his best friend, Capt. Mike Kennedy, risks his life to save him. A Touchstone Pictures/Beacon Pictures production. Released on October 1, 2004. Directed by Jay Russell. Stars John Travolta (Capt. Mike Kennedy), Joaquin Phoenix (Jack Morrison), Balthazar Getty (Ray Gauquin), Robert Patrick (Lenny Richter), Jacinda Barrett (Linda Morrison), Morris Chestnut (Tommy Drake), Jay Hernandez (Keith Perez), Billy Burke (Dennis Gauquin), Tim Guinee (Tony

Corrigan), Kevin Chapman (Frank McKinney), Kevin Daniels (Don Miller). 115 min. Released on video in 2005.

Ladies and the Champ (television) Two-hour television movie airing on *The Wonderful World of Disney* on April 22, 2001. Two elderly women in Younger, Illinois, a retirement town, break all the rules to become boxing managers to a young homeless man, a small-time crook whom the old ladies mistake for a prizefighter. Directed by Jeff Barry. Stars Olympia Dukakis (Sarah Stevenson), Marion Ross (Margaret Smith), David DeLuise (Darold Boyarsky), Sarah Strange (Jenny), Garwin Sanford (Vossbinder), Blu Mankuma (Royal Reynolds), Paul Michael (Hamp Gilliam). Filmed on location in Vancouver, B.C.

Lady Cocker spaniel heroine of *Lady and the Tramp*; voiced by Barbara Luddy.

Lady and the Tramp (film) Lady, a young cocker spaniel from a respectable home, falls in love with Tramp, a mutt who lives in the railroad yards. They enjoy several outings together, including a memorable spaghetti dinner by moonlight at Tony's, but their relationship is strained not only by Lady's loyalty to her human family and their newborn baby, but by Tramp's devil-may-care attitude that at one point gets Lady thrown in the dog pound. Tramp redeems himself by saving the baby from a rat and thereby wins Lady's love and the affection of her human family. The first Disney animated feature filmed in Cinema-Scope, which necessitated extra work in planning scenes and action to fill the entire screen. World premiere in Chicago on June 16, 1955; general release on June 22, 1955. Directed by Hamilton Luske, Clyde Geronimi, Wilfred Jackson. 76 min. The idea for the film came from a short story by Ward Greene entitled "Happy Dan, the Whistling Dog." The film was enlivened by such songs as "He's a Tramp" and "The Siamese Cat Song," by Sonny Burke and Peggy Lee. In early script versions, Tramp was first called Homer, then Rags, then Bozo. A 1940 script introduced the twin Siamese cats eventually known as Si and Am; they were then named Nip and Tuck. The

film stars such voice talents as Barbara Luddy as Lady; Larry Roberts as Tramp; and Peggy Lee as Darling, the Siamese cats, and Peg, the show

dog. Peggy Lee helped promote the film on the Disney television series, explaining her work with the score and singing a few numbers. *Lady and the Tramp* was re-released in theaters in 1962, 1971, 1980, and 1986. Released on video in 1987.

Lady and the Tramp: A Lesson in Sharing Attention Educational film; released in September 1978. The film stresses the importance of sharing attention when a new baby joins a family.

Lady and the Tramp II: Scamp's Adventure (film) Direct-to-video release on February 27, 2001. Lady and Tramp are now parents of Scamp, a mischievous pup who longs for the freedom and excitement of a junkyard dog, but soon discovers that life on the streets is not what he expected and that the love of his family is more valuable than he knew. Scamp has three sisters—Annette, Colette, and Danielle—and while on his jaunt "to see the world," rescues from the dog-catcher and falls in love with an orphan mutt, Angel. Directed by Darrell Rooney. Voices include: Scott Wolf (Scamp), Alyssa Milano (Angel), Jodi Benson (Lady), Jeff Bennett (Tramp, Jock, Trusty, Dogcatcher), Chazz Palminteri (Buster), Bill Fagerbakke (Mooch), Bronson Pinchot (Francois), Mickey Rooney (Sparky). 70 min.

Lady Kluck Maid Marian's lady-in-waiting, a chicken, in *Robin Hood*; voiced by Carole Shelley.

Lady Tremaine Cinderella's evil stepmother; voiced by Eleanor Audley.

Ladykillers, The (film) An eccentric Southern professor assembles a band of less-than-competent thieves to rob a Mississippi riverboat casino. When the gang rents a room from unsuspecting, straitlaced, churchgoing little old Mrs. Munson, they get more than they bargained for, along with a strong reminder that crime does not pay. Directed by Joel Coen and Ethan Coen. A Touchstone Picture. Released on March 26, 2004. Stars Tom Hanks (Prof. G. H. Dorr), Irma P. Hall (Marva Munson), Marlon Wayans (Gawain Mac-Sam), J.K. Simmons (Garth Pancake), Tzi Ma (The General), Ryan Hurst (Lump), George Wallace (Sheriff Wyner), Jason Weaver (Weemack Funthes). 104 min. Inspired by the 1955 film featuring Alec Guinness. It received a screening at the Cannes Film Festival on May 18, 2004. Released on video in 2004.

Lafayette Dog in *The Aristocats*; voiced by George Lindsey.

Lahti, Christine Actress; appeared in *Gross Anatomy* (Rachel Woodruff) and *The Doctor* (Anne), and on Disney Channel in *The Four Diamonds* (Dr. Burke/Raptenahad).

Lake Buena Vista Club See Buena Vista Club.

Lake Buena Vista, Florida Hometown of Walt Disney World.

Lake Buena Vista Office Plaza Building opened at Walt Disney World on July 18, 1978.

Also known as the Sun Bank Building. Sun Bank operates on the ground floor, with Disney offices filling the upper floors.

Lake Buena Vista Village Opened at Walt Disney World on March 22, 1975; name later changed to Walt Disney World Village, Disney Village Marketplace, and Downtown Disney Marketplace. A couple of dozen shops are clustered in a delightful setting along the shores of the lagoon. Over the years, the list of shops has changed many times. See *Downtown Disney Marketplace*.

Lake Titicaca (film) Segment of *Saludos Amigos*, starring Donald Duck high in the Andes; re-released as a short on February 18, 1955.

Lakeside Circle Area at Disney-MGM Studios surrounding Echo Lake.

Lambert, the Sheepish Lion (film) Special cartoon; released on February 8, 1952. Directed by Jack Hannah. A stork delivers a lion cub to a flock of sheep by mistake, which eventually proves fortuitous for the sheep when Lambert

grows up to realize his power and uses it to protect the sheep from a wolf. Nominated for an Academy Award.

Lampwick Boy who tempts *Pinocchio*; voiced by Frankie Darro.

Lancaster, Burt (1913–1994) Actor; appeared in *Tough Guys* (Harry Doyle).

Lanchester, Elsa (1902–1986) Actress; appeared in *Mary Poppins* (Katie Nanna), *That Darn Cat* (Mrs. MacDougal), *Blackbeard's Ghost* (Emily Stowecroft), *Rascal* (Mrs. Satterfield), and on television in *My Dog, the Thief*.

Land, The Pavilion in Future World at Epcot; opened on October 1, 1982, sponsored by Kraft from opening until November 1992, when Nestlé took over. The largest pavilion in Future World, The Land covers six acres. Inside, one can find exhibits and shows about agricultural techniques, the importance of good nutrition, and how humans can effectively manage the land while still maintaining its ecology. Besides the areas that can be seen by guests, there are working greenhouses and laboratories where graduate students in agriculture and other disciplines come together to study the latest processes and ideas.

Land Grille Room, The Restaurant in The Land at Epcot; from May 14, 1986, to October 4, 1993. It was previously named The Good Turn Restaurant, and later became Garden Grill Restaurant.

Land of Enemies, The (television) Television show; episode 4 of *Andy Burnett*.

Landau, Martin Actor; appeared in *Ed Wood* (Bela Lugosi). He won an Academy Award for Best Supporting Actor for the role.

Land's End (television) Hour-long syndicated television series; premiered on September 22, 1995, and ended September 15, 1996. Mike Land, a disillusioned former LAPD detective, joins longtime friend Willis P. Dunleevy in opening a private detective agency in Cabo San Lucas, Mexico. When they are invited to provide security for the Westin Regina, a five-star resort, the cases come rolling in. Stars Fred Dryer (Mike Land), Geoffrey Lewis (Willis P. Dunleevy).

Lane, Diane Actress; appeared in *Indian Summer* (Beth Warden), *Judge Dredd* (Judge Hershey), *Jack* (Karen Powell), and *Under the Tuscan Sun* (Frances Mayes).

Lane, Nathan Actor; voiced the meerkat Timon in *The Lion King*, and played Ed Chapman in *Life with Mikey*. He provides the voice of Spot/Scott in *Teacher's Pet* (for which he won an Emmy Award), and he did the voice of Tom Morrow in Innoventions at Disneyland.

Laney, Charley (1943–1997) Mouseketeer from the 1950s television show,

Lange, Jessica Actress; appeared in and co-produced *Country* (Jewell Ivy), and appeared in *A Thousand Acres* (Ginny).

Langhammer, Fred H. Member of the Disney board of directors beginning in January 2005.

Lansburgh, Larry (1911–2001) Director and producer of animal-themed films for three decades, best known for his horse pictures, including the Academy Award–winning *The Horse with the Flying Tail*. He was named a Disney Legend in 1998.

Lansbury, Angela Actress; appeared in *Bedknobs and Broomsticks* (Eglantine Price) and provided the voice of Mrs. Potts in *Beauty and the Beast*. She was a host of *Fantasia/2000*, and appeared on television in *The Dream Is Alive*. She was named a Disney Legend in 1995.

Lantern Hill (television) A Disney Channel Premiere Film; aired on January 27, 1990. A girl plans to reunite her parents after discovering her father, long thought to be dead, is alive. Directed by Kevin Sullivan. Stars Sam Waterston (Andrew Stuart), Mairon Bennett (Jane), Colleen

Dewhurst, Sarah Polley. 112 min. Released on video in 1991.

Lapland (film) People and Places featurette; released on July 3, 1957. Directed by Ben Sharpsteen. Filmed in CinemaScope. 29 min. High in the frigid zone of the continent of Europe, where the Arctic Circle cuts through the upper tips of Norway, Sweden, Finland, and Russia, is the land of the Lapps—a people privileged to cross these frontiers unrestricted because of their nomadic traditions and their owing allegiance to no one nation. Their economy, dependent on migrating livestock, is explained, as well as their customs and gypsylike existence.

Large Animals of the Arctic (film) Part of *White Wilderness*; released on 16mm for schools in September 1964. The musk ox, caribou, and reindeer grazing on the tundra face constant danger from wolf packs and ferocious wolverines.

Large Animals that Once Roamed the Plains (film) Part of *The Vanishing Prairie*; released on 16mm for schools in September 1962. Few are left of the pronghorn antelope, bighorn sheep, cougar, and coyote, which once roamed the prairie in great numbers.

Larkin, Linda She voiced Jasmine in *Aladdin*.

Larsen, Larry Mouseketeer from the 1950s television show.

Larson, Eric (1905–1988) Animator; one of Walt's "Nine Old Men," he began at the Studio in 1933 and worked on such classics as *Snow White and the Seven Dwarfs*, *Bambi*, *Cinderella*, *The Jungle Book*, and *The Great Mouse Detective* as animator and directing animator. His  patience and skill in explaining animation techniques made him the obvious choice to work with

the training program for new animators in the 1970s, and many of the current animators look to Eric as their mentor. He was honored posthumously with the Disney Legends award in 1989.

Laserdisc The first Disney films were released on disc on December 16, 1978.

Laserphonic Fantasy Show at Epcot; beginning on June 9, 1984, and superseded by Illuminations in 1988. The show was essentially a less sophisticated version of Illuminations, without the spotlighting of the individual countries.

Lasseter, John After a stint in the Disney animation department in the late 1970s and early 1980s, he returned in 1995 as the director of *Toy Story* for Pixar and directed or produced all of the remaining Disney·Pixar releases.

Last Chance Café Restaurant in Frontierland in Disneyland Paris; opened on April 12, 1992.

Last Dance (film) Rick Hayes is a cocky young lawyer from a wealthy family who is assigned the clemency case of Cindy Liggett, a woman on death row. After years of appeals, Cindy no longer wants to fight to save her life. But during the course of Rick's visits and research to prepare a clemency plea, he comes to know a Cindy very different from the teenager who committed murder so many years ago. As they learn to trust each other, they cannot help but acknowledge the love that has grown between them. No matter what the clemency board decides, Rick and Cindy discover and embrace love for the first time in their lives. Released on May 3, 1996. A Touchstone Picture. Directed by Bruce Beresford. Stars Sharon Stone (Cindy), Rob Morrow (Rick), Randy Quaid (Sam Burns), Peter Gallagher (John Hayes), Jack Thompson (Governor), Don Harvey (Doug), Jayne Brook (Jane). 103 min. Set in an unspecified Southern state, the movie was filmed in Nashville and Eddyville, Kentucky; Ridgeland, South Carolina; and briefly at the Taj Mahal in India. At Ridgeland, a brand-new, not-yet-occupied prison was turned into Bridgeland for the film crew. Released on video in 1996.

Last Electric Knight, The (television) Television show; aired on February 16, 1986. Directed by James Fargo. A young martial arts expert searches for a pretend guardian when a social worker tries to take him away from his elderly grandfather. The person he picks happens to be a detective. Pilot for the *Sidekicks* series. Stars Ernie Reyes, Gil Gerard, Keye Luke, Nancy Stafford, Jason Hervey.

Last Flight of Noah's Ark, The (film) An unemployed pilot, fleeing debt collectors, accepts the risky mission of flying an old converted B-29, loaded with farm animals, an attractive young missionary, and two young orphan stowaways, to an island in the Pacific. The plane crash-lands on a small island inhabited by two World War II Japanese naval officers who don't know the war is over. After some confusion, they all end up friends. Converting the plane into a boat, everyone sets sail for Hawaii. After several adventures, they are rescued by the Coast Guard. The pilot and the missionary, with plans to adopt the orphans, are married by the captain. Released on June 25, 1980. Directed by Charles Jarrott. 98 min. Stars Elliott Gould (Noah Dugan), Genevieve Bujold (Bernadette), Ricky Schroder (Bobby), Tammy Lauren (Julie), Vincent Gardenia (Stoney), John Fujioka (Cleveland), Yuki Shimoda (Hiro), John P. Ryan (Coslough), Dana Elcar (Benchley). The film was based on a story by Ernest K. Gann. The movie's song, "Half of Me" was written by Hal David and Maurice Jarre, and performed by Alexandra Brown. Location shooting took place at a dilapidated airfield in the desert near Victorville, California, and on the island of Kauai in Hawaii. For the scene in which the B-29 crashes into the sand, 22 artificial palms were shipped from California to protect the island's ecology. The interior of the plane and many night scenes were filmed on Disney soundstages, and for the underwater scenes, the soundstage tank built for *20,000 Leagues Under The Sea* was utilized. Five B-29's were used in the film, but only one could fly. The others were gathered from remote areas in various dismantled and decaying forms to be rejuvenated, with two sent to the Studio and two sent to Hawaii for an excru- ciatingly difficult rejuvenation process. The U.S. Navy had some rigging and instrumentation on hand; additional equipment was purchased from outside sources, and the rest had to be painstakingly tooled by Disney craftsmen. Besides the human cast, 2 goats, 6 pigs, 5 sheep, 20 chickens, 4 rabbits, 2 grey geese, 4 white ducks, a mallard duck, a cow, and 2 bulls comprised the film's animal cast. Released on video in 1983.

Last Resort, The (television) Reality series; premiered on ABC Family on January 20, 2003. Dysfunctional couples are taken to a Hawaiian island to work out their relationships. From Buena Vista Prods. and Fisher Entertainment in association with Wheeler/Sussman Prods.

Last Shot, The (film) Hollywood screenwriter Steven Schats has long held the great ambition of selling his morbid screenplay, but he has had no success. Then he meets Joe Devine, who represents himself as the man who can green-light Schats's low-budget movie. But Devine is not who he claims to be. In truth, he is not an agent— not of the movie industry variety at least—but rather with the FBI, and he is on a covert mission to ferret out mobsters with criminal ties to Hollywood. Devine is as determined to be a star at the Bureau as Schats is to be one in his industry, and he is just clever enough to make the trusting screenwriter believe that he is at last on the fast track to filmmaking success. A Touchstone Picture in association with Mandeville Films. Directed by Jeff Nathanson. Limited release on September 24, 2004. Stars Matthew Broderick (Steven Schats), Alec Baldwin (Joe Devine), Toni Collette (Emily French), Calista Flockhart (Valerie Weston), Ray Liotta (Jack Devine), Tim Blake Nelson (Marshal Paris), Tony Shalhoub (Tommy Sanz), Buck Henry (Lonnie). Joan Cusack has an uncredited role as Fanny Nash; Pat Morita and Russell Means also have cameo roles playing themselves. 93 min. Based on a true story about aspiring filmmakers, Gary Levy and Dan Lewk, who became unwitting pawns in a covert government operation, as related in the article, "What's Wrong with This Picture?" by Steve Fishman. The working title was *Providence*.

Laugh-O-gram Films Walt Disney's Kansas City company, which made a series of six modernized versions of fairy tales: *The Four Musicians of Bremen*, *Little Red Riding Hood*, *Puss in Boots*, *Jack and the Beanstalk*, *Goldie Locks and the Three Bears*, and *Cinderella*, in 1922. The company had to file for bankruptcy when the distributor defaulted on his payments.

Launchpad McQuack Scrooge's pilot in *Ducktales*, and later in *Darkwing Duck*; voiced by Terence McGovern.

Laurie, Piper Actress; appeared in *Return to Oz* (Aunt Em).

Laurie Hill (television) Television series; aired on ABC from September 30 to October 28, 1992. A family practitioner seesaws between the needs of her writer-husband and her 5-year-old son, and the demands of her work as a physician and partner in a successful medical practice. Stars DeLane Matthews (Laurie Hill), Robert Clohessy (Jeff Hill), Eric Lloyd (Leo Hill), Ellen DeGeneres (Nancy MacIntire).

Lavender Blue (Dilly Dilly) Song from *So Dear to My Heart*, written by Larry Morey and Eliot Daniel. Nominated for an Academy Award.

LaVerne, Lucille (1872–1945) She voiced the Queen/Witch in *Snow White and the Seven Dwarfs*.

Law and Order, Incorporated (television) Television show; episode 4 of *Elfego Baca*.

Lawman or Gunman (television) Television show; episode 3 of *Elfego Baca*.

Lawrence, Andrew Actor; appeared in *Walter and Emily* (Andrew), *Brotherly Love* (Andy Roman), *Horse Sense* and *Jumping Ship* (both as Tommy Biggs), *The Other Me* (Will Browning/Twoie), *Going to the Mat* (Jace Newfield), and provided the voice of T. J. Detweiler on *Recess*.

Lawrence, Joey He voiced Oliver in *Oliver & Company*, and later went on to appear in the pilot for an *Adventures in Babysitting* television series and as Joey Russo in the long-running series *Blossom*. In 1995, he starred in the series *Brotherly Love* with his real-life brothers, Matthew and Andrew. On Disney Channel he was in *Horse Sense* and *Jumping Ship* (both as Michael Woods).

Lawrence, Matthew Actor; appeared in *The Hot Chick* (Billy), on television in *Walter and Emily* (Zack Collins), *Brotherly Love* (Matt Roman), *Boy Meets World* (Jack), and *Angels in the Endzone* (Jesse Harper), and as himself on the *Walt Disney World Happy Easter Parade* (1996). On Disney Channel he was in *H-E-Double Hockey Sticks* (Dave Heinrich) and *Jumping Ship* (Jake Hunter).

Laybourne, Geraldine Hired by Disney in 1996 to be president of Disney/ABC Cable Networks. She had formerly headed Nickelodeon. She left in 1998 to found Oxygen Media.

Le Cellier Buffeteria restaurant in Canada in World Showcase at Epcot; opened on October 1, 1982. Salmon, maple-syrup pie, strawberry-rhubarb cobbler, and other delicacies from north of the border were originally featured. On June 25, 1995, the restaurant reopened after being closed

for nine months, with a new menu featuring deli-style sandwiches and salads. Another change was made as of July 20, 1997, with the restaurant becoming a full-service steakhouse.

Le Fou Gaston's clueless sidekick in *Beauty and the Beast*; voiced by Jesse Corti.

Leachman, Cloris Actress; appeared in *Charley and the Angel* (Nettie Appleby), *The North Avenue Irregulars* (Claire), *Herbie Goes Bananas* (Aunt Louise), *My Boyfriend's Back* (Maggie), and *Sky High* (Nurse Spex), on The Disney Channel in *Spies*, and on television in *Miracle Child* (Doc Betty) and on the series *The Nutt House* (Edwina Nutt), *Walter and Emily* (Emily Collins), *Maybe This Time* (Beasy), and *Thanks* (Grammy).

Learning with Film and Video (film) Educational film; released in September 1986. 15 min. Demonstration of the important role of film and video in the learning experience.

Leave a Legacy Program, beginning October 1, 1999, in the entrance plaza at Epcot whereby guests can have miniature photos of themselves etched in steel on large sculptures.

Ledger, Heath Actor; appeared in *10 Things I Hate About You* (Patrick Verona) and *Casanova* (Giacomo Casanova).

LeDoux, Leone She voiced Minnie Mouse in cartoons of the 1930s and 1940s.

Lee, Jason Actor; appeared in *Enemy of the State* (Zavitz), *Mumford* (Skip Skipperton), *Big Trouble* (Puggy), and provided the voice of Syndrome in *The Incredibles*.

Lee, Jason Scott Actor; appeared in *Rudyard Kipling's The Jungle Book* (Mowgli) and provided the voice of David Kawena in *Lilo & Stitch*.

Lee, Johnny (1898–1965) He voiced Brer Rabbit in *Song of the South*.

Lee, Peggy (1920–2002) She co-wrote songs and voiced Si, Am, Peg, and Darling in *Lady and the Tramp*. Successfully sued Disney almost four decades later for video royalties in a highly publicized case.

Leeds China Co. Chicago manufacturer of ceramic items that was licensed to produce Disney merchandise from 1944 to 1954. Some of their more popular items were various types of vases and planters, and a series of Turnabout cookie jars, each of which consisted of two Disney characters, each facing the opposite way.

Leetch, Tom (1933–1993) Producer, director; he began at Disney in 1955, serving as assistant director on such films as *Mary Poppins*, *Son of Flubber*, and *The Happiest Millionaire*. He produced or directed numerous television shows and films such as *The Sky's the Limit*, *The Whiz Kid and the Carnival Caper*, *The Adventures of Pollyanna*, *Gun Shy*, *The Watcher in the Woods*, and *Night Crossing*.

Leftovers, The (television) Two-hour television movie; aired on November 16, 1986. Directed by Paul Schneider. The unorthodox director of an orphanage, who doesn't believe in strict rules, battles to save the home. The owner wants to develop the land, and the director has to use all his wits to foil him. Stars John Denver, Cindy Williams, George Wyner, Pamela Segall, Andrea Barber, Matthew Brooks, Douglas Emerson, Jason Presson, Jaleel White, Henry Jones, Anne Seymour.

Lefty (television) Television special; aired on October 22, 1980, on NBC. Directed by James E. Thompson. A gymnast with one arm yearns to compete despite her disability. Stars Carol Johnston. Enlarged from an educational film made for the Walt Disney Educational Media Company, entitled *The Truly Exceptional: Carol Johnston.*

Lefty, the Dingaling Lynx (television) Television show; aired on November 28, 1971. Directed by Winston Hibler. A forest ranger befriends a young lynx, who in turn befriends the ranger's Irish setter as its substitute mother. Eventually he has to return the lynx to the wild but the lynx never forgets his dog friend and later helps him when he is lost. Stars Ron Brown, Harrison Tout, Brooks Woolley. Narrated by Mayf Nutter.

Legacy of Walt Disney Display of Walt Disney's awards and other memorabilia along with an exhibit on the California Institute of the Arts, on Main Street at Disneyland from January 15, 1970, to February 11, 1973. Took the former space of the Wurlitzer shop, until the major awards were moved to the Walt Disney Story attractions at Disneyland and the Walt Disney World Magic Kingdom. At that time it became Disneyland Presents a Preview of Coming Attractions (1973–1989).

Legend of Coyote Rock, The (film) Pluto cartoon; released on August 24, 1945. Directed by Charles Nichols. Pluto is charged with guarding lambs, but a coyote lures him far away in the desert. While Pluto is gone, the coyote captures all of the lambs in a cave, except for a little black lamb who manages to escape. Pluto returns to the scene and chases the coyote, who falls off a cliff, knocking over rock formations, and the tumbling rocks settle in his likeness to become Coyote Rock.

Legend of El Blanco, The (television) Television show; aired on September 25, 1966. Directed by Arthur J. Vitarelli. The show is based on an old Aztec legend about a white horse owned by Hernando Cortez, with the narration sung rather than spoken, by the group Los Tres Con Ella. The area has been having a drought, and the natives believe only the return of the white horse can end it. A colt, thought to be the offspring of the legendary horse, is discovered and hidden from an evil horse trader by a peasant. The colt grows up to lead the wild herds. Stars Alfonso Romero, Jose F. Perez.

Legend of Johnny Appleseed (film) Release title of *Johnny Appleseed* for schools.

Legend of Lobo, The (film) With both parents killed by man, Lobo has learned the ways of the hunter and becomes the most hated and sought after wolf in the West. By the time he becomes leader of the pack he has mated and become a father. Man's relentless determination to eliminate the wolves raiding their cattle leads to the capture of Lobo's mate. In the end, Lobo cleverly leads a raid that frees his loved one and then takes his pack into a land so wild man has not yet invaded it. Released on November 7, 1962. Co-produced by James Algar. 67 min. Rex Allen is featured as narrator, with music by Allen and the Sons of the Pioneers; the title song was written by Richard M. Sherman and Robert B. Sherman. The film was based on Ernest Thompson Seton's story, and was produced in the field by Jack Couffer. Released on video in 1985.

Legend of Sleepy Hollow, The (film) Theatrical release of the segment from *The Adventures of Ichabod and Mr. Toad* on November 26, 1958. 33 min. Also shown under this title on television, airing on October 26, 1955. Released on video in 1982 and 1990.

Legend of Tarzan, Disney's The (television) Half-hour television series; premiered on September 3, 2001, on UPN and in syndication. Tarzan returns to the jungle, to succeed Kerchak as Lord of the Jungle. He tests his wits, prowess, and ability as the new leader of the gorilla family alongside his ladylove, Jane. Voices include Michael T. Weiss (Tarzan), Olivia d'Abo (Jane), Jeff Glen Bennett (Archimedes Q. Porter), April Winchell (Terk), Jim Cummings (Tantor). 39 episodes.

Legend of the Boy and the Eagle, The (film) In Arizona, while boys of the Hopi tribe perform a traditional eagle dance, an old man tells how the ritual dance began 500 years ago. He relates the story of Tutuvina, a 10-year-old Native American boy who defied the gods and brought shame to his people by saving the life of his pet, an eagle marked for sacrifice. Today, however, Hopis honor his memory. Featurette released on June 21, 1967. Directed by Norman Tokar. 48 min. Released on video in 1986.

Legend of the Lion King, The Attraction in Fantasyland in Magic Kingdom Park at Walt Disney World; opened on July 8, 1994. After a pre-show featuring Rafiki and "The Circle of Life," costumed characters and puppets combine to present the story of *The Lion King*, in the theater that had originally housed the Mickey Mouse Revue. Sponsored by Kodak. It closed on February 23, 2002, to make way for *Mickey's PhilharMagic*.

Legend of Two Gypsy Dogs, The (television) Television show; aired on March 1, 1964. Directed by Dr. Istvan Homoki-Nagy. Two carefree dogs in Hungary come to the attention of an old fisherman. Later they free a hawk from a cage, and he joins them. They have adventures with a flood, a wild boar, and a cheetah.

Legend of Young Dick Turpin, The (television) Two-part television show; aired on February 13 and 20, 1966. Directed by James Neilson. The life of an English highwayman from the 18th century is chronicled. When he loses his possessions as the result of a fine for poaching, he steals back his horse, only to become sought as a horse thief. Turpin befriends a boy who eventually helps him escape from prison in London, and he is able to clear his name. Stars David Weston, Bernard Lee, George Cole, Maurice Denham, Leonard Whiting. Four years later, Whiting played Romeo in Franco Zefferelli's acclaimed version of *Romeo and Juliet*. Newcomer David Weston was advised by Richard Burton to try a film career.

Leguizamo, John Actor; appeared in *Super Mario Bros.* (Luigi Mario) and *Summer of Sam* (Vinny).

Lemmings and Arctic Bird Life, The (film) Part of *White Wilderness*; released on 16mm for schools in September 1964. The film tells the living legend of the strange migration of the lemmings, along with stories of interesting bird life.

Lend a Paw (film) Pluto cartoon; released on October 3, 1941. Academy Award winner for Best Cartoon. Remake of *Mickey's Pal Pluto* (1933).

Directed by Clyde Geronimi. Pluto's jealousy over a new kitten almost causes it to be drowned, but Pluto's angel self wins out and the kitten is rescued. Dedicated to "The Tailwagger Foundation."

Lenny (television) Television series; aired on CBS from September 19, 1990, to March 9, 1991. There was a preview on September 10, 1990. A hard-working, blue-collar man whose everyday life presents him with a series of ups and downs on which he bases his nonstop, commonsense commentary on such topics as making ends meet and his responsibilities to his wife, kids, parents, and brother. Stars Lenny Clarke (Lenny Callahan), Lee Garlington (Shelly Callahan), Peter Dobson (Eddie Callahan), Eugene Roche (Pat Callahan), Jenna Von Oy (Kelly Callahan), Alexis Caldwell (Tracy).

Leonard, Robert Sean Actor; appeared in *Dead Poets Society* (Neil Perry) and *Swing Kids* (Peter).

Leonardo da Vinci—First Man of the Renaissance (film) Sixteen mm educational film produced by Anthony Corso; released in 1972. The history of the 15th-century genius and his contributions.

Les Chefs de France See Chefs de France, Les

Less than Perfect (television) Half-hour television series on ABC; premiered on October 1,

2002. Claudia ("Claude") Casey, a temp who worked at the GBN Television Network for two years, unexpectedly lands a job on the coveted desk of handsome news anchor Will Butler, where she quickly realizes she may be in over her head. But Claude stands up to her co-workers and battles her own insecurities while refusing to compromise her values. Stars Sara Rue (Claude Casey), Eric Roberts (Will Butler), Zachary Levi (Kipp Romano), Sherri Shepherd (Ramona Platt), Andrea Parker (Lydia West), Andy Dick (Owen Kronsky). From Touchstone Television.

Lessing, Gunther (1886–1965) Lawyer; hired by Walt Disney in 1930 to help protect the copyrights of Mickey Mouse. He eventually became a company vice president and general counsel, and was a member of the board of directors from 1938 to 1964. One of his pre-Disney claims to fame was as an adviser to Mexican revolutionary Pancho Villa.

Lester, Mark Actor; appeared on television in *The Boy Who Stole the Elephant*. Best known for his starring in the title role in the motion picture *Oliver!*

Let's Get Together Song from *The Parent Trap*, written by Richard M. Sherman and Robert B. Sherman.

Let's Go Day Tuesday on the new *Mickey Mouse Club*.

Let's Stick Together (film) Donald Duck cartoon; released on April 25, 1952. Directed by Jack Hannah. Donald and the bee, Spike, reminisce about their early days together and the scrapes they got into.

Levis, Patrick Actor; appeared on Disney Channel in *Brink!* (Peter) and *Miracle in Lane 2* (Seth Yoder), and as a regular on *So Weird* (Jack Phillips).

Lewis, Aylwin Member of the Disney board of directors beginning on January 1, 2004.

Lewis, Nat (1911–1977) He began selling Mickey Mouse–shaped balloons at Disneyland in 1956, and continued providing all balloons for both Disneyland and Walt Disney World until his death in 1977.

Liberators, The (television) Two-hour television movie; aired on February 8, 1987. Directed by Kenneth Johnson. In the years prior to the Civil War, a slave convinces a young man to help him escape to Canada, so he poses as the boy's slave to do so. They meet other escaping slaves and help them get to the Underground Railway in Ohio, where they are helped by a Quaker. Their success convinces them to continue helping slaves escape from bondage. Stars Robert Carradine, Larry B. Scott, Cynthia Dale, Bumper Robinson.

Liberty Arcade Arcade behind the Main Street Shops at Disneyland Paris, on the Frontierland side of the street.

Liberty Belle Riverboat in Magic Kingdom Park at Walt Disney World. Formerly the *Richard F. Irvine*, it was renamed the *Liberty Belle* after an extensive rehab in 1996.

Liberty Inn Fast-food restaurant in The American Adventure complex in World Showcase at Epcot; opened on October 1, 1982. Since each World Showcase country features its own cuisine, hot dogs, hamburgers, french fries, chili, apple pies, and chocolate chip cookies are the standard fare at this large eatery.

Liberty Square Area in Magic Kingdom Park at Walt Disney World, where The Hall of

Presidents and The Haunted Mansion are located. As in Disney's movie, *Johnny Tremain*, there is a liberty tree, with lanterns hanging from its branches. The patriots did the same after they dumped the tea in Boston harbor. The majestic 135-year-old live oak was actually transplanted from another area of the Walt Disney World property, a major feat when you consider that the full-grown tree weighed about 35 tons. But, the Disney designers knew that a sapling simply would not do, so they posed to the landscaping engineers the most difficult task they were ever asked to accomplish.

Liberty Story, The (television) Television show; aired on May 29, 1957. Directed by Hamilton S. Luske, Robert Stevenson. A segment from *Johnny Tremain*, depicting the Boston Tea Party and the battle at Concord, is followed by *Ben and Me*.

Liberty Street In 1956, Walt Disney announced plans for a Liberty Street at Disneyland to be located behind the east side of Main Street. Included would be a Hall of Presidents. But, this was long before Audio-Animatronics figures were invented, so the presidential figures would have been mere mannequins. Other projects occupied Disney's time, while eventually the Audio-Animatronics process was perfected and deemed ideal for the planned Hall of Presidents. However, Liberty Street was never built at Disneyland; instead, it made its debut as Liberty Square at Magic Kingdom Park in Walt Disney World in 1971.

Liberty Tree Tavern Restaurant in Liberty Square in Magic Kingdom Park at Walt Disney World; opened on October 1, 1971. An 18th-century feel is given to the restaurant through the use of antique furniture, oak plank floors, and pewter ware.

Lt. Robin Crusoe, U.S.N. (film) This modern-day Robinson Crusoe is a pilot for the U.S. Navy who is forced to ditch his plane in the Pacific. Rescued from a tropical island a year later, he writes to his fiancée, explaining why he never showed up for their wedding. His story is a humorous one, involving Floyd, a chimpanzee who is an astro-chimp; Wednesday, a beautiful native girl; some lovely maidens; some menacing warriors; and a harrowing escape from the island by helicopter. Released on July 29, 1966. Directed by Byron Paul. The only film on which Walt Disney received a story credit (as Retlaw Yensid). 114 min. Stars Dick Van Dyke (Lt. Robin Crusoe), Nancy Kwan (Wednesday), Akim Tamiroff (Tanamashu), Arthur Malet (Umbrella man), Tyler McVey (Captain). This popular film was reissued theatrically in 1974. Released on video in 1986.

Life Aquatic with Steve Zissou, The (film) Eccentric, down-but-not-out oceanographer Steve Zissou and his motley crew—Team Zissou—find themselves in troubled waters when they attempt to track down the mysterious "jaguar shark" that ate Zissou's partner while filming a documentary of their latest adventure. Adding to his troubles, Zissou must contend with a beautiful journalist assigned to write a profile and a new member of the team who might possibly be his long-lost son. Zissou faces hilarious complications trying to keep his expedition afloat while contending with budgetary woes and a host of other challenges (including a close encounter with marauding pirates). A Touchstone Picture. Directed by Wes Anderson. Released on December 10, 2004 in New York and Los Angeles, and on December 25, 2004 nationwide. Stars Bill Murray (Steve Zissou), Owen Wilson (Ned Plimpton), Cate Blanchett (Jane Winslett-Richardson), Anjelica Huston (Eleanor Zissou), Willem Dafoe (Klaus Daimler), Jeff Goldblum (Alistair Hennessey), Michael Gambon (Oseary Drakoulias), Seu Jorge (Pele dos Santos), Bud Cort (Bill Ubell), Seymour Cassel (Esteban du Plantier). 118 min. Filmed in Rome and other Italian locations in Super 35-Scope. For the boat, the *Belafonte*, the filmmakers found a 50-year-old minesweeper in South Africa and then re-outfitted it to become an oceanographic research ship. Released on video in 2005.

life as we know it (television) Hour-long drama series on ABC; premiered on October 7,

2004, and ended on January 20, 2005. Three hormone-charged teenage boys are trying to do something even harder than losing their virginity, and that's growing up without totally "losing it." There's Dino, the handsome jock with the secret sensitive side; Jonathan, the artist who sees life through a camera lens; and Ben, the straight-A student who still can't make his parents happy. Stars Sean Faris (Dino Whitman), Jon Foster (Ben Connor), Chris Lowell (Jonathan Fields), Missy Peregym (Jackie), Kelly Osbourne (Deborah), D.B. Sweeney (Michael Whitman), Lesa Darr (Annie Whitman), Marguerite Moreau (Monica Young), Jessica Lucas (Sue). Adapted from Melvin Burgess' novel. From Touchstone Television. For legal reasons, the show could not use capital letters in the title. Filmed in Vancouver, British Columbia. The entire series, including two episodes unaired in the United States, was released on DVD in 2005.

Life Is Ruff (television) A Disney Channel Original Movie; debuted on July 15, 2005. Calvin Wheeler, a popular yet unmotivated 13-year-old, has a passion for rare comic books and desires to buy a rare, $3,000 first edition. When he learns of a prestigious dog show with a $5,000 first prize, he enters it. His friend Emily, who volunteers at the local animal shelter, helps him adopt Tyco, a slobbering, lovable stray Labrador retriever/Saint Bernard mix. Tyco wreaks havoc at home, but Calvin cleans up after the playful pup and tries to teach him some new tricks so he can win Best in Show. After enduring various trials and tribulations, Calvin learns to appreciate the value of true friendship, responsibility, and hard work. Directed by Charles Haid. Stars Kyle Massey (Calvin Wheeler), Kay Panabaker (Emily Watson), Mitchel Musso (Raymond Figg), Carter Jenkins (Preston Price), Mark Christopher Lawrence (Mr. Wheeler), Judith Moreland (Mrs. Wheeler), Ibrahim Abdel-Baaith (Rondel). Filmed in Salt Lake City by Davis Entertainment and Salty Pictures.

Life with Bonnie (television) Half-hour television series on ABC; premiered on September 17, 2002, and ended on July 30, 2004. Bonnie Molloy is a woman who creatively balances the roles of wife, mother, and host of the local morning talk show, *Morning Chicago*, with sincerity and humor. Stars Bonnie Hunt (Bonnie Molloy), Mark Derwin (Dr. John Molloy), Marianne Muellerleile (Gloria), Charlie Stewart (Charlie Molloy), Holly Wortell (Holly), Chris Barnes (Marv), Anthony Russell (Tony Russo), David Alan Grier (David Bellows). From Touchstone Television.

Life with Mikey (film) Agent and former television child star Michael Chapman, who is co-running a third-rate talent agency with his brother, finds his big chance with the discovery of a young, streetwise urchin, Angie Vega, who has a fresh, unaffected personality and an ability to act her way out of any situation—including illegal ones. Michael comes to learn that his concern for Angie and her future welfare is more important than his own dreams of success. Released on June 4, 1993. Directed by James Lapine. A Touchstone Picture. 91 min. Stars Michael J. Fox (Michael Chapman), Christina Vidal (Angie Vega), Nathan Lane (Ed Chapman), Cyndi Lauper (Geena Briganti). The "Life with Mikey Theme" was written by Alan Menken, with lyrics by Jack Feldman. Filmed on location in Toronto and New York City. Released on video in 1993.

Life's Work (television) Half-hour television series; premiered on September 17, 1996, on ABC and ended July 29, 1997. When Lisa Hunter becomes an Assistant State's Attorney, in addition to her already hectic roles as wife and mother, she learns that being a full-time attorney and a full-time mother entails more than she had bargained for. Stars Lisa Ann Walter (Lisa Hunter), Michael O'Keefe (Kevin Hunter), Molly Hagan (DeeDee Lucas), Lightfield Lewis (Matt Youngster), Alexa Vega (Tess Hunter), Andrew Lowery (Lyndon Knox), Larry Miller (Jerome Nash).

Life-Size (television) Two-hour television movie; aired on *The Wonderful World of Disney* on March 5, 2000. In trying a magic spell to bring back her deceased mother, lonely 12-year-old Casey accidentally brings to life a beautiful fashion doll, Eve, instead. The doll creates havoc as she tries to fit into the real world. Directed by Mark Rosman. Stars Lindsay Lohan (Casey Mitchell), Tyra Banks (Eve), Jere Burns (Ben Mitchell), Ann Marie Loder (Drew), Garwin Sanford (Richie), Tom Butler (Phil).

Lifestyles of the Rich and Animated (television) Television show (90 min.); aired on August 18, 1991. Ludwig Von Drake takes a look at famous cartoon stars, with new dialogue written for Von Drake animation from previous shows.

Lifetime Television With the purchase of Capital Cities/ABC in 1996, Disney obtained a 50 percent ownership of Lifetime Television, which emphasizes original movies, specials, prime-time signature shows, and unique daytime blocks for women.

Light in the Forest, The (film) In 1764, Col. Henry Bouquet parleys with the Delaware Indians and persuades them to give up their white captives in exchange for peace. Among those freed is Johnny Butler, who despises whites as his enemy and only reaches Fort Pitt, Pennsylvania, after much struggle. He finds the townspeople wary and prejudiced, too, and only after a reckoning with his Uncle Wilse, who, with his gang, has senselessly killed Indians for years, and falling in love with a young indentured girl named Shenandoe, can he settle down to a peaceful life. Released on July 8, 1958. Directed by Herschel Daugherty. 93 min. Stars James MacArthur (Johnny Butler/True Son), Carol Lynley (making her movie debut as Shenandoe), Fess Parker (Del Hardy), Wendell Corey (Wilse Owens). This was television director Daugherty's first feature film after directing such hits as *The Alfred Hitchcock Show* and *Wagon Train*. He shot on location in Tennessee, outside Chattanooga, but the Indian settlement was built in California on the Rowland V. Lee ranch. The song "The Light In The Forest" was written for the film by Paul J. Smith and Gil George. The film was released on video in 1986.

Light Is What You Make It (film) Educational film comparing the human eye to a camera, showing the effect of poor lighting and how eyes can be helped by correcting lighting faults, made for the National Better Light Better Sight Bureau. Delivered on December 3, 1945.

Light Magic Show at Disneyland that replaced the Main Street Electrical Parade; began on May 23, 1997, and ended on September 1, 1997, featuring lights, fiber-optic effects, special effects, music, pixies, and Disney characters, encouraging everyone "to dream and to believe that those dreams can come true." Deemed a spectacular or "streetacular" rather than a parade, the show is presented on four moving floats or stages (each 80 feet long and 11 feet wide) that are set up in between "it's a small world" and the Matterhorn, and again on Main Street.

Lighthouse Keeping (film) Donald Duck cartoon; released on September 20, 1946. Directed by Jack Hannah. Donald is the keeper of a lighthouse who must deal with Marblehead, the pelican, who tries to douse the lighthouse lamp over and over again.

Lights! Camera! Fractions! (film) Educational film; released in August 1984. A blend of live action, stop-motion, and clay animation is used to introduce young math students to the basics of fractions.

Lights, Motors, Action! Extreme Stunt Show Exciting show featuring high-flying, gravity-defying automobile, motorcycle, and high-speed watercraft stunts and centering on the filming of a spy thriller, with production crew members, stunt managers, and a director and

assistant director on the "live" set. Opened at Disney-MGM Studios at Walt Disney World May 5, 2005. The show is inspired by a similar show at Disneyland Resort Paris; see Moteurs . . . Action.

Like Father, Like Son (television) Syndicated television show from 1986; a compilation of animated films.

Like Jake and Me (film) Educational film about how mutual support and understanding turn strangers into a family; released on May 9, 1989. 15 min.

Lilly Belle Name of Walt Disney's locomotive for his backyard railroad, the Carolwood Pacific, built by Disney with the help of technician Roger Broggie and his staff. Also the name of a special, elegantly furnished caboose on the Disneyland Railroad formerly used for transporting VIPs and a locomotive on the Walt Disney World Railroad.

Lilo & Stitch (film) On the Hawaiian Islands, a lonely little girl, Lilo, adopts what she thinks is a dog. She names her pet Stitch, completely unaware that he is a dangerous genetic experiment gone awry who has escaped from an alien planet. Stitch's only interest in Lilo is using her as a human shield to evade the alien bounty hunters who are bent on recapturing him. In the end, Lilo's unwavering faith in "ohana," the Hawaiian tradition of family, unlocks Stitch's heart and gives him the one thing he was never designed to have—the ability to care for someone else. Released on June 21, 2002. Directed by Chris Sanders and Dean DeBlois. 85 min. Voices include Daveigh Chase (Lilo), Tia Carrere (Nani), Ving Rhames (Cobra Bubbles), David Ogden Stiers (Jumba), Kevin McDonald (Pleakley), Jason Scott Lee (David Kawena), Zoe Caldwell (Grand Councilwoman), Kevin Michael Richardson (Captain Gantu). Music by Alan Silvestri. Co-director Chris Sanders also provides the voice of Stitch. Produced primarily at Disney's Feature Animation facility at Walt Disney World in Florida. Nominated for an Academy Award for Best Animated Feature. Released on video in 2002. There was a direct-to-video sequel, *Stitch!*

The Movie in 2003, and another, *Lilo & Stitch 2: Stitch Has a Glitch*, in 2005.

Lilo & Stitch, the Series (television) Half-hour animated series on ABC; premiered on September 20, 2003. Stitch, Dr. Jumba Jookiba's Experiment 626, finds there are 625 other experiments. They land in Hawaii and, one by one, are activated. Each experiment has its own unique set of extreme capabilities, including Stitch's initial penchant for destruction. Lilo and Stitch search out these experiments and help to turn their nature from bad to good, finding places where each can belong and contribute to the community. Voices include Daveigh Chase (Lilo),

Chris Sanders (Stitch), Tia Carrere (Nani), David Ogden Stiers (Jumba), Ving Rhames (Cobra Bubbles), Kevin McDonald (Pleakley), Kevin Michael Richardson (Capt. Gantu), Zoe Caldwell (Grand Councilwoman). 65 episodes.

Lilo & Stitch 2: Stitch Has a Glitch (film) Direct-to-video animated release on August 30, 2005. Stitch, Jumba, and Pleakley have settled into life with their human family, and Stitch blissfully enjoys his new "Ohana" with Lilo and Nani. It seems like paradise, but it appears Stitch's molecular makeup is out of whack, which brings out his worst behavior, and his friendship with Lilo is threatened by misunderstanding. Pleakley, Jumba, and Lilo must find a way to restore his goodness level before he ruins everything, including Lilo's big hula competition—the same competition her mother won years before. Lilo must search within her heart to find the key to help her friend and restore their family. Directed by Tony Leonidis and Michael LaBash. 68 min. Voices include Dakota Fanning (Lilo), Chris Sanders (Stitch), Tia Carrere (Nani), David Ogden Stiers (Jumba), Kevin McDonald (Pleakley), Jason Scott Lee (David).

Lindquist, Jack Lindquist began at Disneyland in 1955 as its first advertising manager. He later took other marketing positions, and was named marketing director of both Disneyland and Walt Disney World in 1971. He brought the Pigskin Classic to Anaheim. In October 1990, he was named president of Disneyland. He retired in 1993 and was named a Disney Legend in 1994.

Lindsey, George Actor; appeared in *Snowball Express* (Double L. Dingman), *Charley and the Angel* (Pete), *Treasure of Matecumbe* (sheriff), and provided the voice of Trigger (*Robin Hood*), Lafayette (*The Aristocats*), and Deadeye, the rabbit (*The Rescuers*). He also appeared on television in *Bristle Face*.

Line of Fire (television) One-hour drama series on ABC; premiered on December 2, 2003, and ended on February 3, 2004, with the final two episodes shown on May 30. On one side of the FBI's fight against organized crime is the Richmond, Virginia–based Malloy Crime Syndicate headed by Jonah Malloy, a charismatic but dangerous father figure. On the other side is the Richmond FBI branch, led by dynamic Special Agent-in-Charge Lisa Cohen, and aided by a new recruit, Paige Van Doren. Stars Leslie Bibb (Paige Van Doren), David Paymer (Jonah Malloy), Leslie Hope (Lisa Cohen), Anson Mount (Roy Ravelle), Jeffrey Sams (Todd Stevens), Brian Goodman (Donovan Stubbin). Produced by DreamWorks Television in association with Touchstone Television. 9 episodes.

Linkletter, Art Television personality who served, with Ronald Reagan and Bob Cummings, as one of the hosts of the television show for the opening of Disneyland on July 17, 1955. He was named a Disney Legend in 2005, after serving as a Disneyland park ambassador during its 50th year.

Linz, Alex D. Young actor; appeared in *Max Keeble's Big Move* (Max), *The Jennie Project* (Andrew Archibald), and *Full Court Miracle* (Alex Schlotsky) on Disney Channel, and provided the voice of the young Tarzan in *Tarzan*.

Lion Around (film) Donald Duck cartoon; released on January 20, 1950. Directed by Jack Hannah. The nephews disguise themselves as a lion to get a pie from Donald, who, when he discovers the trick, chases them and gets mixed up with a real lion to whom he must keep serving pies in order to stay alive.

Lion Down (film) Goofy cartoon; released on January 5, 1951. Directed by Jack Kinney. In his attempt to hang a hammock, Goofy searches for a second tree to hold it up, but the one he finds dislodges a lion, who returns home with Goofy. Soon the lion wants the hammock too, and a battle begins with Goofy emerging the victor.

Lion King, The (film) A young lion cub, Simba, struggles to find his place in nature's "circle of life" and follow in the regal paw prints of his father, the great King Mufasa, after his father is killed by his treacherous uncle, Scar. Scar convinces Simba that he is responsible for his father's death and urges him to run far away from the Pride Lands and never return. A frightened and guilt-stricken Simba flees into exile where he is befriended by a wacky but warmhearted warthog, Pumbaa, and his free-wheeling meerkat companion, Timon. Simba adopts their "hakuna matata" (no worries) attitude toward life, living on a diet of bugs and taking things one day at a time as he matures into a young adult. When his childhood friend Nala arrives on the scene, he is persuaded to return to the Pride Lands, which have fallen into hard times under Scar's reign, and take his rightful place as king. The wise shaman baboon, Rafiki, convinces Simba that his father's spirit lives on in him and that he must accept his responsibility, and when he returns, he manages to defeat Scar and an army of hyenas. Limited release in New York and Los Angeles on June 15, 1994; general release on June 24, 1994. Directed by Roger Allers and Rob Minkoff. 88 min. Voices

include Jonathan Taylor Thomas (young Simba), Matthew Broderick (adult Simba), James Earl Jones (Mufasa), Jeremy Irons (Scar), Niketa Calame (young Nala), Moira Kelly (adult Nala), Ernie Sabella (Pumbaa), Nathan Lane (Timon), Robert Guillaume (Rafiki), Whoopi Goldberg (Shenzi), Cheech Marin (Banzai), Jim Cummings (Ed). The project originated a number of years earlier under the title *King of the Jungle*. When production began, an artistic team traveled to Africa to search for ways to best present the African settings in the film, and the animators studied actual live lions and other animals that were brought to the Studio. Songs were by Elton John and Tim Rice, with a background score by Hans Zimmer. Computer-generated imagery was used to create the dramatic wildebeest stampede, a visual highlight in the film and a new level of sophistication for the art form. The original release was interrupted when kids went back to school in September, to return on November 18, 1994, this time paired with a 3-minute preview of *Pocahontas*. Released on video in 1995. The Lion King became one of the highest-grossing films of all time. The song "Can You Feel the Love Tonight" won a Best Song Oscar for Elton John and Tim

Rice, and a second Oscar was awarded to Hans Zimmer for Best Original Score. A stage show, based on the film, opened at the New Amsterdam Theater in New York City in 1997. The film was re-released in Imax and large-format theaters on December 25, 2002. For the Special Edition Platinum DVD release in 2003, a song written for the stage play, "The Morning Report," by Elton John and Tim Rice, was adapted, animated, and inserted into the body of the original film.

Lion King, The The stage version of the animated film had a pre-Broadway tryout at the Orpheum Theater in Minneapolis beginning on July 8, 1997, before opening in previews at the New Amsterdam Theater on Broadway on October 10 (official opening was November 13). The show earned rave reviews and smashed box office records. Directed by Julie Taymor. The performers utilize a wide array of masks and puppetry techniques to portray the story's 13 characters, as well as dozens of other animals. With a wholly original design, there was no attempt

to re-create the animated look of the feature film. Eight songs were added to the five in the movie. The production was awarded six Tony awards— for Best Choreography (Garth Fagan), Best Costume Design (Julie Taymor), Best Lighting Design (Donald Holder), Best Scenic Design (Richard Hudson), Best Direction of a Musical (Julie Taymor), and Best Musical. The show moved to the Minskoff Theater in June 2006 to make room for *Mary Poppins* at the New Amsterdam.

Lion King, The: A Musical Journey (television) Half-hour television special about the creation of the music in *The Lion King*, including interviews with Elton John and Tim Rice; aired on ABC on June 14, 1994. Directed by John Jopson.

Lion King Celebration, The Parade at Disneyland beginning on July 1, 1994, and ending June 1, 1997. For the first time, Audio-Animatronics–like figures were used on the floats, and remote-controlled crocodiles and large African bugs followed them down the street. There was even a waterfall on a float and rain coming down from the jungle canopy. At intervals, the parade would stop and the performers would put on a brief street show for the guests featuring "Circle of Life."

Lion King Celebration: A Roaring Good Time (television) Half-hour television special on KCAL (Los Angeles); aired on July 24, 1994. A behind-the-scenes look at the making of the movie. Included are highlights of the Hollywood premiere with Whoopi Goldberg, Matthew Broderick, and James Earl Jones, along with a look at the new Disneyland attraction, The Lion King Celebration.

Lion King 1½, The (film) Direct-to-video sequel released on February 10, 2004. The story running parallel to *The Lion King*, yet completely original, depicts the history of Timon and Pumbaa—how they met and became friends, and their behind-the-scenes influence on Simba's rise to the throne. The duo discovers their perfect oasis, but after becoming friends with Simba, they learn the limits of the easy life, and they finally find that the real "hakuna matata" happens only when they leave the oasis and reunite with the ones they love. Directed by Brad Raymond. The voice cast from the original film returns, supplemented by Julie Kavner (Timon's mom), Jerry Stiller (Timon's Uncle Max), and Matt Weinberg (Young Simba).

Lion King II, The: Simba's Pride (film) Direct-to-video release on October 27, 1998, of a sequel to the 1994 feature. An epic story of Simba's infant daughter, Kiara, who is destined to grow into a heroic young lioness and heal the rift in the Pride Lands caused by the banishment of Scar's followers. Meeting Kovu, Scar's hand-picked successor and son of Zira, new leader of the Outlanders, Kiara forges a forbidden bond of friendship, which blossoms into love, honor, and trust. Kiara and Kovu eventually reunite the two

prides, bringing peace to Pride Rock. Directed by Darrell Rooney. Added voices for this video are Suzanne Pleshette (Zira), Neve Campbell (adult Kiara), Jason Marsden (adult Kovu), Michelle Horn (young Kiara), Ryan O'Donahue (young Kovu), Andy Dick (Nuka). 75 min. Included are five new songs, as well as "He Lives in You," from the "Rhythm of the Pridelands" CD.

Lion King's Timon & Pumbaa, The (television) Animated television series; began on September 8, 1995, as part of The Disney Afternoon, with different episodes airing Saturdays on CBS beginning September 16, 1995. The CBS run ended on March 29, 1997, and the syndication on August 25, 1997. Wacky adventures of the wise-cracking meerkat and his good-natured warthog pal. Stars the voices of Nathan Lane and Quinton Flynn (Timon), Ernie Sabella (Pumbaa). 85 episodes.

Lion, the Witch and the Wardrobe, The See *The Chronicles of Narnia*.

Lionel Corp, The Disney licensee in the 1930s of toy railroad handcars and train sets. When they filed for bankruptcy in the mid-1930s, the judge in the court allowed them to produce a Mickey/Minnie handcar for that Christmas season, and the resulting sales pulled them out of bankruptcy. Disney got lots of publicity for having Mickey Mouse save Lionel from bankruptcy.

One of their more valuable items is a Mickey Mouse circus train set. Lionel returned as a licensee beginning in the 1960s.

Listen to the Land Boat ride in The Land at Epcot; open from October 1, 1982 to September

27, 1993. Guests traveled through a greenhouse of the future, with living plants being harvested and served in the pavilion's restaurants. There was an Aquacel environment for the raising of special fish (tilapia) and shrimp, hydroponics displays, and a cruise through three ecological areas—the desert, the rain forest, and the prairie. Superseded by Living with the Land.

Litterbug, The (film) Donald Duck cartoon; released on June 21, 1961. Directed by Hamilton Luske. Donald Duck gives us a graphic demonstration of various types of litterbugs: the unconscious carrier, the sports bug, the sneak bug, the highway bug, the beach bug, and the mountain bug. Perhaps, Donald suggests at the end of his

demonstration, if we start at home, we can stamp out the pest—the litterbug. This was the last Donald Duck cartoon made.

Little April Shower Song from *Bambi*; written by Larry Morey and Frank Churchill.

Little Dog Lost (television) Television show; aired on January 13, 1963. Directed by Walter Perkins. From the well-known book by Newbery Award–winning author Meindert de Jong. Candy, a Welsh Corgi, who is terrified of brooms because of an incident in puppyhood, is separated from his family during a storm, and faces all sorts of dangers. Candy is befriended by an old woman whom he helps save when her cart turns over and traps her, and later by a kindly farmer who helps him get over his fear. Narrated by Winston Hibler. Stars Hollis Black, Margaret Gerrity, Grace Bauer, Priscilla Overton.

Little Einsteins (television) Disney Channel series; premiering on October 9, 2005. Group of four children who, with their musical flying ship Rocket, help preschoolers solve an important mission and learn along the way. Spectacular live-action images of nature, art, and landmarks are combined with character animation. A DVD launched preliminarily on August 23, 2005.

Little Hiawatha (film) Silly Symphony cartoon; released on May 15, 1937. Directed by  Dave Hand. A little Indian boy desires to be a mighty hunter and goes out in the forest to prove it. But he cannot kill a bunny that crosses his path, an act that endears him to the woodland creatures who later rescue him from a grizzly bear. At one time Walt considered making a Hiawatha feature film, but the story never satisfied him, so the idea was shelved.

Little House, The (film) Special cartoon; released on August 8, 1952. Directed by Wilfred Jackson. The little house begins life happily in the country but with "progress" it is soon completely overtaken and surrounded by the encroaching big city. Fortunately, a caring family has her moved back to the country onto a small hill and there the little house is happy once more. From the popular children's book by Virginia Lee Burton.

Little House on the Prairie (television) Five-part six-hour series; aired on *The Wonderful World of Disney* beginning on March 26, 2005, and continuing on April 2, 9, 16, and 23, about a pioneer family's travels across the Kansas Territory at the turn of the century. Directed by David L. Cunningham. Stars Cameron Bancroft (Charles Ingalls), Erin Cottrell (Caroline Ingalls), Danielle Ryan Churchran (Mary), Kyle Chavarria (Laura). From the book by Laura Ingalls Wilder. Filmed near Calgary, Alberta, by Voice Pictures, Inc.

Little Indian, Big City (film) A successful Parisian businessman, Stephan Marchado travels deep into a South American rain forest to obtain a divorce agreement from his wife, Patricia, only to find that he has a young son who has been raised among the natives and given an Indian name, Mimi-Siku. Stephan is coerced into taking the mischievous lad back to Paris, creating a major culture clash that turns Stephan's well-ordered life upside down. But soon the father begins thinking less about maintaining the status quo of his affluent life in Paris and more about nurturing the friendship and love that have grown between him and his son. Released on March 22, 1996. Directed by Hervé Palud. 90 min. U.S. release by Touchstone Pictures of a dubbed version of the French hit comedy, *Un indien dans la ville*, starring Thierry Lhermitte (Stephan Marchado), Miou Miou (Patricia), Ludwig Briand (Mimi-Siku). The U.S. release of this film was a condition for actor-producer Lhermitte selling Touchstone Pictures the remake rights. The remake, which was titled *Jungle 2 Jungle* and starred Tim Allen, was released in 1997. Released on video in 1998.

Little John Robin Hood's bumbling bear pal; voiced by Phil Harris.

Little Kidnappers, The (television) Two mischievous boys "borrow" an abandoned infant, keeping their discovery secret, and set their gruff grandfather's temper aflame in turn-of-the-century Nova Scotia. Directed by Donald Shebib. A Disney Channel Premiere Film; first aired on August 17, 1990. Stars Charlton Heston (James MacKenzie), Patricia Gage (Ruth MacKenzie), Leah Pinsett (Kirsten), Charles Miller (Davy), Leo Wheatley (Harry). 93 min.

Little Lake Bryan Thirty-acre lake on the Walt Disney World property on which Disney built a recreation center for its cast members. The area was extensively remodeled and renamed Mickey's Retreat in 1998. In August 1996, an apartment community opened at the same location. The first development was dubbed Plantation Park, and other apartment communities along with retail and commercial centers are planned.

Little League Moochie (film) Sixteen mm release title of *Moochie of the Little League*.

Little Mermaid, The (film) Animated tale of a beautiful young mermaid, Ariel, who is fascinated by the human world, to the dismay of her father, King Triton. She spies Prince Eric and falls hopelessly in love. Sebastian the crab is sent by the king to keep an eye on Ariel, though he cannot stop her from rescuing the prince during a storm. Ursula the sea witch plots to grant Ariel's wish to be human, in exchange for her beautiful voice, and as part of a larger scheme to gain control of Triton's realm. Eric finds himself falling for the now-human mermaid, but Ursula tricks him and Ariel, now mute, cannot warn him. Finally, Ariel and Eric together foil Ursula's evil plans, save the undersea kingdom, and receive Triton's blessing. Initial release on November 15, 1989, in Los Angeles and New York; general release on November 17, 1989. Directed by John Musker and Ron Clements. 82 min. Voices include Jodi Benson (Ariel), Pat Carroll (Ursula), Christopher Daniel Barnes (Eric), Buddy Hackett (Scuttle), Kenneth Mars (Triton), Samuel E. Wright (Sebastian), Ben Wright (Grimsby), René Auberjonois (Louis). Songs by Howard Ashman and Alan Menken.

The first Disney animated feature based on a classic fairy tale in three decades (since *Sleeping Beauty*), this film turned to the famous story by Hans Christian Andersen. Disney artists had considered an animated film of *The Little Mermaid* in the late 1930s, and illustrator Kay Nielsen prepared a number of striking story sketches in pastels and watercolors. For this film, the artists received inspiration from the Nielsen story sketches that were brought out of the Archives for them to study, and they gave Kay Nielsen a "visual development" credit on the film. Actress Sherri Stoner was the live-action model for Ariel. The film had more effects than probably any animated film since *Fantasia*; nearly 80 percent of the film required some kind of effects work—storms at sea, billowing sails, schools of fish, shadows, raging fire, explosions, magic pixie dust, surface reflections, underwater distortions, ripples, and bubbles. Academy Award winner for best song ("Under the Sea") and best original score. Re-released in theaters in 1997; released on video in 1990 and 1998.

Little Mermaid, The (television) Animated television series premiered on September 12, 1992, on CBS; and ended September 2, 1995. Utilized the voices of Jodi Benson, Pat Carroll, Kenneth Mars, and Samuel E. Wright from the original film, and added others, such as Danny Cooksey (Urchin), Edan Gross (Flounder), and Maurice La Marche (Scuttle). The series continues the stories of Ariel and her rebelling against the rules of her father, though the stories take place prior to the happenings in the motion picture. Urchin is an orphan merboy, full of boyish enthusiasm, who is befriended by Ariel. 31 episodes.

Little Mermaid II, The: Return to the Sea (film) Direct-to-video release on September 19, 2000. Ariel and Prince Eric, living happily married on land, have a feisty daughter, Melody, who is curious about her roots. Melody, venturing into the sea against her parents' wishes, makes new friends of Tip the Penguin and Dash the Walrus, but then becomes a pawn in a plot by Morgana, Ursula's sinister sibling, against Ariel's father, King Triton. Ariel must come to the rescue. Directed by Jim Kammerud. 75 min. Voices include Jodi Benson (Ariel), Tara Charendoff (Melody), Pat Carroll (Morgana), Max Casella (Tip), Stephen Furst (Dash), Samuel E. Wright (Sebastian).

Little Red Riding Hood (film) Laugh-O-gram film made by Walt Disney in Kansas City in 1922.

Little Riders, The (television) A Disney Channel Premiere Film; aired on March 24, 1996. Trapped in Holland during World War II, a young American girl, Joanne Hunter, lives with her Dutch grandparents. Together they must endure—and resist—the Nazi occupation of their village. When Joanne boldly tries to protect the Little Riders, the much beloved symbol of the town, she suddenly finds herself face-to-face with the enemy. Directed by Kevin Connor. Stars Noley Thornton (Joanne Hunter), Rosemary Harris (Juliana Roden), Paul Scofield (Pieter Roden), Malcolm McDowell (Captain Kessel), Benedict Blythe (Lt. Braun). Based on the book by Margaretha Shemin. The film was shot entirely on location in the Netherlands.

Little Shepherd Dog of Catalina, The (television) Television show; aired on March 11, 1973. Directed by Harry Tytle. A champion Shetland sheepdog is lost on Catalina Island, where he swims after being swept off a boat. He is befriended by a farmer, whose stallion he eventually saves. Stars Clint Rowe, William Maxwell, Joe Dawkins.

Little Spies (television) Two-hour television movie; aired on October 5, 1986. Directed by Greg Beeman. A dog gets loose from the pound, but the neighborhood kids save it, and then find a rough nearby gang is involved in a sinister plot to capture dogs and sell them for use in medical experiments. With the help of an old war hero, they plan to save all the dogs. Stars Mickey Rooney, Peter Smith, Robert Costanzo, Candace Cameron, Adam Carl, Sean Hall, Jason Hervey, Scott Nemes, Kevin King Cooper.

Little Toot (film) Segment of *Melody Time* about a little tugboat who is constantly getting into trouble, but who redeems himself by saving a ship from sinking during a big storm. Re-released as a short on August 13, 1954. From a story by Hardie Gramatky. The title song is sung by the Andrews Sisters.

Little Whirlwind, The (film) Mickey Mouse cartoon; released on February 14, 1941. Directed by Riley Thomson. Mickey gives chase to a baby whirlwind when it frustrates him as he tries to clean up Minnie's yard. Mama Whirlwind shows up to save her youngster and proceeds to destroy the yard and the countryside. Minnie is not at all pleased with Mickey's work.

Littlest Horse Thieves, The (film) When, in 1909, the manager of a Yorkshire coal mine decides to replace the pit ponies who pull the ore carts with machinery and have the ponies destroyed, three youngsters, Dave, Tommy, and Alice, get together and daringly kidnap the ponies from the mine. The kids get caught, however, and the ponies seem doomed. An explosion in the mine traps some of the men and they are saved only with the help of one of the ponies, which dies in the attempt. In his honor all the ponies are put out to pasture for life. Released on May 26, 1976, in England as *Escape from the Dark*; U.S. release on March 11, 1977. Directed by Charles Jarrott. 104 min. Stars Alastair Sim (Lord Harrogate), Peter Barkworth (Richard Sandman), Maurice Colbourne (Luke), Susan Tebbs (Violet), Andrew Harrison (Dave), Chloe Franks (Alice), Benjie Bolgar (Tommy), Prunella Scales (Mrs. Sandman). The Grimethorpe Colliery Band provided the music, composed and conducted by Ron Goodwin. The film was shot on location in Yorkshire, England, including Langthwaite Village, the moors, historic Ripley Castle, the Oakworth Railways station, the Thorpe-Hesley colliery, and at Pinewood Studios in London. The actual underground mine workings, including the stables housing the pit ponies, were built by studio craftsmen at Pinewood. The working title of the film had been *Pit Ponies*. Released on video in 1986.

Littlest Outlaw, The (film) Story of a young boy, Pablito, in Mexico who has a great love for a horse named Conquistador, owned by a general, and manages to save its life only by running away with it. When Pablito loses the horse himself, a friendly priest and some gypsies help him find the horse about to be killed in a bullring. He rescues the horse by leaping onto its back and making it jump a high gate. The general has seen this, and acknowledging Pablito's affection for the horse, presents Conquistador as a gift. Released December 22, 1955. Directed by Roberto Galvadon. 73 min. Stars Andrew Velasquez (Pablito), Pedro Armendariz (Gen. Torres), Enriqueta Zazueta (Señora Garcia), Laila Maley (Celita), Margarito Luna (Silvertre), Ricardo Gonzales (Marcos), Rodolfo Acosta (Chato). From a story by Disney animal film expert, Larry Lansburgh, who also produced the movie. Filmed on location in Mexico. Released on video in 1987.

Litvack, Sandy Litvack joined Disney in 1991 as senior vice president and general counsel. He was promoted to executive vice president the same year, and in 1994 he was named senior executive vice president, taking over many of Frank Wells' duties after Wells' death, and later vice chairman of the board. He resigned in December 2000.

Live action Walt Disney experimented with live action along with animation in *The Reluctant Dragon*, *Song of the South*, and *So Dear to My Heart*, but his first completely live-action film was *Treasure Island* (1950). He realized that the financial health of the company would be aided by a program that included live-action features, since animated features took so long to make thus tying up funds for years.

Live with Regis and Kathie Lee (television) Television talk-show series; premeried on September 3, 1988, in syndication. Stars Regis Philbin and Kathie Lee Gifford. The series ended on July 28, 2000, when Kathie Lee left the show; it started as *Live with Regis* on July 31, 2000. On February 12, 2001, Kelly Ripa joined the show, with a new title of *Live with Regis and Kelly*.

Living Desert, The (film) True-Life Adventure feature; released on November 10, 1953. Directed by James Algar. Though the desert to most people represents an area of arid desolation, it is really a place teeming with life, including extraordinary plants, desert tortoises, rattlesnakes, scorpions, kangaroo rats, and roadrunners. A flash flood hits the desert, causing much of the plant life to blossom anew. The film stands as a landmark of factual filmmaking. 69 min. Academy Award winner. As Walt Disney had had a difficult time convincing his distributor, RKO, of the value of the True-Life Adventure featurettes, he had renewed problems when he produced his first feature-length True-Life Adventure. Again

they argued that audiences would not pay money to see a one-hour-plus film about desert creatures. But again, Disney knew they were wrong. This time he went to Roy Disney and together they decided that it was time to part company with RKO and handle the releases of the Disney product themselves. With some trepidation they made the break and set up the Buena Vista Distribution Company, with its first release being *The Living Desert*. This film, made for only about $500,000, went out and made $5 million during its original release, and Walt and Roy knew they had made the right decision. Released on video in 1986.

Living Seas, The Pavilion in Future World at Epcot; opened on January 15, 1986, originally sponsored by United Technologies. Exhibits on man's search to learn the mysteries of the sea (including an actual 11-foot-long model of the *Nautilus* from *20,000 Leagues Under the Sea*) give way to a short film on the importance of the ocean. To the accompaniment of a haunting musical backdrop composed by Russell Brower based on a theme by George Wilkins, guests descend by means of hydrolators to Sea Base Alpha, where they are able to see various marine displays, look into the largest salt water tank in the world (5.7 million gallons) to view the fish and other sea

creatures swimming by, and see Florida manatees up close. Divers demonstrate their equipment after completing their dives in the tank.

Living Seas, The (film) Educational film in the EPCOT Educational Media Collection: Minnie's Science Field Trips series; released in

September 1988. 17 min. Students explore The Living Seas at Epcot.

Living with Change (film) Educational film in the Skills for the New Technology: What a Kid Needs to Know Today series; released in September 1983. A custodian learns that change can mean advances and benefits for society and that he should not fear the future.

Living with Computers (film) Educational film in the Skills for the New Technology: What a Kid Needs to Know Today series; released in September 1983. Elmer the custodian is led on a magical cross-country tour that introduces him to the computer's many applications.

Living with the Land Boat ride in The Land at Epcot; beginning on December 10, 1993. Superseded Listen to the Land.

Livingston, Jerry (1909–1987) Composer; he wrote the *Cinderella* songs.

Lizzie McGuire (television) Half-hour series mixing live action and animation on Disney Channel; premiered on January 19, 2001. The series covers the life of 13-year-old Lizzie McGuire as she stumbles into her adolescence with all its attendant crises and joys. Stars Hilary Duff (Lizzie McGuire), Hallie Todd (Jo McGuire), Robert Carradine (Sam McGuire), Jake Thomas (Matt McGuire). Working title was *What's Lizzie Thinking?* The series began airing as part of ABC's *ABC Kids* Saturday morning lineup on September 20, 2003.

Lizzie McGuire Movie, The (film) Lizzie McGuire and her pals Gordo, Kate, and Ethan go on a class trip to Italy, where Lizzie is mistaken for Isabella (who is part of an Italian pop duo) and begins to fall for Paolo (Isabella's handsome Italian-pop star former boyfriend). When Lizzie's mom, dad, and annoying brother Matt get wind of this, they all jet their way to Italy. In the meantime, Lizzie is transformed from a gawky teen to a beautiful pop star. Gordo struggles to understand his true feelings for her, and a whirlwind of sur-

prising events force Lizzie to find the true meaning of friendship. Released on May 2, 2003. Directed by Jim Fall. Stars Hilary Duff (Lizzie), Adam Lamberg (Gordo), Robert Carradine (Sam McGuire), Hallie Todd (Jo McGuire), Jake Thomas (Matt), Yani Gellman (Paolo), Alex Borstein (Miss Ungermeyer), Clayton Snyder (Ethan), Ashlie Brillault (Kate), Brendan Kelly (Sergei), Carly Schroeder (Melina). 94 min. Filmed on location in Rome, in Super 35-Scope. Released on video in 2003.

Lloyd, Christopher Actor; appeared in *Who Framed Roger Rabbit* (Judge Doom), *Angels in the Outfield* (Al), *Camp Nowhere* (Dennis Van Welker), *My Favorite Martian* (the Martian/Uncle Martin), and provided the voice of Merlock in *Ducktales the Movie*. He received an Emmy Award for Lead Actor in a Drama Series for a guest appearance on *Avonlea* on The Disney Channel. On television he appeared in *Angels in the Endzone* (Al).

Lloyd in Space (television) Half-hour animated television series; premiered on February 3, 2001. Follows the humorous day-to-day dilemmas of Lloyd, a space-station–bound alien teenager who must endure the often confusing transition toward adulthood. Voices include Courtland Mead (Lloyd), Bill Fagerbakke (Kurt), Brian George (Station), April Winchell (Nora), Pam Hayden (Douglas). Created by Paul Germain and Joe Ansolabehere, who also created Disney's *Recess*. 39 episodes.

Loaded Weapon (film) Educational 16mm release in February 1992. 22 min. Illustrates the lethal combination of drinking and driving when a high school girl is killed.

Lockhart, Anne Actress; appeared on television in *Fire on Kelly Mountain*.

Loggia, Robert Actor; appeared in *The Marrying Man* (Lew Horner), *I Love Trouble* (Matt Greenfield), *Holy Man* (McBainbridge), provided the voice of Sykes in *Oliver & Company*, and appeared on television as *Elfego Baca*.

Lohan, Lindsay Actress; appeared in *The Parent Trap* remake (Hallie Parker/Annie James), the *Freaky Friday* remake (Anna), *Confessions of a Teenage Drama Queen* (Lola), *Herbie: Fully Loaded* (Maggie Peyton), and on television in *Life-Size* (Casey Mitchell) and *Get a Clue* (Lexy Gold).

Lomond, Britt Actor; appeared in *Tonka* (Gen. Custer) and on television as Monastario in *Zorro*.

London Connection, The (film) Foreign theatrical version of *The Omega Connection*; released first in England on December 21, 1979. 84 min.

Lone Chipmunks, The (film) Chip and Dale cartoon; released on April 7, 1954. Directed by Jack Kinney. Chip and Dale's game of robber and sheriff turns real when they successfully capture Pete, the infamous bank robber.

Lone Survivor of Custer's Last Stand (television) Television show; part 2 of *Comanche*.

Lonesome Ghosts (film) Mickey Mouse cartoon; released on December 24, 1937. Directed by Burt Gillett. Some overconfident spirits hire professional, but inept, ghost-exterminators Mickey, Donald, and Goofy to try and get rid of them, hoping to have some fun in the process. The exterminators succeed in ridding the house of the ghosts accidentally, after many misadventures in which they crash into molasses and flour and appear more hideous than the ghosts, which scares the ethereal inhabitants into racing out of the house. One of the more interesting inventions of the Disney Animation Department was transparent paint, used effectively for the ghosts in this film.

Long, Shelley Actress; appeared in *Outrageous Fortune* (Lauren) and *Hello Again* (Lucy Chadman), and on television in *The Best of Disney: 50 Years of Disney Magic*, and the remake of *Freaky Friday* (Ellen Andrews).

Long Live the Rightful King (television) Television show; part 3 of *The Prince and the Pauper*.

Longoria, Eva Actress; appeared on television in *Desperate Housewives* (Gabrielle Solis).

Looking for Miracles (television) A teenager's summer as a camp counselor in 1935 is complicated by his stowaway little brother. A Disney Channel Premiere Film; aired on June 3, 1989. Based on the novel by A. E. Hotchner. Directed by Kevin Sullivan. Stars Patricia Phillips (mother), Zachery Bennett (Sullivan), Greg Spottiswood (Ryan), Joe Flaherty (Arnold Berman). 103 min. Greg Spottiswood won the Emmy Award for Outstanding Performer in a Children's Special. Released on video in 1991.

Lord Is Good to Me, The Song from *Johnny Appleseed*, sung by Dennis Day. Written by Kim Gannon and Walter Kent.

Lords & Ladies Current name for His Lordship, shop in United Kingdom in World Showcase at Epcot. Sells English cottage replicas and similar items.

Lorenzo (film) Animated short about a fat and sassy cat terrorized by its own tail into a fit of ballroom dancing. Directed by Mike Gabriel. Premiered at Florida Film Festival 2004 in Orlando on March 6, 2004. Released with *Raising Helen* on May 28, 2004. Based on an original idea by Joe Grant. 5 min. Nominated for an Academy Award.

Loretta Claiborne Story, The (television) Two-hour movie on *The Wonderful World of Disney*; aired on January 16, 2000. The story of a poor, mentally disabled African American girl who goes on to become a champion athlete, teacher, and passionate advocate for those with mental and physical disabilities. Directed by Lee Grant. Stars Kimberly Elise (Loretta), Tina Lifford (Rita), Nicole Ari Parker (Christine), Damon Gupton (Sam), Camryn Manheim (Janet).

L'Originale Alfredo di Roma Ristorante Restaurant in Italy in World Showcase at Epcot; opened on October 1, 1982. Guests partake of fettuccine Alfredo or any number of Italian pastas and other delicacies in this full-service restaurant, surrounded by intriguing trompe l'oeil paintings of Italian scenes. Occasionally, a waiter or two might step aside and belt out an operatic aria in between courses to the delight of guests.

Lorre, Peter (1904–1964) Actor; appeared in *20,000 Leagues Under the Sea* (Conseil) and on television in *Monsters of the Deep*.

Los Angeles International Airport Designers from Walt Disney Imagineering helped in the redesign of the theme restaurant at LAX, which reopened in December 1996. The Encounter Restaurant, originally known as the Theme Building Restaurant, was built in 1961 with a then futuristic look resembling a flying saucer on parabolic stilts.

Lost (television) One-hour drama series on ABC; premiered on September 22, 2004. A plane crashes on a Pacific island, and the 48 survivors, stripped of everything, scavenge what they can from the plane for their survival. Some panic; some pin their hopes on rescue. The band of friends, family, enemies, and strangers must work together against the cruel weather and mysterious opponents. Stars Matthew Fox (Jack), Evangeline Lilly (Kate), Dominic Monaghan (Charlie), Ian Somerhalder (Boone), Jorge Garcia (Hurley), Maggie Grace (Shannon), Malcolm David Kelley (Walt), Naveen Andrews (Sayid), Harold Perrineau (Michael), Josh Holloway (Sawyer), Terry O'Quinn (Locke), Daniel Dae Kim (Jin), Yunjin Kim (Sun). From Touchstone Television. Filmed entirely on location in Hawaii. The show won an Emmy for Best Drama Series in 2005.

Lost at Home (television) Half-hour comedy series on ABC; premiered on April 1, 2003, and ended on April 22. Ad agency superstar Michael Davis is full of ambition, but he is losing touch with his family. The winning strategies that have made him a success at work are surprisingly useless at home. His wife, Rachel, gives him an ultimatum, and he tries to win back his family. Stars Mitch Rouse (Michael), Connie Britton (Rachel), Gregory Hines (Jordan King), Stark Sands (Will), Leah Pipes (Sara), Gavin Fink (Joshua), Aaron Hill (Tucker). From Touchstone Television in association with NBC Studios.

Lost Boys, The Peter Pan's pals in Never Land.

Lost on the Baja Peninsula (television) Television show; part 1 of *Three Without Fear*.

Lost River Cookhouse Counter-service restaurant in the Lost River Delta area of Tokyo DisneySea; opened on July 21, 2005, in conjunction with Raging Spirits.

Lot Like Love, A (film) A pair of dynamic, diametrically opposed twentysomethings—Oliver and Emily—have an initial fateful meeting that sets off sparks, but then seems to go nowhere. Over the next seven years, they continue to meet through changing careers and different relationships. There always seems to be plenty keeping them apart, and yet there is also something utterly inexplicable pulling them together. Released on April 22, 2005. A Touchstone Pictures/Beacon Pictures film. Directed by Nigel Cole. Stars Ashton Kutcher (Oliver Martin), Amanda Peet (Emily

Friehl), Ty Giordano (Graham Martin), Melissa Van der Schyff (Carol Martin), Taryn Manning (Ellen Martin), Kathryn Hahn (Michelle). 107 min. The film uses more than 55 locations, from New York's Chinatown to Los Angeles' El Matador Beach. Released on video in 2005.

Lots of Luck (television) Television movie for The Disney Channel; first aired on February 3, 1985. A housewife's winning lottery ticket starts a lucky streak in the family as everyone starts bringing home prizes, but there are problems that go with this Midas touch. Directed by Peter Baldwin. Stars Annette Funicello (Julie Maris), Martin Mull (Frank Maris), Fred Willard, Polly Holliday. Released on video in 1986.

Lottery, The (film) Short film about a music teacher who finds and loses a winning lottery ticket, illustrating various special-effects techniques for guests at the Backstage Studio Tour, Disney-MGM Studios; opened on May 1, 1989, and ended June 29, 1996. 4 min. Stars Bette Midler.

Lotus Blossom Cafe Fast-food facility in China in World Showcase at Epcot, opened on September 24, 1985.

Louie One of Donald Duck's three nephews.

Louis Frantic cook in *The Little Mermaid*, voiced by René Auberjonois.

Louis L'Amour's The Cherokee Trail See *The Cherokee Trail*.

Lounsbery, John (1911–1976) Animator; one of Walt's "Nine Old Men." He started his career

with Disney in 1935, as an animator on *Snow White and the Seven Dwarfs*. He worked on most of the classic features, as an animator or directing animator, including *Pinocchio*, *Peter Pan*, *Lady and the Tramp*, and *The Rescuers*. He was honored posthumously in 1989 with the Disney Legends award.

Love Song from *Robin Hood*, nominated for an Academy Award; written by Floyd Huddleston and George Bruns.

Love and Duty: Which Comes First? (film) Educational film; using sequences from *Old Yeller*. In the Questions!/Answers? series, released in October 1975. Helps students understand the relationship of duty to feelings of love and loyalty.

Love Bug, The (film) A down-and-out racetrack driver, Jim Douglas acquires a little Volkswagen but doesn't realize that the "bug" is almost human. The car helps Jim to win many races, but runs away, when it feels it is not appreciated, into the clutches of villainous rival Peter Thorndyke. With the help of his friends Tennessee and Carole, Jim changes his attitude, finds the "bug," and apologizes. They win another race—and Jim falls in love with Carole. Released on March 13, 1969. Directed by Robert Stevenson. Stars Dean Jones (Jim Douglas), Michele Lee (Carole), David Tomlinson (Thorndyke), Buddy Hackett (Tennessee), Joe Flynn (Havershaw), Benson Fong (Mr. Wu), Andy Granatelli. The movie was based on the story "Car-Boy-Girl" by Gordon Buford. On-location shooting was done in California in San Francisco, as well as Willow Springs, the Riverside Raceway, and the Monterey Peninsula. 108 min. The highest-grossing film in the U.S. during 1969; the film was so successful that it led to the sequels *Herbie Rides Again*, *Herbie Goes to Monte Carlo*, *Herbie Goes Bananas*, *Herbie: Fully*

Loaded; a limited television series, *Herbie, the Love Bug*; and a 1997 television-movie sequel. Reissued in 1979 and released on video in 1980 and 1992.

Love Bug, The (television) Two-hour television movie; aired on *The Wonderful World of Disney* on November 30, 1997. Now owned by egotistical Englishman Simon Moore III, Herbie is junked when he places last in a big race. The little car is saved from demolition by Hank Cooper, a washed-up racer-turned-mechanic. Hank discovers Herbie's special personality, and Herbie tries to help out Hank in his romance with Alex Davis, while defending himself against Moore's newly created car-with-a-personality—Horace, the Hate Bug. Directed by Peyton Reed. Stars Bruce Campbell (Hank Cooper), John Hannah (Simon Moore), Alexandra Wentworth (Alex Davis), Kevin J. O'Connor (Roddy Martel). Dean Jones returns to play Jim Douglas, Herbie's first owner, three decades after he made the original film.

Love Is a Song Song from *Bambi*; written by Larry Morey and Frank Churchill. Nominated for an Academy Award.

Love Leads the Way (television) Television movie for The Disney Channel; aired on October 7, 1984. A blind man, Morris Frank fights prejudice and skepticism to prove the worth of guide dogs in America in the 1930s. Directed by Delbert Mann. Stars Timothy Bottoms (Morris Frank), Eva Marie Saint (Dorothy Eustis), Ralph Bellamy (Senator), Ernest Borgnine (Senator), Arthur Hill (father), Patricia Neal (mother),

Glynnis O'Connor (Lois), Susan Dey (Beth). Filmed on location in Nashville, Tennessee, and in Washington State. Released on video in 1985.

Low Down Dirty Shame, A (film) Andre Shame has been fired from the police force because of a botched drug bust, so he is now down on his luck, working as a private investigator, taking big risks for small rewards. He has a trusty secretary, Peaches, whose resourcefulness and feistiness are often necessary to get him out of a jam, and he is tough talking and knows the ways of the streets. When he is retained by DEA agent Rothmiller to track down $20 million in missing drug money, he finds himself facing the notorious Ernesto Mendoza, the man he thought he killed in the failed drug raid. Now he has a chance to clear his name as well as shut down Mendoza's illegal operations. Released on November 23, 1994. Directed by Keenen Ivory Wayans. A Hollywood Picture release, in association with Caravan Pictures. 100 min. Stars Keenen Ivory Wayans (Shame), Charles S. Dutton (Rothmiller), Jada Pinkett (Peaches), Salli Richardson (Angela), Andrew Divoff (Mendoza). The final scenes were shot in a closed five-level shopping mall in Scottsdale, Arizona. Wayans did most of his own stunts for the film. Released on video in 1995.

Lowell, Tom Actor; appeared in *That Darn Cat!* (Canoe), *The Gnome-Mobile* (Jasper), and *The Boatniks* (Wagner).

Lozano, Ignacio E., Jr. Member of the Disney board of directors beginning in 1981. He left the board on March 6, 2001.

Lozano, Monica C. Member of the Disney board of directors beginning September 19, 2000.

Lucas, George Noted producer/director, collaborated with Walt Disney Imagineering on five theme park attractions. The first was Captain Eo, which opened at Disneyland in 1986 and later at Epcot. He also co-created Star Tours at Disneyland, Disney-MGM Studios, Tokyo Disneyland,

and Disneyland Paris, Indiana Jones and the Temple of Peril: Backwards! at Disneyland Paris, the Indiana Jones Epic Stunt Spectacular at Disney-MGM Studios, and, most recently, the Indiana Jones Adventure at Disneyland.

Lucca, Tony Actor; appeared on the *Mickey Mouse Club* on The Disney Channel, beginning in 1991.

Lucifer Tough alley-cat character in *Pluto's Kid Brother* (1946).

Lucifer The cat menace in Cinderella's household.

Luck of the Irish, The (television) A Disney Channel Original Movie; aired on March 9, 2001. When junior high basketball star Kyle Johnson questions his heritage, he discovers that his mother is actually a leprechaun, and he is starting to change into one too, all because someone stole his gold Celtic good luck coin. To get it back, and keep him and his family human, Kyle has to ward off an evil, step-dancing leprechaun, Seamus McTiernan, and challenge him to a contest. Directed by Paul Hoen. Stars Ryan Merriman (Kyle Johnson), Alexis Lopez (Bonnie Lopez), Glenndon Chatman (Russell Holloway), Marita Geraghty (Kate Johnson), Paul Kiernan (Bob Johnson), Henry Gibson (Reilly O'Reilly), Timothy Omundson (Seamus McTiernan). Filmed in Salt Lake City, Utah.

Lucky Fortune Cookery, The Chinese food location at Pacific Wharf at Disney's California Adventure; opened on February 8, 2001.

The restaurant has only been open during peak periods.

Lucky Nugget Cafe Restaurant in Westernland at Tokyo Disneyland; opened on April 15, 1983.

Lucky Nugget Saloon, The Restaurant in Frontierland in Disneyland Paris; opened on April 12, 1992. The saloon features a menu typical of the American West.

Lucky Number (film) Donald Duck cartoon; released on July 20, 1951. Directed by Jack Hannah. Donald, unbeknownst to him, has won a new car, and his nephews go to pick it up as a surprise. But when the car arrives, Donald wrecks it thinking his nephews played a trick.

Lucky the Dinosaur The first Audio-Animatronics figure to walk freely and personally interact with park guests, Lucky the Dinosaur was introduced at Disney's California Adventure as a test on August 28, 2003. Lucky, created by Walt Disney Imagineering after five years of effort, walks on two legs, stands approximately nine feet tall and twelve feet long, and pulls a cart of flowers. Lucky next appeared at Disney's Animal Kingdom at Walt Disney World in spring/summer 2005 and later Hong Kong Disneyland.

Luddy, Barbara (1907–1979) She voiced Lady in *Lady and the Tramp*, Kanga in the Winnie the Pooh films, Mother Rabbit in *Robin Hood*, and Merryweather in *Sleeping Beauty*.

Ludwig, Irving (1910–2005) He joined Disney in 1940 to manage the road-show engagements of *Fantasia*, and later became part of the sales administration staff of Walt Disney Productions. He was first vice president and domestic sales manager for the newly formed Buena Vista Distribution Company in 1953. In 1959 he became its president, a post he held until his retirement in 1980. He was honored with the Disney Legends award in 1993.

Ludwig Von Drake Donald Duck's erudite and eccentric uncle who hosted several television shows, debuting in the first show of *Walt Disney's Wonderful World of Color* in 1961: *An Adventure*

in Color. He appeared in a total of 18 shows. The voice was supplied by Paul Frees.

Lukas, Paul (1887–1971) Actor; appeared in *20,000 Leagues Under the Sea* (Prof. Aronnax).

Lullaby Land (film) Silly Symphony cartoon; released on August 19, 1933. Directed by Wilfred Jackson. A little baby and a toy dog have an adventure in a land of patchwork-quilt fields, trees laden with rattles, and magic nursery crockery, safety pins, and bottles of castor oil. Frightened by a Forbidden Garden of penknives, scissors, and matches, the pair are rescued by the sandman and sent back to the cradle on a blanket of flowers. The title song was published on sheet music.

Lulubelle Bongo's girlfriend in the *Bongo* segment of *Fun and Fancy Free*.

Lumiere Enchanted candlestick/butler in *Beauty and the Beast*; voiced by Jerry Orbach.

Lumiere's Kitchen Fast-food facility in Fantasyland in Magic Kingdom Park at Walt Disney World; opened on February 13, 1993. Formerly Gurgi's Munchies and Crunchies.

Luminaria Holiday-themed nighttime show, with fireworks, on the lagoon at Disney's California Adventure, beginning November 9, 2001, for that one Christmas season.

Lumpjaw Bongo's rival in the *Bongo* segment of *Fun and Fancy Free*.

Luna, Ricky Actor; appeared on the *Mickey Mouse Club* on The Disney Channel, beginning in 1990.

Lunch Money (film) Educational film about the necessity of honesty and integrity in dealing with others, from the What Should I Do? series; released in July 1970.

Lund, Sharon Disney See Sharon Disney.

Lundy, Dick (1907–1990) Animator; began at Disney in 1929, he worked on *Snow White and the Seven Dwarfs* and various shorts. He first directed on *Sea Scouts*, and continued directing Donald cartoons in the 1939–43 period. He left Disney in 1943.

Lupton, John (1928–1993) Actor; appeared in *The Great Locomotive Chase* (William Pittenger), *Napoleon and Samantha* (Pete), and *The World's Greatest Athlete*, and on television in *The Secret of Lost Valley*.

Luske, Hamilton "Ham" (1903–1968) He began at Disney in 1931. He animated on cartoons until 1943, when he became a director for training films; later he directed *Ben and Me, Donald in Mathmagic Land, Donald and the Wheel*, and *Scrooge McDuck and Money*. He was supervising director on *Pinocchio*; sequence director on *Fantasia*, *Saludos Amigos*, *Make Mine Music*, *Cinderella*, *Alice in Wonderland*, *Peter Pan*, *Lady and the Tramp*, *One Hundred and One Dalmatians*; cartoon director on *The Reluctant Dragon*, *Fun and Fancy Free*, *Melody Time*, *So Dear to My Heart*, and *Mary Poppins*. He was noted for his animation of Max Hare in *The Tortoise and the Hare*, of Jenny Wren in *Who Killed Cock Robin?*, Elmer in *Elmer Elephant*, and Snow White herself in *Snow White and the Seven Dwarfs*. He shared a Visual Effects Oscar in 1965 for *Mary Poppins* with Peter Ellenshaw and Eustace Lycett, and was named a Disney Legend posthumously in 1999.

Luske, Tommy He voiced Michael in *Peter Pan*. The son of Disney animator and director Ham Luske, he died in a car accident in 1990.

Lynche, Tate Actress; appeared on the *Mickey Mouse Club* on The Disney Channel, beginning in 1993.

Lynton, Michael He joined Disney in 1987 as manager of business development for Consumer Products, moving into the publishing area in 1989. In 1994 he was named president of Hollywood Pictures. He left the company in 1996.

Lyric Street Records Disney announced in 1997 the founding of this new country music label, named after the street on which Walt and Roy Disney used to live. Their first album, *Stepping Stone*, with Lari White, debuted in 1998.

M

M. Mouse Mercantile Souvenir shop on the mezzanine level in the Grand Floridian Resort & Spa at Walt Disney World; opened on June 28, 1988.

MacArthur, James Actor; appeared in *Swiss Family Robinson* (Fritz), *The Light in the Forest* (Johnny Butler/True Son), *Third Man on the Mountain* (Rudi Matt), and *Kidnapped* (David Balfour), and on television in *Willie and the Yank*. His mother, Helen Hayes, had a cameo role in *Third Man on the Mountain* with him.

McCallum, David Actor; appeared in *The Watcher in the Woods* (Paul Curtis).

McClanahan, Rue Actress; appeared on *The Golden Girls* (for which she won the Emmy Award as Outstanding Lead Actress in a Comedy Series in 1987) and *The Golden Palace*, and on *Disneyland's All Star Comedy Circus* and *The Disney-MGM Studios Theme Park Grand Opening*. She appeared on television in *A Saintly Switch* (Aunt Fanny Moye).

McClure, Marc Actor; appeared in *Freaky Friday* (Boris Harris), and on television in *The Sky Trap*. He made a cameo appearance in the 2003 remake of *Freaky Friday* as Boris.

McCrum, Thomas B. Dentist in Kansas City who hired the young Walt Disney to produce a dental training film for him in 1922—*Tommy Tucker's Tooth*. Several years later, after Walt was in California, McCrum commissioned another film, *Clara Cleans Her Teeth*.

McDaniel, Hattie (1895–1952) Actress; portrayed the house servant, Tempy, in *Song of the South*.

Macdonald, Jim ("Jimmy") (1906–1991) Longtime Disney sound-effects wizard, who created sound effects for many of the Disney films beginning in 1934. In 1946, he was asked by Walt to take over the voice of Mickey Mouse, a chore he provided until his retirement three decades later. He was named a Disney Legend in 1993.

McDonald's For many years, Disney has partnered with McDonald's restaurants in marketing its movies. On January 8, 1998, the first McDonald's restaurant opened at a Disney park, at the Downtown Disney Marketplace at Walt Disney World, following the introduction of kiosks selling McDonald's french fries in the Magic Kingdom and at Disneyland Park the previous year.

McDowall, Roddy (1928–1998) Actor; appeared in *That Darn Cat!* (Gregory Benson), *The Adventures of Bullwhip Griffin* (Bullwhip Griffin), *Bedknobs and Broomsticks* (Mr. Jelk), *The Cat from Outer Space* (Mr. Stallwood), and *The Black Hole* (voice of V.I.N.Cent). He appeared in the pilot of *Small and Frye* (Prof. Vermeer), and did the voice of Mr. Soil in *a bug's life* and Proteus in *Gargoyles*.

McEnery, Peter Actor; appeared in *The Moonspinners* (Mark Camford) and *The Fighting Prince of Donegal* (Hugh O'Donnell).

McEveety, Bernard (1924–2004) Director of *The Bears and I, Napoleon and Samantha, One Little Indian*, and *The Boy and the Bronc Buster*. He was one of three brothers who had extensive directing careers at Disney.

McEveety, Joe (1926–1976) Assistant director, director, and writer at Disney beginning in 1957. He wrote scripts for *Now You See Him, Now You Don't, Michael O'Hara IV, The Wacky Zoo of Morgan City, The Computer Wore Tennis Shoes, The Barefoot Executive, The Apple Dumpling Gang*, and *The Strongest Man in the World*.

McEveety, Vince Director; he began at Disney as an assistant director on the *Mickey Mouse Club*, and later directed such films as *The Ballad of Hector the Stowaway Dog, Gus, Treasure of Matecumbe, The Strongest Man in the World, Million Dollar Duck, The Biscuit Eater, Charley and the Angel, Superdad, The Castaway Cowboy*, and *High-Flying Spy*.

McGavin, Darren Actor; appeared in *No Deposit, No Return* (Duke) and *Hot Lead and Cold Feet* (Mayor Ragsdale), and on television in *Small and Frye, Boomerang, Dog of Many Talents, High Flying Spy*, and *Donovan's Kid*. On The Disney Channel he appeared in *Perfect Harmony*.

McGill, Jennifer Actress; appeared on the *Mickey Mouse Club* on The Disney Channel, beginning in 1989.

McGoohan, Patrick Actor; appeared in *The Three Lives of Thomasina* (Andrew MacDhui), *Baby* (Dr. Eric Kiviat), and on television in the title role of *The Scarecrow of Romney Marsh*. He later went on to fame on *The Secret Agent* and *The Prisoner* television series. He provided the voice of Billy Bones in *Treasure Planet*.

McGreevey, Michael Actor; appeared in *The Computer Wore Tennis Shoes, The Strongest Man in the World*, and *Now You See Him, Now You Don't* (Richard Schuyler); *Snowball Express* (Wally Perkins); and *The Shaggy D.A.* (Sheldon), and on television in *For the Love of Willadean, Texas John Slaughter, Sammy, the Way-out Seal, The Wacky Zoo of Morgan City*, and *Michael O'Hara the Fourth*.

McGuire, Dorothy (1916–2001) Actress; appeared in *Swiss Family Robinson* (mother), *Old Yeller* (Katie Coates), and *Summer Magic* (Margaret Carey). On television she narrated part of *The Best Doggoned Dog in the World*.

McIntire, John (1907–1991) Actor; appeared in *The Light in the Forest* (John Elder), *Herbie Rides Again* (Mr. Judson), and as the voices of Rufus in *The Rescuers* and Badger in *The Fox and the Hound*. Appeared on television in *Bayou Boy, Gallegher Goes West*, and *The Mystery of Edward Sims*.

McKennon, Dallas Perennial voice actor for Disney projects for records, movies, and the parks. He appeared in *Son of Flubber* (First Juror), *The Misadventures of Merlin Jones* (Detective Hutchins), *The Cat from Outer Space* (Farmer), and *Hot Lead and Cold Feet* (Saloon Man), and lent his voice to such characters as the Fisherman Bear in *Bedknobs and Broomsticks*, Toughy and Professor in *Lady and the Tramp*, Owl in *Sleeping Beauty*, and several animated characters in *Mary Poppins*. He provided the voice of Ben Franklin in The American Adventure at Epcot, Old Prospector on Big Thunder Mountain Railroad, and several voices in the Country Bear Jamboree.

McKim, Sam (1924–2004) McKim started at Disney in 1955 as a conceptual artist for Disneyland. He sketched attractions for Main Street, U.S.A., and Frontierland, as well as working on Disney films such as *Nikki, Wild Dog of the North* and *The Gnome-Mobile*. He contributed sketches for such Disneyland favorites as Great Moments with Mr. Lincoln, "it's a small world," The Haunted Mansion, the monorail, and the Carousel of Progress. For Walt Disney World, he worked on The Hall of Presidents, Universe of Energy, and Disney-MGM Studios. He retired in 1987. McKim had been charged with creating many of the Disneyland maps that were sold to guests through the years, and they were so highly regarded that he was persuaded to come out of retirement to design a map for Disneyland Paris. He was named a Disney Legend in 1996.

McKinley High School Chicago school where Walt attended his freshman year and served as an artist on the school magazine, *The Voice*. When World War I intervened, Walt left to serve in the Red Cross, and he never returned to school. Some art classes at night school prepared him for his future profession, and an inquiring mind and retentive memory contributed to his lifelong quest for knowledge.

McLeish, John (1916–1968) Narrator of the Goofy "how to" cartoons, as well as *Dumbo*; also known as John Ployardt. According to the story, McLeish was a very serious and dignified person. When the staff realized that his educated voice would be perfect for narrating the Goofy cartoons, they asked him to do it, but did not bother to explain that the erudite narration was really tongue in cheek, and that Goofy would be doing almost exactly the opposite of what was being described. He also provided the voice for the prosecuting attorney in *The Adventures of Ichabod and Mr. Toad* and a barker in *Pinocchio*. McLeish worked at Disney in animation and story from 1939 to 1941.

McLiam, John (1918–1994) Actor; appeared on television in *Shadow of Fear* and *The Mystery of Edward Sims.*

MacManus, Dan (1900–1990) Effects animator; began at the Disney Studio in 1935, and remained until his retirement in 1973, working on most of the Disney features during that period.

McMorehouse Customer in *Pigs Is Pigs* (1954).

MacMurray, Fred (1908–1991) Actor; appeared in *The Shaggy Dog* (Wilson Daniels), *The Absent-Minded Professor* and *Son of Flubber* (Prof. Ned Brainard), *Bon Voyage* (Harry Willard), *Follow Me, Boys!* (Lemuel Siddons), *The Happiest Millionaire* (Anthony J. Drexel Biddle), and *Charley and the Angel* (Charley Appleby). He was named a Disney Legend in 1987.

McNair, Terra Actress; appeared on the *Mickey Mouse Club* on The Disney Channel, from 1991 to 1993.

McNamara, William Actor; appeared in *Stella* (Pat Robbins) and *Aspen Extreme* (Todd Pounds), and in the television series *The Nutt House.*

McPherson, Stephen He served as president of Touchstone Television from 2001 until he was named president of ABC Primetime Entertainment in 2004.

Mad Doctor, The (film) Mickey Mouse cartoon; released on January 21, 1933. Directed by Dave Hand. Pluto is captured by an evil scientist and taken to an old castle. Mickey attempts to rescue him, in spite of bats, skeletons, and a giant skeletal spider. Just as a buzz saw is about to cut Mickey in two, he awakens to a mosquito biting him; it was all a nightmare and Pluto is safe. The British film censor at the time thought the film too frightening for some audiences.

Mad Dog, The (film) Mickey Mouse cartoon; released on March 5, 1932. Directed by Burt Gillett. Pluto learns a lesson in submission when he refuses to be bathed by Mickey. In the resulting tug-of-war, Pluto swallows the soap, is taken by everyone to be a mad dog, and is forced to flee the dogcatcher, Pete. Now humbled, Pluto meekly allows himself to be bathed.

Mad Hatter Character who puts on a tea party in *Alice in Wonderland*, voiced by Ed Wynn. Being somewhat befuddled, he has left the price tag on his hat. The 10/6 is the price, ten shillings sixpence.

Mad Hatter Shop Shop on Main Street at Disneyland from June 1958, located in the Penny Arcade building until 1963 and then in the Opera House building. Guests can buy hats and have their names embroidered on them. Also a shop in Fantasyland, beginning in 1956, and another one in Fantasyland in Magic Kingdom Park at Walt Disney World. Also in Fantasyland at Tokyo Disneyland; opened on April 15, 1983.

Mad Hatter's Tea Cups Attraction in Fantasyland at Disneyland Paris; opened on April 12, 1992. Also at Hong Kong Disneyland; opened on September 12, 2005. For the Disneyland and Walt Disney World attractions, see Mad Tea Party.

Mad Hermit of Chimney Butte, The (television) Television show; aired on April 1, 1960. Directed by Jack Hannah. Donald Duck is the hermit; what led him to that fate is revealed through a series of cartoons.

Mad Love (film) Two teenagers, Matt Leland and Casey Roberts, are involved in a passionate affair, during which Matt abandons everything he has worked for to follow Casey on a cross-country trip. Eventually, he discovers an irrational and dangerous side to Casey, and must find a way to release her from his life. Directed by Antonia Bird. A Touchstone Picture. Released on May 26, 1995. Stars Chris O'Donnell (Matt), Drew Barrymore (Casey), Joan Allen (Margaret), T.J. Lowther (Adam), Amy Sakasitz (Joanna), Jude Ciccolella (Richard), Kevin Dunn (Clifford). 96 min. Released on video in 1995.

Mad Tea Party Fantasyland attraction at Disneyland; opened on July 17, 1955; it was closed in 1982–83 and moved to a new location. Based on the sequence from the 1951 film *Alice in Wonderland*. Guests spin, and can control their speed, in giant tea cups in a ride best not taken just after having eaten lunch. Also, Fantasyland attraction in Magic Kingdom Park at Walt Disney World; opened on October 1, 1971. See also Mad Hatter's Tea Cups and Alice's Tea Party.

Madam Mim Evil witch in *The Sword in the Stone*; voiced by Martha Wentworth.

Madame Adelaide Bonfamille Aristocratic owner of the cats in *The Aristocats*; voiced by Hermione Baddeley.

Madame Medusa Evil pawnshop owner in *The Rescuers*; voiced by Geraldine Page.

Madcap Adventures of Mr. Toad, The (film) Theatrical reissue of the *Wind in the Willows* segment from *The Adventures of Ichabod and Mr. Toad*, on December 25, 1975. 32 min.

Mademoiselle Upanova Ostrich dancer in the *Dance of the Hours* segment of *Fantasia*.

Madigan Men (television) Half-hour television series; running on ABC from October 6 to December 12, 2000. Benjamin, Seamus, and Luke Madigan are three generations of Irishmen trying to make their way in the dating world of New York. Together, they might be able to teach each other something about what it means to be a man in the 21st century. Stars Gabriel Byrne (Benjamin), Roy Dotrice (Seamus), John C. Hensley (Luke), Grant Shaud (Alex Rossetti), Sabrina Lloyd (Wendy Lipton).

Madonna Actress; appeared as Breathless Mahoney in *Dick Tracy* and as Eva Peron in *Evita*.

Maelstrom Boat ride attraction in Norway in World Showcase at Epcot; opened on July 5, 1988. Guests take a short ride through scenes from Norwegian history while being menaced by trolls. A unique element of the journey is when the boats plummet backward down some rapids and narrowly miss going over a waterfall. The boat trip ends at a theater where guests see a short film about Norwegian scenery.

Mafia! See *Jane Austen's Mafia!*

Magellan's Restaurant; opened on September 4, 2001, featuring international cuisine inside the Fortress at Explorers' Landing at Tokyo Disney-Sea. The decor celebrates the exploration of the sea and the discovery of astronomy in the 16th century.

Maggie Bossy and heroic cow character in *Home on the Range*; voiced by Roseanne Barr.

Magic and Music (television) Television show; aired on March 19, 1958. Directed by Hamilton S. Luske. The slave in the Magic Mirror emcees a show on the magic of music, using footage of visual fantasies from *Melody Time* and *Fantasia*. Stars Hans Conried.

Magic Carpet 'Round the World (film) Tour around the world in Circle-Vision, prepared for the Monsanto-sponsored attraction at Walt Disney World; opened on March 16, 1974, and closed on March 14, 1975; later shown at Tokyo Disneyland from April 15, 1983 to May 16, 1986 (including new footage of Europe and the United States).

Magic Carpets of Aladdin, The Attraction in Adventureland in Magic Kingdom Park at Walt Disney World; opened May 23, 2001.

Magic Eye Theater Indoor theater in Tomorrowland at Disneyland taking the place of the Space Stage in 1986, where *Magic Journeys*, *Captain Eo*, and *Honey, I Shrunk the Audience* have been presented. Also the name of the 3-D movie theater in Journey into Imagination at Epcot.

Magic Highway U.S.A. (television) Television show; aired on May 14, 1958. Directed by Ward Kimball. The importance of America's highways is depicted, from the earliest days to the highways (and vehicles) of the future. Narrated by Marvin Miller.

Magic in the Magic Kingdom See Disney's Magic in the Magic Kingdom.

Magic Jersey, The See *The Jersey*.

Magic Journeys (film) 3-D impressionistic view of a child's imagination, for Journey into Imagination, Epcot, opened on October 1, 1982.

Moved to the Fantasyland Theater in Magic Kingdom Park at Walt Disney World from December 15, 1987 until December 1, 1993. Presented by Kodak. Also shown at Disneyland from 1984 to 1986, and in Tokyo Disneyland from 1985 to 1987.

Magic Kingdom Club Created in 1958 under the direction of Milt Albright. Companies and organizations primarily near Disneyland and later Walt Disney World could offer memberships to employees, which gave them discounts at the parks. The club published *Disney News*, later *The Disney Magazine*, before that magazine went national. The club ceased operation in 2000, to be superseded by a membership Disney Club.

Magic Kingdom on Ice See World on Ice.

Magic Kingdom Park Theme park at Walt Disney World, opened on October 1, 1971. The name has been used generally to refer to Disneyland ever since its opening in 1955 (as the Magic Kingdom). The name takes on added importance in Florida, because it to refers to only a part of Walt Disney World.

Magic Kingdom Resorts Hotels at Walt Disney World; consists of the Contemporary Resort, Polynesian Resort, Wilderness Lodge, and Grand Floridian Resort & Spa.

Magic Lamp Theater, The Attraction at Tokyo DisneySea, sponsored by Fuji, opening on September 4, 2001. A magic show, featuring Shaban—"The Greatest Magician in the World." But the real star of the show is the hilarious and unpredictable Genie from Disney's *Aladdin*, brought to life with the latest in 3-D magic.

Magic Mirror Character voiced by Moroni Olsen in *Snow White and the Seven Dwarfs*; later used by Walt as a co-host on his television show with Hans Conried usually playing the part.

Magic Music Days Program begun at Disneyland that gives school choral, band, and other music groups the unique opportunity to perform

at a Disney park as well as learn about musical performance from Disney professionals.

Magic of Disney Animation, The Tour opened at Disney-MGM Studios on May 1, 1989. Featured the film *Back to Neverland* followed by a walking tour through a working animation studio where the processes were explained on video monitors. Elements of the tour changed over the years, especially after animation at the Studio ceased in 2003.

Magic of Disneyland, The (film) Sixteen mm film; released in October 1969. A guided tour of Disneyland, exploring many of the attractions, including Pirates of the Caribbean, PeopleMover, Enchanted Tiki Room, Carousel of Progress, and "it's a small world."

Magic of the Rails (film) Circle-Vision 360 film prepared for the Swiss Federal Railways and shown at an exposition in Lucerne and later in Germany; a train tour around Europe. Released in 1965.

Magic of Walt Disney World, The (film) Documentary; featurette, released on December 20, 1972, with *Snowball Express*. Directed by Tom Leetch. A look at the pleasures of the Disney resort, in the year after its opening. 29 min. An expanded version aired on television, March 31, 1974.

Magic Whistle, The (film) Educational film about a small boy whose wonderful imagination gives magic to an old broken whistle, produced by Dave Bell, released in 1972.

Magica de Spell Evil comic book character, created by Carl Barks, who debuted in *Uncle Scrooge* no. 36 in 1961 and who later appeared in *Ducktales*.

Magical Disney Christmas, A (television) Television show; aired on December 5, 1981. A grouping of holiday cartoons and segments.

Magical World of Disney, The (television) Television series on NBC; from October 9, 1988, to September 9, 1990. The show then moved to The Disney Channel, where it began on September 23, 1990. Michael Eisner hosted.

Magical World of Disney, The (television) Television show; aired on October 9, 1988. The first show of the series with this title, introducing the season's programs. Michael Eisner talks about the return to NBC 27 years after *Walt Disney's Wonderful World of Color* began on the network. Stars Betty White, Harry Anderson. Directed by Max Fader.

Magician Mickey (film) Mickey Mouse cartoon; released on February 6, 1937. Directed by Dave Hand. Donald continually heckles Mickey's magic act, but Mickey bests him at every turn. Donald shoots off a magic pistol that causes all the stage props to fall down on them at the finish of the act.

Magnificent Rebel, The (television) Two-part television show; aired on November 18 and 25, 1962. Directed by Georg Tressler. The life of musical genius and nonconformist composer Ludwig van Beethoven, from his arrival in Vienna in 1792 through the writing of the famous Ninth Symphony, who along the way fought those who opposed something new in music. Rejected by the family of the only woman he truly loved, he devoted himself to music, rising to the height of his career only to be shattered by the loss of hearing. After a period of seclusion, he began anew with a new flood of inspiration that carried him on to even greater acclaim. Stars Karl Boehm, Giulia Rubini, Peter Arens. Boehm was an accomplished pianist and was able to perform his own musical sequences in the film. Filmed in the sumptuous

concert halls of Vienna. This was Walt Disney's first filmmaking venture in Austria, and he chose actual locales, many of them unchanged over the centuries, where Beethoven lived, found inspiration, and worked. Released theatrically abroad.

Magno, Deedee Actress; appeared on the *Mickey Mouse Club* on The Disney Channel, beginning in 1989, and was a member of The Party. Beginning in 2002, she appeared as Jasmine in *Aladdin: A Musical Spectacular* in the Hyperion Theater at Disney's California Adventure.

Magnolia Golf Course Located across from the Polynesian Resort at Walt Disney World. Formerly served by the Disney Inn. Designed by Joe Lee. Provided the setting each year for the final round of the Walt Disney World/Oldsmobile Golf Classic.

Magnolia Tree Terrace When Quaker Oats ceased their sponsorship of Aunt Jemima's Kitchen in Frontierland in 1970, Disneyland changed the name to Magnolia Tree Terrace. The following year, the name was changed again to River Belle Terrace, when Oscar Mayer became the sponsor.

Maharajah Jungle Trek Attraction in the Asia section of Disney's Animal Kingdom at Walt Disney World; opened on March 1, 1999. Guests are able to see such creatures as Komodo dragons, bats, and tigers as they walk through an Asian jungle setting.

Maid Marian Robin Hood's girlfriend, a vixen; voiced by Monica Evans.

Mail Dog (film) Pluto cartoon; released on November 14, 1947. Directed by Charles Nichols. When a pilot has to turn back due to a severe storm, he drops the mail at a remote outpost where it can be delivered by dogsled. The falling mail pouch lands on Pluto, and he sets out to deliver it. He is continually delayed by a rabbit along the way, but, in the end, the rabbit helps Pluto deliver the mail pouch.

Mail Pilot, The (film) Mickey Mouse cartoon; released on May 13, 1933. Directed by Dave Hand. In Mickey's devotion to getting the mail through in his battered little plane, he must fight the elements and Pete, engaging in an aerial battle in which he captures Pete.

Mail to the Chief (television) Two-hour television movie aired on *The Wonderful World of Disney* on April 2, 2000. A struggling president begins an anonymous e-mail correspondence with a middle schooler, Kenny, who is having trouble in his civics class, but provides savvy political advice to the chief executive. Directed by Eric Champnella. Stars Randy Quaid (President Osgood), Bill Switzer (Kenny Witowski), Holland Taylor (Katherine Horner), Dave Nichols (Senator Harris), Ashley Gorrell (Heather). Filmed on location in Toronto.

Main Street Arcade See Penny Arcade.

Main Street Athletic Club Sports clothing shop on Main Street in Magic Kingdom Park at Walt Disney World, opened on June 28, 1995, taking the place of the Penny Arcade, House of Magic, and Main Street Book Shop.

Main Street Bake Shop Shop on Main Street in Magic Kingdom Park at Walt Disney World, opened in 1971. A tearoom that offers pastries, cinnamon rolls, and cookies. Hosted by Nestlé Toll House.

Main Street Cinema Attraction at Disneyland; opened on July 17, 1955. Inside, six screens continuously play selected early cartoons, including *Steamboat Willie*. Also an attraction in  Magic Kingdom Park at Walt Disney World, opened on October 1, 1971; and in World Bazaar at Tokyo Disneyland, opened on April 15, 1983. The Walt Disney World attraction was turned into a shop in June 1998.

Main Street Confectionery Shop on Main Street in Magic Kingdom Park at Walt Disney World; opened on October 1, 1971. Sells many varieties of candy, some of it prepared fresh in the shop.

Main Street Corner Café Table service restaurant at Hong Kong Disneyland featuring Western and Chinese cuisine; opened on September 12, 2005.

Main Street Electrical Parade Parade in summers at Disneyland beginning on June 17, 1972, and ending November 25, 1996. The parade, featuring half a million tiny lights on floats themed primarily to Disney movies, became one of the most beloved traditions at Disneyland. The park's lights were dimmed and the illuminated parade snaked from a gate next to "it's a small world," past the Matterhorn, skirted the hub, and then continued down Main Street to conclude at Town Square. The parade's synthesizer music was based on a piece called "Baroque Hoedown," with themes from Disney songs worked in. The parade did not run in 1975 and 1976 because of America on Parade for the Bicentennial, but it returned in 1977 with a whole new edition. A 108-foot-long "Honor America" finale unit was added in 1979. During 1980 there was a special unit reproducing Sleeping Beauty Castle in honor of the park's 25th anniversary. The parade did not run during the summers of 1983 or 1984. A duplicate version of the Main Street Electrical Parade ran at Magic Kingdom Park at Walt Disney World beginning on June 11, 1977, and ending on September 14, 1991, when it was replaced by Spectromagic. The Walt Disney World parade was moved to Disneyland Paris in April 1992. A version of the parade, called the Tokyo Disneyland Electrical Parade, ran at Tokyo Disneyland from March 9, 1985 to June 21, 1995, being replaced by Disney's Fantillusion. The

Disneyland parade floats were completely refurbished for a move of the parade to Walt Disney World Magic Kingdom Park from May 28, 1999 to April 1, 2001. Then, on July 4, 2001, they made a return to California, this time as Disney's Electrical Parade at Disney's California Adventure. The Tokyo Disneyland Electrical Parade Dream

Lights returned on June 1, 2001. The Disneyland Paris Main Street Electrical Parade ended on March 23, 2003.

Main Street Magic Shop Opened at Disneyland in 1957. At one time, before his career took off, actor Steve Martin worked in this shop. Magic tricks, disguises, and makeup are available, and the shop hosts will often offer a demonstration. See also Merlin's Magic Shop, and House of Magic for the Walt Disney World version.

Main Street Motors Shop/display sponsored by Esso on Main Street at Disneyland Paris.

Main Street Photo Supply See Camera Center.

Main Street, U.S.A. One of the original areas of Disneyland, with its interconnected shops making it one of the world's first "shopping malls." Walt's plan was to present an idealized town at the turn of the century. Such a town never really existed, but if guests were to conjure up their ideal town, it would be something like Main Street, U.S.A. Various towns from Walt Disney's past have claimed that he got the idea for Main Street from them, but the most likely candidate for this honor would be Marceline, Missouri, the town in which Walt spent the formative years

of his childhood. Using forced perspective, the Disney designers gave a fantasy look to the street, making a small place seem large. The ground floors were built at about ⅞ size, with the succeeding floors proportionately smaller. This fudging on the size gives the whole area a fantasy, not-quite-real feeling, which increases one's appreciation of it. Main Street runs from the railroad station and Town Square for two blocks to the Hub. Looking straight down Main Street, guests can catch a glimpse of the castle leading to Fantasyland. On the windows above the ground floor, Disney started a tradition of honoring the men and women who were instrumental in the construction and operation of Disneyland. One of the few exceptions is a window honoring Walt's father, Elias, above the Emporium. The Walt Disney World Magic Kingdom, Disneyland Paris, and Hong Kong Disneyland have their Main Streets, but Tokyo Disneyland opted instead for World Bazaar, which looks very similar except for a roof covering the entire area.

Major Effects (television) Television show; aired on December 16, 1979. Directed by Nicholas Harvey Bennion. Joseph Bottoms as Major Effects explains some of the secrets of special effects in the movies. Mike Jittlov appears with two stop-motion animated films he has made. With Hans Conried.

Make Me Laugh (television) Half-hour game show on Comedy Central; debuted on June 2, 1997, and ended in June 2000, with contestants able to win cash prizes if they can resist the impulse to laugh at the stand-up acts of a series of wisecracking comedians. Host is Ken Ober.

Make Mine Music (film) Ten shorts are combined in a tuneful compilation. Disney's first postwar "package" picture, produced because financial problems prevented Walt Disney from finding enough money to create a full animated feature. By tying a group of shorts together, he was able to get the production into theaters sooner. Premiered in New York on April 20, 1946; general release on August 15, 1946. Production supervisor was Joe Grant; directors were

Jack Kinney, Clyde Geronimi, Hamilton Luske, Robert Cormack, and Joshua Meador. 75 min. Theater program titles are animated to announce the title of the subject that follows. The segments are: (1) *The Martins and the Coys*, which deals with two feuding families who shoot and kill off each other except for Henry Coy and Grace Martin, who fall in love, but continue fighting after marriage (sung by The King's Men); (2) *Blue Bayou*, originally created for *Fantasia* to accompany "Clair de Lune," this short, sung by the Ken Darby Chorus, follows a majestic crane who lands in a bayou, then rises again to join another in the moonlit sky; (3) *All the Cats Join In*, with Benny Goodman and his orchestra playing while animated teenagers go out and dance at a malt shop; (4) *Without You*, in which Andy Russell sings a "Ballad in Blue" as a petal falls, changing to a tear; light reveals a love letter containing lyrics of the song, and rain washes paintings onto a window illustrating the lyrics; (5) *Casey at the Bat*, with Jerry Colonna reciting the sad story of Mighty Casey, a baseball player who loses his touch and can no longer hit the ball; (6) *Two Silhouettes*, with Dinah Shore singing as two figures dance in ballet, the boy meeting, losing, and finding the girl theme (live action dancing was performed by Tania Riabouchinska and David Lichine); (7) *Peter and the Wolf*, told by Sterling Holloway, with Peter going with a duck, cat, and bird to catch

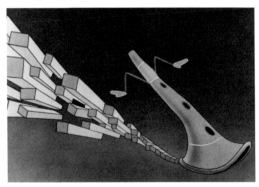

a wolf; (8) *After You've Gone*, with the Benny Goodman Quartet and a musical cartoon fantasy of personalized instruments; (9) *Johnny Fedora and Alice Bluebonnet*, sung by the Andrews Sisters, illustrating the romance between boy and girl hats; and (10) *The Whale Who Wanted to Sing at the Met*, Nelson Eddy tells the story and

sings the songs about a whale who is found singing grand opera with a beautiful voice; a dream sequence shows the whale at the Met as a sensation but the return to reality shows him being harpooned because it is believed he swallowed an opera singer. The film was never theatrically reissued. Many of the individual segments would later be used on television or released theatrically as shorts. Released on video in 2000 minus *The Martins and the Coys*.

Making Friends (film) Educational film, in the Songs for Us series; released in September 1989. 8 min. Songs teach the value of friendship and other relationship skills.

Making of Arachnophobia, The See *Thrills, Chills, and Spiders: The Making of Arachnophobia*.

Making of Me, The (film) Film that answers the question "Where did I come from?" in Wonders of Life, Epcot; opened on October 30, 1989. 15 min. Stars Martin Short. Directed by Glen Gordon Caron.

Making of the NHL's Mighty Ducks, The (television) Television special on KCAL, Los Angeles; aired on October 10, 1993.

Mako Actor; appeared in *The Ugly Dachshund* (Kenji), *Island at the Top of the World* (Oomiak), *Taking Care of Business* (Sakamoto), and *Pearl Harbor* (Admiral Yamamoto).

Malden, Karl Actor; appeared in *Pollyanna* (Rev. Paul Ford) and *The Adventures of Bullwhip Griffin* (Judge Higgins).

Maleficent Evil fairy in *Sleeping Beauty*, voiced by Eleanor Audley.

Malet, Arthur He voiced King Eidilleg in *The Black Cauldron*. Also appeared in *Mary Poppins* (Mr. Dawes, Jr.), *Lt. Robin Crusoe, USN* (Umbrella man), and *Dick Tracy* (diner patron). He appeared on television in *The Further Adventures of Gallegher* (Sir James), *The Nutt House* (Raymond), and *The Fanelli Boys* (Arthur).

Maliboomer Attraction at Paradise Pier at Disney's California Adventure; opened on February 8, 2001. Seated guests catapult 180 feet straight up steel-girder towers in just two seconds, then come down bungee-style in a series of thrilling ups and downs.

Malotte, Albert Hay (1895–1964) Composer; at Disney from 1935 to 1938, he wrote the scores for such award-winning cartoons as *Ferdinand the Bull* and *The Ugly Duckling*. He is probably best known for writing "The Lord's Prayer."

Maltin, Leonard Film historian and commentator; wrote *The Disney Films* (1st edition Crown, 1973), the first filmography to discuss the Disney output of shorts and features. He has appeared as a speaker at Disney conventions, and introduced a series of Walt Disney Treasures DVDs.

Mama Melrose's Ristorante Italiano Restaurant opened at Disney-MGM Studios on September 26, 1991. Formerly The Studio Pizzeria. The restaurant serves pizza and pasta dishes.

Mammoth Records In July 1997, Disney announced the purchase of Mammoth Records, a top independent label in the music industry, based in Carrboro, North Carolina. President and founder Jay Faires entered into a long-term employment contract.

Man and the Moon (television) Television show; aired on December 28, 1955. Directed by

Ward Kimball. Rerun in 1959 as *Tomorrow the Moon*. The show takes a look at how scientists are preparing for a flight to the moon, beginning with a live-action segment and then going into animation as the rocket ship takes off to film the backside of the moon. Dr. Wernher von Braun worked as a technical adviser and appeared in the film.

Man from Bitter Creek, The (television) Television show; episode 5 of *Texas John Slaughter*.

Man in Flight (television) Television show; aired on March 6, 1957. Directed by Hamilton S. Luske. The history of flight, told in a humorous animated sequence using parts of *Victory Through Air Power* with new narration. Walt Disney also takes viewers to Disneyland by helicopter and shows them some of the flying attractions there. A rerun in 1961 replaced some footage to provide a preview of *The Absent-Minded Professor*.

Man in Space (television) Television show; aired on March 9, 1955. Directed by Ward Kimball. Space scientists Willy Ley, Heinz Haber, and Wernher von Braun help explain some of the challenges of space exploration, including a discussion of some of the perceived problems of weightlessness. The history of rockets is shown in animation, beginning with 13th-century Chinese experiments. Von Braun unveils a four-stage, passenger-carrying rocket ship that could break free of the earth's gravitational pull, leading to an animated depiction of man's first trip into space. An abridged version (33 min.) was released theatrically as a featurette on July 18, 1956. This was the first of several Disney shows on space exploration. President Eisenhower requested a print of this film to show the brass at the Pentagon, and it was evidently instrumental in helping to push them into the space program. The doughnut-shaped space station model has been on long-term loan to the National Air and Space Museum in Washington, D.C. Nominated for an Academy Award for Best Short Subject (Documentary). The educational film *All About Weightlessness* was excerpted from this television show.

Man Is His Own Worst Enemy (television) Television show; aired on October 21, 1962. Directed by Hamilton S. Luske. Prof. Ludwig Von Drake tells how people cause most problems, and without them, we wouldn't have any problems. He uses cartoons such as *Reason and Emotion*, *Chicken Little*, and *How to Have an Accident in the Home* to prove his point.

Man, Monsters and Mysteries (film) Foreign release featurette; released first on December 6, 1974, in South Africa. 26 min. A film about Nessie, the Loch Ness monster, revealing the existence of ancient legends and writings previously known only to the Scottish Highlanders. In addition to reproduced photos, there are interviews with citizens, scientists, and even a hypothetical one with Nessie. Directed by Les Clark.

Man of the House (film) A resourceful 11-year-old boy, Ben, tries to scare off his mother's suitor, Jack, a beleaguered federal prosecutor unprepared for stepfatherhood, by forcing him to join the YMCA's Indian Guides program and participate in Native American–inspired rituals and games. The boy's scheme seems to be working until a vengeful indicted mob boss enters the picture and decides to have Jack eliminated. Ultimately, the Guides take on the mob and use their superior wilderness warfare tactics to capture Jack's pursuers. In the process, Jack and the boy forge a bond of friendship, respect, and love. Released on March 3, 1995. Directed by James Orr. 98 min. Stars Chevy Chase (Jack), Jonathan Taylor Thomas (Ben), Farrah Fawcett (Sandy), George Wendt (Chet), Nicholas Garrett (Monroe). Farrah Fawcett's former real-life husband, Ryan O'Neal, has a brief uncredited cameo at the beginning of the movie. Released on video in 1995.

Man on Wheels (television) Television show; aired on March 26, 1967. Directed by Hamilton S. Luske. The effect of the invention of the wheel on society, featuring two featurettes—*Donald and the Wheel* and *Freewayphobia*.

Mang, Mary Anne Beginning in convention and tour sales at Disneyland in 1961, she moved into public and community relations, retiring in 1994 after being instrumental in consolidating the companywide VoluntEars program. She was named a Disney Legend in 2005.

Manhattan Jazz Club The hottest groups perform in the Hotel New York at Disneyland Paris.

Mannequins Nightclub at Pleasure Island at Walt Disney World; opened on May 1, 1989. Features dressed mannequins around the floor, a turntable dance floor, and a sophisticated lighting system.

Man's Best Friend (film) Goofy cartoon; released on April 4, 1952. Directed by Jack Kinney. Goofy acquires a puppy and has difficulties with the neighbors as well as with his attempts to train the puppy to be a watchdog.

Man's Hunting Instinct (television) Television show; aired on January 2, 1982. Used footage from *The Hunting Instinct*.

Mansson, Gunnar He led Disney merchandising in Scandinavia for 26 years, beginning in 1963, and was presented a European Disney Legends award in 1997.

Many Adventures of Winnie the Pooh, The (film) In the Hundred Acre Wood, Winnie the Pooh, the roly-poly little bear, and his animal friends plus Christopher Robin find themselves in one ticklish situation after another. These adventures included a compilation of *Winnie The Pooh and the Honey Tree*, *Winnie The Pooh and the Blustery Day*, and *Winnie the Pooh and Tigger Too*, with newly animated linking material from the original books by A. A. Milne. Released on March 11, 1977. Directed by Wolfgang Reitherman and John Lounsbery. 74 min. Features the voices of Sebastian Cabot, Sterling Holloway, Junius Matthews, Barbara Luddy, Howard Morris, John Fiedler, Ralph Wright, Hal Smith, Clint Howard, Bruce Reitherman, Jon Walmsley, Timothy Turner, and Paul Winchell. Music and lyrics were provided by Richard M. Sherman and Robert B. Sherman, who wrote ten songs for the entire series of Pooh films: "Winnie The Pooh," "Up, Down, and Touch the Ground," "Rumbly In My Tumbly," "Little Black Rain Cloud," "Mind Over Matter," "A Rather Blustery Day,"

"The Wonderful Thing About Tiggers," "The Rain, Rain, Rain Came Down, Down, Down," "Heffalumps and Woozles," and "Hip Hip Pooh-Ray." Released on video in 1981 and 1996.

Many Adventures of Winnie the Pooh, The Attraction in Magic Kingdom Park at Walt Disney World; opened on June 5, 1999, taking the place of Mr. Toad's Wild Ride. Guests board giant honey pots for their journey through famous spots from the Hundred Acre Wood. They then exit through Pooh's Thotful Shop, featuring Pooh-themed merchandise. An attraction with the same name opened at Disneyland, in the former Country Bear Playhouse, on April 11, 2003. Also at Hong Kong Disneyland; opened September 12, 2005. Its vehicles are beehives, rather than honey pots. (For a similar Tokyo Disneyland attraction, see Pooh's Hunny Hunt.)

MAPO Incorporated in 1965, the manufacturing area of WED Enterprises. Named after MAry POppins, successfully released the year before.

Marahute Majestic eagle in *The Rescuers Down Under*.

Marblehead Pelican character in *Lighthouse Keeping* (1946).

Marceline Missouri town where Walt Disney lived during his early childhood. Fearing that crime was becoming rampant in his area of Chicago, Elias Disney decided to move his family to the country. His brother, Robert, owned a farm in Marceline, a small town northeast of Kansas City, so Elias decided to move there too, and he bought a small farm just north of town. He moved his family there in 1906, and the young Walt thrived. He loved the farmyard animals and the rural atmosphere, both of which would figure prominently in his early cartoons. Walt began school in Marceline, and adoringly tagged around after his big brother, Roy. The two brothers found their workload around the farm increased when older brothers, Herb and Ray, tiring of Elias's domination, ran away from home. Walt, punished for drawing on the side of the farmhouse with tar, was given drawing materials by his aunt Margaret, and he began some of his earliest artwork. He even received a small payment for drawing a horse belonging to a neighbor. Eventually, Elias became ill and had to sell the farm. In 1911, he moved the family to Kansas City to begin a new life. The U.S. issued a 6¢ Walt Disney commemorative postage stamp in Marceline on September 11, 1968.

March Hare The Mad Hatter's friend at the tea party in *Alice in Wonderland*; voiced by Jerry Colonna.

Marie Girl kitten in *The Aristocats*; voiced by Liz English.

Marin, Cheech Actor; provided the voices of Banzai in *The Lion King* and Tito in *Oliver & Company*. He also appeared on the television series *The Golden Palace*.

Marin, Jacques Actor; appeared in *Island at the Top of the World* (Capt. Brieux) and *Herbie Goes to Monte Carlo* (Inspector Bouchet).

Marin, Jason He voiced Flounder in *The Little Mermaid*.

Mark Twain and Me (television) A Disney Channel Premiere Film; first aired on November 22, 1991. An 11-year-old girl happens upon her favorite author, Mark Twain, on board the SS *Minnetonka*, sailing from England to America, and they strike up a friendship that will endure until the last days of Twain's life. Directed by Daniel Petrie. Stars Jason Robards (Mark Twain), Amy Stewart (Dorothy Quick), Talia Shire. The show won two Emmy Awards for Best Children's Program and Best Makeup in 1992.

Mark Twain Riverboat Frontierland attraction at Disneyland; opened on July 17, 1955. The Disneyland Publicity Department originally trumpeted the fact that this was the first paddle wheeler built in the United States in 50 years. Its 105-foot-long hull was built at the Todd Shipyards in San Pedro, California, but the superstructure was constructed in a soundstage at the Disney Studio in Burbank, and then trucked down the Santa Ana Freeway to Disneyland. The *Mark Twain* travels around Tom Sawyer Island, seeing views of a Native American village and assorted wildlife, brought to life by the Disney Imagineers. The riverboat weighs 150 tons and is designed to carry 300 passengers. Also a riverboat in Frontierland at Disneyland Paris, opened April 12, 1992, where it shares the Rivers of the Far West with the *Molly Brown*. Also in Westernland at Tokyo Disneyland, opened on April 15, 1983. The Walt Disney World riverboats were the *Admiral Joe Fowler* (retired in 1980) and the *Richard F. Irvine* (later named the *Liberty Belle*).

Market Clearing Price (film) Educational film; from The People on Market Street series, produced by Terry Kahn, released in September 1977. A butcher shop serves as an example for students to learn economic concepts of inventory and the prevention of shortages and surpluses by pricing.

Market House Store on Main Street at Disneyland; originally sponsored by Swift. Also in Magic Kingdom Park at Walt Disney World; opened on October 1, 1971. It is patterned after an old-fashioned general store.

Market House Bakery On Main Street, U.S.A., at Hong Kong Disneyland, hosted by Maxim's. Opened on September 12, 2005.

Market House Deli Restaurant on Main Street in Disneyland Paris; opened on April 12, 1992.

Markham, Monte Actor; appeared on television in *The Ghosts of Buxley Hall*.

Marks, Franklyn (1911–1976) Composer; joined Disney in 1955 and as a staff composer wrote music for many Disney projects, including *Charlie the Lonesome Cougar*, *Sancho, the Homing Steer*, and *The Legend of the Boy and the Eagle*. He retired in 1976.

Marlin Nemo's father in *Finding Nemo*; voiced by Albert Brooks.

Maroon Cartoon Studio Movie studio in *Who Framed Roger Rabbit*.

Marrakesh See Restaurant el Marrakesh.

Marrying Man, The (film) During his bachelor party, Charley Pearl meets and falls for sultry lounge singer Vicki Anderson, girlfriend of mobster Bugsy Siegel. When the gangster catches the new lovebirds together, he forces them to marry at gunpoint, spoiling Charley's wedding plans with his real fiancée, Adele. His life then becomes a series of ups and downs as he and Vicki separate and remarry several times over the next eight tumultuous years, wondering if they will ever get it right. Released on April 5, 1991. Directed by Jerry Rees. A Hollywood Picture. 116 min. Stars Kim Basinger (Vicki Anderson), Alec Baldwin (Charley Pearl), Robert Loggia (Lew Homer), Elisabeth Shue (Adele Homer), Paul Reiser (Phil), Fisher Stevens (Sammy), Peter Dobson (Tony), Armand Assante (Bugsy Siegel). Released on video in 1991.

Mars and Beyond (television) Television show; aired on December 4, 1957. Directed by Ward Kimball. With the help of technical advisers Dr. Wernher von Braun, Dr. Ernst Stuhlinger, and Dr. E. C. Slipher. Walt presents a humorous look at what man might find on Mars, coupled with predictions for the exploration of the planet with an atomic-powered spaceship. Humankind's place in the universe is explored, from early cavemen's awareness of the stars through 20th-century writers and scientists who see Mars as a new frontier for future plans to solve the overpopulation and depletion of resources of Earth. The film was released theatrically as a 49-minute featurette on December 26, 1957. Portions of the film were re-edited into a short, *Cosmic Capers*, in 1979.

Mars, Kenneth Actor; appeared in *The Apple Dumpling Gang Rides Again* (Marshal Woolly Bill Hitchcock), and provided the voice of Triton in *The Little Mermaid.*

Marsden, Jason Actor; provided the voice of Cavin on *Disney's Adventures of the Gummi Bears*, Shnookums in *The Shnookums and Meat Funny Cartoon Show*, Max in *A Goofy Movie*, and young Shere Khan in *Jungle Cubs*, and appeared as Gregory Morgan in the television series *Almost Home*. He appeared in *White Squall* (Shay Jennings) and as Jimmy on the television series *Blossom*. He voiced Tino in *The Weekenders* and the adult Kovu in *The Lion King II: Simba's Pride*. He returned as Max in *An Extremely Goofy Movie* and *Mickey's Twice Upon a Christmas*, and voiced Haku in *Spirited Away.*

Marsh, Jean Actress; appeared in *Return to Oz* and on television in *The Horsemasters*. Much of her fame has come from her starring in the public television miniseries *Upstairs, Downstairs*. She appeared on Disney Channel in *Bejewelled* (Barbara Donaldson) and *Danny, the Champion of the World* (Miss Hunter).

Marshall, Sean Child actor; starred as Pete in *Pete's Dragon* and voiced the boy in *The Small One.*

Marsupilami (television) Animated television series; aired on CBS beginning September 18, 1993, and ending August 27, 1994. Based on a popular European comic book character from the mid-1960s. Marsupilami, called Marsu, and his ape pal, Maurice, don't go looking for trouble, but it usually finds them. *Marsupilami* segments had debuted earlier on *Raw Toonage*. Voices are Steve Mackall (Marsu), Dan Castellaneta (Stuie), Steve Landesberg (Edúardo), Jim Cummings (Norman, Maurice). In 1999, Disney was successfully sued by the European owners of Marsupilami, claiming that Disney failed to adequately promote and merchandise the character. 13 episodes.

Martha (film) "Song-o-reel" film made by Walt Disney for his Laugh-O-gram Films company in Kansas City in 1923. A filmed rendition of the song "Martha: Just a Plain Old-Fashioned Name" by Joe L. Sanders.

Martin, Bill Designer; joined Disney in 1953 to aid in the design effort for Disneyland. He was associated with such attractions as Snow White's Scary Adventures, Peter Pan's Flight, Nature's Wonderland, the Monorail, the Submarine Voyage, Pirates of the Caribbean, and The Haunted Mansion. He was named vice president of design at WED Enterprises in 1971, and assumed responsibility for the master layout of Magic Kingdom Park at Walt Disney World. He helped design Cinderella Castle, the riverboats, and the utilidors beneath the Magic Kingdom. Bill retired in 1977, but returned to WED (later WDI) as a consultant on Epcot and Tokyo Disneyland. He was named a Disney Legend in 1994.

Martin, Dewey Actor; appeared in *Savage Sam* (Lester White) and on television as Daniel Boone.

Martin, Lucille She began at Disney in the steno pool in 1964, and has the distinction of serving with Disney chief executives over four decades. She became one of Walt Disney's two executive assistants shortly before his death. Later she served as Ron Miller's executive secretary and Michael Eisner's administrative assistant. In 1995, she was named vice president and special assistant to the board of directors. She retired in 2005.

Martin, Pete He ghost-wrote Diane Disney Miller's biography of her father.

Martin, Ross (1920–1981) Actor; appeared on television in *Donovan's Kid*, *Zorro*, and *Texas John Slaughter.*

Martin, Steve Actor; appeared in *Father of the Bride* and *Father of the Bride Part II* (George Banks), *A Simple Twist of Fate* (Michael McCann), *Remember the Titans* (Heckler) and *Bringing Down the House* (Peter Sanderson). In *Father of the Bride*, Martin's character name was coincidentally the same as that of the father in *Mary Poppins*. Martin had as a young man worked in the Magic Shop at Disneyland. Also appeared on television in *The Dream Is Alive* and was one of the hosts of *Fantasia/2000.* He appeared with Donald Duck in a film for the Disneyland: The First 50 Magical Years attraction, and was named a Disney Legend in 2005.

Martin, Strother (1919–1980) Actor; appeared in *The Shaggy Dog* (Thurm), and on television in *The Boy and the Bronc Buster.*

Martins and the Coys, The (film) Segment of *Make Mine Music* about two feuding families. Sung by the King's Men. Re-released as a short on June 18, 1954.

Marx, Louis, and Co. Licensee manufacturing Disney toys from 1936 to 1961, and then again beginning in 1968. Some of the more valuable Marx items are the windup or mechanical tin toys, usually sold under the LineMar trademark. The Disneykins, a series of over 100 tiny Disney character figures, were manufactured by Marx, they have become popular with collectors.

Mary Poppins (film) A magical English nanny, Mary Poppins, arrives at the home of Mr. and Mrs. George Banks, facing the park at No. 17, Cherry Tree Lane in London, to the delight of their young children, Jane and Michael. The proper English father is too preoccupied with his responsibility at the bank; the mother, an ardent suffragette, is not really aware that their two children, left in the care of one nanny after another, are unhappy and unable to communicate with the parents they truly love. Mary Poppins has come to change all this. She settles into the house, and soon has everyone wrapped around her little finger. Mary, along with her friend Bert and a host of chimney sweeps, teaches the children how to have fun, and in so doing makes the Banks household a happier place. By the time she opens her umbrella and flies off on a beautiful spring evening, the family is united together in the park, flying a kite. General release on August 29, 1964. Directed by Robert Stevenson. 139 min. This famed Disney masterwork is indeed "practically perfect" in every way from its cast—Julie Andrews (Mary Poppins), Dick Van Dyke (Bert), David Tomlinson (George Banks), Glynis Johns (Mrs.

Banks), Ed Wynn (Uncle Albert), Hermione Baddeley (Ellen), Karen Dotrice (Jane), Matthew Garber (Michael), Elsa Lanchester (Katie Nanna), Arthur Treacher (Constable Jones), Reginald Owen (Admiral Boom), Reta Shaw (Mrs. Brill), Jane Darwell (bird woman)—to its lavish musical score and delightful songs provided by Richard M. Sherman and Robert B. Sherman, which includes such favorites as "Spoonful of Sugar," "Feed the Birds," "Jolly Holiday," "Sister Suffraggette," "The Life I Lead," "Step in Time," "Supercalifragilisticexpialidocious," and "Let's Go Fly a Kite." The Academy of Motion Picture Arts and Sciences agreed too, giving it 13 nominations from which it won five Oscars for Best Actress (Julie Andrews), Best Song ("Chim Chim Cher-ee"), Best Music Score (the Sherman brothers), Best Film Editing (Cotton Warburton), and Best Special Visual Effects (Peter Ellenshaw, Eustace Lycett, and Hamilton Luske). There was also a special Scientific award to Petro Vlahos, Wadsworth E. Pohl, and Ub Iwerks for the creation and application to use of Color Traveling Matte Composite Cinematography, which helped make possible the combination of live action with animated actors in the film. The special-effects work on *Mary Poppins* was the most challenging the studio had ever known. Everything from the two-strip sodium process and piano wire to bungee cords were used to create the magical sequences. The work of the special-effects crew, as well as all the production staff, was the culmination of years of Disney innovation. In fact, only Marc Breaux and Dee Dee Wood, the choreographers, and Irwin Kostal, musical arranger, had to be brought in from the out-

side; Disney staff members could be called upon for all of the other tasks. The entire film was shot on soundstages at the Disney Studio in Burbank. A lavish premiere at Grauman's Chinese Theater on August 27, 1964, began its fabulous box office run that made it Disney's most successful feature until then. P. L. Travers, author of the popular books on which the film is based, continued writing new adventures for Mary Poppins long after the film, and in the late 1980s worked with a Disney screenwriter on a film sequel that never materialized. Reissued theatrically in 1973 and 1980; released on video in 1980 and kept available continuously. In 2004 a stage adaptation of *Mary Poppins* opened in England.

Mary Poppins Stage musical produced by Disney and Cameron Macintosh, opened for previews in England at the Bristol Hippodrome on September 15, 2004, with regular performances beginning September 28. After the Bristol run ended on November 6, the show moved to London for an opening at the Prince Edward Theatre on December 15. Laura Michelle Kelly stars as Mary Poppins with Gavin Lee as Bert. George Stiles and Anthony Drewe wrote six new songs to be included with the original songs by Richard M. Sherman and Robert B. Sherman. The book was by Julian Fellowes, with direction by Richard Eyre and Matthew Bourne. Plans are to open the show at the New Amsterdam Theater on Broadway on November 16, 2006, after previews beginning in mid-October.

Mason, James (1909–1984) Actor; appeared in *20,000 Leagues Under the Sea* (Captain Nemo).

Mason, Marsha Actress; appeared in *Stella* (Janice Morrison) and *I Love Trouble* (Senator Gayle Robbins).

Mastrantonio, Mary Elizabeth Actress; appeared in *The Color of Money* (Carmen) and *Consenting Adults* (Priscilla Parker).

Masur, Richard Actor; appeared in *My Science Project* (Detective Isadore Nulty), *Shoot to Kill* (Norman), *Encino Man* (Mr. Morgan), and *Play It* *to the Bone* (Artie), and on television in *Mr. Boogedy* and *Bride of Boogedy*.

Match Point (television) Serial on the *Mickey Mouse Club* on The Disney Channel; aired from May 22 to June 23, 1989. Archrivals Bart and Jason tangle at the Match Point tennis camp. Stars Brian Krause (Bart), Renee O'Connor (Robin), Anthony Palermo (Jason), Zero Hubbard (Joel), Evan Richards (Runkle), Crystal Justine (Francie).

Matchmaker, The (television) Television show; episode 3 of *Willie and the Yank*.

Matheison, Bob Beginning at Disneyland as a sound coordinator in 1960, he was later selected by Walt Disney to manage Disney's four shows at the New York World's Fair. Involved in the early planning of Walt Disney World, he moved to Florida in 1970 as director of Operations. He became vice president of Operations in 1972, vice president of Magic Kingdom/Epcot in 1984, and executive vice president of Walt Disney World in 1987. He retired in 1994, and was named a Disney Legend in 1996.

Matheson, Tim Actor; appeared in *The Apple Dumpling Gang Rides Again* (Private Jeff Reid). He also appears in Body Wars in Wonders of Life at Epcot. He provided uncredited narration (replacing Deems Taylor) for the 1982 reissue of *Fantasia*.

Matshullat, Robert W. Member of the Disney board of directors beginning December 3, 2002.

Matterhorn Bobsleds Fantasyland attraction with dual bobsled runs at Disneyland; opened on June 14, 1959. The first thrill attraction to be added to Disneyland, based on the Disney film Third Man on the Mountain. The Matterhorn at Disneyland is 147 feet high, about one-hundreth the size of its Swiss counterpart, but to make it look larger, forced perspective was used. The mountain was built of wood and steel, with a plaster coating over a layer of metal mesh. Trees growing on the side of the mountain get progressively smaller as they get higher. The ride was

innovative at the time it opened because it for the first time utilized cylindrical rails and urethane wheels, which have since become standard for roller coasters. An ice cavern, glowing ice crystals, and the Abominable Snowman were added

in 1978, along with a new ride, which featured tandem bobsleds, greatly increasing capacity. Until it was removed in 1994, the Skyway's cable passed directly through the mountain, providing more leisurely views of the Abominable Snowman.

Matthews, Junius C. He voiced Archimedes in *The Sword in the Stone* and Rabbit in *Winnie the Pooh*.

Mattraw, Scotty (1880–1946) He voiced Bashful in *Snow White and the Seven Dwarfs*.

Maude-Roxby, Roddy He voiced Edgar in *The Aristocats*.

Maurice Belle's befuddled father in *Beauty and the Beast*; voiced by Rex Everhart. Tom Bosley originated the role on Broadway.

Max Prince Eric's big shaggy dog in *The Little Mermaid*.

Max Hare Cocky star of *The Tortoise and the Hare* (1935) and its sequel *Toby Tortoise Returns* (1936); he was said to have been the inspiration for Bugs Bunny.

Max Keeble's Big Move (film) After a depressing first day at school, much-bullied seventh grader Max Keeble finds out he's moving to a new city in a week. Rather than put up with the normal routine of school, he starts getting revenge on all the people who have picked on him. After creating all kinds of mayhem, Max finds out he's not moving after all, and he must face up to the consequences of his actions. Directed by Tim Hill. Released on October 5, 2001. Stars Alex D. Linz (Max Keeble), Larry Miller (Jindraike), Jamie Kennedy (Evil Ice Cream Man), Zena Grey (Megan), Josh Peck (Robe), Nora Dunn (Lily), Robert Carradine (Don), Justin Berfield (Caption Writer). 86 min. Released on video in 2002.

Max Q: Emergency Landing (television) Two-hour movie from Jerry Bruckheimer Films, Inc., in association with Touchstone Television; aired on ABC on November 19, 1998. A routine space shuttle mission is struck by a disastrous explosion forcing NASA into fast crisis management to rescue the disabled crew floating perilously in space. ("Max Q" refers to the period of maximum aerodynamic stress during launch.) Directed by Michael Shapiro. Stars Bill Campbell (Clay Jarvis), Paget Brewster (Rena Wynter), Ned Vaughn (Scott Hines), Geoffrey Blake (Jonah Randall), Tasha Smith (Karen Daniels).

Maxwell House Coffee House Restaurant on Town Square at Disneyland; from December 1, 1955 to October 8, 1957. It later became Hills Brothers Coffee House.

Maya Grill Restaurant orginally serving Yucatan specialties and later steaks and fish with a Latin American flair in the Coronado Springs Resort at Walt Disney World, opened on August 1, 1997.

Maybe It's Me (television) Half-hour series on the WB Network; premiered on October 5, 2001, and ended on July 19, 2002. Fifteen-year-old Molly Stage, like most girls her age, feels that she is surrounded by a family of freaks. From Warner Bros. Television and Touchstone Television. Stars Reagan Dale Neis (Molly Stage), Julia Sweeney (Mary Stage), Fred Willard (Jerry Stage), Patrick Levis (Grant Stage), Andrew Walker (Rick Stage), Daniella & Deanna Canterman (Mindy & Cindy

Stage), Vicki Davis (Mia), Ellen Albertini Dow (Grandma), Dabbs Greer (Grandpa), Shaun Sipos (Nick).

Maybe This Time (television) Television series; premiered on ABC on September 16, 1995, after a preview on September 15, and ended February 17, 1996. Comedy about three generations of women working together in their family-owned coffee shop. Stars Marie Osmond (Julia), Betty White (Shirley), Ashley Johnson (Gracie), Craig Ferguson (Logan), Amy Hill (Kay). 18 episodes.

Mazurki, Mike (1907–1990) Actor; appeared in *Davy Crockett* (Bigfoot Mason), *The Adventures of Bullwhip Griffin* (Mountain Ox), and *Dick Tracy* (old man at hotel).

MDs (television) Two San Francisco superdoctors pay little heed to the rules while saving lives and having fun. Hour-long drama series premiered on ABC on September 25, 2002, and ended on December 11, 2002. Stars William Fichtner (Dr. Bruce Kellerman), John Hannah (Dr. Robert Dalgety), Leslie Stefanson (Shelly Pangborn), Aunjanue Ellis (Dr. Quinn Joyner), Jane Lynch (Nurse "Doctor" Poole), Robert Joy (Frank Coones), Michaela Conlin (Dr. Maggie Yang).

Meador, Josh (1911–1965) Longtime Disney special-effects animator and painter, loaned out to create the animation effects for *Forbidden Planet* (1956). He worked at Disney from 1936 until his death in 1965.

Measuring Up (film) Educational film in the Fitness for Living series; released in September 1982. The film explains the reasons behind fitness measurements.

Mechanical Cow, The (film) Oswald the Lucky Rabbit cartoon; released on October 3, 1927.

Meck, Ed (1898–1973) Veteran entertainment publicist who became the head of publicity for Disneyland in 1955, and helped make the world aware of the new park. He retired in 1972, after helping with the opening of Walt Disney World, and passed away a year later. He was named a Disney Legend posthumously in 1995.

Medicine Man (film) In the Amazon rain forest a brilliant but eccentric research scientist, Dr. Robert Campbell, is on the verge of a medical breakthrough, a cure for cancer, but he has lost the formula and must now rediscover the elusive serum. The pharmaceutical corporation sponsoring the research has sent another biochemist, Dr. Rae Crane, to investigate the reclusive genius. A hardheaded female scientist is the last thing Campbell wants around his camp, but Crane refuses to leave and is soon caught up in the quest to find the rare antidote. In a race against time and the coming physical destruction of the jungle, the pair climbs to the tops of the tallest trees in what becomes the most exciting adventure of their lives. Released on February 7, 1992. Directed by John McTiernan. A Hollywood Picture, the first film produced by Cinergi Productions. Filmed in CinemaScope. 104 min. Stars Sean Connery (Dr. Robert Campbell), Lorrraine Bracco (Dr. Rae Crane), and 57 Indian natives from nine Brazilian tribes. The jungle scenes were shot in Catemaco, Mexico. Released on video in 1992.

Mediterranean Cruise (television) Television show; aired on January 19, 1964. Directed by Hamilton S. Luske. Ludwig Von Drake looks at countries around the Mediterranean Sea. In Portugal, we see the Corrida festival. Village singers are featured in Italy, then we go to Africa to learn about the tribes of nomads. Finally, Von Drake leads viewers to Sardinia and a fishing fleet, and to Sicily, where he witnesses a festive parade and dance.

Meeko's Fast-food facility in Fantasyland at Disneyland, formerly called Yumz, opened on June 23, 1995, and closed on September 5, 1997.

Meet Me at Disneyland (television) A summer series of television shows on Los Angeles independent station KTTV; aired live from Disneyland weekly from June 9 to September 8, 1962. The Osmond Brothers made one of their early television appearances on the show.

Meet the Deedles (film) Two surfer dude brothers from Hawaii, Phil and Stew Deedle, have to prove to their millionaire father that they have matured, or risk being disinherited. The guys wind up training as rookie rangers in Yellowstone National Park and soon find themselves in hot water when they uncover a plot by a deranged ranger who plans to steal Old Faithful geyser. Released on March 27, 1998. Directed by Steve Boyum. Stars Dennis Hopper (Frank Slater), Paul Walker IV (Phil), Steve Van Wormer (Stew), John Ashton (Captain Pine), A.J. Langer (Lt. Jesse Ryan). 94 min. Filmed on location in the Wasatch National Forest near Park City, Utah, since the filmmakers could not utilize Yellowstone National Park itself in the heart of the tourist season. A replica of Old Faithful geyser was created utilizing a jet engine on loan from Utah State University to spew water to the requisite height. Released on video in 1998.

Meet the Munceys (television) Television show; aired on May 22, 1988. Directed by Noel Black. A lower-class family moves into a mansion when a maid is left in charge of an elderly woman's fortune. Naturally, the woman's relatives are not at all pleased, and they plot to get rid of the Munceys. It was a pilot for a series. Stars Nana Visitor, Peggy Pope, Carmine Caridi, Dan Gauthier, Mark Neely, Lee Weaver. Vanna White makes a cameo appearance.

Meet the Robinsons (film) A 3-D computer-animated feature; with a planned release in 2006. A boy-genius creates a machine with the fantastic purpose of recovering the lost memory of the past. What he unlocks is time itself, and a visit with a family and a future whose survival all depends upon him. Directed by Steve Anderson. Based on the book by William Joyce.

Meet the World Audio-Animatronics attraction about Japanese history in Tomorrowland at Tokyo Disneyland; opened on April 15, 1983, and closed on June 30, 2002.

Mello Men Singing group that provided vocals in many Disney films and theme park attractions. Consisted of Bill Lee, Max Smith, Bob Stevens,

and Thurl Ravenscroft. They are shown recording the voices of the dogs in the dog pound for
Lady and the Tramp in the television show *Cavalcade of Songs*. Sometimes spelled The Mellomen
or MelloMen.

Megara Character in
Hercules; voiced by
Susan Egan.

Melody See *Adven-
tures in Music: Melody*.

Melody Time (film) An animation/live-action
feature consisting of seven sequences: (1) *Once
Upon a Wintertime*, sung by Frances Langford,
tells of a winter romance by both human and
bunny couples sleighing and skating in the 1800s;
(2) *Bumble Boogie*, played by Freddy Martin and
his orchestra, is a fantasy of a bee's nightmare;
(3) *Johnny Appleseed* in which Dennis Day portrays the characters of the old settler, Johnny
Appleseed, and Johnny's angel, telling the story
of the pioneer who heads out west planting apple
trees as he goes; (4) *Little Toot*, sung by the
Andrews Sisters, tells of a little tugboat who
wants to be like his father, but keeps getting
into trouble; (5) *Trees*, with Fred Waring and his
Pennsylvanians interpreting Joyce Kilmer's poem;
(6) *Blame It on the Samba*, sung by the Dinning
Sisters, in which Donald is taught to samba by
José Carioca, and interacts with Ethel Smith at
the organ; and (7) *Pecos Bill*, told and sung by
Roy Rogers and the Sons of the Pioneers to Luana
Patten and Bobby Driscoll; after singing "Blue
Shadows on the Trail," Roy recounts how the leg-
endary Pecos Bill was born, raised, and fell in
love with Slue Foot Sue. Released on May 27,
1948. Directed by Clyde Geronimi, Hamilton
Luske, Jack Kinney, Wilfred Jackson. 75 min.
Songs include "Melody Time," "The Apple Song,"
"Little Toot," and "Pecos Bill." Many of the seg-
ments were later released separately as shorts.
Released on video in 1998.

Men Against the Arctic (film) People and
Places featurette; released on December 21, 1955.

Directed by Winston Hibler. Academy Award
winner. 30 min. The film shows how icebreakers,
specially constructed ships built by the U.S.
Coast Guard, to make their way through heavy
Arctic icepacks. They maneuver with the aid of
helicopters in their effort to reach the weather
station at Alert, only 400 miles from the Arctic
Circle, in Operation Alert, an annual task.

Menace on the Mountain (television) Two-
part television show; aired on March 1 and 8,
1970. Directed by Vincent McEveety. A boy
struggles to take care of his family during the
Civil War, after his father joins the Confederate
Army. To help pay the taxes, he captures a mountain lion for the bounty, angering another man
who also wanted the money. When the war ends,
outlaws take over the family's ranch and the army
has to come to save the day. Stars Mitch Vogel,
Charles Aidman, Patricia Crowley, Albert Salmi,
Richard Anderson, Dub Taylor, Eric Shea, Jodie
Foster.

Menjou, Adolphe (1890–1963) Actor; appeared
in *Pollyanna* (Mr. Pendergast).

Menken, Alan Composer; joined Disney in
1987 to work on *The Little Mermaid*. Since then,
he has composed the music for Disney classics
such as *Beauty and the Beast* and *Aladdin*, writing
the music for such memorable songs as "Under
the Sea," "Beauty and the Beast," and "A Whole
New World," all of which won him Academy
Awards. Partnered first with Howard Ashman
and later with Tim Rice, he helped engineer the
rebirth of popularity of Disney animation in
the 1980s. He also wrote the music for the songs
in *Newsies* and *Polly*. In 1995, he joined with lyricist Stephen Schwartz to write the songs for *Pocahontas*, winning the Academy Award for the score
and "Colors of the Wind." The following year, he
partnered with Schwartz again for *The Hunchback of Notre Dame* and in 1997 with David Zippel for *Hercules*. He wrote the score and songs
for *Home on the Range*. With eight Oscars for his
Disney work, Alan is second only to Walt Disney.
He was named a Disney Legend in 2001.

Merbabies (film) Silly Symphony cartoon; released on December 9, 1938. Actually produced for Disney by Harman-Ising Studios, directed by Rudolf Ising and supervised for the Walt Disney Studio by Ben Sharpsteen, Dave Hand, Otto Englander, and Walt Disney. The workload at the Disney Studio was getting out of hand, so Walt decided to help his former colleagues (from Laugh-O-grams) by passing some work their way. A sequel to *Water Babies*, in which ocean waves change to form merbabies who are summoned to a playground on the floor of the ocean for an underwater circus. When a whale blows them all to the surface, they disappear into the waves from which they came.

Merchandise Shoppers are so accustomed to seeing the wide variety of Disney merchandise on store shelves today that it is hard to imagine a time before you could buy a Mickey Mouse doll, book, toothbrush, or pair of bedroom slippers. Actually, it all started by chance back in 1929. Walt Disney was walking through a hotel lobby in New York, and a man came up to him asking if he could put Mickey Mouse on a children's pencil tablet he was manufacturing. He offered $300, and as Walt needed the money, he agreed. That tablet began Disney licensing. Within a year, the first Mickey Mouse book and comic strip had been licensed, and other items soon followed.

In 1932, a major change in Disney licensing occurred with the appearance of Kay Kamen. Kamen, a born entrepreneur, convinced Walt that licensing could open up whole new vistas for the company. For the next 17 years, until he died in a plane crash, Kamen handled the licensing of Disney merchandise. Insisting on quality control, Kamen set the standard for character licensing that would later be copied by many others.

Shortly after the opening of Walt Disney World in 1971, Disney founded the Walt Disney Distributing Company, to actually produce merchandise, for sale primarily in the parks. Up until then, Disney had simply licensed the Disney characters to other manufacturers. The WDDC experiment was not successful, but a decade later, the Disney company would try again. This time, the manufacturing was being done for The Disney Store, a chain of outlets for Disney merchandise opening up in malls throughout the country. The Disney Store concept was tremendously successful, and other areas of the company, such as Walt Disney Attractions, the Walt Disney Classics Collection, and Disney Art Editions, were soon following suit and getting into the manufacturing business. While the company is ever wary of oversaturation of the market, that point has evidently not been reached and the various divisions of Disney Consumer Products continue to grow each year. Over six decades after that first pencil tablet, Disney merchandising is still going strong.

Merciful Law of the King (television) Television show; episode 2 of *The Prince and the Pauper.*

Meredith, Burgess (1908–1997) Actor; appeared on television in *The Strange Monster of Strawberry Cove.*

Merkel, Una (1903–1986) Actress; appeared in *The Parent Trap* (Verbena), *Summer Magic* (Maria Popham), and *A Tiger Walks* (Mrs. Watkins).

Merlin Wart's magical mentor in *The Sword in the Stone*; voiced by Karl Swenson.

Merlin's Magic Shop Fantasyland shop at Disneyland; from July 17, 1955 to January 16,

1983. Succeeded by Mickey's Christmas Chalet. Also a Fantasyland shop in Magic Kingdom Park at Walt Disney World, from March 1972 until May 1986. See also Main Street Magic Shop.

Merlin's Treasures Shop in Fantasyland at Hong Kong Disneyland; opened on September 12, 2005.

Merlock Villainous sorcerer in *Ducktales: the Movie*; voiced by Christopher Lloyd.

Mermaid Lagoon Theater Attraction at Tokyo DisneySea; opened on September 4, 2001. Guests enter through the wooden hull of a sunken ship to experience "Under the Sea," featuring puppetry, colorful costumes, amazing special effects, and suspended actors who "swim" above the audience.

Merriman, Ryan Actor; appeared on television in *Smart House* (Ben Cooper), *The Luck of the Irish* (Kyle Johnson), *A Ring of Endless Light* (Adam Eddington), and the series *Veritas* (Nikko).

Merry Dwarfs, The (film) Silly Symphony cartoon; released on December 16, 1929. Directed by Walt Disney. Small bearded dwarfs perform musical numbers in their woodland village.

Merry Mickey Celebration, A (television) Hour-long television special; aired on ABC on December 20, 2003. Celebrities salute Mickey Mouse on the occasion of his 75th anniversary through music and song, and *Mickey's Christmas Carol* is shown.

Merryweather Short, chubby good fairy in *Sleeping Beauty* who wore blue; voiced by Barbara Luddy.

Mestres, Ricardo Joined Disney in 1984, first as vice president of production and then moving to Hollywood Pictures, when it was formed in 1988, where he was made president. He resigned in 1994.

Metro (film) Scott Roper is a fast-talking, wise-cracking hostage negotiator whose unorthodox but winning ways make him the San Francisco Police Department's top arbitrator. But even his silver tongue cannot change his fortune when he and rookie SWAT team sharpshooter Kevin McCall come face-to-face with a psychotic killer in a lethal game of cat and mouse. A Touchstone Picture, in association with Caravan Pictures. Directed by Thomas Carter. Released on January 17, 1997. Stars Eddie Murphy (Scott Roper), Michael Rapaport (Kevin McCall), Michael Wincott (Korda), Carmen Ejogo (Ronnie Tate), Denis Arndt (Capt. Frank Solis), Art Evans (Lt. Sam Baffert), Donal Logue (Earl). Filmed in CinemaScope. 117 min. This is the American film debut for British actress Ejogo. Filming took place over 15 weeks in and around San Francisco, including Chinatown, the Tenderloin, the financial district, Treasure Island, Pier 50, Half Moon Bay, and the former Naval Shipyards at Mare Island, Vallejo, where the film's action-packed finale utilized several of the cavernous dry docks. Released on video in 1997.

Metzler, Jim Actor; appeared in *Tex* (Mason McCormick), and on television in *The Christmas Star.*

Mexico Pavilion in World Showcase at Epcot; opened on October 1, 1982. Inspired by an Aztec pyramid, the central part of the pavilion beckons guests inside to see a display on Mexican history and culture. Farther on is the Plaza de los Amigos, where colorful stalls are situated under a simulated nighttime sky, flanked by other shops. The San Angel Inn, also there, offers guests tempting and authentic Mexican fare. To one side, guests can board a boat for El Río del Tiempo, a tuneful journey celebrating Mexican life. Outside, beside the lagoon, guests can partake of counter-service fare in the Cantina de San Angel.

Miami Rhapsody (film) A young woman is forced to confront the true essence of marriage when her boyfriend finally pops the question. To determine if marriage is worth the impact it will have on her carefree life, she tries to discover what relationships and marriage are all about. Along the way, she discovers that the marriages of her brother, sister, and parents are not as happy as she thought, as each one of them is engaging in an extramarital affair. Limited release in Los Angeles and New York on January 27, 1995; general release on February 3, 1995. Directed by David Frankel. A Hollywood Pictures film. 95 min. Stars Sarah Jessica Parker (Gwyn), Antonio Banderas (Antonio), Gil Bellows (Matt), Mia Farrow (Nina), Carla Gugino (Leslie), Paul Mazursky (Vic), Kevin Pollak (Jordan). Released on video in 1995.

Michael Wendy's younger brother in *Peter Pan*, who clutches his teddy bear; voiced by Tommy Luske.

Michael and Mickey (film) Michael Eisner and Mickey Mouse in a film introducing a changing array of coming-attraction trailers shown at the end of the Backstage Tour, Disney-MGM Studios; opened on May 1, 1989, and ended in 1992. 2 min.

Michael O'Hara the Fourth (television) Two-part television show; aired on March 26 and April 2, 1972. Directed by Robert Totten. Episode titles are *To Trap a Thief* and *The Deceptive Detective*. A police captain's daughter yearns to be a detective and tries to solve some cases regarding counterfeiters and murderers. Her successes impress her father, who had been longing for a son to carry on the family name. Stars Jo Ann Harris, Dan Dailey, Michael McGreevey, Nehemiah Persoff, William Bramley, James Almanzar.

Michelle Kwan: Princess on Ice (television) One-hour television special; aired on ABC on January 20, 2001. Features ice skating to the sounds of hot singing groups, along with songs that feature classic Disney princesses. Stars Michelle Kwan, Dorothy Hamill, Katarina Witt, SHeDAISY, and O-Town.

Michelle Kwan Skates to Disney's Greatest Hits (television) One-hour television special; aired on ABC on March 5, 1999. Stars Olympic medalist Michelle Kwan, along with Oksana Baiul, Ilia Kulik, and Elvis Stojko. Featured is a countdown of the Top Ten Disney songs as voted upon by Internet users on Disney.com.

Mickey and Donald Kidding Around (television) Television show; aired on May 3, 1983. It is an edited version of *Kids Is Kids*.

Mickey and Donald Present Sport Goofy See *Sport Goofy*.

Mickey and Nora (television) An ex-CIA agent can't convince anyone—including his new bride—that he is no longer a spy; pilot for a television series. Aired on CBS on June 26, 1987. Directed by Paul Bogart. Stars Ted Wass, Barbara Treutelaar, George Furth, Nancy Lenehan. 30 min.

Mickey and the Beanstalk (film) Segment of *Fun and Fancy Free*, with Edgar Bergen telling the story. Released on video in 1988.

Mickey and the Seal (film) Mickey Mouse cartoon; released on December 3, 1948. Directed by Charles Nichols. Pluto finds a baby seal in Mickey's basket when he returns from a visit to the zoo, but does not get a chance to tell him until the seal is in the bathtub with Mickey. They return it to the zoo, only to return home and find the bathroom full of seals. Nominated for an Academy Award.

Mickey Cuts Up (film) Mickey Mouse cartoon; released on November 30, 1931. Directed by Burt Gillett. Mickey is mowing Minnie's lawn with Pluto helping to pull the mower. Playing a trick on Minnie, Mickey crawls into her birdhouse, pretending to be a bird, but a cat pounces on him. Pluto causes widespread destruction with the mower attached to him when he chases the cat.

Mickey, Donald and Sport Goofy Show (television) Limited series of three syndicated half-hour television shows featuring cartoons; aired first on September 7, November 17, and December 1, 1984.

Mickey Down Under (film) Mickey Mouse cartoon; released on March 19, 1948. Directed by Charles Nichols. Mickey, in the Australian bush, throws a boomerang that gets caught in Pluto's mouth. Mickey then discovers an egg of an emu. Unfortunately, the parent chases him, but Pluto and the boomerang zoom into his path, leaving the emu all tangled.

Mickey in Arabia Mickey Mouse cartoon; released on July 18, 1932. Directed by Wilfred Jackson. Mickey and Minnie are tourists when an evil sheik, Pete, kidnaps Minnie. Mickey's attempted rescue of Minnie is complicated by a drunken camel. After a furious battle with Pete and his soldiers, a rooftop chase ensues. Mickey and Minnie fall into an awning, but Pete tumbles onto the sand, running off into the desert, after being speared by his own soldiers.

Mickey Mouse Walt Disney's primary cartoon character, who made his debut in *Steamboat Willie* on November 18, 1928, at the Colony Theater in New York. Mickey's heyday was the 1930s; in the 1940s his popularity on the screen was overtaken by Donald Duck and Goofy. In all, there were 120 Mickey Mouse cartoons, with a 30-year gap between *The Simple Things* (1953) and *Mickey's Christmas Carol* (1983). He starred in the *Mickey Mouse Club* television show in the 1950s, appeared on thousands of merchandise items, and acted as chief greeter at the Disney theme parks. Walt Disney provided Mickey Mouse's voice up to 1946, when Jim Macdonald took over until his retirement three decades later. The current voice is Wayne Allwine.

© WALT DISNEY PRODUCTIONS

Mickey Mouse was originally drawn using circles—for head, body, and ears. *The Pointer*, in 1939, was the first cartoon that featured a drastically new design for Mickey. His body became more pear-shaped than round, and pupils were added to his eyes, making them more expressive. In the early 1940s, animators gave him perspective ears—shadowing them to give a three-dimensional effect—but this change was short-lived. Later changes consisted mainly of costume changes, taking him out of his red shorts, for instance, and putting him in more contemporary clothes.

Following is a list of the 120 Mickey Mouse cartoons:

1.	*Steamboat Willie*	1928
2.	*The Gallopin' Gaucho*	1928
3.	*Plane Crazy*	1928
4.	*The Barn Dance*	1928
5.	*The Opry House*	1929
6.	*When the Cat's Away*	1929
7.	*The Barnyard Battle*	1929
8.	*The Plow Boy*	1929
9.	*The Karnival Kid*	1929
10.	*Mickey's Follies*	1929
11.	*Mickey's Choo-Choo*	1929
12.	*The Jazz Fool*	1929
13.	*Jungle Rhythm*	1929
14.	*The Haunted House*	1929
15.	*Wild Waves*	1929
16.	*Just Mickey*	1930
17.	*The Barnyard Concert*	1930
18.	*The Cactus Kid*	1930
19.	*The Fire Fighters*	1930
20.	*The Shindig*	1930
21.	*The Chain Gang*	1930
22.	*The Gorilla Mystery*	1930
23.	*The Picnic*	1930
24.	*Pioneer Days*	1930
25.	*The Birthday Party*	1931
26.	*Traffic Troubles*	1931
27.	*The Castaway*	1931
28.	*The Moose Hunt*	1931
29.	*The Delivery Boy*	1931
30.	*Mickey Steps Out*	1931
31.	*Blue Rhythm*	1931
32.	*Fishin' Around*	1931
33.	*The Barnyard Broadcast*	1931
34.	*The Beach Party*	1931
35.	*Mickey Cuts Up*	1931
36.	*Mickey's Orphans*	1931
37.	*The Duck Hunt*	1932
38.	*The Grocery Boy*	1932
39.	*The Mad Dog*	1932
40.	*Barnyard Olympics*	1932
41.	*Mickey's Revue*	1932
42.	*Musical Farmer*	1932
43.	*Mickey in Arabia*	1932
44.	*Mickey's Nightmare*	1932
45.	*Trader Mickey*	1932
46.	*The Whoopee Party*	1932
47.	*Touchdown Mickey*	1932
48.	*The Wayward Canary*	1932
49.	*The Klondike Kid*	1932
50.	*Mickey's Good Deed*	1932
51.	*Building a Building*	1933
52.	*The Mad Doctor*	1933
53.	*Mickey's Pal Pluto*	1933
54.	*Mickey's Mellerdrammer*	1933
55.	*Ye Olden Days*	1933
56.	*The Mail Pilot*	1933
57.	*Mickey's Mechanical Man*	1933
58.	*Mickey's Gala Premiere*	1933
59.	*Puppy Love*	1933
60.	*The Steeple Chase*	1933
61.	*The Pet Store*	1933
62.	*Giantland*	1933
63.	*Shanghaied*	1934
64.	*Camping Out*	1934
65.	*Playful Pluto*	1934
66.	*Gulliver Mickey*	1934
67.	*Mickey's Steam Roller*	1934
68.	*Orphan's Benefit*	1934
69.	*Mickey Plays Papa*	1934
70.	*The Dognapper*	1934
71.	*Two-Gun Mickey*	1934
72.	*Mickey's Man Friday*	1935
73.	*The Band Concert*	1935—1st color
74.	*Mickey's Service Station*	1935—B & W
75.	*Mickey's Kangaroo*	1935—B & W
76.	*Mickey's Garden*	1935
77.	*Mickey's Fire Brigade*	1935
78.	*Pluto's Judgement Day*	1935
79.	*On Ice*	1935
80.	*Mickey's Polo Team*	1936
81.	*Orphans' Picnic*	1936
82.	*Mickey's Grand Opera*	1936
83.	*Thru the Mirror*	1936
84.	*Mickey's Rival*	1936

85. *Moving Day*	1936
86. *Alpine Climbers*	1936
87. *Mickey's Circus*	1936
88. *Mickey's Elephant*	1936
89. *The Worm Turns*	1937
90. *Magician Mickey*	1937
91. *Moose Hunters*	1937
92. *Mickey's Amateurs*	1937
93. *Hawaiian Holiday*	1937
94. *Clock Cleaners*	1937
95. *Lonesome Ghosts*	1937
96. *Boat Builders*	1938
97. *Mickey's Trailer*	1938
98. *The Whalers*	1938
99. *Mickey's Parrot*	1938
100. *Brave Little Tailor*	1938
101. *Society Dog Show*	1939
102. *The Pointer*	1939
103. *Tugboat Mickey*	1940
104. *Pluto's Dream House*	1940
105. *Mr. Mouse Takes a Trip*	1940
106. *The Little Whirlwind*	1941
107. *The Nifty Nineties*	1941
108. *Orphans' Benefit* (remake)	1941
109. *Mickey's Birthday Party*	1942
110. *Symphony Hour*	1942
111. *Mickey's Delayed Date*	1947
112. *Mickey Down Under*	1948
113. *Mickey and the Seal*	1948
114. *Plutopia*	1951
115. *R'coon Dawg*	1951
116. *Pluto's Party*	1952
117. *Pluto's Christmas Tree*	1952
118. *The Simple Things*	1953
119. *Mickey's Christmas Carol*	1983
120. *Runaway Brain*	1995

Mickey Mouse Anniversary Show, The (television) Television show; aired on December 22, 1968. Directed by Robert Stevenson. Dean Jones hosts a look at Mickey Mouse's 40 years, through film clips, and the return of a group of Mouseketeers.

Mickey Mouse Book The first Disney book; published by Bibo-Lang in 1930.

Mickey Mouse Club In 1929, the Fox Dome Theater in Ocean Park, California, began a Mickey Mouse Club. Soon there were hundreds of other Mickey Mouse Clubs associated with theaters all over the country. These were real clubs, which kids joined. The children attended Saturday meetings where Mickey Mouse cartoons were shown, a Chief Mickey Mouse and a Chief Minnie Mouse were elected, Mickey Mouse credos were recited, and Mickey Mouse Club bands entertained. At the height of their popularity in 1932, these clubs had more than a million members. The television version of the Mickey Mouse Club would not come along until 23 years later.

Mickey Mouse Club (television) One of the most popular children's television series of all time; aired on ABC from October 3, 1955 to September 25, 1959. The show began as an hour-long show Monday through Friday and introduced 24 talented kids, known as Mouseketeers, who performed skits, musical numbers, and introduced special guest stars, serials, and Disney cartoons. Adult leaders were Jimmie Dodd and Roy Williams. Many of the Mouseketeers—including Annette, Tommy, Darlene, Lonnie, Sharon, Sherry, Doreen, Bobby, Cubby, Karen, Dennis, Cheryl— became instantaneous celebrities. Over the next two seasons, 15 additional kids would become Mouseketeers, for a total of 39. Monday was Fun With Music Day; Tuesday was Guest Star Day; Wednesday was Anything Can Happen Day; Thursday was Circus Day; and Friday was Talent Roundup Day. Serials included *The Adventures of Spin and Marty, Border Collie, The Hardy Boys, Clint and Mac, San Juan River Expedition, Adventure in Dairyland, The Boys of the Western Sea, The Secret of Mystery Lake, Corky and White Shadow,* and *Annette. Mickey Mouse Club Newsreels* featured footage sent in by camera crews roaming the world looking for interesting stories featuring kids. Each show began with an animated segment culminating with Donald Duck striking a gong (with a variety of unexpected consequences) and ended with Mousekartoon Time.

The show began as part of Walt Disney's original contract with ABC, which gave him needed money to build Disneyland, a year after the debut of the nighttime *Disneyland* show. In all, 260 one-hour and 130 half-hour shows were produced. *Mickey Mouse Club* returned in syndication from 1962 to 1965 (with some new footage produced) and again in 1975. Because of the popularity of that 1975 syndication a new version of the club, known as the "new" *Mickey Mouse Club*, ran in syndication from January 14, 1977 to December 1, 1978. Twelve children were selected to be Mouseketeers, and the show was updated to appeal more to contemporary kids. The primary change was that the show was videotaped in color. Also, the days were changed—Monday was Who, What, Why, Where, When and How Day; Tuesday was Let's Go Day; Wednesday was Surprise Day; Thursday was Discovery Day; and Friday was Showtime Day. There was only one original serial produced—*The Mystery of Rustler's Cave*—though a number of Disney films were shown in serialized form. Because of high production costs and so-so ratings, the show only ran for two years.

When The Disney Channel began on April 18, 1983, the original *Mickey Mouse Club* episodes were featured daily. The Disney Channel produced its own updated version of the *Mickey Mouse Club* beginning on April 24, 1989, though by then the Mickey Mouse element was no longer emphasized, the kids in the cast no longer wore the distinctive mouse-ear hats, and the show was aimed at a slightly older age group. There were a number of new serials produced: *Teen Angel, Match Point, Teen Angel Returns, Just Perfect, The Secret of Lost Creek, My Life as a Babysitter, Emerald Cove*. The last new episodes of the *Mickey Mouse Club* were taped in the fall of 1994. Responding to the now older ages of the cast members and thus the target audience, the show had a new title, *MMC*, and any references to Mickey Mouse were dropped. See also Mouseketeers.

Mickey Mouse Club Circus Special circus under a tent at Disneyland; from November 24, 1955 to January 8, 1956, starring some of the Mouseketeers who were thrilled to be able to ride horses and work the trapezes. This circus was one of Walt Disney's few failures. He was fascinated by circuses, but guests visiting Disneyland had too many other fun things to see and do to spend their time sitting under a big top seeing a circus. After all, they could see a circus anywhere; there was only one Disneyland. Mickey Mouse Club Circus only lasted over one Christmas season. The tent, which Disney had bought, saw later usage in Holidayland for corporate picnics and other events.

Mickey Mouse Club Headquarters Located in the Opera House at Disneyland in 1963 and 1964. During a period of syndication of the television series, Walt Disney opened up an area where children could sign up and get their own membership cards in the Mickey Mouse Club. At the time of the original run of the show in the 1950s, everyone who watched the show was automatically a member of the club.

Mickey Mouse Club Magazine Quarterly magazine beginning publication at the height of popularity of the Mickey Mouse Club with the Winter 1956 issue. In June 1957, it went bimonthly and changed its name to *Walt Disney's Magazine*. It ceased publication with the October 1959 issue. Included were stories on the Mickey Mouse Club, its stars, and various Disney television and theatrical films of the period.

Mickey Mouse Club Theater Theater in Fantasyland at Disneyland that showed Disney cartoons; opened on August 27, 1955, changed its name to Fantasyland Theater in 1964, and closed on December 20, 1981. At one time, the *3D Jamboree* was featured, and guests donned polarized glasses to watch Mouseketeers and Disney cartoons in 3-D. The cartoon fare in the theater changed from time to time, and the theater itself was only open during busy periods. Before the theater was built in the Opera House as the home to Great Moments with Mr. Lincoln, this was the only auditorium in the park, so it was also used for press conferences and cast member events. It made way for Pinocchio's Daring Journey in the new Fantasyland in 1983.

Mickey Mouse Disco (film) Cartoon compilation featuring footage from a number of cartoons starring Mickey, Donald, and Goofy, re-edited, with a new sound track from the best-selling record album. The project was the birthplace of The Disney Channel's DTV music videos, which also marry classic Disney animation with contemporary songs and artists. Released on June 25, 1980. 7 min.

Mickey Mouse Magazine In January 1933, Kay Kamen created *Mickey Mouse Magazine*, which was a small publication containing short stories, articles, gags, games, and poems. There were nine monthly issues of the magazine, distributed through movie theaters and department stores. In November 1933, a second version of the magazine, in the same format but distributed through dairies, debuted, and continued until October 1935. The dairies would print their name on the cover of the magazine above the title. This dairy magazine was superseded by a

third, and much more elaborate, magazine, which began publication with a large issue in the summer of 1935. In October 1935, it turned into a monthly magazine. Over the years, several different sizes were experimented with, until finally in 1940 the magazine reached the size we know today as the normal comic book size. The last issue of *Mickey Mouse Magazine* was the one

for September 1940. In October 1940, *Walt Disney's Comics and Stories* took over.

Mickey Mouse March Theme song for the *Mickey Mouse Club*; written by Jimmie Dodd.

Mickey Mouse Revue Audio-Animatronics musical attraction in Fantasyland in Magic Kingdom Park at Walt Disney World, from October 1, 1971, until September 14, 1980, when it was removed and the theater was used seasonally as the Fantasyland Theater. The revue featured a large cast of Audio-Animatronics Disney characters performing selections of the most memorable of the Disney songs, with the orchestra led by maestro Mickey Mouse himself. The attraction was removed to Tokyo Disneyland, where it opened on April 15, 1983. *Magic Journeys* was shown for a time in 3-D, and in 1994 *The Legend of the Lion King* opened in the theater. It is the current home of *Mickey's PhilharMagic*.

Mickey Mouse: Safety Belt Expert (television) Educational film; a musical courtroom drama encouraging students to buckle up, released in September 1988. 16 min.

Mickey Mouse Theater of the Air Short-lived radio program on NBC in 1938. Walt Disney provided Mickey's voice.

Mickey MouseWorks (television) Animated television series; premiered on ABC on May 1, 1999, and ended January 6, 2001, with new cartoons starring Mickey, Donald Duck, Goofy, Pluto, and Minnie Mouse of varying lengths (12, 7½, and 6 minutes, and 90 seconds). Executive producers are Roberts Gannaway and Tony Craig.

Mickey Plays Papa (film) Mickey Mouse cartoon; released on September 29, 1934. Directed by Burt Gillett. Mickey discovers a baby on his doorstep and with Pluto's help tries to find different ways to stop its crying by imitating screen greats Charlie Chaplin and Jimmy Durante. An edited version, without Mickey, titled *Pluto and the Baby*, aired on the 1950s *Mickey Mouse Club*.

Mickey Steps Out (film) Mickey Mouse cartoon; released on July 7, 1931. Directed by Burt Gillett. Dressed up and on his way to see Minnie, Mickey falls in some mud, but makes up for his disheveled appearance with some entertaining dance and juggling routines. When Pluto chases a cat into the house, the resulting chaos wrecks the house and covers the inhabitants with soot from the stove.

Mickey's Amateurs (film) Mickey Mouse cartoon; released on April 17, 1937. Walt decided to try using some fresh directors, with storymen Pinto Colvig, Walt Pfeiffer, and Ed Penner handling the chores for this cartoon. When Donald's recitation is booed off Mickey's radio broadcast, Clara Cluck sings, Clarabelle plays the piano, and Goofy performs as a one-man band. But despite these diversions, Donald is back at the end with his recitation.

Mickey's Big Break (film) Short film being a humorous portrayal of Mickey Mouse's interview for a job with Disney, featuring Roy E. Disney portraying Walt Disney. Directed by Rob Minkoff. Cameo roles by Mel Brooks, Ed Begley, Jr., Dom DeLuise. The film was originally known as *Mickey's Audition*, and used during the summer of 1991 at Disney-MGM Studios for a temporary attraction on one of the soundstages. Beginning in 1994, it was shown at the Main Street Cinema in the Magic Kingdom, and in 1998 in the Town Square Exhibition Hall.

Mickey's Birthday Party (film) Mickey Mouse cartoon; released on February 7, 1942. Directed by Riley Thomson. The gang gives Mickey a surprise party that turns into a jam session with everyone playing instruments while Goofy has problems baking the cake.

Mickey's Birthdayland Area near Fantasyland in Magic Kingdom Park at Walt Disney World, created to honor Mickey's 60th birthday, from June 18, 1988 to April 22, 1990. At short notice, Disney executives decided that there should be a special area to honor the landmark birthday. A town, known as Duckburg, was quickly designed, and Disney artists helped the architects make it look cartoony. In order to build Mickey's Birthdayland, the Grand Prix Raceway had to be moved slightly. When it was suggested that there should be a statue to Duckburg's founder, the designers started coming up with ideas as to whom it should be, but one of the artists, Russell Schroeder, reminded them that there already was a founder of Duckburg, Cornelius Coot, in a comic book story, and he already had a statue in that comic book. Thus, the designers unexpectedly had something on which to base their statue. A train station was added along the route of the Walt Disney World Railroad, and special signs and displays lined the tracks leading from the Main Street station to Mickey's Birthdayland. There was Grandma Duck's Farm (a petting farm), a live show featuring Disney characters, Mickey's house, and guests could even visit Mickey himself in his dressing room. After the birthday celebration was over the area became Mickey's Starland, and was remodeled in 1996 as Mickey's Toontown Fair.

Mickey's Character Shop Large store featuring Disney character merchandise at the Disney Village Marketplace at Walt Disney World; open from October 25, 1985 to October 2, 1996.

Mickey's Choo-Choo (film) Mickey Mouse cartoon; released in 1929. Directed by Walt Disney. Train engineer Mickey and his anthropomorphic train share some harrowing adventures with Minnie when one of the cars breaks away from the train with Mickey and Minnie on top.

Mickey's Christmas Carol (film) Mickey Mouse cartoon featurette, premiere in England

on October 20, 1983; U.S. release on December 16, 1983. Directed by Burny Mattinson. 25 min. Dickens' well-known Christmas story is retold with Uncle Scrooge taking the role of Ebenezer Scrooge, Mickey Mouse as Bob Cratchit, Goofy as Jacob Marley's ghost, Donald Duck as nephew Fred, and many other Disney favorites who were returning to the silver screen after quite an absence. Mickey, for instance, had not been seen in a theatrical cartoon since *The Simple Things* in 1953. The film features the voices of Alan Young, Wayne Allwine, Hal Smith, Will Ryan, Eddy Carroll, Patricia Parris, Dick Billingsley, Clarence Nash. The song "Oh, What a Merry Christmas Day" was written by Frederick Searles and Irwin Kostal. The idea for the film was inspired by a 1974 Disney record album of the same name. Director Mattinson was inspired to begin the

project, with the okay from Disney president and chief executive officer Ron Miller, in May 1981. One of the difficult tasks in bringing back such favorite characters as Mickey and Donald was finding the right voices. Clarence "Ducky" Nash was still available to voice Donald as he had since Donald's debut, but Mickey's voice would introduce a new talent— Wayne Allwine. Nominated for an Academy Award as Best Short Film. Released on video in 1984. Began an annual television airing in 1984 on NBC.

Mickey's Christmas Chalet Fantasyland shop featuring Christmas holiday merchandise at Disneyland; open from May 25, 1983 to May 17, 1987. Succeeded by Briar Rose Cottage.

Mickey's Circus (film) Mickey Mouse cartoon; released on August 1, 1936. Directed by Ben Sharpsteen. At a circus benefit, orphans continually give Mickey and Donald trouble. When Donald chases seals who steal fish, orphans shoot him from a cannon onto Mickey's high-wire act. The orphans try to get Mickey and Donald to fall, and

when they do, into the pool below, all the seals jump in to get a fish that a young seal throws into Donald's mouth.

Mickey's Delayed Date (film) Mickey Mouse cartoon; released on October 3, 1947. Directed by Charles Nichols. Minnie phones Mickey from a party to hurry up, and with the aid of Pluto, he gets all dressed up in his tux. But on the way to the party, he and Pluto tangle with a trash can. Minnie sees Mickey with his torn clothes, and, to Mickey's amazement, is not mad, for the party is a "hard times" party. She compliments him on his costume.

Mickey's Elephant (film) Mickey Mouse cartoon; released on October 10, 1936. Directed by Dave Hand. Happy with his gift, Mickey makes a home for Bobo, his new elephant, incurring Pluto's jealousy. Putting pepper in Bobo's trunk, Pluto succeeds in not only getting Bobo's new home blown to bits, but his own doghouse as well.

Mickey's Field Trips Series of four educational films, released in September 1987 and July 1989: *The Police Station, The Fire Station, The Hospital, The United Nations.*

Mickey's 50 (television) Television show (90 min.); aired on November 19, 1978. Dozens of celebrities, many of them in very short cameo appearances, stop by to help wish Mickey a happy birthday. Included

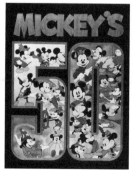

among them are Gerald Ford, Billy Graham, Lawrence Welk, Willie Nelson, Gene Kelly, Roy Rogers and Dale Evans, Edgar Bergen, O. J. Simpson, Jodie Foster, Goldie Hawn, Eva Gabor, Anne Bancroft, Jo Anne Worley, Burt Reynolds. Mike Jittlov provides a stop-motion sequence on Mickey Mouse merchandise through the years, using new merchandise from Disneyland shops and old merchandise from the Walt Disney Archives.

Mickey's Fire Brigade (film) Mickey Mouse cartoon; released on August 3, 1935. Directed by Ben Sharpsteen. Mickey, Donald, and Goofy come to put out a fire in Clarabelle Cow's house. Unaware, she is taking a bath when the trio comes crashing in to the rescue and into her bathtub.

Mickey's Follies (film) Mickey Mouse cartoon; featuring Mickey's theme song "Minnie's Yoo Hoo." Released in 1929. The first cartoon directed by Wilfred Jackson. In the midst of a musical revue, two chickens do an Apache dance, a pig sings opera, and Mickey brings it to a successful finale by singing and dancing on a piano.

Mickey's Gala Premiere (film) Mickey Mouse cartoon; released on July 1, 1933. Directed by Burt Gillett. Mickey and the gang are treated to a lavish premiere of their new picture at which many screen stars—including Greta Garbo, Clark Gable, Charlie Chaplin, Mae West, Laurel and Hardy, Harold Lloyd, and Marlene Dietrich—praise Mickey. But Mickey awakens to find it is only a dream. Spelled *Mickey's Gala Premier* on the film's title card.

Mickey's Garden (film) Mickey Mouse cartoon; released on July 13, 1935. Directed by Wilfred Jackson. Mickey and Pluto as pest exterminators sniffing around when Mickey gets a whiff of his own potent insecticide, and dreams of battles with gigantic insects.

Mickey's Good Deed (film) Mickey Mouse cartoon; released on December 17, 1932. Directed by Burt Gillett. Mickey is a street singer who selflessly sells Pluto to a rich family to raise money for a poor family at Christmas. But Pluto is mistreated and flees, returning to his beloved master.

Mickey's Grand Opera (film) Mickey Mouse cartoon; released on March 7, 1936. Directed by Wilfred Jackson. Mickey conducts the orchestra as Donald Duck and Clara Cluck sing a duet, which is marred by Pluto's antics with a magician's hat and its magical inhabitants.

Mickey's Happy Valentine Special (television) Television show; aired on February 12, 1989. Directed by Scot Garen. Ludwig Von Drake looks at love in this re-edited show told in MTV style.

Mickey's Hollywood Theater Area at Mickey's Starland in Magic Kingdom Park at Walt Disney World; open from June 18, 1988 to March 11, 1996, where guests could go backstage and meet Mickey in his dressing room.

Mickey's House Attraction opened in Mickey's Toontown at Disneyland on January 24, 1993. Guests can walk through the house, seeing Mickey's living quarters, along with memorabilia from his long career. Farther on, they can see a short film then meet Mickey on the set from one of his famous cartoons. There is also a Mickey's House in Mickey's Toontown Fair at the Walt Disney World Magic Kingdom.

Mickey's House of Villains (film) Direct-to-video film pits Mickey Mouse and his friends versus Disney's greatest villains as they try to turn the House of Mouse into the House of Villains. Released on September 3, 2002. 70 min.

Mickey's Kangaroo (film) Mickey Mouse cartoon; released on April 13, 1935. The last black-and-white Disney cartoon. Directed by Dave Hand. Mickey receives a kangaroo from Australia that delights in boxing with him. They make Pluto's life miserable with their antics, but by the end all are good friends.

Mickey's Kitchen The Walt Disney Company's first restaurant venture outside of its theme parks, begun in 1990 with one facility next door to The Disney Store in Montclair, California. A second one was later opened in Schaumburg, Illinois. The fast-food restaurants, which emphasized healthier fare, did not catch on and the two were eventually removed.

Mickey's Magical TV World Show at Mickey's Starland; opened on April 26, 1990, and closed on March 11, 1996. Upon exiting Mickey's House, guests entered the theater where they could watch a live show featuring Disney characters from the television shows. It was formerly Minnie's Surprise Birthday Party.

Mickey's Man Friday (film) Mickey Mouse cartoon; released on January 19, 1935. Directed by Dave Hand. Loosely based on the story of Robinson Crusoe, and one of Mickey's last black-and-white cartoons. Mickey, shipwrecked, lands on an island inhabited by cannibals. He befriends a native who helps him escape in a trick boat.

Mickey's Mart Souvenir store in Tomorrowland in Magic Kingdom Park at Walt Disney World; opened on October 1, 1971, and closed June 27, 1991. Became Mickey's Star Traders.

Mickey's Mechanical Man (film) Mickey Mouse cartoon; released on June 17, 1933. Directed by Wilfred Jackson. Inventor Mickey creates a robot that fights the hairy star of *The Gorilla Mystery* and overpowers him with the help of Minnie, who revives the robot at one point with a horn.

Mickey's Mellerdrammer (film) Mickey Mouse cartoon; released on March 18, 1933. Directed by Wilfred Jackson. Mickey and the gang put on a production of *Uncle Tom's Cabin* with Horace Horsecollar as Simon Legree and Mickey as Uncle Tom. Unfortunately, the bloodhounds in the play become unruly and bring down the curtain early.

Mickey's Nightmare (film) Mickey Mouse cartoon; released on August 13, 1932. Directed by Burt Gillett. Mickey dreams he is married to Minnie, but the dream turns into a nightmare when he is overwhelmed by their children. He happily wakes up to repeated lickings from Pluto.

Mickey's Nutcracker Christmas musical show at Videopolis at Disneyland during the 1991 and 1992 holiday seasons.

Mickey's of Hollywood Clothing shop on Hollywood Blvd. at Disney-MGM Studios; opened on May 1, 1989.

Mickey's Once Upon a Christmas (film) Released on videocassette on November 9, 1999, the 70-minute program includes *Donald Duck: Stuck on Christmas*, *A Very Goofy Christmas*, and *Mickey and Minnie's Gift of the Magi*, tied together with narration by Kelsey Grammer and concluding with a rendition of "Deck the Halls" by the country trio SHeDAISY.

Mickey's Orphans (film) Mickey Mouse cartoon; released on December 9, 1931. Directed by Burt Gillett. Nominated for an Academy Award.

A basket of kittens is left on Minnie's doorstep at Christmas, and Mickey and Minnie charitably bring it inside. But they soon regret their action as the cats wreck the house, strip the tree, and take the gifts and candy.

Mickey's Pal Pluto (film) Mickey Mouse cartoon; released on February 18, 1933. Directed by Burt Gillett. When Mickey and Minnie find some kittens, Pluto is jealous, torn between his angel good and bad consciences. When the cats fall into a well, Pluto and his angel-self rescue them. It was remade as *Lend a Paw* (1941), which won an Academy Award.

Mickey's Parrot (film) Mickey Mouse cartoon; released on September 9, 1938. The first cartoon directed by Bill Roberts. Overhearing a radio broadcast about an escaped killer, Mickey and Pluto hear a voice they assume to be the felon. After a scary few minutes, they discover it is only Mickey's pet parrot and all are relieved, including the parrot.

Mickey's PhilharMagic Computer-animated 3-D film attraction in Magic Kingdom Park at Walt Disney World; opened on September 30, 2003. A Grand Opening ceremony was held on October 8. Donald Duck swipes Mickey's sorcerer's hat, then tries to conduct a symphony, but ends up stumbling into scenes from classic Disney animated features. Also at Hong Kong Disneyland; opened on September 12, 2005.

Mickey's Polo Team (film) Mickey Mouse cartoon; released on January 4, 1936. Directed by Dave Hand. Walt's interest in this sport found its

way into a cartoon that features many Hollywood celebrities versus Disney characters such as the Big Bad Wolf and Mickey. The horses all seem to resemble their riders. By the time the dust settles, the horses are riding the players.

Mickey's Retreat See Little Lake Bryan.

Mickey's Revue (film) Mickey Mouse cartoon; released on May 25, 1932. Directed by Wilfred Jackson. First appearance of the character who would become Goofy; here he is a member of the audience cheering on Mickey's musical comedy. The show is brought to an abrupt end when Pluto creates havoc by chasing cats onstage.

Mickey's Rival (film) Mickey Mouse cartoon; released on June 20, 1936. Directed by Wilfred Jackson. Mickey's rival, Mortimer, strives for Minnie's affections on an afternoon outing. As he woos Minnie, he plays practical jokes on Mickey and even his car threatens Mickey's car. But, when Mortimer is responsible for a bull attacking, it is Mickey who finally rescues Minnie, while Mortimer runs away.

Mickey's Safety Club Series of four educational films released in September 1989: *Halloween Surprises*, *Playground Fun*, *What to Do at Home*, and *Street Safe, Street Smart*.

Mickey's Service Station (film) Mickey Mouse cartoon; released on March 16, 1935. Directed by Ben Sharpsteen. Mickey, Donald, and Goofy are service-station attendants who attempt to fix Pete's car but eventually find the problem is the squeak of a cricket. They do such a poor job putting the car back together again that the furious Pete ends up being chased by the motor.

Mickey's 60th Birthday (television) Television show; aired on November 13, 1988. Directed by Scot Garen. Mickey disappears and everyone is searching for him. The cause? A wizard has punished Mickey for using his magic hat by making everyone forget what he looks like. But finally all is forgiven and there is a big celebration at Disneyland. Stars John Ritter, Jill Eikenberry, Carl Reiner, Cheech Marin, Phylicia Rashad, Charles Fleischer, and a host of other celebrities.

Mickey's Star Traders Souvenir and sun-care-product shop in Tomorrowland in Magic Kingdom Park at Walt Disney World; opened June 28, 1991. Formerly Mickey's Mart. Presented by Coppertone.

Mickey's Starland Area near Fantasyland in Magic Kingdom Park at Walt Disney World; opened on May 26, 1990, taking the place of Mickey's Birthdayland after the conclusion of the 60th-birthday celebrations. Became Mickey's Toontown Fair in 1996.

Mickey's Steam Roller Mickey Mouse cartoon; released on June 16, 1934. Directed by Dave Hand. When Mickey's nephews crawl into his steamroller while he is romancing Minnie, a chase ensues as the machine goes out of control and causes massive destruction until it stops after smashing a hotel.

Mickey's Surprise Party (film) Cartoon commercial starring Minnie and Fifi, made for the National Biscuit Co. for showing at the 1939 New York World's Fair. Delivered on February 18, 1939. Fifi interferes with Minnie's cooking, but Mickey saves the day by his purchase of Nabisco cookies. He uses the opportunity to show Minnie the company's various products.

Mickey's Toontown Area that opened at Disneyland on January 24, 1993. Disney designers Dave Burkhart and Joe Lanzisero looked to the Toon world and created it as the place where Mickey, Minnie, Donald, and the other Disney characters live. There is a downtown section, where guests can have fun pushing buttons, twisting knobs, and opening boxes, all leading to a comic happening—the fireworks factory explodes, the mailbox talks back, weasels make snide comments under the manhole. The Jolly Trolley transports one to the residential area, where guests can visit the characters at their houses. Some, like Goofy's Bounce House, are limited to children only. In back of Mickey's House, one can meet the mouse himself on the set from one of his classic cartoons. Other attractions include Gadget's Go-Coaster and Roger Rabbit's Car Toon Spin, a zany ride through the Toon world. A Toontown opened at Tokyo Disneyland on April 15, 1996, sponsored by Kodansha, with its two main areas reversed from the ones at Disneyland.

Mickey's Toontown Fair Mickey's Starland was remodeled in Magic Kingdom Park at Walt Disney World, opening on June 29, 1996. Now, besides a redesigned Mickey's country house, there is Minnie's country house, Donald's boat, and a roller coaster, The Barnstormer at Goofy's Wise Acres.

Mickey's Trailer (film) Mickey Mouse cartoon; released on May 6, 1938. Directed by Ben Sharpsteen. On their trip out of the city for a vacation, Mickey, Donald, and Goofy plan on having lots of fun and relaxation with their trailer, but all does not go as they plan and they soon have their hands full when the trailer gets away from them. Despite a steep mountain road and a speedy express train, the car and trailer eventually meet

once again. Includes some fun gags about marvelous contraptions built into the trailer.

Mickey's Twice Upon a Christmas (film) Direct-to-video release on November 9, 2004. Directed by Matt O'Callaghan. The Disney gang is presented in computer-generated animation, in five segments about the holiday. Voices include Wayne Allwine (Mickey), Tony Anselmo (Donald), Bill Farmer (Goofy), Tress MacNeille (Daisy), Jason Marsden (Max), Chuck McCann (Santa), Clive Revill (Narrator), Russi Taylor (Minnie Mouse), Alan Young (Scrooge McDuck). 68 min.

MicroAdventure Revised version of *Honey, I Shrunk the Audience*; opened at Tokyo Disneyland on April 15, 1997.

Middleton, Robert (1911—1977) Actor; appeared on television in *Gallegher* and *Texas John Slaughter.*

Midget Autopia Fantasyland attraction at Disneyland; opened on April 23, 1957, and closed on April 3, 1966. Walt supposedly did not like the attraction because only children could ride it. When he had it removed from Disneyland, he donated it to his boyhood hometown of Marceline, Missouri, where it was installed in the Walt Disney Park (though it has not operated for many years).

Midler, Bette Actress; appeared in *Down and Out in Beverly Hills* (Barbara Whiteman), *Ruthless People* (Barbara Stone), *Outrageous Fortune* (Sandy), *Big Business* (Sadie Shelton/Sadie Ratliff), *Beaches* (C. C. Bloom), *Stella* (Stella Claire), *Scenes from a Mall* (Deborah), and *Hocus Pocus* (Winifred), and provided the voice of Georgette in *Oliver & Company*. She also starred in the short demonstration film *The Lottery* at Disney-MGM Studios, and was a host of *Fantasia/2000.*

Midnight in a Toy Shop (film) Silly Symphony cartoon; released on August 16, 1930. Directed by Wilfred Jackson. In its exploration of a toy shop, a spider has unnerving experiences with various activated toys, a lighted candle, and firecrackers.

Midnight Madness (film) A genius grad student organizes an all-night treasure hunt in which five rival teams composed of colorful oddballs furiously match wits with one another while trying to locate and decipher various cryptic clues planted ingeniously around Los Angeles. Released on February 8, 1980. Directed by David Wechter and Michael Nankin. 112 min. Stars David Naughton (Adam), Debra Clinger (Laura), Eddie Deezen (Wesley), Brad Wilkin (Lavitas), Maggie Roswell (Donna), Stephen Furst (Harold), Irene Tedrow (Mrs. Grimhaus), Michael J. Fox (in his Disney and film debut as Scott), Dirk Blocker (Blaylak). The film underwent four title changes during production: *The All-Night Treasure Hunt, The Ultimate Game, The Great All-Nighter,* and finally the final title, which proved most popular in audience research tests. The movie was shot on 25 locations around Los Angeles, from Griffith Park Observatory to the Hollywood Wax Museum, Osko's Disco, Occidental College, Sherman Clay Piano Museum, and the Bonaventure Hotel. Three songs, "Midnight Madness,"

"Don't Know Why I Came," and "Someone New," were written for the movie by David and Julius Wechter. The film was released without the Disney name on it, with the hope that it would reach teenagers and young adults who often shied away from "Disney" films. To build a cast of fresh, new faces, more than 2,000 actors and actresses were interviewed by the directors. Of 25 feature roles, seven were cast from the open call, four others were cast for supporting parts. Released on video in 1985.

Mighty Ducks, The (film) A competitive, aggressive trial lawyer, Gordon Bombay is sentenced to community service—coaching a peewee hockey team full of clumsy misfits. Bombay, who formerly played hockey himself, finds his work cut out for him, as he has to teach the team to skate, to score, and to win. The reluctant coach becomes committed, names his team "The Ducks," and slowly molds his group of losers into a championship team while he himself realizes that the sport may be even more satisfying to him than his chosen profession. Released on October 2, 1992. Directed by Stephen Herek. 103 min. Stars Emilio Estevez (Gordon Bombay), Joss Ackland (Hans), Lane Smith (Coach Reilly). Filmed on location in Minneapolis, Minnesota, the heart of peewee hockey country. Released on video in 1993. Two sequels were released: *D2: The Mighty Ducks* in 1994 and *D3: The Mighty Ducks* in 1996.

Mighty Ducks (television) Animated television series; premiered on September 6, 1996, in syndication and on ABC the following day. The ABC run ended on August 30, 1997. A combination hockey team and band of superheroes, part-duck and part-human, show off their hockey prowess at the Anaheim Pond rink. Elsewhere, they use their high-tech tools and teamwork to save the world from the evil Lord Dragaunus and his henchmen, whom they've followed from the planet Puckworld. The Mighty Ducks team includes the role-model captain Wildwing, his renegade brother Nosedive, martial arts expert Mallory, sylish ex-criminal Duke L'Orange, scientific whiz Tanya, and huge Zen master Grin. The only human who knows the Ducks' true identities is Phil, the team's manager. Voices include Ian Ziering (Wildwing), Steve Mackall (Nosedive), April Winchell (Mallory), Jeff Bennett (Duke L'Orange), Jennifer Hale (Tanya), Brad Garrett (Grin), Jim Belushi (Phil), Tim Curry (Lord Dragaunus). 26 episodes.

Mighty Ducks, The Disney's first entry into the realm of professional sports. In 1992, the company founded the Mighty Ducks hockey team, named for the team in Walt Disney Pictures' *The Mighty Ducks*, as an expansion team in the National Hockey League. They were ready for league play in the 1993–94 season, and their first exhibition game was held on September 18, 1993. They play at the Arrowhead Pond in Anaheim, California. Henry and Susan Samueli agreed to purchase the Mighty Ducks from Disney on February 25, 2005, taking Disney out of the professional sports business two years after selling the Anaheim Angels.

Mighty Ducks the Movie: The First Face-Off (film) Animated movie, tying together television episodes, released on video on April 8, 1997. The evil Lord Dragaunus returns to Puckworld, a peaceful planet of hockey-loving ducks, from a distant galaxy to take revenge against the inhabitants who once banished him. A special strike team of six young courageous superheroes—The Mighty Ducks—is formed to face off against Lord Dragaunus's dark forces. After a fierce battle, Dragaunus manages to escape, and the Ducks must follow him and find themselves transported to the weird, alien metropolis of Anaheim, California. Trapped there, the Ducks build a super-secret headquarters under the Anaheim Pond to thwart Dragaunus's plans to take over the world. Directed by Joe Barruso. 66 min. Stars Ian Ziering (Wildwing), Jim Belushi (Phil), Tim Curry (Lord Dragaunus).

Mighty Joe Young (film) Zoologist Gregg O'Hara is exploring the remote Pangani Mountains in Central Africa when he comes upon an incredible discovery—an awesome 15-foot gorilla. Fearsome and dangerous when provoked, he is tame in the hands of Jill, the 21-year-old orphan who raised the gorilla and named him Joe. When Joe's life is threatened by poachers, Gregg and Jill rescue him by moving him to a California animal preserve. However, Joe is not safe for long. His newfound notoriety makes him a target for an enemy from his past, a ruthless poacher who is eager to steal Joe for his unique value in the endangered species black market. Feeling threatened and confused in his man-made confines, Joe finally escapes from captivity. With only Los Angeles and its terrified residents in his way, this powerful force of nature attempts to traverse a modern metropolis, leaving a trail of destruction and chaos in his wake. Jill and Gregg race to save Joe's life before he is destroyed by the encircling authorities, and the chase culminates in an incredible and selfless display of courage by the mighty Joe, proving that within his fearsome frame beats a noble and heroic heart. Released on December 25, 1998. Directed by Ron Underwood. Stars Bill Paxton (Gregg O'Hara), Charlize Theron (Jill), Rade Sherbedgia (Strasser), Regina King (Cecily Banks), Peter Firth (Garth), David Paymer (Dr. Harry Ruben), Naveen Andrews (Pindi). 115 min. Based on the classic RKO motion picture from 1949. Locations in Hawaii, such as the jungles and mountains of Oahu's Kualoa Valley, doubled for the Pangani

Mountains in Tanzania. Animatronics, and computer graphics, as well as forced perspective and blue-screen camera work with actor John Alexander in a 40 percent scale "Joe" costume, all contributed to the character of the gorilla. Three different hydraulic versions of Joe, as well as the 40 percent scale suits, were created by Academy Award–winning designer, Rick Baker. In scenes where the suits were used, the sets and props also

had to be created at 40 percent size. Released on video in 1999.

Mike & Maty (television) Hour-long daytime television talk show on ABC; premiered on April 11, 1994, and ended on June 7, 1996. The show featured upbeat funny events and stories. Stars Michael Burger and Maty Monfort.

Mike Fink Keel Boats Frontierland attraction in Disneyland; opened on December 25, 1955. Based on the television episode *Davy Crockett's Keel Boat Race.* The boats are the *Gullywhumper*, named for Mike Fink's boat, and the *Bertha Mae*, named for Davy's boat. Fink was the legendary King of the River to go along with his opponent's title of King of the Wild Frontier. The Keel Boats were closed in 1994 but reopened on March 30, 1996. They closed again on May 17, 1997. Also Frontierland attraction in Magic Kingdom Park at Walt Disney World; opened on October 1, 1971. See also River Rogue Keelboats for the Disneyland Paris version.

Mike Wazowski James P. Sullivan's monster friend in *Monsters, Inc.*; voiced by Billy Crystal.

Mike's New Car (film) Short cartoon, made by Pixar and featuring the stars of *Monsters, Inc.*, created as bonus material for the September 17, 2002, DVD release of the feature. Mike Wazowski shows off his new car to his friend James P. "Sulley" Sullivan, but neither knows how to operate it. 4 min. Released initially at the El Capitan Theater in Los Angeles on May 17, 2002, for Academy Award consideration; it received a nomination for Best Animated Short Film.

Mile Long Bar In Frontierland in Magic Kingdom Park at Walt Disney World; opened on October 1, 1971, and closed on January 5, 1998. An ingenious use of mirrors made the bar seem like it was a mile long. Served light fare and cool drinks. Also in Bear Country at Disneyland, opened in

1972. Later named Brer Bar (1989–2002). Also in Westernland at Tokyo Disneyland; opened on April 15, 1983.

Miles, Vera Actress; appeared in *A Tiger Walks* (Dorothy Williams), *Those Calloways* (Liddy Calloway), *Follow Me, Boys!* (Vida Downey), *The Wild Country* (Kate), *One Little Indian* (Doris Melver), and *The Castaway Cowboy* (Henrietta MacAvoy).

Milestones for Mickey (film) Sixteen mm compilation of *Plane Crazy*, *Mickey's Service Station*, *The Band Concert*, *Thru the Mirror*, *Sorcerer's Apprentice*, and the "Mickey Mouse Club March." Released in May 1974.

Milestones in Animation (film) Sixteen mm compilation of *Steamboat Willie*, *The Skeleton Dance*, *Flowers and Trees*, *Three Little Pigs*, *The Old Mill*. Released in March 1973.

Milland, Ray (1905–1986) Actor; appeared in *Escape to Witch Mountain* (Aristotle Bolt).

Millar, Lee (1924–1980) He voiced Jim Dear in *Lady and the Tramp*.

Millennium Celebration To celebrate the new millennium, with a theme of "Celebrate the Future Hand in Hand," Walt Disney World concentrated its efforts on Epcot. There an enormous Mickey Mouse hand held a magic wand that trailed a giant "2000" over the globe of Spaceship Earth for 15 months beginning in October 1999. In World Showcase, the 65,000-square-foot Millennium Village presented exhibits from countries around the world. Additionally, there was a program of pin trading, updated Innoventions and Illuminations, and the opportunity for guests to have their photos etched into steel tiles on 35 granite slabs at Leave a Legacy. After the close of the celebration, the Millennium Village facility was remodeled and opened in 2001 as a convention meeting location.

Miller, Bob Vice president and publisher of Hyperion Books since its creation in 1990.

Miller, Diane Disney See Diane Disney.

Miller, Ilana Actress; appeared on the *Mickey Mouse Club* on The Disney Channel, beginning in 1990.

Miller, Julius Sumner (1909–1987) College professor who, as Professor Wonderful, hosted the Fun with Science segment on the syndicated version of the *Mickey Mouse Club* in the 1964–65 season.

Miller, Roger Singer; he voiced Allan-a-Dale in *Robin Hood*. He narrated on television *Deacon, the High Noon Dog* and *Go West, Young Dog*.

Miller, Ronald W. Walt Disney's son-in-law and the husband of Diane Disney; joined Disney in 1957, served as associate producer of such films as *Bon Voyage*, *Summer Magic*, *Moon Pilot*, and *A Tiger Walks*. He became co-producer with Walt Disney on such films as *The Monkey's Uncle*; *That Darn Cat!*; *Lt. Robin Crusoe, USN*; and *Monkeys, Go Home!* His first full producer credit was on *Never a Dull Moment*. Beginning in 1968, he served 12 years as executive producer of motion pictures and television for the company, then was elected president in 1980. He served as president of Walt Disney Productions from 1980 to 1984. He was a member of the board of directors from 1966 to 1984.

Million Dollar Collar, The (film) Foreign theatrical title of the two-part *Ballad of Hector, the Stowaway Dog*. Released in 1967.

Million Dollar Dixie Deliverance, The (television) Two-hour television movie; aired on February 5, 1978. Directed by Russ Mayberry. A Confederate officer kidnaps for a $1,000,000 ransom five well-to-do children from a Yankee boarding school; a wounded black Union soldier helps them escape after they perform the necessary surgery to remove the bullet from his leg. But they are captured again, and it takes a lucky Union army attack to save them. Stars Brock Peters, Christian Juttner, Chip Courtland, Kyle Richards, Alicia Fleer, Christian Berrigan, Joe Dorsey, Kip Niven.

Million Dollar Duck, The (film) By chance, a white duck in a science lab eats some terrible-tasting applesauce, and is exposed to a radiation beam. The result: the duck lays golden eggs! This upsets the life—and moral values—of a university professor, Albert Dooley, who soon has troubles with his wife, son, and even government T-men. But, after a wild chase and zany court battle, Professor Dooley reforms, and all his problems are solved. Released on June 30, 1971. Directed by Vincent McEveety. 92 min. Stars Dean Jones (Albert Dooley), Sandy Duncan (Katie), Joe Flynn (Finley Hooper), Tony Roberts (Fred), James Gregory (Rutledge), Lee Harcourt Montgomery (Jimmy), Jack Kruschen (Dr. Gottlieb). From the story by Ted Key. The Studio held open auditions for the duck role, with Webfoot Waddle winning the part. The second- and third-place winners Carlos and Jennifer got to be stand-ins. The ducks were given the full Hollywood treatment: their own drinking-water pails, lettuce and chicken scratch, plus evenings and weekends free to rest floating around the Disney studio pond. Also known as *$1,000,000 Duck*. Released on video in 1986.

Mills, Hayley Actress; appeared in *Pollyanna* (Pollyanna), *The Parent Trap* (Sharon McKendrick/Susan Evers), *In Search of the Castaways* (Mary Grant), *Summer Magic* (Nancy Carey), *The Moonspinners* (Nikky Ferris), and *That Darn Cat* (Patti Randall). On television, she appeared in *Disney Animation: the Illusion of Life*; *The Disneyland Tenth Anniversary Show*; *Parent Trap III*; *Parent Trap Hawaiian Honeymoon*; and on The Disney Channel in *Back Home*, *Parent Trap II*, and the series *Good Morning, Miss Bliss*. She is the daughter of actor John Mills. Hayley received a special Academy Award for *Pollyanna*. She was named a Disney Legend in 1998.

Mills, John (1908–2005) Actor; appeared in *Swiss Family Robinson* (Father), *The Disneyland Tenth Anniversary Show*, and *Escape to Paradise*. He was named a Disney Legend in 2002.

Milotte, Alfred and Elma Husband and wife team of cinematographers responsible for creating the True-Life Adventure series of nature films. Walt Disney hired them to film on location in the wilderness of Alaska, and the result was *Seal Island*, the first True-Life Adventure, and *The Alaskan Eskimo*, both of which won Academy Awards. Other award-winning films they helped photograph were *Beaver Valley*, *Bear Country*, *Nature's Half Acre*, *Prowlers of the Everglades*, *Nature's Strangest Creatures*, *Water Birds*, and *The African Lion*. For the latter film, the couple spent 33 months in Africa. They were named Disney Legends in 1998.

Milton Cat nemesis of Pluto, in three cartoons beginning with *Puss-Cafe* (1950).

Mimieux, Yvette Actress; appeared in *Monkeys, Go Home!* (Maria Riserau) and *The Black Hole* (Dr. Kate McCrea).

Min and Bill's Dockside Diner Opened at Disney-MGM Studios on May 1, 1989. A tramp steamer docked at Echo Lake serving sandwiches and other fast-food items, based on the 1930 film starring Marie Dressler and Wallace Beery.

Minado, the Wolverine (television) Television show; aired on November 7, 1965. A young wolverine torments a trapper who has killed the wolverine's mother, by stealing his food, tools, and other supplies, and eventually driving him away. Narrated by Sebastian Cabot.

Mine Train Through Nature's Wonderland Frontierland attraction at Disneyland; open from May 28, 1960 to January 2, 1977. Formerly Rainbow Caverns Mine Train (1956–1959). Guests rode a train through a new wilderness area populated by 204 lifelike bears, beavers, and other critters, then continued through the area of the former attraction—the painted desert and Rainbow Caverns, where the coolness of colored waterfalls and pools were a refreshing respite on a hot day. When Walt was planning this attraction, he was not satisfied with his designers' creations, so he took drawing materials home and drew up the entire ride himself. Today, this drawing is one of the treasures of the Walt Disney Archives. The attraction was removed for construction of Big Thunder Mountain Railroad.

Mineo, Sal (1939–1976) Actor; appeared in *Tonka* (White Bull).

Mineral Hall Shop and display of minerals in Frontierland at Disneyland from July 30, 1956 to 1963. The front part of the shop offered minerals for sale; in back you could see displays of minerals alternately under regular light and black light. It was fun to see how clothing would also glow under the black light.

Mineral King Area in the Sierra Nevada Mountains of California that the U.S. government opened to private development in the 1960s. Walt Disney put in a bid, which was accepted by the government. However, a groundswell of criticism arose over what environmentalists felt would be the desecration of a major untouched wilderness area. While Disney tried to show that their development would enhance the area and enable more people to see its beauty, the critics prevailed. Congress voted to make the Mineral King area part of Sequoia National Park, and no private development was allowed.

Ming-Na See Ming-Na Wen.

Miniatures One of Walt Disney's hobbies was the collecting of miniatures, and this hobby actually helped bring about Disneyland. For years Walt had been collecting tiny furniture and household items and displaying them in little room settings. Out of this collection came an idea for a miniature Americana display with dioramas that would travel the country by truck and teach people about how life in the United States developed to the present. His first completed model was Granny's Cabin, which he exhibited at a Festival of California Living at the Pan Pacific Auditorium in Los Angeles in 1952. Because of the obvious problem of not being able to show dioramas to large numbers of people, Disney put aside his idea of a miniature display and expanded his sights to what eventually became Disneyland.

Minion, The (film) Touchstone Home Video release on July 11, 2000, of a Mahogany Pictures film. A mysterious key is unearthed beneath the streets of New York City and the Minion, a domestic servant of the Antichrist, will do everything in its power to possess the key and see that his master is freed to wreak havoc on the world. Only Lucas, a modern-day warrior trained in the ancient arts, can defeat the ultimate evil. Directed by Jean-Marc Piché. Stars Dolph Lundgren (Lukas), Françoise Robertson (Karen Goodleaf), Roc LaFortune (David Schulman), David Newman (Lt. Roseberry). 96 min.

Minkoff, Rob Animator/director; joined Disney in 1983 and worked as an inbetweener on *The Black Cauldron*. He helped design the characters of Basil in *The Great Mouse Detective* and Ursula in *The Little Mermaid*, before becoming associated with the character Roger Rabbit as the director of *Tummy Trouble* and *Roller Coaster Rabbit* and co-producer of *Trail Mix-up*. He directed *The Lion King* with Roger Allers.

Minnie Mouse Mickey Mouse's girlfriend also made her debut in *Steamboat Willie* on November 18, 1928. She did not have her own cartoon series, but appeared in 73 cartoons with Mickey  Mouse and Pluto. She has been a popular character at the Disney parks, where 1986 was declared Minnie's year, giving her much deserved recognition. The first voice of Minnie Mouse was Marcellite Garner, from the Ink and Paint Department at the Disney Studio. She was succeeded by several others from that department, and currently the voice is supplied by Russi Taylor. Minnie Mouse has two nieces, Millie and Melody, who appeared in one 1962 comic book story.

Minnie's House Attraction opened in Mickey's Toontown at Disneyland on January 24, 1993. The ultra-cartoony style is used to show how

Minnie might live. Also at Mickey's Toontown Fair at the Walt Disney World Magic Kingdom, and at Tokyo Disneyland.

Minnie's Surprise Birthday Party Show at Mickey's Birthdayland from June 18, 1988, until April 22, 1990. Reopened as Mickey's Magical TV World.

Minnie's Yoo Hoo The Mickey Mouse Club theme song from the original club; it was the first Disney song to be released on sheet music, in 1930, and a filmed version, using animation from *Mickey's Follies*, was prepared for showing at Mickey Mouse Club events. Written by Walt Disney and Carl Stalling.

Minor, Jason Actor; appeared on the *Mickey Mouse Club* on The Disney Channel from 1990 to 1993.

Mintz, Margaret Winkler (1895–1990) Film distributor in New York who signed a contract with Walt Disney on October 16, 1923, to distribute the Alice Comedies. She later married Charles Mintz, and let him take over the business.

Miracle (film) In 1980, the U.S. ice hockey team needed a miracle. Coach Herb Brooks was charged with taking his ragtag squad to the Olympic Games at Lake Placid, but even the encouraging coach was not sure what his boys could do against the storied teams from the East-ern bloc countries and the juggernaut from the Soviet Union. Despite long odds, Team USA rose to the occasion in one of the most thrilling moments in the country's sports history. Released on February 6, 2004. Directed by Gavin O'Connor. Stars Kurt Russell (Herb Brooks), Eddie Cahill (Jim Craig), Patricia Clarkson (Patty Brooks), Noah Emmerich (Craig Patrick), Sean McCann (Walter Bush), Kenneth Welsh (Doc Nagobads), Patrick O'Brien Demsey (Mike Eruzione), Michael Mantenuto (Jack O'Callahan), Nathan West (Rob McClanahan), Kenneth Mitchell (Ralph Cox). 136 min. Released on video in 2004.

Miracle at Midnight (television) Two-hour television movie; aired on *The Wonderful World of Disney* on May 17, 1998. During World War II, the members of the Koster family in Denmark risk their lives to help their Jewish countrymen who are about to be arrested by the Nazis occupying their country. Directed by Ken Cameron. Stars Sam Waterston (Dr. Karl Koster), Mia Farrow (Doris Koster), Justin Whalin (Hendrik Koster), Patrick Malahide (Duckwitz), Benedick Blythe (General Best). Since progress has changed Copenhagen and the Danish fishing villages so much in recent years, the filmmakers turned instead to Ireland for their locations. Released on video in 2000.

Miracle Child (television) Two-hour television movie; aired on NBC on April 6, 1993. Lisa Porter is a young mother whose infant daughter miraculously changes her life and the life of a small town. Directed by Michael Pressman. Stars Crystal Bernard (Lisa), Cloris Leachman (Doc Betty), John Terry (Buck Sanders), Graham Sack (Lyle Sanders). Based on the novel *Miracle at Clement's Pond*, by Patricia Pendergraft.

Miracle Down Under (film) Video release title of *The Christmas Visitor*; released on video in 1987.

Miracle in Lane Two (television) Two-hour Disney Channel Original Movie; premiered on May 13, 2000. A heartwarming tale of Justin

Yoder, a courageous 12-year-old kid who has a real zest for life and a wonderful sense of humor, despite being confined to a wheelchair. Against all odds, his talent, perseverance, and enthusiasm take him to the national soapbox derby championships. Directed by Greg Beeman. Stars Frankie Muniz (Justin Yoder), Rick Rossovich (Myron Yoder), Molly Hagan (Sheila Stopher Yoder), Patrick Levis (Seth Yoder), Roger Aaron Brown (Vic Sauder). Released on video in 2000.

Miracle of the White Stallions (film) True story of how Colonel Alois Podhajsky, director of Vienna's world-famous Spanish Riding School, saves the school and its beautiful Lipizzan white horses during World War II. When the bombs start falling on Vienna near the end of the war, Podhajsky secretly defies the Nazis and smuggles the marvelous performing white stallions into rural St. Martin. Meanwhile, the Lipizzan mares, on which the future of the breed depend, are in Czechoslovakia in the path of the advancing Russians who are slaughtering all livestock coming into their hands. Under the direct order of General Patton, an expert horseman, the mares are rescued, reunited with the stallions, and both the Lipizzans and the Spanish Riding School are saved for posterity. Released on March 29, 1963. Directed by Arthur Hiller. 118 min. Stars Robert Taylor (Col. Podhajsky), Lilli Palmer (Vedena Podhajsky), Curt Jurgens (Gen. Tellheim), Eddie Albert (Rider Otto), James Franciscus (Maj. Hoffman), John Larch (Gen. Patton). Based on the book *The Dancing White Horses of Vienna*, by Colonel Podhajsky. Features the song "Just Say Auf Wiedersehen," by Richard M. Sherman and Robert B. Sherman. Released on video in 1987.

Miracle Worker, The (television) Two-hour television movie; aired on *The Wonderful World of Disney* on November 12, 2000. The story of eight-year-old Helen Keller, blind, deaf, and mute, who in 1887 blossoms under the care and teaching of Annie Sullivan, whose groundbreaking techniques for teaching deaf and blind people are still being used today. Directed by Nadia Tass. Stars Hallie Kate Eisenberg (Helen Keller), Alison Elliott (Annie Sullivan), David Strathairn

(Capt. Keller), Lucas Black (James Keller), Kate Greenhouse (Kate Keller). Based on the Tony Award–winning play by William Gibson. Released on video in 2001.

Miracles (television) Hour-long drama series; premiered on ABC on January 27, 2003, and ended March 3, 2003. A former Vatican miracle investigator joins forces with Sodalitas Quaerito, a shadowy organization interested in studying good vs. evil. Stars Skeet Ulrich (Paul Callan), Angus Macfadyen (Alva Keel), Marisa Ramirez (Evelyn Santos). Produced by Touchstone Television in association with Spyglass Entertainment.

Miramax Films Disney bought Miramax Films, founded by Harvey and Bob Weinstein, on June 30, 1993, gaining the rights to its library of more than 200 films. As part of the deal, Disney financed future Miramax productions. Since the Disney purchase, Miramax has released such hits as *The Piano*, *The Crow*, *Little Buddha*, *Pulp Fiction*, *Trainspotting*, *Sling Blade*, *Life Is Beautiful*, *The English Patient* (Best Picture Oscar), *Shakespeare in Love* (Best Picture Oscar), *Good Will Hunting*, *Chicago* (Best Picture Oscar), and *Gangs of New York*. After winning its Academy Award for Best Picture, *Chicago* became Miramax's highest-grossing release ever. Miramax also releases movies under its Dimension Films label. On September 30, 2005, the Weinsteins left Miramax to form their own new company, The Weinstein Company. Disney continued to run Miramax, as well as its own film library.

Misadventures of Chip 'n Dale, The (television) Rerun title of *The Adventures of Chip 'n Dale*.

Misadventures of Merlin Jones, The (film) Merlin Jones is the brightest young student at a small midwestern college. Possessing an extremely high IQ, he is head and shoulders above his fellow classmates, particularly in the field of scientific endeavor. Although admonished by his professor to proceed slowly, he is already applying the results of his research to not only the problems confronting the college, but also to assist some of his fellow students. His efforts as a do-gooder boomerang on all concerned, but eventually everything works out. The application of Merlin's meager knowledge of extrasensory perception and hypnotism results in some way-out hilarious involvements. Released on January 22, 1964. Directed by Robert Stevenson. 91 min. Stars Tommy Kirk (Merlin Jones), Annette Funicello (Jennifer), Leon Ames (Judge Holmby), Stuart Erwin (Capt. Loomis), Alan Hewitt (Prof. Shattuck), Connie Gilchrist (Mrs. Gossett). Features a musical hit for Annette in the form of the title song written by Richard M. Sherman and Robert B. Sherman. This teenage comedy was originally made as a two-parter for the Disney television show, but it turned out so well that Walt decided it deserved a theatrical release, and it was in fact so popular that it led to a sequel—*The Monkey's Uncle.* The film was reissued in 1972 and released on video in 1986.

Misery Loves Company (television) Half hour television series; premiered on Fox on October 1, 1995, and ended on October 23, 1995. Four men, whose dreams of youth have not survived to adulthood, still have their friendship despite divorces and failing marriages. Stars Dennis Boutsikaris (Joe), Christopher Meloni (Mitch), Julius Carry (Perry), Stephen Furst (Lewis), Wesley Jonathan (Connor), Nikki DeLoach (Tracy).

Misner, Terri One of the adult hosts on the *Mickey Mouse Club* on The Disney Channel from 1991 to 1994.

Miss Daisy Attraction opened in Mickey's Toontown at Disneyland on January 24, 1993. Donald's house is actually a boat named the *Miss Daisy*, which fits the nautical theme of a duck who wears a sailor suit.

Mission: SPACE Attraction in Future World at Epcot, taking the place of Horizons, sponsored by Hewlett Packard. Opened August 15, 2003. Guests find themselves 40 years in the future, where spaceflight is routine for ordinary citizens. After a quick course in spaceflight at the ISTC (International Space Training Center), the trainees have a briefing on their training mission and embark for Mars. They experience the sensations and sounds of a shuttle launch, including high g-forces (using centrifuge technology). During the mission, the team encounters challenges and each team member has a task to perform. When they return to Earth, guests move on to interactive experiences in the Advanced Training Lab.

Mission to Mars Updated Flight to the Moon attraction in Tomorrowland at Disneyland; opened on March 21, 1975, and closed on November 2, 1992. Also Tomorrowland attraction in Magic Kingdom Park at Walt Disney World; opened on June 7, 1975, and closed on October 4, 1993. After man set foot on the moon, the Flight to the Moon attraction was passé. Disney designers changed the destination to Mars several years later, and for a few months even utilized some film clips from the Disney television show *Mars and Beyond*, showing fantastic creatures that one might encounter on the red planet. The preflight show was fashioned after Mission Control, utilizing Audio-Animatronics figures.

Mission to Mars (film) In the year 2020, Luke Graham leads the first manned mission to Mars, but his crew is decimated by a catastrophic and mysterious disaster. A rescue mission, co-piloted by Commander Woody Blake and Jim McConnell, is hurriedly launched to investigate the tragedy and bring back any survivors. The astronauts face almost insurmountable dangers on their journey through space, and they make an amazing discovery when they finally reach the red planet. A Touchstone Picture. Directed by Brian De Palma. Released on March 10, 2000. Stars Gary Sinise (Jim McConnell), Don Cheadle (Luke Graham), Connie Nielsen (Terri Fisher), Jerry O'Connell (Phil Ohlmyer). Tim Robbins (Woody Blake), Armin Mueller-Stahl (Ray Beck). 113 min. Filmed in CinemaScope. Photography took place in and around Vancouver, British Columbia, with the Mars surface, at 55 acres, one of the largest sets ever built for a movie, constructed at the Fraser Sand Dunes. Some landscape elements were also filmed in Jordan and the Canary Islands. Released on video in 2000.

Mission Tortilla Factory Attraction at Pacific Wharf at Disney's California Adventure where guests can watch machines turning out tortillas and taste a sample. Sponsored by Mission Foods; opened on February 8, 2001.

Mrs. Beakley The nephews' governess in *Ducktales*; voiced by Joan Gerber.

Mrs. Caloway Regal, hat-wearing cow character in *Home on the Range*; voiced by Judi Dench.

Mrs. Judson Basil's housekeeper in *The Great Mouse Detective*; voiced by Diana Chesney.

Mrs. Jumbo Dumbo's mother.

Mrs. Peabody's Beach (film) Educational film teaching basic economics, produced by Dave Bell; released in 1972. A teenager uses his interest in surfing to create a profitable business, learning valuable lessons in economics.

Mrs. Potts Kindly enchanted teapot/ housekeeper in *Beauty and the Beast*; voiced by Angela Lansbury.

Mr. Boogedy (television) One-hour television movie; aired on April 20, 1986. Directed by Oz Scott. A family finds their new house is haunted by the ghost of a man who loved to leap out and yell "boogedy" at the local children. The family eventually manages to stop him by stealing his magic cloak. Stars Richard Masur, Mimi Kennedy, David Faustino, John Astin, Benjamin Gregory, Kristy Swanson, Howard Witt. See also *Bride of Boogedy*.

Mr. Destiny (film) Larry Burrows is certain that his ultraordinary life is the direct result of losing his high school championship baseball game. Twenty years later, a mysterious stranger, Mr. Destiny, comes along with the power to alter Larry's past. Now, instead of being married to his high school sweetheart, he is the rich husband of prom queen Cindy Jo, father of two spoiled brats, president of the company, and owner of the biggest house in town. And everybody hates him. Realizing that toying with destiny can lead to grave complications, Larry strives to extricate himself from the predicament. Released on October 12, 1990. Directed by James Orr. A Touchstone Picture. 110 min. Stars James Belushi (Larry Burrows), Linda Hamilton (Ellen Burrows), Michael Caine (Mike/Mr. Destiny), Jon Lovitz (Chip Metzler), Hart Bochner (Niles Pender). Filmed at the Biltmore Estate in Asheville, North Carolina. Released on video in 1991.

Mr. Duck Steps Out (film) Donald Duck cartoon; released on June 7, 1940. Directed by Jack King. Donald's frustration level is stretched to the limit when he attempts to court Daisy without the interference of his nephews.

Mr. Headmistress (television) Two-hour television movie; aired on *The Wonderful World of Disney* on March 15, 1998. A notorious con man dresses up as the headmistress of an all-girls boarding school in order to escape two dangerous thugs who are intent on collecting on a bad debt, and in the interim changes the lives of everyone he meets. Directed by James Frawley. Stars Harland Williams (Tucker), Shawna Waldron (Beryl), Duane Martin (Jim), Joel Brooks (Ferguson), Lori Hallier (Sally), Lawrence Dane (Rawlings), Conrad Dunn (Farley), Katey Sagal (Harriet Magnum). The 120-year-old Alma College in St. Thomas, Ontario, Canada, subbed for the fictional Rawlings School for Girls.

Mr. Holland's Opus (film) Glenn Holland is a music teacher who had dreams of composing a great symphony, but life got in the way. His dream was deferred and he came to regard himself as a failure. But, on his last day at Kennedy High School, after 30 years of instilling his vision and imagination into his students, Holland comes to realize that the true measure of a man's success can best be seen through the eyes of those he has aided and inspired. Each student thus became a note in a lasting composition—Mr. Holland's Opus—and they have come to honor their precious and underappreciated teacher. A Hollywood Pictures film from Interscope Communications/PolyGram Filmed Entertainment, in association with the Charlie Mopic Company. Released on January 19, 1996, after a December 29, 1995, release in Los Angeles for Academy Award consideration. Directed by Stephen Herek. Stars Richard Dreyfuss (Glenn Holland), Glenne Headly (Iris Holland), Jay Thomas (Bill Meister), Olympia Dukakis (Principal Jacobs), Alicia Witt (Gertrude Lang). The film was shot on location in and around Portland, Oregon, with Grant High School being the school location. Grant High's drama director brought in many current and former students, who won roles as dancers, musicians, and actors in the film. 145 min. Released on video in 1996.

Mr. Magoo (film) When a stolen and priceless ruby, the Star of Kuristan, lands in the possession of nearsighted millionaire Quincy Magoo, a sinister plot is hatched to steal it back. Perpetually the target of evil culprits, the elderly and bumbling curmudgeon Magoo manages to consistently escape unharmed, totally oblivious to the dangers that surround him. Hunted by robbers and set up by a conniving female thief, the sultry Luanne Leseur, Magoo ultimately nabs the villains with the help of his nephew, Waldo, and his trusty bulldog, Angus, and is hailed a hero. Released on December 25, 1997. Directed by Stanley Tong. Stars Leslie Nielsen (Mr. Magoo), Kelly Lynch (Luanne Leseur), Ernie Hudson (Gus Anders), Stephen Tobolowsky (Chuck Stupak), Nick Chin-

lund (Bob Morgan), Matt Keeslar (Waldo), Malcolm McDowell (Austin Cloquet). 87 min. Angus, Magoo's trusty companion, is an English bulldog, actually played by four different bulldogs, three female and one male, dyed with hair coloring to match each other. Based on the Mr. Magoo cartoons, which were released by UPA Productions beginning in 1949, first in theaters then in a long-running television series. Filming took place on location in Vancouver, British Columbia, Canada. Released on video in 1998.

Mr. Mouse Takes a Trip (film) Mickey Mouse cartoon; released on November 1, 1940. Directed by Clyde Geronimi. Mickey must do some quick thinking and don a few disguises to foil Pete, the train conductor, who wants him off the train for concealing Pluto.

Mr. St. Nick (television) Two-hour television movie; aired on *The Wonderful World of Disney* on November 17, 2002. Nick St. Nicholas, a philanthropist from Florida has a secret—he is the son of Santa Claus. Santa wants to retire and have his son take over, but Nick is too busy being scammed by a holiday charity with the help of a sexy but shady weathercaster, Heidi. Meanwhile, he has a growing affection for his outspoken Venezuelan cook, Lorena, who recognizes Heidi as a phony. Directed by Craig Zisk. Stars Kelsey Grammer (Nick), Charles Durning (Santa), Elaine Hendrix (Heidi Gardelle), Ana Ortiz (Lorena Braga), Brian Bedford (Jasper), Brian Miranda (Danny). Produced by Hallmark Entertainment, and released on video by them in 2003.

Mr. Smee Captain Hook's faithful first mate in *Peter Pan*; voiced by Bill Thompson.

Mr. Snoops Madame Medusa's bumbling assistant in *The Rescuers*; voiced by Joe Flynn. The character was patterned by animator Milt Kahl after author John Culhane.

Mr. 3000 (film) A middle-aged, retired baseball star's record of 3,000 career base hits is in jeopardy when three of those hits are disqualified. Reluctantly getting back into a Milwaukee Brewers uniform to pursue his goal, he rediscovers his love of the game, realizes the importance of teamwork and ethics, and, in the process, falls for a tough-minded sports reporter. A Touchstone Pictures/Spyglass Entertainment production. Released on September 17, 2004. Directed by Charles Stone III. Stars Bernie Mac (Stan Ross), Angela Bassett (Mo Simmons), Dondré T. Whitfield (Skillet), Evan Jones (Fryman), Michael Rispoli (Boca), Amaury Nolasco (Minadeo), Paul Sorvino (Gus Panas), Brian White (T-Rex Pennebaker), Ian Anthony Dale (Fukuda), Earl Billings (Lenny Koron), Chris Noth (Schembri). 103 min. The record of 3,000 career hits is so rare than only 25 men have ever achieved it. Released on video in 2005.

Mr. Toad See J. Thaddeus Toad.

Mr. Toad's Wild Ride Fantasyland attraction at Disneyland; opened on July 17, 1955. One of the original Disneyland dark rides, it was completely remodeled with the new Fantasyland in 1983, with the most obvious change being the exterior. It became Toad Hall itself, rather than just a pavilion from a medieval fair. Based on *The Adventures of Ichabod and Mr. Toad* (1949). Also Fantasyland attraction in Magic Kingdom Park at Walt Disney World; opened on October 1, 1971, and closed on September 7, 1998, being replaced by The Many Adventures of Winnie the Pooh. The Florida attraction featured two separate tracks.

Mr. Toad's Wild Ride (film) Video of an Allied Filmmakers 1996 live-action film originally entitled *The Wind in the Willows*, released on December 8, 1998. Mr. Toad has a passion for motorcars, but crashes every car he buys. In order to finance his mania, Toad has been selling land to the nefarious weasels. Mole, Rat, and Badger try to save their homes and Toad Hall from them. Stars Eric Idle (Rat), Steve Coogan (Mole), Terry Jones (Mr. Toad), Nicol Williamson (Badger). 87 min.

Mr. Wrong (film) Bright and sassy Martha Alston, a '90s woman, has an age-old problem—how to recognize Mr. Right when he comes along. A radio-talk show producer, Martha definitely gets her signals crossed when she suddenly meets Whitman Crawford, a handsome stranger with whom she instantly falls head over heels in love. However, she soon realizes she is dating a guy who is as right on the outside as he is wrong on the inside, and the ratings on this romance quickly plummet. Calamity prevails as she tries to pull the plug on her love life altogether. But Whitman proceeds to prove that too often dream dates become nightmares. A Touchstone Picture. Directed by Nick Castle. Released on February 16, 1996. Stars Ellen DeGeneres (Martha), Bill Pullman (Whitman), Joan Cusack (Inga), Dean Stockwell (Jack Tramonte), Joan Plowright (Mrs. Crawford), Peter White and Polly Holliday (Mr. and Mrs. Alston), Robert Goulet (Dick Braxton). 97 min. Principal photography took place in and around San Diego, where the story is set. Released on video in 1996.

Mitchell, George J. Former U.S. Senate Majority Leader, he was elected to the board of

The Walt Disney Company in 1995, became presiding director on December 3, 2002, and was elected chairman on March 3, 2004.

Mitchell, Keith See Keith Coogan.

Mitsukoshi Department Store In Japan in World Showcase at Epcot; opened on October 1, 1982. One of the larger stores in Epcot, selling Japanese clothing, crafts, toys, and souvenirs.

Mitsukoshi Restaurant In Japan in World Showcase at Epcot; opened on October 1, 1982. Features two areas—Tempura Kiku, where items are deep-fried in the tempura style, and Teppanyaki Dining Room, where the chef chops and stir-frys your food at the table, which usually seats several parties.

Mixed Nuts (television) Rerun title of *The Adventures of Chip 'n Dale*.

Miyazaki, Hayao As part of a distribution deal with the master Japanese animator, Buena Vista Home Video began distributing his films on video in the United States with *Kiki's Delivery Service* in 1998. Miramax released in theaters Miyazaki's *The Princess Mononoke* in 1999, and Disney released *Spirited Away* in 2002 (winning the Oscar for Best Animated Feature) and *Howl's Moving Castle* in 2005.

Mizner's Lounge Library lounge and bar at the Grand Floridian Resort & Spa at Walt Disney World.

MMC See Mickey Mouse Club.

Mobley, Mary Ann Actress; appeared on television in *The Secret of Lost Valley* and *My Dog, the Thief*.

Mobley, Roger Actor; appeared in *Emil and the Detectives* (Gustav) and *The Apple Dumpling Gang Rides Again* (Sentry #1), and on television in *For the Love of Willadean*, *The Treasure of San Bosco Reef*, and in the title role on the *Gallegher* series. After playing Gallegher, Mobley served as a paratrooper and worked in a Texas hospital before returning years later to the Disney Studio to play a bit part of a policeman in *The Kids Who Knew Too Much*. Mobley had actually made his very first Disney appearance on Talent Round-Up Day on the *Mickey Mouse Club*, as part of the Mobley Trio, on January 10, 1958.

Moby Duck Comic book character, one of the many distant relatives of Donald Duck, used only once on film, in the television show *Pacifically Peeking*. A seafarer, Moby Duck had his own comic book series starting in October 1967. He was introduced in a *Donald Duck* comic book, no. 112, in March 1967.

Model Behavior (television) Two-hour television movie on *The Wonderful World of Disney*, airing on March 12, 2000. Directed by Mark Rosman. Two teen girls with strikingly similar looks—one a glasses-wearing self-described geek, and the other a successful fashion model—trade places and turn their mutual lives topsy-turvy. Stars Maggie Lawson (Alex, Janine), Kathie Lee Gifford (Deirdre), Justin Timberlake (Jason). Kathie Lee's son, Cody, appears in the cameo role of Janine's precocious brother, Max. Based on the book *Janine & Alex, Alex & Janine* by Michael Levin. Released on video in 2000.

Modern Inventions (film) Mickey Mouse cartoon; released on May 29, 1937. The first cartoon directed by Jack King. While released as a Mickey cartoon, Mickey does not appear; Donald Duck is the star. A robotic butler continually takes Donald's hat when he doesn't want the butler to have it; Donald keeps pulling new hats out of thin air.

Modine, Matthew Actor; appeared in *Gross Anatomy* (Joe Slovak).

Molly Brown One of two steamboats in Frontierland at Disneyland Paris.

Mom for Christmas, A (television) Television movie; a young girl's Christmas wish magically comes true with the help of a department store mannequin. Aired on NBC on December 17, 1990. Directed by George Miller. 120 min. Stars Olivia Newton-John, Juliet Sorcey, Doug Sheehan, Carmen Argenziano.

Mom's Got a Date with a Vampire (television) A Disney Channel Original Movie; premiered on October 13, 2000. To get their divorced mother out of the house, Adam and Chelsea Hansen hatch a plot, setting her up on a date with Dimitri Dentatos, who just happens to be a vampire. When the kids learn the truth, they try to save their mother from becoming Dimitri's everlasting soul mate. Directed by Steve Boyum. Stars Caroline Rhea (Lynette Hansen), Charles Shaughnessy (Dimitri Dentatos), Matthew O'Leary (Adam), Laura Vandervoort (Chelsea), Myles Jeffrey (Taylor), Robert Carradine (Malachi Van Helsing).

Mondadori, Arnoldo (1889–1971) He secured the license for the Italian *Topolino* magazine in 1935 and continued to publish it throughout his career. He was presented a European Disney Legends award in 1997.

Monday Fun with Music Day on the 1950s *Mickey Mouse Club*. Who, What, Why, Where, When, and How Day on the new *Mickey Mouse Club*.

Money for Nothing (film) When unemployed longshoreman Joey Coyle finds a bag containing $1.2 million in unmarked, untraceable currency that has fallen off an armored truck, he attempts to keep it, only to find that the cash brings myriad unwanted problems. When dedicated detective Pat Laurenzi begins to close in, Joey and his girlfriend attempt to launder the money through an underworld leader, but even that goes awry, and Joey is soon forced to own up to his mistake. Released on September 10, 1993. Directed by Ramon Menendez. A Hollywood Picture. Filmed in CinemaScope. 100 min. Stars John Cusack (Joey Coyle), Debi Mazar (Monica Russo), Michael Madsen (Det. Laurenzi). Filmed on location in Pittsburgh and Philadelphia, Pennsylva-

nia. Joey Coyle, upon whose true-life exploits of finding a fortune on February 26, 1981, this film was based, died shortly before the release. Released on video in 1994.

Monk (television) One-hour television series about a brilliant but obsessive-compulsive private detective; premiered as a two-hour movie on USA Network on July 12, 2002. In an unusual move, it was then picked up by ABC for airing on the network after its cable airing (the first 13 episodes), beginning on August 13, 2002. Due to the tragic unsolved murder of his wife, Adrian Monk has developed an abnormal fear of germs, heights, crowds, and virtually everything else, which cost him his position as a legendary homicide detective on the San Francisco police force, and provides an unusual challenge to solving crimes, not to mention his day-to-day existence. Stars Tony Shalhoub (Adrian Monk), Bitty Schram (Sharona 2002–2004), Ted Levine (Capt. Stottlemeyer), Traylor Howard (Natalie Teeger 2005–). Produced by Mandeville Films in association with Touchstone Television. Tony Shalhoub won an Emmy for Best Actor in a Comedy Series in 2003 and 2005.

Monkey Melodies (film) Silly Symphony cartoon; released on September 26, 1930. Directed by Burt Gillett. Monkeys and other jungle animals sing and dance. A boy and girl monkey continue their romance despite being threatened by an alligator, hippo, snake, and leopard.

Monkeys Monkeys, primarily chimpanzees, were popular for a number of years in Disney features, including *The Barefoot Executive*; *The Misadventures of Merlin Jones*; *The Monkey's Uncle*; *Monkeys, Go Home!*; *Moon Pilot*; *Swiss Family Robinson*; *Toby Tyler*; and *Lt. Robin Crusoe, U.S.N.*

Monkeys, Go Home! (film) A young American, Hank Dussard, inherits a large olive farm in Provence, France. Labor is too costly to harvest the olives, so Hank trains four chimpanzees to do the job, and thus incurs the wrath of the villagers. Eventually, the American foils a local labor leader, wins the girl he loves, and the olives are harvested. Released on February 2, 1967. Directed by Andrew V. McLaglen. Based on the book *The Monkeys* by G. K. Wilkinson. 101 min. Stars Dean Jones (Hank Dussard), Maurice Chevalier (Father Sylvain), Yvette Mimieux (Maria Riserau), Bernard Woringer (Marcel Cartucci), Clement Harari (Emile Paraulis), Yvonne Constant (Yolande Angelli), Darlene Caar (Sidoni Riserau). For the filming at the Walt Disney Studio, a grove of olive trees was planted near the Studio's Animation Building. It remained for years until the space was needed for the Studio's expansion. The film featured the song "Joie de Vivre" by Richard M. Sherman and Robert B. Sherman, which was sung by Chevalier and Darleen Carr. Released on video in 1987.

Monkey's Uncle, The (film) Young Merlin Jones, the legal uncle of his chimpanzee Stanley, devises a "sleep learning" machine to sharpen his "nephew's" intellect. When Midvale College footballers Norm and Leon are in danger of being scrubbed from the team due to poor grades, Merlin produces his sleep-learning machine and the two muscle-bound students soon stun all on campus by walking off with straight A's. After drinking a strength potion and using it to prove man-powered flight in his bicycle-driven contraption in order to gain an endowment for the school from a "crazy" but rich philanthropist, Darius Green, Merlin settles down knowing that football is forever secure at Midvale. Released on June 23, 1965. Directed by Robert Stevenson. 90 min. Stars Tommy Kirk (Merlin Jones), Annette Funicello (Jennifer), Leon Ames (Judge Holmby), Frank Faylen (Mr. Dearborne), Arthur O'Connell (Darius Green III), Leon Tyler (Leon), Norman Grabowski (Norman). The film featured the popular title tune sung by Annette and the Beach Boys, written by Richard M. Sherman and Robert B. Sherman. Released on video in 1986.

Monorail Tomorrowland attraction at Disneyland; opened on June 14, 1959. It was the first daily operating monorail in the country, and was originally known as the Disneyland-Alweg Monorail System, with Alweg being the German company that aided in its design. The Monorail first glided on its beam around Tomorrowland, but it was extended, with new style Mark II trains, to the Disneyland Hotel in 1961. At this time, it was the first monorail in the country to actually cross a public street, and it became more of a transportation system than a theme park ride, serving to deliver hotel guests directly into the park and vice versa. Mark III trains were added in 1968. The Mark IV train was designed in 1971 for Walt Disney World. Mark V trains, at 137 feet long, made their debut in 1986–88. In the 1970s, Disney started a Community Transportation division to market the clean-running and dependable monorails and people-movers to cities, but the only installation was a people-mover at the Houston Intercontinental Airport. Later, the technology was licensed to Bombardier, Inc. At Walt Disney World, a Monorail transportation system, larger in scale, opened on October 1, 1971, connecting the main Ticket and Transportation Center at the parking lot with several of the hotels and the Magic Kingdom. A separate line was built all the way from the Ticket and Transportation Center to Epcot on June 1, 1982.

Monsanto Hall of Chemistry Display in Tomorrowland at Disneyland from July 17, 1955 until September 19, 1966.

Monsanto House of the Future Modernistic house on display in Tomorrowland at Disneyland from June 12, 1957 until December 1967. Built of plastics, the four-winged, cantilevered house featured the latest in furniture and appliances, along with intercoms and other gadgets that were uncommon in the homes of the time. By 1967, the future had caught up with the house, so preparations were made to tear it down. But, it was so well built that when the wrecker's ball struck the house, it merely bounced off. Eventually, the demolition experts had to take their saws and crowbars and pry the place apart piece by piece.

Monsieur D'Arque Fawning head of the lunatic asylum in *Beauty and the Beast*; voiced by Tony Jay.

Monster Sound Show Attraction at Disney-MGM Studios; opened on May 1, 1989. Four audience members are selected to act as Foley artists and add eerie sounds to a creepy comedy film starring Martin Short as a deranged butler who tries to do in insurance salesman Chevy Chase. In the postshow area called Soundworks, guests can create their own sound effects, add their voices to classic movies, and enter the three-dimensional world of Soundsations. Presented by Sony. Adjacent are two state-of-the-art radio broadcast studios, from which stations can air their shows. In July 1997, the attraction became One Saturday Morning, with the film changed to animated offerings from ABC. It was changed again in April 1999, to ABC Sound Studio: Sounds Dangerous, starring Drew Carey.

Monsters, Inc. (film) Monsters, Incorporated is the largest scare factory in the monster world, and James P. (Sulley) Sullivan is one of its top Scarers. Sullivan is a huge, intimidating monster with blue fur, large purple spots, and horns. His Scare Assistant, best friend, and roommate is Mike Wazowski, a green, opinionated, feisty, little one-eyed monster. Visiting from the human world is Boo, a tiny girl, who goes where no human has ever gone before. A Walt Disney Picture, from Pixar Animation Studios. Directed by Pete Docter. Released on November 2, 2001. Voices include John Goodman (James P. [Sulley] Sullivan), Billy Crystal (Mike Wazowski), James Coburn (Henry J. Waternoose), Jennifer Tilly (Celia), Steve Buscemi (Randall Boggs), Mary Gibbs (Boo), John Ratzenberger (Yeti), Bonnie Hunt (Ms. Flint). 92 min. A computer-animated production with a breakthrough achievement being the depiction of hair and fur, which has the shadowing, density, lighting, and movement consistent with the real thing. Music is by Randy Newman. Released with the Pixar animated short *For the Birds* (2000), which won an Oscar for Best Animated Short. *Monsters, Inc.* won the Oscar for Best Song, "If I Didn't Have You," written by Randy Newman, and was nominated for Original Score, Sound Effects Editing, and Animated Feature Film. Released on video in 2002, it became the top-selling title of the year.

Monsters Inc. Mike & Sulley to the Rescue! Attraction in Hollywood Pictures Backlot at Disney's California Adventure; opened to guests in December 2005, with a grand opening in January 2006. Guests boarding a Monstropolis taxicab discover that something is wreaking havoc on the city—a little girl named Boo has escaped into Monstropolis and, without knowing it, is terrorizing the monsters. Friendly monsters Mike and Sulley are determined to get Boo home before any harm comes to her. The attraction took the place of the short-lived Superstar Limo.

Monsters of the Deep (television) Television show; aired on January 19, 1955. Directed by Hamilton S. Luske, Peter Godfrey. Walt discusses historical and mythical monsters, including a look at *20,000 Leagues Under the Sea* and its squid. He also covers dinosaurs, sea serpents, and whales.

Monstro The gigantic whale in *Pinocchio*.

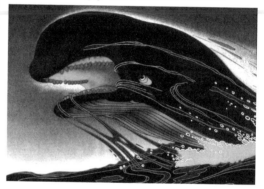

Montalban, Ricardo Actor; appeared on television in *Zorro*.

Monte Sleepwalking pelican in *The Pelican and the Snipe* (1944).

Monterey Jack Sidekick of Chip and Dale in *Chip 'n' Dale's Rescue Rangers*; voiced by Jim Cummings.

Monty (television) Television series on Fox; aired from January 11 to February 15, 1994. A conservative talk show host, Monty Richardson, is a politically incorrect man of the nineties whose opinions are constantly challenged by his liberal-minded wife and children. Stars Henry Winkler (Monty Richardson), Kate Burton (Fran Richardson), David Schwimmer (Greg Richardson), China Kantner (Geena Campbell), David Krumholtz (David Richardson), Tom McGowan (Clifford Walker), Joyce Guy (Rita Simon).

Monty City mouse in *The Country Cousin* (1936).

Moochie of Pop Warner Football (television) Two-part television show; aired on November 20 and 27, 1960. Directed by William Beaudine. Episode titles are *Pee Wees Versus City Hall* and *From Ticonderoga to Disneyland*. Moochie joins a Pop Warner Football team, but has troubles with the mayor's son. When the two make amends, they help the team win and go to the Disneyland Bowl, and get to enjoy a visit to the park. Stars Kevin Corcoran, Dennis Joel, Reginald Owen, John Howard, Alan Hale, Jr., Frances Rafferty. Walt Disney appears in a cameo role in the Disneyland segment.

Moochie of the Little League (television) Two-part television show; aired on October 2 and 9, 1959. Directed by William Beaudine. A young newspaper boy who is on a Little League team works hard to persuade an elderly Englishman, with whom he had a previous run-in, to donate land for a baseball diamond. Stars Kevin Corcoran, Reginald Owen, Alan Hale, Jr., Stuart Erwin, Frances Rafferty, Lee Aaker, Annette Gorman. Sixteen mm release as *Little League Moochie*.

Moody, Ron Actor; appeared in *Unidentified Flying Oddball* (Merlin), and played the same role in *A Kid in King Arthur's Court* years later.

Moon Pilot (film) Richmond Talbot, a young space scientist, is tricked into volunteering for a space trip to the moon. On a last visit to see his mother he is contacted by Lyrae, a messenger from a planet off in space. They know everything and want to help America get there before the Russians. The FBI moves in when Lyrae makes contact, but she slips through their hands. After a series of comical experiences that confound and confuse the Air Force and the FBI, Lyrae winds up in the space capsule in the arms of Richard, culminating the romance that was gathering impetus as the story unfolded. Instead of going to

the moon, they detour to her planet, Beta Lyrae, to meet her folks. Released on February 9, 1962. Directed by James Neilson. 98 min. Stars Tom Tryon (Capt. Richmond Talbot), Brian Keith (Gen. Vanneman), Dany Saval (Lyrae), Tommy Kirk (Walter Talbot), Edmond O'Brien (McClosky), Bob Sweeney (Sen. McGuire), and a mischievous chimp named Cheeta (Charlie). This was the Studio's first feature film about outer space. The songs, written by the Richard M. Sherman and Robert B. Sherman, were "Seven Moons of Beta Lyrae," "True Love's an Apricot," and "The Void." This was Tom Tryon's only Disney feature film, after a long run as Texas John Slaughter on the Disney television series, as well as director Neilson's first of several directing efforts for the Disney Studio. Released on video in 1986.

Mooncussers, The (television) Two-part television show; aired on December 2 and 9, 1962. Directed by James Neilson. Based on Iris Vinton's book, *Flying Ebony*. Episode titles are *Graveyard of Ships* and *Wake of Disaster*. Pirates prey on unsuspecting ships in the 1840s off Long Island, luring them to run aground, but the son of a shipowner and the locals try to outwit them. Stars Oscar Homolka, Kevin Corcoran, Robert Emhardt, Joan Freeman, Erin O'Brien-Moore, Dub Taylor. It won an Emmy for art direction.

Mooney, Andy Joined Disney as president of Consumer Products (coming from Nike) in December 1999; promoted to chairman in May 2003.

Moonlight Mile (film) Joe Nast, recovering from the death of his fiancée, tries to be the perfect would-be son-in-law to Ben and Jojo, while falling in love with another woman. Joe learns to let go and discovers that love comes in the most unexpected circumstances. Directed by Brad Silberling. Limited release on September 27, 2002, with an expanded release on October 4. Stars Jake Gyllenhaal (Joe Nast), Dustin Hoffman (Ben Floss), Susan Sarandon (Jojo Floss), Holly Hunter (Mona Camp), Ellen Pompeo (Bertie Knox), Richard T. Jones (Ty), Allan Corduner (Stan Michaels), Dabney Coleman (Mike Mulcahey). 117 min. Filmed in CinemaScope. Massachusetts towns such as Gloucester and Marblehead filled in for the fictional Cape Anne in the movie. Working title was *Goodbye Hello*. Released on video in 2003.

Moon-Spinners, The (film) On vacation in Greece, an English woman and her young niece, Nikky, stumble into the midst of intrigue involving a young Englishman and jewel thieves who have hidden their loot in the vicinity of the tourist hotel. The young people survive a series of dangerous escapades with desperately serious criminals who try twice to kill. Determination and ingenuity eventually save the day and the youth not only clears his name, but wins the affection of a much-in-love young English lady. Released on July 2, 1964. Directed by James Neilson. 119 min. Based on Mary Stewart's best-selling novel. Stars Hayley Mills (Nikky Ferris), Eli Wallach (Stratos), Pola Negri (Madame Habib), Peter McEnery (Mark Camford), Joan Greenwood (Aunt Frances), Irene Papas (Sophia). Pola Negri, the famous silent film star who had not made a film in over 20 years, was personally coaxed out of retirement by Walt Disney to appear as the treacherous Madame Habib. This was Peter McEnery's Disney film debut, the success of which landed him the title role in *The Fighting Prince of Donegal*. The film features gorgeous on-location photography in Crete by Paul Beeson, and a memorable musical score by Ron Grainer. "The Moon-Spinners Song" was written by Terry Gilkyson. Released on video in 1985.

Moore, Bob (1920–2001) Publicity artist; joined Disney in 1940 in the animation department, but soon moved into the marketing division. He became advertising art director in 1951, a position he held for three decades. He is noted for

designing the 1968 U.S. Disney postage stamp (with Paul Wenzel), and the Eagle Sam character for the Los Angeles Summer Olympics, as well as movie posters, and murals for a number of Walt Disney schools. Moore was one of the artists whom Walt Disney authorized to sign his name, and, being an artist, he could copy it quite well. He was named a Disney Legend in 1996.

Moore, Demi Actress; appeared in *The Scarlet Letter* (Hester Prynne) and *G.I. Jane* (Jordan O'Neil), and voiced Esmeralda in *The Hunchback of Notre Dame*.

Moore, Dudley (1935–2002) Actor; appeared in *Blame It on the Bellboy* (Melvyn Orton).

Moore, Fred (1911–1952) Animator; joined Disney in 1930, and worked on the pigs in *Three Little Pigs*. He is credited with work on *Snow White and the Seven Dwarfs* and with updating Mickey Mouse's appearance in the late 1930s. He served as animator or directing animator for most of the animated features from *Snow White* to *Peter Pan*. He is noted for his work on such characters as the Dwarfs, Lampwick, Timothy, Katrina, and Mr. Smee, giving appeal and charm to his characters. He was named a Disney Legend posthumously in 1995.

Moorehead, Agnes (1906–1974) Actress; appeared in *Pollyanna* (Mrs. Snow), and on television in *The Strange Monster of Strawberry Cove*.

Moose Hunt, The (film) Mickey Mouse cartoon; released on May 3, 1931. The first cartoon where Pluto is known by that name. In their misadventures on a moose hunt, Mickey accidentally shoots Pluto, who only pretends to be harmed, and when the pair are later chased by a moose over a cliff, Pluto saves the day by flying with his ears. Directed by Burt Gillett.

Moose Hunters (film) Mickey Mouse cartoon; released on February 20, 1937. Directed by Ben Sharpsteen. In their search for a moose, Goofy and Donald dress up as a female moose to lure a potential victim. But their plans go too far and

they soon are running for their lives with Mickey not far behind.

Moranis, Rick Actor; appeared as Wayne Szalinski in *Honey, I Shrunk the Kids* and *Honey, I Blew Up the Kid*, and at Epcot in *Honey, I Shrunk the Audience.*

More, Kenneth (1914–1982) Actor; appeared in *Unidentified Flying Oddball* (King Arthur).

More About the Silly Symphonies (television) Television show; aired on April 17, 1957. Directed by Clyde Geronimi. Walt presents a series of Silly Symphonies, explaining how many of them are based on early folktales and stories.

More Kittens (film) Silly Symphony cartoon; released on December 19, 1936. Directed by Dave Hand. In this sequel to *Three Orphan Kittens*, the turned-out kittens seek shelter with a St. Bernard and have more misadventures with a turtle, a bird, and some milk.

Moreno, Rita Actress; appeared on television in episodes of *Zorro.*

Morgan, Harry Actor; appeared in *The Barefoot Executive* (E. J. Crampton), *Scandalous John* (Hector Pippin), *Snowball Express* (Jesse McCord), *Charley and the Angel* (angel), *The Apple Dumpling Gang* (Homer McCoy), *The Cat from Outer Space* (General Stilton), and *The Apple Dumpling Gang Rides Again* (Major Gaskill), and on television in *14 Going on 30.*

Morocco Pavilion in World Showcase at Epcot; opened on September 7, 1984. The first country to be added to World Showcase after its opening. Native craftsmen were brought over to create the intricate tile work, mosaics, and carved plaster throughout the pavilion. This is also the first and only pavilion to have a country as its sponsor, so besides the Restaurant el Marrakesh and the bazaars and shops offering Moroccan crafts, jewelry, clothing, baskets, and brasswork, there is an information center for the Moroccan National Tourist Office.

Morpheus God of night in the *Pastoral* segment of *Fantasia.*

Morris, Matt Actor; appeared on the *Mickey Mouse Club* on The Disney Channel, beginning in 1991.

Morris, the Midget Moose (film) Special cartoon; released on November 24, 1950. Directed by Jack Hannah. Morris is the laughingstock of

the whole moose herd because he is so small but has a full set of antlers. Everything changes, however, when he meets another outcast moose, Balsam, who is huge but has only puny antlers. The two become a great pair, and by getting up on Balsam's back and using his antlers, Morris and Balsam are able to defeat the leader of the herd. Released on video in 1988.

Morrow, Richard T. Attorney; general counsel of the company for many years. He was on the board of directors from 1971 to 1984.

Morrow, Rob Actor; appeared in *Last Dance* (Rick Hayes) and *Quiz Show* (Dick Goodwin).

Morrow, Vic (1932–1982) Actor; appeared in *Treasure of Matecumbe* (Spangler), and on television in *The Ghost of Cypress Swamp.*

Morse, Robert Actor; appeared in *The Boatniks* (Ensign Garland).

Mortensen, Viggo Actor; appeared in *Crimson Tide* (Weps), *G.I. Jane* (Master Chief), and *Hidalgo* (Frank T. Hopkins).

Mortimer Mouse According to legend, Walt Disney had originally wanted to name his mouse star Mortimer, but Mrs. Disney objected and suggested Mickey instead; Disney later used a character named Mortimer Mouse as *Mickey's Rival* (1936).

Morty and Ferdy Mickey Mouse's nephews, first appeared in the Mickey Mouse comic strip on September 18, 1932 (where Ferdie had a different spelling). Their only film appearance was in *Mickey's Steamroller*, in 1934.

Mosby Raiders, The (television) Television show; part 2 of *Willie and the Yank*.

Mosby's Marauders (film) Foreign theatrical release of *Willie and the Yank* television episodes. First released in England in May 1967. 80 min. Released on video in 1987.

Moteurs . . . Action! Stunt Show Spectacular Unique live stunt show featuring cars, motorbikes, and Jet Skis, presented at Walt Disney Studios Paris; opened on March 16, 2002. The action takes place in a 3,000-seat theater facing a Mediterranean-style village complete with shops, street stalls, and cafés, bordering a market square. A similar production, Lights, Motors, Action! Extreme Stunt Show, opened at Disney-MGM Studios at Walt Disney World in May 2005.

Moth and the Flame (film) Silly Symphony cartoon; released on April 1, 1938. Directed by Burt Gillett. A boy and girl moth run away to live in an old costume shop, where the girl is caught by an cruel flame. Only by calling on the aid of his friends can the boy moth save her.

Mother Goose Goes Hollywood (film) Silly Symphony cartoon; released on December 23, 1938. Directed by Wilfred Jackson. Pages from "Mother Goose" come alive with famous motion picture stars, including W. C. Fields, Katharine Hepburn, Spencer Tracy, and Eddie Cantor, caricatured as nursery rhyme characters.

Mother Goose Melodies (film) Silly Symphony cartoon; released on April 16, 1931. Directed by Burt Gillett. The Mother Goose characters come to life to entertain Old King Cole with their nursery rhymes.

Mother Goose Rock 'n' Rhyme (television) A hip musical-comedy retelling of familiar nursery rhymes. A Disney Channel Premiere Film, first aired on May 19, 1990. 77 min. Pat Field won an Emmy Award for costume design. Stars Shelley Duvall (Little Bo Peep), Harry Anderson (Pied Piper), Cyndi Lauper (Mary Had a Little Lamb), Bobby Brown (Three Blind Mice), Art Garfunkel (Georgie Porgie), Teri Garr (Jill of Jack and Jill), Paul Simon (Simple Simon), Woody Harrelson (Lou the Lamb), Deborah Harry (The Old Woman Who Lived in a Shoe), Little Richard (Old King Cole), Howie Mandel (Humpty Dumpty), Cheech Marin (the carnival baker).

Mother Pluto (film) Silly Symphony cartoon; released on November 14, 1936. Directed by Wilfred Jackson. When a family of baby chicks hatch in his doghouse, Pluto feels duty-bound to protect them, despite the many hazards that continue to appear.

Mother's Courage, A: The Mary Thomas Story (television) Two-part television show; aired on December 3 and 10, 1989. Directed by John Patterson. The story of Detroit Pistons basketball star, Isiah Thomas, and the struggles of Isiah's mother in raising him. It takes all her power, and the death of a buddy, to convince him to get out of the local street gang. When he becomes athlete of the year, he publicly thanks his mother for her never-ending confidence in him. Emmy Award winner for Individual Achievement for a Children's Program. Stars Alfre Woodard, A. J. Johnson, Leon, Garland Spencer, Chick Vennera, Larry O. Williams, Jr.

Motion Dance club with the latest videos shown on a massive screen; opened at Downtown Disney Pleasure Island at the Walt Disney World Resort on May 12, 2001.

Motor Boat Cruise Fantasyland attraction at Disneyland; opened in June 1957 and closed on January 11, 1993, with the area becoming Fantasia Gardens. In 1991 (March 15 to November 10) it was redecorated to become a special Motor Boat Cruise to Gummi Glen. This attraction was popular with children, who enjoyed piloting their crafts around the waterways under the Autopia bridges and Monorail beams, but adults found it pretty tame.

Motor Mania (film) Goofy cartoon; released on June 30, 1950. Directed by Jack Kinney. Goofy portrays both the roles of a normal family man, Mr. Walker, who becomes a monster, and Mr. Wheeler, behind the wheel of his car. He changes back to a mild pedestrian attempting to cross the street, only to revert back once again behind the

wheel. This cartoon has long been a favorite one in driver's training classes.

Motocrossed (television) A Disney Channel Original Movie; premiered on February 2, 2001. Motocross is a hot topic for 15-year-old twins Andrew and Andrea Carson, but their father wants Andrea to stick with more feminine pursuits. When Andrew is injured, Andrea sets up a scheme to pose as her brother in an all-important race that's just days away, and into which her father has sunk the family's finances. But she did not reckon with her father finding out or her falling for a fellow competitor. Directed by Steve Boyum. Stars Alana Austin (Andrea Carson), Mary-Margaret Humes (Geneva Carson), Trevor

O'Brien (Andrew Carson), Timothy Carhart (Edward Carson), Scott Terra (Jason Carson), Michael Cunio (Rene Cartier), Riley Smith (Dean Talon). The motocross track used in the film was Barona Oaks, located on an Indian reservation in eastern San Diego County in Southern California. Released on video in 2002.

Mountain Born (television) Television show; aired on January 9, 1972. Directed by James Algar. A boy learns the duties of a shepherd from his idol, the ranch foreman, high in the Colorado mountains. When the foreman becomes ill, the boy has to take the sheep into the mountains where they will graze for the summer season. A fierce storm almost causes tragedy as the boy leads the sheep back home. Stars Sam Austin, Walter Stroud, Jolene Terry.

Mouse Club, The With the growth in interest in the collecting of Disneyana, collectors enjoyed getting together to share stories and buy and sell items for their collections. The Mouse Club was the first major club to begin, in 1980, originally run by Ed and Elaine Levin. The primary activity of the Mouse Club was an annual convention held at a hotel in Anaheim in the summer. In 1985, Kim and Julie McEuen led the club to ever-larger convention events, until its final one was held in 1993. The Mouse Club, along with other Disneyana groups, was not sponsored by Disney; their logo was a certain mouse unrecognizable because it had a paper bag over its head. The Mouse Club is no longer in operation.

Mouse Factory, The (television) Syndicated television series produced and directed by Ward Kimball; aired for two seasons beginning January 26, 1972. There were 43 shows, each featuring classic Disney animated cartoons tied to the appearance of a guest star host or hostess in a specially produced live-action sequence. For example, Jo Anne Worley hosted a show about horses, Jonathan Winters one about space travel, and Bill Dana one about bullfighting. The other hosts were Wally Cox, Pat Buttram, Pat Paulsen, Dom DeLuise, Charles Nelson Reilly, Skiles & Henderson, Johnny Brown, Don Knotts, Phyllis

Diller, John Byner, Jim Backus, Joe Flynn, Harry Morgan, Dave Madden, Henry Gibson, Kurt Russell, John Astin, Nipsey Russell, Shari Lewis, Ken Berry, and Annette Funicello. Shows were 30 min.

Mouse Gear See Centorium.

Mousecar Award, created in the 1940s, consisting of a bronze-colored figure of Mickey Mouse, used by the Disney company to honor its employees and those who have done a service to the company. The name is a reference to the motion picture academy's Oscar. In 1973, at the time of the company's 50th anniversary, special Mouse-cars were given to every employee at the Disney Studio who had worked at the Hyperion Studio—naming them members of the exclusive Hyperion Club. The Donald Duck equivalent to the Mousecar is known as the Duckster.

Mousegetar The original Mousegetar was built specially for Jimmie Dodd to use on the *Mickey Mouse Club* show. It was a four-string instrument, which Jimmie called a tenor guitar. Mattel produced and sold toy versions of the Mousegetar in the late 1950s. The original Mousegetar was donated to the Walt Disney Archives by Jimmie's widow, Ruth Dodd Braun, in the 1980s.

Mousekartoon The final segment of each 1950s *Mickey Mouse Club* show. The Mouseketeers would open the treasure mine and introduce the showing of a Disney cartoon.

Mouseketeer Reunion, The (television) Television show; aired on November 23, 1980. Directed by Tom Trbovich. The original Mouseketeers come back for the 25th anniversary, hosted by Paul Williams. When it was announced to the wire services that the company had found all except 4 of the original 39 Mouseketeers, the story went out and in less than 24 hours the missing "mice" had been found—one in Winnipeg, and the other three nearby in Southern California.

Mouseketeers A total of 39 talented kids originally performed on the 1950s *Mickey Mouse Club*; there were 24 regulars the first season. The 39 Mouseketeers were Nancy Abbate, Don Agrati, Sherry Alberoni, Sharon Baird, Billie Jean Beanblossom, Bobby Burgess, Lonnie Burr, Tommy Cole, Johnny Crawford, Dennis Day, Eileen Diamond, Dickie Dodd, Mary Espinosa, Bonnie Lynn Fields, Annette Funicello, Darlene Gillespie, Judy Harriet, Cheryl Holdridge, Linda Hughes, Dallas Johann, John Lee Johann, Bonni Lou Kern, Charley Laney, Larry Larsen, Cubby O'Brien, Karen Pendleton, Paul Petersen, Lynn Ready, Mickey Rooney, Jr., Tim Rooney, Mary Lynn Sartori, Bronson Scott, Michael Smith, Jay-Jay Solari, Ronald Steiner, Margene Storey, Mark Sutherland, Doreen Tracey, Don Underhill. The adult leaders were Jimmie Dodd and Roy Williams, aided occasionally by Bob Amsberry.

There were 12 Mouseketeers on the new *Mickey Mouse Club* (1977–1978): Billy "Pop" Attmore, Scott Craig, Nita Dee, Mindy Feldman, Angel Florez, Allison Fonte, Shawnte Northcutte, Kelly Parsons, Julie Piekarski, Todd Turquand, Lisa Whelchel, Curtis Wong.

The latest version of the *Mickey Mouse Club* on The Disney Channel (1989–1994) added 34 additional kids to the Mouseketeer list, though they were not actually called Mouseketeers: Josh Ackerman, Christina Aguilera, Lindsey Alley, Rhona Bennett, Nita Booth, Mylin Brooks, Brandy Brown, Blain Carson, J.C. Chasez, Braden Danner, Nikki DeLoach, T.J. Fantini, Albert Fields, Dale Godboldo, Ryan Gosling, Tiffini Hale, Chase Hampton, Roqué Herring, David Kater, Tony Lucca, Ricky Luna, Tate Lynche, Deedee Magno, Jennifer McGill, Terra McNair, Ilana Miller, Jason Minor, Matt Morris, Kevin Osgood, Damon Pampolina, Keri Russell, Britney Spears, Justin Timberlake, Marc Worden. Adult leaders were Fred Newman and Mowava Pryor, with the latter succeeded by Terri Misner in 1991.

Mouseketeers at Walt Disney World, The (television) Television show; aired on November 20, 1977. Directed by John Tracy. The kids from the new *Mickey Mouse Club* head for Florida to do a show. They set up camp at Fort Wilderness, and visit the new River Country. Because of several misadventures, their chaperone has a difficult time keeping them all friends. Stars Jo Anne Worley, Ronnie Schell, Dennis Underwood, the Mouseketeers.

Mousercise (television) Aerobics show on The Disney Channel; premiered on April 18, 1983, starring Kellyn Plasschaert, with Steve Stark and Garett Pearson. 60 episodes.

Mouseterpiece Theater (television) Series of Disney cartoon shows on The Disney Channel; hosted by George Plimpton à la Alistair Cooke on PBS's *Masterpiece Theater*, premiered on April 18, 1983. There were 60 episodes prepared.

Move Along Mustangers (television) Television show; episode 7 of *Elfego Baca*.

Moving Day (film) Mickey Mouse cartoon; released on June 20, 1936. Directed by Ben Sharpsteen. When the sheriff, Pete, evicts them from their home due to overdue rent, Mickey and

Donald get Goofy, an ice man, to help them move out. Soon all is pandemonium with Goofy's struggles with a piano that will not stay in the moving truck and Donald wrestling with various household items. The house is utterly destroyed when Pete strikes a match near a gas leak, resulting in all the belongings being blown into the truck as they drive away.

Mowgli Boy raised by wolves in *The Jungle Book*; voiced by Bruce Reitherman.

Mucha, Zenia She became senior vice president of corporate communications for The Walt Disney Company in May 2002. She had originally joined ABC as senior vice president of communications in February 2001.

Mufasa Lion ruler, and father of Simba, in *The Lion King*; voiced by James Earl Jones.

Mulan (film) Based on a 2,000-year-old Chinese folktale, this animated feature is the story of a young, high-spirited girl who tries hard to please her parents and be the perfect daughter, but who feels that she is always disappointing them. When Mulan's aged father is called to certain death in war, her bold spirit compels her to save his life by disguising herself as a man and joining the Chinese army in his place. Brought to life by Mulan's extraordinary actions, a feisty, flimflam "guardian" dragon, Mushu, joins the heroine's quest and leads her into a series of comic misadventures. At the height of their success, their masquerade unravels and they are banished far, far away from home. When all seems lost, Mulan's irrepressible spirit spurs her once again to courageously fight against all odds, defeat the terrible Hun invaders, and save the Emperor, bringing honor to her beloved parents. Released on June 19, 1998. There was a world premiere at the Hollywood Bowl on June 5. Directed by Barry Cook and Tony Bancroft. Voices include Ming-Na Wen (Mulan speaking), Lea Salonga (Mulan singing), B.D. Wong (Shang speaking), Donny Osmond (Shang singing), Eddie Murphy (Mushu), Miguel Ferrer (Shan-Yu), Harvey Fierstein (Yao), Gedde Watanabe (Ling), Jerry Tondo (Chien-Po), June Foray (Grandmother Fa). 88 min. Five new songs by Matthew Wilder and David Zippel—"Honor to Us All," "Reflection," "I'll Make a Man Out of You," "A Girl Worth Fighting For," and "True to Your Heart." Jerry Goldsmith provided the underscore. *Mulan* was the first feature to be primarily produced at the Disney Feature Animation studio at the Walt Disney World Resort in Florida. In order to prepare the filmmakers for the task, a select group of the film's artistic supervisors made a three-week trip to China to sketch and photograph the intriguing sites, and soak up the culture. Then, under the direction of production designer Hans Bacher, they found a unique look for the film, inspired by the simple graphic style of traditional Chinese art. Released on video in 1999.

Mulan II (film) Direct-to-video animated film premiering on February 1, 2005. Mulan receives a marriage proposal from General Shang, making everyone happy except Mushu, who tries to keep Mulan single on learning he'll lose his guardian job if she marries. With China threatened by a mongol invasion, the emperor calls upon Mulan, Shang, and their lovable "gang of three" friends, Yao, Ling, and Chien-Po, to escort his daughters to arranged marriages with vital allies in the northern provinces. When the three princesses unexpectedly fall in love with the gang of three, Mulan decides to help them, even though this contradicts the emperor's orders and calls Mulan's relationship with Shang into question. Mulan remains true to her heart, however, by solving the problem in her own unique way, saving both the princesses and China. Directed by Darrell Rooney and Lynne Southerland. Voices include Ming-Na (Mulan), Pat Morita (Emperor), B.D. Wong (Shang), Mark Moseley (Mushu), Lucy Liu (Mei), Harvey Fierstein (Yao), Sandra Oh (Ting Ting), Gedde Watanabe (Ling), Lauren Tom (Su), Jerry Tondo (Chien-Po), George Takei (First Ancestor), Michelle Kwan (Shopkeeper), Lea Salonga (singing voice of Mulan).

Mule Pack Frontierland attraction at Disneyland; open from July 17, 1955, to February 1, 1956. Became Rainbow Ridge Pack Mules (1956–1959) and Pack Mules Through Nature's Wonderland (1960–1973). Walt Disney insisted that mules be a part of his Frontierland, even though they were ornery animals that would often nip the guests or refuse to move. Disney felt that they helped give the necessary ambience to the western theme. As new attractions were added to Frontierland, there was more to view while riding the mules.

Mulholland Madness Attraction at Paradise Pier at Disney's California Adventure; opened on February 8, 2001. A mini–roller coaster ride as vehicles careen across a crazy map of the Hollywood Hills and Santa Monica Mountains.

Mulligan, Richard (1932–2000) Actor; appeared on television in *The Deacon Street Deer*, and on the series *Empty Nest*, for which he won the Emmy Award for Best Lead Actor in a Comedy Series in 1989. He provided the voice of Einstein in *Oliver & Company*.

Multiplane camera Camera which gave depth to an animated film by use of layers of backgrounds painted on glass; first used in *The Old Mill* (1937) but used most effectively in the features of the 1940s, such as *Pinocchio*, *Fantasia*, and *Bambi*. It was the invention of Disney staff members under William Garity, and its creators received a special Scientific and Technical–category

Academy Award. The vertical camera stand could hold up to six background layers. Ub Iwerks, who had left the Disney Studio several years earlier, created his own version of a multiplane camera at his studio about the same time, but it was a horizontal arrangement.

Mumford (film) A psychologist named Dr. Mumford hangs out his shingle in a small town that also happens to be named Mumford and begins dispensing no-nonsense advice to an array of quirky locals. Included are a shop-by-mail-addicted housewife, an eccentric young billionaire, and a mild-mannered pharmacist with delusions of lascivious grandeur. Dr. Mumford's unique style of therapy has a surprising effect on the community, sparking romance in some of the most unlikely places. A Touchstone Picture. Directed by Lawrence Kasdan. Released on September 24, 1999. Stars Loren Dean (Mumford), Hope Davis (Sofie Crisp), Mary McDonnell (Althea Brockett), Ted Danson (Jeremy Brockett), Martin Short (Lionel Dillard), David Paymer (Dr. Ernest Delbanco), Alfre Woodard (Lily), Pruitt Taylor Vince (Henry Follett), Jane Adams (Dr. Phyllis Sheeler), Jason Lee (Skip Skipperton). 112 min. Since no one town had all the elements required by the producers to pass for the town of Mumford, they filmed in a total of eleven California locations—St. Helena, Healdsburg, Santa Rosa, Petaluma, Sebastopol, Calistoga, Napa, Guerneville, Sonoma, Kenwood, and Tomales. Filmed in CinemaScope. Released on video in 2000.

Mumford, David (1956–2003) Designer; joined WED Enterprises in 1979 as a show-set draftsman working on The Land at Epcot. He later worked on show set design for several attractions before becoming show producer for Star Tours at Tokyo Disneyland and Aladdin's Oasis at Disneyland. As a Disney aficionado, he became an unofficial historian at Walt Disney Imagineering, writing a number of articles and speaking at Disneyana Conventions with his colleague Bruce Gordon. Together Mumford and Gordon wrote the book *Disneyland: The Nickel Tour.*

Mumy, Bill Actor; appeared in *Rascal* (Sterling), and on television in *For the Love of Willadean* and *Sammy, the Way-out Seal.*

Muncey English sheepdog who appears in *The New Neighbor* (1953).

Munro, Janet (1934–1972) Actress; appeared in *Swiss Family Robinson* (Roberta), *Darby O'Gill and the Little People* (Katie O'Gill), and *Third Man on the Mountain* (Lizbeth Hempel), and on television in *The Horsemasters.*

Muppet Christmas Carol, The (film) Musical version of the Dickens tale about a miserly, unsympathetic old man who learns the true meaning of Christmas with the visitation of three spirits—of Christmases past, present, and future. Enacted by Jim Henson's Muppets, with Kermit the Frog as Bob Cratchit and Miss Piggy as his faithful wife. The Great Gonzo narrates the tale as Charles Dickens himself, with the aid of a hungry rat named Rizzo. Released on December 11, 1992. From Jim Henson Productions. Directed by Brian Henson. 86 min. Stars the Muppets along with Michael Caine as Ebenezer Scrooge. Made at Shepperton Studios, London, England. Released on video in 1993.

Muppet Treasure Island (film) Young Jim Hawkins is given a treasure map by a mysterious sailor, and he sets sail with his pals, Gonzo and Rizzo, on a high-seas adventure. Joining them on the expedition is the Squire Trelawney (Fozzie Bear), the dashing Captain Smollett (Kermit), and the mutinous Long John Silver. When Silver and his crew seize the map and take Jim hostage, it is up to Captain Smollett and his men to come to the rescue. But, first, who will rescue *them* from a tribe of native warthogs, ruled by their queen, Benjamina Gunn (Miss Piggy)? Directed by Brian Henson. Released on February 16, 1996. Stars Tim Curry (Long John Silver), Kevin Bishop (Jim Hawkins), Billy Connolly (Billy Bones), Jennifer Saunders (Mrs. Bluveridge). 99 min. The film was shot over fourteen weeks on seven stages at Shepperton Studios outside London. Released on video in 1996.

Muppet* Vision 3D See *Jim Henson's Muppet* Vision 3D.*

Muppets While working with Jim Henson on the production *Jim Henson's Muppet* Vision 3D,* Disney announced an agreement with Henson to acquire the merchandise, licensing, and publishing rights to the Muppets on August 29, 1989. How-

ever, estate tax problems encountered by Henson's heirs after his unexpected passing in May 1990, caused them to end the deal in December of that year. Finally, four years later, in April 2004, Disney was able to complete an acquisition of the Muppet properties and *Bear in the Big Blue House*.

Muppets at Walt Disney World, The (television) Television show; aired on May 6, 1990. Directed by Peter Harris. Kermit and his friends go to Paradise Swamp in Florida, and then decide to visit the nearby Walt Disney World. They visit many of the attractions, and Mickey Mouse welcomes Kermit as an old friend. Stars Charles Grodin, Raven-Symoné.

Muppets Celebrate Jim Henson, The (television) Television special; a tribute to the Muppet creator. Aired on CBS on November 21, 1990. Directed by Don Mischer. 60 min. Stars Harry Belafonte, Carol Burnett, Ray Charles, John Denver, Steven Spielberg, Frank Oz. The special won an Emmy for Editing of a Miniseries or Special (Multi-Camera Production).

Muppets on Location—The Days of Swine and Roses Live show at Disney-MGM Studios; began on September 16, 1991, and ended on January 23, 1994.

Muppets' Wizard of Oz, The (television) In this fun, contemporary take on a family classic, featuring the Muppets, Dorothy Gale is a teenager with dreams of showbiz that seem far from coming true in the Kansas trailer park where she lives. When she's transported to the magical land of Oz, she and her sidekick, Toto, join the Scarecrow, the Tin Thing, and the Lion to fight the Wicked Witch of the West and find the Wizard who might make her a star. Television movie on ABC; aired on May 20, 2005. Produced by Touchstone Television. Directed by Kirk R. Thatcher. Stars Ashanti (Dorothy), Queen Latifah (Auntie Em), David Alan Grier

(Uncle Henry), Jeffrey Tambor (Wizard). Miss Piggy plays the four witches (two good and two bad), Kermit is the Scarecrow, The Great Gonzo is the Tin Thing, and Fozzie Bear is the Lion. Based on the novel *The Wonderful Wizard of Oz* by L. Frank Baum.

Murder She Purred: A Mrs. Murphy Mystery (television) Two-hour television movie; aired on *The Wonderful World of Disney* on December 13, 1998. Mystery-solving postmistress Mary Minor Haristeen, known to her friends as Harry, has two remarkable pets, a cat named Mrs. Murphy and a Welsh corgi named Tucker, whose detective skills are every bit as keen as her own. When Harry gets mixed up with a man who may be involved in a murder, Mrs. Murphy and Tucker do some snooping on their own. Directed by Simon Wincer. Stars Ricki Lake (Harry), Blythe Danner (Mrs. Murphy), Anthony Clark (Tucker), Linden Ashby (Blair Bainbridge). Based on a novel by Rita Mae Brown. Released on video in 2000.

Murphy, Eddie Actor; appeared in *The Distinguished Gentleman* (Thomas Jefferson Johnson), *Metro* (Scott Roper), *Holy Man* (G), and *The Haunted Mansion* (Jim Evers), and provided the voice for Mushu in *Mulan* and on television for Thurgood Stubbs in *The PJs*.

Murphy, Thomas S. Member of the Disney board of directors from February 9, 1996 to March 3, 2004.

Murray, Bill Actor; appeared in *What About Bob?* (Bob Wiley), *Ed Wood* (Bunny Breckinridge), *Rushmore* (Mr. Blume), *Cradle Will Rock* (Tommy Crickshaw), *The Royal Tenenbaums* (Raleigh St. Clair), and *The Life Aquatic with Steve Zissou* (Steve Zissou).

Murray, Don Actor; appeared on television in *Brand New Life* and *Justin Morgan Had a Horse*.

Murray, Ken (1903–1988) Actor; appeared in *Son of Flubber* (Mr. Hurley) and *Follow Me, Boys!* (Melody Murphy).

Murry, Paul (1911–1989) Comic strip artist; known primarily for his work on the Mickey Mouse comic books.

Mushu Dragon character in *Mulan*; voiced by Eddie Murphy.

Music Music has been an important part of Disney films ever since *Steamboat Willie*. The Silly Symphony series was built around musical themes, and the animated features, beginning with *Snow White and the Seven Dwarfs*, carefully integrated music into the plots. Disney songs were released on sheet music, beginning in 1930 with "Minnie's Yoo Hoo." "Who's Afraid of the Big Bad Wolf" in 1933, from *Three Little Pigs*, was the most popular song to come out of a short cartoon. Practically all of the songs from *Snow White* made it onto the hit parade, and with "When You Wish Upon a Star," Disney songs began receiving Oscar honors. *Snow White* was the first feature film to have a sound track album. Television contributed to the Disney song catalog, with "The Ballad of Davy Crockett" and "The Mickey Mouse Club March" perhaps the most popular. In 1949, Disney established its own Walt Disney Music Company, and soon began releasing its own records. Storyteller albums were introduced, and eventually cassettes and CDs. The establishment of Hollywood Records in 1990 represented a move into the field of contemporary music, primarily unrelated to Disney films. Mammoth Records and Lyric Street Records were added as new labels in 1997.

Music for Everybody (television) Television show; aired on January 30, 1966. Directed by Hamilton S. Luske. Ludwig Von Drake studies the importance of music in people's lives, utilizing sequences from *Melody Time*, *Make Mine Music*, and the "Clair de Lune" sequence originally planned for *Fantasia*. For a 1970 rerun, the latter sequence was deleted to include footage from *Sleeping Beauty*, then having a theatrical reissue.

Music Land (film) Silly Symphony cartoon; released on October 5, 1935. Directed by Wilfred Jackson. In this innovative cartoon; a war between the Land of Symphony and the Isle of Jazz is the background for this musical tale in which Romeo and Juliet–type characters finally help bring about peace and the Bridge of Harmony is established. All the characters are musical instruments, with the "dialogue" furnished in musical sounds.

Music Land (film) A grouping of selected shorts from *Make Mine Music* and *Melody Time*, released by RKO on October 5, 1955.

Music Man, Meredith Willson's The (television) Three-hour presentation of the classic musical; aired on *The Wonderful World of Disney* on February 16, 2003. Matthew Broderick stars as Professor Harold Hill, the charming, fast-talking con man who stops off in River City, Iowa, hoping to make a killing selling band instruments and uniforms for the local kids. The town librarian sees through his scam, but falls in love with him. Directed by Jeff Bleckner. Also stars Kristin Chenoweth (Marian Paroo), Victor Garber (Mayor Shinn), Debra Monk (Mrs. Paroo), Molly Shannon (Eulalie MacKechnie Shinn), David Aaron Baker (Marcellus Washburn), Cameron Monaghan (Winthrop). *The Music Man*, starring Robert Preston as Harold Hill, was a huge hit when it opened on Broadway in 1957, winning six Tony awards. Preston reprised his role in the 1962 film version, which starred Shirley Jones as Marian. Released on video in 2003.

Musical Christmas at Walt Disney World, A (television) Television special; aired on ABC (60 min.) on December 18, 1993. Directed by Jeff Margolis.

Musical Farmer (film) Mickey Mouse cartoon; released on July 9, 1932. Directed by Wilfred Jackson. Mickey and Pluto chase away crows eating their seeds and then wear the scarecrow to tease Minnie. This leads to a musical extravaganza with all the farmyard animals taking part. One of the hens, who has been unable to lay eggs, lays an enormous egg. Mickey takes a picture but uses too much powder, exploding all the feathers off the hens.

Musker, John Animator/director; joined Disney in 1977 where he animated on *The Small One*, *The Fox and the Hound*, and *The Black Cauldron*. He worked on the story of the latter film. He co-directed, with  Ron Clements, *The Great Mouse Detective*, *The Little Mermaid*, *Aladdin*, *Hercules*, and *Treasure Planet*. He left Disney in 2004.

Musse Pigg Swedish name for Mickey Mouse.

Mustang! (television) Two-part television show; aired on October 7 and 21, 1973. Directed by Roy Edward Disney. A Mexican boy saves an injured wild mustang and attempts to train him, but the spirited horse resists. Stars Charles Baca, Flavio Martinez, Ignacio Ramirez.

Mustang Man, Mustang Maid (television) Television show; episode 8 of *Elfego Baca*.

My Adventures in Television See *Wednesday 9:30 (8:30 Central)*.

My Boyfriend's Back (film) A teen, Johnny Dingle, plots a fake robbery so he can "rescue" a pretty girl, Missy, and get a chance to take her out on a date. When the staged robbery turns out to be a real one, Johnny only manages to protect Missy by getting himself shot. But, before he dies, she promises him that elusive date. Now, even death cannot stop Johnny. He comes back as a zombie, and with the help of his parents, who are willing to adapt to his new flesh-eating ways, and a mad doctor, who attempts to find other ways to keep him alive, Johnny does at last manage to go out with Missy. Despite the help he receives, however, he decomposes, and dies once again. But due to a heavenly error, it is found he should not have died at all, so he is brought back to life and to Missy, who has fallen in love with him. Released on August 6, 1993. Directed by Bob Balaban. A Touchstone Picture. 85 min. Stars Andrew Lowery (Johnny), Traci Lind (Missy), Bob Dishy (Murray), Paul Dooley (Big Chuck), Danny Zorn (Eddie), Edward Herrmann (Mr. Dingle), Cloris Leachman (Mrs. Dingle), Austin Pendleton (Dr. Bronson), Jay O. Sanders (Sheriff McCloud), Paxton Whitehead (Judge in heaven). Much of the film was shot in and around Austin, Texas. Released on video in 1994.

My Date with the President's Daughter (television) Two-hour television movie; aired on *The Wonderful World of Disney* on April 19, 1998. Duncan Fletcher, a somewhat shy high school junior, meets a girl at the mall and asks her to the school's spring dance. She agrees, but what he does not know is that she is Hallie Richmond, the daughter of the president of the United States. After picking her up at 1600 Pennsylvania Avenue and the requisite meeting of parents, Duncan is really flustered, and becomes even more so when Hallie tells him the only way they will have fun is to ditch the Secret Service agents. Directed by Alex Zamm. Stars Dabney Coleman (President Richmond), Will Friedle (Duncan Fletcher), Elisabeth Harnois (Hallie Richmond), Mimi Kuzyk (Caroline Richmond), Wanda Cannon (Rita Fletcher), Jay Thomas (Charles Fletcher). Ron Reagan, Jr., plays a cameo role as the White House security guard. Released on video in 2000.

My Dog, the Thief (television) Two-part television show; aired on September 21 and 28, 1969. Directed by Robert Stevenson. A helicopter traffic reporter, Jack Crandall, finds a stowaway St. Bernard, and while he is horrified, the station director and the listening audience is delighted.

After he sneaks the dog, which he names Barabbas, into his rooming house, he discovers the dog is a kleptomaniac. One of the items he steals is a valuable necklace, and the jewel thieves are now after Jack. He eventually manages to capture them and save the day. Stars Dwayne Hickman, Mary Ann Mobley, Elsa Lanchester, Joe Flynn, Roger C. Carmel, Mickey Shaughnessy.

My Family Is a Menagerie (television) Television show; aired on February 11, 1968. A young widow who has a way with animals moves to Northern California and is asked to care for the local strays. A wreck of a circus truck sets a menagerie of circus animals free, and she has to use all her wits to catch them. Only a leopard eludes her, and he is befriended by a local renegade dog. Eventually she is able to trap them and she trains them to be in her animal act. Stars Ann Harrell, Jack Garrity, Kathy Thorn. Narrated by Rex Allen.

My Father the Hero (film) A 14-year-old girl, Nicole, is not happy to be going on a vacation on a tropical island with her dad, André; she is angry at him for being away for so long, and mortified at the thought of spending two weeks with him amongst her peers. But then along comes Ben, a sexy young man whose good looks and charm spin Nicole into impetuous, adolescent love. Determined to impress her boyfriend, Nicole gets carried away with a scheme to attract his attention by appearing sophisticated and alluring. She fabricates an elaborate tale about her life, including the idea that André is really her lover and an international spy, masquerading as her father. Nicole sets in motion a comedy of errors and confusion that wreaks havoc on her budding romance as well as her father's reputation. But Ben eventually does indeed find her more attractive than the indifferent, fickle girls he is used to. Released on February 4, 1994. Directed by Steve Miner. A Touchstone Picture, produced by Cité Films/Film par Film/D.D. Productions, in association with the Edward S. Feldman Company. 90 min. Stars Gérard Depardieu (André), Katherine Heigl (Nicole), Dalton James (Ben), Lauren Hutton (Megan), Faith Prince (Diana). Filmed at Ocean Club, Paradise Island Resort, Nassau, Bahamas. Released on video in 1994.

My Favorite Martian (film) When a Martian's spacecraft accidentally crash lands on Earth, ambitious television reporter Tim O'Hara visualizes his upcoming fame at breaking what he sees as the story of the century. The Martian takes human form and poses as Tim's Uncle Martin. Hoping to repair his ship for a return to Mars, he systematically thwarts all of Tim's attempts to divulge the truth. Eventually the two become friends and decide to work together to outwit scientists who have discovered the Martian's existence. Released on February 12, 1999. Directed by Donald Petrie. Stars Jeff Daniels (Tim O'Hara), Christopher Lloyd (the Martian/Uncle Martin), Elizabeth Hurley (Brace Channing), Daryl Hannah (Lizzie), Wallace Shawn (Coleye Epstein). 93 min. Based on the 1963–66 television series that starred Ray Walston and Bill Bixby. Walston returned for a role (Armitan) in the new movie. Filming took place in Santa Barbara and other areas of Southern California. Released on video in 1999.

My Life as a Babysitter (television) Serial on the *Mickey Mouse Club* on The Disney Channel; aired from October 15 to November 9, 1990. A young man is saddled with babysitting a bratty kid. Stars Jim Calvert (Nick Cramer), Kelli Williams (Kelly), Shane Meier (Ben), Michele Abrams (Jennifer Edwards), Sean Patrick Flannery (Mitch Buckley).

My Science Project (film) High school senior Michael Harlan and his best friend, Vince, must put together a passing science project in two weeks in order to graduate. With the deadline rapidly approaching, Michael risks the wrath of armed military guards and stages a midnight raid on a nearby U.S. Air Force supply dump. They discover a mysterious instrument that can cause a space-time warp. Michael's teacher is sucked into a cosmic whirlpool, and the device madly drains power from the school and then the surrounding city. Michael and his friends try to stop the device, while fighting everything from a Neanderthal man, mutants, gladiators, and Egyptian queens to Vietcong soldiers. Finally, the kids are able to shut off the device and return it to the supply dump. Released on August 9, 1985. Directed by Jonathan Betuel. A Touchstone Picture. 95 min. Stars John Stockwell (Michael Harlan), Danielle Von Zerneck (Ellie Sawyer), Fisher Stevens (Vince Latello), Raphael Sbarge (Sherman), Dennis Hopper (Bob Roberts), Richard Masur (Det. Isadore Nulty), Barry Corbin (Lew Harlan), Ann Wedgeworth (Dolores). The film was shot at the Walt Disney Studio in Burbank and at local Southern California locations, including Van Nuys High School, Alhambra High School, and Portola Highly Gifted Magnet School. The final two weeks of production consisted of night shooting in Tucson, Arizona, where key sequences were filmed amid a thousand acres of decommissioned military aircraft. The elaborate special effects included a Tyrannosaurus rex, which was a complex puppet built and animated by Doug Beswick Productions, Inc. Matte paintings, special lighting effects, miniature photography, and effects animation were also used. The title song, "My Science Project," was written by Bob Held, Michael Colina, and Bill Heller and performed by The Tubes. Released on video in 1986.

My Town (television) Television show; aired on May 25, 1986. Development threatens a small town. Stars Glenn Ford, Meredith Salenger. Directed by Gwen Arner.

My Wife and Kids (television) Half-hour television series; premiered on ABC on March 28, 2001, and ended on August 9, 2005. Michael Kyle, a modern-day man, loving husband, and traditional father, is at the center of his household, ruling with his own distinctive parenting style. Stars Damon Wayans (Michael Kyle), Tisha Campbell-Martin (Janet Kyle), George O. Gore II (Jr. Kyle), Jazz Raycole (Claire Kyle), Parker McKenna Posey (Kady Kyle).

Myhers, John (1921–1992) Actor; appeared in *Now You See Him, Now You Don't* (golfer), *Snowball Express* (Mr. Manescue), *Treasure of Matecumbe* (Captain Boomer), and *The Shaggy D.A.*

(Admiral Brenner), and on television in *The Ghosts of Buxley Hall.*

Mystères du Nautilus, Les *Nautilus* walk-through attraction in Discoveryland in Disneyland Paris; opened on July 4, 1994.

Mysteries of the Deep (film) Documentary featurette; released on December 16, 1959. Production associate Ben Sharpsteen. In this Oscar-nominated short, a submerged reef is the home of many strange creatures of the sea. We see mating, birth, and development of the young into adults, with the laws of nature being fulfilled as the battle for survival goes continually on. One of the shorts in which Walt Disney's nephew Roy E. Disney wrote the narration, photographed by, among others, H. Pederson. 24 min.

Mystery, Alaska (film) Completely isolated by glaciers and vast snowy mountains, the residents of the little town of Mystery are experts at one sport—hockey played on the glacier. The weekly hockey game has become a ritual celebration attended with religious devotion. However, an article in a sports magazine prompts the NHL to send the New York Rangers to challenge these local heroes, and the publicity stunt threatens to change the way of life in Mystery forever. Directed by Jay Roach. Released on October 1, 1999. Stars Russell Crowe (John Biebe), Hank Azaria (Charles Danner), Mary McCormack (Donna Biebe), Lolita Davidovich (Mary Jane Pitcher), Ron Eldard (Skank Marden), Colm Meaney (Scott Pitcher), Maury Chaykin (Bailey Pruitt), Michael McKean (Walsh), Judith Ivey (Joanne Burns), Burt Reynolds (Walter Burns). 119 min. The town of Mystery was built from scratch for the production at the site of a former strip coal mine near Canmore, Alberta. Filmed in CinemaScope. Released on video in 2000.

Mystery in Dracula's Castle, The (television) Two-part television show; aired on January 7 and 14, 1973. Directed by Robert Totten. Two bored kids in a vacation town get involved with thieves when they try to make their own horror movie. They find a stray dog, who brings them a stolen necklace, which they use in their movie. The thieves are then after the kids, but after a series of misadventures they are captured, and the kids finish their movie. Stars Clu Gulager, Mariette Hartley, Johnny Whitaker, Scott Kolden, Mills Watson, John Fieldler, James Callahan, Gerald Michenaud.

Mystery of Edward Sims, The (television) Two-part television show; aired on March 31 and April 7, 1968. Directed by Seymour Robbie. The cub reporter, Gallegher, becomes involved in a land fraud, when some valueless land is sold to a group of Cornish immigrants. A murder implicates one of the immigrants, and it is up to Gallegher to prove that a local resident is actually the murderer and the swindler is a local banker. Stars Roger Mobley, John McIntire, John Dehner, Warren Oates, John McLiam, Jeanette Nolan, Ray Teal. See *Gallegher* for other television shows about the cub reporter.

Mystery of Rustler's Cave, The (television) Serial on the new *Mickey Mouse Club*; aired from February 1 to March 1, 1977. Stars Kim Richards, Robbie Rist, Christian Juttner, Bobby Rolofson, Tony Becker, Ted Gehring, Lou Frizzel, Bing Russell, Dennis Fimple. Directed by Tom Leetch. A motorcycle enthusiast and his sister join with three visiting city kids to chase cattle rustlers.

Mystery of the Applegate Treasure, The (television) Hardy Boys serial on the *Mickey Mouse Club*. 20 episodes.

N

Nabbe, Tom As Disneyland's youngest cast member, he began work there in July 1955 as a "newsie" on Main Street before being selected by Walt Disney to portray Tom Sawyer on Tom Sawyer Island in 1956. Later he worked on other attractions, transferring to Walt Disney World in 1971. He retired in 2003 as manager of distribution services for the Florida resort. He was named a Disney Legend in 2005.

Naboombu Island kingdom ruled by King Leonidas in *Bedknobs and Broomsticks*.

Naismith, Laurence (1908–1996) Actor; appeared in *Third Man on the Mountain* (Teo Zurbriggen), *Greyfriars Bobby* (Mr. Traill), and *The Three Lives of Thomasina* (Rev. Angus Peddie), and on television in *The Prince and the Pauper*.

Najimy, Kathy Actress; appeared in *Sister Act* and *Sister Act 2: Back in the Habit* (Sister Mary Patrick), *Hocus Pocus* (Mary), *It's Pat* (Tippy), on Disney Channel in *Scream Team* (Mariah), on video in *The Jungle Book: Mowgli's Story* (voice of Chil), and in The ExtraTerrestrial Encounter at Walt Disney World (Dr. Femus).

Nala Lioness friend of Simba's in *The Lion King*; voiced by Niketa Calame (young) and Moira Kelly (adult).

Nana Dog nursemaid in the Darling house in *Peter Pan*.

Nanula, Richard He went to work at Disney in 1986 as a senior planning analyst. He was named vice president and treasurer in 1989, senior vice president and chief financial officer in 1991, and executive vice president in 1994. In November 1994, he was named worldwide president of The Disney Store. In February 1996 he was promoted to senior executive vice president as chief financial officer of The Walt Disney Company. He left the company on May 31, 1998.

Napier, Alan (1903–1988) He voiced Sir Pelinore in *The Sword in the Stone*, and appeared on television in *The Golden Dog* (Archie).

Napoleon Dog in *The Aristocats*; voiced by Pat Buttram.

Napoleon and Samantha (film) Upon the death of his grandfather, a young boy inherits a full-grown African lion, who is really a gentle pet. It is impossible to keep the lion in a small town, so the boy and his young girlfriend head for the mountains with the lion to find him a safe home. The trek leads to excitement and danger before all ends happily. Released on July 5, 1972. Directed by Bernard McEveety. 91 min. Stars Johnny Whitaker (Napoleon), Jodie Foster (Samantha), Michael Douglas (Danny), Will Geer (Grandpa), Arch Johnson (Chief of Police), Henry Jones (Mr. Gutteridge). This was Jodie Foster's movie debut. Producer Winston Hibler discovered the beautiful scenery utilized in this film in the Strawberry Mountains wilderness area of eastern Oregon. The rugged 33,000 acres of unspoiled terrain contains the largest stand of Ponderosa pines in the world. Filming also took place in the adjoining picturesque historic gold country towns of John Day and Canyon City. The lion, Major, a 500-pound, 16-year-old, was a film veteran, having appeared in Tarzan movies with Mike Henry and in a television series with Ron Ely. Academy Award nomination for Original Score by Buddy Baker. Released on video in 1986.

Narcoossee's Restaurant in the Grand Floridian Resort & Spa at Walt Disney World; opened on June 28, 1988. Octagon-shaped, it sits near the boat dock and from its open kitchen serves a variety of grilled fare.

Nash, Clarence "Ducky" (1904–1985) Voice of Donald Duck from the character's beginning with *The Wise Little Hen* in 1934 until 1985. Nash did Donald's voice in over 150 shorts and television shows, including dubbing the voice in

foreign languages. He made extensive promotional appearances, including a cross-country trip in 1984 for Donald's 50th anniversary. He was named a Disney Legend posthumously in 1992.

Nashville Coyote, The (television) Television show; aired on October 1, 1972. Directed by Winston Hibler. A surprised coyote stowaway on a freight train ends up in Nashville, where he meets a friendly beagle and an aspiring songwriter. The songwriter is unable to sell his songs, so he returns to California, taking the coyote back to his desert home. Stars Walter Forbes, William Garton, Eugene Scott, Michael Edwards. Narrated by Mayf Nutter.

National Car Rental Operated a locker area on Town Square at Disneyland from 1980 to 1990. The locker area was formerly operated by Bekins and later Global Van Lines.

National Fantasy Fan Club (NFFC) A group of Disney collectors and enthusiasts broke away from the Mouse Club in 1984 and began their own club, called the National Fantasy Fan Club, later shortened to the NFFC. It has operated as a nonprofit organization, not sponsored by Disney, with regular conventions held in Anaheim around the birthday of Disneyland each July, beginning in 1985. In 1993, a mini-convention was added in January. The NFFC publishes a regular newsletter and has chapters all over the country.

National Film Registry The United States Government, through the Library of Congress, has each year since 1989 named 25 films it deems as "culturally, historically, or aesthetically important." Five Disney films have been added to the Registry: *Snow White and the Seven Dwarfs* in 1989, *Fantasia* in 1990, *Pinocchio* in 1994, *Steamboat Willie* in 1998, and *Beauty and the Beast* in 2002.

National Student Fire Safety Test, The (film) Educational film; released in September 1979. The film covers the basics of fire prevention in humorous fashion.

National Student First Aid Test, The (film) Educational film; released in September 1979. The film provides reinforcement of basic first aid procedures.

National Student Recreational Safety Test, The (film) Educational film; released in September 1979. Young people should be aware of their environment while they play.

National Student School Safety Test, The (film) Educational film; released in September 1979. Some school safety precautions do not always occur to youngsters.

National Student Traffic Safety Test, The (film) Educational film; released in September 1979. The film instructs young people on safety habits out on the street.

National Treasure (film) A patriotic, third-generation treasure-hunter, Benjamin Franklin Gates has spent his life searching for a great treasure that no one believed existed. Our Founding Fathers left clues to the treasure's location right before our eyes—from our nation's birthplace, to the nation's Capitol, to clues buried within the symbols on the dollar bill. Gates's journey takes him to the last place anyone thought to look, on the back of the Declaration of Independence. But what he thought was the final clue is only the beginning. Joining with two friends, he realizes that in order to protect the legendary treasure, he must now do the unthinkable: steal the most revered, best-guarded document in American history before it falls into the wrong hands. In a race against time, Gates must elude the FBI, stay one step ahead of a ruthless adversary, decipher the remaining clues, and unlock the mystery behind our greatest national treasure. A Jerry Bruckheimer Films production. Released on November 19, 2004. Directed by Jon Turteltaub. Stars Nicolas Cage (Benjamin Franklin Gates), Jon Voight (Patrick Gates), Justin Bartha (Riley Poole), Diane Kruger (Abigail Chase), Sean Bean (Ian Howe), Harvey Keitel (Sadusky), Christopher Plummer (John Adams Gates). 131 min. Filmed in Super 35-Scope by award-winning cine-matographer Caleb Deschanel. Filming took place at many of the countriy's most hallowed historical sites, including the Library of Congress, Lincoln Memorial, and DAR Building in Washington, and Independence Hall, The Franklin Institute, the Reading Terminal Market, Philadelphia City Hall, and Pine Street Church Cemetery in Philadelphia. Because of ongoing renovations at the National Archives, the filmmakers had to build extensive sets based on reality. Released on video in 2005.

Nature of Things, The—The Camel (film) Jiminy Cricket tells the story of the camel for the *Mickey Mouse Club*; later released in 16mm for schools (June 1956).

Nature of Things, The—The Elephant (film) Jiminy Cricket uses animation and live action to tell the story of the elephant on the *Mickey Mouse Club*; later released in 16mm for schools (June 1956).

Nature's Better Built Homes (television) Television show; aired on March 2, 1969. Directed by Ward Kimball, Hamilton S. Luske. Ranger J. Audubon Woodlore hosts a look at beavers, birds, squirrels, bees, and other animals, with cartoon and live-action film clips. Narrated by Olan Soulé.

Nature's Charter Tours (television) Television show; aired on April 28, 1968. Directed by Hamilton S. Luske. Ranger J. Audubon Woodlore looks at migration, using footage from *White Wilderness* and *Seal Island*.

Nature's Half Acre (film) True-Life Adventure featurette; released on July 28, 1951. Directed by James Algar; photographed by Murl Deusing and eight other photographers; music by Paul Smith; narrated by Winston Hibler. Academy Award winner for Best Two-Reel Short Subject. 33 min. The film tells the story of the amazing amount of life to be found each season in almost any small plot of ground and the way nature maintains her balance in the "grass-roots" world of insects and their ever-present fight for survival. The time-lapse photography by John Nash Ott is particularly notable. Originally released in the United States with *Alice in Wonderland*.

Nature's Strangest Creatures (film) Featurette; released on March 19, 1959. Produced by Ben Sharpsteen. Filmed in Australia by Alfred and Elma Milotte. Since Australia broke from the Asiatic mainland many eons ago, it has developed a unique and exotic population of wildlife, free from outside influences. Such creatures as the giant bat, the duck-billed platypus, kangaroos, wallabies, and the bush-tailed possum pursue their business of survival in this isolated land where nature has preserved a sanctuary for the strangest of its creatures. 16 min.

Nature's Strangest Oddballs (television) Television show; aired on March 29, 1970. Directed by Les Clark, Hamilton S. Luske. Professor Ludwig Von Drake looks at animals who have not changed greatly over the years, such as the platypus, iguana, koala, and anteater. The story of *The Cold-Blooded Penguin* from *The Three Caballeros* and *Goliath II* are also shown.

Nature's Wild Heart (film) Educational film; two city children spend a summer in the Canadian wilderness and learn some of the wonders of the natural world. Released in November 1973. The film is from the television program *Wild Heart*.

Nature's Wonderland See *Mine Train Through Nature's Wonderland*.

Natwick, Grim (1890–1990) Animator; known for designing Betty Boop before coming to Disney in 1934. He specialized in the development of female characters, including animating Snow White in *Snow White and the Seven Dwarfs*. He left the Studio in 1938.

Naughty or Nice (television) Two-hour holiday-themed television movie; aired on *The Wonderful World of Disney* on December 11, 2004. A rude sports-radio DJ, Henry Ramiro gets a lesson on the importance of family and the values of life when a young listener, Michael, with a life threatening illness, forces him into a deal to be nicer on the air for just one day. The episode has a positive effect on Henry's life and those around him. Directed by Eric Laneuville. A von Zerneck-Sertner Films production. Stars George Lopez (Henry Ramiro), James Kirk (Michael), Roger Lodge (The Hitman), Lisa Vidal (Diana), Bianca Collins (Olivia), Chris Collins (Bobby), Dan McLean (Kevin Giles), John Salley (Dion Bailey).

Navajo Adventure (film) Foreign theatrical featurette; released first in France in December 1957. Produced by Ben Sharpsteen. The story of the Navajo, at work and play, in the Southwestern United States, and in particular, in scenic Monument Valley. The film focuses on a typical family, its daily life, struggles, and folkways, as every aspect of living is governed by Navajo gods and legends. See also *The Navajos—Children of the Gods*.

Navajos, The—Children of the Gods (film) Sixteen mm release title of *Navajo Adventure* (foreign release featurette from 1957); released in September 1967.

Navidad Mágica Disney (television) Entertainers appear at the four Walt Disney World parks to help celebrate Christmas, in this hour-long Spanish-language television special airing on December 24, 2001, from Univision. Entertainers include Bobby Pulido, Jaime Camil, Daniela Aedo, Myra, Pablo Montero, and José Feliciano.

Navidad Mágica Disney (television) Hour-long Spanish-language television special, which aired on December 24, 2002. A joint production of Univision and the Walt Disney World Resort. Christmas is celebrated at Walt Disney World, hosted by Karla Martinez and with entertainers including Olga Tañon, Juanes, Jennifer Peña, Odalys, Control, and Mariachi Cobre. Directed by Emilio Pimentel.

NBC Salutes the 25th Anniversary of the Wonderful World of Disney (television) Television special; aired on September 13, 1978.

Directed by Art Fisher. Stars Ron Howard, Suzanne Somers, Fess Parker, Buddy Ebsen, Crystal Gayle, Melissa Gilbert, Gavin MacLeod.

Neary, Kevin Disney cast member and co-author with Dave Smith of *The Ultimate Disney Trivia Book* (1992), *The Ultimate Disney Trivia Book 2* (1994), *The Ultimate Disney Trivia Book 3* (1997), and *The Ultimate Disney Trivia Book 4* (2000).

Neck 'n Neck (film) Oswald the Lucky Rabbit cartoon; released on January 23, 1928.

Neeson, Liam Actor; appeared in *The Good Mother* (Leo), *Before and After* (Ben Ryan), and *Gun Shy* (Charlie Cutter).

Negri, Pola (1895–1987) Actress; appeared in *The Moon-Spinners* (Madame Habib).

Neilson, James (1918–1979) Director of such films as *Moon Pilot*, *Bon Voyage*, *Summer Magic*, *The Scarecrow of Romney Marsh*, *The Moon-Spinners*, and *The Adventures of Bullwhip Griffin*. He retired in 1975.

Nelson, Craig T. Actor; appeared in *Turner & Hooch* (Chief Hyde), and provided the voice of Bob Parr/Mr. Incredible in *The Incredibles*.

Nelson, Gary Director of such films as *Freaky Friday*, *The Black Hole*, *Bayou Boy*, *The Secrets of the Pirate's Inn*, and *The Boy Who Talked to Badgers*.

Nelson, Tim Blake Actor; appeared in *Heavyweights* (Camp Hope salesman), *O Brother, Where Art Thou?* (Delmar), *Holes* (Dr. "Mom" Pendanski), *The Last Shot* (Marshal Paris).

Nemo Clownfish in *Finding Nemo*; voiced by Alexander Gould.

Neon Armadillo Music Saloon Nightclub at Pleasure Island at Walt Disney World; opened on May 1, 1989, and closed in 1998. Country-western music was featured in Southwestern decor. It became the BET Soundstage Club.

Nero and Brutus Madame Medusa's pet crocodiles in *The Rescuers*.

Never a Dull Moment (film) Mistaken for a hired killer, television actor Jack Albany impersonates the man to save his own life. However, he is forced to join a gang of hoodlums attempting to heist an enormous 42-foot-long painting, "A Field of Sunflowers," from the Manhattan Museum of Art. Then the real killer shows up. But Jack outwits him, thwarts the robbery, and also finds time to fall in love. Released on June 26, 1968. Directed by Jerry Paris. 100 min. Stars Edward G. Robinson (Smooth), Dick Van Dyke (Jack Albany), Dorothy Provine (Sally), Jack Elam (Ace Williams). The film was based on the book by John Godey. Released on video in 1985.

Never Cry Wolf (film) A young biologist, Tyler is sent by the Canadian government into the Arctic wilderness to study the wolves, which have been accused of killing off the caribou herds. He suffers hardships in the wilds, but gains a respect for the wolves. He adopts some of their lifestyle and discovers that hunters, and not the wolves, are the main enemy of the caribou. Premiere in Toronto on October 6, 1983; general release on October 7, 1983. Directed by Carroll Ballard. 105 min. Stars Charles Martin Smith (Tyler), Brian Dennehy (Rosie), Zachary Ittimangnaq (Ootek), Samson Jorah (Mike), Hugh Webster (Drunk), Martha Ittimangnaq (Woman). The film is based on the best-selling book by Farley Mowat, published in 1963 and since translated into more than 20 languages. Executive producer Ron Miller had sought the rights to the book for ten years. The movie was shot in the awesome wilderness of Canada's Yukon Territory and in Nome, Alaska, and was more than two years in production. Alan Splet, an Oscar-winning sound-effects editor fashioned a uniquely aural experience for the Arctic wilderness. Released on video in 1984 and 1993.

Never Land Island where Peter Pan lives (not Never-Never Land, which was used in non-Disney versions).

Neverland Club Supervised children's activities are available in this facility at the Polynesian Resort at Walt Disney World.

New Adventures of Spin and Marty, The (television) Serial on the *Mickey Mouse Club* during the 1957–58 season. Directed by Charles Barton. Spin and Marty have an old jalopy, which crashes into the kitchen, and the boys volunteer to raise the money to pay for the damages. Marty tries to tame a wild stallion, and then the guys get the girls to help put on a talent show. Stars Tim Considine (Spin), David Stollery (Marty), Kevin Corcoran, Annette Funicello, Darlene Gillespie, J. Pat O'Malley, Harry Carey, Jr., Roy Barcroft, B. G. Norman, Sammy Ogg, Tim Hartnagel, Don Agrati. 30 episodes.

New Adventures of Spin and Marty, The: Suspect Behavior (television) Two-hour television movie on *The Wonderful World of Disney*; aired on August 13, 2000. Snooty Marty must make a friend while his parents are away, or he'll be sent to a dude ranch for the summer. Enter Spin, the mischievous son of his building superintendent, and the two boys try to crack the case of their creepy neighbors. Directed by Rusty Cundieff. Stars David Gallagher (Marty), Jeremy Foley (Spin), Charles Shaughnessy (Jordon), Judd Nelson (Hulka). This update of the 1950s *Mickey Mouse Club* serial features cameos by the original Spin and Marty as Mayor [Tim] Considine and Commissioner [David] Stollery. Based on the novel *The Undertaker's Gone Bananas* by Paul Zindel.

New Adventures of Winnie the Pooh, The (television) Television series; premiered on January 10, 1988, on The Disney Channel and then on ABC from September 10, 1988 until September 4, 1992. It returned to ABC on January 4, 1997. It won the Emmy Award for Best Animated Program, Daytime, in both 1989 and 1990. Voices are Jim Cummings (Winnie the Pooh, Tigger), Paul Winchell (Tigger), John Fiedler (Piglet), Ken Sansom (Rabbit), Hal Smith (Owl), Peter Cullen (Eeyore), Michael Hough (Gopher), Tim Hoskins (Christopher Robin), Nicholas Melody (Roo), Patty Parris (Kanga). 50 episodes.

New Amsterdam Theater Disney restored and reopened this historic theater on West 42nd Street in New York City, to help with the company's expanding commitment to live entertainment. The theater opened May 18, 1997, with a world-premiere concert performance of *Alan Menken and Tim Rice's King David*, following several previews.

New! Animal World (television) Series on The Disney Channel; premiered on April 18, 1983. Features Bill Burrud traveling the world to search out interesting stories about animals.

New Century Clock Shop Shop on Main Street at Disneyland; opened in January 1972. The shop replaced the Upjohn Pharmacy when Elgin (Bradley) became the licensee for Disney watches and clocks. Later sponsored by Lorus. Also in Magic Kingdom Park at Walt Disney World, from October 1971 until April 1986, and in World Bazaar at Tokyo Disneyland, opened on April 15, 1983.

New Girl, The (film) Educational film about acceptance of differences, from the What Should I Do? series; released in March 1970.

New Kids on the Block at Walt Disney World—Wildest Dreams (television) Television special; aired on ABC on January 21, 1991. Directed by Jim Yukich. 60 min. Stars the New Kids on the Block in concert at Disney-MGM Studios, who share their fantasies about being movie stars.

New Mickey Mouse Club, The See *Mickey Mouse Club*.

New Neighbor, The (film) Donald Duck cartoon; released on August 1, 1953. Directed by

Jack Hannah. Donald tries hard to get along with his new neighbor, Pete, and Pete's terrible dog, but when Pete borrows all of Donald's food and throws stuff in his backyard, the fight is on.

New Orleans Square Land dedicated at Disneyland on July 24, 1966, by Walt Disney and the mayor of New Orleans. Disney had always enjoyed New Orleans, in fact it was in an antique shop there that he found an old windup mechanical bird that would give him the idea for Audio-Animatronics. He felt the unique New Orleans architecture would add an ideal touch along the banks of the Rivers of America, so he set his designers to coming up with a plan. The space they had to work with was not large, so they were ingenious in fitting in everything that they wanted to include. It not only houses the major attractions of Pirates of the Caribbean and The Haunted Mansion, but features shops and restaurants as well. It was also here that Walt wanted his own apartment built (see Disney Gallery). Tucked in, around, underneath, and out of view of the daily guests are offices, kitchens, and a cast-member cafeteria.

New Port South (film) Four high school students, sick of being censored by their teachers, attempt to change things by uncovering a scandal involving an ex-student, resulting in their plotting a revolution at the school. A Touchstone Picture. Very limited theatrical release on September 7, 2001. Directed by Kyle Cooper. Stars Todd Field (Walsh), Chad Christ (Moorehouse), Kevin Christy (Clip), Will Estes (Chris), Melissa George (Amanda), Blake Shields (Maddox), Nick Sandow (Armstrong), Mike Shannon (Stanton), Gabriel Mann (Wilson), Raymond Barry (Principal Edwards). 97 min. Released on video in 2002.

New Spirit, The (film) Donald Duck is persuaded to willingly and promptly pay his income tax in order to help the war effort in this cartoon made for the Treasury Department and distributed by the War Activities Committee of the Motion Picture Industry. Delivered to them on January 23, 1942. Directed by Wilfred Jackson

and Ben Sharpsteen. Nominated for an Academy Award as Best Documentary. Cliff Edwards sings "Yankee Doodle Spirit." The Secretary of the Treasury originally questioned using Donald Duck in this film, but Disney assured him that Donald was the equivalent of MGM offering him Clark Gable. The film caused a commotion in Congress, which balked at paying the high costs, most of which were necessitated by the Treasury Department's insistence on a speedy production period and enough prints to blanket the country. Surveys showed that the film succeeded in convincing Americans to pay their taxes promptly.

New Swiss Family Robinson, The (television) Two-hour television movie; produced by the Total Film Group, which aired on *The Wonderful World of Disney* on January 10, 1999. A contemporary version of the classic family adventure, with the Robinson family, sailing from Singapore to Sydney, being attacked by pirates, and shipwrecked on a deserted tropical island. Directed by Stewart Raffill. Stars Jane Seymour (Anna), James Keach (Jack), David Carradine (Sheldon Blake), Jamie Renee Smith (Elizabeth), Blake Bashoff (Todd), John Mallory Asher (Shane).

New True Life Adventures (television) Premiered on February 14, 2000, in syndication, and was the first of a new True-Life Adventure series. Titles were *Disney Presents Alaska: Dances of the Caribou*, *Disney Presents Elephant Journey*, *Disney Presents Sea of Sharks*, and *Disney Presents The Everglades: Home of the Living Dinosaurs*.

New Year's Eve A popular party begun at Disneyland in 1957, and continued at Magic Kingdom Park at Walt Disney World starting in 1971. Pleasure Island later celebrated New Year's Eve festivities every night of the year.

New Year's Jamboree (film) Shorts program released by RKO in 1953.

New York Stock Exchange Disney stock was first listed on November 12, 1957.

New York Stories (film) Combination of three short stories—*Life Lessons*, *Life Without Zoe*, and *Oedipus Wrecks*—each about life with intriguing characters in New York City. In *Life Lessons*, contemporary New York artist Lionel Dobie is suffering from "painter's block" when his lover-assistant Paulette announces that she is leaving him. He convinces her to stay, and while her coolness to him infuriates him, at the same time it inspires him. The more their relationship deteriorates, the more compelled and creative he becomes, while Paulette doubts her own talents as an artist. Ultimately Paulette leaves, and the successful artist finds a new student to whom he can give "life lessons." In *Life Without Zoe*, 12-year-old Zoe lives on her own at the Sherry Netherland Hotel with her butler, Hector, while her famous parents follow their own separate careers all over the world. Zoe becomes friends with a lonely rich boy, upon hearing him play the flute. She gets involved in a plot between a princess and her jealous husband that might cause Zoe's father harm. Her worldly wisdom and affection for her parents saves the day, and brings mother and father back together again. In *Oedipus Wrecks*, Sheldon is embarrassed by his mother, who doesn't seem to approve of anything about him—especially his shiksa fiancée, Lisa. Sheldon's wish that his mother just "disappear" comes true during a magic show. He is first distraught but then increasingly content with life without Mother. Suddenly, Mother reappears—personality intact, but in a rather different "form"—creating havoc for Sheldon and all the people of New York City. On the advice of his psychiatrist, Sheldon turns to psychic Treva, who tries to return Mother to her original state. The strain is too much for Lisa, and she leaves Sheldon. Treva fears she is a failure at everything, since she hasn't been able to bring Mother back, but Sheldon finds consolation in her, making everyone happy: Sheldon, Treva, and Mother. Premiere in New York on March 1, 1989; general release on March 10, 1989. The three segments were each directed by a different director—Martin Scorsese, Francis Ford Coppola, and Woody Allen respectively. A Touchstone Picture. 124 min. Stars Nick Nolte (Lionel Dobie), Rosanna Arquette (Paulette), Patrick O'Neal (Phillip Fowler), Heather McComb (Zoe), Talia Shire (Charlotte), Woody Allen (Sheldon), Mae Questel (Mother), Mia Farrow (Lisa), Julie Kavner (Treva). Filmed in New York City. Released on video in 1990.

New York Street Area opened at Disney-MGM Studios on May 1, 1989. Miniature skyscrapers provide an illustration of forced perspective at the end of the street. At first the street was only accessible to guests on the tram tours, but later it was opened to pedestrians as new attractions were built around it.

New York World's Fair Two-year exhibition, 1964 and 1965, which included four Disney shows: Ford's Magic Skyway, It's a Small World presented by Pepsi-Cola/UNICEF, General Electric's Progressland, featuring the Carousel of Progress, and the State of Illinois' Great Moments with Mr. Lincoln. The Fair premiered on April 22, 1964. After the opening and success of Disneyland, more and more cities had asked Walt Disney to build a Disneyland in their neighborhoods. He resisted at first, making sure that Disneyland was operating smoothly, but when he began listening to the entreaties from the East Coast, he wondered if Disneyland-style attractions would be popular among the easterners. The Fair provided an opportunity for him to test that popularity. If Disney attractions were popular at the Fair, then they should be popular anywhere on the Eastern seaboard—and they were. The Disney attractions had some of the longest

lines at the Fair. When the Fair closed in 1965, Disney was able to remove his attractions and re-install them at Disneyland. The organizations that sponsored the Fair attractions therefore helped pay for Disney's research and development of the four shows, which featured extensive use of Audio-Animatronics, including human characters for the first time.

Newbern, George Actor; appeared in *Adventures in Babysitting* (Dan), *Father of the Bride* and *Father of the Bride Part II* (Bryan MacKenzie), and on television in *Double Switch* (Bartholomew Holton/Matt Bundy), and on Disney Channel in *Buffalo Dreams* (Dr. Nick Townsend).

Newhart, Bob He voiced Bernard in *The Rescuers* and *The Rescuers Down Under.*

Newman, Fred Actor; adult leader on the *Mickey Mouse Club* on The Disney Channel, from 1989 to 1994. He did voice work for multiple characters on *Brand Spanking New Doug* and *Doug's 1st Movie.*

Newman, Paul Actor; appeared in *The Color of Money* (Eddie) and *Blaze* (Earl Long). He won an Academy Award as Best Actor for the former role.

Newman Laugh-O-grams (film) Short cartoons made for the Newman Theater in Kansas City, Missouri, by Walt Disney in 1920. Typical local problems, such as Kansas City's road conditions and corruption in the police force, were the subjects of the approximately one-minute shorts. These were the first films Disney made.

Newport Bay Club Hotel at Disneyland Paris; opened on April 12, 1992. A convention center was added in 1997. Similar to the Yacht Club Resort at Walt Disney World in theming. The hotel was designed by Robert Stern. A convention center was added in 1997.

Newsies (film) The young newsboys of New York City are dismayed when, in an attempt to squeeze out more profits for his newspaper,

publisher Joseph Pulitzer increases the price they pay for their papers. Led by the spirited Jack Kelly, the newsies set out to challenge the power of the press bosses and go on strike. With the help of reporter Bryan Denton, the newsies get word of the strike out to the whole city, and other child laborers rally to the cause. Jack himself confronts Pulitzer in a battle of wills. The strike is eventually successful, thanks in part to the intervention of Teddy Roosevelt. A musical; released on April 10, 1992. Directed by Kenny Ortega. Filmed in CinemaScope. 121 min. Stars Christian Bale (Jack Kelly), David Moscow (David Jacobs), Max Casella (Racetrack), Marty Belafsky (Crutchy), Bill Pullman (Bryan Denton), Ann-Margret (Medda Larkson), Robert Duvall (Joseph Pulitzer). Original songs by Alan Menken and Jack Feldman. Filmed primarily on the Universal Studios backlot, the first movie shot on their New York street set that had just been rebuilt after a disastrous fire in 1990. (Another Disney film, *Oscar*, was the last film shot on the set before the fire.) Released on video in 1992.

Newsies! Newsies! See All About It (television) Syndicated television special; aired on March 28, 1992. About the making of the movie, *Newsies*. Directed by Gayle Hollenbaugh.

Newton, Robert (1905–1956) Actor; appeared in *Treasure Island* (Long John Silver), one of the classic performances of his career. He was named a Disney Legend posthumously in 2002.

NFFC See National Fantasy Fan Club.

Nichols, Charles ("Nick") (1910–1992) Longtime animation director of shorts and television shows at the Disney Studio beginning there in 1935. He began at the Studio as an animator on the shorts, then moved up to director beginning with *First Aiders* in 1944. He had responsibility for most of the Pluto cartoons and animated the coachman in *Pinocchio*. He left the Studio in 1962.

Nick & Jessica Variety Hour (television) Hour-long television special on ABC; aired on April 11, 2004. Nick Lachey and Jessica Simpson, multi-platinum artists from their hit MTV series, *Newlyweds*, showcase their singing and comedic talents in a series of sketches and musical performances with such guests as Jewel, Kenny Rogers, Johnny Bench, and Muppets stars Kermit and Miss Piggy. From Tenth Planet Productions & JT Television in association with Touchstone Television.

Nick & Jessica's Family Christmas (television) Hour-long television special on ABC; aired on December 1, 2004. Nick Lachey and Jessica Simpson star in a fun-filled family variety hour of comedy and music celebrating the holidays. From Bob Bain Productions & JT Television in association with Touchstone Television.

Nick & Jessica's Tour of Duty (television) Two-hour television special on ABC; aired on May 23, 2005. Nick Lachey and Jessica Simpson perform for more than 6,000 servicemen and servicewomen at the Ramstein Air Base in Germany, with an added special trip to give much needed love and support to those serving our country in Tikrit, Iraq. From Bob Bain Productions & JT Television in association with Touchstone Television.

Nick Price Story of Non-Manipulative Selling, The Series of educational films from 1981: *The Danbury Secret of Flexible Behavior*, *A Better Way to Go*, and *The Voice*.

Nicky and Rock—Working Sheep Dogs (film) Sixteen mm release title of *Arizona Sheepdog*; released in November 1966.

Nielsen, Kay (1886–1957) Sketch artist, story man, and designer; came to Disney in 1939 and worked on concepts for films on *The Little Mermaid* and *Ride of the Valkyries*. He created designs for the *Night on Bald Mountain* segment of *Fantasia*. Nielsen's *Little Mermaid* designs were brought out of the Archives in the 1980s to inspire the artists who were again working on that story, and they thought enough of Nielsen's sketches to give him a film credit. Nielsen left Disney in 1941, and returned briefly in

1952–1953. He is known for his non-Disney work as a book illustrator of such classics as *East of the Sun and West of the Moon*.

Nielsen, Leslie Actor; appeared in *Spy Hard* (Dick Steele) and *Mr. Magoo* (title role), and on television as *The Swamp Fox* and narrated *Wild Heart*. He also appeared on television in *Safety Patrol* (Mr. Penn) and *Santa Who?* (Santa Claus).

Nifty Nineties, The (film) Mickey Mouse cartoon; released on June 20, 1941. Directed by Riley Thomson. Turn-of-the-century Mickey and Minnie attend a vaudeville show and later ride in a new "horsecar" that ends in a wreck when a cow interferes.

Night (film) Silly Symphony cartoon; released on April 28, 1930. Directed by Walt Disney. This early version of *The Old Mill* depicts the musical nighttime frolics of owls, fireflies, frogs, and other inhabitants of an old mill pond.

Night Before Christmas, The (film) Silly Symphony cartoon; released on December 9, 1933. Color. Directed by Wilfred Jackson. In a sequel to *Santa's Workshop*, Santa arrives at a house, setting

up the tree, its trimmings, and toys. The noise awakens the children, who are in time only to see Santa driving away on his sleigh. The 16mm release title was *Santa's Toys*.

Night Crossing (film) Peter Strelzyk and Günter Wetzel hope to escape with their families from East Germany to the freedom of the West. Realizing that a balloon might be the answer, Peter and Günter buy materials and begin building one in secret. The first flight, with just Peter's family—Günter's wife had convinced him to abandon the project—crashes just short of the border. With the police closing in rapidly, the Strelzyks, once more joined by the Wetzels, make a final attempt to fly to freedom and this time achieve success. Released on February 5, 1982. Directed by Delbert Mann. 107 min. Stars John Hurt (Peter Strelzyk), Jane Alexander (Doris), Glynnis O'Connor (Petra), Doug McKeon (Frank), Beau Bridges (Günter Wetzel), Ian Bannen (Josef), Klaus Löwitsch (Schmalk), Anne Stallybrass (Magda Keller), Kay Walsh (Doris's mother). Moved by newspaper accounts of the daring escape, Disney executive Ron Miller and producer Tom Leetch contacted European story editor Eva Redfern with instructions to pursue the film rights. Impressed by the Disney television shows that were beamed from West to East Germany, the two couples accepted Disney's offer. The families flew to California to provide background material with the added inducement of a grand tour of Disneyland. To assure authenticity, the producers decided to film the entire production in West Germany in Landsberg, Muhltal, Harthausen, and Munich. Near the town of Eulenschwang, production designer Rolf Zehetbauer and art director Herbert Strabel spent $300,000 to re-create a half-mile section of the border that separated East and West Germany, authentic down to the wire-mesh fencing, concrete posts, automated shrapnel guns, leashed guard dogs, and impregnable cast-iron barricades. One of the large exhibition halls at the I.B.O. fairgrounds, in Friedrichshafen on Lake Constance, was turned into the world's largest "green set" for filming scenes under controlled conditions. Within the 5,000-square-yard area,

300 pine trees were transplanted for the forest, and to shut out the light from the glass-walled structure, 6,000 square yards of black plastic covered the walls. The final cost for the set was $150,000. At the Bavaria Film Studio, interior filming was done on four soundstages. Gary Cerveny of Balloon Ventures, Inc. of Glendale, California, made and flew a total of seven hot-air balloons for the production. The balloons were re-created as closely as possible to the original. The only changes were in the material used and certain technical improvements to comply with FAA standards. What made the real-life flight all the more miraculous was that the experts say their balloon shouldn't have flown at all. With all the proper equipment, sophisticated electronic devices and human expertise, Cerveny had extreme difficulty getting the exact reproductions airborne. Released on video in 1982.

Night on Bald Mountain (film) Music by Modeste Moussorgsky, a segment of *Fantasia*.

Night Stalker, The (television) One-hour drama series; debuted on ABC on September 29, 2005. When a pregnant woman is snatched from her home, crime reporter Carl Kolchak suspects all is not as it seems. That is because 18 months ago, his wife was killed in a bizarre fashion and he has been the FBI's number-one suspect ever since. Kolchak's determination to find the truth leads him to investigate other crimes that seem to have a supernatural component. But he's trying to piece together a puzzle that keeps changing shape. Who or what is committing these crimes? How are they all related? With sidekick Perri Reed, a sexy if skeptical fellow reporter in tow, Kolchak will go to any lengths to answer these questions. But when he does discover the truth, will anyone believe him? Stars Stuart Townsend (Carl Kolchak), Gabrielle Union (Perri Reed), Eric Jungmann (Jain McManus), Cotter Smith (Tony Vincenzo). From Touchstone Television.

Night Train to Kathmandu (television) Exotic adventure of an American girl on vacation in Nepal and a prince who has left his secret city to explore the real world. A Disney Channel Premiere Film; first aired on June 5, 1988. Directed by Robert Wiemer. 102 min. Stars Pernell Roberts (Professor Hadley-Smythe), Milla Jovovich (Lily), Eddie Castrodad (Prince Johar).

Nightjohn (television) A Disney Channel Premiere Film; first aired on June 1, 1996. In the 1830s, Sarny, a young, black slave girl, meets the mysterious Nightjohn, who freely risks his life to give the girl a gift that white law forbids: the gift of reading and writing. Directed by Charles Burnett. Stars Beau Bridges (Clel Waller), Carl Lumbly (Nightjohn), Allison Jones (Sarny), Lorraine Toussaint (Delie). Based on the novel by Gary Paulsen. 103 min. Filmed entirely on the Rip Raps Plantation in Sumter, South Carolina.

Nightmare Before Christmas, Tim Burton's The (film) Jack Skellington is the Pumpkin King of Halloweentown who, though busy, feels a void in his life. Upon discovering Christmastown, he rejoices with a fervor to take over a new holiday. With the help of three mischievous trick-or-treaters, Lock, Shock, and Barrel, he manages to capture Santa Claus, whom he calls Sandy Claws, and proceeds to turn Halloweentown into a Christmas manufacturing plant. Sally, a lonely ragdoll, who loves Jack, fears his new obsession will bring him trouble. Despite her efforts, Jack and his reindeer, created by the local evil scientist, set off on Christmas Eve with a lot of ghoulish presents. When the world responds with horror to Jack's earnest efforts, and cries for the real Santa Claus, Jack realizes his mistake. He manages to save Sally and Santa Claus from the dangerous Oogie Boogie and restore the Christmas holiday. With his newfound love for Sally, he can happily return to being himself. This film is Tim Burton's tour de force using stop-motion

animation. Initial release in New York on October 13, 1993; general release on October 22, 1993. Directed by Henry Selick. A Touchstone Picture. 76 min. Voices include Chris Sarandon (Jack Skellington), Catherine O'Hara (Sally), Glenn Shadix (Mayor), William Hickey (evil scientist), Ken Page (Oogie Boogie). Tim Burton created the story and characters for the film. The original score was by Danny Elfman, who also provided the singing voice of Jack Skellington. Produced in a studio in San Francisco, utilizing more than 227 animated characters. Released on video in 1994. It has had a limited reissue at Halloween beginning  in 2000, and the film has become a cult classic. For the holiday season in 2001, the Disneyland Haunted Mansion was outfitted with *Nightmare Before Christmas* elements, characters, and scenes, and its popularity ensured its return in ensuing years.

Nightmare Ned (television) Animated series; aired on ABC from April 19 to August 30, 1997. Ned Needlemeyer is a misunderstood, solitary, bespectacled eight-year-old boy, who happens to have wild nightmares. Voices include Courtland Mead (Ned), Brad Garrett (Dad), Victoria Jackson (Mom). 12 episodes.

Nikki, Wild Dog of the North (film) Andre Dupas, a French-Canadian hunter, finds a dead mother-bear, and deciding to save her cub from sure death by raising it himself, ties the cub, Neewa, to his malamute pup, Nikki, and continues paddling down the river. At the rapids, the canoe overturns, and the animals are washed away, still tied together. They discover they have to cooperate to survive, and even though they eventually break loose from each other, they become friends until a winter hibernation leaves Nikki on his own. Nikki grows into a powerful dog, but is captured by a cruel hunter, LeBeau, who makes him into a savage fighter and takes him to the trading post run by Dupas, who has banned the customary dog fighting. LeBeau ignores the ruling, fights Nikki, and is thrown out by Dupas, whom he then shoves into the dog pit, expecting the savage Nikki to tear him to bits. Nikki recognizes his old master, and the enraged LeBeau springs into the pit to kill Dupas himself. When he finds he is losing the battle he treacherously pulls a knife, but Nikki springs on him. LeBeau falls on his own knife, killing himself. Nikki and Dupas are reunited. Released on July 12, 1961. Directed by Jack Couffer and Dan Haldane. The screenplay was based on James Oliver Curwood's book, *Nomads of the North*. 73 min. Stars Jean Coutu (Andre Dupas), Emile Genest (Jacques LeBeau), with narration by Jacques Fauteux. Filmed on location in Canada by two separate film units. The film helped prove that Disney had perfected the method of blending a True-Life Adventure–style nature film with a dramatic story. Released on video in 1986.

Nine Dragons Restaurant Restaurant in China in World Showcase at Epcot; opened on October 23, 1985. It seemed a little odd that World Showcase opened with China but with no Chinese restaurant, because of the popularity of

Chinese cuisine. That omission was remedied three years later, and the resulting restaurant has been honored with awards for its blend of Chinese cuisine from many of the provinces.

Nine Lives of Elfego Baca, The (television) Television show; episode 1 of *Elfego Baca*. See under *Elfego Baca*. Also a foreign and video

release title for an *Elfego Baca* feature. Released on video in 1986.

Nine Old Men Walt called his key animators in the 1950s his Nine Old Men, after Franklin D. Roosevelt's Nine Old Men on the Supreme Court. They were Frank Thomas, Ollie Johnston, John Lounsbery, Marc Davis, Ward Kimball, Woolie Reitherman, Les Clark, Eric Larson, Milt Kahl.

1900 Park Fare Restaurant in the Grand Floridian Resort & Spa at Walt Disney World; opened on June 28, 1988. Food is served buffet style, and there are frequent appearances by Disney characters, as well as entertainment from a huge band organ named Big Bertha.

Niok (film) Featurette; released on August 28, 1957. Directed by Edmond Sechan. Near the region of Angkor Watt, a group of children capture a baby elephant and are just growing attached to it when it is sold to a traveling safari. Pursuing the new owner, a boy manages to steal it back, and the children free it to return to its mother. 29 min.

Niven, David (1910–1983) Actor; appeared in *No Deposit, No Return* (J. W. Osborne) and *Candleshoe* (Priory).

Nixon (film) The political life of Richard Nixon is covered, with flashbacks showing his Quaker upbringings, from his congressional days to Watergate and his resignation, presenting a psychological portrait of the complex public figure and a look at the people who surrounded him. Released on a limited basis on December 20, 1995; expanded release on January 5, 1996. A Hollywood Pictures release of an Andrew G. Vajna presentation of an Illusion Entertainment Group/ Cinergi production. Directed by Oliver Stone. Stars Anthony Hopkins (Richard Nixon), Joan Allen (Pat Nixon), Powers Boothe (Alexander Haig), Ed Harris (E. Howard Hunt), Bob Hoskins (J. Edgar Hoover), E. G. Marshall (John Mitchell), David Paymer (Ron Ziegler), David Hyde Pierce (John Dean), Paul Sorvino (Henry Kissinger), Mary Steenburgen (Hannah Nixon), J. T. Walsh (John Erlichman), James Woods (H. R. Haldeman), Brian Bedford (Clyde Tolson), Ed Herrmann (Nelson Rockefeller), Madeleine Kahn (Margaret Mitchell). 191 min. Filmed in Cinema-Scope. The production was filmed almost exclusively in Southern California, and utilized White House sets that had been built at Sony Studios in Culver City for the movie *The American President*. The wedding scene was shot at the Mission Inn in Riverside, where Richard and Pat Nixon had said their vows. The Nixon family's East Whittier white frame house and grocery store/filling station were re-created on a road running between citrus groves in Redlands. Joan Allen was nominated for the Oscar for Best Supporting Actress. Released on video in 1996, with additional footage included.

Nixon, Richard M. Vice President Nixon first visited Disneyland shortly after its opening in July 1955. He returned with his family on June 14, 1959, to help dedicate the Monorail, and again in August 1968.

No Big Deal (film) Educational video; released in June 1992; 20 min. A story of the dangers of inhalants, and how they can cause paranoia and increased aggression.

No Deposit, No Return (film) Tracy, eleven, and Jay, eight, who would like to be with their mother in Hong Kong, are stuck spending their Easter holiday with their wealthy grandfather in California. When the kids fall in with two bumbling safecrackers, they pretend to be kidnapped to con their grandfather into paying ransom money, which they can use as airfare to Hong Kong. Their ploy backfires with hilarious results, as everyone from the police to the kids' mother tries to rescue them from their "kidnappers." Released on February 11, 1976. Directed by Norman Tokar. 111 min. Stars David Niven (J.S. Osborne), Darren McGavin (Duke), Don Knotts (Bert), Herschel Bernardi (Sgt. Turner), Barbara Feldon (Carolyn), Kim Richards (Tracy), Brad Savage (Jay), John Williams (Jameson), Vic Tayback (Big Joe), Charlie Martin Smith (Longnecker), Bob Hastings (Peter). The story was written by Disney veteran Joe McEveety. Released on video in 1986.

No Hunting (film) Donald Duck cartoon; released on January 14, 1955. Directed by Jack Hannah. Donald is inspired by his Grandpappy's hunting skills to go out with him on a modern-day hunt where the pair spend most of their time avoiding the bullets of the other hunters, and never have a chance to bag any game. Filmed in CinemaScope. Nominated for an Academy Award.

No Sail (film) Donald Duck and Goofy cartoon; released on September 7, 1945. Directed by Jack Hannah. Donald and Goofy are sailing in a rented boat that runs on nickels. When they run out of coins, they are marooned for days until Donald's beak gets caught in the coin slot, starting the boat, and they sail off toward the horizon.

No Smoking (film) Goofy cartoon; released on November 23, 1951. Directed by Jack Kinney. Goofy decides to give up smoking but experiences so many temptations that he grows desperate and gets into various situations trying to get a cigarette.

Noah (television) Two-hour television movie; aired on *The Wonderful World of Disney* on October 11, 1998. Set in modern times, a building contractor, Norman Waters, is asked to build an ark and fill it with animals, two by two. Despite his skepticism, and problems with his three boys, Norman begins the ark and befriends a pet store owner who agrees to supply the animals. Directed by Ken Kwapis. Stars Tony Danza (Norman Waters), Wallace Shawn (Zack), Jane Sibbett (Angela), John Marshall Jones (Ernie), Don McManus (Gavin), Jesse Moss (Levon), Christopher Marquette (Daniel), Michal Suchanek (Benny). For the production, the ark was built in Hoodoo Provincial Park near Drumheller, Alberta, Canada. Released on video in 2000.

Noah's Ark (film) Special featurette; released on November 10, 1959. Directed by Bill Justice. Using the magic of stop-motion animation, X Atencio and a team of artists brought to life a variety of objects normally found in a hardware store as characters in the biblical story of Noah and his ark. With his sons Ham, Shem, and Japheth, Noah manages to cut enough gopher wood to fabricate the ark, preparing to set sail with his family, and inviting various animals to join them and wait out the Great Flood safe in the hold. Nominated for an Academy Award. 21 min. There was also a Silly Symphony cartoon from 1933 entitled *Father Noah's Ark*.

Noises Off (film) A less-than-stellar American acting troupe attempts to put on a wacky British sex farce entitled "Nothing On." The cast lumbers through a last-minute run-through under the direction of the exasperated Lloyd Fellowes, then the camera swings backstage for a behind-the-scenes view of the chaos going on there, as the actors vent their frustrations and jealousies. The play is shown to an unenthusiastic preview audience who barely sit through a disastrous full production complete with missed cues, misplaced props, and missing actors. Thinking that his career will be ruined after the Broadway opening, the director has hidden in a bar until the final curtain when he hears the cheers of approval from the audience. His motley acting crew has somehow turned out a hit after all. Released on March 20, 1992. Directed by Peter Bogdanovich. A Touchstone Picture, with Amblin Entertainment. 104 min. Stars Carol Burnett (Dotty Otley/Mrs. Clackett), Michael Caine (Lloyd Fellowes), Denholm Elliott (Selsdon Mowbray/The Burglar), Julie Hagerty (Poppy Taylor), Marilu Henner (Belinda Blair/Flavia Brent), Mark Linn-Baker (Tim Allgood), Christopher Reeve (Frederick Dallas/Philip Brent), John Ritter (Gary Lejuene/Roger Tramplemain), Nicollette Sheridan (Brooke Aston/Vicki). This was Denholm Elliott's last film; he died shortly after its release. From the Tony Award–nominated play by Michael Frayn. Released on video in 1992.

Nolan, Jeanette (1911–1998) Actress; appeared on television in *Bayou Boy*, *Gallegher Goes West*, *The Sky's the Limit*, and *The Mystery of Edward Sims*, and voiced Ellie Mae in *The Rescuers* and Widow Tweed in *The Fox and the Hound*. She also appeared in *The Horse Whisperer* (Ellen Booker).

Nolan, Lloyd (1902–1985) Actor; appeared on television in *The Sky's the Limit* (Cornwall).

Nolte, Nick Actor; appeared in *Down and Out in Beverly Hills* (Jerry Baskin), *Three Fugitives* (Lucas), *New York Stories* (Lionel Dobie), *I Love Trouble* (Peter Brackett), *Jefferson in Paris* (Thomas Jefferson), *Breakfast of Champions* (Harry Le Sabre), and on television in *The Feather Farm* (Les).

North Avenue Irregulars, The (film) When organized crime hits their town, a reverend and a group of unusual ladies from his church decide to hit back. By posing as knockout performers, masters of disguise, and cunning mistresses of pursuit, they bring the underworld to its knees in a wild and crazy car chase and roundup finale. Released on February 9, 1979. Directed by Bruce Bilson. 100 min. Stars Edward Herrmann (Michael Hill), Barbara Harris (Vickie), Susan Clark (Anne), Karen Valentine (Jane), Michael Constantine (Marv), Patsy Kelly (Rose), Ivor Francis (Rev. Wainwright), Douglas V. Fowley (Delaney), Virginia Capers (Cleo), Steve Franken (Tom), Dena Dietrich (Mrs. Carlisle), Dick Fuchs (Howard), Herb Voland (Dr. Fulton), Alan Hale, Jr. (Harry the Hat), Ruth Buzzi (Dr. Rheems), Cloris Leachman (Claire). The film is based on the book by Rev. Albert Fay Hill. Though many of the incidents in the film are fiction, the story is based on the factual account of Reverend Hill. The group's name comes from the Baker Street Irregulars, a reference to the youth of Victorian London who gathered information for Sherlock Holmes for a pittance. Scenes were filmed on the backlot of the Disney Studio and on 42 separate locations in and around the Los Angeles area from florist shops in Burbank to alleys in Pasadena to desert roads near Newhall to streets in Long Beach. More than $155,000 was paid for cars involved in the filming, 14 automobiles and one motorcycle of which were destroyed in the final scenes. The film was released in other countries under the title *Hill's Angels*. Released on video in 1980 and 1985.

Northcutte, Shawnte Mouseketeer on the new *Mickey Mouse Club*.

Northern Lights (television) A Disney Channel Original Movie; first aired on August 23, 1997. A New York woman goes to her brother's funeral in small-town New England, along with his onetime buddy, Ben, and gets the shock of her life. They are inheriting a young nephew she never knew she had. Directed by Linda Yellen. Stars Diane Keaton (Roberta Blumstein), Joseph Cross (Jack), Maury Chaykin (Ben). 95 min.

Northwest Mercantile Trading Post Shop in Canada in World Showcase at Epcot; opened on October 1, 1982. Harkening back to the early days of the Hudson Bay Company, the trading post offers sheepskins, maple syrup, Native Ameri-

can soapstone carvings, and lumberjack shirts, along with other Canadian wares.

Norton, Edward Actor; appeared in *Keeping the Faith* (Brian) and *25th Hour* (Monty Brogan).

Norway Pavilion in World Showcase at Epcot; opened on May 6, 1988. The most recent country to be added to World Showcase. The focal point is a large stave church, in which one can see displays of Norwegian cultural objects. The architecture reminds the visitor of towns such as Oslo and Bergen, with a castle patterned after Oslo's Akershus from the fourteenth century. The Maelstrom attraction, shops, and a restaurant are the main attractions here.

Norway—the Film (film) Seventy mm. Film on the people and culture of Norway at the conclusion of the Maelstrom attraction at Norway in World Showcase at Epcot; opened on July 5, 1988. 5 min.

Nosey, the Sweetest Skunk in the West (television) Television show; aired on November 19, 1972. An orphaned skunk comes into the lives of an artist and his daughter in a desolate area of Arizona, and he tangles with an owl and a pair of poodles. Stars Jane Biddle, James Chandler, Walter Carlson, Lois Binford. Narrated by Rex Allen.

Not Quite Human (television) A Disney Channel Premiere Film; first aired on June 19, 1987. An android goes to high school with the daughter of his inventor. Directed by Steven H. Stern. 91

min. With Jay Underwood (Chip Carson), Alan Thicke (Dr. Carson), Joe Bologna (Vogel), Robyn Lively (Becky). There were two sequels, *Not Quite Human II* and *Still Not Quite Human*. Released on video in 1993.

Not Quite Human II (television) A Disney Channel Premiere Film; first aired on September 23, 1989. Chip the android goes to college to learn more about human emotions in this sequel, and he meets and falls for an android created by a rival scientist. Directed by Eric Luke. 92 min. Stars Jay Underwood, Alan Thicke, Robyn Lively, Katie Barberi (Roberta). Released on video in 1993.

Not So Lonely Lighthouse Keeper, The (television) Television show; aired on September 17, 1967. This is the story of a lighthouse keeper on Anacapa Island and his pet goat. Progress decrees that the lighthouse give way to an automated beacon, but the keeper is unhappy on the mainland, and he is able to return to the island as a game warden. Stars Clarence Hastings, Ingrid Niemela. Narrated by Roy Barcroft.

Nothing to Lose (film) Things couldn't get any worse for advertising executive Nick Beam, whose life has just completely unraveled when he thinks he has caught his wife being unfaithful to him with his boss. But while he is sitting at a traffic light, in a state of shock and unable to get a grip on reality, a fast-talking carjacker named T. Paul leaps into his car, attempting to rob him. With nothing to lose and on the verge of a nervous breakdown, Nick turns the tables on his mugger, taking him hostage while he decides what to do. An unlikely friendship gradually unfolds between this offbeat pair in a madcap comedy of holdups, high-speed chases, mistaken identities, and revenge. A Touchstone Picture. Directed by Steve Oedekerk. Released on July 18, 1997. Stars Martin Lawrence (T. Paul), Tim Robbins (Nick Beam), John C. McGinley (Rig), Giancarlo Esposito (Charlie), Michael McKean (Philip Barrows), Kelly Preston (Ann Beam). 98 min. Filming began in the desert near Lancaster, California, then continued at locations around Los Angeles. Released on video in 1998.

Novarro, Ramon (1899–1968) Actor; appeared on television in *Elfego Baca*.

Novis, Donald (1906–1966) He sang "Love Is a Song" in *Bambi*; the original silver-toned tenor in the Golden Horseshow Revue at Disneyland.

Novis, Julietta Singer; sang "Ave Maria" in *Fantasia*.

Now I Can Tell You My Secret (film) Educational film; released in August 1984. Shows how children can protect themselves from sexual advances by saying "no," getting away, and telling an adult.

Now You See Him, Now You Don't (film) At Medfield College, Dexter Riley comes up with a lab experiment that produces fantastic results—invisibility! But the magic potion is stolen and is put to use by a bank robber. Nevertheless, Dexter and his pals foil the robbers and recover the potion, which wins an award and saves Medfield from financial ruin and being transformed into a gambling mecca. Premiere in Edmonton, Canada on July 7, 1972; general release on July 12, 1972. Directed by Robert Butler. 88 min. Stars Kurt Russell (Dexter), Joyce Menges (Debbie Dawson), Joe Flynn (Dean Higgins), Cesar Romero (A.J. Arno), William Windom (Lufkin), Jim Backus (Forsythe). Released on video in 1985.

Now You See It (television) Disney Channel Original Film; premiered on January 14, 2005. Aspiring student producer Allyson Miller is producing a new reality show that will search for the world's greatest kid magician. She stumbles upon Danny Sinclair, who becomes one of three finalists. While the other two contestants are good magicians, Danny appears to have something more. When Allyson finally learns that Danny's powers are real, she must protect him from those who want to destroy him. Directed by Duwayne Dunham. Stars Alyson Michalka (Allyson Miller), Johnny Pacar (Danny Sinclair), Frank Langella (Max), Chris Olivero (Hunter), Gabriel Sunday (Brandon), Deneen Tyler (Ms. McAllister), Amanda Shaw (Zoe), Patty French (Madam Susette).

Nowhere Man (television) One-hour psychological suspense television series; premiered on September 4, 1995, on UPN, after a preview on August 28, and ended August 19, 1996. In the course of one evening, a man seemingly has his entire identity erased. Now he is engaged in a life-consuming quest for the truth. Stars Bruce Greenwood (Thomas Veil), and in the premiere episode Megan Gallagher (Alyson Veil), Ted Levine (Dave Powers), Murray Rubenstein (Larry Levy), Michael Tucker (Dr. Bellamy).

N.T.S.B.: The Crash of Flight 323 (television) Two-hour television movie; aired on ABC on March 22, 2004. The National Transportation and Safety Board investigates the fictional crash of a commuter plane in the Colorado mountains, trying to find out what went wrong, and decide whether it was mechanical failure, pilot error, or an act of terrorism. Produced by Omnibus, Inc. and Touchstone Television. Directed by Jeff Bleckner. Stars Mandy Patinkin (Al Cummings), Ted McGinley (Reese Faulkner), Eric Close (N'Tom), Kevin Dunn (Dr. Cyrus Lebow), Tyra Ferrell (Jessamyn). Originally scheduled to air in 2001, but posponed due to the World Trade Center attacks, then a later airdate, in February 2003, was postponed due to the crash of the space shuttle *Columbia*.

Nucci, Danny Actor; appeared in *Alive* (Hugo Diaz), *Crimson Tide* (Danny Rivetti), *The Rock* (Spec. Agent Shepard), and on television in *Brand New Life* (D.J.), *Blossom* (Lou), and *10-8* (Rico Amonte).

Nunis, Dick He began his Disney career in the summer of 1955 at Disneyland as an assistant to Van France in orientation training. He worked up through the ranks as area supervisor, supervisor of the mail-

room and steno pool, director of Disneyland operations (1961), and vice president of Disneyland operations (1968). In 1972, he became executive vice president of both Disneyland and Walt Disney World, and president in 1980. He was a member of the Disney board of directors from 1981 to 1999, and was named chairman of Walt Disney Attractions in 1991. He retired in 1999, and was named a Disney Legend the same year.

Nurses (television) Television series on NBC; from September 14, 1991 to June 18, 1994. A dedicated team of health-care professionals use humor to handle the daily pressures of demanding work and complex personal lives. Stars Stephanie Hodge (Sandy), Arnetia Walker (Anne), Mary Jo Keenen (Julie), Ada Maris (Gina), Kenneth David Gilman (Dr. Kaplan), Carlos LaCamara (Paco). The second season added David Rasche (Jack Trenton), Markus Flanagan (Luke Fitzgerald); the third season added Loni Anderson (Casey MacAfee) as a new, ruthlessly ambitious hospital administrator.

Nutcracker Suite, The (film) Music by Tchaikovsky, a segment of *Fantasia*.

Nutt House, The (television) Television series on NBC; from September 20 to October 25, 1989. The adventures of a zany hotel staff at the Nutt House, a New York hotel owned by elderly Edwina Nutt. Stars Cloris Leachman (Mrs. Frick/Edwina Nutt), Harvey Korman (Reginald J. Tarkington), Brian McNamara (Charles Nutt III), Molly Hagan (Sally Lonnaneck). The television show utilized the expensive replica of the Plaza Hotel lobby that had been built as a set for the Disney feature *Big Business*. The series was created by Mel Brooks and Alan Spencer.

Nye, Bill See *Bill Nye, the Science Guy*.

O

O Brother, Where Art Thou? (film) In the Depression-era Deep South, three escapees from a Mississippi prison chain gang—Everett Ulysses McGill, sweet-and-simple Delmar, and the perpetually angry Pete—embark on the adventure of a lifetime as they set out to pursue their freedom and return to their homes. With nothing to lose and still in shackles, they make a hasty run for their lives and end up on an incredible journey filled with challenging experiences and colorful characters. However, they must also match wits with the cunning and mysterious lawman Cooley, who tracks the men, bent on bringing the trio back to the prison farm. Released on December 22, 2000, in New York and Los Angeles, and elsewhere on December 29 and January 12, 2001. It had earlier been released abroad, first by Bac Films in France on August 30, 2000, after a preview at the Cannes Film Festival on May 13. Directed by Joel Coen. A Touchstone Pictures/Universal co-production. Stars George Clooney (McGill), John Turturro (Pete), Tim Blake Nelson (Delmar), Daniel Van Bargen (Cooley), Charles Durning (Pappy O'Daniel), John Goodman (Big Dan Teague), Holly Hunter (Penny Wharvey). 103 min. Filmed in CinemaScope on location in a 75-mile radius from Jackson, Mississippi, and at Disney's Golden Oak Ranch. Based on Homer's *The Odyssey*. The film was nominated for Academy Awards for Best Screenplay Adaptation and Cinematography. Released on video in 2001.

O, Canada! (film) Glimpses of the beauty of Canada caught by the Circle-Vision cameras for the Canada pavilion at World Showcase, Epcot; opened on October 1, 1982.

Oaks Tavern Frontierland fast-food facility at Disneyland; open from 1956 to September 1978. It later became Stage Door Cafe.

O'Brien, Clay Child actor; appeared in *One Little Indian* (Mark) and *The Apple Dumpling Gang* (Bobby Bradley), and on television in *Hog Wild*, *The Whiz Kid and the Carnival Caper*, and *The Whiz Kid and the Mystery at Riverton*.

O'Brien, Cubby (Carl) Mouseketeer from the 1950s television show.

O'Brien, Edmond (1915–1985) Actor; appeared in *Moon Pilot* (McClosky), on television in the *Gallegher* series.

O'Brien, Ken (1915–1990) He came to Disney as an animator in 1937, working on the animated features from *Snow White and the Seven Dwarfs* to *Sleeping Beauty*. In 1962 he transferred to WED

Enterprises, to help program Audio-Animatronics figures for the New York World's Fair. He continued at WED working on such attractions as Pirates of the Caribbean, The Hall of Presidents, Country Bear Jamboree, and World of Motion. He retired in 1982.

O'Brien, Pat (1899–1983) Actor; appeared on television in *I Captured the King of the Leprechauns* and *The Sky's the Limit* (Abner Therman).

Ocean Hop, The (film) Oswald the Lucky Rabbit cartoon; released on November 14, 1927.

O'Connor, Carroll (1924–2001) Actor; appeared on television in *Ride a Northbound Horse*.

O'Connor, Ken (1908–1998) Layout artist; started working at Disney in 1935 and served as art director or layout man on 13 features and nearly 100 shorts, including *Snow White and the Seven Dwarfs*, *Fantasia*, *Lady and the Tramp*, and the Academy Award–winning *Toot, Whistle, Plunk and Boom*. He retired in 1978 but returned to work on the development of shows such as World of Motion and Universe of Energy at Epcot, and the film *Back to Neverland* for the Animation Tour at Disney-MGM Studios. He was honored with the Disney Legends Award in 1992.

O'Donnell, Chris Actor; appeared in *The Three Musketeers* (D'Artagnan) and *Mad Love* (Matt Leland).

O'Donnell, Rosie Actress; appeared in *Another Stakeout* (Gina Garrett), and provided the voice of Terk in *Tarzan*.

O'Donovan, Leo J., S.J. Member of the Disney board of directors beginning September 30, 1996.

Odyssey Fast-food restaurant located between Future World and World Showcase at Epcot, opened October 1, 1982. The hexagonal restaurant is located on a pool of water, reachable by several bridges/walkways. Closed July 30, 1994, to be used for special events and banquets only.

Of Cats and Men (film) Sixteen mm release of footage from a television show; released in April 1968. Traces the history of the cat—a god in Egyptian days, an evil spirit in the Dark Ages, and a pet today.

Of Horses and Men (film) Educational film; released in August 1968. The film tells the story of the horse and how man has depended upon it.

Off Beat (film) As a favor, library clerk Joe Gower takes the place of his friend police officer Abe Washington at a dance audition for cops. He is supposed to fail, and get his friend out of the show, but he falls in love with his dance partner, hostage negotiator Rachel, who thinks he is really a cop, and passes the audition. Joe continues the impersonation in order to win Rachel, but finally decides to confess. Before he can do so, he is taken hostage—still in uniform—by bank robbers. He foils the robbers, and Rachel learns the truth. They realize their love makes up for his masquerade, and dance together at the policeman's show. Released on April 11, 1986. Directed by Michael Dinner. A Touchstone Picture. 92 min. Stars Judge Reinhold (Joe Gower), Meg Tilly (Rachel Wareham), Cleavant Derricks (Abe Washington), Joe Mantegna (Pete Peterson), Jacques D'Amboise (August), Amy Wright (Mary Ellen Grunewald), John Turturro (Neil Pepper). This was Judge Reinhold's first starring picture. The film was made entirely in New York City at locations ranging from the bustling sections of Midtown Manhattan and Soho to a tree-lined residential section of Brooklyn. Among the key shooting sites were Central Park, the Times Square subway station, the Vivian Beaumont Theatre in Lincoln Center, the New York School of Ballet on the Upper West Side, and the New York Public Library. Released on video in 1986 and 1989.

Off His Rockers (film) Special experimental cartoon, making some use of computer animation; released on July 17, 1992. The magical tale of a young boy who has abandoned his faithful rocking horse playmate in favor of the latest video games. Unwilling to be "put out to pasture," the wooden horse uses some inventive and hilarious means to remind his fickle friend of the great times they used to have when his imagination was free to roam. Soon the boy is back in the saddle again as he gallops off into the sunset in search of exciting new adventures. Directed by Barry Cook. Animated at Disney-MGM Studios in Florida. 5 min.

Off the Page Shop in Hollywood Pictures Backlot at Disney's California Adventure; opened on February 8, 2001. Features animation-related merchandise, books, and artwork.

Officer Duck (film) Donald Duck cartoon; released on October 10, 1939. Directed by Clyde Geronimi. Donald is a cop who has to serve eviction papers on Pete. He finally manages to arrest him by posing as a doorstep baby to get access to the house.

Ogg, Sammy Actor; appeared in *Adventure in Dairyland* and *Spin and Marty* on the *Mickey Mouse Club.*

Oh, Teacher (film) Oswald the Lucky Rabbit cartoon; released on September 19, 1927.

Oh, What a Knight (film) Oswald the Lucky Rabbit cartoon; released in 1928.

'Ohana Restaurant in the Polynesian Resort at Walt Disney World, taking the place of the Papeete Bay Verandah; opened on April 12, 1995. Guests have an interactive dining experience as food is grilled in an 18-foot semicircular fire pit on skewers up to three feet long, and then served family style.

O'Hara, Paige Actress; voiced Belle in *Beauty and the Beast.*

Oilspot and Lipstick (film) Special computer-animated cartoon; released at the SIGGRAPH convention in Anaheim on July 28, 1987. Computer animation is utilized to bring to life objects in a junkyard. The junk monster threatens two small "junk" dogs, but the boy dog (Oilspot) manages to defeat the monster and rescue his girlfriend (Lipstick).

Okun, Erwin (1934–1992) He joined Disney in 1981 to handle corporate communications, became a corporate officer in 1984, and by 1992 was senior vice president. He prepared corporate press releases, dealt with press inquiries, and helped write the company's annual report.

Ol' Swimmin' 'ole, The (film) Oswald the Lucky Rabbit cartoon; released on February 6, 1928.

Old Army Game, The (film) Donald Duck cartoon; released on November 5, 1943. Directed by Jack King. Though Donald is in the Army, he enjoys his evenings out by fooling Sgt. Pete, leaving a snoring record in the barracks. But one evening he is caught, escaping in one of three boxes, which turns into the famous shell game. A chase ensues.

Old Curiosity Shop, The (television) Four-hour Disney Channel Premiere film; first aired on March 19 and 20, 1995. In 19th-century England, Nell's secure and innocent childhood is threatened when the family's curio shop, owned by her compulsive gambling grandfather, is repossessed by the evil moneylender, Daniel Quilp. Nell and her grandfather must take to the road in search of safety and happiness. On their travels, they encounter bizarre and fascinating characters who make the world itself seem like a curiosity shop. Directed by Kevin Connor. Stars Peter Ustinov (Grandfather), Tom Courtenay (Quilp), Sally Walsh (Nell), James Fox (Single Gentleman), William Mannering (Kit). Filming took place at various locales throughout Ireland, with the majority of the film being shot at Ardmore Studios in Dublin. The streets of Dickensian London, as well as Quilp's wharf and dockland, were built entirely for the production and then burned to the ground as part of the film's dramatic conclusion.

Old Key West Resort New name, in January 1996, for the Disney Vacation Club Resort at Walt Disney World. It initially sold out its membership inventory at 25,000 member families in 1998. New accommodations were added in November and December 1999.

Old King Cole (film) Silly Symphony cartoon; released on July 29, 1933. Directed by Dave Hand. King Cole's ball at the castle is attended by the many characters of Mother Goose, emerging from the pages of a large book. Later, problems occur in trying to get all the characters back into the book.

Old MacDonald Duck (film) Donald Duck cartoon; released on September 12, 1941. Directed by Jack King. Donald, to the accompaniment of "Old MacDonald Had a Farm," does chores, and feeds the chickens and pigs. When he attempts to milk a cow, a fly bothers him, and his attempts to combat it causes the pail to be upset and Donald to be kicked by the cow.

Old Mill, The (film) Silly Symphony cartoon; released on November 5, 1937. Directed by Wilfred Jackson. The first film to use the multiplane camera. Night in an old mill is dramatically  depicted in this Oscar-winning short in which the frightened occupants, including birds, timid mice, owls, and other creatures try to stay safe and dry as a storm approaches. As the thunderstorm worsens, the mill wheel begins to turn and the whole mill threatens to blow apart until at last the storm subsides. Besides the award for Best Cartoon, Walt Disney received a second Academy Award, a Scientific and Technical Class II plaque, for the design and application of the multiplane camera.

Old Port Royale Central shop and food service area for the Caribbean Beach Resort at Walt Disney World, featuring a restaurant, food court, the Calypso Trading Post and Straw Market, and a swimming pool.

Old Sequoia (film) Donald Duck cartoon; released on December 21, 1945. Directed by Jack King. Forest ranger Don is charged with guarding a sequoia tree, but he must deal with some troublesome beavers who, despite Donald's pleading and promises, manage to fell the tree. Donald is fired.

Old Yeller (film) In the late 1860s on a ranch in Texas, a big, mongrel yellow dog befriends the Coates family, and in particular the two boys, Travis and Arliss. He proves his loyalty by saving Arliss from a huge bear, Travis from wild pigs, and Mrs. Coates from a wolf infected with hydrophobia. Though Travis shoots the wolf, he must soon after shoot the dog, Old Yeller, who has contracted the dread disease. Travis is inconsolable until he accepts one of Old Yeller's puppies as his own for its uncanny resemblance to Old Yeller. Released December 25, 1957. Directed by Robert Stevenson. 84 min. Based on the well-known book by Fred Gipson, the film grossed over $8 million in its initial release and has proved a perennial Disney favorite. Stars Dorothy McGuire (Katie Coates), Fess Parker (Jim Coates), Tommy Kirk (Travis), Kevin Corcoran (Arliss). The dog who played Old Yeller was named Spike. Gil George and Oliver Wallace wrote the title song. Two educational films were made from the film, *Love and Duty: Which Comes First?* (1975) and an episode in the Films as Literature series. A program on the *Disneyland* television series, *The Best Doggoned Dog in the World*, aired shortly before the film's release to promote the film. *Old Yeller* was reissued in 1965 and 1974. Released on video in 1981 and 1992.

Olde World Antiques Shop in Liberty Square in Magic Kingdom Park at Walt Disney World; opened in March 1972 and closed on January 30,

1996. The antique shop at Disneyland was the One-of-a-Kind Shop.

Oldest Rookie, The (television) Television series; aired on CBS from September 16, 1987 to January 6, 1988. After 25 years on the police force as a senior-ranking public relations officer, Ike Porter decides to hit the streets and is paired with a free-wheeling partner, Tony Jonas, who is half his age. Through a growing mutual respect for each other, their own brand of charm, and unorthodox methods, the two solve more than their share of cases, while driving their superiors crazy. Stars Paul Sorvino (Ike), D. W. Moffett (Tony), Raymond J. Barry (Zaga), Marshall Bell (Lane).

Oliveira, Jose He voiced José Carioca.

Oliver Lead character, a kitten, in *Oliver & Company*; voiced by Joey Lawrence, who went on to star in the television series *Blossom*.

Oliver, Barret Actor; appeared in *Frankenweenie*, and on television in *Spot Marks the X*.

Oliver & Company (film) The Oliver Twist story animated with a twist—the setting is New York and Oliver is a kitten and Fagin the human master of a pack of pickpocket dogs. When a wealthy little girl from Fifth Avenue finds Oliver and takes him uptown to live in her mansion,

Fagin's evil boss, Sykes, steps in and kidnaps the pair. His nasty plan is foiled however, when Oliver's motley crew of dog buddies, aided by Jenny's prissy poodle, Georgette, decide to use their street savoir faire in order to rescue their feline friend. Released on November 18, 1988.

Directed by George Scribner. 72 min. With the voices of Joey Lawrence (Oliver), Billy Joel (Dodger), Cheech Marin (Tito), Richard Mulligan (Einstein), Roscoe Lee Browne (Francis), Sheryl Lee Ralph (Rita), Dom DeLuise (Fagin), Robert Loggia (Sykes), Bette Midler (Georgette). Twelve-year-old Joey Lawrence would later go on to become a teenage heartthrob on *Blossom*. Six supervising animators and a team of over 300 artists and technicians worked for over two and a half years to create this hand-drawn feature film in the time-honored Disney tradition. More than a million story sketches and drawings were required to produce the 119,275 hand-painted cels that comprise the finished film. Designers went to New York and photographed street scenes from a dog's perspective—18 inches off the ground—getting stares from passersby but providing excellent reference material for the layout artists. To give the backgrounds a contemporary and hard-edged look, Xerox overlays were used, the first time for this approach since *One Hundred and One Dalmatians*. Many of the inanimate objects in the film were created and animated on the computer—cars, cabs, buses, Sykes's limousine, Fagin's trike (part scooter and part shopping cart), a cement mixer, a sewer pipe, a spiral staircase, a piano, subway tunnels and trains, cityscapes, and even the Brooklyn Bridge. This was the first film to have its own department set up expressly for the purpose of generating computer animation. Many different songwriters contributed to the production, including Howard Ashman and Barry Mann ("Once Upon a Time in New York City"); Dan Hartman and Charlie Midnight ("Why Should I Worry?"); Barry Manilow, Jack Feldman, and Bruce Sussman ("Perfect Isn't Easy"); and Dean Pitchford and Tom Snow ("Streets of Gold"). Re-released and released on video in 1996.

Oliver Twist (television) Television movie appearing on *The Wonderful World of Disney*; aired on November 16, 1997. An orphaned boy in 19-century England is given shelter and clothed by an old criminal who provides a family-type setting for many orphan boys while preying on their naïveté and teaching them to steal.

Directed by Tony Bill. Stars Richard Dreyfuss (Fagin), Elijah Wood (The Artful Dodger), David O'Hara (Bill Sykes), Alex Trench (Oliver), Antoine Byrne (Nancy). This represents 10-year-old Alex Trench's acting debut. Dreyfuss's young son, Harry, played one of the street urchins. Filming took place at Ardmore Studios in Dublin, and at local locations. Released on video in 1998.

Olivia Flaversham Cute child mouse whose father in kidnapped in *The Great Mouse Detective*; voiced by Susanne Pollatschek.

Olivia's Cafe Restaurant at the Old Key West Resort at Walt Disney World.

Ollie Hopnoodle's Haven of Bliss (television) A Disney Channel Premiere Film; first aired on August 6, 1988. The trials of a family in the 1950s as they prepare for two weeks of vacation. Directed by Dick Bartlett. 90 min. Stars James B. Sikking ("the Old Man"), Dorothy Lyman (Mom), Jerry O'Connell (Ralph), Jason Clarke Adams (Randy). Released on video in 1993.

Olsen, Jack (1923–1980) He joined Disney in 1955 to handle merchandising at Disneyland. He served as the director of merchandise at Disneyland until 1970 when he moved to Florida to begin the merchandise operation at Walt Disney World. He retired in 1977 and was named a Disney Legend in 2005.

Olsen, Moroni (1889–1954) He voiced the Magic Mirror in *Snow White and the Seven Dwarfs*.

Olson, Nancy Actress; appeared in *Pollyanna* (Nancy Furman), *The Absent-Minded Professor* (Betsy Carlisle), *Son of Flubber* (Betsy Brainard), *Smith* (Norah), *Snowball Express* (Sue Baxter), and *Flubber* (cameo as secretary).

Olympic Champ, The (film) Goofy cartoon; released on October 9, 1942. Directed by Jack Kinney. Goofy traces the history of the Olympic Games by demonstrating various events— walking, running, hurdles, pole vaulting, discus, and javelin throwing.

Olympic Elk, The (film) True-Life Adventure featurette; released on February 13, 1952. Directed by James Algar. Depicts the lives of elk living on the Olympia Peninsula in Washington, including their feeding habits, breeding, and battles for supremacy of the herd.

Olympic Games Walt Disney helped produce the pageantry for the Olympic Winter Games in Squaw Valley, California, beginning February 18, 1960.

O'Malley, J. Pat (1901–1985) Actor; appeared in *Son of Flubber* (sign painter), and provided the voices of Walrus, Carpenter, Tweedledee, and Tweedledum in *Alice in Wonderland*, Jasper Badun and the Colonel in *One Hundred and One Dalmatians*, Colonel Hathi and Buzzie in *The Jungle Book*, Otto in *Robin Hood*, and Cyril in *The Adventures of Ichabod and Mr. Toad*. Also appeared on television in *The Swamp Fox* and *The Adventures of Spin and Marty* (Perkins).

Omega Connection, The (television) Two-hour television movie; aired on March 18, 1979. Directed by Robert Clouse. Young American government agent Luther Starlin arrives in London to vacation with a friend, Roger Pike, but immediately gets involved unintentionally with intrigue surrounding a defecting Eastern European scientist. Through the use of James Bond–like inventions, Luther and Roger are able to outwit the international crime organization that is trying to abduct the scientist. Stars Jeffrey Byron, Larry Cedar, Roy Kinnear, Lee Montague, Mona Washbourne, David Kossoff, Frank Windsor. The film was shot on location in London. Released theatrically abroad as *The London Connection*.

Omnibus Main Street vehicles at Disneyland; beginning in 1956. Also in Magic Kingdom Park at Walt Disney World; beginning October 1, 1971. The double-decker buses were urgently needed to transport guests around the World Showcase Lagoon at Epcot, so those from California and the Magic Kingdom were moved to Epcot in the 1980s. Also at World Bazaar at Tokyo Disneyland;

opened on April 15, 1983. At Disneyland Paris; opened on April 12, 1992.

Omnisphere (film) Projected in Omnimax 70mm on hemispherical screens, this film was produced as part of the Horizons attraction at Epcot in Walt Disney World and includes a space shuttle blastoff, a flight over Manhattan, and a computerized journey across the Earth's surface.

On Ice (film) Mickey Mouse cartoon; released on September 28, 1935. Directed by Ben Sharpsteen. Mickey and friends have various levels of enjoyment skating on a frozen river. As Mickey and Minnie glide romantically, Donald plays tricks on Pluto and ends up in trouble himself with a kite, from which Mickey must save him.

On Promised Land (television) A Disney Channel Premiere Film; first aired on April 17, 1994. A poignant drama set in the American South of the 1950s about two families, one black and one white, and the dreams and broken promises that bind them together. Directed by Joan Tewkesbury. Stars Joan Plowright (Mrs. Appletree), Norman D. Golden II, Judith Ivey. 99 min.

On Seal Island See *Seal Island.*

On the Record Stage presentation set in a recording studio, consisting of more than 50 classic Disney songs performed by a cast of singers, dancers, and musicians. Directed by Robert Longbottom. It premiered at the Palace Theater in Cleveland, Ohio, on November 9, 2004, with an official opening of November 19, prior to setting out on a national tour until July 31, 2005. The original cast was headed by Emily Skinner and Brian Sutherland.

On Vacation (television) Television show; aired on March 7, 1956. Directed by Jack Hannah. Some later reruns as *On Vacation with Mickey Mouse and Friends.* Jiminy Cricket hosts and tries

to find the other Disney characters, but they are all on vacation.

On Your Own (film) Educational film; released in September 1985. The film outlines safety measures and self-care skills for children who are home alone, and methods for confronting their fears.

Once and Again (television) One-hour television series on ABC; premiered on September 21, 1999, and ended on May 2, 2001. Two divorced parents meet by chance and start a romance, but are caught in a crossfire of conflicting opinions about their relationship from children, exspouses, and society at large. Stars Bill Campbell (Rick Sammler), Sela Ward (Lily Manning), Shane West (Eli), Julia Whelan (Grace), Susanna Thompson (Karen), Jeffrey Nordling (Jake). Released on DVD in 2002.

Once Upon a Dream Song from *Sleeping Beauty*; written by Sammy Fain and Jack Lawrence, adapted from a theme by Tchaikovsky.

Once Upon a Mattress (television) Two-hour television movie for *The Wonderful World of Disney* aired on ABC on December 18, 2005. A whimsical, fractured telling of the classic fairytale, "The Princess and the Pea," with Prince Dauntless, the handsome hero, desperate to find a wife. Dozens of women have been tested and rejected as unsuitable by his mother, Queen Aggravain, who insists her son must marry a "true princess." The prince comes upon the lovable—and definitely not shy—Princess Winnifred, but the Queen is appalled and conspires to cook up a test for "sensitivity" to get rid of her. What about a pea under 20 mattresses? Directed by Kathleen Marshall. Stars Carol Burnett (Queen Aggravain), Tracey Ullman (Princess Winnifred), Denis O'Hare (Prince Dauntless), Zooey Deschanel (Lady Larken), Michael Boatman (Jester), Edward Hibbert (Wizard), Matthew Morrison (Sir Harry), Tom Smothers (King Sextimus). Carol Burnett originated the role of Princess Winnifred in 1959, when the play debuted Off Broadway and later moved to the Great White Way. It eventually became one of her signature roles, not only on stage, but also in two television productions, in 1964 and 1972. Produced by Mattress Productions, Ltd. in association with Touchstone Television. Released on DVD in 2005.

Once Upon a Mouse (film) Kaleidoscopic magic carpet ride through the world of Disney animation, including segments from hundreds of films shown through the use of montages, collages, computerized optical effects, behind-the-scenes footage, and special tributes to Walt Disney and Mickey. Released on July 10, 1981. Produced by Kramer/Rocklin Studios in association with Walt Disney Productions. 28 min.

Once Upon a Time (film) A 1944 Columbia film; starring Janet Blair and Cary Grant as a free-wheeling promoter who finds a caterpillar who can dance. The caterpillar, Curly, is a child's pet, and the kid does not want to give Curly up for he wants him to go to work for Walt Disney and become famous. An actor (Walter Fenner) portrays Walt Disney in the film.

Once Upon a Time in New York City Song from *Oliver & Company*; written by Howard Ashman and Barry Mann.

Once Upon a Wintertime (film) Frances Langford sings about a boy and girl's outing on the ice in the 1800s in this segment from *Melody Time*. Re-released as a short on  September 17, 1954. The song is by Bobby Worth and Ray Gilbert.

One and Only, Genuine, Original Family Band, The (film) In the year 1888, the eleven members of the Bower family comprise "The One and Only, Genuine, Original Family Band," which is practicing to perform at the Democratic Presidential Convention for Grover Cleveland. But their plans go askew when a young Republican newspaperman, who supports Cleveland's rival, Benjamin Harrison, falls in love with Alice Bower, and convinces even Grandpa that they should move to the Dakota Territory. The family inescapably becomes involved in personal and political problems once they arrive. Difficulties end on Election Day, however, and the family band harmonizes once more. World premiere in New York on March 21, 1968. Directed by Michael O'Herlihy. 110 min. Stars Walter Brennan (Grandpa Bower), Buddy Ebsen (Calvin), Lesley Ann Warren (Alice), John Davidson (Joe Carder), Kurt Russell (Sidney), Janet Blair (Katie), Wally Cox (Mr. Wampler). Goldie Jean Hawn plays a bit part as a giggly girl and later shortened her name as she moved into stardom in a host of films. The film is based on the autobiographical novel by Laura Bower Van Nuys. The musical numbers were choreographed by Hugh Lambert and written by Richard M. Sherman and Robert B. Sherman. The songs include: "Dakota," "The One And Only, Genuine, Original Family Band," "Let's Put it Over with Grover," "Ten Feet Off The Ground," "'Bout Time," "The Happiest Girl Alive," and "West o' the Wide Missouri." Released on video in 1981 and 1985.

One and Only You (film) Educational film about positive self-image and getting along with others, in the Think It Through With Winnie the Pooh series; released in September 1989. 14 min.

One by One (film) On a rainy day, a group of children in a South African township decide to build their own kites. As they complete these kites, the sky starts to clear. The children run out into a field that is now golden with sunshine and proceed to fly their homemade kites. In the end, they release the kites, a metaphor for freedom. Animated short released on *The Lion King 2: Simba's Pride* special edition DVD on August 31, 2004. Directed by Pixote Hunt and David A. Bossert. Music by Lebo M, being a song from the stage production of *The Lion King*. 6 min.

One Day at Teton Marsh (television) Television show; aired on November 8, 1964. Depicts the animal life, including ospreys, otters, beavers, and others, in a small area near the Grand Teton

Mountains. Based on the book by Sally Carrighar. Narrated by Sebastian Cabot.

One Day on Beetle Rock (television) Television show; aired on November 19, 1967. A small area of Sequoia National Park is teeming with wildlife. Narrated by Sebastian Cabot.

One Good Cop (film) New York City police lieutenant Artie Lewis faces a major dilemma in his life when his longtime partner Stevie Diroma is killed in the line of duty. Artie and his wife, Rita, take in Stevie's three orphaned daughters, but cannot make ends meet on a cop's salary. He soon finds himself straddling the fine line between his ethical code as a "good cop" or the temptation of the corrupt ways of the street in order to keep his suddenly enlarged family together. Released on May 3, 1991. Directed by Heywood Gould. A Hollywood Picture. 105 min. Stars Michael Keaton (Artie Lewis), Rene Russo (Rita Lewis), Anthony LaPaglia (Stevie Diroma). Filmed in New York City and Los Angeles. Released on video in 1991.

One Hour in Wonderland (television) The first Disney television show; sponsored by Coca-Cola and shown on December 25, 1950. Directed by Richard Wallace. The show serves as a promo for the upcoming *Alice in Wonderland.* Joining Walt Disney are Edgar Bergen with Charlie McCarthy and Mortimer Snerd, Kathy Beaumont, Bobby Driscoll, and Diane and Sharon Disney. Hans Conried portrays the slave in the Magic Mirror.

One Hundred and One Dalmatians (film) Animated feature about Pongo, a clever Dalmatian, who arranges to get married to the female of his choice, Perdita, and to round things out, gets his master, Roger Radcliff, wed to Perdita's pretty mistress, Anita. Soon Perdita produces 15 puppies, which the evil Cruella De Vil arranges to have kidnapped in her quest to make a fabulous Dalmatian-fur coat, also gathering many other puppies in order to accomplish her aim. Helped by the Twilight Bark, whereby dogs throughout

the city and the countryside pass along the word of the missing puppies by barking, Pongo and Perdita go into action and locate 99 stolen puppies in Cruella's sinister-looking home, Hell Hall. Pongo, Perdita, and the puppies manage to escape and, through various ruses, elude the pursuing Cruella. Cruella and her henchmen, Horace and Jasper Badun, get their just desserts. Roger and Anita adopt the puppies and, with their new family of 101 Dalmatians and Nanny to look after them, plan to build a "Dalmatian Plantation" and live happily ever after. Released on January 25, 1961. Directed by Wolfgang Reitherman, Hamilton Luske, Clyde Geronimi. Based on the book by Dodie Smith. The songs "Cruella De Ville (*sic*)," "Dalmatian Plantation," and "Kanine Krunchies Commercial" were written by Mel Leven. Costing $4 million, the film did phenomenal business on its original release, and in its subsequent reissues in 1969, 1979, 1985, and 1991. Released on video in 1992. It was the first feature to solely use the Xerox process for transferring the animators' drawings to cels. Prior to this, each one of the animators' drawings had to be hand traced in ink onto a cel. The new process sped up production greatly, especially in a film that had so many dogs, and not just dogs, but spotted dogs. It would have been horribly time-consuming to hand-ink each of the cels. Voice actors include Rod Taylor (Pongo), Betty Lou Gerson (Cruella de Vil), Lisa Davis (Anita), Ben Wright (Roger), and Cate Bauer (Perdita). 79 min. The famous Twilight Bark, used to rescue the puppies, was later adopted as the name for the newsletter for Disney Feature Animation. Note the spelling of Dalmatians. This word is probably

the most misspelled Disney word, with most people misspelling it "Dalmations." Dalmatia, however, is a place, so people, and dogs, from there are Dalmatians.

101 Dalmatians (film) Live-action version of the Dodie Smith book and Disney's 1961 animated feature. Anita, who works as a designer for Cruella De Vil, is fired when she will not sell her boss the 15 Dalmatian puppies that have been born to Pongo and Perdy. Not willing to take no for an answer, Cruella arranges to have the puppies stolen by her hapless henchmen, Jasper and Horace, setting in motion a countrywide search. A Walt Disney picture in association with Great Oaks Entertainment. Directed by Stephen Herek. Released on November 27, 1996. Stars Glenn Close (Cruella), Jeff Daniels (Roger), Joely Richardson (Anita), Hugh Laurie and Mark Williams (Jasper and Horace), Joan Plowright (Nanny). 103 min. Filmed on seven soundstages at Shepperton Studios in England, as well as at selected locations in and around London. A major task was the finding and training of over 200 Dalmatian puppies whose welfare was of top concern to the filmmakers. Released on video in 1997.

One Hundred and One Dalmatians: A Lesson in Self-Assertion (film) Educational film; released in September 1981. The film teaches how to stand up to a bully through self-assertion.

101 Dalmatians: The Series (television) Animated television series; in syndication beginning September 1, 1997, and on ABC beginning September 13, 1997. The spotted puppies go on wild adventures that are both entertaining and educational. In a playful, fun, and subtle way, each episode explores an important issue for kids—the perils of exaggerating, the responsibility of babysitting, the true meaning of winning, dealing with a bully, etc. Produced by Walt Disney Television Animation and Jumbo Pictures, Inc. Voices include Pam Segall and Debi Mae West (Lucky), Kath Soucie (Anita, Rolly, and Cadpig), Jeff Bennett (Roger), Tara Charendoff (Spot), April Win-

chell (Cruella De Vil), David Lander (Horace), Michael McKean (Jasper), Charlotte Rae (Nanny), Kevin Schon (Pongo), Pam Dawber (Perdita). 65 episodes.

101 Dalmatians II: Patch's London Adventure (film) An animated direct-to-video sequel to *One Hundred and One Dalmatians*. Patch is accidentally left behind when his family moves to their new farm, and he sets out to meet his hero, canine star Thunderbolt. Thunderbolt uses Patch to help him execute real-life heroics, while Cruella De Vil seeks the puppies—dead or live—as models for a spot-fixated artist, Lars. Released on January 21, 2003. Directed by Jim Kammerud and Brian Smith. Voices include Barry Bostwick (Thunderbolt), Jason Alexander (Lightning), Martin Short (Lars), Susanne Blakeslee (Cruella), Bobby Lockwood (Patch), Samuel West (Pongo), Maurice LaMarche (Horace), Jeff Bennett (Jasper), Jodi Benson (Anita), Tim Bentinck (Roger), Kath Soucie (Perdita), Mary Macleod (Nanny), Michael Lerner (Producer). Original songs by Randy Rogel.

101 Problems of Hercules, The (film) Television show; aired on October 16, 1966. Three mismatched dogs must care for the sheep when the shepherd is injured by Indians, guarding them against the elements, man, and various predators. Stars Harold Reynolds, David Farrow, Elliott Lindsey, Kathe McDowell.

102 Dalmatians (film) Cruella De Vil is released from prison on good behavior, swearing that she will have nothing to do with fur ever again. Everyone marvels at her miraculous transformation, but she, however, cannot keep her promise and soon is plotting another scheme with French fashion designer Jean Pierre Le Pelt to get her ultimate Dalmatian coat, as she and the dogs romp through Paris. Released

on November 22, 2000. Directed by Kevin Lima. Stars Glenn Close (Cruella De Vil), Ioan Gruffudd (Kevin Shepherd), Alice Evans (Chloe Simon), Tim McInnerny (Alonso), Gérard Depardieu (Jean Pierre Le Pelt). 100 min. Filmed in England and France. Nominated for an Academy Award for Costume Design. Released on video in 2001.

100 Lives of Black Jack Savage, The (television) Television series on NBC; premiered as a two-hour pilot on March 31, 1991, and then aired from April 5 to May 26, 1991. Set on the Caribbean island of San Pietro, the story concerns the ghost of a 17th-century pirate who teams up with an exiled billionaire to save 100 lives as atonement for their wrongdoings. In the pilot episode, the unlikely crime fighters set out to solve the mysterious disappearance of the island's fishermen from a remote reef on which Black Jack's treasure is buried. Stars Daniel Hugh Kelly (Barry Tarberry), Steven Williams (Black Jack Savage), Steve Hytner (Logan Murphy), Roma Downey (Danielle St. Claire), Bert Rosario (Abel Vasquez).

100,000,000 Franc Train Robbery (television) Television show; part 1 of *The Horse Without a Head*.

100 Years of Magic Special celebration at Walt Disney World for the 100th anniversary of the birth of Walt Disney in 2001, and extending into 2003. For the first time, four special parades were created, one at each park. The Magic Kingdom had Share A Dream Come True, Epcot had Tapestry of Dreams, Disney's Animal Kingdom had Mickey's Jammin' Jungle Parade, and Disney-MGM Studios had Stars and Motor Cars. There was a special exhibit on Walt Disney's life and career, One Man's Dream, at Disney-MGM.

One Little Indian (film) A story of the army in the Old West. Clint Keys has deserted because soldiers have killed his Indian wife. While fleeing to Mexico with two camels stolen from the army, he becomes friends with Mark, a ten-year-old boy raised by Indians, who is also a fugitive. During

Mark's capture, Clint is almost hanged, but is finally set free. The pair then head for Colorado to find the attractive widow and her daughter they met during their flight from the army. Released on June 20, 1973. Directed by Bernard McEveety. 91 min. Stars James Garner (Clint), Vera Miles (Doris), Clay O'Brien (Mark), Jodie Foster (Martha), Pat Hingle (Capt. Stewart), Morgan Woodward (Sgt. Raines), John Doucette (Sgt. Waller), Jim Davis (trail boss), Jay Silverheels (Jimmy Wolf). Eleven-year-old O'Brien wanted the part so badly that he showed up for auditions in full Indian costume and black wig; only later did the director discover that Clay had blond hair. The film was shot near Kanab, Utah, which is surrounded by the Grand Canyon, Kaibab National Forest, Bryce and Zion National Parks, and Lake Powell. Cooperation was gained with the U.S. Department of the Interior's Bureau of Land Management. The production was constantly delayed by accidents and freak mishaps: lightning struck the plane flying the cast and crew into Kanab; flooding occurred; the truck containing all the props caught fire, destroying both; Jodie Foster sprained an ankle; and stuntmen were injured in the action sequences. Released on video in 1986.

One Magic Christmas (film) Her husband and kids try to cheer up a young mother, Ginnie Grainger, who has lost the spirit of Christmas. Gideon, a Christmas angel, appears to help and causes a number of seeming tragedies in the family's life. He then takes the daughter on a visit to Santa Claus to retrieve a letter the mother had written years before. The letter helps the mother regain her Christmas spirit, and Gideon turns back the clock to negate the tragic events. Released on November 22, 1985. Directed by Phillip Borsos. 89 min. Stars Mary Steenburgen (Ginny Grainger), Harry Dean Stanton (Gideon), Arthur Hill (Caleb Grainger), Elizabeth Harnois (Abbie), Gary Basaraba (Jack), Robbie Magwood (Cal). Walt Disney Pictures agreed to co-finance this film with the participation of Silver Screen Partners II and Telefilm Canada. Filming took place in Toronto. The Christmas spirit prevailed during the early stages of principal photography at a Toronto shopping center when more than 300 extras turned out for a Sunday shoot. At the location, 50 shopkeepers took down their current Valentine's Day decorations and replaced them with Christmas decor. The shopping center also offered a Santa Claus Village complete with Santa, a 20-piece brass band, and an all-girl choir singing Christmas carols. In the Toronto suburb of Scarborough, all the residents in a three-block radius also joined in the true spirit of Christmas and happily bedecked their houses with seasonal decorations for the six days of filming in their area. Throughout the filming, as the production moved to the towns of Owen Sound and Meaford, the inconsistent weather nearly made filming impossible, as the crew faced rain, fog, sleet, blizzard, winds gusting up to 50 mph, mud, 15-foot snow drifts denying access to country locations and, often, zero visibility. Production designer Bill Brodie constructed three major sets: the Grainger house, the grandfather's home, and Santa's workshop and cottage, which was filled with real rare toys, insured for $1 million prior to filming, and 20,000 actual letters to Santa from the Toronto main post office. Released on video in 1986.

One Man's Dream Show at Videopolis at Disneyland from December 16, 1989, to April 29, 1990. Originally produced at Tokyo Disneyland, where it ran from April 15, 1988, to September 3, 1995. Tells Walt Disney's story through his animated triumphs. One unique element of the show was that the beginning was all in black and white; the characters and sets then almost magically changed to full color. The show returned to Tokyo Disneyland on July 3, 2004, as *One Man's Dream II—The Magic Lives On*.

One Man's Dream: 100 Years of Magic (film) Film created in 2001 by Walt Disney Imagineering for an exhibit at Disney-MGM Studios at Walt Disney World for the 100 Years of Magic celebration of the 100th anniversary of the birth of Walt Disney. Michael Eisner introduces and Walt Disney himself, through rare digitally enhanced audio commentary, narrates the film, which documents Walt's life. It also screened at Disney Animation at Disney's California Adventure from December 5, 2001, to April 6, 2005. 16 min.

$1,000,000 Duck See *Million Dollar Duck*.

One More Mountain (television) Two-hour television movie; aired on ABC on March 6, 1994. Margaret Reed, a fragile pioneer woman, struggles to overcome hardships, and keep her family alive, while traveling to California over the Sierra Nevada range during the mid-1800s. Directed by Dick Lowry. Stars Meredith Baxter (Margaret), Chris Cooper (James Reed), Larry Drake (Patrick Breen), Jean Simmons (Sarah Keyes).

One-of-a-Kind Antique shop in New Orleans Square at Disneyland; opened in 1967. Lillian Disney was very fond of antiques, and was supposedly Walt Disney's inspiration for opening this shop. In 1995, the shop began carrying antique reproductions and gifts rather than true antiques. The shop was closed on May 13, 1996, and changed to a gourmet shop. The antique shop at Walt Disney World was called Olde World Antiques.

One of Our Dinosaurs Is Missing (film) Lord Southmere, a British intelligence agent, steals a piece of top secret microfilm, the Lotus X, from a Chinese warlord, and hides it in the skeleton of a dinosaur in a London museum after escaping from a Chinese agent, Hnup Wan, who soon recaptures him. Southmere has told his childhood nanny, Hettie, what has happened and she, aided by a small army of fellow nannies, helps foil the machinations of Hnup and his gang. Released on July 9, 1975. Directed by Robert Stevenson. 94 min. Stars Peter Ustinov (Hnup Wan), Helen Hayes (Hettie), Clive Revill (Quon), Derek Nimmo (Lord Southmere), Joan Sims (Emily), Bernard Bresslaw (Fan Choy), Natasha Pyne (Susan). The film was shot on location in London, including the London Zoo in Regent's Park, the Natural History Museum in Kensington, Hyde Park, and parts of Soho. The movie was based on the book *The Great Dinosaur Robbery* by "David Forrest" who was, in actuality, two authors: David Eliades and Bob Forrest Webb. Art director Michael Stringer engaged a team of six modelers who worked for two months replicating two 75-foot-long dinosaur skeletons weighing several tons, which had necks that could bob up and down during the chase sequence. Adding to the 1920s look of the film is a collection of vintage vehicles ranging from a Daimler for Hnup Wan's limousine to Nanny Emily's 1920 Godfrey-Nash cycle car. Released on video in 1986.

One Saturday Morning (television) Two-hour Saturday morning show on ABC; debuted on September 13, 1997, and included *Brand Spanking New Doug*, *Pepper Ann*, and *Recess*, along with segments featuring the Genie from *Aladdin*, a roving reporter named Manny the Uncanny, the Monkey Boys, Mrs. Munger's Class, and an educational segment. A series of short segments (90 seconds apiece) entitled "Great Minds Think 4 Themselves" aired during the show, featuring Robin Williams as the voice of Genie, taking viewers through a mixed media overview of the life of great Americans who "thought for themselves"—such as John Muir, Jackie Robinson, Clara Barton, Ben Franklin, and Cesar Chavez. These segments received two Emmy nominations in 1998. Various other segments were utilized in succeeding years. The series ended on September 7, 2002.

O'Neal, Shaquille Athlete/actor; appeared in *Kazaam* (title role).

Oo-De-Lally Song from *Robin Hood*; written by Roger Miller.

Open Range (film) In 1882, Charley Waite, Boss Spearman, and Mose Harrison are all men trying to escape their pasts by driving cattle on the open range. They try to avoid violence, but one frontier town that is ruled through fear and tyranny changes their lives and forces them into action. Amidst this turmoil, Charley meets the spirited Sue Barlow, who embraces both his heart and his soul. A Touchstone Picture, in association with Cobalt Media Group. Directed by Kevin Costner. Released on August 15, 2003. Stars Robert Duvall (Boss Spearman), Kevin Costner (Charley Waite), Annette Bening (Sue Barlow), Michael Gambon (Denton Baxter), Michael Jeter

(Percy), Diego Luna (Button), James Russo (Sheriff Poole), Abraham Benrubi (Mose Harrison). 138 min. Based on the novel *The Open Range Men*, by Lauran Paine. Filmed in CinemaScope on location at the Stoney Indian Reservation and other locations in Alberta, Canada. Released on video in 2004.

Operation Dumbo Drop (film) U.S. Army captain Sam Cahill, wrapping up his final tour of duty in Vietnam, finds himself trying to replace a village's prized elephant, which had been caught in crossfire between American troops and the North Vietnamese. The task of moving a grown elephant across 300 miles of mine-laden, enemy-infested jungle is more than Cahill had counted on. When travel by road and river does not work, the intrepid crew decides to parachute the elephant using a very big parachute. Released on July 28, 1995. Directed by Simon Wincer. Stars Danny Glover (Sam Cahill), Ray Liotta (Capt. Doyle), Denis Leary (David Poole), Doug E. Doug (Harvey Ashford), Corin Nemec (Lawrence Farley). Filmed in CinemaScope. 108 min. The 26-year-old elephant star, Tai, weighs 8,000 pounds, is eight and a half feet tall, and had to be transported from the United States to the filming location in Thailand by means of a custom-made steel crate carried in a Korean Airlines 747 jumbo jet. Released on video in 1996.

Operation Undersea (television) Television show; aired on December 8, 1954. Directed by Winston Hibler, Hamilton S. Luske. Walt Disney tells the history of the exploration of the sea, then takes viewers behind the scenes of the making of *20,000 Leagues Under the Sea*, describing new techniques that had to be invented for underwater filming. While this show was essentially an hour-long commercial for the new Disney movie, it was of such excellent quality that it won the Emmy Award for Best Individual Show of the year.

Oprah Winfrey Presents: Their Eyes Were Watching God (television) ABC Premiere Event; aired on March 6, 2005. The story of a beautiful and resilient woman's quest for love, sensual excitement, and spiritual fulfillment, despite society's expectations of a woman of color in 1920s America. Janie Crawford's journey takes her through three marriages with very different men, during which she experiences everything from tremendous success to unspeakable heartbreak. Directed by Darnell Martin. Stars Halle Berry (Janie Crawford), Ruben Santiago-Hudson (Joe Starks), Michael Ealy (Tea Cake), Terrence Howard (Amos Hicks), Lorraine Toussaint (Pearl Stone), Nicki Micheaux (Pheoby Watson), Mel Winkler (Logan Killicks), Ruby Dee (Nanny). Based on the novel by Zora Neale Hurston. Produced by Harpo Films/Touchstone Television.

Opry House, The (film) Mickey Mouse cartoon; released in 1929. Directed by Walt Disney. In the first real Disney musical, Mickey is the proprietor of and pianist for a small town vaudeville show.

Optimist/Pessimist: Which Are You? (film) Educational film using sequences from *Pollyanna*. In the Questions!/Answers? series; released in October 1975. The film shows that negativism is wrong and that one should form healthy attitudes.

Orange Bird Character with the head of an orange created for the Florida Citrus Growers when they signed to sponsor the Tropical Serenade in Magic Kingdom Park at Walt Disney World. He appeared in the educational film *Foods and Fun: A Nutrition Adventure.*

Orange Stinger Attraction at Paradise Pier at Disney's California Adventure; opened on February 8, 2001. Guests whirl like "buzzing bumblebees" inside a giant peeling orange.

Orbach, Jerry (1935–2004) Actor; appeared in *Straight Talk* (Milo Jacoby) and provided the voice of Lumiere in *Beauty and the Beast*, Sa'luk in *Aladdin and the King of Thieves*, and Pierre in The Enchanted Tiki Room—Under New Management at Walt Disney World.

Orbitron—Machines Volantes Attraction in Discoveryland in Disneyland Paris, similar to Rocket Jets and Star Jets; opened on April 12, 1992. Also an attraction at Hong Kong Disneyland (without the French subtitle); opened on September 12, 2005.

Orddu, Orgoch, and Orwen The Witches of Morva in *The Black Cauldron*; voiced respectively by Eda Reiss Merin, Billie Hayes, and Adele Malia-Morey.

Originale Alfredo di Roma Ristorante, L' See L'Originale Alfredo di Roma Ristorante.

Orlando Florida city near which Walt Disney decided to build his East Coast version of Disneyland. After the success of his California park, Walt realized that an East Coast park would likely attract many visitors who would be unable to travel all the way to California. Thus, he searched for the ideal location, eventually deciding on the Orlando area of Central Florida. He was able to amass a huge amount of land southwest of the city, and there built the park that would be known as Walt Disney World. Its announcement, the construction, and the subsequent 1971 opening forever changed the face of Orlando, which quickly grew from a sleepy town to a major metropolis.

Orphan's Benefit (film) Mickey Mouse cartoon; released on August 11, 1934. Directed by Burt Gillett. Donald and Goofy were featured together for the first time as they, Mickey, Horace

Horsecollar, and Clarabelle Cow try to put on a show for orphans. But the mischievous children take delight in taunting the performers, including

eggs that fall on Donald as he tries to recite "Mary Had a Little Lamb." Remade with updated animation and in color, released on August 12, 1941. The remake was directed by Riley Thomson.

Orphan's Picnic (film) Mickey Mouse cartoon; released on February 15, 1936. Directed by Ben Sharpsteen. Donald has problems with rambunctious orphans, as in *Orphan's Benefit*, who tease and torment the poor duck into getting in trouble with a beehive and swallowing a bee.

Orville Baby bird character in *Pluto's Fledgling* (1948).

Orville Inept albatross, proprietor of Albatross Air Charter Service, in *The Rescuers*; voiced by Jim Jordan.

Osberg, Anne She was named president of Disney Consumer Products in 1997. She joined Disney in 1988, and served in various positions in the division, until being named president of U.S. and Canada operations in 1994. She left the company in 1999.

Osborne Family Spectacle of Lights Jennings Osborne, an Arkansas businessman, designed a major holiday light show at his home. In 1995 his show, with millions of bulbs, was moved to Disney-MGM Studios, where it continue to amaze guests each holiday season (except for 2003, when construction prevented its installation).

Oscar (film) At his father's deathbed in 1931, notorious bootlegger Angelo "Snaps" Provolone, in a moment of remorse, agrees to his father's plea that he give up his shameful life, become an honest man, and restore his family's name to honor. The bewildered Snaps tries to go straight, but his new image is far too fantastic for either the cops or new easily bribed banker friends. Things are not helped by Snaps' surroundings—a madhouse of peculiar characters and relatives. Mistaken identities and misplaced suitcases all help add up to a day full of surprises for the former gangster. Released on April 26, 1991. Directed by John Landis. A Touchstone Picture. 109 min. During production, the film crew lost many of its sets, props, and 21 period cars leased for the production in a disastrous fire on the Universal Studios backlot, where the movie was being shot. This necessitated an unexpected move to Orlando, Florida, for filming at both Disney-MGM Studios and Universal/Florida, the first movie shot at the latter studio. Stars Sylvester Stallone (Angelo "Snaps" Provolone), Yvonne DeCarlo (Aunt Rosa), Don Ameche (Father Clemente), Tim Curry (Dr. Poole). Kirk Douglas had an uncredited cameo role as Snaps' dying father. Released on video in 1991.

Osgood, Kevin Actor; appeared on the *Mickey Mouse Club* on The Disney Channel, from 1989 to 1993. He is an accomplished dancer, and was the oldest of the kids to appear on the show.

Osment, Haley Joel Actor; appeared in *The Sixth Sense* (Cole Sear), for which he received an Oscar nomination for Best Supporting Actor, in the videos *Beauty and the Beast: The Enchanted Christmas* (voice of Chip) and *The Hunchback of Notre Dame II* (Zephyr), and on television in *Thunder Alley* (Harry Turner). He provided the voice for Beary Barrington in *Country Bears*, Sora on the *Kingdom Hearts* interactive game, and Mowgli in *The Jungle Book 2*.

Osmond, Donny Actor; provided the singing voice of Shang in *Mulan*.

Osmond Brothers, The Singing group; in 1961, the boys, dressed alike, were noticed by the barbershop quartet on Main Street at Disneyland. When asked if they sang, they agreed to do a number. Each group sang a song and the concert went on for almost an hour, attracting and delighting a large crowd. The Osmonds were then brought to the Disneyland entertainment office where their talents were recognized and they were signed to their first professional contract. Later on they appeared on television in *Meet Me at Disneyland*, *Disneyland After Dark*, and *Disneyland Showtime*.

Osprey Ridge Golf course at Bonnet Creek Golf Club at Walt Disney World, nestled in some of the outer reaches of the resort. Designed by Tom Fazio.

Oswald the Lucky Rabbit Series of 26 silent cartoons made by Walt Disney between 1927 and 1928 for Charles Mintz, who contracted with Universal for the distribution. When Walt lost the rights to Oswald, he came up with the character of Mickey Mouse. The Oswald character was later continued by Walter Lantz. Sound was added by Universal, the copyright holder, to some of the Disney Oswalds in the early days of television. Oswald was the first Disney character to generate merchandise—there was a candy bar, a stencil set, and a pin-back button.

The Oswald cartoons were:

1. *Poor Papa*
2. *Trolley Troubles*
3. *Oh, Teacher*
4. *Great Guns*
5. *The Mechanical Cow*
6. *All Wet*
7. *The Ocean Hop*
8. *The Banker's Daughter*
9. *Harem Scarem*
10. *Rickety Gin*
11. *Neck 'n Neck*
12. *Empty Socks*
13. *The Ol' Swimmin' 'ole*
14. *Africa Before Dark*
15. *Rival Romeos*
16. *Bright Lights*
17. *Sagebrush Sadie*
18. *Ride 'em Plowboy*
19. *Ozzie of the Mounted*
20. *Hungry Hoboes*
21. *Oh, What a Knight*
22. *Sky Scrappers*
23. *The Fox Chase*
24. *Tall Timber*
25. *Sleigh Bells*
26. *Hot Dog*

Other Me, The (television) A Disney Channel Original Movie; debuting on September 8, 2000. Thirteen-year-old Will Browning accidentally clones himself, calling the clone Twoie. Will gets Twoie to go to school in his place, but soon gets bored with the routine and becomes jealous of his twin. The pair may have the same genetic makeup, but Twoie is everything Will is not: popular at school and at home, and a whiz to boot. Directed by Manny Coto. Stars Andrew Lawrence (Will/Twoie), Brenden Jefferson (Chuckie), Lori Hallier (Mom), Mark Taylor (Dad), Alison Pill (Alanna Browning). Based on the book *Me Two* by Mary C. Ryan.

Other Side of Heaven, The (film) Nineteen-year-old John Groberg is sent on a three-year Mormon mission to Tonga, where he finds himself in the midst of a culture as remote to him as the island is to his Idaho Falls home. Not understanding the language, and longing for the girl he left behind, John faces suspicion, distrust, typhoons, mosquitoes, and other perils of man and nature as he reaches out to the people of Tonga. A video release on April 1, 2003, by Walt Disney Home Entertainment after a limited theatrical release by Excel Entertainment beginning December 14, 2001. Directed by Mitch Davis. Stars Christopher Gorham (John Groberg), Anne Hathaway (Jean Sabin), Joe Folau (Feki), Miriama Smith (Lavania). 113 min.

Other Sister, The (film) Carla Tate, while mentally challenged, has matured into a young woman with dreams and ambitions, searching for her independence. But she has a handicap—her mother—who refuses to accept her daughter's personal needs. Carla falls in love for the first time, with a young man who is also mentally challenged, and defies her family in order to prove that, despite all appearances, she has the capacity to be a responsible adult, worthy of being loved. Released on February 26, 1999. Directed by Garry Marshall. A Touchstone Picture. Stars Juliette Lewis (Carla Tate), Diane Keaton (Elizabeth Tate), Tom Skerritt (Radley Tate), Giovanni Ribisi (Danny McMahon). 131 min. Filmed in Cinema-Scope. Released on video in 1999.

O'Toole, Peter Actor; appeared in *Kidnapped* (Robin MacGregor).

Otter in the Family, An (television) Television show; aired on February 21, 1965. A boy in

Wisconsin cares for an injured otter, who is then suspected of stealing eggs. The boy eventually discovers that the real culprits are skunks. Stars Tom Beecham, Mable Beecham, Gary Beecham, Donald Cyr. Narrated by Rex Allen.

Ouimet, Matt He joined Disney in 1989, holding several leadership positions before becoming president of Disney Cruise Line Series in 1999. In October 2003, he was named president of the Disneyland Resort.

Our Friend the Atom (television) Television show; aired on January 23, 1957. Directed by Hamilton S. Luske. Dr. Heinz Haber looks at the atom as a potential power source, stressing that strict controls are necessary. He traces the history of the atom from the tale of "The Fisherman and the Genie" through the days of the ancient Greek philosophers to the discoveries of modern scientists. The film uses excerpts from *20,000 Leagues Under the Sea* as well as new animation sequences. A popular book version of this show by Dr. Haber was published by Golden Press. In 1980, an updated version was produced as an educational film entitled *The Atom: A Closer Look.*

Our Planet Tonight (television) Unsold pilot for a series on NBC, a comedy spoof of television news magazine shows; aired on April 22, 1987. Directed by Louis J. Horvitz. Stars John Houseman, Morgan Fairchild.

Our Shining Moment (television) Television pilot on NBC (60 min.); aired on June 2, 1991. Directed by Mark Tinker. Michael McGuire looks back on his childhood in the 1960s. Stars Cindy Pickett, Max Gail, Jonathan Brandis, Seth Green, Don Ameche.

Our Unsung Villains (television) Television show; aired on February 15, 1956. Directed by Hamilton S. Luske. The Magic Mirror hosts a look at the Disney villains from several different Disney films. Hans Conried played the slave in the mirror.

Out Cold (film) Good-hearted but single-minded teen snowboarding dudes Rick, Luke, Anthony,

and Pig Pen are into extreme boarding, as well as extreme partying in the winter wonderland around their tiny hamlet of Bull Mountain, Alaska. John Majors, a slick Colorado ski mogul, plans to buy Bull Mountain to turn it into a ski resort, and joining him is his beautiful Swiss stepdaughter, Inga. The competitive foursome antagonize each other into a frenzy set into motion by the high expectations of an exotic foreign beauty living in town. A Touchstone Picture in association with Spyglass Entertainment. Directed by Brendan Malloy and Emmett Malloy. Released on November 21, 2001. Stars Flex Alexander (Anthony), A. J. Cook (Jenny), David Denman (Lance), Caroline Dhavernas (Anna), Zach Galifianakis (Luke), Willie Garson (Ted Muntz), Derek Hamilton (Pig Pen), David Koechner (Stumpy), Jason London (Rick Rambis), Thomas Lennon (Eric), Lee Majors (John Majors), Victoria Silvstedt (Inga). 90 min. Filming took place in British Columbia (especially Vancouver and Salmo). Released on video in 2002.

Out of Control (film) Educational video; released in November 1992, 17 min. A boy has a problem with his temper, but after he vandalizes the campsite of a homeless man, he wrestles with his conscience and finds more creative and humorous ways to deal with his anger.

Out of Scale (film) Donald Duck cartoon; released on November 2, 1951. Directed by Jack Hannah. Donald, as engineer of a miniature train in his backyard, runs into difficulties with Chip and Dale when he replaces their oak tree with a miniature one. The only way the clever animals can save their home is by puting a "Giant Red-

wood" sign on it and letting the train pass through a tunnel in its trunk.

Out of the Frying Pan into the Firing Line (film) Made during World War II, the film, starring Minnie Mouse and Pluto, shows the importance of housewives saving waste fats for the purpose of making shells and explosives. Made for the U.S. government; delivered on July 30, 1942. Directed by Ben Sharpsteen.

Out on a Limb (film) Donald Duck cartoon; released on December 15, 1950. Directed by Jack Hannah. In his work as a tree surgeon, Donald discovers the tree home of Chip and Dale and harasses them with a tree pruner they believe to be a monster. They soon realize their error and have the frustrated Donald venting his temper.

Outlaw Cats of Colossal Cave, The (television) Television show; aired on September 28, 1975. Directed by Hank Schloss. A cave guide befriends bobcats he finds living inside the Arizona cave, and eventually transports them to a national park where they will be safe from hunters. Stars Gilbert de la Peña, José Maierhauser.

Outrageous Fortune (film) Two aspiring actresses, rivals in drama class, discover they are also rivals for the affections of the same man. When he disappears, they team up to find him so he can choose between them. When they finally catch him, they discover he is a renegade CIA agent, escaping to the Russian KGB with a dangerous toxin. They team up, as friends now, to thwart their former lover and save the United States. Released on January 30, 1987. Directed by Arthur Hiller. 100 min. Stars Bette Midler (Sandy), Shelley Long (Lauren), Peter Coyote (Michael), Robert Prosky (Stanislov Korzenowski), John Schuck (Atkins), George Carlin (Frank). Filmed in Los Angeles and New York City and in the area around Santa Fe, New Mexico. Released on video in 1987.

Ovitz, Michael In August 1995 he was named the president of The Walt Disney Company, to take office in October. Ovitz had been chairman of the Creative Artists Agency. He left the company on December 27, 1996.

Owen, Reginald (1887–1972) Actor; appeared in *Mary Poppins* (Admiral Boom) and *Bedknobs and Broomsticks* (Gen. Teagler).

Owens, Gary Actor; he made his on-screen film debut in *The Love Bug* as a race announcer and also appeared in *Spy Hard* (MC). He narrated *Wonderful World of Disney* for five years, provided the narration for World of Motion at Epcot, and did voices for numerous cartoon shorts and television programs.

Owl Character in the Winnie the Pooh films; voiced by Hal Smith.

Owl That Didn't Give a Hoot, The (television) Television show; aired on December 15, 1968. A boy cares for an abandoned owl and prepares her for life in the wild. Stars David Potter, Marian Fletcher, John Fetzer. Narrated by Steve Forrest.

Oz See *Rainbow Road to Oz* and *Return to Oz*.

Ozzie of the Mounted (film) Oswald the Lucky Rabbit cartoon; released on April 30, 1928.

P

Pablo Cold-blooded penguin who appeared in *The Three Caballeros.*

Pablo and the Dancing Chihuahua (television) Two-part television show; aired on January 28 and February 4, 1968. Directed by Walter Perkins. A Mexican boy, Pablo, searches for his missing uncle and is joined by a Chihuahua, lost by an American tourist. They have to battle wild pigs, a mountain lion, and a rattlesnake, but finally find the dog's owner, who offers Pablo a place to live. Stars Armando Islas, Francesca Jarvis, Walker Tilley, Manuel Rivera.

Pacific Station (television) Television series on NBC, from September 15, 1991 to January 3, 1992. Stationed in the quirky beach community of Venice, California, by-the-book detective Bob Ballard finds his life is disrupted when he is partnered with Richard Capparelli, an officer full of New Age insights and unorthodox techniques. Stars Robert Guillaume (Bob Ballard), Richard Libertini (Richard Capparelli), Joel Murray (Kenny Epstein), John Hancock (Hal Bishop), Ron Leibman (Al Burkhardt).

Pacific Wharf Café Counter-service restaurant at Pacific Wharf at Disney's California Adventure; opened February 8, 2001.

Pacifically Peeking (television) Television show; aired on October 6, 1968. Directed by Ward Kimball. Moby Duck leads a study of life on several South Pacific islands—including Pitcairn, Fiji, and Hawaii. Paul Frees provided the voice of Moby Duck.

Pacifier, The (film) Assigned to protect the endangered children of an assassinated scientist working on a secret invention, Navy SEAL Shane Wolf is suddenly faced with juggling two incompatible jobs—fighting evil while keeping house. Shane must not only defeat a world-threatening enemy but also wrangle teen rebel Zoe, uplift sullen 14-year-old Seth, and outwit 8-year-old Ninja-wannabe Lulu, simultaneously keeping toddler Peter and baby Tyler out of mischief, not to mention harm's way. Being used to drop zones, demolitions, and the destruction of enemy targets, he has no idea what tough really is until he pits his courage against diapering, denmothering, and driver's education. He is truly out of his element, but this tough-guy loner soon realizes that he is facing the most important mission of his life—becoming part of a family and bringing them all closer together. Directed by Adam Shankman. From Walt Disney Pictures/Spyglass Entertainment. Released on March 4, 2005. Stars Vin Diesel (Shane Wolf), Lauren Graham (Principal Claire Fletcher), Carol Kane (Helga), Faith Ford (Julie Plummer),

Bittany Snow (Zoe), Max Thieriot (Seth), Brad Garrett (Vice-Principal Murney), Morgan York (Lulu), Chris Potter (Capt. Bill Fawcett), Howard Plummer (Tate Donovan). 95 min. Filmed in CinemaScope.

Pacino, Al Actor; appeared as Big Boy Caprice in *Dick Tracy*. Also appeared in *The Insider* (Lowell Bergman) and *The Recruit* (Walter Burke).

Pack Mules Through Nature's Wonderland Frontierland attraction at Disneyland; from June 10, 1960 to 1973. Formerly Mule Pack (1955–1956) and Rainbow Ridge Pack Mules (1956–1959).

Page, Geraldine (1924–1987) Actress; appeared in *The Happiest Millionaire* (Mrs. Duke) and provided the voice of Madame Medusa in *The Rescuers*.

Pal Mickey Interactive Mickey Mouse doll that acts as a tour guide, sharing park tips, fun facts, and jokes, and playing three different games, available for rental or purchase at Walt Disney World in April 2003. A Spanish version was introduced on October 5, 2003. Due to guest preference, while the Mickeys continued to be sold, the rental program ended on December 1, 2004. A new enhanced version of Pal Mickey was released in May 2005 for the Happiest Celebration on Earth.

Palivoda, Armand (1906–1960) He handled the distribution of Disney films in Switzerland from 1937 until his death in 1960. He was presented posthumously with a European Disney Legends award in 1997.

Palm Golf Course Located across from the Polynesian Resort at Walt Disney World, along with the Magnolia Golf Course. Formerly served by the Disney Inn. Designed by Joe Lee. It has been rated by *Golf Digest* as one of the top 25 resort courses.

Palmer, Lilli (1914–1986) Actress; appeared in *Miracle of the White Stallions* (Vedena Podhajsky).

Palmer, Norman "Stormy" Film editor for many years, best known for his work on the True-Life Adventures. He was named a Disney Legend in 1998.

Paltrow, Gwyneth Actress; appeared in *Jefferson in Paris* (Patsy Jefferson), *Duets* (Liv), and *The Royal Tenenbaums* (Margot Tenenbaum).

Pampolina, Damon Actor; appeared on the *Mickey Mouse Club* on The Disney Channel, beginning in 1989, and was a member of The Party.

Pancake Races Held at Disneyland for several years beginning in March 1957. The winners qualified for national races.

Panchito Mexican charro rooster, one of The Three Caballeros; voiced by Joaquin Garay.

Pancho, the Fastest Paw in the West (television) Television show; aired on February 2, 1969. A runaway orphan and his Chesapeake Bay retriever in 1880 are helped by an itinerant peddler, and they help him when his horses are stolen. Stars Armando Islas, Frank Keith, Albert Hachmeister. Based on the book by Bruce Grant. Narrated by Rex Allen.

Pangani Forest Exploration Trail Attraction in Africa at Disney's Animal Kingdom. It opened April 22, 1998, as Gorilla Falls Exploration Trail. The name change was made in July 1998. Guests can view gorillas in a natural habitat, along with hippos, meerkats, and other animals.

Pantry Pirate (film) Pluto cartoon; released on December 27, 1940. Directed by Clyde Geronimi. Pluto has conflicts with the cook when he tries to steal a roast, encountering a troublesome ironing board and soap flakes.

Papeete Bay Verandah Restaurant in the Polynesian Village Resort at Walt Disney World, opened on October 1, 1971, and closed in September 1994 (to reopen the following year as 'Ohana). An elegant restaurant serving Polynesian cuisine with dancers and singers providing entertainment.

Paperino Italian name for Donald Duck.

Parade of the Award Nominees (film) Short animated film produced in color for the November 18, 1932, Academy Awards ceremony held at the Ambassador Hotel, in which Mickey leads a parade of the nominees, including Fredric March turning from Dr. Jekyll to Mr. Hyde. This marked the first animation of Mickey Mouse in color. Released on the laserdisc set *Mickey Mouse: The Black and White Years* in 1993.

Paradise (film) A troubled 10-year-old boy, Willard Young, who wonders why his father hasn't come home for about three months, is packed off by his mother to stay with friends in the rural town of Paradise. Painfully shy, Willard discovers that his new guardians, Ben and Lily Reed, are having deep problems, too. The couple is still grieving over the accidental death of their son, and it is tearing them apart. Willard's presence eventually becomes a healing catalyst for the troubled pair, and they, in turn, along with a sensitive little girl, Billie, help Willard prevail over his greatest fears. Initial release in New York on September 18, 1991; general release on October 4, 1991. Directed by Mary Agnes Donoghue. A Touchstone film. 111 min. Stars Melanie Griffith (Lily Reed), Don Johnson (Ben Reed), Elijah Wood (Willard Young), Thora Birch (Billie Pike). Filmmakers used the town of McClellanville, South Carolina, to double for Paradise. Additional filming was done in other areas around Charleston. Released on video in 1992.

Paradise Pier Area themed to the California beach culture at Disney's California Adventure, with attractions, shops, and food facilities; opened February 8, 2001. The Disney Imagineers got creative when naming the shops (including Man Hat 'n' Beach, Point Mugu Tattoo, Rebound Beach) and food locations (including Burger Invasion, Catch a Flave, Malibu-Ritos, Pizza Oom Mow Mow).

Paradise Pier Hotel, Disney's New name for the Disneyland Pacific Hotel as of October 2000. It was re-themed to tie in with Paradise Pier in Disney's California Adventure across the street.

Parent Trap, The (film) After an imaginative title sequence using stop-motion animation (by experts T. Hee, Bill Justice, and X. Atencio) and the song "The Parent Trap" sung by Annette Funicello and Tommy Sands, the film introduces twins Sharon and Susan, who were separated as children by their divorced parents, and who accidentally meet during a summer at Camp Inch. Determined never to be separated again, the sisters decide to bring their parents, Mitch and Maggie, back together again. In this they have a rival, the devious Vicky, who wants to marry Mitch for his money. But after a fateful camping trip, Vicky finds living with the twins is not worth it and flees, leaving Mitch and Maggie to reunite happily. Released on June 21, 1961. Directed by David Swift. 129 min. Starring Hayley Mills in the dual role of both sisters. The careful use of double-exposure and split-screen shots, as well as a double for Hayley Mills, provided the illusion of the twins. With Maureen O'Hara (Maggie McKendrick), Brian Keith (Mitch Evans), Charlie Ruggles (Charles McKendrick), Joanna Barnes (Vicky Robinson), Una Merkel (Verbena), Leo G. Carroll (Rev. Mosby). Oscar nominations were awarded for Sound, by Robert O. Cook, and for Film Editing, by Philip W. Anderson. Richard M. Sherman and Robert B. Sherman provided the songs, which, besides the title song, included "For Now, For Always," and "Let's Get Together," and these, too, added to the film's enormous popularity. The film was shot mostly in California at various locales, including millionaire Stuyvesant Fish's 5,200-acre ranch in Carmel, Monterey's Pebble Beach golf course, and the Studio's Golden Oak Ranch in Placerita Canyon, where Mitch's ranch was built. It was the design of this set that proved the most popular, and to this day the Walt Disney Archives receives requests for plans of the home's interior design, but there, of course, never was such a house; the set was simply various rooms built on a sound-stage. The film was re-released theatrically in 1968, and released on video in 1984 and 1992. The Studio later produced three television sequels starring Hayley Mills.

Parent Trap, The (film) A remake of the 1961 Hayley Mills film. This time the identical twins are Hallie and Annie, and when they meet for the first time at Camp Walden for Girls in Maine, they conspire to reunite their mom (a wedding-gown designer in London) and dad (a vineyard owner in the Napa Valley), who never should have been apart. Directed by Nancy Meyers. Released on July 29, 1998. Stars Dennis Quaid (Nick Parker), Natasha Richardson (Elizabeth James), Lindsay Lohan (Hallie/Annie), Lisa Ann Walter (Chessy), Elaine Hendrix (Meredith Blake). 128 min. Joanna Barnes, who plays Mrs. Vicki Blake, played the role of Vicky Robinson in the original film. Eleven-year-old newcomer Lohan hails from Long Island. After filming in London, the produc-tion moved to the Staglin family vineyard near Rutherford in California's Napa Valley. Camp Sealey in Crestline, California, doubled for Camp Walden. Special-effects technology has pro-gressed tremendously in the 37 years since the original film, so it was much easier for the cine-matographer, Dean Cundey, to accomplish the more than 100 shots combining both girls. Released on video in 1998.

Parent Trap Hawaiian Honeymoon (televi-sion) Two-part television movie; aired on Novem-ber 19 and 26, 1989. Directed by Mollie Miller. The family has inherited a dilapidated hotel in Hawaii, which they visit and decide to clean up. The triplets practice deception by impersonating each other, and they try to help their father save the hotel from being sold to a developer. Stars Hayley Mills, Barry Bostwick, John M. Jackson, the Creel triplets, Sasha Mitchell, Jayne Meadows.

Parent Trap II, The (television) Mistaken iden-tities once again disrupt the twins' lives 25 years later, as Sharon's daughter, Nikki, turns mischief-making matchmaker for her divorced mother. A Disney Channel Premiere Film; first aired on July 26, 1986. 81 min. Stars Hayley Mills. Directed by Ronald F. Maxwell.

Parent Trap III (television) Two-part television movie; aired on April 9 and 16, 1989. Directed by Mollie Miller. The fiancée of a man with triplet daughters hires one of the twins as an interior decorator. Before long, the decorator steals the man's heart, encouraged by the daughters, who don't like the fiancée. Stars Hayley Mills, Barry Bostwick, Patricia Richardson, the Creel triplets, Ray Baker, Christopher Gartin.

Park, Tom He joined Disney at Walt Disney Imagineering in 1991, headed Walt Disney Art Classics and Disney Direct Marketing from 1996 to 1999, and was then named head of The Disney Store worldwide. He left the company in July 2001.

Parker, Fess Actor; appeared as Davy Crockett on television, and in *The Great Locomotive Chase* (James J. Andrews), *Westward Ho the Wagons* (John Doc Grayson), *Old Yeller* (Jim Coates), and *The Light in the Forest* (Del Hardy), and on television in *Along the Oregon Trail*, *The Fourth Anniversary Show*, and *Behind the Scenes with Fess Parker*. Parker had not been the first one considered for Davy Crockett; James Arness had been recommended to Walt Disney, but when he screened the science-fiction film *Them*, Walt was attracted not to Arness but to another actor in the thriller, Fess Parker. Parker was hired and proved to be perfect as Davy Crockett. He was named a Disney Legend in 1991.

Parker, Sarah Jessica Actress; appeared in *Flight of the Navigator* (Carolyn McAdams), *Hocus Pocus* (Sarah), *Ed Wood* (Dolores), and *Miami Rhapsody* (Gwyn).

Parker Bros. Game manufacturer that has had one of the longest-running Disney merchandise licenses, beginning in 1933. Their popular games and puzzles have featured Disneyland attractions and the standard Disney characters as well as those from the feature films.

Parsons, Kelly Mouseketeer on the new *Mickey Mouse Club*.

Part of Your World Song from *The Little Mermaid*, written by Howard Ashman and Alan Menken.

Partners Bronze statue of Walt Disney and Mickey Mouse installed in the hub at Disneyland park on November 18, 1993, to commemorate the 65th birthday of Mickey Mouse. Master Disney sculptor Blaine Gibson came out of retirement to create the sculpture. Identical statues were installed at Magic Kingdom Park at Walt Disney World on June 19, 1995, at Tokyo Disneyland on April 15, 1998, at Walt Disney Studios Paris on July 19, 2002, and at the Disney Studio in Burbank on February 10, 2003. Many guests wonder about the STR symbol on Walt Disney's tie; it refers to Smoke Tree Ranch, a development in Palm Springs, California, where he had a vacation home. Gibson also sculpted a statue of Walt Disney's brother, Roy O. Disney, on a bench with Minnie Mouse, which was installed in Town Square at Walt Disney World Magic Kingdom Park on October 1, 1999, and dedicated on October 25. A copy of that statue was also installed at the Disney Studio in Burbank on February 10, 2003.

Party, The Singing group composed of cast members of The Disney Channel's *Mickey Mouse Club*—Tiffini Hale, Albert Fields, Deedee Magno, Chase Hampton, and Damon Pampolina. Their first single was "Summer Vacation," which broke into the *Billboard* charts in 1990.

Party Gras Parade Parade at Disneyland from January 11 to November 18, 1990. Disney's version of Mardi Gras in New Orleans, this parade featured large floats, stilt-walkers, dancers, and performers, who would toss special Party Gras coins and strings of beads out to the guests. The parade would stop at intervals and a special performance would be given.

Party Tilyadrop Tour, The (film) Video release; behind the scenes on tour with this musical group from the *Mickey Mouse Club*, released on April 19, 1991. 25 min.

Passed Away (film) During one long weekend, four grown children come together under the family roof for their 70-year-old father's funeral. Each tries to cope with his or her personal failures and the family's expectations. They find themselves confronting each other about past scandals, current secrets, a failing business, an unwed mother, and an illegal alien. Family friction and turmoil rule as the family prepares for the burial. Released on April 24, 1992. Directed by Charlie Peters. A Hollywood Pictures film. 96 min. Stars Bob Hoskins (Johnny Scanlan), Blair Brown (Amy Scanlan), Tim Curry (Boyd Pinter), Frances McDormand (Nora Scanlan), William Petersen (Frank Scanlan), Pamela Reed (Terry Scanlan), Peter Riegert (Peter Scanlan), Maureen Stapleton (Mary Scanlan), Nancy Travis (Cassie Slocombe), Jack Warden (Jack Scanlan). Filmed at various locations in the area of Pittsburgh, Pennsylvania. Released on video in 1992.

Pasta Piazza Ristorante Restaurant in Communicore West at Epcot, from May 1994. It was formerly called Sunrise Terrace Restaurant.

Pastoral Symphony, The Music composed by Ludwig van Beethoven, a segment of *Fantasia*.

Patinkin, Mandy Actor; appeared in *Dick Tracy* (88 Keys), *The Doctor* (Murray), *Life with Mikey* (irate man), and *Squanto; a Warrior's Tale* (friar). He appeared on television in *Criminal Minds* (Jason Gideon).

Patrick, Butch Actor; appeared on television in *The Young Loner* and *Way Down Cellar.*

Patriot, The (film) Non-Disney film from Interlight Pictures and Baldwin/Cohen Productions, released on video by Touchstone Home Video on June 15, 1999. An immunologist, retired to a small Montana town, finds the town infected by a rare virus, and he rushes to discover a cure while fending off the paramilitary group that released it. Directed by Dean Semler. Stars Steven Seagal (Wesley McClaren), Gailard Sartain (Floyd Chisolm), L.Q. Jones (Frank), Silas Weir Mitchell (Pogue), Camilla Belle (Holly), Dan Beene (Richard Bach). Originally released theatrically in Spain on July 10, 1998.

Patten, Luana (1938–1996) Actress; appeared in *Song of the South* (Ginny), *Fun and Fancy Free*, *Melody Time*, *So Dear to My Heart* (Tildy), *Johnny Tremain* (Cilla Lapham), and *Follow Me, Boys!* (Nora White).

Paul Bunyan (film) Special cartoon featurette; released on August 1, 1958. Directed by Les Clark. One day, after a great storm on the coast of Maine, the townspeople found baby Paul Bunyan on the beach where the heavy seas had left him. Paul grows to a great size and becomes a legend with his double-bladed ax and friend, Babe, the Blue Ox. But the prosperity Paul brought to his land

ultimately defeats him when steam saws are produced that can do the job easier and faster than Paul and his ox. 17 min. Released on video in 1983 and 1995.

Pauper King, The (television) Television show; part 1 of *The Prince and the Pauper*.

Pay-TV The first Disney films were shown on pay-TV on April 1, 1978. On April 18, 1983, The Disney Channel began operation.

Payant, Gilles Actor; appeared in *Big Red* (Rene Dumont).

Paying the Price (film) Educational release in March 1991. 17 min. A new teen in town is coerced by friends to shoplift, only to be arrested and forced to face the consequences.

Paymer, David Actor; appeared in *Quiz Show* (Dan Enright), *Nixon* (Ron Ziegler), *The Sixth Man* (Coach Pederson), *Mighty Joe Young* (Harry Ruben), *Mumford* (Dr. Ernest Delbanco), and on television in *Sky High* (Vic), *The Absent-Minded Professor* (Oliphant), and *Rock'n Roll Mom* (Boris). He played Jonah Malloy in the *Line of Fire* television series.

Pays des Contes de Fées, Le Storybook Land attraction in Fantasyland in Disneyland Paris, opened in April 1994.

PB&J Otter (television) Half-hour animated television series on Disney Channel; premiered on March 15, 1998, produced by Jumbo Pictures. The show features the adventures of three young river otters named Peanut, Jelly, and Baby Butter,

and their friends, the Raccoon, Duck, and Beaver families who live in the close-knit community of Lake Hoohaw. Voices include Adam Rose (Peanut), Jenell Slack (Jelly), Gina Marie Tortorici (Baby Butter), Chris Phillips (Ernest), Gwendolyn S. Shepherd (Opal). 65 episodes.

Pearl Harbor (film) On December 7, 1941, squadrons of Japanese warplanes launched a surprise attack on the U.S. armed forces at Pearl Harbor in Hawaii. This infamous day jolted America from peaceful isolationism to total war and altered the course of history. It has an especially devastating impact on two daring young American pilots and a beautiful, dedicated nurse. Directed by Michael Bay. From Touchstone Pictures and Jerry Bruckheimer Films. Released on May 25, 2001, after a May 21 premiere aboard the USS *John C. Stennis*, a nuclear aircraft carrier, at Pearl Harbor. Stars Ben Affleck (Rafe McCawley), Josh Hartnett (Danny Walker), Kate Beckinsale (Evelyn Stewart), Cuba Gooding, Jr. (Dorie Miller), Tom Sizemore (Earl), Jon Voight (President Roosevelt), Colm Feore (Admiral Kimmel), Dan Aykroyd (Capt. Thurmann), Mako (Admiral Yamamoto), Alec Baldwin (Jimmy Doolittle), William Lee Scott (Billy), Mike Shannon (Gooz), Peter Firth (Captain of the *West Virginia*), Scott Wilson (General George Marshall). 183 min. Filmed in CinemaScope on location on Oahu, and in California and Texas. Released on video in 2001. It won the Oscar for Best Sound Editing for 2001 for George Watters II and Christopher Boyes, as well as nominations for Sound, Original Song ("There You'll Be"), and Visual Effects.

Pecos Bill (film) Segment of *Melody Time*, featuring "Blue Shadows on the Trail," sung by Roy Rogers and the Sons of the Pioneers. It was re-released as a short in 1955. 23 min. Released on video in 1983.

Pecos Bill Cafe Restaurant in Frontierland in Magic Kingdom Park at Walt Disney World, opened on October 1, 1971. Served Mexican fare along with hamburgers and grilled chicken breast sandwiches. It closed on January 5, 1998, and was then remodeled and enlarged to become Pecos Bill Tall Tale Inn & Cafe, opening in May 1998. Also in Westernland at Tokyo Disneyland; opened on April 15, 1983.

Peculiar Penguins (film) Silly Symphony cartoon; released on September 1, 1934. Directed by Wilfred Jackson. Peter and Polly Penguin are sweethearts. Their wintry antics include catching fish and escaping the jaws of a hungry shark.

Pedro (film) Segment of *Saludos Amigos*, about a baby airplane carrying the mail. Re-released as a short on May 13, 1955.

Pee Wees vs. City Hall, The (television) Television show; part 1 of *Moochie of Pop Warner Football*.

Peet, Bill (1915–2002) He worked in story at the Disney Studio from 1938 to 1964, with credits on films from *Fantasia* to *The Sword in the Stone*. Peet made a name for himself in later years by writing and illustrating children's books. He wrote his autobiography for Houghton Mifflin in 1989. He was named a Disney Legend in 1996.

Peg Vampish dog in the dog pound in *Lady and the Tramp*; voiced by Peggy Lee.

Pelican and the Snipe, The (film) Special cartoon; released on January 7, 1944. Directed by Hamilton Luske. Vidi, the snipe, tries to stop his pelican friend, Monte, from sleepwalking, which puts him in danger of being killed. But Monte ends up rescuing Vidi in a bombing raid. The film was originally meant to be part of *The Three Caballeros*.

Pélisson, Gilles He was named chairman of Euro Disney in February 1997; he had joined the company as executive vice president in July 1995, and was elevated to president in February 1996, serving in that post until leaving the company in April 2000.

Pendleton, Karen Mouseketeer from the 1950s television show.

Pendleton Woolen Mills Dry Goods Store Shop in Frontierland at Disneyland from July 18, 1955 to April 29, 1990. One of the longest-running original participants of Disneyland, popular for its heavy woolen and leather goods. It later became Bonanza Outfitters.

Pennsylvania Miners' Story, The (television) Two-hour television movie; aired on ABC on November 24, 2002. Based on the summer 2002 rescue of nine coal miners at Quecreek mine, after they had been trapped for 77 hours underground. Directed by David Frankel. Stars Graham Beckel (Randy Fogle), Michael Bowen (Robert Pugh), Tom Bower (John Unger), Dylan Bruno (Blaine Mayhugh), Brad Greenquist (Ronald Hileman), Robert Knepper (Moe Popernack), William Mapother (John Phillippi), John Ratzenberger (Tom Foy), John David Souther (Dennis Hall). Produced by Touchstone Television in association with The Sanitsky Company. Filmed in Valencia, California, and on location in Somerset County, Pennsylvania. Released on video in 2003.

Penny Girl kidnapped by Madame Medusa in *The Rescuers*; voiced by Michelle Stacy.

Penny Arcade Attraction on Main Street at Disneyland; began July 17, 1955. Themed to Main Street's era, the arcade features antique Mutoscopes and Cail-o-Scopes, along with more modern video games. Also on Main Street in Magic Kingdom Park at Walt Disney World, and at Tokyo Disneyland. The latter was open from October 1, 1971 until March 19, 1995, when it closed to become part of the Main Street Athletic Company.

People and Places Series of 17 travelogue featurettes released from 1953 to 1960 (*The Alaskan Eskimo, Siam, Switzerland, Men Against the Arc-*

tic, Sardinia, Disneyland U.S.A., Samoa, The Blue Men of Morocco, Lapland, Portugal, Wales, Scotland, Ama Girls, Seven Cities of Antarctica, Cruise of the Eagle, Japan, The Danube). Three of the films (*The Alaskan Eskimo, Men Against the Arctic,* and *Ama Girls*) won Academy Awards.

People and Places—Tiburon, Sardinia, Morocco, Icebreakers (television) Television show; aired on October 5, 1955. Directed by Winston Hibler. Segments featuring three People and Places films and one that was never completed—*Tiburon*, an island in the Gulf of California inhabited by a tribe of Native Americans.

People of the Desert (television) Television show; aired on April 10, 1957. Includes *Navajo Adventure* and *The Blue Men of Morocco*.

People on Market Street, The (film) Educational film series of seven films released in September 1977: *Wages and Production, Scarcity and Planning, Market Clearing Price, Demand, Cost, Supply, Property Rights and Pollution.*

PeopleMover Tomorrowland attraction at Disneyland; opened on July 2, 1967, with major improvements in 1968. The Superspeed Tunnel was added in 1977; *Tron* footage in 1982. Closed August 21, 1995. By riding the PeopleMover, guests traveled inside several of the Tomorrowland attractions and were thus able to get a preview. The technology, innovative in 1967, featured electric motors in the track itself which propelled the vehicles. Disney's Community Transportation division used this same technology to build a PeopleMover at the Houston International Airport. See also WEDway PeopleMover.

Pepper Ann (television) Animated series about a spunky, quirky 12-year-old girl in an eternal quest for coolness, but caught between childhood and adulthood, which debuted on *One Saturday Morning* on ABC on September 13, 1997. Voices include Kathleen Wilhoite (Pepper Ann), April Winchell (Lydia), Pam Segall (Moose), Clea Lewis (Nicky), Danny Cooksey (Milo), Jenna von Oy (Trinket). 65 episodes.

Pepper, John E., Jr. Member of the Disney board of directors beginning January 1, 2006.

Pepper Market Food court at the Coronado Springs Resort at Walt Disney World; opened on August 1, 1997.

Percival McLeach Poacher villain in *The Rescuers Down Under*; voiced by George C. Scott.

Percy Governor Ratcliffe's pampered dog in *Pocahontas*.

Perdita Female lead Dalmatian in *One Hundred and One Dalmatians*; voiced by Cate Bauer and Lisa Daniels. Perdita had a litter of 15 puppies.

Perfect Game (film) Direct-to-video release by Buena Vista Home Entertainment on April 18, 2000, of a film by Up to Bat Productions. When 11-year-old Kanin gets a new coach for his Little League baseball team, he discovers that the coach thinks him a terrible player and spends all his time coaching the good players. Kanin and some other "Little League losers" fire their coach and set their sights on the championship with the aid of Kanin's mom and a retired high school coach. Directed by Dan Guntzelman. Stars Ed Asner (Billy Hicks), Patrick Duffy (Bobby Geiser), Cameron Finley (Kanin), Tracy Nelson (Diane), Drake Bell (Bobby Jr.). 99 min.

Perfect Harmony (television) Two young men at a Southern prep school overcome the boundaries of racism to pursue a friendship based on their love of music. A Disney Channel Premiere Film;

first aired on March 31, 1991. Directed by Will MacKenzie. Stars Justin Whalin (Taylor Bradshaw), Eugene Byrd (Landy Allen), David Faustino (Paul Bain), Cleavon Little (Rev. Clarence Branch), Peter Scolari (Derek Sanders), Darren McGavin (Roland Hobbs). 93 min. Filmed at Berry College in Rome, Georgia. Released on video in 1993.

Perfect Isn't Easy Song from *Oliver & Company*, sung by the pampered poodle, Georgette; voiced by Bette Midler, written by Jack Feldman, Bruce Sussman, and Barry Manilow.

Perilous Assignment (television) Television show; aired on November 6, 1959. Directed by Hamilton S. Luske. Behind the scenes of the filming of *Third Man on the Mountain* on location in Zermatt, Switzerland, where the cast and crew endure many hardships.

Perils of a Homesick Steer, The (television) Television show; part 2 of *Sancho, the Homing Steer*.

Perkins, Anthony (1932–1992) Actor; appeared in *The Black Hole* (Dr. Alex Durant).

Perkins, Elizabeth Actress; appeared in *The Doctor* (June) and *Indian Summer* (Jennifer Morton). She also provided the voice of Coral in *Finding Nemo*.

Perkins, Les He originated the Disney Character Voices department in 1988 to standardize the character voices; voiced Mickey Mouse on two television specials and Toad in *Who Framed Roger Rabbit*.

Perrault, Charles (1628–1703) Author of *Cinderella* and *Sleeping Beauty*.

Perri (film) The first, and only, True-Life Fantasy. Directed by N. Paul Kenworthy, Jr. and Ralph Wright. Released on August 28, 1957. The story of a little pine squirrel named Perri and her life from childhood to maturity. When Perri's life is threatened by a marten, her father sacrifices his life to lure it away from Perri's nest. Now alone with her brothers, she seeks a new nest of her own, and even falls in love with Porro, all the while dodging marten and wildcat. Based on a story by Felix Salten, who had written *Bambi*, the film was shot in Jackson Hole, Wyoming, and the Uintah National Forest in Utah. 74 min. Nominated for an Academy Award. Animated effects were credited to Joshua Meador, Ub Iwerks, and Peter Ellenshaw, and Paul Smith wrote the musical score. Roy E. Disney, Walt's nephew, contributed some of the footage.

Persephone Female lead character in *The Goddess of Spring* (1934) which may have been an attempt by the Disney animators to practice animating a human character before *Snow White and the Seven Dwarfs*.

Persoff, Nehemiah Actor; appeared on television in *Michael O'Hara IV* and *The Treasure of San Bosco Reef*.

Pesci, Joe Actor; appeared in *Betsy's Wedding* (Oscar Henner) and *Gone Fishin'* (Joe Waters).

Pests of the West (film) Pluto cartoon; released on July 21, 1950. Directed by Charles Nichols. Bent-Tail, the coyote, and his son, Junior, try again to steal what  Pluto guards, this time chickens in a henhouse, but this proves as unsuccessful as their previous outing in *Sheep Dog* (1949).

Pet Store, The (film) Mickey Mouse cartoon; released on October 28, 1933. Directed by Wilfred Jackson. Working in a pet store, Mickey, with the help of the store animals, saves Minnie from a gorilla that escapes from its cage. In the fight, the store is trashed. Mickey quits and he and Minnie leave just before Tony, the owner, returns.

Petal to the Metal (film) Special cartoon, starring Bonkers; released on August 7, 1992. Directed by David Block. A production of Walt

Disney Television Animation. 8 min. In delivering a bouquet of flowers across town to a stunning starlet named Fawn Deer, a delirious delivery cat named Bonkers D. Bobcat turns a relatively easy assignment into a catalog of catastrophes. Racing against the clock to meet his five-minute delivery deadline and keep his job, Bonkers encounters a wide array of ridiculous roadblocks, ranging from banana peels to the world's slowest taxi driver. Released with *3 Ninjas*. While the original pre-production work took place in California, the animation was done in France.

Pete Also known as Peg Leg Pete and Black Pete, this gruff, cat-like character appeared first in the Alice Comedies in 1925, but soon became better known as Mickey Mouse's and later Donald Duck's primary nemesis. Since *Steamboat Willie*, Pete appeared in 31 cartoons. In the earliest cartoons he had a peg leg, but that was dispensed with in his later appearances when the animators found it too hard to handle in the stories.

Peter and the Wolf (film) Segment of *Make Mine Music*, told by Sterling Holloway, about the brave young boy who goes with a duck, cat, and bird to catch the wolf, with each character represented by a musical instrument in the orchestra. Peter is represented by a string quartet; Sasha the bird by a flute, Sonia the duck by an oboe, Ivan the cat by a clarinet, Grandpa by a bassoon, and the hunters by kettle drums. The music is by Prokofiev. It was re-released as a short on September 14, 1955. 16 min. Released on video in 1982 and 1991.

Peter Pan (film) Story of the magical boy who wouldn't grow up who teaches the three Darling children—Wendy, John, and Michael—to fly to

Never Land with him where they embark on adventures with the chief inhabitants, Captain Hook and his crew of pirates. The fairy, Tinker Bell, is jealous of Peter's attentions to Wendy, and is duped into helping Captain Hook. After rescuing the Indian princess, Tiger Lily, Peter must save his band, the Lost Boys, and the Darlings from Hook. Released on February 5, 1953. Directed by Hamilton Luske, Clyde Geronimi, Wilfred Jackson. Features the voices of Bobby Driscoll as Peter, Kathryn Beaumont as Wendy, Hans Conried as Captain Hook and Mr. Darling, and Bill Thompson as Mr. Smee, the Captain's only friend. 77 min. Features the songs "You Can Fly, You Can Fly, You Can Fly," "The Second Star to the Right," and "Your Mother and Mine" by Sammy Cahn and Sammy Fain. Walt Disney planned as early as 1935 to make this film, arranging in 1939 with the Great Ormond Street Hospi-

tal in London (who had the rights to the play bequeathed by author James M. Barrie) for permission, but it was not until 1949 that production actually began. It was re-released in theaters in 1958, 1969, 1976, 1982, and 1989. Released on video in 1990.

Peter Pan Story, The (film) Made in the early days of television, this promotional film for *Peter Pan* took audiences behind the scenes; released in 1952. 12 min.

Peter Pan's Flight Fantasyland attraction at Disneyland; opened on July 17, 1955, and redesigned in 1983. Also Fantasyland attraction in Magic Kingdom Park at Walt Disney World, opened October 3, 1971, and at Tokyo Disneyland, opened April 15, 1983. Also in Fantasyland

at Disneyland Paris, opened April 12, 1992. Based on Disney's 1953 film. The attraction is different because the vehicles are suspended from an overhead rail, giving guests the feeling of flying through the evening skies over London and Never Land. Makes use of black light and fiber optics.

Peter Penguin Star of *Peculiar Penguins* (1934).

Peter Tchaikovsky Story, The (television) Television show; aired on January 30, 1959. Directed by Charles Barton. Background information on Tchaikovsky gathered during the making of *Sleeping Beauty* led to this biographical show, telling stories of the life of the great Russian composer from a child, born in 1840, to adulthood. The film covers his education and early displays of musical genius. Later, after a number of rebuffs by the public and a great disappointment in love, young Tchaikovsky has a stunning success with his "Sleeping Beauty Ballet" whose premiere he directs himself. Stars Grant Williams, Rex Hill, Lilyan Chauvin, Leon Askin. This was the first television show ever to be simulcast in stereo. An FM radio had to be placed near the television set to get the full effect. The film was released theatrically abroad.

Peters, Brock Actor; appeared on television in *The Million Dollar Dixie Deliverance* and *Polly*. He also did the voice of Druid Chief in *DuckTales*.

Petersen, Paul He was hired as a Mouseketeer for the *Mickey Mouse Club* in 1955 but let go shortly afterward. He wrote the book *Walt, Mickey and Me* (Dell, 1977), about the club and his experiences with it.

Pete's Dragon (film) Lively musical comedy in which a magical and sometimes mischievous dragon, Elliott, inadvertently causes chaos and confusion in Passamaquoddy, a Maine fishing village. To help the young orphan Pete break away from his evil foster parents the Gogans and find a happy home with Nora and her father Lampie in their lighthouse, Elliott must avoid the clutches of the greedy Dr. Terminus, who wants to exploit him. Premiered on November 3, 1977; general release on December 16, 1977. Directed by Don Chaffey. 135 min. Stars Helen Reddy (Nora), Mickey Rooney (Lampie), Jim Dale (Dr. Terminus), Red Buttons (Hoagy), Shelley Winters (Lena Gogan), Sean Marshall (Pete), Jane Kean (Miss Taylor), Jim Backus (Mayor), Charles Tyner (Merle), Gary Morgan (Grover), Jeff Conaway (Willie), Cal Bartlett (Paul), and featuring the voice of Charlie Callas as Elliott the dragon. This was internationally known vocalist Helen Reddy's first starring role, and the film debut of Sean Marshall, as Pete, who went on to provide the voice for the boy in *The Small One*. The musical score was written by Al Kasha and Joel Hirschhorn and included "Candle on the Water," "It's Not Easy," "There's Room For Everyone," "Brazzle Dazzle Day," "In These Hills," "Every Little Piece," and "Passamaschloddy." Animation art director Ken Anderson, animation director Don Bluth, and effects animator Dorse A. Lanpher were responsible for the ebullient animated dragon and his memorable interactions with the live actors. The story originated from writers Seton I. Miller and S. S. Field, who brought the property to Disney, where it had been purchased years earlier, but it was not until 1975 that producer Jerome Courtland asked screenwriter Malcolm Marmorstein to adapt a screenplay. The Passamaquoddy town square and wharf area was constructed on the Disney Burbank Studio lot partly from the old Western set. Jack Martin Smith, the art director, face-lifted 30 existing buildings and constructed 8 more, with interiors designed on the Disney soundstages. The lighthouse for the film was built on a point above Morro Bay, California, substituting for Maine. It was equipped with a large Fresnell-type lighthouse lens, with a wickstand inside that caused a beacon of from 18 to 24 miles. In fact, it worked so well that Disney had to get special permission from the Coast Guard to operate it, since it would have confused passing ships. The domestic gross on the film's initial release was $18 million, a disappointment to the Disney Studio, which had hoped for another *Mary Poppins* success. The movie was nominated for Best Original Song ("Candle on the Water") and Best Original Song Score, by Al Kasha, Joel

Hirschhorn, and Irwin Kostal. Because of the disappointing box office, the film was cut from its original 135 minutes to 129 minutes during its initial run. A reissue appeared in 1984 that was edited further to 106 minutes. Released on video in 1980 and 1991.

Petit Train du Cirque, Le Casey Jr. attraction in Fantasyland in Disneyland Paris; opened in April 1994.

Pfeiffer, Michelle Actress; starred in *Dangerous Minds* (LouAnne Johnson), *Up Close and Personal* (Tally Atwater), and *A Thousand Acres* (Rose Cook Lewis).

Pfeiffer, Walt (1901–1976) Childhood friend of Walt Disney's from Kansas City; Walt Disney considered the Pfeiffer home as his "laughing place." The two boys would put on acts in vaudeville theaters as "The Two Walts." Pfeiffer was employed by Walt Disney Productions in various capacities from 1935 until his retirement in 1972.

Phantom Boats Tomorrowland attraction at Disneyland in 1956. The boats sported large fins.

Phantom Manor The Haunted Mansion attraction in Frontierland at Disneyland Paris; opened April 12, 1992.

Phantom of the Megaplex (television) A Disney Channel Original Film; first aired on November 10, 2000. A teenage boy, Pete Riley, is proud of his responsibilities as assistant manager at a megaplex, until a special premiere night is sabotaged by a mysterious figure. Directed by Blair Treu. Stars Taylor Handley (Pete Riley), Jacob

Smith (Brian Riley), Caitlin Wachs (Karen Riley), Corinne Bohrer (Julie Riley), Richard Hutchman (Shawn MacGibbon), Mickey Rooney (Movie Mason). Filmed at the ten-screen Eaton Center in Toronto.

Phenomenon (film) George Malley, a regular guy, finds his life turned upside down when he is struck by a blinding white light on his 37th birthday. Suddenly George has a newfound intelligence and an insatiable appetite for learning, and rapidly becomes a genius. Through a series of unusual situations, he gains widespread attention. Renowned scientists want to meet him, the military wants to control him, and people all over the country seek his counsel. The townspeople, on the other hand, afraid and in awe of George's genius, turn their backs on him. But, as his intellectual powers grow, so does his understanding of humanity. A Touchstone Picture. Directed by Jon Turteltaub. Released on July 3, 1996. Stars John Travolta (George), Kyra Sedgwick (Lace), Robert Duvall (Doc), Forest Whitaker (Nate Pope), Richard Kiley (Dr. Wellin). Filmed in CinemaScope. 123 min. The town of Auburn, California, doubled for the fictional town of Harmon, but it was extensively redesigned, with practically every facade altered. Farmhouses were utilized in Petaluma and Bodega Bay. Released on video in 1997.

Phenomenon II (television) Two-hour made-for-television movie; aired on *The Wonderful World of Disney* on November 1, 2003. Based on the 1996 motion picture, the story continues with George Malley, who miraculously gained increased mental and physical powers, escaping to San Francisco and beginning a new life under an assumed identity. As he adjusts to life in the big city, he senses other people may share his newfound abilities. Directed by Ken Olin. Stars Christopher Shyer (George Malley), Jill Clayburgh (Nora Malley), Peter Coyote (Dr. John Ringold), Terry O'Quinn (Jack Hatch), Gina Tognoni (Claire), Stoney Westmoreland (Nate Pope). Produced by Touchstone Television.

Phil of the Future (television) A Disney Channel original series; debuting on June 18, 2004.

Also aired as part of *ABC Kids* beginning in fall 2004. Phil Diffy, a teen from the year 2121, gets stranded in the present day when his family's time machine malfunctions during a vacation. Phil has to handle universal issues like being the new kid in school and making friends, while also needing to learn how to get along in a new century and keep his family's future origins a secret. Stars Ricky Ullman (Phil Diffy), Alyson Michalka (Keely Teslow), Craig Anton (Lloyd), Lise Simms (Barbara), Amy Bruckner (Pim), JP Manoux (Curtis).

Philippe Maurice's horse in *Beauty and the Beast*.

Phillips, Frank (1912–1994) Director of cinematography on dozens of Disney television shows and features during the 1960s and 1970s, including *The Apple Dumpling Gang*, *Bedknobs and Broomsticks*, *Escape to Witch Mountain*, *Herbie Rides Again*, *Pete's Dragon*, *The Mouse Factory*, and *High Flying Spy*.

Philoctetes Character in *Hercules* known as Phil, a hero-training satyr; voiced by Danny DeVito.

Phipps, William He voiced Prince Charming in *Cinderella*, and acted in a *Texas John Slaughter* episode ("Wild Horse Revenge").

Phoebus Character in *The Hunchback of Notre Dame*; voiced by Kevin Kline.

Phoenix, Joaquin Actor; appeared in *Signs* (Merrill Hess), *The Village* (Lucius Walker), and *Ladder 49* (Jack Morrison), and provided the voice of Kenai in *Brother Bear*.

Physical Fitness (film) Educational film from the Fun to Be Fit series; released in March 1983. The film defines fitness and shows the need for developing it to improve the quality of studying, working, and playing.

Physical Fitness and Good Health (film) Educational film made for Upjohn's Triangle of Health series; released in August 1969. Exercise, rest, and proper diet are essential for physical fitness.

Pickens, Slim (1919–1983) Character actor, appeared in *The Great Locomotive Chase* (Pete Bracken), *Tonka* (Ace), *Savage Sam* (Wily Crup), *Never a Dull Moment* (Cowboy Schaeffer), and *The Apple Dumpling Gang* (Frank Stillwell), and on television in *Bristle Face*; *The Saga of Andy Burnett*; *Stub, the Best Cowdog in the West*; *The Swamp Fox*; and *Runaway on the Rogue River*.

Pickett, Cindy Actress; appeared in *Son-in-Law* (Connie), and on television in *Plymouth* (Addy Mathewson), *The Cherokee Trail* (Mary Breydon), and *Our Shining Moment* (Betty).

Pickett Suite Resort Hotel in Lake Buena Vista at Walt Disney World; opened on March 15, 1987. The name later changed to Guest Quarters Suite Resort.

Picnic, The (film) Mickey Mouse cartoon; released on October 23, 1930. Directed by Burt Gillett. Mickey and Minnie are having a troubled picnic with Minnie's big dog, Rover, the biggest nuisance. But the loyal animal proves its worth in a thunderstorm by providing its tail as a windshield wiper.

Pidgeon, Walter (1897–1984) Actor; appeared in *Big Red* (James Haggin) and as the voice of Sterling North in *Rascal*.

Pied Piper, The (film) Silly Symphony cartoon; released on September 16, 1933. Directed by Wilfred Jackson. When the Pied Piper lures the rats from Hamelin Town but is not paid in gold by the mayor as promised, he lures all the children of the town to

the magical Garden of Happiness on a mountain to punish the parents.

Piekarski, Julie Mouseketeer on the new *Mickey Mouse Club*.

Pierce, Bradley Michael He voiced Chip in *Beauty and the Beast*.

Pierce, David Hyde Actor; appeared in *Nixon* (John Dean), and provided the voices of Slim in *a bug's life* and Dr. Doppler in *Treasure Planet*, as well as Daedalus in the television series *Hercules*.

Pigeon that Worked a Miracle, The (television) Television show; aired on October 10, 1958. Directed by Walter Perkins. A boy, Chad, confined to a wheelchair, raises pigeons, and they are the therapy that he needs to walk again, when he forgets his own troubles to try to save his favorite pigeon. Stars Bradley Payne, Winifred Davenport.

Piglet Pig character in the *Winnie the Pooh* films; voiced by John Fiedler.

Piglet's Big Movie (film) Piglet gets an inferior feeling when his friends begin a "honey harvest" and he is told that he is too small to help. When Piglet disappears, the others use his scrapbook as a map to find him, and in the process discover that this "very small animal" has been a big hero in a lot of ways. After an eventful search and a dramatic climax, Piglet once again demonstrates how large an influence he has been on his pals. Released on March 21, 2003. Directed by Francis Glebas. Voices include Jim Cummings (Winnie the Pooh and Tigger), John Fiedler (Piglet), Ken Sansom (Rabbit), Nikita Hopkins (Roo), Kath Soucie (Kanga), Peter Cullen (Eeyore), André Stojka (Owl), Tom Wheatley (Christopher Robin). 75 min. The film features several new songs written and performed by Carly Simon, including "If I Wasn't So Small (The Piglet Song)," "Mother's

Intuition," and "With a Few Good Friends." A production of DisneyToon Studios, a division of Walt Disney Feature Animation. Pre-production work was done in Burbank, but the film was animated primarily by Walt Disney Animation Japan. Released on video in 2003.

Pigs Is Pigs (film) Special cartoon; released on May 21, 1954. Directed by Jack Kinney. Backgrounds by Eyvind Earle. McMorehouse goes to collect his two guinea pigs from stationmaster Flannery and argues the animals are pets and not pigs, and therefore the shipping charges should be cheaper. While the dispute goes on, the pigs multiply, McMorehouse leaves, and Flannery sends all the pigs to the main office. Produced in the popular UPA style of limited animation. Nominated for an Academy Award.

Pin trading Program begun at Walt Disney World in October 1999, at Disneyland in April 2000, at Tokyo Disneyland in November 2000, and at Disneyland Paris in October 2001, whereby guests and cast members exchange Disney pins among each other at special pin stations and throughout the parks.

Pinchot, Bronson Actor; appeared in *Blame It on the Bellboy* (bellboy). He provided the voice of Francois in *Lady and the Tramp II: Scamp's Adventure*.

Pinocchio (film) A wooden puppet is brought to life by the Blue Fairy, with the promise that he can become a real boy if he earns it. He is led astray by the wicked Honest John and his companion, Gideon, who turn him over to an evil puppeteer, Stromboli. Pinocchio is sent to Pleasure Island, where the wicked boys are turned into donkeys, but he escapes with the aid of his friend and conscience Jiminy Cricket, and eventually redeems himself by saving his father, Geppetto, who had been swallowed by Monstro, the whale. The Blue Fairy rewards Pinocchio by turning him into a real boy. From an original serialized story written for a children's magazine by Collodi (the pen name of Carlo Lorenzini) in 1881. Premiered in New York on February 7, 1940. Directed by

Ben Sharpsteen and Hamilton Luske. Voices include Dickie Jones (Pinocchio), Cliff Edwards (Jiminy Cricket), Christian Rub (Geppetto), Evelyn Venable (Blue Fairy). 87 min. The film

required the talents of 750 artists, including animators, assistants, inbetweeners, layout artists, background painters, special-effects animators, and inkers and painters, who produced more than 2 million drawings and used some 1,500 shades of paint for the Technicolor production. Jiminy Cricket became the film's most popular and enduring character, appearing in subsequent Disney films and television shows, including *Fun and Fancy Free* and the *Mickey Mouse Club*. The character, brought to life by animator Ward Kimball, was only a minor one in Collodi's tale, in which he was eventually squashed by Pinocchio. The Disney film gave him a much more important role. Gustaf Tenggren, an award-winning illustrator, was assigned to the production to give the film the kind of lavish European storybook flavor that Walt Disney envisioned. Academy Award winner for Best Score and Best Song ("When You Wish Upon a Star"). Other songs include "Hi Diddle Dee Dee" and "I've Got No Strings." Many film historians describe the film as the most beautifully realized and technically perfect of all the Disney animated features. The film cost $2.6 million in 1940, but using the same techniques and processes, it would cost well over $100 million today. *Pinocchio* was re-released theatrically in 1945, 1954, 1962, 1971, 1978, and 1984. In 1992 it again returned to theaters in a new, painstakingly restored print by Buena Vista Worldwide Services and YCM Labs of Burbank. It was released on video in 1985 and 1993.

Pinocchio Cartoon character; voiced by Dickie Jones.

Pinocchio: A Lesson in Honesty (film) Educational film; released in September 1978. A boy who plays hooky from school learns that lies only increase a problem.

Pinocchio Village Haus Fast-food facility in Fantasyland in Magic Kingdom Park at Walt Disney World; opened on October 1, 1971. Murals and furnishings are modeled after the *Pinocchio* film.

Pinocchio's Daring Journey Fantasyland dark-ride attraction at Tokyo Disneyland, opened on April 15, 1983; also at Disneyland, opened on May 25, 1983. See also Les Voyages

de Pinocchio for the Disneyland Paris version. This attraction had been in design at WED Enterprises for many years, with a plan of putting it at Disneyland, but the schedules for the new Fantasyland there and the Tokyo Disneyland park resulted in the attraction premiering in Tokyo a month before it opened at Disneyland. Makes ample use of special effects, including holograms and fiber optics.

Pioneer Days (film) Mickey Mouse cartoon; released on December 5, 1930. Directed by Burt Gillett. As Mickey and Minnie head west in a covered wagon, they are set upon by Indians who capture Minnie. Mickey rescues her and when they return they frighten off the Indians from the pioneer encampment by pretending to be an army of soldiers.

Pioneer Hall Located at Fort Wilderness at Walt Disney World; opened on April 1, 1974. Features the Hoop-Dee-Doo musical revue and dining facilities.

Pioneer Trails, Indian Lore and Bird Life of the Plains (film) Includes part of *Vanishing Prairie*; released on 16mm for schools in September 1962. Shows the wagon trails made by the pioneers, explains the origins of Native American dance forms, and describes the types of bird life on the prairie.

Pirates of the Caribbean New Orleans Square attraction at Disneyland; opened on March 18, 1967. One of the most elaborate uses of Audio-Animatronics figures ever attempted by Disney, and still considered the favorite attraction by many guests. Walt Disney worked extensively on this attraction, but passed away before it was finished. Guests travel by boat through scenes of pirate treasure, ghost ships, and a Caribbean town being plundered by an inept bunch of brigands, to the sounds of the attraction's theme song, "Yo

Ho, (A Pirate's Life for Me)." Also in Adventureland in Magic Kingdom Park at Walt Disney

World, opened on December 15, 1973; at Tokyo Disneyland, opened on April 15, 1983; and at Disneyland Paris, opened on April 12, 1992.

Pirates of the Caribbean: Dead Man's Chest (film) First sequel to *Pirates of the Caribbean: The Curse of the Black Pearl*. A Walt Disney Pictures film in association with Jerry Bruckheimer Films. Directed by Gore Verbinski. Released July 7, 2006. Stars Johnny Depp, Orlando Bloom, Keira Knightley, Stellan Skarsgard, Bill Nighy, Jack Davenport, Jonathan Pryce, Kevin McNally, Naomie Harris, Tom Hollander, Lee Arenberg, Mackenzie Crook. Began filming at the Disney Studio in Burbank on February 28, 2005.

Pirates of the Caribbean: The Curse of the Black Pearl (film) In the 18th century, Captain Jack Sparrow is roguish yet charming, as he sails the Caribbean. But Jack's idyllic life capsizes after his nemesis, the wily Captain Barbossa, steals his ship, the *Black Pearl*, and later attacks the town of Port Royal, kidnapping the Governor's beautiful daughter, Elizabeth Swann. Elizabeth's childhood friend, Will Turner, joins forces with Jack to commandeer the fastest ship in the British fleet, the HMS *Interceptor*, in a gallant attempt to rescue her and recapture the *Black Pearl*. The duo and their motley crew are pursued by Elizabeth's betrothed, the debonair, ambitious Commodore Norrington, aboard the HMS *Dauntless*. Unbeknownst to Will, whose father once served with the crew, there is a curse that has doomed Barbossa and his men to live forever as the undead, where, under moonlight, they are transformed into living skeletons. The curse they carry can only be broken if a once-plundered treasure is restored and blood is spilt. Released on July 9, 2003. A Walt Disney Pictures film in association with Jerry Bruckheimer Films. Directed by Gore Verbinski. Stars Johnny Depp (Captain Jack Sparrow), Geoffrey Rush (Captain Barbossa), Orlando Bloom (Will Turner), Jonathan Pryce (Governor Swann), Keira Knightley (Elizabeth Swann), Jack Davenport (Commodore Norrington). 143 min. Filmed in Super 35-Scope. The set for Port Royal's Fort

Charles was built on a bluff at Palos Verdes, California; Caribbean filming took place at St. Vincent and the Grenadines. Since the film is an homage to the popular Disneyland attraction, the film's premiere was held at Disneyland on June 28, 2003. The film eventually grossed over $300 million, placing it right behind *Finding Nemo* as the #3 film of the year. It received five Academy Award nominations (Best Actor [Johnny Depp], Sound Mixing, Sound Editing, Visual Effects, and Makeup). Released on video in 2003.

Pirouettes de Vieux Moulin, Les Ferris wheel attached to an old mill in Fantasyland at Disneyland Paris, opened June 6, 1993.

Pixar Animation Studios Pixar, located in Emeryville, California, produced *Toy Story* (the first full-length animated feature produced entirely by computer) for Disney and in February 1997 signed a five-picture deal with Disney, with Disney agreeing to purchase up to 5% of Pixar stock. Additional productions have included *Toy Story 2*, *a bug's life*, *Monsters, Inc.*, *Finding Nemo*, and *The Incredibles*. On January 24, 2006, Disney announced an agreement to purchase Pixar.

Pixel Perfect (television) A Disney Channel Original Movie; premiering on January 16, 2004. Techno-wiz Roscoe sees his friend Samantha's band, the Zettabytes, floundering because they don't have the right image, so he uses computer technology designed by his dad to craft singer Loretta Modern—a perfect rockin' hologram who fronts the band and makes it an overnight success. But Roscoe's good deed backfires when Samantha starts to feel like an outsider in the group. Meanwhile Loretta has the world at her feet but knows it doesn't compare to being "real." At the height of the Zettabytes' success, Roscoe struggles with newfound feelings for Samantha, a lack of nurturing from his father, and Loretta's quest to become an individual. Directed by Mark A. Z. Dippé. Stars Ricky Ullman (Roscoe), Leah Pipes (Samantha), Spencer Redford (Loretta Modern), Chris Williams (Daryl Fibbs), Brett Cullen (Xander), Tania Gunadi (Cindy), Porscha Coleman (Rachel).

Pizzafari Restaurant on Discovery Island at Disney's Animal Kingdom; opened April 22, 1998.

Pizzeria Bella Notte Restaurant in Fantasyland at Disneyland Paris; opened on April 12, 1992.

PJs, The (television) Half-hour television comedy series; debuted on Fox on January 12, 1999, after a preview on January 10, and ended on June 17, 2001. Produced in a stop-motion animation technique called "foamation," the series is set in a big-city housing project, and takes a satirical look at urban family values through the eyes of Thurgood Stubbs, the cantankerous superintendent of the Hilton-Jacobs Projects, his wife, relatives, and friends. Voices include Eddie Murphy (Thurgood Stubbs),

Loretta Devine (Muriel Stubbs), James Black (Tarnell), Michael Paul Chan (Jimmy), Ja'net DuBois (Mrs. Avery). The animation is produced by Will Vinton Studios.

Place, Mary Kay Actress; appeared in *Captain Ron* (Katherine Harvey) and *Sweet Home Alabama* (Pearl) and on television in *The Girl Who Spelled Freedom* (Prissy Thrash).

Plane Crazy (film) The first Mickey Mouse cartoon made, but the third one released, after sound was added, in 1929. Directed by Walt Disney. Inspired by Charles Lindbergh's exploits. With the help of his farm-

yard friends, Mickey builds a plane and goes on an adventurous flight with Minnie until an unwilling cow passenger and an unwanted kiss end the trip. Also later released as part of *Milestones for Mickey* (1974).

Plane Crazy Musical show at Videopolis at Disneyland from March 15 to October 31, 1991. Fat Cat and Don Karnage battle it out with Baloo, Chip and Dale, and Launchpad McQuack in this comedy/mystery musical adventure. It was the first Disneyland show to feature primarily original music.

Planes (film) Educational film in the Goofy's Field Trips series; released on August 18, 1989. 15 min. Goofy shows two children what it's like behind the scenes at an airport.

Planet Hollywood 400-seat spherical entertainment restaurant, featuring displays of movie memorabilia, at Pleasure Island at Walt Disney World, opened on December 18, 1994. Another Planet Hollywood opened in Disney Village at Disneyland Paris in the summer of 1996.

Planning for Good Eating (film) Educational film produced under the auspices of the Coordinator of Inter-American Affairs. Delivered on April 3, 1946. Careless Charlie is utilized to teach a family all about good dietary habits.

Plantation Park See Little Lake Bryan.

Plastics Inventor, The (film) Donald Duck cartoon; released on September 1, 1944. Directed by Jack King. Donald bakes a plastic airplane from radio instructions and proudly goes to try it out. But it melts in a storm, coming down on a flock of blackbirds like a pie.

Platt, Oliver Actor; appeared in *The Three Musketeers* (Porthos), *Tall Tale* (Paul Bunyan), *Funny Bones* (Tommy Fawkes), *Simon Birch* (Ben Goodrich), *Bicentennial Man* (Rupert Burns), *Gun Shy* (Fulvio Nesstra), *Hope Springs* (Doug Reed), *Casanova* (Papprizzio).

Plausible Impossible, The (television) Television show; aired on October 31, 1956. Directed by Wilfred Jackson, William Beaudine. Walt Disney explains some of the techniques of animation, and includes for the first time the pencil test footage of the "Soup Eating Sequence" from *Snow White and the Seven Dwarfs*. Disney used a prop book in the show called *The Art of Animation*, and many people expected to be able to find it in their bookstores, but the book was never completed quite in the manner he foresaw; instead, Bob Thomas used that title two years later on a book to tie in with the upcoming release of *Sleeping Beauty*.

Play It to the Bone (film) Best friends and professional boxing rivals Vince Boudreau and Caesar Dominguez have not worked in years. Finally, from out of the blue, they get the chance of a lifetime: an assignment to work together in Las Vegas. The job promises big money, but there's a hitch: they have to be there immediately. They quickly hit the road with Grace Pasic at the wheel, embarking on a circuitous route through the sizzling desert. Sparks fly as the competitive Vince and Caesar antagonize each other to a frenzy matched only by Grace's own combative temper. The going gets rougher when they pick up a sultry hitchhiker, Lia, whose presence throws the trio into further upheaval. A riotous race ensues as Vince and Caesar scramble to make it to Vegas for their big showdown. A Touchstone Picture. Released on December 25, 1999, in Los Angeles, and elsewhere on January 21, 2000. Directed by Ron Shelton. Stars Woody Harrelson (Vince Boudreau), Antonio Banderas (Caesar Dominguez), Lolita Davidovich (Grace Pasic), Lucy Liu (Lia). 125 min. Filmed in CinemaScope. Released on video in 2000.

Playful Pan (film) Silly Symphony cartoon; released on December 27, 1930. Directed by Burt Gillett. Pan's musical pipe causes flowers and trees to come to life, and also saves the woodland creatures by extinguishing a fire that threatens to destroy the forest by luring the flames into the water as the animals take refuge on an island.

Playful Pluto (film) Mickey Mouse cartoon; released on March 3, 1934. Directed by Burt Gillett. Pluto tries to help Mickey with his spring cleaning but instead becomes a nuisance and ends up caught in flypaper. The flypaper-gag sequence, animated by Norm Ferguson, has been praised as a masterful piece of animation.

Playground Fun (film) Educational film with safety experts Huey, Dewey, and Louie introducing safe ways to have fun, in the Mickey's Safety Club series; released in September 1989. 20 min.

Playhouse Disney—Live on Stage Attraction at Disney-MGM Studios; opened on October 1, 2001. A similar attraction opened at Disney's California Adventure on April 11, 2003. Segments from *Rolie Polie Olie*, *Stanley*, *The Book of Pooh*, and *Bear in the Big Blue House* help provide life lessons to kids.

Playing God (film) Stripped of his medical license after performing an operation while high on amphetamines, famed L.A. surgeon Dr. Eugene Sands abandons his former life only to find himself crossing paths with Raymond Blossom, a ruthless criminal. Raymond hires Eugene as his "gunshot doctor," treating associates who cannot risk visiting a hospital. Lured deeper and deeper into the dangerous underworld and growing treacherously close to Claire, Raymond's seductive girlfriend, Eugene is faced with his most challenging decision—to continue a life on the run or to face his demons and regain control of his destiny. A Touchstone film. Directed by Andy Wilson. Released on October 17, 1997. Stars David Duchovny (Eugene Sands), Timothy Hutton (Raymond Blossom), Angelina Jolie (Claire). 93 min. Set in Los Angeles in the 1990s, the film used locations all around the city. Released on video in 1998.

Playing Mona Lisa (film) Claire Goldstein, a brilliant 23-year-old pianist living in San Francisco, suddenly finds her life in a downward spiral. Her own misfortunes are the catalyst for introspection in those around her and, as she picks up the pieces of her own life, she finds that no one has a perfect life—they are just hiding behind contrived smiles, playing Mona Lisa. Directed by Matthew Huffman. Very limited theatrical release, opening on October 27, 2000, in San Francisco. Released without a label. Stars Alicia Witt (Claire), Harvey Fierstein (Bennett), Brooke Langton (Sabrina Pagniatti), Johnny Galecki (Arthur Kapp), Elliott Gould (Bernie Goldstein), Marlo Thomas (Sheila Goldstein), Ivan Sergei (Eddie). Based on the play *Two Goldsteins on Acid*, by Marni Freedman. 93 min. Released on video in 2001.

Plaza East and Plaza West Boutiques Shops on Main Street in Disneyland Paris; opened on April 12, 1992.

Plaza Gardens Restaurant Located on Main Street in Disneyland Paris; opened on April 12, 1992.

Plaza Inn Restaurant on the hub at Disneyland; opened July 18, 1965. It was formerly called the Red Wagon Inn. One of the most attractively decorated restaurants at Disneyland, this buffeteria is furnished with authentic antiques, stained glass, crystal chandeliers and sconces, and tufted velvet upholstery. Also a restaurant at Hong Kong Disneyland, hosted by Maxim's; opened on September 12, 2005. It features Chinese cuisine.

Plaza Pavilion Buffeteria restaurant on the hub at Disneyland; opened July 17, 1955. Before the Tahitian Terrace Restaurant was built on the backside of its building, guests could take their meals from the Plaza Pavilion to tables on a terrace overlooking the Jungle Cruise. An early specialty was a French dip beef sandwich. Open only during summer and holiday seasons. It closed in July 1998 and became an annual passport processing center in November 2000. Also in Westernland at Tokyo Disneyland; opened on April 15, 1983.

Plaza Restaurant Located at Tokyo Disneyland; opened on April 15, 1983. There is also a Plaza Restaurant in Magic Kingdom Park at Walt Disney World.

Plaza Swan Boats Attraction on the hub in Magic Kingdom Park at Walt Disney World, opening May 20, 1973, and operating occasionally during peak periods until August 1983.

Pleasence, Donald (1919–1995) Actor; appeared in *Escape to Witch Mountain* (Deranian), and on television in *The Horsemasters*. He appeared on The Disney Channel in *Black Arrow*.

Pleasure Island Evening entertainment area; opened at Walt Disney World on May 1, 1989. Disney Imagineers felt that there should be a place where guests staying on the property could find nighttime entertainment without having to travel into Orlando. This was one of the first Disney attractions that came with a mythology all its own, about the recent discovery of an abandoned shipbuilding operation of one Merriweather Adam Pleasure that the Disney designers decided to restore. It is now the location of a group of nightclubs, restaurants, a multiplex movie theater, and shops, with entertainment culminating in a New Year's Eve celebration every night. *The Empress Lilly* has become part of Pleasure Island. There is an entrance fee to the island only in the evenings; during the day guests can wander around the shops at leisure. In 1996, Pleasure Island became part of the Downtown Disney complex.

Pleshette, Suzanne Actress; appeared in *The Ugly Dachshund* (Fran Garrison), *The Adventures of Bullwhip Griffin* (Arabella Flagg), *Blackbeard's Ghost* (Jo Anne Baker), and *The Shaggy D.A.* (Betty Daniels). She provided the voice of Zira in *The Lion King II: Simba's Pride* and Yubaba and Zeniba in *Spirited Away*, and appeared in *8 Simple Rules for Dating My Teenage Daughter* (Laura Hennessy)

Plowboy, The (film) Mickey Mouse cartoon; released in 1929. Directed by Walt Disney. When

Mickey and Minnie attempt to milk a cow, they meet Clarabelle Cow and Horace Horsecollar (in their first cartoon), and the two couples play tricks on each other.

Plowright, Joan Actress; appeared in *A Pyromaniac's Love Story* (Mrs. Linzer), *The Scarlet Letter* (Harriet Hibbons), *Mr. Wrong* (Mrs. Crawford), *101 Dalmatians* (live action—Nanny), *Bringing Down the House* (Mrs. Arness); provided the voice of Baylene in *Dinosaur*, and appeared on television in *On Promised Land* (Mrs. Appletree) and *Bailey's Mistake* (Aunt Angie).

Ployardt, John See John McLeish.

Plumb, Ed (1907–1958) He joined Disney in 1938 and served as musical director on *Fantasia*. He later served as co-musical director on such films as *Bambi*, *Saludos Amigos*, and *The Three Caballeros*, and worked on orchestration on such films as *Song of the South*, *Peter Pan*, *The Living Desert*, *Lady and the Tramp*, *Davy Crockett*, *Secrets of Life*, and *Johnny Tremain*.

Plume et Palette Shop in France in World Showcase at Epcot; opened on October 1, 1982. Art, Limoges porcelain, and crystal are featured in this shop designed with beautiful wood paneling and cabinets, and wrought-iron balustrades. Fine paintings by French artists are shown on the mezzanine.

Pluto Mickey's faithful pet dog starred in 48 of his own cartoons, but also appeared along with Mickey Mouse and Donald Duck in many of their cartoons. Pluto was created as an actual

dog character, with no speaking voice, as opposed to Goofy, who was created as a human character. The dog who would eventually evolve into Pluto made his debut as a bloodhound in the Mickey Mouse cartoon, *The Chain Gang*, in 1930. Later that year he appeared as Minnie Mouse's dog, Rover, in *The Picnic*, and the following year finally became Mickey's dog Pluto in *The Moose Hunt*.

The 48 Pluto cartoons are as follows:

1.	*Pluto's Quin-Puplets*	1937
2.	*Bone Trouble*	1940
3.	*Pantry Pirate*	1940
4.	*Pluto's Playmate*	1941
5.	*A Gentlemen's Gentleman*	1941
6.	*Canine Caddy*	1941
7.	*Lend a Paw*	1941
8.	*Pluto, Junior*	1942
9.	*The Army Mascot*	1942
10.	*The Sleepwalker*	1942
11.	*T-Bone for Two*	1942
12.	*Pluto at the Zoo*	1942
13.	*Pluto and the Armadillo*	1943
14.	*Private Pluto*	1943
15.	*Springtime for Pluto*	1944
16.	*First Aiders*	1944
17.	*Dog Watch*	1945
18.	*Canine Casanova*	1945
19.	*The Legend of Coyote Rock*	1945
20.	*Canine Patrol*	1945
21.	*Pluto's Kid Brother*	1946
22.	*In Dutch*	1946
23.	*Squatter's Rights*	1946
24.	*The Purloined Pup*	1946
25.	*Pluto's Housewarming*	1947
26.	*Rescue Dog*	1947
27.	*Mail Dog*	1947
28.	*Pluto's Blue Note*	1947
29.	*Bone Bandit*	1948

Pluto (devil) The king of the underworld, who menaced Persephone in *The Goddess of Spring* (1934).

Pluto and His Friends (television) Television show (30 min.); aired on July 31, 1982. A salute to Pluto, with four cartoons. Narrated by Gary Owens.

Pluto and the Armadillo (film) Pluto cartoon; released on February 19, 1943. Directed by Clyde Geronimi. Mickey and Pluto are in South America, where they meet a playful friend for Pluto—an armadillo. When Pluto plays too

rough, it hides, but finally returns to join Pluto and Mickey on the plane back home.

Pluto and the Baby (film) Title of an edited version of *Mickey Plays Papa*, which aired on the *Mickey Mouse Club* in the 1950s; all scenes of Mickey are edited out.

Pluto and the Gopher (film) Pluto cartoon; released on February 10, 1950. Directed by Charles Nichols. Pluto digs up Minnie's garden and destroys her house in order to catch a pesky gopher—in spite of Minnie's scoldings.

Pluto at the Zoo (film) Pluto cartoon; released on November 20, 1942. Directed by Clyde Geronimi. Pluto is disgusted with his small bone when he sees a huge one in a lion's cage. He manages to get it away from the lion, but has conflicts with other zoo animals in an exhausting attempt to keep the bone. Finally he props the lion's jaw open with the bone and leaves the zoo happy with his small bone.

Pluto Gets the Paper: Spaceship (film) While fetching the newspaper for Mickey, Pluto is abducted by an alien spaceship and subjected to a number of humorous experiments. Directed by William Speers. Released on February 12, 1999. 2 min. From the *MouseWorks* television series. Released with *My Favorite Martian*.

Pluto, Junior (film) Pluto cartoon; released on February 28, 1942. Directed by Clyde Geronimi. Pluto's rest is continually disturbed by scrapes an energetic puppy gets into, including the puppy's troubles with a worm and a goofy bird.

Plutopia (film) Mickey Mouse and Pluto cartoon; released on May 18, 1951. Directed by Charles Nichols. While on vacation at a mountain resort with Mickey, Pluto dreams he is in Utopia with an overly obsequious cat acting as his butler. The butler will perform anything Pluto's heart desires, when Pluto bites his tail. Awakening, Pluto bites a nearby cat's tail and a furious battle ensues.

Pluto's Blue Note (film) Pluto cartoon; released on December 26, 1947. Directed by Charles Nichols. When Pluto's singing annoys everyone, he entices female dogs by miming to a record (the song is "You Belong to My Heart," from *The Three Caballeros*). Nominated for an Academy Award.

Pluto's Christmas Tree (film) Mickey Mouse cartoon; released on November 21, 1952.

Directed by Jack Hannah. The tree that Mickey chops down to bring home for Christmas turns out to be the home of Chip and Dale. In discovering the chipmunks' presence and trying to get them out of the trimmed tree, Pluto destroys it.

Pluto's Day (television) Television show; aired on December 12, 1956. Directed by Wolfgang Reitherman. Walt Disney presents a typical day in Pluto's life through several cartoons.

Pluto's Dream House (film) Mickey Mouse cartoon; released on August 30, 1940. Directed

by Clyde Geronimi. Mickey wishes on a magic lamp to build an ideal doghouse and to bathe Pluto, but his plans go awry when garbled radio announcements interfere with the lamp's instructions.

Pluto's Fledgling (film) Pluto cartoon; released on September 10, 1948. Directed by Charles Nichols. Pluto tries to teach Orville, a baby bird, how to fly with some tricks of his own.

Pluto's Heart Throb (film) Pluto cartoon; released on January 6, 1950. Directed by Charles Nichols. When Butch and Pluto vie for Dinah's attention, it appears the brute strength of the bulldog will vanquish Pluto until Dinah must be

rescued from a swimming pool. Only Pluto manages to rescue her and, in doing so, wins her.

Pluto's Housewarming (film) Pluto cartoon; released on February 21, 1947. Directed by Charles Nichols. Pluto moves into his new house, only to find Butch the bulldog and a turtle have also taken up residence there. With the help of the turtle, they get rid of Butch and live happily together.

Pluto's Judgement Day (film) Mickey Mouse cartoon; released on August 31, 1935. Directed by Dave Hand. Mickey chastises Pluto for chasing a kitten, which causes Pluto to have a nightmare in which cats try him in court for his crimes against the feline world. As he is sentenced to a grisly end, he awakens to make amends with the kitten.

Pluto's Kid Brother (film) Pluto cartoon; released on April 12, 1946. Directed by Charles Nichols. Pluto and his kid brother have many adventures together trying to keep some stolen wieners, including eluding a bulldog and the dogcatcher.

Pluto's Party (film) Mickey Mouse cartoon; released on September 19, 1952. Directed by Milt Schaffer. At his own birthday party, Pluto gets pushed around by the nephews and cannot even get any of his own cake until after the party, when Mickey presents him with a piece he had saved.

Pluto's Playmate (film) Pluto cartoon; released on January 24, 1941. Directed by Norm Ferguson. Pluto thinks he has an enemy when a baby seal steals his ball on the beach, but when the seal rescues him from a squid, they soon become fast friends.

Pluto's Purchase (film) Pluto cartoon; released on July 9, 1948. Directed by Charles Nichols. Pluto is in for a surprise when Mickey sends him to buy a salami at the butcher shop, and he has to fight to keep Butch the bulldog from stealing it. When Pluto gets home with the salami, Mickey presents it to Butch as a birthday gift.

Pluto's Quin-Puplets (film) Pluto cartoon; released on November 26, 1937. Directed by Ben Sharpsteen. Left in charge of five pups when Fifi goes out, Pluto has his hands (paws?) full when he gets drunk, and the puppies get mixed up in paint spray. Disgusted, Fifi shoves them all out of the doghouse to sleep in a barrel.

Pluto's Surprise Package (film) Pluto cartoon; released on March 4, 1949. Directed by Charles Nichols. Pluto has quite a time getting Mickey's mail into the house, what with the wind blowing the letters about and a turtle emerging from one package.

Pluto's Sweater (film) Pluto cartoon; released on April 29, 1949. Directed by Charles Nichols. Minnie knits Pluto a sweater that he hates, and he tries everything in his power to get it off. When it gets wet and shrinks to a tiny size, Minnie gives it to a disgusted Figaro instead.

Plymouth (television) Two-hour television movie; aired on ABC on May 26, 1991. Directed by Lee David Zlotoff. Residents of a Pacific Northwest town resettle on the moon but find living con-

ditions there difficult. Stars Cindy Pickett, Richard Hamilton, Matthew Brown.

Pocahontas (film) The first Disney animated feature based on historical fact, *Pocahontas* tells the story of the meeting of the English settlers in Jamestown with the local tribe of Powhatan Indians. The adventurous young woman, Pocahontas, along with her constant companions, Meeko, a raccoon, and Flit, a hummingbird, visit Grandmother Willow, a counseling tree spirit, because she is uncertain about the path her life should take. She soon meets the brave English captain John Smith, and while opening his eyes to an understanding and respect for the world around him, the two fall in love. The other English settlers, led by Governor Ratcliffe, are intent on finding gold in the New World and become convinced the Native Americans are hiding the precious substance from them. Thomas, an inexperienced settler, kills the brave, Kocoum, but Smith lets the Native Americans think he is responsible, so he is condemned to death. In begging her father, Chief Powhatan, to spare Smith's life, Pocahontas finds that her path in life is to be instrumental in establishing the early

peace between the Jamestown settlers and her tribe. Smith, however, is severely wounded by an enraged Ratcliffe and must return to England. Pocahontas and he part, each knowing their lives are richer for the love they share. Directed by Mike Gabriel and Eric Goldberg. Limited release on June 16; general release on June 23, 1995. Voices include Irene Bedard (Pocahontas speaking), Judy Kuhn (Pocahontas singing), Mel Gibson (Capt. John Smith), David Ogden Stiers (Ratcliffe/ Wiggins), Linda Hunt (Grandmother Willow), Christian Bale (Thomas), Russell Means (Chief Powhatan). 81 min. Music is by Alan Menken, with lyrics by Stephen Schwartz. Songs include "Just Around the Riverbend," "Steady as the Beating Drum," and "Colors of the Wind." The look and style of the film were inspired by the filmmakers' numerous visits to Jamestown, Virginia, as well as by extensive research into the Colonial period. The use of strong vertical and horizontal imagery in the design springs from the tall, vertical shapes of the Virginia pine forests and the vast horizontal landscapes. At various stages of the production, the creative team consulted with Native American scholars and storytellers to incorporate authentic aspects of the Powhatan culture into the film. The film had an outdoor premiere in New York's Central Park on June 10, 1995. Alan Menken and Stephen Schwartz were presented Oscars for Best Song ("Colors of the Wind") and Menken won for Best Score. Released on video in 1996.

Pocahontas II: Journey to a New World (film) Direct-to-video sequel to the *Pocahontas* film. Pocahontas sets sail for England on an important mission of peace, escorted by a dashing English diplomat, John Rolfe; her bodyguard, Uti; and stowaways Meeko, Percy, and Flit. She is awed by London, and the Londoners by her. Ratcliffe plots against Pocahontas, and she is eventually saved by Rolfe and John Smith. Released on September 5, 1998. Directed by Bradley Raymond and Tom Ellery. Voices include actors from the original film, along with Billy Zane (John Rolfe), Jean Stapleton (Mrs. Jenkins), Donal Gibson (John Smith), Finola Hughes (Queen Anne). 72 min. Donal Gibson is the brother of Mel Gibson, who voiced John Smith in the original film.

Pointer, The (film) Mickey Mouse cartoon; released on July 21, 1939. Directed by Clyde Geronimi. Mickey tries to teach Pluto to be a

pointer in their hunt for quail. But they have a harrowing encounter with a huge bear, and Pluto points instead to a can of beans—their dinner. Nominated for an Academy Award. It was in this cartoon that the public saw for the first time a redesigned Mickey Mouse, supervised by animator Fred Moore. Most noticeable were his eyes—now they had pupils in a white eye where before they were simple black ovals.

Poitier, Sidney Actor; appeared in *Shoot to Kill* (Warren Stantin). He was named to the Disney board of directors on November 22, 1994, to fill the vacancy caused by the death of Frank Wells, and held the post until March 19, 2003.

Polar Trappers (film) Donald Duck cartoon; released on June 17, 1938. Directed by Ben Sharpsteen. Goofy tries to trap a walrus but echoes and icicles in a cave are his downfall. Donald uses Pied Piper tactics to try to trap a colony of penguins, but ends up destroying the trappers' camp.

Police Station, The (film) Educational film in which Mickey meets and learns from a police officer, in the Mickey's Field Trips series, released in September 1987. 11 min.

Pollard, Michael J. Actor; appeared in *Summer Magic* (Digby Popham) and *Dick Tracy* (Bug Bailey).

Pollatschek, Susanne She voiced Olivia Flaversham in *The Great Mouse Detective.*

Polley, Sarah Actress; appeared in *Lantern Hill* and *Avonlea* (Sara Stanley) on The Disney Channel.

Polly (television) Two-hour television movie; aired on November 12, 1989. Directed by Debbie Allen. An adaptation of the Pollyanna story as a musical with an African American cast. Stars Keshia Knight Pulliam (Polly), Phylicia Rashad (Aunt Polly), Dorian Harewood (Dr. Shannon), Barbara Montgomery (Mrs. Conley), T. K. Carter (George), Brandon Adams (Jimmy Bean), Butterfly McQueen (Miss Priss), Brock Peters (Eban

Pendergast), Celeste Holm (Miss Snow). The repeat airing of *Polly* on September 9, 1990, marked the final episode of the *Magical World of Disney*.

Polly—Comin' Home (television) Television movie; aired on NBC on November 18, 1990. Polly restores racial and political harmony in a town split in two in this musical sequel. 120 min. Directed by Debbie Allen. Stars Keshia Knight Pulliam (Polly), Phylicia Rashad (Aunt Polly), Dorian Harewood (Dr. Shannon), Barbara Montgomery (Mrs. Conley), Brandon Adams (Jimmy Bean), Celeste Holm (Miss Snow), Anthony Newley (Dabney Mayhew).

Polly Penguin Co-star of *Peculiar Penguins* (1934).

Pollyanna (film) Orphaned Pollyanna, coming to live with Aunt Polly Harrington who sternly runs her small New England town, brings her cheerful philosophy to the grim household and eventually to the whole town. With her "Glad Game" she intrigues Mr. Pendergast, an old hermit, who shows the kids his glass prisms and eventually decides to adopt orphan Jimmy Bean; coaxes Mrs. Snow, a crotchety hypochondriac, from her sickbed; teaches the Reverend Ford to stand up for himself; and revives a romance between Aunt Polly and Dr. Edmund Chilton. Under the girl's influence, the town resists Aunt Polly, and stages its own benefit for building a new orphanage. When Pollyanna is severely injured while trying to join the festivities, the accident gives Aunt Polly a whole new outlook. This wins her the goodwill of the town and the love of the doctor who will restore Pollyanna's health. Directed by David Swift. Released May 19, 1960. 134 min. Stars Hayley Mills (Pollyanna), Jane Wyman (Aunt Polly), Richard Egan (Dr. Edmund Chilton), Karl Malden (Rev. Paul Ford), Agnes Moorehead (Mrs. Snow), Nancy Olsen (Nancy Furman), Adolphe Menjou (Mr. Pendergast), Donald Crisp (Mayor Karl Warren), Kevin Corcoran (Jimmy Bean). This was Hayley Mills's first film for Disney, and she immediately became the Studio's newest star. She won an Academy

Award for the most outstanding juvenile performance of 1960. Wyman and Moorehead had earlier appeared together in *Johnny Belinda*, a film for which both were nominated for Academy Awards—Wyman won the Oscar. Based on the book by Eleanor H. Porter, published in 1913, it became perhaps the best-known American novel since *Uncle Tom's Cabin*. It was so popular that the word *Pollyanna* even got into everyday usage and eventually the dictionary, meaning someone who looks for the best in things. The film was director Swift's first Disney feature and, in fact, he appears briefly as the fireman scolding Jimmy Bean. With a then-lavish $2.5 million budget, Swift gathered a crew and cast unlike any other in a Disney live-action feature. Disney set decorator Emile Kuri was on hand, but outsiders Walter Plunkett (costumes), Russell Harlan (cinematographer), and art directors Carroll Clark and Robert Clatworthy came from established careers at other studios. To find a house to use as the residence of Aunt Polly, Walt Disney had to go far afield from his Studio in Burbank. An ideal house was found in Santa Rosa, near the famed Napa Valley. It occupied a full block in the center of the town, and was surrounded by spacious lawns and gardens. It was built in 1877 as a replica of an old Natchez, Mississippi, antebellum house. The vintage train station and water hole were also filmed in Santa Rosa, but the interiors were completed at the Disney Studio. The film was released on video in 1982 and 1993. For television productions, see *The Adventures of Pollyanna*, along with *Polly* and *Polly—Comin' Home*.

Polo Walt Disney became interested in polo in 1932 and enlisted several Disney staff members and his brother Roy to join in. Walt eventually had a stable of seven polo ponies, named June, Slim, Nava, Arrow, Pardner, Tacky, and Tommy. The Disney team competed in matches at the Riviera Country Club against such luminaries as Spencer Tracy, Darryl F. Zanuck, and Will Rogers. The film *Mickey's Polo Team* reflected the Disney staff's interest in the sport.

Polynesian Resort Hotel at Walt Disney World; opened on October 1, 1971. The hotel is

one of the two original Disney hotels on the property, and features lush vegetation filling much of the lobby in the Great Ceremonial House. The hotel rooms are in several longhouses, named for Pacific islands, such as Samoa, Oahu, Bali Hai, and Tonga. The Monorail stops at the hotel, making it convenient to get around. Perhaps because of the South Seas theme, the hotel seems more restful than some of the others.

Polynesian Revue Luau show at the Polynesian Resort at Walt Disney World; beginning in October 1971. Also known as Kaui-Pono Polynesian Revue and Polynesian Luau. The luau had its last performance on January 4, 2003, to make way for a new tropical-themed dinner show, the Spirit of Aloha Dinner Show, which began on February 25, 2003.

Polynesian Terrace Restaurant Located in Adventureland at Tokyo Disneyland; opened on April 15, 1983.

Pompano Grill Restaurant in the Buena Vista Club; previously and later known as the Lake Buena Vista Club Restaurant.

Pongo Male lead Dalmatian in *One Hundred and One Dalmatians*; voiced by Rod Taylor.

Pony Farm Home of the stables for Disneyland, behind Frontierland and Fantasyland, begun by Dolly and Owen Pope before Disney-

land opened. Name changed to Circle D Corral in 1980. At Walt Disney World, stables at Fort Wilderness are known as the Tri Circle D Ranch.

Pooch and the Pauper, The (television) Television movie; aired on *The Wonderful World of Disney* on July 16, 2000. The president's pampered pet bulldog, Liberty, accidentally swaps places with a scrappy look-alike, Moocher, from the wrong side of the tracks. Stars Richard Karn (Drainville), Fred Willard (President Caldwell), George Wendt (Sparks), Cody Jones (Nate). Released on video in 2000.

Poof Point, The (television) A Disney Channel Original Movie; premiered on September 14, 2001. Two teenage siblings must save the lives of their inventor parents after mom and dad's time-machine experiment goes awry and they become younger versions of themselves. Directed by Neal Israel. Stars Taj Mowry (Eddie Ballard), Dawnn Lewis (Marigold Ballard), Raquel Lee (Marie Ballard), Mark Curry (Norton Ballard).

Pooh Corner Shop in Critter Country at Disneyland; opened in 1995. Also in Fantasyland at Tokyo Disneyland; opened July 14, 2000; and at Hong Kong Disneyland; opened September 12, 2005.

Pooh's Grand Adventure: The Search for Christopher Robin (film) Direct-to-video release on August 5, 1997. The group of animals in the Hundred Acre Wood misunderstand that Christopher Robin has gone away to school, and they head off on a grand journey to find their childhood friend. Directed by Karl Geurs. Voices include Jim Cummings (Pooh), Paul Winchell (Tigger), John Fiedler (Piglet), Brady Bluhm (Christopher Robin), Ken Sansom (Rabbit), Andre Stojka (Owl), David Warner (narrator). 70 min.

Pooh's Great School Bus Adventure (film) Educational film; released in September 1986. Hundred Acre Wood characters illustrate rules for bus safety.

Pooh's Heffalump Halloween Movie (film) Direct-to-video animated film; released on September 13, 2005. At Halloween, Roo's best pal Lumpy is excited to trick-or-treat for the first time. That is, until Tigger warns them about the dreaded Gobloon who will turn you into a jaggedy lantern if he catches you. But if they catch the Gobloon before it catches them, they get to make a wish. When Pooh eats all the Halloween candy, Lumpy and Roo decide to be brave and catch the Gobloon. Directed by Saul Blinkoff and Elliot Bour. Voices include Kyle Stanger (Lumpy), Nikita Hopkins (Roo), Jim Cummings (Pooh/Tigger), John Fiedler (Piglet). 66 min.

Pooh's Heffalump Movie (film) An animated feature created by DisneyToon Studios. Roo, the half-pint kangaroo, sets off on a solo journey to face and capture the dreaded Heffalump. While the older characters head off to save Roo from certain peril by setting makeshift traps to thwart the Heffalumps, Roo comes upon a young, playful Heffalump and makes friends with him. The Heffalump's name is Heffridge Trumpler Brompet Heffalump III, known as Lumpy. Roo discovers that Heffalumps are nothing like the creatures of the ominous stories he has been told, and that the creature is equally afraid of his silly pals. Roo and Lumpy work together to dispel the unfounded fears of their respective friends and families. Directed by Frank Nissen. Released in the U.S. on February 11, 2005, after initial releases on February 4 in Iceland and Poland. 68 min. Voices include Jim Cummings (Winnie the Pooh/Tigger), Nikita Hopkins (Roo), Kath Soucie (Kanga), Ken Sansom (Rabbit), Peter Cullen (Eeyore), Brenda Blethyn (Mama Heffalump), Kyle Stanger (Lumpy). Heffalumps and Woozles made their first Disney appearance in *Winnie the Pooh and the Blustery Day.* Carly Simon composed six new songs for the film. Released on video in 2005.

Pooh's Hunny Hunt Attraction at Tokyo Disneyland; opened on September 1, 2000. Guests enter the world of Winnie the Pooh in large hunny pot vehicles through the pages of a giant storybook, experiencing scenes from the animated films. The attraction is more elaborate than its Walt Disney World counterpart. (For the Walt Disney World attraction, see The Many Adventures of Winnie the Pooh.)

Poor Papa (film) Oswald the Lucky Rabbit cartoon, the first made but not the first released. Released on June 11, 1928.

Pop Century Resort, Disney's 5,760-room value resort planned for opening adjacent to Disney's Wide World of Sports complex at Walt Disney World in 2002, but postponed due to a slowdown in Florida tourism after the New York terrorist attack. The theming highlights the toys, fads, technology breakthroughs, dance crazes, and catchphrases that defined each decade of the 20th century. Larger-than-life pop icons include the Big Wheel, Play-Doh, Rubik's Cube, Duncan Yo-Yo, bowling pins, a laptop computer, and cellular phones. There will be two phases, each with 2,880 rooms: the "Legendary Years" (1900s to 1940s) and the "Classic Years" (1950s to 1990s). The first phase, the Classic Years, opened December 14, 2003.

Pop Warner Football See *Moochie of Pop Warner Football.*

Pope, Owen (1910–2000) The Popes, Owen and Dolly, were hired by Walt Disney in November 1951 to start putting together some livestock for his future park. They first lived in a trailer at the Studio, where they raised and trained the first horses and helped build wagons and coaches. During the construction of Disneyland, Disney gave them their choice of the houses being moved on the property, and they staked out a 10-acre site for the Pony Farm. Three days before the park opened, they moved to Disneyland but had to live in their trailer for a while until their house was ready. They were Disneyland's only residents. The Popes continued with the company, running the Disneyland Pony Farm and then moving to Florida in 1971 to start the Tri Circle D Ranch there. They retired in 1975.

Popeye (film) The cartoon character comes to life in this joint Disney/Paramount musical fantasy. Popeye blows into Sweethaven on the heels of a story. He is looking for his long-lost dad but ends up mopping up various town bullies, falling for Olive Oyl, adopting an abandoned baby, and fighting an undersea battle with Bluto and a giant octopus. Original theatrical release by Paramount in December 1980. Directed by Robert Altman. Music by Harry Nilsson. Stars Robin Williams (Popeye), Shelley Duvall (Olive Oyl), Ray Walston (Pappy), Paul Dooley (Wimpy). Filmed on location in Malta, where the coast of Anchor Bay was transformed into the make-believe harbortown of Sweethaven. Sixteen-mm release by Disney on September 15, 1981.

Popular (television) One-hour series on the WB network; airing first on September 29, 1999, and ending on May 18, 2001. A series about popularity in high school, and the students' constant struggle to define themselves. Stars Leslie Bibb (Brooke McQueen), Carly Pope (Sam McPherson), Tamara Mello (Lily Esposito), Christopher Gorham (Harrison John), Bryce Johnson (Josh Ford), Tammy Lynn Michaels (Nicole Julian), Ron Lester (Mike Bernadino), Sara Rue (Carmen Ferrara), Lisa Darr (Jane McPherson), Scott Bryce (Mike McQueen), Leslie Grossman (Mary Cherry). In the second season Diane Delano (Bobbi Glass) joined the cast as a regular. From Touchstone Television.

Port of Entry Shop in World Showcase Plaza at Epcot; opened on March 28, 1987. Includes merchandise from many countries, including those not featured in World Showcase.

Port Orleans Resort Hotel at Walt Disney World; opened on May 17, 1991. Themed after the French Quarter in New Orleans, this hotel has 1,008 rooms. One could eat at Bonfamille's Cafe or select from the fare at the Sassagoula Floatworks and Food Factory. The swimming pool is called Doubloon Lagoon, and it is built around a sea serpent. The Dixie Landings Resort was combined with the Port Orleans Resort on April 1, 2001.

Porter, Hank (1900–1951) Artist; came to Disney in 1936 as a publicity artist. He designed posters, penciled and inked several Sunday comic pages, and, during World War II, designed many insignias for military units. He was one of the first to be authorized to sign Walt Disney's name for him, and his stylized signature was found for years on fan cards and other items. He left Disney in 1950.

Portobello Road Title of a song in *Bedknobs and Broomsticks*, written by Richard M. Sherman and Robert B. Sherman; the location where Eglantine Price and the kids go searching for a rare book. Portobello Road is an actual place in London, site of a famous weekly Saturday flea market.

Portraits of Canada (film) Circle-Vision film tour of Canada prepared for Expo '86 in Vancouver in conjunction with Telecom Canada; released on May 2, 1986.

Portugal (film) People and Places featurette, released on December 25, 1957. Directed by Ben Sharpsteen. Filmed in CinemaScope. 30 min. Opening with animation showing the adventurous and courageous Portuguese explorers and the routes they traveled, this film then looks at some of the main elements of the Portuguese people's economy—shipping, harvesting grapes for wine, marketing of cork, as well as the country's bullfighting traditions.

Portuguese Reading Film See *A Historia de José* and *José Come Bien*.

Potter, William E. ("Joe") (1905–1988) Retired Army major general and Panama Canal Zone governor who was hired by Walt Disney in 1965 to direct construction of the infrastructure for Walt Disney World, utilizing techniques that were considered revolutionary at the time. After the park's opening he became its senior vice president. He retired in 1974. He was named a Disney Legend posthumously in 1996.

Powder (film) An enigmatic young man with startlingly white skin and extraordinary abilities is discovered living in the cellar of a remote farmhouse and brought to live in a community that does not quite know what to make of him. Befriended by the head of a school for troubled youths and an enthusiastic science teacher, the young man, known as Powder, demonstrates an astoundingly high IQ and a tremendous compassion to persist regardless of the distrust, hatred, and fear that his presence seems to generate. Ultimately, Powder has a profound effect on all who come in contact with him, but learns that he is the only one who can help himself. A Hollywood Pictures film in association with Caravan Pictures. Directed by Victor Salva. Released on October 27, 1995. Stars Sean Patrick Flannery (Powder), Mary Steenburgen (Jessie), Jeff Goldblum (Donald Ripley), Lance Henriksen (Sheriff Barnum). 111 min. Filmed in and around Houston, Texas. Special makeup for Powder was created by the Burman Studio, and was applied with an airbrush. It took from two to three and a half hours to apply each day, and another hour to remove. Released on video in 1996.

Power Rangers (television) Disney acquired *Power Rangers*, and the brand's merchandising rights, when the company purchased Fox Family Channel in 2001. *Power Rangers Ninja Storm*, which debuted in 2003, was the first production solely managed by Disney. Production moved to New Zealand and included a new producer, cast, and crew. Power Rangers first appeared on American television in 1993.

Powers, Mala Actress; appeared on television in *Daniel Boone*.

Powers, Stefanie Actress; appeared in *The Boatniks* (Kate) and *Herbie Rides Again* (Nicole).

Practical Pig, The (film) Silly Symphony cartoon; released on February 24, 1939. Directed by Dick Rickard. The two foolish pigs are captured by the Big Bad Wolf and almost made into pork pies by the three little wolves when Practical Pig comes to save them with the use of an inventive lie detector machine.

Prairie Outpost Supply Shop in Frontierland in Magic Kingdom Park at Walt Disney World; opened February 26, 1991. Formerly Bearly Country. Features decorative gifts and clothing themed to the Southwest.

Prairie/Seal Island (television) Television show; aired on November 10, 1954. Directed by James Algar, Richard Bare. Walt Disney introduces Jim Algar who hosts behind-the-scenes footage of *The Vanishing Prairie* and *Seal Island*. Winston Hibler also appears on the show.

Pratt, Judson (1916–2002) Actor; appeared in *The Barefoot Executive* (policeman), and on television in *The Flight of the Grey Wolf*, *Texas John Slaughter*, *The Wacky Zoo of Morgan City*, and *The Tenderfoot*.

Preacher's Wife, The (film) A preacher, Henry Biggs, is having problems with his church, seeing its congregation declining while its debts are mounting, along with a general feeling of inadequacy that causes problems in his personal life. When he asks for divine intervention, he and his gospel-singing wife, Julia, are visited by an angel, Dudley, and Dudley soon becomes both the source of and solution to their problems. Directed by Penny Marshall. A Touchstone Picture. Released on December 13, 1996. Stars Whitney Houston (Julia), Courtney B. Vance (Henry Biggs), Denzel Washington (Dudley), Gregory Hines (Joe Hamilton), Jenifer Lewis (Marguerite Coleman), Loretta Devine (Beverly), Lionel Richie (Britsloe). 124 min. Whitney Houston's mother, famed gospel singer, Cissy Houston, appeared as choir member Mrs. Havergal. Doubling as the exterior of Rev. Biggs's church, St. Matthew's, was the Good Shepherd Presbyterian Church in the Nodine Hill District of Yonkers, New York. The interiors were filmed at the Trinity United Methodist Church in Newark. The church's choir was made up of members of the Georgia Mass Choir, founded by Rev. Milton Biggham. Other filming took place in Jersey City and Paterson, New Jersey; Portland, Maine (where the ice-skating sequence was filmed on a local pond); and New York City (with an abandoned jazz club in Greenwich Village providing the setting for Jazzie's). Based on *The Bishop's Wife* (RKO, 1947). When Walt Disney and his wife saw that film shortly after its opening, he wrote a warm letter of praise to the producer, Samuel Goldwyn, noting that the movie was in "excellent taste and interspersed with superb light, humorous touches" leaving you with "a very good feeling." Released on video in 1997.

Predators of the Desert (film) Segment from *The Living Desert*; released on 16mm for schools in November 1974. Shows nature's impartiality, as predator and prey combat each other in a struggle for survival.

Prefontaine (film) The inspiring true-life story of an incomparable athlete who attained greatness, challenged defeat, and transformed adversity into personal triumph. From early childhood, the handsome, charismatic, brash, "Pre"—as he was affectionately known throughout his life— was filled with determination to succeed at the highest level no matter the odds. He began distance running in his home state in high school and at the University of Oregon, and gained worldwide popularity with his participation in the 1972 Munich Olympics. Losing a race there, he became an activist, championing rights for sports figures. And though his life was tragically cut short, at age 24, in a car accident in 1975, Steve Prefontaine not only became a sports legend, but he also changed the sport of distance running forever. A Hollywood Pictures film. Directed by Steve James. Limited release on January 24, 1997. Stars Jared Leto (Steve Prefontaine), R. Lee Ermey (Coach Bill Bowerman), Ed O'Neill (Bill Dellinger), Breckin Meyer (Pat Tyson), Lindsay Crouse (Elfriede Prefontaine), Amy Locane (Nancy Alleman). 106 min. Some of the members of the production company had worked on an award-winning Steve Prefontaine documentary, *Fire on the Track*, which aired on CBS in 1995. For the feature film, the producers decided to photograph it in Super 16mm film stock, designed to be enlarged to 35mm for theatrical exhibition, in order to give it a documentary feel, and to employ intercut interviews. The locale selected for the filming was Seattle and its environs. Released on video in 1997.

Prejudice: Hatred or Ignorance (film) Educational film; using sequences from *Light in the Forest*. In the Questions!/Answers? series, released in 1976. A young man tries to overcome prejudice—is it hatred, misunderstanding, or ignorance?

Pre-Opening Report from Disneyland, A Alternate title of *A Further Report on Disneyland*.

Prescot Press (television) Serialized sitcom on the *MMC* show, beginning September 19, 1992, running for 14 episodes; humorous happenings on the school newspaper. Stars Terra McNair (Katie), Keri Russell (Heather), Jennifer McGill (Tracy), Tony Lucca (Tommy), Dale Godboldo (Brian), Marc Worden (Arthur), Lindsey Alley (Kelly), Kevin Osgood (Dennis).

Present for Donald, A (television) Television show; aired on December 22, 1954. Walt Disney presents a Christmas show, with footage primarily from *The Three Caballeros*.

Presidential Medal of Freedom Presented to Walt Disney by President Lyndon B. Johnson at the White House on September 14, 1964.

Pressler, Paul He began at Disney in 1987 in the Consumer Products Division, with general responsibilities for merchandise licensing; he was promoted to head of The Disney Stores beginning in 1992. He was named president of the Disneyland Resort on November 7, 1994. In 1998, he was named president of Walt Disney Attractions, and in 2000 he became chairman. He left Disney in September 2002.

Pretty Irish Girl Song from *Darby O'Gill and the Little People*, written by Lawrence Edward Watkin and Oliver Wallace.

Pretty Woman (film) Corporate mogul Edward Lewis finds himself in Los Angeles and needing a female companion for some business get-togethers. When a chance encounter with a prostitute, Vivian, brings them together, Edward offers her the job for a week, promising a $3,000 fee. His friendly takeover of her life introduces Vivian to a fantasy world of power and privilege, and thanks to Edward's extravagance, her natural charm and grace emerge. Edward is soon captivated by his prize Cinderella, and romance comes out of what was a purely business arrangement. Released on March 23, 1990. Directed by Garry Marshall. A Touchstone film. 119 min. Stars Richard Gere (Edward Lewis), Julia Roberts (Vivian Ward), Ralph Bellamy (James Morse), Jason Alexander (Philip Stuckey), Hector Elizondo (hotel manager). Filmed at various locations around Los Angeles. Released on video in 1990.

Prevention and Control of Distortion in Arc Welding (film) Training film made for the Lincoln Electric Co.; delivered on April 12, 1945. Using educational film techniques perfected during World War II, Disney animators show the methods of proper welding.

Preview Center Walt Disney World preview exhibits; open from January 10, 1970 until September 30, 1971. Because of the interest in the project that was under construction in Florida, Disney opened a preview center where guests could learn about the project firsthand. Besides the displays of models and drawings, there was a short filmed presentation, along with a snack bar and merchandise shop. The Preview Center itself had a higher attendance during the short time it was open than many major attractions in Florida.

Price, Harrison "Buzz" A research economist, he was given the task, while working for Stanford Research Institute, of determining the economic feasibility and surveying the ideal location for Walt Disney's Disneyland park. In 1958, Walt Disney encouraged him to form his own company, which became Economics Research Associates (ERA). ERA was involved in many studies leading to the building and expansion of Walt Disney World, and others for CalArts, Mineral King, and Tokyo Disneyland. He was named a Disney Legend in 2003.

Price, Vincent (1911–1993) He voiced Ratigan in *The Great Mouse Detective* and inspired Tim Burton to produce *Vincent*, which he narrated.

Pride & Joy (television) Television series; aired from March 21 to July 11, 1995, on NBC. A young New York couple, Amy and Greg Sherman, with a six-month-old son, experience the humorous side of the anguish, tumult, and guilt that accompanies the love and joy of starting a new family. Stars Julie Warner (Amy Sherman), Craig Bierko (Greg Sherman), Jeremy Piven (Nathan Green), Caroline Rhea (Carol Green), Natasha Pavlovic (Katya).

Priestley, Jason Actor; appeared in *Tombstone* (Billy Breckenridge) and on The Disney Channel's *Mickey Mouse Club* serial as Teen Angel.

Prima, Louis (1910–1978) He voiced King Louie in *The Jungle Book*.

Primeval Whirl Attraction at Chester & Hester's Dino-Rama! in Disney's Animal Kingdom; opened April 18, 2002.

Primeval World Diorama on the Santa Fe and Disneyland Railroad, opening on July 1, 1966. The display used elements from the Ford Magic Skyway at the New York World's Fair. Several varieties of prehistoric creatures are represented by Audio-Animatronics, set in a misty swamp. The brontosaurus snacks on greenery from the swamp while nearby a stegasaurus and a Tyrannosaurus rex ready themselves for battle. The Ford pavilion at the Fair also included cavemen, but the humans did not make it to the Disneyland attraction. Also on the Western River Railroad at Tokyo Disneyland.

Primitive Pluto (film) Pluto cartoon; released on May 19, 1950. Directed by Charles Nichols.

Pluto's Primitive Instinct, in the form of a little wolf, Primo, convinces Pluto to hunt for food like a wild dog. When Pluto is unable to catch anything, he returns to his food, only to find Primo has eaten it.

Primo Pluto's Primitive Instinct, in the form of a little wolf, in *Primitive Pluto* (1950).

Prince Character in *Snow White and the Seven Dwarfs* who did not have a name; voiced by Harry Stockwell.

Prince Ali Song from *Aladdin*; written by Howard Ashman and Alan Menken.

Prince and the Pauper, The (film) Animated featurette; released on November 16, 1990. 25 min. Directed by George Scribner. Mickey Mouse plays the classic  dual roles of the impoverished youth and the prince who discover they look exactly alike. When the prince suggests they change places for a day, the evil captain of the guards, Pete, plots to take over the country after the king's death. But the prince, aided by Donald Duck and Mickey and his pals Goofy and Pluto, manages to save the day. Voices include Wayne Allwine (Mickey/Prince), Bill Farmer (Goofy), Arthur Burghardt (Captain Pete), Tony Anselmo (Donald), Roy Dotrice (narrator). Released with *The Rescuers Down Under*, and included an additional ten minutes of intermission animation, tying the two films together. Released on video in 1991.

Prince and the Pauper, The (television) Three-part television show; aired on March 11, 18, and 25, 1962. Directed by Don Chaffey. The three episodes were titled "The Pauper King," "The Merciful Law of the King," and "Long Live the Rightful King." The classic Mark Twain story of the poor boy who trades places with the prince, filmed on location in England. Stars Guy Williams,

Sean Scully (who plays both title roles), Laurence Naismith, Donald Houston, Niall MacGinnis.

Prince Charming The handsome prince in *Cinderella*; speaking voice by William Phipps and singing voice by Mike Douglas.

Prince Eric Prince who falls for the mermaid in *The Little Mermaid*; voiced by Christopher Daniel Barnes.

Prince John Spineless ruler of England, portrayed as a scrawny lion in *Robin Hood*; voiced by Peter Ustinov.

Prince Phillip Handsome prince in *Sleeping Beauty*; voiced by Bill Shirley.

Princess Aurora Lead character in *Sleeping Beauty*; voiced by Mary Costa. When she was disguised by the fairies, she was known as Briar Rose.

Princess Diaries, The (film) Shy San Francisco teenager, Mia Thermopolis, receives the astonishing news that she is a real-life princess, the heir apparent to the crown of Genovia, a small European principality. Her strict and formidable grandmother, Queen Clarisse Renaldi, arrives to give her "princess lessons," but the two clash because Mia has no intention of leaving her normal life, and a budding romance, to become the ruler of a far-off country. Directed by Garry Marshall. Released on August 3, 2001. Stars Anne Hathaway (Mia Thermopolis), Caroline Goodall (Helen), Hector Elizondo (Joseph), Robert Schwartzman (Michael), Heather Matarazzo (Lilly), Mandy Moore (Lana), Sean O'Bryan (O'Connell), Sandra Oh (Vice Principal Gupta), Eric Von Detten (Josh), Julie Andrews (Queen Clarisse Renaldi). 115 min. Based on the novel by Meg Cabot. Released on video in 2001.

Princess Diaries 2: Royal Engagement (film) Mia is ready to assume her role as princess of Genovia, but no sooner has she moved into the royal palace with her beautiful, wise grandmother, Queen Clarisse, than she learns her days as a princess are numbered—Mia has to take the crown herself. And, according to Genovian law, princesses must be married before being crowned, so Mia faces a parade of suitors who would all like to be her king. Released on August 11, 2004. Directed by Garry Marshall. Stars Anne Hathaway (Mia Thermopolis), Julie Andrews (Queen Clarisse), Hector Elizondo (Joseph), Heather Matarazzo (Lilly), John Rhys-Davies (Viscount Mabrey), Chris Pine (Nicholas Devereaux), Callum Blue (Andrew Jacoby), Kathleen Marshall (Charlotte Kutaway), Tom Poston (Lord Palimore), Asana (Raven). 113 min. According to Garry Marshall, the mythical Genovia "is probably somewhere between Spain and Italy." The film was shot in Southern California; the enormous palace set was built at the Disney Golden Oak Ranch. Released on video in 2004.

Princess of Thieves (television) Two-hour television movie on *The Wonderful World of Disney* on March 11, 2001. Robin Hood's daughter, Gwyn, against her father's wishes, goes to battle against the evil Sheriff of Nottingham in order to bring the crown to Prince Philip, heir of King Richard. Produced by Granada Entertainment U.S.A. Directed by Peter Hewitt. Stars Malcolm McDowell (Sheriff of Nottingham), Stuart Wilson (Robin Hood), Jonathan Hyde (Prince John), Keira Knightley (Gwyn), Stephen Moyer (Prince Philip), Del Synnott (Froderick). Filmed in Romania. Released on video in 2001.

Principal Takes a Holiday (television) Two-hour television movie; aired on *The Wonderful World of Disney* on January 4, 1998. A notorious high school prankster, John Scaduto, has to make it through his senior year without any demerits in order to claim a $10,000 inheritance. So he engineers his first prank of the year and recruits a scruffy, unconventional drifter, Franklin Fitz, to pose as a substitute principal of the conservative private school in order to obtain access to the school's computer records and remove the demerits. Directed by Robert King. Stars Kevin Nealon (Franklin Fitz), Zachery Ty Bryan (John Scaduto), Jessica Steen (Celia Shine), Rashaan H. Nall (Peter Heath), Kurt Fuller (Principal Hockenberry). Point Grey High School in Vancouver, British Columbia, doubled for the film's fictitious Patton High.

Pringle of Scotland Shop in United Kingdom in World Showcase at Epcot; opened October 1, 1982. Scottish woolens and cashmere are the highlight here, and you can purchase something with your family tartan.

Private Pluto (film) Pluto cartoon; released on April 2, 1943. Directed by Clyde Geronimi. Pluto gets mixed up in his drilling by Sergeant Pete and is ordered to guard a pillbox that two pesky chipmunks are using for acorn storage. First appearance of the as-yet-unnamed Chip and Dale.

Professor Barnaby Owl's Photographic Art Studio Facility opened at the exit of Splash Mountain at Disneyland on January 31, 1992. A camera was added in the attraction, so that each log full of guests is photographed as it plummets down the long drop. The photos are then ready for viewing when guests exit.

Professor Owl Zany teacher in *Adventures in Music: Melody* and *Toot, Whistle, Plunk and Boom* (both 1953). Voiced by Bill Thompson.

Professor Porter's Trading Post Shop in Adventureland at Hong Kong Disneyland; opened September 12, 2005.

Program, The (film) Darnell Jefferson has just been inducted into the football program at Eastern State University. With his great skills on the field, and a lovely girl, Autumn Haley, to show him around the college, Darnell intends to enjoy himself. But his severe academic problems, and a heated rivalry with Ray Griffen for the starting tailback position and for Autumn's affection, makes him realize that things will not be so easy. Darnell and his teammates discover the intense pressures, both on and off the field, of being on the football team. Released on September 24, 1993. Directed by David S. Ward. A Touchstone film. 112 min. (Edited from a 115-min. version a month after its release after several people had imitated the dangerous stunt of lying down in the middle of a busy highway that was depicted in the film.) Stars James Caan (Coach Winters), Halle Berry (Autumn), Omar Epps (Darnell Jefferson), Craig Sheffer (Joe Kane), Kristy Swanson (Camille). Duke University in Durham, North Carolina, doubled for the fictional Eastern State University, and locations were also used at the University of South Carolina in Columbia. The crew was allowed exactly 14 minutes to film during halftime at an actual South Carolina/Tennessee game in the University of South Carolina's 78,000-seat William Brice Stadium, and nine plays had to be worked out with precision to fit within the allotted time. Released on video in 1994.

Progress Report, A/Nature's Half Acre (television) Television show; aired on February 9, 1955. Directed by Winston Hibler, Al Teeter. Walt Disney takes his viewers by helicopter to Anaheim and shows them some previews of Dis-

neyland park, including stop-motion photography of construction, a model of Main Street, U.S.A., and a drive by car through the yet-to-be-filled Jungle Cruise riverbed, followed by the True-Life Adventure film *Nature's Half Acre*.

Project, The (film) Educational film to help develop attitudes about the need for involvement and cooperation, from the What Should I Do? series; released in December 1970.

Project Florida (film) Marketing film for Walt Disney World showing the creation of the new theme park, with footage of WED designers at work, actual construction, scale models, the Preview Center, and Walt Disney discussing his hopes for the project from an earlier 1966 film. 16mm release in 1971. Directed by James Algar.

Promised Land, The (television) Television show; episode 4 of *Daniel Boone*.

Property Rights and Pollution (film) Educational film; from The People on Market Street series, produced by Terry Kahn; released in September 1977. The economic concepts of property rights and pollution are discussed, focusing on the theft of a bicycle.

Prospect Studios Built in 1919 as the Vitagraph Studios, the complex, just a few blocks from Walt Disney's uncle's home, is the longest-operating studio in Hollywood, and eventually became a home to ABC. The news broadcasts originated there for many  years, and the soundstages housed soaps such as *General Hospital* and *Port Charles*. The Studios experienced a major renovation in 2002.

Proud Bird from Shanghai, The (television) Television show; aired on December 16, 1973. Directed by Harry Tytle. Chinese pheasants set loose in Oregon in 1881 find it difficult to survive in their new home, where there are different kinds of predators, but eventually they multiply and create a breed of ring-necked pheasants that can be found throughout the country.

Proud Family, The (television) An animated sitcom on Disney Channel that follows the adventures and misadventures of Penny, a 14-year-old African American girl, along with her best friend, the sassy and scheming Dijonay. Premiered on September 21, 2001. Voices include Kyla Pratt (Penny Proud), Tommy Davidson (Oscar Proud), Paula Jai Parker (Trudy Proud), Jo Marie Payton (Suga Mama), Karen Malina White (Dijonay), Orlando Brown (Sticky), Alisa Reyes (LaCienega Boulevardez), Soleil Moon Frye (Zoey).

Provine, Dorothy Actress; appeared in *That Darn Cat!* (Ingrid Randall) and *Never a Dull Moment* (Sally Inwood).

Provost, Jon Actor; appeared in *The Computer Wore Tennis Shoes* (Bradley). He was perhaps best known for appearing as a child in the *Lassie* television series.

Prowlers of the Everglades (film) True-Life Adventure featurette; released on July 23, 1953. Directed by James Algar. Story of the vast and primitive Everglades in Florida, told through the lives of its animal inhabitants, including alligators, raccoons, skunks, otters, and birds. 32 min.

Pryce, Jonathan Actor; appeared in *Something Wicked This Way Comes* (Mr. Dark), *Evita* (Juan Perón), *Confessions of an Ugly Stepsister* (The Master), and the *Pirates of the Caribbean* trilogy (Governor Wetherby Swann).

Pryor, Mowava Actress; adult leader on the *Mickey Mouse Club* on The Disney Channel from 1989 to 1991.

PSP Disney released its first two films, *Pirates of the Caribbean: Curse of the Black Pearl* and *Kill Bill Vol. 1* (from Miramax), on Sony's PSP (PlayStation Portable) video-game format on

April 19, 2005. PSP uses a Universal Media Disc, which is about two inches in diameter.

Pueblo Pluto (film) Pluto cartoon; released on January 14, 1949. Directed by Charles Nichols. Pluto and Ronnie the pup fight and chase each other for possession of a bone until they end up in a cactus bed and Ronnie must lead Pluto out, ending the argument and restoring peace.

Pueblo Trading Post Shop in Frontierland in Disneyland Paris; opened on April 12, 1992.

Puffin Bakery Shop on Main Street at Disneyland from July 18, 1955 to June 3, 1960. It later became Sunkist Citrus House.

Puffin's Roost Shop in Norway in World Showcase at Epcot; opened on May 6, 1988.

Pullman, Bill Actor; appeared in *Ruthless People* (Earl), *Newsies* (Bryan Denton), *While You Were Sleeping* (Jack), and *Mr. Wrong* (Whitman Crawford), and on Disney Channel in *Tiger Cruise* (Cmdr. Gary Dolan).

Pumbaa Warthog in *The Lion King*; voiced by Ernie Sabella.

P.U.N.K.S. (television) A Disney Channel Original Movie; premiering on September 4, 1999. Five 13-year-old underdogs band together in a club whose name is an acronym formed from the initials of their last names. Their mission is to protect others and maintain peace. When they discover that Edward Crow, the evil head of Crow, Inc., plans to test a new invention called the Augmentor on the engineer father of one of the kids, they realize the invention is not perfected and could cause death. They try to overcome their fears in order to steal the device and stop the potentially deadly experiment. Directed by Sean McNamara. Stars Randy Quaid (Pat Utley), Tim Redwine (Drew Utley), Henry Winkler (Edward Crow), Kenneth

Brown IV (Miles Kitchen), Patrick Renna (Lanny Nygren), Brandon Baker (Jonny Pasiotopolis), Jessica Alba (Samantha Swaboda).

Puppet Masters, Robert A. Heinlein's The (film) When a local television station reports that something strange has landed in the small town of Ambrose, Iowa, the government's covert Office of Scientific Intelligence is called upon to investigate. Andrew Nivens, his son Sam, and NASA scientist Mary Sefton are the team who make the frightening discovery: alien creatures have taken over and are rapidly multiplying and spreading beyond the borders of cities and states. Against impossible odds, Nivens, Sam, and Mary must find a way to eliminate the aliens who seem unstoppable—without killing the innocent human hosts. Released on October 21, 1994. Directed by Stuart Orme. A Hollywood Pictures film. Filmed in CinemaScope. 109 min. Stars Donald Sutherland (Andrew Nivens), Eric Thal (Sam Nivens), Julie Warner (Mary Sefton), Yaphet Kotto (Ressler). Based on the novel by Robert A. Heinlein. Filmed primarily in Los Angeles and Fresno, California. Released on video in 1995.

Puppy Love (film) Mickey Mouse cartoon; released on September 2, 1933. Directed by Wilfred Jackson. When Mickey and Pluto mix up their gifts to their sweethearts, Minnie and Fifi, all sorts of romantic complications ensue over Fifi receiving a box of candy and Minnie a bone. Minnie is enraged until she sees the mistake, and there is a happy reunion for both couples.

Purloined Pup, The (film) Pluto cartoon; released on July 19, 1946. Directed by Charles Nichols. Pluto is a rookie policeman who saves a cuddly pup named Ronnie from Butch, a kidnapper. Together the pair send Butch to jail.

Push, Nevada (television) Mild-mannered IRS agent Jim Prufrock travels to a remote desert town in search of missing money, and stumbles upon a place where mystery, danger, and peculiar characters lurk around every corner. Everyone has a secret in Push, Nevada, but no one is talking. One-hour television series, premiered on September 19, 2002, after a preview on September 17, and ended on October 24. Stars Derek Cecil (Jim Prufrock), Scarlett Chorvat (Mary), Liz Vassey (Dawn), Eric Allan Kramer (Sheriff Gaines), Melora Walters (Grace), Raymond J. Barry (Sloman). Executive producers include Matt Damon and Ben Affleck. From Touchstone Television. The show featured a contest in which a viewer could win a million-dollar prize. The final clue was broadcast live on Monday Night Football, and the winner was Mark Nakamoto, of West New York, NJ.

Puss in Boots (film) Laugh-O-gram film made by Walt in Kansas City in 1922. A young man is kicked out of the palace when he tries to see the princess. His cat, in exchange for his buying her a pair of boots, comes up with a plan for him to win a bullfight and thus the princess.

Puss-Cafe (film) Pluto cartoon; released on June 9, 1950. Directed by Charles Nichols. Two cats disturb Pluto's napping by trying to help themselves to the milk on the back step, and to birds and fish in his yard. Pluto continually chases them away, finally chasing them all the way back to their alley, where a huge third cat chases Pluto away.

Put-Put Troubles (film) Donald Duck cartoon; released on July 19, 1940. Directed by Riley Thomson. Pluto tangles with a spring coil on land while Donald has trouble starting the outboard motor on his boat. In the finale, the motor clamps onto Donald's tail and drags Pluto, surfboard fashion.

Pyle, Denver (1920–1997) Actor; appeared in *Escape to Witch Mountain* (Uncle Bene), and on television in *The Boy Who Talked to Badgers*, *Three on the Run*, and *Hog Wild*.

Pyromaniac's Love Story, A (film) After being dumped by his girlfriend, arsonist Garet Lumpke burns down a pastry shop. Garet's wealthy father tries to get the shop's employee, Sergio, to take the blame, but he refuses until the owner himself is accused and he decides to be gallant. But this makes Garet mad, because he wants the blame so he can show his girlfriend he can be passionate about something. The police do not believe the owner, so then his wife steps forward to confess. The resulting clash of confessed arsonists and hopelessly devoted lovers confounds everyone. Directed by Joshua Brand. A Hollywood Pictures film. Released on April 28, 1995. 96 min. Stars William Baldwin (Garet), John Leguizamo (Sergio), Erika Eleniak (Stephanie), Sadie Frost (Haltie), Armin Mueller-Stahl (Mr. Linzer), Joan Plowright (Mrs. Linzer). Though filmed in many locations around Toronto, the filmmakers tried to ensure the neighborhood looked anonymous. Released on video in 1995.

Q

Quack Pack (television) Animated television series; premiered on September 3, 1996, as part of The Disney Afternoon. Donald Duck is a cameraman chasing after compelling stories for a TV entertainment/news show, *What in the World*. Daisy Duck is a field reporter, and they work with an insufferably pompous anchorman, Kent Powers. Operating from their Duckburg home base, the crew is constantly on the move in a mobile video van, visiting far-flung locales. Don also has the responsibility of riding herd on his three rebellious teenage nephews, Huey, Dewey, and Louie. Voices include Tony Anselmo (Donald), Kath Soucie (Daisy), Roger Rose (Kent Powers), Jeanne Elias (Huey), E. G. Daily (Louie), Pam Segall (Dewey). 39 episodes.

Quaid, Dennis Actor; appeared in *D.O.A.* (Dexter Cornell), *The Parent Trap* (Nick Parker), *The Rookie* (Jim Morris), *Cold Creek Manor* (Cooper Tilson), and *The Alamo* (Sam Houston).

Quaid, Randy Actor; appeared in *Last Dance* (Sam Burns), *Frank McKlusky, C.I.* (Madman McKlusky), and on television in *P.U.N.K.S.* (Pat Utley) and *Mail to the Chief* (President Osgood). He provided the voice of Slim in *Home on the Range*.

Quasimodo Lead character in *The Hunchback of Notre Dame*; voiced by Tom Hulce.

Queen Mary When Disney purchased the Wrather Corporation to acquire the Disneyland Hotel in 1988, it also obtained Wrather's lease to operate the *Queen Mary* in Long Beach, along with the adjacent Spruce Goose Dome and small village of shops. For several years, Disney tried to enhance the guest's experience at the monumental ocean liner, offering special entertainment, such as a lengthy and elaborate "Voyage to 1939" celebration, and upgrading the restaurants and shops. The Spruce Goose Dome, where Howard Hughes's gigantic wooden airplane was displayed, also hosted exhibits, and a stage was built for regular shows. But Disney was never able to help the *Queen Mary* turn a profit, so when the DisneySea project in Long Beach fell through, the lease was not renewed. The City of Long Beach took over the lease for the ship, and the "Spruce Goose" was moved to an aviation museum in Oregon.

Queen Moustoria Ruler of the country who Ratigan wants to get out of the way in *The Great Mouse Detective*; voiced by Eve Brenner.

Queen of Hearts Pompous character, known for yelling "off with her head," in *Alice in Wonderland*; voiced by Verna Felton.

Queen of Hearts Banquet Hall Restaurant in Fantasyland at Tokyo Disneyland; opened November 13, 1998.

Queen: The Days of Our Lives (television) Syndicated television special; aired on August 11, 1991. Axl Rose hosts a show about the musical group Queen, with interviews and concert footage. Directed by Rudi Dolezal and Hannes Rossacher.

Questions!/Answers? Series of ten educational films, utilizing segments from earlier Disney films, released in October 1975: *Alcoholism*, *Stepparents*, *Responsibility*, *Love and Duty*, *Optimist/Pessimist*, *Death*, *Prejudice*, *Your Career*, *Being Right*, *Ambition*.

Quints (television) A Disney Channel Original Movie; first airing on August 18, 2000. Jamie Grover, 13, was the center of her parents' world until suddenly her mother gave birth to quintuplets. At first Jamie is thrilled to escape her parents' constant doting, but soon she feels neglected and unappreciated as the quints take up all of her parents' time. Directed by Bill Corcoran. Stars Kimberly J. Brown (Jamie Grover), Daniel Roebuck (Jim Grover), Elizabeth Morehead (Nancy Grover), Shadia Simmons (Zoe), Jake Epstein (Brad), Don Knotts (Governor Healy).

Quiz Show (film) Herb Stempel, a contestant on the popular television quiz show *Twenty-One* in 1958, is persuaded to lose to Columbia University English instructor Charles Van Doren, who becomes the nation's darling as he continues week after week answering difficult questions. A disgruntled Stempel blows the whistle—he reveals that the quiz show is rigged. The contestants are given the answers in advance. Congressional investigator Richard Goodwin likes Van Doren and his Pulitzer Prize–winning father, Mark, but he still doggedly pursues the investigation, and when the deception is exposed, shock waves are sent reverberating across America. Limited release in New York on September 14, 1994; general release on September 16, 1994. Directed by Robert Redford. A Hollywood Pictures film. 133 min. Stars John Turturro (Herb Stempel), Rob Morrow (Dick Goodwin), Ralph Fiennes (Charles Van Doren), David Paymer (Dan Enright), Paul Scofield (Mark Van Doren). Based on the book *Remembering America: A Voice from the Sixties* by Richard N. Goodwin. Filmed on location in New York. Nominated for an Academy Award for Best Picture, as well as for Best Supporting Actor (Paul Scofield), Best Director, and Best Screenplay Adaptation. Released on video in 1995.

R

R'coon Dawg (film) Mickey Mouse cartoon; released on August 10, 1951. Directed by Charles Nichols. Mickey is 'coon hunting with Pluto, tracking the animal that tricks the pair into believing Mickey's raccoon hat is its baby. Mickey and Pluto apologize and leave quietly as the "baby" waves good-bye.

Race for Survival (television) Television show; aired on March 5, 1978. When a game warden crashes in East Africa, his greyhound goes for help, only to find unexpected assistance from an aging lion. Directed by Jack Couffer. Stars Bosco Hogan, Peter Lukoye, Saeed Jaffrey, Dick Thomsett. Narrated by Peter Graves.

Rachel and Marla (film) Educational film that explores physical and emotional abuse in a story of friendship between two girls; released on July 5, 1990. 24 min.

Radio There was a short-lived Disney radio program, the *Mickey Mouse Theater of the Air*, which was broadcast on NBC in 1938. Walt Disney did the voice of Mickey Mouse.

Radio Disney A live 24-hour music-intensive radio network, produced and distributed by ABC Radio Networks, debuted on November 18, 1996. Targeting children under 12 and their families, the network features an educational and entertaining Top 40–style music format from a variety of genres: pop, oldies, sound tracks, and kid songs, as well as contests and short-form features, such as ABC News for Kids and ESPN Sports for Kids.

Rafiki Baboon in *The Lion King*; voiced by Robert Guillaume.

Rafiki's Planet Watch New name for Conservation Station at Disney's Animal Kingdom beginning in October 2000.

Rafts to Tom Sawyer Island Frontierland attraction at Disneyland; opened on June 16, 1956. The dock where the guests board the rafts has moved several times over the years as construction has changed the face of Frontierland. See also Tom Sawyer Island Rafts for the Walt Disney World and Tokyo Disneyland versions.

Rag, a Bone, a Box of Junk, A (television) Television show; aired on October 11, 1964. Directed by Bill Justice. A lesson on stop-motion animation, as used in the titles for *The Parent Trap*, the cartoon *Noah's Ark*, and the Ludwig Von Drake–hosted featurette *A Symposium on Popular Songs*.

Raging Spirits Roller coaster attraction at Tokyo DisneySea; opened on July 21, 2005, in the Lost River Delta area. Guests take a high-speed ride through the ruins of an ancient ceremonial site, passing by vengeful statues and bursts of water and flame before experiencing a 360-degree loop followed by a hair-raising plunge into a steam-filled sinkhole.

Raglan Road Irish Pub and Restaurant Restaurant featuring an Irish-themed menu; opened at Pleasure Island at the Walt Disney World Resort on October 21, 2005.

Rainbow Caverns Mine Train Frontierland attraction at Disneyland, from July 2, 1956 to October 11, 1959. Later became Mine Train Through Nature's Wonderland (1960–77). The caverns held beautiful colored pools and small waterfalls set among stalagmites and stalactites.

Rainbow Mountain Stage Coaches Frontierland attraction at Disneyland, from June 26, 1956 to September 13, 1959. It was formerly Stage Coach (1955–56). The stagecoaches were removed after the horses became spooked by the Disneyland Railroad trains that traveled nearby.

Rainbow Ridge Pack Mules Frontierland attraction at Disneyland, from June 26, 1956 to October 2, 1959. Earlier Mule Pack (1955–56) and later Pack Mules Through Nature's Wonderland (1960–73).

Rainbow Road to Oz Walt had originally planned to make a movie using L. Frank Baum's Oz stories that would be called *Rainbow Road to Oz*. It was even previewed on his television *Fourth Anniversary Show*, with the Mouseketeers playing all the roles. The movie was never made, however, and many years would pass before the Disney Studios would produce *Return to Oz*, finally fulfilling that early dream of Walt Disney's. See also *Return to Oz*.

Rainforest Cafe Environmentally friendly, this 450-seat restaurant and retail emporium opened at the Downtown Disney Marketplace on August 6, 1996. Taking the place of Chef Mickey's, the restaurant features cascading waterfalls, tropical showers, and an erupting volcano. A second Rainforest Cafe opened at Disney's Animal Kingdom in 1998.

Raising Helen (film) A career-minded head of a top Manhattan modeling agency and party girl, Helen Harris finds herself plunged into motherhood when her sister's three children come to live with her, bringing her carefree lifestyle to a screeching halt. She learns that staying up and dancing till 3 A.M. doesn't mix with getting the kids ready for school on time. Along the way, Helen finds support from Dan Parker, the handsome young pastor and principal of the kids' new school. Directed by Garry Marshall. A Touchstone Picture. Released on May 28, 2004. Stars Kate Hudson (Helen Harris), John Corbett (Dan Parker), Joan Cusack (Jenny Portman), Hayden Panettiere (Audrey Davis), Spencer Breslin (Henry Davis), Abigail Breslin (Sarah Davis), Hector Elizondo (Mickey Massey), Helen Mirren (Dominique). 119 min. Filmed at locations in New York and Los Angeles.

Raize, Jason (1975–2004) Actor; portrayed Simba in the original cast of *The Lion King* on Broadway, and provided the voice of Denahi in *Brother Bear*.

Rajah Jasmine's tiger bodyguard in *Aladdin*.

Ralph, Sheryl Lee She voiced Rita in *Oliver & Company*. She also appeared in *The Distinguished Gentleman* (Miss Loretta), *Sister Act 2: Back in the Habit* (Florence Watson), and on Disney Channel in *The Jennie Project* (Dr. Pamela Prentiss).

Rancho del Zocalo Restaurant in Frontierland at Disneyland, built on the site of the former Casa Mexicana; opened February 6, 2001, featuring both Mexican and barbecue offerings. In November 2004 the restaurant switched to an all-Mexican menu.

Randall, Ethan Actor; appeared in *A Far Off Place* (Harry Winslow). He changed his name to Ethan Embry and appeared in *White Squall* (Tracy Lapchick) and *Sweet Home Alabama* (Bobby Ray), and on television in *Celeste in the City* (Kyle).

Randall, Tony (1920–2004) Actor; appeared on television in *Sunday Drive* and *Walt Disney World Celebrity Circus*, and on The Disney Channel in *Save the Dog*.

Ranft, Joe (1960–2005) Story artist, joined Disney in 1980 working on such films as *Oliver & Company*, *Who Framed Roger Rabbit*, *Beauty and the Beast*, and *The Lion King*. In 1992, he joined his schoolmate John Lasseter at Pixar where he made significant contributions to each of their features beginning with *Toy Story*, not only in story development, but also by providing such voices as Heimlich in *a bug's life* and Jacques in *Finding Nemo*. Ranft was considered by many to be one of the best story men in the business.

Range War at Tombstone (television) Television show; Episode 8 of *Texas John Slaughter*.

Ranger Fussy character named J. Audubon Woodlore; in five shorts with Donald Duck and Humphrey, beginning with *Grin and Bear It* (1954).

Ranger of Brownstone, The (television) Television show; aired on March 17, 1968.

Directed by Hamilton S. Luske. A selection of cartoons with Ranger J. Audubon Woodlore and Humphrey the Bear.

Ranger's Guide to Nature, The (television) Television show; aired on November 13, 1966. Directed by Hamilton S. Luske. Walt introduces the Ranger's new "book" about nature, which acts as the theme for a series of cartoons and live-action nature footage.

Ransom (film) Maverick New York tycoon Tom Mullen is used to mediating tough business deals for his high-tech corporation, and he seems to have it made with a position in New York society, a Fifth Avenue penthouse, and a beautiful wife and son. But when his son, Sean, is kidnapped, and an FBI ransom drop goes awry, Tom must mastermind a daring countermeasure to get his son back. With time running out, and his wife horrified by her husband's shocking plans, Tom faces the most difficult negotiation of his life and the possibility that his strategy, of turning the ransom into a bounty on the kidnappers, may have already backfired. A Touchstone picture. Directed by Ron Howard. Released on November 8, 1996. Stars Mel Gibson (Tom), Rene Russo (Kate Mullen), Gary Sinise (Jimmy Shaker), Delroy Lindo (Lonnie Hawkins), Lili Taylor (Maris), Evan Handler (Miles), Liev Schreiber (Clark), Donnie Wahlberg (Cubby), Brawley Nolte (Sean). Brawley Nolte is the son of actor Nick Nolte; Donnie Wahlberg is a former member of the musical group New Kids on the Block. 121 min. Filming took place on soundstages in Queens and other locations around New York City. Released on video in 1997.

Rapids Ahead/Bear Country (television) Television show; aired on October 16, 1960. Directed by William Beaudine. Walt presents a behind-the-scenes look at the filming of *Ten Who Dared* on the Colorado River, along with the True-Life Adventure *Bear Country*.

Rapp, Anthony Actor; appeared in *Adventures in Babysitting* (Daryl), and on television in *Sky High*.

Rapunzel Unbraided (film) CG-animated feature planned for a 2008 release. Directed by Glen Keane.

Rascal (film) The voice of 60-year-old Sterling North recalls his youth in the Wisconsin heartland when he found a raccoon kit, named it Rascal, and took it home. During a summer in central Wisconsin, the boy and raccoon have many adventures; and Rascal even helps a friend—a horse—to win a race against a Stanley Steamer. But, eventually, young Sterling lets Rascal seek his freedom. Released on June 11, 1969. Directed by Norman Tokar. 85 min. Stars Steve Forrest (Willard North), Bill Mumy (Sterling), Pamela Toll (Theo), Elsa Lanchester (Mrs. Satterfield), Henry Jones (Garth), Bettye Ackerman (Miss Whalen), Jonathan Daly (Rev. Thurman), and narrated by Walter Pidgeon. The story was based on the book by Sterling North, and features the song "Summer Sweet," by Bobby Russell. 2002 video release.

Rasulo, Jay Named executive vice president of Disneyland Paris in 1998, president in 1999, and chairman in 2000. He joined Disney in 1986 and worked in corporate alliances and strategic planning be-

fore moving in 1995 to Disney Regional Entertainment, where he was responsible for helping to develop and launch Club Disney. He was promoted to president of Walt Disney Parks and Resorts in 2002.

Rathbone, Basil (1892–1976) Narrator of the Mr. Toad segment of *The Adventures of Ichabod and Mr. Toad.*

Ratigan Evil denizen of the sewers who aspires to rule in *The Great Mouse Detective*; voiced by Vincent Price.

Ratings After the Motion Picture Association of America created its rating system in 1968, Disney, with its long tradition of "family entertainment," attempted to maintain a G rating for all of its releases. In a few cases when earlier films such as *Treasure Island* were reissued, they had to be slightly edited to qualify for the G rating. However, as the motion picture business and tastes of the public changed in the 1970s, Disney released its first PG-rated film, *The Black Hole*, in 1979. *The Black Cauldron*, in 1985, was the first animated feature to receive a PG rating. The first PG-13 film did not occur until 2003 with *Pirates of the Caribbean: The Curse of the Black Pearl*. After the management change that brought Michael Eisner in to head the company, and the move into more adult-themed motion pictures being released under the Touchstone label, the first R-rated film, *Down and Out in Beverly Hills*, came along in 1986. *Adventures in Babysitting*, in 1987, was Touchstone's first PG-13 rating. No Disney film has ever received an NC-17 or X rating. Some earlier films have been rated PG for video release. For ratings of individual films, see Features.

Ratzenberger, John Actor; provided voices in *Toy Story* and *Toy Story 2* (Hamm), *a bug's life* (P.T. Flea), *Monsters, Inc.* (Yeti), *Finding Nemo* (Moonfish), *The Incredibles* (The Underminer), and *Spirited Away* (Assistant Manager), and appeared in *Disneyland's 35th Anniversary Celebration*, *Mickey's 60th Birthday*, *Disney's Magic in the Magic Kingdom*, *That Darn Cat* (remake—Dusty), and *The Pennsylvania Miner's Story* (Tom Foy).

Ravenscroft, Thurl (1914–2005) Bass singer with the Mello Men, whose deep voice was utilized in many Disney films and park projects. His bust in the graveyard scene in the The Haunted Mansion at Disneyland is often mistakenly identified as a bust of Walt Disney. He was named a Disney Legend in 1995.

Raw Toonage (television) Animated television series; aired on CBS from September 19, 1992 to September 11, 1993. A Disney cartoon star is guest host for each show, which includes animated parodies, kid-oriented music videos, and original cartoon shorts of *Bonkers* and *Marsupilami*. Voices include *Bonkers*—Jeff Bennett (Jitters), Rodger Bumpass (Grumbles), Nancy Cartwright (Fawn Deer), Jim Cummings (Bonkers); *Marsupilami*—Jim Cummings (Norman, Maurice), Steve Mackall (Marsupilami). 12 episodes.

Rea, Stephen Actor; appeared in *Angie* (Noel).

Reaching Out: A Story About Main-streaming (film) Educational film produced by Dave Bell; released in September 1981. Multi-handicapped, Mary faces much curiosity and uneasiness as she enters a regular classroom, but her determination wins the support and friend-ship of her classmates.

Reading Magic with Figment and Peter Pan (film) Educational film in the Epcot Educa-tional Media Collection; released in August 1989. 16 min. Figment and Wendy show Peter Pan the value and fun of learning to read.

Ready, Lynn Mouseketeer in the 1950s televi-sion show.

Ready to Run (television) A Disney Channel Original Movie; first airing on July 14, 2000. Fourteen-year-old Corrie Ortiz discovers she has the ability to talk to horses, and Thunderjam, her thoroughbred racehorse, becomes her best buddy. With a dream of standing proudly in the winner's circle, she and Thunderjam team up. Directed by Duwayne Dunham. Stars Krissy Perez (Corrie), Nestor Serrano (Machado), Theresa Saldana (Sonja), Lillian Hurst (Lourdes), Cristian Guerrero (Gabby).

Reagan, Ronald Long before he became pres-ident of the United States, Reagan, a friend of Walt Disney, served as one of the emcees for the television show on the opening day of Disney-land, July 17, 1955. As president, he attended a second Inaugural Celebration at America Gar-dens at Epcot on May 27, 1985. This was due to extremely cold weather having canceled many of the originally planned events in Washington, D.C., in January. In 1990, he returned to Disneyland,

with his co-emcees Art Linkletter and Bob Cum-mings, for its 35th anniversary.

Reason and Emotion (film) Special cartoon; released on August 27, 1943. Directed by Bill Roberts. A morale-building wartime film, pre-senting an explanation and demonstration of how reason combats emotion within our minds. Illus-trations show how the two could work together in winning the war against the Axis. Nominated for an Academy Award.

Recess (television) Animated series about a quirky group of fourth graders who make friends, learn how to get along with each other, and discover that cool things happen at recess. It debuted on *One Saturday Morning* on ABC on September 13, 1997. From the team who helped produce the award-winning *Rugrats*, Paul Germain and Joe Anso-labehere. Voices include Andy Lawrence (T.J.), Rickey D'Shon Collins (Vince), Pamela Segall (Spinelli), Jason Davis (Mikey), Ashley John-son (Gretchen), Court-land Mead (Gus), April Winchell (Miss Finster), Dabney Coleman (Principal Prickly), Allyce Beasley (Miss Grotke), Glenne Headley (Miss Salamone). 65 episodes.

Recess: School's Out! (film) T.J. Detweiler, whose friends are all at summer camp, is bored until he uncovers a plot by the school's former principal to do away with summer vacation, by using a laser beam to alter the weather and create permanent winter. T.J. calls in his friends to help, and eventually the faculty joins in to save sum-mer vacation. Released on February 16, 2001. Directed by Chuck Sheetz. Voices include Andy Lawrence (T.J.), Rickey D'Shon Collins (Vince), Pamela Segall (Spinelli), Jason Davis (Mikey), Ashley Johnson (Gretchen), Courtland Mead (Gus), James Woods (Dr. Benedict), Melissa Joan Hart (Becky), Peter MacNicol (Fenwick), Dab-ney Coleman (Principal Prickly), April Winchell

(Miss Finster). 83 min. Based on the animated television show. Released on video in 2001.

Recruit, The (film) James Clayton joins the CIA and is sent to their ultrasecret training facility, known as The Farm. There the recruit comes under the supervision of instructor Walter Burke, who tries to mold him into a seasoned veteran. When Clayton starts to question his role and his cat-and-mouse relationship with his mentor, Burke taps him for a special assignment to root out a mole. Released on January 31, 2003. From Touchstone Pictures and Spyglass Entertainment. Directed by Roger Donaldson. Stars Al Pacino (Walter Burke), Colin Farrell (James Clayton), Bridget Moynahan (Layla), Gabriel Macht (Zack), Mike Realba (Ronnie). 115 min. Filmed in Super 35 widescreen. Released on video in 2003.

Recycle Rex (film) Educational release on February 5, 1993 (California version), 12 min.; February 26, 1993 (generic version), 11 min. An animated program about a group of dinosaur friends who learn about recycling.

Red Cross During World War I, Walt Disney's brothers were in the army and the navy, and he wanted to do his part for his country, too. He was too young, at 16, to get into the military, but a Red Cross unit that would take 17-year-olds seemed ideal. Walt felt he could pass for 17. After a little discreet forgery on his passport application, Walt became a 17-year-old, and he was accepted for the Red Cross on September 16, 1918. After training at Sound Beach, Connecticut, he was sent over to France one week after the Armistice was signed. Landing at Le Havre, Walt took the train to Paris, and was then stationed at St. Cyr, near Versailles. Two weeks later he had his 17th birthday. Walt was first assigned to driving ambulances for Evacuation Hospital no. 5 in Paris, and later to a motor pool. In his spare time, he drew. A local canteen had him make up some posters. An enterprising friend had the idea of searching dumps for discarded German Army helmets, then having Walt paint on camouflage to make them into snipers' helmets. These would then be sold to raw recruits coming in on the troop trains. While Walt enjoyed his time in France, the American troops were quickly being sent home, and by September 1919, there were few American faces to be seen in Paris. Walt put in for a discharge and was sent home late that month.

Red Wagon Inn Restaurant on the hub at Disneyland; opened on July 17, 1955; became Plaza Inn in 1965. The restaurant was sponsored by Swift and named after their logo—a red delivery wagon.

Redcoat Strategy (television) Television show; episode 5 of *The Swamp Fox.*

Redd Rockett's Pizza Port Restaurant; opened on May 22, 1998, in the new Tomorrowland at Disneyland. Located in the former Mission to Mars attraction, the restaurant serves a variety of pasta, pizza, and salads. In front is a 50-foot replica of the original red-and-white Moonliner rocket ship that was an icon at Disneyland from 1955 to 1966.

Reddy, Helen Actress; appeared in *Pete's Dragon* (Nora).

Redford, Robert Actor; he appeared in *Up Close and Personal* (Warren Justice), *The Horse Whisperer* (Tom Booker), and narrated *Sacred Planet.*

Redux Riding Hood (film) In this quirky 1997 short cartoon sequel to the classic fairy tale, the wolf is obsessed with his failure to catch Red Riding Hood. He can't sleep, he is mocked by his co-workers, and he's driving his wife crazy. He ultimately devises an outrageous plan to rectify the situation—including the use of a time machine. Directed by Steve Moore. It was released theatrically only for Academy Award consideration in Encino, California, on August 5, 1997. Voices include Garrison Keillor (narrator), Michael Richards (wolf), Mia Farrow (Doris), Don Rickles (wolf's boss), Lacey Chabert (Red Riding Hood), Adam West (Leonard Fox), Fabio (woodsman), June Foray (grandma), Jim Cummings (Thompkins). Produced by Walt Disney Television Animation. Nominated for an Academy Award.

Reedy Creek Improvement District In 1967 the Florida legislature created this district, having most of the powers of a county, to encompass the Walt Disney World property. The district has its own building code, supervises construction projects, and runs the fire department. An associated company, the Reedy Creek Utilities Company, provides the utilities for Walt Disney World.

Ref, The (film) An inept cat burglar, Gus, sets off a booby-trapped alarm system and in his haste to escape, grabs two obnoxious hostages, Caroline and Lloyd Chasseur, both of whom argue incessantly, playing one-upsmanship to see who can be the most abusive. Gus's hoped-for heist turns into a visit with the family from hell. There is a rebel son, Jesse, along with an abominable, money-pinching matriarch, Rose, and a coterie of contemptuous relatives coming over for a Christmas Eve dinner. Soon Gus finds that his survival necessitates that he become a referee for the domestic disputes. Limited release in Los Angeles and New York on March 9, 1994; general release on March 11, 1994. Directed by Ted Demme. A Touchstone film. 97 min. Stars Denis Leary (Gus), Judy Davis (Caroline), Kevin Spacey (Lloyd), Glynis Johns (Rose), Raymond J. Barry (Huff), Robert J. Steinmiller, Jr. (Jesse). Glynis Johns had made her first film for Disney, *The Sword and the Rose*, four decades earlier. Even though the film was set on Christmas Eve, it was filmed in and around Toronto in July, so the filmmakers had to create over 400 feet of snowbanks, using chicken wire and burlap sprayed with insulation foam. They also used 3,200 pounds of dry, bleached wood pulp for flocking. The snowbanks were then moved from location to location. Released on video in 1994.

Reflections of China (film) Circle-Vision film replacing *Wonders of China* in China at Epcot in May 2003. The film features updated footage of many of the cities and landmarks shown in the original film, as well as additions, including Hong Kong and Macau, which are now part of China. Shanghai, especially, has dramatically changed over the past 20 years, and now has a stunning, ultramodern skyline. Directed by Jeff Blyth. 13 min.

Reflections on Ice: Michelle Kwan Skates to the Music of Disney's Mulan (television) Special; airing on ABC on June 16, 1998, with skaters Michelle Kwan and Michael Weiss spotlighting music from the animated feature. Directed by Steve Binder.

Refreshment Corner See Coca-Cola Refreshment Corner.

Refreshment Outpost Snack bar in the area reserved for a future African pavilion in World Showcase at Epcot; opened on June 11, 1983.

Regular Joe (television) Half-hour comedy series on ABC; premiering on March 28, 2003, and ending on April 18. Recent widower Joe Binder has his hands full as he tries to run a household composed of a teenage son, Grant, and a college freshman daughter, Joanie, who is a single mother. Complicating his life further are his well-meaning but intrusive father, Baxter, and a high-strung employee at his hardware store. Stars Daniel Stern (Joe Binder), John Francis Daley (Grant), Kelly Karbacz (Joanie), Judd Hirsch (Baxter), Brian George (Sitvar). Produced by Touchstone Television.

Reid, Elliott Actor; appeared in *The Absent-Minded Professor* and *Son of Flubber* (Shelby Ashton), *Follow Me, Boys!* (Ralph Hastings), and *Blackbeard's Ghost* (TV commentator).

Reign of Fire (film) In present-day London, 12-year-old Quinn watches as his mother, a construction engineer, inadvertently awakens an enormous fire-breathing beast from its centuries-long slumber. Twenty years later, much of the world has been scarred by the beast and its offspring. As a fire chief, Quinn is responsible for warding off the beasts and keeping a small community alive as they eke out a meager existence. Into their midst comes a hotshot American, Denton Van Zan, who says he has a way to kill the beasts and save mankind. Directed by Rob Bowman. A Touchstone Picture from Spyglass Entertainment. Released on July 12, 2002. Stars Matthew McConaughey (Van Zan), Christian Bale (Quinn), Izabella Scorupco (Alex), Gerard Butler (Creedy), Scott James Moutter (Jared Wilke), David Kennedy (Eddie Stax). 102 min. Filmed in CinemaScope on location in Ireland. Released on video in 2002.

Reinhold, Judge Actor; appeared in *Off Beat* (Joe Gower), *Ruthless People* (Ken Kessler), and *The Santa Clause* and *The Santa Clause 2* (Neal).

Reitherman, Bruce He voiced Christopher Robin in *Winnie the Pooh and the Honey Tree* and Mowgli in *The Jungle Book*; son of Disney animator/director Wolfgang Reitherman. Much later he produced and filmed *Alaska: Dances of the Caribou.*

Reitherman, Robert He provided part of the voice of Arthur in *The Sword in the Stone*; son of Disney animator/director Wolfgang Reitherman.

Reitherman, Wolfgang ("Woolie") (1909–1985) Animator/director; began at Disney in 1933. He was one of the "Nine Old Men." He first tried his hand at directing on *Sleeping Beauty*,  and he was one of the first of the directing animators to be given the directorial reins of an entire animated feature, with *The Sword in the Stone.*

After Walt's passing, he took over the producing and directing of all the animated features until his retirement in 1980. He was honored posthumously with the Disney Legends Award in 1989.

Reluctant Dragon, The (film) Feature in which Robert Benchley visits the Disney Studio in Burbank to sell Walt Disney on the idea of making a film of Kenneth Grahame's book, *The Reluctant Dragon*. After explorations of an art class, dialogue stage, sound-effects stage, multiplane camera department, story and animation departments, he discovers Walt has already finished the cartoon version of his story. In the story department, actor Alan Ladd, portraying a Disney storyman, tells of Baby Weems, a child prodigy whose fame takes him away from his parents until a serious illness makes him a regular baby once more. In the final segment, the audience learns about the poetry-writing dragon who must prove his mettle if he wants to co-exist with a neighboring village. He and Sir Giles stage a mock battle in order to show everyone that the dragon really is fierce.  Released on June 20, 1941. Directed by Alfred Werker. Begins in black and white and then switches to color. For the opening credits, storyman T. Hee prepared clever caricatures of Studio staff. 73 min. Cartoon segments include *Casey, Jr., Old MacDonald Duck,* and *How to Ride a Horse.* The animated *Reluctant Dragon* segment by itself was released on 16mm in October 1975, and on video in 1987. The full feature was released on video in 1998.

Remember . . . Dreams Come True Fireworks show at Disneyland for the 50th anniversary; debuting on May 5, 2005. Sponsor was American Honda Motor Co.

Remember the Titans (film) In Alexandria, Virginia, in 1971, high school football was everything to the city. But when the local school board was forced to integrate an all-black school with an all-white school, the very foundation of football's great tradition was put to the test. Herman Boone, a young African American coach new to the community, was hired as head coach of the T.C. Williams High Titans over Bill Yoast, a white man with several year's seniority, a steadfast following, and a tradition of winning. As the pair learned to work together, they found they had much more than football in common. Although from vastly different backgrounds, these two coaches not only molded a group of angry, unfocused boys into a dynamic, winning team, but helped guide them into becoming responsible young men, and along the way initiated a lifelong friendship. Released on September 29, 2000, after a September 23 world premiere at the Rose Bowl in Pasadena, California. Directed by Boaz Yakin. A Walt Disney Pictures/Jerry Bruckheimer Films production. Stars Denzel Washington (Herman Boone), Will Patton (Bill Yoast), Donald Faison (Petey Jones), Wood Harris (Julius Campbell), Ryan Hurst (Gerry Bertier), Ethan Suplee (Louie Lastik), Hayden Panettiere (Cheryl Yoast), Ryan Gosling (Alan Bosley). 113 min. Filmed in CinemaScope. Released on video in 2001.

Renaday, Pete He did many acting and voice roles for Disney films and park attractions in the 1970s and 1980s while heading the script morgue at the Disney Studio. His real name is Pete Renoudet.

Renaissance Man (film) When a middle-aged advertising executive, Bill Rago, loses his job, he realizes that he is not really qualified to do anything else. Finally, an imperious unemployment-office counselor finds Bill a short-term assignment teaching basic comprehension to a group of borderline washouts at a nearby army post. Hesitantly, Bill accepts the job, but then has difficulty adjusting to the regimentation of life on an army base and in communicating with the recruits. When he accidentally brings a copy of *Hamlet* to class, the students get involved and Bill begins to inspire and motivate them with Shakespeare. He eventually proves to them and to himself that

they can achieve more than they ever dreamed. Released on June 3, 1994. Directed by Penny Marshall. A Touchstone film. 128 min. Stars Danny DeVito (Bill Rago), Gregory Hines (Sgt. Cass), James Remar (Capt. Murdoch), Cliff Robertson (Col. James), Ed Begley, Jr. (Jack Markin). Also in the cast as one of the recruits is Mark Wahlberg in his film debut. Filmed primarily at Fort Jackson, South Carolina, with generous cooperation from military officials. The film received a short test run in Seattle in September 1994, under the title *By the Book*. Released on video in 1995.

Rendez-Vous des Stars Restaurant Buffet-style restaurant, seating 300, at Walt Disney Studios Paris; opened March 16, 2002.

Renfro, Brad Actor; appeared in *Tom and Huck* (Huckleberry Finn).

Rennie, Michael (1909–1971) Actor; appeared in *Third Man on the Mountain* (Capt. John Winter).

Rescue, The (film) When a group of Navy SEAL officers are captured while on a secret mission off North Korea, the U.S. government hesitates to use force to rescue them, despite the threat of their impending execution as spies. So, at the Navy base, the men's children steal a top secret plan and go off to rescue their fathers on their own. Sneaking into North Korea, but spurned by South Korean intelligence operatives because of their ages, the kids manage to break into a high-security prison by themselves and effect the rescue under cover of a barrage of fireworks. Released on August 5, 1988. Directed by Ferdinand Fairfax. A Touchstone film. 97 min. Stars Kevin Dillon (J.J. Merrill), Christina Harnos (Adrian Phillips), Marc Price (Max Rothman), Ned Vaughn (Shawn Howard), Ian Giatti (Bobby Howard), Charles Haid (Cmdr. Howard), Edward Albert (Cmdr. Merrill). Filmed entirely on location in Queenstown (and its nearby Whenuapai Air Force Base) and Auckland, New Zealand, and in Hong Kong and Macau. Released on video in 1988.

Rescue Dog (film)
Pluto cartoon; released
on March 21, 1947.
Directed by Charles
Nichols. Pluto loses his
brandy keg to a baby
seal and gives chase.
But when Pluto falls
through the ice and
must be rescued by the
seal, they become friends.

Rescue Rangers Fire Safety Adventure
(film) Educational release in 16mm in August
1991. 14 min. Rescue Rangers Chip and Dale,
along with their friends, must foil the plans of Fat
Cat as he leaves a trail of fire hazards throughout
the fire station and neighboring bank.

Rescue Rangers Raceway Dressed-up
Fantasyland Autopia at Disneyland for a special
Disney Afternoon promotion from March 15 to
November 10, 1991. Cutouts of the cartoon char-
acters were placed throughout the attraction.

Rescuers, The (film) The Rescue Aid Society,
an international organization of mice, with headquarters in the basement of the United Nations
building, receives a plea for help from a little
orphan girl named Penny. Penny has been kidnapped by an evil woman, Madame Medusa, who
intends to use her to retrieve a fabulous diamond,
the Devil's Eye, from a pirate cave. The case is
taken by lovely Bianca and Rescue Aid Society
custodian Bernard, who becomes her shy assistant. Together, after avoiding two brutish alligators, enlisting the help of the local swamp folk,
and turning Medusa and her henchman Snoops
against themselves, they rescue Penny and the
diamond. Released on June 22, 1977. Directed by
Wolfgang Reitherman, John Lounsbery, Art
Stevens. 76 min. Featuring the voices of Eva Gabor
(Bianca), Bob Newhart (Bernard), Geraldine
Page (Madame Medusa), Jim Jordan (Orville),
John McIntire (Rufus), James Macdonald (Evin-
rude), Michelle Stacy (Penny), Bernard Fox
(Chairmouse), Larry Clemmons (Gramps), George
Lindsey (Deadeye), Dub Taylor (Digger), John

Fiedler (Deacon), and Pat Buttram (Luke), the
animated film was based on two books by
Margery Sharp: *The Rescuers* and *Miss Bianca*.
The film was nominated for an Academy Award
for "Someone's Waiting For You," as Best Song,
written by Sammy Fain, Carol Connors, and Ayn
Robbins. The other songs, by Connors and Robbins, were "The Journey," "Rescue Aid Society,"
and "Tomorrow Is Another Day." The film was
four years in the making, with the combined talents of 250 people, including 40 animators who
produced approximately 330,000 drawings; there
were 14 sequences with 1,039 separate scenes and
750 backgrounds. The film was re-released in theaters in 1983 and 1989. Released on video in 1992
and 1999. *The Rescuers Down Under* was the
sequel, released in 1990.

Rescuers Down Under, The (film) In Aus-
tralia, the young Cody discovers that evil Percival
McLeach has captured the magnificent eagle,
Marahute. He manages to set her free only to
be kidnapped himself, and later to see her re-
captured. A frantic call for help goes out to the
Rescue Aid Society, which sends the intrepid
Bernard and Miss Bianca to help. They are aided
by Wilbur from Albatross Air Lines, and in Aus-
tralia are joined by Jake and frill-necked lizard
Frank, in trying to outwit McLeach and save
Marahute. Released on November 16, 1990.
Directed by Hendel Butoy and Mike Gabriel.
74 min. Features the voice talents of Bob
Newhart (Bernard), Eva Gabor (Bianca), John
Candy (Wilbur), Tristan Rogers (Jake), Adam
Ryen (Cody), Wayne Robson (Frank), George C.
Scott (Percival McLeach), Douglas Seale
(Krebs), Frank Welker (Joanna). The first

Disney animated classic essentially to be a sequel, to the 1977 hit film *The Rescuers*. The production required a team of more than 415 artists and technicians. Five key members of the creative team traveled to the Australian outback to observe for themselves its unique beauty, which they wanted to capture on film. They came home with hundreds of photographs of Ayers Rock, Katherine Gorge, and Kakadu National Park, and countless filled sketchbooks. Since Jim Jordan, who had voiced the albatross Orville in the original *The Rescuers*, had passed away, it was Roy E. Disney who suggested the character of Wilbur, Orville's brother, as a replacement. The names, of course, were a play on the Wright Brothers. While the animation itself would be done by hand as it always has been, for the first time computer technology took the place of the Xerox process and the hand painting of cels (and it also enabled the inclusion of several spectacular visuals). The marketing effort for the film did not call attention to the fact that cels were not used, so that the film would be reviewed on its own merits and not in comparison to earlier Disney films. Released on video in 1991.

Residential Street Area opened at Disney-MGM Studios on May 1, 1989. Part of the Backstage tour, it featured the *Golden Girls* house, among others.

Responsibility: What Are Its Limits? (film) Educational film; using sequences from *Those Calloways*. In the Questions!/Answers? series; released in October 1975. The film helps present the personal quality of responsibility.

Responsible Persons (film) Educational film in which Pooh and friends demonstrate responsibility and promote interpersonal skills, in the Think It Through With Winnie the Pooh series, released in September 1989. 15 min.

Restaurant Akershus Located in Norway in World Showcase at Epcot; opened on May 6, 1988. Differing from the other restaurants at World Showcase, Akershus features a koldtbord, or buffet, with both hot and cold dishes. Pickled

herring, meatballs, cold cuts, and salads are featured. The building is patterned after a medieval fortress in Oslo.

Restaurant el Marrakesh Restaurant in Morocco in World Showcase at Epcot; opened on September 16, 1984. Moroccan cuisine, with its couscous, lamb and chicken dishes, and bastila,

is quite different from what most Americans eat, so here it is possible to really try something exotic. Guests can also watch the belly dancers who entertain the diners.

Restaurant Hokusai Located in World Bazaar at Tokyo Disneyland; opened in July 1984. Tokyo Disneyland had opened without a restaurant serving Japanese cuisine, but there turned out to be a demand by many of the Japanese visitors, especially elderly ones, so this restaurant was added a little over a year later.

Restaurant Sakura Restaurant in the American Waterfront area of Tokyo DisneySea; opened on September 4, 2001, with guests finding the atmosphere of a turn-of-the-century wharfside fish market. There is traditional Japanese cuisine along with new dishes that combine tastes of Japan with flavors from around the world.

Restaurantosaurus Fast-food restaurant, sponsored by McDonald's, in DinoLand U.S.A., at Disney's Animal Kingdom; opened April 22, 1998.

Restless Sea, The (television) The story of the sea, in live action and animation, prepared for the Bell System Science Series on television. It depicts the beginnings of the sea and primal life, the sea's chemical composition, continental drift, and the effect of gravitational pull on tides and currents. Aired on January 24, 1964. A revised version was released as an educational film in September 1979 and aired on The Disney Channel in 1983.

Retlaw Enterprises The family corporation of the Walt Disney family, with the name being *Walter* spelled backward. Retlaw took over the family interests when Walt Disney sold his original WED Enterprises holdings to Walt Disney Productions in 1965.

Return from Witch Mountain (film) Sequel to *Escape to Witch Mountain*, in which the two extraterrestrial youngsters, Tony and Tia, return to Earth for a vacation in Los Angeles. Tony is kidnapped by an evil scientist, Dr. Victor Gannon, who discovers Tony's amazing psychic powers and wishes to control him with his mind-control device. As Tia searches for her brother, with the aid of a group of kids named the Earthquake Gang, Dr. Gannon's greedy partner, Letha, uses Tony to steal gold bars from a museum. Using telepathy, Tia finds Gannon's subterranean lab and is also kidnapped. Gannon's master plan is, with Tony's help, to seize a plutonium processing plant, and he vows to destroy it unless $5 million is brought to him. Tia manages to thwart the scheme with the help of the Earthquake Gang, but not before there's a fantastic contest of psychic strength with the brain-controlled Tony. Once Gannon's mind-control device is destroyed, the villains are vanquished, and Tony and Tia are free to return to Witch Mountain. Released on March 10, 1978. Directed by John Hough. 94 min. Stars

Bette Davis (in her Disney film debut and 83rd picture, as Letha), Christopher Lee (Victor), Ike Eisenmann (Tony), Kim Richards (Tia), Jack Soo (Yokomoto), Anthony James (Sickle), Dick Bakalyan (Eddie), Christian Juttner (Dazzler), Brad Savage (Muscles), Poindexter (Crusher), Jeffrey Jacquet (Rocky). The film was based on the characters created by Alexander Key. On location filming was done in downtown Los Angeles; in the Hollywood Hills, at "Wolf House," built in the 1920s (used as Dr. Gannon's mansion); in a dilapidated Victorian mansion near Union Station that was built in 1887 (used as the Earthquake Gang's hideout); and in the Museum of Natural History in Exposition Park, where the gold heist took place. Finally, a rocket-missile testing facility in the San Fernando Valley and a steam-generating plant in Wilmington were combined to create the nuclear processing plant. Released on video in 1986.

Return of Jafar, The (film) Video release on May 20, 1994. Directed by Toby Shelton, Tad Stones, Alan Zaslove. A made-for-video sequel to *Aladdin*, which picks up where the feature left off—with the evil Jafar trapped inside a magic lamp. A clumsy thief, Abis Mal, inadvertently unleashes the now ultrapowerful "genie Jafar," who proceeds to plot his revenge against Aladdin. It is up to Aladdin and his friends to foil Jafar and save their home. Scott Weinger, Brad Kane, Linda Larkin, Gilbert Gottfried, and Jonathan Freeman reprise their voice roles from the feature, with Val Bettin (Sultan), Liz Calloway (Jasmine singing), and Dan Castellaneta (Genie) added to their ranks. It became one of the top-selling videos of all time within weeks of its release.

Return of the Big Cat (television) Two-part television show; aired on October 6 and 13, 1974. Directed by Tom Leetch. A boy, Leroy McClaren, trains a wild dog to hunt the cougar that has been threatening his family. Stars Christian Juttner, Jeremy Slate, Patricia Crowley, David Wayne, Kim Richards, Ted Gehring, Jeff East.

Return of the Shaggy Dog, The (television) Two-hour television movie; aired on November 1, 1987. Directed by Stuart Gillard. The magic ring's spell still turns Wilby into a dog, much to his consternation, and he has to battle a pair of wicked servants who want to use the ring's power. Stars Gary Kroeger, Todd Waring, Michelle Little, Cindy Morgan, Jane Carr, Gavin Reed.

Return of True Son (television) Television show; part 1 of the television airing of *The Light in the Forest.*

Return to Never Land (film) During World War II, Wendy has grown up and had children of her own. Her daughter, Jane, is kidnapped by Captain Hook and taken to Never Land. He thought she was Wendy, and hoped to use her as bait to catch Peter Pan. Peter rescues Jane, and they, along with Tinker Bell and the Lost Boys, defeat the old pirate. Jane eventually realizes that with faith, trust, and pixie dust, anything is possible. Released on February 15, 2002. Directed by Robin Budd; co-director Donovan Cook. Voices include Harriet Kate Owen (Jane), Blayne Weaver (Peter Pan), Corey Burton (Captain Hook), Jeff Bennett (Smee), Kath Soucie (Wendy), Roger Rees (Edward), Spencer Breslin (Cubby). 72 min. Produced by Walt Disney Television Animation. Released on video in 2002.

Return to Oz (film) Dorothy Gale, thought to have psychological problems because of her tales of Oz, is sent to an institution and is about to receive shock treatment when a lightning storm enables her to escape down a raging river. She awakens the next day in Oz. But her happiness in returning to Oz soon dissolves into horror as she finds the magical land in ruins, and the Emerald City a wasteland. The kingdom is now ruled by the Nome King and the wicked Princess Mombi, who captures Dorothy. But she escapes with the aid of new friends: Tik-Tok; Billina, a talking hen; Jack Pumpkinhead; and the Gump. They travel to the Nome King's mountain in the Deadly Desert to find the Scarecrow, and must play a nightmarish game with the evil monarch to save their friend. Dorothy manages to emerge victori-

ous, save her friends, and rescue the mystical princess Ozma, thereby restoring Oz to its former glory. Released on June 21, 1985. Directed by Walter Murch. 109 min. Stars Nicol Williamson (Dr. Worley/Nome King), Fairuza Balk (Dorothy), Jean Marsh (Nurse Wilson/Princess Mombi), Piper Laurie (Aunt Em), Matt Clark (Uncle Henry), Emma Ridley (Ozma), Michael Sundin (Tik-Tok puppeteer), Peter Elliot (Wheeler), Pons Maar (Lead Wheeler), Justin Case (Scarecrow), John Alexander (Cowardly Lion), Deep Roy (Tin Man), and puppet performers Brian Henson and Mac Wilson. The production marked the culmination of three years of preparatory work and research in the United States and Britain. New systems of remote control, stop-motion photography, and a pioneering clay animation process created a wonderland that blended the realistic with the surreal. Sixteen weeks of shooting included interior work on five Elstree stages and filming on the studio lot. There was an additional location on Salisbury Plain, the site of Stonehenge. The production was the realization of Walt Disney's personal interest in the Oz stories by L. Frank Baum. On November 16, 1954, Disney purchased the rights to 11 of Baum's books from the author's son, Robert S. Baum. Originally the Oz stories were considered as the basis for a two-part television show in the *Disneyland* series and in April 1957 the Studio hired Dorothy Cooper to write a preliminary outline of the story. Her original storyline was called *Dorothy Returns to Oz.* The title changed in August to *The Rainbow Road to Oz,* and it was largely based on *The Patchwork Girl of Oz.* Disney realized that his Oz film had become too ambitious a project for television. He announced in November of that same year that a multimillion-dollar live-action musical feature was underway. Bill Walsh was named as producer and Sid Miller as director. Miller wrote songs and musical numbers with Tom Adair and Buddy Baker. To arouse public interest in the project, Disney featured a short *Rainbow Road to Oz* segment on one of his television shows (*The Fourth Anniversary Show* of *Disneyland* on September 11, 1957), which featured two production numbers on three sets, including 120 feet of Yellow Brick Road. Fearing another studio might rush out an

Oz film, Disney bought a 12th title from Lippert Pictures, paying almost as much for it as he had for the ones he already owned. By February 1958, however, the project had died because of Disney's frustrations with the script and designs, and perhaps fear of competing with the 1939 MGM musical, which was gaining renewed popularity via television exposure at that time. Unfortunately, the Disney film was not a box office success, though it was nominated for an Academy Award for Best Visual Effects by Will Vinton, Ian Wingrove, Zoran Perisic, and Michael Lloyd. Released on video in 1985.

Return to Sender (film) Educational release in 16mm in March 1991. 13 min. A young girl learns about the problems that result when many people litter.

Return to Snowy River (film) Jim Craig, the "Man from Snowy River," returns to his homeland with a herd of wild horses, to claim the woman he loves and set up his stake as a horse breeder. Jessica's father still opposes the match, as does her would-be suitor, Alistair Patton. Jessica defies her father and goes with Jim, but Patton, bitter at his loss, steals Jim's herd. When Jim follows, Patton and his gang shoot his horse, leaving it to die in the wilderness. A mysterious black stallion comes to Jim's aid, along with Jessica and her father and his men, and together they rescue the herd. Jessica is reunited with her father and her lover, and they begin their new life in Snowy River. Released on April 15, 1988. Directed by Geoff Burrowes. A sequel to the non-Disney *The Man from Snowy River*. 99 min. Stars Tom Burlinson (Jim), Sigrid Thornton (Jessica), Brian Dennehy (Harrison), Nicholas Eadie (Alistair Patton), Bryan Marshall (Hawker), Mark Hembrow (Seb). Filmed on location in Australia. Released on video in 1988 and 1992.

Return to Treasure Island (film) Ten-hour mini-series on The Disney Channel, premiering on April 5, 1986. Directed by Piers Haggard. The one-legged pirate, Long John Silver, has plans for retrieving the remaining treasure he and his young shipmate, Jim Hawkins, left on Treasure Island ten years before. They join forces and embark on a voyage filled with danger, romance, excitement, and suspense. Stars Brian Blessed (Long John Silver), Christopher Guard (Jim Hawkins), Kenneth Colley (Ben Gunn), Morgan Sheppard (Boakes). Filmed on location in Spain, Jamaica, and the United Kingdom.

Reubens, Paul Actor; provided the voice of Rex in Star Tours at the Disney parks, appeared in *Midnight Madness* (pinball proprietor), and provided voices in *The Nightmare Before Christmas* (Lock), *Beauty and the Beast: The Enchanted Christmas* (Fife), and *Teacher's Pet* (Dennis).

Reunion, The (film) Educational film on career awareness produced by Glenn Johnson Prods.; released in September 1976. Shows sixth graders and their career choices ten years later.

Reyes, Ernie, Jr. Actor; appeared on television in *The Last Electric Knight*, the series *Sidekicks*, and *Secret Bodyguard* (Ernie) on *The Mickey Mouse Club* on The Disney Channel.

Reynolds, Debbie Actress; starred in *Halloweentown*, *Halloweentown II: Kalabar's Revenge*, and *Halloweentown High* (Aggie Cromwell) on Disney Channel. She also guested as Truby on television in *The Golden Girls*.

Rhys-Davies, John Actor; appeared in *The Princess Diaries 2* (Viscount Mabrey), on The Disney Channel in *Great Expectations* (Joe Gargery), and as Sallah in the pre-show film for the Indiana Jones Adventure at Disneyland.

Ribbons & Bows Hat Shop Shop on Main Street in Disneyland Paris; opened on April 12, 1992.

Rice, Joan (1930–1997) Actress; appeared in *The Story of Robin Hood* (Maid Marian).

Rice, Tim Lyricist; joined Disney to work on the lyrics for *Aladdin* after the death of Howard Ashman. Wrote songs for *Beauty and the Beast*, *Evita*, and *The Lion King*, as well as for the stage shows

The Lion King, Aida, and *King David.* He received Oscars for "You Must Love Me," "A Whole New World," and "Can You Feel the Love Tonight?" He was named a Disney Legend in 2002.

Rich, Adam Actor; appeared in *The Devil and Max Devlin* (Toby Hart), and on television in *Gun Shy.*

Rich Man's Wife, The (film) Josie, who is married to a successful television producer, Tony, has been unhappy in her marriage. First she has an affair with a restaurant owner, Jake Golden, and later offhandedly remarks to a sympathetic stranger that she wishes she were "free" of her estranged husband. When her husband is murdered, Josie is the primary suspect and soon the victim of blackmail, with no one to turn to. A Hollywood Pictures presentation in association with Caravan Pictures. Released on September 13, 1996. Directed by Amy Holden Jones. Stars Halle Berry (Josie Potenza), Clive Owen (Jake Golden), Peter Greene (Cole Wilson), Christopher McDonald (Tony Potenza). 95 min. For Tony's house, the filmmakers found a modern Spanish mansion in Malibu, California. A mountain cabin was located after a long search at a Seattle Council Boy Scout Camp in the Cascade Mountains of Washington. Released on video in 1997.

Richard F. Irvine Riverboat Liberty Square attraction in Magic Kingdom Park at Walt Disney World; opening May 20, 1973. Dick Irvine was one of the early Disney designers and one of the first executives of WED Enterprises. The boat is an authentic steamboat, in which the steam helps turn the huge paddle wheel. The riverboat was renamed the *Liberty Belle* after a rehab in 1996.

Richards, Beah (1926–2000) Actress; appeared in *The Biscuit Eater* (Charity Tomlin) and *Beloved* (Baby Suggs).

Richards, Evan Actor; appeared in *Down and Out in Beverly Hills* (Max Whiteman) and in the same role in the television series of the same name, also appeared in *Match Point* on the *Mickey Mouse Club* on The Disney Channel.

Richards, Kim Child actress; appeared in *Escape to Witch Mountain* and *Return from Witch Mountain* (Tia) and *No Deposit, No Return* (Tracy), and on television in *Hog Wild, Return of the Big Cat, The Whiz Kid and the Carnival Caper, The Whiz Kid and the Mystery at Riverton,* and *The Mystery of Rustler's Cave.*

Richardson, Lloyd (1915–2002) Film editor from 1937 to 1980, with some of his best work on the True-Life Adventures. He was named a Disney Legend in 1998.

Richardson, Patricia Actress; appeared on television in *Home Improvement* and in *Parent Trap III.*

Richest Cat in the World, The (film) Two-hour television movie; aired on March 9, 1986. Directed by Greg Beeman. A wealthy man leaves his fortune to his cat, but his relatives plot the cat's demise because they are next in line. It turns out the cat can talk, and he befriends the son of one of the servants. Stars Brandon Call, Kellie Martin, Ramon Bieri, Steven Kampmann, Caroline McWilliams.

Rick, You're In: A Story About Mainstreaming (film) Educational film produced by Dave Bell; released in September 1980. Confined to a wheelchair, a handicapped student enters a regular high school, and in trying to be accepted has both triumphs and frustrations.

Rickety Gin (film) Oswald the Lucky Rabbit cartoon; released on December 26, 1927.

Riddle of Robin Hood, The (film) Promotional film for *The Story of Robin Hood,* featuring Walt Disney and production personnel; released in 1952. 15 min.

Ride a Northbound Horse (television) Two-part television show; aired on March 16 and 23, 1969. Directed by Robert Totten. An orphan boy, Cav Rand, saves to buy a horse, but others plot to get it. Stars Carroll O'Connor, Michael Shea, Ben Johnson, Dub Taylor, Andy Devine, Harry Carey,

Jr., Jack Elam, Edith Atwater. Carroll O'Connor later went on to fame in the role of Archie Bunker on television's *All in the Family*.

Ride a Wild Pony (film) In Australia, a wild 13-year-old boy, Scott Pirie, who is poor, and a haughty, crippled teenage girl named Josie Ellison, who is rich, find themselves at odds over the ownership of a beloved pony. The boy calls the Welsh pony Taff and uses it to get to school, while Josie loves the pony as well for its wild spirit and names it Bo. Since she is a victim of polio, Bo allows her to get around in a pony cart. The children's fight for the animal leads to the courtroom where it is decided that it is up to the pony to decide who its owner should be. The pony hesitantly picks Scotty, but also comforts Josie. The Ellisons bring feed for Taff to the Pirie ranch, and Josie invites the boy and horse to visit her often in the future. They become friends, and the bond in the relationship is the pony. The first Disney feature filmed in Australia. Initial release in Los Angeles on December 25, 1975; general release on March 26, 1976. Directed by Don Chaffey. 91 min. Stars Michael Craig (James), John Meillon (Charles Quayle), Robert Bettles (Scott), Eva Griffith (Josie), Graham Rouse (Bluey), Peter Gwynne (Sgt. Collins), John Meillon, Jr. (Kit Quayle), Alfred Bell (Angus Pirie), Melissa Jaffer (Mrs. Pirie). The film was based on the novel *A Sporting Proposition* by James Aldridge, and shot on location in Australia in Victoria and New South Wales. The ideal location for the derelict Pirie farm was found in the Horton Valley, but the nearest towns were 60 miles away, so the cast and crew were divided between Barraba and Bingara. For the Ellison ranch, the crew used the historic Belltrees, an expansive 20,000-acre country estate, which was available only after His Royal Highness Prince Charles ended his vacationing there. The small Victorian town of Chiltern was also used as the town of Barambogie, after considerable restoration of the storefronts and pouring tons of earth over the paved roads. An old K-class steam locomotive and coach cars were brought out of mothballs, spruced up, and transported from Melbourne, more than 200 miles away. Most of Chiltern's population signed on as extras. Released on video in 1987.

Ride 'em Plowboy (film) Oswald the Lucky Rabbit cartoon; released on April 16, 1928.

Ridgway, Charlie Publicity director for Walt Disney World beginning two years before its opening. He had earlier started in publicity at Disneyland in 1963. Ridgway was instrumental in arranging for so much free publicity for the opening of Walt Disney World that paid advertising was felt unnecessary. He oversaw all of the major press events for the openings of Walt Disney World parks and hotels over the next two decades, retiring in 1994. He was named a Disney Legend in 1999.

Rigdon, Cicely After joining Disneyland as a ticket seller in 1957, she joined the tour guide department in 1959, being responsible for initiating its growth and development, and later all of guest relations and ticket sales. From 1982 until her retirement in 1994, she headed the Disneyland Ambassador program. She was named a Disney Legend in 2005.

Right of Dissent, The (film) Educational film in the History Alive! series, produced by Turnley Walker; released in 1972. Should a private citizen have the right to criticize the president, as shown in the story of John Adams vs. Matthew Lyon, 1798.

Right of Petition, The (film) Educational film in the History Alive! series, produced by Turnley Walker; released in 1972. John Quincy Adams and Thomas Marshall clash over a gag rule preventing antislavery petitions from being introduced in the House.

Right on Track (television) A Disney Channel Original Movie; first airing on March 21, 2003. When Erica Enders enters the male-dominated world of drag racing at the age of eight, she quickly becomes a force to be reckoned with on the drag strip. Her younger sister, Courtney, follows in her footsteps, helping make Enders a household name in the world of drag racing, though not without challenges from their fierce competitors who would rather not have girl drivers winning in their sport. Directed by Duwayne Dunham. Stars Beverley Mitchell (Erica Enders), Jon Robert Lindstrom (Gregg Enders), Brie Larson (Courtney Enders), Marcus Toji (Randy Jones), Jodi Russell (Janet Lee Enders). 88 min. Based on a true story. The real Erica and Courtney Enders are featured in cameo roles.

Right Spark Plug in the Right Place, The (film) Training film made for the Electric Auto-Lite Company; delivered to them on February 12, 1945. The film stresses the need to keep spark plugs in good order to keep in harmony with the ignition system.

Ring of Endless Light, A (television) A Disney Channel Original Movie; first airing on August 23, 2002. When three kids go to visit their grandfather for the summer, they meet a boy who is studying dolphins and trying to save them from fishermen using illegal methods. Sixteen-year-old Vicky discovers she has a unique ability to communicate with the dolphins, and she confronts her growing feelings for Adam while maintaining her friendship with the previous summer's boyfriend, Zachary. Directed by Greg Beeman. Stars Mischa Barton (Vicky Austin), Ryan Merriman (Adam Eddington), Jared Padelecki (Zachary Gary), James Whitmore (Rev. Eaton), Scarlett Pomers (Suzy Austin), Soren Fulton (Rob Austin). Based on the book by Madeline L'Engle.

Ringmaster Character in *Dumbo*; voiced by Herman Bing.

Ringo, the Refugee Raccoon (television) Television show; aired on March 3, 1974. A raccoon's habitat is destroyed by construction of a new shopping center, and he gets into all sorts of trouble trying to find a new place to live. Finally, he is transported to the forest by the Humane Society. Stars William Hochstrasser, the Foutz family. Directed by Roy Edward Disney.

Ringwald, Molly Actress; appeared in *Betsy's Wedding* (Betsy Hopper).

Rip Girls (television) A Disney Channel Original Movie; first airing on April 22, 2000. Thirteen-year-old Sydney returns to her native Hawaii to claim an inheritance consisting of a faded plantation set on several acres of pristine beachfront property. As the sole heir, she has to decide whether to sell the plantation to land developers or keep it. While at the house, she befriends some local kids and comes to fall in love with the island paradise. Directed by Joyce Chopra. Stars Camilla Belle (Sydney), Dwier Brown (Ben), Stacie Hess (Gia), Brian Christopher Mark (Kona), Jeanne Mori (Malia), Lauren Sinclair (Elizabeth), Keone Young (Bo Kauihau), Kanoa Chung (Kai), Meleana White (Mele).

Ristorante di Canaletto Restaurant overlooking the Palazzo Canals of Mediterranean Harbor at Tokyo DisneySea, featuring Italian cuisine with decor based on the Italian artist Giovanni Antonio Canal, nicknamed "Canaletto." Opened on September 4, 2001.

Rita Sensuous Afghan hound in *Oliver & Company*; voiced by Sheryl Lee Ralph.

Rite of Spring (film) Music by Igor Stravinsky; a segment of *Fantasia*.

Ritter, John (1948–2003) Actor; appeared in *The Barefoot Executive* (Roger), *Scandalous John*, and *Noises Off* (Garry Lejeune), and on television in *Celebrate the Spirit*, *Mickey's 60th Birthday*, *The Disney-MGM Studios Theme Park Grand Opening*, *8 Simple Rules for Dating My Teenage*

Daughter (Paul Hennessy), also guested on *Felicity* as Ben's father.

Rival Romeos (film) Oswald the Lucky Rabbit cartoon; released on March 5, 1928.

River Belle Terrace Frontierland restaurant at Disneyland; opened in 1971 with Oscar Mayer Co. as sponsor. Formerly Aunt Jemima's Pancake House, Aunt Jemima's Kitchen, and Magnolia Tree Terrace. Later sponsored by Hormel and Sunkist. Pancakes have always been the specialty for breakfast here, and the kids can even get one shaped like Mickey Mouse.

River Country Water park; opened at Walt Disney World on June 20, 1976, and closed September 1, 2001. The Disney designers longed for an old-fashioned swimming hole, so they created one next to Fort Wilderness campground. It meant building miniature mountains for the waterslides, since Florida has no mountains to offer. Bay Cove, the swimming hole, was actually part of Bay Lake and held 330,000 gallons of water. The popularity of River Country convinced Disney executives to build Typhoon Lagoon some years later, to be followed by Blizzard Beach.

River Rogue Keelboats Located in Frontierland at Disneyland Paris; opened April 12, 1992.

River View Café Restaurant in Adventureland at Hong Kong Disneyland; opened September 12, 2005. It serves Chinese cuisine, family style.

Riverboats See *Mark Twain, Admiral Joe Fowler, Richard F. Irvine, Molly Brown, Liberty Belle.*

Rivers of America Waterways in Frontierland at Disneyland, Tokyo Disneyland, and Magic Kingdom Park at Walt Disney World. The waterways flow around Tom Sawyer Island. At Disneyland Paris, the waterways are called Rivers of the Far West.

Riveter, The (film) Donald Duck cartoon; released on March 15, 1940. Directed by Dick Lundy. Donald is a riveter who has trouble with the riveting gun, heights, and the foreman, Pete. Pete chases him throughout the construction site, causing the building to collapse. Donald runs away while Pete is trapped in cement, holding a water hose in the pose of a statue.

RKO Distributor of the Disney cartoons from 1937 to 1956 and features from 1937 to 1954. In 1953, as they were losing the Disney license, they released six shorts programs: *Christmas Jollities, New Year's Jamboree, 4th of July Firecrackers, Halloween Hilarities, Fall Varieties,* and *Thanksgiving Day Mirthquakes.* In 1955, they released another—*Music Land.*

Rob Roy, the Highland Rogue (film) Rob Roy, leader of the rebel Highlanders in Scotland, manages to elude the English again and again as he weds his sweetheart Helen Mary, but he inadvertently causes his mother's death when the English try to capture her instead. In revenge, he captures Inversnaid Fort and plans to continue the fight until Helen Mary pleads for an end to the bloodshed. When he surrenders to George I, the king is so impressed he pardons Rob Roy and his clan. Released on February 4, 1954. Directed by Harold French. 83 min. Richard Todd's third Disney movie co-starred Glynis Johns (Helen Mary MacGregor), James Robertson Justice (Duke of Argyll), and Finlay Currie (Hamish MacPherson). It would be Disney's last United Kingdom production until *Kidnapped,* in 1960. The Argyll and Sutherland Highlanders who simulated the English redcoats and the Blues were loaned to Disney for the occasion by the Scottish Command of the British War Office. Released on video in 1985.

Robards, Jason (1922–2000) Actor; appeared in *Something Wicked This Way Comes* (Charles Halloway), *The Good Mother* (Muth), *The Adventures of Huck Finn* (The King), *Crimson Tide* (unbilled cameo as an admiral), *A Thousand Acres* (Larry Cook), *Beloved* (Mr. Bodwin), and *Enemy of the State* (unbilled cameo as Congressman), and on The Disney Channel in *Mark Twain and Me* (Mark Twain) and *Heidi* (grandfather).

Robber Kitten, The (film) Silly Symphony cartoon; released on April 20, 1935. Directed by Dave Hand. An adventurous young male kitten runs away from home to become a robber and joins up with a notorious badman. When he is robbed and nearly frightened out of his wits, he returns home and even submits to a bath.

Robber Stallion, The (television) Television show; episode 7 of *Texas John Slaughter*.

Robert A. Heinlein's The Puppet Masters See *The Puppet Masters*.

Roberts, Dodie She spent 45 years in Disney's Ink and Paint Department, the last decade of which she was supervisor of the paint lab. She retired in 1984, and was named a Disney Legend in 2000.

Roberts, Julia Actress; appeared in *Pretty Woman* (Vivian Ward), *I Love Trouble* (Sabrina Peterson), and *Runaway Bride* (Maggie).

Roberts, Larry He voiced Tramp in *Lady and the Tramp*.

Robertson, Cliff Actor; appeared in *Wild Hearts Can't Be Broken* (Dr. Carver) and *Renaissance Man* (Colonel James).

Robin Hood (film) Story of England's legendary hero of the common people is told by traveling minstrel Allan-a-Dale. The story is enacted by an assortment of cartoon animal characters (Robin Hood and Maid Marian are foxes, Little John is a bear, King Richard and Prince John are lions, etc.). Robin Hood rebels against the villainy of Prince John, and his accomplices, Sir Hiss and the Sheriff of Notting-

ham. Prince John has usurped the throne of King Richard, his brother, who was captured on the Crusades. With Little John, Friar Tuck, and the townspeople of Nottingham, Robin defeats the runty prince and his minions, and Richard is free to return and reclaim his kingdom. Released on November 8, 1973. Directed by Wolfgang Reitherman. 83 min. Features the voices of Phil Harris (Little John), Brian Bedford (Robin Hood), Roger Miller (Allan-a-Dale), Peter Ustinov (Prince John/King Richard), Terry-Thomas (Sir Hiss), Andy Devine (Friar Tuck), Monica Evans (Maid Marian), Pat Buttram (Sheriff of Nottingham), George Lindsey (Trigger), Ken Curtis (Nutsy), Carole Shelley (Lady Kluck). The songs, by Johnny Mercer, George Bruns, Roger Miller, and Floyd Huddleston include "Whistle-Stop," "The Phony King of England," "Love," "Oo-de-lally," and "Not in Nottingham." The song "Love," by George Bruns and Floyd Huddleston, was nominated for an Academy Award. In several sequences, George Bruns sought to capture the flavor of the period by using medieval instruments such as French horns and harpsichords, and occasionally just a mandolin. The Robin Hood legend has long been popular with moviemakers, from the silent version starring Douglas Fairbanks, the Errol Flynn classic of 1938, Disney's own live-action version *The Story of Robin Hood and His Merrie Men* in 1952, Sean Connery and Audrey Hepburn's *Robin and Marian* in 1976, to Kevin Costner's version in 1991. Some 350,000 drawings were made for the production, with over 100,000 painted cels and 800 painted backgrounds. The film was re-released in theaters in 1982. Released on video in 1984 and 1991.

Robinson, Edward G. (1893–1973) Actor; appeared in *Never a Dull Moment* (Smooth).

Robson, Wayne He voiced Frank in *The Rescuers Down Under*. Also appeared in *One Magic Christmas* (Harry Dickens), *In the Nick of Time* (Melvin), *Murder She Purred* (Ben Seifert), and *Cold Creek Manor* (Stan Holland).

Rock, The (film) Brigadier General Francis X. Hummel, a legendary military hero, and his crack team of commandos seize control of Alcatraz, taking a group of tourists hostage, threatening to launch poison gas missiles on San Francisco if their demands of restitution for the families of his men who lost their lives during highly covert military operations are not met. The city's only chance for survival is a young FBI chemical weapons expert, Stanley Goodspeed, and a federal prisoner, John Patrick Mason, who also happens to be the only known convict to have escaped the island prison. With the clock ticking, they embark on a desperate bid to sneak onto the island and detoxify the weapons before disaster strikes. A Hollywood Picture. Directed by Michael Bay. Released on June 7, 1996. Stars Sean Connery (Mason), Nicolas Cage (Goodspeed), Ed Harris (Hummel), Michael Biehn (Anderson), William Forsythe (Paxton). Filmed in Cinema-Scope. 136 min. The production company filmed extensively on almost every area of Alcatraz Island, for both interiors and exteriors. In fact, some areas, such as the laundry and industries building, had been closed to public tours for years because they contained hazardous materials. The moviemakers undertook the expense and effort to clean up the hazardous waste, and in so doing, enabled the National Park Service to expand their public tour into areas that were once restricted. The tunnels of Alcatraz were built in the huge, 30-foot-deep tank under the floor of Stage 30 at Sony Studios; this was the tank, when the studio was the MGM Studios, where Esther Williams did much of her swimming and diving work for the MGM musicals. Five hundred invited guests attended a world premiere of the film on Alcatraz Island on June 3, 1996. Released on video in 1996.

Rock 'n Roll America 1950s to 1990s rock music performed in a nightclub in Disney Village at Disneyland Paris.

Rock 'n' Roll Mom (television) Two-hour television movie, aired on February 7, 1988. Directed by Michael Schultz. A suburban mother, Annie, who loves rock music is discovered while singing at a local club, and is given a new identity as Mystere. When her secret is discovered, Annie has to be persuaded to come back, agreeing only if her children can join her act. Stars Dyan Cannon, Michael Brandon, Telma Hopkins, Nancy Lenehan, Josh Blake, Amy Lynne, Alex Rocco, Heather Locklear.

Rock 'N Roller Coaster Attraction at the Disney-MGM Studios that is the first at the Walt Disney World Resort to feature a high-speed launch and multiple complete inversions. Guests take a twisting, turning journey through a Hollywood night in a stretch limo booming to the driving beat of rock 'n roll music. Dedicated on July 29, 1999, and opened to the public the next day. Another Rock 'N Roller Coaster opened at Walt Disney Studios Park in Paris on March 16, 2002.

Rockefeller, Nelson See South America.

Rocket Jets Tomorrowland attraction at Disneyland; opened on July 2, 1967. Followed Astro-Jets and Tomorrowland Jets. The attraction afforded a great view over the park, since the guests could adjust the height of their jets as they circled the towering rocket. The Rocket Jets closed on January 6, 1997, to be replaced by the similar Astro Orbiter in 1998. See Star Jets for the Walt Disney World (later Astro Orbiter) and Tokyo Disneyland attractions.

Rocket Rods High-speed attraction in Tomorrowland at Disneyland, built on the site of the former PeopleMover; opened on May 22, 1998, and closed September 5, 2000. The five-passenger modernistic vehicles whisked guests at high speeds, the fastest at Disneyland, on nearly a mile of roadway.

Rocket to the Moon Tomorrowland attraction at Disneyland, from July 22, 1955 to September 5, 1966. Sponsored by TWA from 1955 to 1961 and McDonnell Douglas from June 8, 1962 to 1966. Later became Flight to the Moon (1967–1975) and Mission to Mars (1975–1992). Space flight was still years away when Disneyland opened in 1955, so the Rocket to the Moon experience was a big thrill to park guests. They would sit in a pseudo-rocket and live through a simulated trip to observe the far side of the moon. Projections above and below enabled guests to see where they were going and where they had been. It was always impressive to see Disneyland and then the

Earth getting smaller and smaller as the rocket left for the moon. After American astronauts actually set foot on the moon, the Disneyland attraction became outdated, and by 1975 it became a trip to Mars instead. The icon for the attraction was a huge standing rocket, at first labeled TWA and later Douglas. The rocket was destroyed when Tomorrowland was totally remodeled in 1966.

Rocketeer, The (film) In 1938, a young air racing pilot, Cliff Secord, and his partner, Peevy, discover a secret rocket pack that enables a man to fly. They quickly become entangled in international intrigue in their attempts to keep the device away from Nazi spies and other villains, including Hollywood matinee idol Neville Sinclair. With the help of his actress girlfriend, Jenny

Blake, Cliff, dubbed "The Rocketeer" by the press, embarks on a mission that could alter the course of history and make him a true hero. Released on June 21, 1991. Directed by Joe Johnston. 108 min. Stars Bill Campbell (Cliff Secord), Jennifer Connelly (Jenny Blake), Alan Arkin (Peevy), Paul Sorvino (Eddie Valentine), Timothy Dalton (Neville Sinclair). Based on a comic character created by Dave Stevens. The airport scenes were filmed in Santa Maria, California, where an airport was built in an area that could pass for Los Angeles in 1938. The Bulldog Cafe was based on an actual restau-

rant in Los Angeles built in the 1920s. Released on video in 1992.

Rocketeer: Excitement in the Air (television) Syndicated television special; aired on June 19, 1991. Directed by Douglas Burnet. Bill Campbell, star of *The Rocketeer*, hosts a look at the movie.

Rocketeer Gallery Display of props and costumes from the film at Disney-MGM Studios from July to September 1991. Replaced by Studio Showcase.

RocketMan (film) When a member of the first manned mission searching for life on Mars is injured during training, NASA turns to a very unlikely replacement, the designer of the ship's operating system, Fred Z. Randall, who, for a rocket scientist . . . is no rocket scientist. Comic chaos ensues en route to the Red Planet, as Fred butts heads with no-nonsense crew captain William Overbeck, falls hopelessly in love with beautiful, but humorless, Officer Julie Ford, and teams up with Ulysses, a trained chimpanzee. Directed by Stuart Gillard. Released on October 10, 1997. Stars Harland Williams (Fred Z. Randall), Jessica Lundy (Julie Ford), William Sadler (William Overbeck), Jeffrey DeMunn (Paul Wick), Beau Bridges (Bud Nesbitt). Ulysses is played by Raven, a three-year-old female chimpanzee, whose principal trainer was Advid Allsberry. 94 min. Location filming took place in and around Houston, Texas, so the filmmakers could utilize NASA's Johnson Space Center and the Sonny Carter Training Facility for authenticity. For the surface of Mars, the filmmakers moved to Moab, Utah, where they found giant cliffs, red rocks, a lack of vegetation, and the overall scale of what could be a distant planet. Released on video in 1998.

Rodney (television) Half-hour comedy series on ABC; premiered on September 21, 2004. Rodney Hamilton is getting fired from jobs he hates while doing stand-up comedy in dive bars at night. He may not have much money, but he still finds comedy exciting, and hopes to make stand-up his career. Stars Rodney Carrington (Rodney Hamilton), Jennifer Aspen (Trina Hamilton), Amy Pietz (Charlie), Nick Searcy (Barry), Oliver Davis (Jack Hamilton), Matthew Josten (Bo Hamilton). From Touchstone Television.

Roger and Anita Radcliff Humans who owned the Dalmatians in *One Hundred and One Dalmatians*; voiced by Ben Wright and Lisa Davis.

Roger Rabbit Frantic star of *Who Framed Roger Rabbit*, along with the cartoons *Roller Coaster Rabbit*, *Tummy Trouble*, and *Trail Mix-up*; voiced by Charles Fleischer.

Roger Rabbit & the Secrets of Toon Town (television) Television special on CBS on September 13, 1988. 60 min. Directed by Les Mayfield. Behind the scenes of the filming of *Who Framed Roger Rabbit*, hosted by Joanna Cassidy. Actors and crew members are interviewed.

Roger Rabbit's Car Toon Spin Attraction opened in Mickey's Toontown at Disneyland on January 26, 1994. The first new dark ride built at Disneyland in a decade, Car Toon Spin takes guests in Lenny (not Benny) the Cab on a joyride through Roger's milieu, with all sorts of intriguing effects. For the first time in a Disney dark ride, the rider can turn the steering wheel of the cab and change the direction in which the cab is pointing. For example, with a little effort, guests can go through much of the attraction backward if they so desire, and because of this, the designers had to create things to see in all directions.

This attraction did not open until a year after the rest of Mickey's Toontown. Also at Tokyo Disneyland; opened April 15, 1996.

Rogers, Roy (1911–1998) Cowboy actor; appeared in *Melody Time* with the Sons of the Pioneers, singing the hauntingly beautiful "Blue Shadows on the Trail" to introduce the story of Pecos Bill.

Rogers, Tristan He voiced Jake in *The Rescuers Down Under*.

Rogers, Wathel (1919–2000) Artist/sculptor; started at Disney in 1939 in animation, and sculpted on his own time. He animated on the animated feature films between *Pinocchio* and *Sleeping Beauty*, and created props and miniatures for such films as *Darby O'Gill and the Little People* and *The Absent-Minded Professor*, and television shows such as the *Mickey Mouse Club* and *Zorro*. In 1954, Wathel was one of three founding members of the WED model shop, where he assisted in the construction of architectural models for Disneyland. He participated in Project Little Man, leading to Audio-Animatronics, which he programmed for many years for Disneyland, Walt Disney World, the New York World's Fair, and Epcot attractions. He retired in 1987. He was named a Disney Legend in 1995.

Rogers, Wayne Actor; appeared on television in *The Girl Who Spelled Freedom*.

Rogers, William, and Son Company also known as International Silver; produced a number of pieces of Disney silverware, cups, and bowls from 1931 to 1939. A Mickey Mouse spoon, designated Branford Silver Plate on the verso of the handle, is one of the most common items of Disney merchandise from the 1930s. It was sold as a premium by Post Toasties—you sent in 25 cents and a box top and you got a spoon.

Rohde, Joe Imagineer at Walt Disney Imagineering since 1980, working on such projects as Mexico, Norway, *Captain Eo*, and Pleasure Island. He served as executive designer on Disney's Animal Kingdom Park.

Rolie Polie Olie (television) Animated series on Disney Channel; created by William Joyce, debuting on October 4, 1998. The world of Olie, a simple six-year-old boy who  lives in a magical, all-robot, all-round world. Produced by Nelvana Ltd./Metal Hurlant Productions in association with Disney Channel. Cole Caplan provides the voice of Olie.

Roller Coaster Rabbit (film) Roger Rabbit cartoon; released on June 15, 1990. Directed by Rob Minkoff. Roger is drafted into service as Baby Herman's babysitter during a visit to the county fair. When the infant goes off in search of his airborne balloon, Roger has to follow him on a perilous course that takes them through a volley of darts and a shooting gallery into a close encounter with a bull, and ultimately onto the wildest roller coaster ride ever captured on film. Charles Fleischer provides the voice of Roger Rabbit. A Touchstone film.

Romero, Cesar (1907–1994) Actor; appeared in *The Computer Wore Tennis Shoes*, *The Strongest Man in the World*, and *Now You See Him, Now You Don't*, all as A. J. Arno.

Romy and Michele: In the Beginning (television) Television movie; premiering on ABC Family on May 30, 2005. Before they rocked their high school reunion, Romy and Michele took a rocking road trip to Hollywood. It's ten years ago, and all Romy and Michele have is a destination and a dream. Soon they are dipping their toes in the Pacific, but they can't even set foot in Ozone, the coolest club in town. With their future on the line, they are sabotaged by a crazed PR agent and a super-needy supermodel until their California dreaming seems to be coming to a very un-Hollywood ending. Are they destined for drabness or can a little help from some lucky shoes, unlikely friends, and their idol Paula Abdul show them what it really means to be a star? Directed by Robin Schiff. Stars Katherine Heigl (Romy White), Alex Breckinridge (Michele Weinberger), Nat Faxon (Chad), Scott Vickaryous (Taylor), Kelly Brook (Linda), Dania (Elena), Alexandra Billings (Donna), Rhea Seehorn (Ashley Schwartz), Paula Abdul (herself). A prequel to the 1997 film, *Romy and Michele's High School Reunion*. From Touchstone Television.

Romy and Michele's High School Reunion (film) With their ten-year high school reunion fast approaching, best friends and party girls Romy and Michele review their lives since high school and are surprised to find them sorely lacking. They were misfits in high school, so they decide to re-invent themselves, concocting fantasies of wealth and success to impress their former classmates. The scheme unfolds perfectly, until Heather Mooney shows up—she knows their real stories. Directed by David Mirkin. A Touchstone film. Released on April 25, 1997. Stars Mira Sorvino (Romy), Lisa Kudrow (Michele), Alan Cumming (Sandy Frink), Julia Campbell (Christie), Janeane Garofalo (Heather Mooney). 91 min. The characters of Romy and Michele were created nearly a decade earlier in the play *Ladies Room*, by playwright Robin Schiff, who focuses exclusively on the play's two most popular characters in her screenplay for this movie. Lisa Kudrow originated the role of Michele in the play before moving to the film. Released on video in 1997.

Ronnie Saint Bernard puppy, first appearing in *The Purloined Pup* (1946).

Roo Baby kangaroo character in the Winnie the Pooh films.

Rookie, The (film) A shoulder injury ended a pitcher's career in the minor leagues twelve years ago; now he, Jim Morris, is a high school chemistry teacher and baseball coach in Big Lake, Texas. Jim's team makes a deal with him—if they win the district championship, Jim will try out with a major-league organization. The bet proves incentive enough for the team, and they go from worst to first. Jim, forced to live up to his deal, is nearly laughed off the try-out field, until he gets onto the mound and throws successive 98 mph fastballs, enough for a minor-league contract with the Tampa Bay Devil Rays. Directed by John Lee Hancock. Released on March 29, 2002, after a special world premiere at the Loews Astor Plaza in New York attended by a large group of baseball legends, Olympic medalists, and other sports personalities. Stars Dennis Quaid (Jim Morris), Rachel Griffiths (Lorri), Jay Hernandez (Joaquin "Wack" Campos), Beth Grant (Jimmy's mother), Angus T. Jones (Hunter), Brian Cox (Jim, Sr.). Filmed in CinemaScope. 128 min. Filmed on location in and around Austin, Texas, with the town of Thorndale doubling for Big Lake. Based on a true story. Released on video in 2002.

Room for Heroes (film) Educational film describing the exploits of American heroes such as Johnny Appleseed, Davy Crockett, Pecos Bill, and Casey Jones; released in August 1971.

Roommates (film) An irascible but lovable elderly grandfather, Rocky Holeczek, plays an important role in the life of his grandson, Michael. At 107, Rocky is the oldest employed baker in Pittsburgh, and this saga, covering 30 years of his life, shows how he raises Michael from childhood and continues to guide him into manhood as he marries, has children, and embarks on a busy career in medicine. The relationship makes a powerful statement about the value of family, as Rocky is determined to stick around for as long as it takes to teach Michael what he needs to know about living. Released on March 3, 1995. Directed by Peter Yates. A Hollywood Pictures film. Stars Peter Falk (Rocky Holeczek), D.B. Sweeney (Michael), Julianne Moore (Beth), Jan Rubes (Bolek Krupa), Ellen Burstyn (Judith). 109 min. The film's inspiration was the real-life, unconventional relationship between the author, Max Apple, and his grandfather. Filmed in Pittsburgh, encompassing the blue-collar world of Polish Hill and the fashionable community of Sewickley Heights, the

movie's time span covering four decades created many challenges for the production designer, Dan Bishop. Perhaps the most arduous element of the production was the makeup—aging Peter Falk from 75 to 107, with the actor having to put up with sitting under layers of latex for hours at a time. Released on video in 1995.

Rooney, Mickey Actor; appeared in *Pete's Dragon* (Lampie) and provided the voice of the adult Tod in *The Fox and the Hound*. Appeared on television in *Donovan's Kid* and *Little Spies*. On Disney Channel he was in *Phantom of the Megaplex* (Movie Mason), and he did the voice of Sparky in *Lady and the Tramp II: Scamp's Adventure*.

Rooney, Mickey, Jr. He was hired as a Mouseketeer for the 1950s *Mickey Mouse Club*, but was fired shortly afterward.

Rooney, Tim He was hired as a Mouseketeer for the 1950s *Mickey Mouse Club*, but he was fired shortly afterward along with his brother, Mickey.

Roquefort Polite mouse character voiced by Sterling Holloway in *The Aristocats*.

Roscoe and DeSoto Sykes's Doberman henchmen in *Oliver & Company*; voiced by Taurean Blaque and Carl Weintraub.

Rose & Crown Pub & Dining Room Restaurant in United Kingdom in World Showcase at Epcot; opened on October 1, 1982. For those who like fish-and-chips or steak and kidney pie, with trifle for dessert, this is the place to go.

In the pub section, you can order your English ale or stout. The Rose & Crown combines the styles of several kinds of pubs, from the normal street-side ones in the cities and country towns to London's famed Ye Olde Cheshire Cheese.

Ross, Rich He was named president of Disney Channel Worldwide in 2004. He had originally joined Disney Channel in 1996 as senior vice president.

Roth, Joe He came to Disney in 1992 with a contract to produce films under the Caravan Pictures label. Roth was named chairman of the Walt Disney Motion Pictures Group in 1994 on the resignation of Jeffrey Katzenberg. In April 1996 he was named chairman of Walt Disney Studios, adding television and video production responsibilities. He left the company in January 2000.

Royal Banquet Hall Restaurant in Fantasyland in Hong Kong Disneyland; opened September 12, 2005, and featuring a food court with four specialized show kitchens.

Royal Plaza Hotel in Lake Buena Vista at Walt Disney World; opened in January 1973. The Royal Plaza has 17 stories and 396 rooms.

Royal Street Veranda Restaurant in Adventureland at Tokyo Disneyland; opened on April 15, 1983.

Royal Tenenbaums, The (film) Royal Tenenbaum and his wife, Etheline, had three children—Chas, who became a real estate mogul with a deep understanding of international finance; Richie, a champion tennis player; and Margot, a gifted playwright. But the brilliance of the young Tenenbaums is erased over two decades of betrayal, failure, and disaster, mostly attributable to their father. One winter, the family has a sudden, unexpected reunion. Directed by Wes Anderson. A Touchstone Picture. Released on December 14, 2001, in New York and Los Angeles, with general release on December 21. Stars Gene Hackman (Royal Tenenbaum), Angelica Huston (Etheline), Ben Stiller (Chas), Gwyneth Paltrow (Margot), Owen Wilson (Eli Cash), Danny Glover (Henry Sherman), Bill Murray (Raleigh St. Clair), Luke Wilson (Richie Tenenbaum). 110 min. Filmed in CinemaScope on location in New York City. The filmmakers discovered a dilapidated limestone mini-mansion in a historic neighborhood of Harlem called Hamilton Heights to use as the Tenenbaum house. The film received an Academy Award nomination for Best Original Screenplay. Released on video in 2002.

Rub, Christian (1887–1956) Voice of Geppetto in *Pinocchio*.

Ruby Bridges (television) Two-hour television movie; aired on *The Wonderful World of Disney* on January 18, 1998. The poignant story of a six-year-old girl's struggle for equality during the tumultuous American civil rights movement of the 1960s, as one of the first African American students to be integrated into the New Orleans public schools. Stars Chaz Monét (Ruby), Penelope Ann Miller (Barbara Henry), Kevin Pollak (Dr. Robert Coles), Michael Beach (Abon Bridges), Jean Louisa Kelly (Jane Coles), Peter Francis James (Dr. Broyard), Patrika Darbo (Jill), Diana Scarwid (Miss Woodmore), Lela Rochon (Lucielle Bridges). Shot entirely on location in Wilmington, North Carolina. As a first for Disney, President Bill Clinton joined Michael Eisner in introducing the show; the two men were taped in the Cabinet Room at the White House. Released on video in 2000.

Rufus Elderly cat in the orphanage in *The Rescuers*; voiced by John McIntire.

Rugged Bear (film) Donald Duck cartoon; released on October 23, 1953. Directed by Jack Hannah. When hunting season opens, a terrified bear hides in Donald's cabin and endures the torture of being a household bear rug until

the season closes. Nominated for an Academy Award.

Ruggles, Charlie (1886–1970) Actor; appeared in *The Parent Trap* (Charles McKendrick), *Son of Flubber* (Judge Murdock), *The Ugly Dachshund* (Dr. Pruitt), and *Follow Me, Boys!* (John Everett Hughes). He did the voice of Ben Franklin in *Ben and Me*.

Ruggles China and Glass House Shop on Main Street at Disneyland, from July 17, 1955 to March 1964.

Rummell, Peter He came to Disney as president of the Disney Development Company in 1985; he had been an officer with the Arvida Corporation, which Disney had bought. Rummell was later promoted to the head of Disney Design and Development, which encompassed both Walt Disney Imagineering and the Disney Development Company. When Walt Disney Imagineering and Disney Development Company merged in 1996, Rummell was named chairman of the new organization. He left the company in 1997.

Run (film) A carefree summer road trip turns into a living nightmare for a law school student, Charlie Farrow, when he accidentally kills the son of a notorious mobster. Stranded in a small New England town, Charlie becomes the target of both the cold-blooded mob and a corrupt police force, and is on the run. With a single ally, Karen Landers, a pretty casino card dealer, Charlie struggles to stay one step ahead of his pursuers. Released on February 1, 1991. Directed by Geoff Burrowes. A Hollywood Picture. 91 min. Stars Patrick

Dempsey (Charlie Farrow), Kelly Preston (Karen Landers), Ken Pogue (Halloran). Vancouver, British Columbia, doubled for the fictitious city of Sawtucket. Released on video in 1991.

Run, Appaloosa, Run (film) Featurette about Mary, a beautiful Nez Perce Indian girl in Northwest Idaho who raises a motherless Appaloosa colt, Sky Dancer, one of the unique, spotted horses developed by the tribe. The girl and horse are separated, but after a series of adventures they are reunited at a rodeo, which leads to their entry in the dangerous Hell's Mountain Suicide Relay Race. Released on July 29, 1966, on a bill with *Lt. Robin Crusoe, U.S.N.* Directed by Larry Lansburgh. 48 min. Stars Adele Palacios, Wilbur Plaugher, Jerry Gatlin. Released on video in 1986.

Run, Cougar, Run (film) When a professional hunter and two sportsmen use a helicopter to scout for big game in the southwestern wilderness of the United States, Seeta, a tawny, 3-year-old mountain lion, her mate, and their three kits are endangered, and Seeta has to struggle to protect her family from these dangerous intruders. Released on October 18, 1972. Directed by Jerome Courtland. 87 min. Stars Stuart Whitman (Hugh McRae), Lonny Chapman (Harry Walker), Douglas V. Fowley (Joe Bickley), Harry Carey, Jr. (Barney), Alfonso Arau (Etie). The film's song, "Let Her Alone," was written by Terry Gilkyson and sung by Ian & Sylvia. The movie was narrated by Ian Tyson and filmed entirely on location in the Great Southwest, along the Colorado River in Utah and Arizona.

Run, Light Buck, Run (television) Television show; aired on March 13, 1966. A grizzled, backwoods prospector in the wild mesa country north of Arizona's Grand Canyon twice helps a young antelope, and the animal becomes a pet. Eventually he meets another antelope and heads back to the wild. Stars Al Niemela.

Runaway Brain (film) Mickey Mouse cartoon. Dr. Frankenollie, a mad scientist, transplants Mickey's brain into a monster's body and vice

versa. The monster-ized Mickey, known as Julius, becomes obsessed with pursuing Minnie, and Mickey, whose intentions are misun-derstood because he is in the monster's body, tries to save her. Released on August 11, 1995, with *A Kid in King Arthur's Court*. Directed by Chris Bailey. Voices are Wayne Allwine, Russi Taylor, Kelsey Gram-mer, Jim Cummings, Bill Farmer. The name of Dr. Frankenollie was inspired by the famed animators Frank Thomas and Ollie Johnston. The cartoon was nominated for an Academy Award. 8 min.

Runaway Bride (film) Touchstone Pictures and Paramount jointly produced for release on July 30, 1999, this story of Maggie Carpenter, a Maryland woman who has a penchant for leaving grooms at the altar. Ike Graham is a reporter who tries to uncover Maggie's story, with the two fated to end up together. Directed by Garry Marshall. Stars Julia Roberts (Maggie Carpenter), Richard Gere (Ike Graham), Joan Cusack (Peggy), Hector Elizondo (Fisher). 116 min. This film reunited Roberts, Gere, Elizondo, and director Marshall for the first time since their hit, *Pretty Woman*, in 1990. Most of the filming took place in and around Baltimore, Maryland, with the small East-ern shore town of Berlin portraying the fictitious Hale. Released on video by Paramount in 2000.

Runaway on the Rogue River (television) Television show; aired on December 1, 1974. Directed by Larry Lansburgh. A boy, Jeff, comes upon a runaway elephant while fishing. He has adventures taking the elephant to show his father, and the elephant ends up helping to save the father's life. Stars Slim Pickens, Willie Aames, Denis Arndt.

Running Brave (film) Not made by Disney, but distributed by Buena Vista Distribution Co. The true story of Marine Corps Lt. Billy Mills, a rank outsider and half-Sioux Indian who won Amer-ica's first and only top award in the 10,000-meter

race during the Olympic Games in Tokyo in 1964. Directed by D.S. Everett. Released in November 1983. 107 min. Stars Robby Benson (Billy Mills), Pat Hingle, Claudia Cron, Jeff McCracken. Released on video in 1984.

Rush, Barbara Actress; appeared in *Superdad* (Sue McCready).

Rush, Geoffrey Actor; portrayed Captain Bar-bossa in the *Pirates of the Caribbean* trilogy, and provided the voice of Nigel in *Finding Nemo*.

Rushin' River Outfitters Shop in Golden State at Disney's California Adventure; opened on February 8, 2001.

Rushmore (film) A chronicle of a year in the life of 15-year-old student Max Fischer at Rush-more Academy, one of the finest schools in the country. Max loves his prestigious school, is editor of the school paper, and is involved in practically every student organization. Because of all his extracurricular activities, he is also one of the worst students in the school. Threatened with expulsion, he begins a new interest—pursuing a first-grade teacher. When Max's tycoon mentor starts an affair with the same teacher, it triggers a war between Max and his friend. Released for one week on December 11, 1998, in Los Angeles and New York for Academy Award considera-tion, on a limited basis on February 5, 1999, and then nationwide on February 12, 1999. Directed by Wes Anderson. Stars Jason Schwartzman (Max Fischer), Olivia Williams (Miss Cross), Brian Cox (Dr. Guggenheim), Seymour Cassell (Bert Fischer), Mason Gamble (Dirk Calloway), Bill Murray (Mr. Blume). 93 min. Filmed in Cinema-Scope. Doubling for the fictional Rushmore was St. John's School in Houston, Texas, the alma mater of director/co-writer Wes Anderson. The public school scenes at "Grover Cleveland" were actually filmed at Lamar High School, across the street from St. John's. Released on video in 1999.

Russell, Bryan Child actor; appeared in *Babes in Toyland* (boy), *Emil and the Detectives* (Emil), and *The Adventures of Bullwhip Griffin* (Jack Flagg), and on television in *Gallegher* and *Kilroy*.

Russell, Irwin E. He was named to the Disney board of directors in 1987, where he remained until March 6, 2001.

Russell, Keri Actress; appeared on the *Mickey Mouse Club* on The Disney Channel, beginning in 1991. She also had the starring role in *Felicity* on television, and appeared as Mandy in *Honey I Blew Up the Kid*.

Russell, Kurt Actor; appeared in *Follow Me, Boys!* (Whitey), *The One and Only, Genuine, Original Family Band* (Sidney Bower), *The Horse in the Gray Flannel Suit* (Ronnie Gardner), *The Barefoot Executive* (Steven Post), *Charley and the Angel* (Ray Ferris), *Superdad* (Bart), *Captain Ron* (Ron), *Tombstone* (Wyatt Earp), *Miracle* (Herb Brooks), *Sky High* (Steve Stronghold/The Commander), and as Dexter Riley in *The Computer Wore Tennis Shoes, The Strongest Man in the World*, and *Now You See Him, Now You Don't*. On television he appeared in *Disneyland Showtime, Willie and the Yank*, and *The Secret of Boyne Castle*. He voiced the older Copper in *The Fox and the Hound*, and narrated *Dad, Can I Borrow the Car?* Russell was one of the few child stars to make a successful transition to adult film roles. He was named a Disney Legend in 1998.

Rustler Roundup Shootin' Gallery Located in Frontierland at Disneyland Paris; opened April 12, 1992.

Rusty and the Falcon (television) Television show; aired on October 24, 1958. Directed by N. Paul Kenworthy. Jerome Courtland describes falconry and then helps tell the story of a boy who finds an injured falcon and tries to train him. Stars Rudy Lee, Jay W. Lee.

Ruthless People (film) A husband plans to murder his loud, overweight wife, but before he can carry out his plan, she is kidnapped. The inept kidnappers keep lowering their ransom demands when the husband refuses to pay. The wife takes advantage of her confinement to go on a crash reducing program, and she eventually teams with the kidnappers against her husband. Released on June 27, 1986. Directed by Jim Abrahams, David Zucker, Jerry Zucker. A Touchstone film. 94 min. Stars Danny DeVito (Sam Stone), Bette Midler (Barbara Stone), Judge Reinhold (Ken Kessler), Helen Slater (Sandy Kessler). Filmed at various Southern California locations. Released on video in 1987.

Ryan, Meg Actress; appeared in *D.O.A.* (Sydney Fuller) and *When a Man Loves a Woman* (Alice Green), and on television in *Wildside*.

Ryan, Will He voiced Pete and Willie the Giant in *Mickey's Christmas Carol*, the sea horse in *The Little Mermaid*, Rabbit in *Winnie the Pooh and a Day for Eeyore*, as well as many voices for Disney television animation and Disney records.

Ryen, Adam He voiced Cody in *The Rescuers Down Under*.

Ryman, Herb (1910–1989) Art director and designer; Herbert Dickens Ryman came to the Studio in 1954 to help Walt Disney by drawing the original concept for Disneyland so Roy O. Disney could use it to help sell investors. He designed Sleeping Beauty Castle for Disneyland and over the years worked on various Imagineering projects until he retired in 1971, but he continued on after that as a consultant. He was working on Euro Disneyland plans when he died in 1989. Lithographs of a number of his concept paintings have been sold by the Disney Gallery at Disneyland. He was named a Disney Legend posthumously in 1990.

Sabella, Ernie Actor; appeared in *Tough Guys* (hotel clerk), *Roommates* (Stash), *Quiz Show* (car salesman), and voiced the warthog Pumbaa in *The Lion King*.

Sacred Planet (film) An inspiring journey around the world viewing the landscape, the people, and the animals indigenous to the land, showcasing the natural beauty of our planet's diverse regions. Released on April 22, 2004, in large format/IMAX theaters. Filmed in 70mm. Directed by Jon Long. 47 min. Narrated by Robert Redford.

Safari Outpost Adventureland shop at Disneyland; opened March 1, 1986.

Safari Shooting Gallery Adventureland attraction at Disneyland from 1962 to 1982; also known as Big Game Safari Shooting Gallery and Big Game Shooting Gallery. The area later was remodeled with several shops.

Safari Village Island in the midst of Disney's Animal Kingdom, dominated by the majestic Tree of Life, from where bridges provide access to The Oasis, Camp Minnie-Mickey, Africa, Asia, and DinoLand U.S.A. The island also features dining (Pizzafari and Flame Tree Barbecue) and shopping (Beastly Bazaar, Creature Comforts, Disney Outfitters, and Island Mercantile) opportunities.

Safety Patrol (television) Two-hour television movie; aired on *The Wonderful World of Disney* on March 29, 1998. Eleven-year-old Scout Bozell is a safety fanatic, whose lifelong dream is to become a member of his school's Safety Patrol. While clumsy and accident-prone, he still manages to outwit the school bullies—who make up the patrol at Laurelview Middle School—and a couple of evil adults, and become a hero. Directed by Savage Steve Holland. Stars Bug Hall (Scout Bozell), Lainie Kazan (Mrs. Day), Curtis Armstrong (Mr. Miller), Leslie Nielsen (Mr. Penn), Stephanie Faracy (Principal Marlow), Alex McKenna (Hannah), Ed McMahon (Grandpa). Filmed in Los Angeles. Released on video in 1999.

Saga of Andy Burnett (Episode 1), The: Andy's Initiation (television) Television show; aired on October 2, 1957. Directed by Lewis R. Foster. Episode 1 set in 1820, in which Andy, an Easterner, is introduced; his ambition is to become a farmer, but a penniless mountain man convinces him that is not the life for him. His band puts Andy through a series of tests to see if he has what it takes to become a mountain man. Stars Jerome Courtland (Andy Burnett), Jeff York (Joe Crane), Slim Pickens (Old Bill Williams), Andrew Duggan (Joe Kelly), Robert J. Wilke (Ben Tilton), Iron Eyes Cody (Mad Wolf),

Abel Fernández (Kiasax), John War Eagle (Chief Matosuki), Ralph Valencia (Small Eagle).

Saga of Andy Burnett (Episode 2), The: Andy's First Chore (television) Television show; aired on October 9, 1957. Directed by Lewis R. Foster. Andy is educated by the mountain men, who are asked by Senator Tom Benton to deliver an urgent message to Santa Fe. They are tracked by a rough band of men led by Bill Sublette, who Andy helps outwit by turning some unfriendly Indians in their direction.

Saga of Andy Burnett (Episode 3), The: Andy's Love Affair (television) Television show; aired on October 16, 1957. Directed by Lewis R. Foster. On their way to Santa Fe, the mountain men have problems with the Spanish border patrol, and Andy makes the *capitán* jealous by falling in love with his sweetheart. But she is only using Andy for her own purposes; when he discovers that, he and the other mountain men leave the city to return to the wilds of the mountains.

Saga of Andy Burnett (Episode 4), The: The Land of Enemies (television) Television show; aired on February 26, 1958. Directed by Lewis R. Foster. Andy and his friends continue their trip to Taos into Indian territory, where they are attacked. But Andy kills a white buffalo, making him almost a god to the Indians, and he learns sign language in order to communicate with them.

Saga of Andy Burnett (Episode 5), The: White Man's Medicine (television) Television show; aired on March 5, 1958. Directed by Lewis R. Foster. Still captured by Indians, Andy has to use his wiles to save his life and those of his companions.

Saga of Andy Burnett (Episode 6), The: The Big Council (television) Television show; aired on March 12, 1958. Directed by Lewis R. Foster. In this final chapter, Andy and the mountain men are held captive by the Indians, and only because Andy saves the chief's son's life are they able to escape. Eventually the Indians and the mountain men smoke the peace pipe.

Saga of Windwagon Smith, The (film) Special cartoon; released on March 16, 1961. Directed by Charles Nichols. Capt. Windwagon Smith rigs a Conestoga prairie wagon like a schooner with sails and tiller, and sweeps into a Kansas town where he meets the mayor's lovely daughter, Molly, and falls in love. The townspeople are transfixed with Smith's new form of transportation, and build a super windwagon only to have a hurricane sail it off, with the Captain and Molly aboard, into the skies never to be seen again—except when the sunset turns to gold: only then can they be seen. Look for Jasper and Horace Badun from *One Hundred and One Dalmatians* who put in an anonymous appearance. 13 min.

Sagal, Katey Actress; appeared in *The Good Mother* (Ursula), and on television in *Mr. Headmistress* (Harriet Magnum), *Smart House* (PAT), and as a regular on *Imagine That* (Barb) and *8 Simple Rules for Dating My Teenage Daughter* (Cate Hennessy).

Sagebrush Sadie (film) Oswald the Lucky Rabbit cartoon; released on April 2, 1928.

Saintly Switch, A (television) Two-hour television movie; aired on *The Wonderful World of Disney* on January 24, 1999. A pro quarterback dad and feminist mom literally exchange personalities—but not bodies—thanks to their meddling children and some good old-fashioned voodoo magic. Directed by Peter Bogdanovich. Stars Vivica A. Fox (Sara Anderson), David Alan Grier (Dan Anderson), Al Waxman (Coach Beasily), Scott Owen Cumberbatch (Clarke), Shadia Simmons (Annette), David Keeley (Otis), Rue McClanahan (Aunt Fanny). Released on video in 2000.

Salenger, Meredith Actress; appeared as Natty Gann in *The Journey of Natty Gann*, and on television in *My Town*.

Salonga, Lea Broadway singing star of *Miss Saigon* fame who did the singing voice of Jasmine in *Aladdin* and the title character in *Mulan*.

Salten, Felix (1869–1945) Born in Budapest and educated in Vienna, he wrote several adult novels and plays, but he is best known for *Bambi*, first published in English in 1928. Disney later also adapted his *Perri* for the screen. Most fans of the classic comedy *The Shaggy Dog* do not realize that it is from a Salten story, *The Hound of Florence*.

Salty Seal who appears with Pluto in *Rescue Dog* (1947).

Salty, the Hijacked Harbor Seal (television) Television show; aired on December 17, 1972. Directed by Harry Tytle. A biologist helps save a young seal who was caught in a fishing net, but the seal hides in a small boat, not knowing that it is about to be towed far from the bay. The seal causes all sorts of trouble, until the biologist takes him back to the bay. Stars John Waugh, Doug Grey, Lance Rasmussen, Bud Sheble, Hal Stein.

Saludos Amigos (film) Animated feature film about Latin America, made up of four animated segments tied together by live-action footage of the activities of Walt Disney and his artists on their trip. The segments are *Lake Titicaca*, chronicling Donald's exploration of the Andes; *Pedro*, the story of a baby airplane who replaces his father in getting the mail through; *Aquarela do Brasil*, with art showing the various landscapes of Brazil and José Carioca, the parrot, teaching Donald to dance the samba; and *El Gaucho Goofy*, in which American cowboy Goofy becomes a gaucho on the Argentine pampas, learning the habits through offstage narration. World premiere in Rio de Janeiro on August 24, 1942; released in the U.S. on February 6, 1943. It was re-released in 1949. Animation directed by Bill Roberts, Jack King, Hamilton Luske, and Wilfred Jackson. 42 min. While the film is shorter than a normal feature film, it has always been grouped with the Disney animated classic features. C. O. Slyfield received an Academy Award nomination for Best Sound, and addi-

tional nominations went to Charles Wolcott and Ned Washington for Best Song ("Saludos Amigos") and to Edward H. Plumb, Paul J. Smith, and Charles Wolcott for Best Scoring of a Musical Picture. Released on laser disc in 1995.

Salute to Alaska, A (television) Television show; aired on April 2, 1967. Directed by Hamilton S. Luske and Ward Kimball. Celebrating Alaska's 100th birthday, Walt Disney looks at Alaska's past.

Salute to Father, A (television) Television show; aired on January 22, 1961. Directed by Wolfgang Reitherman. Some reruns aired as *Goofy's Salute to Father*. Various Goofy cartoons, showing him as a father, are featured as Walt Disney dedicates the show to all fathers.

Sammy, the Way-Out Seal (television) Two-part television show; aired on October 28 and November 4, 1962. Directed by Norman Tokar. Two brothers adopt an injured seal on their vacation and decide to bring it home. The seal causes disaster at an outdoor party and a supermarket, which makes the boys decide that he has to go back to the ocean. Stars Michael McGreevey, Billy Mumy, Jack Carson, Robert Culp, Patricia Barry, Elisabeth Fraser, Ann Jilliann. Note that Ann Jilliann wears a Camp Inch sweatshirt, left over in the Studio's wardrobe department from *The Parent Trap*.

Samoa (film) People and Places featurette; released on December 25, 1956. Directed by Ben Sharpsteen. Filmed in CinemaScope. 32 min. The story of a happy people on an island paradise begins with a description of life and cultural events in the communities. There are glimpses of fishing and local foods being prepared, and the building of a guest house (*fale tele*) is shown with the resulting housewarming festivities climaxed by an evening *fia fia*, or happy time, including ritual dances.

San Angel Inn Restaurant in Mexico in World Showcase at Epcot; opened on October 1, 1982. With an atmosphere similar to that of the Blue

Bayou at Disneyland, set under a simulated evening sky, this attractive restaurant serves authentic Mexican food, much of which is unfamiliar to most Americans who are used to the Tex-Mex style. There are such dishes as mole poblano—chicken covered in a sauce that combines chocolate and chilies—and pollo en pipina—chicken simmered in a pumpkin seed sauce. The restaurant is operated by the company that runs the San Angel Inn in Mexico City.

San Diego Zoo (film) Educational film in the EPCOT Educational Media Collection: Minnie's Science Field Trips series; released in September 1988. 16 min. Behind the scenes at the world-renowned zoo.

San Juan River Expedition (television) Serial on the *Mickey Mouse Club* during the 1955–56 season. Narrated by Alvy Moore. Directed by Al Teeter. Youngsters touring the San Juan River by boat learn about the Native Americans who used to live in the area, and the explorers who came later. 5 episodes.

Sancho on the Rancho...and Elsewhere (television) Television show; Part 1 of *Sancho, the Homing Steer.*

Sancho, the Homing Steer (television) Two-part television show; aired on January 21 and 28, 1962. Directed by Tom McGowan. The two episodes were titled *Sancho on the Rancho... and Elsewhere* and *The Perils of a Homesick Steer.* A pet steer, Sancho, is awkward to keep when it is full grown at the rancho, and he almost ruins a cattle drive. Sancho heads off toward home by himself, a journey of 1,200 miles, finding many obstacles along the way. Stars Bill Shurley, Rosita Fernandez, Arthur Curtis.

Sanders, George (1906–1972) Actor; appeared in *In Search of the Castaways* (Thomas Ayerton) and provided the voice of Shere Khan in *The Jungle Book.*

Sanders, Richie He voiced Toby Turtle in *Robin Hood.*

Sands, Tommy Actor; appeared in *Babes in Toyland* (Tom Piper), and recorded the title song for *The Parent Trap* with Annette Funicello.

Sandy in Disneyland (television) Television special taped at Disneyland; aired on April 10, 1974. Directed by Marty Pasetta. Sandy Duncan visits Disneyland. Stars also Ernest Borgnine, Ruth Buzzi, Ted Knight, John Davidson, Lorne Greene, The Jackson Five, Kenny Loggins, Doc Severinson.

Santa Clause, The (film) Scott Calvin is a divorced father whose strained relationship with his 8-year-old son, Charlie, begins to mend only after a bizarre twist of fate transforms him into the new Santa. When the current Santa Claus falls off his roof on Christmas Eve, Scott dons Santa's suit, and soon he and his son are whisked off to the North Pole. The head elf, Bernard, tells Scott about the clause, a contract stating that whoever puts on the Santa suit must also take on all the responsibilities that go with the position. While Scott is not too thrilled, Charlie is overjoyed. Over twelve months, Scott puts on an enormous amount of weight and sprouts a full white beard, and when Christmas comes, it becomes clear that Scott is the real Santa. Released on November 11, 1994. Directed by John Pasquin. 97 min. Stars Tim Allen (Scott Calvin), Judge Reinhold (Dr. Neal Miller), Wendy Crewson (Laura Calvin), David Krumholtz (Bernard), Peter Boyle (Mr. Whittle), Eric Lloyd (Charlie Calvin). For the elves, the filmmakers selected 125 children ranging in age from 2 to 13 years, but even though they happen to look like children, they are supposed to be hundreds of years old. Through makeup and "fat suits," Tim Allen changes from a 32- to a 53-inch waist during the course of the production. The film was shot on location in Oakville, Ontario, Canada, and at the Raleigh Studios in Hollywood. Released on video in 1995.

Santa Clause 2, The (film) Scott Calvin has been Santa Claus for the past eight years, and his loyal elves consider him the best Santa ever. Then he gets bad news: not only has his son, Charlie, landed on this year's "naughty" list, but if Scott doesn't marry by Christmas Eve, he'll stop being Santa forever. (It's right in his contract—the "Mrs. Clause.") Desperate, Scott turns to the elves' new invention, a machine that can replicate anything, to create Santa II, a toy version of himself, whom he leaves in charge. Things get worse when Santa II institutes some strange redefinitions of what's naughty and nice, and when Scott finally falls for a potential Mrs. Claus, she threatens to drive a wedge between him and Charlie. In a climactic battle pitting Santa, Charlie, the new Mrs. Claus, and the elves against Santa II and his army of tin soldiers, the future of Scott's family, the North Pole, and Christmas itself hang in the balance. Directed by Michael Lembeck. Released on November 1, 2002. Stars Tim Allen (Scott Calvin/Santa), Spencer Breslin (Curtis), Judge Reinhold (Neal Miller), Wendy Crewson (Laura Miller), Elizabeth Mitchell (Carol), David Krumholtz (Bernard), Eric Lloyd (Charlie Calvin), Liliana Mumy (Lucy Miller). 104 min. Released on video in 2003.

Santa Clause 3, The (film) Directed by Michael Lembeck. Stars Tim Allen (Scott Calvin). Planned for a holiday 2006 release.

Santa Fe and Disneyland Railroad Disneyland attraction; opened July 17, 1955. See Disneyland Railroad.

Santa Who? (television) Two-hour movie on *The Wonderful World of Disney* on November 19, 2000. Two days before Christmas, Santa Claus accidentally falls out of his sleigh and develops amnesia. It is up to Santa's head elf, Max, to find the missing man and save Christmas. Directed by William Dear. Produced by Gleneagle Prods. in association with Hearst Entertainment, Inc. Stars Leslie Nielsen (Santa Claus), Steven Eckholdt (Peter Albright), Robyn Lively (Claire Dreyer), Tommy Davidson (Max), Max Morrow (Zack). Released on video in 2001.

Santa's Toys (film) Sixteen mm release title of 1933 Silly Symphony cartoon *The Night Before Christmas*; released in October 1974.

Santa's Workshop (film) Silly Symphony cartoon; released on December 10, 1932. Directed by Wilfred Jackson. Santa is assisted by his elves

in preparing for the famous sleigh ride on Christmas Eve. As the toys are finished, they come to life and march into Santa's big bag. Its sequel is *The Night Before Christmas* (1933).

Sarabi Simba's mother in *The Lion King*; voiced by Madge Sinclair.

Sarafina! (film) Set in turbulent South Africa, the movie tells of a young student in Soweto who is inspired by a teacher, Mary Masembuko, to take pride in herself and her heritage. When Mary is sent to prison for stepping outside the prescribed curriculum, Sarafina and her schoolmates must choose between violence and nonviolent means of protest. A school musical production celebrating the life of Nelson Mandela, with Sarafina in the lead, eventually does take place amid the burnt ruins of the schoolyard. Initial release on September 18, 1992; general release on September 25, 1992. Directed by Darrell James Roodt. A Hollywood Pictures film, in association with Miramax Films, Videovision Enterprises, Les Films Ariane, Vanguard Films, and the BBC. 101 min. Stars Whoopi Goldberg (Mary Masembuko), Miriam Makeba (Angelina), John Kani (School Principal), Mbongeni Ngema (Sabela), Leleti Khumalo (Sarafina). Based on the play by Mbongeni Ngema. Filmed on location in Soweto, South Africa. Released on video in 1993. The director's cut was released on laser disc, adding about 20 minutes to the length.

Saratoga Springs Resort & Spa Vacation Club resort that opened at Walt Disney World on May 17, 2004, on the site of the former Disney Institute with 184 units in 2004, expanding to 552 in early 2005. The architecture was inspired by the upstate New York country retreats of the late 1800s and designed around the themes of natural springs and Saratoga's tradition of horse racing. An expansion of another 644 units is planned by 2007.

Sardinia (film) People and Places featurette; released on February 15, 1956. Directed by Ben Sharpsteen. 30 min. A train ride takes the audience through the rugged countryside to see the Sardinian people of today. Their independence and self-reliance is emphasized. Sheep are tended and the treatment of their wool is depicted. A wedding and a funeral service are shown, as well as the annual "Ardia" festival with horsemen commemorating historical events.

Sartori, Mary Lynn Mouseketeer from the 1950s television show. One of two Marys on the show—the other was Mary Espinosa. This was the only name duplication among the Mouseketeers.

Sasha Bird friend of Peter in *Peter and the Wolf*, represented by a flute.

Sassagoula Floatworks and Food Factory Food court at the Port Orleans Resort at Walt Disney World; opened on May 17, 1991.

Satellite View of America See Space Station X-1.

Saturday Night at the Movies with Disney (television) Series of 11 programs on NBC from 1974 to 1977.

Savage, Ben Actor; appeared on television as the title character in *Boy Meets World.*

Savage, Brad Actor; appeared in *The Apple Dumpling Gang* (Clovis Bradley), *No Deposit, No Return* (Jay), and *Return from Witch Mountain*

(Muscles), and on television in *The Secret of Lost Valley.*

Savage Sam (film) In this sequel to *Old Yeller*, Travis, now 18, and Arliss, 12, are alone at the homestead while their parents are away. Bud Searcy arrives with Lisbeth, his 16-year-old daughter, to announce the presence of marauding Indians in the vicinity while Arliss and his beloved dog, Savage Sam, a son of the famous hound dog, Old Yeller, are out hunting. Travis and Lisbeth locate him just as the Indians appear. The kids are taken prisoner and the Indians take off on their horses on the trek back to their distant village. Savage Sam, who had been knocked on his head by one of the braves and left for dead, now comes to life. It is he who leads Beck Coates, the boys' uncle, and a party of men on the trail of the Indians. After a wild chase of several days duration, Savage Sam leads the rescue party to the camp-out of the warriors, and after a furious battle, Arliss, Travis, and Lisbeth are rescued. Released on June 1, 1963. Directed by Norman Tokar. 103 min. Stars Brian Keith (Uncle Beck), Tommy Kirk (Travis), Kevin Corcoran (Arliss), Dewey Martin (Lester White), Jeff York (Bud Searcy), Marta Kristen (Lisbeth Searcy). The film was based on Fred Gipson's book, but was not as successful at the box office as its predecessor. Released on video in 1986.

Saval, Dany Actress; appeared in *Moon Pilot* (Lyrae).

Save the Dog (television) An out-of-work actress comes to her sick dog's rescue and gets her big break at the same time. A Disney Channel Premiere Film. First aired on March 19, 1988. 87 min. Stars Cindy Williams (Becky Dale), Tony Randall (Oliver Bishop), Katherine Helmond (Maude).

Saved by the Bell See *Good Morning, Miss Bliss.*

Sayers, Jack (1914–1986) He joined Disney in 1955 as director of customer relations for Disneyland. He served as chairman of the Park

Operating Committee from 1956 to 1959, and then became director and later vice president of lessee relations. He retired in 1975.

Scamp One of Lady and Tramp's puppies in *Lady and the Tramp*. He first appeared in comic strips in the Treasury of Classic Tales Lady and the Tramp strip for July 10, 1955. His own daily strip began on October 31, 1955, and the Sunday color page on January 15, 1956. The character is not named in the movie.

Scandalous John (film) In modern times, a rip-snorting, 79-year-old western rancher, with the prettiest granddaughter; ugliest horse; scrawniest herd; and puniest partner, a Mexican handyman; go on a cattle drive (of one cow) and do battle against a wealthy, land-grabbing industrialist. After an adventurous (and humorous) trek, à la *Don Quixote*, the rancher confronts the villain in a shootout that parallels the classic struggle of good and evil in the Old West. Released on June 22, 1971 (a rather limited release; it never played New York City). Directed by Robert Butler. Filmed in CinemaScope. 114 min. Stars Brian Keith (John McCanless), Alfonso Arau (Paco), Michele Carey (Amanda), Rick Lenz (Jimmy), Harry Morgan (Hector Pippin), Simon Oakland (Whitaker), Bill Williams (Sheriff Hart), John Ritter (Wendell). The film was based on the book by Richard Gardner. Rod McKuen composed the musical score and sang the theme song, "Pastures Green," which interprets the hero's love of open land. Location scenes were filmed in Alamogordo, White Sands National Monument, and near Las Cruces, New Mexico; at the western town of Old Tucson, Arizona; and along the tenmile route of an 1880-period train from Hill City to Keystone, South Dakota. Released on video in 1986.

Scar Lion villain in *The Lion King*; voiced by Jeremy Irons.

Scarcity and Planning (film) Educational film from The People on Market Street series, produced by Terry Kahn; released in September 1977.

Economic concepts of scarcity and planning are explored using the visit of a man and his wife to a clinic as an example.

Scarecrow of Romney Marsh, The (television) Three-part television show; aired on February 9, 16, and 23, 1964. Directed by James Neilson. Adapted from the book *Christopher Syn* by Russell Thorndike and William Buchanan. The adventures of a disguised vicar who fights for justice in 18th-century England. The people in Kent and Sussex have turned to smuggling to get around unjust and heavy import taxes. The Vicar of Dymchurch disguises himself as a scarecrow to help the people against the king's men, eventually aided by one of the royal officers. Stars Patrick McGoohan (Dr. Christopher Syn), George Cole (Mr. Mipps), Tony Britton (Simon Bates), Michael Hordern (Squire Banks), Geoffrey Keen (General Pugh), Kay Walsh (Mrs. Waggett), Sean Scully (John Banks). Filmed on location in England, including the actual Romney Marsh. A theatrical version was called *Dr. Syn, Alias the Scarecrow*.

Scarlet Letter, The (film) A retelling of Nathaniel Hawthorne's timeless classic. Set in puritanical 17th-century Boston, this romantic drama follows the sensational life of a bright and beautiful woman who becomes a social outcast when she bears the child of a respected reverend and refuses to divulge the name of the father. Shunned by the townspeople for her indiscretion and threatened with the loss of her child, she bravely bears the mark of disgrace—a scarlet "A"—until an Indian attack unites the Puritans and causes them to reevaluate their attitudes and laws. Directed by Roland Joffe. A Hollywood Pictures film. Released on October 13, 1995. Stars Demi Moore (Hester Prynne), Gary Oldman (Rev. Arthur Dimmesdale), Robert Duvall (Roger Prynne). 135 min. The production was filmed on Vancouver Island, British Columbia, and in Shelburne, Nova Scotia, where a small maritime fishing village was turned into a replica of 17th-century New England. Filmed in CinemaScope. Released on video in 1996.

Scat Cat Led the jazz band of cats in *The Aristocats*; voiced by Scatman Crothers.

Scenes from a Mall (film) A modern couple—she, Deborah, a successful psychologist who has recently written a best-selling book on marriage, and he, Nick, a high-powered sports lawyer—embark on their 16th wedding anniversary by going to the local mall for party supplies. Nick decides to put his wife's modern mating theories to the test by revealing that he has just ended a six-month affair with a younger woman. Deborah, shocked and hostile, parries with some equally astonishing revelations of her own. The twin true confessions lead to a major verbal battle, until the underlying love the couple has for each other wins out. Released on February 22, 1991. Directed by Paul Mazursky. A Touchstone film. 87 min. Stars Bette Midler (Deborah), Woody Allen (Nick), Bill Irwin (Mime). Filmed on location at Stamford Town Center in Stamford, Connecticut, and at the Beverly Center in Los Angeles. A two-story reproduction of the Stamford mall was also created on a huge soundstage at Kaufman Astoria Studios in New York, since it was determined that it would be impossible to shoot the entire film in a mall that was open for business. Released on video in 1991.

Schallert, William Actor; appeared as Professor Quigley in *The Computer Wore Tennis Shoes* and *The Strongest Man in the World*, and on television in *Elfego Baca* and *The Torkelsons*.

Scheider, Roy Actor; appeared in *Tiger Town* (Billy Young).

Schell, Maximilian Actor; appeared in *The Black Hole* (Dr. Hans Reinhardt) and *A Far Off Place* (Col. Mopani Theron).

Schell, Ronnie Actor; appeared in *Gus* (Joe Barnsdale), *The Shaggy D.A.* (Television Director), *The Cat from Outer Space* (Sgt. Duffy), and *The Devil and Max Devlin* (Greg Weems), and on television in *The Mouseketeers at Walt Disney World* and *The Whiz Kid and the Carnival Caper*.

Scheme of Things, The (television) Series on The Disney Channel, hosted by James MacArthur and Mark Shaw, examining the world

of science. 65 episodes. Debuted on April 18, 1983.

Schiffer, Bob (1916–2005) Makeup artist, joined Disney in 1968 after a successful career at MGM and other studios, and was in charge of makeup for almost every subsequent Disney feature into the 1980s. He retired in 2001.

Schmid Bros., Inc. Licensee of collectible Disney merchandise, often dated or limited edition items, beginning in 1970. Their series of Christmas plates, first sold in 1973, have become popular, with the first one bringing several hundreds of dollars. Through Hudson Pewter they also distributed a series of popular pewter figures. When the Walt Disney Classics Collection was begun in the 1990s, Schmid was chosen to handle the distribution, a relationship which continued until 1995.

Schneider, Peter Named president of feature animation in 1992, he had joined Disney in 1985 as vice president of Feature Animation. He played a key role in the revitalization of the animation division. He was promoted to president of The Walt Disney Studios in January 1999 and chairman in January 2000, adding other Disney-branded films, television, and park entertainment to his responsibilities. He left the company in June 2001.

Schneider, Rob Actor; appeared in *Judge Dredd* (Fergie), *The Waterboy* (Townie), *The Hot Chick* (Clive), *Around the World in 80 Days* (San Francisco hobo), and played the title role in both *Deuce Bigalow: Male Gigolo* and *Deuce Bigalow: European Gigolo*.

School Hero (A Story About Staying in School) (film) Educational film in the EPCOT Educational Media Collection; released in August 1988. 20 min. A custodian impresses upon a student the importance of sticking with school.

Schroeder, Russell Disney artist; began at Walt Disney World in 1971, eventually moving into Marketing Art as a character artist. Later he joined Disney Publishing in California overseeing character art for Disney books. He has written and illustrated a number of books and comic books, including *Mickey Mouse: My Life in Pictures*, *Walt Disney: His Life in Pictures*, and *Disney: The Ultimate Visual Guide*.

Schuck, John Actor; appeared in *Outrageous Fortune* (Atkins), *Dick Tracy* (reporter), and *Holy Matrimony* (Markowski).

Schumacher, Thomas He joined Disney in 1988 to serve as producer of *The Rescuers Down Under*, and later was executive producer of *The Lion King*. He served as executive vice president of Feature Animation for several years, and in January 1999 was promoted to president. He left animation to concentrate on Disney stage productions in 2003.

Schumann China Corp. One of the earliest of the Disney licensees, the company had a license from 1932 to 1934 to sell Disney chinaware they had manufactured in Bavaria. These early dishes are quite collectible today.

Schwartz, Stephen Lyricist; wrote the words for the songs in *Pocahontas* and *The Hunchback of Notre Dame*.

Schwartzman, Jason Actor; appeared in *Rushmore* (Max Fischer) and *Shopgirl* (Jeremy).

Sci-Fi Dine-In Theater Restaurant Opened at Disney-MGM Studios on April 20, 1991. The restaurant re-creates a 1950s drive-in theater, as guests sit in pseudo-convertibles under an eve-

ning sky facing a huge drive-in movie screen on which clips of B-movie trailers and intermission animation are shown. The titles of some dishes on the original menu included Monster Mash (turkey Sloppy Joe), Tossed in Space (chef's salad), and When Berries Collide (strawberry shortcake).

Scotland (film) People and Places featurette; released on June 11, 1958. Directed by Geoffrey Foot. Scotland is a country of three distinct regions—the highlands, the islands, and the lowlands. These regions are examined, showing how the isolated people contact the outside world with their use of channel boats called "Puffers," how they observe the customs of the seasons, and how the various clans and regiments celebrate their history at the Edinburgh Festival. Filmed in CinemaScope. 25 min.

Scott, Bronson The youngest Mouseketeer from the 1950s television show.

Scott, George C. (1927–1999) Actor; provided the voice of Percival McLeach in *The Rescuers Down Under*, and appeared in *The Whipping Boy* on The Disney Channel.

Scott (Worcester), Retta (1916–1990) The first woman animator at the Disney Studio, first receiving screen credit on *Bambi*. After six years at the Studio, she left Disney, but continued to illustrate Disney books as a freelance artist. She was named a Disney Legend posthumously in 2000.

Scream Team, The (television) A Disney Channel Original Movie, premiering on October 4, 2002. With Halloween looming, teenagers Ian and Claire Carlyle accompany their father to his childhood home of Steeple Falls for their grandfather's funeral. The kids make a startling discovery that ghosts flock to the town as it is a "soul processing center," and an angry spirit won't allow their late grandfather's soul to rest. Soon, the siblings get some supernatural help from a trio of bumbling, yet well-meaning spirits, The Scream Team, who are assigned to police the district. Directed by Stuart Gillard. Stars Tommy Davidson (Jumper),

Kathy Najimy (Mariah), Eric Idle (Coffin Ed), Mark Rendall (Ian), Kat Dennings (Claire), Kim Coates (Zachariah Kull), Robert Bockstael (Richard Carlyle), Nigel Bennett (Warner MacDonald), Gary Reineke (Grandpa Frank).

Scrooge McDuck Donald Duck's popular rich uncle; created by Carl Barks in a 1947 comic book story, "Christmas on Bear Mountain," and soon starred in his own comic series. He went on to star in the films *Scrooge McDuck and Money* and *Mickey's Christmas Carol* (Ebenezer Scrooge), and the television series, *Ducktales*.

Scrooge McDuck and Money (film) Special cartoon featurette; released on March 23, 1967. Directed by Hamilton Luske. Scrooge McDuck is visited by his nephews, who wish to become as wealthy as their uncle. In an illustrated lecture,  punctuated by song, Scrooge tells about the history of money, and explains how budgeting works, for both home and country. He says money should be wisely invested and should circulate. And he charges his nephews three cents for this good advice, "for nothing good is ever free." This was Scrooge McDuck's theatrical debut. 17 min.

Scrubs (television) A new doctor and his fellow first-year medical interns navigate the transition from medical school to practicing in a busy teaching hospital, with the help and sometimes hindrance of two seasoned doctors and a sympathetic nurse. Half-hour television series on NBC, premiering on September 25, 2001. Stars Zach Braff (John "J.D" Dorian), Sarah Chalke (Elliot Reid), Donald Faison (Chris Turk), Ken Jenkins (Dr. Bob Kelso), John C. McGinley (Dr. Perry Cox), Judy Reyes (Carla Espinosa). Produced by Touchstone Television.

Scully, Sean Actor; appeared in *Almost Angels* (Peter Schaefer), and on television in *The*

Prince and the Pauper (both title roles) and *The Scarecrow of Romney Marsh.*

Scuttle Seagull in *The Little Mermaid* who shows off to Ariel his false knowledge of humans; voiced by Buddy Hackett.

Scuttle's Scooters Attraction in Mermaid Lagoon at Tokyo DisneySea, opening September 4, 2001. Guests travel in comical hermit crab vehicles.

Sea of Sharks (television) The mysteries of the volcanic islands of the Pacific, home to a rich panoply of marine life—including the giant manta ray, green turtle, humpback whale, and the shark—are plumbed in this New True Life Adventure documentary. Produced by Pete Zuccarini. Aired in syndication beginning July 24, 2000.

Sea Salts (film) Donald Duck cartoon; released on April 8, 1949. Directed by Jack Hannah. Bootle Beetle reminisces about his relation-

ship with Donald through the years, including the time they were shipwrecked and the time the Duck cheated him out of a soda.

Sea Scouts (film) Donald Duck cartoon; released on June 30, 1939. The first cartoon directed by Dick Lundy. Donald is an admiral on a seagoing voyage with his nephews in which they encounter a ravenous shark.

Seal Island (film) The first True-Life Adventure featurette. The fur seals arrive on the fogbound islands known as the Pribilofs to mate and bear pups. The young "bachelors" challenge the older bulls for their harems of females, which results in a terrific fight. In the fall, the herd sets out on a long migration into the Pacific Ocean to spend the winter. Initial release on December 21, 1948; general release on May 4, 1949. Directed by James Algar. 27 min. Alfred and Elma Milotte shot the fascinating footage that formed the beginning of the True-Life Adventure series. Walt Disney had hired them to do some filming for him in Alaska, but as he studied the footage they sent back to the Studio, he zeroed in on the seal footage as having the most promise. He asked them to emphasize the life cycle of the seals, and not show any indication of man's presence. The resulting film did not appeal to RKO, the Disney distributor, who felt that no one would want to sit in a theater for half an hour watching a nature film, so Walt had a friend of his, who ran the Crown Theater in Pasadena, run the film for a week in order to qualify for an Academy Award. Sure enough, it won the award for Best Documentary. According to legend, Walt took the Oscar down to Roy Disney's office and said, "Here, Roy, take this over to RKO and bang them over the head with it." As one could expect, RKO was soon clamoring for more of the True-Life Adventures.

Seale, Douglas (1913–1999) He voiced Krebbs in *The Rescuers Down Under* and the Sultan in *Aladdin*. He also appeared in *Ernest Saves Christmas* (Santa) and *Mr. Destiny* (Boswell).

Searching for Nature's Mysteries (television) Television show; aired on September 26,

1956. Directed by Winston Hibler. Winston Hibler describes the cameras and special techniques developed for nature photography, illustrating his points with segments from the True-Life Adventures.

Seas, The (film) Story of the ocean's mysterious depths and its effect on our lives, for The Living Seas, Epcot, opened on January 15, 1986. Directed by Paul Gerber.

Seasons of the Vine (film) Attraction at the Golden Vine Winery in Disney's California Adventure; opened February 8, 2001. Guests view a film about wine making, from spring vine cutting to bountiful harvest.

Sebastian Crab who is court composer and serves at King Triton's bidding in *The Little Mermaid*; voiced by Samuel E. Wright. The crab's full name is Horatio Felonious Ignacious Crustaceous Sebastian.

Second Star to the Right, The Song from *Peter Pan*; written by Sammy Cahn and Sammy Fain.

Secret Bodyguard (television) Serial on the Mickey Mouse Club on The Disney Channel beginning on September 9, 1991. A wealthy father is protective of his daughter, who is entering a regular high school for the first time, so he hires a teenage martial arts expert to be her bodyguard (without her being aware of it). Stars Ernie Reyes, Jr. (Ernie), Heather Campbell (Brittany Belmont), Stephen Burton (Rick), Johnny Moran (Kevin), James O'Sullivan (Mr. Belmont).

Secret Lab, The See Dream Quest Images.

Secret Mission (television) Television show; Part 1 of *Andrew's Raiders*.

Secret of Boyne Castle, The (television) Three-part television show, aired on February 9, 16, and 23, 1969. A later rerun was under the title *Spybusters*. Directed by Robert Butler. A young American studying in Ireland, Rich Evans, becomes involved with Russian agents and a defecting scientist, after he hears a warning from a dying man. It seems that Rich's brother, Tom, is an American agent trying to meet a defecting scientist, and the Russians are trying to stop the meeting before it happens. Stars Glenn Corbett (Tom Evans), Kurt Russell (Rich Evans), Alfred Burke (Kersner), Patrick Dawson (Sean O'Connor), Patrick Barr (Lord Boyne), Hugh McDermott (Carleton). Released theatrically abroad as *Guns in the Heather*.

Secret of Lost Creek, The (television) Serial on the *Mickey Mouse Club* on The Disney Channel, aired from October 30 to November 27, 1989. Two kids, Jeannie Fogle and her brother, Robert, reluctantly go to visit their grandparents for the summer in the High Sierra town of Lost Creek. Jeannie digs up a story about a lost treasure and is soon involved in intrigue about an illegal mining operation. Stars Shannon Doherty (Jeannie), Scott Bremner (Robert), Jody Montana (Travis), Dabbs Greer (Grandpa).

Secret of Lost Valley, The (television) Two-part television show; aired on April 27 and May 4, 1980. Directed by Vic Morrow. While on a family outing, a boy, Adam, gets lost in the forest and discovers a wild boy there. Communicating by sign language, they become friends. When the wild boy is captured by scientists, Adam helps him escape. Stars Gary Collins, Mary Ann Mobley, Brad Savage, Eddie Marquez, Tom Simcox, Barry Sullivan, Jackson Bostwick, John Lupton.

Secret of Mystery Lake, The (television) Serial on the *Mickey Mouse Club* during the 1956–57 season. Directed by Larry Lansburgh. A naturalist finds a mystery when he goes to study a remote swamp area of northeastern Tennessee.

Stars George Fenneman, Gloria Marshall, Bogue Bell, R. P. Alexander. 7 episodes.

Secret of Old Glory Mine, The (television) Television show; aired on October 31, 1976. Directed by Fred R. Krug. An old prospector, Charlie, living alone with his burro in Arizona, tries to keep a rich silver vein a secret. He takes out only enough to pay his expenses. When another miner arrives, Charlie tries to dissuade him from finding the vein, but when he saves Charlie's life, the two decide to share the secret. Stars Rowan Pease, Barry Dowell.

Secret of the Pond, The (television) Two-part television show; aired on October 5 and 12, 1975. Directed by Robert Day. A spoiled city boy, Joey, doesn't know the ways of the backwaters of Virginia when he goes there on vacation. He makes friends with two local boys whose alcoholic father is secretly poaching alligators. Stars Anthony Zerbe, Ike Eisenmann, Eric Shea, John McLiam, Moses Gunn, Rex Corley.

Secrets of Life (film) True-Life Adventure feature; released on November 6, 1956. Directed by James Algar. A look at nature's endless variety of species' common problem—that of reproduction and survival. In order to show the vastness and minuteness of nature, the technique of time-lapse photography is utilized. We see plants growing, and learn about such creatures as the stickleback fish and the diving spider. The film impressively switches to CinemaScope for the final segment on volcanoes. 70 min. Released on video in 1985.

Secrets of the Animal Kingdom (television) Syndicated half-hour television series, which aired from September 18, 1998 to September 13, 1999, and served as a vehicle to teach kids about the life and habits of animals. Stars Brian Donnelly, Talia Osteen. Taped at Disney's Animal Kingdom, it was the first and only series produced by Walt Disney Attractions Television.

Secrets of the Ant and Insect World (film) Educational film comprising part of *Secrets of*

Life, released in September 1960. Microphotography reveals that the ant society offers many parallels to human society.

Secrets of the Bee World (film) Educational film comprising part of *Secrets of Life*, released in September 1960. Tells the story of a bee colony with the queen bee reproducing the species and the workers building the honeycombs.

Secrets of the Pirate's Inn, The (television) Two-part television show; aired on November 23 and 30, 1969. Directed by Gary Nelson. A man, Dennis McCarthy, in Louisiana, befriends three kids and enlists them to help search for Jean Lafitte's treasure. An unscrupulous newspaper reporter is also searching, and when the kids and McCarthy find the treasure, he takes it from them by force. Stars Ed Begley, Jimmy Bracken, Annie McEveety, Patrick Creamer, Charles Aidman.

Secrets of the Plant World (film) Educational film comprising part of *Secrets of Life*, released in September 1960. Time-lapse photography shows the germinating of seeds and the growth of plants.

Secrets of the Underwater World (film) Educational film comprising part of *Secrets of Life*, released in September 1960. A study of the intriguing life beneath the water's surface where lives a whole world of bizarre creatures.

Secrets, Stories & Magic of the Happiest Place on Earth (film) Direct-to-DVD release of a documentary prepared for the fiftieth anniversary of Disneyland, featuring interviews with dozens of Imagineers, cast members, and Disneyland enthusiasts. Planned for release in 2006. Produced by Jim Garber.

Seeing Eye, The (television) Television show; part 3 of *Atta Girl Kelly*.

Seems There Was This Moose (television) Television show; aired on October 19, 1975. Directed by Roy Edward Disney. A moose has problems when he stumbles into civilization,

including managing to destroy the local market, so he heads back to the forest. Stars Bob Cox, Ron Brown.

Seiberling Latex Products Co. A Disney licensee from 1934 to 1942, they made rubber figures of various characters. Their Mickey Mouse figures are fairly common, as are those of the Seven Dwarfs. However, Snow White herself from the latter set is almost impossible to find. She was made of hollow rubber; the Dwarfs were solid. While the Dwarfs have survived, it is sad to see the few remaining Snow Whites, which have in most cases collapsed into themselves from age.

Self Control (film) Donald Duck cartoon; released on February 11, 1938. Directed by Jack King. Though he tries to take radio philosopher Uncle Smiley's advice about controlling his temper, Donald soon flies into a rage when his rest is upset by various pests, including a woodpecker and an incooperative hammock.

Selleck, Tom Actor; appeared in *Three Men and a Baby* and *Three Men and a Little Lady* (Peter) and *An Innocent Man* (Jimmie Rainwood).

Selma, Lord, Selma (television) Two-hour television movie, aired on *The Wonderful World of Disney* on January 17, 1999. Two little girls remember the infamous and violent Bloody Sunday in Selma, Alabama, during the tumultuous American civil rights movement of the 1960s, when freedom fighters organize a black registration march amidst Southern violence, hatred, racial prejudice, and the ever-present threat of the Ku Klux Klan. Directed by Charles Burnett. Stars Mackenzie Astin (Jonathan Daniels), Jurnee Smollett (Sheyann Webb), Clifton Powell (Martin Luther King, Jr.), Ella Joyce (Betty Webb), Yolanda King (Miss Bright), Stephanie Peyton (Rachel West). Ms. King is the daughter of Martin Luther King, Jr. Released on video in 2000.

Sequels Even though Walt Disney professed that he did not like to make sequels, he was occasionally persuaded by economic reality to make them against his better judgment. One of the first of his films to lead to sequels was the cartoon *Three Little Pigs*; the pigs were brought back for *The Big Bad Wolf*, *Three Little Wolves*, and *The Practical Pig*. *Three Orphan Kittens* had *More Kittens* as a sequel. Some Disney features also had sequels, such as *Old Yeller* (sequel was *Savage Sam*), *The Misadventures of Merlin Jones* (*The Monkey's Uncle*), and *The Absent-Minded Professor* (*Son of Flubber*). In recent years, sequels have been a little more common, with *The Love Bug* (*Herbie Rides Again*, *Herbie Goes to Monte Carlo*, *Herbie Goes Bananas*), *Escape to Witch Mountain* (*Return from Witch Mountain*), *The Apple Dumpling Gang* (*The Apple Dumpling Gang Rides Again*), *Three Men and a Baby* (*Three Men and a Little Lady*), *Honey, I Shrunk the Kids* (*Honey, I Blew Up the Kid*), *White Fang* (*White Fang 2*), *The Mighty Ducks* (*D2* and *D3*), *Stakeout* (*Another Stakeout*), *Sister Act* (*Sister Act 2*), *The Princess Diaries* (*The Princess Diaries 2*) not to mention the *Ernest* films. Only one animated feature has had a theatrical sequel—*The Rescuers* (*The Rescuers Down Under*)—unless one counts computer animation, with *Toy Story* and *Toy Story 2*. There have been a number of television sequels to theatrical features, such as *The Love Bug* and *The Parent Trap*, and to other television shows, such as *Davy Crockett* and *Not Quite Human*. In recent years there have been a number of sequels to the classic animated features, a few released in theaters, but most direct-to-video.

Sequoia Lodge Hotel at Disneyland Paris; opened on May 27, 1992. It was the only hotel there not to open with the others on the park's opening day. Reminiscent of some of the National Park hotels in the United States. Designed by Antoine Grumbach.

Sequoyah (film) Educational film about the Cherokee silversmith who singlehandedly created a written language, produced by Anthony Corso; released in September 1974.

Servants' Entrance (film) 20th Century Fox film starring Janet Gaynor containing a Disney cartoon insert of a nightmare sequence featuring kitchen utensils; released in 1934.

Seven Cities of Antarctica (film) People and Places featurette; released on December 25, 1958. Directed by Winston Hibler. The biography of earth's final frontier, Antarctica, and how this last of our planet's continents was finally opened up by humans after millions of years of seclusion. The picture ends with a summary of Antarctica's future potentials as a source of natural wealth, and as a strategic hub for air travel in the Southern Hemisphere. Filmed in CinemaScope. Footage was obtained when Walt Disney sent cameramen Lloyd Beebe and Elmo Jones with Navy photographers to capture the U.S. expedition "Operation Deepfreeze" on film. 30 min.

Seven Dwarfs Doc, Sleepy, Happy, Grumpy, Sneezy, Bashful, Dopey.

Seven Seas Lagoon Body of water between the Ticket and Transportation Center and Magic Kingdom Park at Walt Disney World. A ferry crosses the Seven Seas Lagoon, providing an alternative to the monorail. Disney's Contemporary Resort, Polynesian Resort, and Grand Floridian Beach Resort are all located around the lagoon, with the latter two having boat docks. (The dock for the Contemporary Resort is on Bay Lake.)

7 Wise Dwarfs (film) The film shows the advisability and necessity of purchasing Canadian war bonds. Made for the National Film Board of Canada. Delivered to them on December 12, 1941. The Dwarfs wisely invest in war bonds with their diamonds, with revamped lyrics to "Heigh Ho."

Seymour, Anne (1909–1988) Actress; appeared on television in *The Leftovers* and *The Wacky Zoo of Morgan City*.

Shades of Green at Walt Disney World Resort R&R hotel leased by the U.S. government for military personnel on February 1, 1994, and purchased by them on January 12, 1996. Formerly The Golf Resort and The Disney Inn. It is no longer available to non-military guests, although the golf courses are. The Army has a 100-year lease on the land from Disney.

Shadow Conspiracy (film) A trusted presidential adviser, Bobby Bishop, suddenly finds himself a murder suspect and his own life threatened by a ruthless professional killer. He goes underground with former girlfriend and ace reporter Amanda Givens and uncovers a plot to assassinate the president, with conspirators including the vice president and the crafty chief of staff, who feel the chief executive has become too liberal. A Hollywood Picture from Cinergi Pictures Entertainment. Directed by George P. Cosmatos. Released on January 31, 1997, after earlier releases in Europe and Asia (December 20, 1996, in Taiwan). Stars Charlie Sheen (Bobby Bishop), Sam Waterston (President), Linda Hamilton (Amanda Givens), Stephen Lang (the Agent), Donald Sutherland (Jake Conrad), Theodore Bikel (Yuri Pochenko), Ben Gazzara (Saxon). Gore Vidal has a cameo role as a crooked congressman. 103 min. Filming took place, mostly at night, in Washington, D.C., as well as in Baltimore, Maryland, and Richmond, Virginia. A total of 85 locations were utilized over 12 weeks of filming. Filmed in CinemaScope. Released on video in 1997.

Shadow of Fear (television) Two-part television show; aired on January 28 and February 4, 1979. Directed by Noel Nosseck. A boy turns to his pets after his father dies, and on a visit to his great-uncle in the Amish country, he learns their legends and superstitions. He soon discovers he has the power to make mind contact with the animals. Stars Ike Eisenmann, John Anderson, Peter Haskell, Joyce Van Patten, Lisa Whelchel, Kip Niven, John McLiam, Charles Tyner.

Shaggy D.A., The (film) In this sequel to the hit film *The Shaggy Dog*, Wilby Daniels, his wife, and their son return from a vacation to find their home stripped bare by housebreakers. Angry, Wilby decides to run against the rascally incumbent district attorney, "Honest John" Slade, and he launches a fumbling campaign. When an ice cream man, who innocently bought a mysterious scarab ring from the thieves, recites the Latin inscription, Wilby once again turns into a shaggy dog. A mad chase ensues as everyone realizes the worth of the ring and searches for it, even

through a huge stack of cherry pies. Slade confiscates the ring and sends Wilby to the pound, where the cunning dog masterminds a breakout. There are still more misadventures, but eventually "Honest John" and his slippery sidekick are brought to heel, and Wilby and his family adopt the gallant dogs from the pound who helped him to become district attorney. Released on December 18, 1976. Directed by Robert Stevenson. 92 min. Stars Dean Jones (Wilby Daniels), Tim Conway (Tim), Suzanne Pleshette (Betty), Keenan Wynn (John Slade), Jo Anne Worley (in her motion picture debut as Katrinka), Dick Van Patten (Raymond), Shane Sinutko (Brian Daniels), Vic Tayback (Eddie Roschak). The film was suggested by *The Hound of Florence* by Felix Salten, author of *Bambi*. The song "The Shaggy D.A.," written by Shane Tatum and Richard McKinley, was sung by Dean Jones. The amusing special effects were provided by Eustace Lycett, Art Cruickshank, and Danny Lee. Released on video in 1985.

Shaggy Dog, The (film) Young misfit teenager Wilby Daniels accidentally discovers a magic ring in a museum, and, by repeating the Latin inscription, he becomes a large and clumsy Bratislavian sheep dog. This amuses his younger brother, Moochie, but shocks his parents, and endears him to lovely neighbor girl Franceska, who thinks he is her dog, Chiffon. But when her father turns out to be a Russian spy, it is up to Wilby to capture the gang, which he manages to do after a hair-raising chase. Unfortunately it is Franceska's Chiffon who gets all the attention and credit at the end—for who would believe Wilby's story? Released March 19, 1959. Directed by Charles Barton in black and white. One of the biggest and most unexpected film milestones in Disney history, the Studio's first live-action comedy set the formula for many Disney movies to come: youngsters, animals, strange—sometimes magical—events, music, and a catchy main title sequence. 101 min. Stars Fred MacMurray (Wilson Daniels), Jean Hagen (Frieda Daniels), Tommy Kirk (Wilby Daniels), Annette Funicello (Allison D'Allessio), Tim Considine (Buzz Miller), Roberta Shore (Franceska Andrassy), Kevin Corcoran (Moochie). The first

Disney film starring Fred MacMurray. The film has grossed over $12 million, and spawned two sequels: *The Shaggy D.A.* (1976) and *The Return of The Shaggy Dog*, a television movie in 1987, and two remakes (for television in 1994 and for theaters in 2005). The film was originally devised for the Disney television series. Released on video in 1981 and 1993.

Shaggy Dog, The (television) A remake of the 1959 film, with various changes to the storyline, aired as a two-hour movie on ABC on November 12, 1994, starring Scott Weinger (Wilby), Ed Begley, Jr. (Mr. Daniels), and Jordan Blake Warkol (Moochie). It was directed by Dennis Dugan.

Shaggy Dog, The (film) Directed by Brian Robbins. Stars Tim Allen, Robert Downey, Jr., Danny Glover, Kristin Davis. Filming began in November 2004.

Shan-Yu The ruthless leader of the Huns in *Mulan*; voiced by Miguel Ferrer. The name means "Invader from the North."

Shang The disciplined Chinese army captain in *Mulan*; voiced by B. D. Wong (speaking) and Donny Osmond (singing).

Shanghai Knights (film) After taming the Wild West in *Shanghai Noon*, Chon Wang and Roy O'Bannon are out to settle a score in civilized London in this sequel. When Chon's estranged father is mysteriously murdered, Chon and Roy make their way to London to track down the killer. Chon's sister, Lin, has the same idea, and uncovers a worldwide conspiracy to murder the royal family—but almost no one will believe her. With the help of a kindly Scotland Yard inspector and a ten-year-old street urchin, the acrobatic Chon uses his high-flying martial arts skills in Victorian Britain as he attempts to avenge his father's death—and keep the romance-minded Roy away from his sister. A Touchstone/Spyglass Entertainment film. Directed by David Dobkin. Released on February 7, 2003. Stars Jackie Chan (Chon Wang), Owen Wilson (Roy O'Bannon), Aaron Johnson (Charlie), Thomas Fisher (Artie Doyle), Aidan Gillen (Rathbone), Fann Wong (Chon Lin), Donnie Yen (Wu Chan). 114 min. The production utilized locations throughout the Czech Republic. Filmed in CinemaScope. Released on video in 2003.

Shanghai Noon (film) The Wild West meets the Far East in a battle for honor, royalty, and a trunk full of gold when acrobatic Imperial Guard Chon Wang comes to Nevada in the 1890s to rescue a beautiful kidnapped Chinese princess. With the help of a partner he does not trust, a wife he does not want, a horse he cannot ride, and martial arts moves that no one can believe, Wang finds himself facing the meanest gunslingers in the West. Directed by Tom Dey. A Touchstone Pictures/Spyglass Entertainment production. Released on May 26, 2000. Stars Jackie Chan (Chon Wang), Owen Wilson (Roy O'Bannon), Lucy Liu (Princess Pei Pei), Roger Yuan (Lo Fong), Xander Berkeley (Van Cleef). 110 min. Doubling for Nevada was the Drumheller area, near Calgary, Alberta, Canada. Filmed in CinemaScope. Released on video in 2000.

Shanghaied (film) Mickey Mouse cartoon; released on January 13, 1934. Directed by Burt Gillett. In this pirate adventure, Mickey saves Minnie from Peg Leg Pete and his crew with the aid of a stuffed swordfish, taking over the ship in the process.

Sharif, Omar Actor; appeared in *The 13th Warrior* (Melchisidek) and *Hidalgo* (Sheik).

Sharing and Cooperation (film) Educational film in the Songs for Us series; released in September 1989. 8 min. The film shows through songs the importance of sharing and cooperation.

Shark Reef Snorkel pool at Typhoon Lagoon at Walt Disney World where guests can swim among the fish, and sharks (though they aren't the dangerous type).

Sharpe, Albert (1885–1970) Actor; appeared in *Darby O'Gill and the Little People* (Darby).

Sharpsteen, Ben (1895–1980) Animator/director; joined Disney in 1929 and left in 1959. He animated on shorts until 1934 when he became a director for the next four years. He was a sequence director on *Snow White and the Seven Dwarfs*, supervising co-director on *Pinocchio*, supervising director on *Dumbo*, production supervisor on *Fantasia, Fun and Fancy Free, Cinderella, Alice in Wonderland*, and several of the True-Life Adventures, and was considered one of Walt's right-hand men. He directed *Water Birds* and served as associate producer or producer on several other of the nature and People and Places films, and television shows. He received an Oscar for *The Ama Girls*. He was named a Disney Legend in 1998.

Shaughnessy, Mickey (1920–1985) Actor; appeared in *Never a Dull Moment* (Francis) and *The Boatniks* (Charlie), and on television in *A Boy Called Nuthin'* and *My Dog, the Thief*.

Shaw, Mel Shaw was hired by Disney in 1937, and worked on story for *Fantasia, Bambi*, and *The Adventures of Ichabod and Mr. Toad*. After leaving the Studio for many years, he returned in the mid-1970s to work on story for *The Rescuers, The Fox and the Hound, The Great Mouse Detective, Beauty and the Beast*, and *The Lion King*. He was named a Disney Legend in 2004.

Shaw, Reta Actress; appeared in *Pollyanna* (Tillie Lagerlof), *Mary Poppins* (Mrs. Brill), and *Escape to Witch Mountain* (Mrs. Grindley).

Shaw, Steve (1965–1990) Child actor; appeared on television in *Child of Glass* (Alexander).

Shawn, Wallace Actor; appeared in *The Cemetery Club* (Larry), *My Favorite Martian* (Coleye Epstein), and *The Haunted Mansion* (Ezra), on television in *Noah* (Zack) and *Mr. St. Nick* (Mimir), and did the voice of Principal Mazur in *A Goofy Movie*, Principal Strickler in *Teacher's Pet*, Rex in *Toy Story* and *Toy Story 2*, Gilbert Huph in *The Incredibles*, and Principal Fetchit in *Chicken Little*.

She Stood Alone (television) Television movie; one woman's battle in 1832 to establish America's first black female academy. Aired on NBC on April 15, 1991. Directed by Jack Gold. 120 min. Stars Mare Winningham, Ben Cross, Robert Desiderio.

Shea, Eric Child actor; appeared in *The Castaway Cowboy* (Booten MacAvoy), and on television in *Menace on the Mountain, The Whiz Kid and the Carnival Caper, The Whiz Kid and the Mystery at Riverton*, and *The Secret of the Pond*.

Sheedy, Ally Actress; appeared in *Betsy's Wedding* (Connie Hopper).

Sheen, Charlie Actor; appeared in *The Three Musketeers* (Aramis), *Shadow Conspiracy* (Bobby Bishop), and *Terminal Velocity* (Ditch Brodie).

Sheep Dog (film) Pluto cartoon; released on November 4, 1949. Directed by Charles Nichols. Bent-Tail, the coyote, tries to teach his son to steal sheep from Pluto's flock, but when the two attempt it, Bent-Tail runs away with a sheep, which turns out to be his son in disguise.

Sheldon, Gene (1909–1982) Actor; appeared in *Toby Tyler* (Sam Treat), *Babes in Toyland* (Roderigo), and on television in *The Golden Horseshoe Revue* and in *Zorro* as Bernardo.

Shelley, Carole She voiced Amelia Gabble (*The Aristocats*), Lady Kluck (*Robin Hood*), and

Fate (*Hercules*). She also appeared in *Quiz Show* (Cornwall aunt) and *Jungle 2 Jungle* (Fiona).

Shepard, Sam Actor; appeared in *Country* (Gil Ivy).

Shere Khan Sneering tiger in *The Jungle Book*; voiced by George Sanders.

Sheridan, Nicolette Actress; appeared in *Noises Off* (Brooke Ashton/Vickie) and *Spy Hard* (Veronique Ukrinsky), and on television in *Desperate Housewives* (Edie Britt).

Sheridan, Susan She voiced Eilonwy in *The Black Cauldron*.

Sheriff of Nottingham Character portrayed as a wolf in *Robin Hood*; voiced by Pat Buttram.

Sherman, Richard M., and Robert B. Songwriters; known primarily for their Disney work, they first wrote pop songs for Annette Funicello, beginning with "Tall Paul." The record sold 700,000 singles. Later they wrote songs for Disney films such as *The Parent Trap*, *Summer Magic*, *Winnie the Pooh and the Honey Tree*, *That Darn Cat!*, *The Jungle Book*, *The Aristocats*, *Mary Poppins*, *The Happiest Millionaire*, *Bedknobs and Broomsticks*, and *The Tigger Movie*. It was their songs for *Mary Poppins* that gave them their big break, and two Academy Awards. In all, they wrote over 200 songs featured in 27 films and two dozen television productions, and received nine Academy Award nominations. Some of their most popular songs include "Supercalifragilistic-expialidocious," "Spoonful of Sugar," "I Wan'na Be Like You," and "Winnie the Pooh." Probably their best-known song was not for a film at all, but for a Disney attraction at the 1964–1965 New York World's Fair—"It's a Small World (After All)." Also for the Fair, they wrote "There's a Great Big Beautiful Tomorrow" for the GE Carousel of Progress. Their last Disney projects were songs for Epcot in 1982. They were named Disney Legends in 1990. In 1992 Disney Records released a special retrospective collection on CD entitled "The Sherman Brothers: Walt Disney's 'Supercalifragilistic' Songwriting Team."

Shindig, The (film) Mickey Mouse cartoon; released on July 29, 1930. Directed by Burt Gillett. At a barn dance, Mickey, Minnie, and the gang perform and dance. Mickey dances with several partners, including a dachshund and a hippo.

Ships (film) Educational film; Goofy escorts two children on a tour of a passenger ship, in the Goofy's Field Trips series; released on August 7, 1989. 15 min.

Shipwrecked (film) A 14-year-old, Hakon Hakonsen, bravely agrees to become a sailor in order to help pay his parents' debts. But danger comes as Hakon's ship is hijacked by a mysterious stranger, Merrick, who charts a course for a South Seas island where he has hidden a fortune in stolen treasure. A fierce hurricane scuttles the ship, and Hakon and a young stowaway girl,

Mary, find themselves marooned on a tropical island paradise. The two must now face the unknown perils of the jungle, and the eventual return of Merrick, as he comes looking for his treasure, and to take the young adventurers prisoner. Released on March 1, 1991. Directed by Nils Gaup. 93 min. Stars Stian Smestad (Hakon Hakonsen), Gabriel Byrne (Merrick), Louisa Haigh (Mary), Trond Peter Stamso Munch (Jens). Based on the classic Norwegian novel, *Haakon Haakonsen*, by Oluf Vilhelm Falck-Ytter. The filming took place in Norway, England, Spain, and Fiji. Released on video in 1991.

Shirley, Bill (1921–1989) He voiced Prince Phillip in *Sleeping Beauty*.

Shnookums & Meat Funny Cartoon Show, The (television) Syndicated television series; debuted on January 2, 1995, and ended on August 28, 1995. Three different animated comedy shorts mixing nutty gags, bad puns, weird events, surrealistic flavor, and wacky storylines in a fast-paced half hour of humor. The segments are *Shnookums and Meat*, with Shnookums a cat and Meat a dog, who are both friends and enemies; *Pith Possum: Super Dynamic Possum of Tomorrow*, a satire of the superhero genre; and *Tex Tinstar: the Best in the West*, with Tex a frontier sheriff who faces certain destruction in each episode. Voices include: *Shnookums and Meat*—Jason Marsden (Shnookums), Frank Welker (Meat), Tress MacNeille (Wife), Steve Mackall (Husband); *Pith Possum*—Jeff Bennett (Pith/Peter Possum), Brad Garrett (Comm. Stress), Jess Harnell (Lt. Tension), April Winchell (Doris Deer), Patric Zimmerman (Obediah); *Tex Tinstar*—Charlie Adler (Chafe), Jeff Bennett (Tex Tinstar), Corey Burton (Ian), Jim Cummings (Narrator), Brad Garrett (Wrongo). 13 episodes.

Shokee, the Everglades Panther (television) Television show; aired on September 29, 1974. Directed by Roy Edward Disney. A Native American boy spending the summer alone in the Everglades as a rite of passage helps a lost panther cub survive, but the village does not welcome him when he follows the boy home. The

boy has to steal an airboat to take the panther deep into the swamp. Stars Curtis Osceola.

Shoot to Kill (film) FBI agent Warren Stantin is in pursuit of a ruthless murderer/extortionist who is fleeing the country by posing as one of a group of fishermen on a trek through the mountains near the Canadian border. In order to track his man in the rugged wilderness, Stantin teams up with Jonathan Knox, the loner partner/boyfriend of the fishermen's guide, Sarah. Knox is angry about being saddled with a tenderfoot whose inexperience in the wild might keep him from reaching Sarah until it is too late, but he and Stantin gradually come to rely on each other. The pursuit continues to Vancouver, but here Stantin is on *his* turf and takes the lead in an exciting chase and climax. Released on February 12, 1988. Directed by Roger Spottiswoode. A Touchstone film. 106 min. Stars Sidney Poitier (Warren Stantin), Tom Berenger (Jonathan Knox), Kirstie Alley (Sarah). Filmed primarily in Vancouver, British Columbia and its environs. Released on video in 1988.

Shooting Gallery Frontierland gallery at Disneyland; opened July 12, 1957. Remodeled as Frontierland Shootin' Arcade in March 1985.

Shopgirl (film) Mirabelle is a "plain Jane" overseeing the rarely frequented glove counter at Saks Fifth Avenue in Beverly Hills. An artist struggling to keep up with even the minimum payment on her credit card and student loans, she keeps to herself until a rich, handsome fiftysomething named Ray Porter sweeps her off her feet. Simultaneously Mirabelle is being pursued by Jeremy, a bachelor who is not quite as cultured and successful as Ray. The film is a glimpse inside the lives of three very different people on diverse paths, but all in search of love. A Touchstone Picture in association with Hyde Park Entertainment. Directed by Anand Tucker. Limited release on October 21, 2005, in Los Angeles, New York, and Toronto; general release on October 28, 2005. Original release on November 11, 2004, in Russia. Stars Steve Martin (Ray Porter), Claire Danes (Mirabelle Buttersfield), Jason Schwartzman (Jeremy), Bridgette Wilson-Sampras (Lisa Cramer), Frances Conroy

(Catherine Buttersfield), Sam Bottoms (Dan Buttersfield), Rebecca Pidgeon (Christie Richards). 106 min. Based on Steve Martin's best-selling novella. Filmed in CinemaScope.

Shore, Dinah (1917–1994) She narrates *Bongo* in *Fun and Fancy Free* and sings "Two Silhouettes" in *Make Mine Music*.

Shore, Pauly Actor; appeared in *Encino Man* (Stoney Brown), *Son-in-Law* (Crawl), and *In the Army Now* (Bones Conway). He provided the voice of Bobby in *An Extremely Goofy Movie*.

Shore, Roberta Actress; appeared in *The Shaggy Dog* (Franceska Andrassy), and on television in the *Annette* serial on the *Mickey Mouse Club*.

Short, Martin Actor; appeared in *Three Fugitives* (Perry), *Father of the Bride* and *Father of the Bride Part II* (Franck Eggelhoffer), *Jungle 2 Jungle* (Richard), *Mumford* (Lionel Dillard), *Captain Ron* (Martin Harvey), and in *The Making of Me* at Epcot. He provided the voice of B.E.N. in *Treasure Planet* and Lars in *101 Dalmatians II: Patch's London Adventure*.

Shot Heard 'Round the World, The (film) Sixteen mm release title of a portion of *Johnny Tremain*; released in May 1966. The Sons of Liberty supply information about British plans which enable Paul Revere to alert the Minutemen to take up arms. Also the television title of Part 2.

Show Biz Is Show in Tomorrowland in Magic Kingdom Park at Walt Disney World, beginning on July 12, 1983, and running until September 27, 1985. The Kids of the Kingdom starred in a revue of Broadway and movie tunes.

Show Me America Entertainment event at Disneyland in the summer of 1970, helping to celebrate the Park's 15th anniversary. The fast-paced show combined favorite tunes, old and new, with plenty of humor, lavish costumes, and spectacular sets.

Showdown at Sandoval (television) Television show; Episode 4 of *Texas John Slaughter*.

Showdown with the Sundown Kid (television) Television show; Part 1 of *Gallegher Goes West*.

Showman of the World Award presented by the National Association of Theater Owners; Walt Disney was the first recipient on October 1, 1966.

Showtime Day Friday on the new *Mickey Mouse Club*.

Shue, Elizabeth Actress; appeared in *Adventures in Babysitting* (Chris), *Cocktail* (Jordan Mooney), and *The Marrying Man* (Adele Horner), and on television in *Double Switch*. She also appears in *Body Wars* in Wonders of Life at Epcot, and narrated *Tuck Everlasting*.

Si and Am The mean Siamese cats owned by Aunt Sarah in *Lady and the Tramp*; voiced by Peggy Lee.

Siam (film) People and Places featurette; released on December 24, 1954. Photographed by Herb and Trudy Knapp. Directed by Ralph Wright. 32 min. The featurette shows the everyday lives of the people of Siam, their classic dances, how they avoid the monsoon rains, a visit to a teak camp with elephants at work as well as a visit to Bangkok, the "Venice of the Orient."

Sid Cahuenga's One-of-a-Kind Shop on Hollywood Boulevard at Disney-MGM Studios that sells movie memorabilia; opened May 1,

1989. The shop's buyers scour the memorabilia auctions and sales to find interesting items to sell in the shop, whether it be a movie star's autograph or a costume or a prop from a film. Occasionally, there will be an authentic Walt Disney autograph in stock, often priced well over a thousand dollars. This is the only place in a Disney park where you can purchase a photograph of Walt Disney; there is a selection available. Usually, there will also be stills, posters, and press kits from Disney movies of the past.

Sidekicks (television) Television series on ABC; aired from September 26, 1986 to June 27, 1987. The pilot movie was called *The Last Electric Knight*, which aired first on February 16, 1986, and was repeated, under the title *Sidekicks*, on September 19, 1986. The evolving relationship between Ernie, an 11-year-old mystically gifted martial arts expert, and Jake Rizzo, the hard-nosed but soft-hearted homicide detective who takes Ernie into his home. Stars Gil Gerard (Jake), Keye Luke (Sabasan), Ernie Reyes, Jr. (Ernie), Nancy Stafford (Patricia Blake).

Sigman, Paula An archivist at the Walt Disney Archives for 15 years, she later was the founding head of the Walt Disney Collectors Society.

Sign of Zorro, The (film) Theatrical compilation of several *Zorro* shows, released first in Japan in November 1958, and in the U.S. on June 11, 1960; an edited version was released on June 9, 1978. Directed by Norman Foster and Lewis R. Foster. Don Diego returns to the pueblo of Los Angeles after completing his schooling in Spain. At home he challenges the cruel tyranny of Monastario, becoming the secret savior of the oppressed, but outwardly playing the fop. When he is captured, he turns the tables on Monastario by revealing his true identity to his friend, the Viceroy from Spain. 90 min. Black and white. Stars Guy Williams (Zorro), Henry Calvin (Sgt. Garcia), Gene Sheldon (Bernardo), Britt Lomond (Monastario). Released on video in 1982.

Signs (film) In Bucks County, Pennsylvania, a mysterious intricate 500-foot design of circles and lines appears carved into a family's crops. Graham Hess, the family patriarch, still bereft over the accidental death of his wife, is tested in his journey to find the truth behind the unfolding mystery. Directed by M. Night Shyamalan. A Touchstone Picture. Released on August 2, 2002. Stars Mel Gibson (Graham Hess), Joaquin Phoenix (Merrill Hess), Cherry Jones (Officer Paski), Rory Culkin (Morgan Hess), Abigail Breslin (Bo Hess), Patricia Kalember (Colleen Hess). The director himself plays the role of Ray Reddy. 107 min. Filmed on location in Pennsylvania. Released on video in 2003.

Silent Trigger (film) Direct-to-video release on September 16, 1997, by Hollywood Pictures of a Dolph Lundgren action-adventure feature co-starring Gina Bellman, Conrad Dunn, and Christopher Heyerdahl. A professional government hit man partners with a novice young woman for a final hit from the top of a still unfinished skyscraper, only to discover that there are plans to make them the victims. Directed by Russell Mulcahy. 98 min.

Silly Symphony A series of 75 cartoons, beginning with *The Skeleton Dance* in 1929. Composer Carl Stalling suggested to Walt Disney that there be a second cartoon series to be different from the Mickey Mouse series, which was based on comedic action centered around one character. The Silly Symphonies would be based on musical themes, and each would feature a different cast of characters. The series served as the training ground for the animators and other Disney artists as they prepared for the feature films. Seven Silly Symphonies won Academy Awards for best cartoon. The complete list of Silly Symphony cartoons follows:

1.	*The Skeleton Dance*	1929
2.	*El Terrible Toreador*	1929
3.	*Springtime*	1929
4.	*Hell's Bells*	1929
5.	*The Merry Dwarfs*	1929
6.	*Summer*	1930
7.	*Autumn*	1930
8.	*Cannibal Capers*	1930

9. *Night* 1930
10. *Frolicking Fish* 1930
11. *Arctic Antics* 1930
12. *Midnight in a Toy Shop* 1930
13. *Monkey Melodies* 1930
14. *Winter* 1930
15. *Playful Pan* 1930
16. *Birds of a Feather* 1931
17. *Mother Goose Melodies* 1931
18. *The China Plate* 1931
19. *The Busy Beavers* 1931
20. *The Cat's Out* 1931
21. *Egyptian Melodies* 1931
22. *The Clock Store* 1931
23. *The Spider and the Fly* 1931
24. *The Fox Hunt* 1931
25. *The Ugly Duckling* 1931
26. *The Bird Store* 1932
27. *The Bears and Bees* 1932
28. *Just Dogs* 1932
29. *Flowers and Trees*
    (1st color) 1932
30. *King Neptune* 1932
31. *Bugs in Love* 1932
32. *Babes in the Woods* 1932
33. *Santa's Workshop* 1932
34. *Birds in the Spring* 1933
35. *Father Noah's Ark* 1933
36. *Three Little Pigs* 1933
37. *Old King Cole* 1933
38. *Lullaby Land* 1933
39. *The Pied Piper* 1933
40. *The Night Before*
    Christmas 1933
41. *The China Shop* 1934
42. *Grasshopper*
    and the Ants 1934
43. *Funny Little Bunnies* 1934
44. *The Big Bad Wolf* 1934
45. *The Wise Little Hen* 1934
46. *The Flying Mouse* 1934
47. *Peculiar Penguins* 1934
48. *The Goddess of Spring* 1934
49. *The Tortoise and*
    the Hare 1935
50. *The Golden Touch* 1935
51. *The Robber Kitten* 1935
52. *Water Babies* 1935
53. *The Cookie Carnival* 1935
54. *Who Killed Cock Robin?* 1935
55. *Music Land* 1935
56. *Three Orphan Kittens* 1935
57. *Cock o' the Walk* 1935
58. *Broken Toys* 1935
59. *Elmer Elephant* 1936
60. *Three Little Wolves* 1936
61. *Toby Tortoise Returns* 1936
62. *Three Blind*
    Mouseketeers 1936
63. *The Country Cousin* 1936
64. *Mother Pluto* 1936
65. *More Kittens* 1936
66. *Woodland Cafe* 1937
67. *Little Hiawatha* 1937
68. *The Old Mill* 1937
69. *Moth and the Flame* 1938
70. *Wynken, Blynken*
    and Nod 1938
71. *Farmyard Symphony* 1938
72. *Merbabies* 1938
73. *Mother Goose Goes*
    Hollywood 1938
74. *The Practical Pig* 1939
75. *The Ugly Duckling*
    (remake) 1939

Note: *Ferdinand the Bull*, originally planned as a Silly Symphony, was released instead as a special short.

Silver Fox and Sam Davenport, The (television) Television show; aired on October 14, 1962. Field producer was Hank Schloss. A fox stows away in a farmer's wagon and is soon mistakenly accused of being a chicken thief. Stars Gordon Perry (Sam).

Silver Screen Partners A limited partnership formed to put up money for the production costs of films, with the investors recouping their investment from the gross amounts the films earned in all their markets and forms. The partners were guaranteed their principal back five years after a film's initial theatrical release. There have been three offerings, all with shares priced at $500 per unit: Silver Screen Partners II began in January 1985, and raised $193 million. Its 28,000 investors put money into such films as *The Color of Money*, *Down and Out in Beverly Hills*, and *Ruthless People*. Silver Screen Partners III began in January 1987 and raised $300 million through 44,000 investors. Their films included *Good Morning, Vietnam*; *Three Men and a Baby*; *Who Framed Roger Rabbit*; and *Honey, I Shrunk the Kids*. Silver Screen Partners IV began in June 1988 and through 52,000 investors raised $400 million. Their films included *The Good Mother*, *Beaches*, *Dead Poets Society*, *Turner & Hooch*, and *The Little Mermaid*. (There was a Silver Screen Partners I, but it invested in HBO films, not in Disney.) The successor to Silver Screen Partners for Disney films was Touchwood Pacific Partners.

Silver Spur Steakhouse Restaurant in Frontierland in Disneyland Paris; opened on April 12, 1992.

Silvers, Phil (1912–1985) Actor; appeared in *The Boatniks* (Harry Simmons) and *The Strongest Man in the World* (Krinkle).

Sim, Alastair (1900–1976) Actor; appeared in *The Littlest Horse Thieves* (Lord Harrogate).

Simba Lion hero of *The Lion King*; voiced by Jonathan Taylor Thomas (young) and Matthew Broderick (adult).

Simmons, Jean Actress; appeared on The Disney Channel in *Great Expectations* (Miss Havisham) and in the television movie *One More Mountain*.

Simon Birch (film) Simon Birch is the smallest baby ever born at Gravestown Memorial Hospital, and as he gets older, he remains small. Certain he is going to become a hero, he argues about faith with his Sunday school teacher and priest, and pals around with his best friend, Joe. However, when his first hit in a baseball game, a high foul ball, accidentally kills Joe's mother, the destinies of the two boys become linked. Simon helps Joe look for his father, while trying to figure out how he is supposed to become a hero. A Hollywood Pictures film in association with Caravan Pictures. Released on September 11, 1998. Directed by Mark Steven Johnson. Stars Ian Michael Smith (Simon Birch), Joseph Mazzello (Joe Wenteworth), Ashley Judd (Rebecca Wenteworth), Oliver Platt (Ben Goodrich), David Strathairn (Rev. Russell), Jan Hoods (Miss Leavey). Jim Carrey appears briefly as the adult Joe Wenteworth and narrator. Eleven-year-old Smith is afflicted with Morquio's syndrome, a rare genetic disorder that causes dwarfism. 114 min. Suggested by John Irving's best-selling novel *A Prayer for Owen Meany*. Filmed on location mostly in Canada, ranging from Toronto to Lunenburg, Nova Scotia. The bus accident was filmed both in the French River, 250 miles north of Toronto, and, to get underwater close-ups safely, in the USC Olympic Stadium pool in Los Angeles. Released on video in 1999.

Simple Machines: A Moving Experience (film) Educational film; released in March 1986. 15 min. Introduction to basic concepts of mechanical physics using simple machines and mimes performing the same movements.

Simple Things, The (film) Mickey Mouse cartoon; released on April 18, 1953. Directed by Charles Nichols. While Mickey fishes at the beach, Pluto has bad encounters with a clam and then a seagull that also steals Mickey's bait and fish. The pair are eventually chased away by all the gull's friends. The last Mickey Mouse cartoon for thirty years (until *Mickey's Christmas Carol*).

Simple Twist of Fate, A (film) Cabinetmaker Michael McCann has withdrawn from society to lead a solitary, unencumbered life, but one fateful winter's night, the beguiling baby daughter of a young mother who has died in the snow wanders into Michael's secluded cabin. As a result, his life changes forever. A strong attachment develops between the man and the girl, and he legally adopts her, naming her Mathilda McCann. Together, they begin life anew, thriving on mutual devotion. But, unknown to Michael, his daughter's biological father is a local politician who observes the girl's progress from a distance, while making plans of his own for the child's future. When he eventually comes forth and demands custody, a bitter controversy ensues. Released on September 2, 1994. Directed by Gillies MacKinnon. A Touchstone film. 106 min. Stars Steve Martin (Michael McCann), Gabriel Byrne (John Newland), Catherine O'Hara (Mrs. Simon), Stephen Baldwin (Tanny Newland). Written by Steve Martin, who was inspired by the nineteenth-century novel *Silas Marner*, by George Eliot. Filmed on location in the area of Atlanta, Georgia. Released on video in 1995.

Simply Mad About the Mouse (video) Classic Disney songs sung to a modern beat, with singers surrounded by animated backgrounds and special effects. Directed by Scot Garen. Features Billy Joel, Ric Ocasek, LL Cool J, The Gipsy Kings, Harry Connick, Jr., Bobby McFerrin, Soul II Soul, Michael Bolton. Video release on September 27, 1991. 35 min.

Sinbad Actor; starred in *Houseguest* (Kevin Franklin), *First Kid* (Sam Simms), and on television in *The Sinbad Show*.

Sinbad Show, The (television) Television series, airing on Fox from September 16, 1993 to July 28, 1994. When David Bryan, a young and single computer graphics designer with no thoughts beyond next Saturday night's date, takes in two foster children, he slowly realizes that he has kissed his carefree bachelor life good-bye. Stars Sinbad (David Bryan), T.K. Carter (Clarence), Willie Norwood (Little John), Erin Davis (Zana), Hal Williams (Rudy Bryan).

Sinclair, Madge Actress; voiced Sarabi in *The Lion King*.

Sindbad's Seven Voyages Attraction in the Arabian Coast area at Tokyo DisneySea, spon-

sored by Nippon Express, opening on September 4, 2001. Guests embark on an enchanting boat ride experiencing fantastic realms, unknown dangers, and unimaginable riches in the fabled lands of the Arabian Nights.

Sinden, Donald Actor; appeared in *Island at the Top of the World* (Sir Anthony Ross).

Sing Me a Story: with Belle See *Disney's Sing Me a Story: with Belle.*

Singer & Sons (television) Television series on NBC from June 9 to 27, 1990. A contemporary comedy in the nostalgic setting of a kosher delicatessen on New York's Upper East Side, it chronicles the day-to-day comic crises of an aging Jewish deli owner who hires his African American housekeeper's two sons as his partners in the family business. Stars Harold Gould (Nathan Singer), Esther Rolle (Mrs. Patterson), Bobby Hosea (Mitchell Patterson), Tommy Ford (Reggie Patterson), Fred Stoller (Sheldon Singer), Arnetia Walker (Claudia James).

Sir Ector Wart's foster father in *The Sword in the Stone*; voiced by Sebastian Cabot (who also narrated the film).

Sir Giles The "brave" knight in *The Reluctant Dragon*; voiced by Claud Allister.

Sir Hiss Prince John's right-hand snake in *Robin Hood*; voiced by Terry-Thomas.

Sir Kay Sir Ector's oafish son in *The Sword in the Stone*; voiced by Norman Alden.

Sir Pelinore Knight in *The Sword in the Stone*; voiced by Alan Napier.

Siskel & Ebert (television) Syndicated television series beginning September 18, 1986. Chicago film critics Gene Siskel and Roger Ebert reviewed current films each week. Originally aired as *Siskel & Ebert at the Movies*. Gene Siskel passed away in February 1999. For the 1999–2000 season, beginning September 4, 1999, the title of the show was changed to *Roger Ebert & the Movies*. In 2000 it became *Ebert & Roeper and the Movies* when Richard Roeper joined the cast.

Siskel & Ebert, the Future of the Movies with Steven Spielberg, George Lucas and Martin Scorsese (television) Syndicated television special; aired on May 21, 1990, on CBS. 60 min.

Sister Act (film) When a second-rate lounge singer in a Reno casino, Deloris Van Cartier, accidentally witnesses a murder at the hands of her mobster boyfriend, Vince LaRocca, she finds herself on the run. A smart cop out to nab LaRocca places Deloris in the witness protection program, hiding her out in a convent of nuns. The Mother Superior insists that Deloris—now Sister Mary Clarence—take a job in the convent and she becomes the new choir director. In no time at all she has the group singing hymns with a 1960s beat, spurring unheard-of attendance at Sunday Masses. When Deloris is kidnapped and taken back to Reno, the nuns effect a rescue in the heart of the gambling city. With LaRocca captured, Deloris is free to go on her way, but she stays with the nuns long enough to appear in a special performance for the pope. Released on May 29, 1992. Directed by Emile Ardolino. A Touchstone film. 100 min. Stars Whoopi Goldberg (Deloris), Maggie Smith (Mother Superior), Harvey Keitel (Vince LaRocca), Kathy Najimy (Sister Mary Patrick), Mary Wickes (Sister Mary Lazarus). Filmed in Los Angeles and San Francisco, California, and Reno, Nevada. Released on video in 1992.

Sister Act 2: Back in the Habit (film) This sequel has Deloris Van Cartier as a successful Las Vegas nightclub singer being asked by the nuns of St. Catherine's Convent to lead a choir in an inner-city school in San Francisco. Having trouble with rowdy teenagers and shrinking budgets, the Sisters enlist Deloris to masquerade as Sister Mary Clarence and help save the school from being closed. She transforms her music class into a first-rate choir, and enters them in a Los Ange-

les choral competition where they go all out to win first prize. Released on December 10, 1993. Directed by Bill Duke. A Touchstone film. 107 min. Stars Whoopi Goldberg (Deloris), Kathy Najimy (Sister Mary Patrick), James Coburn (Mr. Crisp), Barnard Hughes (Father Maurice), Mary Wickes (Sister Mary Lazarus), Lauryn Hill (Rita Louise Watson). Two of the kids in the choir are played by David Kater and DeeDee Magno, who had been Mouseketeers on The Disney Channel's *Mickey Mouse Club*. Released on video in 1994.

Six Days, Seven Nights (film) Quinn Harris is a rough-hewn cargo pilot who makes his living flying freight in his weather-beaten old plane. His life changes when he meets Robin Monroe, a sharp, driven, magazine editor on holiday with her new fiancé, Frank Martin. When an unexpected editorial deadline requires Robin to be in Tahiti, she reluctantly bribes Quinn to fly her there. Forced down in a storm, the two suddenly find themselves stranded on a deserted island, where over the next week danger and romance ensue as the two castaways are thrown into a series of adventures conquering the wilds, evading pirates, and trying to find a way to get off the island. A Touchstone Pictures film, in association with Caravan Pictures. Directed by Ivan Reitman. Released on June 12, 1998. Stars Harrison Ford (Quinn Harris), Anne Heche (Robin Monroe), David Schwimmer (Frank Martin), Jacqueline Obradors (Angelica). 102 min. The production filmed for two months on the island of Kauai, with additional filming in Burbank and New York City. As a trained pilot, Ford did some of his own flying in the film. Filmed in CinemaScope. Released on video in 1998.

Six Gun Law (film) Foreign theatrical compilation of *Elfego Baca* episodes. First released in England in December 1962. 78 min. Stars Robert Loggia. Released on video in 1986.

Sixth Man, The (film) Just as college basketball star Antoine Tyler is about to realize his dream of making it to the NCAA Championships, he dies, leaving his brother Kenny to lead the Washington Huskies to victory. Heartbroken, scared, and lonely, Kenny loses his drive to win until Antoine's ghost appears, determined to take his team all the way. Kenny finds his self-confidence and comes to realize he must ask "The Sixth Man" to leave the team so he and his teammates can play fair and square. A Mandeville Films Production from Touchstone Pictures. Directed by Randall Miller. Released on March 28, 1997. Stars Marlon Wayans (Kenny Tyler), Kadeem Hardison (Antoine Tyler), Kevin Dunn (Mikulski), Michael Michele (R.C. St. John), David Paymer (Gunnar Peterson). 108 min. Filming took place at the University of Washington, and at locations in Seattle and Vancouver. Released on video in 1997.

Sixth Sense, The (film) Cole Sear, an 8-year-old boy, is haunted by his ability to "see dead people." A helpless and reluctant channel, Cole is terrified by threatening visitations from those with unresolved problems who appear from the shadows. Confused by his paranormal powers, Cole is too young to understand his purpose, and too terrified to tell anyone, except child psychologist Dr. Malcolm Crowe, about his torment. As Dr. Crowe tries to uncover the ominous truth about Cole's supernatural abilities, they both receive a jolt that awakens them to something harrowing and unexplainable. Directed by M. Night Shyamalan. A Hollywood Pictures/Spyglass Entertainment presentation. Released on August 6, 1999. Stars Bruce Willis (Malcolm Crowe), Toni Collette (Lynn Sear), Olivia Williams (Anna Crowe), Haley Joel Osment (Cole Sear), Donnie Wahlberg (Vincent Gray). 107 min. The film was produced at various locations in Shyamalan's hometown, Philadelphia, and it went on to do phenomenal business at the box office, becoming Disney's highest grossing live-action motion picture. It also received six Academy Award nominations, including Best Picture, Best Supporting Actor (Haley Joel Osment), and Best Supporting Actress (Toni Collette). Released on video in 2000.

Skeleton Dance, The (film) The first Silly Symphony cartoon; released on August 22, 1929. Directed by Walt Disney. At midnight, skeletons in a cemetery perform a macabre, often humor-

ous, dance before scurrying back to their graves when the cock crows the approach of dawn. It was later featured on the 16mm release *Milestones in Animation* (1973).

Skelton, Red (1913–1997) See America on Parade.

Skills for the New Technology: What a Kid Needs to Know Today (film) Series of three educational films; released in September 1983.

Skin Deep (film) Educational film; released on October 4, 1993. 26 min. The film educates about eating disorders, for teenagers.

Skippy Bunny in *Robin Hood*; voiced by Billy Whitaker.

Sklar, Marty Vice chairman of Walt Disney Imagineering, involved with concepts and writing contributions for most Disney theme park shows. He joined Disney in 1956, and helped develop *Vacationland* magazine. He moved over to WED Enterprises in 1961 to develop shows for the New York World's Fair. Sklar became a vice president, concepts/planning of WED in 1974, was made vice president of creative devel-  opment in 1979, and in 1982 became executive vice president. He was named president in 1987. He was promoted to vice chairman when Walt Disney Imagineering and Disney Development Company merged in 1996. He had originally worked at Disneyland for a month in 1955 while a UCLA student. He was named a Disney Legend in 2001.

Sky High (television) Three-hour television show; aired on March 11 (120 min.) and August 26, 1990 (60 min.) Directed by James Whitmore, Jr., James Fargo. Two teenagers find themselves the owners of a 1917 biplane and they learn to fly it. They get into various adventures as they fly around the country. Stars Damon Martin, Anthony Rapp, James Whitmore, Traci Lind, Page Hannah, Annie Oringer, David Paymer, Barney Martin, Heidi Kozak. These three hour-long shows were meant to be the start of a series that never happened.

Sky High (film) When you are the son of the world's most legendary superheroes, The Commander and Jetstream, there is only one school for you—Sky High, an elite high school that is entrusted with the responsibility of molding today's power-gifted students into tomorrow's superheroes. The problem is that Will Stronghold is starting with no superpowers of his own and, worst of all, instead of joining the ranks of the "hero" class, he finds himself relegated to being a "sidekick." Now he must somehow survive his freshman year while dealing with an overbearing gym coach, a bully with superspeed, and a dangerous rebel with a grudge (and the ability to shoot fire from his hands) . . . not to mention the usual angst, parental expectations, and girl problems that accompany teenage life. But when an evil villain threatens his family, friends, and the very sanctity of Sky High, Will must use his newfound superpowers to save the day and prove himself a "hero" worthy of the family tradition. Directed by Mike Mitchell. A Touchstone Pictures/Gunn Films presentation. Released on July 29, 2005. Stars Kurt Russell (Steve Stronghold/The Commander), Kelly Preston (Josie Stronghold/Jetstream), Michael Angarano (Will Stronghold), Danielle Panabaker (Layla), Mary Elizabeth Winstead (Gwen Grayson/Royal Pain), Bruce Campbell (Coach Boomer), Lynda Carter (Principal Towers), Dave Foley (Mr. Boy), Steven Strait (Warren Peace), Nicholas Braun (Zach), Kevin McDonald (Mr. Medulla), Cloris Leachman (Nurse Spex). 99 min. Filmed in Super 35 Scope. Released on DVD in 2005.

Sky Scrappers (film) Oswald the Lucky Rabbit cartoon; released on June 11, 1928.

Sky Trap, The (television) Two-hour television movie; aired on May 13, 1979. Directed by Jerome Courtland. A young man in Arizona, trying to save his mother's business, takes off in a sailplane and finds a secret landing strip. He discovers that it is being used by drug smugglers, and he works to catch them. Stars Jim Hutton, Marc McClure, Patricia Crowley, Kitty Ruth, John Crawford, Kip Niven.

Sky Trooper (film) Donald Duck cartoon; released on November 6, 1942. Directed by Jack King. In his desire to be an Army pilot, Donald is tricked into being a paratrooper by Pete. In Donald's battle with Pete to avoid jumping, they dislodge a bomb from under the plane that destroys the General's headquarters. As a result, both end up doing KP duty.

Skyfest The city of Anaheim saluted Disneyland on Walt Disney's birthday, December 5, in 1985 with a world-record release of 1,000,000 balloons. Seven thousand pounds of helium were used, enough to lift 190 people.

Sky's the Limit, The (television) Two-part television show; aired on January 19 and 26, 1975. Directed by Tom Leetch. A boy, Abner, at an English boarding school, resists visiting his grandfather's California farm, but when he does, he is intrigued to find the old man's ancient airplane, which they fix up and fly. Stars Richard Arlen (Grimes), Norman Bartold (Capt. Willoughby), Ike Eisenmann (Three), Huntz Hall (Hitchhiker), Pat O'Brien (Abner Therman), Lloyd Nolan (Cornwall), Ike Eisenmann (Abner III), Jeanette Nolan (Gertie), Robert Sampson (Two).

Skyway to Fantasyland Tomorrowland attraction at Disneyland; opened on June 23, 1956. Four-passenger buckets were suspended from a 2,400-foot-long cable, traveling between

Tomorrowland and Fantasyland. The Tomorrowland station was very modernistic; the Fantasyland station resembled a mountain chalet. In the early days of Disneyland, guests could purchase either a one-way or round-trip ticket. Later, it was one-way only. The attraction closed on November 10, 1994. Also a Tomorrowland attraction in Magic Kingdom Park at Walt Disney World, opened on October 1, 1971, and closed on November 9, 1999. Also in Tomorrowland at Tokyo Disneyland; opened on April 15, 1983, and closed November 3, 1998.

Skyway to Tomorrowland Fantasyland attraction at Disneyland; opened on June 23, 1956. There were 44 gondolas on the cable, passing through the Matterhorn on the way to Tomorrowland. It was the first ride of its kind to be built in the United States. The attraction closed on November 10, 1994. Also a Fantasyland attraction in Magic Kingdom Park at Walt Disney World; opened on October 1, 1971, and closed on November 9, 1999. Also in Fantasyland at Tokyo Disneyland; opened on April 15, 1983, and closed November 3, 1998.

Slam Dunk Ernest (film) The lovable Ernest P. Worrell becomes a basketball star. A direct-to-video release from Touchstone Home Video. Directed by John Cherry. Released on June 20, 1995. Stars Jim Varney (Ernest P. Worrell), Jay Brazeau, Kareem Abdul-Jabbar. 93 min.

Slater, Helen Actress; appeared in *Ruthless People* (Sandy Kessler).

Slaughter Trail, The (television) Television show; episode 6 of *Texas John Slaughter*.

Sleeping Beauty (film) In spectacular style, the film recounts the simple story of Princess Aurora, who is cursed by the evil fairy Maleficent to die before the sun sets on her sixteenth birthday by pricking her finger on the spindle of a spinning wheel. Despite the loving attempts of the three good but often bumbling fairies, Flora, Fauna, and Merryweather, the curse is fulfilled. The good fairies put everyone in the castle into a deep sleep until the spell can be broken. It is only with the aid of Prince Phillip that Maleficent, transformed into a towering, fire-breathing dragon, is destroyed, and the Sleeping Beauty is awakened by a kiss. Released January 29, 1959. Supervising director Clyde Geronimi. In Technirama 70. 75 min. The voice talents include Mary Costa (Princess Aurora), Bill Shirley (Prince Phillip), Eleanor Audley (Maleficent), Verna Felton (Flora), Barbara Luddy (Merryweather), Barbara Jo Allen (Fauna), Candy Candido (Goons). George Bruns's orchestral score, which was nominated for an Academy Award, expertly blended famous themes from Tchaikovsky's ballet. Sammy Fain, Jack Lawrence, Tom Adair, Winston Hibler,

Erdman Penner, and Ted Sears wrote lyrics to such songs as "I Wonder" and "Once Upon a Dream." Based upon the Charles Perrault version of "Sleeping Beauty," the film had an overall stylistic look conceived by artist Eyvind Earle, today known for his paintings and Christmas card designs. With a budget that exceeded $6 million in 1959, this was Walt Disney's most lavish and expensive animated feature to date. Though not an initial box office success, the film has proven to be a unique asset with popular reissues in 1970, 1979, and 1986. Released on home video in 1986 and 1997.

Sleeping Beauty Castle Fantasyland landmark at Disneyland. On opening day, the drawbridge was lowered for the only time until the new Fantasyland opened in 1983. In order to use wasted space, the interior of the castle was opened as a walk-through attraction featuring dioramas telling the *Sleeping Beauty* story on April 29, 1957, with Shirley Temple making the dedication. The interior was expanded in 1968 and redesigned in November 1977. It has been questioned why Walt Disney built the castle relatively small (it only rises 77 feet above the moat), but he actually had a very good reason. He recalled that the tyrants in Europe built huge, imposing castles in order to intimidate the peasants. Walt wanted his castle to be friendly, so it was built on a smaller scale. While it looks in many ways similar to Neuschwanstein castle in Bavaria, actually a number of medieval European castles provided a model for this one. The faux building stones give a forced perspective, making the castle seem larger than it is, with larger ones at the bottom and smaller ones above. After his death a few

years ago, a tree was planted in front of the castle in honor of Herb Ryman, the Disneyland designer extraordinaire, who was responsible for much of the look of the castle. At Hong Kong Disneyland there is a Sleeping Beauty Castle patterned after the one at Disneyland.

See also Le Château de la Belle au Bois Dormant for the Disneyland Paris version.

Sleepwalker, The (film) Pluto cartoon; released on July 3, 1942. Directed by Clyde Geronimi. Walking in his sleep, Pluto presents a female dachshund with a bone but wants it back when he awakens, until he realizes the dog and her family of puppies need it more than he does.

Sleepy One of the Seven Dwarfs; voiced by Pinto Colvig.

Sleepy Time Donald (film) Donald Duck cartoon; released on May 9, 1947. Directed by Jack King. Donald is a sleepwalker. When he sleepwalks to Daisy's house, she humors him and gets him home only to have him wake up and accuse her of sleepwalking.

Sleigh Bells (film) Oswald the Lucky Rabbit cartoon, released on July 23, 1928.

Slezak, Walter (1902–1983) Actor; appeared in *Emil and the Detectives* (Baron).

Slide, Donald, Slide (film) Donald Duck cartoon; released on November 25, 1949. Directed by Jack Hannah. A fight between Donald and a bee over which radio program to listen to (Donald wants a baseball game; the bee wants a classical music concert) ends up with Donald locked in the shower, stung, and the bee happily listening to his favorite program.

Slue Foot Sue Pecos Bill's girlfriend, in the *Melody Time* segment.

Small and Frye (television) Limited television series of six episodes, airing from March 7 to June 15, 1983, on CBS. A detective has the ability to shrink to six inches in height. Stars Darren McGavin, Jack Blassing, Debbie Zipp, Bill Daily, Warren Berlinger, Kristoffer Tabori.

Small Animals of the Plains (film) Part of *The Vanishing Prairie*; released on 16mm for schools in September 1962. Tells of prairie dogs, badgers, cottontails, porcupines, and other small animals in their daily struggle against predators.

Small One, The (film) Special cartoon featurette telling a Christmas story; released on December 16, 1978. Directed by Don Bluth.

Ordered by his father to sell his old, small donkey, Small One, a Hebrew boy in ancient Israel takes the donkey to the Jerusalem market. Finding no buyers there for Small One, the boy is about to give up when he meets a kind man named Joseph. Joseph buys Small One and uses him to take his pregnant wife Mary to Bethlehem. 25 min. Featuring the voices of Sean Marshall (Small One), Olan Soule (Father), Joe Higgins (Roman guard), William Woodson (tanner), Hal Smith (auctioneer), Gordon Jump (Joseph). Based on a story by Charles Tazewell, published in 1947. In 1960, rights to the book were bought by Walt Disney, but the property was never developed. Then, in 1973, Disney writer/artist Pete Young re-discovered the book in the studio library and fell in love with it. When the project was approved by Ron Miller, vice president in charge of productions, Young and writer Vance Gerry further developed the script. After several delays, actual production began in 1977. This was the first Disney production created exclusively by the new generation of animators at the studio, except for "old timer" directing animator Cliff Nordberg, to prove their ability to create a success. More than 150 artists and technicians were involved in the production. Nearly 100,000 final drawings were used in the finished film, with at least triple that number drawn as sketches, pencil tests, and for rough animation. The three songs—

"The Small One," "A Friendly Face," and "The Market Song"—were written by Don Bluth and Richard Rich. For the first time since *Sleeping Beauty*, a choral sound was extensively used consisting of a 12-voice choir and a 42-piece orchestra. Released on video in 1985.

Small World Restaurant Located in Fantasyland at Tokyo Disneyland; opened on April 15, 1983, as Four Corners Food Faire. The name changed to Small World Restaurant in March 1987.

Smart Guy (television) Half-hour television series, premiering on The WB Network on April 2, 1997, and ending on August 1, 1999. T.J. Henderson is a 10-year-old genius, who leaps from the fourth grade to high school, while in other respects remaining a typical kid. It is difficult for T.J.'s family to adjust to the need to live with and raise a child prodigy, leading to often unpredictable and hilarious situations. Stars Tahj Mowry (T.J. Henderson), John Marshall Jones (Floyd Henderson), Jason Weaver (Marcus Henderson), Essence Atkins (Yvette Henderson), Anne-Marie Johnson (Denise Williams). Omar Gooding became a regular in the 1997–98 season as Morris "Mo" L. Tibbs.

Smart House (television) Two-hour Disney Channel Original Movie, airing first on June 26, 1999. Ben Cooper, a 13-year-old computer whiz, helps his widowed father win a computerized house named PAT (Personal Applied Technology) to take care of their every need. To prevent his father from dating, Ben tries programming PAT to become a surrogate mom, but things get wildly out of hand and PAT literally takes on a life of her own, becoming very overbearing. As chaos ensues, Ben has to outsmart the house, realizing that a computer cannot take the place of a real person. Directed by LeVar Burton. Stars Katey Sagal (PAT), Ryan Merriman (Ben Cooper), Kevin Kliner (Nick Cooper), Jessica Steen (Sara Barnes), Katie Volding (Angie Cooper). Released on video in 2000.

Smestad, Stian Actor; appeared in *Shipwrecked* (Hakon Hakonsen).

Smith, Alexis Actress; appeared in *Tough Guys* (Belle).

Smith, Charles Martin Actor; appeared in *Herbie Goes Bananas* (D.J.), *No Deposit, No*

Return (Longnecker), *I Love Trouble* (Rick Medwick), and *Never Cry Wolf* (Tyler).

Smith, Dave Established the Walt Disney Archives in 1970 and continues to serve as  Archives director. He has written numerous articles on Disney subjects as the company's official historian, a regular column in *The Disney Channel Magazine* and *Disney Magazine*, and, besides writing *Disney A to Z*, has co-authored *The Ultimate Disney Trivia Book* (1992), *The Ultimate Disney Trivia Book 2* (1994), *The Ultimate Disney Trivia Book 3* (1997), and *The Ultimate Disney Trivia Book 4* (2000) with Kevin Neary. He co-authored *Disney: The First 100 Years* (1999) with Steven Clark, and its updates, and compiled *The Quotable Walt* (2001). He has also been a featured speaker at the Disneyana Conventions, and was honored as a Disney Legend by the NFFC.

Smith, Dodie (1896–1990) Playwright and author, wrote *The Hundred and One Dalmatians*.

Smith, Lane (1936–2005) Actor; appeared in *The Mighty Ducks* (Coach Reilly), *The Distinguished Gentleman* (Dick Dodge), and *Son-in-Law* (Walter).

Smith, Maggie Actress; appeared as the Mother Superior in *Sister Act* and *Sister Act 2: Back in the Habit*, and in *Washington Square* (Aunt Lavinia Penniman).

Smith, Michael (1945–1983) Mouseketeer from the 1950s television show.

Smith, Orin C. Member of the Disney board of directors beginning January 1, 2006.

Smith, Paul (1906–1985) Composer; joined Disney in 1934. He won an Academy Award for the score of *Pinocchio*, along with nominations for scores of such classics as *Snow White and the Seven Dwarfs*, *Cinderella*, *Song of the South*, *Saludos Amigos*, and *The Three Caballeros*. He wrote the background music for almost all of the True-Life Adventures and nearly 70 animated short subjects. He left Disney in 1962. He was named a Disney Legend posthumously in 1994.

Smith, Webb Story man at the Disney Studio beginning in 1931. He is credited with coming up with the idea of the storyboards, used for planning an animated film instead of a script. He left Disney in 1942.

Smith! (film) A rancher, Smith, who is trying to make a go of a small spread, sometimes aggravates his family with his lackadaisical ways and his friendship with the local Nez Perce Indians. When one of them, Gabriel Jimmyboy, is falsely accused of murder, Smith comes to the rescue at the trial. The accused is freed and the Indians are grateful, coming to the Smith ranch to help with the cutting of the hay crop, and to train Smith's son, Albie's, prize Appaloosa. Released on March 21, 1969. Directed by Michael O'Herlihy. 102 min. Stars Glenn Ford (Smith), Nancy Olson (Norah), Dean Jagger (Judge), Chief Dan George (Ol' Antoine), Keenan Wynn (Vince Heber), Warren Oates (Walter), Frank Ramirez (Gabriel Jimmyboy), Christopher Shea (Albie). Based on *Breaking Smith's Quarter Horse*, by Paul St. Pierre. The song "The Ballad of Smith and Gabriel Jimmyboy" was written by Bobby Russell. Released on video in 1987.

Smoke (television) Two-part television show; aired on February 1 and 8, 1970. Directed by Vincent McEveety. A boy, Chris, mourning the loss of his father cares for an injured dog named Smoke. When he finds out the dog's real owner may be around, he runs away, only to become a hero by saving an elderly couple from a fire. Stars Earl Holliman (Cal Finch), Ronny Howard (Chris), Jacqueline Scott (Fran Fitch), Shug Fisher (Leroy), Andy Devine (Mr. Stone), Pamelyn Ferdin (Susie), Kelly Thordsen (Mr. Horn).

Smoke Signals (film) A dramatic educational film for children about cigarette smoking. 18 min. Released in January 1995.

Smoke Tree Ranch Walt Disney had a vacation home at this ranch, located in Palm Springs, California, and he often wore a necktie emblazoned with a stylized STR emblem.

Smokeless Tobacco: The Sean Marsee Story (film) Educational film, a true story about the dangers of snuff; released in September 1986. 16 min.

Smoking: The Choice Is Yours (film) Educational film, produced by Reynolds Film Export, John Ewing; released in September 1981. The film deals with problems of self-image and peer pressure that influence students to begin smoking.

Snake Eyes (film) A joint production between Touchstone Pictures and Paramount (with Buena Vista International handling foreign distribution) of a Brian DePalma-directed film. An Atlantic City police detective, Rick Santoro, joins an old friend, Navy Commander Kevin Dunne, who is working with the Secretary of Defense, at a heavyweight boxing match. Suddenly the secretary is assassinated, and Santoro and Dunne join forces to investigate the murder. Released August 7, 1998. Stars Nicolas Cage (Rick Santoro), Gary Sinise (Kevin Dunne), John Heard (Gilbert Powell), Carla Gugino (Julia Costello), Stan Shaw (Lincoln Tyler). 98 min. Released on video.

Sneezy One of the Seven Dwarfs; voiced by Billy Gilbert.

Snow (television) A two-hour ABC Family original movie; premiered on December 12, 2004. In a reinvention of the Santa Claus myth, Nick Snowden reluctantly takes over the family business. But, with only three days before the big night, one of Nick's young reindeer is captured by a hunter and taken to a zoo. Not only must Nick rescue the reindeer in time to complete his Christmas deliveries, he must do it before the young buck learns to fly and the zoo realizes what it has. In the course of his adventures, Nick touches the lives of those at a boarding house, including Sandy, who works at the zoo and has lost heart during the holidays since the death of her parents, and eight-year-old Hector, who lives there with his mom. Nick tries to bring back the spirit of Christmas they lost long ago. Directed by Alex Zamm. Stars Tom Cavanagh (Nick Snowden), Ashley Williams (Sandy), Patrick Fabian (Buck Seger), Bobb'e J. Thompson (Hector).

Snow Bear (television) Two-part television show; aired on November 1 and 8, 1970. Directed by Gunther Von Fritsch. A polar bear cub is befriended by Timko, a teenage Eskimo boy, while he is on a year's self-imposed exile from his community, learning the art of the hunt. The soon grown bear has to be returned to the wilds after it destroys the village's meager supply of food. Stars Steve Kalcak, Rossman Peetook, Laura Itta. Filmed on location in Point Barrow and other Alaskan sites. Released for schools on 16mm film as *The Track of the Giant Snow Bear*.

Snow Dogs (film) When Miami dentist Ted Brooks finds out that he has been named in a will, he travels to Tolketna, Alaska, to claim his inheritance. However, he discovers that he has been left a mischievous team of sled dogs, who have got it in for him. A crusty mountain man, Thunder Jack, also has it in for the city slicker. Wanting to claim the dogs for himself, he urges Ted to return to warmer climates. Released on January 18, 2002. Directed by Brian Levant. Stars Cuba Gooding, Jr. (Ted Brooks), James Coburn (Thunder Jack), Sisqo (Dr. Rupert Brooks), Nichelle Nichols (Amelia), Graham Greene (Peter Yellowbear), Brian Doyle-Murray (Ernie), Joanna Bacalso (Barb), M. Emmet Walsh (George). 99 min. For the filming, the town of Canmore, Alberta,

Canada, doubled for the fictitious town of Tolketna. Released on video in 2002.

Snow White Lead character in *Snow White and the Seven Dwarfs*; voiced by Adriana Caselotti.

Snow White: A Lesson in Cooperation

(film) Educational film; released in September 1978. Cooperating, even in chores, can be a rewarding experience.

Snow White—An Enchanting New Musical

Stage show, a 28-minute adaptation of the film, premiering on February 23, 2003, at the Fantasyland Theater at Disneyland, being the most elaborate stage show to be produced exclusively for that theater. Directed by Eric Schaeffer. Patrick Stewart provided the voice of the slave in the Magic Mirror.

Snow White and the Seven Dwarfs (film)

A beautiful girl, Snow White, takes refuge in the forest in the house of Seven Dwarfs to hide from her stepmother, the wicked Queen. The Queen is jealous because she wants to be known as the fairest in the land, and Snow White's beauty surpasses her own. The Dwarfs grow to love their unexpected visitor, who cleans their house and

cooks their meals. But one day when they are at their diamond mine, the Queen arrives at the cottage, disguised as an old peddler woman, and she persuades Snow White to bite into a poisoned apple. The Dwarfs, warned by the forest animals, rush home to chase the witch away, but they are too late to save Snow White. They place her in a glass coffin in the woods, and mourn for her. The Prince, who has fallen for Snow White, happens by and awakens her from the wicked Queen's deathlike spell by "love's first kiss." Supervising director was David Hand. Premiered on December 21, 1937, at the Carthay Circle Theater in Hollywood, it was the first animated feature film. The film cost $1.4 million, and featured such classic songs as "Someday My Prince Will Come," "Heigh Ho," and "Whistle While You Work." More than 750 artists worked on the film, which took three years to produce. Of many who auditioned for the voice of Snow White (Walt Disney turned down Deanna Durbin), he chose the young singer Adriana Caselotti. Harry Stockwell, the father of Dean Stockwell, did the voice of the Prince, and many radio and screen personalities were selected for other roles, such as Lucille LaVerne as the Queen and Billy Gilbert as Sneezy. Pinto Colvig (Goofy) voiced two of the Dwarfs. Walt had gotten the idea for the film when he was a newsboy in Kansas City, and he saw a major presentation of a silent film version of the story starring Marguerite Clark. The screening was held at the city's Convention Hall in February 1917, and the film was projected onto a four-sided screen using four separate projectors. The movie made a tremendous impression on the 15-year-old viewer because he was sitting where he could see two sides of the screen at once, and they were not quite in sync.

The film received a special Academy Award in 1939 consisting of one full-size Oscar and seven dwarf Oscars, presented to Walt Disney by Shirley Temple. For a while after its release, the film became the highest-grossing motion picture of all time, until finally surpassed by *Gone With the Wind* a couple of years later. This statistic is all the more surprising when one realizes that children were paying a dime to get into the theaters in 1937, and the film, of course, had great appeal to that age group. The original worldwide gross was $8.5 million, a figure that would translate into several hundreds of millions in today's dollars. In England, the film was deemed too scary for children, and those under 16 had to be accompanied by a parent. 83 min. A stage version of the movie played at Radio City Music Hall in New York in 1979. For its 1993 reissue, the film was completely restored, being the first ever to be completely digitized by computer, cleaned up, and then printed back to film. The film was reissued eight times, in 1944, 1952, 1958, 1967, 1975, 1983, 1987, and 1993, and released on video in 1994. In 1978, a 16mm release, *Snow White: A Lesson in Cooperation*, was released for schools. For the television show on the 1983 reissue, see *The Fairest of Them All*, and for the one for the 50th Anniversary reissue in 1987, see *Golden Anniversary of Snow White and the Seven Dwarfs.*

Snow White and the Seven Dwarfs (stage show) (television) Taped version of the production at Radio City Music Hall, which added four songs to those in the motion-picture score; released in December 1980 on Pay-TV and then on video. Aired on The Disney Channel in 1987 as *Snow White Live*.

Snow White Grotto Marble figures of the Snow White characters from Italy displayed just outside Sleeping Beauty Castle at Disneyland; opened on March 27, 1961. Disney designer John Hench was dismayed when he was given the figures by Walt Disney to display—Snow White was the same size as the Dwarfs. Hench solved the problem by placing her above the rest of the characters, so her small size is not noticeable. Also at Tokyo Disneyland and Hong Kong Disneyland.

Snow White: The Fairest of Them All (television) A two-hour movie from Hallmark Entertainment, airing on *The Wonderful World of Disney* on March 17, 2002. Directed by Caroline Thompson. A gothic version of the classic tale from the Brothers Grimm. After Snow White's mother's death, her father, John, is granted three wishes and becomes king, though soon finds himself under the spell of Queen Elspeth, who becomes Snow White's stepmother. The queen is obsessed with being "fairest of them all," and is reassured by her towering hall of mirrors, until Snow White's growing beauty surpasses her own. Stars Kristin Kreuk (Snow White), Tom Irwin (John), Miranda Richardson (Elspeth), Tyron Leitso (Prince Alfred). The Dwarfs are named after the days of the week. Originally aired on television in Israel in October 2001.

Snow White's Adventures Fantasyland attraction at Disneyland; opened on July 17, 1955. One of the original dark rides in Fantasyland. The original attraction used to have a large sign out in front, featuring the Witch, warning guests that the attraction was scary. When the attraction was rebuilt for new Fantasyland, it was renamed Snow White's Scary Adventures, opening on May 25, 1983. Also Fantasyland attraction in Magic Kingdom Park at Walt Disney World; opened October 1, 1971. This attraction received extensive renovations in 1994, to actually put the character of Snow White into the ride for the first time, and it reopened on December 16. Also an attraction at Tokyo Disneyland; opened April 15, 1983. See also *Blanche-Neige et les Sept Nains* for the Disneyland Paris version.

Snow White's Scary Adventures Snow White's Adventures (1955–1982) was renamed at Disneyland for its reopening as a remodeled attraction in New Fantasyland on May 25, 1983.

Snowball Express (film) A New Yorker unexpectedly inherits the "Grand Imperial Hotel" in Colorado, so he quits his job and takes his family west, only to discover that the hotel does not live up to its name at all and in fact is a dilapidated ruin. But the New Yorker perseveres and turns the hotel into a colorful ski lodge. However, he has to enter a cross-country snowmobile race and thwart the local banker in order to do it. Released on December 20, 1972. Directed by Norman Tokar. 93 min. Stars Dean Jones (Johnny Baxter), Nancy Olson (Sue), Harry Morgan (Jesse McCord), Keenan Wynn (Martin Ridgeway). Filmed on location in the Colorado Rockies. A city ordinance banning snowmobiles on the main street of Crested Butte had to be temporarily suspended in order to allow the Disney crew to film the snowmobile race sequence. Released on video in 1982.

So Dear to My Heart (film) Jeremiah Kincaid lives on his grandmother's farm, adopts a baby black lamb, and names him Danny. When Uncle Hiram tells him of the prizes sheep can win at the fair, Jeremiah begins to train Danny to be a champion, although once too often the sheep runs afoul of Granny because of his destructive tendencies. But they do go to the fair where the lamb wins a special award. Contains several animated sequences that teach Jeremiah lessons such as "It's Whatcha Do with Whatcha Got" and "Stick-to-it-ivity." Released on January 19, 1949. Directed by Harold Schuster. 82 min. Stars Burl Ives (Uncle Hiram), Beulah Bondi (Granny Kincaid), Bobby Driscoll (Jeremiah Kincaid), Luana Patten (Tildy). Ives sings the famous "Lavender Blue (Dilly Dilly)" by Larry Morey and Eliot Daniel (adapted from a folk song) nominated for an Academy Award for Best Song. Bobby Driscoll, the young lead, received a special outstanding juvenile Oscar for his movies that year (which included the non-Disney film, *The Window*). Filmed in Sequoia National Park and the San Joaquin Valley of California. The train station used on the set had another life after the film was shot. Disney artist Ward Kimball was given the station by Walt Disney to install at his Southern California home. Kimball was an avid railroad buff who had railroad tracks running down his driveway, and he enjoyed surprising new neighbors by stoking up his full-size locomotive on a Sunday afternoon. The film was reissued in 1964 and released on video in 1986 and 1992.

So This Is Love Song from *Cinderella*; written by Mack David, Al Hoffman, and Jerry Livingston.

So Weird (television) Series on Disney Channel that explores various mysteries of the paranormal with musician Molly Phillips, her family,

and their friends, the Bells, as they travel across the country. Premiered on January 18, 1999, and ended September 2, 2001. Stars Cara DeLizia (Fi Phillips), Mackenzie Phillips (Molly Phillips), Patrick Levis (Jack Phillips), Erik von Detten (Clu Bell). In the third season, Alexz Johnson (Annie Thelan) joined the cast in place of Cara DeLizia as Fi went off to school. 65 episodes.

SoapNet Launched by Disney/ABC on January 24, 2000, the first and only cable channel dedicated to soap operas. The channel features same-day episodes of daytime dramas, as well as original soap-related programming and acquired dramatic series.

Soarin' Over California (film) Film attraction at Disney's California Adventure; opened February 8, 2001. Guests are lifted up to 40 feet in the air, and surrounded by a giant projection dome. They then get a birds-eye view of much of the beauty and wonder of California, with an extraordinary sensation of free flight, accompanied by a musical score by Jerry Goldsmith. 4 min. Walt Disney Imagineering ride engineer Mark Summer came up with the idea of the unique ride system one weekend by building a model with an erector set he had at home. A similar attraction called Soarin' opened as part of The Land at Epcot on May 5, 2005.

Soccermania See *An All New Adventure of Disney's Sport Goofy Featuring Sport Goofy in Soccermania.*

Social Lion (film) Special cartoon; released on October 15, 1954. Directed by Jack Kinney. A lion, feared by all in the wilds of Africa, learns that no one fears him when he escapes in the big city after being captured. However, when he tries to dress up like a human, everyone then recognizes him as a lion and is terrified. The lion ends up in the zoo, scaring all the zoo visitors.

Social Side of Health, The (film) Educational film made for Upjohn's Triangle of Health series; released in August 1969. The film focuses on learning how to live with others while retaining one's own individuality.

Social Studies (television) Half-hour television series, debuting on UPN on March 18, 1997, and ending on August 5, 1997. Manhattan's once-posh Woodridge girls' boarding school has its financial problems and tries to weather them by becoming coeducational and taking in students of greater financial, cultural, and ethnic diversity. Stars Bonnie McFarlane (Katherine "Kit" Weaver), Adam Ferrara (Dan Rossini), Julia Duffy (Frances Harmon), Lisa Wilhoit (Madison Lewis), Vanessa Evigan (Sara Valentine), Corbin Allred (Chip Wigley).

Society Dog Show (film) Mickey Mouse cartoon; released on February 3, 1939. Directed by Bill Roberts. Mickey enters Pluto in a dog show, but they are thrown out when Pluto bites the judge. When a fire starts, Pluto saves a female dog, Fifi, and receives a medal for his heroism.

Solari, Jay-Jay (John Joseph) Mouseketeer from the 1950s television show.

Solomon, the Sea Turtle (television) Television show; aired on January 5, 1969. Scientists study the migratory habits of the green sea turtles, attaching a transmitter to the shell of Solomon, a 350-pound example. Solomon has to fight storms and a tiger shark as he migrates from the Virgin Islands to his birthplace far across the Caribbean. Stars Dr. Archie Carr (himself), Henry Del Giudice (Dr. Hamilton), Steve Weinstock (Mark).

Some Day My Prince Will Come Song from *Snow White and the Seven Dwarfs*; written by Larry Morey and Frank Churchill.

Someone Like Me (television) Television series on NBC, from March 14 to April 25, 1994. Comedy focusing on an 11-year-old girl's realistic views of today's fast-changing world. Stars Gaby Hoffman (Gaby), Patricia Heaton (Jean), Anthony Tyler Quinn (Steven), Nikki Cox (Sam), Raegan Kotz (Jane), Joseph Tello (Evan), Matthew Thomas Carey (Neal).

Someone's Waiting for You Song from *The Rescuers*; written by Carol Connors, Ayn Robbins, and Sammy Fain. Nominated for an Academy Award.

Something Wicked This Way Comes (film) The ominous arrival of Dark's Pandemonium Carnival in Green Town sparks the curiosity of two boys, Will Halloway and Jim Nightshade. Dark transforms some of the townspeople as the boys try to find out the secret of the carnival. The boys hide from Dark, who threatens Will's father, the town librarian, who in turn finally helps good triumph over evil as he saves the boys and causes the destruction of the ominous carnival. Released on April 29, 1983. Directed by Jack Clayton. 95 min. Stars Jason Robards (Charles Halloway), Jonathan Pryce (Mr. Dark), Diane Ladd (Mrs. Nightshade), Pam Grier (Dust Witch), Royal Dano (Tom Fury), Vidal Peterson (Will), Shawn Carson (Jim). The film began life as a short story in a publication called *Weird Tales* in May 1948, then called "Black Ferris," written by famed science fiction author Ray Bradbury. It became his favorite work and when he saw Gene Kelly's direction of *Invitation to a Dance*, he personally delivered the story to the star's home in order to work for and with Kelly on a film version of his story. Kelly agreed, but failed to raise the necessary funding. Over the next several years Bradbury converted his screenplay into the novel that was published in 1962 as *Something Wicked This Way Comes*, and was an immediate, and enduring, best seller. Producers

Robert Chartoff and Irwin Winkler and directors Sam Peckinpah, Mark Rydell, and Steven Spielberg are among those who were associated with the property over the years. Producer Peter Vincent Douglas's fascination with Bradbury's works culminated in a chance meeting with the celebrated author in 1976, in a bookstore, where Douglas discovered the rights to the novel were available again. Acquiring them, he met with director Clayton and over the next several years, they worked on a script. In 1980, Disney production vice president Tom Wilhite expressed an interest in the project, and in September 1981 the production went before the cameras. Green Town was created on the Disney Studio's backlot, after the long-standing generic town square set was bulldozed. It took nearly 200 construction workers to build the one-acre set featuring the elaborate, Victorian-style town. The carnival, a tent, and caravan-lined midway covering two acres was likewise constructed on the Disney lot. Some sequences were shot on location in Vermont to provide the proper atmosphere. Live tarantulas were provided for the movie by Animal Actors of Hollywood, and though they performed dutifully, Studio veterans claim that a few got loose on the lot, causing consternation wherever they turned up. Released on video in 1983.

Something You Didn't Eat (film) Educational film depicting the dangers of an unbalanced diet; made for the Cereal Institute, O.W.I., War Food Administration. The film was delivered on June 11, 1945.

Somethin's Cookin' (film) Maroon Cartoon starring Roger Rabbit and Baby Herman that opened the feature film *Who Framed Roger Rabbit*. Roger, left as a babysitter, has to try to save Baby Herman from destroying the kitchen and himself.

Son-in-Law (film) When a college coed, Rebecca Warner, brings her weird resident adviser, Crawl, home to South Dakota for Thanksgiving, the traditional-minded family is horrified, but slowly he is accepted by them as he helps each learn the value of his or her own individuality.

Released on July 2, 1993. Directed by Steve Rash. A Hollywood Pictures film. 95 min. Stars Pauly Shore (Crawl), Carla Gugino (Rebecca), Lane Smith (Walter). The college scenes were filmed at California State University, Northridge, whose campus would be devastated by an earthquake six months after the film's release. A farm in Visalia, California, doubled for the South Dakota farm in the story. Released on video in 1994.

Son of Flubber (film) In this sequel to *The Absent-Minded Professor*, the unpredictable Ned Brainard continues his scientific ventures at Medfield College. The professor's use of a Flubber by-product, his efforts in controlling the weather with "dry rain," and his assistant's discovery of Flubber-gas result in a series of climactic incidents that add up to a hilarious finale. Released on January 18, 1963. Directed by Robert Stevenson in black and white. 102 min. Stars Fred MacMurray (Ned Brainard), Nancy Olson (Betsy), Keenan Wynn (A.J. Allen), Tommy Kirk (Biff Hawk), Elliott Reid (Shelby Ashton), and many others from the cast of *The Absent-Minded Professor*. Walt Disney's grandson, Walter Elias Disney Miller, makes a short appearance as a baby in a television commercial. For the football game in the film, exterior shooting was prohibitive because of the special effects and trick shots involved in the sequence. So, a section of the stadium and a major part of the field were reproduced on one of Disney's largest soundstages. It was exact in every detail, from the transplanted green sod and the goal posts to the cheering spectators and the enthusiastic cheerleaders. Since the team opposing Medfield College was composed of professional football players and not actors, they were surprised to be asked to play indoors. Released on video in 1984.

Song of the South (film) Live-action feature about a boy learning about life through the stories of Uncle Remus, which are shown in animated segments. Little Johnny is taken to his grandmother's plantation where he meets Uncle Remus and is guided by his stories ("Running Away," "The Tar Baby," and "The Laughing Place") about Brer Rabbit, Brer Fox, and Brer Bear. Johnny finds friendship with a local girl,

Ginny Favers, but is bullied by her cruel brothers. When he is accidentally gored by a bull,

it takes more than Uncle Remus to save him. His parents must reunite, creating a happy family once more. The film was nominated for Best Scoring of a Musical Picture and received an Oscar for Best Song ("Zip-A-Dee-Doo-Dah") and an honorary Oscar to James Baskett for his portrayal of Uncle Remus. Premiered on November 12, 1946, at Loew's Grand in Atlanta. Directed by Harve Foster; cartoon direction by Wilfred Jackson. 94 min. Stars Ruth Warrick (Sally), Bobby Driscoll (Johnny), James Baskett (Uncle Remus), Luana Patten (Ginny), Hattie McDaniel (Tempy). Based on the stories of Joel Chandler Harris. Other songs included "Uncle Remus Said," "How Do You Do?" and "Ev'rybody's Got a Laughing Place." The film and its songs provided the inspiration for the Splash Mountain attractions in the Disney parks. Bobby Driscoll and Luana Patten were Disney's first contract players, since this was the Studio's first major plunge into live-action filmmaking. But since Walt Disney was considered an animated film producer, it was felt that the film should contain at least some animated sequences. Thus, Uncle Remus's stories are shown in animation, along with some clever combinations of the live action and animated characters. The film was reissued in 1956, 1972, 1980, and 1986.

Songs for Us (film) Series of three educational films: *Appreciating Differences*, *Making Friends*, and *Sharing and Cooperation*; released in September 1989.

Songs for Us: Part 2 (film) A three-part educational music video for young children, covers ethnic songs. 10 min. Released in January 1995.

Sonia Duck friend of Peter in *Peter and the Wolf*, represented by an oboe.

Sons of the Pioneers Singing group; appeared with Roy Rogers in *Melody Time* introducing the *Pecos Bill* segment and also recorded songs for such films as *The Saga of Andy Burnett*; *The Swamp Fox*; *Sancho, the Homing Steer*; *The Legend of Lobo*; *Johnny Shiloh*; and *The Saga of Windwagon Smith*.

Sorcerer's Apprentice, The (film) Music by Paul Dukas; a segment of *Fantasia*. The film was originally meant to be released as a short cartoon, but since it turned out to be so elaborate (and expensive), it was combined with other segments into the feature film.

Sorcery in the Sky Fireworks show presented at Disney-MGM Studios, featuring a large inflatable Mickey Mouse with fireworks shooting from his pointing finger.

Sorensen, Ricky (1946–1994) He did the voice of Wart (Arthur) in *The Sword in the Stone*.

Sorority Boys (film) Dave, Adam, and Doofer, three college playboy chauvinists, are strapped for cash, and find one last, desperate hope for free housing—one of the campus sororities, Delta Omicron Gamma (i.e. DOG). The boys go undercover as Daisy, Adina, and Roberta, and everything goes well until Dave falls for Leah. The boys, with a long history of treating women badly, see firsthand how the other half lives. Dave wants to tell Leah who he is, but without destroying Daisy's relationship with the girl of his dreams. A Touchstone Picture. Released on March 22, 2002. Directed by Wally Wolodarsky. Stars Barry Watson (Dave/Daisy), Harland Williams (Doofer/Roberta), Michael Rosenbaum (Adam/Adina),

Melissa Sagemiller (Leah), Heather Matarazzo (Katie), Brad Beyer (Spence), Tony Denman (Jimmy), Kathryn Stockwood (Patty). 94 min. Released on video in 2002.

Sorvino, Paul Actor; appeared in *Dick Tracy* (Lips Manlis), *The Rocketeer* (Eddie Valentine), *Nixon* (Henry Kissinger), *Mr. 3000* (Gus Panas), and on television in *The Oldest Rookie* (Ike Porter).

Soul Man (television) Comedy series premiering on ABC on April 15, 1997, and ending on August 25, 1988. Reverend Mike Weber is a widowed Episcopalian minister who is trying to raise four rambunctious children. He is also unorthodox, rides a motorcycle, and is constantly stymied in trying to lead his kids down the straight and narrow path. Stars Dan Aykroyd (Mike Weber), Dakin Matthews (the bishop), Kevin Sheridan (Kenny), Brendon Ryan Barrett (Andy), Courtney Chase (Meredith), Spencer Breslin (Fred).

Sounder (television) Two-hour television movie, aired on *The Wonderful World of Disney* on January 19, 2003. The classic story of an 11-year-old boy who grows into manhood while on a years-long search for his beloved father, who has been sentenced to five years of hard labor for stealing a ham to help feed his family. The family includes a young coon-dog puppy, Sounder, a loyal friend to the boy and an enthusiastic hunter. Directed by Kevin Hooks. Stars Carl Lumbly (Father), Suzzanne Douglass (Mother), Daniel Lee Robertson III (Boy), Paul Winfield (Teacher), Peter MacNeill (Sheriff), Bill Lake (Deputy). Hooks and Winfield starred in the original 1972 Oscar-nominated feature film from 20th Century Fox. Produced by Touchstone Television in association with Jaffe/Braunstein Films. Released on video in 2003.

Soundstage Restaurant Opened at Disney-MGM Studios on May 1, 1989, and closed on November 14, 1998. At opening, this restaurant was set up as the Plaza Hotel set from the movie *Big Business*, as if it was the movie's wrap party. Later on, it was themed to *Beauty and the Beast* and to Agrabah, from *Aladdin*.

Soundstages See Walt Disney Studio.

Soup's On (film) Donald Duck cartoon; released on October 15, 1948. Directed by Jack Hannah. Donald is soon chasing after his nephews when they steal his prepared supper. But when he falls over a cliff and is knocked out, the nephews trick him into believing that he is an angel. They soon regret their ruse. Features the song "Zip-A-Dee-Doo-Dah."

South America In the early 1940s as Europe was moving deeply into World War II, America was not yet involved, but dark clouds were gathering on the horizon. President Franklin D. Roosevelt was worried about the influence of Nazi Germany extending to our neighbors in South America. As part of the government's Good Neighbor Policy, Nelson Rockefeller, then Coordinator of Inter-American Affairs, asked Walt Disney if he would travel to Latin America on a goodwill tour. Walt argued that he did not want to go on a handshaking trip—but he was willing to take some of his artists and make some animated cartoons about the area. This was agreeable to Rockefeller, so the Disney contingent set off on August 17, 1941, for Argentina, Brazil, and Chile, bringing back to Hollywood sketches, songs, and impressions of the South American life and culture. Two feature films came out of the trip: *Saludos Amigos* and *The Three Caballeros*. Both proved so successful with theater audiences that Walt did not need the subsidy promised him by the government. In addition to the films for theaters, Disney made a number of educational films for the South American market, in the Health for the Americas series. *Saludos Amigos* and *The Three Caballeros* were released on laser disc in 1995.

South of the Border with Disney (film) Documentary featurette; a 16mm film about the visit of a group of the Disney artists to Brazil, Argentina, Uruguay, and Chile. The artists react to the beauty of the Latin American countries through their sketches. The film emphasizes local customs and ends with the group returning with souvenirs. Produced under the auspices of the

Coordinator of Inter-American Affairs, to help promote unity between the United States and South America. It was delivered on November 23, 1942. Directed by Norm Ferguson.

South Pacific (television) Three-hour television special on ABC on March 26, 2001, of the classic Rodgers and Hammerstein musical set against the backdrop of World War II. A nurse falls in love with a local planter, and is devastated when he is sent on a dangerous mission. A young naval officer falls for a beautiful native girl, daughter of the local promoter, Bloody Mary. Directed by Richard Pearce. Produced for Touchstone Television by John Braunstein Films in association with Trillium Productions and White Cap Productions. Stars Glenn Close (Ensign Forbush), Rade Sherbedgia (Emile de Becque), Harry Connick, Jr. (Lt. Cable), Robert Pastorelli (Luther Billis), Lori Tan Chinn (Bloody Mary). Released on video in 2001.

South Seas Traders Adventureland shop at Disneyland; opened June 30, 1984. Carries South Seas-themed wearing apparel.

Space Mountain Tomorrowland attraction in Magic Kingdom Park at Walt Disney World; opened on January 15, 1975. Hoping to appeal to young people who like thrill rides, Space Mountain is a unique type of roller coaster. It is designed so that one rides inside, in the dark. Since you are unable to see which way the tracks are going, it is hard to brace yourself for the drops and turns, adding to the thrill. Comets, shooting stars, and other outer-space effects add interest. A moving sidewalk at the exit leads one past displays of how  electronics might affect us in the future. The mountain itself is over 180 feet high, and 300 feet in diameter. Also, a Tomorrowland attraction at Disneyland; opened May 4, 1977. First sponsored by RCA at Walt Disney World; Federal Express became the sponsor in both parks from 1993 to 2003. Also a Tomorrowland attraction at Tokyo Disneyland; opened April 15, 1983; and at Hong Kong Disneyland; opened September 12, 2005. At Disneyland Paris, Space Mountain: de la Terre à la Lune opened on June 1, 1995. The Disneyland attraction closed for a major rebuild on April 10, 2003 and reopened on July 16, 2005. The Disneyland Resort Paris attraction was redesigned in 2005 as Space Mountain: Mission 2.

Space Place, The Large 670-seat fast-food facility in the Space Mountain complex in Tomorrowland at Disneyland beginning in 1977.

Space Place FoodPort Restaurant in Tomorrowland at Tokyo Disneyland; opened on April 15, 1983.

Space Stage Outdoor stage with 1,100 seats in Tomorrowland at Disneyland from 1977 until 1986. The stage was replaced by the Magic Eye Theater where *Captain Eo* and later *Honey, I Shrunk the Audience* were shown, and the outdoor shows moved to Videopolis.

Space Station X-1 Tomorrowland exhibit at Disneyland, open from July 17, 1955 to February 17, 1960. Beginning in 1957 it was known as Satellite View of America. Guests viewed a shaped scenic painting of Earth as if it was being viewed from space. The attraction was created by artist Peter Ellenshaw.

Space Traders Shop in Tomorrowland at Hong Kong Disneyland; opened September 12, 2005.

Spaced Invaders (film) On Halloween, a group of Martians intercept a 50th anniversary rebroadcast of Orson Welles's dramatic "War of the Worlds," and misinterpret it as their cue to attack Earth. The small town of Big Bean, Illinois, happens to be their destination. Ten-year-old resident Kathy Hoxly is unfazed by the pint-sized invaders, and with the help of her friend Brian, her father, and Old Man Wrenchmuller, she rescues the Martians from a frenzied posse of townsfolk, saves the Earth from the aliens' blitz, and helps blast the visitors back to their planet. Released on April 27, 1990. Directed by Patrick Read Johnson. A Touchstone film. 102 min. Stars Douglas Barr (Sam), Royal Dano (Wrenchmuller), Ariana Richards (Kathy), J.J. Anderson (Brian). The "aliens" had electronically controlled heads made of foam, latex, and fiberglass. Unfortunately, the actors could not see out of the elaborate heads, so they were in constant contact with the director by way of wireless headphones. Released on video in 1990.

Spacek, Sissy Actress; appeared in *The Straight Story* (Rose) and *Tuck Everlasting* (Mae Tuck), and as a guest on *Disney's Captain Eo Grand Opening*.

Spaceman and King Arthur, The (film) Foreign theatrical title of *Unidentified Flying Oddball.*

Spaceman in King Arthur's Court, The (television) Television title of *Unidentified Flying Oddball*; shown in two parts in 1982.

Spaceship Earth Geodesic globe attraction, the symbol of Epcot; opened on October 1, 1982. Sponsored by AT&T from 1982 to 2002. A new narration script with Walter Cronkite was added on May 29, 1986. The geosphere is 165 feet in diameter, standing 15 feet above the ground on 6 legs. In its more than two million cubic feet of space, guests ride upward in a journey that passes the highlights of communication history through the years from cavemen to the present and into the future. At the very top of the sphere is a majestic star field. The show received major renovations in 1994, reopening on November 23. Jeremy Irons now provides the narration, from concepts by Ray Bradbury and a host of advisers to the Disney designers.

Spacey, Kevin Actor; appeared in *Consenting Adults* (Eddy Otis), *Iron Will* (Harry Kingsley), *The Ref* (Lloyd), and provided the voice of Hopper in *a bug's life.*

Spade, David Actor; provided the voice of Kuzco in *The Emperor's New Groove*, and appeared as C.J. on *8 Simple Rules.*

Spanjers, Martin Actor; appeared in *Max Keeble's Big Move* (Runty Band Member), and on television in *Daddio* (Max Woods) and *8 Simple Rules for Dating My Teenage Daughter* (Rory).

Spare the Rod (film) Donald Duck cartoon; released on Janaury 15, 1954. Directed by Jack Hannah. Donald's conscience, in the form of a "guidance counselor duck," advises him to deal with his nephews' misbehavior psychologically, rather than physically. Donald mistakes some pygmy cannibals, who have escaped from the circus, for his nephews playing in disguise. Donald spanks one pygmy who bites (tastes) Donald. Tired of its interference, Donald takes his conscience out to the woodshed.

Speaking of Weather (film) Educational film; released in September 1982. The film shows basic weather.

Spears, Britney Actress; appeared on the *Mickey Mouse Club* on The Disney Channel, beginning in 1993. She later became a top-selling pop vocalist.

SpectroMagic Parade in Magic Kingdom Park at Walt Disney World, beginning on October 1, 1991. The new parade was designed so the old Main Street Electrical Parade could be sent to Disneyland Paris. SpectroMagic differs from the Electrical Parade in that there is increased use of fiber optics and there are a number of newly created characters. It ended its run on May 22, 1999, for the Main Street Electrical Parade, and then returned on March 26, 2001.

Spellbinder (television) Polish-born Australian actors Zybch Trofimiuk and Gosia Piotrowska star as Paul Reynolds and Riana in this 26-episode Disney Channel series that began airing on February 5, 1996. A mischievous student, Paul, involved in a prank, interacts with a solar eclipse, a strange electrical storm, and a mysterious magnetic field, and finds himself transported into another dimension. Lost in this parallel world, he discovers people living in a time when the industrial revolution did not occur, exploited by a ruthless elite called Spellbinders. With the help of the resourceful and strong-willed Riana, Paul attempts to outwit the Spellbinders and return to his world. Also stars Brian Rooney (Alex), Michela Noonan (Katrina).

Spencer, Fred (1904–1938) Animator; helped create the characters of Donald Duck and Dopey. He was known as one of the best animators on Donald Duck. He was hired by Disney in 1931 and worked at the Studio until he was killed in a car accident in 1938.

Spider and the Fly, The (film) Silly Symphony cartoon; released on October 23, 1931. Directed by Wilfred Jackson. To defend themselves from a hungry spider, flies enlist all of their kin, including horseflies and dragonflies. In the battle, a boy fly manages to save a captured girl fly and the spider is caught on flypaper.

Spies (television) A Disney Channel Premiere Film; first aired on March 7, 1993. In 1942, 12-year-old Harry Prescott, who has lost his brother in wartime service, and Harry's English refugee pal stumble upon a Nazi plot to assassinate President Franklin D. Roosevelt—but no one will listen to them. Shiloh Strong (Harry Prescott), David Dukes (Robert Prescott), Cloris Leachman (Pamela Beale). 88 min. Filmed aboard the USS *North Carolina.* Directed by Kevin Connor.

Spike See Buzz-Buzz.

Spin and Marty See *The Adventures of Spin and Marty* and *The New Adventures of Spin and Marty: Suspect Behavior.*

Spirit of Aloha Dinner Show See Polynesian Revue.

Spirit of '43, The (film) A sequel to *The New Spirit,* made for the U.S. Treasury Department. Delivered on January 7, 1943. Directed by Jack King. Donald stars to teach the general public to be careful with their money and save it for increased income taxes needed to fight World War II.

Spirit of Pocahontas, The Stage show at the Fantasyland Theater at Disneyland; opened on June 23, 1995, and closed on September 4, 1997. Also played at Disney-MGM Studios, where it closed February 24, 1996.

Spirited Away (film) A ten-year-old girl, Chihiro, discovers a secret world when she and her family get lost and venture through a hillside tunnel. When her parents undergo a mysterious transformation, Chihiro must fend for herself as she encounters strange spirits, assorted creatures, and a grumpy sorceress who seeks to prevent her from returning to the human world. Directed by Hayao Miyazaki. Limited North American release on September 20, 2002, with an expanded release on September 27. 125 min. Produced by Studio Ghibli in Japan; John Lasseter of Pixar supervised the dubbed version for American audiences. Voices include Daveigh Chase (Chihiro), Suzanne Pleshette (Yubaba, Zeniba), Jason Marsden (Haku), Susan Egan (Lin), David Ogden Stiers (Kamaji), Lauren Holly (Chihiro's mother), Michael Chiklin (Chihiro's father), John Ratzenberger (Assistant Manager), Tara Strong (Boh). Originally released in Japan on July 20, 2001, as *Sen to Chihiro no kamikakushi.* The film was the highest-grossing film in Japan in 2001. It won the Academy Award as Best Animated Feature. Released on video in 2003.

Splash (film) Allen Bauer discovers a mermaid, whom he had originally seen as a child, at Cape Cod. She goes to New York to find him, and on land, her tail transforms into legs. Allen and the mermaid, who calls herself Madison, fall in love, and he tries to teach her the ways of human life. Scientists capture Madison, but she is saved by Allen and his philandering brother, Freddie. Allen and Madison finally elude their captors by leaping into the ocean. Released on March 9, 1984. The first Touchstone film. Directed by Ron Howard. 110 min. Stars Tom Hanks (Allen Bauer), Daryl Hannah (Madison), Eugene Levy (Walter Kornbluth), John Candy (Freddie Bauer), Dody Goodman (Mrs. Stimler), Shecky Greene (Mr. Buyrite), Richard B. Shull (Dr.

Ross), Bobby Di Cicco (Jerry), Howard Morris (Dr. Zidell), Tony Di Benedetto (Tim). The production took 17 days of principal photography on location in New York City, filming at such landmarks as the Statue of Liberty, the Museum of Natural History and its renowned whale room, Bloomingdale's department store, and Columbus Circle. When Rockefeller Center's ice skating rink closed prematurely for reconstruction, the production was granted permission to build a special rink and film in Central Park. The production then moved to Los Angeles for additional filming at locations throughout Southern California before traveling to the Bahamas for the underwater sequences. Producer Brian Grazer spent much of four years exploring various approaches to the undersea filming. He opted for the real thing, filming 50 feet down in the Caribbean waters surrounding the Bahamas. The actors received special training in diving and adapting to their confining locations. Each was required to swim from one safety diver to

another, through a shot, for their supply of air. Noted underwater cinematographer Jordan Klein storyboarded each frame of film they would be shooting. The director and producer were so pleased with Daryl Hannah's swimming that they allowed her to do all her own stunts. The film was nominated for an Academy Award for Best Screenplay Written Directly for the Screen. Released on video in 1984. The television sequel was *Splash, Too*.

Splash Mountain Critter Country flume attraction at Disneyland; opened on July 17, 1989. Based on animated sequences and characters from *Song of the South*. Many of the Audio-

Animatronics characters from the closed America Sings attraction were renovated and placed in Splash Mountain. Some new ones were added

also, namely Brer Bear, Brer Fox, and Brer Rabbit, making a total of 103. Guests travel through backwoods swamps and bayous in their hollowed-out log. The culmination is a high-speed 52-foot flume drop, at a 45-degree angle, which can almost assure the guests of getting splashed. At opening, it was the longest flume chute in the world. Disney designer Tony Baxter came up with the idea for the attraction while stuck in his car during rush-hour traffic in 1983. Also Frontierland attraction in Magic Kingdom Park at Walt Disney World opening on July 17, 1992; and in Critter Country at Tokyo Disneyland opening on October 1, 1992.

Splash, Too (television) Two-part television show; aired on May 1 and 8, 1988. Directed by Greg Antonacci. Sequel to the 1984 feature, with Allen and the mermaid, Madison, returning to New York to help Allen's brother, who is in danger of losing the family business. Madison plots to save a dolphin from the aquarium, when she discovers it is going to be used for scientific experiments. Stars Todd Waring, Amy Yasbeck, Donovan Scott, Rita Taggart, Noble Willingham, Dody Goodman, Joey Travolta. This was the first motion picture to film at the new Disney-MGM Studios in Florida.

Splashdown Photos Photo shop at Splash Mountain in Magic Kingdom Park at Walt Disney World; opened on June 1, 1993. The shop is the same as the Professor Barnaby Owl's Photography Studio at Disneyland.

Spoodles Restaurant at the BoardWalk Resort at Walt Disney World; opened July 1, 1996.

Spoon, Mickey Mouse See *William Rogers and Son*.

Spooner (television) An escaped convict starts a new life as a Texas high school English teacher and wrestling coach, attempting to turn a fledgling team into a championship squad. He tries to make a difference in the life of a tough juvenile delinquent and falls in love with a fellow teacher, all while trying to keep out of sight of pursuing lawmen. A Disney Channel Premiere Film; first aired on December 2, 1989. Directed by George Miller. Stars Robert Urich (Michael Gillette/Harry Spooner), Jane Kaczmarek (Gail), Brent Fraser (Shane). 98 min.

Spoonful of Sugar, A Song from *Mary Poppins*, sung by Julie Andrews; written by Richard M. Sherman and Robert B. Sherman.

Sport Goofy (television) Syndicated television specials; aired on May 21, September 16, and November 24, 1983. Also known as *Walt Disney's Mickey and Donald Present Sport Goofy.*

Sport Goofy in Soccermania See *An All New Adventure of Disney's Sport Goofy Featuring Sport Goofy in Soccermania.*

Sports End-Zone Food Court Located at the All-Star Sports Resort at Walt Disney World; opened in 1994.

Sports Night (television) Half-hour television series, debuting on ABC on September 22, 1998, which looks at the professional and personal lives of the people who produce a live, nightly cable sports-news show. It ended on May 16, 2000. Stars Josh Charles (Dan Rydell), Peter Krause (Casey McCall), Felicity Huffman (Dana Whitaker), Joshua Malina (Jeremy Goodwin), Sabrina Lloyd (Natalie Rosen), Robert Guillaume (Isaac Jaffee). Released on DVD in 2002.

Spot Marks the X (television) An adopted dog with a checkered past leads his new young owner on a wild chase after buried loot. A Disney Channel Premiere Film; first aired on October 18, 1986. Directed by Mark Rosman. 90 min. Stars Barret Oliver (Ken), Geoffrey Lewis (Dog Pound Attendant), Natalie Gregory (Kathy), David Huddleston (Ross), Mike the Dog (Capone).

Spottiswood, Greg Actor; appeared in *Looking for Miracles* on The Disney Channel, for which he won the Emmy Award in 1990 as Outstanding Performer in a Children's Special.

Spring Fling Entertainment event, first held at Disneyland on April 14, 1962, featuring top bands, and continuing for the next decade.

Springtime (film) Silly Symphony cartoon; released on October 24, 1929. Directed by Walt Disney. In the first of a series of Silly Symphonies based on the seasons, a fantasy of spring is portrayed through the lives of woodland creatures.

Springtime for Pluto (film) Pluto cartoon; released on June 23, 1944. The first cartoon directed by Charles Nichols. Pluto is awakened by the Spirit of Spring, which causes him to dance about, getting mixed up with angry bees and poison ivy. Out for revenge, he goes after the spirit.

Spy Hard (film) Dick Steele, Agent WD-40, is lured back to active service by the Agency's director as the only man who can stop the evil General Rancor. Rancor, a malevolent madman presumed dead after losing two limbs in an explosive altercation with Steele 15 years earlier, is alive. He's mad as hell—armless but still dangerous. Steele joins forces with the mysterious and beautiful Agent 3.14 to thwart his old nemesis's diabolical scheme for global power. Together they elude Rancor's henchmen, escape speeding vehicles, and evade kidnap attempts as they make their way to General Rancor's lair. A Hollywood Picture. Directed by Rick Friedberg. Released on May 24, 1996. Stars Leslie Nielsen (Steele), Andy Griffith (Rancor), Nicollette Sheridan (Agent 3.14), Charles Durning (Director), John Ales (Kabul), Barry Bostwick (Coleman). 81 min. Completely filmed in Los Angeles area locations. Released on video in 1996.

Spy in the Sky (television) Television show; aired on April 1, 1962. Directed by Harmon Jones and Ward Kimball. Walt Disney presents a preview of *Moon Pilot*, with some behind-the-scenes footage, and then shows *Eyes in Outer Space*.

Spybusters Alternate title of *The Secret of Boyne Castle*.

Spyglass Entertainment Successor company to Caravan Pictures, with Roger Birnbaum teaming up with Gary Barber. They had a co-financing and distribution deal with Disney, their first and biggest release being *The Sixth Sense*, with Bruce Willis, in 1999.

Squanto: A Warrior's Tale (film) Cultures collide when English explorers and traders sail to the New World and encounter the friendly native peoples of the land. But the wayfarers violate the Indians' trust by abducting two braves—Squanto and Epenow—whom they intend to take back to England to display as exotic examples of primitive life. Driven by a passion for freedom, Squanto makes a dramatic escape and, against nearly impossible odds, survives a long and perilous journey back to his homeland. Upon his return, however, he discovers that everything has changed during his absence—his noble tribe has been wiped out by disease and the Mayflower pilgrims have settled into what little remains of Squanto's village. Squanto must summon all he has learned over the course of his travels about goodwill and understanding if he is to survive.

And the colonists, unprepared for the struggle they face, must learn to trust Squanto, the only man who can help them survive and broker a peace that will enable them to coexist with the Native people. Released on October 28, 1994. Directed by Xavier Koller. 102 min. Stars Adam Beach (Squanto), Michael Gambon (Sir George), Nathaniel Parker (Thomas Dormer), Mandy Patinkin (Brother Daniel). Beach is one of the first Native American actors to have the lead in a major motion picture. Filmed on location in Canada, primarily at the restored Fortress of Louisbourg and elsewhere in Nova Scotia and in Quebec. Released on video in 1995.

Square Peg in a Round Hole, A (television) Television show; aired on March 3, 1963. Directed by Hamilton S. Luske. A later rerun was titled *Goofing Around with Donald Duck*. Ludwig Von Drake studies psychology this time, by looking at several Donald Duck and Goofy cartoons.

Squatter's Rights (film) Pluto cartoon; released on June 7, 1946. Directed by Jack Hannah. Chip and Dale battle Mickey and Pluto to keep an old stove as their home in a cabin Mickey is using for vacation. The chipmunks trick Mickey and Pluto into thinking Pluto has accidentally been shot. Nominated for an Academy Award.

S.S. Columbia Dining Room Restaurant on the third deck of the ocean liner docked in New York Harbor in the American Waterfront area of Tokyo DisneySea; opened on September 4, 2001. Guests find the service and quality of the dining experience just as it might have been on one of the great luxury liners of yesteryear during a transatlantic crossing.

Stacy, Michelle She voiced Penny in *The Rescuers*.

Stage Coach Frontierland attraction at Disneyland, from July 17, 1955 to February 1, 1956. It became Rainbow Mountain Stage Coaches, which operated until 1959. The stagecoaches were removed because the horses were spooked by the Disneyland Railroad trains that traveled nearby.

Stage Door Cafe Restaurant opened in Frontierland at Disneyland in September 1978. Formerly Oaks Tavern.

Staggs, Thomas O. He joined Disney in strategic planning in 1990 and was a key member of the team that put together the acquisition of Capital Cities/ABC. He was named executive vice president and chief financial officer of The Walt Disney Company in May 1998.

Stainton, David President of Walt Disney Animation, beginning in 2003. He had started with Disney in 1989, and in 2002 was named president of Walt Disney Television Animation.

Stakeout (film) Seattle detectives Chris Lecce and Bill Reimers pull an unwanted assignment— the nightshift stakeout of the home of an ex-girlfriend of a vicious escaped convict. Lecce becomes smitten by the object of their stakeout, Maria McGuire, and soon is bending rules and having dinner with her. Eventually the convict arrives, kidnaps Lecce and McGuire, and sets off a frantic chase. Released on August 5, 1987. Directed by John Badham. A Touchstone film. 117 min. Stars Richard Dreyfuss (Chris Lecce), Emilio Estevez (Bill Reimers), Madeleine Stowe (Maria McGuire), Aidan Quinn (Richard "Stick"

Mongomery). Filmed in and around Vancouver, British Columbia, Canada. Released on video in 1988. *Another Stakeout* was a sequel.

Stalling, Carl (1891–1972) Musician/composer; Walt Disney knew him in Kansas City in the 1920s when he was a theater organist. When Disney decided to add a sound track to *Steamboat Willie*, he turned to Stalling. Stalling came out to the Disney Studio beginning in 1928, and remained for a little over a year before beginning a long career in the animation department at Warner Bros. It was Stalling who gave Walt the idea for the Silly Symphony series.

Stallone, Sylvester Actor; appeared in *Oscar* (Angelo "Snaps" Provolone), *Judge Dredd* (Judge Dredd), and *An Alan Smithee Film: Burn Hollywood Burn* (as himself).

Stalmaster, Hal Actor; appeared in *Johnny Tremain* (Johnny), and on television in *The Swamp Fox* (Gwynn).

Stampede at Bitter Creek (film) Foreign theatrical compilation of *Texas John Slaughter* episodes. First released in Mexico in November 1962. 80 min. Stars Tom Tryon. Released on video in 1986.

Stamps The first Disney postage stamp was a 6-cent commemorative issued by the United States to honor Walt Disney on September 11, 1968. The stamp featured children from all over the world streaming from the Disneyland castle, along with a portrait of Disney. Designers were Bob Moore (castle and children) and Paul Wenzel (portrait). The first-day ceremonies were held in Marceline, Missouri. It was followed in 1971 by a set of ten stamps from the tiny Republic of San Marino. After some unauthorized Disney stamps from Persian Gulf shiekdoms in the 1970s (legal proceedings eventually stopped their distribution), in 1979 the Inter-Governmental Philatelic Corp. in New York was licensed to use Disney characters on the stamps that they produced for a number of small countries around the world. This created a whole new stamp collecting subfield, with special albums, newsletters, and catalogs created for those interested in the Disney stamps. In 2004, the U.S. Postal Service partnered with Disney for a series of "Art of Disney" Disney-themed 37-cent postage stamps. The first set of four sold more than 250 million stamps. A second set followed in 2005 and a third in 2006.

Stand by Me See *Disney's Timon and Pumbaa in Stand by Me.*

Stanley (television) Animated, interactive series on Disney Channel follows the adventures of six-year-old Stanley Griff, an extremely imaginative and creative little boy who is wild about animals. He loves to make simple drawings of his favorite animals and to do research using his *Great Big Book of Everything.* Premiered on September 15, 2001 with the last original episode airing on November 26, 2004. Voices include Jessica D. Stone (Stanley), Charles Shaughnessy (Dennis), Ari Myers (Mom), David Landsberg (Dad), Rene Mujica (Harry), Hynden Walch (Elsie).

Stanley, Helene (1928–1990) Actress; appeared in *Davy Crockett* (Polly Crockett). She was also the live-action model of Cinderella and Sleeping Beauty for the animators.

Stanton, Harry Dean Actor; appeared in *One Magic Christmas* (Gideon) and *The Straight Story* (Lyle Straight).

Stapleton, Maureen Actress; appeared in *Passed Away* (Mary Scanlan).

Star Command Suppliers Shop in Tomorrowland at Hong Kong Disneyland; opened on September 12, 2005.

Star Jets Tomorrowland attraction in Magic Kingdom Park at Walt Disney World; opened on November 28, 1974. Star Jets closed in 1994 and a new attraction, Astro Orbiter, was built as part of a general renovation of Tomorrowland. Also in Tomorrowland at Tokyo Disneyland as StarJets; opened on April 15, 1983. See Rocket Jets for the Disneyland attraction.

Star Today Program at Disney-MGM Studios where motion picture and television stars make personal appearances, participate in interviews, and put their handprints in the cement in front of the Chinese Theater.

Star Tours Tomorrowland attraction at Disneyland, created in cooperation with George Lucas; opened on January 9, 1987. Opened at Disney-MGM Studios on December 15, 1989, and on July 12, 1989, in Tomorrowland at Tokyo Disneyland. Also in Discoveryland in Disneyland Paris; opened on April 12, 1992. Guests travel in vehicles called StarSpeeders, each holding 40 passengers, to the Moon of Endor and beyond. In the pre-show area, one can watch R2-D2 and C-3PO from the *Star Wars* films working to service the fleet of StarSpeeders. The voice of the trainee pilot, REX, is provided by Paul Reubens.

Star Traders Large souvenir shop in Tomorrowland at Disneyland; opened on November 21, 1986. Formerly The Character Shop.

Starcade Video arcade in Tomorrowland at Disneyland; opened on May 4, 1977. Originally covered two floors, with an escalator taking guests to the upper level, but now uses only the lower level. Also in Tomorrowland at Tokyo Disneyland; opened on April 15, 1983.

Stargate Fast-food facility in Communicore East at Epcot, from October 1, 1982 to April 10, 1994. It later became Electric Umbrella.

Starliner Diner Counter-service restaurant in Tomorrowland at Hong Kong Disneyland; opened on September 12, 2005. It features American-style cuisine.

Starring Rolls Café Food facility on Hollywood Blvd. at Disney-MGM Studios; opened on May 1, 1989.

Starship Troopers (film) A handful of dedicated young soldiers must rise to the challenge of intergalactic warfare against a species of terrifying giant alien insects that threaten to eliminate the human race. Johnny Rico, a Mobile Infantry squad leader, who is disillusioned and about to resign, finds his home city attacked and destroyed, so he determines to remain in the Mobile Infantry and fight to destroy the insect threat to human civilization. A co-production of Tristar and Touchstone Pictures, distributed abroad by Buena Vista International. Released in the U.S. on November 7, 1997. Directed by Paul Verhoeven. Stars Casper Van Dien (Johnny Rico), Dina Meyer (Dizzy Flores), Denise Richards (Carmen Ibanez), Jake Busey (Ace Levy), Neil Patrick Harris (Carl Jenkins), Michael Ironside (Jean Rasczak). 129 min. From the novel by Robert A. Heinlein.

STAT (television) Television series; aired on ABC from April 16 to May 21, 1991. Irreverent, frenetic, and wildly comic, the show takes a look at life in a big-city trauma center staffed by highly skilled, fiercely dedicated nurses and doctors whose offbeat senses of humor are often their only weapon against the struggle to save lives. Stars Dennis Boutsikaris (Dr. Tony Menzies), Alison LaPlaca (Dr. Elizabeth Newberry), Casey Biggs (Dr. Lewis Droniger), Alex Elias (Jeanette Lemp).

State Fair Entertainment spectacular at Disneyland in the fall of 1987 and 1988. Fair-style game and food booths were set up around the hub, and there were displays of quilts and other homemade items. There was a "Come to the Fair" parade, along with pig races and thrilling daredevil feats.

States' Rights (film) Educational film in the History Alive! series, produced by Turnley Walker; released in 1972. The film documents Andrew Jackson's fight with John C. Calhoun over a tariff law in 1832.

Steakhouse, The Restaurant in Disney Village at Disneyland Paris; opened on April 12, 1992.

Steamboat Ventures Venture capital arm of The Walt Disney Company, formed in September 2000, to invest in early to mid-stage technology-focused companies that are pursuing opportunities in emerging media and entertainment markets.

Steamboat Willie (film) The first Mickey Mouse cartoon released, and the first cartoon with synchronized sound. Directed by Walt Disney. After unsuccessfully trying to make a deal to record through RCA or Western Electric, Disney contracted with the bootleg Powers Cinephone process and, after an initial disastrous recording session, finally recorded the sound track with a 15-piece band and his own squeaks for Mickey. Released at the Colony Theater in New York on November 18, 1928, the date used for the birth of Mickey Mouse. As a mischievous deckhand on a riverboat, Mickey, to Minnie's delight, plays "Turkey in the Straw" utilizing an animal menagerie as his instruments. The tyrannical Captain Pete is not amused, and Mickey ends up peeling potatoes in the galley. Later released on the 16mm compilation *Milestones in Animation* (1973).

Steel and America (film) Donald Duck stars in this educational film telling the story of steel from the ore to the finished product, along with its effect on America's growth and economy, produced for the American Iron & Steel Institute. Released on 16mm in 1965. Revised version released in 1974 as *Steel and America—A New Look.*

Steel Chariots (television) One-hour pilot, airing on the Fox network on September 23, 1997. A high school drama set at a NASCAR stock car race track. Directed by Tommy Lee Wallace. Stars John Beck (Dale), Ben Browder (DJ), Scott Gurney (Brett), Heidi Mark (Amber), Kathleen Nolan (Ethyl), Heather Stephens (Josie), Randy Travis (Jones), Brian Van Holt (Franklin).

Steele, Tommy Actor; appeared in *The Happiest Millionaire* (John Lawless).

Steenburgen, Mary Actress; appeared in *One Magic Christmas* (Ginny Grainger), *Powder* (Jessie), *Nixon* (Hannah Nixon), and *Hope Springs* (Joanie Fisher).

Steeplechase, The (film) Mickey Mouse cartoon; released on September 30, 1933. Directed by Burt Gillett. Mickey is a jockey getting ready for the big race when he finds his horse is drunk.

Swiftly he has two stable boys dress up in a horse costume and manages to win the race with the aid of angry hornets.

Steiner, Ronnie Mouseketeer from the 1950s television show.

Stella (film) Fiercely independent Stella, a wisecracking bartender, refuses to marry the doctor, Stephen Dallas, who gets her pregnant. Instead she decides to raise their daughter, Jenny, single-handedly. Through the years, Stella and Jenny share a special bond of friendship, but as Jenny blooms into a precocious young woman, Stella is confronted with the reality of their lower-class existence. Realizing that Jenny's wealthy father could offer Jenny a much better life, Stella decides to make the ultimate sacrifice in order to give her daughter the life she never had. Released on February 2, 1990. Directed by John Erman. A Touchstone film, in association with the Samuel Goldwyn Company. 106 min. Stars Bette Midler

(Stella Claire), John Goodman (Ed Munn), Trini Alvarado (Jenny Claire), Stephen Collins (Stephen Dallas). Based on the novel *Stella Dallas* by Olive Higgins Prouty. A remake of two previous Samuel Goldwyn films (in 1925 and 1937, the latter the classic starring Barbara Stanwyck and Anne Shirley). Filmed on location in Toronto; Boca Raton, Florida; and New York City. Released on video in 1990.

Stephanie Miller Show, The (television) Syndicated television talk show, beginning on September 15, 1995, and ending January 20, 1996.

Stephen King's Kingdom Hospital (television) Drama series on ABC, debuting on March 3, 2004, and ending July 15, 2004. A hospital built on the exact site of the Gates Falls Mills, where a mysterious fire killed scores of children laboring in the basement in 1869, seems to be haunted. Certain patients hear the tortured sounds of a little girl crying in the elevator shaft. The hospital staff, trained as rational scientists, dismiss the report of ghosts as foolish superstition, but do so at their own peril. Stars Andrew McCarthy (Dr. Hook), Bruce Davison (Dr. Stegman), Ed Begley, Jr. (Dr. Jesse James). Based on the Danish mini-series *Riget*. From Sony Pictures/Touchstone Television.

Stepparents: Where Is the Love? (film) Educational film, using sequences from the television show *Smoke*. In the Questions!/Answers? series; released in October 1975. The film depicts the adjustments and understanding needed to build a positive stepfamily relationship.

Steps Toward Maturity and Health (film) Educational film, made for Upjohn's Triangle of Health series; released in June 1968. Tracing human life from birth to adolescence, the film shows how a sound mind, a sound body, and social adjustment form the Triangle of Health.

Stepsister from Planet Weird (television) A Disney Channel Original Movie, debuting on

June 17, 2000. Fourteen-year-old Megan Larsen is stunned to discover that her mother's exuberant new fiancé and his seemingly perfect daughter are actually aliens who have taken sanctuary on Earth. Directed by Steve Boyum. Stars Courtnee Draper (Megan Larsen), Tamara Hope (Ariel Cola), Khrystyne Haje (Kathy Larson), Lance Guest (Cosmo Cola), Myles Jeffrey (Trevor Larson). Based on the book by Frances Lantz.

Stepsisters Anastasia and Drizella made life difficult for Cinderella; voiced by Lucille Bliss and Rhoda Williams.

Stern, Daniel Actor, appeared in *Celtic Pride* (Mike O'Hara) and *D.O.A.* (Hal Petersham), and on television in *Tourist Trap* (George Piper) and *Regular Joe* (Joe Binder).

Stern, Robert A. M. Architect; designed the Yacht and Beach Club Resorts at Walt Disney World and the Hotel Cheyenne and the Newport Bay Club at Disneyland Resort Paris. He was named to the board of directors of The Walt Disney Company in 1992. He designed the new animation building at the Disney Studio that opened in December 1994.

Steven Banks Show, The (television) Unsold pilot for a cable television series; reality and fantasy merge in this comedy about a bachelor copywriter's life at work and at home. First aired on Showtime on January 12, 1991. Directed by Tom McLoughlin. 30 min. Stars Steven Banks, David Byrd, Signy Coleman, Alex Nevil.

Stevens, Art Co-director, with Woolie Reitherman and John Lounsbery, of *The Rescuers*, and producer and co-director of *The Fox and the Hound*, he had started at the studio in 1939 and among other films received credit as an animator on *Peter Pan*, *One Hundred and One Dalmatians*, *Bedknobs and Broomsticks*, *Robin Hood*, and *The Many Adventures of Winnie the Pooh*. He contributed story concepts and animation to the *Man in Space* films for television in the 1950s. He retired in 1983.

Stevens, Fisher Actor; appeared in *My Science Project* (Vince Latello), *The Marrying Man* (Sammy), and *Super Mario Bros.* (Iggy).

Stevenson, Robert (1905–1986) Extremely prolific and successful director of Disney live-action films, including some of the most popular box-office hits—*Johnny Tremain*, *Old Yeller*, *Darby O'Gill and the Little People*, *Kidnapped*, *The Absent-Minded Professor*, *In Search of the Castaways*, *Son of Flubber*, *The Misadventures of Merlin Jones*, *Mary Poppins*, *The Monkey's Uncle*, *That Darn Cat!*, *The Gnome-mobile*, *Blackbeard's Ghost*, *The Love Bug*, *Bedknobs and Broomsticks*, *Herbie Rides Again*, *The Island at the Top of the World*, *One of Our Dinosaurs Is Missing*, *The Shaggy D.A.* In 1977 he was labeled "the most commercially successful director in the history of films" by *Variety*. He was named a Disney Legend in 2002.

Stewart, Nicodemus (1910–2000) He voiced Brer Bear in *Song of the South*.

Stick It (film) A Touchstone Picture in conjunction with Happy Landing Productions and Spyglass Entertainment. Directed by Jessica Bendinger. Stars Jeff Bridges, Missy Peregrym, Vanessa Lengies, Nikki Soohoo, Maddy Curley, Kellan Lutz, John Patrick Amendori, Jon Greis, Gia Carides. Filming began in June 2005 in Los Angeles.

Stiers, David Ogden Actor; narrated and voiced Cogsworth in *Beauty and the Beast*, and voiced Governor Ratcliffe and Wiggins in *Pocahontas* and the Archdeacon in *The Hunchback of Notre Dame*. He provided the voice for Mr. Jolly in *Teacher's Pet*, Fenton Q. Harcourt in *Atlantis*, Jumba in *Lilo & Stitch*, Kamaji in *Spirited Away*, and King Cole and Prime Minister in *The Cat that Looked at a King*. He also appeared in *Iron Will* (J. P. Harper), *Bad Company* (Judge Beach), *Jungle 2 Jungle* (Jovanovic), and *Krippendorf's Tribe* (Henry Spivey).

Still Not Quite Human (television) Further adventures of the teenage android, who first appeared in *Not Quite Human*. Chip discovers, after Dr. Carson's mysterious disappearance while attending a scientific conference, that something is now "not quite human" about his dad. A Disney Channel Premiere Film, first aired on May 31, 1992. Stars Jay Underwood (Chip), Alan Thicke (Dr. Carson). Directed by Eric Luke.

Still the Beaver (television) Series on The Disney Channel, premiering on November 7, 1984, which continued *Leave It to Beaver*. Barbara Billingsley (Mrs. Cleaver), Tony Dow (Wally), Ken Osmond (Eddie Haskell), and Jerry Mathers (the Beaver) all returned, with the addition of Janice Kent (Mary Ellen Rogers Cleaver), Kaleena Kiff (Kelly Cleaver), John Snee (Oliver Cleaver), Eric Osmond (Freddie Haskell), and Kipp Marcus (Kip Cleaver).

Still Waters (film) Educational film for teenagers about the effect of alcohol on family communication. 26 min. Released in January 1995.

Stitch! The Movie (film) Direct-to-video sequel to *Lilo & Stitch*, released on August 26, 2003. Stitch was Experiment 626; now 625 other alien experiments are landing on earth and it is up to Lilo and Stitch to rescue these outrageous cousins and change them from bad to good, before they are captured by evil captain Gantu. For example, Experiment 221 causes island-wide power surges and Experiment 625, a lazy yellow Stitch look-alike makes great sandwiches. Directed by Tony Craig and Roberts Gannaway. Voices include Daveigh Chase (Lilo), Tia Carrere (Nani), Zoe Caldwell (Grand Councilwoman), Ving Rhames (Cobra Bubbles), David Ogden Stiers (Jumba), Kevin MacDonald (Pleakley), Chris Sanders (Stitch).

Stitch's Great Escape Attraction in Tomorrowland at Magic Kingdom Park in Walt Disney World; opened November 16, 2004. Stitch has been captured by the Galactic Federation and Park guests are asked to provide security. They aren't very good security guards, and Stitch escapes. Replaced The ExtraTERRORestrial Alien Encounter.

Stock The first prospectus to sell Disney common stock was April 2, 1940. The stock was listed on the New York Stock Exchange on November 12, 1957.

Stockwell, Guy Actor; appeared on television in *The Ballad of Hector the Stowaway Dog.*

Stockwell, Harry (1902–1984) The voice of the Prince in *Snow White and the Seven Dwarfs.* He was the father of actors Guy and Dean Stockwell.

Stokowski, Leopold (1882–1977) Conductor of the Philadelphia Orchestra, selected by Walt Disney to conduct the music for *Fantasia.* He and his colleagues won a special Academy Award for their work on that film.

Stollery, David Actor; appeared in *Westward Ho the Wagons* (Dan Thompson) and *Ten Who Dared* (Andrew Hall). On television, he appeared as Joel Chandler Harris in *A Tribute to Joel Chandler Harris*, was Marty in the *Spin and Marty* serials, and appeared in the *Annette* serial on the *Mickey Mouse Club*. He provided a voice for *Boys of the Western Sea.*

Stone, Sharon Actress; appeared in *Last Dance* (Cindy Liggett) and *Cold Creek Manor* (Leah Tilson).

Stop that Tank (film) Humorous cartoon segment included in a wartime training film on the *Boys Anti-tank Rifle*, made for the National Film Board of Canada in 1942.

Storey, Margene Mouseketeer from the 1950s television show.

Storm Called Maria, A (television) Television show; aired on November 27, 1959. Directed by Ken Nelson. Covers the birth and development of a major storm in the Sierra Nevada Mountains, creating increasing danger for the people in the area, based on the book *Storm*, by George R. Stewart.

Stormalong Bay Unique swimming pool area at the Yacht and Beach Club Resorts at Walt Disney World, with meandering waterways, waterslides, and other fun activities for the aquatic-minded.

StormRider Attraction in the Port Discovery area of Tokyo DisneySea, opening on September 4, 2001. Aboard a new class of flying weather laboratory, guests join a mission and embark on a flight right into the middle of the storm of the century, experiencing a harrowing encounter with the forces of nature.

Storms (film) Educational film; released in March 1986. 14 min.

Stormy, the Thoroughbred with an Inferiority Complex (film) Featurette; released on March 12, 1954. Directed by Larry Lansburgh. 46 min. Stormy, a handsome colt with a famous bloodline, is sold to a cattle ranch when he misses his chance to be a glamorous race horse, but soon he accepts and enjoys his new life. He proves his thoroughbred training when  he is bought by a famous polo player and helps his master win a game. Lansburgh later produced many animal featurettes for the Studio.

Story Book Shop Located on Main Street at Disneyland, from July 17, 1955 to April 1995. Western Publishing Co., sponsor of this shop, was one of the few companies that invested in what was in 1955 thought to be Walt Disney's risky venture.

Story of Anyburg, U.S.A., The (film) Special cartoon; released on June 19, 1957. Directed by Clyde Geronimi. The problems of traffic are examined by the city of Anyburg in judicial court as several automobiles are tried for various crimes and declared "not guilty" since it is the people driving them who must admit their guilt and promise to drive carefully.

Story of Dogs, A (television) Television show; aired on December 1, 1954. Directed by Clyde Geronimi, C. August Nichols, and Robert Florey. A look behind the scenes at *Lady and the Tramp*, with information on the work of the animators, director, voice artists, background artists, inkers and painters, and camera operators, along with a group of Pluto cartoons.

Story of Donald Duck, The Alternate title of *The Donald Duck Story*.

Story of Menstruation, The (film) Educational film, made for International Cellucotton Co.; delivered on October 18, 1946. Through animation and diagrams, the film discusses the female reproductive organs and functions and follows development from babyhood to motherhood. A popular Disney film for girls in school for several decades.

Story of Robin Hood and His Merrie Men, The (film) When King Richard the Lionhearted leaves England for the Crusades, his evil brother, Prince John, conspires for the throne with the Sheriff of Nottingham. But loyal Robin Hood and his followers defy them with the aid of Maid Marian, ward of King Richard, raising the ransom when the King is held prisoner in Germany. When Richard returns, he rewards Robin by making him earl of Locksley and giving him the hand of Maid Marian in marriage. Released on June 26, 1952. Directed by Ken Annakin. 84 min. Stars Richard Todd as Robin, Joan Rice as Maid Marian, Peter Finch as the Sheriff, Hubert Gregg as Prince John, and Patrick Barr as King Richard. The second Disney fully live-action feature, produced at Denham Studios in England with blocked funds that Walt Disney had been unable to get out of the country. Early plans had called for the film to be cast with actors from *Treasure Island*, including Bobby Driscoll as a member of Robin's band and Robert Newton as Friar Tuck. Released on video in 1987 and 1992. See also *Robin Hood* (the title of the 1973 animated film).

Story of the Animated Drawing, The (television) Television show; aired on November 30, 1955. Directed by Wilfred Jackson and William Beaudine. Walt discusses the history of animation, beginning with J. Stuart Blackton and his *Humorous Phases of Funny Faces* in 1906, and including *Gertie the Dinosaur* (Winsor McCay). Disney composer Oliver Wallace, who at one time accompanied silent films on the organ in movie theaters, re-creates a scene featuring a Koko the Clown cartoon.

Story of the Silly Symphony, The (television) Television show; aired on October 19, 1955. Directed by Clyde Geronimi. Walt Disney provides a look at some of the Silly Symphony cartoons, while explaining how newly learned techniques were later used by his artists on the animated features.

Storyboards Disney storyman Webb Smith is credited with coming up with the idea of storyboards in the early 1930s. These 4x8-foot boards had story sketches pinned up on them in order,

and the Disney artists found it much easier to visualize a story this way than to read a script. Since the 1930s, storyboards as invented at the Disney Studio have come into general usage throughout the motion-picture industry, especially for filmmakers planning commercials and action sequences of live-action films.

Storybook Land Canal Boats Fantasyland attraction at Disneyland; opened June 16, 1956. Formerly Canal Boats of the World (1955). Boats cruise past miniature scenes from Disney movies, from the homes of the Three Pigs to Geppetto's Village. Above on the hill is Cinderella Castle, with the pumpkin coach visible on its way up the winding road. In July 1994 the attraction was renovated, removing Toad Hall and adding Agrabah from *Aladdin* and scenes from *The Little Mermaid*. See *Le Pays de Contes de Fées* for the Disneyland Paris version.

Storybook Shoppe Store in Fantasyland at Hong Kong Disneyland; opened September 12, 2005.

Storybook Store, The Shop in World Bazaar at Tokyo Disneyland; opened April 15, 1983, and on Main Street in Disneyland Paris, opened on April 12, 1992.

Storybook Theater In Fantasyland at Hong Kong Disneyland; opened on September 12, 2005, with "The Golden Mickeys."

Stoyanov, Michael Actor; appeared on television in *Blossom* and *Exile*.

Straight Shooters (film) Donald Duck cartoon; released on April 18, 1947. Directed by Jack King. Don is a barker in a shooting gallery, where he has troubles with his nephews who retaliate for being cheated by him by dressing up first as a female duck and then a mummy to get the candy prizes.

Straight Story, The (film) Alvin Straight, a 73-year-old man with failing eyesight who uses two canes to walk, receives a call that his brother, Lyle, several hundred miles away, has suffered  a stroke. Without a driver's license, the eccentric Alvin sets out, at five miles an hour, to get to his brother aboard his 1966 John Deere lawn mower. On his difficult odyssey, Alvin encounters a number of strangers with whom he shares his life's earned wisdom in the form of simple stories, and has a profound impact on their lives. Released in New York, Los Angeles, and Chicago on October 15, 1999. Directed by David Lynch. Stars Richard Farnsworth (Alvin Straight), Sissy Spacek (Rose Straight), Harry Dean Stanton (Lyle Straight). 112 min. Filmed in CinemaScope. Based on the true story of Alvin Straight's 260-mile journey in 1994 from Laurens, Iowa, to Mt. Zion, Wisconsin, which was discovered by the producers in a *New York Times* article. They eventually filmed the story in the actual area where it had happened. The film was a hit at the 1999 Cannes Film Festival, and Richard Farnsworth received an Academy Award nomination as Best Actor. Released on video in 2000.

Straight Talk (film) Shirlee Kenyon, a small-town dance instructor, gets fired because she spends more time counseling her customers than teaching them to dance. She heads to Chicago to make a fresh start and gets a job as the receptionist at the WNDY radio station. While looking for the coffee room on a break, she is mistakenly identified as the station's new on-air radio psychologist. Her warm heart and common sense make her an instant celebrity, arousing the suspicions of news reporter Jack Russell, whose secret assignment is to woo her in order to discredit her in a newspaper exposé. The more Jack learns about Shirlee, the harder he falls for her charms, falls in love, and ultimately gives up the story. Released on April 3, 1992. Directed by Barnet Kellman. A Hollywood Picture. 90 min. Stars Dolly Parton (Shirlee), James Woods (Jack), Griffin Dunne (Alan), Michael Madsen (Steve). Filmed on location in Chicago and its environs. Released on video in 1992.

Strange Companions (television) A veteran bush pilot and an orphan stowaway crash in a dense Canadian forest, encounter many hardships, and are finally rescued many months later. Prepared for American television, but did not air. First aired in Canada on December 4, 1983. Directed by Frank Zuniga. Later shown on The Disney Channel. Stars Doug McClure (Archie), Michael Sharrett (David), Marj Dusay (Mae).

Strange Monster of Strawberry Cove, The (television) Two-part television show; aired on October 31 and November 7, 1971. Directed by Jack Shea. Three kids building a fake sea monster stumble upon a smuggling operation, but cannot get the sheriff to believe them, so they have to try to catch the smugglers themselves. Stars Burgess Meredith, Agnes Moorehead, Annie McEveety, Jimmy Bracken, Patrick Creamer, Larry D. Mann, Parley Baer, Skip Homeier, Bill Zuckert, Kelly Thordsen.

Stranger Among Us, A (film) Emily Eden is a New York City police detective absorbed by her career and emotionally detached from the violence she sees in daily life. Her routine investigation of a missing person report develops into a complex undercover murder case in the Hassidic Jewish community. She meets Ariel, a spiritual young man destined to be the community's next rabbi, and learns from him the centuries-old Jewish traditions while the two of them struggle with their growing but forbidden feelings for one another. With Ariel's help, Emily eventually solves the case of murder and diamond theft, and the two of them part ways—each with a better understanding of life and of their distinct worlds. Released on July 17, 1992. Directed by Sidney Lumet. A Hollywood Pictures film. 109 min. Stars Melanie Griffith (Emily Eden), Eric Thal (Ariel). Filmed on location in New York. Released on video in 1993.

Strassman, Marcia Actress; appeared in *Honey, I Shrunk the Kids* and *Honey, I Blew Up the Kid* (Diane Szalinski) and *Another Stakeout* (Pam O'Hara).

Streep, Meryl Actress; appeared in *Before and After* (Carolyn Ryan).

Street Safe, Street Smart (film) Educational film with Mickey and friends taking a close look at important street safety situations, in the Mickey's Safety Club series; released in September 1989. 13 min.

Streetmosphere At Disney-MGM Studios, actors on Hollywood Blvd. portray taxi cab drivers, policemen, starlets, casting directors, and avid autograph seekers to provide comic entertainment while one strolls down the street.

Stromboli Puppet-show proprietor in *Pinocchio*; voiced by Charles Judels.

Strongest Man in the World, The (film) Medfield College science student Dexter Riley eats a bowl of cereal accidentally containing a chemical compound he has been working on. He develops superhuman strength, which he mistakenly attributes to a vitamin formula devised by a fellow student. Two cereal companies compete for ownership of the secret ingredient and back a weight-lifting contest between Medfield and rival State College. Medfield is losing badly when Dexter realizes his compound, not the other student's, is the secret of his strength, and he leads his team to victory. Released on February 6, 1975. Directed by Vincent McEveety. 92 min. Stars Kurt Russell (Dexter), Joe Flynn (Dean Higgins), Eve Arden (Harriet), Cesar Romero (A.J. Arno), Phil Silvers (Krinkle), Dick Van Patten (Harry), Harold Gould (Dietz). The main building of Medfield College, the setting for numerous Disney movies, including *The Computer Wore Tennis Shoes* and *Now You See Him, Now You Don't*, was, in fact, the Animation Building on the Disney Studio lot in Burbank. Location shooting was done on this film in New Chinatown, Griffith Park, Echo Park, and the federal penitentiary, all in Los Angeles. Robert F. Brunner composed the music score, which included a running theme, called "Instant Muscle," featuring jazz and Oriental themes, as well as two school marching band songs. Released on video in 1998.

Stub, the Best Cowdog in the West (television) Television show; aired on December 8, 1974. Directed by Larry Lansburgh. A wild Brahma bull is endangering the herds, so a ranch owner and his daughter track him down. An Australian herding dog helps out, and years later its offspring are still active in the area. Stars Slim Pickens, Jay Sisler, Mike Hebert, Luann Beach. An updated version of the featurette *Cow Dog* (1956).

Stuck in the Suburbs (television) A Disney Channel Original Movie, premiering on July 16, 2004. Two tween girls are bored with their suburban lives until a famous pop singing/dancing sensation arrives in their area and his Personal Digital Assistant (PDA) falls into their hands. As they attempt to return it to him, the girls discover that the singing sensation's entire image is manufactured by his record company, despite his true artistic singer/songwriter style. When they set out to reveal his authentic persona, they discover that it doesn't matter where you live or what you do, as long as you are true to yourself and others.

Directed by Savage Steve Holland. Stars Danielle Panabaker (Brittany Aarons), Brenda Song (Natasha), Taran Killam (Jordan Cahill), Ryan Belleville (Eddie), Amanda Shaw (Kaylee), CiCi Hedgpeth (Ashley), Jennie Garland (Olivia), Kirsten Nelson (Susan Aarons), Todd Stashwick (Len), Corri English (Jessie Aarons), Ric Reitz (David Aarons). Filmed in and around New Orleans, Louisiana.

Student Exchange (television) Two-hour television show, aired on November 29 and December 6, 1987. Directed by Mollie Miller. Carol and Neil are nobodies, whom no one notices in their high school, but when they plot to exchange places with two arriving French and Italian exchange students who are suddenly transferred to another school, they take their school by storm and cause no end of trouble for the vice principal. Stars Viveka Davis (Carol/Simone), Todd Field (Neil/Adriano), Mitchell Anderson (Rod), Heather Graham (Dorie), Maura Tierney (Kathy), Gavin MacLeod (Dupiner).

Studio See Backlot, Walt Disney Studio.

Studio Catering Co. Food facility opened at Disney-MGM Studios on May 1, 1989. Snacks are available here, at the end of the Backstage Studio Tour tram excursion. Hosted by Coca-Cola.

Studio Pizzeria, The Restaurant opened at Disney-MGM Studios on June 15, 1991. The name changed in September 1991 to Mama Melrose's Ristorante Italiano.

Studio Showcase Attraction opened at Disney-MGM Studios on September 29, 1991. Shows props, costumes, and other memorabilia from today's biggest movies.

Studio Tram Tour—Behind the Magic Behind-the-scenes attraction at Walt Disney Studios Paris, featuring Catastrophe Canyon; opened March 16, 2002. See also Backstage Studio Tour.

Style and Substance (television) Half-hour television series, which debuted on CBS on January 5, 1998, and ended on September 9, 1998. Chelsea Stevens has written books and produced videotapes on home decorating and entertaining, and even has her own television show. She lives in an efficiently ordered world, totally oblivious to the chaotic and hysterical reality surrounding her. Jane Sokol comes onboard as the new manager of Chelsea's business enterprises, and they collide on an almost daily basis. Stars Jean Smart (Chelsea Stevens), Nancy McKeon (Jane Sokol), Heath Hyche (Terry), Linda Kash (Trudy), Joseph Maher (Mr. John), Alan Autry (Earl).

Submarine Voyage Tomorrowland attraction at Disneyland; opened June 6, 1959, and was dedicated on June 14. It closed on September 7, 1998. Billed as a voyage through "liquid space." New animation was added in 1961. Originally the eight submarines were painted gray, based on America's newest nuclear submarines, and named after them—*Nautilus*, *Seawolf*, *Skate*, *Skipjack*. The subs were 52 feet long and held a pilot and 38 passengers, each with a porthole for viewing the underwater wonders, from fish and mermaids to a giant sea serpent and the lost city of Atlantis. In the 1980s, the subs were repainted bright yellow to resemble scientific research vessels, and renamed. The Walt Disney World attraction was 20,000 Leagues Under the Sea, with subs patterned after Captain Nemo's *Nautilus*; it closed in 1994.

Suite Life of Zack & Cody, The (television) Comedy series debuting on Disney Channel on March 18, 2005. Twin 12-year-old boys, Zack and Cody, have a single mom who is a headlining singer at the Tipton, an upscale hotel in Boston. As part of her contract, she is given an upper-floor suite in the hotel, where the family lives. To the chagrin of the hotel manager, Mr. Moseby, the twins turn the hotel into their playground, and the staff and guests into unwitting participants in the outrageous situations they manage to create. Stars Cole Sprouse (Cody Martin), Dylan Sprouse (Zack Martin), Ashley Tinsdale (Maddie Fitzpatrick), Brenda Song (London Tipton), Phill Lewis (Mr. Moseby), Kim Rhodes (Carey Martin), Estelle Harris (Murielle), Adrian R'Mante

(Esteban). Also aired on *ABC Kids* beginning September 17, 2005.

Suited for the Sea (film) The evolution of dive-suit technology, from the early diving bell to the Deep Rover, for The Living Seas, Epcot; opened on January 15, 1986.

Sullivan, Bill ("Sully") He joined the staff at Disneyland in 1955, progressing from ticket taker to ride operator to operations supervisor. He assisted in the pageantry for the 1960 Olympic Winter Games in Squaw Valley and the Disney attractions for the New York World's Fair in 1964. Sullivan relocated to Florida to help open Walt Disney World and remained there as an executive in operations until his retirement in 1993. He was named a Disney Legend in 2005.

Sultan Ruler of Agrabah in *Aladdin*; voiced by Douglas Seale.

Sultan and the Rock Star (television) Television show; aired on April 20, 1980. Rerun as *The Hunter and the Rock Star*. Directed by Ed Abroms. A gentle tiger is taken to an island to become the object of a hunting party, but they don't reckon on a popular rock star escaping from his adoring public for a few days and helping the tiger. Stars Timothy Hutton, Ken Swofford, Bruce Glover, Ned Romero.

Summer (film) Silly Symphony cartoon; released on January 16, 1930. Directed by Ub Iwerks. In this summer fantasy, the woodland animals, bugs, and flowers celebrate the season.

Summer Magic (film) Based on the novel *Mother Carey's Chickens* by Kate Douglas Wiggin, which has become an American classic, the film tells the story of how the recently widowed Margaret Carey and her brood of three lively children, Nancy, Peter, and Gilly, left almost penniless when her late husband's investments prove worthless, leave their lovely Boston home to make a new life in a quaint rural town in Maine. Osh Popham, the local postmaster, sets them up in an empty home owned by the mysterious Mr. Hamilton, who turns up only to fall in love with Nancy. When their snobbish cousin, Julia, comes to visit, she too soon becomes one of the family, and falls in love with the new schoolteacher, Charles Bryan. Released on July 7, 1963. Directed by James Neilson. 109 min. Stars Hayley Mills (Nancy Carey), Burl Ives (Osh Popham), Dorothy McGuire (Margaret Carey), Deborah Walley (Julia), Eddie Hodges (Gilly), Jimmy Mathers (Peter), Peter Brown (Tom Hamilton). One of the earliest Disney "musicals," the film features songs written by Richard M. Sherman and Robert B. Sherman, highlighted by Burl Ives's rendition of "The Ugly Bug Ball." Other songs include "Flitterin'," "Beautiful Beulah," "Summer Magic," "The Pink of Perfection," "On the Front Porch," and "Femininity." Released on video in 1985.

Summer of Sam (film) During the summer of 1977, the serial killer dubbed the Son of Sam begins terrorizing New York City. With the media playing an integral role in creating mass fear and paranoia, the whole city becomes a hotbed of trepidation and panic. As the vicious murderer, preying on young women, stalks his way through the Italian-American section of the Bronx, a 32-year-old thug, Joey T., and his gang of flunkies begin a witch hunt for the murderer, obsessed with the idea that he is someone from "the neighborhood." Directed by Spike Lee. Released on July 2, 1999. Stars John Leguizamo (Vinny), Adrien Brody (Ritchie), Jennifer Esposito (Ruby), Ben Gazzara (Luigi), Bebe Neuwirth (Gloria), Patti LuPone (Helen), Anthony LaPaglia (Petrocelli), Mira Sorvino (Dionna), Michael Rispoli (Joey T.). 142 min. Released on video in 1999.

Summer of the Monkeys (film) Non-Disney film from Edge Productions released on video on December 18, 1998, as "Disney's Summer of the Monkeys" by Walt Disney Home Video. A 12-year-old boy tries to capture four runaway circus chimps for the reward money. Directed by Michael Anderson. Stars Michael Ontkean (John Lee), Leslie Hope (Sara Lee), Wilford Brimley (Grandpa), Corey Sevier (Jay Berry Lee). 101 min.

Sun Bank Building See Lake Buena Vista Office Plaza.

Sun Wheel Ferris wheel attraction at Paradise Pier at Disney's California Adventure; opened February 8, 2001. Huge A-frame struts hold a giant, 168-feet-in-diameter wheel that takes passengers for a ride in gondolas, some just swinging but others zigzagging toward the hub in a perpetual state of centrifugal excitement.

Sunday Drive (television) Two-hour television movie; aired on November 30, 1986. Two bored children, Christine and John, are mistakenly left behind at a restaurant while on a Sunday drive with their aunt and uncle, due to two identical cars. Everyone has a hassle trying to get back together. Stars Tony Randall, Ted Wass, Carrie Fisher, Audra Lindley, Claudia Cron, Norman Alden. Directed by Mark Cullingham.

Sunkist Citrus House Shop on Main Street at Disneyland, from July 31, 1960 to January 3, 1989. Originally took the place of Puffin Bakery; became Blue Ribbon Bakery.

Sunrise Terrace Restaurant Fast-food facility in Communicore West at Epcot; opened on October 23, 1982. Name changed to Pasta Piazza Ristorante in May 1994.

Sunset Boulevard Opened at Disney-MGM Studios in 1994. The street contains shops and eating facilities, and leads off of Hollywood Boulevard to the The Twilight Zone Tower of Terror and Rock 'N Roller Coaster.

Sunset Ranch Market Food area on Sunset Blvd. at Disney-MGM Studios, featur-

ing Anaheim Produce Company, Catalina Eddie's, Fairfax Fries, Hollywood Scoops, Rosie's All-American Café, and Toluca Legs Turkey Co. Opened in June 1994.

Sunshine Pavilion Adventureland attraction in Magic Kingdom Park at Walt Disney World; opened October 1, 1971. Originally sponsored by the Florida Citrus Growers. Also known as Tropical Serenade and The Enchanted Tiki Birds. The Florida equivalent of the Enchanted Tiki Room at Disneyland. Originally sponsored by the Florida Citrus Growers. It closed on September 1, 1997, for extensive renovations to the show, to reopen in the spring of 1998 as The Enchanted Tiki Room—Under New Management.

Sunshine Season Food Fair Fast-food court in The Land at Epcot; opened November 9, 1993. It was formerly called Farmers Market and after April 2005 known simply as Sunshine Season.

Super Duck Tales (television) Two-hour animated show, aired on March 26, 1989. Directed by James T. Walker. Scrooge McDuck's new accountant, Fenton Crackshell, becomes a superhero by means of a robotic suit. He fights the Beagle Boys' attempt to steal Scrooge's fortune by building a highway through the site of the money vault. The battle continues at the bottom of the sea and in outer space.

Super Goof He made his debut in *Donald Duck* comic no. 102 in July 1965, and had his own comic series from November of that year until 1972.

Super Mario Bros. (film) Brother plumbers Mario and Luigi enter a subterranean kingdom, a world of men evolved from dinosaurs, where they attempt to rescue a pretty college student with an interesting heritage from King Koopa, the sinister ruler of the underground. Released on May 28, 1993. Directed by Rocky Morton and Annabel Jankel. A Hollywood Pictures film. 104 min. Stars Bob Hoskins (Mario Mario), John Leguizamo (Luigi Mario), Dennis Hopper (King Koopa), Samantha Mathis (Daisy), Fisher Stevens (Iggy), Fiona Shaw (Lena), Richard Edson (Spike).

Based on the characters from the Nintendo video game. Filming took place in Wilmington, North Carolina. Released on video in 1993.

Super Robot Monkey Team Hyperforce Go! (television) A sci-fi anime adventure series in which a young teen named Chiro, teamed up with five high-tech cyborg monkeys, becomes the brave fighter, bold leader, and great hero he always wanted to be. Premiered on ABC Family in the Jetix programming block on September 18, 2004, and on Toon Disney on September 20. Voices include Greg Cipes (Chiro), Kevin Michael Richardson (Antauri), Kari Wahlgren (Nova), Corey Feldman (SPRX-77), Tom Kenny (Gibson), Clancy Brown (Otto), Mark Hamill (Skeleton King). The first original Jetix property from Walt Disney Television Animation. 26 episodes.

Supercalifragilisticexpialidocious Song from *Mary Poppins*; written by Richard M. Sherman and Robert B. Sherman.

Superdad (film) Successful lawyer Charlie McCready has big plans for his teenage daughter, Wendy: the right college, the right people, and Mr. Right for her perfect future. These plans do not include her current boyfriend, Bart. But the "generation gap" is happily closed when Charlie realizes his daughter will be happiest going to college with Bart and marrying him rather than going away to fashionable Huntington College with a stuffy law student or becoming engaged to the radical artist Klutch. Released in Los Angeles on December 14, 1973; general release on January 18, 1974. Directed by Vincent McEveety. 95 min. Stars Bob Crane (Charlie), Barbara Rush (Sue), Kurt Russell (Bart), Kathleen Cody (Wendy), Joe Flynn (Hershberger), B. Kirby, Jr. (Stanley Schlimmer), Joby Baker (Klutch), Dick Van Patten (Ira Kershaw), Nicholas Hammond (Roger Rhinehurst). The movie was filmed on the hills of San Francisco, along its famed Fisherman's Wharf, across the bay among the houseboats of Waldo Point in picturesque Sausalito, and at the Wedge at Newport Beach and the area's Back Bay. The church used for the wedding scene was the First Christian Church in Pasadena. The songs, written by Shane Tatum, are "These Are the Best Times," sung by Bobby Goldsboro, "Los Angeles," and "When I'm Near You." The former has become a perennially popular song for weddings, since it was used in the film's wedding scene. Released on video in 1985.

Superstar Goofy (television) Television show; aired on July 25, 1976. Features Goofy sports cartoons and tied in to the 1976 Olympics.

Superstar Limo Dark ride attraction at Hollywood Pictures Backlot at Disney's California Adventure; opened February 8, 2001, and closed January 11, 2002. Guests took a wild ride in purple limousines through Tinsel Town amid a sea of colorful signs, caricatures of real celebrities, and cartoonish Hollywood landmarks.

SuperStar Television Opened at Disney-MGM Studios on May 1, 1989. Audience members co-star in memorable scenes from such television shows as *I Love Lucy*, *Cheers*, *The Tonight Show*, *Gilligan's Island*, and *The Golden Girls*. Presented by Sony. It closed on September 26, 1998, to be replaced by Disney's Doug Live.

Supply (film) Educational film; from The People on Market Street series, produced by Terry Kahn; released in September 1977. The factors that influence supply are surveyed, as well as production costs and rate of production, using an ant farm as an example.

Surprise Celebration Parade Located in Magic Kingdom Park at Walt Disney World; beginning September 22, 1991, and ending June 4, 1994. Similar to the Party Gras parade at Disneyland.

Surprise Day Wednesday on the new *Mickey Mouse Club*.

Surreys Main Street vehicles at Disneyland in the early years. Eventually motorized vehicles took over everything except the horse-drawn streetcars.

Survival in Nature (television) Television show; aired on February 8, 1956. Directed by Winston Hibler. The show teaches about survival of the fittest in nature.

Survival of Sam the Pelican, The (television) Television show; aired on February 29, 1976. Directed by Roy Edward Disney. A listless teenager, Rick, gets a job helping with a survey of the pelican population in Florida; he finds an injured bird and nurses it back to health. Stars Kim Friese, Scott Lee, Bill DeHollander.

Susie Determined mother bird in *Wet Paint* (1946).

Susie, the Little Blue Coupe (film) Special cartoon; released on June 6, 1952. Directed by Clyde Geronimi. Susie, in an auto showroom, is bought by a man who takes good care of her, but as time passes she grows older and her owner

trades her in. She has a succession of unfortunate owners who mistreat her, and just as she is about to be abandoned in a junkyard, an eager young man buys her, tinkers with her, and soon has her running again.

Süssigkeiten Shop selling cookies, chocolates, and candies in Germany in World Showcase at Epcot, presented by Bahlsen of America, Inc. Opened October 1, 1982.

Sutherland, Donald Actor; appeared in *The Puppet Masters* (Andrew Nivens), *Shadow Con-*

spiracy (Conrad), and *Instinct* (Ben Hillard), and on television in *Commander in Chief* (Nathan Templeton).

Sutherland, Kiefer Actor; appeared in *The Three Musketeers* (Athos) and *Woman Wanted* (Wendall Goddard).

Sutherland, Mark Mouseketeer from the 1950s television show.

Swamp Fox (Episode 1), The: Birth of the Swamp Fox (television) Television show; aired on October 23, 1959. Directed by Harry Keller. The first episode telling the story of the patriot, Francis Marion, who fought the British using unusual methods during the Revolutionary War. Marion learns that the British are about to attack Charleston, and he helps by leading the governor and his party safely out of the city. Eluding Tarleton in the swamps, Marion becomes known as the Swamp Fox, as he works with a band of loyal colonists to save a group of captured patriots. Stars Leslie Nielsen, Joy Page, Tim Considine, John Sutton, Dick Foran, Patrick Macnee, Louise Beavers.

Swamp Fox (Episode 2), The: Brother Against Brother (television) Television show; aired on October 30, 1959. Directed by Harry Keller. The Tories stage raids against their patriot neighbors, but leave standing the Videaux mansion. Marion is enamored with Mary Videaux, even through her parents are Tory sympathizers, and he stops the patriots from taking revenge and burning her place when she agrees to provide valuable information. On hearing that Tarleton is about to transfer a group of American prisoners, Marion plots to free them. Stars Leslie Nielsen, Joy Page, John Sutton, Dick Foran, Richard Erdman, Tim Considine.

Swamp Fox (Episode 3), The: Tory Vengeance (television) Television show; aired on January 1, 1960. Directed by Louis King. Marion gathers information from informers, but the British begin to suspect his friend, Mary Videaux.

Marion's nephew, Gabe, joins the army, but he is captured, tortured, and eventually killed. Marion vows vengeance. Stars Leslie Nielsen, John Sutton, Henry Daniell, Barbara Eiler, Dick Foran, Tim Considine, Myron Healey.

Swamp Fox (Episode 4), The: Day of Reckoning (television) Television show; aired on January 8, 1960. Directed by Louis King. Marion vows revenge on the man, Amos Briggs, who killed his nephew, Gabe, and in searching for him, helps the patriots acquire some needed quinine from the British. Later, a boy, Gwynn, attacks Marion, believing he was responsible for killing his family, when it was really Briggs. Gwynn kills Briggs and later saves Marion's life. Stars Leslie Nielsen, John Sutton, Barbara Eiler, Henry Daniell, Rhys Williams, Slim Pickens, Hal Stalmaster. Stalmaster, who plays Gwynn, had starred as Johnny Tremain for Disney.

Swamp Fox (Episode 5), The: Redcoat Strategy (television) Television show; aired on January 15, 1960. Directed by Louis King. Marion captures a British colonel, and later battles Colonel Tarleton, who has orders to capture the Swamp Fox or else. Tarleton invades the Marion home, but the servants manage to outwit him. Stars Leslie Nielsen, Robert Douglas, John Sutton, Barbara Eiler, Myron Healey, Henry Daniell, Jordan Whitfield, Louise Beavers, Eleanor Audley.

Swamp Fox (Episode 6), The: A Case of Treason (television) Television show; aired on January 22, 1960. Directed by Louis King. Tarleton discovers Mary Videaux's spying and arrests her, hoping that Marion will try to rescue her. Using various ruses, Marion enters Charleston and shows up at a masked ball where Mary is in attendance, only to be captured himself. His men free him and Mary, and she sails for New Orleans and safety. Stars Leslie Nielsen, Robert Douglas, Barbara Eiler, John Sutton, Myron Healey, J. Pat O'Malley, Hal Stalmaster, Slim Pickens.

Swamp Fox (Episode 7), The: A Woman's Courage (television) Television show; aired on January 8, 1961. Directed by Lewis R. Foster. Marion and his men outwit the British forces, who follow them out of Charleston. Mary Videaux, hiding on a ship in Charleston harbor, discovers a ship full of prisoners and tries to help them, at great peril to herself. Stars Leslie Nielsen, Barbara Eiler, Arthur Hunnicutt, Sean McClory, J. Pat O'Malley, Jordan Whitfield.

Swamp Fox (Episode 8), The: Horses for Greene (television) Television show; aired on January 15, 1961. Directed by Lewis R. Foster. In the final episode, Marion plots to steal horses from the British, eventually getting them to stampede through the streets of Charleston. Stars Leslie Nielsen, Barbara Eiler, Arthur Hunnicutt, Ralph Clanton, J. Pat O'Malley, Jordan Whitfield, Slim Pickens.

Swayze, Patrick Actor; appeared in *Father Hood* (Jack Charles) and *Tall Tale* (Pecos Bill).

Sweatbox, The (film) Documentary about production problems during the making of *The Emperor's New Groove*. Directed by John-Paul Davidson and Trudie Styler. Produced by Xingu Films; distributed by Buena Vista Films. Premiered on September 13, 2002, at the Toronto Film Festival. 86 min., rated PG-13. Styler is the wife of Sting, who wrote the music for *The Emperor's New Groove*.

Sweeney, Anne Hired by Disney in 1996 to be president of The Disney Channel and executive vice president of Disney/ABC Cable Networks.

 She was promoted to president, Disney/ABC Cable Networks in 1998 and president, ABC Cable Networks Group/ Disney Channel Worldwide in 2000. In 2004 she became co-chairman of Disney Media Networks and president of Disney-ABC Television Group.

Sweeney, Bob (1918–1992) Actor; appeared in *Toby Tyler* (Harry Tupper), *Moon Pilot* (Senator McGuire), and *Son of Flubber* (Mr. Harker).

Sweeney, D.B. Actor; provided the voice of Aladar in *Dinosaurs*, and appeared in *Roommates* (Michael). He was a regular on *Life As We Know It* (Michael Whitman), and appeared on Disney Channel in *Going to the Mat* (Coach Rice).

Sweet Home Alabama (film) New York fashion designer Melanie Carmichael suddenly finds herself engaged to the city's most eligible bachelor. But Melanie's past holds many secrets, including Jake, the redneck husband she married in high school, who refuses to divorce her. Bound and determined to end their contentious relationship once and for all, Melanie sneaks back home to Alabama to confront her past. A Touchstone Picture. Released on September 27, 2002. Directed by Andy Tennant. Stars Reese Witherspoon (Melanie Carmichael), Fred Ward (Earl), Mary Kay Place (Pearl), Patrick Dempsey (Andrew), Josh Lucas (Jake), Jean Smart (Stella Kay), Candice Bergen (Kate), Ethan Embry (Bobby Ray). 109 min. Ethan Embry, as Ethan Randall, starred with Reese Witherspoon years earlier in *A Far Off Place*. The film crew was one of the few ever allowed to film in Tiffany & Co. in New York City. Filmed in CinemaScope. Released on video in 2003.

Swenson, Karl (1908–1978) He voiced Merlin in *The Sword in the Stone*, and appeared in *The Wild Country* (Jensen).

Swift, David (1919–2001) He initially worked for the Disney Studio in the 1930s, first as an office boy and then as an animator and assistant to Ward Kimball, but left in the 1940s, establishing himself in television directing the successful series *Mr. Peepers*. He returned as a director and screenwriter of *Pollyanna* and *The Parent Trap*.

Swing Kids (film) In 1939, German youths Peter and Thomas enjoy American swing music, despite its illegality under Hitler's regime. Hitler's harsh discipline, which crushes individuality, is sweeping Germany as the country prepares for full-scale war, and the two friends fight to remain loyal to their music. But soon Thomas is drawn into the Hitler Youth, absorbing Nazi principles and growing antagonistic toward his still independent friend Peter. A Nazi official takes an interest in Peter's family, and talks Peter into joining the Hitler Youth also. For a brief time, Peter and Thomas believe they can have it all—Hitler Youth by day and Swing Kids by night. When a mutual friend, Arvid, who has remained a rebel, commits suicide after being badly beaten by Nazis, Peter realizes he cannot live contrary to his conscience. He rebels and is arrested. Released on March 5, 1993. Directed by Thomas Carter. A Hollywood Picture. 114 min. Stars Christian Bale (Thomas), Robert Sean Leonard (Peter), Frank Whaley (Arvid), Barbara Hershey (Frau Muller). Musical score by James Horner. Kenneth Branagh played an uncredited role as the Nazi official. Since Germany has changed drastically over the years, the filmmakers turned instead to the Czech Republic, and filmed in a studio and on location in Prague. Released on video in 1993.

Swiss Family Robinson (film) The members of a Swiss family are the sole survivors of a shipwreck on an uncharted tropical island. With great courage and ingenuity, they use the salvage from the wreck to build a home in a huge tree, raise food, and protect themselves from a raiding band of pirates. The rescue of the granddaughter of a sea captain from pirates precipitates the ultimate attack by the buccaneers. The furious battle is almost won by the brigands when her grandfather's ship arrives and routs the attackers. The romance between the eldest Robinson boy and the granddaughter culminates in their marriage. The new couple and much of the family decide to stay on the island paradise, but scholarly brother Ernst decides to go back on the ship to civilization. Released on December 21, 1960. Directed by Ken Annakin. 126 min. Stars John Mills (Father), Dorothy McGuire (Mother), James MacArthur (Fritz), Tommy Kirk (Ernst), Kevin Corcoran (Francis), Janet Munro (Roberta), Sessue Hayakawa (Pirate Chief). The film was based on the book by Johann Wyss, written to preserve the tales he and his sons made up while imagining themselves in Robinson Crusoe's predicament. Not originally intended for publication, the narrative was later edited and illustrated by Wyss's descendants. Filmed on the Caribbean island of Tobago, the motion picture's lavish preproduction planning and on-location shooting (22 weeks) resulted in a budget that exceeded $4 million, but the extraordinary box office returns, subsequent popular reissues in 1969, 1972, 1975, 1981, and a release on home video in 1982 has made it one of Disney's top-grossing films. The creation of an intriguing tree house, matching the one in the movie, through which guests can climb in the Disney parks, has increased and perpetuated the popularity of the film.

Swiss Family Treehouse Adventureland attraction at Disneyland; opened on November 18, 1962. John Mills, daughter Hayley, and the rest of the family were there for the dedication with Walt Disney. Mills had starred in the Disney 1960 film *Swiss Family Robinson*. The tree has been called a *Disneyodendron semperflorens grandis* (translated as large ever-blooming Disney tree), and is entirely man-made. The roots are concrete and the limbs are steel, covered in concrete. The 300,000 plastic leaves all had to be attached by hand. The Swiss flag flies from the top of the tree house. This is one of the few Disneyland attractions where guests have to walk (or more appropriately, climb) through to view the rooms that the Robinson family built in the tree. A fascinating pulley system, using bamboo buckets and a waterwheel, provides water high up in the tree. It closed March 8, 1999, to become Tarzan's Treehouse. Also, an Adventureland attraction in Magic Kingdom Park at Walt Disney World; opened October 1, 1971. In Florida, the tree is known as a *Disneyodendron eximus* (or out-of-the-ordinary Disney tree). A Tokyo Disneyland version opened on July 21, 1993. See also *La Cabane des Robinson* for the Disneyland Paris version.

Swit, Loretta Actress; appeared on television in *14 Going on 30*.

Switching Goals (television) Two-hour television movie produced by Dualstar Productions and Warner Bros. Television for airing on *The Wonderful World of Disney* on May 26, 2002.

Twin sisters switch places on the soccer field to help their father's youth soccer team win the championship. Directed by David Steinberg. Stars Mary-Kate Olsen (Sam), Ashley Olsen (Emma), Eric Lutes (Jerry Stanton), Kathryn Greenwood (Denise), Trevor Blumas (Greg Jeffries).

Switzerland (film) People and Places featurette; released on June 16, 1955. Directed by Ben Sharpsteen. Filmed in CinemaScope. 33 min. The film visits cities and small towns of Switzerland to explore the local customs and activities during the seasons. The climax is a climb to the top of the Matterhorn with three mountaineers. Along with *Third Man on the Mountain*, it was this film that helped inspire Walt to build a Matterhorn at Disneyland.

Sword and the Rose, The (film) An adventure tale set in England during the reign of King Henry VIII. Charles Brandon, a handsome young commoner, becomes attached to the court and falls in love with the King's sister and political pawn, Mary Tudor. When Henry discovers this, Brandon is banished and Mary is sent off to marry the aging Louis of France, but when the French king dies, Mary extracts a promise from Henry to let her choose her second husband and she happily marries Brandon. Released on July 23, 1953. Directed by Ken Annakin. 92 min. Despite its historical inaccuracy, the film was a success due to the acting talents of Richard Todd (Charles Brandon), Glynis Johns (Mary Tudor), James Robertson Justice (Duke of Buckingham), Michael Gough (Louis VII), Jean Mercure (Louis VII), and the wizardry of over 60 matte paintings by Peter Ellenshaw that helped give the film the feel of Tudor England. It was the third and most elaborate of the Disney live-action features made in England to use up blocked funds that Disney could not take out of the country. It aired on television in 1956 as *When Knighthood Was in Flower*, the title of the book on which the film was based. Released on video in 1985 and 1993.

Sword in the Stone, The (film) An animated feature, set in the medieval era at a time when the English king dies leaving no heir. In the churchyard of a cathedral in London a sword appears imbedded in a stone, inscribed: "Who so pulleth out this sword of this stone and anvil is rightwise king born of England." Although many

try, no one can budge the sword from the stone. Deep in the dark woods, kindly but absent-minded Merlin the Magician begins to teach 11-year-old Arthur who is called "Wart" and who lives in the castle of Sir Ector where he is an apprentice squire to burly, oafish Sir Kay when he is not washing mounds of pots and pans in the scullery. By being changed by Merlin into various animals, Wart learns the basic truths of life, but he also runs into the evil Madam Mim, who tries to destroy him. Merlin and Mim have a Wizard's Duel during which each changes into various creatures, with Merlin using his wits to win. On New Year's Day a great tournament is held in London to pick a new king. Wart, attending as Kay's squire, forgets Kay's sword, and runs back to the inn to get it, but the inn is locked. Seeing the sword in the stone, Wart innocently, and easily, pulls it out. When the knights marvel at the wondrous sword, and question where he got it, Wart has to prove himself all over again, and again he pulls the sword from the stone. Wart is proclaimed king by the marveling warriors. Wart as King Arthur is apprehensive of his ability to govern, but Merlin returns to reassure him. Released on December 25, 1963. Directed by Wolfgang Reitherman. Based on a book by

T. H. White. 79 min. Features the voices of Ricky Sorensen (Wart), Sebastian Cabot (Narrator), Karl Swenson (Merlin), Junius Matthews (Archimedes), Norman Alden (Sir Kay), Martha Wentworth (Madam Mim, Granny Squirrel, Scullery Maid). The film marked Wolfgang Reitherman's first solo directorial effort for a feature film. The movie is somewhat dated, being filled with 1960s references, but it has some wonderful moments, especially the highly imaginative Wizard's Duel. The songs, including "A Most Befuddling Thing," "That's What Makes the World Go Round," "Higitus Figitus," and "The Legend of the Sword in the Stone," were written by Richard M. Sherman and Robert B. Sherman. The motion picture was re-released theatrically in 1972 and 1983, and inspired the Sword in the Stone ceremony at the Disney theme parks. Released on video in 1986.

Sword in the Stone Ceremony, The Merlin challenges young guests to pull the sword from the stone in regular presentations; in Fantasyland at Disneyland and in Magic Kingdom Park in Walt Disney World. Opened in California in 1983 and in Florida in 1994.

Sykes Villain in *Oliver & Company*; voiced by Robert Loggia.

Symbiosis (film) Film about the delicate balance between technological progress and environmental integrity, for The Land, Epcot; opened on October 1, 1982, and closed on January 1, 1995. Replaced by *Circle of Life*.

Symphony Hour (film) Mickey Mouse cartoon; released on March 20, 1942. Directed by Riley

Thomson. Mickey's radio orchestra is to present an interpretation of the "Light Cavalry Overture" when Goofy smashes the instruments in an elevator. Sponsor Pete's fury subsides when the rendition is a success due to Mickey's improvisation.

Symposium on Popular Songs, A (film) Special cartoon featurette; released on December 19, 1962. Directed by Bill Justice. Nominated for an Academy Award as Best Cartoon Short Subject. Ludwig Von Drake invites the audience into his home where he tells all about popular music, introducing several songs illustrated with stop-motion photography. 20 min.

T

Tag Team (television) Unsold pilot for a television series about a couple of ex-pro-wrestlers who become Los Angeles city cops; aired on ABC on January 26, 1991. Directed by Paul Krasny. 60 min. Stars Jesse Ventura, Roddy Piper, Phill Lewis.

Tahitian Terrace Adventureland restaurant at Disneyland; opened in June 1962. A Polynesian-themed show entertained diners. During construction, Walt Disney was a little dismayed by the short height of the man-made tree that forms the backdrop for the small stage. When his designers were baffled as to how to rectify the problem, Walt posed the obvious solution. Just slice the tree horizontally in the center, lift up the top, and add some more cement trunk. The designers were thinking of it as a real tree, and had been wondering how they could raise the entire thing. The restaurant closed on April 17, 1993, and replaced by Aladdin's Oasis. There is a Tahitian Terrace restaurant at Hong Kong Disneyland, serving South Asian and Cantonese cuisine; opened on September 12, 2005.

Takahashi, Masatomo (1913–2000) As president of the Oriental Land Co., he was instrumental in convincing Disney to build Tokyo Disneyland. He was named a Disney Legend at a special ceremony in Japan in 1998.

Take Down (film) A disillusioned teenager's bitterness and defeatism is turned around by the girl who loves him and the hopelessly overmatched high school wrestling team that only he can lead to victory. Not a Disney film, but a Buena Vista release of an American Film Consortium production in 1979. Directed by Kieth Merrill. Stars Edward Herrmann, Kathleen Lloyd, Lorenzo Lamas, Maureen McCormick, Nick Beauvy, Stephen Furst, Kevin Hooks. 107 min.

Take Flight See Delta Dreamflight.

Taking Care of Business (film) Petty criminal and Chicago Cubs fan Jimmy Dworski has won tickets to the World Series. The only obstacle standing in his way is that the game is scheduled for the day before he gets released on parole from prison. Scheming his way out early, he finds the lost daily planner of ultraorganized business executive Spencer Barnes, complete with credit cards, keys to a mansion, and everything he needs for an all-expenses-paid weekend of luxury. Spencer, meanwhile, is hopelessly lost without his organizer, not even being able to prove his identity, while Jimmy passes himself off as Spencer at important business meetings. After crossing paths and missing signals, the two men end up at the ball game together, having made discoveries about themselves. Released on August 17, 1990. Directed by Arthur Hiller. A Hollywood Pictures film. 108 min. Stars James Belushi (Jimmy), Charles Grodin (Spencer), Anne DeSalvo (Debbie), Mako (Sakamoto), Veronica Hamel (Elizabeth), Hector Elizondo (Warden). Filmed at various locations around the Los Angeles area. Released on video in 1991.

Tale of Two Critters, A (film) Featurette about a bear cub and a young raccoon accidentally thrown together who become friends; released on June 22, 1977, on a bill with *The Rescuers*. 48 min. Released on video in 1982.

Tale Spin (television) Animated television series; premiered on May 5, 1990, on The Disney Channel and syndicated beginning September 10, 1990, and ending September 2, 1994. Ace cargo pilot Baloo is teamed with feisty Kit Cloudkicker, pitted against a band of air pirates led by Don Karnage. Louie the ape is a music-loving nightclub owner. They find mystery, intrigue, and humor in the exotic setting of Cape Suzette, a huge, bustling city in a tropic zone. Voices include Ed Gilbert (Baloo), Sally Struthers (Rebecca Cunningham), Jim Cummings (Louie, Don Karnage), Pat Fraley (Wildcat), Tony Jay (Shere Khan), R. J. Williams (Kit). The theme song was written by Michael and Patty Silversher. 65 episodes. A syndicated television special serving as a preview to the series was *Disney's Tale Spin: Plunder and Lightning*; aired on September 7, 1990.

Talent Roundup Day Friday on the 1950s *Mickey Mouse Club*. The Mouseketeers wore Western outfits.

Tales of Texas John Slaughter, The See *Texas John Slaughter*.

Tales of the Apple Dumpling Gang (television) Television show; aired on January 16, 1982. Directed by E. W. Swackhamer. Remake of the 1975 feature *The Apple Dumpling Gang*, used as a pilot for a series. The resulting limited series had a different cast, and was titled *Gun Shy*. Russell Donavan in Quake City becomes the unwilling guardian of two children, Clovis and Celia. Stars John Bennett Perry, Sandra Kearns, Ed Begley Jr., Henry Jones, Arte Johnson, Keith Mitchell, Sara Abeles, William Smith.

Taliaferro, Al (1905–1969) Comic strip artist; joined Disney in 1931 as an assistant to Floyd Gottfredson on the Mickey Mouse comic strip, and then worked on the Silly Symphonies Sunday comic page. He originated the Donald Duck daily strip in February 1938, and the Sunday page in December 1939, and continued with these two for three decades. He was named a Disney Legend posthumously in 2003.

Talk to Me (television) Ensemble comedy series premiering on ABC on April 11, 2000, and ending after three episodes on April 25, about the life of Janey Munro, a successful radio talk show host in New York. Stars Kyra Sedgwick (Janey Munro), Beverly D'Angelo (Dr. Debra), David Newsom (Rob), Nicole Sullivan (Kat), Peter Jacobson (Sandy), Max Baker (Marshall), Michael J. Estime (Cam).

Tall Tale (film) A strong-willed boy conjures up a trio of legendary Old West characters—John Henry, Paul Bunyan, and Pecos Bill—to help him save the family farm and their entire way of life on the American frontier. With the help of his larger-than-life pals and a steadfast determination, the boy heroically confronts the archetypal bad guy, J.P. Stiles, to achieve the impossible. Released on March 24, 1995. Directed by Jeremiah Chechik. In association with Caravan Pictures. Stars Scott Glenn (J.P. Stiles), Oliver Platt (Paul Bunyan), Stephen Lang (Jonas Hackett), Roger Aaron Brown (John Henry), Nick Stahl (Daniel Hackett), Catherine O'Hara (Calamity Jane), Patrick Swayze (Pecos Bill). Filmed in CinemaScope. 96 min. Locations throughout the West included the Roaring Fork Valley of Colorado, Monument Valley in Utah, Lake Powell and Glen Canyon in Arizona, and Death Valley in California. Released on video in 1995. Advertised with the title: *Tall Tale: The Unbelievable Adventures of Pecos Bill*.

Tall Timber (film) Oswald the Lucky Rabbit cartoon; released on July 9, 1928.

Tally Ho (television) Television show; part 2 of *The Horsemasters*.

Tamblyn, Russ Actor; appeared in *Cabin Boy* (Chocki).

Tamiroff, Akim (1899–1972) Actor; appeared in *Lt. Robin Crusoe, USN* (Tanamashu).

Tandy, Jessica (1909–1994) Actress; appeared in *The Light in the Forest* (Myra Butler).

Tangaroa Terrace Restaurant in the Polynesian Village Resort at Walt Disney World; closed in June 1996.

Taran Boy pig-keeper in *The Black Cauldron*; voiced by Grant Bardsley.

Tarzan (film) From the classic tale by Edgar Rice Burroughs, this animated feature traces the story of a baby who is orphaned in the African jungle and raised by a family of gorillas, led by Kerchak and his mate, Kala. Tarzan matures into a young man with all the instincts of a jungle animal and the physical prowess of an athletic superstar, befriending a garrulous gorilla named Terk and a neurotic elephant named Tantor. He is even able to use his cunning and strength to defeat the bloodthirsty leopard, Sabor, who had killed his parents. But Tarzan's peaceful and sheltered world is turned upside down by the arrival of a human expedition, led by an arrogant adventurer, Clayton, and including Professor Porter, a noted authority on gorillas, and his dynamic and beautiful daughter, Jane. Tarzan spies on them, and soon comes to the revelation that he is one of them. As he struggles to decide which "family" he belongs with, his dilemma is further complicated by his feelings for Jane and the discovery that Clayton is plotting to harm the gorillas. Directed by Chris Buck, Kevin Lima. General

release on June 18, 1999, after a world premiere at the El Capitan Theater in Hollywood on June 12 and a limited release in that theater only beginning on June 16. (The film began its run in

Malaysia, Singapore, and Israel on June 17.) Voices include Tony Goldwyn (Tarzan), Glenn Close (Kala), Rosie O'Donnell (Terk), Minnie Driver (Jane), Nigel Hawthorne (Prof. Porter), Brian Blessed (Clayton), Wayne Knight (Tantor), Alex D. Linz (young Tarzan), Lance Henriksen (Kerchak). 88 min. Includes five songs by Phil Collins (singing four of them himself—"Two Worlds," "You'll Be in My Heart," "Son of Man," and "Strangers Like Me") and a score by Mark Mancina. "You'll Be in My Heart" won the Oscar for Best Song. Disney also received an Academy Award in 2003 for the Deep Canvas software that enabled dimensional effects. Animator Glen Keane designed the character of Tarzan, drawing inspiration for Tarzan's persona from his teenage son, Max, who loved performing fearless skateboarding stunts and watching extreme sports, such as snowboarding. Thus, Tarzan seems to "surf" through the trees. The directors and artistic supervisors received inspiration by taking an African safari to study the jungles, the animal reserves, and the domain of the mountain gorillas first hand. Released on video in 2000. There was also a television series, *The Legend of Tarzan*, and a video sequel, *Tarzan II*. A stage production, *Disney Presents Tarzan,* is planned for Broadway in 2006 with previews beginning March 24 at the Richard Rodgers Theater leading up to an official opening on May 10. Book is by David Henry Hwang with Bob Crowley as director as well as set and costume designer.

Tarzan and Jane (film) A direct-to-video release on July 23, 2002. As Tarzan and Jane's one-year marriage anniversary approaches, Jane searches the jungle for the perfect gift for Tarzan, enlisting the help of Terk and Tantor. As they recall the many adventures they have shared so far, Jane realizes what an exciting year it has been in the jungle. But Tarzan also has a surprise for Jane that will show her just how much he understands her world. Supervising director Steve Loter. Voices include Michael T. Weiss (Tarzan), Olivia d'Abo (Jane), Jeff Bennett (Prof. Porter), Jim Cummings (Tantor), April Winchell (Terk). 75 min.

Tarzan Rocks Show in the Theater in the Wild in DinoLand U.S.A. at Disney's Animal Kingdom; opened on July 2, 1999. In the 30-minute rock concert, singers, dancers, gymnasts, aerialists, and in-line skaters join Tarzan, Jane, and Terk.

Tarzan II (film) Direct-to-video animated feature; released on June 14, 2005. As a child, Tarzan feels like the worst ape ever. Kala reassures him that his differences will one day be his strengths, but these very differences cause an accident that leaves Kala injured, and Tarzan missing and presumed dead. Convinced that everyone would be better off without him, Tarzan sets off to find his place in the world. A dramatic encounter with an outcast family of gorillas sends Tarzan up to Dark Mountain, where he uncovers the myth of the dreaded Zugor, a legendary monster who turns out to be nothing more than a cranky old hermit ape. With Zugor's help, Tarzan is able to find his own set of remarkable jungle skills. Glenn Close and Lance Henriksen return to provide the voices of Kala and Kerchak; other voices include Harrison Chad (Tarzan), Brenda Grate (Terk), Harrison Fahn (Tantor), Estelle Harris (Mama Gunda), Brad Garrett (Uto), Ron Perlman (Kago), George Carlin (Zugor). Featured are two original songs by Phil Collins.

Tarzan's Treehouse Adventureland attraction in Disneyland; opened on June 23, 1999, taking the place of the Swiss Family Treehouse. Guests climb a wooden staircase made from salvaged items from a shipwreck, cross an aged suspension bridge, then in the moss and vine-covered tree find the homes of Tarzan's human parents, of his foster mother Kala, as well as the main hut where Tarzan lives. An interactive play area is at the base of the tree. Also at Hong Kong Disneyland; opened on September 12, 2005.

Taste of Melon, A (television) Television show; part 1 of *For the Love of Willadean*.

Taste Pilots' Grill Quick service restaurant at Condor Flats in Disney's California Adventure; opened on February 8, 2001.

Tattooed Police Horse, The (film) Featurette; released on December 18, 1964. Directed by Larry Lansburgh. Registered trotting horse Jolly Roger is thrown out of racing for speeding into a gallop whenever he races. Bought by a Boston police captain, the horse manages to redeem himself by winning and becoming a champion racer. 48 min. Stars Sandy Saunders, Charles Steel, Shirley Skiles.

Tatum, Donn B. (1913–1993) He came to Walt Disney Productions as production business manager in 1956 and was later executive vice president of Disneyland, Inc. After 1960, he returned to the Studio where he was vice president of television sales and vice president of administration. He served as president of Walt Disney Productions from 1968 to 1971 and succeeded Roy O. Disney as chairman of the board and chief executive officer, serving from 1971 to 1980. He became chairman of the executive committee from 1980 to 1983. He was a member of the board of directors beginning in 1964, until his resignation in 1992, at which time he was named director emeritus. He was well known by stockholders for his adeptness in handling the corporate annual meetings. With Card Walker, he ably led the company after Roy O. Disney's death. He was posthumously named a Disney Legend the same year.

Tayback, Vic (1929–1990) Actor; appeared in *No Deposit, No Return* (Big Joe) and *The Shaggy D.A.* (Eddie Roschak).

Taylor, Betty Performer in the Golden Horseshoe Revue at Disneyland, from 1956 until the show's final curtain in 1987. As Slue Foot Sue, she personified the spunky leader of a troupe of Western dance hall girls and as Pecos Bill's sweetheart. She was named a Disney Legend in 1995.

Taylor, Dub (1907–1994) Actor; appeared in *The Adventures of Bullwhip Griffin* (timekeeper), *The Wild Country* (Phil), *Treasure of Matecumbe* (Sheriff Forbes), and provided the voice of Digger in *The Rescuers*. On television he appeared in *Menace on the Mountain*, *Ride a Northbound Horse*, and *The Mooncussers*.

Taylor, Robert (1911–1969) Actor; appeared in *The Miracle of the White Stallions* (Colonel Podhajsky).

Taylor, Rod He voiced Pongo in *One Hundred and One Dalmatians*.

Taylor, Russi She currently voices Minnie Mouse; also did Webbigail Vanderquack, Huey, Dewey, and Louie, and many others.

T-Bone for Two (film) Pluto cartoon; released on August 14, 1942. Directed by Clyde Geronimi. When Pluto steals a bone from Butch, the bulldog, he has a difficult time keeping hold of it.

Tea for Two Hundred (film) Donald Duck cartoon; released on December 24, 1948. Directed by Jack Hannah. Donald is at war with an army of ants who are after his picnic food, but it is a losing battle from the start and soon the ants have even taken his clothes. Nominated for an Academy Award.

Teachers Are People (film) Goofy cartoon; released on June 27, 1952. Directed by Jack Kinney. Goofy is a teacher with a class of children so full of mischief that by the end of the day Goofy is exhausted—and wiser.

Teacher's Pet (television) Animated series created by Gary Baseman; part of *One Saturday Morning* on ABC; debuted on September 9, 2000. A tale of boy and his dog, Spot—a talking canine that yearns for the education afforded his master. Spot disguises himself as a boy in order to attend school and becomes the teacher's pet. Voices include Nathan Lane (Spot/Scott), Debra Jo Rupp (Mrs. Helperman), Wallace Shawn (Principal Strickler), David Ogden Stiers (Mr. Jolly), Shaun Fleming (Leonard), Jerry Stiller (Pretty Boy), Rob Paulsen (Ian). Emmy Award winner. 39 episodes.

Teacher's Pet (film) Spot, a talking canine, has the ultimate wish of becoming a real boy. When the opportunity presents itself, through the DNA manipulations of wacko scientist Dr. Ivan Krank, Spot quickly follows his family to Florida in order to make the evolution to human form. However, Dr. Krank's experiments have had far-from-perfect results and, although Spot's transformation to human is complete, not all the calculations are exactly correct. It will take his best buddy Leonard and his quirky pet pals, Mr. Jolly (a cat) and Pretty Boy (a bird), to help him out of his tight spot and try to right this genetic wrong. Directed by Timothy Björklund. Released on January 16, 2004. Voices include Nathan Lane (Spot/Scott), Kelsey Grammer (Dr. Krank), Shaun Fleming (Leonard), Debra Jo Rupp (Mrs. Helperman), David Ogden Stiers (Jolly), Jerry Stiller (Pretty Boy), Paul Reubens (Dennis), Megan Mullaly (Adele), Rob Paulsen (Ian), Wallace Shawn (Principal Strickler), Estelle Harris (Mrs. Boogin), Barry Anger (Jay Thomas). 74 min. Based on the television series created by Gary Baseman. Released on video in 2004.

Team Disney Building Corporate headquarters at the Disney Studios in California since 1990, designed by Michael Graves, and featuring huge statues of the Seven Dwarfs holding up the roof. There is also a Team Disney building at Walt Disney World designed by Arata Isozaki; it opened in 1991. It is themed after a huge sundial, and serves as an administration building. A Team Disney Anaheim building, designed by Frank O. Gehry, opened in early 1996 to house all of the Disneyland administrative staff, for the first time in one facility.

Team Mickey's Athletic Club Shop selling sports fashions at the Downtown Disney Marketplace at Walt Disney World; opened on April 19, 1987.

Teamo Supremo (television) Animated series, part of *One Saturday Morning* on ABC; debuted on January 19, 2002. A quirky triumvirate of superheroes—Captain Crandall, Rope Girl, and Skate Lad—are sworn to protect their state from the forces of evil . . . and still finish all their homework. Voices include Spencer Breslin (Crandall), Alanna Ubach (Brenda, Hector), Martin Mull (Gov. Kevin), Fred Willard (Paulsen), Brian Doyle Murray (Chief). 39 episodes.

Technicolor Walt Disney had the foresight to sign an exclusive two-year contract for the use of Technicolor's new three-color process in cartoons, and he first used it in *Flowers and Trees* (1932). For the first time it brought full color to cartoons. The first Mickey Mouse cartoon in color was *The Band Concert* (1935). See also Color.

Teddi Barra's Swingin' Arcade Critter Country game arcade at Disneyland, featuring games with a distinctive backwoods flavor; opened in 1972.

Teddybär, Der See Der Teddybär.

Tedrow, Irene (1907–1995) Actress; appeared in *Midnight Madness* (Mrs. Grimhaus), and on television in *14 Going on 30* and *Child of Glass*.

Teen Angel (television) Serial on the *Mickey Mouse Club* on The Disney Channel; aired from April 24 to May 19, 1989. Guardian angel Buzz Gunderson receives his first assignment: to help a shy misfit named Dennis Mullen gain self-confidence, not to mention the love of the beautiful Nancy Nichols. Only Dennis can see the angel, who has to succeed with his task in order to get into heaven. Stars Jason Priestley (Buzz), Adam Biesk (Dennis), Renee O'Connor (Nancy).

Teen Angel (television) Half-hour comedy series on ABC; aired from September 26, 1997 to September 11, 1998. As high school buddies, Marty, who prefers partying over studying, and Steve, a guy who plays by the rules, couldn't be more different. When Marty dies from eating a tainted hamburger, he learns from the Court of Eternal Judgement that he must prove himself worthy of entry into Heaven by serving as his friend's guardian angel. Invisible to everyone but Steve, Marty helps his friend navigate the pitfalls of high school life while getting himself into trouble with his newfound celestial powers. Stars Mike Damus (Marty DePolo), Corbin Allred (Steve Beauchamp), Maureen McCormick (Judy Beauchamp), Katie Volding (Katie Beauchamp), Jordan Brower (Jordan Lubell), Ron Glass (Head), Conchata Ferrell (Pam). At mid-season, Maureen McCormick was dropped and Tommy Hinkley and Jerry Van Dyke were added as Steve's father and grandfather.

Teen Angel Returns (television) Serial on the *Mickey Mouse Club* on The Disney Channel; aired from October 2 to 27, 1989. Guardian angel Buzz decides to help Cindy, the daughter of a friend whose gas station is threatened by a cruel developer. The developer's kids constantly hassle Cindy, who initially refuses to believe in her angel, but eventually he helps her gain the self-confidence she needs to save the gas station and win over her boyfriend. Stars Jason Priestley (Buzz), Robyn Lively (Cindy), Scott Reeves (Brian), Jennie Garth (Karrie).

Teen Win, Lose or Draw (television) Disney Channel series, hosted by Marc Price and his Dalmatian pup, Tyler, with teen guest stars competing in drawing clues for contestants to decipher; first aired on May 6, 1989. The show was a spin-off from *Win, Lose or Draw.*

Teenage Mutant Ninja Turtles They appeared at Disney-MGM Studios demonstrating some of their karate moves and signing autographs beginning on July 1, 1990.

Teenage Substance Abuse: An Open Forum with John Callahan (film) Educational film; released in November 1989. 23 min. A wheelchair-bound recovering alcoholic tells his story to teenagers.

Teeth Are for Chewing (film) Educational film; released in September 1971. Designed to make children aware of the unique functions human teeth perform and the importance of good dental safety habits.

Television Walt Disney was one of the first of the major movie producers to go into television. He started with Christmas specials in 1950 (*One Hour in Wonderland*) and 1951 (*Walt Disney Christmas Show*), and then began his regular series on October 27, 1954. Disney was persuaded to begin the series on ABC because he knew he could use it to help sell his movies, and, especially, because ABC offered to advance money to help him build Disneyland park. The evening series remained on the air for 29 seasons, airing on all three networks during this period. This made it the longest-running prime-time show of all time. While there were a few other series during the first three decades, notably the *Mickey Mouse Club* and *Zorro*, beginning in the 1980s, Disney became a mainstream producer of series for television. The complete list of Disney television series follows:

1. *Disneyland* [ABC]   10/27/54–9/3/58
   Walt Disney   9/12/58–9/17/61
   Presents [ABC]
   Walt Disney's   9/24/61–9/7/69
   Wonderful World
   of Color [NBC]
   The Wonderful   9/14/69–9/2/79
   World of Disney
   [NBC]
   Disney's Wonderful   9/9/79–9/13/81
   World [NBC]
   Walt Disney [CBS]   9/26/81–9/24/83
2. *Mickey Mouse*   10/3/55–9/25/59
   Club [ABC]
3. *Zorro*   10/10/57–9/28/59
   (78 episodes)
   [ABC]
4. *The Mouse Factory*   1/26/72–1973
   (43 episodes)
   [syndicated]

5. *Saturday Night*   2/23/74–1/29/77
   at the Movies
   with Disney
   (11 programs)
   [NBC]
6. *[New] Mickey*   1/17/77–12/1/78
   Mouse Club
   [syndicated]
7. *Herbie the Love*   3/17/82–4/14/82
   Bug (5 episodes)
   [CBS]
8. *Small and Frye*   3/7/83–6/15/83
   (6 episodes)
   [CBS]
9. *Gun Shy*   3/25/83–4/19/83
   (6 episodes)
   [CBS]
10. *Zorro and Son*   4/6/83–6/1/83
    (5 episodes)
    [CBS]
11. *Wildside*   3/21/85–4/25/85
    (6 episodes)
    [ABC]
12. *The Golden Girls*   9/14/85–9/12/92
    [NBC]
13. *Disney's Adventures*   9/14/85–9/2/89
    of the Gummi
    Bears
    [NBC]
    [ABC]   9/9/89–9/8/90
    [syndicated]   9/10/90–9/6/91
14. *Disney's Wuzzles*   9/14/85–9/6/86
    [CBS]
    [ABC]   9/13/86–5/16/87
15. *The Disney*   2/2/86–9/11/88
    Sunday Movie
    [ABC]
16. *The Wonderful*   9/4/86–
    World of Disney
    [syndicated]
17. *Disney Magic*   9/8/86–
    [syndicated]
18. *Siskel & Ebert*   9/18/86–8/29/99
    at the Movies
    [syndicated]
(Became *Roger Ebert & the Movies* 9/5/99–8/20/00, and *Ebert & Roeper and the Movies* 8/27/00–)

19. *The Ellen Burstyn* 9/20/86–11/15/86,
 Show [ABC] 8/8/87–9/12/87
20. *Sidekicks* [ABC] 9/26/86–6/27/87
21. *Today's Business* 9/26/86–4/26/87
 [syndicated]
22. *Harry* [ABC] 3/4/87–3/25/87
23. *Down and Out in* 7/25/87–9/12/87
 Beverly Hills [Fox]
24. *Win, Lose or Draw* 8/7/87–9/1/89
 [NBC]
 [syndicated] 8/7/87–8/31/90
25. *Ducktales* 9/21/87–9/5/92,
 [syndicated] 9/1/97–
 [ABC] 4/19/97–8/30/97
26. *The Oldest Rookie* 9/16/87–1/6/88
 [CBS]
27. *Live with Regis* 9/3/88–7/28/00
 and Kathie Lee
 [syndicated]
(Became *Live with Regis* 7/31/00–2/9/01,
 and *Live with* 2/12/02–)
 Regis & Kelly
28. *The New* 9/10/88–9/4/92
 Adventures of
 Winnie the Pooh
 [ABC]
 (Premiered 1/4/97–
 1/10/88 on The Disney Channel)
29. *Empty Nest* [NBC] 10/8/88–7/8/95
30. *The Magical World* 10/9/88–9/9/90
 of Disney [NBC]
31. *Hard Time on* 3/1/89–7/5/89
 Planet Earth [CBS]
32. *Chip 'n' Dale's* 9/18/89–9/3/93
 Rescue Rangers
 [syndicated]
(Premiered 3/4/89 on The Disney
Channel)
33. *The Nutt House* 9/20/89–10/25/89
 [NBC]
34. *Carol & Co.* 3/31/90–8/19/91
 [NBC]
35. *Singer & Sons* 6/9/90–6/27/90
 [NBC]
36. *The Challengers* 9/3/90–8/30/91
 [syndicated]
37. *The Fanelli Boys* 9/8/90–2/16/91
 [NBC]

38. *Tale Spin* 9/10/90–9/2/94
 [syndicated]
(Premiered 5/5/90 on The Disney Channel;
*Ducktales, Gummi Bears, Chip 'n' Dale's
Rescue Rangers*, and *TaleSpin* made up *The
Disney Afternoon* syndicated package,
9/10/90)
39. *Lenny* [CBS] 9/19/90–3/9/91
 (preview was 9/10/90)
40. *Hull High* [NBC] 9/23/90–12/30/90
 (preview was 8/20/90 &
 9/15/90)
41. *Blossom* [NBC] 1/3/91–6/5/95
42. *The 100 Lives of* 3/31/91
 Black Jack Savage
 (pilot) (2 hours)
 [NBC]
 [NBC] (series) 4/5/91–5/26/91
43. *STAT* [ABC] 4/16/91–5/21/91
44. *Dinosaurs* [ABC] 4/26/91–9/20/94
45. *Darkwing Duck* 9/7/91–9/11/93
 [ABC]
 [syndicated] 9/9/91–9/1/95,
 9/2/96–8/29/97
(Premiered 4/6/91 on The Disney Channel;
Darkwing Duck replaced *Gummi Bears*
in *The Disney Afternoon* syndicated
package; the network show ran concurrently with *The Disney Afternoon*
version)
46. *Herman's Head* 9/8/91–6/16/94
 [FOX]
47. *Nurses* [NBC] 9/14/91–6/18/94
48. *Pacific Station* 9/15/91–1/3/92
 [NBC]
49. *Home Improvement* 9/17/91–9/17/99
 [ABC]
50. *The Torkelsons* 9/21/91–6/20/92
 [NBC]
51. *Good and Evil* 9/25/91–10/31/91
 [ABC]
52. *The Carol Burnett* 11/1/91–12/27/91
 Show [CBS]
53. *Walter and Emily* 11/16/91–2/22/92
 [NBC]
54. *Goof Troop* 9/7/92–8/30/96
 [syndicated]
 [ABC] 9/12/92–9/11/93

(Premiered 4/20/92 on The Disney Channel; *Goof Troop* replaced *Duck Tales* in *The Disney Afternoon* syndicated package; the network show ran concurrently with *The Disney Afternoon* version)

55. *Disney's The Little Mermaid* [CBS] — 9/12/92–9/2/95

56. *The Golden Palace* [CBS] — 9/18/92–8/6/93

57. *Raw Toonage* [CBS] — 9/19/92–9/11/93

58. *Laurie Hill* [ABC] — 9/30/92–10/28/92

59. *Woops!* [FOX] — 9/27/92–12/6/92

60. *Almost Home* [NBC] (Formerly *The Torkelsons*) — 2/6/93–7/3/93

61. *Where I Live* [ABC] — 3/5/93–11/20/93

62. *Cutters* [CBS] — 6/11/93–7/9/93

63. *Bonkers* [syndicated] — 9/6/93–8/30/96

(Premiered 2/28/93 on The Disney Channel; *Bonkers* replaced *Chip 'n' Dale's Rescue Rangers* in *The Disney Afternoon* package; *Chip 'n' Dale's Rescue Rangers* ran on Saturdays)

64. *Bill Nye–The Science Guy* [syndicated] — 9/10/93–

65. *The Crusaders* [syndicated] — 9/10/93–1/21/95

66. *Disney's Adventures in Wonderland* [syndicated] — 9/6/93–9/10/95

(Premiered 3/23/92 on The Disney Channel)

67. *Bakersfield P.D.* [FOX] — 9/14/93–1/4/94

68. *The Sinbad Show* [FOX] — 9/16/93–7/28/94

69. *Countdown at the Neon Armadillo* [syndicated] — 9/17/93–12/12/93

70. *Marsupilami* [CBS] — 9/18/93–8/27/94

71. *Boy Meets World* [ABC] — 9/24/93–9/8/00

72. *The Good Life* [NBC] — 1/3/94–4/12/94

73. *Monty* [FOX] — 1/11/94–2/15/94

74. *Thunder Alley* [ABC] — 3/9/94–7/25/95

75. *Ellen* [ABC] — 3/9/94–7/29/98

(Aired as *These Friends of Mine*, 3/9/94–5/24/94; began airing as *Ellen* 8/2/94)

76. *Someone Like Me* [NBC] — 3/14/94–4/25/94

77. *Mike & Maty* [ABC] — 4/11/94–6/7/96

78. *Hardball* [FOX] — 9/4/94–10/23/94

79. *Disney's Aladdin* [syndicated] — 9/5/94–8/29/97
    [CBS] — 9/17/94–8/24/96

(Replaced *Tale Spin* on *The Disney Afternoon*, which then consisted of *Darkwing Duck*, *Goof Troop*, *Bonkers*, and *Disney's Aladdin*)

80. *Judge for Yourself* [syndicated] — 9/12/94–4/7/95

81. *All–American Girl* [ABC] — 9/14/94–3/22/95

82. *Gargoyles* [syndicated] — 10/24/94–8/29/97

83. *Shnookums & Meat Funny Cartoon Show* [syndicated] — 1/2/95–8/28/95

84. *Unhappily Ever After* [WB] — 1/11/95–9/19/99

85. *The George Wendt Show* [CBS] — 3/8/95–4/12/95

86. *Pride & Joy* [NBC] — 3/21/95–7/11/95

87. *Nowhere Man* [UPN] — 9/4/95–8/19/96
    (previewed on 8/28/95)

88. *The Lion King's Timon & Pumbaa* [syndicated] — 9/8/95–8/29/97
    (part of *The Disney Afternoon*) [CBS] — 9/16/95–3/29/97

89. *Disney's Sing Me a Story: with Belle* [syndicated] — 9/9/95–

90. *Danny!* [syndicated] — 9/11/95–2/2/96

91. *The Stephanie*   9/15/95–1/20/96
    Miller Show
    [syndicated]
92. *Maybe This Time*   9/16/95–2/17/96
    [ABC]
    (previewed on 9/15/95)
93. *If Not for You*   9/18/95–10/9/95
    [CBS]
94. *Land's End*   9/22/95–9/15/96
    [syndicated]
95. *Brotherly Love*   9/24/95–4/1/96
    [NBC]
    (previewed on   9/15/96–6/1/97
    9/16/95) [WB]
96. *Misery Loves*   10/1/95–10/23/95
    Company [FOX]
97. *Buddies* [ABC]   3/5/96–3/27/96
98. *Debt* [Lifetime]   6/3/96–7/3/98
99. *Homeboys in*   8/27/96–5/13/97
    Outer Space [UPN]
100. *Quack Pack*   9/3/96–
    [syndicated]
101. *The Mighty Ducks*   9/6/96–
    [syndicated]
    [ABC]   9/7/96–8/30/97
(*The Mighty Ducks* and *Quack Pack* were
added to *The Disney Afternoon*)
102. *Gargoyles: The*   9/7/96–4/12/97
    Goliath Chronicles
    [ABC]
103. *Brand Spanking*   9/7/96–
    New Doug [ABC]
(New title: *Disney's Doug*, syndicated
8/31/98; see also entry for One Saturday
Morning)
104. *Life's Work* [ABC]   9/17/96–7/29/97
105. *Dangerous Minds*   9/30/96–7/12/97
    [ABC]
106. *Jungle Cubs* [ABC]   10/5/96–9/5/98
107. *Vital Signs* [ABC]   2/27/97–7/3/97
108. *Social Studies*   3/18/97–8/5/97
    [UPN]
109. *Smart Guy* [WB]   4/2/97–8/1/99
110. *Soul Man* [ABC]   4/15/97–8/25/98
111. *Nightmare Ned*   4/19/97–8/30/97
    [ABC]
112. *Make Me Laugh*   6/2/97–
    [Comedy Central]

113. *Win Ben Stein's*   7/28/97–
    Money [Comedy
    Central]
114. *The Keenan Ivory*   8/4/97–4/24/98
    Wayans Show
    [syndicated]
115. *101 Dalmatians:*   9/1/97–
    The Series
    [syndicated]
    [ABC]   9/13/97–
116. *One Saturday*   9/13/97–9/7/02
    Morning [ABC]
117. *Recess* [ABC]   9/13/97–
    (part of *One*
    Saturday Morning)
    [syndicated]
118. *Pepper Ann* [ABC]   9/13/97–
    (part of *One*
    Saturday Morning)
    [syndicated]
119. *Honey, I Shrunk*   9/22/97– 5/20/00
    the Kids
    [syndicated]
120. *Hiller and Diller*   9/23/97–3/13/98
    [ABC]
121. *Teen Angel* [ABC]   9/26/97–9/11/98
122. *You Wish* [ABC]   9/26/97–9/4/98
123. *The Wonderful*   9/28/97–
    World of Disney
    [ABC]
124. *Style and Substance*   1/5/98–9/9/98
    [CBS]
125. *Hercules*   8/31/98–
    [syndicated]
126. *Costello* [FOX]   9/8/98–10/13/98
127. *Secrets of the*   9/18/98–9/13/99
    Animal Kingdom
    [syndicated]
128. *Sports Night* [ABC]   9/22/98–5/16/00
129. *Felicity* [WB]   9/29/98–5/22/02
130. *The PJs* [FOX]   1/12/99–6/17/01
131. *Zoe, Duncan,*   1/17/99–7/18/99
    Jack & Jane [WB]
132. *Mickey's Mouse*   5/1/99–1/6/01
    Works [ABC]
133. *Thanks* [CBS]   8/2/99–9/6/99
134. *Who Wants to Be*   8/16/99–6/27/02
    a Millionaire [ABC]

135. *Disney's One Two*   9/6/99–9/1/02
     [UPN & syndicated]
136. *Once and Again*   9/21/99–5/2/01
     [ABC]
137. *Your Big Break*   9/23/99–
     [syndicated]
138. *Popular* [WB]   9/29/99–5/18/01
139. *The Ainsley*   1/10/00–9/15/00
     Harriott Show
     [syndicated]
140. *Brutally Normal*   1/24/00–2/14/00
     [WB]
141. *The Weekenders*   2/26/00–
     [ABC]
     (part of *One*
     Saturday Morning)
     [syndicated]
142. *Daddio* [NBC]   3/23/00–
                   10/13/00
143. *Wonderland*   3/30/00–4/6/00
     [ABC]
144. *Talk to Me* [ABC]   4/11/00–4/25/00
145. *Clerks* [ABC]   5/31/00–6/7/00
146. *Teacher's Pet*   9/9/00–
     [ABC]
     (part of *One*
     Saturday Morning)
     [syndicated]
147. *House Calls*   9/11/00–2001
     [syndicated]
148. *Buzz Lightyear of*   10/14/00–
     Star Command
     [ABC]
     (part of *One*
     Saturday Morning)
     [UPN &   10/2/00–
     syndicated]
149. *Madigan Men*   10/6/00–12/12/00
     [ABC]
150. *The Geena Davis*   10/10/00–7/12/01
     Show [ABC]
151. *Gideon's Crossing*   10/18/00–4/9/01
     [ABC]
152. *Disney's House of*   1/13/01–
     Mouse [ABC]
     [syndicated]
153. *Disney's Lloyd in*   2/3/01–
     Space [ABC]

     (part of *One*
     Saturday Morning)
     [syndicated]
154. *The Job* [ABC]   3/14/01–4/24/02
155. *My Wife and Kids*   3/28/01–8/9/05
     [ABC]
156. *Go Fish* [NBC]   6/19/01–7/3/01
157. *The Beast* [ABC]   6/20/01–7/18/01
158. *The Wayne Brady*   8/8//01–9/19/01
     Show [ABC]
     [syndicated]   9/2/02–5/04
159. *Iyanla* [syndicated]   8/13/01–
160. *The Legend of*   9/3/01–
     Tarzan [UPN &
     syndicated]
161. *The Amazing*   9/5/01–
     Race [CBS]
162. *Alias* [ABC]   9/30/01–
163. *Bob Patterson*   10/2/01–10/31/01
     [ABC]
164. *Scrubs* [NBC]   10/2/01–
165. *According to Jim*   10/3/01–
     [ABC]
166. *Maybe It's Me*   10/5/01–7/19/02
     [WB]
167. *Imagine That*   1/8/02–1/15/02
     [NBC]
168. *Teamo Supremo*   1/19/02–
     [ABC]
     (part of *One*
     Saturday Morning)
     [syndicated]
169. *The Court* [ABC]   3/26/02–4/9/02
170. *Wednesday 9:30*   3/27/02–6/12/02
     (8:30 Central)
     [ABC]
171. *Monk* [USA]   7/12/02–
172. *ABC Kids* [ABC]   9/14/02–
     (includes *Fillmore*)
173. *8 Simple Rules*   9/17/02–8/19/05
     for Dating My
     Teenage Daughter
     [ABC]
174. *Life with Bonnie*   9/17/02–7/30/04
     [ABC]
175. *Push, Nevada*   9/17/02–10/24/02
     [ABC]
176. *MDs* [ABC]   9/25/02–12/11/02

177. *That Was Then* [ABC] — 9/27/02–10/18/02
178. *Less Than Perfect* [ABC] — 10/1/02–
179. *Dinotopia* [ABC] — 11/28/02–12/26/02
180. *The Last Resort* [ABC Family] — 1/20/03–
181. *Jimmy Kimmel Live* [ABC] — 1/26/03–
182. *Miracles* [ABC] — 1/27/03–3/3/03
183. *Veritas: The Quest* [ABC] — 1/27/03–3/10/03
184. *The Family* [ABC] — 3/4/03–9/10/03
185. *Regular Joe* [ABC] — 3/28/03–4/18/03
186. *Lost at Home* [ABC] — 4/1/03–4/22/03
187. *Threat Matrix* [ABC] — 9/18/03–1/29/04
188. *Lilo & Stitch, The Series* [ABC] — 9/20/03–
189. *Hope & Faith* [ABC] — 9/26/03–
190. *10–8* [ABC] — 9/28/03–1/25/04
191. *It's All Relative* [ABC] — 10/1/03–4/6/04
192. *Line of Fire* [ABC] — 12/2/03–2/3/04
193. *Stephen King's Kingdom Hospital* [ABC] — 3/3/04–7/15/04
194. *The Tony Danza Show* [syndicated] — 9/13/04–
195. *Rodney* [ABC] — 9/21/04–
196. *Lost* [ABC] — 9/22/04–
197. *Kevin Hill* [UPN] — 9/29/04–6/8/05
198. *Desperate Housewives* [ABC] — 10/3/04–
199. *life as we know it* [ABC] — 10/7/04–1/20/05
200. *W.I.T.C.H.* [ABC Family] — 1/15/05–
201. *Grey's Anatomy* [ABC] — 3/27/05–
202. *Empire* [ABC] — 6/28/05–7/26/05
203. *Criminal Minds* [CBS] — 9/22/05–
204. *Inconceivable* [NBC] — 9/23/05–
205. *Ghost Whisperer* [CBS] — 9/23/05–
206. *Commander in Chief* [ABC] — 9/27/05–
207. *The Night Stalker* [ABC] — 9/29/05–
208. *In Justice* [ABC] — 1/1/06–
209. *Crumbs* [ABC] — 1/12/06–
210. *Courting Alex* [CBS] — 1/23/06–

Temple, Shirley See Shirley Temple Black.

Tempura Kiku Tempura bar in the Mitsukoshi restaurant in Japan in World Showcase at Epcot; opened on October 1, 1982. Seafood, vegetables, chicken, and beef are battered and deep-fried in the crisp tempura style.

10-8 (television) One-hour drama series on ABC; aired from September 28, 2003 to January 25, 2004. As a graduate of the Los Angeles County Sheriff's academy, Rico Amonte, former Brooklyn bad boy, becomes a deputy sheriff trainee, but he is totally unprepared for the hazing he gets from his own department. And his training officer, John Henry Barnes, is the meanest, toughest veteran on the force, determined to hammer the rookie into a by-the-book officer of the law. Stars Danny Nucci (Rico Amonte), Ernie Hudson (John Henry Barnes), Indigo (Tisha Graves), Scott William Winters (Matt Jablonski), Mercedes Colón (Sheryl Torres), Travis Schuldt (Chase Williams). From Spelling Television and Touchstone Television.

10 Things I Hate About You (film) Bianca and Kat Stratford are sisters, but there the similarity ends. Bianca, a popular and attractive Padua High School sophomore, is unable to date until older sister Kat does so, but Kat is so ill-tempered she alienates any boy who might be remotely interested in her. So, Bianca and her hoped-for boyfriend concoct a scheme to match Kat with someone with whom she might be compatible. Directed by Gil Junger. A Touchstone Picture. Released on March 31, 1999. Stars Larisa Oleynik (Bianca), Julia Stiles (Kat), Joseph Gordon-Levitt (Cameron James), Heath Ledger (Patrick Verona),

Andrew Keegan (Joey Donner), David Krumholtz (Michael Eckman), Susan May Pratt (Mandela), Gabrielle Union (Chastity). 97 min. Based on Shakespeare's "The Taming of the Shrew," which is set in Padua, Italy. Stadium High School in Tacoma, Washington, became Padua High for the film, and the Stratford family home was found nearby. Additional photography took place in Seattle. Released on video in 1999.

Ten Who Dared (film) The film is based on the journal of Maj. John Wesley Powell, who led the expedition that made the journey, hitherto thought impossible, down the Grand Canyon of the Colorado River in 1869. It is both a reenactment of this historical scientific expedition, and a dramatic story of the struggles, dangers, and conflicts of the ten men who made the trip. A prominent character in the story is a small dog that is responsible for the rescue of the major just before the boats shoot the final treacherous rapids. Released on October 18, 1960. Directed by William Beaudine. 92 min. Stars Brian Keith (Bill Dunn), John Beal (Maj. John Wesley Powell), James Drury (Walter Powell), R. G. Armstrong (Oramel Howland), David Stollery (Andy Hall). Beal had years earlier done voice work for the animation in *So Dear to My Heart*. Songs in the film include "Ten Who Dared," "Roll Along," and "Jolly Rovers" by Lawrence E. Watkin and Stan Jones. Released on video in 1986.

Tencennial Parade Event in Magic Kingdom Park at Walt Disney World from October 1, 1981 to September 30, 1982, celebrating the 10th anniversary of Walt Disney World. Disneyland celebrated its Tencennial earlier with yearlong festivities in 1965.

Tenderfoot, The (television) Three-part television show; aired on October 18, 25, and November 1, 1964. Directed by Byron Paul. Natural dangers and hostile Indians create problems for travelers in the West in the 1850s; a young man almost killed in an Indian raid looks to a frontier scout, Mose Carson, for an education. They get involved in a plan to sell wild mustangs to the Army. Brian Keith (Mose Carson), Brandon de Wilde (Jim Tevis), James Whitmore (Capt. Ewell),

Richard Long (Paul Durand), Rafael Campos (Juarez), Donald May (Phineas Thatcher), Christopher Dark (Pike), Judson Pratt (Sergeant).

Tenggren, Gustav (1896–1970) Swedish sketch artist; worked at Disney from 1936 to 1939 doing early concept paintings for *Snow White and the Seven Dwarfs* and *Pinocchio*. For the former film he created the design for the one-sheet poster used to promote the film, and illustrated several children's storybooks.

Tennis Racquet (film) Goofy cartoon; released on August 26, 1949. Directed by Jack Kinney. Goofy's game of tennis confounds the sports announcer and the crowd, but one player does indeed win the gigantic trophy.

Tennisland Racquet Club Tennis courts at Disney's Vacationland Campground, across the street from Disneyland. It closed in November 1994.

Teppanyaki Dining Rooms Restaurant in Japan in World Showcase at Epcot; opened on October 1, 1982. A number of guests sit together around a table where a chef prepares the stir-fried meal on a grill in front of them.

Terk Gorilla and best friend of Tarzan; voiced by Rosie O'Donnell.

Terminal Velocity (film) A devil-may-care professional skydiving instructor, Richard "Ditch" Brodie finds himself hurled into a world of international espionage and intrigue when a beautiful and mysterious woman named Chris signs up for a parachute jump and during her initial free fall, the chute fails to open. When the FAA unjustly blames Ditch for the woman's death and closes down his business, the hotshot instructor takes it upon himself to discover the truth behind the bizarre incident. However, he soon learns that nothing is as it seems—least of all Chris, who turns up alive, and is revealed to be a former deep-cover KGB espionage agent. A Hollywood Pictures film. Filmed in CinemaScope. Released on September 23, 1994. Directed by Deran Sarafian. 102 min. Stars Charlie Sheen (Ditch Brodie), Nastassja Kinski (Chris Morrow), James Gandolfini (Ben Pinkwater), Christopher McDonald (Kerr). Filmed on location in Tucson and Phoenix, Arizona; San Bernardino, California, and the Mojave Desert; and in Moscow. Released on video in 1995.

Terrible Toreador, El See *El Terrible Toreador.*

Terry-Thomas (1911–1990) Actor; voiced Sir Hiss in *Robin Hood,* a character given the same gap between his front teeth as the actor has.

Test Pilot Donald (film) Donald Duck cartoon; released on June 8, 1951. Directed by Jack Hannah. Chip and Dale fight Donald over possession of his model airplane.

Test Track General Motors attraction at Epcot, which took the place of World of Motion. Soft openings began in December 1998, a year and a half after the original opening had been announced, with the grand opening on March 17, 1999. Guests experience the exhilarating twists and turns in a General Motors test vehicle as it steers through Disney's longest and fastest attraction. At a length of just a fraction less than a mile from start to finish, the test track winds through the pavilion and then on a loop outside reaching speeds of up to 65 miles per hour. Up to six guests in each vehicle.

Tetti Tatti Impresario who harpoons the whale in *The Whale Who Wanted to Sing at the Met.*

Tex (film) Fifteen-year-old Tex McCormick and his 17-year-old brother Mason are trying to make it on their own in the absence of their rodeo-riding father. Mason takes over running the household and, to make ends meet, sells Tex's beloved horse, Rowdy. Tex gets mad at Mason and heedlessly tumbles into scrape after scrape. When his Pop comes home, Tex is shocked to learn that he isn't his real father. But Tex realizes that Mason and Pop do love him, and it is time to start growing up. Released on July 30, 1982, briefly, then withdrawn and released again on September 24, 1982. Directed by Tim Hunter. 103 min. Stars Matt Dillon (Tex McCormick), Jim Metzler (Mason), Meg Tilly (Jamie), Bill McKinney (Pop), Frances Lee McCain (Mrs. Johnson), Ben Johnson (Cole), Emilio Estevez (Johnny Collins). *Tex* represented the film debuts of both Meg Tilly and Emilio Estevez. The film is based on the novel by S.E. Hinton. *Tex* was an experiment by the Disney Studio to reach a new generation of teenagers who often abandoned Disney films for more "realistic" live-action fare, and this accounts for the PG rating. The movie represents a faithful adaptation of the novel where teen problems are confronted directly and honestly with no easy solutions or false hopes necessarily offered. Aware that Disney was seeking to broaden the content horizon of their films, it was director and screenwriter Tim Hunter who originally recommended *Tex* to the studio, suggesting Matt Dillon (a fan of Miss Hinton's books, which included *The Outsiders*) as the lead. Hunter viewed the association between Disney and Hinton as "a lucky convergence that compromises neither the book nor the studio's high standards for family entertainment." But the experiment was not a box office success, despite the time, care, and talent that went into the production. Released on video in 1983.

Texas John Slaughter (film) Theatrical compilation of several television episodes; released first in Malaysia in April 1960. Directed by Harry Keller. In 1870, Slaughter rides into Friotown, kills two gunmen, and is asked to join the Texas

Rangers. He initially refuses, but when his herd is stolen by the Davis gang, he becomes a Ranger fighting many spectacular battles with the gang. Eventually, Davis overplays his hand and dies by Slaughter's gun in the great climactic battle. 74 min. Stars Tom Tryon (Texas John Slaughter), Robert Middleton (Frank Davis), Norma Moore (Adeline Harris).

Texas John Slaughter (Episode 1) (television) Television show; aired on October 31, 1958. Directed by Harry Keller. Slaughter is persuaded by circumstances to enlist in the Texas Rangers and to go after a local outlaw. Stars Tom Tryon, Robert Middleton, Norma Moore, Harry Carey, Jr., Judson Pratt, Robert J. Wilke, Edward Platt. First episode of the series of 17 shows about a Texas Ranger. This was the longest miniseries to air on the Disney television anthology show. Tom Tryon later went on to become a best-selling author.

Texas John Slaughter (Episode 2): Ambush at Laredo (television) Television show; aired on November 14, 1958. Directed by Harry Keller. Gang leader Frank Davis is out on bail and being followed by Slaughter. Davis plans to divide the area into separate spheres of influence, each to be under a different gang leader, but first he yearns to get rid of Slaughter. Slaughter just misses being killed by gunmen and ambushed by Davis, but he manages to vanquish his foes. Episode 1 (titled *Texas John Slaughter*) and this episode of the television show were edited together to become a foreign feature entitled *Texas John Slaughter*. Stars Tom Tryon, Robert Middleton, Harry Carey, Jr., Norma Moore, Judson Pratt.

Texas John Slaughter (Episode 3): Killers from Kansas (television) Television show; aired on January 9, 1959. Directed by Harry Keller. Slaughter is wounded in a bank robbery, but still goes after the Barko gang that was responsible. They are finally trapped at Slaughter's fiancée's house, and she barely escapes. Stars Tom Tryon, Lyle Bettger, Beverly Garland, Norma Moore, Harry Carey, Jr., Judson Pratt, Don Haggerty.

Texas John Slaughter (Episode 4): Showdown at Sandoval (television) Television show; aired on January 23, 1959. Directed by Harry Keller. Slaughter and a group of Rangers pose as the Barko gang to get the confidence of a major outlaw. The deception works but Slaughter has to duel with the outlaw and then steal their booty out from under their noses. Stars Tom Tryon, Dan Duryea, Beverly Garland, Norma Moore, Harry Carey, Jr., Judson Pratt.

Texas John Slaughter (Episode 5): The Man from Bitter Creek (television) Television show; aired on March 6, 1959. Directed by Harry Keller. Slaughter has resigned from the Texas Rangers, but he still has to fight to keep his ranch's water supply and to bring a herd of cattle from Mexico. Stars Tom Tryon, Stephen McNally, Sidney Blackmer, Bill Williams, John Larch, Norma Moore.

Texas John Slaughter (Episode 6): The Slaughter Trail (television) Television show; aired on March 20, 1959. Directed by Harry Keller. Slaughter and a neighboring rancher agree to combine their herds on a drive to market, but they head down a new trail through Indian country. After an Indian attack and Slaughter's false arrest for murder, he hears that his wife is seriously ill, but she dies before he can rush home. Stars Tom Tryon, Sidney Blackmer, Bill Williams, John Larch, Norma Moore, Grant Williams.

Texas John Slaughter (Episode 7): The Robber Stallion (television) Television show; aired on December 4, 1959. Directed by Harry Keller. Slaughter meets Ashley Carstairs and decides to help him capture some mustangs. But they didn't reckon on Jason Kemp who tries to get rid of the two men. Stars Tom Tryon, Darryl Hickman, Barton MacLane, John Vivyan, Jean Inness.

Texas John Slaughter (Episode 7A): Wild Horse Revenge (television) Television show; aired on December 11, 1959. Directed by Harry Keller. Slaughter continues trying to capture a wild mustang, while being opposed by a local rancher. Stars Tom Tryon, Darryl Hickman,

Barton MacLane, John Vivyan, William Phipps, Bing Russell.

Texas John Slaughter (Episode 8): Range War at Tombstone (television) Television show; aired on December 18, 1959. Directed by Harry Keller. Slaughter and his friend Ashley are accused of being thieves by a girl, Viola, but eventually they help her and her parents. A local cattleman battles them when they try to settle on land he covets. Viola turns down Ashley's proposal, but Slaughter begins to get interested in her himself. Stars Tom Tryon, Darryl Hickman, Betty Lynn, Regis Toomey, Jan Merlin, James Westerfield.

Texas John Slaughter (Episode 9): Desperado from Tombstone (television) Television show; aired on February 12, 1960. Directed by Harry Keller. Slaughter is overjoyed that his children are coming to live with him, but neighbor Viola argues that the frontier is no place for a single father to raise children. A local cattle rustler is giving Slaughter trouble at the same time that his children arrive, so he has to juggle caring for them with trying to capture the outlaw. The kids find it hard to adjust, but they are attracted to Viola, and even Slaughter begins to fall in love. Stars Tom Tryon, Gene Evans, Regis Toomey, Betty Lynn, Brian Corcoran, Annette Gorman, Don Haggerty.

Texas John Slaughter (Episode 10): Apache Friendship (television) Television show; aired on February 19, 1960. Directed by Harry Keller. Slaughter is looking for a mother for his children, and woos Viola Howell. She will consider marrying but wants him to give up his guns; when he does that, he is set upon by an escaped outlaw, Crispin, while he is unarmed. He finally takes up his guns again, and manages to capture Crispin; Viola admits her mistake and the wedding is planned. Stars Tom Tryon, Gene Evans, Regis Toomey, Betty Lynn, Brian Corcoran, Jay Silverheels.

Texas John Slaughter (Episode 11): Kentucky Gunslick (television) Television show; aired on February 26, 1960. Directed by Harry Keller. Slaughter saves a man from gunmen, only to discover that it is the former beau, Ashley Carstairs, of Slaughter's wife. Johnson sets up ranching in the area, but causes no end of trouble, with Slaughter constantly having to save him. Stars Tom Tryon, Darryl Hickman, Betty Lynn, Brian Corcoran, Allan Lane, Don Haggerty, Jay Silverheels.

Texas John Slaughter (Episode 12): Geronimo's Revenge (television) Television show; aired on March 4, 1960. Directed by Harry Keller. Geronimo is an outcast from his tribe, hating the settlers, and especially Slaughter. He lures him away from his ranch in order to attack, but Slaughter's family manages to hold out until help arrives. Stars Tom Tryon, Darryl Hickman, Betty Lynn, Brian Corcoran, Jay Silverheels, Pat Hogan.

Texas John Slaughter (Episode 13): End of the Trail (television) Television show; aired on January 29, 1961. Directed by James Neilson. Slaughter agrees to help the army search for the Apache Geronimo, who has been terrorizing the populace, but he takes refuge in Mexico, where the army cannot follow. Slaughter lures him back across the border and eventually captures him. Stars Tom Tryon, Betty Lynn, Onslow Stevens, Harry Carey, Jr., Pat Hogan, Brian Corcoran.

Texas John Slaughter (Episode 14): A Holster Full of Law (television) Television show; aired on February 5, 1961. Directed by James Neilson. Slaughter's cattle are rustled, and when the sheriff is powerless to do anything about it, Slaughter is elected sheriff himself. With a band of skilled deputies, he brings law and order to Tombstone, and eventually settles his feud with the cattle rustler. Stars Tom Tryon, Betty Lynn, R. G. Armstrong, Jim Beck, Robert Burton, Brian Corcoran, Ross Martin.

Texas John Slaughter (Episode 15): Trip to Tucson (television) Television show; aired on April 16, 1961. Directed by James Neilson. The people in Tombstone are not happy with Sheriff Slaughter's harsh ways, but he enjoys the reputation, for it makes the outlaws fear him. He tricks his wife into going on vacation to Tucson, but it is really to catch a wanted killer.

Stars Tom Tryon, Betty Lynn, Joe Maross, Jim Beck, Brian Corcoran, Peggy Knudsen, Annette Gorman.

Texas John Slaughter (Episode 16): Frank Clell's in Town (television) Television show; aired on April 23, 1961. Directed by James Neilson. Some of the businessmen in Tombstone long for the return of the desperadoes Slaughter has run out of town, for they had helped the town's economy. A saloon keeper hires a notorious killer to kill Slaughter, but the sheriff finally wins the battle. Stars Tom Tryon, Betty Lynn, Brian Corcoran, Jim Beck, Robert Burton, Michael McGreevey, Ralph Meeker, Raymond Bailey.

Thanks (television) A satirical comedy skewering contemporary life as it looks as the venerable Pilgrims whose landing at Plymouth Rock in 1620 literally got this country going. A half-hour television series; aired on CBS on August 2, 1999 and ended September 6. Stars Tim Dutton (James Winthrop), Kirsten Nelson (Polly Winthrop), Jim Rash (Cotton), Erika Christensen (Abigail Winthrop), Amy Centner (Elizabeth Winthrop), Andrew Ducote (William Winthrop), Cloris Leachman (Grammy).

Thanksgiving Day Mirthquakes (film) Shorts program; released by RKO in 1953.

Thanksgiving Promise, The (television) Television show; aired on November 23, 1986. A boy must care for an injured Canada goose until it is ready to grace the table at Thanksgiving. However, he becomes attached to his new companion and must decide whether to break his promise or lose his new friend. Stars Lloyd, Beau, and Jordan Bridges (three generations of the same family). Directed by Beau Bridges.

That Darn Cat! (film) A Siamese cat named D.C. stumbles upon the hideout where two bank robbers are keeping a woman bank teller prisoner. When the woman manages to slip her wristwatch around his neck, D.C. saunters from the hideout to the Randall family with whom he lives.

When 19-year-old Patti Randall recognizes the wristwatch as belonging to the woman teller, the FBI is called in to watch D.C.'s every move. The young FBI agent working the case follows D.C., despite his allergic reaction to the animal, and in due time the bank robbers are collared and their prisoner set free. Released on December 2, 1965. Directed by Robert Stevenson. 116 min. Stars Hayley Mills (Patti Randall), Dean Jones (Zeke Kelso),  Dorothy Provine (Ingrid Randall), Roddy McDowall (Gregory Benson), Neville Brand (Dan), Elsa Lanchester (Mrs. MacDougall), Ed Wynn (Mr. Hofstedder), William Demarest (Mr. MacDougall). The film was a big Christmas release, grossing more than $9 million at the box office, due in part to a screenplay that was written by the original authors of the story *Undercover Cat*, Millie and Gordon Gordon, along with Bill Walsh, and a popular title tune written by Richard M. Sherman and Robert B. Sherman. One of the featured cats was actually Tao from Disney's *The Incredible Journey*. Released on video in 1985 and 1993.

That Darn Cat (film) Updated remake of the 1965 feature. Sixteen-year-old Patti Randall is totally bored with her sleepy hometown, but she awakens to feverish excitement when her tomcat, D.C. (Darn Cat), delivers an important clue in a mysterious kidnapping of a wealthy family's maid. With inept novice FBI agent Zeke Kelso at her side, she must track D.C. through all his favorite hangouts, hoping to solve the mystery. Directed by Bob Spiers. Released on February 14, 1997. 89 min. Stars Christina Ricci (Patti Randall), Doug E. Doug (Kelso), Dean Jones (Mr. Flint), George Dzundza (Boetticher), Peter Boyle (Pa), Michael McKean (Peter Randall), Bess Armstrong (Judy Randall), Dyan Cannon (Mrs. Flint), John Ratzenberger (Dusty), Estelle Parsons (Old Lady McCracken). Based on the novel *Undercover Cat* by the Gordons and the screenplay by the Gordons and Bill Walsh for the 1965 Disney film. Dean Jones, who starred as Kelso in the earlier film, returned for a role in this version. The star cat, Elvis, was discovered by his trainer, Larry Madrid, at the North Hollywood animal shelter. Elvis was actually selected because he was a perfect double for some other cats selected earlier, but Elvis turned out to be the star himself. And he hardly needed any doubles; he did 98 percent of the work himself. Edgefield, South Carolina, was selected to portray the fictional Massachusetts town in the movie, with the filmmakers even changing the town name to match the filming location. Released on video in 1997.

That Was Then (television) Hour-long series; aired on ABC from September 27, 2002 to October 18. Travis Glass, about to turn 30, and unhappy with his life, makes a wish during a lightning storm and is jolted back in time to when he was 16. He has a chance to try again to woo the girl of his dreams. Stars James Bulliard (Travis Glass), Tyler Labine (Donnie Pinkus), Kiele Sanchez (Claudia Wills-Glass), Brad Raider (Gregg Glass), Tricia O'Kelley (Sophie Frisch), Andrea Bowen (Zooey Glass), Bess Armstrong (Mickey Glass), Jeffrey Tambor (Gary Glass). From Touchstone Television.

That's So Raven (television) Comedy series; airing in the United States on Disney Channel beginning on January 17, 2003, after a September 2, 2002, debut in Britain. Raven Baxter is a teen whose ability to glimpse flashes of the future often gets her into hot water, as she tries to alter the course of future events. She is aided by her loyal best friends, Eddie and Chelsea.  Luckily her parents and little brother are always there to set Raven on the right course. Stars Raven (Raven Baxter), Orlando Brown (Eddie Thomas), Kyle Orlando Massey (Cory Baxter), Anneliese van der Pol (Chelsea Daniels), T'Keyah Crystal Keymáh (Tonya Baxter), Rondell Sheridan (Victor Baxter). Raven was formerly known as Raven-Symone. The show began airing on ABC's *ABC Kids* Saturday morning lineup on September 20, 2003.

Theater in the Wild Theater in DinoLand U.S.A. at Disney's Animal Kingdom; opened in 1998 with *Journey into Jungle Book* and changing in 1999 to *Tarzan Rocks*. At Hong Kong Disneyland, the theater features *Festival of the Lion King.*

Theater of the Stars Located on Hollywood Boulevard at Disney-MGM Studios from May 1, 1989 to May 2, 1993. It was moved to a location on Sunset Boulevard.

Their Eyes Were Watching God See *Oprah Winfrey Presents: Their Eyes Were Watching God.*

There's a Great Big Beautiful Tomorrow "Shining at the end of every day," which is how the song, written by Richard M. Sherman and Robert B. Sherman, began. It was written for the G.E. Carousel of Progress built by Disney at the 1964–1965 New York World's Fair, and it followed the attraction when it moved to Disneyland. Due to a change in corporate philosophy at General Electric, however, the song was dropped when the attraction moved to Magic Kingdom Park at Walt Disney World in 1975. Instead, a new song, "The Best Time of Your Life," was commissioned. But by then, the original song was a favorite among many parkgoers, and its return in November 1993, marked a historic moment for those who recalled the original show.

These Friends of Mine (television) Television series; premiered on ABC on March 9, 1994. Retitled *Ellen* in the Summer of 1994 (see also under that title). The series features a close-knit group of spirited singles who look out for each other. Stars Ellen DeGeneres, Arye Gross (Adam Green), Holly Fulger (Holly), Maggie Wheeler (Anita).

They're Off Goofy cartoon; released on January 23, 1948. Directed by Jack Hannah. At a horse race, the expert bets on the favorite, Snapshot, and the novice bets on the long shot, Old Moe. After a series of racing misadventures, Old Moe wins by a nose when Snapshot turns his head to pose for the camera.

Thicke, Alan Actor; appeared on television in *14 Going on 30*, and as the father, Dr. Carson, in the *Not Quite Human* films for The Disney Channel. He also appeared in *Raising Helen* (Hockey Cantor).

Thimble Drome Flight Circle See Flight Circle.

Think It Through With Winnie the Pooh (film) Series of two educational films: *Responsible Persons*, and *One and Only You*; released in September 1989.

Third Man on the Mountain (film) In 1865, as young kitchen helper Rudi Matt climbs the unconquered Citadel, he rescues Captain John Winter, a famous English climber, and discloses that his father was legendary guide Joseph Matt, who, like many others, had tried to reach the top of the mountain, but was killed. Despite his inexperience, he is chosen to scale the mountain with Winter, his Uncle Lerner, and Saxo, a guide from a rival village. Rudi, sure his father had discovered a route to the summit, wins permission to climb a deep cleft, bringing the others behind. He succeeds, and the climb goes on. Near the top Rudi must master his desire to reach the summit in order to save Saxo from death. Winter and Lerner make the top, and plant Joseph Matt's revered red shirt and alpenstock like a banner atop the now conquered mountain. Released on November 10, 1959. Directed by Ken Annakin. 107 min. Stars James MacArthur (Rudi Matt), Michael Rennie (Capt. John Winter), Janet Munro (Lizbeth Hempel), James Donald (Franz Lerner), Herbert Lom (Emil Saxo). Walt Disney's interest at the time in Switzerland (he took his family there on summer vacation) not only brought about this "Tom Sawyer in the Alps" (*Time* magazine), but later, the popular Matterhorn Bobsleds attraction at Disneyland. Aired on television in two parts in 1963 as *Banner in the Sky*, which was the name of the original book by James Ramsey Ullman. (Ullman happened to be vacationing in Zermatt at the foot of the Matterhorn while the film was being made, and the director gave him a cameo role as an American tourist, as he did with revered actress Helen Hayes, MacArthur's mother.) Released on video in 1986.

13th Warrior, The (film) When an important emissary from Baghdad, Ibn Fahdlan, accompanied by his manservent, Melchisidek, is abducted by a band of Viking warriors, he is forced to join their quest to battle cannibal creatures legendary for consuming every living thing in their path. Ibn realizes he must conquer his fear and go to battle with the warriors or face being devoured as well. A Touchstone Picture. Directed by John McTiernan. Released on August 27, 1999. Stars Antonio Banderas (Ahmed Ibn Fahdlan), Diane Venora (Queen Weilew), Omar Sharif (Melchisidek), Vladimir Kulich (Buliwyf), Dennis Storhoi (Herger the Joyous), Sven Wollter (King Hrothgar). 103 min. Based on the novel *Eaters of the Dead* by Michael Crichton. In searching for the perfect Northern setting, the filmmakers traveled extensively before settling on the North Central coast of Vancouver Island, near Campbell River, British Columbia, at Elk Bay. Filmed in CinemaScope. Released on video in 2000.

Thirteenth Year, The (television) A Disney Channel original movie; debuted on May 15, 1999. A young boy, Cody, begins to experience an unusual phenomenon as he approaches his 13th birthday. He gets scales and fins, begins to breathe underwater, and communicates with fish. Cody soon discovers the real reason for the unusual changes—he is the child of a mermaid and is transforming into a "merboy." Directed by Duwayne Dunham. Stars Chez Starbuck (Cody Griffin), Dave Coulier (Whit Griffin), Lisa Stahl Sullivan (Sharon Griffin), Brent Briscoe (Big John Wheatley).

This Is You See *You* (educational films).

This Is Your Life, Donald Duck (television) Television show; aired on March 11, 1960. Directed by Jack Hannah, C. August Nichols. Walt Disney turns the show over to Jiminy Cricket who presents a tribute to Donald Duck, using a number of his cartoons.

Thomas, Bob Author; wrote several books on Disney—*The Art of Animation*; *Walt Disney: Magician of the Movies*; *Walt Disney, an American Original* (the most authoritative biography of Walt Disney); *Building a Company: Roy O. Disney and the Creation of an Entertainment Empire*; and *The Art of Animation, from Mickey Mouse to Beauty and the Beast*, and its revision, *The Art of Animation, from Mickey Mouse to Hercules*. He was issued a special commendation at the Disney Legends ceremony in 2001.

Thomas, Frank (1912–2004) Animator and author; one of Walt's "Nine Old Men." He joined Disney in 1934 as an assistant animator. He animated on such shorts as *Mickey's Circus* and *Little Hiawatha*. He worked on *Snow White and the Seven Dwarfs* and went on to work on 18 more features, through *The Fox and the Hound*. Some of his most memorable sequences are Bambi and Thumper on the ice and Lady and Tramp eating spaghetti. He retired in 1978 but then embarked upon a writing career with his long-

time friend and colleague, Ollie Johnston, turning out *Disney Animation: The Illusion of Life* (the ultimate treatise on Disney-style animation); *Too Funny for Words*; *The Disney Villain*; and *Bambi: The Story and the Film*. He was honored with the Disney Legends award in 1989. He and Ollie Johnston were profiled in the documentary *Frank and Ollie*, made by his son, Ted Thomas.

Thomas, Jonathan Taylor Child actor; appeared in *Home Improvement* (Randy) and pro-

vided the voice of the young Simba in *The Lion King*. He also appeared in *Man of the House* (Ben), *Tom and Huck* (Tom Sawyer), and *I'll Be Home for Christmas* (Jake).

Thomas O'Malley Alley cat who helps Duchess and her kittens in *The Aristocats*; voiced by Phil Harris. The cat's full name is Abraham de Lacy Giuseppe Casey Thomas O'Malley.

Thompson, Bill (1913–1971) Popular Disney voice actor, with characters such as the White Rabbit and Dodo in *Alice in Wonderland*; Mr. Smee in *Peter Pan*; Joe, Bull, Dachsie, and Jock in *Lady and the Tramp*; King Hubert in *Sleeping Beauty*; Uncle Waldo in *The Aristocats*; Professor Owl, and Ranger J. Audubon Woodlore.

Thompson, Emma Actress; appeared (uncredited) in *My Father the Hero* (Andre's girlfriend) and did the voice of Captain Amelia in *Treasure Planet*.

Thornton, Billy Bob Actor; appeared in *Bound by Honor* (Lightning); *Tombstone* (Johnny Tyler); *An Alan Smithee Film: Burn Hollywood Burn* (himself); *Armageddon* (Dan Truman); and *The Alamo* (Davy Crockett).

Thornton, Randy Senior producer at Walt Disney Records, best known for his work digitally restoring the classic Disney sound tracks. With Walt Disney Records since 1986, he also produces their spoken-word projects, and has been honored with many awards.

Those Calloways (film) New England trapper Cam Calloway, a poor provider for his wife and son, dreams of the day he can build a sanctuary for migrating geese. Using the money his son earned as a fur trapper, Calloway buys a lake and plants it with corn to attract the migrating birds. Learning that two rascally operators want the lake as a resort site, Calloway sets his corn afire, and then is shot by one of the operators. Later, with the area declared a sanctuary by officials, Calloway is able to see his dream realized when the geese come to the lake. Released on January 28, 1965. Directed by Norman Tokar. 131 min. Stars Brian Keith (Cam Calloway), Vera Miles (Liddy Calloway), Brandon de Wilde (Bucky Calloway), Walter Brennan (Alf Simes), Ed Wynn (Ed Parker), Philip Abbot (Dell Fraser), Tom Skerritt (Whit Turner), John Larkin (Jim Mellot). The cast includes Linda Evans as Bridie Mellot in one of her first film appearances. Most of the film takes place during the fall folliage season. After beautiful establishing shots were filmed in Vermont, some extra work was needed to turn the Disney Studio backlot, where the lake, Calloway cabin, and village were created, into a similar setting. Since California is not known for its fall colors, 280,000 handpainted leaves and bushes had to be meticulously prepared to match the Vermont scenes. The film marked the only time the prominent film composer Max Steiner, of *Gone With The Wind* and *Casablanca* fame, produced a score for Disney. There were also two songs, "The Cabin-Raising Song" and "Rhyme-Around," written by Richard M. Sherman and Robert B. Sherman. Released on video in 1985.

Thousand Acres, A (film) The saga of the Cook family, headed by the indomitable patriarch, Larry Cook. Cook's kingdom is a fertile farm that spans 1,000 acres, but the seeds of its destruction are sown when he impulsively decides to distribute it among his three daughters, Ginny, Rose, and Caroline. The apportioned land soon begins to divide the family. Long-guarded secrets, unspoken rivalries, and denied desires lay buried just beneath the surface and are unwillingly unearthed with profound, catastrophic, and ultimately liberating repercussions. A Touchstone Picture. Directed by Jocelyn Moorhouse. Released on September 19, 1997. Stars Jessica Lange (Ginny), Michelle Pfeiffer (Rose), Jennifer Jason Leigh (Caroline), Jason Robards (Larry Cook), Keith Carradine (Ty Smith), Kevin Anderson (Peter Lewis), Colin Firth (Jess Clark). 105 min. Based on the Pulitzer Prize–winning novel by Jane Smi-

ley, who told the *King Lear* story from the outlook of the daughters. Although the story is set in Iowa, most of the location filming took place on several farms in the area of Rochelle, Illinois. Released on video in 1998.

Threat Matrix (television) One-hour drama series; aired on ABC from September 18, 2003 to January 29, 2004. To guard against terrorist threats, the Homeland Security Department has created a highly specialized, elite task force trained and equipped to counter anyone or anything that threatens our nation. The head of this supersecret team is Special Agent John Kilmer, who reports only to the president and has authority to call upon the technical skills, firepower, and specialist agents of the FBI, CIA, and NSA. Stars Jamie Denton (John Kilmer), Kelly Rutherford (Frankie Ellroy Kilmer), Will Lyman (Col. Roger Atkins), Kurt Caceres (Tim Serrano), Mahershalalhashbaz Ali (Jelani), Melora Walters (Anne Larken), Anthony Azizi (Mo), Shoshannah Stern (Holly Brodeen). From Touchstone Television and Industry Television.

Three Blind Mouseketeers (film) Silly Symphony cartoon; released on September 26, 1936. Directed by Dave Hand. In their quest for survival, three mice continually outwit Captain Katt. While he is in pursuit of them, the mice get mixed up in a collection of bottles that serve to increase their number, confusing Captain Katt and causing him to be caught in his own traps.

Three Caballeros, The (film) Four short films on Latin America, in a story about Donald Duck receiving birthday gifts from his Latin American amigos, José Carioca, the parrot, and Panchito, the Mexican charro rooster. He unwraps a 16mm projector and views *The Cold-Blooded Penguin* about Pablo Penguin, who flees the cold for a tropical isle and then misses the winter. Then he views *The Flying Gauchito*, about a racing donkey with wings; *Baia*, in which Donald and José go to Baia, meet a cookie girl, and dance; and *La Piñata*, in which Donald learns of Las Posadas, the children's procession before Christmas, and finds friendly shelter and the breaking of the piñata. Interspersed throughout the film is live action of native dancing and Latin American songs. The world premiere was in Mexico City on December 21, 1944; released in the United States on February 3, 1945. Directed by Norm Ferguson. 71 min. It was re-released in theaters in an abridged version in 1977 at a time when the film had gained increased awareness because of its almost psychedelic sequences. Released on video in 1982. Aurora Miranda, sister of Hollywood Star Carmen, dances with Donald in the *Baia* sequence, showing how far the Studio had advanced the art of combining animation with live actors. This is the first time Walt Disney had attempted the technique since the Alice Comedies in the 1920s. Songs from the film include "You Belong to My Heart," "Baia," and "The Three Caballeros." Parts of the film were released

separately as shorts and extracts appeared in the educational film *Creative Film Adventures, No. 1* in 1976. The motion picture was nominated for two Academy Awards—Best Sound (C. O. Slyfield) and Best Scoring of a Musical Picture (Edward H. Plumb, Paul J. Smith, Charles Wolcott).

3D Jamboree (film) Special cartoon; shown only in the Fantasyland Theater at Disneyland beginning on June 16, 1956, containing footage of the Mouseketeers along with *Working for Peanuts* and *Adventures in Music: Melody*. Filmed in 3-D. Besides these, there were no other Disney 3-D films until *Magic Journeys* was produced for Epcot 25 years later.

Three for Breakfast (film) Donald Duck cartoon; released on November 5, 1948. Directed by

Jack Hannah. In their attempt to steal Donald's pancakes, Chip and Dale are fooled into taking rubber ones until they realize their mistake and trick Donald out of his meal.

Three Fugitives (film) Newly released from prison, former bank robber Lucas has decided to go straight. As he is trying to deposit his prison paycheck in a local bank, Ned Perry, an inept but desperate robber, stumbles into the bank and takes him hostage. Because of Lucas's notorious reputation, the police think he masterminded the robbery, and when Perry endangers everyone with a live grenade, Lucas reluctantly takes charge of the situation and engineers their escape. The fugitives are joined by Perry's cute but troubled six-year-old daughter, who hasn't spoken in the two years since her mother died and for whose special schooling he needed the money. Soon a genuine friendship grows between these unlikely partners in crime, as Lucas tries to prove his innocence and Perry tries to provide a better life for his daughter. Released on January 27, 1989. Directed by Francis Veber. A Touchstone Picture. 96 min. Stars Nick Nolte (Lucas), Martin Short (Perry), James Earl Jones (Dugan), Sarah Rowland Doroff (Meg). Filmed in Los Angeles and in Tacoma, Washington. The prison scenes were shot at McNeil Island Prison. Released on video in 1989.

Three Little Pigs (film) Silly Symphony cartoon; released on May 27, 1933. Directed by Burt Gillett. While two happy-go-lucky pigs frolic and

build flimsy houses of straw and sticks, the third pig toils at building a secure brick dwelling. The

Big Bad Wolf manages to huff and puff and blow down the first two houses, but meets his match at the third. When he tries to slide down the chimney, he is scalded by landing in a boiling pot. When released in 1933, this cartoon not only strengthened Depression-weary audiences, who made the theme song, "Who's Afraid of the Big Bad Wolf?," their anthem, but it proved to be another milestone of Disney animation in the scope of characterization, as well as in score and song. Walt Disney entrusted Frank Churchill with the score for the picture and Fred Moore with animating the pigs, and, justifiably proud, said, "At last we have achieved true personality in a whole picture." The film became so popular that it often ranked higher on the marquee than the accompanying feature, and often stayed long after feature films came and went. At one New York theater, the manager had beards put on the pigs' faces that grew longer as the short's run extended. One of the most famous cartoons of all time, it won the Academy Award for Best Cartoon. A major merchandising campaign led to many items featuring the Big Bad Wolf and the Three Little Pigs. The film is included in *Milestones in Animation* (1973). The names of the pigs were Fiddler Pig, Fifer Pig, and Practical Pig. The writing of the song was re-enacted in the television show *Cavalcade of Songs* (1955). The popularity of the film led to three sequels: *The Big Bad Wolf, Three Little Wolves,* and *The Practical Pig.*

Three Little Pigs (film) Twenty-six-minute animated film made by Disney Television Animation, and released in one theater for Academy Award consideration on October 21, 1997. Directed by Darrell Rooney. When the Three Little Pigs allow Barnabas the Wolf, a professed vegan, to become their roommate, they quickly become paranoid after a series of misunderstandings that could only have one explanation—the Wolf intends to make the Pigs his protein source. Part of a Twisted Tales series, which included *Redux Riding Hood.*

Three Little Wolves (film) Silly Symphony cartoon; released on April 14, 1936. Directed by Dave Hand. In this second sequel to *Three Little Pigs,* the frivolous pigs blow the Practical Pig's

wolf horn one too many times, and he refuses to come when they are actually captured by the Big Bad Wolf and Three Little Wolves. Practical Pig manages to save them in the nick of time with a "Wolf Pacifier."

Three Lives of Thomasina, The (film) Thomasina, a big, four-year-old ginger cat, comes to live with widowed veterinary surgeon Andrew MacDhui and his five-year-old daughter Mary, in a little village in Scotland. When the cat is hurt, Andrew "puts her to sleep." Mary is so heartbroken she accuses her father of killing her beloved pet. So far as Mary is concerned, her father is dead, too. But Thomasina has not died. She has been discovered, still breathing, by Lori MacGregor, a beautiful but mysterious young woman who loves animals and has an almost supernatural ability to cure their ills. Lori brings Thomasina back to life, eventually brings Andrew and little Mary together again, and becomes Andrew's wife and mother for the little girl. But it is really Thomasina, home again with the MacDhuis, who rules the family. Initial release in New York on December 11, 1963; general release on June 6, 1964. Directed by Don Chaffey. 97 min. Based on Paul Gallico's story. Stars Patrick McGoohan (Andrew MacDhui), Susan Hampshire (Lori MacGregor), Karen Dotrice (Mary MacDhui), Matthew Garber (Geordie), Vincent Winter (Hughie Stirling), Finlay Currie (Grandpa Stirling), Laurence Naismith (Rev. Angus Peddie), and Espeth March as the voice of Thomasina. Dotrice and Garber were selected by Walt Disney for the major roles of the children in *Mary Poppins* after he witnessed their performances in this film. Shot at Pinewood Studio, in England, where the entire village of Inveranoch was built, with leftover sets from Disney's *Horse Without A Head.* The song "Thomasina" was written by Terry Gilkyson. Released on video in 1985 and 1993.

Three Men and a Baby (film) Happy-go-lucky bachelors, Peter, Michael, and Jack, live together in an avant-garde apartment in New York City. When Jack goes off on a trip telling his roommates to expect a package, the two are amazed to find a baby on their doorstep. Totally inexperienced at caring for a baby, Peter and Michael learn quickly and soon find themselves becoming very protective of "their" baby, as does Jack when he returns. Meanwhile, drug dealers who are after the real package threaten the baby's safety. The trio foil the dealers, and arrange for baby Mary—and her mother—to live with them permanently. Released on November 25, 1987. Directed by Leonard Nimoy. A Touchstone Picture. 102 min. Stars Tom Selleck (Peter), Steve Guttenberg (Michael), Ted Danson (Jack), Nancy Travis (Sylvia). Filmed primarily in Toronto, with some sequences shot in New York City. A wild rumor ran rampant after the film's release and moviegoers caught a glimpse of what was reported to be a ghostly figure in the background of one shot. The rumor was that it was the ghost of a child who had lived in the house where the filming took place. The rumor was false. There was no house; the set was built on a soundstage, and the "ghost" turned out to be a prop left inadvertently where it could be seen in the shot. Released on video in 1988.

Three Men and a Little Lady (film) A sequel to *Three Men and a Baby*, taking up the story five years later, with the three bachelors—Peter, Michael, and Jack—having settled into a comfortable functioning household with the little girl, Mary, and her single mom, Sylvia. Their five-part harmony is shaken when Sylvia agrees to appear in a play in London, directed by the man she has decided to marry, and to take Mary with her to live there permanently. The three men soon discover how empty their lives are without Mary and go to great lengths to stop the wedding, bring Mary back to New York, and, coincidentally, find the perfect husband for Sylvia. Released on November 21, 1990. Directed by Emile Ardolino. A Touchstone Picture. 100 min. Stars Tom Selleck (Peter), Steve Guttenberg (Michael), Ted Danson (Jack), Nancy Travis (Sylvia), Christopher Cazenove (Edward), Fiona Shaw (Miss Lomax), Sheila Hancock (Vera). Filmed in the Los Angeles and New York areas, and in London and Banbury in Britain's Cotswolds. Released on video in 1991.

Three Musketeers, The (film) The classic story of the young D'Artagnan journeying to Paris to join the King's Musketeers, only to find the powerful Cardinal Richelieu plotting against them and attempting to make himself king. Richelieu is thwarted in this action by the three remaining Musketeers, Athos, Porthos, and Aramis. The cardinal dispatches the Count De Rochefort, a nefarious former Musketeer, to kill them, and arranges for his cohort, Milady De Winter, to travel to England to make a secret treaty with the Duke of Buckingham, the true ruler of England. On the young king's birthday, Richelieu plans to have him murdered, and rule himself with Queen Anne. The Musketeers and D'Artagnan come through, capturing Milady and then boldly gathering up the old Musketeer regiment to finally conquer Richelieu. Released on November 12, 1993. Produced in association with Caravan Pictures. Directed by Stephen Herek. 105 min. Stars Charlie Sheen (Aramis), Kiefer Sutherland (Athos), Chris O'Donnell (D'Artagnan), Oliver Platt (Porthos), Tim Curry (Cardinal Richelieu), Rebecca De Mornay (Milady De Winter), Gabrielle Anwar (Queen Anne). Based on the novel by Alexandre Dumas. Filmed on location in Austria. Released on video in 1994.

Three Musketeers, The (film) Direct-to-video release from DisneyToon Studios on August 17, 2004. Working as janitors at Musketeer headquarters, Mickey, Donald, and Goofy dream of becoming Musketeers. Peg Leg Pete, the Captain of the Musketeers, and his sinister lieutenant Clarabelle, have a dastardly plot to rid the kingdom of the Princess Minnie so Pete can take over the throne. Pete makes the trio official Musketeers and assigns them to "protect" the princess, assuming they will fail to get the job done. But, Mickey, Donald, and Goofy learn an invaluable lesson about friendship, teamwork, and the true meaning of "All for one and one for all!" Directed by Donovan Cook. Voices include Wayne Allwine (Mickey), Tony Anselmo (Donald), Bill Farmer (Goofy), Russi Taylor (Minnie), Tress MacNeille (Daisy), Jim Cummings (Peg Leg Pete), April Winchell (Clarabelle Cow), Jeff Bennett & Maurice LaMarche (the Beagle Boys), Rob Paulsen (Troubadour). 68 min.

3 Ninjas (film) Three young boys who feel neglected by their FBI-agent father spend their summer learning the ways of the ninja from their grandfather. The old man also teaches them to rely upon themselves and each other. But when an evil arms dealer decides to kidnap the boys to keep their father from thwarting his illegal business deal, the boys dodge their kidnappers and realize that their family ties are just as important as their ninja skills. Released on August 7, 1992. Directed by Jon Turteltaub. A Touchstone Picture. 84 min. Stars Victor Wong (Grandpa), Michael Treanor (Rocky), Max Elliott Slade (Colt), Chad Power (Tum Tum). Filmed on locations in Los Angeles by an American, European, and Far Eastern crew. Released on video in 1993. Two sequels, *3 Ninjas Kick Back* and *3 Ninjas Knuckle Up*, were made in 1994 and 1995 by Tri-Star.

Three on the Run (television) Television show; aired on January 8, 1978. Directed by William Beaudine, Jr. Two brothers enter an annual sled dog race to try to match their deceased father's record. They eventually win, thanks to a grumpy bear who gives the inept dogs the incentive to increase their speed. Stars Denver Pyle, Davey Davison, Brett McGuire, Donald Williams, Ron Brown, Peggy Rea.

Three Orphan Kittens (film) Silly Symphony cartoon; released on October 26, 1935. Directed by Dave Hand. Remarkable animation design and perspective was created by artist Ken Anderson for this cartoon, which tells the story of three

castaway kittens who find refuge in a warm house and get into trouble with the occupant in antics with the furniture and a grand piano. Academy Award winner for Best Cartoon. The film led to a sequel, *More Kittens*.

Three Skrinks, The (television) Serialized version of *Emil and the Detectives* on the new *Mickey Mouse Club*.

Three Tall Tales (television) Television show; aired on January 6, 1963. Directed by Hamilton S. Luske. Walt Disney explains about Baron Munchausen and his tall tales, then Ludwig Von Drake tells the stories of *Casey at the Bat, The Saga of Windwagon Smith*, and *Paul Bunyan*.

Three Without Fear (television) Two-part television show; aired on January 3 and 10, 1971. The two episodes are titled *Lost on the Baja Peninsula* and *In the Land of the Desert Whales*. Two Mexican orphans help save the life of an American boy, Dave, stranded by a plane crash, who has been bitten by a scorpion. The orphans are being tracked by an evil guardian, and Dave volunteers to help them. Narrated by Hugh Cherry. Stars Bart Orlando, Pablo Lopez, Marion Valjalo, Claude Earls.

Thrifty Pig, The (film) Shows the advisability and necessity of purchasing Canadian War Bonds. Footage from *Three Little Pigs* was reanimated, with the wolf as a Nazi and the pigs' house being made of bricks made from Canadian War Savings Certificates. The song "Who's Afraid of the Big Bad Wolf?" is used with new lyrics. Made for the National Film Board of Canada. The film was delivered on November 19, 1941.

Thrills, Chills & Spiders: The Making of Arachnophobia (television) Syndicated television special; aired on July 15, 1990. Directed by John Schultz. A behind-the-scenes look at the making of *Arachnophobia*, hosted by Mark Taylor.

Thru the Mirror (film) Mickey Mouse cartoon; released on May 30, 1936. Directed by Dave Hand. Mickey dreams he steps through his bedroom mirror into a land where all the furnishings and objects are animated and he can interact with them. But they are not all friendly, and after Mickey dances with the queen in a deck of playing cards, making the king jealous, they attack

him and send him back through the mirror as the alarm clock wakes him up. Based on the "Alice Through the Looking Glass" story.

Thumper Rabbit friend of Bambi; voiced as a youngster by Peter Behn.

Thunder Alley (television) Television series; aired on ABC from March 9, 1994 to July 25, 1995. A divorced liberal 1990s mom is raising her three children in a household headed by her father, a crusty retired stock car racer. She experiences a clash of child-rearing styles when she and her children move in with her traditionalist father, in his home above the garage where he works—his refuge since his days on the track. Stars Edward Asner (Gil Jones), Diane Venora (Bobbi Turner), Jim Beaver (Leland), Lindsay Felton (Jenny Turner), Haley Joel Osment (Harry Turner), Kelly Vint (Claudine Turner), Andrew Keegan (Jack Kelly). After eight episodes, Robin Riker took over the role of Bobbi.

Thunder Mesa Mercantile Building Located in Frontierland in Disneyland Paris; opened on April 12, 1992. Contains Bonanza Outfitters, Eureka Mining Supplies and Assay Office, Frontierland Traders, and Tobias Norton & Sons.

Thunder Mesa Riverboat Landing Located in Frontierland at Disneyland Paris; opened on

April 12, 1992. Port for the *Mark Twain* and the *Molly Brown*.

Thursday Circus Day on the 1950s *Mickey Mouse Club*. Discovery Day on the new *Mickey Mouse Club*.

Tiburon See *People and Places—Tiburon, Sardinia, Morocco, Icebreakers*.

Ticket books Disneyland began offering ticket books to guests on October 11, 1955. The first books cost $2.50 for an adult for a day at the park, and consisted of A, B, and C tickets for the different attractions. A D ticket was added in 1956 and an E ticket in 1959. Ticket books were phased out in favor of all-inclusive passports in 1982. Tokyo Disneyland continued to utilize

ticket books until March 31, 2001. Annual passports were available at Walt Disney World starting on September 28, 1982; at Disneyland they were first offered to Magic Kingdom Club members exclusively in June 1983, but in the following year they were made available to all guests. See also E ticket.

Tickets Please (television) Unsold television pilot; aired on CBS on September 6, 1988. Directed by Art Dielhenn. Life of a group of regulars on the commuter trains of New York City. 30 min. Stars Cleavon Little, Marcia Strassman, Joe Guzaldo, David Marciano, Yeardley Smith, Harold Gould, Bill Macy.

Tie That Binds, The (film) An attractive and loving couple, the Cliftons decide to adopt a child, and after visiting an adoption agency, they are immediately bewitched by a beautiful but shy six-year-old girl, Janie. But, it turns out that Janie already has parents, the Netherwoods, who happen to be drifters and dangerous criminals. The Netherwoods appear to reclaim their child, and they will stop at nothing, including murder, in their quest. The Cliftons are forced to fight for their very lives to protect their daughter. Released on September 8, 1995. A Hollywood Pictures film. Directed by Wesley Strick. Stars Vincent Spano (Russell Clifton), Moira Kelly (Dana Clifton), Julia Devin (Janie), Daryl Hannah (Leann Netherwood), Keith Carradine (John Netherwood). 98 min. Filming took place around the Los Angeles area. Released on video in 1996.

Tieman, Robert Archives manager; joined the Walt Disney Archives in 1990 after several years as a photo librarian with The Disney Channel. He has spoken at Disneyana gatherings and on the Disney Cruise Line about the Archives' collections, and wrote the books *Disney's Photomosaics* (1998), *The Disney Treasures* (2003), *The Disney Keepsakes* (2005), and *Quintessential Disney* (2005).

Tiger Cruise (television) Disney Channel Original Film; premiered on August 6, 2004. Operation Tiger allows sailors to invite their families to ship out with them for a week to learn what their loved ones do in the military. But in 2001, when teen Maddie Dolan embarks on a weeklong tour with a mission to persuade her father, the ship's executive officer, to give up his military career and come home, she and other families are trapped aboard when the USS *Constellation* is mobilized in full combat alert after the terrorist attacks of 9/11. Maddie thus sees firsthand her father's courage, honor, and commitment to those aboard his ship. Directed by Duwayne Dunham. Stars Bill Pullman (Cmdr. Gary Dolan), Hayden Panettiere (Maddie Dolan), Bianca Collins (Tina Torres), Nathaniel Lee, Jr. (Anthony), Mehcad Brooks (Kenny), Mercedes Colon (Grace Torres), Jansen Panettiere (Joey), Lisa Dean Ryan (Diane

Coleman), Ty O'Neal (Danny Horner), Troy Evans (Chuck Horner), Gary Weeks (Lt. Tom Hillman). Filmed aboard the USS *John C. Stennis*, which was docked in San Diego, and aboard the USS *Nimitz* at sea.

Tiger Lily Indian princess in Never Land in *Peter Pan*.

Tiger Town (television) Twelve-year-old Alex is a die-hard Tiger fan who is convinced that a true believer can make anything happen. He idolizes aging baseball star Billy Young, who dreams of winning the pennant. When Alex is in the stands, watching and wishing, Billy suddenly begins playing a winning game, and the Tigers come closer to the pennant. Alex continues to believe in Billy, and the Tigers do indeed win the championship. The first motion picture created exclusively for The Disney Channel, on which it aired on October 9, 1983; the film had a brief theatrical release only in Detroit beginning on June 8, 1984. Directed by Alan Shapiro. 76 min. Stars Justin Henry (Alex), Roy Scheider (Billy Young), Ron McClarty (Buddy), Bethany Carpenter (Mother). Filmed at Tiger Stadium and at other landmarks in Detroit. Released on video in 1984.

Tiger Trouble (film) Goofy cartoon; released on January 5, 1945. Directed by Jack Kinney. Goofy and his elephant get into all sorts of trouble when they attempt to catch a tiger while on safari.

Tiger Walks, A (film) A drunken truck driver accidentally permits a mistreated tiger to escape from captivity while the circus wagon is undergoing repairs in a small country town garage. This animal, never out of captivity, escapes into the countryside, hungry, frightened, and incapable of coping with this new way of life. Julie, the young daughter of the local sheriff, realizes that the gathering hordes of local hunters, the Army, and her father's deputies will kill the tiger, who does not belong in the wilds but back in captivity. She succeeds in winning over her father, who decides to send for a tranquilizer gun located in a nearby city in an effort to capture the animal peacefully before it is killed by an aroused and panic-stricken community. In the end, the animal is spared and returned to the only life it knows, at the local zoo. Released on March 12, 1964. Directed by Norman Tokar. 91 min. Stars Brian Keith (Pete Williams), Vera Miles (Dorothy Williams), Pamela Franklin (Julie Williams), Sabu (Ram Singh), Kevin Corcoran (Tom Hadley), Peter Brown (Vern Goodman). One of the highlights of this film is the truly extraordinary supporting cast, which featured such favorites as Una Merkel (Mrs. Watkins), Connie Gilchrist (Lewis' wife), Frank McHugh (Bill Watkins), Edward Andrews (Governor), Doodles Weaver (Bob Evans), Jack Albertson (Sam Grant), Arthur Hunnicutt (Lewis), and Hal Peary (Uncle Harry). This was Sabu's last film role. With sets built at the Walt Disney Studio in Burbank, things got a little exciting during filming when at one point the trained tiger leapt through a sheet of plate glass that had been placed between him and the camera. But the trainers soon had him back under control before anyone was injured. Because of the serious subject matter and the unflattering look at small-town life, the film was only moderately successful. Released on video in 1986.

Tigger Tiger who first appeared in *Winnie the Pooh and the Blustery Day* (1968); voiced by Paul Winchell. According to Tigger, the most wonderful thing about Tiggers is that he is the only one.

Tigger Movie, The (film) As the gang is busy preparing a suitable winter home for Eeyore, Tigger interrupts their efforts with his boisterous bouncing. Rabbit suggests Tigger find some other tiggers to bounce with. Tigger thinks the suggestion absurd, since he is the only one, but then he decides that being the one and only can be kind of lonely. So he begins thinking that there must be other tiggers out there. This leads him on an amazing journey through the Hundred Acre Wood in search of the "biggest and bestest" family tree around. When his search proves fruitless, Tigger's pals try to cheer him up by masquerading as his family and dressing up in tigger costumes. This only serves to deepen Tigger's longing and he stubbornly bounces off into a cold winter storm to find his reclusive relatives. Pooh, Piglet, Rabbit, Roo, and Eeyore become concerned and form a search party to find him. In the end, Tigger's heart leads him home and he comes to realize that his family has always been with him—those friends who love and care for him. Directed by Jun Falkenstein. Released on February 11, 2000. Voices include Jim Cummings (Tigger, Pooh), Nikita Hopkins (Roo), Ken Sansom (Rabbit), John Fiedler (Piglet), Eeyore (Peter Cullen), André Stojka (Owl), Kath Soucie (Kanga), Tom Attenborough (Christopher Robin), John Hurt (narrator). 77 min. Included are six new songs by Richard M. Sherman and Robert B. Sherman. Released on video in 2000.

Tillie Tiger Character saved by Elmer Elephant in the 1936 Silly Symphony *Elmer Elephant*; voiced by Alice Ardell.

Tilly, Meg Actress; appeared in *Tex* (Jamie Collins) and *Off Beat* (Rachel Wareham).

Tim Allen Presents: A User's Guide to Home Improvement (television) Allen presents his own favorite clips, show bloopers, and personal reflections on the long-running series; aired on ABC on May 4, 2003. Directed by Andy Cadiff. Stars Tim Allen, Richard Karn, Debbe Dunning. From Touchstone Television.

Tim Burton's The Nightmare Before Christmas See *The Nightmare Before Christmas.*

Timber (film) Donald Duck cartoon; released on January 10, 1941. Directed by Jack King. In payment for stealing food, Donald is forced by Pierre, alias Pete, to chop down trees, and he gets involved in close encounters with axes and saws, and a furious chase on railroad handcars.

Timberlake, Justin Actor; appeared on the *Mickey Mouse Club* on The Disney Channel, beginning in 1993. He was later a member of the boy band 'NSYNC. He appeared as Jason in *Model Behavior*.

Time Flyer (television) Television title in 1986 of *The Blue Yonder*.

Time for Table Manners (film) Educational film; released in September 1987. 6 min. The film teaches standard etiquette and cleanliness at meal time.

Time to Tell, A: Teen Sexual Abuse (film) Educational film; released in September 1985. Adolescents in a peer support group share their experiences of being sexually molested and learn how to protect themselves.

Time Traveler's Guide to Energy, The (film) Educational film; released in September 1983. A boy from the future accidentally erases computer data on 20th-century energy history, so he calls upon a student to help him re-create it.

Timekeeper, The Attraction in Tomorrowland in Magic Kingdom Park at Walt Disney World; opened on November 21, 1994. Presents the Circle-Vision show *From Time to Time* from Visionarium at Disneyland Paris, changing the language to English and adding in some U.S. footage. Robin Williams provides the voice of Timekeeper, Rhea Perlman that of 9-Eye. It closed on April 29, 2001, but continued to operate seasonally.

Times Square Studios Located at 1500 Broadway between 43rd and 44th streets in New York City, this 46,750-square-foot multiuse production facility, which opened on September 13, 1999, spans three floors, including two studios, office space, extensive production support facilities, production control room, radio broadcast studio, green room, and dressing rooms. As the home for ABC News's *Good Morning America*, it features glass walls to utilize Times Square as a live backdrop.

Timon Wisecracking meerkat in *The Lion King*; voiced by Nathan Lane.

Timothy Q. Mouse Dumbo's friend; voiced by Ed Brophy.

Tin Men (film) In Baltimore in 1963, two rival aluminum siding salesmen ("tin men"), Bill (BB) Babowsky and Ernest Tilley, start feuding when Tilley runs into BB's brand-new Cadillac. Their feud escalates until finally BB plays what he thinks is a winning card: he seduces Tilley's wife, Nora. BB's plan backfires because Tilley is glad to be rid of Nora, and BB finds himself falling in love with her. In addition to BB's and Tilley's personal struggles, the IRS is after Tilley, and both men face losing their licenses because of unscrupulous sales practices. But BB and Tilley are survivors, and together they face the future with new dreams. Released on March 6, 1987. Directed by Barry Levinson. A Touchstone Picture. 112 min. Stars Richard Dreyfuss (Bill Babowsky), Danny DeVito (Ernest Tilley), Barbara Hershey (Nora Tilley). Filmed on location in Baltimore, where Levinson had filmed his earlier *Diner*. Released on video in 1987.

Tinker Bell Pixie character who tries to protect Peter Pan, modeled after actress Margaret Kerry (not Marilyn Monroe as frequently written). Tinker Bell began flying above Sleeping Beauty Castle preceding the Fantasy in  the Sky fireworks at Disneyland in 1961. Contrary to frequent usage, Tinker Bell is two words; in *Peter Pan* she is referred to as Miss Bell.

Tinker Bell Toy Shoppe Fantasyland shop at Disneyland; opened in 1957, and changed its name to Once Upon a Time in July 2002. Also a shop in Fantasyland in Magic Kingdom Park at Walt Disney World; opened in November 1971 and became Tinker Bell's Treasures on December 6, 1992. Also in Fantasyland at Tokyo Disneyland; opened on April 15, 1983.

Tinker Bell's Treasures See Tinker Bell Toy Shoppe.

Title Makers, The/Nature's Half Acre (television) Television show; aired on June 11, 1961. Directed by Robert Stevenson, James Algar. The show explains how Bill Justice, X. Atencio, and T. Hee prepared the titles for *The Parent Trap* by using stop-motion animation, and Tommy Sands and Annette Funicello recorded the title song. The end of the program shows the True-Life Adventure *Nature's Half Acre*.

Tito Little Chihuahua in *Oliver & Company*; voiced by Cheech Marin. His full name is Ignacio Alonzo Julio Federico De Tito.

To Conquer the Mountain (television) Television show; part 1 of *Banner in the Sky*, the television airing of *Third Man on the Mountain*.

To My Daughter, with Love (television) Two-hour television movie; aired on NBC on January 24, 1994. A young father's tragic loss of his wife turns to crisis when his in-laws try to take custody of his child. Directed by Kevin Hooks. Stars Rick Schroder (Joey), Lawrence Pressman (Arthur), Khandi Alexander (Harriet), Megan Gallivan (Alice), Keith Amos (Tim), Ashley Malinger (Emily), Linda Gray (Eleanor).

To the South Pole for Science (television) Television show; aired on November 13, 1957. Directed and narrated by Winston Hibler. The program shows how scientists struggled to construct five bases in Antarctica during the International Geophysical Year. The other shows on the subject were *Antarctica: Past and Present* and *Antarctica: Operation Deepfreeze*.

To Trap a Thief (television) Television show; episode 1 of *Michael O'Hara IV*.

Toad Hall Restaurant Located in Fantasyland at Disneyland Paris; opened on April 12, 1992.

Toby Overgrown puppy in *The Great Mouse Detective*.

Toby Tortoise Plodding but persistent star of *The Tortoise and the Hare* (1935) and its sequel, *Toby Tortoise Returns* (1936).

Toby Tortoise Returns (film) Silly Symphony cartoon; released on August 22, 1936. Directed by Wilfred Jackson. Max Hare and Toby Tortoise are opponents in a boxing match. Max becomes frustrated when Toby retreats into his shell during punches. Max cheats by dumping fireworks into Toby's shell, but the plan backfires when it helps Toby win. A sequel to *The Tortoise and the Hare*.

Toby Turtle Friend of Skippy in *Robin Hood*; voiced by Richie Sanders.

Toby Tyler, or Ten Weeks with a Circus (film) Toby, a 12-year-old orphan, believing his aunt and uncle do not want him, runs away and joins a circus. He is exploited by Harry, the concessionaire, helped by Ben, the strong man, and becomes fast friends with Mr. Stubbs, the chimp. When the boy equestrian is hurt, Toby takes his place, becoming a tremendous success when Mr. Stubbs joins the act. He is reunited with his now understanding guardians. Released January 21, 1960. Directed by Charles Barton. 95 min. Stars Kevin Corcoran (Toby Tyler), Bob Sweeney (Harry Tupper), Henry Calvin (Ben Cotter), Gene Sheldon (Sam Treat), Barbara Beaird (Mademoiselle Jeanette). Note the final credits "introducing Ollie Wallace." This referred to the circus bandleader, played by the veteran Disney composer. Based on the novel by James Otis Kaler. Disney donated the authentic, restored circus wagons used in the film to the

Circus World Museum in Baraboo, Wisconsin. Released on video in 1986.

Toccata and Fugue in D Minor Music composed by Johann Sebastian Bach; a segment of *Fantasia*. The piece was also played on the organ by Captain Nemo in his parlor in the *Nautilus* in *20,000 Leagues Under the Sea*.

Tod Lead fox character in *The Fox and the Hound*; voiced by Keith Mitchell (young) and Mickey Rooney (older).

Today's Business (television) Syndicated television show; aired from September 26, 1986 to April 26, 1987. Consuelo Mack anchored this daily early morning business news show.

Todd, Richard Actor; appeared in the leading roles in *The Story of Robin Hood* (Robin Hood), *The Sword and the Rose* (Charles Brandon), and *Rob Roy* (Rob Roy). He was named a Disney Legend in 2002.

Tokar, Norman (1920–1979) Prolific director of Disney live-action films; signed by Disney in 1961 to direct *Big Red*, and he remained at the studio from then until his death in 1979. Among his films were *Savage Sam; A Tiger Walks; Those Calloways; The Ugly Dachshund; Follow Me, Boys!; The Happiest Millionaire; Candleshoe; The Cat from Outer Space; No Deposit, No Return; The Apple Dumpling Gang; Snowball Express; The Boatniks; Rascal; The Horse in the Gray Flannel Suit*; as well as the featurette *The Legend of the Boy and the Eagle*.

Tokyo Disneyland Park; opened on April 15, 1983, in Urayasu, just outside of Tokyo. After the success of the American Disney parks, many different countries made entreaties to Disney about building Disneylands in their countries. It was only after Disneyland park and the Walt Disney World resort were running smoothly that the Disney executives decided to listen to some of the requests. Japan's request seemed eminently feasible. The Oriental Land Company had some land, reclaimed from Tokyo Bay, which had to be used for a recreational purpose, and there was a huge local population within a 30-mile radius. A Disneyland would be a perfect fit for the site. The Japanese had long been enamored with Disneyland, and when contracts were signed, it was determined that they did not want an Oriental version of Disneyland; they wanted an American park. So, Disney Imagineers worked carefully to design an ideal park for the Japanese site. Because of more inclement weather, the Main Street area was redesigned as World Bazaar, with a roof over it. There was one Audio-Animatronics attraction that dealt with Japanese history, Meet the World. The park had a successful opening and ever since has attracted more than 10 million visitors a year. Over the years, many new attractions, such as Big Thunder Mountain Railway, Star Tours, and Splash Mountain, have been added to encourage repeat visitors. Tokyo Disneyland welcomed its 250 millionth visitor, Mrs. Hisae Do, on July 14, 2000, and its 300 millionth (combined with Tokyo DisneySea), Mrs. Yoko Kusunoki, on November 8, 2002.

Tokyo DisneySea One-hundred-acre aquatic-themed park opened next to Tokyo Disneyland; opened on September 4, 2001. On entering and viewing a unique AquaSphere, guests choose between seven distinct "ports of call"—Mediterranean Harbor, Mysterious Island, Mermaid Lagoon, Arabian Coast, Lost River Delta, Port Discovery, and American Waterfront. Attractions, dining, and shopping experiences immerse guests in ocean life and lore. The 10 millionth guest, Tetsuya Goto, arrived on July 7, 2002. Included within the park is the new Tokyo DisneySea Hotel MiraCosta, with 502 guest rooms.

Tom and Huck (film) Tom Sawyer and Huck Finn team up to steal a pirate's treasure map from Injun Joe in order to save an innocent man from being wrongly convicted in court. Witnessing a heinous crime, they are forced to run away from home. Presumed lost in the Mississippi River, they must decide whether to come forward and save the innocent man or risk retribution from Injun Joe. Released on December 22, 1995. Directed by Peter Hewitt. Stars Jonathan Taylor Thomas (Tom), Brad Renfro (Huck), Eric Schweig (Injun Joe), Charles Rocket (Judge Thatcher), Amy Wright (Aunt Polly), Michael McShane (Muff Potter), Marian Seldes (Widow Douglas). Filmed in CinemaScope. 92 min. Based on the Mark Twain book *The Adventures of Tom Sawyer*. For the movie, the town of Mooresville, Alabama, doubles for Hannibal, Missouri, which today looks too polished as a tourist attraction. Cathedral Caverns served as the location for Injun Joe's cave. Ike Eisenmann, of Disney's *Witch Mountain* fame, has a bit part as a taverner. For its original release, it was combined on a program with *Disney's Timon and Pumbaa in Stand by Me*. Released on video in 1996.

Tom Sawyer Island Frontierland attraction at Disneyland; opened on June 16, 1956. Guests can explore at their leisure, after reaching the island by raft. Some of the points of interest are the Suspension Bridge, Barrel Bridge, Injun Joe's Cave, Castle Rock Ridge with its Teeter-Totter Rock and Merry-Go-Round Rock, and Fort Wilderness. Also in Magic Kingdom Park at Walt Disney World; opened on May 20, 1973. The fort in Florida is Fort Langhorne (formerly Fort Sam Clemens). Aunt Polly's Landing (in 1995 it

became Aunt Polly's Dockside Inn) sells refreshments on the island. Both islands were in the middle of their respective Rivers of America on opening day, but the attractions were not built until many months later. Also in Westernland at Tokyo Disneyland.

Tom Sawyer Island Rafts Frontierland attraction in Magic Kingdom Park at Walt Disney World; opened on May 20, 1973. See also Rafts to Tom Sawyer Island (Disneyland). Also in Westernland at Tokyo Disneyland; opened on April 15, 1983.

Tombstone (film) Wyatt Earp and his wife Mattie arrive in the booming silver town of Tombstone intending to settle down with the rest of the Earp clan. Leaving his violent life as a Kansas lawman behind, Wyatt wants nothing more than to run a gambling establishment with his brothers, Virgil and Morgan. But peace for the Earps is not to be. A feud between the Earp brothers and an evil gang, the "Cowboys," culminates with the gunfight at the O.K. Corral, but the victorious Earps are hunted by the surviving Cowboys, headed by Johnny Ringo and Curly Bill, who seek revenge. Wyatt gathers a posse to destroy the Cowboys, and with the help of his friend, Doc Holliday, the last members of the gang are killed and Wyatt is vindicated. Released on December 25, 1993. Directed by George P. Cosmatos. A Hollywood Pictures film. 128 min. Stars Kurt Russell (Wyatt Earp), Val Kilmer (Doc Holliday), Michael Biehn (Ringo), Powers Boothe (Curly Bill), Robert Burke (Frank McLaury), Dana Delany (Josephine), Sam Elliott (Virgil Earp), Stephen Lang (Ike Clanton), Joanna Pacula (Kate), Bill Paxton (Morgan Earp), Jason Priestley (Billy Breckenridge), Michael Rooker (Sherman McMasters), Jon Tenney (Behan), Billy Zane (Mr. Fabian), Charlton Heston (Henry Hooker). Filmed on locations in and around Tucson, Arizona. Released on video in 1994.

Tomei, Marisa Actress; appeared in *Oscar* (Lisa Provolone).

Tomlin, Lily Actress; appeared in dual roles in *Big Business* (Rose Shelton/Rose Ratliff), *Krippendorf's Tribe* (Ruth Allen), and *Disney's The Kid* (Janet).

Tomlinson, David (1917–2000) Actor; appeared in *Mary Poppins* (George Banks), *The Love Bug*

(Thorndyke), and *Bedknobs and Broomsticks* (Emelius Brown). A veteran of over 35 British films, Tomlinson had never sung on screen before making *Mary Poppins*. A little polishing of his fine baritone voice soon had him singing like a pro. He was named a Disney Legend posthumously in 2002.

Tommy Tucker's Tooth (film) Dental training film made by Walt Disney for Dr. Thomas B. McCrum in Kansas City in 1922. Tommy Tucker takes pride in his appearance and very good care of his teeth, but Jimmie Jones is careless about his appearance and neglects his teeth. The first Disney educational film.

Tomorrow the Moon Alternate title of *Man and the Moon*.

Tomorrow We Diet (film) Goofy cartoon; released on June 29, 1951. Directed by Jack Kinney. Goofy's willpower to diet is quashed by a voice from the mirror that tells him to eat, drink, and be merry—and tomorrow we'll diet.

Tomorrowland One of the original lands at Disneyland. It was completely remodeled in 1967, adding new attractions, after tomorrow had caught up with it. Tomorrowland was repeated at Walt Disney World, Tokyo Disneyland, and Hong Kong Disneyland, but replaced by Discoveryland at Disneyland Paris. The Tomorrowland in the Walt Disney World Magic Kingdom was completely remodeled in 1994–1995, giving the land the look of a city like those imagined by sci-fi writers and moviemakers of the 1920s and 1930s. An extensively remodeled Tomorrowland at Disneyland opened in May 1998.

Tomorrowland Boats Attraction at Disneyland; from July 30, 1955 to January 15, 1956. Located between Tomorrowland and Fantasyland. Later became Phantom Boats. The Motor Boat Cruise, Boat Cruise to Gummi Glen, and Fantasia Gardens, located in the same space, were usually considered as Fantasyland attractions.

Tomorrowland Indy Speedway New name, in 1999, for the Tomorrowland Speedway.

Tomorrowland Jets See Astro-Jets.

Tomorrowland Speedway New name, beginning on September 28, 1996, of the Grand Prix Raceway in Magic Kingdom Park at Walt Disney World. In 1999 it became Tomorrowland Indy Speedway.

Tomorrowland Terrace Fast-food facility with bandstand; opened July 2, 1967, at Disneyland, and closed in June 2001 to become Club Buzz. There is a popular dance floor, and the bandstand is constructed so that the bands can arrange themselves in the basement level, then the stage is raised to the restaurant level. Also in Magic Kingdom Park at Walt Disney World and at Tokyo Disneyland. The Walt Disney World facility closed in September 1994 to become Cosmic Ray's Starlight Cafe in December 1994.

Tomorrowland Transit Authority Attraction in Magic Kingdom Park at Walt Disney World (1994), formerly the WEDway People-Mover.

Tomorrow's Harvest Guided walking tour in The Land at Epcot; from October 1, 1982 to September 27, 1993. Became Greenhouse Tours on December 10, 1993.

Tompson, Ruthie After appearing as an extra in the Alice Comedies as a child in the 1920s, she joined the Studio's Ink and Paint Department in 1937, eventually becoming supervisor of the

Scene Planning Department. She retired in 1975 and was named a Disney Legend in 2000.

Tonka (film) In the territory of the Dakotas in the 1870s, a young brave, White Bull, captures a wild stallion and decides to keep him as his own, naming him Tonka Wakan—The Great One. Yellow Bull, the brave's cousin, is envious and through rank acquires him, but mistreats him so that White Bull frees the horse once more. The horse's new master, Capt. Myles Keogh, rides him into battle with General Custer against the Sioux in the Battle of the Little Big Horn, where Keogh is killed by Yellow Bull, but in retaliation is stomped upon and killed by Tonka. Tonka survives, and is officially retired by the U.S. Seventh Cavalry on April 10, 1878, to be ridden only by his exercise boy, his beloved master, White Bull. Directed by Lewis R. Foster. Based on the novel by David Appel. Released on December 25, 1958. 96 min. Stars Sal Mineo (White Bull), Philip Carey (Capt. Myles Keogh), Jerome Courtland (Lt. Henry Nowlan), H.M. Wynant (Yellow Bull). The picture was filmed at the Warm Springs Indian Reservation in Oregon. The title song was written by Gil George and George Bruns. The remarkable photography was by Loyal Griggs, who had filmed such famous westerns as *Shane*. Released on video in 1986. It aired on television as *Comanche*, and was serialized on the new *Mickey Mouse Club* as *A Horse Called Comanche*.

Tony Proprietor of the Italian restaurant where Lady and Tramp get a meal of spaghetti in *Lady and the Tramp*; voiced by George Givot. He is aided by Joe; voiced by Bill Thompson.

Tony Awards With the success of *Beauty and the Beast* on Broadway, Disney began qualifying for Tony Awards. The winners have been:

1994—*Beauty and the Beast* (Ann Hould-Ward, Costume Design)

1998—*The Lion King* (Garth Fagan, Choreography)

1998—*The Lion King* (Julie Taymor, Costume Design)

1998—*The Lion King* (Donald Holder, Lighting Design)

1998—*The Lion King* (Richard Hudson, Scenic Design)

1998—*The Lion King* (Julie Taymor, Director of a Musical)

1998—*The Lion King* (Musical)

2000—*Aida* (Elton John, Tim Rice, Original Score)

2000—*Aida* (Heather Headley, Actress in a Musical)

2000—*Aida* (Bob Crowley, Scenic Design)

2000—*Aida* (Natasha Katz, Lighting Design)

Tony Danza Show, The (television) Syndicated talk show; premiered on September 13, 2004, from Buena Vista Television.

Tony's Town Square Restaurant Located on Town Square in Magic Kingdom Park at Walt Disney World; opened on July 24, 1989. Themed to characters from *Lady and the Tramp*, featuring Italian dishes. Formerly Town Square Cafe.

Too Smart for Strangers, with Winnie the Pooh (film) Educational home video release, warning children about strangers; released in June 1985.

Toon Disney A 24-hour cable network that launched on April 18, 1998, offering cartoons and animated television shows from the vast Disney library.

Toontown Residence of toon characters in *Who Framed Roger Rabbit*. See also *Mickey's Toontown*.

Toontown Hall of Fame Location in Mickey's Toontown Fair at Walt Disney World where guests can have their pictures taken with the Disney characters; opened in June 1996.

Toontown Railroad Station Opened on November 25, 1992, at Disneyland; formerly the Fantasyland Railroad Station and Videopolis Railroad Station.

Toot, Whistle, Plunk and Boom (film) Special cartoon; released on November 10, 1953. Directed by Charles Nichols and Ward Kimball. Academy Award winner for Best Cartoon. Prof. Owl explains to his students about musical instruments, illustrating with the song "Toot, Whistle, Plunk and Boom." From the cave dwellers to modern times, we find that all instruments are based on the toot, the whistle, and so on, and they finally evolve into modern musical instruments. First cartoon filmed in CinemaScope. The unique backgrounds were devised by artist Eyvind Earle who would later give *Sleeping Beauty* its distinctive look. The first short cartoon released by Buena Vista. 10 min.

Toot, Whistle, Plunk and Boom (television) Television show; aired on March 27, 1959. Directed by Wilfred Jackson. The Academy Award–winning cartoon is shown, along with several others that use music to tell a story.

Toothless (television) Two-hour television movie; aired on *The Wonderful World of Disney* on October 5, 1997. Dr. Katherine Lewis is an attractive, successful dentist who has fulfilled her career dream, but in reality leads a very empty life. While walking down the street one day, she gets hit by a bicycle messenger and is killed. Ending up in a place called Limbo, she finds she must atone for inflicting pain on her patients through the years by becoming the Tooth Fairy. But when she gets involved in the life of a 12-year-old boy, she risks not going to heaven. Directed by Melanie Mayron. Stars Kirstie Alley (Katherine Lewis), Dale Midkiff (Thomas Jameson), Ross Malinger (Bobby Jameson), Daryl Mitchell (Raul), Lynn Redgrave (Mrs. Rogers). Interiors were filmed in the historic former I. Magnin department store building on Wilshire Blvd. in Los Angeles.

Tootsie Title star of *Donald's Penguin* (1939).

Top of the World Nightclub/restaurant on the 15th floor in the Contemporary Resort at Walt Disney World; open from October 1, 1971 until September 30, 1993. The view over Seven Seas Lagoon toward the Magic Kingdom is spectacular. The longtime dinner show presented twice nightly was "Broadway at the Top," with talented performers singing hit numbers from Broadway shows, and the all-you-can-eat Sunday brunch was also popular. The restaurant was replaced by the California Grill in May 1995.

Topolino Italian name for Mickey Mouse, and the title of an Italian comic book that began publication in December 1932, making it the first of the Disney comic books.

Torkelsons, The (television) Television series; aired on NBC from September 21, 1991 to June 20, 1992. Continued in 1993 with story changes as *Almost Home* (see also that entry). An eccentric but lovable single mother and her brood of five, headed by Millicent Torkelson's wistful eldest daughter Dorothy Jane, in Pyramid Corners, Oklahoma. Like most 14-year-olds, she is perpetually embarrassed by her mother. Sharing the Torkelson house is a lodger, the grandfatherly Wesley Hodges. Stars Connie Ray (Millicent Torkelson), Olivia Burnette (Dorothy Jane), Aaron Michael Melchik (Steven Floyd), Lee Norris (Chuckie Lee), Rachel Duncan (Mary Sue), William Shallert (Wesley Hodges).

Tornado Name of Zorro's majestic black stallion. (Zorro also had a white horse, named Phantom, in a few episodes.)

Tortoise and the Hare, The (film) Silly Symphony cartoon; released on January 5, 1935. Directed by Wilfred Jackson. Overconfident Max Hare races against Toby Tortoise. In his belief that he can win the race no matter what, Max spends his time entertaining the female rabbits

while persistent Toby comes from behind and wins the race. Academy Award winner for Best Cartoon. An educational version was titled *Aesop's Hare and the Tortoise*.

Tory Vengeance (television) Television show; episode 3 of *The Swamp Fox*.

Totally Circus (television) Half-hour documentary/adventure series on Disney Channel; premiered on June 16, 2000. Features the 37 kids, ages 9–19, of the Vermont-based traveling Circus Smirkus, learning the circus acts and putting on performances. 15 episodes.

Totally Hoops (television) Half-hour reality series on Disney Channel; premiered on January 7, 2001. Follows the lives of the Dayton Lady Hoopstars, eleven 13- and 14-year-old girls, as they head for the state championships and a national tournament.

Totally in Tune (television) Half-hour reality series on Disney Channel; premiered on June 17, 2002. Cameras followed kids at Los Angeles's Hamilton High magnet program for music.

Totally Minnie See *Disney's Totally Minnie*.

Totally Minnie Parade Event at Disneyland in the summer of 1986. Minnie Mouse was given her due, updated with 1980s fashions and a rocking theme song, in this parade with over 100 performers.

Touchdown Mickey (film) Mickey Mouse cartoon; released on October 15, 1932. Directed by Wilfred Jackson. In a spirited game of football between Mickey and the gang and local alley cats, both sides share misadventures with the ball, but Mickey is undeniably the hero by single-handedly winning the game.

Touchstone Pictures New label created at the Disney Studio by Ron Miller for films that had more mature themes than the standard "Disney" film; the first film to be released as a Touchstone Picture was *Splash* in 1984. Eventually, Touchstone would have its own production personnel, and when the number of films being released greatly increased, another label, Hollywood Pictures, was established to spread out the work. For a list of films made by Touchstone Pictures, see Features.

Touchwood Pacific Partners I Limited partnership formed in October 1990, to finance live-action films at Disney, with the $600 million equity underwritten by Japanese financial institutions. It succeeded Silver Screen Partners IV. Its films included *Billy Bathgate, Captain Ron, Encino Man, Father of the Bride, Homeward Bound: the Incredible Journey, Newsies, Sister Act,* and *What About Bob?*

Tough Guys (film) Two train robbers of the old school, Harry Doyle and Archie Long, are released from prison, but they find it very difficult adjusting to modern society. They come to realize that their age has caught up to them, but desire one more moment of glory. Aided by their probation officer who has hero-worshipped them for years, they attempt to pull off one last train robbery—on the final run of the train they had failed to rob 18 years before. Premiere in San Luis Obispo, California, on September 30, 1986; general release on October 3, 1986. Directed by Jeff Kanew. A Touchstone Picture. 103 min. Stars Burt Lancaster (Harry Doyle), Kirk Douglas (Archie Long), Charles Durning (Deke Yablonski), Alexis Smith (Belle), Dana Carvey (in his motion picture debut as Richie Evans), Eli Wallach (Leon B. Little). The train used in the film is

Southern Pacific's steam engine 4449, an oil-burning locomotive constructed in 1940 and designed for passenger trains on the Los Angeles-San Francisco run. The engine had been retired in 1957 and placed on display in Oaks Park in Portland, Oregon. As it traveled south to the Los Angeles area for the filming, thousands of train buffs frequently lined the route to catch a glimpse of the venerable old locomotive. The climactic railroad sequences were filmed south of Palm Springs on the Eagle Mountain line. Released on video in 1987.

Toulouse Aspiring artist kitten in *The Aristocats*; voiced by Gary Dubin.

Tour of the West, A See *Circarama, U.S.A.*

Tourist Trap (television) Two-hour television movie; aired on *The Wonderful World of Disney* on April 5, 1998. Bored banker George Piper takes his reluctant family on a motor-home vacation to retrace the footsteps of his heroic ancestor and idol, Jeremiah Piper, who fought during the Civil War. Hoping to bond his family, George instead finds them facing a series of misadventures and unexpected dangers before they realize that they really are a close-knit family. Directed by Richard Benjamin. Stars Daniel Stern (George Piper), Julie Hagerty (Bess), David Rasche (Derek Early), Paul Giamatti (Jeremiah), Margot Finley (Rachel), Blair Slater (Josh), Rodney Eastman (Stork), Ryan Reynolds (Wade Early). Filming took place on location around Vancouver, British Columbia. Released on video in 2000.

Tournament of Roses Parade Walt Disney served as grand marshal for the Pasadena, California, parade on January 1, 1966. Disney had a *Snow White* float in the 1938 parade, and broke a height record (100 ft.) with a Tower of Terror float in the 2004 parade. Roy E. Disney was grand marshal in 2000. Mickey Mouse was grand marshal in 2005, and Disneyland had a float that year for its 50th anniversary. There were Disney Parks, Little Einstein, and ESPN/ABC Sports floats in 2006.

Tower of Terror See The Twilight Zone Tower of Terror.

Tower of Terror (television) Two-hour made-for-television movie; aired on *The Wonderful World of Disney* on October 26, 1997. When lightning strikes the deluxe Hollywood Tower Hotel in 1939, five people, including child superstar Sally Shine, suddenly vanish from an elevator en route to a Halloween gala at the Tip Top Club on the top floor. Haunted by the incident, the swank hotel closes overnight and falls into disrepair. Nearly 60 years later, a down-on-his-luck journalist, Buzzy Crocker, with help from his spunky niece, Anna, and former boss/old flame Jill Whitman, is suddenly given reason to believe he can solve the mystery. Directed by D.J. MacHale. Stars Lindsay Ridgeway (Sally Shine), Steve Guttenberg (Buzzy Crocker), Kirsten Dunst (Anna Petterson), Nia Peeples (Jill Whitman). This movie is perhaps the first to be based on a theme park attraction, rather than vice versa. However, since it was not possible to film in The Twilight Zone Tower of Terror at the Disney-MGM Studios (in the film, the lobby had to be shown in its 1939 splendor and then aged to 1997), an accurate replica was built in a warehouse. Released on video in 1999.

Town Square Cafe Restaurant at Disneyland; open from winter 1976 to spring 1978. Formerly Maxwell House Coffee House and Hills Brothers Coffee House. It became the American Egg House (1978–1983). On October 1, 1983, it became Town Square Cafe again, and it closed on August 23, 1992. It is also on Town Square in Magic Kingdom Park at Walt Disney World; opened on October 1, 1971, and later became Tony's Town Square Restaurant.

Town Square Exhibition Hall Area on Town Square in Magic Kingdom Park at Walt Disney World housing the Camera Center; opened on August 27, 1998.

Toy Soldier, The Shop in United Kingdom in World Showcase at Epcot; opened October 1, 1982. A favorite sight is the diorama just inside the entrance of a medieval banquet hall and its royal court.

Toy Story (film) Andy's toys are fearful of being replaced when the boy's birthday comes along. Woody, his favorite toy, a pull-string cowboy doll, discovers the boy has a new toy—Buzz Lightyear, the latest, greatest action figure, complete with pop-out wings and laser action. Woody's plan to get rid of Buzz backfires, and he finds himself lost in the world outside of Andy's room, with Buzz as his only companion. Together they must try to find their way back to Andy. Directed by John Lasseter. Released on November 22, 1995. Voices provided by Tom Hanks (Woody), Tim Allen (Buzz Lightyear), Jim Varney (Slinky Dog), Don Rickles (Mr. Potato Head), John Ratzenberger (Hamm), Annie Potts (Bo Peep), Wallace Shawn (Rex). Songs by Randy Newman. 81 min. The film is the first animated feature ever generated completely on computers, produced as part of a partnership between Disney and Northern California–based Pixar. John Lasseter was presented a special Academy Award for "the development and inspired application of techniques that have made possible the first feature-length computer-animated film." Released on video in 1996.

Toy Story 2 (film) Andy goes off to summer cowboy camp, and the toys are left to their own devices. When an obsessive toy collector, Al McWhiggin, kidnaps Woody, who, unbeknownst to him is a highly valued collectible, it's up to Buzz Lightyear and the gang from Andy's room to spring into action and save their pal from winding up as a museum piece. The toys get into one predicament after another in their daring race to get Woody home before Andy returns. Released on November 24, 1999, after a November 19 release at the El Capitan in Hollywood. Directed by John Lasseter. Voices include Tom Hanks (Woody), Tim Allen (Buzz Lightyear), Don Rickles (Mr. Potato Head), Jim Varney (Slinky Dog), Wallace Shawn (Rex), John Ratzenberger (Hamm), Annie Potts (Bo Peep), Kelsey Grammer (Stinky Pete, the Prospector), Joan Cusack (Jessie), Wayne Knight (Al McWhiggin), Estelle Harris (Mrs. Potato Head). 92 min. Produced as a partnership between Walt Disney Pictures and Pixar Animation Studios. Composer Randy Newman added two new songs, "When She Loved Me" and "Woody's Roundup," with the former nominated for an Academy Award for Best Original Song. Improved computer programs and controls gave the animators more flexibility in moving the characters and allowed more subtle articulation than ever before. The film did phenomenal business, and became Disney's third-highest-grossing film ever (after *The Lion King* and *The Sixth Sense*). Released on video in 2000.

Toy Tinkers (film) Donald Duck cartoon; released on December 16, 1949. Directed by Jack Hannah. Chip and Dale invade Donald's home for his Christmas goodies. This turns into an all-out war, with the chipmunks victorious, leaving with a convoy of nuts and candies. Nominated for an Academy Award. Sixteen mm release title was *Christmas Capers*.

Toys Fantastique Toy store presented by Mattel in the Downtown Disney Marketplace at Walt Disney World.

Tracey, Doreen Mouseketeer from the 1950s television show.

Track of the African Bongo, The (television) Television show; aired on April 3, 1977.

Directed by Frank Zuniga. A young Kenyan boy, Kamua, spots a rare African antelope, protects the animal from hunters, and helps save the breed. Stars Johnny Ngaya, Oliver Litondo, Tony Parkinson. Narrated by Michael Jackson (not the singer but the L.A. talk-show host).

Track of the Giant Snow Bear (film) Sixteen mm release title of *Snow Bear*; released in March 1972.

Trader Mickey (film) Mickey Mouse cartoon; released on August 20, 1932. The first cartoon directed by Dave Hand. In the midst of their African safari, Mickey and Pluto are captured by a native tribe. To save themselves from the cannibals, Mickey and Pluto perform an impromptu jam session with musical instruments in their canoe.

Traffic Troubles (film) Mickey Mouse cartoon; released on March 17, 1931. Directed by Burt Gillett. Mickey is a reckless taxi driver who has a series of hilarious adventures involving a flat tire, a medicine man, a cow, and a collision with a barn.

Tragedy on the Trail (television) Television show; episode 3 of *Gallegher Goes West*.

Trail Mix-Up (film) Roger Rabbit cartoon; released on March 12, 1993. Directed by Barry Cook. Roger Rabbit is left to care for Baby Herman in Yellowstone National Park. When Baby Herman's curiosity gets the better of him, Roger is plunged into all sorts of zany adventures. He upsets a beehive, meets a tree-hungry beaver, and has several misadventures with a sawmill that conclude with Roger being sawed into hundreds of tiny Rogers. Roger, Baby Herman, the beaver, and an angry bear are saved from going over a waterfall only to plummet over a cliff. They land on a geyser that shoots them all into the faces carved on Mount Rushmore, ruining the national landmark. Voices by Charles Fleischer, Kathleen Turner, April Winchell. Produced at Disney-MGM Studios in Florida. Originally released with *A Far Off Place*.

Trail of Danger (television) Two-part television show; aired on March 12 and 19, 1978.

Directed by Andrew V. McLaglen. Two men taking horses to market run afoul of angry sheep herders and are hampered by a lack of water for the horses. Stars Larry Wilcox, Jim Davis, Robert Donner, David Ireland.

Trailer Horn (film) Donald Duck cartoon; released on April 28, 1950. Directed by Jack Hannah. Donald and the chipmunks, Chip and Dale, are after each other again, this time when they come upon Donald vacationing in a trailer. When he goes swimming, they fool him by moving the diving board and end up wrecking his car.

Trains (film) Educational film in the Goofy's Field Trips series; released on August 10, 1989. 14 min. Goofy takes two kids on a field trip to learn about trains.

Tramp Happy-go-lucky mutt hero of *Lady and the Tramp*; voiced by Larry Roberts.

Transcenter Automotive display at the exit of World of Motion in Future World at Epcot; opened on October 1, 1982. General Motors changed the displays over the years. The display featured films and shows such as *The Bird and the Robot* and *The Water Engine*, future vehicles, and the latest models from General Motors. Closed on January 2, 1996.

Trauth, AJ Actor; appeared on Disney Channel in *Even Stevens* and *The Even Stevens Movie* (Alan Twitty), *You Wish* (Alex Lansing), and does the voice of Josh on *Kim Possible*.

TraveLodge Hotel in Lake Buena Vista at Walt Disney World. From 1984 to 1989 it changed its name to the Viscount.

TravelPort Attraction in Communicore East at Epcot sponsored by American Express; open from October 1, 1982 to April 27, 1992. Guests could touch a television screen to preview vacation trips to many areas of the world or ask for help from the American Express personnel.

Travers, P. L. (1899–1996) Australian-born English author of the Mary Poppins books, with the first one published in 1934. While she admired Walt Disney, she never quite approved of the film he made about her fictional nanny.

Travis, Nancy Actress; appeared in *Three Men and a Baby*, *Three Men and a Little Lady* (Sylvia), and *Passed Away* (Cassie Slocombe).

Travolta, John Actor; appeared in *Phenomenon* (George Malley), *A Civil Action* (Jan Schlictmann), and *Ladder 49* (Capt. Mike Kennedy).

Treacher, Arthur (1894–1975) Actor; appeared in *Mary Poppins* (Constable Jones).

Treasure from the Sea (film) Educational film demonstrating the benefits of magnesium, which, because of its lightness, can save energy. The film was made for Dow Chemical Co.; delivered on September 30, 1946.

Treasure in the Haunted House (television) Television show; part 2 of *For the Love of Willadean.*

Treasure Island (film) Young Jim Hawkins, possessor of a map to buried treasure, and his friends, Squire Trelawney and Dr. Livesey, plan to travel to Treasure Island to hunt for the treasure. Captain Smollett rounds up a crew that includes Long John Silver, who secretly plots a mutiny to secure the map and treasure for himself. When the mutiny fails, Silver escapes, taking Jim with him. When they reach the island, Jim gets away

and meets a strange old hermit named Ben Gunn, who helps him return to his crewmates, now battling the pirates led by Silver. Finally, the Squire, Smollett, and Gunn disarm Silver, and Gunn leads them to the treasure he had rehidden years earlier. With their captive and the treasure, the crew rows back to the ship, only to have Silver escape with the rowboat, aided by Jim, who has a grudging affection for the rascally pirate. Released on July 19, 1950. Based on the book published in 1881 by Robert Louis Stevenson. Directed by Byron Haskin. The first Disney live-action film without any animation. Also the first Disney film shot in England, in locations off the Cornish coast and Falmouth Bay. 96 min. Stars Bobby Driscoll (Jim Hawkins), Robert Newton (Long John Silver), Basil Sydney (Capt. Smollett), Finlay Currie (Capt. Bones), Walter Fitzgerald (Squire Trelawney), Denis O'Dea (Dr. Livesey), Geoffrey Wilkinson (Ben Gunn). The Disney company had "blocked funds" in England after the war, money that Disney films had earned in the country, which could not be exported due to currency regulations. Walt Disney decided that he could use the money to make some films in England, but since he could not find trained animators there to produce his usual fare, he decided to turn to live action instead. Over the next few years, four live-action films would be made in England. Disney found itself in trouble with British child labor laws when they imported an American boy to star in the film, and it took a bit of deception and cunning to get the film completed. The film was cut for its 1975 re-release in order to gain a G rating, but the so-called violent scenes were restored on a later video release. Released on video in 1981 and 1992.

Treasure Island Nature preserve at Walt Disney World; opened on April 8, 1974. It became Discovery Island in 1977.

Treasure of Matecumbe (film) Shortly after the Civil War, two 13-year-old boys—one white, the other black—set out from Kentucky to seek a treasure buried in a Florida swamp. During the course of their exciting and often hilarious experiences, they acquire three colorful traveling companions—a dashing adventurer, a tart-tongued Southern belle, and a jaunty old medicine man. It takes the talents and ingenuity of all five to overcome the sinister forces working against them. Released on July 9, 1976. Directed by Vincent McEveety. 116 min. Stars Robert Foxworth (Jim), Joan Hackett (Lauriette), Peter Ustinov (Dr. Snodgrass), Vic Morrow (Spangler), Johnny Doran (David), Billy Attmore (Thad), Jane Wyatt (Aunt Effie), Don Knight (Skaggs), Val De Vargas (Charlie), Dub Taylor (Sheriff Forbes), Dick Van Patten (Gambler). The movie was based on the book *A Journey to Matecumbe* by Robert Lewis Taylor. The song "Matecumbe" was written by Richard McKinley and Shane Tatum. Danville, Kentucky, was chosen for the opening scenes, and an old 217-acre plantation estate, built around 1830, became "Grassy." The Sacramento River above Colusa, California, became the Mississippi, but the actual Everglades of Florida were used as such in the film, with the cast setting up production headquarters in Kissimmee. The man-made hurricane was shot in part of a rain forest inhabited by ancient Seminole Indians, and made by using giant wind machines and tons of water pumped in and blasted at the cast by airplane engines. The last night of the disaster sequence Ustinov was struck by a wave, fell, and was hospitalized with pulled ligaments in his left ankle. The company then moved to a beach at Walt Disney World, where final scenes in the picture were filmed. Released on video in 1986.

Treasure of San Bosco Reef, The (television) Two-part television show; aired on November 24 and December 1, 1968. Directed by Robert L. Friend. A young man, Dave Jones, visiting his uncle in Italy becomes involved with smugglers as they explore a sunken wreck and learn of stolen artifacts. Stars Roger Mobley,

James Daly, Nehemiah Persoff, John van Dreelen. The star, Roger Mobley, moved on to this show directly after his work on the *Gallegher* series.

Treasure Planet (film) With a nod to Robert Louis Stevenson's *Treasure Island*, this animated feature follows 15-year-old Jim Hawkins's amazing journey across a fantasy universe as cabin boy aboard a glittering solar galleon, *RLS Legacy*. Befriended by the ship's cyborg cook (part man, part machine), John Silver, Jim thrives under his guidance, showing the makings of a fine spacer. As the story unfolds, he and the all-alien crew battle supernovas, black holes, and ferocious space storms. But even greater dangers lie ahead when Jim discovers that his trusted mentor Silver is actually a scheming pirate with mutiny in mind. Confronted with a betrayal that cuts deep to his soul, Jim is transformed from boy to man as he finds the strength to face down the mutineers and discovers a "treasure" greater than he had ever imagined. Directed by John Musker and Ron Clements. Released on November 27, 2002, simultaneously in regular and large-screen theaters, after a world premiere on November 5 in Paris and a release beginning there November 6. Voices include Martin Short (B.E.N.), David Hyde Pierce (Doctor Doppler), Emma Thompson (Captain Amelia), Joseph Gordon-Levitt (Jim), Brian Murray (John Silver), Michael Wincott (Scroop), Michael McShane (Hands), Roscoe Lee Browne (Mr. Arrow), Corey Burton (Onus), Tony Jay (Narrator), Austin Majors (young Jim), Patrick McGoohan (Billy Bones). 95 min. This was the first animated feature where the backgrounds were all painted in the computer. While most of the characters were drawn by hand, John Silver was a complicated blend of hand-drawn and computer animation. Nominated for an Academy Award for Best Animated Feature. Released on video in 2003.

Tree of Life Located in Safari Village at the hub of Disney's Animal Kingdom at Walt Disney World, the tree towers 14 stories above the landscape and is 50 feet wide and sprawls to 170 feet in diameter at its base. The trunk of the tree is intricately carved with a swirling tapestry of animal forms that symbolize the richness and diversity of animal life on Earth. Inside, guests experience a 3-D adventure about insects, entitled *It's Tough To Be A Bug.*

Treehouse Villas Accommodations at Lake Buena Vista, built on pedestals in forested glens; opened in 1975 and closed in 2002. Became part of The Disney Institute in February 1996.

Trees (film) Segment of *Melody Time*; 16mm release in November 1971.

Trenchcoat (film) While vacationing in Malta, aspiring mystery writer Mickey Raymond gets mixed up with disappearing corpses, disbelieving police, a federal agent in disguise, kidnappers, terrorists, and stolen plutonium. She and the federal agent—with whom she is becoming romantically involved—narrowly escape an explosion set to kill them, and they capture the terrorists instead. Released on March 11, 1983. Directed by Michael Tuchner. 92 min. Stars Margot Kidder (Mickey), Robert Hays (Terry), David Suchet (Inspector Stagnos), Gila Von Weitershausen (Eva Warner), Ronald Lacey (Princess Aida), Donald Faraldo (Nino), John Justin (Marquis de Pena). Before the creation of the Touchstone label, of which this would most likely have been an example, the film was simply not released as a "Disney" film. The film was shot on location on the island of Malta, in the town of Valletta, Verdala Castle, Hagar Qim Temple, the Grand Master's Palace Armory, the Mosta Dome, St. Paul's Catacombs, and the Dragonara Palace Hotel and Casino. Released on video in 1983.

Tri Circle D Ranch Located at Fort Wilderness at Walt Disney World; guests can rent horses for trail rides in the area.

Trial by Terror (television) Television show; episode 4 of *Gallegher Goes West.*

Trial of Donald Duck, The (film) Donald Duck cartoon; released on July 30, 1948. Directed by Jack King. Donald refuses to pay his $35 lunch bill at a swanky restaurant and is sentenced in court to washing dishes, which he smashes in revenge.

Triangle of Health (film) Series of four educational films made for Upjohn in 1968 and 1969: *Steps Toward Maturity and Health, Understanding Stresses and Strains, Physical Fitness and Good Health, The Social Side of Health.*

Triangle of Health: Keeping the Balance (film) Educational release in November 1992. 11 min. A girl at camp puts herself on a rigorous training schedule that excludes all other activities, and she becomes ill. She has to learn how to maintain a balance in all areas of life.

Triangle of Health: Moving On (film) Educational release in November 1992. 11 min. A young boy becomes sullen and depressed when he learns his family is moving.

Triangle of Health: Personal Challenge (film) Educational release in November 1992. 10 min. A boy's best friend at camp helps him with a strict training program so he can compete in a race.

Triangle of Health: True Friends (film) Educational release in November 1992. 10 min. A Hungarian girl feels ostracized because she is unfamiliar with American ways at summer camp, and she loses her only friend, who doesn't want to be ostracized either.

Tribute to Joel Chandler Harris, A (television) Television show; aired on January 18, 1956. Directed by William Beaudine, Clyde Geronimi.

Harris's early years as apprentice to a printer and budding writer are re-created, then the *Tar Baby* sequence of *Song of the South* is shown. Stars David Stollery (Joel Chandler Harris), Jonathan Hale (J.A. Turner), Sam McDaniel (Herbert), Harry Shannon (Mr. Wilson), Barbara Woodell (Mrs. Harris).

Tribute to Mickey Mouse (television) Sequence featuring Mickey Mouse cartoons included in the television shows *The Disneyland Story* and *A Further Report on Disneyland*.

TriceraTop Spin Attraction at Chester & Hester's Dino-Rama! at Disney's Animal Kingdom; opened on November 18, 2001. Guests in four-person vehicles based on old-fashioned tin toys move up and down and spin like a giant top.

Trick or Treat (film) Donald Duck cartoon; released on October 10, 1952. Directed by Jack Hannah. When the nephews come to Donald's house in their Halloween costumes, he plays tricks on them until Witch Hazel joins up with them and with her magical powers teaches Donald a lesson.

Tricks of Our Trade (television) Television show; aired on February 13, 1957. Directed by Wilfred Jackson. Walt Disney explains some of the techniques of animation, including exaggeration, pantomime, effects animation, caricature, and the multiplane camera.

Trigger and Nutsy Two vulture soldiers of the sheriff in *Robin Hood*; voiced by George Lindsey and Ken Curtis.

Trip Thru Adventureland, A/Water Birds (television) Television show; aired on February 29, 1956. Directed by Winston Hibler. A visit to the Jungle Cruise and the rest of Adventureland at Disneyland, plus the True-Life Adventure *Water Birds*.

Trip to Tucson (television) Television show; episode 15 of *Texas John Slaughter*.

Triton Gardens A King Triton leap-frog fountain is the centerpiece of this garden opened in February 1996, on the site of the former Alpine Gardens (where the Monsanto House of the Future once stood) at Disneyland.

Triton's Kingdom Attraction in King Triton Castle at Mermaid Lagoon at Tokyo DisneySea, consisting of The Whirlpool, Blowfish Balloon Race, and Jumpin' Jellyfish; opened on September 4, 2001.

Triviateers Name by which the finalists of the Disney Store National Trivia Competition were known. From 1989 to 1999, the Store held an annual trivia showdown for its cast members, with the finalists going to Disneyland in the fall to compete for a trophy. Of the 50 Disney experts who competed for their stores, only 11 became national champs: Tony Anderson, Michael McNiel, Kevin Neary, Tim Huebner, Tom Byerly, Tony Davis, Yvonne Mercer, John Kurowski, Antonio Ruberto, Carol Dobson, and Kevin Burk.

Trolley Troubles (film) Oswald the Lucky Rabbit cartoon; the first released, on September 5, 1927.

Trombone Trouble (film) Donald Duck cartoon; released on Febuary 18, 1944. Directed by Jack King. The gods Vulcan and Jupiter are disturbed by Pete's sour trombone playing, so they give Donald the power to stop him. After Donald wins, he picks up the trombone and starts playing it himself.

Tron (film) Flynn, a young computer genius, breaks into the ENCOM computer looking for evidence that the video game programs he wrote were stolen by Dillinger, an ENCOM executive. Dillinger's Master Control Program must stop Flynn, and it blasts him into its own computer dimension. Flynn awakens in an electronic world, where computer programs are the alter egos of the programmers who created them, and he is sentenced to die on the video game grid. Together with Tron, an electronic security program, Flynn escapes, destroys the MCP, and is able to return to the "real" world. Released on July 9, 1982. Directed by Steven Lisberger. 96 min. Photographed in Super Panavision 70mm, this special effects tour de force stars Jeff Bridges (Kevin Flynn/Clu), Bruce Boxleitner (Alan/Tron), David Warner (Dillinger/Sark), Cindy Morgan (Lora/Nori), Barnard Hughes (Dr. Walter/Gibbs), Dan Shor (Ram), Peter Jurasik (Crom), Tony Stephano (Peter/Sark's Lt.). The idea for *Tron* grew out of director Lisberger's pas-

sion for computer games. He and producer Donald Kushner spent two years researching the technology to make the film, on which he made his live-action directorial debut. The film was the first motion picture to make extensive use of computer imagery, requiring much expertise and imagination. Though computer imagery had been previously seen as an effect in motion pictures such as *Star Wars* and *West World*, *Tron* was the first film to use the technique to create a three-dimensional world. The special-effects team was headed by futuristic industrial designer Syd Mead, comic artist "Moebius" Giraud, and high-tech commercial artist Peter Lloyd. Harrison Ellenshaw supervised the effects with Richard Taylor. Computer graphics were first applied to aerospace and scientific research in the mid-1960s, when methods of simulating objects digitally in their dimensions proved as effective as building models. The technology was then diverted into the entertainment field. Information

International Inc. (Triple-I) and Robert Able & Associates of Los Angeles, and the Mathematic Applications Group Inc. (MAGI) and Digital Effects of New York produced the computer imagery for the film. MAGI, the single largest contributor of computer imagery, speeded up the process of supplying its work to Disney Studios in Burbank by a transcontinental computer hookup. The computer link cut between 2½ to 5 days from the creation of each scene. The electronic world was shot on soundstages at the Disney Studio in Burbank. Photography for the real world took place at locations around Los Angeles, and at the U.S. Government's futuristic Lawrence Livermore Laboratory outside Oakland, California. The film was not the box office bonanza the Studio had hoped for, but it did spawn a number of popular video games. *Tron* was nominated for an Academy Award for Sound, by Michael, Bob, and Lee Minkler and Jim La Rue, and for Costume Design by Elois Jenssen and Rosanna Norton. Released on video in 1982 and 1993.

Tropical Serenade See Sunshine Pavilion.

Troubadour Tavern Located in Fantasyland at Tokyo Disneyland; opened on April 15, 1983.

Trout, Dink (1898–1950) He voiced Bootle Beetle and the King of Hearts in *Alice in Wonderland*.

Tru Confessions (television) A Disney Channel Original Movie; premiered on April 5, 2002. High school freshman Trudy "Tru" Walker aspires to have her own television show, and, to enter a cable television contest that awards a television hosting job, she produces a documentary about her twin brother, Eddie, a boy with a developmental disability. The filmmaking process becomes a perfect outlet for Tru to express herself and discover a greater appreciation for Eddie. Stars Clara Bryant (Tru Walker), Shia LaBeouf (Eddie Walker), Mare Winningham (Ginny Walker), William Francis McGuire (Bob Walker).

Truant Officer Donald (film) Donald Duck cartoon; released on August 1, 1941. Directed by

Jack King. Donald, as a truant officer, battles with his nephews to force them to go to school. When Donald finally wins and they reach the schoolhouse, he is embarrassed to learn that it is closed for summer vacation. Nominated for an Academy Award.

True Identity (film) After a long series of discouraging auditions, an aspiring African American actor, Miles Pope, takes a flight home. When his plane begins to crash, the passenger in the seat next to him confesses that he is the infamous mob boss Frank Luchino, a man the FBI believes to be dead. The airplane eventually lands safely, but Miles's relief is short-lived. He is the only man alive who knows the truth about Luchino and he soon becomes the target of a contract hit man. Forced to hide his true identity under a parade of new disguises, including changing his skin color to white, Miles sets out to protect his life, reveal the crime lord's secret, and realize his dream of being a great actor. Released on August 23, 1991. Directed by Charles Lane. A Touchstone Picture. 93 min. Stars Lenny Henry (Miles), Frank Langella (Frank Luchino/Leland Carver), Charles Lane (Duane). Filmed at locations in New York and Los Angeles. Released on video in 1992.

True Son's Revenge (television) Television show; part 2 of the television airing of *The Light in the Forest.*

True-Life Adventure Festival (film) Reissues of the True-Life Adventure films in six packages in the summer of 1964.

True-Life Adventures (film) Series of 13 nature films between 1948 and 1960, including 7 featurettes (*Seal Island, Beaver Valley, Nature's Half Acre, The Olympic Elk, Water Birds, Bear Country, Prowlers of the Everglades*) and 6 features (*The Living Desert, The Vanishing Prairie, The African Lion, Secrets of Life, White Wilderness, Jungle Cat*); 8 of them won Academy

Awards. See also *Seal Island* for more history of the series. A new series, called New True Life Adventures, began airing in syndication in February 2000.

Truly Exceptional, The: Carol Johnston (film) Educational film; released in September 1979. The film depicts the story of a top-ranked gymnast with only one arm and her struggle toward a national championship. Aired as a television special as *Lefty.*

Truly Exceptional, The: Dan Haley (film) Educational film; released in September 1979. A blind 16-year-old overcomes seemingly insurmountable obstacles, giving other students a clearer sense of individual human potential.

Truly Exceptional, The: Tom and Virl Osmond (film) Educational film; released in September 1979. Two young men, deaf since birth, have not let their deafness hinder their success in helping to manage the Osmond family entertainment business.

Truman, Harry S. Former President Truman visited Disneyland in November 1957.

Trust in Me Song from *The Jungle Book*; written by Richard M. Sherman and Robert B. Sherman.

Trusty Lady's plodding bloodhound friend in *Lady and the Tramp*; voiced by Bill Baucom.

Truth About Mother Goose, The (film) Special cartoon featurette; released on August 28, 1957. Directed by Wolfgang Reitherman and Bill Justice. Tells the historical stories behind three popular nursery rhymes (Little Jack Horner; Mary, Mary Quite Contrary; and London Bridge). 15 min. Nominated for an Academy Award.

Truth About Mother Goose, The (television) Television show; aired on November 17, 1963. Directed by Hamilton S. Luske. Prof. Ludwig Von Drake and his co-host, Herman, present the theatrical featurette, plus sequences from other Disney films, including *Mickey and the Beanstalk.*

Tryon, Tom (1919–1991) Actor; appeared in *Moon Pilot* (Capt. Richmond Talbot), and on television as *Texas John Slaughter*, and later became a best-selling novelist.

Tuberculosis (film) Educational film. Produced under the auspices of the Coordinator of Inter-American Affairs. Delivered on August 13, 1945. The film describes tuberculosis as man's deadliest enemy and tells how it can be cured. It stresses prevention and communication.

Tuck Everlasting (film) Teenager Winnie Foster longs for a life outside the control of her domineering mother, and when lost in the woods near her home, she happens upon Jesse Tuck, a boy unlike any she has ever met before. He and his family are kind and generous, and they immediately take her in as one of their own. However, the Tucks hold a powerful secret, that of immortality, and with the mysterious Man in the Yellow Suit tracking them down, they fear that their world could end. Ultimately Winnie must decide whether to return to her life or stay with her beloved Jesse and his family forever. Released on October 11, 2002. Directed by Jay Russell. Stars Alexis Bledel (Winnie Foster), Ben Kingsley (Man in the Yellow Suit), Sissy Spacek (Mae Tuck), Amy Irving (Mother Foster), Victor Garber (Robert Foster), Jonathan Jackson (Jesse Tuck), Scott Bairstow (Miles Tuck), William Hurt (Angus Tuck). Narrated by Elizabeth Shue. 90 min. Based on the book by Natalie Babbitt. Filmed in CinemaScope. Released on video in 2003.

Tucker, Forrest (1919–1986) Actor; appeared on television in *A Boy Called Nuthin'*.

Tuesday Guest Star Day on the 1950s *Mickey Mouse Club*. Let's Go Day on the new *Mickey Mouse Club*.

Tugboat Mickey (film) Mickey Mouse cartoon; released on April 26, 1940. Directed by

Clyde Geronimi. Captain Mickey issues orders to shipmates Donald and Goofy to respond to an SOS. But in getting the ship underway, it explodes. Later, they find out the cry for help was only a radio show.

Tummy Trouble (film) Roger Rabbit cartoon; released on June 23, 1989. Directed by Rob Minkoff. Roger Rabbit is left to babysit with the mischievous Baby Herman. The infant swallows a toy rattle, which is just the beginning of Roger's troubles. When he rushes the baby to the hospital, the duo gets involved in a multitude of misadventures. Voices by Charles Fleischer (Roger Rabbit), Kathleen Turner (Jessica), April Winchell/Lou Hirsch (Baby Herman). The first short cartoon made by the Disney Studio in 24 years. Released on video in 1990 with *Honey, I Shrunk the Kids.*

Turnabout cookie jars See Leeds China Co.

Turner, Kathleen Actress; appeared in *V. I. Warshawski* (Vic), and provided the voice (uncredited) of Jessica Rabbit in *Who Framed Roger Rabbit.* She is credited in later Roger Rabbit shorts.

Turner & Hooch (film) Small-town police detective Scott Turner's life is suddenly turned around when an elderly friend is murdered and Turner unwillingly takes in Hooch, the friend's huge, sloppy, ill-mannered dog, who is the only witness to the murder. Soon Hooch has completely wrecked Turner's house and complicated his budding romance with veterinarian Emily Carson, but the mismatched pair eventually form a partnership in outwitting the crooks. Released on July 28, 1989. Directed by Roger Spottiswoode. A Touchstone Picture 98 min. Stars Tom Hanks (Scott Turner), Mare Winningham (Emily Carson). Hooch was portrayed by Beasley, a dog of the French breed called the De Bordeaux. Filmed on Terminal Island near Los Angeles, in San Pedro, and on the Monterey Peninsula. Released on video in 1990.

Turner & Hooch (television) Unsold pilot for a television series based on the 1989 Touchstone feature about a detective with an unruly St. Bernard for a partner; aired on NBC on July 9, 1990. Directed by Donald Petrie. 30 min. Stars Tom Wilson, Wendee Pratt, Bradley Mott, Al Fann, John Anthony.

Turquand, Todd Mouseketeer on the new *Mickey Mouse Club.*

Turtle Talk with Crush Attraction within The Living Seas at Epcot; opened in November 2004. By the use of digital projection and voice-activated animation, Crush, the sea turtle from *Finding Nemo*, interacts with guests. Also opened in Disney Animation at Disney's California Adventure on July 15, 2005.

Turturro, John Actor; appeared in *Off Beat* (Neil Pepper), *The Color of Money* (Julian), *Quiz Show* (Herbert Stempel), *Unstrung Heroes* (Sid), *He Got Game* (Coach Billy Sunday), *O Brother, Where Art Thou?* (Pete), and *Cradle Will Rock* (Aldo Silvano).

Tusker House Restaurant Fast-food restaurant in Harambe at Disney's Animal Kingdom; opened on April 22, 1998.

TWA Rocket to the Moon See Rocket to the Moon.

'Twas the Night (television) A Disney Channel Original Movie; premiered on December 7, 2001. Fourteen-year-old Danny Wrigley and his irresponsible but well-meaning Uncle Nick almost ruin Christmas when they decide to take Santa's new hi-tech sleigh for a joyride. When they discover that Santa, on Christmas eve, has been temporarily knocked out by an accident on the family's roof, they decide to take the holiday into their own hands and even out the inequities of Christmas once and for all. Directed by Nick Castle. Stars Bryan Cranston (Nick Wrigley), Josh Zuckerman (Danny Wrigley), Jefferson Mappin (Santa), Brenda Grate (Kaitlin Wrigley), Rhys Williams (Peter Wrigley), Barclay Hope (John Wrigley), Torri Higginson (Abby Wrigley).

Tweedledum and Tweedledee Obnoxious twins in *Alice in Wonderland*; voiced by J. Pat O'Malley.

25th Anniversary of the Wonderful World of Disney See *NBC Salutes the 25th Anniversary of the Wonderful World of Disney.*

25th Hour (film) In 24 hours, Monty Brogan, New York City highflier, is off to jail for seven years. On his last day, he tries to reconnect with his father and gets together with his two closest friends, Jacob and Slaughtery. Plus, there is his girlfriend, Naturelle, who might have been the one who tipped off the cops. Time is running out, and Monty has some tricks up his sleeve. Limited release in Los Angeles and New York on December 19, 2002; expanded release on January 10, 2003. A Touchstone Picture. Directed by Spike Lee. Stars Edward Norton (Monty Brogan), Philip Seymour Hoffman (Jacob Elinsky), Barry Pepper (Francis Xavier Slaughtery), Rosario Dawson (Naturelle Riviera), Anna Paquin (Mary D'Annunzio), Brian Cox (James Brogan). Filmed in Super 35 wide-screen on location in the five boroughs of New York City. 135 min. Released on video in 2003.

20,000 Leagues Under the Sea (film) In 1868, an armed frigate sent to seek out a fabled destroyer of ships is itself sunk, and three passengers from the frigate—a harpooner, Ned Land, along with a professor who is an expert on the creatures of the sea and his assistant—are rescued. They discover that the "monster" they searched for is in reality the first man-made submarine, the *Nautilus*, commanded by Captain Nemo, a madman who is willing to share his secrets of nuclear energy with the world only on his own terms. Land rescues Nemo from the clutches of a giant squid and eventually manages to alert the outside world as to the location of Nemo's secret island base. Nemo and his creations are destroyed. Released on December 23, 1954. Based on the classic story by Jules Verne.

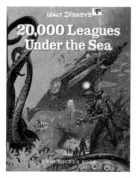

Academy Award winner for Best Special Effects and Best Art Decoration/Set Decoration (John Meehan and Emile Kuri); nominated also for Best Film Editing. 127 min. The first Disney feature filmed in CinemaScope. Disney special-effects wizards constructed the giant squid of rubber, steel spring, flexible tubing, glass cloth, Lucite, and plastic, with tentacles measuring 40 feet with two feelers of 50 feet. It could rear up eight feet out of water, its tentacles and feelers moving with frightening realism. It took a staff of 28 men to operate the intricate remote controls. Using hydraulics, electronics, and compressed air, they succeeded in giving a lifelike appearance to the squid. But there were problems. The squid fight had to be filmed a second time after Walt Disney and the director, Richard Fleischer, were unhappy with the initial results. It had been filmed in a special tank on brand-new soundstage 3 at the Disney Studio as if it was sunset on a placid sea; unfortunately this allowed viewers to see too much of the mechanics that enabled the squid to move, and it looked too fake. Instead, the scene was shot a second time, as if it was a stormy night, with 100 backstage workers on hand providing the needed lightning, rain, turbulent seas, and hurricane winds, and everything worked much better. The movie featured the song "A Whale of a Tale" by Al Hoffman and Norman Gimbel. Director Fleischer was the son of Walt's early animation rival, Max Fleischer, who created the *Out of the Inkwell* and *Betty Boop* cartoons, and Disney made sure that Max did not object before he hired his son. Stars James Mason (Capt. Nemo), Kirk Douglas (Ned

Land), Paul Lukas (Prof. Aronnax), Peter Lorre (Conseil). Locations for the film included the Disney and 20th Century Fox lots in California, and various locales in the Bahamas and Jamaica. The *Nautilus* was designed by Harper Goff. Reissued in theaters in 1963 and 1971. Released on video in 1980, 1985, and 1992. A television show on the making of the film, *Operation Undersea*, won the Emmy for best television program of the year. The *Nautilus* set was displayed for a time at Disneyland.

20,000 Leagues Under the Sea Fantasyland submarine attraction in Magic Kingdom Park at Walt Disney World; opened on October 14, 1971, and closed on September 5, 1994. While Disneyland had based its submarine attraction on the nuclear submarines that had been so much in the news in the late 1950s, by the time Walt Disney World was planned, the designers decided instead to pattern their 12 submarines after Capt. Nemo's *Nautilus*. It quickly became one of the most popular attractions in the park. While the attraction closed in 1994, demolition did not occur until the summer of 2004.

20,000 Leagues Under the Sea. Attraction at Tokyo DisneySea; opened on September 4, 2001. Sponsored by Coca-Cola. Guests join Captain Nemo's crew and undertake a mysterious deep-sea exploration mission aboard a six-passenger submarine boat, encountering shipwrecks, sea monsters, and the lost continent of Atlantis.

20,000 Leagues Under the Sea Exhibit Display of sets from the movie; located in Tomorrowland at Disneyland from August 3, 1955, to August 28, 1966. When Walt Disney was rushed to finish Disneyland on time, he fell behind on Tomorrowland. So, since the movie *20,000 Leagues Under the Sea* was so successful, he decided to display the original sets there. The stopgap attraction turned out to be one of the more popular ones at Disneyland, so it remained for 11 years. The popularity of movie sets was proven again when Disney-MGM Studios opened in Florida in 1989. In 1994, Disneyland Paris opened a walk-through attraction, Les Mystères du Nautilus, similar to the one that had been at Disneyland, but this time most of the set pieces had to be reconstructed.

Twilight Bark, The The barking of dogs that sounds the alert about the missing puppies in *One Hundred and One Dalmatians*. The phrase was used years later as the title of Disney Feature Animation's weekly employee newsletter.

Twilight Zone Tower of Terror, The Attraction on Sunset Boulevard at Disney-MGM Studios; opened on July 22, 1994. Guests take a strange odyssey through the remains of a decaying Hollywood hotel, visiting the lobby, the library, where Rod Serling on a television set helps get visitors in the proper mood, and the boiler room. The adventure climaxes in a 13-story drop in a runaway service elevator. Over the next two years, the experience was enhanced by the addition of two more drops on the elevator. In

1999, even more drops were added to the experience, and on December 31, 2002, the drops became random, controlled by the attraction itself. A similar attraction, The Hollywood Tower of Terror, 183 feet in height, at Disney's California Adventure opened on May 5, 2004.

Twister, Bull from the Sky (television) Television show; aired on January 4, 1976. Directed by Larry Lansburgh. A young man raises a cast-off Brahma calf to become a champion bucking bull, but to lighten a disabled plane's load, the bull has to be pushed out while harnessed into three parachutes. The bull lands in a wildlife safari park and is endangered because of the wild

animals there. Stars Larry Wilcox, Willie Aames, Keith Andes, Denis Arndt.

Twitches (television) A Disney Channel Original Movie; premiered on October 14, 2005. Twin sisters, Alex and Camryn, were separated shortly after birth in the otherworldly kingdom of Coventry and quickly sent to Earth to escape the dangers of an evil force. At birth, their wizard father assigned each twin a protector, Ileana and Karsh, and from there, each girl was adopted and raised in wildly disparate homes. When they finally meet each other on their twenty-first birthday, they learn they have extraordinary, mysterious powers. Now, Alex and Camryn struggle to accept the truth about their past and the extent of their magic, and set out to find their birth mother. But when they learn they are the only hope to save Coventry, the sisters must battle the evil forces of Darkness that once threatened to destroy them. Directed by Stuart Gillard. Stars Tia Mowry (Alex), Tamara Mowry (Camryn), Kristen Wilson (Miranda), Patrick Fabian (Thantos), Pat Kelly (Karsh). 86 min.

Two Against the Arctic (television) Two-part television show; aired on October 20 and 27, 1974. Directed by Robert Clouse. Two Eskimo children are stranded on an ice cap with little food. They struggle not only with nature but with polar bears and wolves as they head toward home. Stars Susie Silook, Marty Smith, Rossman Peetook.

2½ Dads (television) Television show; aired on February 16, 1986. Faced with rising housing costs, a widower father with two kids, a divorced dad with three, and a bachelor friend hit on an ingenious solution: they decide to share a house. As the kids try to adjust to their new "siblings," the three men struggle to cope with running the household. Stars George Dzundza, Lenore Kasdorf, Marissa Mendenhall. Directed by Tony Bill.

Two Chips and a Miss (film) Chip and Dale cartoon; released on March 21, 1952. Directed by Jack Hannah. Chip and Dale attend a nightclub and fall in love with the female entertainer, another chipmunk named Clarice, who divides her attention between the two.

Two for the Record (film) Special cartoon combining *After You've Gone* and *All the Cats Join In* from *Make Mine Music*; released on April 23, 1954.

Two Gun Goofy (film) Goofy cartoon; released on May 16, 1952. Directed by Jack Kinney. Goofy, by accident, becomes a hero and a sheriff when he interrupts a stagecoach robbery.

Two-Gun Mickey (film) Mickey Mouse cartoon; released on December 15, 1934. The first cartoon directed by Ben Sharpsteen. In this Western adventure, Pete and his bandits rob and fire on Minnie before she is rescued by Mickey, who disposes of the gang.

Two Happy Amigos (television) Television show; aired on February 5, 1960. Directed by Jack Hannah, C. August Nichols. Walt introduces a visit by José Carioca in a show that combines Donald Duck and other cartoons.

Two Much (film) A struggling art gallery owner in Miami, Art Dodge works a scam of trying to get widowed spouses of recently deceased men to pay for paintings the men allegedly purchased. But he gets into trouble when one of his patsies turns out to be the widow of a purported mob boss, and Art finds himself in the middle of a wacky romantic triangle involving the man's son and ex-wife. The wealthy ex-wife, Betty, announces her intention to marry Art, and he is not turned off by the thought of her money, but he really loves Betty's sister, Liz, an art instructor. Since Liz will have nothing to do with this supposed fortune hunter, Art creates a new persona of a long-lost twin brother, Bart, who is free to pursue Liz. Needless to say, this leads to chaos. Released on March 15, 1996. Directed by Fernando Trueba. A Touchstone Pictures presentation of an Interscope Communications production, in association with Occidental Media. Stars Antonio Banderas (Art/Bart), Danny Aiello (Gene), Melanie Griffith (Betty), Daryl Hannah (Liz), Eli Wallach (Sheldon Dodge), Joan Cusack (Gloria Fletcher). 118 min. Filmed in CinemaScope. Based on the novel by Donald E. Westlake. The movie was based on a script originally created in Spain by Fernando and David Trueba, and filmed on location in Miami. Released on video in 1996.

Two Silhouettes (film) Segment of *Make Mine Music*, "Ballade Ballet," featuring Tania Riabouchinska and David Lichine dancing and Dinah Shore singing. The song is by Charles Wolcott and Ray Gilbert.

Two Weeks Vacation (film) Goofy cartoon; released on October 31, 1952. Directed by Jack Kinney. Goofy goes on his vacation but gets tangled up with a trailer and has various other mishaps until he ends up peacefully in jail.

Tyner, Charles Actor; appeared in *Pete's Dragon* (Merle), and on television in *Shadow of Fear*.

Typhoon Lagoon Fifty-six–acre water park at Walt Disney World; opened on June 1, 1989. After the popularity of River Country, Disney designers decided that another aquatic experience was needed, and they tried to outdo their former effort. The mythology of the place is that a typhoon hit the town in the past, marooning a shrimp boat, the *Miss Tilly*, perched precariously atop magical Mt. Mayday and leaving all in ruins. Now, with the water park, guests climb Mt. Mayday to slide down the slides into the pools below. Highlights are Castaway Creek, Shark Reef, Ketchakiddie Creek, and the water slides Humunga Kowabunga, Keelhall Falls,

Gangplank Falls, Mayday Falls, Jib Jammer, Stern Burner, and Rudder Buster. The main lagoon features the world's largest artificially created waves. Refreshments are available at Leaning Palms and Typhoon Tilly's Galley & Grog.

Tytla, Vladimir ("Bill") (1904–1968) Highly regarded animator; at Disney from 1934 to 1943. He animated on the shorts, then on *Snow White and the Seven Dwarfs*, *Pinocchio*, *Fantasia* (the devil on Bald Mountain), and *Dumbo*. He was named a Disney Legend in 1998.

Tytle, Harry (1909–2004) He joined Disney in 1936 in the Animation Department, where he served as an assistant director. Tytle moved up through the ranks to production manager in 1944, shorts manager in 1946, cartoon production manager in 1955, and production coordinator in 1963. In the 1970s, he became a producer of such films as *Chandar, the Black Leopard of Ceylon; Salty, the Hijacked Harbor Seal; The Little Shepherd Dog of Catalina; Barry of the Great St. Bernard;* and *The Proud Bird from Shanghai.* For a number of years, he served as the Disney representative in Europe for the projects that were being filmed there. In 1998 he wrote his autobiography entitled *One of Walt's Boys.*

U

U.S. Junior Tournament; World Junior Tennis Tournament (television) Two 2-hour syndicated television specials commemorating the national and international Sport Goofy Junior Tennis Championships; aired in September and December 1983. The show is hosted by Dick and Patti Van Patten.

Ugly Dachshund, The (film) When a Great Dane puppy is put into a litter of dachshunds, the puppy grows up thinking he's a dachshund, too, thereafter causing no end of humorous complications in the lives of Mark Garrison, a magazine illustrator, and his lovely wife, Fran. The Great Dane finally proves his worth, realizing just what kind of an animal he is, and peace once more descends on the Garrison household. Released on February 4, 1966. Directed by Norman Tokar. 93 min. Stars Dean Jones (Mark Garrison), Suzanne Pleshette (Fran Garrison) in her Disney debut, along with Charlie Ruggles (Dr. Pruitt), Kelly Thordsen (Officer Carmody), and Parley Baer (Mel Chadwick). For the title role of Brutus, the animal trainer found a three-year-old prizewinning Great Dane named Diego of Martincrest. But needing a dog with more experience for some of the more demanding scenes, he found a double in Duke, whom he had used earlier as one of the Great Danes in *Swiss Family Robinson*. Released on video in 1986.

Ugly Duckling, The (film) Silly Symphony cartoon; released on December 17, 1931. Directed by Wilfred Jackson. When a mother hen scorns a little duckling, it runs away in dismay. But when a tornado dumps her chicks into the flooded river, the duckling saves them from going over the waterfall. A hero, he is now one of the family. The film is from a story by Hans Christian Andersen. Remade in color as the last Silly Symphony, released on April 7, 1939. Directed by Jack Cutting. The remake changed the story to have a baby "duckling" shunned by his family because of his ugliness until a mother swan recognizes him as a swan and adopts him as one of her brood. It won an Academy Award as Best Cartoon. An educational version was entitled *Hans Christian Andersen's The Ugly Duckling*.

Ullman, Ricky Actor; starred in the title role in the *Phil of the Future* series, and played Roscoe in *Pixel Perfect* on Disney Channel.

Ultimate Christmas Present, The (television) A Disney Channel Original Movie; premiered on December 1, 2000. In Los Angeles, 13-year-old Allie Thompson and her friend Sam find a discarded contraption that turns out to be Santa Claus's weather-making machine. They decide to use it to make it snow so they can get a school snow day and not have to turn in an assignment. But the machine gets out of hand and causes no end of problems that threaten to ruin Christmas. Allie and Sam team up with Santa in an attempt to save the day. Directed by Greg Beeman. Stars Hallie Hirsh (Allie Thompson), Brenda Song (Samantha Kwan), Peter Scolari (Edwin Hadley), Hallie Todd (Michelle Thompson), John B. Lowe (Santa Claus), Bill Fagerbakke (Sparky), John Salley (Crumpet), Spencer Breslin (Joey Thompson). Vancouver, British Columbia, substituted for Los Angeles for the filming.

Ultimate X See *ESPN's Ultimate X.*

Unbirthday Song, The Song from *Alice in Wonderland*; written by Mack David, Al Hoffman, and Jerry Livingston.

Unbreakable (film) David Dunn is the sole survivor of a devastating train wreck. Elijah Price is a mysterious stranger who offers a bizarre explanation as to why David escaped without a single scratch, an explanation that threatens to change David's family and life forever. Released on November 22, 2000. A Touchstone Picture. Directed by M. Night Shyamalan. Stars Bruce Willis (David Dunn), Samuel L. Jackson (Elijah Price), Robin Wright Penn (Audrey Dunn), Charlayne Woodard (Elijah's mother), Spencer Treat Clark (Joseph Dunn). 107 min. Filmed in CinemaScope. Shot on location in and around Philadelphia. Released on video in 2001.

Uncle Donald's Ants (film) Donald Duck cartoon; released on July 18, 1952. Directed by Jack Hannah. Donald has ant trouble when sugar spills from a bag he is carrying. This leads to a battle with the ants at his home over a jug of maple syrup, eventually resulting in Donald's car exploding and the ants enjoying the syrup.

Uncle Remus Character created by Joel Chandler Harris and played by James Baskett in *Song of the South*.

Uncle Scrooge See Scrooge McDuck.

Under the Gun (film) Dramatic educational film for children about handgun violence, produced in cooperation with the Center to Prevent Handgun Violence and sponsored by MetLife. 26 min. Released in January 1995.

Under the Sea Song from *The Little Mermaid*; written by Howard Ashman and Alan Menken. Academy Award winner.

Under the Tuscan Sun (film) Freshly divorced San Francisco writer Frances Mayes is depressed, but her best friend, Patti, offers a gift to try to shake Frances out of her lethargy—a ten-day trip to Tuscany, in the heart of Italy. Once there, under the Tuscan sun, Frances impulsively buys a run-down villa named "Bramasole," literally "something that yearns for the sun." As she embraces the local ways and devotes herself to the restoration of her new home, Frances finds herself forming close bonds with people around her and slowly rediscovers the pleasures of laughter, friendship, and romance. A Touchstone Picture. Directed by Audrey Wells. Released on September 26, 2003. Stars Diane Lane (Frances Mayes), Sandra Oh (Patti), Lindsay Duncan (Katherine), Raoul Bova (Marcello), Vincent Riotta (Martini). 115 min. Based on the book by Frances Mayes. Filmed on location in Cortona, Positano, Rome, and Florence, Italy. Released on video in 2004.

Under Wraps (television) A Disney Channel original movie; first aired on October 25, 1997. Three kids find a 3,000-year-old mummy on Halloween and accidentally set him free. They discover that they must return their new friend to his resting place before midnight or he will turn to dust and lose his immortal soul. Directed by Greg Beeman. Stars Maria Yedidia (Marshall), Adam Wylie (Gilbert), Clara Bryant (Clara), Bill Fagerbakke (mummy).

Undergrads, The (television) A 68-year-old enrolls with his grandson, Jody, at a local university after Jody spirits him away from a rest home to which he has been sent by his son. He finds his study skills have rusted over the years. A pay-TV movie for The Disney Channel, first aired on May 5, 1985. 101 min. Directed by Steven H. Stern. Stars Art Carney (Mel Adler), Chris Makepeace (Jody), Len Birman (Verne), Lesleh Donaldson, Jackie Burroughs. The film was shot in Canada, with the University of Toronto a major location. Released on video in 1987.

Underhill, Don Mouseketeer from the 1950s television show.

Understanding Alcohol Use and Abuse (film) Educational film produced by Reynolds Film Export, John Ewing; released in September 1979. The dangers of alcohol abuse are shown through animation.

Understanding Stresses and Strains (film) Educational film made for Upjohn's Triangle of Health series; released in June 1968. The film suggests the use of common sense to minimize the normal stresses and strains of life.

Underwood, Jay Actor; appeared on The Disney Channel in *Not Quite Human, Not Quite Human II*, and *Still Not Quite Human* (Chip Carson).

Unhappily Ever After (television) Television series; debuted on the WB network on January 11, 1995, and ended September 19, 1999. Used-car salesman Jack Mulloy is getting a divorce from his wife, Jennie, after 16 years, and their three self-centered kids hope they will be spoiled rotten by their competing parents. Jack's only confidant is an old stuffed bunny—a parting gift from his eight-year-old son—that just happens to talk. Stars Geoff Pierson (Jack), Stephanie Hodge (Jennie), Joyce Van Patten (Maureen), Justin Berfield (Ross), Kevin Connolly (Ryan), Nikki Cox (Tiffany). Bobcat Goldthwait provides the voice of Mr. Floppy, the talking bunny.

Unidentified Flying Oddball (film) In this updated adaptation of Mark Twain's *A Connecticut Yankee in King Arthur's Court*, an astronaut and his robot companion accidentally fly backward in time and end up as prisoners at the court of King Arthur. A jealous Merlin and Mordred plot to overthrow the king, but thanks to modern technology, the knights of the round table are able to defeat the evil forces in a rousing climactic battle. Released first in England as *The Spaceman and King Arthur* on July 10, 1979; U.S. release on July 26, 1979. Directed by Russ Mayberry. 93 min. The television title was *The Spaceman in King Arthur's Court*. Stars Dennis Dugan (Tom), Jim Dale (Sir Mordred), Ron Moody (Merlin), Kenneth More (King Arthur), Rodney Bewes (Clarence), John Le Mesurier (Sir Gawain), Sheila White (Alisande). The film was shot on location at Alnwick Castle and at Pinewood Studios, London, England. Alnwick Castle, which dates back to the eleventh century, doubled for Camelot. A banquet hall within the castle walls was converted into a commissary to provide meals for the more than 150 filmmakers and 1,000 extras. All of the extras were rounded up from within a 50-mile radius, including the people of the historic market town of Alnwick. A large special-effects team headed by Cliff Culley and Ron Ballanger created Hermes, the robot; laser guns; a jet-pack that flies; a magnetized sword; and a 25-foot-long space shuttle aircraft with a retractable ramp and compact four-foot moon rover that expands to seven feet, with various screens, a solar disc, and a large hydraulic arm that emerges and operates on cue. When space suits designed by NASA proved impractical, a space-garb specialist, Olinkha Horne, was put to work to create new costumes. Released on video in 1986.

United Artists Distributor of the Disney cartoons from 1932 to 1937, along with *Victory Through Air Power* in 1943.

United Kingdom Pavilion in World Showcase at Epcot; opened on October 1, 1982. A street winding past buildings that evoke the small towns of England leads guests to a series of shops selling typical wares. In the square, the Old Globe Players entice passersby into participating in their little comedies.

United Nations, The (film) Educational film, in Mickey's Field Trips series; released on July 27, 1989. 16 min. It provides a guided tour through the United Nations complex.

Universe of Energy Pavilion in Future World at Epcot; opened on October 1, 1982. It was sponsored by Exxon from 1982 to 2004. On the roof of the pavilion are two acres of solar panels that generate enough electricity to power much of the attraction. Inside, guests learn about energy in a series of films and a trip into the prehistoric past. For the latter, they ride in 30,000-pound traveling theater cars, which hold 96 passengers each and are guided along a very thin wire embedded in the concrete floor. The show was updated beginning on September 15, 1996, incorporating *Ellen's Energy Adventure*, starring Ellen DeGeneres.

Unstrung Heroes (film) Steven Lidz is 12 years old and his world is falling apart. Overwhelmed by his life with an ailing mother and an emotionally disturbed father, Steven runs off to live with his two wildly eccentric uncles, Danny and Arthur. Baffled by the tragedies surrounding him, Steven finds solace in the idiosyncrasies of his uncles' strange and wonderful world, and begins understanding his life. Limited release on September 15, 1995; general release on September 22. A Hollywood Pictures film. Directed by Diane Keaton. Stars Andie MacDowell (Selma Lidz), John Turturro (Sid Lidz), Michael Richards (Danny), Maury Chaykin (Arthur), Nathan Watt (Steven). 93 min. Filmed on location in Los Angeles and Pasadena, California. Released on video in 1996.

Up a Tree (film) Donald Duck cartoon; released on September 23, 1955. Directed by Jack Hannah. Donald Duck, a logger in a logging camp, is getting ready to topple a tree that is the home of Chip and Dale, who quickly get revenge that ultimately leads to the destruction of Donald's house.

Up Close and Personal (film) Tally Atwater is determined to capture the coveted news anchor position, a spot many assured her she would never achieve. Blazing a trail from small-town weather girl to prime-time anchor, she has a meteoric rise to fame which causes her to collide with Warren Justice, a brilliant older newsman who becomes her mentor and lover. As their relationship grows, so, too, does Tally's celebrity, to the point where her popularity begins to eclipse Warren's. A Touchstone Picture in association with Cinergi Pictures Entertainment. Directed by Jon Avnet. Released on March 1, 1996. Stars Robert Redford (Warren Justice), Michelle Pfeiffer (Tally Atwater), Stockard Channing (Marcia McGrath), Joe Mantegna (Bucky Terranova), Kate Nelligan (Joanna Kennelly), Glenn Plummer (Ned), James Rebhorn (John Merino). 124 min. Suggested by the book *Golden Girl: The Story of Jessica Savitch* by Alanna Nash. The movie filmed in such disparate settings as the Orange Bowl, Holmesburg Prison in Philadelphia, and Hollywood soundstages. Released on video in 1996.

Up, Up and Away (television) A Disney Channel original movie; first aired on January 22, 2000.

Scott Marshall, approaching his 14th birthday and the supposed arrival of superpowers like the rest of his superhero family, exhibits no signs of extraordinary behavior of any kind. When the family is captured by a criminal mastermind intent on taking over the world, it is up to Scott to use his brains instead of supernatural brawn to stop the evil plan and save humankind. Directed by Robert Townsend. Stars Robert Townsend (Jim), Michael J. Pagan (Scott), Alex Datcher (Judy), Sherman Hemsley (Edward), Kasan Butcher (Adam).

Upjohn See Triangle of Health.

Upjohn Pharmacy Drugstore display on Main Street at Disneyland; open from July 1955 to September 1970. Decorated like a turn-of-the-century pharmacy, it was primarily a display, though in early days guests could pick up tiny free sample bottles of vitamins. Became the New Century Clock Shop.

Ursula Sea witch villain in *The Little Mermaid*; voiced by Pat Carroll.

Ursus H. Bear's Wilderness Outpost Shop in Bear Country at Disneyland; opened in 1972. Became Crocodile Mercantile in 1988.

Using Simple Machines (film) Educational film; released in September 1986. 14 min. The film explains basic concepts of mechanical physics.

Ustinov, Peter (1921–2004) Actor; appeared in *Blackbeard's Ghost* (Blackbeard), *One of Our Dinosaurs Is Missing* (Hnup Wan), *Treasure of Matecumbe* (Dr. Snodgrass), and provided the voices of Prince John and King Richard in *Robin Hood*. On The Disney Channel, he played the grandfather in *The Old Curiosity Shop*.

Utilidors Web of tunnels, called Utilidors, which connect all areas of Magic Kingdom Park at Walt Disney World. Actually, because of the high water table in Florida, the Utilidors had to be built on top of the ground. Then the park was added on top of that, essentially putting it on the second floor. The Utilidors allow easy maintenance, stocking of shops, and movement of costumed cast members from place to place, without disturbing the guests or disrupting the ambiance in the park.

V

Vacation Club Resort Time-share hotel facility at Walt Disney World; opened on October 1, 1991. Guests can learn about time-share ownership in the Commodore House. The resort includes dining at Olivia's Cafe and shopping at the Conch Flats General Store. In January 1996 it was renamed Disney's Old Key West Resort.

Vacation Club Resort, Hilton Head Island, South Carolina This 102-unit resort opened on March 1, 1996. Adjacent to Shelter Cove Harbour along the intracoastal waterway, it was designed as a 1940s Carolina Lowcountry vacation lodge. Separate from the lodge itself but part of the resort is Disney's Beach House in Palmetto Dunes, featuring private access to a 12-mile beach.

Vacation Club Resort, Vero Beach, Florida Ground was broken on July 28, 1994, for a new Vacation Club Resort located in Vero Beach. This was the first Disney resort built separately from a Disney park. It opened on October 1, 1995, consists of an inn and villas, and includes Shutters restaurant, Bleachers Bar & Grill, and The Green Cabin Lounge.

Vacation Villas Opened in December 1971 as town houses primarily for lease to corporations, the original 27 units were eventually expanded to 133. By 1977, the town houses were known as Vacation Villas, and were available for overnight guest rentals. They became part of The Disney Institute in 1996 and were removed in 2002 to make way for the Saratoga Springs Resort.

Vacationland Campground Campground across West Street from Disneyland. It closed at the end of 1996 to make way for construction on the Disneyland Resort.

Val d'Europe Shopping center, and eventual town, being constructed next to Disneyland Paris. The 1-million-square-foot International Shopping Center, with an adjacent factory outlet mall, opened on October 25, 2000. The 60-acre site has been leased to SEGECE, a Paris-based company.

Valentine, Karen Actress; appeared in *Hot Lead and Cold Feet* (Jenny) and *The North Avenue Irregulars* (Jane), and on television in *A Fighting Choice*.

Valentine from Disney, A (television) Television show; aired on February 8, 1983. A salute to romance, with clips from a number of animated films.

Valiant (film) In England during World War II, a young pigeon, Valiant, inspired by the heroic exploits of squadron leader Gutsy of the Royal Homing Pigeon Service, decides to join up. In Trafalgar Square, Valiant meets up with a Cockney con-bird, Bugsy, who also enlists. After a rigorous training period, they and their Squadron F are sent to France to collect a message from the Resistance despite attacks by a brigade of vicious enemy falcons, led by the ruthless General Von Talon. A CGI-animated film from Touchstone Pictures, Vanguard Animation, and Ealing Studios, released in the United States by Buena Vista on August 19, 2005. Originally released in the United Kingdom on March 25, 2005. Directed by Gary Chapman. Voices include Ewan McGregor (Valiant), Ricky Gervais (Bugsy), Tim Curry (General Von Talon), Jim Broadbent (Sergeant), Hugh Laurie (Gutsy), John Cleese (Mercury), John Hurt (Felix). 76 min. Released on DVD.

Van de Kamp, Andrea L. Member of the Disney board of directors from September 29, 1998 to March 19, 2003.

Van Dyke, Barry Actor; appeared on television in *Gun Shy.*

Van Dyke, Dick Actor; appeared in *Mary Poppins* (Bert, Mr. Dawes, Sr.), *Lt. Robin Crusoe, USN* (Lt. Robin Crusoe), *Never a Dull Moment* (Jack Albany), and *Dick Tracy* (D.A. Fletcher), and on television in *The Best of Disney: 50 Years of Magic, Walt Disney—One Man's Dream, Golden Anniversary of Snow White and the Seven Dwarfs,* and *Donald Duck's 50th Birthday.* He was named a Disney Legend in 1998.

Van Patten, Dick Actor; appeared in *Snowball Express* (Mr. Carruthers), *Superdad* (Ira Kershaw), *The Strongest Man in the World* (Harry), *Gus* (Cal Wilson), *Treasure of Matecumbe* (gambler), *The Shaggy D.A.* (Raymont), and *Freaky Friday* (Harold Jennings), and on television in *14 Going on 30.*

Van Patten, Jimmy Actor; appeared in *Freaky Friday* (cashier), *Hot Lead and Cold Feet*

(Jake), and *The Apple Dumpling Gang Rides Again* (Soldier #1).

Van Patten, Vincent Actor; appeared in *Charley and the Angel* (Willie Appleby), and on television in *The Boy and the Bronc Buster* and *High Flying Spy.* The son of actor Dick Van Patten, Vincent went on to become a top-seeded tennis pro.

Vance, Courtney B. Actor; appeared in *The Adventures of Huck Finn* (Jim), *Holy Matrimony* (Cooper), and *The Preacher's Wife* (Henry Biggs).

Vanessa Ursula's human guise to get the prince to marry her, in *The Little Mermaid.*

Vanishing Prairie, The (film) True-Life Adventure feature, released on August 16, 1954. Directed by James Algar. Academy Award winner. 71 min. Story of the pronghorn antelope, the prairie dog, the bighorn sheep, the mountain lion, the buffalo, and numerous other creatures that once made the prairie their home, and how the animals survived through the seasons. A team of 12 photographers, led by Tom McHugh, filmed in the wilderness from the Mississippi to the Rockies and from the Gulf of Mexico to the plains of Canada. Released on video in 1985.

Vanishing Private, The (film) Donald Duck cartoon; released on September 25, 1942. Directed by Jack King. After Donald camouflages a cannon with invisible paint, Pete tries to catch him, so he makes himself invisible. The general sees Pete chasing nothing and puts him in a straitjacket, with Donald guarding him.

Vanneste, André (1927–1995) He handled Disney licensing and publications in Belgium for 40 years, beginning in 1953, and was presented a

European Disney Legends award posthumously in 1997.

Varda, the Peregrine Falcon (television) Television show; aired on November 16, 1969. A Seminole Indian captures a falcon on its yearly migration, but it yearns to be free. Stars Peter de Manio, Noreen Klincko, Denise Grisco. Narrated by Hugh Cherry.

Varney, Jim (1949–2000) He appeared as Ernest P. Worrell in *Ernest Goes to Camp*, *Ernest Saves Christmas*, *Ernest Goes to Jail*, and *Ernest Scared Stupid*. Also played the roles of Mr. Nash and Auntie Nelda in *Ernest Goes to Jail*. He appeared on television in *Disneyland's 35th Anniversary Celebration* and *Walt Disney World Celebrity Circus*. He provided the voice for Slinky Dog in *Toy Story* and *Toy Story 2* and Cookie in *Atlantis*.

VD Attack Plan Animated educational film; released in January 1973. Directed by Les Clark. The film explores the dangers of venereal disease, where to go for help, how to cure it, and how to prevent it. Narrated by Keenan Wynn.

Venable, Evelyn (1913–1993) Actress; she voiced the Blue Fairy in *Pinocchio*.

Venetian Gondolas Attraction at Tokyo DisneySea; opened on September 4, 2001. Guests in Palazzo Canals can tour this Mediterranean Harbor neighborhood aboard an Italian gondola.

Veritas: The Quest (television) Hour-long, action-adventure drama series; premiered on ABC on January 27, 2003, and ended on March 10. After being kicked out of an expensive private school, Nikko Zond discovers that his estranged father, Solomon, is not just an archaeology professor, but is secretly leading an international search for the truth about a civilization that vanished long before known history began. Stars Ryan Merriman (Nikko Zond), Alex Carter (Solomon Zond), Eric Balfour (Calvin Banks), Cynthia Martells (Maggie), Cobie Smulders (Juliet Droil), Arnold Vosloo (Vincent Siminou). Filmed in Montreal and Toronto. Produced by Touchstone Television in association with Storline Entertainment and Massett/Zinman Productions.

Vernon Kilns Manufacturer of licensed Disney ceramics from 1940 to 1942. They produced figurines from only three films—*Fantasia*, *Dumbo*, and the *Baby Weems* segment of *The Reluctant Dragon*. Their set of 36 *Fantasia* figurines, featuring such characters as hippos, ostriches, sprites, elephants, and mushrooms, is especially noteworthy. Besides the figurines, they produced dinnerware in eight different *Fantasia* patterns, as well as a series of vases and bowls.

Vero Beach, Florida See Vacation Club Resort, Vero Beach, Florida.

Veronica Guerin (film) Veronica Guerin, a journalist covering the crime beat in Dublin in the 1990s, starts a crusade to expose local drug dealers, and in doing so she neglects her family and is accused of glory-seeking. Guerin relentlessly pursues her mission, and her obsession eventually leads to her murder. A Touchstone Picture with Jerry Bruckheimer Films. Released in the U.S. on October 17, 2003, after a premiere (July 8) and initial release (July 11) in Ireland. Directed by Joel Schumacher. Stars Cate Blanchett (Veronica Guerin), Brenda Fricker (Bernie Guerin), Ciaran Hinds (John Traynor), Gerard McSorley (John Gilligan), Barry Barnes (Graham Turley), Joe Hanley (Eugene "Dutchie" Holland), David Murray (Charles Bowden), David Herlihy (Peter "Fatso" Mitchell). 98 min. Filmed on location in Ireland in Super 35-Scope. Released on video in 2004.

Very Merry Christmas Parade Event at Disneyland from 1977 to 1979 and 1987 to 1994. Beginning in 1995 the parade was A Christmas Fantasy.

V.I. Warshawski (film) A tough-talking, fiercely independent female private investigator (with a weakness for pretty shoes), Warshawski is often forced to play hardball with Chicago's crime element. When her new flame, ex-hockey player Boom-Boom Grafalk turns up murdered, his 13-year-old daughter Kat hires V.I. to find her father's killer. She soon uncovers a startling conspiracy for murder and money. Released on July 26, 1991. Directed by Jeff Kanew. A Hollywood Pictures film. 89 min. Stars Kathleen Turner (Vic), Jay O. Sanders (Murray), Charles Durning (Lt. Mallory). Based on the novels by Sara Paretsky. Filmed on location in Chicago. Released on video in 1991.

Victoria and Albert's The most elegant restaurant at Walt Disney World, located in the Grand Floridian Beach Resort; opened on June 28, 1988. All the waitresses are Victoria and the waiters, Albert. The chef prepares a special selection of gourmet dishes each evening, which are described by the waitstaff and later in the individually inscribed menus that are delivered to each diner. A harpist provides background music.

Victoria's Home-Style Cooking Restaurant on Main Street in Disneyland Paris; opened on April 12, 1992.

Victory Through Air Power (film) Based on Maj. Alexander P. de Seversky's book of the same title, the film shows how long-range air power could cause the defeat of the Axis and Japan during World War II. It opens with an animated history of aviation, followed by scenes of Major de Seversky expressing his theories about air power and its further development. Filmmakers use animation to produce strikingly vivid graphics of the Allied forces pounding the Axis strongholds. To the strains of a stirring "Song of the Eagle," an animated eagle is dramatically shown attacking the heart of Japan with a dagger. Released on July 17, 1943, by United Artists, although all

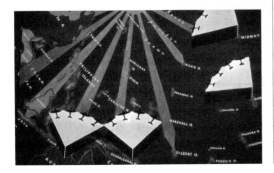

other Disney films at the time were being released by RKO. Sequence directors were Clyde Geronimi, Jack Kinney, James Algar. Animation supervisor was David Hand. 65 min. Nominated for an Academy Award for Best Scoring of a Dramatic or Comedy Picture. The history of aviation sequences were reissued as part of *Man in Flight* and *Fly with Von Drake* on television, and as an educational film, *History of Aviation*.

Victory Vehicles (film) Goofy cartoon; released on July 30, 1943. Directed by Jack Kinney. Goofy demonstrates, with offscreen narration, various devices used to replace the automobile during wartime, finally ending up with a pogo stick.

Video After initial reticence to release its films on videocassette for home usage, Disney finally released its first videos, for rental and sale, in both Beta and VHS format, in October 1980. Besides some cartoon compilations, among the ten features released that month were *The Apple Dumpling Gang*, *The Black Hole*, *The Love Bug*, and *Escape to Witch Mountain*. *Dumbo* was the first of the animated classics to be released, in June 1981, for rental only. *Alice in Wonderland* followed, for rental only, in October 1981. Both films were released for sale in 1982, but it was not until July 1985 that Disney dipped into its library of top-ranked animated features, with the release of *Pinocchio*. Following the success of that film on video, other animated features followed on a regular basis. Each film would be available for a limited time only, then would go into a moratorium period with plans made to re-release it at a future date. While the earliest video releases were expected to be primarily for rental through video dealers, the desire of consumers to actually own private copies of Disney films moved the company to offer selected videos at a sell-through price. With its growing acceptance, some features have been produced directly for video, bypassing a theatrical or television release. The direct-to-video features have been:

1. *Breakin' Through* (1985)
2. *The Return of Jafar* (1994)
3. *Aladdin and the King of Thieves* (1996)
4. *Honey, We Shrunk Ourselves* (1997)

5. *Mighty Ducks the Movie: The First Face-Off* (1997)
6. *Pooh's Grand Adventure: The Search for Christopher Robin* (1997)
7. *Beauty and the Beast: The Enchanted Christmas* (1997)
8. *Belle's Magical World* (1998)
9. *Air Bud: Golden Receiver* (1998)
10. *Pocahontas II: Journey to a New World* (1998)
11. *The Jungle Book: Mowgli's Story* (1998)
12. *The Lion King II: Simba's Pride* (1998)
13. *The Wonderful Ice Cream Suit* (Touchstone)(1999)
14. *Hercules: Zero to Hero* (1999)
15. *Belle's Tales of Friendship* (1999)
16. *Mickey's Once Upon a Christmas* (1999)
17. *Winnie the Pooh: Seasons of Giving* (1999)
18. *An Extremely Goofy Movie* (2000)
19. *Buzz Lightyear of Star Command: The Adventure Begins* (2000)
20. *The Litle Mermaid II: Return to the Sea* (2000)
21. *Air Bud: World Pup* (2000)
22. *Lady and the Tramp II: Scamp's Adventure* (2001)
23. *The Book of Pooh: Stories from the Heart* (2001)
24. *Cinderella II: Dreams Come True* (2002)
25. *The Hunchback of Notre Dame II* (2002)
26. *Air Bud: Seventh Inning Fetch* (2002)
27. *Tarzan and Jane* (2002)
28. *Winnie the Pooh: A Very Merry Pooh Year* (2002)
29. 101 *Dalmatians II: Patch's London Adventure* (2003)
30. *Inspector Gadget 2* (2003)
31. *Atlantis: Milo's Return* (2003)
32. *Air Bud Spikes Back* (2003)
33. *Stitch! The Movie* (2003)
34. *Kim Possible: The Secret Files* (2003)
35. *George of the Jungle II* (2003)
36. *The Lion King 1½* (2004)
37. *Winnie the Pooh: Springtime with Roo* (2004)
38. *The Three Musketeers* (2004)
39. *Mickey's Twice Upon a Christmas* (2004)
40. *Mulan II* (2005)
41. *Tarzan II* (2005)
42. *Lilo & Stitch 2: Stitch Has a Glitch* (2005)
43. *Pooh's Heffalump Halloween Movie* (2005)
44. *Kronk's New Groove* (2005)

Videopolis Opened next to Fantasyland at Disneyland on June 22, 1985, as a high-tech teen dance area, with a 5,000-square-foot dance floor and 70 television monitors offering popular music videos; later seats covered the dance floor, and Videopolis was used for outdoor stage shows such as "One Man's Dream," "Dick Tracy," and "Beauty and the Beast." The name of the amphitheater was changed to Fantasyland Theater on June 23, 1995, with the opening of "The Spirit of Pocahontas." Also stage in Discoveryland in Disneyland Paris; opened on April 12, 1992. The building features a re-creation of the *Hyperion* from *Island at the Top of the World*. Videopolis East was briefly a nightclub in Pleasure Island at Walt Disney World.

Videopolis Railroad Station The renamed Fantasyland Railroad Station at Disneyland; opened on June 30, 1988. It became the Toontown Railroad Station in 1992.

Vidi Protective snipe in *The Pelican and the Snipe* (1944).

Vienna Boys Choir They appeared in *Almost Angels*.

Viewliner Tomorrowland train at Disneyland, from June 26, 1957 to September 15, 1958. This modernistic train traveled around Tomorrowland for little more than a year.

Village, The (film) In 1897 a close-knit community lives with the frightening knowledge that a mythical race of creatures resides in the woods around them. The evil and foreboding force is so unnerving that none dare venture beyond the borders of the village and into the woods. But when curious, headstrong Lucius Hunt plans to step beyond the boundaries of the town and into the unknown, his bold move threatens to forever change the future of the village. Directed by M. Night Shyamalan. A Touchstone Picture. Released on July 30, 2004. Stars Joaquin Phoenix (Lucius Hunt), Bryce Dallas Howard (Ivy Walker), Adrien Brody (Noah Percy), William Hurt (Edward Walker), Sigourney Weaver (Alice Hunt), Brendan Gleeson (August Nicholson). 108 min. Bryce Dallas Howard is the daughter of producer Ron Howard. Filmed in and around Philadelphia. Nominated for an Academy Award for Best Score (James Newton Howard). Released on video in 2005.

Village Haus Restaurant Located in Fantasyland at Disneyland; opened on May 25, 1983. First known as Village Inn Restaurant. Themed after *Pinocchio*, this restaurant began serving pizza and pasta along with hamburgers in 1994.

Village Resorts Located at Walt Disney World, near the Downtown Disney Marketplace, the resort began in December 1971 with 27 town houses for lease primarily to corporations. Eventually, they became known as Vacation Villas and Treehouses. Fairway Villas and Club Lake Villas were added. By 1977 the focus had changed to overnight rentals to Walt Disney World guests. In 1996, the Village Resorts became part of The Disney Institute.

Village Restaurant, The Located at the Downtown Disney Marketplace at Walt Disney World, from 1975 until July 1990. Became Chef Mickey's.

Village Smithy, The (film) Donald Duck cartoon; released on January 16, 1942. Directed by Dick Lundy. Donald's pride in his trade is put to the test when he attempts to work with a cartwheel and to shoe Jenny the donkey.

Village Traders African-themed shop in World Showcase at Epcot; opened on November 12, 1993. An African pavilion has been talked about for years, but this shop and a snack bar are the only representations so far.

Villain's Lair Shop in Fantasyland at Disneyland; opened on October 2, 1998 and closed on July 1, 2004.

Vincent (film) Special cartoon about 7-year-old Vincent Malloy who would rather be Vincent Price than a little boy, and his fantasies turn his life into scenes from a horror film—much to the dismay of his mother. Released in New York on October 1, 1982. Directed by Tim Burton. Narrated by Vincent Price, this black-and-white film uses three-

dimensional models and animation. The animation work was done by Stephen Chiodo. The short was popular enough to Disney for the Studio to back such later Burton creations as *Frankenweenie* and *The Nightmare Before Christmas*, which use some of the same techniques.

Vincent, Jan-Michael Actor; appeared in *The World's Greatest Athlete* (Nanu).

Vincent, Virginia Actress; appeared in *$1,000,000 Duck* (Eunice Hooper), *Amy* (Edna Hancock), and *Treasure of Matecumbe* (Aunt Lou).

Visionarium, Le Circle-Vision attraction, with added Audio-Animatronics of Timekeeper and 9-Eye, who interact with the film *From Time to Time* featuring Jules Verne; in Discoveryland in Disneyland Paris; opened on April 12, 1992. Also at Tokyo Disneyland, from 1993 to 2002.

Visit to EPCOT Center, A (film) Sixteen-mm film released in September 1983.

Vista-United Telecommunications Partnership between Disney and United Telephone System (originally known as Vista-Florida Telephone System when created in 1971) to handle the telephone needs of the Walt Disney World Resort, but after industry deregulation in 1981 it began selling systems to customers around the country, including Disneyland and the Walt Disney Studio. Vista-United was the first phone company to use fiber-optic cable commercially, installed the first computer-controlled telephone operating center, began the first 911 emergency telephone system in Florida, and in 1986 became the first fully digital phone company.

Vital Signs (television) One-hour dramatic medical reality series, showcasing doctors who race against time to solve baffling medical mysteries. The stories were told in the first person by physicians, and were accompanied by re-enactments of the events. Debuted on ABC on February 27, 1997, and ended on July 3, 1997. Host was Robert Urich. The re-enactments were shot in an actual, though recently closed, hospital—the Tustin Medical Center in California.

Vixey Cute female fox in *The Fox and the Hound*; voiced by Sandy Duncan.

Vogel, David President of Buena Vista Motion Pictures Group, encompassing the Disney, Touchstone, and Hollywood Pictures labels, in 1998. He had joined Walt Disney Pictures in 1989 where he served under various capacities. He left the company in 1999.

Vogel, Mitch Child actor; appeared on television in *Bayou Boy* and *Menace on the Mountain.*

Voght (Scott), Dolores (1897–1981) Longtime executive secretary to Walt Disney, from 1930 until her retirement in 1965.

Voice, The: Questions that Help You Sell (film) Educational film from The Nick Price Story of Non-Manipulative Selling series; released in February 1981. Communication with customers is important and keeps them coming back.

Voices on the Road Back: A Program About Drugs (film) Educational film; released in October 1990. 15 min. The film includes interviews with teenagers who began using drugs at an early age.

Voight, Jon Actor; appeared in *Enemy of the State* (Reynolds), *Pearl Harbor* (President Roosevelt), *Holes* (Mr. Sir), *National Treasure* (Patrick Gates), and *Glory Road* (Adolph Rupp).

Volunteer Worker, The (film) Community Chest trailer; starring Donald Duck. Delivered on September 1, 1940. Donald has a hard time collecting for charity, when he meets a kindly ditchdigger.

von Detten, Erik Actor; provided the voices of Sid in *Toy Story*, Croney #1 in *Tarzan*, and on television as Flynt in *The Legend of Tarzan*. He appeared in *The Princess Diaries* (Josh Bryant) and the television series *Dinotopia* (Karl Scott), as a regular on Disney Channel in *So Weird* (Clu Bell), and in the Disney Channel Original Movie *Brink* (Andy Brinker). He was Danny in the 1995 television remake of *Escape to Witch Mountain*.

Von Drake in Spain (television) Television show; aired on April 8, 1962. Directed by Norman Foster. Ludwig Von Drake looks at the dances and customs of Spain. Guest stars Jose Greco, along with many other Spanish dancers, including Rafael de Cordova, Pedro Azorin, Oscar Herrera, Mariemma, Lola de Ronda.

Von Oy, Jenna Actress; appeared in the television series *Blossom* and *Lenny*.

Voyage of the Little Mermaid Multimedia show featuring animation, live performers, puppetry, lasers, and special effects taking you under the sea to Ariel's domain. Opened at the Disney-MGM Studios on January 7, 1992. Replaced Here Come the Muppets.

Voyages de Pinocchio, Les Located in Fantasyland at Disneyland Paris; opened on April 12, 1992.

Wacky Zoo of Morgan City, The (television) Two-part television show; aired on October 18 and 25, 1970. Directed by Marvin Chomsky. Based on Charles Goodrum's book, *I'll Trade You an Elk*. The mayor wants to close down the run-down city zoo and use the site for a museum, but an accountant and his children fight to save it. Stars Hal Holbrook, Joe Flynn, Cecil Kellaway, Wally Cox, Mary LaRoche, Michael-James Wixted, Anne Seymour, Michael McGreevey, Christina Anderson, Annie McEveety, Judson Pratt. The film was shot on the site of the former Los Angeles Zoo, after the animals had all been moved to a new zoo nearby.

Waco & Rhinehart (television) Two unorthodox U.S. marshals search for the person who killed a member of their unique agency. An unsold pilot for a proposed television series. Aired on ABC on March 27, 1987. Directed by Christian I. Nyby. 90 min. Stars Charles C. Hill, Justin Deas, Bill Hootkins, Bob Tzudiker, Kathleen Lloyd.

Wages and Production (film) Educational film; from The People on Market Street series, produced by Terry Kahn; released in September 1977. A visit to a furniture company helps students understand the concept of labor as a salable service.

Waging Peace (film) Educational film, premiered on The Disney Channel on November 6, 1996. Produced by Disney Educational Productions in association with Jazbo Productions. Based on the Elie Wiesel Foundation for Humanity's "Tomorrow's Leaders" conference held in Venice, Italy, the film documents the meeting of world leaders, conflict resolution facilitators, and 30 teenagers, representing divergent points of view from some of the world's most serious crisis regions, with a goal of working toward mutual understanding and peace. Follow-up trips to each area provide a series of profiles showing the reality of the lives of a group of young people.

Wagner, Jack (1925–1995) Actor; for two decades, beginning in 1970, he was the "voice of Disneyland." Wagner's familiar voice was heard in most recorded announcements at the park, as well as narrating several of the attractions. He also did work for Walt Disney World, Tokyo Disneyland, and Disneyland Paris, and his voice is featured on the shuttles at the Orlando and Houston airports. Jack prepared most of his recordings in a state-of-the-art studio at his Anaheim, California, home. He was named a Disney Legend in 2005.

Wahlberg, Mark Actor; appeared in *Renaissance Man* (Tommy Lee Haywood). Wahlberg, as Marky Mark, had made a sensation on the musical scene, becoming an advertising model for Calvin Klein underwear after his trademark lowering of his pants on stage.

Wahoo Bobcat, The (television) Television show; aired on October 20, 1963. An old fisherman in the Okefenokee Swamp befriends an aging bobcat. But the bobcat has no place in civilization, so the fisherman transports him to a deserted island where he can live out his days. Narrated by Rex Allen. Stars Jock MacGregor, Bill Dunnagan, Lloyd Shelton.

Wake of Disaster (television) Television show; part 2 of *The Mooncussers*.

Wales (film) People and Places featurette; released on June 10, 1958. Directed by Geoffrey Foot. Wales prides herself in her wealth of natural resources, foundries, mills, and factories. Beyond this modern facade lies another treasure—a rich historical background and ancient lore. The great granite fortresses still remain as reminders that from the struggle and strife was born a pure and distinctive national culture. Filmed in CinemaScope. 25 min.

Walk Around the World Pathway that will encircle the Seven Seas Lagoon at Walt Disney World. In 1994 it was announced that individuals could sponsor a 10-inch hexagonal brick in the pathway, which would be inscribed with the sponsor's name, for a fee of $96.

Walker, E. Cardon ("Card") (1916–2005) He served as president of Walt Disney Productions from 1971 to 1980 and chairman of the board from 1980 to 1983. He originally began with the company in 1938 delivering the mail, and worked his way up in the company in the camera and story departments, finally moving into advertising. In 1956 he was named vice president of advertising and sales, and he joined the board of directors in 1960. In 1965 he was appointed vice president of marketing. He became executive vice president and chief operating officer in 1968. It was Walker who, with Donn Tatum, ably led the company after Roy O. Disney's death, and who, in 1975,

announced plans to commence with Walt's plans for EPCOT. He was elected president in 1971 and became chief executive officer in 1976. In this capacity, he oversaw its design and construction of EPCOT. In 1980 he was named chairman of the board. He retired in 1983 after supervising the opening of EPCOT Center, Tokyo Disneyland, and the launch of The Disney Channel. He remained on the company's board of directors until 1999, qualifying for his 50-year service award in 1988. He received the Disney Legend Award in 1993.

Walker, Tommy (1922–1986) Showman; served as director of entertainment at Disneyland from 1955 to 1967. Besides the park's parades and fireworks spectaculars, he was in charge of many special events, including the grand opening ceremonies for Disneyland, and later the pageantry for the 1960 Winter Olympics in Squaw Valley. He was the son of Vesey Walker.

Walker, Vesey (1893–1977) Original director of the Disneyland Band from 1955. He led the band in thousands of parades and concerts during his years at the park. He was named "founding director" and retired in 1967, but he remained available as a guest conductor and for special appearances. He was named a Disney Legend in 2005.

Walker Ranch See The Disney Wilderness Preserve.

Wallace, Oliver (1887–1963) Composer; he worked on the scores for many Disney films, including *Dumbo* (he won an Academy Award), *Cinderella*, *Peter Pan*, *Alice in Wonderland*, *Lady and the Tramp*, plus dozens of shorts. He began at Disney in 1936.

Wallach, Eli Actor; appeared in *The Moon-Spinners* (Stratos), *Tough Guys* (Leon B. Little), *The Associate* (Frank), *Two Much* (Sheldon), and *Keeping the Faith* (Rabbi Lewis).

Walley, Deborah (1943–2001) Actress; appeared in *Bon Voyage* (Amy Willard) and *Summer Magic* (Cousin Julia).

Walmsley, Jon Actor; appeared in *The One and Only, Genuine, Original Family Band* (Quinn Bower), and provided the voice of Christopher Robin in *Winnie the Pooh and the Blustery Day*. Walmsley later went on to fame in the role as Jason Walton on *The Waltons*.

Walrus and the Carpenter Characters in the tale of the gullible oysters in *Alice in Wonderland*; voiced by J. Pat O'Malley.

Walsh, Bill (1913–1975) Producer; joined Disney in 1943 as a writer for the Mickey Mouse comic strip, later moving into television and films. In 1950 Walt Disney selected Bill to write and produce the first Disney television show, *One Hour in Wonderland*. He later produced the spec-

tacularly successful *Davy Crockett* and *Mickey Mouse Club* shows. In 1956, he became a movie producer, soon reaching the ranks of one of the most successful producers of all time with such titles as *Westward Ho the Wagons!*, *The Shaggy Dog*, *Toby Tyler, The Absent-Minded Professor, That Darn Cat!, Blackbeard's Ghost, Mary Poppins, The Love Bug*, and *Bedknobs and Broomsticks*. He was named a Disney Legend posthumously in 1991.

Walsh, Kay (1914–2005) Actress; appeared in *Greyfriars Bobby* (Mrs. Brown), *Night Crossing* (Doris's mother), and on television in *The Scarecrow of Romney Marsh* (Mrs. Waggett).

Walston, Ray (1914–2001) Actor; appeared in *My Favorite Martian* (Martin), and on television in *Ask Max* (Harmon).

Walt Disney (television) Name of the television series on CBS, from September 26, 1981 to September 24, 1983. The series was not renewed at that time, so it would not conflict with The Disney Channel.

Walt Disney—A Golden Anniversary Salute (television) Television tribute to Walt Disney Productions' 50th anniversary on ABC's *Wide World of Entertainment*; aired on October 23, 1973. Directed by Lou Tedesco.

Walt Disney Archives Founded on June 22, 1970, with Dave Smith as the archivist, to collect, preserve, and make available for use the various historical materials of The Walt Disney Company. While the Archives works primarily with departments of The Walt Disney Company, it also handles mail, e-mail, and telephone inquiries relating to Disney history.

Walt Disney Christmas Show (television) Television show promo for *Peter Pan*, starring Walt Disney, Kathy Beaumont, Bobby Driscoll, and the Magic Mirror (Hans Conried), sponsored by Johnson and Johnson; aired on December 25, 1951. Directed by Robert Florey.

Walt Disney Classics Collection, The Premiered in 1992 as the first line of fine animation art sculptures produced directly by the Walt Disney Studios. Licensees took over in 2001. It uses authentic Disney animation principles and materials to bring to life memorable moments and characters from Disney animated classics. The meticulously crafted figurines, created from a special low-fire porcelain, can be displayed singly or grouped to re-create entire scenes, and some have been plussed with materials such as crystal, blown glass, and precious metals. Each sculpture bears a special symbol connoting the year in which it was made, along with a backstamp featuring Walt Disney's signature. Since its introduction, the collection has become highly popular because of its attention to quality and because early pieces produced in limited editions have increased dramatically in value. Numerous clubs of Classics Collection collectors have sprung up around the country, as well as the official one, The Walt Disney Collectors Society.

Walt Disney Collectors Society, The Launched in 1993 to support the Walt Disney Classics Collection, this society is the first official membership organization for Disney fans and enthusiasts sponsored by Disney itself. Headed originally by Paula Sigman, the Society publishes *Sketches* as its quarterly magazine and offers member-only Classics Collection pieces.

Walt Disney Company, The Corporate name of the company as of February 6, 1986. It was formerly Walt Disney Productions.

Walt Disney Educational Materials Co. Incorporated on June 25, 1969; later known as Walt Disney Educational Media Co. and Disney Educational Productions.

Walt Disney Enterprises The entity of the Disney company during the 1930s which handled the licensing of character merchandise. It was consolidated to become a part of Walt Disney Productions on September 30, 1938.

Walt Disney Gallery, The A new concept in retail merchandising began on November 4, 1994, with the opening of the first Walt Disney Gallery connected to a Disney Store at Main Place in Santa Ana, California. The Gallery featured collectibles, artwork, and other special items of Disneyana in an attractively designed setting.

Walt Disney Imagineering New name, as of January 1986, of WED Enterprises. In 1996, Walt Disney Imagineering merged with the Disney Development Company, the Disney company's real estate development subsidiary.

Walt Disney Motion Pictures Group Division of The Walt Disney Company established in 1994 with Joe Roth as chairman.

Walt Disney Music Company Formed in October 1949, to publish and license Disney songs. It was affiliated with ASCAP, while its sister music publishing arm at Disney, the Wonderland Music Co., formed in 1952, was affiliated with BMI. The first songs published by Walt Disney Music Company were those from *Cinderella* (1950).

Walt Disney—One Man's Dream (television) Two-hour television movie; aired on December 12, 1981. Directed by Dwight Hemion. A look at Walt Disney's life leading up to the building of EPCOT Center. The story emphasizes the many times that Walt refused to listen to advisers and critics who tried to tell him that his plans would not work. But he was an innovator and continued to dream. And most of his dreams came true. Stars Christian Hoff, Michael Landon, Mac Davis, Dick Van Dyke, Marie Osmond, Carl Reiner, Ben Vereen, Julie Andrews, and many other stars in cameo roles. Hoff was the first actor to portray Walt Disney in a Disney film, albeit as a child.

Walt Disney Presents (television) Television series on ABC, from September 12, 1958 to September 17, 1961.

Walt Disney Productions Corporate name of the Walt Disney company until changed to The Walt Disney Company on February 6, 1986. The company began on October 16, 1923, when Walt Disney signed his first contract to produce the Alice Comedies. On December 16, 1929, the company was incorporated, taking over the assets previously held as a partnership between Walt and Roy Disney.

Walt Disney Records After its success in the early 1950s with music publishing, the Walt Disney Music Company entered the phonograph record business in 1956. The "Disneyland" record label was created for the new record line, with the first release in 1956 being "A Child's Garden of Verses." Walt Disney himself narrated one of the earliest LPs, *Walt Disney Takes You to Disneyland.* There was a WDL series for sound tracks, an ST series for Storytellers, and an MM series for music from the *Mickey Mouse Club* television show. Non-Disney music was included in the line with adult easy listening and novelty records. In 1959, the Buena Vista label began a more prestigious line, and in 1964 had a huge hit with the *Mary Poppins* sound track (14 weeks as number one on the Billboard chart, and two Grammy awards). Forty-five-rpm singles promoted songs from Disney films and heralded performances by Annette Funicello, Darlene Gillespie, Fess Parker, and other Disney stars. A popular LLP (Little Long Playing) series began in 1967. The Disney records have earned a large number of gold records, with one of the biggest sellers being the 1979 *Mickey Mouse Disco*. The CD revolution reached Disney in 1988 with the release of its last 12-inch vinyl record—the *Oliver & Company* sound track. The following year, Disneyland/Vista Records changed its name to Walt Disney Records, which today continues to represent a broad and diverse selection of audio entertainment for the family.

Walt Disney Story, The Main Street attraction at Disneyland, in the Opera House; opened on April 8, 1973, taking the place of Great Moments with Mr. Lincoln. A movie, narrated by Walt himself, told his life story. Many guests missed Lincoln, however, so the movie closed on February 12, 1975, enabling Great Moments with Mr. Lincoln to return to the theater. A Lincoln display and a model of the Capitol replaced some of the Walt Disney display in 1985. Memorabilia related to Walt Disney from the Walt Disney Archives is displayed, including awards, letters written to Walt Disney by famous people, and even an exact reproduction of his offices from the Disney Studio in Burbank. The offices were reconstructed from photographs and accurate blueprints, and furnished with the same pieces that had graced the offices originally. The scene outside the window is a photographic backdrop which had been used at the Studio when a replica of Disney's office was built on a soundstage for him to use on some of his television lead-ins. The *Walt Disney Story* film, which uses Walt Disney interviews and other recordings for the narration and features rare stills and film clips, was eventually released as an educational film and in 1994 on videocassette for purchase in the parks. Also an attraction on Main Street in Magic Kingdom Park at Walt Disney World, from April 15, 1973 until October 5, 1992. The post-show area included an EPCOT Center preview in 1981–82 and a Disney-MGM Studios preview in 1987–89. The Walt Disney Story display area was reopened in 1993 to serve as a center for annual passport redemption.

Walt Disney Studios The Disney corporate headquarters, located at the corner of Buena Vista and Alameda in Burbank, California, at 500 South Buena Vista Street. Built in 1940, the Studio covers 44 acres. There are buildings for animation, camera, sound recording, live-action production, editing, costume, music, marketing, and so on. There were originally backlot sets, but these have given way to offices (see *Backlot*). One soundstage was built in 1940, and three more were added over the next two decades (stage four was eventually divided into two separate stages). Two more soundstages were added in 1997. The most famous landmark is a signpost at the corner of Mickey Avenue and Dopey Drive. It was placed there for the Studio tour segment of *The Reluctant Dragon* in 1941 and never removed. There were earlier Disney Studios on Kingswell Avenue (1923) and Hyperion Avenue (1926).

Walt Disney Studios Park Theme park that opened adjacent to Disneyland Paris on March 16, 2002, giving guests an insight into movies, animation, and television. The Park's inspiration is

the classic Hollywood movie studios from the 1920s to today. After passing through the main entrance, with a fountain featuring Mickey as the Sorcerer's Apprentice, guests can choose from four different areas to explore: Front Lot, Animation Courtyard, Production Courtyard, and Backlot.

Walt Disney Television Animation Department formed in November 1984, with Gary Krisel as president, to produce special animation for television. Their first series were *Disney's Adventures of the Gummi Bears* and *The Wuzzles*. A decade later, they were producing 150 half-hour episodes of programing a year, plus specials, movies, direct-to-video features, music videos, featurettes, and commercials. A Japanese branch, Walt Disney Animation (Japan), which opened in 1989, closed in 2003. In November 2005 Walt Disney Television Animation became part of Disney Channel Worldwide. See also DisneyToon Studios.

Walt Disney Television Studios Guests can get a behind-the-scenes view of the Disney Channel France production facility in the Production Courtyard at Walt Disney Studios Paris; opened on March 16, 2002.

Walt Disney Travel Co. Company begun in Florida in 1972 to work with travel agents and individuals planning vacations to Walt Disney World, with expansion that same year to California for Disneyland vacations.

Walt Disney World See Walt Disney World Resort.

Walt Disney World at Home: Garden Magic (film) Video release of step-by-step gardening tips from the gardens of the Walt Disney World Resort. Segments are Telling the Story with Plants, Portable Gardens, Parterre Gardens, Topiary, and Environmental Gardening. 55 min. Released in 1996.

Walt Disney World Casting Center Building opened on March 27, 1989. With its diamond-shaped decorations, it has been called a giant argyle sock. It is here that those hopeful of working for Walt Disney World put in their applications.

Walt Disney World Celebrity Circus (television) Television special; aired on November 27, 1987. Directed by Marty Pasetta. Stars Tony Randall as host, with Allyce Beasley, Tim Conway, Kim Fields, Jim Varney, Malcolm-Jamal Warner.

Walt Disney World Conference Center Building opened in August 1980. Surrounded by the Club Lake Suites, it offered meeting facilities. In 1996 it became part of The Disney Institute.

Walt Disney World Dolphin Hotel at Walt Disney World, near Epcot, originally operated by Sheraton and later by Starwood Lodging. It was designed by Michael Graves and opened on June 4, 1990.

Walt Disney World 4th of July Spectacular (television) Television special; aired in syndication on July 3, 1988. Directed by Don Ohlmeyer. 120 min. Hosted by Tempestt Bledsoe and Marc Summers, with Burt Reynolds, Carol Burnett, Rita Moreno, Tommy Tune, the Beach Boys, Mark Price, Willard Scott. This show marked the first of an annual July 4th holiday special through 1992.

Walt Disney World Golf Classic Beginning in its first year, 1971, Walt Disney World, at the urging of then-Disney president and golf enthusiast Card Walker, sponsored the Walt Disney World Golf Classic. It has been an individual tourney each year, except for 1974 to 1981 when it served as the venue for the PGA Tour's two-man National Team Championship. The winner of the tournament the first three years was Jack Nicklaus. Walt Disney World has hosted a PGA Tour event every year since 1971.

Walt Disney World Happy Easter Parade (television) The first of many annual television specials aired on ABC on April 7, 1985. Directed by Paul Miller. Hosted by Rick Dees and Joan

Lunden. Only in 1986 did the Walt Disney World Easter Parade appear as part of *The CBS Easter Parade* (March 30, 1986), which switched between the Walt Disney World parade and one on Fifth Avenue in New York City. The 1988 parade was hosted by Joan Lunden, Alan Thicke, and Regis Philbin. The telecasts continued until 1999.

Walt Disney World Inside-Out (film) Series on The Disney Channel; premiered on June 7, 1994. Stars Scott Herriott in a wacky, witty, off-beat look at life in Walt Disney World. A new version of the show, featuring J.D. Roth and Brianne Leary, with commentary by George Foreman, began on December 12, 1995. One show a month originated from Disneyland.

Walt Disney World Marching Band Formed in 1971, the band performs concerts in Town Square and occasionally at Fantasy Faire in Fantasyland, as well as in various parades.

Walt Disney World—Phase I (film) Film prepared for a Florida press conference held on April 30, 1969.

Walt Disney World Railroad Attraction in Magic Kingdom Park at Walt Disney World, opening on October 1, 1971. The four locomotives are the *Walter E. Disney*, the *Roy O. Disney*, the *Lilly Belle*, and the *Roger Broggie*, all discovered in the Yucatan where they hauled freight and passengers. (Lilly was Walt Disney's wife, and Broggie was a Disney engineer who helped Walt with his miniature railroad hobby.) The railroad tracks circle the park, and provide a good introduction to a visit, on a 15-minute journey.

Walt Disney World Resort Opened near Orlando, Florida, on October 1, 1971, with the Magic Kingdom and two hotels. After the success of Disneyland in California, Walt Disney was besieged by suggestions for a second park. Everyone wanted this new park to be built in *their* hometown—especially when observing the growth of the economy of Anaheim after Disneyland opened there in 1955. Disney bided his time, however. First of all, he wanted Disneyland to be running smoothly before he considered another site, and second, he wanted to be sure that he selected the right place. Starting in the early 1960s, Walt and Roy Disney began searching for an area on the East Coast where they could build a new Disney park. They knew their second park should be east of the Mississippi, where it could draw from a different segment of the population than did Disneyland. Walt Disney also knew he needed a site with a pleasant climate. Many other factors were considered, such as land cost, population density, and accessibility. In Florida, the climate seemed the best for year-round operation, and there was land available, so they secretly began buying up land. Learning their lesson from the urban clutter that had been built up around Disneyland park in California, the Disneys wanted enough land to insulate their development. After coming up with roughly 17,000 acres, they were offered a huge 10,000-acre parcel. Roy balked at first, but when Walt asked him what he would do if he had an extra 10,000 acres around Disneyland, he realized that they should go ahead. They ended up with 27,500 acres, a parcel twice the size of Manhattan island. While they were able to buy most of the land they needed before the word leaked out who the mysterious buyer was, eventually a newspaper reporter dug out the story. Hurriedly, a press conference was put together at the Cherry Plaza Hotel in Orlando, and Walt and Roy announced their plans publicly on November 15, 1965. It was a major shock for the Disney company when Walt Disney died suddenly a year later, in December 1966. Roy, who was 73 years old, was ready to retire, but decided to stay on the job long enough to see that Walt's final project was built. Construction progressed, and the costs eventually rose to $400 million, but due to Roy's business acumen, the park was able to open in 1971 with the company having no outstanding debt. Roy presided at the grand opening in October and he passed away in December. In size, the Magic Kingdom park was similar to Disneyland, but there was more—two luxury hotels, golf courses, lakes and lagoons offering fishing and water sports, and a campground. The Magic Kingdom opened with some attractions similar to those at Disneyland, but also with its own unique attractions. The Country Bear Jamboree first made its appearance there, as did The Hall of Presidents and the Mickey Mouse Revue. Since 1971, the Walt Disney World Resort has had a steady growth, highlighted by the opening of Epcot in 1982, of Disney-MGM Studio in 1989, and Disney's Animal Kingdom Park in 1998. Over the years, additional hotels, sports and entertainment facilities, and shopping areas have made Walt Disney World the premier destination resort in the world.

The special record-breaking guests at Walt Disney World have been:

1st guest—October 1, 1971
   William Windsor, Jr.
50,000,000th guest—March 2, 1976
   Susan Brummer
100,000,000th guest—October 22, 1979
   Kurt Miller
150,000,000th guest—April 7, 1983
   Carrie Stahl
200,000,000th guest—July 20, 1985
   Virgil Waytes, Jr.
300,000,000th guest—June 21, 1989
   Matt Gleason
400,000,000th guest—August 5, 1992
   Brandon Adams
500,000,000th guest—October 13, 1995
   Michelle Davi
600,000,000th guest—June 24, 1998
   Jacqueline D'Ambrosi

In 1994 Walt Disney World welcomed the one billionth guest worldwide to enter a Disney park (Mary Pat Smith of Decatur, Illinois); the 500,000,000th guest had been welcomed only nine years earlier, on March 25, 1986 (Don McGrath of Millis, Massachusetts).

Walt Disney World Speedway Built in a corner of the Walt Disney World Magic Kingdom parking lot and dedicated on November 28, 1995, the one-mile racetrack is used for various speed events, beginning with a Formula Ford 2000 support race on January 26, 1996, and the Indy Racing League's Indy 200 on January 27. Beginning February 7, 1997, the Richard Petty

Driving Experience offered behind-the-wheel and ride-along experiences in stock cars on the speedway.

Walt Disney World Swan Hotel at Walt Disney World; near Epcot, operated initially by Westin, and then by Starwood Lodging. It was designed by Michael Graves and opened on November 22, 1989.

Walt Disney World 'Twas the Night Before Christmas (television) Two-hour television special; aired on *The Wonderful World of Disney* on December 24, 2000, taking the place of the annual Christmas Day parade. Frankie Muniz, Ryan Stiles, Wayne Brady, and Colin Mochrie are part of a Santa tracking team that follows his progress around the world. Musical performers and variety elements, including Jessica Simpson, 'N Sync, and Monica, emanate from both Walt Disney World and Disneyland.

Walt Disney World—Vacation Kingdom (film) Sixteen-mm promotional film for the Florida park; released in September 1969.

Walt Disney World Village New name in 1977 for Lake Buena Vista Village, which had opened in March 1975. A large outdoor mall, with specialty shops all built by Disney designers. See Downtown Disney Marketplace.

Walt Disney World's 10th Anniversary See *Kraft Salutes Walt Disney World's 10th Anniversary.*

Walt Disney World's 25th Anniversary Party (television) Special airing on ABC on February 28, 1997, with Melissa Joan Hart and Will Friedle hosting. Drew Carey takes viewers on a behind-the-scenes tour of the parks, and Gloria Estefan performs "Remember the Magic." Also stars Michael J. Fox, Rosie O'Donnell, Donna Summer, the Village People, and Hillary Rodham Clinton.

Walt Disney World's Very Merry Christmas Parade (television) Now a Christmas tradition, a television special that first aired on

Christmas Day in 1983 on ABC, hosted by Joan Lunden and Mike Douglas. In 1984 it was Joan Lunden, Bruce Jenner, and Regis Philbin; in 1985 and 1986 it was Joan Lunden, Ben Vereen, and Regis Philbin. The 1999 parade was the first one to be taped at night. The parade was not televised in 2000, but it returned in 2001 with Regis Philbin and Kelly Ripa as hosts. Also known as *Walt Disney World Christmas Day Parade* (2002–05).

Walt Disney's Comics and Stories Comic book first published in October 1940. The original price was 10 cents.

Walt Disney's Mickey and Donald (television) Television show; aired on January 1, 1983 (30 min. format), and on September 24, 1983 (60 min. format). The show is a grouping of cartoons.

Walt Disney's Parade of Dreams Special parade for the 50th anniversary of Disneyland debuting on May 5, 2005, and featuring a large number of Disney characters along with dancers, rhythmic gymnasts, trampoline performers, and aerial artists. The parade floats, some nearly 20 feet high, act as rolling stages and feature jumping fountains, confetti blasts, and wafting bubbles. There are four performance stops along the parade route, with large musical production numbers being performed at each one.

Walt Disney's Wet and Wild (television) Hour-long syndicated television special. This animation compilation features cartoons showing ways of getting wet. First aired on October 1, 1986.

Walt Disney's Wonderful World of Color (television) Television series on NBC, from September 24, 1961 to September 7, 1969.

Walt: The Man Behind the Myth (television) Two-hour documentary about the life of Walt Disney, told through rare film clips and still photos, and by interviews with co-workers, historians, and celebrities. Dick Van Dyke narrates. Directed by Jean-Pierre Isbouts. Aired on the *Wonderful World of Disney* on September 16, 2001, to help celebrate the one hundredth anniversary of Walt Disney's birth. Released on video in 2001.

Walter and Emily (television) Television series on NBC; aired from November 16, 1991 to February 22, 1992. After 40 years of marriage, Walter and Emily Collins still bicker, but this disguises their deep love for each other. Their divorced son moves back in with them, bringing his 11-year-old son, Zack, and hoping that Walter and Emily will help care for him. Stars Cloris Leachman (Emily Collins), Brian Keith (Walter Collins), Christopher McDonald (Matt Collins), Matthew Lawrence (Zack Collins), Edan Gross (Hartley Thompson).

Walt's—an American Restaurant Located on Main Street in Disneyland Paris; opened on April 12, 1992.

Waltz King, The (television) Two-part television show; aired on October 27 and November 3, 1963. Directed by Steve Previn. A look at the life of Johann Strauss, Jr., beginning when, as a boy, he earns his famous father's displeasure when he tries his hand at composing. But he eventually proves to his father and the world that he is a fine musician. Stars Kerwin Mathews, Senta Berger, Brian Aherne, Peter Kraus, Fritz Eckhardt. The show was filmed on location in Europe, utilizing some of the continent's most ornate concert halls. It was released as a feature abroad, and on video in 1986.

War at Home, The (film) A Vietnam veteran, Jeremy Collier has returned to his Texas hometown, but a year later, at Thanksgiving 1973, he has still been unable to forget his traumatic experiences during the war. His family does not know how to deal with him. During the Thanksgiving weekend, Jeremy's rancour ignites a family confrontation that shakes the Colliers down to their very foundation as a family. A Touchstone Picture, in association with Avatar Entertainment and the Motion Picture Corporation of America. Directed by Emilio Estevez. Limited release in New York and Los Angeles on November 22,

1996. Stars Emilio Estevez (Jeremy Collier), Kathy Bates (Maurine Collier), Martin Sheen (Bob Collier), Kimberly Williams (Karen Collier). 124 min. Based on the 1984 Broadway play *Homefront*, by James Duff. Filmed on location in Austin, Texas. Released on video in 1997.

War bond certificate During World War II, to encourage parents to purchase war bonds in the names of their children, the Treasury Department had Disney artists design a colorful certificate, featuring many of the Disney characters around the perimeter, that would be given to each child in whose name a war bond was bought. These certificates are intriguing collectibles today, though some people erroneously think that they are the bonds themselves and can be cashed.

Warburton, Cotton (1911–1982) Film editor at the Disney Studios for 22 years beginning in 1955, he won an Academy Award for his editing of *Mary Poppins*. He also edited such films as *The Love Bug* and *The Absent-Minded Professor*. Before his Disney years, Warburton had gained fame as an all-American quarterback in the early 1930s, leading the USC Trojans during a 27-game winning streak, which remained a school record until 1980.

Warden, Jack Actor; appeared in *Passed Away* (Jack Scanlan), *Guilty as Sin* (Moe), and *While You Were Sleeping* (Saul), and on television in *Gallegher*.

Wardrobe One of the enchanted objects in *Beauty and the Beast;* voiced by Jo Anne Worley.

Waring, Todd Actor; appeared on television in *The Return of the Shaggy Dog* and *Splash, Too.*

Warren, Lesley Ann Actress; appeared in *The Happiest Millionaire* (Cornelia Drexel Biddle), *The One and Only, Genuine, Original Family Band* (Alice Bower), and *Color of Night* (Sandra).

Warrick, Ruth (1915–2005) Actress who played Johnny's (Bobby Driscoll) mother, Sally, in *Song of the South.*

Warrior's Path, The (television) Television show; part 1 of *Daniel Boone*.

Wart Nickname for Arthur in *The Sword in the Stone.*

Washington, Denzel Actor; starred in *Crimson Tide* (Hunter), *The Preacher's Wife* (Dudley), *He Got Game* (Jake Shuttlesworth), *The Hurricane* (Rubin Carter), and *Remember the Titans* (Herman Boone).

Washington, Ned (1901–1976) Lyricist; worked at Disney from 1938 to 1940, during which time he wrote songs for *Pinocchio, Saludos Amigos,* and *Dumbo*. "When You Wish Upon a Star" and the score from *Pinocchio* won him two Oscars. He was named a Disney Legend in 2001.

Washington Square (film) In 1850s New York, shy and awkward Catherine Sloper, the daughter of a wealthy and distinguished physician, and favored by neither beauty nor brilliance, is tottering into spinsterhood when she falls wildly and tempestuously in love with the smooth and dashing wastrel Morris Townsend. She is encouraged by her incurably romantic and sympathetic aunt Lavinia. Catherine is heir to an imposing fortune, and her father, who does not hold a high opinion of his daughter, is highly suspicious of the young man's intentions, feeling that he is only after her money. He does not see how a man of such youthful charm could possibly be in love with his daughter. Thus, Catherine is forced to make a fateful choice that will affect her happiness and the rest of her life. A Hollywood Pictures film in association with Caravan Pictures. Directed by Agnieszka Holland. Released in New York on October 5, 1997, and in an additional limited number of cities on October 10. Stars Jennifer Jason Leigh (Catherine Sloper), Albert

Finney (Dr. Austin Sloper), Ben Chaplin (Morris Townsend), Maggie Smith (Aunt Lavinia Penniman), Judith Ivey (Aunt Elizabeth Almond). 115 min. From Henry James's classic novella, which had previously been adapted for Broadway in 1947 and as William Wyler's 1949 film *The Heiress*, with Olivia de Havilland winning an Oscar for her portrayal of Catherine Sloper. Since Washington Square in New York City no longer looks anything like it did in the 1850s, the filmmakers turned instead to classic Union Square in Baltimore, Maryland, for their location filming. Released on video in 1998.

Watcher in the Woods, The (film) When an American composer and his family rent a foreboding house in England from an eccentric recluse, Mrs. Aylwood, a series of terrifying events occur, primarily to 17-year-old Jan. It turns out that the eerie experiences are connected to Mrs. Aylwood's teenage daughter's disappearance 30 years earlier. A reenactment of the disappearance unexpectedly reveals the secret of the unknown force. Released on October 7, 1981. An earlier version premiered April 16, 1980, in New York but was withdrawn so a new ending could be filmed. Directed by John Hough. 84 min. Stars Bette Davis (Mrs. Aylwood), Carroll Baker (Helen), David McCallum (Paul), Lynn-Holly Johnson (Jan Curtis), Kyle Richards (Ellie), Ian Bannen (John Keller), Richard Pasco (Tom Colley), Frances Cuka (Mary Fleming), Benedict Taylor (Mike Fleming), Eleanor Summerfield (Mrs. Thayer), Georgina Hale (young Mrs. Aylwood). The film was based on the novel *A Watcher in the Woods*, by Florence Engel Randall. St. Hubert's Manor, a huge estate situated near Ivor Heath, Buckinghamshire, was used as the site of the Curtises' vacation dwelling. Ettington Park Manor, a Gothic mansion, and an old stone chapel nearby were also used in the film. Scenes were also filmed at Pinewood Studios, London. Art Cruickshank and Bob Broughton supervised the supernatural effects, utilizing Disney's ACES (Automated Camera Effects System), which culminated in the finale. However, when early audiences in New York saw its premiere and disliked that special-effects–laden ending, the Studio cut it. *Mary Pop-*

pins was re-released to fill the gap, while a new ending was filmed and the movie was released again in October 1981. But it was too late, and the film generally failed at the box office despite the wonderfully eerie direction, music, and Bette Davis's performance. Released on video in 1982.

Watches The original Mickey Mouse watch was manufactured by Ingersoll in 1933, and sold for $3.25, later lowered to $2.95. They also made a pocket watch at the same time, selling for $1.50. The original wristwatch had a round dial, and featured three tiny Mickeys on a disk that indicated the seconds. These early watches have become some of the most sought-after types of Disneyana collectibles. The Mickey Mouse watch has been made continuously since 1933, though there was a period in the 1960s when only the words "Mickey Mouse" appeared on the dial. Ingersoll became U.S. Time, which became Timex. One of the more interesting watches was a backward Goofy watch. The numbers were placed in backward order and Goofy's hands moved backward as well. It took some effort to learn how to tell time backward, but the watches became popular collectibles after their 1972 man-

ufacture by Helbros. It originally cost $19.95 and within two decades was up to about $700 on the collector market. In a program of reproducing some of the classic Disney watches, The Disney Store selected the backward Goofy watch as the first in their series of reproductions. In 1972, Bradley, a division of Elgin National Industries, Inc., took over the manufacture of Disney watches, and in 1987 the contract went to Lorus. Today a number of different companies make Disney watches.

Water Babies (film) Silly Symphony cartoon; released on May 11, 1935. Directed by Wilfred Jackson. In this musical water fantasy based on Charles Kingsley's story, myriad tiny fairy folk find fun in riding rodeo style on frogs, flying with birds, and sailing in lily pad boats. *Merbabies* in 1938 was a sequel.

Water Birds (film) True-Life Adventure featurette; released on June 26, 1952. Directed by Ben Sharpsteen. Vignettes depict the lives of waterbirds, showing how Nature has adapted each of them to meet the problems of survival, such as different types of beaks and bodies, and describe their feeding habits and courtships. Academy Award winner. 31 min.

Water, Friend or Enemy (film) Educational film produced under the auspices of the Coordinator of Inter-American Affairs, the film shows the benefits derived from water, cautions against polluting drinking water, and teaches how to avoid cholera, typhoid, and dysentery. Delivered on May 1, 1943.

Waterboy, The (film) Lowly water boy Bobby Boucher is 31 years old, overly protected by his mother, and socially inept but he loves his job with the university football team, even though he is constantly the target of gross jokes and public humiliation. When he is unceremoniously fired for his ineptitude, he gets a chance with a team that is as clumsy as he is. Surprisingly, Bobby is discovered to have a dazzling talent for tackling, and is quickly signed to a college athletic scholarship, though inadvertently he wreaks havoc in the classroom and on the gridiron. A Touchstone Picture. Directed by Frank Coraci. Released on November 6, 1998. Stars Adam Sandler (Bobby Boucher), Kathy Bates (Mama Boucher), Fairuza Balk (Vicki Vallencourt), Jerry Reed (Red Beaulieu), Henry Winkler (Coach Klein). 90 min. The

nine-week shooting schedule for the film took place in and around Orlando, Florida. Released on video in 1999.

Watson, Raymond L. Member of the Disney board of directors beginning in 1974. When Card Walker retired in 1983, Watson was asked to take over as chairman of the board, a post which he held until Michael Eisner arrived in September 1984. He left the board in 2004.

Way Down Cellar (television) Two-part television show; aired on January 7 and 14, 1968. Directed by Robert Totten. Three friends find a secret tunnel under a destroyed church that leads them to a supposedly haunted house and, incidentally, a group of counterfeiters. Stars Butch Patrick, Sheldon Collins, Lundy Davis, Frank McHugh, Richard Bakalyan, David McLean, Ben Wright.

Wayans, Damon Actor; appeared in *Celtic Pride* (Lewis Scott), and on television in *My Wife and Kids* (Michael Kyle).

Wayans, Keenen Ivory Actor; starred in *A Low Down Dirty Shame* (Shame), and appeared on television in the syndicated *Keenen Ivory Wayans Show*.

Wayne, David (1914–1995) Actor; appeared in *The Apple Dumpling Gang* (Col. T. R. Clydesdale), and on television in *The Boy Who Stole the Elephant* and *Return of the Big Cat*.

Wayne, Patrick Actor; appeared in *The Bears and I* (Bob Leslie).

Wayne Brady Show, The (television) A series featuring comedy skits and musical numbers, starring Wayne Brady. Included are special guests and improv, with audience participation; premiered on ABC on August 8, 2001, and ended on September 19, 2001. The cast includes Brooke Dillman, Jonathan Mangum, J. P. Manoux, Missi Pyle. A new show with the same title, and being a one-hour entertainment talk/variety show, premiered in syndication on September 2, 2002, in a limited rollout to about half the country; it launched nationally on September 1, 2003, and was canceled in May 2004.

Wayward Canary, The (film) Mickey Mouse cartoon; released on November 12, 1932. Directed by Burt Gillett. Minnie is thrilled with Mickey's gift of a pet bird. But the mischievous bird escapes, takes a bath in ink, and is only saved from being a cat's lunch by Pluto's quick action.

Weasel Family, The (film) Educational film; released in May 1968. The film tells of the habits and traits of the weasel, otter, mink, marten, skunk, and wolverine.

Weaver, Doodles (1911–1983) Actor; appeared in *A Tiger Walks* (Bob Evans).

Webbigail Vanderquack Companion of the nephews in *Ducktales*; voiced by Russi Taylor.

WED Enterprises Design and development organization founded by Walt Disney in December 1952, to help him create Disneyland. Walt sold his interest in WED Enterprises in February 1965. Originally at the Disney Studio in Burbank, WED moved to facilities in Glendale in 1961. It later became known as Walt Disney Imagineering (1986).

Wedding Pavilion After starting to promote weddings at Walt Disney World with a Fairy Tale Weddings department in 1991, the park opened a special Wedding Pavilion on July 15, 1995, featuring a view of Cinderella Castle and seating for up to 250 guests. The Pavilion actually had its first wedding, and a preview, on *Weddings of a*

Lifetime on the Lifetime cable network on June 18, 1995, when David Cobb and Susanne Mackie were married there. The pavilion is located on an island near the Grand Floridian Resort & Spa, and adjacent to it is Franck's, a wedding salon where couples can make their wedding plans.

Wednesday Anything Can Happen Day on the 1950s *Mickey Mouse Club*. Surprise Day on the new *Mickey Mouse Club*.

Wednesday 9:30 (8:30 Central) (television) A half-hour series about IBS, a fledgling television network trying its best to be number one. Behind its walls are some of the craziest, quirkiest, and somewhat damaged personalities that have ever paraded through the executive halls of Hollywood. Premiered on ABC on March 27, 2002, and ended on June 12, 2002. Stars Ivan Sergei (David Weiss), Ed Begley, Jr. (Paul Weffler), Melinda McGraw (Lindsay Urich), Sherri Shepherd-Tarpley (Joanne Waters), James McCauley (Mike McClarren). Because the title was deemed too quirky, the show returned after a hiatus as *My Adventures in Television*. Working title was *The Web*.

WEDway PeopleMover Tomorrowland attraction in Magic Kingdom Park at Walt Disney World; opened on July 1, 1975. It became Tomorrowland Transit Authority in 1994. At Disneyland, known as the PeopleMover. A journey in the five-car trains, powered by environmentally correct linear induction motors, provides a visit inside a number of the Tomorrowland attractions.

Weekenders, The (television) Animated series debuting on February 26, 2000, as part of *One Saturday Morning*. Four friends, Tino, Carver, Lor, and Tish, spend each weekend discovering and creating new levels of fun, while negotiating the obligatory obstacles of adolescence. Voices include Jason Marsden (Tino Tonitini), Phil LaMarr (Carver Descartes), Kath Soucie (Tish Katsufrakis), Grey Delisle (Lor MacQuarrie), Lisa Kaplan (Tino's mom). 39 episodes.

Weems Family name in the Baby Weems segment of *The Reluctant Dragon*.

Weinger, Scott He voiced Aladdin and played Wilby in the television remake of *The Shaggy Dog*.

Weinkeller Shop selling wines, accessories, and cheeses in Germany in World Showcase at Epcot, presented by H. Schmitt Söhne GmbH; opened on October 1, 1982.

Weinrib, Lennie He voiced King Leonidas and the Secretary Bird in *Bedknobs and Broomsticks*.

Weiss, Al President of Walt Disney World in 1996. He had joined Walt Disney World in 1972 in the accounting department, and held various positions over the years in the finance and resort management areas, being elevated to executive vice president in 1994. He was promoted to president of worldwide operations for Walt Disney Theme Parks and Resorts in November 2005.

Welcome to Pooh Corner (television) Show on The Disney Channel, featuring life-size puppets of the favorite Pooh characters performing in storybook settings and discovering the values of friendship, honesty, and cooperation; debuted on April 18, 1983. The puppets are what is known as "advanced puppetronics"—live performers in costumes and masks whose facial expressions are controlled by sophisticated electronic circuitry.

Welcome to the "World" (television) Television show; aired on March 23, 1975. Directed by Marty Pasetta. Entertainers perform at Walt Disney World for the opening of Space Mountain. The attraction is dedicated by former astronauts L. Gordon Cooper, Scott Carpenter, and Jim Irwin, and featured is a band composed of 2,000 instrumentalists along with daytime fireworks. Stars Lucie Arnaz, Lyle Waggoner, Tommy Tune, Scotty Plummer.

Welker, Frank Actor; appeared in *The Computer Wore Tennis Shoes* (Henry), *Now You See Him, Now You Don't* (Myles), and provided voices in *My Science Project* (alien), *Oliver & Company*, *The Rescuers Down Under* (Joanna and others), *Beauty and the Beast, The Gun in*

Betty Lou's Handbag (Scarlet's vocals), *Aladdin* (Abu), *Homeward Bound: The Incredible Journey, Super Mario Bros., A Goofy Movie*, and *The Hunchback of Notre Dame*. On television he did voices for a number of characters in such shows as *Gargoyles, Ducktales, Bonkers*, and *Goof Troop*. He has become one of the most prolific Disney voice actors, heard in dozens of projects.

We'll Take Manhattan (television) Pilot (30 min.) for a television series. Seeking to make it big-time in New York, two very different women—a street-smart singer and a gullible country girl who wants to become an actress—become roommates. Aired on NBC on June 16, 1990. Directed by Andy Cadiff. Stars Jackée, Karin Bohrer, Edan Gross, Joel Brooks. 30 min.

Wells, Frank G. (1932–1994) Formerly at Warner Bros., he served as president of The Walt Disney Company from September 22, 1984, until his death in a helicopter accident on April 3, 1994. He is noted for his attempt to climb the highest peaks on each continent, failing only to conquer Mt. Everest. An extremely adept businessman who aided Michael Eisner in bringing Disney back to its former glory, he was named a Disney Legend posthumously in 1994. Frank Wells was also honored by having a new office building at the Disney Studio in Burbank named for him. The Frank G. Wells Building opened in 1997, with tenants including the Disney University, Walt Disney Archives, and Television Animation.

Wen, Ming-Na Actress; appeared in *The Joy Luck Club* (June) and provided the speaking voice of the title character in *Mulan*. She appeared on television in *Inconceivable* (Rachel Lew). She later shortened her name to Ming-Na.

Wendt, George Actor; starred in *Man of the House* (Chet), and in *The George Wendt Show* and *The Pooch and the Pauper* (Sparks) on television. He also appears in Cranium Command in Wonders of Life at Epcot.

Wendy Character visited by Peter Pan and brought back to Never Land to tell stories to the Lost Boys; voiced by Kathryn Beaumont.

Wentworth, Martha (1889–1974) She voiced Jenny Wren in *Who Killed Cock Robin?* and Madam Mim in *The Sword in the Stone*, among several other Disney voices.

Wesson, Dick (1919–1979) He served as the program announcer for the Disney television show from 1954 until his death. His easily recognized voice would introduce the show and Walt Disney at the beginning and give details on the next week's show at the conclusion.

Western Publishing Co., Inc. One of the earliest Disney licensees, producing Disney books (primarily under the Whitman and Golden Press imprints) beginning in 1933. Western sponsored the Story Book Shop at Disneyland and was one of the original investors in the park.

Western River Railroad Located in Adventureland at Tokyo Disneyland; opened on April 15, 1983.

Westernland Frontierland at Tokyo Disneyland. The concept of the frontier has no meaning to the Japanese, so the name of the land was changed.

Westernland Shootin' Gallery Located in Westerland at Tokyo Disneyland; opened on April 15, 1983.

Westward Ho the Wagons! (film) A wagon train composed of a number of emigrant families is making the crossing from the Missouri River to the rich farming country of the Pacific Northwest in 1844. Despite raids and misunderstandings with the Pawnee tribe, Captain Stephen's leadership of the train with the help of a veteran scout, and especially Dr. John Grayson's medical skills, see them through on their westward trek. Released December 20, 1956. Directed by William Beaudine. Filmed in CinemaScope on location at the Conejo Ranch at Thousand Oaks, California. 86 min. Includes the popular song "Wringle Wrangle," by Stan Jones. Stars Fess Parker (John Grayson), Kathleen Crowley (Laura Thompson), George Reeves (James Stephen), and features several cast members of the *Mickey Mouse Club*, including Tommy Cole (Jim Stephen), Karen Pendleton (Myra Thompson), David Stollery (Dan Thompson), Cubby O'Brien (Jerry Stephen), and Doreen Tracey (Bobo Stephen). The film was promoted on television by the show *Along the Oregon Trail*. Released on video in 1986.

Westward Ho Trading Co. Shop in Frontierland at Disneyland; opened on September 2, 1987. It was formerly the Frontier Trading Post.

Wet Paint (film) Donald Duck cartoon; released on August 9, 1946. Directed by Jack King. A bird, Susie, ruins Donald's new paint job on his car, damages his upholstery, and unravels his hat while gathering nest material. He is about to get her with an ax when he sees Susie's babies and gives up.

Wetback Hound, The (film) Featurette; released on June 19, 1957. Directed by Larry Lansburgh. Paco is a young hound owned by mountain lion hunters in Sonora, Mexico. When he is mistreated, he runs away, and even swims across a river to enter the United States in his search for a kindly master. He finds one, and in saving a little doe from a lion, ensures himself a home. 18 min. An expanded version was shown on television on April 24, 1959. Academy Award winner for Best Live Action Short Subject. Also won numerous other awards, including ones from the Southern California Motion Picture Council and the Berlin International Film Festival.

Whale of a Tale, A Song from *20,000 Leagues Under the Sea*; sung by Kirk Douglas, written by Al Hoffman and Norman Gimbel.

Whale Who Wanted to Sing at the Met, The (film) Segment of *Make Mine Music*, an "Opera Pathetique," sung by Nelson Eddy, about an opera-singing whale; also known as *Willie the Operatic Whale*.

Whalers, The (film) Mickey Mouse cartoon; released on August 19, 1938. The first cartoon directed by Dick Huemer. Mickey, Donald, and Goofy are on a tramp steamer when a whale is sighted. Mickey must come to the rescue when Goofy is swallowed by the whale and the boat is destroyed.

Whale's Tooth, The (television) A South Sea islander boy receives his first outrigger canoe and tries to save a sacred talisman that is stolen by enemy warriors. It was prepared for the American television show, but did not air; first aired in Canada on October 22, 1983. It was later shown on The Disney Channel. Directed by Roy Edward Disney.

What About Bob? (film) Saddled with a multitude of phobias, quirky Bob Wiley enlists the help of sane and sensible psychiatrist Dr. Leo Marvin. But Leo soon discovers that he does not want to be the new "best friend" of his obsessive/compulsive patient. Skipping town for a restful summer holiday with his family, Leo is dismayed when the panicked Bob tracks down the family's private vacation hideaway and insinuates himself into their lives. The family comes to adore the guest who won't leave, all except Leo who is driven frantic, to the point where one wonders who is really the crazy one. Released on May 17, 1991. Directed by Frank Oz. A Touchstone Picture. 99 min. Stars Bill Murray (Bob Wiley), Richard Dreyfuss (Dr. Leo Marvin), Julie Hagerty (Fay Marvin), Charlie Korsmo (Siggy Marvin). Filmed in New York, and at Smith Mountain Lake, Virginia, which doubled for the

New Hampshire resort depicted in the story. Released on video in 1991.

What About Brian (television) One-hour drama series planned for ABC in January 2006. At 34, Brian is the last single guy in his group of friends, a serial monogamist who still hopes that one day he will open a door and be blinded by love. But questions arise in his mind: Is there such a thing as Miss Right? Why does love have to be so complicated? What is his problem with commitment? And the most pressing question of all, could all his problems stem from the fact that he is harboring a crush on his best friend's girl? Stars Barry Watson (Brian), Matthew Davis (Adam), Polly Shannon (Marjorie), Rick Gomez (Dave), Amanda Detmer (Deena), Raoul Bova (Angelo), Rosanna Arquette (Nic). From Touchstone Television and Bad Robot.

What Can You See by Looking? (film) Educational film about critical thinking and observation skills through rhymes, anagrams, puzzles, and other brainteasers, in the EPCOT Educational Media Collection: Language Arts Through Imagination series; released in September 1988. 15 min.

What I Want to Be (television) Serial on the *Mickey Mouse Club*, beginning on October 3, 1955, and running for 10 episodes. It was filmed at the TWA headquarters in Kansas City and depicted the special training procedures for becoming an airline pilot and flight attendant.

What Is a Desert? (film) Segment from *The Living Desert*; released on 16mm for schools in November 1974. Explains the geographic features that cause a desert and shows how weather affects it.

What Is Disease? (film) Educational film produced under the auspices of the Coordinator of Inter-American Affairs and delivered on August 13, 1945. The film explains that disease is caused by microbes, and shows how to take the necessary precautions to keep one's body free from them.

What Is Disneyland? See *The Disneyland Story*.

What Is Fitness Exercise? (film) Educational film in the Fitness and Me series; released in March 1984. A good sorceress teaches a scrawny knight the value of physical fitness.

What Is Physical Fitness? (film) Educational film in the Fitness for Living series; released in September 1982. The film demonstrates cardiorespiratory endurance, muscle strength, muscle endurance, flexibility, and body composition, the five elements of physical fitness.

What Should I Do? (film) Series of five educational films released in 1969–70: *The Fight*, *The Game*, *The New Girl*, *Lunch Money*, *The Project*. The series was revised and updated in 1992 (see following entries).

What Should I Do? The Baseball Card (film) Educational release in August 1992. 8 min. When a boy steals a friend's valuable baseball card, he gets caught in a lie; the action freezes as he considers various decisions and consequences to his actions.

What Should I Do? The Fight (film) Educational release in August 1992. 8 min. Kids get into a fistfight after a water balloon is thrown. This film is different from the previous film entitled *The Fight* in the What Should I Do? series.

What Should I Do? The Game (film) Educational release in August 1992. 8 min. An overweight girl considers the strategies to become accepted by her peers. This film is different from the previous film entitled *The Game* in the What Should I Do? series.

What Should I Do? The Lunch Group (film) Educational release in August 1992. 8 min. Students make fun of a girl from El Salvador because she is different.

What Should I Do? The Mural (film) Educational release in August 1992. 8 min. Three friends painting a school mural shun a boy because they consider him a geek.

What Should I Do? The Play (film) Educational release in August 1992. 9 min. A wheelchair-bound girl is told she cannot help construct a set for the school play because of her disability.

What to Do at Home (film) Educational film in the Mickey's Safety Club series; released in September 1989. 16 min. The film gives home-safety information and tips to children home alone.

What's an Abra Without a Cadabra? (film) Educational film; a magical lesson about antonyms, homonyms, synonyms, and rhymes, in the Language Arts Through Imagination series; released in September 1989. 15 min.

What's Love Got to Do with It (film) The story of singer Tina Turner's tumultous life. She meets Ike Turner in a local nightclub. Ike is attracted to her and impressed with her powerful voice. With his help, the couple shoot straight to the top of the music world. Tina marries Ike and seems to have it all, but Ike becomes a brooding, brutal husband who threatens to destroy both their careers. With great courage, and the help of religious meditation, she leaves Ike and their career behind, and starts over again by herself. Slowly and steadily she succeeds, but not without interference from Ike, who believes her popularity is entirely due to him and that she will return to him. As Tina's personal successes mount, Ike realizes that she can indeed do it alone, reaching even greater heights of success and fulfillment. Initial release on June 9, 1993; general release on June 11, 1993. Directed by Brian Gibson. A Touchstone Picture. 118 min. Stars Angela Bassett (Tina Turner), Laurence Fishburne (Ike Turner). Based on Tina Turner's autobiography, *I, Tina*. Rather than construct a film set, the producers used Ike and Tina Turner's actual California home. Tina Turner recorded the songs for the film herself. Released on video in 1994.

What's Wrong With This Picture? (film) Educational release in 16mm in August 1991. 19

min. A teen has behavioral problems because of low self-esteem resulting from a difficult home life. He improves his self-image through group counseling.

Whelchel, Lisa Mouseketeer on the new *Mickey Mouse Club*. She later appeared on television in *Shadow of Fear* and starred on the non-Disney series *The Facts of Life*. She also appeared in *The Facts of Life Reunion* (Blair) on *The Wonderful World of Disney*.

When a Man Loves a Woman (film) Alice and Michael Green have a marriage filled with genuine passion, caring, and sharing, as they are raising two beautiful young daughters. However, beneath the surface of their loving family relationship simmers a painful personal secret Alice has been keeping, not only from her loved ones, but also from herself. She is an alcoholic, and when the family realizes this, they must embark on a courageous struggle to pick up the pieces of their lives and deal head-on with Alice's problem. Limited release in New York and Los Angeles on April 29, 1994; general release on May 13, 1994. Directed by Luis Mandoki. A Touchstone Picture. 126 min. Stars Andy Garcia (Michael Green), Meg Ryan (Alice Green), Lauren Tom (Amy), Ellen Burstyn (Emily). Filmed in Los Angeles and San Francisco, California. The hotel utilized for filming the vacation sequence was La Casa Que Canta Hotel in Zihuatanejo, Mexico. Released on video in 1994.

When Knighthood Was in Flower (television) Two-part television show; aired on January 4 and 11, 1956. The television airing of *The Sword and the Rose*.

When the Cat's Away (film) Mickey Mouse cartoon; released in 1929. Directed by Walt Disney. Mickey with Minnie and his band of mice raise havoc in a cat's house, including a tap dance on a piano keyboard.

When You Wish Upon a Star Song from *Pinocchio*, written by Ned Washington and Leigh Harline. It won the Academy Award for Best

Song, and has become almost a theme song for The Walt Disney Company. For years it opened the Disneyland television show, and is played as guests enter the castle at Disneyland.

Where Do the Stories Come From? (television) Television show; aired on April 4, 1956. Directed by Jack Hannah. Walt Disney explains how the hobbies of his staff provide ideas for cartoons. *Crazy Over Daisy* was born from a song written by composer Oliver Wallace. The True-Life Adventure films led to *R'Coon Dawg*, and wartime experiences of the staff led to a number of cartoons featuring Donald Duck. The scale-model train hobbies of animators Ward Kimball and Ollie Johnston, and of Walt Disney himself, led to *Out of Scale*. Footage is shown of Disney's backyard train, the Carolwood-Pacific Railroad.

Where Does Time Fly? (film) Educational film teaching past, present, and future vocabulary words in a time travel adventure, in the Language Arts Through Imagination series; released in September 1989. 17 min.

Where I Live (television) Television series; aired on ABC from March 5 to November 20, 1993. With the support of his family and friends, offbeat teenager Doug St. Martin learns the fundamental lessons about life as he enters adulthood in his Harlem neighborhood. Stars Doug E. Doug (Douglas St. Martin), Flex (Reggie Coltrane), Shaun Baker (Malcolm), Yanoka Doyle (Sharon St. Martin), Jason Bose Smith (Kwanzie), Sullivan Walker (James St. Martin).

Where the Heart Is (film) Demolition contractor Stewart McBain's three spoiled children have grown up in the lap of luxury and are none too anxious to leave their extravagant lifestyle. But McBain is determined to teach them a lesson in self-sufficiency, so he turns them out of the family home. Forced to live in a dilapidated Brooklyn tenement, the siblings struggle to survive. When McBain's business goes under, he must move in with his children, and together they learn lessons on where their real family values lie. Released on February 23, 1990. Directed by John Boorman. A Touchstone Picture. 107 min. Stars Dabney Coleman (Stewart McBain), Uma Thurman (Daphne), Joanna Cassidy (Jean), Crispin Glover (Lionel), Suzy Amis (Chloe), Christopher Plummer (the !#&@). Filmed primarily on location in Toronto. The film had only a limited theatrical release. Released on video in 1990.

Where the Heck Is Hector? (television) Television show; part 1 of *The Ballad of Hector the Stowaway Dog.*

Where the Red Fern Grows (film) Video release on December 21, 2004, by Walt Disney Home Entertainment of a film made by Crusader Entertainment, Elixir Films, and Bob Yari Productions. Based on the best-selling novel by Wilson Rawls, the story follows a young boy named Billy Coleman whose hard work and determination help him realize his dream of buying a pair of Redbone Coon Hounds. Billy and his hounds become an inseparable trio, as he trains them to become the best hunting dogs in the state. Directed by Lyman Dayton and Sam Pillsbury. Stars Dave Matthews (Will Coleman), Dabney Coleman (Grandpa), Joseph Ashton (Billy Coleman), Ned Beatty (Sheriff), Renee Faia (Jenny Coleman), Kris Kristofferson (older Billy Coleman). Originally shown at the Tribeca Film Festival on May 3, 2003.

While You Were Sleeping (film) Lucy Moderatz is a subway token booth worker at the Chicago Transit Authority who falls in love with a stranger from afar. When he (Peter Callaghan) is mugged on Christmas Day, Lucy saves his life and then finds herself mistaken as Peter's fiancée when he is hospitalized in a coma. Welcomed into the close-knit Callaghan family through the holidays, she brings new life to the household. But Lucy has misgivings about taking advantage of the misunderstanding, and begins to question her

infatuation as she learns more about the man in a coma and finds herself falling in love with Peter's brother, Jack. Released on April 21, 1995. A Hollywood Pictures film, in association with Caravan Pictures. Directed by Jon Turteltaub. 103 min. Stars Sandra Bullock (Lucy), Peter Gallagher (Peter Callaghan), Glynis Johns (Elsie), Micole Mercurio (Midge), Monica Keena (Mary), Jack Warden (Saul Tuttle), Bill Pullman (Jack). Released on video in 1995.

Whipping Boy, The (television) A Disney Channel Premiere Film; first aired on July 31, 1994. In the mid-18th century, a bratty prince seizes an urchin from the town to be his new whipping boy, but when the prince runs away from home with the whipping boy, they go through many adventures and learn to accept each other as friends. Stars Truan Munro (Jemmy), Nic Knight (Prince Horace), George C. Scott (Blind George), Kevin Conway (Hold Your Nose Billy), Vincent Schiavelli (Cutwater), Karen Salt (Annyrose), Mathilda May (gypsy). Adaptation of the Newbery Award–winning novel by Sid Fleischman. Directed by Syd MacArtney.

Whispering Canyon Cafe Restaurant serving food family style at the Wilderness Lodge at Walt Disney World. Skillets of food are placed on the table, and diners are welcome to all they can eat.

Whispers: an Elephant's Tale (film) A baby elephant, Whispers, separated from his mother, searches desperately for her, but finds instead the sassy and fiercely independent Groove, an outcast from her own herd and the last elephant in the world ever to be a substitute mom. Whispers takes hold of her tail and refuses to let go, and the two join to make an unlikely family as they brave the hidden dangers of the dark forest and make their way toward The Great River, a rumored paradise for elephants. Very limited release, opening in Denver on March 10, 2000, and in New York on October 13, 2000. Directed by Dereck Joubert. Voices include Angela Bassett (Groove), Debi Derryberry (Whispers), Anne Archer (Gentle Heart), Joanna Lumley (Half Tusk), Kat Cressida (Princess). 72 min. The film takes its plot entirely from real elephant behavior, with 80 percent being footage of elephants in the wild and 20 percent being footage of trained elephants. The filmmakers made an effort not to fake anything the elephants did, with the exception of giving them human voices. Filmed entirely in and around Chobe National Park in Botswana by Emmy Award–winning naturalist and cinematographer, Dereck Joubert, and his wife, Beverly, who have lived and worked together in the wild for over 20 years. Released on video in 2001.

Whistle While You Work Song from *Snow White and the Seven Dwarfs*; written by Larry Morey and Frank Churchill.

Whitaker, Billy He voiced Skippy in *Robin Hood*.

Whitaker, Forest Actor; appeared in *The Color of Money* (Amos), *Good Morning, Vietnam* (Edward Garlick), *Stakeout* (Jack Pismo), *Consenting Adults* (David Duttonville), and *Phenomenon* (Nate Pope).

Whitaker, Johnny Actor; appeared in *The Biscuit Eater* (Lonnie McNeil), *Napoleon and Samantha* (Napoleon), and *Snowball Express* (Richard Baxter), and on television in *The Mystery in Dracula's Castle*.

White, Betty Actress; appeared on television in *The Golden Girls* (for which she won the Emmy Award as Outstanding Lead Actress in a Comedy Series in 1986), *The Golden Palace*, *The Magical World of Disney*, and *Maybe This Time*. She also appeared in *Holy Man* (herself), *Bringing Down the House* (Mrs. Kline), and did the voice of Round in *Whispers: an Elephant's Tale*.

White, Jesse (1918–1997) Actor; appeared in *The Cat from Outer Space* (Earnest Ernie).

White, Richard Broadway actor; voiced Gaston in *Beauty and the Beast*.

White Fang (film) A young adventurer, Jack Conroy, in the harsh wilderness of Alaska, along with Klondike prospector Alex Larson, come upon a wolf-dog, White Fang, who has been raised by an Indian. White Fang, through deception, becomes the property of the devious Beauty Smith, who mistreats him. Jack rescues the animal and patiently begins to rebuild his spirit and trust. Jack learns the ways of the wilderness as he and White Fang risk their lives for each other. Released on January 18, 1991. Directed by Randal Kleiser. 109 min. Stars Klaus Maria Brandauer (Alex Larson), Ethan Hawke (Jack Conroy), Seymour Cassel (Skunker), James Remar (Beauty Smith), Susan Hogan (Belinda). Based on the novel by Jack London. Filmed on location in Alaska. Released on video in 1991. A sequel, *White Fang 2: The Myth of the White Wolf*, was released in 1994.

White Fang (film) Educational production; released on laser disc in March 1995. A companion to the laser disc of the Disney film, containing an interview with the screenwriter and segments on wolves, Jack London, and the native people of the Yukon.

White Fang 2: The Myth of the White Wolf (film) Young prospector Henry Casey, along with his magnificent half-wolf/half-dog named White Fang, is set to make his fortune during the Alaskan gold rush. After being separated from White Fang after a canoe accident, Henry is found and nursed back to health by a beautiful Native American girl named Lily and her uncle Moses. Moses tries to convince Henry that he carries the spirit of the White Wolf and should stay with the starving tribe because he may have the power to bring back the caribou. When White Fang reappears, the natives feel sure that Henry and the wolf have been sent to save them. It turns out that a crook running a mining operation is trying to starve the tribe off its land by blocking the caribou's migration path. It is up to Henry and White Fang to outwit the villain and save Lily and her people. Released on April 15, 1994. Directed by Ken Olin. 106 min. Stars Scott Bairstow (Henry Casey), Charmaine Craig (Lily Joseph), Alfred Molina (Rev. Leland Drury), Geoffrey Lewis (Heath). Filmed entirely on location in Aspen, Colorado, and in Vancouver, Squamish, Whistler, and Hope, British Columbia. The replica of the Haida Indian village was built on the banks of the Squamish River. Sequel to *White Fang*. Released on video in 1994.

White Man's Medicine (television) Television show; episode 5 of *Andy Burnett*. Also used as the title of part 2 of the television airing of *Westward Ho the Wagons*.

White Rabbit Flighty character chased by Alice in *Alice in Wonderland*; voiced by Bill Thompson.

White Squall (film) A recounting of a 1961 adventure-filled ordeal of a sea captain and a group of teenage boys who set off on a brigantine sailing school called *The Albatross* for an eight-month Caribbean voyage. When a freak storm sinks their ship, the survivors are forced to confront their tragic situation and discover their own inner strengths. The survivors are rescued by a tramp steamer and returned to Florida, but in the aftermath of their ill-fated voyage and the ensuing Coast Guard inquest, they come to some important realizations about themselves. A Hollywood Pictures film. Directed by Ridley Scott. Released on February 2, 1996. Stars Jeff Bridges (Sheldon), Caroline Goodall (Dr. Alice Sheldon), John Savage (McCrea), Scott Wolf (Chuck Gieg), Balthazar Getty (Tod Johnstone). 128 min. Filmed in CinemaScope. Released on video in 1996. Filming took place in the Caribbean, and utilized the islands of St. Vincent, St. Lucia, and Grenada. Additional filming was done in a water tank on Malta; near Cape Town, South Africa; and in the United States. The boat used as *The Albatross* was the *Eye of the Wind*, a 110-foot topsail schooner built in Germany.

White Wilderness film) True-Life Adventure feature; released on August 12, 1958. Directed by James Algar. Academy Award winner. 72 min. A dozen photographers, including Hugh A. Wilmar, Herb and Lois Crisler, and James R. Simon, cre-

ated this film after spending nearly three years in the Arctic, diligently filming animals in their natural habitat. The narrator's foreword describes the nature and origin of some of the largest and most savage beasts on the North American continent. The dramatic setting for the wildlife spectacle is Canada's subarctic and Alaska's arctic wilds. Successive scenes depict the various animals and birds in battle, play, and migration. Included among the larger of the predatory beasts are polar bears, gray wolves, and wolverines; among the migratory animals are the musk ox, caribou, and reindeer; and in the icy seas are the walrus, ring seal, and white beluga whales. The film was reissued in 1972. Released on video in 1985.

Whitman, Stuart Actor; appeared in *Run, Cougar, Run* (Hugh McRae), and on television in *High Flying Spy*.

Whitman Publishing Co. See Western Publishing Co., Inc.

Whitmore, James Actor; appeared on television in *Sky High* and *The Tenderfoot*, and in *A Ring of Endless Light* (Rev. Eaton) on Disney Channel.

Whiz Kid and the Carnival Caper, The (television) Two-part television show; aired on January 11 and 18, 1976. Directed by Tom Leetch. A young inventor, Alvin, and his friends run into bank robbers using a carnival as a front. Alvin volunteers his skills in rebuilding an aging sideshow robot. The kids learn of the plot to rob the bank, but cannot get anyone to listen to them, so they try to get more evidence, which gets them in more danger. Stars Jack Kruschen, John Colicos, Jaclyn Smith, Eric Shea, Clay O'Brien, Kim Richards, Dick Bakalyan, Ronnie Schell, Ted Gehring, John Lupton. A sequel to *The Whiz Kid and the Mystery at Riverton*.

Whiz Kid and the Mystery at Riverton, The (television) Two-part television show; aired on January 6 and 13, 1974. Directed by Tom Leetch. A young inventor, Alvin Fernald, learns that the city treasurer is a crook while gathering information for an essay on city government. Only in winning the essay contest and becoming mayor for the day does Alvin get access to city files to help prove his case against the treasurer. Stars Edward Andrews, John Fiedler, Eric Shea, Clay O'Brien, Kim Richards, Lonny Chapman, Ted Gehring, Larry J. Blake. Based on books by Clifford B. Hicks.

Who Framed Roger Rabbit (film) Roger Rabbit is a toon, an animated star at Maroon Cartoon Studio. After an opening cartoon, *Somethin's Cookin'*, we discover that Roger is suspected of the murder of Marvin Acme, who owned Toontown and the company that makes all cartoon props, and who had been flirting with Roger's wife, Jessica. Down-on-his-luck private detective Eddie Valiant is asked by Roger to find the real culprit. He reluctantly agrees and soon discovers that there is more to the mysterious Judge Doom than meets the eye. Chased by Doom's weasel henchmen, Eddie visits Toontown, with its many well-known toon inhabitants, before discovering the identity of the murderer. Premiered at Radio City Music Hall on June 21, 1988; general release on June 22, 1988. Directed by Robert Zemeckis. A Touchstone Picture in association with Steven Spielberg. 103 min. Stars Bob Hoskins (Eddie Valiant), Christopher Lloyd (Judge Doom), Joanna Cassidy (Dolores), Stubby Kaye (Marvin Acme). Charles Fleischer provided the voice of Roger Rabbit. Based on the novel *Who Censored Roger Rabbit?*, by Gary K. Wolf. Original work on the film began many years before it was produced. The expected high costs for the necessary special effects made Disney executives move cautiously, and it was only when Steven Spielberg and Robert Zemeckis became

interested in the project that the green light was given. They were excited by the prospect of creating a Toon community, with a variety of cartoon characters, culled from different studios, and presented together on screen for the first time. It was Spielberg who was able to help along the complicated negotiations necessary to bring the classic animated personalities together. Zemeckis welcomed the chance to create a new cartoon character, Roger Rabbit. He joked that the character was a combination of "a Disney body, a Warner's head, and a Tex Avery attitude." It was filmed in Los Angeles, and at Elstree Studios in London. Richard Williams headed the large staff of animators at a new studio set up in London, with some additional animation done in Burbank. The special visual effects were created by Industrial Light & Magic. The film won four Academy Awards, the most for a Disney film since *Mary Poppins*. They were for Film Editing (Arthur Schmidt), Sound Effects Editing (Charles L. Campbell, Louis L. Edemann), Visual Effects (Ken Ralston, Richard Williams, Edward Jones, George Gibbs), and an award for Special Achievement in Animation Direction to Richard Williams. Released on video in 1989.

Who Killed Cock Robin? (film) Silly Symphony cartoon; released on June 29, 1935. Directed by Dave Hand. Cock Robin was shot while singing to Jenny Wren (a clever caricature of Mae West), and the court is convened to try the suspects. But it is found that it was only Cupid's arrow that pierced Robin and he is revived by Jenny's kiss.

Who Owns the Sun? (film) Educational film about the son of a plantation slave learning about prejudice, freedom, and self-respect; released on August 14, 1990. 18 min.

Who the Heck Is Hector? (television) Television show; part 2 of *The Ballad of Hector the Stowaway Dog.*

Who Wants to Be a Millionaire (television) Game show on ABC, hosted by Regis Philbin, in which contestants answer multiple-choice questions on the way to a possible $1 million payoff. Aired nightly for two weeks, from August 16 to 29, 1999, and returned from November 7 to 21, then continued airing several nights a week. It ended as a regular prime-time series on June 27, 2002. Based on a hit British series, it became a nationwide phenomenon, pushing ABC to the top of the ratings in 1999–2000. A syndicated show, featuring Meredith Vieira as host, premiered on September 16, 2002. Park attractions based on the television series, entitled Who Wants to Be a Millionaire—Play It, opened at Disney-MGM Studios on April 7, 2001, and at Disney's California Adventure on September 14, 2001 (where it closed August 20, 2004).

Who, What, Why, Where, When and How Day Monday on the new *Mickey Mouse Club.*

Whole New World, A Song from *Aladdin*; written by Alan Menken and Tim Rice. Academy Award winner.

Whoop-'N-Holler Hollow Man-made ridge from which swimmers could ride the flumes at River Country at Walt Disney World.

Whoopee Party, The (film) Mickey Mouse cartoon; released on September 17, 1932. Directed by Wilfred Jackson. After a buffet supper, Mickey and the gang engage in a red-hot treatment of "Running Wild." The rhythm is so catchy that the furniture, household items, and even cops sent to quiet the noise get caught up in the revelry.

Who's Afraid of the Big Bad Wolf? Popular song hit from the 1933 cartoon *Three Little Pigs*, probably the most famous song to come out of a short cartoon. It was written by Disney composer Frank Churchill. Walt Disney re-created the writing of the song for *Cavalcade of Songs* on his television show two decades later.

Why Be Physically Fit? (film) Educational film from the Fun to Be Fit series; released in March 1983. Shows students how being fit can help them have more energy, look better, and cope with stress.

Why Exercise? (film) Educational film in the Fitness and Me series, released in March 1984. The adventures of two knights show students that exercise strengthens the heart, muscles, and other body systems, giving more energy for work and play.

Why We Fight (film) Frank Capra–made series during World War II, containing animated graphs, arrows, and other effects that were supplied by Disney.

Wickes, Mary (1916–1995) Actress; appeared in *Napoleon and Samantha* (clerk), *Snowball Express* (Miss Wigginton), *Sister Act* and *Sister Act 2: Back in the Habit* (Sister Mary Lazarus), and on television in the *Annette* serial on the *Mickey Mouse Club*. She voices Laverne in *The Hunchback of Notre Dame.*

Wide Open Spaces (film) Donald Duck cartoon; released on September 12, 1947. Directed by Jack King. Donald tries to get accommodations at a motel, and is told he can sleep on the porch for $16. When he complains, he is kicked out. He tries an air mattress, which flies through the air and onto the porch, where he again confronts the manager and ends up in a cactus bed.

Wide World of Sports, Disney's Opening in 1997, this complex accommodates professional-caliber training and competition, festival and tournament-type events, and vacation-fitness activities in more than 25 individual and team sports. It includes classrooms, office space, and media facilities, and serves as headquarters for sporting events taking place elsewhere throughout the Walt Disney World Resort. Facilities include a 7,000-seat baseball stadium, a 5,000-seat field house, Major League practice fields, Little League fields, tennis courts, volleyball courts, a track-and-field complex, and a golf driving range. In February 1996 the Atlanta Braves signed a 20-year agreement to use the complex as their spring training base, and the Harlem Globetrotters selected it as their headquarters. The complex had its grand opening on March 28, 1997, with an exhibition baseball game between the Atlanta Braves and the Cincinnati Reds.

Widow Tweed Kindly farm woman who adopts Tod, the fox, in *The Fox and the Hound*; voiced by Jeanette Nolan.

Widowmaker Pecos Bill's horse.

Wiest, Dianne Actress; appeared in *The Associate* (Sally) and *The Horse Whisperer* (Diane Booker).

Wilbur An albatross, Orville's brother, in *The Rescuers Down Under*; voiced by John Candy.

Wilck, Tommie Personal secretary to Walt Disney from 1958 to 1966. She remained at Disney until 1968, playing a major role in the development of the California Institute of the Arts.

Wilcox, Larry Actor; appeared on television in *Fire on Kelly Mountain; Twister, the Bull from the Sky*; and *Trail of Danger*.

Wild Burro of the West (television) Television show; aired on January 29, 1960. Directed by Walter Perkins. A stolen burro in Mexico escapes from her captors and tries to find her way home across the desert, having adventures with an old prospector and a herd of wild burros. Stars Bill Keys, Bill Pace, Jim Burch. Narrated by Winston Hibler.

Wild Cat Family, The—The Cougar (film) Educational film, made up from stock footage from various Disney nature films, released in May 1968. Shows the family life and hunting habits of the cougar, and tells how it fits into the world family of cats.

Wild Country, The (film) The Tanner family comes from the East to a broken-down homestead in Wyoming, and, in trying to make a go of it, face hardship and opposition from man and nature as they struggle for their water rights and survive cyclone and fire. In the process, they persevere and mature. And, after "bringing the law to Jackson's Hole," they face a happier future. Released on January 20, 1971. Directed by Robert Totten. 100 min. Stars Steve Forrest (Jim), Jack Elam (Thompson), Ron Howard (Virgil), Frank de Kova (Two Dog), Morgan Woodward (Ab), Vera Miles (Kate), Clint Howard (Andrew), Dub Taylor (Phil). This film marked the first time in a theatrical film that three members of the Howard family acted together—father, Rance, and sons, Ron and Clint. Based on the book *Little Britches* by Ralph Moody, the movie was filmed almost in its entirety in Jackson Hole, Wyoming, the original locale of the story. The diverse scenery provided all the needed locations for the seven-week exterior shooting schedule. Only one day of inclement weather sent the Disney company to a covered set erected in a barn. The spectacular twister that plagues the pioneer family was manufactured by seven wind machines from the Disney Studio in Burbank, assisted by three snowplanes from Jackson Hole. Together they stirred up dark clouds of dust that could be seen for thirty miles. For the drought sequence, 80 acres of green alfalfa had to be browned with a mixture of white paint, yellow vegetable dye, and chocolate dye, plus the necessary paint thinners. "And to get it we cleaned out all the paint stores in Jackson and Idaho Falls, and an entire paint factory in Salt Lake City," said production designer Robert Clatworthy. Released on video in 1986.

Wild Dog Family, The—The Coyote (film) Educational film, made up of stock footage from other Disney nature films; released in April 1968. This is the story of the intelligent wild dog of the West and how it has survived and adjusted to encroaching civilization.

Wild Geese Calling (television) Television show; aired on September 14, 1969. A boy, Dan Tolliver, discovers an injured Canadian gander shot by a hunter and nurses it back to health. He then sadly bids it good-bye as it flies south with the other geese for the winter. Stars Carl Draper, Persis Overton. Narrated by Steve Forrest.

Wild Heart (television) Television show; aired on March 10, 1968. Directed by Jack Couffer. Two Canadian children have adventures with an injured sea lion, a red-tailed hawk, and a seagull when they visit their aunt and uncle on Puget Sound. Stars Andrew Penn, Kitty Porteous, Stanley Bowles. Narrated by Leslie Nielsen. Released as an educational film with the title *Nature's Wild Heart*.

Wild Hearts Can't Be Broken (film) During the Depression, Sonora Webster, growing up in rural Georgia, longs for more excitement. With the stubborn confidence of a young woman determined to prove she can do anything she sets her mind to, Sonora answers a newspaper ad for a diving girl, one who leaps, astride a horse, from a 40-foot tower platform into a tank of water. Despite early rejection by the owner of the traveling stunt show, W.F. Carver, Sonora sets out to prove she has star quality. Despite setbacks, including sudden blindness, Sonora's spirit and determination make her a legendary attraction at Atlantic City's Steel Pier. Released on May 24, 1991. Directed by Steve Miner. 89 min. Stars Gabrielle Anwar (Sonora Webster), Cliff Robert-

son (Dr. W. F. Carver), Michael Schoeffling (Al Carver). Based on the life story of Sonora Webster Carver, whose autobiography, *A Girl and Five Brave Horses*, was published in 1961. Filmed at location sites in South Carolina. The Atlantic City set was built in Myrtle Beach. Released on video in 1992.

Wild Horse Revenge (television) Television show; episode 7A of *Texas John Slaughter*.

Wild Jack (television) Television miniseries; aired on January 15, July 9, and July 16, 1989. An Alaskan wilderness guide becomes the unwilling trustee of a publishing empire. Stars John Schneider (Jack McCall), Carol Huston (Constance Fielding). Directed by Harry Harris and James Quinn.

Wild Waves (film) Mickey Mouse cartoon; released on April 25, 1930. The first cartoon directed by Burt Gillett. Mickey and Minnie's fun day at the beach is spoiled when Minnie is swept out to sea and Mickey must save her.

Wilderness Lodge Mercantile Shop at the Wilderness Lodge Resort at Walt Disney World; opened in May 1994.

Wilderness Lodge Resort Hotel at Walt Disney World; opened in May 1994. Fashioned after the fine rustic National Park hotels in the West, such as the Old Faithful Inn in Yellowstone. There are two restaurants, a snack bar (plus another at the swimming pool), and outside the Firerock Geyser, which erupts high in the air on a regular hourly schedule. The majestic timbered lobby rivals that of the Grand Floridian Beach Resort for its grandeur.

Wilderness Road, The (television) Television show; episode 3 of *Daniel Boone*.

Wildhorse Saloon At Downtown Disney Pleasure Island, a 27,000-square-foot entertainment venue features live music and concert performances by rising country artists, while dancers teach new dance steps to guests. Opened May 31, 1998 and closed May 11, 2001.

Wildside (television) Limited hour-long television adventure series of six episodes; aired from March 21 to April 25, 1985, on ABC. A group of five men calling themselves the Wildside Chamber of Commerce work to rid the town of the criminal element in order to make it a better place to live. Stars Howard Rollins, William Smith, J. Eddie Peck, John DiAquino, Terry Funk, Sandy McPeak, Meg Ryan, Jason Hervey.

Wilhite, Tom He joined Disney in 1977 as director of television publicity and later of motion pictures as well, and then director of creative affairs. In 1980 he became vice president of creative development for motion pictures and television, and in 1982 he became vice president of production. He left the Studio in 1983.

Williams, Bill (1916–1992) Actor; appeared in *Scandalous John*, and on television in *Chester, Yesterday's Horse; Gallegher Goes West*; and *The Flight of the Grey Wolf.*

Williams, Cindy Actress; appeared on television in *The Leftovers* and *Help Wanted: Kids*, and on The Disney Channel in *Save the Dog* and *Just Like Family.*

Williams, Guy (1924–1989) Actor; starred on television as Zorro and in *The Prince and the Pauper.* He later played in *Lost in Space* on television and retired to Buenos Aires, Argentina.

Williams, Kimberly Actress; appeared in *Indian Summer* (Gwen Daugherty), *Father of the Bride* and *Father of the Bride Part II* (Annie Banks), and *The War at Home* (Karen Collier).

Williams, R.J. Child actor; the voice of Cavin in the *Gummi Bears* and Kit Cloudkicker in *Tale Spin.*

Williams, Rhoda She voiced the stepsister Drizella in *Cinderella.*

Williams, Robin Actor; appeared in *Good Morning, Vietnam* (Adrian Cronauer), *Dead Poets Society* (John Keating), *Jack* (Jack Powell), *Flubber* (Phillip Brainard), *Bicentennial Man* (Andrew Martin), and voiced the Genie in *Aladdin* and the direct-to-video *Aladdin and the King of Thieves.* Appeared in *Back to Neverland* for the Disney-MGM Studios Animation Tour, and provided the voice of The Timekeeper for the attraction of that name at Walt Disney World.

Williams, Roy (1907–1976) Adult Mouseketeer on the 1950s *Mickey Mouse Club*, known as the Big Mooseketeer because of his size. A Disney Studio cartoon story man, comic strip story man, and publicity representative beginning in 1930 and popular caricaturist at Disneyland. He designed the *Mickey Mouse Club* ears. He was named a Disney Legend posthumously in 1992.

Williams, Samuel L. (1933–1994) Lawyer; named to the Disney board of directors in 1983.

Willie and the Yank (television) Three-part television show, aired on January 8, 15, and 22, 1967. Directed by Michael O'Herlihy. The three episodes are *The Deserter, The Mosby Raiders*, and *The Matchmaker.* A lonely Confederate guard, Willie Prentiss, befriends his Union counterpart, Henry Jenkins, across the river and their friendship lasts through many incidents. Henry helps Willie escape after he accidentally wounds his commanding officer, Lieutenant Mosby, but he is arrested as a spy. When he escapes, he joins Mosby's band in trying to capture a Union general. Jenkins is captured, and falls for Willie's cousin, Oralee. Stars James MacArthur, Nick Adams, Kurt Russell, Jack Ging, Peggy Lipton, Jeanne Cooper. Released theatrically abroad as *Mosby's Marauders.*

Willie the Giant Character in *Mickey and the Beanstalk* segment of *Fun and Fancy Free*; voiced by Billy Gilbert. Also appeared in *Mickey's Christmas Carol*; voiced by Will Ryan.

Willie the Operatic Whale (film) Re-release title (on August 17, 1954) of *The Whale Who Wanted to Sing at the Met*. Released on 16mm for schools in 1959 and on video in 1991.

Willis, Bruce Actor; appeared in *Billy Bathgate* (Bo Weinberg), *Color of Night* (Capa), *Armageddon* (Harry Stamper), *Breakfast of Champions* (Dwayne Hoover), *The Sixth Sense* (Malcolm Crowe), *Disney's The Kid* (Russ), and *Unbreakable* (David Dunn).

Wilson, Gary He joined Disney in 1985 as chief financial officer and a member of the board of directors, and left in 1990, but he remained a member of the board. Oversaw the financial arrangements for Euro Disney.

Wilson, Owen Actor; appeared in *Armageddon* (Oscar Choi), *Breakfast of Champions* (Monte Rapid), *Shanghai Noon* and *Shanghai Knights* (Roy O'Bannon), *The Royal Tenenbaums* (Eli Cash), *Around the World in 80 Days* (Wilbur Wright), and *The Life Aquatic with Steve Zissou* (Ned Plimpton).

Win Ben Stein's Money (television) Game show on Comedy Central, beginning July 28, 1997, in which contestants are pitted against host Ben Stein to win $5,000 of his money in a test of knowledge.

Win, Lose or Draw (television) Television game show; aired in syndication from September 7, 1987 to August 31, 1990 (570 episodes), and on NBC from September 7, 1987 to September 1, 1989 (505 episodes). Bert Convy hosted the syndicated show, while Vicki Lawrence was the host on NBC. The game, based on charades, had contestants and celebrity players sketch clues rather than acting them out. The game was played by separate teams of men and women, with two celebrities and a contestant on each. The executive producers were Bert Convy and Burt Reynolds. The show spawned a Disney Channel spinoff called *Teen Win, Lose or Draw*.

Winchell, Paul (1922–2005) He voiced Tigger in the *Winnie the Pooh* films, Boomer in *The Fox and the Hound*, and the Chinese Cat in *The Aristocats*.

Wind in the Willows (film) Segment of *The Adventures of Ichabod and Mr. Toad*. U.S. theatrical release as *The Madcap Adventures of Mr. Toad*. Educational release as *The Adventures of J. Thaddeus Toad*. Released on video in 1982 and 1988.

Wind in the Willows (television) Airing February 2, 1955, this television show was devoted to the British writer, Kenneth Grahame, featuring the Disney versions of his *The Reluctant Dragon* and *Wind in the Willows*.

Windom, William Actor; appeared in *Now You See Him, Now You Don't* (Lufkin), and on television in *The Bluegrass Special*.

Window Cleaners (film) Donald Duck cartoon; released on September 20, 1940. Directed by Jack King. Donald is having enough trouble with his helper, Pluto, in washing the windows of a tall building when a bee, goaded by Donald, enters the scene and causes total disaster.

Windwagon Smith Eccentric lunk in *The Saga of Windwagon Smith* (1961).

Winebaum, Jake He started *Family PC* magazine in a joint venture deal with Disney in 1993. In 1995, he was named president of Disney Online, and in 1997 his duties were expanded as president of Buena Vista Internet Services. In 1999, as chairman of Buena Vista Internet Group, he left to form eCompanies, an Internet start-up and development company in which Disney and EarthLink are founding investors.

Winfrey, Oprah Actress; starred in *Beloved* (Sethe) after entering an exclusive overall deal with Walt Disney Studios in 1995.

Winged Scourge, The (film) Educational film; produced under the auspices of the Coordinator of Inter-American Affairs. Delivered on January 15, 1943. Directed by Bill Roberts. To protect themselves from the mosquito, a malaria-carrying parasite, the Seven Dwarfs show effective methods of mosquito control. The first and most elaborate of the health films produced for the CIAA.

Winkie Villain who acquires Toad Hall in *The Adventures of Ichabod and Mr. Toad*; voiced by Alec Harford. Also at times spelled Winkey and Winky.

Winkler, Margaret See Margaret Winkler Mintz.

Winkler, Paul (1898–1981) He began promoting Mickey Mouse in France in 1930, and in 1934 began *Le Journal de Mickey*. He was presented posthumously with a European Disney Legends Award in 1997.

Winnie the Pooh A.A. Milne character first animated by Disney artists in *Winnie the Pooh and the Honey Tree* (1966), and later appearing in three additional theatrical featurettes, along with educational films and television series. Pooh became one of the more popular Disney characters on merchandise, due to an early exclusive marketing agreement with Sears. Voiced by Sterling Holloway and later Hal Smith and Jim Cummings. Three of the featurettes were combined, with connecting animation, and released as a feature—*The Many Adventures of Winnie the Pooh*. See *The New Adventures of Winnie the Pooh* for the televi-

sion version and three features (*The Tigger Movie*, *Piglet's Big Movie*, and *Pooh's Heffalump Movie*).

Winnie the Pooh, a Valentine for You (television) Half-hour television special; aired on ABC on February 13, 1999. Pooh and his friends worry that because Christopher Robin is making a valentine for someone else, he is now lovesick and will no longer have time for them. They search for a Smitten, whose "love bug bite" will cure Christopher Robin of his new affection. But, eventually they realize that the heart has room for new friends and old. Voices include: Jim Cummings (Winnie the Pooh), Paul Winchell (Tigger), John Fiedler (Piglet), Peter Cullen (Eeyore), Brady Bluhm (Christopher Robin), David Warner (narrator).

Winnie the Pooh: A Very Merry Pooh Year (film) Video; released on November 12, 2002. All of Pooh's friends gather for fond recollections of a Christmas past, and then the New Year's countdown begins. Directed by Gary Katona and Ed Wexler. Voices include Jim Cummings (Winnie the Pooh/Tigger), Paul Winchell (Tigger, in the Christmas portion only), John Fiedler (Piglet), Peter Cullen (Eeyore), Michael Gough (Gopher), Ken Sansom (Rabbit), Nikita Hopkins (Roo), Michael Green (Christopher Robin), Michael York (narrator). 65 minutes.

Winnie the Pooh and a Day for Eeyore (film) Special cartoon featurette; released on March 11, 1983. Directed by Rick Reinert. Winnie the Pooh is teaching his friends how to play "Pooh Sticks" under a bridge when Eeyore floats by. It is his birthday and no one has remembered. That is soon remedied and the gang gathers with a party, presents, and a cake. Featuring the voices of Hal Smith (Pooh), Ralph Wright (Eeyore), John Fiedler (Piglet), Will Ryan (Rabbit), Kim Christianson (Christopher Robin), Dick Billingsley (Roo), Julie McWhirter Dees (Kanga), Paul Winchell (Tigger), this fourth installment of the Disney *Pooh* films was, like the others, based on the stories written by A.A. Milne, specifically "In Which Eeyore Has a Birthday and Gets Two

Presents" and "Pooh Invents a New Game and Eeyore Joins In." However, the film lacks some of the major voice talents used in the other featurettes, most notably Sebastian Cabot as narrator and Sterling Holloway as Pooh. 24 min. Released on video in 1984.

Winnie the Pooh and Christmas Too (television) Television special on ABC; first aired on December 14, 1991. Supervising director was Ken Kessell. When Winnie the Pooh and Piglet retrieve a letter to Santa, in hopes of adding some forgotten Christmas wishes, their plans go awry. Realizing now that the letter won't find its way to the North Pole on time, Pooh and Piglet decide to play Santa with some decidedly comic results. Voices are Jim Cummings (Winnie the Pooh), Peter Cullen (Eeyore), John Fiedler (Piglet), Michael Gough (Gopher), Ken Sansom (Rabbit), Paul Winchell (Tigger), Edan Gross (Christopher Robin).

Winnie the Pooh and Friends (television) Television show; aired on December 11, 1982. Directed by John Lounsbery. Pooh footage is combined with segments from other Disney cartoons.

Winnie the Pooh and the Blustery Day (film) Special cartoon featurette; released on December 20, 1968. Directed by Wolfgang Reitherman. A blustery day turns into a storm for Winnie the Pooh and his friends in the Hundred Acre Wood. They seek safety at Christopher Robin's, but Pooh and Piglet are washed away in a flood, and Owl's house is lost. But, before the day is over, Owl finds a new home, and Pooh and Piglet become heroes. Featuring the voices of Sterling Holloway (Pooh), Sebastian Cabot (narrator), Jon Walmsley (Christopher Robin), Ralph Wright (Eeyore), Howard Morris (Gopher), Barbara Luddy (Kanga), Hal Smith (Owl), John Fiedler (Piglet), Junius Matthews (Rabbit), Paul Winchell (Tigger), and Sterling Holloway (Pooh), the film proved a bigger success than its predecessor, *Winnie The Pooh and the Honey Tree*, by winning an Academy Award as Best Cartoon Short Subject. In its most imaginative sequence, Pooh has a nightmare inhabited by such fantastic creatures as Heffalumps and Woozles. The film was based on the stories of A.A. Milne. 25 min. Released on video in 1981. See also *Pooh's Heffalump Movie*.

Winnie the Pooh and the Honey Tree (film) Special cartoon featurette; released on February 4, 1966. Directed by Wolfgang Reitherman. The Studio's first animated treatment of the famous children books written by A.A. Milne. Winnie the Pooh and his friends, Christopher Robin, Eeyore the donkey, Owl, Kanga, and baby Roo, as well as Rabbit and Gopher, encounter a swarm of bees and a fabulous honey tree. Little modification was done on the original stories of the most famous teddy bear in the world. The most noticeable change was the introduction of a new character—Gopher. Sebastian Cabot narrated the story, and the theme song was written Richard M. Sherman and Robert B. Sherman.

Voices include Bruce Reitherman (Christopher Robin), Ralph Wright (Eeyore), Howard Morris (Gopher), Barbara Luddy (Kanga), Hal Smith (Owl), Junius Matthews (Rabbit), Clint Howard (Roo). Sterling Holloway was perfectly cast as voice of Pooh, and added to the popularity of the short, which inspired many sequels. 26 min. Released on video in 1981.

Winnie the Pooh and Tigger Too (film) Special cartoon featurette; released on December 20, 1974. Directed John Lounsbery. Inhabitants of the Hundred Acre Wood have a problem. Ebullient Tigger, has been getting on everyone's nerves, introducing himself about the Wood and then turning to mischief. Rabbit calls a protest meeting and it is decided to lose Tigger in the woods. But they in fact become lost, and it is up to Tigger to rescue them. When Tigger then bounces himself and little Roo onto a high tree limb, he must promise to never bounce again to be rescued. When he is, Rabbit holds him to his promise, and Tigger is heartbroken. Pressure from the others causes Rabbit to relent, admitting that he, too, liked the old bouncy Tigger better. 26 min. Featuring the voices of Sebastian Cabot (narrator), Sterling Holloway (Pooh), Junius Matthews (Rabbit), Paul Winchell (Tigger), John Fiedler (Piglet), Barbara Luddy (Kanga), Dori Whitaker (Roo), and Timothy Turner (Christopher Robin), this was the third installment in the Winnie the Pooh animated series, based on A.A. Milne's classic children's tales. Music and lyrics are by Richard M. Sherman and Robert B. Sherman. The film was nominated as Best Animated Short Film by the Academy of Motion Picture Arts and Sciences. Released on video in 1981.

Winnie the Pooh Discovers the Seasons (film) Educational film; released in September 1981. In discussing seasons, the film covers animal behavior, hibernation, temperature, and weather patterns. Voices include Ronald Feinberg (Eeyore), Hal Smith (Pooh, Tigger, and Owl), Kim Christenson (Christopher Robin), John Fiedler (Piglet), Ray Earlenborn (Rabbit).

Winnie the Pooh for President Days Event held at Disneyland in October 1972, and repeated in October 1976. Winnie the Pooh was touted as a presidential candidate to tie in with the national elections. The event had originally been part of On Stage U.S.A. in 1968.

Winnie the Pooh: Seasons of Giving (film) Direct-to-video movie; released on November 9, 1999. Pooh and friends set out on a quest for winter, leading to a wild search for the perfect ingredients for a festive Thanksgiving dinner, and finally to Christmas. 70 min.

Winnie the Pooh: Springtime with Roo (film) Direct-to-video movie; released on March 9, 2004. Every year Rabbit plays the Easter bunny, but not this year. Instead Rabbit expects

the gang to spring into action: scrubbing, dusting, sweeping, and mopping. But Roo's love and wisdom show Rabbit that special days are to be shared in special ways. Directed by Elliot M. Bour and Saul Andrew Blinkoff. Voices include Jim Cummings (Winnie the Pooh and Tigger), Ken Sansom (Rabbit), Jimmy Bennett (Roo), David Ogden Stiers (narrator), Kath Soucie (Kanga), John Fiedler (Piglet), Peter Cullen (Eeyore). 65 min.

Winnie the Pooh Thanksgiving, A (television) Thirty-minute animated special; aired on ABC on November 26, 1998. Pooh and the gang go on a wild search for the ingredients for a perfect Thanksgiving feast. When the search goes awry, Pooh and his pals frantically assemble a hysterically untraditional dinner, and ultimately realize that Thanksgiving isn't about the trimmings but about family, friends, and the blessings you already have. Directed by Jun Falkenstein. Voices include Jim Cummings (Winnie the Pooh), Paul Winchell (Tigger), John Fiedler (Piglet), Peter Cullen (Eeyore), Brady Bluhm (Christopher Robin), David Warner (narrator).

Winnie the Pooh's ABC of Me (film) Educational film; released on January 18, 1990. 12 min. Learn the alphabet by associating each letter with sounds or words.

Winningham, Mare Actress; appeared in *Turner & Hooch* (Emily Carson), and on television in *She Stood Alone*. She was in *Tru Confessions* (Ginny Walker) on Disney Channel.

Winston Chauffeur in *Oliver & Company*; voiced by William Glover.

Winter, Vincent (1947–1998) Actor; appeared in *Greyfriars Bobby* (Tammy), *Almost Angels* (Toni Fiala), and *The Three Lives of Thomasina* (Hughie Stirling), and on television in *The Horse Without a Head*.

Winter (film) Silly Symphony cartoon; released on October 30, 1930. Directed by Burt Gillett. Despite the cold wind and snow, woodland animals come out from their shelters to dance and skate until threatening clouds cause them to scamper back to their homes.

Winter Storage (film) Donald Duck cartoon; released on June 3, 1949. Directed by Jack Hannah. When Chip and Dale can find no more acorns, they go after the supply Donald is using to reseed the area. Though he manages to trap them, they escape and take revenge on Donald.

Winters, Jonathan Actor; appeared on television in *Halloween Hall of Fame*.

Winters, Shelley (1920–2006) Actress; appeared in *Pete's Dragon* (Lena Gogan).

Winwood, Estelle (1883–1984) Actress; appeared in *Darby O'Gill and the Little People* (Sheelah).

Wise Little Hen, The (film) Silly Symphony cartoon; released on June 9, 1934. Directed by Wilfred Jackson. Donald Duck made his debut in this fable about a mother hen who needs help planting corn and harvesting it. When Donald and his friend, Peter Pig, sole members of the Idle Hour Club, refuse, she does it herself with the help of her chicks. When all is finished, and various types of corn delicacies are on the table, Donald and Peter, now interested, are not invited.

Wise One, The (television) A Native American chief and his grandson pursue a rare black beaver through the Rocky Mountain wilderness. It was prepared for the American television show, but did not air. First aired in Canada on December 31, 1983. Later shown on The Disney Channel. Directed by Frank Zuniga.

Wish Upon a Star (television) Series on The Disney Channel; debuted on April 19, 1983. Joyce Little and Sharon Brown give kids a chance to act out their fantasies. 26 episodes.

Wishes: A Magical Gathering of Disney Dreams Fireworks spectacular in Magic Kingdom Park at Walt Disney World, taking the place of the long-running Fantasy in the Sky in October 2003. A similar Wishes fireworks show premiered on July 16, 2005, at Disneyland Resort Paris.

Witch Character in *Snow White and the Seven Dwarfs*; voiced by Lucille LaVerne.

W.I.T.C.H. (television) In Candracar, a team of 13- and 14-year-old girls, W.I.T.C.H. (acronym of their names—Will, Irma, Taranee, Cornelia, Hay Lin), has magical powers. The girls, a new generation of an ancient and venerable group, the Guardians of the Veil, stress the positive values of courage, loyalty, togetherness, tolerance, and team spirit as they are charged with protecting their world from the evil warlord, Prince Phobos, in a parallel universe. When the girls are at home and school, they face very contemporary and universal teen issues. Created by Disney Publishing Worldwide, launched in Italy in 2001, and appearing first in international magazines, W.I.T.C.H. debuted in the United States in a series of nine paperback books in April 2004, and in an animated television series airing as part of Jetix on ABC Family beginning January 15, 2005 (after a preview on ABC on December 18, 2004).

Witch Hazel Witch star of *Trick or Treat* (1952); voiced by June Foray.

Witches of Morva, The Orddu, Orgoch, and Orwen have hidden the cauldron in *The Black Cauldron*.

Witherspoon, Reese Actress; appeared in *A Far Off Place* (Nonnie Parker) and *Sweet Home Alabama* (Melanie).

Without You (film) Segment of *Make Mine Music*, subtitled "A Ballad in Blue." Written by Osvaldo Farres, with English lyrics by Ray Gilbert; sung by Andy Russell.

Witt, Alicia Actress; appeared in *Mr. Holland's Opus* (Gertrude Lang) and *Playing Mona Lisa* (Claire Goldstein).

Wolcott, Charles (1906–1987) Composer; came to Disney in 1938 as an arranger; accompanied Walt and a group of artists to South America in 1941 in order to study the music of the Latin American countries. He wrote songs for or arranged film scores for *The Reluctant Dragon*, *Bambi*, *Saludos Amigos*, *The Three Caballeros*, *Song of the South*, and *Fun and Fancy Free*. He left Disney in 1949.

Woman Wanted (film) Direct-to-video release by Touchstone Home Video on January 25, 2000, of a Phoenician Entertainment/Annex Entertainment production. In a house divided by rivalry and burning resentment, a wealthy widower and his son maintain a lonely, uneasy existence. Then, as tensions rise, the mysterious Emma enters their lives and immediately creates a complex romantic triangle. Directed by Kiefer Sutherland. Stars Holly Hunter (Emma), Kiefer Sutherland (Wendell Goddard), Michael Moriarty (Richard Goddard). 110 min.

Woman's Courage, A (television) Television show; episode 7 of *The Swamp Fox*.

Wonder Dog (film) Pluto cartoon; released on April 7, 1950. Directed by Charles Nichols. Pluto tries to become Dinah's dream of Wonder Dog, despite Butch's interference, and he does indeed prove himself by performing various circus stunts, to his own wonderment as well as Dinah's.

Wonderful Ice Cream Suit, The (film) Direct-to-video release by Touchstone Home Video on March 16, 1999, of a film based on a Ray Bradbury story, directed by Stuart Gordon and produced by Gordon and Roy E. Disney. The lives of five Latino men are changed when they, all being approximately the same size and weight, jointly purchase a gorgeous white suit in a local clothing store and wear it in the barrio. Stars Joe Mantegna (Gomez), Esai Morales (Dominguez), Edward James Olmos (Vamenos), Clifton Gonzalez Gonzalez (Martinez), Gregory Sierra (Villanazul), Sid Caesar (Leo Zellman). 77 min.

Wonderful Thing About Tiggers, The Song from *Winnie the Pooh and the Blustery Day*, written by Richard M. Sherman and Robert B. Sherman.

Wonderful World of Color See Walt Disney's Wonderful World of Color.

Wonderful World of Disney, The (television) Television series on NBC; aired from September 14, 1969 to September 2, 1979. Also the title of a syndication package of television shows, and a Disney Channel series. *The Wonderful World of Disney* returned to the air on ABC on September 28, 1997.

Wonderful World of Disney: 40 Years of Television Magic (television) Two-hour television special; aired on ABC on December 10, 1994. Directed by Frank Martin. Kirstie Alley is the host, with celebrity interviews and reminiscences by such people as Debbie Allen, Bobby Burgess, Margaret Cho, Roy Disney,

George Foreman, Hugh Hefner, Ward Kimball, James MacArthur, Hayley Mills, Fess Parker, Jim Varney.

Wonderful World of Disney: 25th Anniversary See *NBC Salutes the 25th Anniversary of the Wonderful World of Disney.*

Wonderland (television) One-hour television drama; debuted on ABC on March 30, 2000. Delves into the lives of the doctors manning Rivervue Hospital's psychiatric and emergency programs. The series ended on April 6 after two episodes had aired. Stars Ted Levine (Dr. Robert Banger), Martin Donovan (Dr. Neil Harrison), Michelle Forbes (Dr. Lyla Garrity), Billy Burke (Dr. Abe Matthews), Michael Jai White (Dr. Derrick Hatcher), Joelle Carter (Dr. Heather Miles).

Wonders of China (film) Circle-Vision 360 film tour of China for the China pavilion at World Showcase, Epcot; opened on October 1, 1982. It also alternated with *American Journeys* in the Circle-Vision theater in Tomorrowland at Disneyland from 1984 to 1996. It ended its run at Epcot on March 26, 2003, to be replaced by *Reflections of China.*

Wonders of Life Pavilion in Future World at Epcot, sponsored by Metropolitan Life Insurance Co. from 1989 to 2000; opened on October 19, 1989. This major pavilion in Future World provides a fun look at health and fitness. Guests can try out various fitness machines and computers, or go to the Cranium Command or Body Wars attractions. *Goofy Over Health* and *The Making of Me* are film shows. The pavilion closed in January 2004 to begin seasonal operation.

Wonders of Life (film) Series of three educational films released in January 1990: *The Bones and Muscles Get Rhythm*, *The Brain and the Nervous System Think Science*, *The Heart and Lungs Play Ball.*

Wonders of the Water World (television) Television show; aired on May 21, 1961. Directed and narrated by Winston Hibler. A look at water and its importance to people, as well as fish. From a storm cloud, rain falls and forms streams, which become rivers, eventually reaching the sea.

Wonders of Walt Disney World Series of classes on ecology, creative arts, energy, and entertainment offered for children whose parents have taken them out of school for a trip to Walt Disney World. The classes have been prepared by the Walt Disney World staff in cooperation with educators and have been so highly regarded that many school districts provide excused absences and credit for participation in the classes.

Wong, B.D. Actor; appeared in *Father of the Bride* and *Father of the Bride Part II* (Howard Weinstein) and provided the speaking voice of Shang in *Mulan*. On television, he appeared as Bradd Wong in *Double Switch* (waiter) and in *All-American Girl* (Stuart).

Wong, Curtis Mouseketeer on the new *Mickey Mouse Club.*

Wong, Tyrus Inspirational artist with Disney from 1938 to 1941, with his concepts primarily responsible for the look of *Bambi*. He was named a Disney Legend in 2001.

Wood, C.V., Jr. (1921–1992) Walt Disney hired Wood from the Stanford Research Institute in 1954 to be vice president and general manager of Disneyland, Inc., a post he held for 22 months. During this period, Wood supervised the site selection and land purchase, and the first year of operation of the park. He left in 1956 to become a consultant to the leisure industry.

Wood, Elijah Child actor; appeared in *Paradise* (Willard Young) and *The Adventures of Huck Finn* (Huck Finn), and on television in *Day-o* and *Oliver Twist* (Artful Dodger).

Woodard, Alfre Actress; appeared in *The Gun in Betty Lou's Handbag* (Ann) and *Mumford* (Lily), and on television in *A Mother's Courage*. She provided the voice of Plio in *Dinosaur*, and narrated and did the voice of Polly in *John Henry*. She joined the cast of *Desperate Housewives* at the end of the first season as Betty Applewhite.

Woodland Cafe (film) Silly Symphony cartoon; released on March 13, 1937. Directed by Wilfred Jackson. At a popular bug nightclub, various caterpillars, fireflies, spiders, and other insects dance the evening away. Some even look like famous Hollywood celebrities, including Lionel Barrymore.

Woods, Ilene Walt Disney selected Ilene to be the voice of Cinderella. In later years, she appeared at various special events commemorating that film. She was named a Disney Legend in 2003.

Woods, James Actor; appeared in *Straight Talk* (Jack) and *Nixon* (H.R. Haldeman), and provided the voice of Hades in *Hercules* and Dr. Benedict in *Recess: School's Out*.

Woodward, Morgan Actor; appeared in *The Great Locomotive Chase* (Alex), *Westward Ho the Wagons!* (Obie Foster), *The Wild Country* (Ab Cross), and *One Little Indian* (Sgt. Raines).

Woolverton, Linda Writer; wrote the screenplay for *Homeward Bound: The Incredible Journey* and *Beauty and the Beast*, co-wrote the screenplay for *The Lion King*, and did pre-production story work on *Aladdin*. She also adapted her *Beauty and the Beast* screenplay for the stage.

Woops! (television) Television series; aired on Fox from September 27 to December 6, 1992. Humankind gets a chance to start over in this comedy about the unlikely survivors of an accidental nuclear war who set about the task of re-creating society. Stars Fred Applegate (Jack Connors), Lane Davies (Curtis Thorpe), Cleavant Derricks (Dr. Frederick Ross), Meagen Fay (Alice McConnell), Evan Handler (Mark Braddock).

Worden, Marc Actor; appeared on the *Mickey Mouse Club* on The Disney Channel, beginning in 1990.

Working for Peanuts (film) Donald Duck cartoon; released on November 11, 1953. Directed by Jack Hannah. Filmed in 3-D. Chip and Dale steal peanuts from an elephant, Dolores, until zookeeper Donald comes to the rescue. Chip and Dale win eventually, getting all the peanuts they can eat by using white paint to pass themselves off as rare albino chipmunks. Shown at Disneyland as part of *3D Jamboree*, and later in Magic Kingdom Park at Walt Disney World with *Magic Journeys*.

World According to Goofy Parade Event at Disneyland from June 19 to November 15, 1992. Mounted in honor of Goofy's 60th birthday.

World Bazaar Covered Main Street area of Tokyo Disneyland.

World Beneath Us, The (film) Film show sponsored by Richfield Oil in Tomorrowland at Disneyland for several years beginning in 1955. It described the search for oil, by use of Disney animation.

World Is Born, A (film) The Stravinsky segment *Rite of Spring*, taken from *Fantasia* and released in July 1955, on 16mm for schools.

World Junior Tennis Tournament (television) Two-hour syndicated television special commemorating the national and international Sport Goofy Junior Tennis Championships; aired in September 1983. Directed by Andrew Young.

World News Center Television monitors providing top news stories, formerly pre-show for Electronic Forum in Communicore East at Epcot; opened on March 17, 1991.

World of Disney The largest, at 50,000 square feet, Disney merchandise location in the world opened on October 3, 1996, in the Downtown Disney Marketplace at Walt Disney World. A store also opened in Downtown Disney at the Disneyland Resort in 2001, and in 2004, with the sale of the Disney Stores, the flagship store on Fifth Avenue in New York became a World of Disney. At the New York store, little girls can participate in a role-playing romp entitled Cinderella's Princess Court.

World of Motion Pavilion in Future World at Epcot, sponsored by General Motors; opened on October 1, 1982. The attraction offered a ride through the history of automobiles. The Transcenter at the conclusion of the ride featured the latest technology for cars of the future. The original attraction closed on January 2, 1996, superseded by Test Track.

World on Ice The first edition of Walt Disney's World on Ice premiered in an arena in East Rutherford, New Jersey, on July 14, 1981. The show was produced by Ringling Bros. and Barnum & Bailey Combined Shows, Inc. (Irvin and Kenneth Feld), and combined the Disney characters and stories and the best in musical theater with championship skating, touring 20 major markets in the United States. Spotlighted in the first show was skater Linda Fratianne. Each year since 1981, a new touring live ice show has been mounted, usually tied to a specific Disney theme or movie, such as *Peter Pan*, *Beauty and the Beast*, *Aladdin*, Mickey Mouse's Diamond Jubilee, and *Snow White and the Seven Dwarfs*. Walt Disney's World on Ice became international in 1986, performing first in Japan. In 1994, there were seven productions touring on six continents simultaneously, including dual companies of both *Beauty and the Beast* and *Aladdin* because of their unprecedented popularity. Annual attendance numbers upward of ten million people worldwide. Through 1985, the shows were also called Walt Disney's Magic Kingdom on Ice and Walt Disney's Great Ice Odyssey. In 1996 the show title became Disney on Ice. (In the early 1950s, the Ice Capades had mounted Disney-themed segments in their shows, and it was in fact from the Ice Capades that Walt Disney had borrowed Disney character costumes to use for the opening of Disneyland.)

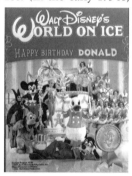

World Owes Me a Living, The Popular song hit from *Grasshopper and the Ants* (1934) that became Goofy's theme song, composed by Larry Morey and Leigh Harline.

World Premiere Circle-Vision Tomorrowland attraction at Disneyland; sponsored by PSA from its opening on July 4, 1984, until July 17, 1989, when Delta took over. Showed the *American Journeys* 360° film, alternated later with *Wonders of China* until July 1996, when *America the Beautiful* was brought back. The attraction closed on September 7, 1997. Originally *Circarama*, and *America the Beautiful*. The words "World Premiere" were later dropped from the name. Delta ended its sponsorship on January 1, 1996.

World Showcase Located at Epcot at Walt Disney World, the major area surrounding a lagoon where 11 countries celebrate their cultures, wares, and cuisines. The countries of World Showcase are Canada, United Kingdom, France, Morocco, Japan, United States (The American Adventure), Italy, Germany, China, Norway, and Mexico. The World Showcase Promenade, 1.3 miles in length, links the countries. There is an entrance into Epcot from the Epcot Resorts between France and England through the International Gateway.

World War I Toward the end of the war, the young Walt Disney, wanting to do his part for his country, tried to enlist in the military, but he was too young. Instead, he managed to join a Red Cross unit, and was sent to France just as the war concluded. For nine months, he drove an ambulance, chauffered dignitaries, and did other cleanup chores as the troops were getting ready to come home.

World War II The day after Pearl Harbor, the military moved onto the Disney Studio lot in Burbank, utilizing the soundstage and parking sheds for automotive maintenance and ammunition storage facilities. But they also turned to Disney for the production of training and propaganda films, and for the duration of the war, 93 percent of the company's output was war-related. The films did not feature the normal Disney characters, but rather used graphics, maps, diagrams, and simple animation to get across their points. To help entertain those on the home front, the Disney characters went to war too, with such cartoons as *Donald Gets Drafted*, *The Old Army Game*, and *Private Pluto*. Films were also produced for other agencies, such as *The New Spirit* for the Treasury Department, and as his contribution to the war effort, Walt had his artists design 1,200 insignias for military units at no charge to the units. Many ships, planes, and the jackets of soldiers featured decals and patches with illustrations of Donald Duck, Pluto, and other characters.

World's Greatest Athlete, The (film) Discovered in Africa by two U.S. college sports coaches, Nanu, a blond boy raised by natives after the death of his missionary parents, is an incredible athlete. Entered in a Los Angeles NCAA track-and-field competition, he wins all the events despite voodoo magic being used against him. Released on February 1, 1973. Directed by Robert Scheerer. 92 min. Stars Tim Conway (Milo), Jan-Michael Vincent (Nanu), John Amos (Coach Archer), Roscoe Lee Browne (Gazenga), Dayle Haddon (Jane), Billy De Wolfe (Maxwell), Nancy Walker (Mrs. Peterson), Danny Goldman (Leopold Maxwell). Bill Toomey, a world and Olympic decathlon champion, acted as a technical adviser to the film crew. The film also included sportscaster favorites Howard Cosell, Bud Palmer, Frank Gifford, and Jim McKay. For one scene in which a 3-inch-tall Tim Conway, under a spell by Nanu's witch-doctor godfather, falls into a lady's handbag, Disney propmakers fashioned a number of giant props—lipstick, compact, hairpins, needle and thread, safety pins, reading glasses, comb and brush, pills, keys, and matches. Ordinary items, but these particular ones were 24 times normal size, weighed 1 ton, and cost over $15,000. In other scenes, Conway encountered many other giant props: a huge telephone cost the studio $7,900. A cocktail glass was 7 feet tall and held a 1,245-gallon old-fashioned displaced by ice cubes 2 feet square. As the Disney press release quipped: "At 40 shots to a quart, consider the possibilities!" The movie was filmed at Caswell Memorial State Park, near Stockton, California, and at Lion Country Safari south of Disneyland, which doubled for Zambia. Scenes were also shot in Merrivale and Newhall, California. Released on video in 1986.

Worley, Jo Anne Actress; appeared in *The Shaggy D.A.* (Katrinka Muggleberg), on television in *The Mouseketeers at Walt Disney World*, and provided the voice of the wardrobe in *Beauty and the Beast* and Hoppopotamus on *The Wuzzles*. She was a guest hostess on *The Mouse Factory*.

Worm Turns, The (film) Mickey Mouse cartoon; released on January 2, 1937. Directed by Ben Sharpsteen. Mickey mixes together a magic potion that gives both strength and courage. The potion allows a series of "underdogs"—a fly, a mouse, and a cat—to get their revenge on their enemies, and finally it enables Pluto to get the best of dogcatcher Pete.

Would You Eat a Blue Potato? (film) Educational film about color and its effect on everything we see, in the EPCOT Educational Media Collection: Language Arts Through Imagination series; released in September 1988. 15 min.

Wrather Corporation Company headed by Jack Wrather that built and ran the Disneyland Hotel; acquired by the Disney company in 1988.

Wright, Ben (1915–1989) Actor; voiced Roger Radcliff in *One Hundred and One Dalmatians*, a wolf in *The Jungle Book*, and Grimsby in *The Little Mermaid*. He also acted on television in *Way Down Cellar*.

Wright, Ralph Actor; voiced Eeyore in the *Winnie the Pooh* films.

Wright, Samuel E. Actor; voiced Sebastian in *The Little Mermaid*, Kron in *Dinosaur*, and starred as Mufasa in *The Lion King* on Broadway, for which he garnered a Tony nomination.

Wrinkle in Time, A (television) Three-hour *Wonderful World of Disney* presentation; aired on May 10, 2004. When astrophysicist Dr. Jack Murry disappears without a trace, his children, Meg and Charles Wallace, and neighbor Calvin, take it upon themselves to find him. Guided by Mrs. Whatsit, Mrs. Who, and Mrs. Which, the children embark on a cosmic quest before finally reaching the dark planet Camazotz, where they encounter a society of human beings controlled by an evil force. They must use collective and personal strengths to find Dr. Murry and save their own lives. Directed by John Kent Harrison. Stars Alfre Woodard (Mrs. Whatsit), Kate Nelligan (Mrs. Which), Alison Elliott (Mrs. Who), Kyle Secor (the Prime Coordinator), Chris Potter (Jack Murry), Sarah-Jane Redmond (Dana Murry), David Dorfman (Charles Wallace), Katie Stuart (Meg), Gregory Smith (Calvin O'Keefe). Based on the Newbery Award–winning book by Madeleine L'Engle. Produced by BLT Productions and Fireworks International, and distributed by Miramax Television in association with Dimension. Originally aired in Canada on April 25, 2003.

Writing Magic: With Figment and Alice in Wonderland (film) Educational film, in the EPCOT Educational Media Collection; released in August 1989. 16 min. Brainstorming, writing, and rewriting are the keys to solving Alice's dilemma.

Writing Process, The: A Conversation with Mavis Jukes (film) Educational film; released on July 3, 1989. 20 min. The award-winning author shares her perspectives on creative writing.

Wrong Way Moochie (television) Television show; part 2 of *Moochie of the Little League*.

Wrubel, Allie (1905–1973) Songwriter; won an Academy Award for "Zip-A-Dee-Doo-Dah," and wrote songs also for *Make Mine Music* and *Melody Time*.

Wurlitzer Music Hall Shop on Main Street at Disneyland from July 1955 to September 1968. A fondly remembered shop where you could hear pianos, player pianos, and organs demonstrated, or buy rolls for your own player piano.

Wuzzles, The Odd group of characters, each two animals in one, living on the Isle of Wuz, created for a 1985 television series. Names included Bumblelion, Eleroo, Hoppopotamus, Moosel, Rhinokey, and Butterbear. Voices include Brian

Cummings (Bumblelion), Jo Anne Worley (Hoppopotamus), Henry Gibson (Eleroo), Bill Scott (Moosel), Allen Oppenheimer (Rhinokey).

Wuzzles: Birds of a Feather, The (film) Foreign theatrical release of the television cartoon, first in England on March 21, 1986. Everything's fine with the fanciful Wuzzles in the Land of Wuz until Eleroo accidentally causes a Brahma Bullfinch to hatch prematurely. The villainous Croc tries to steal the baby for its valuable feathers, but the Wuzzles outwit him and the baby is reunited with its mama.

Wyatt, Jane Actress; appeared in *Treasure of Matecumbe* (Aunt Effie).

Wyman, Jane Actress; appeared in *Pollyanna* (Aunt Polly) and *Bon Voyage* (Katie Willard).

Wyndham Palace Resort and Spa Hotel at Downtown Disney at Walt Disney World on November 1, 1998; formerly (1983–1998) known as the Buena Vista Palace.

Wynken, Blynken and Nod (film) Silly Symphony cartoon; released on May 27, 1938. Directed by Graham Heid. In this fanciful dream

fantasy, three babies float among the clouds in the night sky in a wooden ship, fishing for stars and even a comet, which speeds them on. When a storm breaks, they slide down to earth

on moonbeams and into the cradle of one sleepyhead.

Wynn, Ed (1886–1966) Actor; a Disney favorite who appeared in *The Absent-Minded Professor* (fire chief), *Babes in Toyland* (toymaker), *Son of Flubber* (A. J. Allen), *Mary Poppins* (Uncle Albert), *Those Calloways* (Ed Parker), *That Darn Cat!* (Mr. Hofstedder), *The Gnome-Mobile* (Rufus), and provided the voice of the Mad Hatter in *Alice in Wonderland*. He appeared on television in *Backstage Party*, *The Golden Horseshoe Revue*, and *For the Love of Willadean*.

Wynn, Keenan (1916–1986) Actor; appeared in *The Absent-Minded Professor*, *Son of Flubber*, and *Herbie Rides Again* (Alonzo Hawk), *Smith* (Vince Heber), *Snowball Express* (Martin Ridgeway), and *The Shaggy D.A.* (John Slade). He narrated the educational film *VD Attack Plan*.

X

Xerox process Electrostatic process adapted for transferring animators' pencil drawings to cels. It was tested in *Sleeping Beauty*, and used in *Goliath II* and *One Hundred and One Dalmatians*. The process was then used in practically every Disney animated film up through *The Little Mermaid*, after which the computer obviated the need for cels.

X-Team (television) Two-hour movie; aired on ABC on January 9, 2003. The X-team is an elite rescue and extraction team made up of world-class athletes whose ability to navigate impossible terrain makes them the final option to free hostages or political prisoners. Team member R.J. is kidnapped along with a trio of businessmen on an exotic ski vacation in New Zealand. One of the group, it turns out, has developed a computer program that will revolutionize the Internet. R.J. manages to send out a radio signal seeking help from her colleagues. Directed by Leslie Libman. Stars Bai Ling (R.J. Fillmore), Scott Paulin (Harris Beckett), Paul Francis (Rasputin Wojohovitz), Elizabeth Lackey (Palmer Marix), Eric Mabius (Darby Gibson), Chris Pratt (Keenan Kranjac), Clarence Williams III (Pat Zachary). From Mandalay Television Productions in association with Touchstone Television. Filmed in New Zealand.

XZFR Rock & Roll Beach Club Nightclub at Pleasure Island at Walt Disney World; opened on May 1, 1989, originally as XZFR Rockin' Rollerdrome. The roller skating was a novelty, but it was a little too dangerous, so it was removed in favor of the beach club theme.

Y

Yacht Bar Fast-food facility in Tomorrowland at Disneyland; open from summer 1955 until September 6, 1966.

Yacht Club Galley Restaurant in the Yacht Club Resort at Walt Disney World.

Yacht Club Resort An Epcot Resort; opened at Walt Disney World on November 5, 1990. Robert A.M. Stern designed a 635-room hotel in the style of New England shore hotels of the 1880s. The nautical theme is everywhere. In the Yachtsman Steakhouse, guests can select their own cut of meat, or can eat more leisurely in the Yacht Club Galley. Adjoins the Beach Club Resort.

Yachtsman Steakhouse Fine restaurant for dinner at the Yacht Club Resort at Walt Disney World.

Yakitori House Fast-food restaurant in Japan in World Showcase at Epcot; opened on October 1, 1982. Located in the midst of a Japanese garden, the restaurant is named after the skewered chicken dish served here.

Yankee Trader, The Shop in Liberty Square in Magic Kingdom Park at Walt Disney World selling culinary aids; opened in September 1973.

Ye Olden Days (film) Mickey Mouse cartoon; released on April 8, 1933. Directed by Burt Gillett. Princess Minnie is locked in a tower when

she refuses to marry the prince, Dippy Dog (Goofy), chosen by her father. Mickey, a wandering minstrel, rescues Minnie and wins a joust with the prince in order to marry her.

Year of 100 Million Smiles Disneyland anxiously awaited the arrival of its 100 millionth guest in 1971. The day came on June 17, 1971, when, at 11:13 A.M., Valerie Suldo from New Brunswick, New Jersey, walked through the turnstiles. The 200 millionth guest, Gert Schelvis, arrived on January 8, 1981.

Yellowstone Cubs (film) Tuffy and Tubby, bear cubs of insatiable curiosity, are trapped during their investigation of a tourist's car at Yellowstone Park. In attempting their rescue, their mother is branded a "dangerous bear," and is taken to the outskirts of the park. By the time she finds her mischievous progeny they have just about the whole park in an uproar. Produced by Charles Draper. Released on June 13, 1963. 48 min. Released on video in 1986.

Yellowstone Story/Bear Country (television) Television show; aired on May 1, 1957. Directed by James Algar. Walt Disney tells about the search for far-off locations for the True-Life Adventures, then lets Jim Algar tell about the history and geography of Yellowstone National Park, where *Bear Country* was filmed. He then shows the Academy Award–winning True-Life Adventure.

Yen Sid Sorcerer in *The Sorcerer's Apprentice* segment of *Fantasia*. His name is "Disney" spelled backward.

Yensid, Retlaw Walt Disney's name spelled backward, used for the story credit for *Lt. Robin Crusoe, U.S.N.*

Yippies Group of protestors who invaded Disneyland on August 6, 1970, causing the Park to close early.

Yokoyama, Matsuo Beginning in 1961, Yokoyama helped create the foundation for Disney's

merchandise licensing business in Japan. He retired in 1994 as chairman of Walt Disney Enterprises of Japan, but continued to work as a consultant. He was named a Disney Legend at a special ceremony in Japan in 1998.

Yong Feng Shangdian Shopping gallery in China in World Showcase at Epcot; opened on April 3, 1983.

York, Jeff (1912–1995) Actor; appeared in *The Great Locomotive Chase* (William Campbell), *Davy Crockett and the River Pirates* (Mike Fink), *Westward Ho the Wagons!* (Hank Breckenridge), *Johnny Tremain* (James Otis), and *Old Yeller* and *Savage Sam* (Bud Searcy), and on television in *The Saga of Andy Burnett*.

You and Me Kid Shop offering children's games, toys, and clothing at Downtown Disney Marketplace in Walt Disney World; open from 1988 to 1995.

You and Me, Kid (television) Series on The Disney Channel; premiered on April 18, 1983, with host Sonny Melendrez. Parents and children participate in games and easy-to-learn activities together, enhancing the youngsters' self-awareness and physical coordination. The show featured occasional guest appearances by celebrities with their children.

You—and Your Ears (film) Cartoon made for the *Mickey Mouse Club* and later released, in May 1957, in 16mm for schools. Jiminy Cricket presents the structure of the ear, traces a sound wave through the three parts of the ear, and gives care rules. An updated version was released in March 1990.

You—and Your Eyes (film) Cartoon made for the *Mickey Mouse Club* and later released, in May 1957, in 16mm for schools. Jiminy Cricket explains the structure of the eyes, the mechanics of seeing, and the rules for the proper care and safety of the eyes. An updated version was released in March 1990.

You—and Your Five Senses (film) Cartoon made for the *Mickey Mouse Club* and later released, in May 1956, in 16mm for schools. Jiminy Cricket explains and compares human responses to stimuli, and how they are highly developed because of his reasoning power. This reasoning ability separates humans from other animals that have senses. An updated version was released on August 23, 1990.

You—and Your Food (film) Cartoon made for the *Mickey Mouse Club* and later released, in December 1958, in 16mm for schools. Jiminy Cricket shows the value of food—the important role of a well-balanced diet in being healthy and active. An updated version was released on August 23, 1990.

You—and Your Sense of Smell and Taste (film) Cartoon prepared for the *Mickey Mouse Club* and later released, in September 1962, on 16mm for schools. These two senses work together, producing the sensation of flavor. An updated version was released in March 1990.

You—and Your Sense of Touch (film) Cartoon prepared for the *Mickey Mouse Club* and later released, in September 1962, on 16mm for schools. Touch is really four sensations and our skin is the special receptor for all. An updated version was released in March 1990.

You Can Always Be #1 (film) Sport Goofy theme song, featuring Goofy in various sports predicaments; released as a music video in February 1982. Composed by Dale Gonyea.

You Can Fly! You Can Fly! You Can Fly! Song from *Peter Pan*; written by Sammy Cahn and Sammy Fain.

You Lucky Dog (television) A Disney Channel Original Movie about a dog therapist, Jack Morgan, charged in a rich man's will to care for his dog, Lucky, who has inherited the $64 million estate. The man's relatives are furious and determined to put an end to both Jack and Lucky. First

aired on June 27, 1998. Directed by Paul Schneider. Stars Kirk Cameron (Jack Morgan), Chelsea Noble (Alison), James Avery (Calvin), Christine Healey (Margaret), John de Lancie (Lyle), Taylor Negron (Reuben). 90 min.

You Must Love Me Song from *Evita*, by Andrew Lloyd Webber and Tim Rice, which won the Oscar as Best Song for 1996.

You Ruined My Life (film) Two-hour television movie; aired on February 1, 1987. Directed by David Ashwell. Minerva, the unruly niece of a casino owner, comes to visit her uncle in Las Vegas. A fired teacher tries to beat the odds at blackjack with a portable computer, but he is caught and is forced to tutor Minerva, since he cannot pay back the money he owes. Stars Soleil Moon Frye (Minerva), Paul Reiser (Dexter Bunche), Mimi Rogers (Charlotte Waring), Allen Garfield (Howie Edwards), Edith Fields (Aunt Hermione), Yoshi Hoover (Yaki), Tony Burton (Moustache), John Putch (Winston), Peter Lind Hayes (Congressman Riley), Mary Healy (Mrs. Riley).

You—the Human Animal (film) Cartoon made for the *Mickey Mouse Club* and later released, in May 1956, in 16mm for schools. Jiminy Cricket shows people's unique ability to reason and think, which sets humans apart from all other living creatures. He explains humans' adaptability, language skills, and intelligence. An updated version was released on August 23, 1990.

You—the Living Machine (film) Cartoon made for the *Mickey Mouse Club* and later released, in December 1958, in 16mm for schools. Host Jiminy Cricket discusses the "human machine" and how it converts food into energy to perform properly. An updated version was released on August 23, 1990.

You Wish (television) Television series; premiered on ABC on September 26, 1997, and ended on September 4, 1998. Gillian Apple is trying her best to balance postdivorce parenting and a career when a shopping trip changes her life forever. When she is haggling for a rug in a store stocked with old-world wares, the rug's design of a man magically comes to life in the form of a genie. The genie is anxious for a new master, but cannot get Gillian to make a wish binding him to her forever. Stars Harley Jane Kozak (Gillian Apple), John Ales (genie), Nathan Lawrence (Travis), Alex McKenna (Mickey), Jerry Van Dyke (Grandpa Max).

You Wish! (television) A Disney Channel Original Movie; premiered on January 10, 2003. Alex, a 16-year-old, wishes that his tagalong younger brother, Stevie, would disappear, and his wish comes true after he acquires a magical coin. Alex's life is suddenly transformed, with wealthy parents, improved athletic skills, the dog he always wanted, and even a popular girlfriend. But no Stevie, who has been transformed into a child star with his own television show. Soon, Alex realizes that his new life is not as great as he thought it might be; he misses his brother, and searches for a way to bring him back. Directed by Paul Hoen. Based on the novel by Jackie French Koller. Stars AJ Trauth (Alex Lansing), Spencer Breslin (Stevie Lansing/Terence Russell McCormack), Lalaine (Abby Richardson), Tim Reid (Larry), Peter Feeney (Dave Lansing), Sally Stockwell (Pam Lansing), Ari Boyland (James), Emma Lahana (Fiona), Joshua Leys (Gary), Jay Bunyan (Charles). Filmed in New Zealand.

You'll Be in My Heart Academy Award–winning song from *Tarzan*; words and music by Phil Collins.

Young, Alan Actor; appeared in *The Cat from Outer Space* (Dr. Wenger) and provided the voice of Flaversham in *The Great Mouse Detective* and Scrooge McDuck in *Mickey's Christmas Carol*, *Ducktales*, and *Ducktales the Movie*.

Young, Sean Actress; appeared in *Baby* (Susan Matthews-Loomis) and *Fire Birds* (Billie Lee Guthrie).

Young Again (television) Two-hour television movie; aired on May 11, 1986. A 40-year-old man

wishes he was 17 again. When his wish is granted by an angel, he returns to his hometown to attempt to recapture his long-lost love but their age difference now makes that impossible. In the end, he learns that happiness is not restricted to any particular age. Directed by Steven H. Stern. Stars Lindsay Wagner, Jack Gilford, Robert Urich, Jessica Steen, Jason Nicoloff, Peter Spence, Jeremy Ratchford, Jonathan Welsh, and introducing Keanu Reeves.

Young Black Stallion, The (film) This prequel to the 1979 classic film presents the horse's adventures with a young girl named Neera, who has been separated from her family in Arabia by World War II. Left alone in the desert, she befriends the wild colt, which she names Shetan ("the devil"). Once reunited with her grandfather, however, Neera remains haunted by images of the "lost horse of the desert," one of a few stallions of legend, rumored to be "born of the sands, sired by the night sky, drinkers of the wind." Neera devises a plan to race the wild Shetan in the annual horse race and help restore her grandfather's reputation. Staking everything on the race, Neera finds her iron will and courage is combined with Shetan's untamed power and determination. Released on December 25, 2003. Directed by Simon Wincer. Stars Richard Romanus (Ben Ishak), Biana G. Tamimi (Neera), Patrick Elyas (Aden), Gerard Rudolf (Rhamon), Ali al Ameri (Mansoor), Andries Rossouw (Kadir). 50 min. Disney's first dramatic feature filmed in 70mm specifically for IMAX and other large-format theaters. Based on the book by Walter Farley and Steven Farley. Filmed on location in Namibia and South Africa.

Young Harry Houdini (television) Two-hour television show; aired on March 15, 1987. A young magician and escape artist runs off to join a traveling carnival. Stars Wil Wheaton. Directed by James Orr.

Young Loner, The (television) Two-part television show; aired on February 25 and March 3, 1968. Directed by Michael O'Herlihy. A young migrant worker is injured in an accident and ends up at a ranch to recover. He runs away, but realizes that his heart is not in traveling and that he needs to settle down, so he returns to a job as shepherd at the ranch. Stars Kim Hunter, Frank Silvera, Butch Patrick, Edward Andrews, Jane Zachary.

Young Musicians Symphony Orchestra Annual program, begun in 1992, where musicians under the age of 12 gather at a remarkable music camp. There they rehearse, listen to guest lecturers, and prepare for a concert that is televised on The Disney Channel.

Young Runaways, The (television) Two-hour television movie; aired on May 28, 1978. Directed by Russ Mayberry. Uncaring parents leave two of their four children with foster parents as they leave for Alaska, but the children plot to get back together, in the meantime running into bank robbers. Stars Gary Collins, Anne Francis, Sharon Farrell, Robert Webber, Alicia Fleer, Chip Courtland, Tommy Crebbs, Pat Delany, Dick Bakalyan, Barbara Hale, Lucille Benson.

Your Big Break (television) Syndicated series in which ordinary people with extraordinary voices fulfill their musical fantasies on an innovative talent show. Produced by dick clark productions, inc. and ENDEMOL Entertainment for Buena Vista Television. The series launched on September 23, 1999. Host was Christopher "Kid" Reid.

Your Career: Your Decision? (film) Educational film; using sequences from *Ballerina*. In the Questions!/Answers? series released in 1976. A girl wants to be a ballerina despite opposition from her mother.

Your Host, Donald Duck (television) Television show; aired on January 16, 1957. Directed by Jack Hannah. Walt Disney allows Donald to host the show, and he shows several cartoon clips tied in with the Disneyland theme of Fantasyland, Frontierland, Tomorrowland, and Adventureland.

You're Nothin' but a Nothin' Popular song hit from *The Flying Mouse* (1934); composed by Larry Morey and Frank Churchill.

Yumz Fast-food facility at Videopolis at Disneyland; opened on June 19, 1985. On June 23, 1995, the name was changed to Meeko's, with the opening of "The Spirit of Pocahontas."

Yzma Evil, plotting adviser in *The Emperor's New Groove*; voiced by Eartha Kitt.

Z

Zazu Bird in *The Lion King*, the Pride Lands' chief of protocol; voiced by Rowan Atkinson.

Zegers, Kevin Actor; appeared in *Life with Mikey* (Little Mikey), and *Air Bud*, *Air Bud: Golden Receiver*, and *Air Bud: World Pup* (Josh Framm).

Zemekis, Robert Director of *Who Framed Roger Rabbit*. Enlisted by Steven Spielberg and Disney, he insisted the illusion of animated characters interacting in a live-action setting be realistic, and the resulting film represented a tremendous leap forward in animation art.

Zenon: Girl of the 21st Century (television) A Disney Channel Original Movie; aired on January 23, 1999. Zenon, a mischievous 13-year-old girl, has lived most of her life in a space station with her family. Her curiosity gets her in trouble once too often and she's grounded, which in her world means she's sent to Earth. The horrified Zenon has to learn how to handle gravity, Earth culture, and being an outsider with Earthside teens, as well as having to thwart a sinister plot to destroy her space station. Directed by Kenneth Johnson. Stars Kirsten Storms (Zenon Kar), Raven-Symone (Nebula), Greg Smith (Greg),

Holly Fulger (Aunt Judy), Phillip Rhys (Proto Zoa). Filmed in Vancouver.

Zenon: The Zequel (television) A Disney Channel Original Movie; aired on January 12, 2001. Zenon and Nebula are back to their old tricks, and as punishment for an "innocent" accident, Zenon is given the most boring job in the world—working in the Alien Patrol Room. Boring, because aliens never contact them. But Zenon soon finds herself on a mission to help out some homeless aliens. Directed by Manny Coto. Stars Kirsten Storms (Zenon), Shadia Simmons (Nebula), Holly Fulger (Aunt Judy), Phillip Rhys (Proto Zoa), Stuart Pankin (Commander Plank). Shadia Simmons takes the role of Nebula played by Raven-Symone in the first film. Since sets from the original movie were not saved, new sets had to be constructed for the filming, which took place in Auckland, New Zealand. Released on video in 2002.

Zenon: Z3 (television) A Disney Channel Original Movie; aired on June 11, 2004. Zenon Kar is competing to win the Galactic Teen Supreme contest and celebrate at the Moonstock Festival in 2054. However, she is torn when her need to beat handsome competitor Bronley Hale runs headlong into moon activist Sage Borealis. Sage is desperate to keep the moon from being colonized and wants Zenon's help. Stars Kirsten Storms (Zenon), Alyson Morgan (Dasha), Glenn McMillan (Bronley Hale), Benjamin J. Easter (Sage Borealis), Raven (Nebula Wade), Lauren Maltby (Margie Hammond), Phumi Mthembo (Cassiopeia Wade), Stuart Pankin (Commander Plank), Holly Fulger (Aunt Judy), Nathan Anderson (Proto Zoa), Carol Becker (Selena).

Zip-A-Dee-Doo-Dah Oscar-winning song from *Song of the South*; sung by James Baskett as Uncle Remus. Written by Ray Gilbert and Allie Wrubel.

Zipper Housefly character in *Chip 'n' Dale's Rescue Rangers*; voiced by Corey Burton.

Zoe, Duncan, Jack & Jane (television) Half-hour comedy television series; debuted on the WB Network on January 17, 1999 and ran until July 18, 1999. Four teenage friends come of age in New York City. Stars Selma Blair (Zoe Bean), Michael Rosenbaum (Jack Cooper), David Moscow (Duncan Milch), Azura Skye (Jane Cooper), Mary Page Keller (Iris Bean). The show was sold to Warner Bros., which continued production.

Zorro (television) Television series about a masked avenger, the alter ego of the mild-mannered Don Diego de la Vega, defending the poor and acting as the scourge of military tyrants on his black stallion, Tornado, in early California. A total of 78 episodes aired from October 10, 1957 to September 28, 1959. Zorro's trademark was the ragged "Z" symbol, which he slashed with his sword. The series was inspired by the stories of Johnston McCulley. Four hour-long episodes were later filmed for airing on the Sunday night show, and episodes of the half-hour show were compiled into theatrical features for domestic (*The Sign of Zorro*) and foreign (*Zorro the Avenger*) audiences. Stars Guy Williams (Don Diego de la Vega/Zorro), Henry Calvin (Sgt. Demetrio Lopez Garcia), Gene Sheldon (Bernardo). The popular title song was by director Norman Foster and George Bruns. The cast and crew of the television series, and subsequent

films, had an unusual amount of experience with the Zorro legend: George Lewis, who plays Zorro's father, starred in the 1944 *Zorro's Black Whip*, and William Lava, who composed the score for the television series also wrote the music for the Republic *Zorro* serial. The show was syndicated for years, and returned to a regular time slot on The Disney Channel beginning on April 18, 1983. It was especially popular in Latin America, and the star, Guy Williams, retired to Argentina partly because of his fame there. In the 1990s, The Disney Channel had the black-and-white episodes successfully colorized and they were able to reach an even wider audience.

Zorro: Adios El Cuchillo (television) Television hour; aired on November 6, 1960. Zorro battles a bandit named El Cuchillo, played by Gilbert Roland. Directed by William Witney. Also starred Guy Williams, Henry Calvin, Gene Sheldon, Rita Moreno. Continuation of *Zorro: El Bandido*. El Cuchillo manages to discover the identity of Zorro through numerous encounters with him, but "honor among thieves" prevents him from revealing the truth when he is finally captured.

Zorro and Son (television) Limited television series of five episodes; aired from April 6 to June 1, 1983, on CBS. A comedy version of the *Zorro* theme. Stars Henry Darrow, Paul Regina, Bill Dana, Gregory Sierra, Richard Beauchamp, Barney Martin, John Moschitta, Jr.

Zorro: Auld Acquaintance (television) Television hour; aired on April 2, 1961. Directed by James Neilson. Two bandits attempt to steal the army's payroll, and Zorro's identity is almost compromised, until he uses his wits to foil the bandits and ruin their credibility. Stars Guy Williams, Henry Calvin, Gene Sheldon, Ricardo Montalban, Ross Martin, Suzanne Lloyd.

Zorro: El Bandido (television) Television hour; aired on October 30, 1960. Directed by William Witney. A band of Mexican outlaws, led by El Cuchillo, is tempted by riches in Los Angeles, but they did not reckon on Zorro. The story is concluded in *Adios El Cuchillo*.

Zorro the Avenger (film) Foreign theatrical compilation of several *Zorro* episodes; released first in Japan on September 10, 1959. With the success of *The Sign of Zorro*, director Charles Barton returned to direct this sequel, again pieced together from the popular Disney television series. Zorro and his sidekick, Bernardo, must defeat the wicked "Eagle," who has taken over the commandant post of Los Angeles, by destroying the conspiracy with swordplay and trickery until the flag of Spain can fly once more over the plaza. 97 min. Stars Guy Williams, Henry Calvin, Gene Sheldon.

Zorro: The Postponed Wedding (television) Television hour; aired on January 1, 1961. Directed by James Neilson. Constancia de la Torre returns to the pueblo to get married, carrying a bag full of jewels as her dowry. But her intended wants the jewels more than he wants the girl. Zorro discovers the plot and comes to help. Stars Guy Williams, Annette Funicello, Henry Calvin, Gene Sheldon, Mark Damon, Carlos Romero.

Zort Sorts (film) Educational release in 16mm in May 1991. 16 min. Zort is an alien who comes to earth to learn how earthlings deal with garbage.

Selected Bibliography

Bailey, Adrian. *Walt Disney's World of Fantasy* (New York: Everest House, 1982).

Bain, David, and Bruce Harris, eds. *Mickey Mouse: Fifty Happy Years* (New York: Harmony Books, 1977).

Beard, Richard R. *Walt Disney's EPCOT Center* (New York: Abrams, 1982).

Birnbaum's Walt Disney World and *Birnbaum's Disneyland* (New York: Disney Editions, 2005). Both books are updated annually.

Blitz, Marcia. *Donald Duck* (New York: Harmony Books, 1979).

Brandon, Pam. *Where Magic Lives: Walt Disney World* (New York: Disney Editions, 2003).

Bright, Randy. *Disneyland: Inside Story* (New York: Abrams, 1987).

Broggie, Michael. *Walt Disney's Railroad Story* (Pasadena, CA: Pentrex, 1997).

Burnes, Brian, et al. *Walt Disney's Missouri* (Kansas City: Kansas City Star Books, 2002).

Canemaker, John. *Before the Animation Begins: The Art and Lives of Disney Inspirational Sketch Artists* (New York: Hyperion, 1997).

———. *Paper Dreams: the Art and Artists of Disney Storyboards* (New York: Hyperion, 1999).

———. *Walt Disney's Nine Old Men and the Art of Animation* (New York: Disney Editions, 2001).

———. *The Art and Flair of Mary Blair* (New York: Disney Editions, 2003).

Cotter, Bill. *The Wonderful World of Disney Television* (New York: Hyperion, 1992).

Culhane, John. *Aladdin: The Making of an Animated Film* (New York: Hyperion, 1992).

———. *Fantasia* (New York: Abrams, 1983).

Donald Duck, 50 Years of Happy Frustration (Tucson: HP Books, 1984).

Dunlop, Beth. *Building a Dream: The Art of Disney Architecture* (New York: Abrams, 1996).

Eisner, Michael, and Tony Schwartz. *Work in Progress* (New York: Random House, 1998).

Feild, Robert D. *The Art of Walt Disney* (New York: Macmillan, 1942).

Finch, Christopher. *The Art of Walt Disney* (New York: Abrams, 1973, 2004).

———. *Walt Disney's America* (New York: Abbeville, 1978).

———. *The Art of The Lion King* (New York: Hyperion, 1994).

Flower, Joe. *Prince of the Magic Kingdom: Michael Eisner and the Re-Making of Disney* (New York: Wiley, 1991).

France, Van. *Window on Main Street* (Nashua, NH: Laughter Publications, 1991).

Frantz, Donald. *Beauty and the Beast: A Celebration of the Broadway Musical* (New York: Hyperion, 1995).

Goofy, the Good Sport (Tucson: HP Books, 1985).

Gordon, Bruce, and David Mumford. *Disneyland: The Nickel Tour* (Santa Clarita, CA: Camphor House, 1995).

———, and Tim O'Day. *Disneyland Then, Now, and Forever* (New York: Disney Editions, 2005)

Grant, John. *Encyclopedia of Walt Disney's Animated Characters: From Mickey Mouse to Hercules* (New York: Hyperion, 1998).

Green, Howard. *The Tarzan Chronicles* (New York: Hyperion, 1999).

————, and Amy Boothe Green. *Remembering Walt* (New York: Hyperion, 1999).

Greene, Katherine, and Richard Greene. *The Man Behind the Magic: The Story of Walt Disney* (New York: Viking, 1991).

————. *Inside the Dream; The Personal Story of Walt Disney* (New York: Disney Editions, 2001).

Grover, Ron. *The Disney Touch* (Homewood, IL: Business One Irwin, 1991).

Hansford, Dee. *Gardens of the Walt Disney World Resort* (Lake Buena Vista, FL: Walt Disney World, 1988).

Heide, Robert, and John Gilman. *Disneyana: Classic Collectibles 1928–1958* (New York: Hyperion, 1994).

————. with Monique Peterson and Patrick White. *Mickey Mouse; the Evolution, the Legend, the Phenomenon!* (New York: Disney Editions, 2001).

Hench, John, with Peggy Van Pelt. *Designing Disney: Imagineering and the Art of the Show* (New York: Disney Editions, 2003).

Hollis, Richard, and Brian Sibley. *Snow White and the Seven Dwarfs & the Making of the Classic Film* (New York: Simon & Schuster, 1987; Hyperion, 1994).

————. *The Disney Studio Story* (New York: Crown, 1988).

The Illustrated Treasury of Disney Songs (New York: Hyperion, 1993).

Isbouts, Jean-Pierre. *Discovering Walt* (New York: Disney Editions, 2001).

Iwerks, Leslie, and John Kenworthy. *The Hand Behind the Mouse: An Intimate Biography of Ub Iwerks* (New York: Disney Editions, 2001).

Jackson, Kathy Merlock. *Walt Disney: a Bio-Bibliography* (Westport, CT: Greenwood Press, 1993).

Johnston, Ollie, and Frank Thomas. *The Disney Villain* (New York: Hyperion, 1993).

————. *Walt Disney's Bambi: The Story and the Film* (New York: Stewart, Tabori & Chang, 1990).

Justice, Bill. *Justice for Disney* (Dayton, OH: Tomart, 1992).

Keller, Keith. *The Mickey Mouse Club Scrapbook* (New York: Grosset & Dunlap, 1975).

Kinney, Jack. *Walt Disney and Assorted Other Characters* (New York: Harmony, 1988).

Koehler, William R. *The Wonderful World of Disney Animals* (New York: Howell Book House, 1979).

Koenig, David. *Mouse Tales: A Behind-the-Ears Look at Disneyland* (Irvine, CA: Bonaventure Press, 1994).

————. *More Mouse Tales* (Irvine, CA: Bonaventure Press, 1999).

————. *Mouse Under Glass* (Irvine, CA: Bonaventure Press, 1997, 2001).

Krause, Martin, and Linda Witkowski. *Snow White and the Seven Dwarfs: An Art in the Making* (New York: Hyperion, 1994).

Kurtti, Jeff. *Since the World Began: Walt Disney World's First 25 Years* (New York: Hyperion, 1996).

————. *The Art of Mulan* (New York: Hyperion, 1998).

————. *A Bug's Life: The Art and Making of an Epic of Miniature Proportions* (New York: Hyperion, 1998).

————. *Treasure Planet: A Voyage of Discovery* (New York: Disney Editions, 2002).

Kurtti, Jeff, and Bruce Gordon. *The Art of Disneyland.* (New York: Disney Editions, 2005).

Lassell, Michael. *Disney on Broadway* (New York: Disney Editions, 2002).

Leebron, Elizabeth, and Lynn Gartley. *Walt Disney: A Guide to References and Resources* (Boston: G.K. Hall, 1979).

Littaye, Alain, and Didier Ghez. *Disneyland Paris: From Sketch to Reality* (Paris: Nouveau Millénaire Editions, 2002).

Malmberg, Melody. *The Making of Disney's Animal Kingdom* (New York: Hyperion, 1998).

Maltin, Leonard. *The Disney Films* (New York: Crown, 1973, 1984; Hyperion, 1995; Disney Editions, 2000).

Marling, Karal Ann, ed. *Designing Disney's Theme Parks* (New York: Flammarion, 1997).

Mickey Mouse, His Life and Times (New York: Harper & Row, 1986).

Mickey Mouse in Color (New York: Pantheon Books, 1988).

Mickey Mouse Memorabilia (New York: Abrams, 1986).

Miller, Diane Disney, and Pete Martin. *The Story of Walt Disney* (New York: Holt, 1957; Disney Editions, 2005).

Munsey, Cecil. *Disneyana: Walt Disney Collectibles* (New York: Hawthorn, 1974).

Neary, Kevin, and Dave Smith. *The Ultimate Disney Trivia Book* (New York: Hyperion, 1992).

————. *The Ultimate Disney Trivia Book 2* (New York: Hyperion, 1994).

————. *The Ultimate Disney Trivia Book 3* (New York: Hyperion, 1997).

————. *The Ultimate Disney Trivia Book 4* (New York: Disney Editions, 2000).

O'Day, Tim. *Disneyland—Celebrating 45 Years of Magic* (New York: Disney Editions, 2000).

————, and Lorraine Santoli. *Disneyland Resort: Magical Memories for a Lifetime* (New York: Disney Editions, 2002).

Rawls, Walton. *Disney Dons Dogtags: The Best of Disney Military Insignia from World War II* (New York: Abbeville, 1992).

Rebello, Stephen. *The Art of The Hunchback of Notre Dame* (New York: Hyperion, 1996).

———. *The Art of Pocahontas* (New York: Hyperion, 1995).

———, and Jane Healey. *The Art of Hercules* (New York: Hyperion, 1997).

Ryman, Herbert. *A Brush with Disney* (Santa Clarita, CA: Camphor Tree Publishers, 2000).

Santoli, Lorraine. *The Official Mickey Mouse Club Book* (New York: Hyperion, 1995).

Schickel, Richard. *The Disney Version* (New York: Simon & Schuster, 1968, 1985).

Schroeder, Russell, ed. *Walt Disney: His Life in Pictures* (New York: Disney Press, 1996).

———. *Mickey Mouse: His Life in Pictures* (New York: Disney Press, 1997).

———. *Disney: The Ultimate Disney Guide* (New York: DK Publications, 2002).

Shale, Richard. *Donald Duck Joins Up: The Walt Disney Studio During World War II* (Ann Arbor: UMI Research Press, 1982).

Sherman, Robert B., and Richard M. Sherman. *Walt's Time* (Santa Clarita, CA: Camphor Tree, 1998).

Smith, Dave, ed. *The Quotable Walt Disney* (New York: Disney Editions, 2001).

———, and Steven Clark. *Disney: The First 100 Years* (New York: Hyperion, 1999; Disney Editions, 2002).

Solomon, Charles. *The Disney That Never Was* (New York: Hyperion, 1995).

Surrell, Jason. *The Haunted Mansion: From the Magic Kingdom to the Movies* (New York: Disney Editions, 2003).

———, *Pirates of the Carribean: From the Magic Kingdom to the Movies* (New York: Disney Editions, 2005)

Taylor, John. *Storming the Magic Kingdom* (New York: Knopf, 1987).

Thomas, Bob. *The Art of Animation* (New York: Simon & Schuster, 1958).

———. *Art of Animation: From Mickey Mouse to Beauty and the Beast* (New York: Hyperion, 1991).

———. *Art of Animation from Mickey Mouse to Hercules* (New York: Hyperion, 1997).

———. *Building a Company: Roy O. Disney and the Creation of an Entertainment Empire* (New York: Hyperion, 1998).

———. *Walt Disney: An American Original* (New York: Simon & Schuster, 1976; new edition Hyperion, 1994).

Thomas, Frank, and Ollie Johnston. *Disney Animation: The Illusion of Life* (New York: Abbeville Press, 1981; Hyperion, 1995).

———. *Too Funny for Words: Disney's Greatest Sight Gags* (New York: Abbeville, 1987).

Tieman, Robert. *The Disney Treasures* (New York: Disney Editions, 2003).

———. *Disney Keepsakes, The* (New York: Disney Editions, 2005).

Tietyen, David. *The Musical World of Walt Disney* (Milwaukee: Hal Leonard, 1990).

Treasures of Disney Animation Art (New York: Abbeville, 1982).

Tumbusch, Tom. *Disneyana Catalog and Price Guide* (Dayton, OH: Tomart, 1985–89).

Vaz, Mark Cotta. *The Art of Finding Nemo* (San Francisco: Chronicle Books, 2003).

———. *The Art of The Incredibles* (San Francisco: Chronicle Books, 2004).

Walt Disney Imagineering: A Behind the Dreams Look at Making the Magic Real (New York: Hyperion, 1996).

Walt Disney's Christmas Treasury (New York: Abbeville, 1978).

Watts, Steven. *The Magic Kingdom: Walt Disney and the American Way of Life* (Boston: Houghton Mifflin, 1997).

West, John. *The Disney Live-Action Films* (Milton, WA: Hawthorne & Peabody, 1994).

Williams, Pat. *How to Be Like Walt* (Deerfield Beach, FL: Health Communications, 2004).